W9-AOY-589

ANNUAL REVIEW OF PSYCHOLOGY

ANNUAL REVIEW OF PSYCHOLOGY

VOLUME 48, 1997

JANET T. SPENCE, *Editor*
University of Texas, Austin

JOHN M. DARLEY, *Associate Editor*
Princeton University

DONALD J. FOSS, *Associate Editor*
Florida State University

http://annurev.org science@annurev.org 415-493-4400
ANNUAL REVIEWS INC. 4139 EL CAMINO WAY P.O. BOX 10139 PALO ALTO, CALIFORNIA 94303-0139

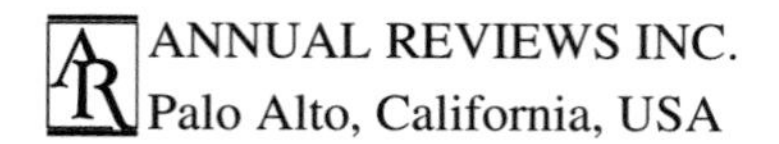

ANNUAL REVIEWS INC.
Palo Alto, California, USA

International Standard Serial Number: 0066-4308
International Standard Book Number: 0-8243-0248-6
Library of Congress Catalog Card Number: 50-13143

The paper used in this publication meets the minimum requirements of American National Standards for Information Sciences—Permanence of Paper for Printed Library Materials, ANZI Z39.48-1984

Typesetting by Ruth McCue Saavedra and the Annual Reviews Inc. Editorial Staff

PRINTED AND BOUND IN THE UNITED STATES OF AMERICA

ANNUAL REVIEWS INC. is a nonprofit scientific publisher established to promote the advancement of the sciences. Beginning in 1932 with the *Annual Review of Biochemistry,* the Company has pursued as its principal function the publication of high-quality, reasonably priced *Annual Review* volumes. The volumes are organized by Editors and Editorial Committees who invite qualified authors to contribute critical articles reviewing significant developments within each major discipline. The Editor-in-Chief invites those interested in serving as future Editorial Committee members to communicate directly with him. Annual Reviews Inc. is administered by a Board of Directors, whose members serve without compensation.

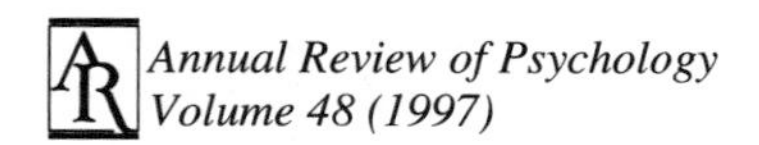
Annual Review of Psychology
Volume 48 (1997)

CONTENTS

SOME RELATED ARTICLES IN OTHER *ANNUAL REVIEWS*

From the *Annual Review of Anthropology,* Volume 25 (1996)

Narrating the Self, Elinor Ochs and Lisa Capps

From the *Annual Review of Neuroscience,* Volume 19 (1996)

Addictive Drugs and Brain, R. A. Wise
Visual Object Recognition, Nikos K. Logothetis and David L. Sheinberg

From the *Annual Review of Public Health,* Volume 17 (1996)

Understanding Research Synthesis (Meta-Analysis), Frederick Mosteller and Graham A. Colditz

From the *Annual Review of Sociology,* Volume 22 (1996)

Innovations in Experimental Design in Attitude Surveys, Paul Sniderman and Douglas B. Grob
Adult Child-Parent Relationships, Diane N. Lye
Mass Effects on Violent Behavior, Richard B. Felson

William J. McGuire

Annu. Rev. Psychol. 1997. 48:1–30

CREATIVE HYPOTHESIS GENERATING IN PSYCHOLOGY: Some Useful Heuristics

William J. McGuire

Yale University, Department of Psychology, P.O. Box 208205, 2 Hillhouse Avenue, New Haven, Connecticut 06520-8205

KEY WORDS: creativity, heuristics, methodology, theory construction

ABSTRACT

To correct a common imbalance in methodology courses, focusing almost entirely on hypothesis-testing issues to the neglect of hypothesis-generating issues which are at least as important, 49 creative heuristics are described, divided into 5 categories and 14 subcategories. Each of these heuristics has often been used to generate hypotheses in psychological research, and each is teachable to students. The 49 heuristics range from common sense perceptiveness of the oddity of natural occurrences to use of sophisticated quantitative data analyses in ways that provoke new insights.

CONTENTS

0084-6570/97/0201-0001$08.00

INTRODUCTION

Psychologists know well that research involves generating hypotheses and theories as well as testing them. However, our methods courses and textbooks concentrate heavily on procedures for testing hypotheses (e.g. measurement, experimental design, manipulating and controlling variables, statistical analysis, etc) and they largely ignore procedures for generating them. This pedagogic neglect probably reflects, not failure to appreciate the importance of creative hypothesis generating, but despair of teaching or even describing it. I have contended (McGuire 1973, 1983) that creative hypothesis-generating aspects of research on both strategic and tactical levels can be taught. While in the past (McGuire 1989) I have discussed creative hypothesis generation on the strategic level, here I address it at the tactical level by describing a variety of creative heuristics psychologists have used and that can also be taught.

My "Yin and Yang" article (McGuire 1973) gave some examples of hypothesis-generating techniques that can be described and taught. Shortly after that article appeared I was surprised to receive a curt note from an annoyed reader pointing out that in my article I mentioned having taught a "dozen" such creative techniques but then in the article I gave only nine examples. Where, this reader wanted to know, were the other three? The request struck me as a bit pedantic, but before I could reply "Who's counting?" I received two more inquiries from readers demanding, "Where are your other three examples?" My articles usually evoke at most a few reprint-request postcards from East Europe, so the receipt of three letters of complaint seemed like a mass protest and raised the specter that I might be called before some ethics committee for giving short weight. In a nervous rush to write down a few more examples of creative heuristics, so that I could send a baker's dozen to any future inquirer, I overshot the target and generated dozen after dozen until the list grew to the 49 heuristics shown in Table 1.

Any list with 49 items would be cruelly long if left unorganized. Therefore, in Table 1 these creative, hypothesis-generating techniques are grouped into five increasingly demanding categories, each with subcategories. Category I includes nine observational heuristics that simply require sensitivity to provocative natural occurrences (e.g. Subcategory IA calls for noticing and accounting for the provocative oddity of exceptional occurrences). Categories II and III call for going beyond observational sensitivity by requiring also conceptual analysis, either by direct inference, such as accounting for the contrary of a banal hypothesis (Category II), or by more complicated mediated inference, such as using a thought-diversifying structure (Category III). The final two categories, IV and V, go beyond a priori conceptual analysis by requiring some wrestling with empirical data, either by retrospectively examining past studies, such as by decomposing a complex obtained relation into multiple simpler components (Category IV), or by prospectively reanalyzing old data or collecting new data, such as by content-analyzing participants' open-ended responses to obtain new insights (Category V). For each of the fourteen A through N subtypes of these five categories (see Table 1), I describe one illustrative heuristic with examples of its uses in psychology and then mention more briefly additional heuristics within the subcategory.

I. HEURISTICS REQUIRING SENSITIVITY TO PROVOCATIVE NATURAL OCCURRENCES

The relatively simple heuristics in Category I require no special training in subject matter (e.g. psychology) or in formal analysis (e.g. statistics) but call only for cultivating habits of observation that focus one's attention on fertile aspects of natural experience. Everyone tends to focus on unexpected nonobvious relations (McGuire 1984), but appropriate training may strengthen and refine this productive tendency. Table 1 groups simple observational techniques for producing new insights into four subcategories of increasing complexity and deliberateness.

The simplest, Subcategory A, involves responding to the provocative oddity of exceptional occurrences. The slightly more complex Subcategory B requires introspective self-analyses in addition to external observation. Subcategory C calls for retrospective comparisons such as extrapolating from similar problems already solved. To use heuristics in these first three subcategories, it is sufficient to react to fortuitous experience, but Subcategory ID requires deliberately immersing oneself in sustained, purposeful observation, such as compiling intensive case studies. Nine heuristics are grouped within these four (A through D) subcategories.

A. Recognizing and Accounting for the Oddity of Occurrences

1. ACCOUNTING FOR DEVIATIONS FROM THE GENERAL TREND Researchers tend to be so preoccupied with searching for regularities that they tend to

Table 1 Creative heuristics used to generate psychological hypotheses

I. Heuristics Simply Calling for Sensitivity to Provocative Natural Occurrences
- A. Recognizing and Accounting for the Oddity of Occurrences
  - 1. Accounting for deviations from the general trend
  - 2. Accounting for the oddity of the general trend itself
- B. Introspective Self-Analysis
  - 3. Analyzing one's own behavior in similar situations
  - 4. Role playing one's own behavior in the situation
- C. Retrospective Comparison
  - 5. Extrapolating from similar problems already solved
  - 6. Juxtaposing opposite problems to suggest reciprocal solutions
- D. Sustained, Deliberate Observation
  - 7. Intensive case studies
  - 8. Participant observation
  - 9. Assembling propositional inventories

II. Heuristics Involving Simple Conceptual Analysis (Direct Inference)
- E. Simple Conversions of a Banal Proposition
  - 10. Accounting for the contrary of a trite hypothesis
  - 11. Reversing the plausible direction of causality
  - 12. Pushing an obvious hypothesis to an implausible extreme
  - 13. Imagining the effects of reducing a variable to zero
  - 14. Conjecturing interaction variables that qualify a relation
- F. Multiplying Insights by Conceptual Division
  - 15. Linguistic explorations
  - 16. Alternative manipulations of the independent variable
  - 17. Dividing the dependent variable into subscales
  - 18. Arranging output subcomponents into a sequence
- G. Jolting One's Conceptualizing Out of its Usual Ruts
  - 19. Shifting attention to an opposite pole of the problem
  - 20. Alternating preferred with nonpreferred research styles
  - 21. Expressing one's hypothesis in multiple modalities
  - 22. Disrupting ordinary states of consciousness

III. Heuristics Calling for Complex Conceptual Analysis (Mediated Inference)
- H. Deductive Reasoning Procedures
  - 23. Generating multiple explanations for a given relation
  - 24. Alternating induction and deduction
  - 25. Identifying counterforces obscuring an obvious relation
  - 26. Hypothetico-deductive sets of postulates
- I. Using Thought-Diversifying Structures
  - 27. Using an idea-stimulating checklist
  - 28. Constructing provocative complex generating structures
  - 29. Formalizing explanatory accounts
- J. Using Metatheories as Thought Evokers
  - 30. The evolutionary functionalism (adaptivity) paradigm
  - 31. Transferring conceptualizations analogously

Table 1 (*continued*)

32. Quixotic defense of a theory
IV. Heuristics Demanding Reinterpretations of Past Research
K. Delving into Single Past Studies
33. Accounting for irregularities in an obtained relation
34. Decomposing nonmonotonic into simpler relations
35. Deviant-case analysis
36. Interpreting serendipitous interaction effects
L. Discovery by Integrating Multiple Past Studies
37. Reconciling conflicting outcomes or nonreplications
38. Bringing together complementary past experiments
39. Reviewing and organizing current knowledge in an area
V. Heuristics Necessitating Collecting New or Reanalyzing Old Data
M. Qualitative Analyses
40. Allowing open-ended responses for content analysis
41. Participating actively in the research routine
42. Exploring a glamorous technique
43. Including low-cost interaction variables in the design
44. Pitting confounded factors against one another
45. Strategic planning of programmatic research
N. Quantitative Analyses
46. Multivariate fishing expeditions
47. Subtracting out the effect of a known mediator
48. Computer simulation
49. Mathematical modeling

suppress exceptions to the general trend as distracting aberrations. Heuristic A1 calls for a two-step analysis of experience, beginning with the usual teasing out of a general relation followed by noticing and accounting for deviant cases.

The challenge to use exceptions creatively can vary over several levels of difficulty. A relatively easy subtype is when the exceptionality receives wide publicity and discussion, in which case the researcher need not discover the oddity but only accept the challenge to account for the aberration, e.g. the paradoxically greater resistance to extinction of habits established by partial reinforcement than by 100% reinforcement. A more demanding variant of this heuristic calls for the researcher's actively seeking out nonsalient exceptions, as when a developmental psychologist, aware that children with traumatic childhoods tend to grow into disturbed, noncontributing adults, selects out for special study cases of traumatized children who in maturity became exceptionally high contributors to society. A third, still more demanding variant of heuristic A1 requires that the researcher show initiative in recognizing that an event is unusual. For example, all great cultural ages are by definition exceptional, but most are readily accounted for by unusually favorable circumstances (e.g. there is an *embarrass de richesses* to explain the greatness of Periclean Athens, Medician Tuscany, Elizabethan England). However, more interesting and creatively provocative are more puzzling cultural flourishings (e.g. *fin-de-siècle* Hapsburg Vienna, which was so productive in music, psychoanalysis, philosophy of science, Zionism, etc), which occurred under conditions that seem especially inauspicious and constitute exceptions even among the exceptional eras and so especially invite notice and explanation.

Students can be trained in the creative use of heuristic A1 by exercises that guide them through a series of steps that differ slightly among the three variants just mentioned. In general, a training trial consists of showing the students a scatter plot and regression line depicting a relation in the domain under study. For example, in a US presidential-performance study the abscissa might be labeled "Age at which first elected to the presidency" (the independent variable) and the ordinate might be labeled "Rated level of achievement in office" (the dependent variable) with 25 dots distributed in the quadrant space, each labeled by the name of one of the 25 most recent US presidents. The trainee is given the open-ended task of interpreting the scatter plot to indicate what questions it raises and what answers it suggests. In some training conditions the student is given a series of probes that guide him or her first to report the general relation indicated by the graphed data, and then (specific to heuristic A1) to note outliers and conjecture multiple situational and dispositional variables that might account for that president's deviation from the general trend line. (In other training conditions the student is not given a guiding probe, but instead his or her free responses are later given a critique that covers the same steps.)

Typically, the trainee goes through three such 15-min trials. Each trial presents a new scatter plot, relating a new pair of independent and dependent variables. At a fourth meeting, the trainee is given a test trial, without prompts, and again two months later a delayed test trial (to evaluate longer-term effects of the training). The test performances of students serving in different training conditions (and in control, no-training conditions) are also evaluated for (*a*) the extent to which that training procedure enhances use of heuristic A1, and (*b*) the extent to which the training (and use of heuristic A1) enhances the creativity exhibited by the trainee in his or her two test performances, as scored by trained judges on various indices of creativity.

I have developed training procedures for each of the heuristics shown in Table 1, but space limits here restrict me to illustrate training procedures only for heuristic A1. For each of the remaining 48 heuristics I describe only what it entails and illustrate some of its uses in psychological research, without describing further how students can be trained to use it creatively.

2. ACCOUNTING FOR THE ODDITY OF THE GENERAL TREND ITSELF Further to save space, only one heuristic in each of the 14 subcategories A through N is described in any detail, so only a brief description can be given of heuristic A2, which concerns situations in which it is the general trend itself, rather than the deviant case, that needs to be recognized as provocatively paradoxical. Often the mere familiarity of the odd general trend hides its peculiar violation of some common sense principle, as in the case of the prevalence of punishing nightmares, recognized by Freud as violating the obvious pleasure principle he was loathe to abandon. Indeed, critics from Aristotle to today's cineastes have wondered at the popularity of tragedies, tearjerkers, and horror movies. Tragedy and terror may be unavoidable in the real world, but why seek them in fantasy? This odd tendency to seek out punishing effects in fantasy has provoked ego psychologists to conjecture a dozen ways in which apparently self-punishing fantasies like nightmares can be reinforcing, and these conjectures have deepened our appreciation of human needs. Festinger's (1957) dissonance-theory formulation was similarly provoked in part by his noticing and conjecturing why actual catastrophes tend to be followed by punishing rumors that further disasters are immanent, rather than by reassuring rumors of impending relief.

B. Introspective Self-Analysis

The heuristics in Subcategory IB are available especially to researchers in the human sciences whose profession it is to think about thinking and who are therefore in the noetically privileged position of being able to introspect on the processes to be explained, a hermeneutic luxury rarely available to physical scientists whose conjectures tend to be irrelevant or even contrary to phenomenal experience (e.g. when they conjecture laws of motion in a frictionless vacuum).

3. ANALYZING ONE'S OWN BEHAVIOR IN SIMILAR SITUATIONS The gist of heuristic B3 is to provoke and deepen insights into a specified human situation by recalling how and why one behaved on past occasions in similar situations. Empirical evidence suggests that people's insight into the reasons for their own behavior is highly flawed (Nisbett & Wilson 1977), but here I discuss techniques for generating hypotheses, not for collecting data to test them. One should retrieve more than a single self-experienced incident of the type in question to recall a set of such experiences, partitioning them into subsets in which one made contrasting types of responses. An illustration is Freud's development of his early psychoanalytic insights by self-analysis in his Fliess letters and in the numerous personal examples that Freud used in his early monographs on wit, dreams, and psychopathology of everyday life (Anzieu 1986).

4. ROLE PLAYING ONE'S OWN BEHAVIOR IN THE SITUATION Introspective heuristic B4 is like B3 except that it does not require that the researcher has actually experienced situations of the type in question. Instead, it suffices for the researcher to do thought experiments, imagining variants of the situation and imagining how she or he would behave in each variant type, thus getting some insight into what changes in the situation would be necessary for behavior to change. For example, the editors of Abelson et al (1968) expanded the richness of Heider's rather banal A-B-X balance theory by imagining triadic relations that, while technically unbalanced, would seem not to be bothersome (e.g. Ted loves Mary, Mary likes knitting, Ted dislikes knitting). These editors then conjectured why each of these imbalanced situations would not be troublesome, thus generating reconceptualizations (e.g. sex-role appropriateness) and interactional qualifications that made balance theory more subtle.

C. Retrospective Comparison

Subcategory C heuristics are slightly more demanding than heuristics in subcategories A and B in that they call for going beyond current observation or imagination to retrieve and compare past experiences.

5. EXTRAPOLATING FROM SIMILAR PROBLEMS ALREADY SOLVED Use of this creative technique is inhibited by researchers' liking to feel that their current thinking is dramatically novel. This enhances its excitingness but at the cost of increasing the difficulty of transferring to it insights from similar problems solved in the past. Possibilities and problems of using this transfer technique are illustrated by my experience while participating in an interdisciplinary conference on hypertension convened to solve the problem that most hypertensives do not adhere to the pharmaceutical regimen prescribed for them. The conference organizers asked us to focus on the reinforcement difficulty that hypertension itself causes little direct discomfort while the prescribed drugs often do produce bothersome side effects. Their question was, is there some way to motivate patients to adhere to a punishing drug-taking regimen to reduce a nonpunishing condition.

Using this C5 heuristic, I mentioned at the conference that there may be some lessons in the success of many birth-control campaigns, which faced an analogous problem in that the condition to be corrected, fertility, causes no direct discomfort while recommended contraception procedures often do have some bothersome side effects. It is revealing that later in the day a physician at the conference gently explained to me that as a social scientist I was quite understandably unaware of an essential difference between the two conditions that caused my analogy to limp, namely, that hypertension involves the circulatory system whereas fertility involves the endocrine. Use of this transfer heuristic comes more readily to researchers whose own interests have shifted among areas, as when Hovland et al (1949) looked for delayed-action "sleeper effects" in persuasion that would be analogous to the delayed-action reminiscence effects in the rote-memory phenomena they had previously investigated.

6. JUXTAPOSING OPPOSITE PROBLEMS TO SUGGEST RECIPROCAL SOLUTIONS The related C6 heuristic in this subcategory calls for juxtaposing the problem at hand with a seemingly opposite problem and examining how each of these contrary problems suggests solutions to the other. For example, the above-mentioned nonadherence by hypertensives to their prescribed medication can be brought into confrontation with the opposite problem of excessive self-drugging in America (e.g. elderly peoples' overdosing on useless or harmful arthritic medications). It is a paradoxical contrast that one segment of the afflicted public won't take drugs they need while another segment won't stop squandering money for drugs that are harming them. An understanding of what causes each of these opposite problems can provoke insights into how the contrasting problem might be mitigated.

D. Sustained, Deliberate Observation

The three subcategories of observational heuristics discussed so far depend on incidental discovery by fortuitous observation or post factum retrospections on past experiences. The observational heuristics in Subcategory D, however, are more purposeful and programmatic in that they involve sustained observation deliberately undertaken to evoke insights into the topic under study. They include case studies, participant observations, and propositional inventories.

7. INTENSIVE CASE STUDIES Case-study analysis has long been used by decision makers in the governmental and private sectors for informal policy guidance; by historians, political scientists, and other academics for analysis and exposition (Neustadt & May 1986); and in medical, law, and business schools as a favorite teaching method that allows students actively to abstract principles, even principles that the instructor is unable to articulate. Students often regard case histories as interesting teaching materials, although Jung, an old pro, complained in his letters to Freud that case histories are "unbelievably monotonous."

Creative insights can be derived from each of three phases of case-history development, namely, selecting which cases to write up, deciding how to write them, and devising ways of using the case studies once written.

(*a*.) The criteria for selecting which occurrences will make provocative case histories are so unclear that it may be cost-effective to settle for whichever cases happen to be already available. Choosing familiar cases (e.g. Piaget's observing cognitive development in his own children or Freud's using data from his patients) entails surplus knowledge that can be a danger in critical thinking but an advantage in creative thinking. It may be optimal to use cases with intermediate puzzlingness, not so obvious as to be devoid of new information and not so obscure as to be baffling. Contrasting paired cases that are superficially similar but which had opposite outcomes may be especially provocative.

(*b*.) Research is also needed on how to write up the history, however the case is selected. One suspects that 90% of the details could be omitted with little loss, but which 90%? As the researcher accumulates experience at the task, a standard format for writing up cases develops, but standardization might adversely effect provocativeness and novelty.

(*c*.) Finally, how case histories should be used, once written up, to maximize their creative evocativeness can be studied by evaluating the productiveness of a variety of case studies used in law and business school curricula, where credible evaluation criteria (starting with student ratings) may be available. The challenge and promise of developing teaching procedures that will exploit the creative potential of this one heuristic, case histories, warrants a whole program of research by itself.

8.–9. OTHER SUSTAINED OBSERVATIONAL HEURISTICS Besides case histories, other examples of sustained observational procedures that can be deliberately and programmatically undertaken to promote hypothesis generation include A8, participant observation, and A9, assembling propositional inventories. Cultural anthropologists and sociologists often use participant observation as their method of choice. Its unsystematic open-endedness, which arouses worries when used to collect evidence for hypothesis testing, makes it a rich source of new hypotheses (e.g. E Goffman's observations of what constitutes total institutions and how they affect inmates). Psychologists might find it provocative to leave their computer terminals, laboratories, and books more often to observe the variables of interest operating in the complex natural environment. Heuristic A9, collecting propositional inventories, can be a rich source of new insights, especially when the topic has a long tradition of practitioner interest relatively isolated from basic research, as is the case with attitude change. Quintilian, in his *Institutio oratoria,* takes four volumes to present the rules of thumb of Hellenic and Roman classical practitioners of persuasive oratory, providing a gold mine of provocative hypotheses largely neglected by attitude-change researchers. Hovland and his colleagues in their 1940s attitude-change research used politicians' working assumptions as springboards for deriving testable hypotheses, and Cialdini (1993) has pulled together practitioners' compliance-gaining tactics such as "low-balling," "foot-in-the-door," "and "door-in-the-face."

II. HEURISTICS INVOLVING SIMPLE CONCEPTUAL ANALYSIS (DIRECT INFERENCE)

Heuristics in Category I above require simply observing and interpreting natural occurrences, while heuristics in Category II, to which we now turn, are more demanding in that they require thought experiments consisting of simple, direct conceptual manipulations. Such direct-inference procedures will be grouped here into three increasingly demanding subcategories: E, simple conversions of a banal hypothesis; F, multiplying insights by conceptual division; and G, jolting one's conceptualizing out of its usual ruts.

E. Simple Conversions of a Banal Proposition

10. ACCOUNTING FOR THE CONTRARY OF A TRITE HYPOTHESIS A dramatically effective, readily available simple thought experiment for evoking creative hypotheses is to convert an initially obvious hypothesis about the relation between two variables into a more exciting conjecture by standing it on its head, as Marx did Hegel, and thinking of circumstances in which the contrary relation would likely obtain between the variables. Simone Weil (1952) epitomized this process: "Method of investigation: as soon as we have thought something, try to see in what way the contrary is true." Even if the initial banal direction of the relation has wider ecological validity, and its counterintuitive contrary obtains only in exceptional circumstances, these exceptional cases will disclose overlooked mediators that operate to some extent even in the typical situation, where they will be manifested in interaction predictions that interestingly modify the initial banal hypothesis. This heuristic is a key component in a "perspectivist" strategy (McGuire 1989) for creating programs of research. For example, one might start with the banal prediction that the more likable the perceived source of a persuasive communication, the more attitude change this source produces. One then uses this E10 heuristic by generating counterexamples, special circumstances in which a less-liked source will paradoxically be more persuasive (e.g. in situations involving praise from a stranger, identification with the aggressor, traumatic initiation, daring to deviate, insufficient justification, ingratiation attribution, etc).

11.–14. OTHER HYPOTHESIS-GENERATING SIMPLE CONVERSIONS OF BANAL HYPOTHESES Space limitations restrict me to mentioning only briefly four other types of creative thought experiments in Subcategory E. Heuristic E11 involves conceptually reversing the direction of causality of a banal hypothesis. For example, the hypothesis that watching TV violence increases viewers' aggression is converted to the reverse causality hypothesis that viewers' aggressiveness increases their watching of TV violence. The researcher then conjectures explanations of why the relation may operate in the reverse causal direction as well (e.g. because of ostracism, esthetic predilection, etc). An underlying assumption is that an adaptive level of cognitive and social stability is maintained by establishing reciprocal causal links. Festinger and his followers in the dissonance movement revitalized the attitude-change area by reversing the trite hypothesis that attitude change produces behavioral change and exploiting the reversed hypothesis that behavioral change leads to attitude change.

Heuristic E12, the thought experiment that involves pushing a reasonable hypothesis to an implausible extreme, can be illustrated by the familiar hypothesis that eye contact increases liking, which is plausible because as eye contact varies from 10 to 20 to 30% of the time, increasing eye contact is likely to be interpreted as interest and liking. However, as eye contact becomes extreme, increasing from 70 to 80 to 90% of the time, liking will tend to decrease. Such intense scrutiny suggests hostility, pathology, and privacy invasion. This implies new mediational and interaction hypotheses, as well as that the main effect of eye contact on liking will be nonmonotonic. A "golden mean" metatheorizing underlies the power of this nonmonotonic, pushing-to-an-extreme type of thought experiment.

Heuristic E13 involves arithmetical thought experiments such as imagining the effect on the dependent variable of reducing each conjectured antecedent to zero, thus helping the theorist decide whether each antecedent is a necessary or contributing cause. Examples include Clark Hull's exploration of whether "habit strength" and "drive" combine additively or multiplicatively to affect behavior, and NH Anderson's (1982) development of a cognitive algebra that could handle the "set size" effect.

Heuristic E14, conjecturing interactional multipliers of the banal hypothesis, serves as a final example of these Subcategory E "Simple Conversion" hypothesis-generating techniques. The thought experiment here involves mentally multiplying banal hypotheses by potential interaction variables. For example, starting with the banal hypothesis that the more similar the other person, then the greater one's liking for her or him, we then elaborate it by conjecturing how various situational and dispositional interacting variables would affect the parameters of the similarity-liking relation and why. Along these lines Byrne (1971) explored whether issue importance affected the height or the slope of the similarity-liking relation to discover the extent to which interpersonal similarity operates as a cue versus as a reinforcement.

F. Multiplying Insights by Conceptual Division

Defining a hypothesis as the assertion of a relation between variables clarifies the difference between Subcategories E and F heuristics. The five Subcategory E thought-experiment heuristics just considered all involve some mental manipulation of the relational component of the hypothesis (e.g. reversing its sign or its causal direction). In contrast, the four heuristics in this Subcategory F all involve mentally manipulating the hypothesis's variables rather than the relation between them. They involve playing some kind of word game to analyze a gross conventional variable into components that relate differently to the other variable in the hypothesis. Thus one multiplies relations by dividing variables. These verbal divisions that multiply insights can be done on any of the five logical types of variables that enter one's experimental designs (dependent, independent, mediating, interactional, and controlled variables). The word games proposed in the Subcategory F heuristics F15–F18 help bridge the gap between one's insight per se and the words one uses to express this insight to oneself and others by playing with labeling the variables in order to grasp more fully one's initial thought, much of which is lost in any given labeling discussed in McGuire (1989).

15. LINGUISTIC EXPLORATIONS The labels one initially uses for one's variables can usually be much improved by a variety of verbal explorations that provide a fuller grasp of one's initial insight. For example, one can develop alternative formal definitions in terms of genus and specific differences and examine which best catches the variable's crucial aspect that best accounts for its hypothesized relation to the other variable in the hypothesis. Alternatively, connotative definitions can be used by generating (or picking out of a thesaurus) synonyms (and antonyms) for the label. One can then "explore the limits" by examining which synonyms do versus do not enter easily into the hypothesized relation and analyzing why some synonyms fit better than others. One can then organize the sufficing synonyms by grouping and subordination, as when Campbell (1963) listed and organized multiple terms used interchangeably with attitudes. It is also clarifying to list attributes of the concept and rate them for centrality or organize them into a tree diagram.

A more complex variant is to list and organize alternative distinctions that have been made between one's own label and similar others, as McGuire (1985) did for the distinctions that have been drawn between attitudes and opinions. More formally, one can do a categorical meta-analysis, as in Johnson & Eagly's (1990) analysis of how persuasive impact is affected by different senses of involvement. One can also list and analyze conceptual distinctions that have been drawn by different researchers, e.g. McGuire's (1986) analysis of six quite varied characteristics that have been proposed to determine when social cognition or social representations are indeed social.

Denotive definitions also can be used, as when one analyzes what one means by "conservatism" by assigning familiar political figures to the different locations on the conservatism variable and then conjectures which of each politician's characteristics has determined one's perception of his or her location on the variable. Other wordplay usable as discovery tools are free associating to the label, analyzing its metaphorical or other figurative transformations, or tracing its etymology. This F15 heuristic includes word games so diverse that it probably should be divided into several distinct heuristics, each deserving its own training regimen.

16.–18. OTHER HYPOTHESIS-GENERATING CONCEPTUAL DIVISIONS Brief mention will be made of three other, more specific heuristics of this linguistic/conceptual analysis type as listed under Subcategory F in Table 1. F16 focuses on the independent variable of a banal hypothesis and conjectures alternative partial definitions in terms of which to vary it. For example, starting with the trite hypothesis that the credibility of a message's source enhances her or his persuasive impact, one can devise interesting partial definitions of credibility by reviewing a list of nonverbal cues—visual and vocalic—and noting or conjecturing which ones people use to infer a speaker's knowledgeability or trustworthiness.

Heuristic F17 focuses on the dependent rather than independent variable of the banal hypothesis, typically by selecting several alternative subscales for measuring it. For example, in the familiar hypothesis that frustration leads to aggression, one can generate a varied list of aggression measures and conjecture how they are differently affected by frustration and thus gain new insights into the meaning of aggression (e.g. it can even take the form of gift-giving as among the Kwakiutl, and can be turned inward as well as outward).

Heuristic F18 goes further in analyzing the dependent variables, not just into parallel subtypes as in F17, but into sequential steps. For example, one can analyze the output side of the communication/persuasion input/output matrix (McGuire 1985) by analyzing the persuasion process into its successive mediating substeps (exposure, attention, comprehension, agreement, etc) and conjecturing how one's independent communication variable of interest (e.g. the message's humorousness) will affect ultimate persuasive impact via its effect on each of these contributing mediating substeps. This often leads to predicting a nonmonotonic overall relation between the gross independent and dependent variables, and to predicting a plethora of interaction effects on the curve's parameters (McGuire 1968).

G. Jolting One's Conceptualizing Out of Its Usual Ruts

Subcategory G, the third subcategory of simple reconceptualizing procedures for generating new insights, includes four heuristics, G19–G22, that involve propelling one's thoughts out of their accustomed ruts by diverse modes that vary from simple mental gymnastics to dangerous pharmaceutical roulette.

19. SHIFTING ATTENTION TO AN OPPOSITE POLE OF THE PROBLEM This heuristic of reversing one's focus of attention (e.g. from the independent to the dependent variable of one's hypothesis, or from costs to benefits of a behavior, etc) is particularly useful when one's thoughts tend to be constrained within a conventional channel by barriers due to habituation, limited knowledge, emotional blocks, or cognitive styles that make it difficult to generate a diverse range of ideas about the hypothesis as initially approached. For example, if one is trying to develop a persuasion campaign to deter heroin abuse, one tends to do a "Casablanca" routine of rounding up the usual suspects by focusing on the drug's negative effects (physiological damage, diminished control by the addict over his or her life, dangerous illegality, overdosing, etc). However, these negatives are already well known by most addicts and are not deterring their doing heroin. Heuristic 19 calls for shifting one's thinking to an opposite pole by considering not the costs of heroin but the benefits that attract so many users to it. By understanding its attractions to users, one's campaign against heroin abuse can be made more relevant.

However, this conceptual shift from the costs to the benefits of a practice one regards as repulsive may itself arouse other creativity-stifling emotional blocks. Thinking creatively about appealing aspects of heinous behaviors such as heroin addiction, child abuse, or rape is distasteful, even if one is trying to appreciate their appeals the better to fight them. One can usually think of a few salient benefits, but it may be difficult to sustain enthusiasm for the task. To sidestep this new block one can shift perspectives from focusing on the dependent variable (requiring that one generate heroin addiction's benefits) to focusing on the independent variable (allowing one to go through one of the many lists of human motives or needs and conjecturing regarding each need how a life on heroin might be satisfying it). By diversifying and propelling one's thoughts by using such an available list of heterogeneous needs, one is provoked to recognize a wide spectrum of gratifications that might be obtained (at least in the short term) from using heroin. One's antiheroin campaign can then be made more sophisticated by taking those gratifications into account and showing their inadequacy. Another variant of this reversal heuristic is to start at the desired end state and work back to the current problem situation, as when Max Planck developed his revolutionary 1900 law of heat radiation by working backward from the desired explanation (Heilbron 1986).

20.–22. OTHER HEURISTICS FOR GETTING OUT OF ONE'S USUAL RUTS There is room here for only a brief description of three other Subcategory G techniques (listed in Table 1) for jolting one's thinking out of well-worn ruts. Heuristic G20 involves deliberately reversing one's accustomed thinking style. If ordinarily one goes for depth, then switch to seeking breadth. For example, when trying to identify origins of substance abuse, if ordinarily one would plunge deeply into a single category such as peer pressure, then this heuristic G20 calls for deliberately switching to considering less deeply each of a wide variety of causes such as peer pressure, mass media, physiological deficits, and lack of purpose. Or, if one is chronically a splitter and sees differences (e.g. between legal tobacco addiction and illegal cannabis addiction), then one might deliberately switch to being a lumper by considering how findings about abuse of one substance may be generalized to abuse of quite different substances. Training in use of this heuristic should start with diagnosing one's customary thought style and recognizing and trying out alternatives.

Heuristic G21 involves reexpressing one's hypothesis in multiple modalities [verbal, pictorial, logistical, symbolic, tabular, etc (McGuire 1989)]. Social scientists tend to be verbal types but should practice expressing hypothetical insights in other modalities, as when Petty & Cacioppo (1986) represent their evaluation-likelihood model as a flow chart. Some modalities may be especially apt for expressing certain insights or for certain purposes, and an individual researcher may resonate best with communicating her or his insights to self or others in one preferred modality. However, translating from one to another modality in either direction is likely to be provocative, so the researcher should work at gaining facility in moving among modalities in either direction, even though chronically each researcher will tend to use his or her most ego-syntonic modality.

Heuristic G22 involves using some physiological prod to jolt one's thinking out of the usual ruts. Chemical stimulants might be legal and conventional like caffeine, or illegal and stigmatized like LSD. If one is to use chemicals as a jolt to enhance hypothesis generating, one should lower one's base level of the substance so that when needed it will make a difference (e.g. one should forego drinking coffee until one needs it to keep alert through an all-nighter). Instead of chemical doses, one can use behavioral prods like hyperventilation or jogger's high, or purportedly mind-altering meditation tricks, or musical backgrounds, or massed practice to extinguish responses normally prepotent in the habit-family hierarchy. Low-inhibition states such as daydreams or even night dreams may allow elusive insights to surface, as when Kekulé formulated the hexagonal-ring model of the benzene molecule after dreaming of a serpent biting its own tail.

III. HEURISTICS CALLING FOR COMPLEX CONCEPTUAL ANALYSIS (MEDIATED INFERENCE)

Category III includes 10 heuristics that, like those in Category II, require conceptual analyses that go beyond the simple perceptual processes used in Category I but that do not require further analyzing of old or collecting of new data (as do the heuristics in Categories IV and V below). The 13 Category II heuristics above require only direct conceptual analyses in the form of thought experiments that take an isolated banal hypothesis and transform it by some simple mental operation such as asserting its contrary. The 10 Category III heuristics use conceptual analyses of more complex mediated types that bring the initial hypothesis into confrontation with additional propositions that allow mediated derivation of new insights. Three increasingly demanding subcategories of Category III heuristics are described in turn: H involves various uses of deductive reasoning from general propositions; I involves using conceptual structures to generate and diversify ideas; J uses general general metatheoretical intellectual schemata as scaffolding for building new conceptual structures.

H. Deductive Reasoning Procedures

23. GENERATING MULTIPLE EXPLANATIONS FOR A GIVEN RELATION Vienna Circle logical empiricism has, since the 1930s, habituated psychologists to recognizing that scientific hypotheses should be embedded in broader theoretical explanations rather than being investigated as isolated ad hoc assertions. Unfortunately, the search for at least one explanation tends to become a search for at most one explanation, in violation of the perspectivist tenet (McGuire 1983, 1989) that any relation is best thought of as obtaining for a multiplicity of reasons. Explaining relations once is not enough; the researcher should routinely go beyond a first explanation by using the "method of strong inference" to test not if a given explanation does or does not account for a significant proportion of the variance in the hypothesized relation, but to test to what extent the relation is accounted for by each of several explanations. In their World War II army indoctrination studies, Hovland et al (1949) accounted for purported delayed-action persuasion effects not only by the "discounting cue" explanation that has received a great deal of subsequent attention (Pratkanis et al 1988), but also by another half-dozen promising explanations such as sensitization, consistency, and two-step flow. That the field subsequently focused almost exclusively on the discounting cue explanation illustrates how needed this heuristic is, in that even when the initial report of a relation proposed multiple theoretical explanations, follow-up researchers tend to overcongregate on just one explanation.

24.–26. OTHER DEDUCTIVE-REASONING HEURISTICS Heuristic H24 involves alternating induction with deduction. One starts with a purported relation, e.g. the report by Hornstein et al (1975) that people become more helpful after hearing good news of a dramatic rescue from danger. One can induce several different principles that explain the relation, such as an affective principle (e.g. that helpfulness is promoted by people's tendency to act in accordance with their hedonic good mood, here induced by hearing of the happy escape) and a cognitive principle (e.g. that people tend to be more helpful to one another when they perceive human beings as generally helpful, as in the brave rescue report). After inducing such explanatory principles—affective and cognitive—one then shifts direction from induction to deduction by inferring new specific hypotheses. By reiterative inductions and deductions one can generate a program of research designed to exploit the ways in which altruism is an affectively and a cognitively determined process.

Heuristic H25, identifying and subtracting obscuring counterforces, is particularly useful in those all-too-common awkward histories where researchers have been testing a hypothesis that is so obvious that they have to apologize for bothering to test it, only to be further embarrassed when their obvious hypothesis fails to receive confirmation. An example is the hypothesis that the higher the perceived credibility of the source of a persuasive message then the more attitude change the message will induce, a hypothesis that might seem trivially obvious but that often fails to be confirmed in empirical tests. Using heuristic H25, one first abstracts the obvious mediator that makes the prediction trite (e.g. that more expert sources are more persuasive because they are perceived as knowing better the facts on the issue). One then conjectures counteroperating mediators (e.g. that the source's expertise evokes an audience's suspicion of guilty knowledgeability and prejudicial involvement, that the source is remote and unlike the audience members, etc) that tend to reduce persuasive impact. One then measures or manipulates the contrasting mediators and derives distinctive interaction predictions of each, e.g. when a highly expert source is shown taking a ludicrous but humanizing pratfall (Deaux 1972) his or her persuasive impact increases. Application of heuristic 25 to the credibility/persuasiveness relation provoked Petty & Cacioppo's (1986) evaluation-likelihood model and their theorizing about alternative paths to persuasion.

Heuristic H26, the hypothetico-deductive method, is more demanding of deductive elegance, calling for the researcher's generating a set of axioms (often obvious ones) covering the domain of inquiry and from their combinations deducing new, often surprising theorems for testing. The classical example is Euclid's geometry. A prime psychological example is Clark Hull's (1940, 1952) axiomatic rote-learning and behavioristic theories, from whose obvious general postulates were derived nonobvious predictions such as the reminiscence, asymmetrical serial position, partial reinforcement, and goal-gradient effects.

I. Using Thought-Diversifying Structures

This second type of Category III complex-inferential heuristics encourages constructing or borrowing a conceptual framework (ranging from a simple checklist to a formal polysyllogism and input-output matrix structure) and using it to propel and diversify one's thinking on a topic.

27. USING AN IDEA-STIMULATING CHECKLIST The utility of checklists for propelling and diversifying thought is recognized in a variety of practical undertakings and deserves more explicit consideration in scientific methodology. The researcher may take over a list, intact or with modifications, or may construct a new list during his or her continuing work in an area. For example, a health psychologist trying to select appeals that will be useful in a public health campaign may borrow an available list of wants [e.g. the Rokeach (1973) list of 16 instrumental and 16 terminal values] or may develop his or her own list, as was done by McGuire (1985) when he developed 2^4 partial views of human nature and used each to suggest health appeals. Each item in one's list can be divided into sublists, thus allowing the researcher either to keep a broad perspective on the big picture by using the first-order list or to fine-tune some specific aspect of the campaign by focusing on a sublist. Cross-fertilization among the sublists can improve each. For example, Table 1 lists five broad categories (I–V) divided into subcategories on different bases, thus offering the possibility of cross-fertilization (e.g. Category IV heuristics are subdivided into those involving single vs multiple studies while Category V heuristics are divided into qualitative vs quantitative). New heuristics might be suggested for each category if one interchanges their basis of division.

Constructing a new checklist calls for creatively developing a tool to augment creativity. With experience in an area one tends to develop a favorite checklist, but one should be on guard against drifting into a petrified routine that makes mechanical use of a once-successful type of list that blinds one to alternative ways of slicing the process. There may be a common danger that creative heuristics carry within themselves the seeds of their own destruction, in that as experience in their use makes one more sophisticated at constructing lists or case histories or whatever, one becomes increasingly stereotyped in using the technique, with the result that it eventually ends up narrowing rather than diversifying one's thoughts.

28.–29. OTHER HEURISTICS USING THOUGHT-DIVERSIFYING STRUCTURES Checklists are the most familiar thought-diversifying structures, but other, more elaborate structures can be still more provocative. Heuristic I28 involves converting simple checklists into more elegant structures, such as input/output matrices, tree diagrams, and flow charts. For example, McGuire (1985) combined diverse partial views of the person into a 2^4 matrix that can be used to generate motivational appeals in persuasive communications. Heuristic I29 involves formalizing the logical structure of one's conceptualization, e.g. into a formal polysyllogism. Some researchers regard logical formalization of a theory as antithetical to creative freedom, or at best as a postcreative cleaning-up for publication. However, McGuire (1989) shows how a theory's creative provocativeness is enhanced by formalization into a polysyllogism, each premise of which constitutes a creative catapult for generating new situational and dispositional interaction hypotheses.

J. Using Metatheories as Thought Evokers

A final triad of complex mediated-inference heuristics—J30, J31, and J32—encourages the researcher to exploit his or her preferred metatheoretical orientation to generate further insights.

30. THE EVOLUTIONARY FUNCTIONALISM (ADAPTIVITY) PARADIGM A functional, adaptivity orientation deriving from evolutionary presuppositions is probably the most common metatheory guiding contemporary psychologists, at least implicitly. When used to promote creative insights into behavior, this approach begins with considering the needs and capacities of human beings in relation to the opportunities and demands of environments in which the species has evolved and the individual has matured. One then conjectures behavioral principles by which people must be operating to have survived and evolved under such phylogenetic and ontogenetic conditions. Functional analysis often yields obvious propositions, such as that people behave in ways for which they have been rewarded for behaving in the past, but propositions that are individually trite can jointly yield unexpected theorems (e.g. Hull et al 1940). Further, not all functional postulates are individually obvious when one thinks dialectically. For example, even obvious behavioristic postulates (e.g. that reinforced performance strengthens habits and that unreinforced performance extinguishes habits) may have to be supplemented by corrective counterpostulates such as reactive inhibition and spontaneous recovery.

Thinkers who resonate with evolutionary adaptivity theorizing can enhance its provocativeness by considering behaviors like altruism and homosexuality, which paradoxically persist even though they seem to impose a reproductive disadvantage. It is accounting for these hard cases that guides the thinker in expanding his or her concept of adaptive selectivity [e.g. adding to it mechanisms like inclusive fitness, reciprocity, cognitive distortions, etc (A McGuire 1994)], which makes the concept more provocative. Evolutionary metatheorizing can lead the researcher into the political minefields of social Darwinism and sociobiology, but it would be maladaptive to abandon all use of intellectual tools that could lead to error or be politically incorrect.

31.–32. OTHER HEURISTICS USING METATHEORIES The evolutionary (functional, adaptivity) approach is not the only type of metatheorizing that can be used as a creative device. Heuristic J31, analogy, is the conceptual transformation most commonly used for creative hypothesis generating. My own most sustained use of this heuristic (McGuire 1964) chose biological inoculation (as in vaccination against smallpox, where an overprotected organism is preexposed to a weakened virus strong enough to stimulate but not strong enough to overcome the organism's immune system). I used biological inoculation as an analog for building up the belief defenses of a person raised in an ideological "germ-free" environment. I exposed the believer to a weakened dose of the attacking arguments, strong enough to stimulate without overcoming belief defenses before exposing the believer to a massive attack. The analogy suggested numerous hypotheses about inducing resistance to persuasion. Analogs may involve methods as well as substance, as when graph theory, previously used for analyzing interpersonal social systems (e.g. to predict how the group members will divide into cliques) is transferred analogously for use in analyzing intrapersonal cognitive systems (e.g. to predict how the person's thoughts will be partitioned into logic-tight compartments). Some analogs are widely shared by researchers in an era, as when the reflex arc metaphor underlying stimulus-response theorizing was used early in the twentieth century and then by midcentury had been largely replaced by the computer flowchart in cognitive theorizing.

The odd-sounding heuristic J32, quixotic defense of a theory, probably receives more use as a creative technique than is recognized. It involves embracing and sticking with a theory, continuing to derive testable implications from it despite its superficial implausibility, its obvious oversimplification, or its poor empirical track record. For example, Max Plank ended up with a fuller grasp of the revolutionary quality of the elementary quantum construct by his creative conservatism in stubbornly and unsuccessfully trying to fit the construct into classical physics theory. Greenwald et al (1986) discussed circumstances when it is productive to stonewall in defense of a nonconfirmed theory, in their case the discounting cue theory of delayed-action effects in persuasion. Not uncommon are prolonged Stakhanovite attempts to make do with an overly simplistic principle, as when congruity theorists (Estes 1950) maintained their revolutionary austere position in insisting that mere contiguity, without adverting to reward or punishment concepts, sufficed to explain learning. Attempts to make do with the linear operator model (Bush & Mosteller 1955) or signal-detection theory are other examples of the creative provocativeness of seeing how far one can get with a simplistic theory.

IV. HEURISTICS DEMANDING REINTERPRETATIONS OF PAST RESEARCH

Category IV heuristics, more than those in the preceding three categories, call for a professional background in that researchers using them must have some facility for working creatively with the area's research literature. Heuristics in a first Subcategory K call for delving into single past studies, while heuristics in a more complicated Subcategory L require bringing together multiple past studies.

K. Delving into Single Past Studies

33. ACCOUNTING FOR IRREGULARITIES IN AN OBTAINED RELATION Esthetic preference, such as a predilection for austere elegance, can serve as a creative tool. Such a minimalist esthete, when he or she finds that two variables are related by some complex function that looks like George Washington's profile, typically tries to decompose this complex relation into several rectilinear components. For example, dissonance theorists exhibited such an esthetic when they accounted for the several peaks and troughs in the relation between postchoice time passage and liking for a chosen alternative (Festinger 1964) or again, in accounting for the complex relation between confidence in one's own belief and avoiding exposure to counterarguments. In each of these cases the complex obtained relation was accounted for by multiple monotonic mediating relations. My rule of thumb is to decompose a tortuous obtained function into N + 1 underlying (mediational) processes, where N is the number of inflection points in the gross functional relation between the independent and dependent variables under study.

This research strategy may be carried out by one researcher or by an invisible college of researchers working on different ranges of a relation, as in the case of visual-perception researchers studying the relation between I and ΔI, where ΔI is the proportional change in illumination level (I) needed to produce a just-noticeable brightness difference. The complex relation between I and ΔI/I was gradually accounted for by successive conceptual decompositions. First, rod-vs-cone subprocesses were teased out to take into account what appeared to be two successive negatively accelerated curves; then special processes were postulated at very high and low illumination levels to account for observed oddities in the relation at both extremes of illumination; and then logarithmic and other scaling transformations were used to flatten out nonrectilinear functions, until the unwieldy ΔI/I curve was decomposed into an austere set of straight lines.

Such a search for monotonic and rectilinear parsimony is less a logical necessity than an esthetic preference. Even as an esthetic criterion, the austerity of rectilinearity is only one preference among many. Contemporary science may reflect a taste for austere simplicity but a zest for baroque, even rococo, may reassert itself, as when a new generation prefers not the Danish furniture cathected by their parents, but the beaded lampshades beloved by their grandparents. In the discovery phase of science, esthetic predilection, however arbitrary, can be valuable in pushing thinking in fertile new directions. Each scientist should be allowed, *de gustibus,* to follow his or her own esthetic radar for detecting the signal masked by a crescendo of noise. It is probably desirable that the Establishment esthetic criterion shifts periodically (e.g. either tactically, as between a preference for negatively accelerated growth curves vs one for sigmoid curves, or by a strategic shift, as when preference shifts between continuous vs discontinuous relations).

34.–36. OTHER HEURISTICS INVOLVING DELVING INTO SINGLE PAST STUDIES
Heuristic K34 is a specific subtype of K33 that deserves separate mention because the opportunity to use it occurs often and is simple to exploit creatively. It arises in the common case where a nonmonotonic inverted-U relation is found between independent and dependent variables. Such relations can be creatively interpreted as the resultant of two opposed mediating processes, both monotonic. For example, the finding that persuadability has an inverted-U relation to many personality variables suggests (McGuire 1968) that it is the resultant of two opposed underlying processes (e.g. self-esteem tends to enhance persuadability via the argument-comprehension mediator and to reduce persuadability via the argument-acceptance mediator). Heuristic 34 has been used creatively on inverted-U relations in the case of the reminiscence phenomenon, the serial-position curve, and the sleeper effect.

Heuristic K35, deviant case analysis, corrects the tendency of published studies to stress the overall obtained relation (as indicated by the regression line or by the piling up of cases in one diagonal of a 2 × 2 cross-tabulation) while downplaying outliers, the deviant cases that lie far off the secular trend line. McClelland's (1961) analyses showed that emphasis on achievement themes in nations' school storybooks in 1950 predicted the nations' economic growth from 1952 to 1958. Use of heuristic K35 involves going further by interpreting the outcome, not only as regards this general trend, but also as regards the deviant cases, the exceptional nations that fall far off the trend line, and so suggest new corrective insights (e.g. by considering why Poland, low in schoolbook achievement themes, showed high productivity growth, while Tunisia, high in achievement themes, showed low growth).

A fourth heuristic in this Subcategory K36, interpreting serendipitous interaction effects, exploits the fact that experimental procedures almost inevitably introduce into the design powerfully diagnostic variables (e.g. sex of participant, first vs second half of the trials, etc) that have a good track record for producing sizable main and interaction effects. Heuristic K36 calls for systematically analyzing and interpreting effects of these variables and cross-validating any post factum discoveries in subsequent studies.

L. Discovery by Integrating Multiple Past Studies

The four Subcategory K heuristics discussed above invite one to delve into results obtained within a single past experiment for discovery purposes. The three heuristics that illustrate Subcategory L, to which I now turn, are more demanding in that they require not simply reaching to one study but actively bringing together results of multiple past experiments.

37. RECONCILING CONFLICTING OUTCOMES OR NONREPLICATIONS Grim experience so accustoms psychologists to failures to replicate and even to seemingly opposite outcomes in similar studies that it takes an effort to regard such disappointments as particularly interesting. Yet conflicting results can reward closer scrutiny, especially when the conflicting studies are carried out by researchers with solid track records. When sets of conflicting studies are closely compared (either informally or in a meta-analysis) differences may be detected in definitions, measures, procedures, samples, etc, that suggest explanations of the conflicting outcomes and the relation's overlooked interactional boundaries. Most researchers can recall advances made in their area by reconciling conflicting outcomes. Examples from the attitude-change area with which I am fairly familiar include discrepancies between laboratory and field persuasion studies (Hovland 1959), the forced-compliance studies on whether the size of the inducement for public counterattitudinal advocacy increases or decreases internalized attitude change (Collins & Hoyt 1972), sex difference in persuadability (McGuire 1968), the selective-exposure prediction that people avoid belief-discrepant material, and delayed-action persuasive effects (Pratkanis et al 1988). Analyses of different experimental conditions that might reconcile conflicting results tend to reveal overlooked mediational and interactional variables. More elegantly, meta-analyses can be used creatively for across-study investigation of interaction variables that may affect the relation between the variables initially under study, as when Eagly & Carli (1981) used meta-analysis to investigate whether the sex difference in persuadability differed between public and private conformity conditions.

38.–39. OTHER HEURISTICS INVOLVING INTEGRATING MULTIPLE PAST STUDIES Several other heuristics that involve bringing together the results of multiple past studies will be mentioned briefly. Heuristic L38, creative exploitation of the complementarity of past studies, is more difficult to use than L37 because it is harder to detect complementarity than conflict among past studies. At least five subtypes of complementarity among studies can be looked for and exploited: (*a*) a moderating subtype, as when Milgram (1976) confronted obedience-to-authority studies with unresponsive-bystander studies; (*b*) a parallel subtype, as when Hull (1933) applied known principles of memorization to hypnotic phenomenon; (*c*) a differentiation subtype, as when one partitions a previously lumped set of studies into two distinctive subtypes (such as motor vs sensory suggestibility); (*d*) a mediational subtype, as when Petty & Cacioppo

(1986) distinguished between attitude-change studies in which central vs peripheral processing is involved; and (*e*) a labeling subtype, as when "foot in the door" studies are irresistibly contrasted with "door-in-the-face" studies.

This subcategory includes also heuristic L39, writing a review of the area in question. Reviewing the literature or writing a theoretical integration requires one to organize and integrate a heterogeneous set of studies, interpreting them creatively so that the whole set is more meaningful than the sum of the individual studies, as patterns emerge and new integrating and bridging hypotheses suggest themselves. Festinger (1957) developed dissonance theory while writing a review of the literature on rumors. Another illustration is the academic joke that if a professor wants to learn about a new area, she or he signs up to teach a course on it.

V. HEURISTICS NECESSITATING COLLECTING NEW DATA OR REANALYZING OLD DATA

This fifth broad category includes creative heuristics more demanding of professionalism than are categories I to IV in that they call for collecting new data or at least reanalyzing old data. I group these heuristics in qualitative Subcategory M and quantitative Subcategory N.

M. Qualitative Analyses

Six Subcategory M qualitative-analysis heuristics are listed in Table 1 in order of increasing demandingness of a priori theoretical guidance, beginning with simply allowing participants more freedom in expressing their responses to carrying out an elaborate strategy for developing a whole program of research.

40. ALLOWING OPEN-ENDED RESPONSES FOR CONTENT ANALYSIS A simple but productive way of obtaining revealing data is for the researcher to present a low profile, allowing the participant more leeway in responding. Research on a popular topic tends to be channeled into ruts worn by constant use of a few familiar manipulations and a few reactive scales that measure some conventional researcher-chosen dimensions. Stifling examples are the long preoccupation of human learning and memory research with nonsense-syllable material, and the confinement of self-concept research to the one dimension of self-esteem (as if people think of themselves only in terms of how good or bad they are). Such reactive measures provide as-if information on where the respondent would place the stimulus on the researchers' favorite dimension were the respondent ever to use that dimension, but fail to provide crucial as-is salience information on the extent to which the respondent actually does use this dimension. Reactive measures have an attractive economy when one wants to measure stimuli on the

popular dimension. Self-esteem is admittedly an important dimension of the self-concept, and if one insists on studying self-esteem it is efficient to use a reactive measure focused on it, rather than a less focused, laborious open-ended "Tell me about yourself" probe. Still, open-ended responses should be collected and analyzed at least occasionally (even though content-analysis systems are laborious to develop and use), because they tend to suggest neglected dimensions and provide insights into people's own phenomenological world as well as to the field's currently fashionable issues (McGuire 1984).

41.–45. OTHER QUALITATIVE ANALYSIS HEURISTICS Space limitations allow only brief mention of five other hypothesis-generating heuristics (M41–M45), which fall into the qualitative-data-analysis Subcategory M. Heuristic M41 calls for more hands-on participation by the principal investigator in the research routine (e.g. constructing stimulus and response material, collecting and entering data, talking with the subjects, etc) rather than leaving these tasks wholly to assistants. Such routine tasks serve to keep one's attention focused on the topic under study but also are undemanding enough to allow insight-provoking reverie that may enable the researcher to pick up unsuspected response patterns.

Heuristic M42, applying a current enthusiasm, does carry the risk of encouraging researchers to follow current fashions, applying some fad mechanically to diverse issues in a "have technique, will travel" style that is a bit ludicrous though sometimes useful. The enthusiasm may be for a new independent variable (e.g. nonverbal cues, facial neoteny), or a new dependent variable measure (e.g. facial EMG, magnetic resonance imaging), or a new explanatory mediational variable (e.g. implicit stereotypes, mood congruence), or a new analytic technique (meta-analysis, structural equation models). A slight variant, heuristic M43, encourages the enthusiast to ride off in all directions on his or her hobbyhorse, routinely introducing some favored variable (sex stereotypy, cognitive complexity, reaction times, etc) into the experimental design of every study, analyzing for new main and especially interaction effects. In the long run such enthusiasms are self-correcting, either paying off in revelations or losing the interest of the field (and perhaps even of the enthusiast).

Heuristic M44 involves pitting confounded factors against each other, as when Brock (1965) weighed source expertise against source similarity or when Argyll & Cook (1976) investigated the trade-off between interpersonal distance and eye contact as mutually substitutable nonverbal channels for communicating intimacy. Particularly provocative is heuristic M45, strategic planning of programs of research. McGuire (1989) has pointed out how our methodological books and courses focus almost entirely on tactical issues that arise in individual experiments (e.g. manipulating and controlling variables, measurement, statistical analysis, etc) to the neglect of strategic issues that arise in planning multiexperimental programs of research. McGuire (1989) describes how training in strategic planning of multiexperiment research programs can be carried out and how it is particularly effective in generating and testing new hypotheses, as well as in testing the initial hypotheses in more meaningful contexts.

N. Quantitative Analyses

Subcategory N moves beyond the qualitative heuristics for generating new hypotheses described above in Subcategory M. It includes heuristics demanding quantitative sophistication such as the four, N46–N49, ordered in Table 1 according to their increasing demandingness of a priori theorizing.

46. MULTIVARIATE FISHING EXPEDITIONS Multivariate analysis can focus narrowly on whether a conventional variable such as self-esteem is a unitary trait or whether self-esteem as regards physical appearance, intelligence, social acceptance, etc, might be at least partially independent and so relate differently to other variables. Multivariate analysis can also be used for the broader task of getting insight into a large, amorphous domain, as when one begins a program of research on nonverbal behavior by reducing the dozens of interrelated nonverbal behaviors to a more manageable subset of factors that not only achieves economy of grouping but also suggests underlying latent variables (e.g. intimacy, vocalic fluency) that mediate the effects of nonverbal cues on other variables. Analytical procedures such as factor analyses and structural equation modeling may serve better for testing among explicit a priori theories than for discovering new theories (Breckler 1984), but they also have their uses for discovering new relations (which can then be validated in subsequent studies).

OTHER QUANTATIVE ANALYSIS HEURISTICS The three other Subcategory N heuristics call for progressively more a priori theorizing and greater knowledge of quantitative methods. Heuristic N47 involves subtracting out of a relation the covariance due to a powerful, well-recognized mediator whose effect is so large that it obscures the lesser roles of other mediators of more theoretical interest. An example is Hovland's (1952) approach to concept learning by subtracting out the amount of information actually contained in positive vs negative instances, thus making it possible to analyze the remaining covariance to test for asymmetries in how well people can actually process equal units of affirmational vs negational information. Similarly, to study how message variables affect attitude change, it is revealing to subtract out the overpowering mediating effect of the amount of learning of message content, to determine the additional mediating role of cognitive elaboration (as emphasized by the cognitive-response theorists), or the role of source perception (as stressed by Eagly 1974).

Heuristic N48, computer simulation, is a discovery process that is becoming increasingly available and suited to problem areas that have resisted natural language and mathematical analyses (Ostrom 1988), as in Rumelhart & McClelland's (1986) exploration of whether and how children's mastery of regular and irregular English verb forms can be accounted for by associations, without recourse to rule learning. Researchers drawn to computer simulation of actual human processes must resist the danger of drifting into an artificial intelligence effort to describe an ideal operator, and the danger of settling for a product rather than process simulation of actual cognition.

Similarly demanding is heuristic N49, mathematical modeling, which is doubly suggestive in indicating both how well the model accounts for the relation in question and also what covariation remains (indicating the involvement of further independent variables) after adjusting for the account given by the mathematical model. For example, rich implications can be drawn regarding how well a simple model (like signal-detection theory) or a complex model (like a LISREL formulation) can account for obtained relations among variables of interest; and then still more novel inferences can be drawn to account for the covariations that remain after adjustment for the variance explained by the mathematical model.

FUTURE DIRECTIONS

In assembling this long list of techniques for creative hypothesis generating I have tried to be inclusive, allowing some of the heuristics to overlap, e.g. several heuristics use variants of interaction effects or of deviant-case analysis as a creative device. A vigorous shaking down may reduce the list to a slightly smaller set of more independent techniques. Conversely, the list could be expanded, both by subdividing some of the present heuristics (e.g. D7 or L38) and by adding new ones.

In addition, the classification system that I use to order and group the heuristics is sometimes based on superficial descriptive criteria. Other classifications might be more provocative or might better reflect intellectual processes involved in discovery and the means by which researchers can be trained in using these heuristics creatively. One elegant advance would be to organize the list into a matrix with current Categories I to V as the five row headings, and then to identify column headings that cross all five of the categories similarly, with the separate heuristics constituting cell entries.

The heuristics have been described in isolation, but they work synergistically, so that some combinations can together augment creativity more than the sum of their individual effects. How several heuristics can be combined into an effective programmatic strategy has been described in McGuire (1989).

Also needed are descriptions of how each heuristic can be effectively taught. I have developed training procedures for these 49 heuristics that use worksheet exercises to teach students each of the steps that the heuristic involves. Space limitations preclude my describing these training procedures here, except for giving some illustrative training procedures specifically for heuristic A1.

There is a need for more empirical work to test the heuristics' usefulness in creative hypothesis generating. I have done informal pedagogical evaluations of the training procedures for some of the heuristics with encouraging results, but systematic evaluation studies are needed to determine if each heuristic is effective in enhancing creativity, under what conditions, for whom, and for what reasons. Two training questions need answering: Do the training procedures enhance students' use of a given heuristic? Does enhanced use of the heuristic increase the creativity of the student's thinking? Such research could be productive, not only for the practical end of enhancing scientists' creativity but also for a basic theoretical yield of clarifying the nature of thinking.

Literature Cited

Abelson RP, Aronson E, McGuire WJ, Newcomb TM, Rosenberg MJ, Tannenbaum PH, eds. 1968. *Theories of Cognitive Consistency.* Chicago: Rand-McNally

Anderson NH. 1982. *Methods of Information Integration Theory.* New York: Academic

Anzieu D. 1986. *Freud's Self-Analysis.* Madison, CT: Int. Univ. Press

Argylle M, Cook M. 1976. *Gaze and Mutual Gaze.* Cambridge: Cambridge Univ. Press

Breckler SJ. 1984. Empirical validation of affect, behavior, and cognition as distinct components of attitude. *J. Pers. Soc. Psychol.* 47:1191–205

Brock TC. 1965. Communicator-recipient similarity and decision change. *J. Pers. Soc. Psychol.* 1:650–54

Bush RR, Mosteller F. 1955. *Stochastic Models for Learning.* New York: Wiley

Byrne D. 1971. *The Attraction Paradigm.* New York: Academic

Campbell DT. 1963. Social attitudes and other acquired behavioral dispositions. In *Psychology: A Study of a Science,* ed. S Koch, 6:94–172. New York: McGraw-Hill

Cialdini RB. 1993. *Influence: Science and Practice.* New York: Harper Collins. 3rd ed.

Collins BE, Hoyt MF. 1972. Personal responsibility-for-consequences: an integration and extension of the "forced compliance" literature. *J. Exp. Soc. Psychol.* 8:558–93

Deaux K. 1972. To err is humanizing: but sex makes a difference. *Represent. Res. Soc. Psychol.* 3:20–28

Eagly AH. 1974. Comprehensibility of persuasive arguments as a determinant of opinion change. *J. Pers. Soc. Psychol.* 29:758–73

Eagly AH, Carli LL. 1981. Sex of researchers and sex-typed communications as determinants of sex differences in influenceability: a meta-analysis of social influence studies. *Psychol. Bull.* 90:1–20

Estes WK. 1950. Toward a statistical theory of learning. *Psychol. Rev.* 57:94–107

Festinger L. 1957. *A Theory of Cognitive Dissonance.* Stanford, CA: Stanford Univ. Press

Festinger L. 1964. *Conflict, Decision, and Dissonance.* Stanford, CA: Stanford Univ. Press

Greenwald AG, Pratkanis AR, Leippe MR, Baumgardner MH. 1986. Under what conditions does theory obstruct research progress? *Psychol. Rev.* 93:216–29

Heilbron JL. 1986. *The Dilemmas of an Upright Man: Max Planck as Spokesman for German Science.* Berkeley, CA: Univ. Calif. Press

Hornstein HA, LaKind E, Frankel G, Manne S. 1975. Effects of knowledge about remote social events on prosocial behavior, social conception, and mood. *J. Pers. Soc. Psychol.* 32:1038–46

Hovland CI. 1952. A "communication analy-

sis" of concept learning. *Psychol. Rev.* 59: 461–72
Hovland CI. 1959. Reconciling conflicting results derived from experimental and field studies of attitude change. *Am. Psychol.* 14: 8–17
Hovland CI, Lumsdaine AA, Sheffield FD. 1949. *Studies in Social Psychology in World War II,* Vol. 3, *Experiments on Mass Communication.* Princeton, NJ: Princeton Univ. Press
Hull CL. 1933. *Hypnosis and Suggestibility.* New York: Appleton-Century
Hull CL. 1952. *A Behavior System.* New Haven, CT: Yale Univ. Press
Hull CL, Hovland CI, Ross RT, Hall M, Perkins DT, Fitch FB. 1940. *Mathematico-deductive Theory of Rote Learning.* New Haven, CT: Yale Univ. Press
Johnson BT, Eagly AH. 1990. Involvement and persuasion: types, traditions, and the evidence. *Psychol. Bull.* 107:375–84
McClelland DC. 1961. *The Achieving Society.* Princeton, NJ: Van Nostrand
McGuire AM. 1994. Helping behaviors in the natural environment: dimensions and correlates of helping. *Pers. Soc. Psychol. Bull.* 20:45–56
McGuire WJ. 1964. Inducing resistance to persuasion. In *Advances in Experimental Social Psychology,* ed. L Berkowitz, 1: 191–229. New York: Academic
McGuire WJ. 1968. Personality and susceptibility to social influence. In *Handbook of Personality Theory and Research,* ed. EF Borgatta, WW Lambert, pp. 1130–87. Chicago: Rand-McNally
McGuire WJ. 1973. The yin and yang of progress in social psychology: seven koan. *J. Pers. Soc. Psychol.* 26:446–56
McGuire WJ. 1983. A contextualist theory of knowledge: its implications for innovation and reform in psychological research. In *Advances in Experimental Social Psychology,* ed. L Berkowitz, 16:1–47. New York: Academic
McGuire WJ. 1984. Search for the self: going beyond self-esteem and the reactive self. In *Personality and the Prediction of Behavior,* ed. RA Zucker, J Aronoff, AI Rabin, pp. 73–120. New York: Academic
McGuire WJ. 1985. Attitudes and attitude change. In *Handbook of Social Psychology,* ed. G Lindsey, E Aronson, pp. 3:233–346. New York: Random House. 3rd ed.
McGuire WJ. 1986. The vicissitudes of attitudes and similar representational constructs in twentieth century psychology. *Eur. J. Soc. Psychol.* 16:89–130
McGuire WJ. 1989. A perspectivist approach to the strategic planning of programmatic scientific research. In *The Psychology of Science: Contributions to Metascience,* ed. B Gholson, A Houts, R Neimeyer, WR Shadish, pp. 214–45. New York: Cambridge Univ. Press
Milgram S. 1976. Interview. In *The Making of Psychology,* ed. RI Evans, pp. 187–97. New York: Knopf
Neustadt RE, May ER. 1986. *Thinking in Time: the Uses of History for Decision Makers.* New York: Free Press
Nisbett RE, Wilson TD. 1977. Telling more than we can know: verbal report on mental processes. *Psychol. Rev.* 84:231–59
Ostrom TM. 1988. Computer simulation: the third symbol system. *J. Exp. Soc. Psychol.* 24:381–92
Petty RE, Cacioppo J. 1986. *Communication and Persuasion: Central and Peripheral Routes to Attitude Change.* New York: Springer-Verlag
Pratkanis AR, Greenwald AG, Leippe MR, Baumgardner MH. 1988. In search of reliable persuasion effects. III. The sleeper effect is dead. Long live the sleeper effect. *J. Pers. Soc. Psychol.* 54:203–18
Rokeach M. 1973. *The Nature of Human Values.* New York: Free Press
Rumelhart DE, McClelland JL. 1986. On learning the past tenses of English verbs. In *Parallel Distributed Processing,* ed. DE Rumelhart, JL McClelland, 2:216–71. Cambridge, MA: MIT Press
Weil S. 1952. (1947). *Gravity and Grace.* London: Routledge & Kegan Paul

Annu. Rev. Psychol. 1997. 48:31–59

WOMEN AND CAREER DEVELOPMENT: A Decade of Research

Susan D. Phillips and Anne R. Imhoff

Department of Counseling Psychology, University at Albany, State University of New York, Albany, New York 12222

KEY WORDS: vocational behavior, gender issues, career counseling, occupational choice

ABSTRACT

This chapter reviews the vocational experiences of women as they have been revealed in the literature during the past decade. The review considers primarily empirical literature; findings are sampled relative to women's self-concept development, readiness for vocational choices, actual choices made, work-force entry, experiences at work, and retirement. Suggestions are made regarding the next generation of research on women and career development.

0084-6570/97/0201-0031$08.00

INTRODUCTION

Counseling psychologists have a long and rich tradition of studying questions of career development: how individuals explore their options, plan their directions, and enter and progress in their chosen vocational roles. Combined with attention to individuality and diversity (Betz & Fitzgerald 1993), this tradition has yielded a vast literature on how these questions are addressed concerning women. The research focusing specifically on gender issues in career development has undergone a veritable information explosion. In this chapter, we examine the vocational experiences of women as they have been articulated in the empirical literature of the past decade.

Some psychologists might argue that a chapter devoted solely to the vocational experiences of women might erroneously support the impression that the issues encountered in this literature are solely women's issues, rather than societal issues that have been studied among women. Others have argued for reframing the literature around gender as a social construct (e.g. Gilbert 1992). Although we tend to agree with these perspectives, we also think that it is necessary and informative to assess what we have learned about women and work, and to reset our sights on what we still need to know.

About a decade ago, Betz & Fitzgerald (1987) provided counseling psychology with a comprehensive and rigorous summary of the state of our knowledge about the career psychology of women. In their now-classic volume, they traced the literature from its infancy (when the primary question was "Why do women work?") to its more mature study of factors that affect women in their vocational lives. Their work served to cull from the literature important evidence that women's talents were underutilized in the paid work force and that there were powerful individual and environmental barriers to satisfying choices and occupational advancement. Now, a decade later, we return to the literature to determine how a decade of study has added to our understanding of work in the lives of women.

Early in our approach to this task, we identified thousands of relevant articles. It is possible to argue that the literature in this area has grown beyond the point where a comprehensive review is even feasible. Consequently, we have circumscribed our review to include reports of original research published in primary journals from 1986 through 1995. Given that the breadth of our task necessitated a certain selectivity, we acknowledge the hundreds of authors whose vital work we were unable to cite directly.

We have sampled the research findings to determine the direction of research in the past decade. In contrast with many reviews that focus on particular constructs or theories, we organize our observations according to issues raised during a woman's life span. That is, we have drawn from the literature those investigations that provide clues about what affects women in each of the various phases of their lives. This approach has naturally exposed areas in women's career development that have not been explored, and it helps us identify directions for future research. However, it may also obscure some potentially important features of the vocational experiences of particular groups of women. Although the women in the surveyed literature represent a broad array of circumstances, ethnicities, and cultures, we have focused on gender as the critical factor. We have, however, noted when certain findings implicate other important contextual variables.

We begin by summarizing the literature that has attempted to articulate those factors that likely influence the development of a woman's sense of herself and her possibilities. Next, we examine the literature relevant to women's decision making and their readiness to choose. We then review new knowledge about the actual choices women make, and about their entry into the work force. Last, women's experiences at work—as an adult in the paid work force—are examined, as well as their disengagement and retirement from their active work roles. We close with a postscript about the decade under review.

SELF-CONCEPT DEVELOPMENT

Underlying all subsequent aspects of women's vocational experiences are the following formative questions: "Who am I?" "How far can I go?" "What can I, as a woman, do?" Answers to these questions are generated early in life, well before the point of choice and implementation. The literature has offered both novel and familiar perspectives on these questions during the past decade.

Development of an Individual Identity

Among the more novel approaches in the literature has been the renewed focus on delineating just how identity develops for women (Jordan et al 1991), and how such relational perspectives on development help to explain women's vocational experiences (Forrest & Mikolaitis 1986). The empirical literature has elaborated these views, consistently showing that interpersonal and familial domains appear to be uniquely central to the development of identity for women (e.g. Bilsker et al 1988).

A more familiar topic for investigation is the emergence of the gender role aspects of the self-concept. Not unexpectedly, the formation of a child's gender role self-concepts, values, and career orientation has been traced to the achievement, attitudinal, and cultural characteristics of the home environment (e.g. Leong & Tata 1990, Sandberg et al 1987, Serbin et al 1993). In addition, studies continue to show that females develop more flexible self-concepts than males (e.g. Bridges 1989, Etaugh & Liss 1992), and that they consider themselves in a broader array of life domains (Curry et al 1994).

Development of Educational and Occupational Aspirations

Although women continue to have generally lower career aspirations than do comparably talented males (Leung et al 1994), there is some indication that women's aspirations have substantially increased over the past several decades (Gerstein et al 1988).

In exploring what accounts for the level of women's aspirations, several environmental factors have been implicated, including cultural and ethnic background (e.g. Evans & Herr 1991, Murrell et al 1991) among other factors (e.g. Hackett et al 1989). Individual differences are also influential. Many researchers have observed, for example, that the relative traditionality of gender role attitudes and occupational plans may limit the level of women's vocational and educational aspirations (e.g. Holms & Esses 1988, Murrell et al 1991).

Although studying individual or environmental factors alone has been fruitful, more promising and integrative have been a number of attempts to capture the broader complexity that surrounds women's aspirations. Harmon (1989), for example, demonstrated that aspects of women's aspirations can be traced to both individual development and sociocultural factors.

Considerable research has been devoted to tests of two major theoretical models of women's vocational aspirations proposed by Gottfredson (1981) and by Hackett & Betz (1981). Gottfredson's (1981) proposals about the gender-related circumscription of alternatives has received both support (e.g. Hannah & Kahn 1989, Lapan & Jingelski 1992) and challenge (e.g. Henderson et al 1988, Leung & Harmon 1990, Leung & Plake 1990). In particular, a number of studies have failed to support the prediction that the sex type of an occupation would be the most resistant to compromise (Hesketh et al 1990, Leung 1993).

The second major model—Hackett & Betz's (1981) application of the self-efficacy concept to the career development of women—has received more uniform support. Lent & Hackett (1987) provided a thorough review and critique of the early self-efficacy literature. Subsequent research has documented strong support for the tenets of this social cognitive theory (e.g. Hackett et al 1990, Lent et al 1991, Scheye & Gilroy 1994). Differences in self-efficacy have also been traced to gender and ethnicity (e.g. Gorrell & Shaw 1988, Hackett et al 1992, Lauver & Jones 1991). Women continue to show higher self-efficacy for female-dominated pursuits than for less traditional activities (e.g. Bridges 1988, Matsui 1994).

Despite voluminous research on the factors that influence the development of educational and occupational aspirations, remarkably few interventions have been reported that might facilitate this aspect of development. Betz (1992) outlined how interventions for women might be organized around the antecedents of self-efficacy. Also, a number of intervention strategies have been suggested to prevent underachievement among talented females, often considered an "at risk" group (e.g. McCormick & Wolf 1993). Most recently, Shamai (1994) demonstrated that a program aimed at reducing gender stereotypes for elementary school teachers produced higher aspirations among their male and female pupils.

Ideas About What Women Can Do

Ideas about what vocational roles are appropriate for women and men are formed early and are evident in children's stories, activities, and attributions (e.g. Trepanier-Street et al 1990, Weisner & Wilson-Mitchell 1990). Restrictive ideas about appropriate roles remain evident during the secondary and college years (Taber 1992, Ward 1991). There is some evidence that boys are more restrictive in their ideas about appropriate roles for either gender (e.g. Alpert & Breen 1989), and that ideas about what is appropriate for males are more rigidly held than ideas about what is appropriate about females (Henshaw et al 1992). However, despite what may be seen as increasing flexibility about women's roles, significant negative consequences can still be expected if women engage in gender role deviant behavior, such as academic achievement or career success (Janman 1989, Pfost & Fiore 1990).

The role of the media in forming—or at least in reflecting—expectations about social and occupational roles has received considerable inquiry. Although several studies have documented that the media depiction of women has moved toward less stereotyping and more accuracy about the diversity of women's roles (e.g. Chafetz et al 1993, Sullivan & O'Connor 1988), the dominant conclusion derived from the study of general publications, television, and children's materials (e.g. Heintz 1987, Lovdal 1989) is that the portrayal of men and women continues to be quite traditional. Further, media may exert a demonstrable impact on children's occupational knowledge and role identification (Wroblewski & Huston 1987).

In a separate line of research, a number of investigators have studied gender-linked perceptions about occupations. They find that while gender stereotyping of occupations is still present, ratings are significantly less stereotyped from those reported in the past (e.g. Beggs & Doolittle 1993). However, it has also been noted that adolescent and adult males tend to stereotype more in their judgments about occupations than females, that older adults tend to stereotype more than younger adults, and that increased information about actual job activity information may elicit less stereotypical responses (e.g. Clarke 1989, Jessell & Beymer 1992).

Given changing percentages of men and women within selected occupations, would the desirability and prestige of such occupations change because of an increase in the minority incumbents? Although early studies indicated no differential desirability of occupations with increased minority representation (Johnson 1986, Shaffer et al 1986), subsequent studies have suggested that an increase in women in a previously male-dominated occupation would result in an upgrade in occupational desirability to women but not necessarily to men (Johnson 1991, 1992).

Although a certain narrowness in ideas about what women can do appears quite pervasive, some efforts to broaden such ideas have been successful among children and adolescents. Cognitive training (Bigler & Liben 1990, 1992) and purposeful exposure to models (Bailey & Nihlen 1990, Smith & Erb 1986, Tozzo & Golub 1990) have been effective in reducing gender role stereotyping associated with occupational activities.

READINESS TO CHOOSE

Where issues of self-concept development focus on the factors that influence how a woman defines herself, the issue of readiness to choose focuses more on the processes through which she prepares herself to make educational and vocational choices. In contrast with most other areas of inquiry in women's career development, questions of readiness have received considerably less attention in the literature.

Vocational Maturity

Central to the question of readiness is vocational maturity, or how well individuals are prepared to address the choices and tasks of their life stage. The past decade has produced some interesting controversy about gender differences in vocational maturity. Although some investigators report greater female maturity (e.g. Munson 1992, Westbrook et al 1988), others report no gender differences (e.g. Westbrook & Sanford 1993). More specifically, the results of several investigations suggest that females may be more advanced in particular aspects of maturity, such as in active involvement in planning and exploring (Fouad 1988, Stumpf & Lockhart 1987) and in considering the affective elements of career information (Bailey & Nihlen 1989). Consistent with some of the relational perspectives on women's development, career exploration and maturity among females appears to be tied to optimal family cohesion and individual independence (Fullinwider-Bush & Jacobvitz 1993, King 1989). In addition, there is evidence that being more vocationally mature facilitates the quality of women's occupational choices (Raphael & Gorman 1986, Westbrook & Sanford 1993).

Barriers to Effective Decision Making

Women may experience a number of barriers in preparing for career decisions. Although women perceive different barriers than men (Swanson & Tokar 1991), there appear to be no clear gender differences in the nature or level of indecision (e.g. Hartman et al 1987, Rojewski 1994) or in coping with indecision (O'Hare & Beutell 1987). Rather, decisional difficulties may be more expectable for those individuals of either gender who have less traditional gender-related characteristics and attitudes (Fassinger 1995, Gianakos & Subich 1986, Hetherington & Orzek 1989).

In contrast with the findings about overall indecision, researchers have found consistent differences in the way individuals organize their occupational knowledge. In particular, males show greater cognitive differentiation than females, who in turn show greater cognitive integration than males (e.g. Brown 1987, Neimeyer et al 1989, Neimeyer & Metzler 1987).

Helping Women Become Ready to Choose

Although the literature on factors affecting women's readiness to choose is limited, there has been considerably greater focus on developing interventions that might help women become ready. Effective means of enhancing women's readiness through group interventions have been documented by Rodriguez & Blocher (1988) and Mawson & Kahn (1993), and a number of perspectives have been advanced regarding strategies for broadening the array of options explored by women (e.g. Brooks 1988, Richman 1988). Furthermore, individual barriers to decision making were demonstrably reduced for college women by focusing the intervention on the particular challenges of women's career development (Foss & Slaney 1986). It is interesting to note that while a group intervention for gifted college students reduced indecision, it also increased awareness of external barriers and intrapersonal conflicts for the female participants (Schroer & Dorn 1986).

Despite increased awareness of the need for counselors and others to be particularly careful to avoid gender bias, evidence continues to suggest that many counseling tools and interventions restrict the options considered by women. For example, Hansen et al (1993) documented gender differences in the structure of interests, which raises questions about the applicability of Holland's theory—and its derivative tools—for women. Others have argued for caution in using interest inventories with women, given their tendency to perpetuate existing sex segregation (e.g. Lancaster & Drasgow 1994). Unfortunately, gender-based stereotypes continue to be evident in the recommendations of some counselors and teachers (Hopkins-Best 1987, Stewart et al 1989).

THE CHOICE MADE

By far the majority of the literature on women's preimplementation vocational experiences has focused on the choices made by women. These choices concern not only what occupation will be pursued but also how multiple life roles will be integrated into a woman's life plans.

Occupational Choices

Given the longstanding concern that women's choices have been restricted to those occupations and activities that are "traditional" for women, the dimension receiving almost exclusive attention is the degree of traditionality of the occupational pursuits that women choose. A number of factors, reviewed below, are predictors of the degree of traditionality in a woman's vocational choices. In considering this literature, however, note that terms such as "nontraditional," "pioneer," "innovative," and the like may have very different actual definitions from study to study (Hayes 1986).

SELF-REFERENCED THOUGHT Focusing specifically on the beliefs held by individuals about what they can do, a number of investigators have studied the role of self-efficacy, self-esteem, and other self-perceptions in determining the traditionality of what is chosen, with generally uniform results. Males and females continue to differ in their self-efficacy and expectations for success for traditionally male-dominated occupations (Brooks & Betz 1990, Post-Kammer & Smith 1986), although there is some question about whether this prevents women from considering such occupations (e.g. Clement 1987). Self-referenced thought has been implicated in the range of careers considered (e.g. Church et al 1992, Rotberg et al 1987), in the level of interest expressed (e.g. Lapan et al 1989), and in the level of performance achieved (e.g. Hackett et al 1992). There is also some indication that self-efficacy expectations may be a stronger predictor of choice than are past performance or achievement (Hackett & Betz 1989). Drawing upon findings such as these, Lent et al (1994) proposed an integrative framework from which to predict interest, choices, and performance. Their model builds on Bandura's (1986) social cognitive model, and it highlights the importance of reciprocal influence among behavior, person, and environment.

GENDER-REFERENCED CHARACTERISTICS AND ATTITUDES Gender-referenced personal characteristics and gender role attitudes have also received considerable attention. In this regard, the literature continues to document that gender-referenced characteristics and gender role attitudes play an important role in the choices women make. Women who report more instrumental traits, together with more expressive traits, are more likely to express interest in or choose more nontraditional fields (e.g. Gianakos & Subich 1988, Kapalka & Lachenmeyer 1988, Mazen & Lemkau 1990), and they tend to make decisions that enable them to use their abilities (Betz et al 1990). Similarly, women with more egalitarian attitudes about women's roles more often engage in nontraditional occupational pursuits (Chatterjee & McCarrey 1989). In addition, Eccles (1987) offered a useful way to conceptualize the role of various gender role–related factors in women's choices, and Fassinger (1990) and O'Brien & Fassinger (1993) provided compelling data to support and refine their comprehensive model of individual and environmental factors in women's occupational choices.

SCHOOL AND FAMILY Parental attitude continues to be implicated in the degree of traditionality of a child's choices and accomplishments (e.g. Davey & Stoppard 1993, Mau et al 1995, Serbin et al 1993), particularly for the more nontraditional choices (Fitzpatrick & Silverman 1989). A number of investigators have also attempted to identify the separate influences of mothers and fathers, with conflicting results (e.g. Barak et al 1991, Hoffman et al 1992). Concerning the school environment, teachers are clearly influential in women's nontraditional choices (e.g. Fitzpatrick & Silverman 1989), as are opportunities for elective science and technology courses (Farmer et al 1995). In addition, childhood playmates and play activities may set the stage for developing the skills and attitudes necessary to pursue nontraditional occupations (e.g. Cooper & Robinson 1989).

INTERVENTIONS AND ASSISTANCE Numerous authors have offered ideas about how teachers, counselors, and employers can help to broaden the options chosen by women (e.g. McCormick 1990, Noble 1987, Soldwedel 1988). Although Betz (1989) highlighted the need for such positive action in her discussion of the inherently discriminatory character of the "null environment," there has been relatively little evidence that such interventions work. Direct short-term interventions (Cini & Baker 1987), interventions with teachers (Shamai 1994), and videotaped models (VanBuren et al 1993) have been among the less successful attempts to increase the diversity of alternatives chosen by women. In a novel approach that involves teaching children about decision rules, Bigler & Liben (1990) demonstrated that although the intervention was successful in altering ideas about what women can do, it was unsuccessful in broadening personal alternatives. Somewhat more successful was Foss & Slaney's (1986) focus on the broad scope of women's choices and lifestyle options, and Rea-Poteat & Martin's (1991) intensive program exposing girls to nontraditional options and experiences.

Planning for Multiple Roles

According to the literature published during the past decade, women appear to be placing increased importance on goals in the work domain. This change has not detracted from the importance women give to the home and family domain, nor diminished the expected conflicts among roles (e.g. Fiorentine 1988, Morgan 1992). As might be expected, this shift has presented women with additional challenges in their career planning. Women appear to be alert to these challenges early in their planning (e.g. Russell & Rush 1987); at least one intervention strategy, however, has been reported to enhance this awareness (Gerken et al 1988).

Where previous literature tended to examine primarily the stressors associated with enacting multiple life roles, the past decade has witnessed an increased emphasis on planning for, and choices about, those roles. Furthermore, several authors have offered models or measures to help to organize and study issues associated with multiple life roles, including expectations about various life roles (Amatea et al 1986), home-career conflict (Tipping & Farmer 1991), and multiple role realism (Weitzman 1994). Although it may be too soon to know the consequences of such efforts, there is some evidence that planning may pay off and result in lower role conflict and more effective problem solving (Steffy & Ashbaugh 1986).

Prominent in the area of multiple roles has been examination of gender differences in orientations toward work and relational roles (Cook 1993). Although Super's (1980) articulation of a life-space model of career development highlighted multiple role salience as a factor for both men and women, it has been repeatedly demonstrated that there are persistent gender differences in thoughts about how work and family roles are conducted (e.g. Covin & Brush 1991, DiBenedetto & Tittle 1990, Lips 1992, Livingston & Burley 1991, Schroeder et al 1993). Although young men and women may demonstrate comparable career commitment (Katz 1986) and similar attitudes about the occurrence of various adult roles (Sullivan 1992), there are also notable gender differences in time perspective, in role expectations, and in implicit ideas about what adulthood will be like (Greene & Wheatley 1992, Stevens et al 1992).

In addition, researchers have attempted to identify the factors contributing to a woman's work orientation. In this vein, a strong orientation toward work has been linked to such individual factors as vocational maturity (Nevill & Super 1988), self-efficacy (Stickel & Bonett 1991), personality and attitudinal factors (Douce & Hansen 1990, Keith 1988), and religious orientation (Morgan & Scanzoni 1987). Similarly, the importance of significant others has also been demonstrated (e.g. Hackett et al 1989). Illustrating the complexity of multiple life commitments, conflicting findings have been reported about the relationship between a nontraditional occupational choice and plans for a strong commitment to home or traditional life roles (e.g. O'Connell et al 1989). Fassinger (1990) offered a comprehensive illustration about how multiple factors are important to the prediction of career orientation for women. Finally, several authors have examined possible ethnic factors associated with women's orientation toward work and education (e.g. Cardoza 1991, Granrose & Cunningham 1988, Murrell et al 1991, Weathers et al 1994).

ENTERING THE WORK FORCE

As is true with many other stages of women's career development, entry into the work force seems to be more complex for women than for men, given gender discrimination and stereotyping, and the demands of multiple roles.

Barriers to Entry

Researchers have traced the effects of gender on several aspects of accessing the work force, from evaluations of one's resume (e.g. Ryland & Rosen 1987) to men's attributions about job acquisition (e.g. Goudge & Littrell 1989). Although there is considerable evidence of gender-based stereotyping and discrimination (e.g. Reskin & Padavic 1988), a number of investigators have found that previous experience with (or information about) a successful woman in a traditionally male occupation decreases gender bias in evaluation and selection decisions made by both student and professional judges (e.g. Glick et al 1988, Heilman et al 1988). From a different perspective, Betz & Hackett (1987) highlighted the agentic behaviors that women may use to reduce barriers to career entry and to create educational and vocational opportunities for themselves.

Reentering the Work Force

One aspect of career development more typical to women than men is role exiting and reentry. Rather than going directly from school to work, many women first engage in full-time family roles, returning to school or work later in their lives. As such, the characteristics of women who reenter school and work roles has been the subject of some investigation, though the research is limited (e.g. Breese & O'Toole 1995, Clayton & Smith 1987, MacKinnon-Slaney et al 1988).

A comparatively larger body of literature has developed around the issue of interventions designed to support the career development of reentry women. Several intervention programs were described in the early part of the decade, many of which focus on specific populations of reentry women, including women entering nontraditional and professional careers (e.g. Towns & Gentzler 1986), displaced homemakers (VanAllen & Wilford 1986), reentry college women (Roy 1986), and women who have lost low-skill jobs (Freeman & Haring-Hidore 1988). In addition to describing reentry intervention programs, some authors have tested the efficacy of their interventions. For example, Slaney & Lewis (1986) compared the effects of administering two different interest measures, finding both equally effective and satisfying for reentry college women.

EXPERIENCES AT WORK

The literature on women's experiences at work has grown exponentially in the past decade and has yielded numerous studies on topics including women's participation in the labor force, management of stress and role conflict, and barriers to women's career advancement.

Work-Force Participation: Continuity, Discontinuity and Change

A variety of factors have been studied about the continuity, discontinuity, and change in women's careers. To integrate those found to influence women's participation in the work force, a number of conceptual models have been introduced and tested. Among them are models that attempt to account for the complexity of women's development, the multiple determinants of career continuity and discontinuity, and the different, interconnected life cycles that seem to characterize women's career development (e.g. Evans 1985, Seiden 1989). Other authors have focused more specifically on testing developmental models of women's career attitudes and intentions (Ornstein & Isabella 1990) or on new ways of understanding career commitment (e.g. Chusmir 1986, Lopata 1993, Schaubroeck et al 1989), job change, and turnover (e.g. Chusid & Cochran 1989, Schaubroeck et al 1989).

INDIVIDUAL AND OCCUPATIONAL FACTORS There is considerable evidence that women's career patterns are changing to reflect higher levels of employment, role innovation, and education, and smaller families started later in life (e.g. Tangri & Jenkins 1986). Along with these changes is a continuing recognition of the influence of family factors on women's careers (e.g. Tangri & Jenkins 1986, Scott & Hatalla 1990). As such, a number of researchers have attempted to isolate the contributions of personal and family factors affecting the work-force participation, work continuity, and role commitment. Variables of interest have included mother's attitudes toward childcare (Kirschenbaum & Merl 1987), marital and family status (Duncan et al 1993, Stohs 1992), husband's career type (Tesch et al 1992), husband's attitude toward wife's employment (Stoltz-Loike 1992), and individual characteristics (Stohs 1991, Stoltz-Loike 1992). Investigators have also focused attention on the effects of gender on job change (e.g. Weisberg & Kirschenbaum 1993) and the effects of educational level and gender role attitudes on women's career commitment (Matsui et al 1991).

Comparatively few studies have isolated occupational characteristics alone as correlates of women's career continuity. The primary feature of occupations studied in this way is the relative traditionality of the work (e.g. Olson et al 1990). More often, in studying women's intentions to change or leave jobs, researchers have considered the role of family factors (e.g. parental status) in combination with specific work variables like opportunity for advancement and office politics (Rosin & Korabik 1990), job rewards (Rosenfeld & Spenner 1992), or satisfaction with pay (Roberts & Chonko 1994). Isolating the relative weight of family and work variables seems to get at the matter of role conflict, and how one's subjective sense of work vs family conflict affects intentions to leave work. These variables, along with job satisfaction and commitment, were investigated specifically by Good et al (1988). Others have attempted to explain women's career patterns in general by focusing on relative role priorities for family and work (e.g. Kahn & Lichty 1987).

ASSISTANCE AND INTERVENTION EFFORTS Considering the evidence that there has been a great deal of change in women's career patterns over the years, and the subsequent balancing and changing of life roles, one might expect that the empirical literature on interventions in this area would be growing at a rapid pace. Surprisingly, there appears to be a dearth of such literature. What has been published seems to reflect the needs of special populations of women (e.g. Melcher 1987). More broadly applicable, however, is the recent work in the area of career counseling with couples (e.g. Benjamin 1992).

Stress, Conflict, and Coping

One area that has received considerable emphasis during the past decade is the literature on gender differences in stress, work-family conflict, and coping. Broadly, the research has related various individual, family, and work factors to psychological and physical well-being. Indices of psychological "well-being" have included burnout (e.g. Burke & Greenglass 1989), stress and strain (e.g. Niles & Anderson 1993), and self-esteem and depression (e.g. Baruch & Barnett 1986). Variables thought to influence well-being include ethnicity, husbands' views about women's employment, household assistance, occupational rank, and traditionality of the woman's occupation (e.g. Geller & Hobfoll 1994, Harlan & Jansen 1987, Pines & Guendelman 1995, Richard & Krieshok 1989).

MANAGING MULTIPLE ROLES Within the stress and coping literature, one area that seems to hold particular relevance for working women is the research on combining multiple roles. In particular, the question has been raised about the possible reciprocal effects of combining life roles and physical and emotional well-being (e.g. Aryee 1992, Gilbert & Rachlin 1987). The evidence to date suggests that combining multiple roles may compromise neither a woman's physical health (e.g. Hibbard & Pope 1991) nor her psychological well-being (e.g. Baruch & Barnett 1986) and may in fact be associated with higher self-esteem (Pietromonaco et al 1986).

Work-family conflict Sources of conflict between work and family roles have become the subject of intense investigation in the past ten years (e.g. Beutell & O'Hare 1987, Loerch et al 1989). Specific factors found to influence women's work-family conflict include gender role attitudes (Izraeli 1993), family climate and cooperation regarding domestic responsibilities (Wiersma & Van den Berg 1991), and perceived gender role attitudes of significant others in a woman's life (Tipping & Farmer 1991). In addition to family and individual factors, a number of researchers have considered the role of various work characteristics on the relative difficulty of combining career and family roles (e.g. Olson et al 1990). Gilbert (1994) provided an updated discussion of work-family conflict and sources of support.

Sharing domestic responsibilities Another area of particular relevance for dual-earner couples is research on how couples share household and childcare responsibilities. Research has documented the relationship between marital satisfaction and couples' perceptions of how equitably household work and parenting is divided (e.g. Dancer & Gilbert 1993). As such, many researchers have attempted to discover the determinants of household division of labor. Predictors have included the number of hours a wife works, the relative income of the two spouses, (e.g. Deutsch et al 1993), the educational attainment of the partners, and the gender-related attributes of the husband (e.g. Kiker & Ying 1990). Still, a number of studies indicate that while women have taken on additional roles outside the home, their level of involvement with childcare and household responsibilities has not changed relative to their husbands (e.g. Duxbury & Higgins 1991). Apparently women are still involved in more childcare than men, even in dual-income households (e.g. Leslie et al 1991).

SUPPORT AND COPING Given the stress and conflict inherent in the dual-worker lifestyle, a number of investigators have attempted to identify the kinds of coping strategies used by such couples (e.g. Wiersma 1994), and some have found a significant relationship between types of coping and marital satisfaction (Houser et al 1990). Researchers have attempted to link use of various types of coping strategies with gender (e.g. Anderson & Leslie 1991). Others have focused on the issue of social support, specifically whether social support influences coping (Greenglass 1993) and what factors influence the provision of social support in dual-earner families (Granrose et al 1992). Several authors have suggested coping strategies to help women balance their multiple roles (e.g. Paddock & Schwartz 1986).

Among the research on support and coping, we found that an impressive body of literature has developed in the area of interventions for helping women and dual-career couples cope with role stress and conflicts (e.g. Avis 1986, Sperry 1993, Wilcox-Matthew & Minor 1989). Finally, a small group of comparative outcome studies demonstrated the efficacy of different interventions for working women (e.g. Higgins 1986, King et al 1986).

Women's Career Development at Work

CAREER ADVANCEMENT That the career experiences and advancement of women is different from those of men has been documented across many professional areas, with most studies finding that men advance faster, further, and with greater compensation (e.g. Cohen & Gutek 1991, Jagacinski et al 1987, Morgan et al 1993, Schneer & Reitman 1995). Several investigators have attempted to explain these gender differences in career advancement. For example, Lassalle & Spokane (1987) studied labor force participation patterns and found that more consistent labor force participation was associated with enhanced occupational advancement. However, women did not appear to move in and out of the work force as often as expected. Others have confirmed that gender differences in career advancement cannot be solely explained by intermittent work-force participation by women (e.g. Jagacinski et al 1987).

The issue of tokenism has also been empirically explored regarding women's career development, and mounting evidence suggests that gender and tokenism interact to effect differential career advancement. Specifically, it has been repeatedly suggested that "standing out" as a male in a female-dominated field may have career advantages for men, although the reverse may not be true for women (e.g. Ott 1989).

Salary In the research addressing specific aspects of career advancement of men and women, "advancement" has commonly been operationalized according to salary. Research has consistently found significant disparities between the salaries of working men and women (e.g. Corzine et al 1994, Stroh et al 1992). Often these differences are found even when controlling for education, age, experience, and performance (e.g. Cox & Harquail 1991). To explain these salary differences, researchers have considered the influence of multiple roles. Apparently the number of roles may interact with sex, so that marriage and parenthood is associated with higher salaries for men but lower salaries for women (e.g. Cooney & Uhlenberg 1991). Another hypothesis is that the gender wage gap is due to women's disinclination to negotiate over salary; however, empirical evidence fails to support this notion (Gerhart & Rynes 1991). Finally, a number of researchers have studied the relationship between job evaluations and gender type of jobs, arguing that bias in job evaluations explains the lower salaries associated with female-typed jobs (e.g. Mount & Ellis 1989).

Occupational status Evidence consistently suggests that despite comparable educational qualifications, tenure, and occupational attitudes, women have not achieved occupational status comparable to that of men (e.g. Robinson & McIlwee 1991). Researchers have attempted to explain differential attainment of occupational status by focusing on gender-related traits (e.g. Fagenson 1990), or on family variables like marital status, parental status, and educational level (Airsman & Sharda 1993). One explanation for women's lower occupational status may be that men, currently in higher-ranking positions, prefer to promote other men. In an analog investigation by Saal & Moore (1993), the promotion of a same-sex candidate over an opposite-sex candidate was perceived as more fair than was the reverse.

Performance evaluations Much of the discrepancy between salaries and occupational status between men and women may hinge on gender differences in performance evaluations. As such, this area has come into sharper focus in the late 1980s and early 1990s, and investigators have found a relationship between gender, or perceived masculinity/femininity, and performance evaluations (e.g. Comer 1992, Maurer & Taylor 1994). Some evidence suggests that exposure to women in professional occupations may help reduce some of the negative evaluations of women in professional careers (Fandt & Stevens 1991).

BARRIERS TO ADVANCEMENT The literature on barriers to women's career advancement has continued to grow since Betz & Fitzgerald's (1987) review. Among the noteworthy discussions of gender issues in career development are Borman & Guido-DiBrito (1986) and Solomon et al (1986). Other research has focused more specifically on the types of barriers that inhibit the career progress of working women.

Stereotyping and sexual discrimination Recently Melamed (1995) examined a number of explanations for gender differences in career success and salary level among British workers and found that between 55 and 62% of the variance in career success could be attributed to sex discrimination. Not surprisingly, past experience with female coworkers has a positive effect on male coworkers' and supervisors' attitudes toward female coworkers (Palmer & Lee 1990).

A subgroup of research focusing on perceptions of discrimination suggests that not all individuals (men and women) believe that women experience inequality of opportunities (e.g. Crosby & Herek 1986). This area of research conveys a recognition by researchers that there is some variety in the number and types of potential barriers perceived by women. One contribution toward assessing these barriers was offered by Swanson & Tokar (1991) in their development of the Career Barriers Inventory.

Sex segregation There is substantial evidence that the work force remains highly sex segregated (e.g. Jacobsen 1994). Some authors have tested the hypothesis that women are more highly concentrated in jobs that have lower penalties for job interruptions, that is, that female type jobs are more compatible with parenting roles. However, research has not supported this hypothesis (e.g. Glass & Camarigg 1992), which suggests that discrimination may play a larger role in sex segregation than choice. For a more extensive review of this topic, the reader is directed to Gutek (1988).

Sexual harassment Perhaps one of the most aversive barriers to women's career advancement, sexual harassment, has been documented across a number of occupations, from blue-collar jobs (e.g. Mansfield et al 1991) to careers in medicine (e.g. Phillips & Schneider 1993). Perceptions of sexual harassment have been associated with the status difference between the initiator and the recipient (e.g. Tata 1993), type of workplace (e.g. Sheffey & Tindale 1992), whether the female complainant was in competition with the accused and whether she was a feminist (Summers 1991), and normative beliefs about sexual harassment (Ellis et al 1991). In addition, the past decade of research in this area has focused less exclusively on prevalence and perceptions of sexual harassment and more on developing sophisticated, multilayered organizational and policy analyses of antecedents and consequences of sexual harassment (e.g. Fitzgerald 1993, Fitzgerald & Shullman 1993, Fitzgerald et al 1995).

RESOURCES FOR ADVANCEMENT Resources for women's career advancement may not be categorically different from those that assist men. However, some evidence suggests that the experience of resources like mentoring, social support, and networking is qualitatively different for men and women.

Mentoring and other social support As has been shown in the literature on men, having a mentor has a positive effect on career advancement for women, and gender may not moderate the positive effects of mentoring on career outcomes (Dreher & Ash 1990). In fact, gender-related traits may play a larger role in predicting mentorship than biological sex (Scandura & Ragins 1993). However, researchers consistently find that women experience barriers to gaining a mentor (e.g. Ragins & Cotton 1991). Sex of the mentoring dyad also appears to affect the experience or outcomes of mentoring. For example, although many of the benefits of mentoring are experienced by female protégés with both male and female mentors, having a female mentor may offer the additional function of serving as a role model to a female protégé (Gaskill 1991).

In addition to the literature on mentoring, a small group of studies have surfaced on networking (Campbell 1988) and social support (South et al 1987) for working women. South et al (1987) found that individuals receive more support for advancement from same-sex coworkers, and that men give more support to other male coworkers but women support their male and female coworkers equally.

Assistance and interventions In the literature addressing specific career interventions for helping women cope with barriers to advancement, most authors have focused on special groups (e.g. Richie 1992). On a more general level, Hammer-Higgins & Atwood (1989) described a simulation management game for counseling women about internal and external barriers to career achievement.

Satisfaction

The areas of job, life, and marital satisfaction have received considerable research attention in the past decade, as illustrated below.

SATISFACTION WITH WORK ROLES Researchers have found no consistent, direct relationship between gender and job satisfaction (e.g. Loscocco 1990, Schneer & Reitman 1994). For example, in his study of gender and reactions to jobs, Lefkowitz (1994) concluded that when differences in job types, tenure, occupational and educational level, and income are controlled, gender differences in satisfaction disappear. Other evidence points to a stronger relationship between gender role traits and work satisfaction than between biological sex and satisfaction (e.g. Jagacinski 1987).

Family variables (e.g. Rudd & McKenry 1986) and role conflict (e.g. Zahrly & Tosi 1988, Schaubroeck et al 1989) have also become productive lines of inquiry to explain relative job satisfaction. Also, a small group of studies focusing on mentoring and social support (e.g. Corzine et al 1994, Schaubroeck et al 1989) have found that both of these variables play an important role in job satisfaction.

SATISFACTION WITH NONWORK ROLES Research in the area of satisfaction with nonwork roles has focused on marital, family, and life satisfaction. Flexible gender-related characteristics and sharing have been consistently related to marital satisfaction (e.g. House 1986, Nicola & Hawkes 1986). The degree to which dual-career couples perceive that they have support from their spouses and families also appears to play an important role in marital and life satisfaction (Holtzman & Gilbert 1987, Ray 1988). Research has also explored the effect of role conflict (e.g. Beutell & O'Hare 1987) and number of roles (e.g. Pietromonaco et al 1986) on satisfaction and well-being. Considerable evidence now suggests that, contrary to popular notions, having multiple roles is not correlated with higher levels of stress and may be associated with enhanced well-being in working women (e.g. Pietromonaco et al 1986).

RETIREMENT

In contrast with the other phases of women's lives, the literature on women's retirement is extremely scant and fragmented. A number of articles focus specifically on gender differences in satisfaction with retirement. This work suggests that the determinants of satisfaction may be the same for women and men, but may be largely a function of income. For example, women's participation in sex-segregated occupations is associated with a work history marked by lower pay and may result in a financially insecure retirement (Perkins 1993). Similarly, Seccombe & Lee (1986) found that although women may be less satisfied with retirement than men, this gender difference may be explained by women's lower income. In addition to money matters, social contact patterns have been associated with greater retirement satisfaction (Reeves & Darville 1994).

POSTSCRIPT

We began this review with the question of what the decade of research has added to our understanding of career development in women's lives. As we have sampled the literature of the past ten years, several conclusions seem evident. Foremost among these is the simple statement that women's lives are complex. Although this statement is hardly novel, it is worth noting that the decade has taken important steps toward capturing this complexity. The increase in the sophistication of questions that are asked, the development of integrative models, and the capability of researchers to embed their studies and findings in larger individual and environmental contexts are all significant accomplishments. We applaud these efforts and also issue a note of caution to those who are tempted to focus on single-factor explanations, to ask fragmentary questions, or to decontextualize a problem. If nothing else, this review should illustrate that such approaches are severely limited.

From a more theoretical perspective, we found some constructs in need of more careful conceptualization. For example, it is clear that there is far more recording of gender and gender role differences than there is exploring the meaning of those differences and the circumstances that keep those differences in place—or, for that matter, the conditions under which no differences occur. Similarly, the notion of "traditional" or "nontraditional" pursuits—although useful in many ways—could benefit from some thoughtful analysis about the assumptions we make when we define some activity as "traditional" or otherwise. The notion of traditionality also probably needs updating to reflect the definitional permutations made possible by increased access to formerly nontraditional fields (e.g. pursuing a nontraditional field in a traditional way). Some effort dedicated to expanding our understanding of constructs such as these would enrich our understanding of the role of gender in career development.

In contrast, the literature concerning social variables in women's career development has advanced considerably. In the formation of a self-concept, in becoming ready to choose, in forming a firm decision about life plans, and in accessing support for executing those multifaceted plans, the woman portrayed during this decade is clearly seen in a social, relational context. Social variables have long been recognized as central in women's careeer development. However, one particular contribution of the research of this decade has been to highlight the benefits derived from those connections rather than focusing solely on the limitations that social contexts impose. This seems a promising perspective in our search for what facilitates women's development over the life span.

Our tour through the literature of the decade has also revealed some critical gaps in the research. One such gap is the limited knowledge we have about the changes and transitions in women's vocational lives. Apparently we have been so focused on issues relating to women being able to access work roles that we have neglected to attend to what happens—or needs to happen—for women when roles are acquired or discarded. As such, we know little about a woman's efforts to enter the work force, and about what helps her negotiate this transition well. We know even less about work-force exits, be they partial, temporary, permanent, or at retirement. Another conspicuous gap is the limited attention given to interventions. That is, despite extensive documentation of problems for women in their career development, there is little in the literature describing and evaluating interventions designed to support the career development of women over the life span. The need for effective assistance is clear in all aspects of career development, and it is particularly critical in helping women broaden the personal array of alternatives; prepare for the complex and constantly changing array of choices, roles, and commitments; and negotiate the challenges of the workplace and of multiple life roles in creative ways.

Finally, in our review we have paused to examine the new knowledge at each phase of a woman's life, from self-concept development through retirement. It is clear that in each phase, the literature reflects that work is only one of many life roles that women plan and negotiate. The empirical attention devoted to the problems raised by multiple life roles for both women and men has increased dramatically, and it represents an important contribution. It is also a contribution that will yield a more comprehensive and contextual view of "work in people's lives" (Richardson 1993) as we launch the next decade of research in career development.

ACKNOWLEDGMENTS

The authors thank Nancy E. Betz, Linda Brooks, and Linda Forrest for their comments and critiques of an earlier version of this review.

Literature Cited

Airsman LA, Sharda BD. 1993. A comparative study of the occupational attainment processes of white men and women in the United Sates: the effects of having ever married, spousal education, children and having ever divorced. *J. Comp. Fam. Stud.* 24:171–87

Alpert D, Breen DT. 1989. "Liberality" in children and adolescents. *J. Vocat. Behav.* 34: 154–60

Amatea ES, Cross EG, Clark JE, Bobby CL. 1986. Assessing the work and family role expectations of career-oriented men and women: the Life Role Salience Scales. *J. Marriage Fam.* 48:831–38

Anderson EA, Leslie LA. 1991. Coping with employment and family stress: employment arrangement and gender differences. *Sex Roles* 24:223–37

Aryee S. 1992. Antecedents and outcomes of work-family conflict among married professional women: evidence from Singapore. *Hum. Relat.* 45:813–37

Avis JM. 1986. "Working Together": an enrichment program for dual-career couples. *J. Psychother. Fam.* 2:29–45

Bailey BA, Nihlen AS. 1989. Elementary school children's perceptions of the world of work. *Elem. Sch. Guid. Couns.* 24: 135–45

Bailey BA, Nihlen AS. 1990. Effect of experience with nontraditional workers on psychological and social dimensions of occupational sex-role stereotyping by elementary school children. *Psychol. Rep.* 66: 1273–82

Bandura A. 1986. *Social Foundations of Thought and Action: A Social Cognitive Theory.* Englewood Cliffs, NJ: Prentice-Hall

Barak A, Feldman S, Noy A. 1991. Traditionality of children's interests as related to their parents' gender stereotypes and traditionality of occupations. *Sex Roles* 24: 511–24

Baruch GK, Barnett R. 1986. Role quality, multiple role involvement, and psychological well-being in midlife women. *J. Pers. Soc. Psychol.* 51:578–85

Beggs JM, Doolittle DC. 1993. Perceptions of now and then of occupational sex typing: a replication of Shinar's 1975 study. *J. Appl. Soc. Psychol.* 23:1435–53

Benjamin BA. 1992. Career counseling with couples. *J. Couns. Dev.* 70:544–49

Betz NE. 1989. Implications of the null environment hypothesis for women's career development and for counseling psychology. *Couns. Psychol.* 17:136–44

Betz NE. 1992. Counseling uses of career self-efficacy theory. *Career Dev. Q.* 41: 22–26

Betz NE, Fitzgerald LF. 1987. *The Career Psychology of Women.* New York: Academic

Betz NE, Fitzgerald LF. 1993. Individuality and diversity: theory and research in counseling psychology. *Annu. Rev. Psychol.* 44: 343–81

Betz NE, Hackett G. 1987. Concept of agency in educational and career development. *J. Couns. Psychol.* 34:299–308

Betz NE, Heesacker RS, Shuttleworth C. 1990. Moderators of the congruence and realism of major and occupational plans in college students: a replication and extension. *J. Couns. Psychol.* 37:269–76

Beutell NJ, O'Hare MM. 1987. Work-nonwork conflict among MBAs: sex differences in role stressors and life satisfaction. *Work Stress* 1:35–41

Bigler RS, Liben LS. 1990. The role of attitudes and interventions in gender-schematic processing. *Child Dev.* 61:1440–52

Bigler RS, Liben LS. 1992. Cognitive mechanisms in children's gender stereotyping: theoretical and educational implications of a cognitive-based intervention. *Child Dev.* 63:1351–63

Bilsker D, Schiedel D, Marcia J. 1988. Sex differences in identity status. *Sex Roles* 18: 231–36

Borman CA, Guido-DiBrito F. 1986. The career development of women: helping Cinderella lose her complex. *J. Career Dev.* 12:250–61

Breese JR, O'Toole R. 1995. Role exit theory: applications to adult women college students. *Career Dev. Q.* 44:12–25

Bridges JS. 1988. Sex differences in occupational performance expectations. *Psychol. Women Q.* 12:75–90

Bridges JS. 1989. Sex differences in occupational values. *Sex Roles* 20:205–11

Brooks L. 1988. Encouraging women's motivation for nontraditional career and lifestyle options: a model for assessment and intervention. *J. Career Dev.* 14:223–41

Brooks L, Betz NE. 1990. Utility of expectancy theory in predicting occupational choices in college students. *J. Couns. Psychol.* 37:57–64

Brown MT. 1987. A comparison of two approaches to the Cognitive Differentiation Grid. *J. Vocat. Behav.* 30:155–66

Burke RJ, Greenglass ER. 1989. Sex differences in psychological burnout in teachers. *Psychol. Rep.* 65:55–63

Campbell KE. 1988. Gender differences in job-related networks. *Work Occup.* 15: 179–200

Cardoza D. 1991. College attendance and persistence among Hispanic women: an examination of some contributing factors. *Sex Roles* 24:133–47

Chafetz JS, Lorence J, Larosa C. 1993. Gender depictions of the professionally employed: a content analysis of trade publications 1960–1990. *Sociol. Perspect.* 36:63–82

Chatterjee J, McCarrey M. 1989. Sex role attitudes of self and those inferred of peers, performance, and career opportunities as reported by women in nontraditional vs. traditional training programs. *Sex Roles* 21: 653–69

Church AT, Teresa JS, Rosebrook R, Szendre D. 1992. Self-efficacy for careers and occupational consideration in minority high school equivalency students. *J. Couns. Psychol.* 39:498–508

Chusid H, Cochran L. 1989. Meaning of career change from the perspective of family roles and dramas. *J. Couns. Psychol.* 36:34–41

Chusmir LH. 1986. Gender differences in variables affecting job commitment among working men and women. *J. Soc. Psychol.* 126:87–94

Cini MA, Baker SB. 1987. Enhancing rural female adolescents' awareness of nontraditional careers. *Career Dev. Q.* 35:316–25

Clarke VA. 1989. Occupational sex-typing: A declining problem in Australia. *Psychol. Rep.* 65:1011–16

Clayton DE, Smith MM. 1987. Motivational typology of reentry women. *Adult Educ. Q.* 37:90–104

Clement S. 1987. The self-efficacy expectations and occupational preferences of females and males. *J. Occup. Psychol.* 60: 257–65

Cohen AG, Gutek BA. 1991. Sex differences in the career experiences of members of two APA division. *Am. Psychol.* 46: 1292–98

Comer LB. 1992. Gender differences in sales managers' perceptions of occupational gender stereotypes. *Percept. Mot. Skills* 74: 995–1002

Cook EP. 1993. The gendered context of life: implications for women's and men's career-life plans. *Career Dev. Q.* 41:227–37

Cooney TM, Uhlenberg P. 1991. Changes in work-family connections among highly educated men and women: 1970 to 1980. *J. Fam. Issues* 12:69–90

Cooper SE, Robinson DA. 1989. Childhood play activities of women and men entering engineering and science careers. *Sch. Couns.* 36:338–42

Corzine JB, Buntzman GF, Busch ET. 1994. Mentoring, downsizing, gender and career outcomes. *J. Soc. Behav. Pers.* 9:517–28

Covin TJ, Brush CC. 1991. An examination of male and female attitudes toward career and family issues. *Sex Roles* 25:393–415

Cox TH, Harquail CV. 1991. Career paths and career success in the early career stages of male and female MBAs. *J. Vocat. Behav.* 39:54–75

Crosby F, Herek GM. 1986. Male sympathy with the situation of women: Does personal experience make a difference? *J. Soc. Issues* 42:55–66

Curry C, Trew K, Turner I, Hunter J. 1994. The effect of life domains on girls' possible selves. *Adolescence* 29:133–50

Dancer LS, Gilbert LA. 1993. Spouses' family work participation and its relations to wives' occupational level. *Sex Roles* 28: 127–45

Davey FH, Stoppard JM. 1993. Some factors

affecting the occupational expectations of female adolescents. *J. Vocat. Behav.* 43: 235–50

Deutsch FM, Lussier JB, Servis LJ. 1993. Husbands at home: predictors of paternal participation in childcare and housework. *J. Pers. Soc. Psychol.* 65:1154–66

DiBenedetto B, Tittle CK. 1990. Gender and adult roles: role commitment of women and men in a job-family trade-off context. *J. Couns. Psychol.* 37:41–48

Douce LA, Hansen JC. 1990. Willingness to take risks and college women's career choice. *J. Vocat. Behav.* 36:258–73

Dreher GF, Ash RA. 1990. A comparative study of mentoring among men and women in managerial, professional, and technical positions. *J. Appl. Psychol.* 75:539–46

Duncan KC, Prus MJ, Sandy JG. 1993. Marital status, children and women's labor market choices. *J. Sociol. Econ.* 22:277–88

Duxbury LE, Higgins CA. 1991. Gender differences in work-family conflict. *J. Appl. Psychol.* 76:60–73

Eccles JS. 1987. Gender roles and women's achievement-related decisions. *Psychol. Women Q.* 11:135–71

Ellis S, Barak A, Pinto A. 1991. Moderating effects of personal cognitions on experienced and perceived sexual harassment of women at the workplace. *J. Appl. Soc. Psychol.* 21:1320–37

Etaugh C, Liss MB. 1992. Home, school, and playroom: training grounds for adult gender roles. *Sex Roles* 26:129–47

Evans KM, Herr EL. 1991. The influence of racism and sexism in the career development of African American women. *J. Multicult. Couns. Dev.* 19:130–35

Evans NJ. 1985. Women's development across the life span. *New Direct. Stud. Serv.* 29: 9–27

Fagenson EA. 1990. Perceived masculine and feminine attributes examined as a function of individuals' sex and level in the organizational power hierarchy: a test of four theoretical perspectives. *J. Appl. Psychol.* 75:204–11

Fandt PM, Stevens GE. 1991. Evaluation bias in the business classroom: evidence relating to the effects of previous experiences. *J. Psychol.* 125:469–77

Farmer HS, Wardrop JL, Anderson MZ, Risinger R. 1995. Women's career choices: focus on science, math, and technology careers. *J. Couns. Psychol.* 42:155–70

Fassinger RE. 1990. Causal models of career choice in two samples of college women. *J. Vocat. Behav.* 36:225–48

Fassinger RE. 1995. From invisibility to integration: lesbian identity in the workplace. *Career Dev. Q.* 44:148–67

Fiorentine R. 1988. Increasing similarity in the values and life plans of male and female college students? Evidence and implications. *Sex Roles* 18:143–58

Fitzgerald LF. 1993. Sexual harassment: violence against women in the workplace. *Am. Psychol.* 48:1070–76

Fitzgerald LF, Shullman SL. 1993. Sexual harassment: a research analysis and agenda for the 1990's. *J. Vocat. Behav.* 42: 5–27

Fitzgerald LF, Swan S, Fischer K. 1995. Why didn't she just report him? The psychological and legal implications of women's responses to sexual harassment. *J. Soc. Issues* 51:117–38

Fitzpatrick JL, Silverman T. 1989. Women's selection of careers in engineering: So traditional-nontraditional differences still exist? *J. Vocat. Behav.* 34:266–78

Forrest L, Mikolaitis N. 1986. The relational component of identity: an expansion of career development theory. *Career Dev. Q.* 35:76–88

Foss CJ, Slaney RB. 1986. Increasing nontraditional career choices in women: relation of attitudes toward women and responses to a career intervention. *J. Vocat. Behav.* 28:191–202

Fouad NA. 1988. The construct of career maturity in the United States and Israel. *J. Vocat. Behav.* 32:49–59

Freeman SC, Haring-Hidore M. 1988. Outplacement for underserved women workers. *J. Career Dev.* 14:287–93

Fullinwider-Bush N, Jacobvitz DB. 1993. The transition to young adulthood: generational boundary dissolution and female identity development. *Fam. Process* 31:87–103

Gaskill LR. 1991. Same-sex and cross-sex mentoring of female proteges: a comparative analysis. *Career Dev. Q.* 40:48–63

Geller PA, Hobfoll SE. 1994. Gender differences in job stress, tedium and social support in the workplace. *J. Soc. Pers. Relat.* 11:555–72

Gerhart B, Rynes S. 1991. Determinants and consequences of salary negotiations by male and female MBA graduates. *J. Appl. Psychol.* 76:256–62

Gerken D, Reardon R, Bash R. 1988. Revitalizing a career course: the gender roles infusion. *J. Career Dev.* 14:269–78

Gerstein M, Lichtman M, Barokas JU. 1988. Occupational plans of adolescent women compared to men: a cross-sectional examination. *Career Dev. Q.* 36:222–30

Gianakos I, Subich LM. 1986. The relationship of gender and sex-role orientation to vocational undecidedness. *J. Vocat. Behav.* 29: 42–50

Gianakos I, Subich LM. 1988. Student sex and sex role in relation to college major choice. *Career Dev. Q.* 36:259–68

Gilbert LA. 1992. Gender and counseling psychology: current knowledge and directions for research and social action. In *Handbook of Counseling Psychology,* ed. SD Brown, RW Lent, pp. 383–416. New York: Wiley. 2nd ed.
Gilbert LA. 1994. Current perspectives on dual-career families. *Curr. Direct. Psychol. Sci.* 3:101–5
Gilbert LA, Rachlin V. 1987. Mental health and psychological functioning of dual-career families. *Couns. Psychol.* 15:7–49
Glass J, Camarigg V. 1992. Gender, parenthood, and job-family compatibility. *Am. J. Sociol.* 98:131–51
Glick P, Zion C, Nelson C. 1988. What mediates sex discrimination in hiring decisions? *J. Pers. Soc. Psychol.* 55:178–86
Good LK, Sisler GF, Gentry JW. 1988. Antecedents of turnover intentions among retail management personnel. *J. Retail.* 64: 295–314
Gorrell J, Shaw EL. 1988. Upper elementary and high school students' attitudes toward gender-typed occupations. *J. Adolesc. Res.* 3:189–99
Gottfredson LS. 1981. Circumscription and compromise: a developmental theory of occupational aspirations. *J. Couns. Psychol.* 28:545–79
Goudge BS, Littrell MA. 1989. Attributions for job acquisition: job skills, dress, and luck of female job applicants. *Cloth. Text. Res. J.* 7:19–26
Granrose CS, Cunningham EA. 1988. Post partum work intentions among black and white college women. *Career Dev. Q.* 37: 149–64
Granrose CS, Parasuraman S, Greenhaus JH. 1992. A proposed model of support provided by two earner couples. *Hum. Relat.* 45:1367–93
Greene AL, Wheatley SM. 1992. "I've got a lot to do and I don't think I'll have time": gender differences in late adolescents' narratives of the future. *J. Youth Adolesc.* 21: 667–86
Greenglass ER. 1993. The contribution of social support to coping strategies. *Appl. Psychol.* 42:323–40
Gutek BA. 1988. Sex segregation and women at work: a selective review. *Appl. Psychol.* 37:103–20
Hackett G, Betz NE. 1981. A self-efficacy approach to the career development of women. *J. Vocat. Behav.* 18:326–39
Hackett G, Betz NE. 1989. An exploration of the mathematics self-efficacy/mathematics performance correspondence. *J. Res. Math. Educ.* 20:261–73
Hackett G, Betz NE, Casas JM, Rocha-Singh IA. 1992. Gender, ethnicity, and social cognitive factors predicting the academic achievement of students in engineering. *J. Couns. Psychol.* 39:527–38
Hackett G, Betz NE, O'Halloran MS, Romac DS. 1990. Effects of verbal and mathematics task performance on task and career self-efficacy and interest. *J. Couns. Psychol.* 37:169–77
Hackett G, Esposito D, O'Halloran MS. 1989. The relationship of role model influences to the career salience and educational and career plans of college women. *J. Vocat. Behav.* 35:164–80
Hammer-Higgins P, Atwood VA. 1989. The Management Game: an educational intervention for counseling women with nontraditional career goals. *Career Dev. Q.* 38: 6–23
Hannah JS, Kahn SE. 1989. The relationship of socioeconomic status and gender to the occupational choices of Grade 12 students. *J. Vocat. Behav.* 34:161–78
Hansen JC, Collins RC, Swanson JL, Fouad NA. 1993. Gender differences in the structure of interests. *J. Vocat. Behav.* 42: 200–11
Harlan CL, Jansen MA. 1987. The psychological and physical well-being of women in sex-stereotyped occupations. *J. Employ. Couns.* 24:31–39
Harmon LW. 1989. Longitudinal changes in women's career aspirations: developmental or historical? *J. Vocat. Behav.* 35:46–63
Hartman BW, Jenkins SJ, Fuqua DR, Sutherland VE. 1987. An analysis of gender differences in the factor structure of the Career Decision Scale. *Educ. Psychol. Meas.* 47:1099–106
Hayes R. 1986. Gender nontraditional or sex atypical or gender dominant or...research: Are we measuring the same thing? *J. Vocat. Behav.* 29:79–88
Heilman ME, Martell RF, Simon MC. 1988. The vagaries of sex bias: conditions regulating the undervaluation, equivaluation, and overvaluation of female job applicants. *Organ. Behav. Hum. Decis. Process.* 41: 98–110
Heintz KE. 1987. An examination of sex and occupational-role presentations of female characters in children's picture books. *Women's Stud. Commun.* 10:67–78
Henderson S, Hesketh B, Tuffin K. 1988. A test of Gottfredson's theory of circumscription. *J. Vocat. Behav.* 32:37–48
Henshaw A, Kelly J, Gratton C. 1992. Skipping's for girls: children's perceptions of gender roles and gender preferences. *Educ. Res.* 34:229–35
Hesketh B, Elmslie S, Kaldor W. 1990. Career compromise: an alternative account to Gottfredson's theory. *J. Couns. Psychol.* 37:49–56

Hetherington C, Orzek A. 1989. Career counseling and life planning with lesbian women. *J. Couns. Dev.* 68:52–57

Hibbard JH, Pope CR. 1991. Effect of domestic and occupational roles on morbidity and mortality. *Soc. Sci. Med.* 32:805–11

Higgins NC. 1986. Occupational stress and working women: the effectiveness of two stress reduction programs. *J. Vocat. Behav.* 29:66–78

Hoffman JJ, Goldsmith EB, Hofacker CF. 1992. The influence of parents on female business students' salary and work hour expectations. *J. Employ. Couns.* 29:79–83

Holmes VL, Esses LM. 1988. Factors influencing Canadian high school girls' career motivation. *Psychol. Women Q.* 12:313–28

Holtzman EH, Gilbert LA. 1987. Social support networks for parenting and psychological well-being among dual-earner Mexican-American families. *J. Community Psychol.* 15:176–86

Hopkins-Best M. 1987. The effect of students' sex and desirability on counselors' agreement with postsecondary career goals. *Sch. Couns.* 35:28–33

House EA. 1986. Sex role orientation and marital satisfaction in dual- and one-provider couples. *Sex Roles* 15:245–59

Houser R, Konstam V, Ham M. 1990. Coping and marital satisfaction in dual-career couples: early stage dual-career couples—wives as college students. *J. Coll. Stud. Dev.* 31:325–29

Izraeli DN. 1993. Work/family conflict among women and men managers in dual-career couples in Israel. *J. Soc. Behav. Pers.* 8: 371–85

Jacobsen JP. 1994. Sex segregation at work: trends and predictions. *Soc. Sci. J.* 31: 153–69

Jagacinski CM. 1987. Androgyny in a male-dominated field: the relationship of sex-typed traits to performance and satisfaction in engineering. *Sex Roles* 17:529–47

Jagacinski CM, LeBold WK, Linden KW. 1987. The relative career advancement of men and women engineers in the United States. *Work Stress* 1:235–47

Janman K. 1989. One step behind: current stereotypes of women, achievement, and work. *Sex Roles* 21:209–30

Jessell JC, Beymer L. 1992. The effects of job title vs. job description on occupational sex typing. *Sex Roles* 27:73–83

Johnson RD. 1986. The influence of gender composition on evaluation of professions. *J. Soc. Psychol.* 126:161–67

Johnson RD. 1991. The influence of time-frame for achieving gender neutrality on evaluations of a male-dominated profession. *J. Soc. Behav. Pers.* 6:833–42

Johnson RD. 1992. A note on the effect of increasing female representation on the evaluation of a previously male-dominated profession. *J. Psychol.* 126:211–15

Jordan JV, Kaplan AG, Miller JB, Stiver IP, Surrey JL. 1991. *Women's Growth in Connection.* New York: Wiley. 310 pp.

Kahn SE, Lichty JM. 1987. The career plans of women. *Int. J. Adv. Couns.* 10:123–30

Kapalka GM, Lachenmeyer JR. 1988. Sex-role flexibility, locus of control, and occupational status. *Sex Roles* 19:417–27

Katz M. 1986. Career and family values for males and females. *Coll. Stud. J.* 20: 66–76

Keith PM. 1988. The relationship of self-esteem, maternal employment, and work-family plans to sex role orientations of late adolescents. *Adolescence* 23:959–66

Kiker BF, Ying CN. 1990. A simultaneous equation model of spousal time allocation. *Soc. Sci. Res.* 19:132–52

King AC, Winett RA, Lovett SB. 1986. Enhancing coping behaviors in at-risk populations: the effects of time-management instruction and social support in women from dual-earner families. *Behav. Ther.* 17: 57–66

King S. 1989. Sex differences in a causal model of career maturity. *J. Couns. Dev.* 68:208–15

Kirschenbaum A, Merl S. 1987. Childcare and labor force activity. *Isr. Soc. Sci. Res.* 5: 44–59

Lancaster AR, Drasgow F. 1994. Choosing a norm group for counseling: legislation, regulation, and nontraditional careers. *Psychol. Assess.* 6:313–20

Lapan RT, Boggs KR, Morrill WH. 1989. Self-efficacy as a mediator of investigative and realistic general occupational themes on the Strong-Campbell Interest Inventory. *J. Couns. Psychol.* 36:176–82

Lapan RT, Jingelski J. 1992. Circumscribing vocational aspirations in junior high school. *J. Couns. Psychol.* 39:81–90

Lassalle AD, Spokane AR. 1987. Patterns of early labor force participation of American women. *Career Dev. Q.* 36:55–65

Lauver PJ, Jones RM. 1991. Factors associated with perceived career options in American Indian, white, and Hispanic rural high school students. *J. Couns. Psychol.* 38: 159–66

Lefkowitz J. 1994. Sex-related differences in job attitudes and dispositional variables: now you see them,... *Acad. Manage. J.* 37: 323–49

Lent RW, Brown SD, Hackett G. 1994. Toward a unifying social cognitive theory of careeer and academic interest, choice, and performance. *J. Vocat. Behav.* 45:79–122

Lent RW, Hackett G. 1987. Career self-efficacy: empirical status and future directions. *J. Vocat. Behav.* 30:347–82

Lent RW, Lopez FG, Bieschke KJ. 1991. Mathematics self-efficacy: sources and relation to science-based career choice. *J. Couns. Psychol.* 38:424–30

Leong FT, Tata SP. 1990. Sex and acculturation differences in occupational values among Chinese-American children. *J. Couns. Psychol.* 37:208–12

Leslie LA, Anderson EA, Branson MP. 1991. Responsibility for children: the role of gender and employment. *J. Fam. Issues* 12: 197–210

Leung SA. 1993. Circumscription and compromise: a replication study with Asian Americans. *J. Couns. Psychol.* 40:188–93

Leung SA, Conoley CW, Scheel MJ. 1994. The career and educational aspirations of gifted high school students: a retrospective study. *J. Couns. Dev.* 72:298–303

Leung SA, Harmon LW. 1990. Individual and sex differences in the zone of acceptable alternatives. *J. Couns. Psychol.* 37: 153–59

Leung SA, Plake BS. 1990. A choice dilemma approach for examining the relative importance of sex type and prestige preferences in the process of career choice compromise. *J. Couns. Psychol.* 37:399–406

Lips HM. 1992. Gender- and science-related attitudes as predictors of college students' academic choices. *J. Vocat. Behav.* 40: 62–81

Livingston MM, Burley KA. 1991. Surprising initial findings regarding sex, sex role, and anticipated work-family conflict. *Psychol. Rep.* 68:735–38

Loerch KJ, Russell JE, Rush MC. 1989. The relationships among family domain variables and work family conflict for men and women. *J. Vocat. Behav.* 35:288–308

Lopata HZ. 1993. Career commitments of American women: the issue of side bets. *Sociol. Q.* 34:257–77

Loscocco KA. 1990. Reactions to blue-collar work: a comparison of women and men. *Work Occup.* 17:152–77

Lovdal LT. 1989. Sex role messages in television commercials: an update. *Sex Roles* 21: 715–24

MacKinnon-Slaney F, Barber SL, Slaney RB. 1988. Marital status as a mediating factor on career aspirations of re-entry female students. *J. Coll. Stud. Dev.* 29:327–34

Mansfield PK, Koch PB, Henderson J, Vicary JR, Cohn M, Young EW. 1991. The job climate for women in traditionally male blue-collar occupations. *Sex Roles* 25: 63–79

Matsui T. 1994. Mechanisms underlying sex differences in career self-efficacy expectations of university students. *J. Vocat. Behav.* 45:177–84

Matsui T, Ohsawa T, Onglatco ML. 1991. Personality and career commitment among Japanese female clerical employees. *J. Vocat. Behav.* 38:351–60

Mau WC, Domnick M, Ellsworth RA. 1995. Characteristics of female students who aspire to science and engineering or homemaking occupations. *Career Dev. Q.* 43: 323–37

Maurer TJ, Taylor MA. 1994. Is sex by itself enough? An explanation of gender bias issues in performance appraisal. *Organ. Behav. Hum. Decis. Process.* 60:231–51

Mawson DL, Kahn SE. 1993. Group process in a women's career intervention. *Career Dev. Q.* 41:238–45

Mazen AM, Lemkau JP. 1990. Personality profiles of women in traditional and nontraditional occupations. *J. Vocat. Behav.* 37: 46–59

McCormick ME, Wolf JS. 1993. Intervention programs for gifted girls. *Roeper Rev.* 16: 85–88

McCormick TE. 1990. Counselor-teacher interface: promoting nonsexist education and career development. *J. Multicult. Couns. Dev.* 18:2–10

Melamed T. 1995. Barriers to women's career success: human capital, career choices, structural determinants, or simply sex discrimination. *Appl. Psychol.* 44:295–314

Melcher CR. 1987. Career counseling tailored to the evangelical Christian woman at midlife. *J. Psychol. Theol.* 15:113–23

Morgan CS. 1992. College students' perceptions of barriers to women in science and engineering. *Youth Soc.* 24:228–36

Morgan MY, Scanzoni J. 1987. Religious orientations and women's expected continuity in the labor force. *J. Marriage Fam.* 49: 367–79

Morgan S, Schor SM, Martin LR. 1993. Gender differences in career paths in banking. *Career Dev. Q.* 41:375–82

Mount MK, Ellis RA. 1989. Sources of bias in job evaluation: a review and critique of research. *J. Soc. Issues* 45:153–67

Munson WW. 1992. Self-esteem, vocational identity, and career salience in high school students. *Career Dev. Q.* 40:361–68

Murrell AJ, Frieze IH, Frost JL. 1991. Aspiring to careers in male- and female-dominated professions: a study of black and white college women. *Psychol. Women Q.* 15: 103–26

Neimeyer GJ, Brown MT, Metzler AE, Hagans C, Tanguy M. 1989. The impact of sex, sex-role orientation, and construct type on vocational differentiation, integration, and conflict. *J. Vocat. Behav.* 34:236–51

Neimeyer GJ, Metzler AE. 1987. Sex differences in vocational integration and differentiation. *J. Vocat. Behav.* 30:167–74

Nevill DD, Super DE. 1988. Career maturity

and commitment to work in university students. *J. Vocat. Behav.* 32:139–51
Nicola JS, Hawkes GR. 1986. Marital satisfaction of dual-career couples: Does sharing increase happiness? *J. Soc. Behav. Pers.* 1:47–60
Niles SG, Anderson WP. 1993. Career development and adjustment: the relation between concerns and stress. *J. Employ. Couns.* 30:79–87
Noble KD. 1987. The dilemma of the gifted woman. *Psychol. Women Q.* 11:367–78
O'Brien KM, Fassinger RE. 1993. A causal model of the career orientation and career choice of adolescent women. *J. Couns. Psychol.* 40:456–69
O'Connell L, Betz M, Kurth S. 1989. Plans for balancing work and family life: Do women pursuing nontraditional and traditional occupations differ? *Sex Roles* 20:35–45
O'Hare MM, Beutell NJ. 1987. Sex differences in coping with career decision making. *J. Vocat. Behav.* 31:174–81
Olson JE, Frieze IH, Detlefsen EG. 1990. Having it all? Combining work and family in a male and female profession. *Sex Roles* 23: 515–33
Ornstein S, Isabella LA. 1990. Age vs stage models of career attitudes of women: a partial replication and extension. *J. Vocat. Behav.* 36:1–19
Ott EM. 1989. Effects of the male-female ratio at work: policewomen and male nurses. *Psychol. Women Q.* 13:41–57
Paddock JR, Schwartz KM. 1986. Rituals for dual-career couples. *Psychotherapy* 23: 453–59
Palmer HT, Lee JA. 1990. Female workers' acceptance in traditionally male-dominated blue-collar jobs. *Sex Roles* 22:607–26
Perkins K. 1993. Working-class women and retirement. *J. Gerontol. Soc. Work* 20: 129–46
Pfost KS, Fiore M. 1990. Pursuit of nontraditional occupations: fear of success or fear of not being chosen? *Sex Roles* 23:15–24
Phillips SP, Schneider MS. 1993. Sexual harassment of female doctors by patients. *N. Engl. J. Med.* 329:1936–39
Pietromonaco PR, Manis J, Frohardt-Lane K. 1986. Psychological consequences of multiple social roles. *Psychol. Women Q.* 10: 373–82
Pines A, Guendelman S. 1995. Exploring the relevance of burnout to Mexican blue collar women. *J. Vocat. Behav.* 47:1–20
Post-Kammer P, Smith PL. 1986. Sex differences in math and science career self-efficacy among disadvantaged students. *J. Vocat. Behav.* 29:89–101
Ragins BR, Cotton JL. 1991. Easier said than done: gender differences in perceived barriers to gaining a mentor. *Acad. Manage. J.* 34:939–51
Raphael KG, Gorman BS. 1986. College women's Holland-theme congruence: effects of self-knowledge and subjective occupational structure. *J. Couns. Psychol.* 33: 143–47
Ray JA. 1988. Marital satisfaction in dual-career couples. *J. Indep. Soc. Work* 3:39–55
Rea-Poteat MB, Martin PF. 1991. Taking your place: a summer program to encourage nontraditional career choices for adolescent girls. *Career Dev. Q.* 40:182–88
Reeves JB, Darville RL. 1994. Social contact patterns and satisfaction with retirement of women in dual-career/earner families. *Int. J. Aging Hum. Dev.* 39:163–75
Reskin BF, Padavic I. 1988. Supervisors as gatekeepers: male supervisors' response to women's integration in plant jobs. *Soc. Probl.* 35:536–50
Richard GV, Krieshok TS. 1989. Occupational stress, strain, and coping in university faculty. *J. Vocat. Behav.* 34:117–32
Richardson MS. 1993. Work in people's lives: a location for counseling psychologists. *J. Couns. Psychol.* 40:425–33
Richie BS. 1992. Coping with work: interventions with African-American women. *Women Ther.* 12:97–111
Richman DR. 1988. Cognitive career counseling for women. *J. Ration. Emot. Cogn. Behav. Ther.* 6:50–65
Roberts JA, Chonko LB. 1994. Sex differences in the effect of satisfaction with pay on sales force turnover. *J. Soc. Behav. Pers.* 9:507–16
Robinson JG, McIlwee JS. 1991. Men, women, and the culture of engineering. *Sociol. Q.* 32:403–21
Rodriguez M, Blocher D. 1988. A comparison of two approaches to enhancing career maturity in Puerto Rican college women. *J. Couns. Psychol.* 35:275–80
Rojewski JW. 1994. Career indecision types for rural adolescents from disadvantaged and nondisadvantaged backgrounds. *J. Couns. Psychol.* 41:356–63
Rosenfeld RA, Spenner KI. 1992. Occupational sex segregation and women's early career job shifts. *Work Occup.* 19:424–49
Rosin HM, Korabik K. 1990. Marital and family correlates of women managers' attrition from organizations. *J. Vocat. Behav.* 37: 104–20
Rotberg HL, Brown D, Ware WB. 1987. Career self-efficacy expectations and perceived range of career options in community college students. *J. Couns. Psychol.* 34:164–70
Roy SW. 1986. Programming for returning women students. *J. Coll. Stud. Pers.* 27: 75–76

Rudd NM, McKenry PC. 1986. Family influences on the job satisfaction of employed mothers. *Psychol. Women Q.* 10:363–71

Russell JE, Rush MC. 1987. A comparative study of age-related variation in women's views of a career in management. *J. Vocat. Behav.* 30:280–94

Ryland EK, Rosen B. 1987. Personnel professionals' reactions to chronological and functional resume formats. *Career Dev. Q.* 35: 228–38

Saal FE, Moore SC. 1993. Perceptions of promotion fairness and promotion candidates' qualifications. *J. Appl. Psychol.* 78:105–10

Sandberg DE, Ehrhardt AA, Mellins CA, Ince SE, Meyer-Bahlberg HFL. 1987. The influence of individual and family characteristics upon career aspirations of girls during childhood and adolescence. *Sex Roles* 16:649–68

Scandura TA, Ragins BR. 1993. The effects of sex and gender role orientation on mentorship in male-dominated occupations. *J. Vocat. Behav.* 43:251–65

Schaubroeck J, Cotton JL, Jennings KR. 1989. Antecedents and consequences of role stress: a covariance structure analysis. *J. Organ. Behav.* 10:35–58

Scheye PA, Gilroy FD. 1994. College women's career self-efficacy and educational environments. *Career Dev. Q.* 42: 244–51

Schneer JA, Reitman F. 1994. The importance of gender in mid-career: a longitudinal study of MBAs. *J. Organ. Behav.* 15: 199–207

Schneer JA, Reitman F. 1995. The impact of gender as managerial careers unfold. *J. Vocat. Behav.* 47:290–315

Schroeder KA, Blood LL, Maluso D. 1993. Gender differences and similarities between male and female undergraduate students regarding expectations for career and family roles. *Coll. Stud. J.* 27:237–49

Schroer AC, Dorn FJ. 1986. Enhancing the career and personal development of gifted college students. *J. Couns. Dev.* 64:567–71

Scott J, Hatalla J. 1990. The influence of chance and contingency factors on career patterns of college educated women. *Career Dev. Q.* 39:18–30

Seccombe K, Lee GR. 1986. Gender differences in retirement satisfaction. *Res. Aging* 8:426–40

Seiden AM. 1989. Psychological issues affecting women throughout the life cycle. *Psychiatr. Clin. North Am.* 12:1–24

Serbin LA, Powlishta KK, Gulko J. 1993. The development of sex typing in middle childhood. *Monogr. Soc. Res. Child Dev.* 58(2): v–74

Shaffer DR, Gresham A, Clary EG, Thielman TJ. 1986. Sex-ratios as a basis for occupational evaluations: a contemporary view. *Soc. Behav. Pers.* 14:77–83

Shamai S. 1994. Possibilities and limitations of a gender stereotypes intervention program. *Adolescence* 29:665–80

Sheffey S, Tindale RS. 1992. Perceptions of sexual harassment in the workplace. *J. Appl. Soc. Psychol.* 22:1502–20

Slaney RB, Lewis ET. 1986. Effects of career exploration on career undecided reentry women: an intervention and follow-up study. *J. Vocat. Behav.* 28:97–109

Smith WS, Erb TO. 1986. Effect of women science career role models on early adolescents' attitudes toward scientists and women in science. *J. Res. Sci. Teach.* 23: 667–76

Soldwedel BJ. 1988. The role of the employment counselor in promoting sex equity and nontraditional careers. *J. Employ. Couns.* 25:119–21

Solomon EE, Bishop RC, Bresser RK. 1986. Organization moderators of gender differences in career development: a facet classification. *J. Vocat. Behav.* 29:27–41

South SJ, Markham WT, Bonjean CM, Corder J. 1987. Sex differences in support for organizational advancement. *Work Occup.* 14:261–85

Sperry L. 1993. Tailoring treatment with dual-career couples. *Am. J. Fam. Ther.* 21: 51–59

Steffy BD, Ashbaugh D. 1986. Dual-career planning, marital satisfaction and job stress among women in dual-career marriages. *J. Bus. Psychol.* 1:114–23

Stevens CJ, Puchtell LA, Ryu S, Mortimer JT. 1992. Adolescent work and boys' and girls' orientations to the future. *Sociol. Q.* 33:153–69

Stewart E, Hutchinson NL, Hemingway P, Bessai F. 1989. The effects of student gender, race, and achievement on career exploration advice given by Canadian preservice teachers. *Sex Roles* 21:247–62

Stickel SA, Bonett RM. 1991. Gender differences in career self-efficacy: combining a career with home and family. *J. Coll. Stud. Dev.* 32:297–301

Stohs JH. 1991. Moving beyond women's career choices: factors associated with career continuity among female former art students. *J. Career Dev.* 18:123–38

Stohs JH. 1992. Career patterns and family status of women and men artists. *Career Dev. Q.* 40:223–33

Stoltz-Loike M. 1992. The working family: helping women balance the roles of wife, mother, and career woman. *Career Dev. Q.* 40:244–56

Stroh LK, Brett JM, Reilly AH. 1992. All the right stuff: a comparison of female and male managers' career progression. *J. Appl. Psychol.* 77:251–60

Stumpf SA, Lockhart MC. 1987. Career exploration: work-role salience, work preferences, beliefs, and behavior. *J. Vocat. Behav.* 30:258–69

Sullivan GL, O'Connor PJ. 1988. Women's role portrayals in magazine advertising: 1958–1983. *Sex Roles* 18:181–88

Sullivan SE. 1992. Is there a time for everything? Attitudes related to women's sequencing of career and family. *Career Dev. Q.* 40:234–43

Summers RJ. 1991. Determinants of judgements of and responses to a complaint of sexual harassment. *Sex Roles* 25:379–92

Super DE. 1980. A life-span, life-space approach to career development. *J. Vocat. Behav.* 13:282–98

Swanson JL, Tokar DM. 1991. Development and initial validation of the Career Barriers Inventory. *J. Vocat. Behav.* 39:344–61

Taber KS. 1992. Science-relatedness and gender-appropriateness of careers: some pupil perceptions. *Res. Sci. Technol. Educ.* 10: 105–15

Tangri SS, Jenkins SR. 1986. Stability and change in role innovation and life plans. *Sex Roles* 14:647–62

Tata J. 1993. The structure and phenomenon of sexual harassment: impact of category of sexually harassing behavior, gender and hierarchical level. *J. Appl. Soc. Psychol.* 23: 199–211

Tesch BJ, Osborne J, Simpson DE, Murray SF, Spiro J. 1992. Women physicians in dual-physician relationships compared with those in other dual career relationships. *Acad. Med.* 67:542–44

Tipping LM, Farmer HS. 1991. A home-career conflict measure: career counseling implications. *Meas. Eval. Couns. Dev.* 24: 111–18

Towns K, Gentzler R. 1986. Empowering reentry women: an organizational case study: the story of PROBE. *Women Ther.* 5:159–66

Tozzo SG, Golub S. 1990. Playing nurse and playing cop: Do they change children's perceptions of sex-role stereotypes? *J. Res. Child. Educ.* 4:123–29

Trepanier-Street ML, Romatowski JA, McNair S. 1990. Children's written responses to stereotypical and nonstereotypical story starters. *J. Res. Child. Educ.* 5:60–72

VanAllen GH, Wilford N. 1986. "Your Place": developmental program for displaced homemakers. *J. Coll. Stud. Pers.* 27: 278–79

VanBuren JB, Kelly KR, Hall AS. 1993. Modeling nontraditional career choices: effects of gender and school location on response to a brief videotape. *J. Couns. Dev.* 72: 101–4

Ward NJ. 1991. Occupational suitability bias for full-time and part-time employment in sex-typed jobs. *Sex Roles* 25:81–89

Weathers PL, Thompson CE, Robert S, Rodriguez J. 1994. Black college women's career values: a preliminary investigation. *J. Multicult. Couns. Dev.* 22:96–105

Weisberg J, Kirschenbaum A. 1993. Gender and turnover: a re-examination of the impact of sex on intent and actual job changes. *Hum. Relat.* 46:987–1006

Weisner TS, Wilson-Mitchell JE. 1990. Nonconventional family life-styles and sex typing in six-year-olds. *Child Dev.* 61: 1915–33

Weitzman LM. 1994. Multiple-role realism: a theoretical framework for the process of planning to combine career and family roles. *Appl. Prev. Psychol.* 3:15–25

Westbrook BW, Sanford EE. 1993. Relation between self-appraisal and appropriateness of career choices of male and female adolescents. *Educ. Psychol. Meas.* 53:291–99

Westbrook BW, Sanford EE, Gilleland K, Fleenor J, Merwin G. 1988. Career maturity in Grade 9: the relationship between accuracy of self-appraisal and ability to appraise the career-relevant capabilities of others. *J. Vocat. Behav.* 32:269–83

Wiersma UJ. 1994. A taxonomy of behavioral strategies for coping with work-home role conflict. *Hum. Relat.* 47:211–21

Wiersma UJ, Van den Berg P. 1991. Work-home role conflict, family climate, and domestic responsibilities among men and women in dual-earner families. *J. Appl. Soc. Psychol.* 21:1207–17

Wilcox-Matthew L, Minor CW. 1989. The dual career couple: concerns, benefits, and counseling implications. *J. Couns. Dev.* 68: 194–98

Wroblewski R, Huston AC. 1987. Televised occupational stereotypes and their effects on early adolescents: Are they changing? *J. Early Adolesc.* 7:283–97

Zahrly J, Tosi H. 1988. Comparative analysis of the influence of stress-related variables on adaptation to a new work setting. *Psychol. Rep.* 63:767–77

Annu. Rev. Psychol. 1997. 48:61–83

HUMAN-COMPUTER INTERACTION: Psychology as a Science of Design

John M. Carroll

Computer Science Department and Center for Human-Computer Interaction, Virginia Tech, Blacksburg, Virginia 24061-0106

KEY WORDS: usability, design, user models, applied psychology, human factors

ABSTRACT

Human-computer interaction (HCI) study is the region of intersection between psychology and the social sciences, on the one hand, and computer science and technology, on the other. HCI researchers analyze and design specific user interface technologies (e.g. pointing devices). They study and improve the processes of technology development (e.g. task analysis, design rationale). They develop and evaluate new applications of technology (e.g. word processors, digital libraries). Throughout the past two decades, HCI has progressively integrated its scientific concerns with the engineering goal of improving the *usability* of computer systems and applications, which has resulted in a body of technical knowledge and methodology. HCI continues to provide a challenging test domain for applying and developing psychological and social theory in the context of technology development and use.

CONTENTS

0084-6570/97/0201-0061$08.00

THE EMERGENCE OF USABILITY

Human-computer interaction (HCI) has emerged relatively recently as a highly successful area of computer science research and development and of applied psychology. Some of the reasons for this success are clearly technical. HCI has evoked many difficult problems and elegant solutions in the recent history of computing, e.g. in work on direct manipulation interfaces, user interface management systems, task-oriented help and instruction, and computer-supported collaborative work. Other reasons for its success are broadly cultural: The province of HCI is the view the nonspecialist public has of computer and information technology and its impact on their lives; HCI is the visible part of computer science. The most recent reasons for the success of HCI are commercial: As the underlying technologies of computing become commodities, inscribed on generic chips, the noncommodity value of computer products resides in applications and user interfaces, that is, in HCI.

HCI has evolved rapidly in the past two decades as it has struggled to develop a scientific basis and utility in system and software development. In this chapter, I review the progression of HCI toward a science of design. My touchstone is Simon's (1969) provocative book *The Sciences of the Artificial.* The book entirely predates HCI, and many of its specific characterizations and claims about design are no longer authoritative (see Ehn 1988). Nevertheless, two of Simon's themes echo through the history of HCI and still provide guidance in charting its continuing development.

Early in the book, Simon discussed the apparently complex path of an ant traversing a beach, observing that the structure of the ant's behavior derives chiefly from the beach; the ant pursues a relatively simple goal and accommodates to whatever the beach presents. The external world, including technology human beings create, should be expected to play a powerful role in structuring human behavior and experience. Late in the book, Simon sounds the second theme: the need for a science of design, a research paradigm and university curriculum directed at understanding, furthering, and disseminating design knowledge. He lamented the tendency of engineering disciplines to adopt goals and methodologies from the natural sciences, to their detriment with respect to design.

HCI is a science of design. It seeks to understand and support human beings interacting with and through technology. Much of the structure of this interaction derives from the technology, and many of the interventions must be made through the design of technology. HCI is not merely applied psychology. It has guided and developed the basic science as much as it has taken direction from it. It illustrates possibilities of psychology as a design science.

Software Psychology

The work that constitutes the historical foundation of HCI was called "software psychology" in the 1970s (e.g. Shneiderman 1980). The goal then was to establish the utility of a behavioral approach to understanding software design, programming, and the use of interactive systems, and to motivate and guide system developers to consider the characteristics of human beings. Software psychology had two distinct methodological axioms. The first assumed the validity of a received view of system and software development, namely the so-called waterfall model of top-down decomposition and discretely sequenced stages with well-specified hand-offs (e.g. Royce 1970). The second assumed two central roles for psychology within this context: (*a*) to produce general descriptions of human beings interacting with systems and software, which could be synthesized as guidelines for developers; and (*b*) to directly verify the usability of systems and software as (or more typically, after) they were developed.

Software psychology inaugurated a variety of technical projects pertaining to what we now call the *usability* of systems and software: assessing the relative complexity of syntactic constructions in programming languages (e.g. Sime et al 1973), classifying people's errors in specifying queries and procedures (Miller 1974), describing the utility of mnemonic variable names and in-line program comments (Weissman 1974), and explicating how flowcharts serve as a programming aid (Shneiderman et al 1977). This work inspired many industrial human-factors groups to expand the scope of their responsibilities to include support for programming groups and the usability of software.

The basic axioms of software psychology proved to be problematic. The waterfall idealization of design work is infeasible and ineffective (e.g. Brooks 1975/1995). It is only observed when enforced, and it is best regarded as a crude management tool for very large-scale, long-term projects. As computer research and development diversified in the 1970s and 1980s, small and distributed personal work organizations became more commonplace. Product development cycles were often compressed to less than a year.

The two roles assigned to software psychologists were also problematic and resulted in a division of labor. Researchers, mainly in universities, developed general descriptions of users and framed them as general guidelines. Human-factors specialists in industry tried to apply these guidelines in specific projects. This division did not work particularly well. From the standpoint of practical goals, the research of this period tended to focus on unrepresentative situations (e.g. undergraduates standing in for programmers, 50-line programs standing in for business systems, and teletypes standing in for display tubes). To obtain statistically stable results, researchers often created outrageous contrasts (organized versus disorganized menus, structured versus scrambled programs). The researchers sometimes understood little about the users of their guidelines and proffered superfluous advice.

Psychologists and others playing the human-factors specialist role in industry were frustrated trying to use and encourage use of these guidelines. They were also frustrated in their other role of verifying the usability of finished systems, because the research tools they had (formal experiments aimed at specific differences among alternatives) were too costly and too uninformative to allow them to serve as anything more than gatekeepers. Human-factors specialists were often seen as imposing bureaucratic obstacles blocking heroic developers.

The origins of HCI in software psychology posed two central problems for the field in the 1980s. One problem was to better describe design and development work and to understand how it could be supported. The other problem was to better specify the role that psychology, in particular, and social and behavioral science, more broadly, should play in HCI.

Iterative Development

Starting in the 1970s, empirical studies of the design process began to explicate the difficulties of the waterfall model. Design work is frequently piecemeal, concrete, and iterative. Designers may work on a single requirement at a time, embody it in a scenario of user interaction to understand it, reason about and develop a partial solution to address it, and then test the partial solution—all quite tentatively—before moving on to consider other requirements. During this process, they sometimes radically reformulate the fundamental goals and constraints of the problem. Rather than a chaos, it is a highly involuted, highly structured process of problem discovery and clarification in the context of unbounded complexity (e.g. Carroll et al 1979, Curtis et al 1988, Malhotra et al 1980).

The leading idea is that designers often need to do design to adequately understand design problems. One prominent empirical case was Brooks's (1975/1995) analysis of the development of the IBM 360 Operating System, one of the largest and most scrupulously planned software design projects of its era. Brooks, the project manager, concluded that system and software designers should always "plan to throw one away" (pp. 116–23). This was a striking lesson to draw and carried with it many implications. For example, formal and comprehensive planning and specification aids (such as detailed flowcharts) will have limited utility in supporting such an iterative design process.

This reformulation of design created an opening for new ideas. Noteworthy inspiration came from the work of the great industrial designer Henry Dreyfuss, who had pioneered an empirical approach in the 1940s (Dreyfuss 1955).

Dreyfuss's approach institutionalizes an accommodation to designers' propensity for concrete, incremental reasoning and testing. It incorporates four central ideas: (*a*) early prototyping with (*b*) the involvement of real users, (*c*) introduction of new functions through familiar "survival forms," and (*d*) many cycles of design iteration. Dreyfuss pushed beyond the designer's need for prototyping and iteration as a means of clarifying the design problem (also emphasized by Brooks 1975/1995) to the user's knowledge, experience, and involvement to constrain design solutions.

A typical example is Dreyfuss's design work on airplane interiors for Lockheed. Dreyfuss sent two associates back and forth across the United States on commercial flights to inventory passenger experiences. They found that passengers were often baffled by design details like water taps that were unnecessarily novel. They were impressed that people wanted to think of airplane seats as armchairs and not as "devices." Initial designs were prototyped in a Manhattan warehouse, and a full flight of "passengers" was hired to occupy the mock-up for 10 hours: to store carry-on luggage, to eat meals, to use lavatories. These tests concretized requirements for seating, storage space, lavatory-door latches, and so forth, and permitted low-cost, iterative reworking of the original designs.

In the 1980s, the inevitability of an empirical orientation toward system and software design rapidly evolved from a somewhat revolutionary perspective to the establishment view. This development provided early and critical motivation and direction for research on user interface management systems to enable prototyping (Tanner & Buxton 1985), it encouraged user participation in design (Gould & Boies 1983, Nygaard 1979, Pava 1983), it emphasized user interface metaphors for presenting novel functionality through familiar concepts (Carroll & Thomas 1982, Smith et al 1982), and it made "rapid prototyping" a standard system development methodology (Wasserman & Shewmake 1982, 1985).

Iterative development shifted the focus of usability evaluation from summative to formative (Scriven 1967). Formal experiments are fine for determining which of two designs are better on a set of a priori dimensions, but they are neither flexible nor rich enough to guide continual redesign. "Thinking aloud" had been pioneered by deGroot (1965) and Newell & Simon (1972) in the study of puzzles and games, and it had been shown to vividly illuminate strategic thought (Ericsson & Simon 1985). In the 1980s, thinking aloud became the central empirical, formative evaluation method in HCI (e.g. Mack et al 1983, Wright & Converse 1992).

User Models

The second problem area bequeathed to HCI by software psychology was to characterize a robust science base that could underwrite system development.

The cornerstone in this effort was the GOMS project of Card et al (1983). GOMS (Goals, Operators, Methods, and Selection rules) provided a framework for systematically analyzing the goals, methods, and actions that comprise routine human-computer interactions. This was an advance on prior human-factors modeling, which did not address the cognitive structures underlying manifest behavior. Indeed, it was an advance on the cognitive psychology of the time: It explicitly integrated many components of skilled performance to produce predictions about real tasks. At first, GOMS appeared to promise a comprehensive paradigm for scientifically grounded HCI design (Newell & Card 1985, but cf Carroll & Campbell 1986). The actual impact of these models has been more narrow, although they have been usefully applied in domains where user performance efficiency is the critical usability variable [e.g. modeling telephone operator scripts (Gray et al 1992)].

One salient limitation of GOMS models is that they do not describe learning, yet the problems of new users beginning with computer systems was perhaps *the* technical focus of the 1980s. The learning problem was conceived as a matter of coordinating knowledge in two domains: the task and the device. The user learns mappings between goals in the task domain and actions in the device domain, between events in the device domain and effects in the task domain (Moran 1983, Payne et al 1990). Much of this discussion focused on the "consistency" of mappings from commands and other user interface actions to application functions (e.g. Payne & Green 1989). For example, learning a command named "pull" is facilitated by a complementary command named "push" (versus, say, one named "grab"); commands like "edit data_file" and "remove data_file" are mutually facilitative (see also Esper 1925). Consistency turned out to be highly intentional (Carroll 1985), significantly idiosyncratic (Furnas et al 1983), and even questionable as a general design objective (Grudin 1989). Nevertheless, promoting consistency in user interface and application design remains a prominent practical issue (Nielsen 1989), and these models are the foundation for our understanding of it.

The role of prior knowledge in learning to use computer systems was another focus of user modeling work. It was widely noted that new users tried to understand computers as analogical extensions of familiar activities and objects (e.g. Douglas & Moran 1983, Mack et al 1983). This observation led to a variety of user interface "metaphors," such as the now pervasive desktop interface, and a paradigm for user interface control and display called "direct manipulation," which was gradually articulated through the 1980s (Hutchins et al 1986, Shneiderman 1983). It also led to theories of user interface metaphor (Carroll et al 1988).

A second limitation of the early GOMS-style cognitive models is that they do not address nonroutine problem solving and error. Studies showed that new users spent a third to a half of their time in error recovery (e.g. Mack et al 1983). More significantly, these studies showed that often the dispositions that make people good sense makers are also causes for characteristic learner problems (Carroll 1990): People want to learn by doing, but this inclines them to opportunistically jump around in sometimes brittle learning sequences. They want to reason things out and construct their own understandings, but they are not always planful, and they often draw incorrect inferences. They try to engage and extend prior knowledge and skill, which can lead to interference or overgeneralization. They try to learn through error diagnosis and recovery, but errors can be subtle, can tangle, and can become intractable obstacles to comprehension and to motivation.

This work entrained the conception of the "active user," improvising, hypothesizing, trying to make sense of a very complex environment. It led to emphases on designing for learning-by-doing and for error (Carroll 1990, Lewis & Norman 1986). For example, Carroll & Carrithers (1984) created a "training wheels" interface in which attempted departures from a correct action path are blocked. Users are informed that the action is not appropriate and are permitted to try again without penalty. This kind of design supports sense-making but not necessarily efficient performance. The active user was somewhat of an alternative to the GOMS conception of the user as an information processor.

USER-CENTERED SYSTEM DEVELOPMENT

In the early days of HCI, the notion that computer systems and software should be designed and developed with explicit consideration of the needs, abilities, and preferences of their ultimate users was not taken seriously. Most writings about computing from the mid-1970s are stunningly dismissive of usability and rather patronizing of users. After only a decade, the computer industry and the discipline of computer science were transformed. The case had been made for a user-centered system development process, a process in which usability was a primary goal. People began to distinguish sharply between technology-driven exploratory development, which is now often accompanied by explicit disclaimers about usability, and "real" system development, in which empirically verified usability is the final arbiter.

With the advent of the 1990s, HCI research had become relatively well integrated in computer science. A 1988 Association for Computing Machinery (ACM) task force listed HCI as one of nine core areas of the computer science discipline (Denning et al 1989). A joint curriculum task force of the ACM and the Institute of Electrical and Electronic Engineers (IEEE) recommended the inclusion of HCI as a common requirement in computer science programs (Tucker & Turner 1991). HCI was included as one of ten major sections of the first *Handbook of Computer Science and Engineering* (Tucker 1997). In the 1990s, computer science students and the corporations that hire them are demanding HCI courses in university curricula. Several major computer science departments have designated HCI as a research focus. Two comprehensive undergraduate texts have appeared (Dix et al 1993, Preece et al 1994).

In industry, HCI practitioners have become well integrated in system development. HCI specialists have moved into a great variety of roles beyond human-factors assurance. They have been routinely included in customer/user interactions to understand the need for new products, product planning, and specification; the development and evaluation of prototypes; the design of documentation and training; and installation and user support. There has been an obvious trend for HCI specialists to be promoted into project management. None of these trends impugns the psychological nature of HCI; rather, they indicate that it has been a practical success. In addition, they remind us that successful applied work involves more than merely applying lab-based theories and results, a theme that continues to be articulated in the current era.

HCI remains an emerging area in computer science. As an applied area of social and behavioral science, it continues to broaden. The issues raised in the early days of software psychology are still being resolved and elaborated: How can iterative development be supported and improved? How should we manage resources in iterative development to optimize cost benefit? How should we expand the scope and richness of the early cognitive user models? How can we cumulate and develop technical lessons learned in iterative development? What role can HCI play in broadening, grounding, and invigorating the development of the social and behavioral science base?

These issues have been pursued through refinements in the original notions of iterative development and user models, discussed below in the sections Usability Engineering, Design Rationale, and Cooperative Activity.

Usability Engineering

Iterative development is consistent with the real nature of design. It emphasizes the discovery of new goals, the role of prototyping and evaluation, and the importance of involving diverse stakeholders, including users. But what makes iterative development more than merely well-intentioned trial and error?

"Usability engineering" became the banner under which diverse methodological endeavors were carried out in the 1980s (Nielsen 1993, Whiteside et al 1988). There were three key notions: First, it was proposed that iterative development be managed according to explicit and measurable objectives, called "usability specifications" (Carroll & Rosson 1985; see also Bennett 1984, Butler 1985). Thus, in designing a word-processing program, one would iteratively design and redesign, prototype and evaluate, include real secretaries in the design deliberations, but also make explicit commitments to precisely operationalized goals such as "two thirds of users will be able to prepare a two-page business letter in less than ten minutes with fewer than three errors after 30 minutes training." Usability specifications are now standard practice in HCI development.

The second key notion in usability engineering was a call to broaden the empirical scope of design. A variety of approaches and techniques for user participation were developed, many of which emphasized "low-tech," cooperative activities to facilitate collaboration between users, who bring expertise on the work situation, and developers, who bring expertise on technology (Greenbaum & Kyng 1991, Kuhn & Muller 1993, Schuler & Namioka 1993). This approach went beyond prior formulations of user involvement by describing broader and more active roles for users. In "participatory design," as the approach is now known, users are involved in setting design goals and planning prototypes, instead of becoming involved only after initial prototypes exist.

Field-study approaches to characterizing the users' real needs and circumstances also became prominent (Whiteside & Wixon 1987). This emphasis came to be known as "contextual design" (Wixon et al 1990). It overturned the laboratory bias inherited by HCI from cognitive psychology by arguing that laboratory situations are often not controlled simulacrums of real situations but are better regarded as distinct but eccentric situations in their own right. Note that field-study approaches are not equivalent to user participation: Often field studies bring to light facts in the background of the context of use, circumstances of which the users themselves are unaware. Conversely, field studies cannot reveal the perspectives and insights users bring to the development process as designers.

In the early 1990s, contextual design converged with a line of ethnographic research that had produced edifying descriptions of use contexts, but which had generally eschewed direct involvement in design (e.g. Suchman 1987). This combination, sometimes called "ethnographically-informed design" (Bentley et al 1992), has become quite prominent. Like participatory design, it pushes a specific methodological commitment a step further by advocating very detailed observation of behavior in real situations. In practice, ethnographically informed design is frequently aimed at characterizing unarticulated power relations, organizational assumptions, and practical know-how that organize the workplace (Blomberg 1995). A complementary stream of work, sometimes called "conversation analysis," addresses itself to finer-grained behavioral structure (Greatbatch et al 1995). The commitment to revelatory interpretation of situated behavior sometimes engenders a behaviorism that gives too little weight to what people experience and report (Nardi 1995b).

The third key notion in usability engineering was cost effectiveness. It is expensive to carry out many cycles of prototyping, evaluation, and redesign. Developers need to employ efficient methods throughout and to know when they have reached diminishing returns. In the 1980s, much HCI work was directed at creating better prototyping tools and environments. An early theme in this work was the *separation* of user interface software from application software (i.e. system functionality) to modularize redesign of the user interface in user interface management systems (e.g. Tanner & Buxton 1985). Subsequent work emphasized the *coordination* of user interface and application software development to facilitate the creation of task-transparent user interfaces (Sukaviriya et al 1993, Szekely et al 1993). Concerns about ease of *implementation* motivated a family of prototyping tools based on the premise that user interface software could be directly created "by demonstration" (Cypher et al 1993).

The issue of cost effectiveness also guided methodological work on usability evaluation. Indeed, the earliest refinement of the GOMS model was a keystroke-counting approximation (Card et al 1983). Frequently, methodological shortcuts were grounded in the exigencies of system development. For example, thinking aloud protocols had become a standard empirical method, but they were generally not analyzed at the level of detail typical in cognitive psychology. Often, they were merely gleaned for critical incidents: episodes of use in which something goes unexpectedly well or badly (Flanagan 1954, Shattuck & Woods 1994).

Methodological work on usability evaluation sought to develop systematic techniques to ensure cost effectiveness (Bias & Mayhew 1994). Good et al (1986) developed "impact analysis," in which a variety of user performance factors are repeatedly measured throughout the development process to identify those factors that offer the greatest potential impact with respect to given usability specifications. Williges et al (1993) developed a statistical meta-strategy for reducing the factorial space of experimental studies through sequential estimates of relationships among large sets of independent variables.

The cost of user studies became a central issue. Many proposals were made for "heuristic" evaluation, checklist and script-oriented approaches to supplement or even replace direct user testing (Nielsen & Mack 1994, Nielsen & Mollich 1990). Other work examined the empirical parameters for user studies. Nielsen (1994) found that HCI practitioners were able to run only an average of 9 subjects in laboratory usability evaluations. Direct cost-benefit studies determined that only 4–5 experimental subjects found 80% of usability problems (Nielsen 1994, Virzi 1992). [Indeed, there have been recent discussions of "quick and dirty" ethnography (Hughes et al 1994).]

The cost of analytical techniques also became an issue. The assumption made in GOMS that actions are independent and additive rendered GOMS incapable of describing the co-articulation of concurrent activities. These limitations were acknowledged by Card et al (1983); for all these limitations, GOMS was also difficult to apply. John (1990) extended GOMS for tasks involving parallel activities by incorporating the concept of critical path. Kieras (1988) developed a simplified and explicit method for building GOMS analyses through top-down, breadth-first expansion of goals into methods to the level desired. Other simplified cognitive approaches were proposed. "Claims analysis" was suggested to integrate design rationale (see section below) and user modeling in analytic evaluation (Carroll & Rosson 1991). "Cognitive walkthrough" was proposed as heuristic evaluation grounded in simplified cognitive theory (Polson et al 1992). Comparative cost-benefit research is needed and is beginning to appear (Jeffries et al 1991, Karat et al 1992, Nielsen & Phillips 1993).

The term "usability engineering" connotes a practice that is broader and more systematic than is the case. HCI is largely a first-generation field in which various pioneers tend to follow the practices they helped to originate, not always the more eclectic best practices. The pioneer zeitgeist of the field needs to be smoothed and consolidated with increased emphasis on synthesis and integration. For example, although it has been shown that different evaluation methods identify different kinds of usability problems (Jeffries et al 1991), there are no schemes for integrating different types of evaluation data (e.g. quantitative performance data and qualitative protocol data) or for integrating evaluation data collected at different points in the iterative development process. Practitioners do not always differentiate among the variety of evaluation goals they must manage (Carroll & Rosson 1995).

A variety of such integration questions remains at the center of usability engineering. How can user models of the most technical sort (GOMS) be used in participatory design processes? Participatory design and usability engineering are sometimes considered alternative technical approaches (e.g. Monk et al 1993). Can broader user participation improve the cost effectiveness of usability engineering? Can users help to critique or even write usability specifications, heuristic evaluation checklists, walk-through scenarios, and design rationales? Cost-benefit analysis often views benefit fairly narrowly; in the long-term, part of the benefit could be the development of user models and design rationale from the specific results of usability evaluations. Can we develop means of estimating these more profound benefits? Can the development of user models and design rationale be (partially) automated as a by-product of usability engineering activities? How directly can ethnographic analysis guide design work?

Design Rationale

A computer system does not itself elucidate the motivations that initiated its design; the user requirements it was intended to address; the discussions, debates, and negotiations that determined its organization; the reasons for its particular features; the reasons against features it does not have; the weighing of trade-offs; and so forth. Such information can be critical to the variety of stakeholders in a design process: customers, users, servicers, and marketers, as well as designers who want to build upon the system and the ideas it embodies. This information comprises the design rationale of the system (Moran & Carroll 1996).

Approaches to design rationale can be divided into those that describe the design *solution* and those that describe the design *process*. The former approach seeks to position a given design in a larger context of issues and alternative designs. For example, MacLean et al (1991) developed an approach that explicates the design "space" surrounding a given design by enumerating the issues designers identified, the options they considered in responding to these issues, and the criteria they used in weighing the options. Thus, a window interface incorporating a particular technique for scrolling window contents can be located in a design space of other scrolling techniques.

Carroll & Rosson (1991) developed an approach that considers systems to be "embodied" social and behavioral claims about the needs, abilities, and activities of their users. Their approach seeks to articulate the social and behavioral theory implicit in a design. Thus, a programming environment can be seen as embodying a range of claims about what programmers know, what they do, and what they experience, and about the nature of programming tasks and the contexts within which these tasks are carried out.

These approaches make it easy to succinctly summarize the critical usability trade-offs of a particular usage situation, and to link these issues closely with specific features of the computer artifact in use. For example, including animated demonstrations as a self-instruction resource in a programming environment may intrinsically motivate learners and support learning about appropriate goals, but the demonstrations may also place learners in a passive role and suggest goals that are too difficult or nonproductive (e.g. the goal of altering the demonstration itself).

Many process-oriented approaches to design rationale are based on the issue-based information system (IBIS) developed by Rittel (e.g. Rittel & Weber 1973). In this approach, design deliberations are described according to the issues that arise during the design process, the various positions raised in response to the issues, and the arguments for and against each position. Conklin & Yakemovic (1991) showed how such a design rationale could be captured and used in a large commercial project, though they also emphasized the considerable work involved in coding this rationale. Other process-oriented approaches to rationale emphasize capturing less coded information, such as sketches and design notes, or videotaped self-disclosures by system developers (e.g. Carroll et al 1994).

The emergent nature of the design process makes design rationale both important and difficult. It is a tool for managing the complexity of a process in which everything, including the problem definition, constantly changes. Design rationale can track the consideration of various subproblems, trade-offs, and partial solutions, the reasons for changes and decisions, and the status of assumptions and issues. It can help design teams structure their problem-solving efforts and avoid thrashing. But how much of the design process can be usefully represented, and who will do the work of creating and maintaining this design rationale? Often design rationale is most useful to those who were not even involved with the project when the rationale was created (Grudin 1994). Should every developer have an analyst noting every hypothetical and every train of thought, videotaping every chance encounter in the hall, collecting every sketch and every note?

Current work on design rationale is concerned with assessing and supporting its efficacy. Empirical studies of designers and project teams are investigating how design rationale techniques can be learned and used (e.g. Buckingham Shum 1996). Other work is experimenting with software tools to support the creation of and access to rationales (Conklin & Begeman 1988, Fischer et al 1991, Rosson & Carroll 1995).

Design rationale integrates advances in iterative development and user models. Making the process and outcomes of design more explicit allows iterative development to be more systematic and more manageable. However, it also creates an explicit design representation, a "theory" of the artifact and its use tested by formative and summative evaluation throughout the iterative development process. This theory is not a classic user model; it describes specific situations of use, not purportedly general information processes and cognitive structures. However, this specificity makes it more powerful within the immediate design context, and schemes have been proposed for generalizing such situated theories (e.g. Carroll et al 1992). This integrative role of design rationale exemplifies what Scriven (1967) called "mediated evaluation," an approach in which design analysis of implicit goals and positions on inherent trade-offs among goals is used to guide design evaluation of user performance and experience.

Design rationale can be a language for stakeholders in the design, but these different stakeholders often speak different disciplinary languages, are motivated by different values, and see different technical issues when looking at the "same" design problem. Can everyone use the same design rationale information? Will gathering and codifying rationale alter the design process? Will it interfere? Who should have access to the design rationale that is created? There are potential conflicts between privacy rights and access rights of stakeholders. For example, it is useful for developers to be candid about trade-offs they managed, but are users entitled to this information?

Cooperative Activity

A trend to the social has gradually developed in HCI over the past 15 years, a development that has markedly accelerated, deepened, and diversified in the past five (Hiltz & Turoff 1978/1993). This recent trend is actually a nexus of at least four logically independent developments. First, there was a clear consensus by 1990 that the cognitive modeling approach had failed to provide a comprehensive paradigm. Second, many voices suggested a more socially or organizationally oriented approach was required to supplement or replace the cognitive paradigm. Third, the growing technical prominence of HCI attracted a sociopolitical critique of usability as a potential apology for de-skilling and other unpleasant aspects of industrial restructuring. Fourth, new technologies for communication and collaborative activity swept through the computing industry and raised significantly new challenges and opportunities for HCI.

It was somewhat an accident of history that the original foundations of HCI are so strongly in cognitive psychology. The research agenda opened up by the pioneers of software psychology, together with the new opportunities occasioned by personal and distributed computing, attracted a core of cognitive psychologists, who attracted even more. HCI emerged from what in retrospect seems to have been the evangelical heyday of the cognitive paradigm. The initial euphoria with models of ideal performance time was soon displaced by frustration with the limitations of these models, particularly regarding learning in context, error and error recovery, preference, fatigue, work context and collaboration, and individual differences. In 1990 and 1991 the major international conferences in HCI featured panels addressed to the failure of theory (Monk et al 1990, Sutcliffe et al 1991). Recent reformulations of the role of cognitive user modeling position it more eclectically within usability engineering (Nielsen 1993, Preece et al 1994).

In the 1990s, new voices entered the HCI discussion, urging a stronger social and contextual orientation. Anthropologists and sociologists joined what had been largely a cognitive psychology project (Bowker et al 1995, Thomas 1995). European perspectives on technology and work began to penetrate the discourse of what had been a somewhat insular American and British endeavor (Bjerknes et al 1987, Greenbaum & Kyng 1991). Concepts from activity theory, work psychology, and the labor movement became well known (Bødker 1991, Carroll 1991, Ehn 1988, Nardi 1995a). More research attention was directed at understanding situated and distributed cognition (Carroll & Rosson

1992, Norman 1991, Suchman 1995, Zuboff 1988). As part of a larger paradigmatic restructuring of social and behavioral science, traditions that had sought to study individuals in isolation from their contexts, and social phenomena in isolation from individuals, were declining (Knorr-Cetina 1981).

By far the most theoretically rich alternate paradigm is activity theory, derived from the work of Vygotsky (Nardi 1995a, Wertsch 1985). The object of description in this approach is an "activity system," the ensemble of technological factors with social factors and of individual attitudes, experiences, and actions with community practices, traditions, and values. Activity theory emphasizes that these ensembles are inherently contingent and changing, that human activities are mediated and transformed by human creations, such as technologies, and that people make themselves through their use of tools. The tensions and contradictions within an activity system at a given point define a "zone of proximal development" within which people can effect changes (Engestrom 1993). Activity theory shifts attention from characterizing static and individual competencies to characterizing how people can negotiate with the social and technological environment to solve problems and learn, which subsumes many of the issues of situated and distributed cognition.

Kuutti & Arvonen (1992) showed how the design of a medical information system reintegrated the activity system of health professionals in a medical center, a hospital, and throughout the larger community by enabling a shared concept of total patient care, supported by electronic tools and new practices (see also Bødker 1991). Activity theory subsumes many of the methodological issues about participatory design. The user community needs to be receptive to change; the tensions and inconsistencies in the current activity system must be made visible and questioned, that is, brought into the zone of proximal development. It subsumes ethnography: One must study communities of practice in situ and in detail to understand their zone of proximal development. A critical unanswered question about activity theory is whether it can be codified as a (predictive) engineering model (e.g. Blackler 1995), or whether part of the thrust of activity theory is to emphasize aspects of usability that are not susceptible to engineering models.

The social and organizational perspective brought with it a new critique of technology development in HCI. One theme is that different perspectives are inevitable and that conflict must be systemically accommodated and managed. HCI concepts and techniques through the 1980s tended to be directed at a naive notion of engineering optimality. The 1990s brought the view that stakeholder interests often conflict profoundly (e.g. Suchman 1995). Some of the most significant conflicts and misunderstandings are not between users and designers—the hallmark concern of participatory design—but between different constituencies of users (e.g. Blomberg 1995). These conflicts typically involve power relations between higher- and lower-status employees, between managers and their subordinates, and between teachers and students. Conflicts can of course be salutary for group decision-making (Kling 1991); the point is that they must be addressed.

The second theme of the sociopolitical critique was the potential for usability to unwittingly become a vehicle for de-skilling and disempowering workers. Making someone's work easier reduces the skill required to perform the work; in a given organizational context, it may reduce status, pay, and even job security. The effects can be subtle and complex because the workers themselves may not recognize the potential for such an outcome and may participate in their own de-skilling. This level of analysis received very little attention in the 1980s by the mainstream involved in HCI. Thus, the malaise regarding cognitive user models arose in doubts that the paradigm could achieve more than performance modeling, not in worries that minimizing low-level actions might be fundamentally the wrong goal to pursue. Recent work has explored the dynamic co-design of new technology and new social and organizational structures (Gasser 1986, Kling & Jewett 1994).

New HCI technologies to support meetings and other collaborative activity have encouraged the development of social and contextual analysis. Through the 1980s, electronic mail became an increasingly common communication tool, and other internet tools like newsgroups, multi-user domains, and real-time chat became less arcane. A variety of environments for collaborative problem solving were investigated, including electronic meeting rooms (Nunamaker et al 1991), two-way video "media-spaces" (Bly et al 1993), and three-dimensional "virtual reality" simulations (Leigh et al 1996). The portrait of a solitary user finding and creating information in a computer became background to the portrait of several to many people working together at a variety of times and places. Speculation about new paradigms for education, work, and leisure activity have become rampant in the field and in the culture at large.

The shift of focus in HCI toward cooperative activity raises many methodological issues. As suggested above, the concept of usability becomes more multifarious and therefore susceptible to a multitude of distortions. Agre (1995) discussed a case in which a usability analysis devolved into a study of the malleability of user perceptions about privacy. Grudin (1994) raised the issue that the people who do the work in a group-oriented system may not be the ones who enjoy the benefits. Most of what we know of usability pertains to information creation and management tasks, but in future systems interpersonal communication tasks may become more central than information access. How are various types of cooperative activity affected by various paradigms for computer-mediated communication? Most of our knowledge pertains to the relatively primitive paradigms based on electronic mail (Hiltz & Turoff 1978/1993, Sproull & Kiesler 1991). What kinds of human communities will be favored by a computer network infrastructure; what kinds will be weakened? Will worldwide interest groups supplant physical neighborhoods as our primary communities? Will our neighborhoods become transformed into local networks (Schuler 1994)?

SYNTHESIZING A DISCIPLINE

In *Sciences of the Artificial,* Simon wrote that "the proper study of mankind is the science of design." The design of human activities and the technologies that support them are a special case of "design" in this broad sense.

HCI has made steady and sometimes dramatic progress as a science of design. It has become a major research area in computer science and the very fulcrum of information technology development. However, the emergence of HCI is ongoing. Perhaps the most impressive current feature of the area is its fragmentation. The paradigmatic consensus of 1970s software psychology and of 1980s cognitive HCI is gone. This is not necessarily bad. Some of the current rifts may help set the agenda for the future. For example, a strong form of contextualism asserts that there is no role for controlled research in HCI (Carroll 1989, Whiteside & Wixon 1987). This is a potentially constructive challenge to the HCI research community. Other rifts are more a matter of mutual neglect. For example, after a brief period of confrontation in the mid-1980s, the proponents of cognitive user modeling have largely disconnected from programmatic discussions of activity theory, and conversely as well.

Mainly, this fragmentation reflects the difficulty of assimilating the great variety of methodologies, theoretical perspectives, driving problems, and people that have become part of HCI. Today's HCI researchers and practitioners are, after all, immigrants from other disciplines and backgrounds. It is not surprising that they often continue to favor what they know how to do. Younger people now entering the field will bring a broader foundation of knowledge and skill, and it is likely that the potential for a broader HCI will be advanced through them.

The recent past suggests three specific technical themes for the near-term future. First, the engineering scope of HCI will continue to broaden beyond user interface interactions. Designing human activities and appropriate technology to support them is likely to become a more integrated endeavor. Second, the success of HCI in generic applications is likely to bolster further domain-specific work, in particular complex application areas. Finally, the impact of HCI on psychology itself, perhaps the strongest fulfillment of Simon's vision of a design science, is likely to progress more concertedly, given recent developments in ecological and rational psychology, and given a political context that increasingly questions the use of science.

Activity theory emphasizes that the purview of usability is the totality of what people do and experience, and that the diverse facets of usability are interdependent and co-evolve with technology. It has begun to play a role in guiding the envisionment of new technology (e.g. Kuutti & Arvonen 1992). However, it needs to be cultivated as a more comprehensive foundation for the development process: requirements gathering, participatory interaction, software analysis and design, specification and prototyping, system implementation, documentation and instruction design, and usability evaluation. Scenario-based design, a fusion of activity theory with object-oriented software engineering in which narratives of use situations represent software and systems, is one proposal for how this might be achieved (Carroll 1995).

HCI has focused on common denominator technical domains: mass-market applications like word processors and spreadsheets, standard graphical user interfaces, like the Macintosh and Windows, and generic techniques like menu hierarchies, direct manipulation, and programming by demonstration. In the 1980s there were so many studies of user issues in text editing that it was called the "white rat" of HCI. As in the psychology of learning, paradigmatic focus yields a technical coherence, but at the price of confounding eccentricities. In the near future, there is likely to be more HCI research directed at specific technical domains; for example, user interfaces for typesetters (Bødker et al 1987) or petroleum engineers (Brooks 1993), and software tools and environments for teachers and students (Soloway et al 1994) or for scientists and engineers (Gallopoulos et al 1994).

The emergence of HCI in the past two decades illustrates the possibility of psychological inquiry in the context of system development and of progress with fundamental issues joined with engineering design. It demonstrates, for example, how the complex problem-solving of system development is not a straightforward scaling of laboratory-based studies of puzzles. Laboratory situations, after all, are models of real situations in which people are deprived of social and tool resources that constitute those situations. As emphasized by activity theory, human behavior and experience both adapt to and transform social and technological context. Human activities motivate the creation of new tools, but these in turn alter activities, which in time motivates further tools. The context of behavior and experience is changing more rapidly, more incessantly, perhaps more profoundly than ever before in history. HCI design provides an opportunity fundamentally to expand traditional ecological and recent rational approaches to psychology. These approaches consider the environment a causal factor in psychological explanation, but they have generally ignored the evolution of the environment itself (Anderson 1990, Brunswick 1956, Gibson 1979).

It is exciting to see that the emerging role of social and cognitive science in computer science and the computer industry is far more diverse, pervasive, and critical than imagined in the 1970s. As it has turned out, that role was not to support a received view of design but to help overturn it and help clarify the real nature of design. Nor was that role to recast psychological laws as human-factors guidelines; it was indeed to play a part in driving the evolution of social and cognitive science, and the recognition that computers can be deliberately designed to facilitate human activity and experience only when social and cognitive requirements drive the design process throughout. There is unprecedented potential for interdisciplinary synergy here. Social science has always borne the vision of what human society might become, but it has typically lacked the means to be constructive. Computer science—quite the converse—cannot avoid causing substantial social restructuring. An integrated and effective HCI can be a turning point in both disciplines and, perhaps, in human history.

ACKNOWLEDGMENTS

Some parts of the section on The Emergence of Usability are adapted from Carroll (1992). Some parts of the section on Design Rationale are adapted from the Introduction to Moran & Carroll (1996).

Literature Cited

Agre P. 1995. Conceptions of the user in computer systems design. See Thomas 1995, pp. 67–106

Anderson JR. 1990. *The Adaptive Character of Thought.* Hillsdale, NJ: Erlbaum

Bennett JB. 1984. Managing to meet usability requirements: establishing and meeting software development goals. In *Visual Display Terminals,* ed. J Bennett, D Case, J Sandelin, M Smith, pp. 161–84. Englewood Cliffs, NJ: Prentice-Hall

Bentley R, Hughes JA, Randall D, Rodden T, Sawyer P, et al. 1992. Ethnographically-informed system design for air traffic control. *Proc. CSCW 1994 Conf. Comput.-Support Coop. Work,* Toronto, pp. 123–29. New York: Assoc. Comput. Mach.

Bias RG, Mayhew DJ, eds. 1994. *Cost-Justifying Usability.* Boston: Academic

Bjerknes G, Ehn P, Kyng M, eds. 1987. *Computers and Democracy: A Scandinavian Challenge.* Brookfield, VT: Avebury

Blackler F. 1995. Activity theory, CSCW and organizations. See Monk & Gilbert 1995, pp. 223–48

Blomberg JL. 1995. Ethnography: aligning field studies of work and system design. See Monk & Gilbert 1995, pp. 175–97

Bly S, Harrison S, Irwin S. 1993. Media spaces: bringing people together in a video, audio, and computing environment. *Commun. Assoc. Comput. Mach.* 36(1):28–47

Bødker S. 1991. *Through the Interface: A Human Activity Approach to User Interface Design.* Hillsdale, NJ: Erlbaum

Bødker S, Ehn P, Kammersgaard J, Kyng M, Sundblad Y. 1987. A utopian experience. See Bjerknes et al 1987, pp. 251–78

Bowker G, Star SL, Gasser L, Turner B, eds. 1995. *Social Science Research, Technical Systems and Cooperative Work.* Mahwah, NJ: Erlbaum

Brooks FP. 1975/1995. *The Mythical Man-Month: Essays on Software Engineering.* Reading, MA: Addison-Wesley

Brooks R. 1993. The case for the specialized interface. *IEEE Softw.* 10(2):86–88

Brunswick E. 1956. *Perception and the Representative Design of Psychological Experiments.* Berkeley: Univ. Calif. Press

Buckingham Shum S. 1996. Analyzing the usability of a design rationale notation. In *Design Rationale: Concepts, Techniques, and Use,* ed. TP Moran, JM Carroll, pp. 185–215. Mahwah, NJ: Erlbaum

Butler KA. 1985. Connecting theory and practice: a case study of achieving usability goals. *Proc. CHI'85 Hum. Factors Comput. Syst., San Francisco,* pp. 85–88. New York: Assoc. Comput. Mach.

Card SK, Moran TP, Newell A. 1983. *The Psychology of Human-Computer Interaction.* Hillsdale, NJ: Erlbaum

Carroll JM. 1985. *What's in a Name? An Essay in the Psychology of Reference.* New York: Freeman

Carroll JM. 1989. Evaluation, description and invention: paradigms for human-computer interaction. In *Advances in Computers,* ed. M Yovits, 29:47–77. San Diego: Academic

Carroll JM. 1990. *The Nurnberg Funnel: Designing Minimalist Instruction for Practical Computer Skill.* Cambridge, MA: MIT Press

Carroll JM, ed. 1991. *Designing Interaction: Psychology at the Human-Computer Interface.* New York: Cambridge Univ. Press

Carroll JM. 1992. Creating a design science of human-computer interaction. In *Future Tendencies in Computer Science, Control, and Applied Mathematics: 25th Anniversary of INRIA,* ed. A Bensoussan, J-P Verjus, pp. 205–15. New York: Springer-Verlag

Carroll JM, Alpert SR, Karat J, Van Deusen M, Rosson MB. 1994. Capturing design history and rationale in multimedia narratives. In *Proc. CHI'94: Hum. Factors Comput. Syst., Boston,* pp. 192–97. New York: Assoc. Comput. Mach./Addison-Wesley

Carroll JM, Campbell RL. 1986. Softening up hard science: reply to Newell and Card. *Hum.-Comput. Interact.* 2:227–49

Carroll JM, Carrithers C. 1984. Blocking learner errors in a training wheels system. *Hum. Factors* 26(4):377–89

Carroll JM, Mack RL, Kellogg WA. 1988. Interface metaphors and user interface design. See Helander 1988, pp. 67–85

Carroll JM, Rosson MB. 1985. Usability specifications as a tool in iterative development. In *Advances in Human-Computer Interaction,* ed. HR Hartson, 1:1–28. Norwood, NJ: Ablex

Carroll JM, Rosson MB. 1991. Deliberated evolution: stalking the View Matcher in design space. *Hum.-Comput. Interact.* 6: 281–318

Carroll JM, Rosson MB. 1992. Getting around the task-artifact cycle: how to make claims and design by scenario. *Assoc. Comput. Mach. Trans. Inf. Syst.* 10:181–212

Carroll JM, Rosson MB. 1995. Managing evaluation goals for training. *Commun. Assoc. Comput. Mach.* 38(7):40–48

Carroll JM, Singley MK, Rosson MB. 1992. Integrating theory development with design evaluation. *Behav. Inf. Technol.* 11: 247–255

Carroll JM, Thomas JC. 1982. Metaphor and the cognitive representation of computing systems. *IEEE Trans. Syst., Man Cybern.* 12:107–16

Carroll JM, Thomas JC, Malhotra A. 1979. A clinical-experimental analysis of design problem solving. *Design Stud.* 1:84–92

Conklin J, Begeman M. 1988. gIBIS: a hypertext tool for exploratory policy discussion. *Assoc. Comput. Mach. Trans. Off. Inf. Syst.* 6(4):303–31

Conklin J, Yakemovic KCB. 1991. A process-oriented approach to design rationale. *Hum.-Comput. Interact.* 6:357–91

Curtis B, Krasner H, Iscoe N. 1988. A field study of the software design process for large systems. *Commun. Assoc. Comput. Mach.* 31:1268–87

Cypher A, Halbert D, Kurlander D, Lieberman H, Maulsby D, et al, eds. 1993. *Watch What I Do: Programming by Demonstration.* Cambridge, MA: MIT Press

deGroot AD. 1965. *Thought and Choice in Chess.* Paris: Mouton

Denning PJ, Comer DE, Gries D, Mulder MC, Tucker AB, et al. 1989. Computing as a discipline. *Commun. Assoc. Comput. Mach.* 32:9–23

Dix A, Finlay J, Abowd G, Beale R. 1993. *Human-Computer Interaction.* Englewood Cliffs, NJ: Prentice-Hall

Douglas SA, Moran TP. 1983. Learning text editor semantics by analogy. *Proc. CHI'83 Conf. Hum. Factors Comput. Syst., Boston,* pp. 207–11. New York: Assoc. Comput. Mach.

Dreyfuss H. 1955. *Designing for People.* New York: Simon & Schuster

Ehn P. 1988. *Work-Oriented Design of Computer Artifacts.* Stockholm: Arbetslivscentrum

Engestrom Y. 1993. Developmental work research: reconstructing expertise through expansive learning. In *Human Jobs and Computer Interfaces,* ed. M Nurminen, G Weir. Amsterdam: Elsevier

Ericsson KA, Simon HA. 1985. *Protocol Analysis: Verbal Reports as Data.* Cambridge, MA: MIT Press

Esper EA. 1925. A technique for the experimental investigation of associative interference in artificial linguistic material. *Lang. Monogr.* 1:1–47

Fischer G, Lemke AC, McCall R, Morch AI. 1991. Making argumentation serve design. *Hum.-Comput. Interact.* 6(3/4):393–419

Flanagan JC. 1954. The critical incident technique. *Psychol. Bull.* 51:28–35

Furnas G, Landauer TK, Gomez L, Dumais S. 1983. Statistical semantics: analysis of the potential performance of keyword information systems. *Bell Syst. Tech. J.* 62: 1753–806

Gallopoulos E, Houstis E, Rice JR. 1994. Computer as thinker/doer: problem-solving environments for computational science. *IEEE Comput. Sci. Eng.* 1(1):11–23

Gasser L. 1986. The integration of computing and routine work. *Assoc. Comput. Mach. Trans. Off. Inf. Syst.* 4(3):205–25

Gibson JJ. 1979. *The Ecological Approach to Visual Perception.* Boston: Houghton Mifflin

Good M, Spine TM, Whiteside J, George P. 1986. User-derived impact analysis as a tool for usability engineering. *Proc. CHI'86 Conf. Hum. Factors Comput. Syst., Boston,* pp. 241–46. New York: Assoc. Comput. Mach.

Gould JD, Boies SJ. 1983. Human factors challenges in creating a principal support office system: the speech filing approach. *Assoc. Comput. Mach. Trans. Off. Inf. Syst.* 1: 273–98

Gray WD, John BE, Atwood ME. 1992. The précis of project Ernestine, or, An overview of a validation of GOMS. *Proc. CHI'92 Conf. Hum. Factors Comput. Syst., Monterey, CA,* pp. 307–12. New York: Assoc. Comput. Mach.

Greatbatch D, Heath C, Luff P, Campion P. 1995. Conversation analysis: human-computer interaction and the general practice consultation. See Monk & Gilbert 1995, pp. 199–222

Greenbaum J, Kyng M, eds. 1991. *Design at Work: Cooperative Design of Computer Systems.* Hillsdale, NJ: Erlbaum

Grudin J. 1989. The case against user interface consistency. *Commun. Assoc. Comput. Mach.* 32:1164–73

Grudin J. 1994. Groupware and social dynamics: eight challenges for developers. *Commun. Assoc. Comput. Mach.* 37(1):92–105

Helander M, ed. 1988. *Handbook of Human-Computer Interaction.* Amsterdam: North-Holland

Hiltz SR, Turoff M. 1978/1993. *The Network Nation: Human Communication via Computer.* Cambridge: MIT Press

Hughes J, King V, Rodden T, Anderson H. 1994. Moving out from the control room: ethnography in system design. *Proc. CSCW'94 Conf. Comput.-Support. Coop. Work, Chapel Hill, NC,* pp. 429–39. New York: Assoc. Comput. Mach.

Hutchins E, Hollan J, Norman DA. 1986. Direct manipulation interfaces. See Norman & Draper 1986, pp. 87–124

Jeffries RJ, Miller JR, Wharton C, Uyeda KM. 1991. User interface evaluation in the real world: a comparison of four techniques. *Proc. CHI'91 Hum. Factors Comput. Syst., New Orleans,* pp. 119–24. New York: Assoc. Comput. Mach.

John BE. 1990. Extensions of GOMS analyses to expert performance requiring perception of dynamic visual and auditory information. *Proc. CHI'90 Hum. Factors Comput. Syst., Seattle,* pp. 107–15. New York: Assoc. Comput. Mach.

Karat CM, Campbell RL, Fiegel T. 1992. Comparison of empirical testing and walkthrough methods in user interface evaluation. *Proc. CHI'92 Hum. Factors Comput. Syst., Monterrey, CA,* pp. 397–404. New York: Assoc. Comput. Mach.

Kieras DE. 1988. Towards a practical GOMS model methodology for user interface design. See Helander 1988, pp. 135–57

Kling R. 1991. Cooperation, coordination and control in computer-supported work. *Commun. Assoc. Comput. Mach.* 34(12):83–88

Kling R, Jewett T. 1994. The social design of worklife with computers and networks: a natural systems perspective. In *Advances in Computers,* ed. M Yovits, 39:239–93. Orlando: Academic

Knorr-Cetina KD. 1981. The micro-sociological challenge of macro-sociology: towards a reconstruction of social theory and methodology. In *Advances in Social Theory and Methodology: Towards an Integration of Micro- and Macro-Sociologies,* ed. KD Knorr-Cetina, A Cicourel. London: Routledge & Kegan Paul

Kuhn S, Muller MJ, eds. 1993. Special section on participatory design. *Commun. Assoc. Comput. Mach.* 36(4):24–103

Kuutti K, Arvonen T. 1992. Identifying CSCW applications by means of activity theory concepts: a case example. *Proc. CSCW'92 Comput.-Support. Coop. Work, Toronto,* pp. 233–40. New York: Assoc. Comput. Mach.

Leigh J, Johnson AE, Vasilakis CA, DeFanti TA. 1996. Multi-perspective collaborative design in persistent networked virtual environments. *Proc. IEEE Virtual Reality Annu. Int. Symp., VRAIS 96,* Santa Clara, CA. In press

Lewis CH, Norman DA. 1986. Designing for error. See Norman & Draper 1986, pp. 411–32

Mack RL, Lewis CH, Carroll JM. 1983. Learning to use office systems: problems and prospects. *Assoc. Comput. Mach. Trans. Off. Inf. Syst.* 1:254–71

MacLean A, Young RM, Bellotti VME, Moran TP. 1991. Questions, options, and criteria: elements of design space analysis. *Hum.-Comput. Interact.* 6:201–50

Malhotra A, Thomas JC, Carroll JM, Miller LA. 1980. Cognitive processes in design. *Int. J. Man-Mach. Interact.* 12:119–40

Miller LA. 1974. Programming by nonprogrammers. *Int. J. Man-Mach. Stud.* 6: 237–60

Monk AM, Carroll JM, Harrison M, Long J, Young RM. 1990. New approaches to theory in HCI: How should we judge their acceptability? *Proc. INTERACT'90 Hum.-Comput. Interact., Cambridge,* pp. 1055–58. Amsterdam: North-Holland

Monk AM, Gilbert N, eds. 1995. *Perspectives on HCI: Diverse Approaches.* London: Academic

Monk AM, Nardi B, Gilbert N, Mantei M, McCarthy J. 1993. Mixing oil and water? Ethnography versus experimental psychology in the study of computer-mediated communication. *Proc. INTERCHI'93 Hum. Factors Comput. Syst., Amsterdam,* pp. 3–6. New York: Assoc. Comput. Mach.

Moran TP. 1983. Getting into a system: external-internal task mapping analysis. *Proc. CHI'83 Hum. Factors Comput. Syst., Boston,* pp. 45–49. New York: Assoc. Comput. Mach.

Moran TP, Carroll JM, eds. 1996. *Design Rationale: Concepts, Techniques, and Use.* Mahwah, NJ: Erlbaum

Nardi BA, ed. 1995a. *Context and Consciousness: Activity Theory and Human-Computer Interaction.* Cambridge, MA: MIT Press

Nardi BA. 1995b. Studying context: a comparison of activity theory, situated action models and distributed cognition. See Nardi 1995a, pp. 69–102

Newell A, Card SK. 1985. The prospects for psychological science in Human-Computer Interaction. *Hum.-Comput. Interact.* 1: 209–42

Newell A, Simon HA. 1972. *Human Problem Solving.* Englewood Cliffs, NJ: Prentice-Hall

Nielsen J, ed. 1989. *Coordinating User Interfaces for Consistency.* New York: Academic

Nielsen J. 1993. *Usability Engineering.* Boston: Academic

Nielsen J. 1994. Estimating the number of subjects needed for a thinking aloud test. *Int. J. Hum.-Comput. Stud.* 41:385–97

Nielsen J, Mack RL, eds. 1994. *Usability Inspection Methods.* New York: Wiley

Nielsen J, Mollich R. 1990. Heuristic evaluation of user interfaces. *Proc. CHI'90 Conf. Hum. Factors Comput. Syst., Seattle,* pp. 249–56. New York: Assoc. Comput. Mach.

Nielsen J, Phillips VL. 1993. Estimating the relative usability of two interfaces: heuristic, formal and empirical methods compared. *Proc. INTERCHI'93 Conf. Hum. Factors Comput. Syst., Amsterdam,* pp. 214–21. New York: Assoc. Comput. Mach.

Norman DA. 1991. Cognitive artifacts. See Carroll 1991, pp. 17–38

Norman DA, Draper SW, eds. 1986. *User Centered System Design.* Hillsdale, NJ: Erlbaum

Nunamaker J, Dennis A, Valacich J, Vogel D, George J. 1991. Electronic meeting systems to support group work. *Commun. Assoc. Comput. Mach.* 34(7):40–61

Nygaard K. 1979. The iron and metal project: trade union participation. In *Computers Dividing Man and Work: Recent Scandinavian Research on Planning and Computers from a Trade Union Perspective,* ed. A Sandberg, p. 98. Malmö: Arbetslivscentrum

Pava CHP. 1983. *Managing New Office Technology: An Organizational Strategy.* New York: Free Press

Payne SJ, Green TRG. 1989. Task-Action Grammars: the model and its developments. In *Task Analysis for Human-Computer Interaction,* ed. D Diaper, pp. 75–107. Chichester: Ellis Horwood

Payne SJ, Squibb H, Howes A. 1990. The nature of device models: the yoked state space hypothesis and some experiments with text editors. *Hum.-Comput. Interact.* 5:415–44

Polson PG, Lewis CH, Rieman J, Wharton C. 1992. Cognitive walkthroughs: a method for theory-based evaluation of user interfaces. *Int. J. Man-Mach. Stud.* 36:741–73

Preece J, Rogers Y, Sharp H, Benyon D, Holland S, Carey T. 1994. *Human-Computer Interaction.* Reading, MA: Addison-Wesley

Rittel H, Webber M. 1973. Dilemmas in a general theory of planning. *Policy Sci.* 4: 155–69

Rosson MB, Carroll JM. 1995. Narrowing the specification-implementation gap in scenario-based design. In *Scenario-Based Design: Envisioning Work and Technology in System Development,* ed. JM Carroll, pp. 247–78. New York: Wiley

Royce WW. 1970. Managing the development of large software systems: concepts and techniques. *Proc. West. Electr. Show Conv., WESTCON, Los Angeles,* pp. (A/1)1-9. Reprinted in *Proc. Int. Conf. Softw. Eng., 11th, Pittsburgh,* May 1989, pp. 328–38

Schuler D. 1994. Community networks: building a new participatory medium. *Commun. Assoc. Comput. Mach.* 37(1):39–51

Schuler D, Namioka A, eds. 1993. *Participatory Design: Principles and Practices.* Hillsdale, NJ: Erlbaum

Scriven M. 1967. The methodology of evaluation. In *Perspectives of Curriculum Evaluation,* ed. R Tyler, R Gagne, M Scriven, pp. 39–83. Chicago: Rand McNally

Shattuck L, Woods D. 1994. The critical incident technique: 40 years later. *Proc. Hum. Factors Ergon. Soc. Annu. Meet., 38th, Nashville,* pp. 1080–84. Santa Monica, CA: Hum. Factors Ergon. Soc.

Shneiderman B. 1980. *Software Psychology: Human Factors in Computer and Information Systems.* Cambridge, MA: Winthrop

Shneiderman B. 1983. Direct manipulation: a step beyond programming languages. *IEEE Comput.* 16(8):57–62

Shneiderman B, Mayer R, McKay D, Heller P. 1977. Experimental investigations of the utility of detailed flowcharts in programming. *Commun. Assoc. Comput. Mach.* 20: 373–81

Sime ME, Green TRG, Guest DJ. 1973. Psychological evaluation of two conditional constructions used in computer languages. *Int. J. Man-Mach. Stud.* 5:105–13

Simon HA. 1969. *The Sciences of the Artificial.* Cambridge: MIT Press

Smith DC, Irby C, Kimball R, Verplank B, Harslem E. 1982. Designing the Star user interface. *Byte* 7(4):242–82

Soloway E, Guzdial M, Hay KE. 1994. Learner-centered design: the challenge for HCI in the 21st Century. *Interactions* 1(2): 36–48

Sproull L, Kiesler S. 1991. *Connections: New Ways of Working in A Networked Organization.* Cambridge: MIT Press

Suchman LA. 1987. *Plans and Situated Actions: The Problem of Human-Machine Communication.* New York: Cambridge Univ. Press

Suchman LA, ed. 1995. Special section on representations of work. *Commun. Assoc. Comput. Mach.* 38(9):33–68

Sukaviriya P, Foley JD, Griffith T. 1993. A second-generation user interface design environment: the model and runtime architecture. *Proc. INTERCHI'93 Conf. Hum. Factors Comput. Syst., Amsterdam,* pp. 375–82. New York: Assoc. Comput. Mach.

Sutcliffe A, Carroll JM, Young RM, Long J. 1991. HCI theory on trial. *Proc. INTERCHI'93 Conf. Hum. Factors Comput. Syst., Amsterdam,* pp. 375–82. New York: Assoc. Comput. Mach.

Szekely P, Luo P, Neches R. 1993. Beyond interface builders: model-based interface tools. *Proc. CHI'91 Conf. Hum. Factors Comput. Syst., New Orleans,* pp. 399–401. New York: Assoc. Comput. Mach.

Tanner PP, Buxton WAS. 1985. Some issues in future user interface management system (UIMS) development. In *User Interface Management Systems: Proc. Workshop User Interface Management Syst., Seehiem, Ger., 1983,* ed. GE Pfaff, 67–79. New York: Springer-Verlag

Thomas PJ, ed. 1995. *The Social and Interactional Dimensions of Human-Computer Interact.* New York: Cambridge Univ. Press

Tucker AB, ed. 1997. *The Handbook of Computer Science and Engineering.* Boca Raton, FL: CRC Press

Tucker AB, Turner AJ. 1991. A summary of the ACM/IEEE-CS Joint Curriculum Task Force Report: computing Curricula 1991. *Commun. Assoc. Comput. Mach.* 34:68–84

Virzi RA. 1992. Refining the test phase of usability evaluation: how many subjects is enough? *Hum. Factors* 34:457–68

Wasserman AI, Shewmake DT. 1982. Rapid prototyping of interactive information systems. *Assoc. Comput. Mach. Softw. Eng. Notes* 7:171–80

Wasserman AI, Shewmake DT. 1985. The role of prototypes in the User Software Engineering (USE) methodology. In *Advances in Human-Computer Interaction,* ed. HR Hartson, 1:191–209. Norwood, NJ: Ablex

Weissman L. 1974. *A methodology for studying the psychological complexity of computer programs.* PhD thesis. Univ. Toronto, Toronto

Wertsch J. 1985. *Vygotsky and the Social Formation of Mind.* Cambridge, MA: Harvard Univ. Press

Whiteside J, Bennett J, Holtzblatt K. 1988. Usability engineering: our experience and evolution. See Helander 1988, pp. 791–817

Whiteside J, Wixon D. 1987. Improving human-computer interaction: a quest for cognitive science. In *Interfacing Thought: Cognitive Aspects of Human-Computer Interaction,* ed. JM Carroll, pp. 337–52. Cambridge, MA: Bradford/MIT Press

Williges RC, Williges BH, Han SH. 1993. Sequential experimentation in human-computer interface design. In *Advances in Human-Computer Interaction,* ed. HR Hartson, D Hix, 4:1–30. Norwood, NJ: Ablex

Wixon D, Holtzblatt K, Knox S. 1990. Contextual design: an emergent view of system design. In *Proc. CHI '90: Hum. Factors Comput. Sys.,* Seattle, pp. 329–36. New York: Assoc. Comput. Mach.

Wright RB, Converse SA. 1992. Method bias and concurrent verbal protocol in software usability testing. *Proc. Hum. Factors Ergon. Soc. Annu. Meet., 36th, Atlanta,* pp. 891–912. Santa Monica, CA: Hum. Factors Ergon. Soc.

Zuboff Z. 1988. *In the Age of the Smart Machine: The Future of Work and Power.* New York: Basic Books

Annu. Rev. Psychol. 1997. 48:85–114

NEUROBIOLOGICAL CONSTRAINTS ON BEHAVIORAL MODELS OF MOTIVATION

Karim Nader,[1] *Antoine Bechara,*[2] *and Derek van der Kooy*[1]

[1]Neurobiology Research Group, Department of Anatomy and Cell Biology, University of Toronto, Toronto, Ontario, Canada M5S 1A8

[2]Department of Neurology, University of Iowa Hospitals and Clinics, Iowa City, Iowa 52242

KEY WORDS: reward, aversion, hedonics, dopamine, deprivation

ABSTRACT

The application of neurobiological tools to behavioral questions has produced a number of working models of the mechanisms mediating the rewarding and aversive properties of stimuli. The authors review and compare three models that differ in the nature and number of the processes identified. The dopamine hypothesis, a single system model, posits that the neurotransmitter dopamine plays a fundamental role in mediating the rewarding properties of all classes of stimuli. In contrast, both nondeprived/deprived and saliency attribution models claim that separate systems make independent contributions to reward. The former identifies the psychological boundary defined by the two systems as being between states of nondeprivation (e.g. food sated) and deprivation (e.g. hunger). The latter identifies a boundary between liking and wanting systems. Neurobiological dissociations provide tests of and explanatory power for behavioral theories of goal-directed behavior.

CONTENTS

INTRODUCTION

The study of motivation focuses on why animals do what they do, when they do it. Out of all the possible responses that an animal can make, why does feeding behavior have a greater probability of occurring in food-deprived animals than other competing behaviors? Similarly, the probability that animals will freeze is much greater on presentation of a tone that predicts shock as opposed to presentation of a tone that has no such predictive value. Thus, motivation can be conceptually described as a continuum along which stimuli can either reinforce or punish responses to other stimuli. Behaviorally, stimuli that reinforce are called rewarding and those that punish aversive (Skinner 1953). Although reward and aversion (collectively called motivational properties in this chapter) describe the impact a stimulus has on behavior, they do not address why we approach some stimuli and not others. Work on this question was greatly impeded by Skinner's behaviorism. Skinner (1953) argued that if psychology was to be a natural science in the same way as physics or chemistry, it too must restrain itself to a quantitative methodology. Thus, the appropriate study area for psychology was an examination of how environmental variables influenced behavior. Skinner argued that in a functional analysis of behavior it was heuristically bankrupt to invoke inner causes as explanatory constructs. To say that a person eats because s/he is hungry, for example, is circular because we infer a state of hunger from the behavior (eating) that we are trying to explain. "If this state [hunger] is purely inferential—if no dimensions are assigned to it which would make direct observation possible—it cannot serve as an explanation" (Skinner 1953, p. 33). Hunger is simply a ghost that we've created and, in turn, projected onto the machine. This is what Skinner is referring to in his observing that the constructs invoked always seem to have the exact qualities necessary to explain the behavior at hand. Further, Skinner (1953) is right to say that even a complete understanding at the neural level of behavior would not bring anything new to a functional analysis of behavior. Even if we knew the exact neural mechanisms that produced hunger, this information is not directly observable to us in normal settings. Therefore, it would not preclude the need to know the antecedent conditions (e.g. number of hours of food deprivation) to predict the probability that a person will eat.

Neurobiology, however, can impact the study of behavior in two significant ways. First, it can test the existence of inferential constructs and directly determine the dimensions of their contribution to the behavior under examination. Second, neurobiological tools can be used to deconstruct behavior into its component processes and then test how these processes interact to create a behavior. For example, any number of hypothetical constructs can be invoked to explain why an individual eats; the food may be rewarding or palatable, or perhaps the individual is hungry. In all cases, the causal analysis refers to some nonquantifiable inferential process, which Skinner argued against. If hunger does influence feeding behavior, then it must be possible to identify the underlying neural substrates mediating hunger. By manipulating the neural mechanisms mediating hunger we can directly test the conditions under which they make a contribution to feeding. In this way, hunger can be reclaimed from limbo, given definable behavioral dimensions, and placed back into the animal. The findings from this neurobiological approach can then be used to constrain or inform the implementation of hunger constructs in behavioral theories of feeding behavior. Furthermore, feeding can be the result of either a single or multiple process(es). By using neurobiological tools, the nature and number of the processes can be identified. For example, if hunger and palatability constructs referred to the same underlying process, then any neural manipulation affecting measures of palatability should similarly affect measures of hunger. Such a finding would question a behavioral theory that defined these two psychological processes separately, and could force the development of a more parsimonious description of the process identified. Conversely, if these two constructs make completely independent contributions to feeding behavior, then manipulations that affect palatability should not affect measurements of hunger, and manipulations affecting hunger should not affect measurements of palatability. This would double dissociate the mechanisms mediating palatability and hunger and define them as two independent processes.

By applying this strategy to rewarding and aversive stimuli, we can test whether common processes mediate the reward properties of different classes of stimuli. Furthermore, if systems can be double dissociated, then we can ask questions about the psychological boundary identified. This chapter reviews three neurobiological models that have developed from such a neurobiological approach and how their findings relate to current psychological theories of goal-directed behavior. These are by no means the only models that have been proposed. They have been chosen because the psychological boundaries identified and the proposed nature of the processes provide interesting studies in contrast.

MODELS OF MOTIVATION

The Dopamine Hypothesis

One of the early successes in the strategy of looking to neurobiology to identify the mechanisms that make stimuli reinforcing was the demonstration by Olds & Milner (1954) that electrical stimulation of different sites in the brain could act as reinforcing, neutral, or punishing events. In one animal, bar press responses reached a rate of 1920 responses/h for delivery of stimulation to the mammilothalamic tract. One of the most important implications of these findings is that pathways in the brain are organized topographically, with psychological boundaries that can be identified behaviorally. Furthermore, in identifying the sites involved in mediating the reinforcing properties of self-stimulation, it was now possible to ask questions about the physiological events that are necessary and sufficient for reinforcement to occur, and whether these same sites are involved in mediating the reinforcing effects of stimuli such as food, water, sex, and even drugs of abuse. Indeed, Rolls et al (1974) showed that regardless of whether the site of stimulation was the nucleus accumbens, septal area, hippocampus, anterior hypothalamus, or ventral tegmental area, systematic administration of spiroperidol (an antagonist at synapses using dopamine as a neurotransmitter) was effective at decreasing the rates of self-stimulation. In addition, spiroperidol also attenuated the rate of responses when the reinforcers were food and water, which suggests the possibility that dopamine might be a common mechanism by which reward is produced.

More recently, dopamine antagonists have been shown in operant paradigms to attenuate the reinforcing properties of food, water, opiates, and intravenous psychostimulants such as amphetamine and cocaine (e.g. Ettenberg et al 1982, Geary & Smith 1985, Gerber et al 1981, Rolls et al 1974, Schneider et al 1990, Yokel & Wise 1975, 1976). Furthermore, the behavior of animals that were pretreated with low doses of dopamine antagonists was often similar to the behavior seen during extinction (when presentation of the stimulus is withheld) (Fouriezos & Wise 1976, Rolls et al 1974, Wise et al 1978, Yokel & Wise 1975, 1976). For example, when response-contingent presentation of amphetamine is withheld, animals show a temporary initial increase in their rate of responding (Pickens & Harris 1968, Pickens & Thompson 1971), which is termed a frustration effect (Amsel & Roussel 1952). Administration of low doses of dopamine antagonists to animals bar-pressing for amphetamine causes similar increases (Yokel & Wise 1975, 1976). Given that dopamine-pretreated animals were competent to respond at elevated rates, the authors suggested that the processes being manipulated were motivational, as opposed to motoric in nature (for alternate interpretations based on motoric deficits, see Ettenberg 1989, Ettenberg et al 1981, Fibiger et al 1976, Tombaugh et al 1980). Such demonstrations contributed to the formulation of the anhedonia hypothesis, which states that dopamine was a critical link in the unconditioned (Wise 1982, Wise et al 1978) and conditioned (Beninger 1983, Gray & Wise 1980) reward properties of all stimuli.

Another line of evidence supporting a role for dopamine in the motivational properties of stimuli comes from the place-conditioning paradigm (Carr et al 1989, Mucha & Iversen 1984, van der Kooy 1987). This paradigm treats the increase in amount of time spent in an environment that has been paired with an unconditioned stimulus as an index of the stimulus's reward properties. Alternatively, if animals avoid the environment because of multiple environment-stimulus pairings, the stimulus is inferred to be aversive. Rats trained using this paradigm show a preference for an environment that has been previously paired with drugs, rewarding brain stimulation, or natural reinforcers (Carr et al 1989). If dopamine antagonists are administered before each conditioning session with amphetamine, then the normal amphetamine-conditioned place preferences are blocked (i.e. when tested, animals spend an equivalent amount of time in both the saline-paired and amphetamine-paired environments) (Hiroi et al 1990, Mackey & van der Kooy 1985, Mithani et al 1986, Spyraki et al 1982b). These findings are not interpretable in terms of a general learning deficit because animals pretreated with the same dopamine antagonists can acquire normal conditioned place aversions to environments paired with lithium chloride (LiCl), which demonstrates that animals can form normal CS-US associations in place conditioning (Bechara & van der Kooy 1986, Shippenberg & Herz 1988). Thus, dopamine antagonist pretreatment blocked the rewarding properties of amphetamine. Dopamine antagonist pretreatment has also been reported to block the acquisition of conditioned place preferences for environments that have been paired with heroin (Bozarth & Wise 1981, Hand et al 1989, Spyraki et al 1983), morphine (Acquas & Di Chiara 1994, Leone & Di Chiara 1987, Shippenberg et al 1993, Shippenberg & Herz 1988; however, see next section for contradictory results), and food (Spyraki et al 1982a).

These findings suggest that normal dopamine transmission is necessary for the rewarding properties of stimuli to occur. Studies using dopamine agonists have also shown that stimulation of dopaminergic receptors is sufficient to reproduce these motivational effects. The direct dopamine agonist apomorphine can act as an effective reinforcer in maintaining self-administration behavior (Baxter et al 1974, Roberts et al 1980, Wise et al 1976) and producing conditioned place preferences (Spyraki et al 1982b, van der Kooy et al 1983). Thus, under certain conditions dopamine stimulation is both necessary and sufficient to produce reward.

Anatomical and physiological manipulations (for a review of the physiological studies, see Milner 1991, Wise 1996) have identified the mesolimbic dopaminergic system that projects from the ventral tegmental area (VTA) neuronal cell bodies rostrally to the nucleus accumbens as a primary link in the reward pathway (Wise & Bozarth 1987). Lesions of the nucleus accumbens with 6-hydroxydopamine, which destroys dopaminergic terminals, attenuate operant responding for morphine (Smith et al 1985), cocaine (Pettit et al 1984, Roberts et al 1977, 1980), amphetamine (Lyness et al 1979), and nicotine (Corrigal et al 1992). Microinjections of dopamine antagonists directly into the nucleus accumbens have also been shown to attenuate responding for electrical stimulation of the VTA (Mogenson et al 1979), oral ethanol self-administration (Rassnick et al 1992), as well as amphetamine (Phillips et al 1994) and cocaine self-administration (Caine & Koob 1993, McGregor & Roberts 1993, Robledo et al 1992). Furthermore, microinjections of morphine directly into the VTA can support the acquisition of both operants (Devine & Wise 1994, Welz et al 1989) and conditioned place preferences (Bozarth 1987).

Thus, a great deal of convergent data (for a review, see Wise & Rompre 1989) support the involvement of the dopaminergic neurons originating in the VTA and projecting to the nucleus accumbens in mediating the reward effects of stimuli. However, difficulties remain in understanding the extent of dopamine's role in motivation. If the dopaminergic pathway from the VTA to the nucleus accumbens is a primary link in the pathways mediating the motivational properties of stimuli, then examples of dopamine-independent reward should be nonexistent. There are a number of examples, however, of stimuli that possess reinforcing properties independent of dopamine. For instance, dopamine antagonist pretreatment or 6-OHDA lesions of the nucleus accumbens have been reported to have no effect on morphine or heroin self-administration (Dworkin et al 1988, Ettenberg et al 1982, Pettit et al 1984). Furthermore, ethanol place preferences are unaffected by pretreatment with the dopamine antagonist halperidol (Cunningham et al 1992, Risinger et al 1992). Indeed, 6-OHDA lesions of the nucleus accumbens have been reported to spare ethanol oral self-administration (Rassnick et al 1993). Work done with cocaine has also revealed a lack of dopaminergic involvement in cocaine place preferences (Mackey & van der Kooy 1985, Spyraki et al 1982c), and direct microinjections of cocaine into the nucleus accumbens, its putative site of action (Caine & Koob 1993, Koob & Bloom 1988), fail to condition a place preference (Hemby et al 1992) or support self-administration behavior (Goeders & Smith 1983). Furthermore, under some conditions, opiate place preferences can be demonstrated to be dopamine independent (Bechara et al 1992, Mackey & van der Kooy 1985, Nader et al 1994). These examples of dopamine-independent motivated behavior seriously question the original dopamine hypothesis that suggested dopamine is a final common pathway in the processes mediating reinforcement.

It is critical to resolve whether these examples of dopamine-independent rewarding effects involve procedural problems or are real indications that other pathways or systems exist that can also mediate reward. Indeed, if there are multiple reward pathways, then the interactions of these other reward pathways with the mesolimbic system need to be identified, and the parameters within which each pathway plays a primary role in reward must be described. One attempt at reconciling demonstrations of dopamine-independent reward with the dopamine hypothesis has been to posit that a single reward system exists, of which the VTA dopaminergic neurons are a component. It is suggested that stimuli may activate this system either upstream or downstream of the dopaminergic neurons themselves (Wise & Rompre 1989). Thus, even though reward may not be mediated by a single neurotransmitter, it may be mediated by a single neural system. Whether other demonstrations of dopamine-independent reward can be incorporated into a similar framework remains unclear.

Nondeprived/Deprived Hypothesis

In contrast with the dopamine hypothesis (a single-system model of reward), the nondeprived/deprived model claims that two separate neurobiological reward systems can be double dissociated, each of which makes a significant contribution to motivated behavior depending on deprivation state. Instead of defining a boundary between stimulus classes such as opiates and food, this model defines a boundary between nondeprived (e.g. drug-naive or food-sated) and deprived (e.g. food-deprived or drug-dependent and withdrawn) motivational states. This distinction is analogous to situations in which one indulges in dessert after having just completed a meal (an example of nondeprived reward), as opposed to situations in which an individual eats because they are food deprived (an example of deprived reward). Food-sated and drug-naive rats show place preferences for environments paired with the presence of food or a drug injection, respectively (Bechara et al 1992, Bechara & van der Kooy 1992a). Bilateral lesions of the brainstem tegmental pedunculopontine nucleus (TPP) before training block the acquisition of preferences for environments paired with food in food-sated rats (Bechara et al 1992, Bechara & van der Kooy 1992a), morphine (Bechara et al 1992, Bechara & van der Kooy 1989, Olmstead & Franklin 1993), and amphetamine (Bechara & van der Kooy 1989, Olmstead & Franklin 1994) in drug-naive animals. When animals were either put into a deprived motivational state by 18 h of food deprivation or by being made opiate dependent and then allowed to go into spontaneous withdrawal, TPP lesions had no effect on the normal acquisition of conditioned place aversions to environments paired with either food deprivation (hunger) or deprivation from opiates in opiate-dependent rats (withdrawal) (Bechara et al 1992). In addition, TPP lesions did not block place preferences for environments paired with opiate alleviation of opiate withdrawal (Bechara et al 1992, Bechara & van der Kooy 1992a). Thus, the TPP is argued to be a critical link in mediating the motivational effects of stimuli only when animals are in a nondeprived state.

Pretreatment with the broad spectrum dopamine antagonist alpha-flupentixol during training produces exactly the opposite pattern of results. The acquisition of conditioned place preferences for environments paired with the presence of food in food-sated rats (Bechara et al 1992, Harrington & van der Kooy 1992) or an injection of morphine (Bechara et al 1992, Mackey & van der Kooy 1985) in drug-naive rats were unaffected by alpha-flupentixol pretreatment. Conversely, place preferences for environments paired with the alleviation of withdrawal were dopamine dependent, as evidenced by alpha-flupentixol blockade (Bechara et al 1992, Nader et al 1994). Furthermore, the acquisition of conditioned place aversions to environments paired with either opiate withdrawal or food deprivation were blocked by dopamine antagonist pretreatment during training (Bechara et al 1992, Harrington & van der Kooy 1992). Taken together, alpha-flupentixol pretreatment and TPP lesions double dissociate two independent systems (acting in nondeprived and deprived states) that mediate the reward properties of both opiates and food.

The identical dissociation can be demonstrated even when rats are conditioned with morphine injected directly into the VTA. Lesions of the TPP, but not alpha-flupentixol administration, blocked the acquisition of intra-VTA morphine place preferences when animals were conditioned drug naive. When using the same paradigm, the opposite pattern of results was found when separate groups of animals were trained while in a state of opiate dependence and withdrawal. In this case, alpha-flupentixol administration, but not TPP lesions, blocked the acquisition of conditioned place preferences for environments paired with morphine in animals that were in a state of opiate dependence and withdrawal (Nader & van der Kooy 1995). Therefore, even within the VTA itself, two independent motivational substrates can be demonstrated to exist.

These findings have two important implications. First, the relationship between the two systems appears to be mutually exclusive. A state of deprivation inhibits the nondeprived TPP-dependent system. This system can be disinhibited or reactivated by giving opiate-dependent animals that are in withdrawal a dose of morphine that is sufficient to bring them out of that withdrawal. While they are in this state of opiate dependence (but in the absence of withdrawal), morphine place preferences are completely blocked by lesions of the TPP (Bechara & van der Kooy 1992b). Similarly, if animals are allowed to recover (over weeks) from dependence and withdrawal, the motivational substrates again switch from a dopamine to a TPP-dependent substrate (Nader et al 1994, Nader & van der Kooy 1995). Thus, the differential activation of the two systems is predicated specifically on whether animals are in a state of withdrawal or not. The second implication is that a state of deprivation engages a second neurobiologically distinct motivational system, a component of which is dopamine. Indeed, the presence of an opiate-deprived motivational state also engages the noradrenergic system into contributing to the rewarding properties of morphine. The ability of clonidine, an α_2-noradrenergic agonist that decreases noradrenaline release, to block the acquisition of morphine-conditioned place preferences was contingent on whether animals were in morphine withdrawal or not. Clonidine pretreatment blocked morphine's rewarding properties only in opiate-dependent and withdrawn rats, and not in previously drug-naive rats (Nader & van der Kooy 1996).

The finding that states of deprivation can switch the neurobiological substrates mediating the motivational properties of stimuli provides a framework for reconciling discrepant results in the literature. For example, pretreatment with serotonin or CCK_A antagonists blocked the acquisition of conditioned place preferences for environments paired with morphine in previously drug-naive animals (Higgins et al 1994a,b), but it had no effect on heroin self-administration behavior in rats that had acquired a stable baseline before challenge (Higgins et al 1992a,b). In an explicit comparison between the exposure to heroin required to induce dependence and the exposure to heroin during the acquisition of self-administration behavior, it was concluded that once rats have acquired a stable baseline of responding they are opiate dependent (Nader et al 1994). The lack of effects of both serotonin and CCK_A antagonists then can be explained in terms of motivational systems that are neurochemically distinct and activated under different conditions. Serotonin and CCK_A may be components of a system that is responsible for mediating the rewarding properties of opiates when animals are in nondeprived motivational states. The same analysis can be applied across self-administration studies. The nondeprived/deprived model predicts that the acquisition of opiate self-administration (when animals have had minimal drug exposure) will be blocked by lesions of the TPP but will be insensitive to dopamine antagonist pretreatment. Once animals have acquired a stable baseline of operant responding, however, then dopamine antagonist pretreatment but not TPP lesions will block operant responding. Indeed, this pattern of results can be found in the literature. Pretreatment with the D1 dopamine antagonist SCH 23390 blocked the reinforcing properties of heroin only when a stable baseline of responding had first been established (Nakajima & Wise 1987; however, see Ettenberg et al 1982), but it had no effect on the acquisition of heroin self-administration (Gerrits et al 1994). Conversely, lesions of the TPP had no effect on the rate of responses of rats that had acquired a stable baseline of heroin responding (Nader et al 1994) but blocked the acquisition of heroin self-administration behavior (Olmstead et al 1993).

According to the nondeprived/deprived model, dopamine should be involved in mediating the reinforcing or rewarding properties of opiates only when rats are in opiate withdrawal. As mentioned in the preceding section, however, there have been a number of reports demonstrating that dopamine antagonists block the acquisition of opiate place preferences in previously drug-naive animals (Acquas & Di Chiara 1994, Bozarth & Wise 1981, Hand et al 1989, Leone & Di Chiara 1987, Shippenberg et al 1993, Shippenberg & Herz 1988, Spyraki et al 1983). In a study that reexamined dopamine's contribution to heroin reward (Nader et al 1994), it was demonstrated that the 0.5 mg/kg and 2 mg/kg doses used in previous studies (Bozarth & Wise 1981, Spyraki et al 1983) were sufficient to induce states of dependence and withdrawal. Furthermore, the dopamine antagonists used in most of these studies possess unconditioned aversive properties that could mask the rewarding properties of heroin or morphine during conditioning (Nader et al 1994, Shippenberg & Herz 1988). Indeed, alpha-flupentixol pretreatment, at a time and with a dose that has no unconditioned motivational properties, did not affect the normal acquisition of conditioned place preferences for environments paired with a low dose of heroin (0.05 mg/kg) (Nader et al 1994). This dose of heroin was an order of magnitude smaller than the heroin conditioning dose used in earlier studies (Bozarth & Wise 1981, Spyraki et al 1983). The rewarding properties of this low dose of heroin, which does not induce dependence during the conditioning period, were blocked by TPP lesions (Nader et al 1994). Thus, when the dose of opiate and the unconditioned properties of the dopamine antagonist are controlled for, dopamine's participation in opiate reward is restricted to instances when animals are in a state of deprivation.

A central issue for all models of motivation that posit common substrates for mediating the rewarding properties of various classes of stimuli, such as food, fluid, or drugs, is whether there is any inherent microstructure to the motivational substrates. For example, is there a subpopulation of neurons in the mesolimbic system that in the deprived state specifically mediates the rewarding properties of food, and another subpopulation that specifically mediates the rewarding effects of water? Or rather, are these stimuli equivalent at the level of reward? One way of addressing this issue is to take advantage of the double dissociation between motivational states. If there is specific stimulus organization to the underlying motivational substrates, then food deprivation should only inhibit the mechanisms that normally mediate the rewarding properties of food when animals are food sated. Therefore, in food-deprived animals morphine reward should still be sensitive to manipulations of the TPP. If, however, the motivational substrates have no inherent stimulus specificity, then food deprivation should generally inhibit the mechanisms that normally mediate the rewarding value of food and nonfood stimuli when animals are in a nondeprived state. In this case, morphine's rewarding properties in a morphine-naive, but food-deprived, animal should be dopamine mediated. A test of these two possibilities revealed that in food-deprived animals morphine produced its rewarding properties through a dopaminergic substrate. Indeed, lesions of the TPP had no effect on the acquisition of conditioned place preferences for environments previously paired with morphine and food deprivation over an environment previously paired with food deprivation alone (Nader & van der Kooy 1994). Thus, morphine reward can substitute for the rewarding properties of food in food-deprived animals, demonstrating the lack of any stimulus microstructure within the motivational systems. These data are consonant with the findings that morphine decreases feeding in food-deprived (Kunihara et al 1983, Sanger & McCarthy 1980) but not food-sated rats (Kunihara et al 1983, Lowy et al 1981, Sanger & McCarthy 1980, 1981), and that food deprivation increases instrumental performance for psychoactive drugs (see Kanarek & Marks-Kaufman 1988).

The obvious question that arises from this model is whether all motivated behaviors can be considered to have a nondeprived and a deprived component. For example, can pain be discussed in terms of a nondeprived and a deprived motivational system? Do some stimuli only work through one of the two systems? For example, dopamine antagonist pretreatment and TPP lesions block amphetamine-induced conditioned-place preferences in previously drug-naive rats (Bechara & van der Kooy 1989, Mackey & van der Kooy 1985). Conversely, neither TPP lesions nor pretreatment with alpha-flupentixol block the acquisition of cocaine place preferences (Mackey & van der Kooy 1985, Parker & van der Kooy 1995), which demonstrates that the motivational substrates may perform differently in mediating the rewarding effects of other (nonopiate and nonfood) classes of stimuli.

Saliency Attribution

The discussion thus far has used the term reward in the narrow sense of being able to change behavior through learning. No reference to the qualitative nature of rewards has been introduced. This is necessarily the case because laboratory rats cannot convey their subjective experiences to us. Reports on the qualitative nature of reward from human beings, however, usually include descriptors such as liking and wanting. Although these terms are frequently used interchangeably, the saliency attribution model claims that liking and wanting are two separate components of reward and that these processes are mediated by separate brain systems (Berridge et al 1989, Berridge 1996).

Liking is defined as the immediate evaluation of how pleasurable a stimulus is, whereas wanting is defined as a process that mediates our attraction toward stimuli in the environment (Berridge et al 1989, Berridge 1996).

Although one cannot ask an animal whether it likes a particular stimulus or not, one can create a context within which an animal's hedonic evaluation of a stimulus can be inferred. For example, if while sitting in a restaurant one sees someone spitting out their soup, it is safe to assume the soup brought the person no pleasure, even though one has not asked the person directly. Similarly, direct infusions of a fluid into a rat's mouth will elicit a series of stereotyped orofacial behaviors that range from ingestive or hedonic reactions to negative or aversive reactions, the most extreme of which is expulsion. Since this paradigm was first developed by Grill & Norgren (1978a), a number of studies have demonstrated that the profile of taste reactivity responses elicited by a taste stimulus is not constant but rather is influenced by physiological states such as hunger (Berridge et al 1984), or the previous associations between that flavor and a toxin (Grill & Norgren 1978b). These changes in pattern of taste reactivity to the same stimulus under different conditions are presented as evidence that the responses are evaluative and not reflexive in nature (Berridge & Peciña 1995). Conversely, paradigms that measure changes in behavior directed at getting food are argued to be measuring wanting. It is this requirement, that animals approach a stimulus, that defines wanting measures (Berridge 1996).

Selective lesions of the substantia nigra or VTA dopaminergic cells are known to render rats aphagic (a state characterized by the absence of food-directed behavior) (Ungersteadt 1971). If wanting and hedonics refer to a common process, then manipulations that affect the approach to food also should affect taste reactivity responses to a given taste stimulus in rats. Surprisingly, lesions that either selectively killed dopaminergic neurons in the substantia nigra or reduced dopamine levels in the striatum and nucleus accumbens by 95–99% had no effect on the profile of taste reactivity responses to various flavors, even though these animals were aphagic (Berridge et al 1989, Berridge 1996). Flavor-toxin pairing shifted the profile of taste reactivity scores for a sweet taste from hedonic to aversive reactions in aphagic and controls equally, which demonstrates that the processes mediating hedonics are capable of responding normally in the absence of dopaminergic mechanisms (as reported in Berridge 1996). Furthermore, pretreatment with dopamine antagonists known to decrease the reward properties of food (see Smith 1995) had no effect on the hedonic reactions of rats to infused flavors as measured by taste reactivity (Treit & Berridge 1990). Together, these results demonstrate the independence of the mechanisms mediating the hedonic properties of taste from the mechanisms required for approach behavior toward food.

The results of a study that examined the effects of stimulation of the hypothalamus on the hedonic responses of rats in the taste reactivity further supports this distinction. It is well documented that feeding behavior is one of the behaviors that can be induced by stimulation of the hypothalamus (Glickman & Schiff 1967). Feeding induced by stimulation of the lateral hypothalamus is also known to be sensitive to dopaminergic manipulation (Jenk et al 1986, Phillips & Nikaido 1975, Streather & Bozarth 1987). If this enhanced feeding were due to increased hedonic evaluations of taste stimuli, then animals undergoing lateral-hypothalamic stimulation should show increased ingestive or hedonic responses to fluids. Surprisingly, exactly the opposite pattern of results was found. Stimulation of the lateral-hypothalamus that induced strong stimulus-bound feeding decreased the ingestive responses to fluids (Berridge 1991). Therefore, stimulation-induced feeding must be working through nonhedonic processes to produce this behavior. The fact that the processes mediating feeding and hedonics responded in opposite directions to the electrical stimulation supports the claim for a neurobiologically based distinction between the behaviorally defined liking and wanting processes.

The brainstem has been implicated as the site mediating the unconditioned hedonic reactions to taste stimuli. Decerebration—separating the caudal brainstem from the forebrain—did not affect taste reactivity responses to taste stimuli even though it renders animals aphagic (Grill & Norgren 1978b,c). Indeed, pretreatment with benzodiazepine, which increases the hedonic reaction to taste stimuli in intact animals, also produced hedonic enhancement in decerebrate rats (Berridge 1988). The sites contributing to the evaluation of taste stimuli include the nucleus of the solitary tract and the parabrachial nucleus. Lesions of these gustatory relay nuclei attenuated both the hedonic responses to sucrose and the aversive responses to quinine (Flynn et al 1991). Similar lesions, however, did not affect the animal's ability to regulate food consumption in response to insulin, 2-deoxy-D-glucose injections, or stomach loading (Flynn 1991), which shows that the wanting mechanisms are independent and still intact.

The VTA and substantia nigra dopaminergic afferents to the nucleus accumbens and striatum, however, are claimed to mediate a process that attributes acquired value to a CS that has come to predict a US. This value acquired by the CS, in turn, is what makes it wanted. Furthermore, the stimuli on which saliency will be conferred is directed or controlled by associatively learned relationships between neutral and hedonically salient stimuli (Berridge 1996, Berridge & Valenstein 1991). By manipulating the mesolimbic dopaminergic system, the value that is attributed to stimuli can be directly modulated. For example, animals will bar press when the reinforcer is a light (CS) that has been previously paired with food. The ability of this CS to reinforce a new response makes it a conditioned reinforcer (Mackintosh 1974). In this case, the qualitative property that maintains an animal's responding for a conditioned reinforcer is the value or incentive properties that the CS has acquired through Pavlovian conditioning with the food. Administration of the indirect dopamine agonist, amphetamine, potentiates responding on the lever associated with presentation of a conditioned reinforcer (e.g. Beninger & Ranaldi 1992, Mazurski & Beninger 1986, Robbins et al 1983). This same potentiation is observed if amphetamine is injected directly into the nucleus accumbens (Phillips et al 1994, Taylor & Robbins 1984). Conversely, lesions of the dopaminergic terminals in the nucleus accumbens block amphetamine's ability to increase responding for the conditioned reinforcer (Taylor & Robbins 1986). Therefore, manipulations affecting the mesolimbic dopamine pathway can alter the value attributed to a CS (Beninger et al 1989).

An important question that needs to be addressed by this model is how significant are the contributions of liking to feeding behavior. If liking and wanting are dissociable processes, then liking should be able to influence feeding behavior in the absence of wanting. The demonstration that 6-hydroxydopamine lesions of the wanting system produce *aphagia,* even though the liking system was still intact, would suggest that liking is not sufficient to elicit feeding. It could be argued, however, that in addition to a deficit in wanting, these lesions also induced motoric impairments that prevented the rats from consuming hedonically salient fluids. Results from studies examining the effects of amygdala lesions on sodium appetite, however, also support the suggestion that liking is not a sufficient condition for feeding to occur. Lesions of the central nucleus of the amygdala, which do not produce aphagia, block the normal increased consumption of sodium chloride (NaCl) when rats are in a state of sodium depletion (Galaverna et al 1991). The lesions, however, had no effect on sodium depletion's ability to both potentiate the number of ingestive and decrease the number of aversive scores in response to intraoral NaCl (Galaverna et al 1993). Even when NaCl was presented intra-orally, rats with lesions of the central nucleus of the amygdala failed to increase their consumption when sodium depleted (Seeley et al 1993). Although these data support a distinction between hedonics and wanting mechanisms, they also highlight the inability of hedonics to influence feeding in the absence of wanting.

ARE THE MODELS OF MOTIVATION REDUCIBLE TO ONE ANOTHER?

Using neurobiological tools, the three models discussed have identified different psychological processes. The challenge for neurobiologists is to test whether the psychological boundaries defined in these different models are isomorphic to, or distinct from, one another. Although there is overwhelming evidence that dopamine plays a central role in the rewarding properties of various classes of stimuli, the findings that reward can be engendered via dopamine-independent substrates undermine the strong version of the anhedonia hypothesis (Wise 1982). Furthermore, the proposition that reward can be mediated at different levels of a single reward pathway of which dopamine is one component (Wise & Rompre 1989), also is compromised by the findings that multiple motivational systems can be double dissociated. Thus, the dopamine hypothesis, a single system model, cannot incorporate the findings of multiple system models. However, both the nondeprived/deprived and saliency attribution hypotheses can incorporate the findings of the dopamine hypothesis. The saliency attribution hypothesis redefines the purported reward process that is mediated by dopamine into a wanting process. The nondeprived/deprived model, however, maintains the nature of dopamine's involvement in opiate and food reward processes but constrains dopamine's participation to instances during which animals are in a deprived motivational state.

Can the nondeprived/deprived and hedonic/wanting boundaries be reduced to one another? While these models have some similarities on both the behavioral and neurobiological levels of analysis, the processes posited by these two models are psychologically distinct. On the neurobiological level, both models have identified separate dopamine-dependent and dopa mine-independent systems. Similarly, on a behavioral level of analysis, the wanting and deprived motivational systems are critical for mediating approach behavior. The similarities, however, end here. The first difference between the two models is that the processes referred to as liking and nondeprived reward are not equivalent. In fact, given the nature of the measures used to assay nondeprived rewarding effects (approach to environments paired with a US), this system would be defined as a wanting system within the saliency attribution model. A second point of conflict is that the saliency attribution model proposes the existence of a single wanting system that mediates approach behavior, whereas the nondeprived/deprived model posits the existence of two independent mechanisms that are competent to mediate approach behaviors under different physiological conditions. The last significant difference is that both liking and wanting mechanisms can be concurrently active, as in the case where a pharmacological manipulation both increases a rat's hedonic response to a taste stimulus and potentiates feeding (Peciña & Berridge 1995). In the nondeprived/deprived model, however, only one system is active at a time (Bechara & van der Kooy 1992b). In fact, the nondeprived system is inhibited or masked while animals are in a state of deprivation (Bechara & van der Kooy 1992b).

Given that the saliency attribution model posits that approach to stimuli is mediated by a single neural system, it cannot explain the results of the nondeprived/deprived model, which has identified two such mechanisms. Conversely, in order for the nondeprived/deprived model to explain saliency attribution, it must address the contribution of the liking system. As previously mentioned, due to the nature of the behaviors measured and the interaction between systems, the liking and nondeprived reward systems appear to be different. An alternative interpretation derives from the demonstrations of increased hedonics in the absence of increased ingestion mentioned in the preceding section. If the processes mediating the orofacial response in rats to flavors have motivational or reward value, then by definition they should be able to influence an animal's behavior. However, given the demonstrated inability of the liking system to independently initiate feeding behavior, it is possible that the taste reactivity paradigm is a better measure of food's subjective sensory, as opposed to hedonic, properties. In this case, what has been identified as a liking system is really a sensory system mediating the discriminative taste properties of food. This model would be consistent with both the implication of gustatory relay nuclei as sites mediating the hedonic reactions and the findings that positive hedonic reactions are not sufficient to control behavior. Thus, the existence of a liking sensory system would not be a challenge to the nondeprived/deprived model if it could be demonstrated that the discriminative and motivational properties of stimuli are separable.

A number of findings support such a distinction. Pretreatment with a dose of the dopamine antagonist pimozide, which decreased the reinforcing properties of sucrose (Muscat & Willner 1989, Towel et al 1987), did not interfere with the ability of rats to discriminate either between different concentrations of sucrose or between sucrose and water (Willner et al 1990). In this study, different concentrations of sucrose and water served as discriminative cues with which rats learned to turn left or right in a T-maze for reinforcement. Even under a high dose of pimozide, rats were as accurate as saline-pretreated animals in solving the discrimination when the cues were water and a 0.0024% sucrose solution. Thus, although dopamine antagonists block the reinforcing properties of sucrose, they do not interfere with the discriminative properties of that same stimulus, which suggests that the mechanisms mediating discrimination and motivation are indeed separable.

Other demonstrations of dissociations between the discriminative and motivational properties of stimuli come from work done with drugs of abuse and physiological states such as hunger. Lesions of the TPP that blocked the rewarding properties of morphine in previously drug-naive animals had no effect on morphine's ability to act as a cue in a discrimination paradigm in which a cue predicts whether a target solution will be followed by illness

(Martin et al 1991). In fact, morphine microinjections into the brainstem parabrachial nucleus produced cueing properties that could be used to solve a similar discrimination task (Jaeger & van der Kooy 1993) but did not produce conditioned place or flavor preferences or conditioned flavor aversions (all measures of the motivational properties of a stimulus) (Jaeger & van der Kooy 1996). Conversely, morphine microinjections into the VTA produced conditioned place preferences and flavor aversions but did not support discrimination learning (Jaeger & van der Kooy 1996). Similar results were obtained in a study using a two-lever food-reinforced discrimination paradigm. Morphine microinjections into the VTA did not substitute for a previously trained systemic heroin cue, nor did opiate antagonist microinjections into the VTA block the discriminative properties of systemic heroin (Shaham & Stewart 1995). However, under certain conditions activation of opiate receptors in the VTA can make a contribution to the discriminative properties of opiates (Shoaib & Spanagel 1994). The most parsimonious interpretation of these findings is that the discriminative effects of morphine are more analogous to a compound stimulus than to an elemental stimulus, with the components of the compound stimulus mediated by a number of distributed neural substrates (Colpaert 1978). Therefore, opiate receptor activation in the VTA may be sufficient in some cases, but not necessary, for producing discriminative properties of opiates. This would still imply that motivation and discrimination are different. Congruent with this hypothesis are the findings that lesions of the hippocampus block the interoceptive cues that result from food deprivation (Davidson 1993) but have no effect on the acquisition of conditioned place aversions to environments paired with food deprivation (K Nader, D Skinner & D van der Kooy, unpublished observations). Similarly, studies with human beings have shown that behavior can be affected in the absence of any subjective awareness of the reinforcing event. For example, recovered addicts will voluntarily press a lever for an infusion of a dose of morphine that they cannot introspectively detect (Lamb et al 1991).

The first implication of such a dissociation is that we do not have direct introspective access to the causal (motivational) events that shape our behavior. Second, the discriminative properties of stimuli have no inherent ability to modify behavior; they are simply subjective sensory events. Only through subsequent associations with the rewarding or aversive properties of stimuli can these sensory events have an influence on behavior. For example, a saccharin-LiCl CTA would be the result of the representation of the taste of saccharin forming an association with the aversive effects of LiCl. When animals are presented with saccharin on test day, the first few licks will produce the normal representation of the saccharin taste. This representation will elicit conditioned aversive effects that will decrease consumption, as well as other conditioned responses such as the oro-facial behaviors that taste reactivity measures. Explicit in this formulation is that the hedonic shift seen after saccharin-LiCl pairings is correlative but not causal to the decreased consumption seen after conditioning. Consistent with this position are the findings that the conditioned taste aversions to flavors paired with drugs of abuse are not correlated with changes in taste reactivity scores (Parker 1991). Thus, if discriminative is a better description than hedonic of the process identified by taste reactivity measures, then this would change the identified process from a reward process to a sensory process. The nondeprived/deprived model would not be challenged by the existence of such a sensory mechanism any more than it is challenged by the existence of visual and auditory pathways.

IMPLICATIONS FOR BEHAVIORAL THEORIES OF GOAL-DIRECTED BEHAVIOR

Bindra's Incentive Motivation Model

In all three models of motivation, the processes identified and the underlying neurobiological substrates mediating either reward or components of reward cross stimulus boundaries. One of the implications of these findings is that there is essentially nothing unique about the rewarding properties of food and water (a kind of reward equivalence). Reward is, by nature, a generic product. Although these findings are exciting because of their potential to elucidate critical substrates involved in reinforcement, they are problematic for current psychological theories of goal-directed behaviors. Incentive motivational theories of goal-directed behavior propose that specificity or direction in behavior is the product of a motivational state (or central motive state) (Bindra 1974, 1978; Toates 1986). This state is produced by the interaction of the central representation of incentive stimuli (such as food) with physiological states such as hunger. Contrary to previous theories that defined the contribution made by motivation as one of either drive reduction or incentive, neither of these variables alone is normally sufficient to create a central motive state. For example, in a hungry animal, the central representation of food would interact with the physiological state of food deprivation to create a feeding central motive state. In turn, this state would feed forward and further excite the representation of food, which would cause the animal to attend to the food stimulus and approach it. Similarly, when a neutral stimulus (CS) predicts the presence of food, presentation of the CS alone will excite a central representation of that food. In the presence of the appropriate physiological conditions, presentation of this CS will create a feeding motivational state. This state will then excite first the representation of food and second the representation of the CS. In this framework, the incentive object both creates and is the object of the central motive state (Bindra 1974, 1978; Toates 1986). "Thus, in the present scheme there is no special problem of integrating the appropriate goal object with a given motivational state; normally the goal object provides the incentive stimuli that, together with the organismic condition, create the central motive state that influences behavior in relation to those stimuli" (Bindra 1976, p. 190).

The difficulty for such a model is that it assumes an inherent neurobiological microstructure with regard to which stimuli interact with which physiological conditions. If food reward and water reward are equivalent, then there is no inherent microstructure in the motivational systems with regard to which stimulus can interact with a particular physiological state. By saying that the representation of food interacts with the physiological state of feeding, we have essentially imposed distinctions and created categories where none exist. Consider, for example, a situation in which a food-deprived animal is confronted with the presence of food and water. According to the incentive motivational model, food deprivation interacts with the representation of food to create a feeding central motive state, which in turn feeds forward to further excite the representation of food. But if there is equivalence in reward, then the feeding physiological state is equally capable of interacting with both of these stimuli, only one of which is biologically appropriate.

This problem is nicely exemplified in studies testing for irrelevant incentive effects, in which concurrent instrumental tasks were reinforced with different incentive stimuli. In these studies, animals are trained while under one particular state such as hunger and are tested under extinction conditions while in a different physiological state such as thirst. For example, Dickinson & Dawson (1988, 1989) trained food-deprived animals with concurrent instrumental tasks that were reinforced with liquid sucrose and solid food. Bindra's incentive motivation model predicts that shifting rats to a state of water deprivation should increase the instrumental responses performed that previously led to sucrose presentation. This is because the physiological state of thirst should gate or facilitate the ability of stimuli in the environment that predict fluid (such as the flavor of the sucrose solution or the task performed in order to receive sucrose) to induce a central drinking motive state. This state will subsequently feed forward and make fluid-associated cues more attractive than food-associated cues. What Dickinson & Dawson found, however, was that animals tested (water deprived) under extinction conditions performed both the food and sucrose-reinforced operants equivalent amounts. Nevertheless, this is exactly what one would predict if the motivational substrates do not differentiate between stimuli. What is needed is something that can be used as a cue by the animal to direct its behavior to the appropriate stimulus.

Interospective Cues as Behavioral Guideposts

Historically, the percepts resultant from deprivation states have been used in various models to instill direction into behavior. One of the earliest models proposed that painful stomach contractions that occur after a period of fasting are the cues that direct us to search out food (Canon 1920). "Hunger, in other words, is normally the signal that the stomach is contracted for action; the unpleasantness of hunger leads to eating; eating starts gastric distention, and abolishes the sensation" (p. 264). This conceptualization was quickly abandoned, primarily because the majority of feeding occurred in the absence of distinctive stomach pains (Skinner 1953). The largest obstacle faced by most theories that postulated a cueing role for interoceptive states was the lack of empirical support demonstrating that such stimuli could gain conditional control over behavior (Webb 1955).

More recently, however, there have been a number of convincing demonstrations of the ability of interoceptive cues to acquire control over behavior (Capaldi et al 1981, Corwin et al 1990, Davidson 1987, Davidson et al 1992, Schuh et al 1994). Using the fear conditioning paradigm, Davidson (1987) conditioned animals such that either a high or low deprivation condition predicted shock, while the second deprivation condition predicted the absence of shock. When animals were tested under the two deprivation states, rats froze significantly more under the deprivation state that was paired with shock than in the deprivation state that was paired with the absence of shock. Furthermore, in a subsequent experiment the nature of the CS predicting shock was verified as being the interoceptive cues due to food deprivation as opposed to other stimuli in the environment. In this study (Davidson 1987), one group of rats was conditioned such that 6 h of food deprivation predicted shock and 23 h of food deprivation predicted the absence of shock. A second group was conditioned using the reversed food-deprivation/shock contingency. All rats were then deprived of food for 22 h and given either sham or condensed milk intubation 1 h before testing. Rats that received 23 h of food-deprivation/shock pairings froze significantly less after condensed milk intubation than after sham intubation. Rats in the 6-h food-deprivation/shock condition, however, froze significantly more after the condensed milk intubation compared with sham intubation. This is exactly what would be predicted if the cues that the animals were using to predict shock were produced by different levels of food deprivation. Furthermore, differential conditioning could be acquired when the difference between interoceptive cues was only 4 h of food deprivation. Thus, not only could animals use and differentiate between interoceptive cues arising from different levels of food deprivation, but these cues could be used to predict the occurrence of events that were irrelevant to the physiological state of the animals.

Because the interoceptive cues of food deprivation can control instrumental responding and enter into association with unconditioned stimuli of a different class, Davidson has suggested recently that interoceptive cues should be revived as critical variables that contribute to the control of food-seeking behavior (Davidson 1993). While maintaining an incentive motivational framework, Davidson argues that the interoceptive cues act as occasion setters or conditioned modulators that, when present, further decrease the threshold for activation of the US by conditioned stimuli in the environment. In contrast with earlier theories of discriminative control of behavior, the interoceptive cues in Davidson's model do not provide direction, but rather they control how vigorously an animal will pursue a goal. The mechanisms controlling the direction of behavior are the same as in traditional incentive motivational models. For this reason, however, Davidson's model suffers from the same shortfalls as incentive motivational theories. If the motivational properties of food and water reward are isomorphic, then prepositional statements such as "food deprivation state cues signal when and if external CSs related to food will be followed by pleasant postingestive consequences" (Davidson 1993, p. 651) are rendered meaningless. Furthermore, such a model predicts that in the irrelevant incentive experiments cited above, a shift in an animal's physiological state should automatically increase responding in the task that delivers the stimulus appropriate for that state, a prediction opposite to the results obtained (Dickinson & Dawson 1988, 1989).

A Neurobiologically Constrained Learning Model of Goal-Directed Behavior

Based on the findings both that the rewarding properties of different classes of stimuli are equivalent and that the mechanisms mediating the discriminative and motivational properties of stimuli are separate, it has been proposed that goal-directed behaviors are necessarily learned phenomena (Nader & van der Kooy 1994). If the products of the activity within motivational substrates are not introspectively accessible, then they cannot guide behavior directly in any meaningful psychological sense. Rather, interoceptive or discriminative events must act as cues with which to direct behavior through previous associations between the discriminative and motivational properties of stimuli. Such a learning mechanism could underlie the specificity in goal-directed behavior. With regard to food, an animal's physiological condition normally fluctuates over various degrees of food deprivation, depending on the absence or presence of food in the environment. As the physiological state fluctuates, the discriminative and motivational effects of deprivation will co-vary, which makes the discriminative properties of deprivation excellent predictors of the underlying deprived motivational state of the animal. Stimuli that alleviate the discriminative properties of food deprivation will become good conditioned predictors of stimuli that alleviate the motivational properties of food deprivation, and thus stimuli (food) that alleviate the discriminative properties of food deprivation will come to be approached. The specificity of goal-directed behavior arises naturally from this model, because even though other stimuli such as water may have the same reward properties as food to food-deprived animals, the other stimuli are incapable of alleviating the discriminative properties of food deprivation. Therefore, animals will maintain behavior directed at stimuli that are capable of alleviating the interoceptive properties of hunger. This position avoids the dilemma faced by reward equivalence. Although stimuli may lack uniqueness at the motivational level, they do not at the perceptual or discriminative level. Inherent to this position is the conclusion that any discussion of specificity in goal-directed behavior is restricted to times when animals are in a deprived motivational state that produces both discriminative cues and aversive motivational effects. Animals in a nondeprived state should engage in behaviors that are more exploratory in nature rather than in behaviors directed at any specific goal stimulus.

In this framework, the interoceptive cues of hunger would direct behavior on the basis of learned expectations of what stimuli in the environment alleviate those cues. This formulation is very reminiscent of the position proposed by Hull (1943), who claimed that associations between the discriminative (drive stimulus) properties of a drive state, such as hunger, and stimuli capable of decreasing the underlying drive contributed to providing behavior with direction. The drive stimulus in this model was purely sensory in nature. Drive itself, however, served an energizing function for responses but did not have any directional qualities itself. In the same way that reward is generic, so too was Hull's drive construct. Hull's model was eventually abandoned for two main reasons. First, as previously mentioned, there was little corroborating evidence at the time to support the idea of drive stimuli gaining control over behavior. Second, drive reduction as the primary motivational construct was replaced with incentive motivational theories that had more generality (Bolles 1975). Given the numerous demonstrations of interoceptive cues gaining control over behavior, the first criticism is no longer valid. The second criticism is more significant. Drive constructs have been found to be inadequate, and often unnecessary, to explain many behaviors (Bolles 1975).

One way of reconciling the constraints identified neurobiologically (i.e. reward equivalence and a distinction between the discrimination and motivation) with behavioral models that posit a process of incentive motivation, as opposed to drive reduction, as the primary motivational construct is to posit the occurrence of two types of learned associations: one that allows interoceptive cues to predict the appropriate incentive stimulus to approach under conditions of deprivation and one that mediates the learning about instrumental contingencies. Indeed, the incentive learning theory proposed by Dickinson & Balleine (1994) suggests that goal-directed behavior is accomplished by the interaction of two separate learned associations. First, instrumental actions are controlled by an expectation of the rewarding properties that will result from an action. Second, through a process of incentive learning, interoceptive properties of deprivation predict that the rewarding properties of a stimulus are enhanced in that state. Therefore, interoceptive cues can influence instrumental performance by predicting a greater reward outcome resulting from the instrumental act. For example, Balleine (1992) trained animals to press a lever for a novel food reward while they were food sated and then tested them in extinction conditions while they were food deprived. Similar early studies that used the animal's normal dietary food as the reinforcer reported that shifting deprivation state directly affected rate of responding in the extinction test (e.g. Perin 1942). When a novel food was used as the reinforcer, however, shifting animals into a state of food deprivation and testing had no effect on the rate of responding (Balleine 1992). However, if animals are simply exposed to the novel food while in a state of food deprivation before testing under the same conditions, then the rate at which rats respond is significantly greater than that for animals that were not preexposed to the food while hungry. The interpretation offered for these findings is that during the food deprivation exposure, the discriminative properties of the motivational state (hunger) enter into an association with the increased value of the novel food outcome in a state of hunger (Balleine 1992). In turn, when animals are then tested in a state of food deprivation, the discriminative properties of hunger predict an increased value of that particular novel food. Thus, the early demonstrations of a direct effect of shifting deprivation levels on response rate under extinction conditions are argued to be byproducts of the familiar food used. In the absence of the opportunity to learn about the value of the new food under conditions of food deprivation, instrumental performance was controlled only by the previously learned value of the outcome. Motivational states in this model are claimed to perform two functions. The first is to directly determine the reward value of the reinforcer. Second, motivational states gain conditional control over instrumental performance once animals have experienced the outcome of a stimulus in different levels of deprivation (Dickinson & Balleine 1994).

Although Dickinson & Balleine (1994) do not address whether these two motivational functions are the product of a single or multiple process(es), this dual role of motivational states may be congruent with a framework that identifies discriminative and motivational components of stimuli as distinct processes (Martin et al 1991, Nader & van der Kooy 1994). In this case, the overall motivational state is not a single process, but rather it has separate discriminative and motivational components. Contingent on the physiological state of the animal, either the nondeprived or deprived motivational pathways determine the value of an outcome. If animals are trained while food sated, then the TPP-mediated nondeprived reward system will determine the motivational value of the outcome. Conversely, in animals trained while deprived, determination of the outcome's motivational value will be dopamine dependent. The discriminative process, however, is required to mediate the interoceptive cues that can come to predict the motivational value of an outcome in any particular deprivation state. This framework provides an explanation for why a change in motivational state (such as the degree of hunger) does not directly affect instrumental responding. The discriminative properties of states such as hunger are sensory events that have no more ability to unconditionally affect behavior than a tone.

There are several advantages to this revised model. First, it is not rooted only to drive reduction as the main motivational construct but allows for conditioned incentive control of behavior. Indeed, the existence of the TPP reward pathway that is active in the absence of deprivation provides the neurobiological bases for stimuli to affect behavior in the absence of drive reduction. Second, it can easily incorporate a distinction between the discriminative and motivational properties of stimuli. Third, this framework does not presuppose that food reward is qualitatively different from water reward. Its only assumption is that animals can learn that food produces more reward in hungry animals than water. Thus, not only does this model respect the constraints imposed by the neurobiological findings, the dissociations identified using neurobiological methods also have explanatory power for the separate learned associations that can be identified behaviorally.

CONCLUSION

Neurobiology can bring more to a functional analysis of behavior than a simple description of the underlying pathways mediating various behaviors. It can dissociate constructs into component psychological processes that make independent contributions to the control of behavior. Furthermore, the dissociations identified neurobiologically can have explanatory value for behavioral models. The three models reviewed differ in the number and nature of the systems that they have identified. It is interesting to note that the motivational processes identified by all three models obey psychological as opposed to simple external stimulus (food vs drugs) boundaries. The challenge now is to test whether the individual systems identified in the different models, such as liking and nondeprived reward, are reducible to one another or represent distinct mechanisms that contribute to the control of behavior.

ACKNOWLEDGMENTS

We would like to thank Darlene Skinner for reading an early version of this manuscript.

Literature Cited

Acquas E, Di Chiara G. 1994. D1 receptor blockade stereospecifically impairs the acquisition of drug-conditioned place preference and place-aversion. *Behav. Pharmacol.* 5:555–69

Amsel A, Rousell J. 1952. Motivational properties of frustration. I. Effect on a running response of the addition of frustration to the motivational complex. *J. Exp. Psychol.* 43:363–68

Balleine B. 1992. Instrumental performance following a shift in primary motivation depends on incentive learning. *J. Exp. Psychol.: Anim. Behav. Process.* 18:236–50

Baxter BL, Gluckman MI, Stein L, Scerni RA. 1974. Self-injection of apomorphine in the rat: positive reinforcement by a dopamine receptor stimulant. *Phamacol. Biochem. Behav.* 2:387–91

Bechara A, Harrington F, Nader K, van der Kooy D. 1992. The neurobiology of motivation: double dissociation of two motivational mechanisms mediating opiate reward in naive versus drug-dependent animals. *Behav. Neurosci.* 106:798–807

Bechara A, van der Kooy D. 1986. Lesions of a brainstem output of the limbic system abolishes the rewarding properties of psychoactive drugs. *Soc. Neurosci. Abstr.* 12:936

Bechara A, van der Kooy D. 1989. The tegmental pedunculopontine nucleus: a brainstem output of the limbic system critical for the conditioned place preferences produced by morphine and amphetamine. *J. Neurosci.* 9:3400–9

Bechara A, van der Kooy D. 1992a. A single brain substrate mediates the motivational effects of both opiates and food in nondeprived, but not in deprived animals. *Behav. Neurosci.* 106:351–63

Bechara A, van der Kooy D. 1992b. Chronic exposure to morphine does not alter the neural tissue subserving its acute rewarding properties: apparent tolerance is overshadowing. *Behav. Neurosci.* 106:364–74

Beninger RJ. 1983. The role of dopamine in locomotor activity and learning. *Brain Res. Rev.* 6:173–96

Beninger RJ, Hoffman DC, Mazurski EJ. 1989. Receptor subtype-specific dopaminergic agents and conditioned behavior. *Neurosci. Biobehav. Rev.* 13:113–22

Beninger RJ, Ranaldi R. 1992. The effects of amphetamine, apomorphine, SKF 38393, quinpirole and bromocriptine on responding for conditioned reward in rats. *Behav. Pharmacol.* 3:155–63

Berridge KC. 1988. Brainstem systems mediate the enhancement of palatability by chlordiazepoxide. *Brain Res.* 447:262–68

Berridge KC. 1991. Modulation of taste affect by hunger, caloric satiety, and sensory-specific satiety in the rat. *Appetite* 16:103–20

Berridge KC. 1996. Food reward: brain substrates of wanting and liking. *Neurosci. Biobehav. Rev.* 20:1–25

Berridge KC, Flynn FW, Sculkin J, Grill HJ. 1984. Sodium depletion enhances salt palatability in rats. *Behav. Neurosci.* 98: 652–60

Berridge KC, Peciña S. 1995. Benzodiazepines, appetite, and taste palatability. *Neurosci. Biobehav. Rev.* 19:121–31

Berridge KC, Valenstein ES. 1991. What psychological process mediates feeding evoked by electrical stimulation of the lateral hypothalamus. *Behav. Neurosci.* 105: 3–14

Berridge KC, Venier IL, Robinson TE. 1989. Taste reactivity analysis of 6-hydroxydopamine-induced aphagia: implications for arousal and anhedonia hypotheses of dopamine function. *Behav. Neurosci.* 103: 36–45

Bindra D. 1974. Motivational view of learning, performance, and behavior modification. *Psychol. Rev.* 81:199–213

Bindra D. 1976. *A Theory of Intelligent Behavior*. New York: Wiley

Bindra D. 1978. How adaptive behavior is produced: a perceptual-motivational alternative to response-reinforcement. *Behav. Brain Sci.* 1:41–91

Bolles RC. 1975. *Theory of Motivation.* New York: Harper & Row

Bozarth MA. 1987. Neuroanatomical boundaries of the reward-relevant opiate-receptor field in the ventral tegmental area as mapped by the conditioned place preference method in rats. *Brain Res.* 414:77–84

Bozarth MA, Wise RA. 1981. Heroin reward is dependent on a dopaminergic substrate. *Life Sci.* 29:1881–86

Caine SB, Koob GF. 1993. Modulation of cocaine self-administration in the rat through D-3 dopamine receptors. *Science* 260: 1814–16

Canon WB. 1920. *Bodily Changes in Pain, Hunger, Fear and Rage.* New York: Appleton

Capaldi ED, Viveiros DM, Davidson TL. 1981. Deprivation stimulus intensity and incentive factors in the control of instrumental responding. *J. Exp. Psychol.: Anim. Behav. Proc.* 7:140–49

Carr GD, Fibiger H, Phillips AG. 1989. Conditioned place preference as a measure of drug reward. In *Oxford Reviews in Psychopharmacology,* ed. JM Leibman, SJ Cooper, pp. 264–319. Oxford: Oxford Univ. Press

Colpaert FC. 1978. Theoretical review: discriminative stimulus properties of narcotic analgesic drugs. *Pharmacol. Biochem. Behav.* 9:863–87

Corrigall WA, Franklin KBJ, Coen KM, Clarke PBS. 1992. The mesolimbic dopaminergic system is implicated in the reinforcing effects of nicotine. *Psychopharmacology* 107:285–89

Corwin RL, Woolverton WL, Schuster CR. 1990. Effects of cholecystokinin, d-amphetamine and fenfluramine in rats trained to discriminate 3 from 22 hr of food deprivation. *J. Pharmacol. Exp. Ther.* 253: 720–28

Cunningham CL, Malott DH, Dickinson SD, Risinger FO. 1992. Halperidol does not alter expression of ethanol-induced conditioned place preference. *Behav. Brain Res.* 50:1–5

Davidson TL. 1987. Learning about deprivation intensity stimuli. *Behav. Neurosci.* 101:198–208

Davidson TL. 1993. The nature and function of interoceptive signals to feed: toward integration of physiological and learning perspectives. *Psychol. Rev.* 100:640–57

Davidson TL, Flynn FW, Jarrard LE. 1992. Potency of food deprivation intensity cues as discriminative stimuli. *J. Exp. Psychol.: Anim. Behav. Process.* 18:174–81

Devine DP, Wise RA. 1994. Self-administration of morphine, DAMGO, and DPDPE into the ventral tegmental area of rats. *J. Neurosci.* 14:1978–84

Dickinson A, Balleine BW. 1994. Motivational control of goal-directed action. *Anim. Learn. Behav.* 22:1–18

Dickinson A, Dawson GR. 1988. Motivational control of instrumental performance: the role of prior experience of the reinforcer. *Q. J. Exp. Psychol.* 40:113–34

Dickinson A, Dawson GR. 1989. Incentive learning and the motivational control of instrumental performance. *Q. J. Exp. Psychol.* 41:99–112

Dworkin SI, Guerin GF, Co C, Goeders NE, Smith JE. 1988. Lack of an effect of 6-hydroxydopamine lesions of the nucleus accumbens on intravenous morphine self-administration. *Pharmacol. Biochem. Behav.* 30:1051–57

Ettenberg A. 1989. Dopamine, neuroleptics and reinforced behavior. *Neurosci. Biobehav. Rev.* 13:105–11

Ettenberg A, Koob GF, Bloom FE. 1981. Response artifact in the measurement of neuroleptic-induced anhedonia. *Science* 213:357–59

Ettenberg A, Pettit HO, Bloom FE, Koob GF. 1982. Heroin and cocaine intravenous self-administration in rats: mediation by separate neural systems. *Psychopharmacology* 78:204–9

Fibiger HC, Carter DA, Phillips AG. 1976. Decreased intracranial self-stimulation after neuroleptics or 6-hydroxydopamine: evidence for mediation by motor deficits rather than by reduced reward. *Psychopharmacology* 47:21–27

Flynn FW. 1991. Central gustatory lesions. II. Effects on sodium appetite, taste aversion learning, and feeding behavior. *Behav. Neurosci.* 105:944–54

Flynn FW, Grill HJ, Schwartz GJ, Norgren R. 1991. Central gustatory lesions. I. Preference and taste reactivity tests. *Behav. Neurosci.* 105:933–43

Fouriezos G, Wise RA. 1976. Pimozide-induced extinction of intracranial self-stimulation: response patterns rule out motor performance deficits. *Brain Res.* 103: 377–80

Galaverna O, De Luca LA, Schulkin J, Yao SZ, Epstein AN. 1991. Deficits in NaCl ingestion after damage to the central nucleus of the amygdala in the rat. *Brain Res. Bull.* 28:89–98

Galaverna OG, Seeley RJ, Berridge KC, Grill HJ, Epstein AN, et al. 1993. Lesions of the central nucleus of the amygdala. I. Effects on taste reactivity, taste aversion learning and sodium appetite. *Behav. Brain Res.* 59: 11–17

Geary N, Smith GP. 1985. Pimozide decreases

the positive reinforcing effects of sham-fed sucrose in the rat. *Pharmacol. Biochem. Behav.* 22:787–90

Gerber GJ, Sing J, Wise RA. 1981. Pimozide attenuates lever-pressing for water reinforcement in rats. *Pharmacol. Biochem. Behav.* 14:201–5

Gerrits M, Ramsey NF, Wolternink G, van Ree JM. 1994. Lack of evidence for an involvement of the nucleus accumbens dopamine D_1 receptors in the initiation of heroin self-administration in the rat. *Psychopharmacology* 114:486–94

Glickman SE, Schiff BB. 1967. A biological theory of reinforcement. *Psychol. Rev.* 74: 81–100

Goeders NE, Smith JE. 1983. Cortical dopa minergic involvement in cocaine reinforcement. *Science* 221:773–75

Gray T, Wise RA. 1980. Effects of pimozide on lever pressing behavior maintained on an intermittent reinforcement schedule. *Pharmacol. Biochem. Behav.* 12:931–35

Grill HJ, Norgren R. 1978a. The taste reactivity test. I. Mimetic responses to gustatory stimuli in neurologically normal rats. *Brain Res.* 143:263–79

Grill HJ, Norgren R. 1978b. Chronically decerebrate rats demonstrate satiation but not bait shyness. *Science* 201:267–69

Grill HJ, Norgren R. 1978c. The taste reactivity test. II. Mimetic responses to gustatory stimuli in chronic thalamic and chronic decerebrate rats. *Brain Res.* 143:281–97

Hand TH, Stinus L, Le Moal M. 1989. Differential mechanisms in the acquisition and expression of heroin-induced place preference. *Psychopharmacology* 98:61–67

Harrington F, van der Kooy D. 1992. Deprivation state determines the motivational effects of neuroleptics in rats. *Psychobiology* 20:294–99

Hemby SE, Jones GH, Justice JB Jr, Neil DB. 1992. Conditioned locomotor activity but not conditioned place preference following intra-accumbens infusions of cocaine. *Psychopharmacology* 106:330–36

Higgins GA, Joharchi N, Nguyen P, Sellers EM. 1992a. Effect of the 5-HT_3 receptor antagonists, MDL 72222 and ondansetron on morphine place conditioning. *Psychopharmacology* 106:315–20

Higgins GA, Joharchi N, Wang Y, Corrigall WA, Sellers EM. 1994b. The CCK_A receptor antagonist devazepide does not modify opioid self-administration or drug discrimination: comparison with the dopamine antagonist halperidol. *Brain Res.* 640:246–54

Higgins GA, Nguyen P, Sellers EM. 1992b. Morphine place conditioning is differentially affected by CCK_A and CCK_B receptor antagonists. *Brain Res.* 572:208–15

Higgins GA, Wang Y, Corrigall WA, Sellers EM. 1994a. Influence of 5-HT_3 receptor antagonists and indirect 5-HT agonist, dexfenfluramine, on heroin self-administration in rats. *Psychopharmacology* 114:611–19

Hiroi N, McDonald RJ, White NM. 1990. The reserpine sensitive dopamine pool mediates (+)-amphetamine conditioned reward in the place preference paradigm. *Brain Res.* 510: 33–42

Hull CL. 1943. *Principles of Behavior.* New York: Appleton-Century-Crofts

Jaeger TV, van der Kooy D. 1993. Morphine acts in the parabrachial nucleus, a pontine viscerosensory relay, to produce discriminative effects. *Psychopharmacology* 110: 76–84

Jaeger TV, van der Kooy D. 1996. Separate neural substrates mediate the motivating and discriminative properties of morphine. *Behav. Neurosci.* 110:181–201

Jenk J, Gratton A, Wise RA. 1986. Effects of pimozide and naloxone on latency for hypothalamically induced eating. *Brain Res.* 375:329–37

Kanarek RB, Marks-Kaufman R. 1988. Animal models of appetitive behavior: interaction of nutritional factors and drug seeking behavior. In *Control of Appetite,* ed. M. Winick, pp. 1–25. New York: Wiley

Koob GF, Bloom FE. 1988. Cellular and molecular mechanisms of drug dependence. *Science* 242:715–23

Kunihara M, Kanbayashi M, Ohshima T. 1983. Opposite effects of morphine on feeding and drinking in rats relative to administration time. *Jpn. J. Pharmacol.* 33:829–35

Lamb RJ, Preston KL, Schindler C, Meisch RA, Davis F, et al. 1991. The reinforcing and subjective effects of morphine in post-addicts: a dose-response study. *J. Pharmacol. Exp. Ther.* 259:1165–73

Leone P, Di Chiara G. 1987. Blockade of D1 receptors by SCH 23390 antagonizes morphine and amphetamine induced place preference conditioning. *Eur. J. Pharmacol.* 135:251–54

Lowy MT, Starkey TC, Yim GKW. 1981. Stereoselective effects of opiate agonists on ingestive behavior in rats. *Pharmacol. Biochem. Behav.* 15:591–96

Lyness WH, Friedle NM, Moore KE. 1979. Destruction of dopaminergic nerve terminals in nucleus accumbens: effect on *d*-amphetamine self-administration. *Pharmacol. Biochem. Behav.* 11:553–56

Mackey WB, van der Kooy D. 1985. Neuroleptics block the positive reinforcing effects of amphetamine but not morphine as measured by place conditioning. *Pharmacol. Biochem. Behav.* 22:101–5

Mackintosh NJ. 1974. *The Psychology of Animal Learning.* New York: Academic

Martin GM, Bechara A, van der Kooy D. 1991.

The perception of emotion: parallel neural processing of the affective and discriminative properties of opiates. *Psychobiology* 19:147–52

Mazurski EJ, Beninger RJ. 1986. The effects of (+)-amphetamine and apomorphine on responding for a conditioned reinforcer. *Psychopharmacology* 90:239–43

McGregor A, Roberts DCS. 1993. Dopaminergic antagonism within the nucleus accumbens or the amygdala produces differential effects on the intravenous cocaine self-administration under fixed and progressive ratio schedules of reinforcement. *Brain Res.* 624:245–52

Milner PM. 1991. Brain stimulation reward: a review. *Can. J. Psychol.* 45:1–36

Mithani S, Martin-Iverson MT, Phillips AG, Fibiger HC. 1986. The effects of halperidol on amphetamine- and methylphenidate-induced conditioned place preferences and locomotor activity. *Psychopharmacology* 90:247–52

Mogenson GJ, Takigawa M, Robertson A, Wu M. 1979. Self-stimulation of the nucleus accumbens and ventral tegmental area of Tsai attenuated by microinjections of spiroperidol into the nucleus accumbens. *Brain Res.* 171:247–59

Mucha RF, Iversen SD. 1984. Reinforcing properties of morphine and naloxone revealed by conditioned place preferences: a procedural examination. *Psychopharmacology* 82:241–47

Muscat R, Willner P. 1989. Effects of dopamine receptor antagonist on sucrose consumption and preference. *Psychopharmacology* 99:98–102

Nader K, Harrington F, Bechara A, van der Kooy D. 1994. Neuroleptics block high but not low dose heroin place preferences: further evidence for a two system model of motivation. *Behav. Neurosci.* 108:1128–38

Nader K, van der Kooy D. 1994. The motivation produced by morphine and food is isomorphic: approaches to specific motivational stimuli are learned. *Psychobiology* 22:68–76

Nader K, van der Kooy D. 1995. Morphine microinjections into the ventral tegmental area produce dopamine independent conditioned place preferences. *Soc. Neurosci. Abstr.* 21:733

Nader K, van der Kooy D. 1996. Clonidine antagonizes the aversive effects of opiate withdrawal and the rewarding effects of morphine only in opiate withdrawn rats. *Behav. Neurosci.* 110:1–12

Nakajima S, Wise RA. 1987. Heroin self-administration in the rat suppressed by SCH 23390. *Soc. Neurosci. Abstr.* 13:1545

Olds J, Milner P. 1954. Positive reinforcement produced by electrical stimulation of septal area and other regions of rat brain. *J. Comp. Physiol. Psychol.* 47:419–27

Olmstead MC, Franklin KBJ. 1993. Effects of pedunculopontine tegmental nucleus lesions on morphine-induced conditioned place preference and analgesia in the formalin test. *Neuroscience* 57:411–18

Olmstead MC, Franklin KBJ. 1994. Lesions of the pedunculopontine tegmental nucleus block drug-induced reinforcement but not amphetamine-induced locomotion. *Brain Res.* 638:29–35

Olmstead MC, Munn EM, Wise RA. 1993. Effects of pedunculopontine nucleus (PPN) lesions on the acquisition of iv heroin self-administration. *Soc. Neurosci. Abstr.* 19: 1023

Parker JL, van der Kooy D. 1995. Tegmental pedunculopontine nucleus lesions do not block cocain reward. *Pharmacol. Biochem. Behav.* 52:77–83

Parker LA. 1991. Taste reactivity responses elicited by reinforcing drugs: a dose-response analysis. *Behav. Neurosci.* 105: 955–64

Peciña S, Berridge KC. 1995. Comparison of systemic and intracranial administration of morphine: effects on hedonic taste reactivity (in rats). *Soc. Neurosci. Abstr.* 21:1460

Perin CT. 1942. Behavior potentiality as a joint function of the amount of training and the degree of hunger at the time of extinction. *J. Exp. Psychol.* 30:93–113

Pettit HO, Ettenberg A, Bloom FE, Koob GF. 1984. Destruction of dopamine in the nucleus accumbens selectively attenuates cocaine but not heroin self-administration in rats. *Psychopharmacology* 84:167–73

Phillips AG, Nikaido RS. 1975. Disruption of brain stimulation–induced feeding by dopamine receptor blockade. *Nature* 258: 750–51

Phillips GD, Robbins TW, Everitt BJ. 1994. Mesoaccumbens dopamine-opiate interactions in the control over behavior by a conditioned reinforcer. *Psychopharmacology* 114:345–59

Phillips GD, Robbins TW, Everitt BJ. 1994. Bilateral intra-accumbens self-administration of *d*-amphetamine: antagonism with intra-accumbens SCH 23390 and sulpiride. *Psychopharmacology* 114:477–85

Pickens R, Harris WC. 1968. Self-administration of *d*-amphetamine by rats. *Psychopharmacology* 12:158–63

Pickens R, Thompson T. 1971. Characteristics of stimulant reinforcement. In *Stimulus Properties of Drugs,* ed. T Thompson, R Pickens, pp. 177–92. New York: Appleton-Century-Crofts

Rassnick S, Pulvirenti L, Koob GF. 1992. Oral ethanol self-administration in rats is reduced by the administration of dopamine and glutamate receptor antagonists into the nucleus accumbens. *Psychopharmacology* 109:92–98

Rassnick S, Stinus L, Koob GF. 1993. The effects of 6-hydroxydopamine lesions of the nucleus accumbens and the mesolimbic dopamine system on oral self-administration of ethanol in the rat. *Brain Res.* 623: 16–24

Risinger FO, Dickinson SD, Cunningham CL. 1992. Halperidol reduces ethanol-induced motor activity stimulation but not conditioned place preference. *Psychopharmacology* 107:453–56

Robbins TW, Watson BA, Gaskin M, Ennis C. 1983. Contrasting interactions of pipradrol, *d*-amphetamine, cocaine, cocaine analogues, apomorphine and other drugs with conditioned reinforcement. *Psychopharmacology* 80:113–19

Roberts DCS, Corcoran ME, Fibiger HC. 1977. On the role of ascending catecholaminergic systems in intravenous self-administration of cocaine. *Pharmacol. Biochem. Behav.* 6:615–20

Roberts DCS, Koob GF, Klonoff P, Fibiger HC. 1980. Extinction and recovery of cocaine self-administration following intraventricular 6-hydroxydopamine lesions of the nucleus accumbens. *Pharmacol. Biochem. Behav.* 24:881–87

Robledo P, Maldonado-Lopez R, Koob GF. 1992. Role of dopamine receptors in the nucleus accumbens. *Ann. NY Acad. Sci.* 654:509–12

Rolls ET, Rolls BJ, Kelly PH, Shaw SG, Wood RJ, Dale R. 1974. The relative attenuation of self-stimulation, eating and drinking produced by dopamine-receptor blockade. *Psychopharmacologia* 38:219–30

Sanger DJ, McCarthy PS. 1980. Differential effects of morphine on food and water intake in food deprived and freely-feeding rats. *Psychopharmacology* 72:103–6

Sanger DJ, McCarthy PS. 1981. Increased food and water intake produced in rats by opiate receptor agonists. *Psychopharmacology* 74:217–20

Schneider LH, Davis JD, Watson CA, Smith GP. 1990. Similar effect of raclopride and reduced sucrose concentration on the microstructure of sucrose sham feeding. *Eur. J. Pharmacol.* 186:61–70

Schuh KJ, Schaal DW, Thompson T, Cleary JP, Billington CJ, Levine AS. 1994. Insulin, 2-deoxy-D-glucose. *Pharmacol. Biochem. Behav.* 47:317–24

Seeley RJ, Galaverna OG, Schulkin J, Epstein AN, Grill HJ. 1993. Lesions of the central nucleus of the amygdala. II. Effects on intraoral NaCl intake. *Behav. Brain Res.* 59: 19–25

Shaham Y, Stewart J. 1995. Effects of restraint stress and intra-ventral tegmental area injections of morphine and methyl naltrexone on the discriminative stimulus effects of heroin in the rat. *Pharmacol. Biochem. Behav.* 51:491–98

Shippenberg TS, Bals-Kubik R, Herz A. 1993. Examination of the neurochemical substrates mediating the motivational effects of opioids: role of the mesolimbic dopamine system and D1 vs D2 dopamine receptors. *J. Pharmacol. Exp. Ther.* 265: 53–59

Shippenberg TS, Herz A. 1988. Motivational effects of opioids: influence of D1 versus D2 receptor antagonists. *Eur. J. Pharmacol.* 151:233–42

Shoaib M, Spanagel R. 1994. Mesolimbic sites mediate the discriminative stimulus effects of morphine. *Eur. J. Pharmacol.* 252: 69–75

Skinner BF. 1953. *Science and Human Behavior.* New York: Macmillan

Smith GP. 1995. Dopamine and food reward. *Progr. Psychobiol. Physiol. Psychol.* 16: 83–144

Smith JE, Guerin GF, Co C, Barr TS, Lane J. 1985. Effects of 6-OHDA lesions of the central medial nucleus accumbens on rat intravenous morphine self-administration. *Pharmacol. Biochem. Behav.* 23:843–49

Spyraki C, Fibiger HC, Phillips AG. 1982a. Attenuation by halperidol of place preference conditioning using food reinforcement. *Psychopharmacology* 77:379–82

Spyraki C, Fibiger HC, Phillips AG. 1982b. Dopaminergic substrates of amphetamine-induced place preference conditioning. *Brain Res.* 253:185–93

Spyraki C, Fibiger HC, Phillips AG. 1982c. Cocaine-induced place preference conditioning: lack of effects of neuroleptics and 6-hydroxydopamine lesions. *Brain Res.* 253:195–203

Spyraki C, Fibiger HC, Phillips AG. 1983. Attenuation of heroin reward in rats by disruption of the mesolimbic dopamine system. *Psychopharmacology* 79:278–83

Streather A, Bozarth MA. 1987. Effect of dopamine-receptor blockade on stimulation-induced feeding. *Pharmacol. Biochem. Behav.* 27:521–24

Taylor JR, Robbins TW. 1984. Enhanced behavioral control by conditioned reinforcers following microinjections of *d*-amphetamine into the nucleus accumbens. *Psychopharmacology* 84:405–12

Taylor JR, Robbins TW. 1986. 6-hydroxydopamine lesions of the nucleus accumbens, but not of the caudate nucleus, attenuate enhanced responding with reward-related stimuli produced by intra-accumbens. *Psychopharmacology* 90: 390–97

Toates FM. 1986. *Motivational Systems*. Cambridge: Cambridge Univ. Press

Tombaugh TN, Anisman H, Tombaugh J. 1980. Extinction and dopamine receptor blockade after intermittent reinforcement training: failure to observe functional equivalence. *Psychopharmacology* 70: 19–28

Towel A, Muscat R, Willner P. 1987. Effects of pimozide on sucrose consumption and preference. *Psychopharmacology* 92: 262–64

Treit D, Berridge KC. 1990. A comparison of benzodiazepine, serotonin, and dopamine agents in the taste reactivity paradigm. *Pharmacol. Biochem. Behav.* 37:451–56

Ungersteadt U. 1971. Adipsia and aphagia after 6-hydroxydopamine induced degeneration of the nigro-striatal dopamine system. *Acta Physiol. Scand.* 367:95–122

van der Kooy D. 1987. Place conditioning: a simple and effective method for assessing the motivational properties of drugs. In *Methods of Assessing the Reinforcing Properties of Drugs of Abuse,* ed. MA Bozarth, pp. 229–40. New York: Springer-Verlag

van der Kooy D, Swerdlow N, Koob GF. 1983. Paradoxical reinforcing properties of apomorphine: effects of nucleus accumbens and area postrema lesions. *Brain Res.* 259: 111–18

Webb WB. 1955. Drive stimuli as cues. *Psychol. Rep.* 1:287–98

Welz H, Kuhn G, Huston JP. 1989. Self-administration of small amounts of morphine through glass micropipettes into the ventral tegmental area of the rat. *Neuropharmacology* 28:1017–23

Willner P, Papp M, Phillips G, Maleeh M, Muscat R. 1990. Pimozide does not impair sweetness discrimination. *Psychopharmacology* 102:278–82

Wise RA. 1982. Neuroleptics and operant behavior: the anhedonia hypothesis. *Behav. Brain Sci.* 5:39–87

Wise RA. 1996. Addictive drugs and brain stimulation reward. *Annu. Rev. Neurosci.* 19:319–40

Wise RA, Bozarth MA. 1987. A psychostimulant theory of addiction. *Psychol. Rev.* 94: 1–24

Wise RA, Rompre PP. 1989. Brain dopamine and reward. *Annu. Rev. Psychol.* 40: 191–225

Wise RA, Spindler J, DeWit H, Gerber GJ. 1978. Neuroleptic-induced "anhedonia" in rats: pimozide blocks reward quality of food. *Science* 201:262–64

Wise RA, Yokel RA, DeWit H. 1976. Both positive reinforcement and conditioned taste aversion from amphetamine and apomorphine in rats. *Science* 191:1273

Yokel RA, Wise RA. 1975. Increased lever pressing for amphetamine after pimozide in rats: implications for a dopamine theory of reward. *Science* 187:547–49

Yokel RA, Wise RA. 1976. Attenuation of amphetamine reinforcement by central dopamine blockade in rats. *Psychopharmacology* 48:311–18

Annu. Rev. Psychol. 1997. 48:115–38

MUSIC PERFORMANCE

Caroline Palmer

Department of Psychology, The Ohio State University, Columbus, Ohio 43210

KEY WORDS: skilled performance, musical memory, sequence production, music perception, motor skills

ABSTRACT

Music performance provides a rich domain for study of both cognitive and motor skills. Empirical research in music performance is summarized, with particular emphasis on factors that contribute to the formation of conceptual interpretations, retrieval from memory of musical structures, and transformation into appropriate motor actions. For example, structural and emotional factors that contribute to performers' conceptual interpretations are considered. Research on the planning of musical sequences for production is reviewed, including hierarchical and associative retrieval influences, style-specific syntactic influences, and constraints on the range of planning. The fine motor control evidenced in music performance is discussed in terms of internal timekeeper models, motor programs, and kinematic models. The perceptual consequences of music performance are highlighted, including the successful communication of interpretations, resolution of structural ambiguities, and concordance with listeners' expectations. Parallels with other domains support the conclusion that music performance is not unique in its underlying cognitive mechanisms.

CONTENTS

0084-6570/97/0201-0115$08.00

INTRODUCTION

Music performance provides a rich domain for study of both cognitive and motor skills. Performers dominate many aspects of our musical culture today. Concert attendance and recording sales, for example, often reflect listeners' preferences for performers and abilities to distinguish among performances. Although public consumption of music tends to highlight performance differences, there are also strong commonalities across performances that reflect cognitive functions of grouping, unit identification, thematic abstraction, elaboration, and hierarchical nesting. Thus, music performance is based on both individualistic aspects that differentiate performers and normative aspects shared by performers. Both the commonalities and differences among music performances can be modeled theoretically in terms of general cognitive abilities.

The majority of studies focus on the performance of musical compositions for which notation is available, thus providing unambiguous performance goals. The focus has also been on piano performance, in which pitch and timing measurements are simplified. Common forms of music performance in the Western tonal tradition include sight-reading (performing unfamiliar music from notation), performing well-learned (prepared) music from memory or from notation, improvising, and playing by ear (performing music from aural presentation). Correlations among these abilities tend to be high and to increase with training (McPherson 1995, Nuki 1984), although some studies show differences in abilities across performers. For instance, accompanists perform better than soloists on some sight-reading tasks (Lehmann & Ericsson 1993). Although there are few studies of long-term changes in performance ability, diary and interview studies suggest that differences in performance levels across individuals are largely a function of experience and practice (Ericsson et al 1993, Sloboda et al 1996).

Psychological studies of music performance aim to develop theories of performance mechanisms (what cognitive or motor constraints influence performance). A second aim is to explain the treatment of structural ambiguities (in what contexts do ambiguities arise, what kinds of choices do performers make). A third aim is to understand relationships between performance and perception (how are listeners influenced by performance aspects). During a performance, musical structures and units are retrieved from memory according to the performer's conceptual interpretation, and are then prepared for production and transformed into appropriate movements. The following sections of the review—Interpretation, Planning, and Movement—focus on these components of performance. Topics that are covered elsewhere include stylistic performance conventions, expertise and skill development (Ericsson & Lehmann 1996), sight-reading and improvising (Sloboda 1985b), and social and evaluative aspects of performance (Gabrielsson 1997). This chapter reviews only those perceptual studies that address performance issues.

Serial Order and Timing Issues

Speaking, typing, and performing music are among the most complex forms of skilled serial action produced by human beings. Seminal theories of motor control (Bernstein 1967, Lashley 1951) often use music performance as the ultimate example of human motor skill. Based on capacities such as the trilling speed of concert pianists (on the order of 16 notes/s), Lashley (1951) suggested that successive elements of this kind of activity must be centrally linked; a centrally controlled mechanism determines movements in a predetermined order. This open-loop (motor program) theory is based on two types of evidence: There is little time for feedback to affect the planning of the next movement (Keele 1968), and some skills can be performed in the absence of kinesthetic feedback (Keele & Summers 1976, Lashley 1951).

The control of complex, temporally structured behaviors such as speech production or music performance embodies two problems: the serial order of sequence elements, and their relative timing. The serial order problem arises from the fact that chain-like organization of behavior is inadequate to explain certain serial order effects in sequence perception and production. For instance, strong constraints on the order of words within phrases and of phonemes within words must be met for speech to be acceptable. Musical and linguistic sequences that are well-formed in their serial order, however, are often not understandable unless additional constraints hold on the relative timing of the individual sequence elements. Music performed without accurate temporal control is considered deficient because it lacks the property of rhythm, in which the timing of elements is influenced by the timing of other (adjacent and nonadjacent) elements (Vorberg & Hambuch 1978). The domain of music performance is ideal for developing models of timing mechanisms because it offers theoretical consensus on the nature of the temporal relationships that must be present for a sequence to be considered accurate. Questions of serial order, relative timing, and how rhythm (temporal patterning) constrains the planning and production of musical sequences are addressed below.

Methodological Issues

Several methodological issues influence the interpretation of research in music performance. First, the wealth of data from a single performance (roughly 3000 pieces of information in one second of digital audio sound recorded at a low sampling rate) results in problems of separating signal from noise. Carl Seashore (1936, 1938), one of the first to conduct psychological studies of music performance, developed a piano camera system to record only gestural (movement-based) data from hammer and foot-pedal movements, greatly reducing the amount of data necessary to capture essential performance aspects. Current computer music technology relies heavily on movement-based information and records only event onsets, offsets, and their relative intensities from electronic- or computer-monitored musical instruments.

Despite the reduction of information, problems with separating the signal—performance expression—from random noise fluctuations remain. Performance expression refers to the large and small variations in timing, intensity or dynamics, timbre, and pitch that form the microstructure of a performance and differentiate it from another performance of the same music. Musicians can replicate their expressive patterns of timing and dynamics for a given musical piece with high precision (Gabrielsson 1987a, Henderson 1936, Seashore 1938, Shaffer & Todd 1987), and attempts to play without expression significantly dampen these patterns but do not remove them altogether (Bengtsson & Gabrielsson 1983, Palmer 1989, Seashore 1938), which suggests that some variations are intentional. Expression is often analyzed according to the deviation of performed events from their fixed or regular values as notated in a musical score (Gabrielsson 1987a, HG Seashore 1936). However, performance can be expressive without reference to a score (as in musical improvisation). Expression can also be analyzed relative to the performance itself; for instance, expression within a unit such as a phrase is the pattern of deviations of its parts with respect to the unit itself (Desain & Honing 1991). Consequently, measurements of performance expression sometimes differ across studies, which makes comparisons difficult.

A second methodological problem is determining which performances should be considered representative, given the large variations that can occur among competent performances of the same music. There are few objective criteria for performance success; most experimenters opt for a recognized level of performer expertise. Large samples of famous performers are hard to find, however, and exploratory (nonexperimental) methods or case study methods are often used. A similar representativeness problem arises in choice of musical stimuli. Because of complexity issues, experimenters often use simplified or reduced musical compositions. For these reasons, the domain of music performance relies heavily on converging evidence from both small and large sample studies conducted with different musical stimuli.

INTERPRETATION

Music performance is often viewed as part of a system of communication in which composers code musical ideas in notation, performers recode from the notation to acoustical signal, and listeners recode from the acoustical signal to ideas (Kendall & Carterette 1990). Each performer has intentions to convey; the communicative content in music performance includes the performers' conceptual interpretation of the musical composition. Western tonal music has developed a notation that represents pitch and duration information fairly explicitly but intensity and tone quality only approximately. Other relationships, such as group boundaries, metrical levels higher than the measure, and patterns of motion, tension, and relaxation are unspecified or only implicitly specified in notation. Thus, ambiguities in musical notation allow a performer considerable freedom in deciding how to interpret the music's content. Interpretation refers to performers' individualistic modeling of a piece according to their own ideas or musical intentions. Differences in interpretation can account for why the same musical score is performed differently by different performers or why the same performer may perform a piece differently on separate occasions.

As in other art forms, there is no single ideal interpretation for a given musical piece; every performance involves some kind of interpretation or analysis (Cone 1968, Levy 1995, Meyer 1973). The field of music analysis offers various explanations for the content of a given composition. For instance, a piece can be viewed as a hierarchy of part/whole relationships, as a linear course that follows the harmonic tension, or as a series of moods that result in a unity of character (Sundin 1984). However, music analysis does not indicate how a performer actually produces a desired interpretation (Dunsby 1989). One goal of interpretation is to convey the meaning of the music. Definitions of musical meaning abound, but several theorists define it as having major components that relate to structure, emotion, and physical movement (Gabrielsson 1982, Meyer 1956), which contribute to performers' interpretations.

One function of interpretation is to highlight particular structural content (Clarke 1987). Some experimental work evaluates the effects of individual performers' structural interpretations on performance expression. Nakamura (1987) compared musicians' performances of a baroque sonata with their notated interpretations of musical dynamics (patterns of intensity changes). Performers' notated intentions generally corresponded to changes in sound level. Listeners' perceived dynamics matched performers' intended dynamics fairly well, even when underlying acoustic changes were not identifiable. Palmer (1989) compared pianists' notated interpretations of phrase structure and melody with expressive timing patterns. Onsets of the melodic voice preceded other voice onsets in notated simultaneities (termed melody leads), and slowing in tempo was greatest at phrase boundaries. Expressive timing patterns decreased when pianists attempted to play without interpretation, and these patterns increased in exaggerated interpretations, similar to other findings of modulations in expressive level (Kendall & Carterette 1990, Seashore 1938). Further studies indicated that the expressive timing patterns increased from novices to experts, increased during practice of an unfamiliar piece, and changed across different interpretations of the same piece performed by the same pianist (Palmer 1988).

Interpretations of structural content affect both the expressive marking of individual events and the likelihood that events will be correctly retrieved and produced. Error analyses (based on comparison with the notated score) of piano performances with different phrase structure interpretations indicated that pitch deletions tended to occur within phrases and perseverations at phrase boundaries, which suggests that interpretations strengthen phrase boundaries relative to other locations (Palmer 1992). These findings were replicated in later experiments, which also indicated that melodic interpretations increased the likelihood that melodic events were correctly retrieved and produced relative to nonmelodic events (Palmer & van de Sande 1993, 1995).

Another function of interpretation is to highlight particular emotional content of the music. An extreme view holds that the structure of music is isomorphic to the structure of moods or feelings; music should sound the way moods feel (Langer 1953). Gabrielsson (1995) compared performers' interpretations of emotional content with their use of expression. Flute and violin performances of the same music interpreted with different emotional characters indicated general patterns of change in expression. Performances of happy and angry emotions were played with faster tempo and larger dynamic range, whereas soft and sad emotions were performed with slower tempo and smaller dynamic range. Tone onsets were abrupt in the angry version and more gradual in the sad version. Related patterns of performance expression were found in violin performances of a Beethoven theme with tender or aggressive interpretations (Askenfelt 1986). Later experiments replicated these patterns, and most of the emotion categories were accurately conveyed to listeners (Gabrielsson & Juslin 1996). The emotional content of music has also been examined recently in terms of narrative, with emphasis on dramatic characterization, thematic content, and conceptions of large-scale structures (Schmalfeldt 1985, Shaffer 1995).

Musical experience enhances both performers' use of expression to emphasize interpretations and listeners' ability to identify interpretations and expressive aspects of performance (Geringer & Madsen 1987, Johnson 1996, Palmer 1988, Sloboda 1985a). Listeners without musical experience do pick up some interpretive aspects. Nonmusician listeners were able to discern general differences among mechanical (inexpressive), expressive, and exaggerated levels of performance as accurately as musician listeners (Kendall & Carterette 1990). Some evidence suggests that type of musical experience matters: All musician listeners were influenced by expressive timing cues when asked to choose the intended phrase structure in piano performances, but only listeners with piano training were influenced by expressive timing cues (melody leads) when choosing among melody interpretations (Palmer 1988, 1996b). Although these studies address the sufficiency of expressive features to convey performers' interpretations, they do not address how necessary they are (see section below on Perception of Performance Expression).

PLANNING

Planning and memory retrieval processes in music performance reflect multi-dimensional relationships among melodic, harmonic, and diatonic elements. In Western tonal music, individual pitches, chords, and keys are posited as conceptually distinct units of knowledge, that reflect levels of melodic, harmonic, and diatonic structure, respectively. Some compositional structures, such as homophonic music, emphasize across-voice (chordal) associations between melody and accompaniment, whereas others, such as polyphonic structure, emphasize within-voice (single-note) associations among multiple important voices. Analyses of piano performances indicated that chord errors occurred more often in homophonic styles and that single-note errors occurred more often in polyphonic styles, which suggests that the relevant musical units change across different musical contexts (Palmer & van de Sande 1993, 1995). Knowledge of diatonic and harmonic structure influences performance as well. Mistakes were more likely to originate from the key of the piece than from another key and to be of the same chord type as what was intended (Palmer & van de Sande 1993). Child singers' pitch errors were also likely to be harmonically related to intended events (Moore 1994), and pianists' errors during sight-reading of pieces in which deliberate pitch alterations had been placed indicated tacit knowledge of likely melodic and harmonic relationships (Sloboda 1976).

Theories of skilled performance often assume that people prepare complex sequences for production by partitioning them into shorter subsequences (cf van Galen & Wing 1984). Phrase structure is one feature that influences the partitioning of musical sequences; evidence from performance timing and errors suggests that musical sequences are partitioned during planning into phrase segments (Palmer & van de Sande 1995). Errors that replaced intended pitches in piano performances were more likely to originate from the same phrase as the intended event than from different phrases. Interacting elements rarely crossed phrase boundaries, similar to findings in speech errors (Garcia-Albea et al 1989, Garrett 1980). Segmentation during performance planning is also influenced by relationships among musical accent structures. Adult pianists' and children's abilities to reproduce melodies were increasingly disrupted the more that melodic, metrical, and rhythmic grouping accents were shifted out of alignment in the performed tunes (Drake et al 1991).

Both structural relations and the serial distance between sequence events influence the range over which performers can plan, presumably because of limitations on memory capacity. Supporting evidence is seen in eye-hand span tasks, in which pianists reproduced briefly presented musical sequences. The mean eye-hand span was 7–8 events beyond the location at which the notation disappeared, and it tended to extend only to phrase boundaries (Sloboda 1974, 1977). However, eye-hand span measures may reflect effects of both memory capacity and anticipatory eye movements. Range of planning in memorized piano performances (with no notation) was affected by both serial distance and structural relations among sequence elements (Palmer & van de Sande 1995). Errors and timing measures indicated that the planning of current elements was affected by elements that spanned larger serial distances in the absence rather than in the presence of intervening phrase boundaries, similar to interactions of distance and structural constraints in language production (Garcia-Albea et al 1989). These findings suggest two possible invariants in the planning of complex serial behaviors in many domains: the co-occurrence during planning of elements that share structural features, and constraints of structural boundaries on serial distances over which elements are concurrently planned.

Syntax of Musical Structure

The performance of music is also constrained by style-specific syntactic properties that transcend individual interpretations. Many theories of Western tonal music have meter and grouping as their primary syntactic elements (Cooper & Meyer 1960, Lerdahl & Jackendoff 1983). Meter refers to periodic features: the regular alternation of strong and weak beats. Positions of metrical accents form hierarchical levels, with different periodicities represented at each level. Meter provides a temporal framework in performance for when to do what, as supported by evidence that only those rhythmic patterns that can be accommodated to a metrical framework are correctly reproduced (Povel 1981, Povel & Essens 1985), and the same duration pattern is performed with different expressive timing when placed in different metrical contexts (Clarke 1985). Grouping refers to the segmentation of a sequence into smaller subsequences that also form hierarchical levels, based largely on pitch relationships (Lerdahl & Jackendoff 1983). Some metrical and grouping levels are more salient than others. Tactus refers to the most salient periodicity or metrical level, which corresponds to the rate at which one might tap a foot to the music (Fraisse 1982), and phrases are thought to be the most salient level of grouping structure. Events at the most salient levels are commonly emphasized in performance (cf Repp 1992b, Todd 1985) and may be most precisely or consistently produced and perceived (see section below on Timekeeper Models).

Probably the most widespread structural characteristic of Western music is its hierarchical nature; both pitch and rhythm structures are represented in a series of levels, between which relationships of reduction or elaboration operate (cf Clarke 1988, Lerdahl & Jackendoff 1983, Schenker 1969). For instance, Schenker's (1969) music theory views the melodic and harmonic organization of a musical piece as a series of progressively more complex elaborations of a simple foundation, the background, from which the surface level or foreground (the note-to-note aspects of the musical score) is generated. These hierarchical levels not only embody music-theoretic principles but also have implications for perceptual and cognitive processes, such as the prediction that more important events are processed at deeper levels and thus memory should be facilitated for those events.

Improvisation tasks have been used to address hierarchical implications for music performance. Pianists' improvisations on a musical theme tended to retain from the theme only structurally important events from abstract hierarchical levels of reduction (Large et al 1995). A neural network model trained to produce reduced memory representations represented structurally important events more efficiently than others, by accounting for the musical reduction in terms of a recursive auto-associative mechanism. The network's weightings of relative importance corresponded with both the musical events retained across improvisations and the predictions of structural importance from a reductionist music theory (Lerdahl & Jackendoff 1983), which suggests that reduction may be a natural consequence of hierarchical encodings of musical structure (Large et al 1995). Schmuckler (1990) used an improvisation task to test performers' expectancies for which events would follow in open-ended musical fragments. Performers' improvised continuations reflected influences of both the contents of the musical fragments and the abstract tonal and metrical hierarchies typical of Western music (Krumhansl & Kessler 1982, Lerdahl & Jackendoff 1983). Other studies indicated a correspondence between the events most often produced in improvisations and listeners' ratings of how highly expected those events were (Schmuckler 1989). These findings suggest that music perception and performance are both influenced by the hierarchical properties of musical styles.

Structure-Expression Relationships

Many findings have established a causal relationship between musical structure and patterns of performance expression (Clarke 1988, Palmer 1989, Sloboda 1983). One of the most well-documented relationships is the marking of group boundaries, especially phrases, with decreases in tempo and dynamics (Henderson 1936). Patterns of rubato (tempo modulations) often indicate a hierarchy of phrases, with amount of slowing at a boundary reflecting the depth of embedding (Shaffer & Todd 1987; Todd 1985, 1989). The more important the musical segment, based on a hierarchical analysis of meter and grouping principles (Lerdahl & Jackendoff 1983), the greater the phrase-final lengthening. The greatest correspondence between expressive timing and intensity in performance is found at an intermediate phrase level (Palmer 1996a, Todd 1992), and performers' notated and sounded interpretations tend to differ most at levels lower than the phrase (Palmer 1989, Repp 1992b).

Metrical structure also influences performance expression. Metrical accents (events aligned with strong beats as implied by notated metrical information) are often emphasized by lengthened durations and delayed onsets in piano performance (Henderson 1936) and in vocal performance (Palmer & Kelly 1992). Pianists presented with the same melodies in different notated metrical contexts played events aligned with metrical accents louder, with longer durations, and with more legato (smooth) articulation (Sloboda 1983, 1985a). Listeners' subsequent judgments of meter for the different performances aligned with performers' metrical intentions most often for the most experienced pianists' performances (whose expressive markings of meter were clearer) (Sloboda 1983). When the different expressive cues were independently manipulated in computer-generated simulations, listeners most often chose the intended meter primarily on the basis of articulation cues. Loudness cues alone communicated meter also, but they were not present in all performances (Sloboda 1985a). In all, these findings suggest that there is no one set of necessary and sufficient expressive cues to denote meter.

One of the first types of musical structure for which systematic patterns of performance expression were documented is the duration patterns that form characteristic rhythms (Bengtsson & Gabrielsson 1977). An example is the Viennese waltz (based on a repeating pattern of three equal-duration beats with a metrical accent on the first beat), typically performed with a short first beat and a long second beat (Askenfelt 1986, Bengtsson & Gabrielsson 1977). Gabrielsson (1974) documented systematic deviations in the note durations and amplitudes of pianists' and percussionists' performances of repeating rhythmic patterns to a metronomic tempo; the first note of each measure was louder, and notated duration ratio relationships were increased. Listeners' ratings of similarity among these performed rhythms (Gabrielsson 1973a) and performances of polyphonic (multivoiced) rhythms (Gabrielsson 1973b) suggested that the expressive timing patterns can be grouped according to three factors: structure, motion, and emotion. Structure included meter, accent pattern, and simplicity (of duration ratios). Motion included rapidity (sound event density), tempo, and forward movement. Emotion included vitality, excitedness, and playfulness (Gabrielsson 1982). Factor analyses of the timing profiles from piano performances of a Mozart sonata replicated some of the same structure-expression relationships found with the simpler rhythm patterns, in which other types of musical structure were not present (Gabrielsson 1987a).

The mapping between structure and expression is modulated by several factors, however, including the musical context. Drake & Palmer (1993) examined whether accents associated with different musical structures affect performance expression independently or interactively. Three types of structure were systematically combined in melodies presented to pianists: meter, rhythmic grouping, and melodic accents (pitch jumps and contour changes). Performance expression corresponding to rhythmic grouping and meter remained the same when those two structures were presented separately or combined, and they remained the same when the two structures coincided or conflicted (Drake & Palmer 1993). Expression associated with melodic accents and sometimes metrical accents, however, was altered by the presence or absence of other accents. These findings suggest again that the mapping between particular musical structures and performance expression is not consistent across contexts.

Performance expression also serves to differentiate among simultaneously occurring voices in multivoiced music. Voices can be distinguished by their intensity or timing. Early analyses of Duo-art (player piano) rolls indicated that pianists played tones comprising the melodic voice sooner than other tones notated as simultaneous (Vernon 1936). Recordings of wind, string, and recorder ensembles also indicated asynchronies among the voices for notated simultaneities, with a spread of 30–50 ms and a small relative lead (7 ms) of the instrument leading the ensemble (Rasch 1979). The amount of spread was larger for instruments whose rise (attack) time was longer, which suggests that musicians may adjust the asynchronies to establish appropriate timing of perceptual onsets. Measurements of both acoustic and electronic piano performances indicated a 20–50 ms lead of the melody over other voices (Palmer 1989, 1996b), longer than the 20 ms needed for listeners to determine the order of two isolated tone onsets (Hirsh 1959). As interpretations of the melodic voice changed across performances, the voice that preceded other notated simultaneities changed accordingly (Palmer 1996b). Melody leads may serve to separate voices perceptually. Experiments with simple tone sequences indicate that tones that are temporally offset tend to be perceived as belonging to separate streams (Bregman & Pinker 1978).

Do performers use a syntax or formal set of rules to generate expression? According to the view that musical structure is related to performance expression in terms of explicit generative principles, systematic patterns of expression result from transformations of the performer's internal representation of musical structure (Clarke 1993, 1995). Three types of evidence support the view that structure systematically generates expression: the ability to replicate the same expressive timing profile with very small variability across performances (cf Henderson 1936, Seashore 1938), the ability to change an interpretation of a piece and produce different expression with little practice (Palmer 1989, 1996b), and the ability to perform unfamiliar music from notation (sight-read) with appropriate expression (Palmer 1988, Shaffer 1981, Sloboda 1983).

Structure-expression relationships have been formalized in computational models that apply rules to input structural descriptions of musical scores (Sundberg et al 1983a,b). In one model, three types of rules affect event durations, intensities, pitch tunings, and vibrato. Differentiation rules enhance differences among categories, grouping rules segment the music, and ensemble rules coordinate multiple voices or parts (Sundberg et al 1991). Another computational model of performance expression formalizes the inner pulses (reflecting individuality and viewpoint) of individual nineteenth-century composers (Clynes 1986); pulses defined at different levels of musical structure are applied similarly to all pieces by a given composer to generate performance expression (Clynes 1977, 1983). Perceptual judgments of model-generated simulations (Clynes 1995, Repp 1989, Thompson 1989, Thompson et al 1989) and comparisons with live performance expression (Repp 1990) provide some support for these models, but they indicate in general that piece-specific factors contribute to performance expression as much as the piece-transcendent factors captured by the models' rules.

The view that musical structure generates expression also predicts that performers should find it more difficult to imitate a performance that contains an arbitrary relationship between expression and structure than a conventional one. In fact, pianists most accurately imitated a performance that contained a conventional relationship between phrase structure and phrase-final lengthening, but they could also reproduce synthesized versions that contained distorted structure-expression relationships (Clarke 1993, Clarke & Baker-Short 1987). Reproduction accuracy worsened with increasingly disrupted structure-expression relationships, although accuracy improved over repeated attempts even for the most distorted timing patterns. Listeners' ratings of the quality of the performances decreased as the structure-expression relationship became more disrupted (Clarke 1993). Evidence that performers can imitate expressive timing patterns that have an arbitrary relationship to the musical structure suggests that performance expression is not generated solely from structural relationships (Clarke 1993).

Perception of Performance Expression

What perceptual functions do expressive aspects of performance serve? Performance expression can communicate particular interpretations and resolve structural ambiguities, as suggested by the studies reviewed above. Performance expression may also function to compensate for perceptual constraints of the auditory system. According to a bottom-up argument based on psychoacoustic mechanisms, musicians play some events louder or longer because they are heard as softer or shorter otherwise (Drake 1993). Listeners showed decreased detection accuracy for experimentally lengthened events placed right before a long duration in simple rhythmic patterns (Drake 1993), the same locations at which performers tended to lengthen events in richer musical contexts (Drake & Palmer 1993, Palmer 1996a). Similar findings have been noted for intensity changes. Under instructions to play melodic tones with equal intensity, pianists systematically intensified the second tone of each group of four tones (Kurakata et al 1993), contrary to predictions of metrical accentuation on the first tone of each group. Perceptual ratings of the same sequences indicated that the tones in original performances as well as simulated equal-intensity versions were judged to have equal intensities, compared with simulated versions of randomized or altered intensities (Kurakata et al 1993). These initial findings suggest that perceptual sensitivity to temporal and intensity changes is modulated by structural aspects of musical sequences, and performance expression may compensate for those modulations.

The compensatory psychoacoustic explanation of performance expression can be contrasted with a top-down explanation that musical structure elicits expectations via listeners' internal representation of structure-expression rules (Repp 1992c). Listeners' detection of a single lengthened event in an otherwise temporally uniform (computer-generated) performance indicated that lengthening was more difficult to detect in places where it was expected to occur (at ends of structural units, strong metrical positions, and points of harmonic tension) (Repp 1992c). Furthermore, listeners' detection accuracy (percent correct per event location) for lengthened events was inversely correlated with a performer's natural use of expressive lengthening in the same musical piece. Detection accuracy also correlated with bottom-up acoustic properties of musical stimuli, including intensity and tone density characteristics inherent in the musical score. These findings were taken to reflect both top-down and bottom-up influences on the perception of performance expression (Repp 1992c). Further experiments replicated the detection findings for lengthenings and extended the detection paradigm to intensity changes (Repp 1995a). Although bottom-up and top-down explanations cannot be completely separated, the findings suggest that the structure given in a musical composition has inherent relational properties that constrain both perception and performance, rather than perception simply constraining performance or vice versa (Repp 1995a; see also Jones 1987).

Psychological tests of music-theoretic models of musical expectancy and tension-relaxation point to a similar explanation of the influence of compositional structure in perception and performance. Narmour's (1990, 1996) model of melodic expectancy predicts which events are most likely to occur in a given musical context. The more expected events are those that match their preceding contextual implications. Lerdahl's (1996) model predicts patterns of tonal tension and relaxation that arise from harmonic relationships across large musical sections. Both music theories are based on a combination of bottom-up (hard-wired) and top-down (acquired) processes that account for listeners' expectations. Perceptual experiments suggest that listeners can apprehend the music-theoretic predictions of melodic expectancies (Cuddy & Lunney 1995, Krumhansl 1995) and tension-relaxation (Krumhansl 1996) from just the categorical score information presented in computer-generated (expressionless) performances. Comparisons of the music-theoretic predictions with piano performance indicate that expressive cues emphasize melodic expectancies and tension-relaxation (Palmer 1996a). Unexpected events were played louder than expected events, and events with higher tension were performed with longer durations. These findings suggest that performers' and listeners' interpretations of certain structural relationships are constrained in similar ways by the musical composition.

MOVEMENT

After musical structures and units are retrieved from memory according to a performer's conceptual interpretation, they must be transformed into appropriate movements. Movement plays many roles in theories of music and its performance; for example, musical rhythm is often defined relative to body movement (Fraisse 1982, Gabrielsson 1982). Different views exist on the causal relationships between musical rhythm and movement in performance. For instance, movement can generate rhythm and timing, or rhythm and timing can generate movement (Clarke 1997). These two views are considered below.

Timekeeper Models

Movement generating timing is the motor control view: Structural information (such as a sequence's rhythm) may be the input to a motor system, which then produces some kind of temporally structured behavior, perhaps with the use of internal clocks or timekeepers. Internal clocks were proposed to account for behaviors such as the anticipation and coordination of gestures or acts, e.g. accompanying musical sounds with tapping. Accompaniment reflects a synchronization between perception and production that requires the anticipation of upcoming events. In music performance, motor systems are thought to construct the information for upcoming movements on the basis of internal clocks, which act as timekeepers by controlling the time scale of movement trajectories (Shaffer 1981). A clock constructs beats at an abstract level that provide temporal reference points for future movements. The primary role of an internal clock is to regulate and coordinate complex time series such as those produced between hands or between performers.

Evidence to support clock models comes mainly from reproduction tasks, in which subjects hear and then reproduce musical rhythms by tapping. People are more accurate at reproducing musical rhythms whose interonset intervals are based on 1:1 or 2:1 ratios than on other ratios (Essens & Povel 1985, Povel 1981). Both musicians and nonmusicians reproduce duration patterns most accurately when the durations are related in integer ratio relationships (Essens 1986). Early models of the temporal control of rhythmic sequences posited a single clock (Essens & Povel 1985, Povel & Essens 1985), whereas others contrasted multiple timekeepers (Vorberg & Hambuch 1984; for a review, see Jones 1990). Because reproduction tasks combine perceptual and motor processes, some models of reproduction timing attribute internal timekeeping to perceptual encoding (Povel & Essens 1985), whereas others attribute it to production mechanisms (Vorberg & Hambuch 1978).

At what hierarchical level of musical time does an internal clock operate? Most clock models exert their influence at the level of the tactus, or most salient metrical level in a musical sequence (Essens & Povel 1985, Parncutt 1994). Evidence from some tasks suggests that 600 ms may be the preferred pace of the tactus: People most often generate beat patterns around 600 ms in spontaneous rhythmic tapping tasks (Fraisse 1982), the typical interstep interval found in neutral walking is 540 ms (Fraisse 1982, Nilsson & Thorstensson 1989), and listeners most often use motion terms to describe rhythmic patterns whose interbeat intervals center around 650 ms (Sundberg et al 1993). Most internal clock models applied to music performance produce time periods greater than or less than the primary timing level by concatenating or dividing beat periods, rather than by positing additional clocks (Clarke 1997, Shaffer 1982).

A further implication of a motor system paced by an internal timekeeper or clock is that temporal variance in performed event durations may be attributable to the timekeeper or to the executing motor system. Early models of the timing mechanisms underlying tapping behaviors partitioned the temporal variance into lack of precision due to an internal timekeeper and due to motor response delays, based on covariance analyses of the interresponse intervals (Wing & Kristofferson 1973a,b). Extensions of this model were developed to test hierarchical organizations of timekeepers operating at multiple metrical levels or beat periods in single rhythms (Vorberg & Hambuch 1978) and in polyrhythms (Jagacinski et al 1988). Covariance analyses also allow comparison of whether the timing of event durations is constructed directly or indirectly; performed durations at the metrical level directly controlled by a timekeeper should be less variable than the durations of residual nested events within that level.

Tests of hierarchical clock models operating at various metrical levels, based on covariance analyses, were applied to music performance. Comparisons of temporal variance in skilled piano performances indicated that timekeeping was most directly controlled (least variable) at intermediate metrical levels of the subbeat (below the tactus), the beat, or the bar (Shaffer 1980, Shaffer et al 1985). Further tests of solo piano performances indicated that timing was directly controlled at the beat level (above the level of individual notes), which allowed the two hands some temporal independence in coordinating note events below the beat level that differed in duration (Shaffer 1984). In extensions of covariance analyses, Shaffer (1981) concluded that separate timekeepers controlled the timing of individual hands in piano performance. Duet performances indicated that each pianist's timing had highest precision (least variance) at the bar level, which suggests how performers might coordinate in the absence of an external conductor (Shaffer 1984). Although covariance analyses rely on an assumption of constant global tempo that is rarely seen in music performance, these findings suggest that temporal precision in performance is influenced by the structure of the sequence—in particular, the salience of the beat level or tactus.

Performance timing can also exhibit stability at more abstract hierarchical levels, such as entire musical pieces. The durations of string quartets over repeated performances by the same performers were highly consistent (Clynes & Walker 1986). The standard deviation of the total piece duration (30–45 min) was about 1%, smaller than that of individual movements within the piece. If one movement was shortened, another compensated in duration, which suggests temporal control at a level higher than the individual movements. A related theory predicts that the performance tempos of successive sections of music form simple integer ratios, called proportional tempos (Epstein 1995). The various periodicities that comprise a performance display phase synchrony, particularly at structural boundaries. Like Clynes & Walker (1986), Epstein proposed oscillator mechanisms that track periodicities of tempo in performance and perception and specify relationships among successive movement durations and tempo changes in quantized steps. Similar mechanisms have been proposed in a model of rhythmic attending, based on internal referent periods (preferred attentional periodicities) that may be shared by performers and perceivers (Jones 1987). However, large-scale tempo measurements may reflect performers' memory for tempo (Levitin & Cook 1996) as well as timekeeper stability, and findings based on live performances (Clynes & Walker 1986) are limited by practical constraints such as concert hall rental periods. Nevertheless, these theories do suggest that a large range of periodicities influences the timing of music performance.

Motor Programs

Another theory of temporal control of performance stems from motor programming views. A motor program contains representations of an intended action and processes that translate these into a movement sequence (Keele & Summers 1976, Shaffer 1981). The basic idea is that a sequence of movements can be coordinated in advance of its execution. The goal of motor programming is to account for motor equivalence across contexts, the fact that the same sequence can be performed with different actions and retain its fluency, expressivity, and adaptivity. One view accounts for performers' ability to produce the same sequence in different ways with a single generalized schema that takes parameters (Rosenbaum et al 1986, Schmidt 1975). Changes in global tempo across performances of the same musical piece have been conceptualized in terms of a parameter change. If timing of music performance is relationally invariant across tempo changes, then a change in tempo amounts to multiplying all event durations by a constant value. Relational invariance would support the existence of a generalized motor program, in which a variable rate parameter accounts for performers' ability to produce the same sequence at different rates. Tests of relational invariance for speech, typing, and walking have produced mixed results (cf Gentner 1987).

Tests of relational invariance in music performance generally indicate that the relative durations of note events tend to vary across performances of the same music played at different tempi by the same performer (Clarke 1982, Desain & Honing 1994, MacKenzie & van Eerd 1990, Repp 1995b), although in some cases the relative timing patterns remain highly similar (Repp 1994). One hypothesis for the relative timing changes across tempi is that structural interpretation does not remain constant across performance tempo; for instance, the number of group boundaries increased with slower tempo in piano performances of the same musical piece (Clarke 1982). Lack of relational invariance suggests a failure of transfer of learning; practicing a pattern at a different rate than the intended performance rate might be counterproductive. These findings also warn against drawing structural conclusions based on performance data averaged or normalized across tempi.

Is the perception of musical structure invariant across tempo changes? Perceptual experiments with performed monorhythms (Gabrielsson 1973a) and polyrhythms (Handel & Lawson 1983) suggest that tempo changes do affect the perception of duration patterns. If performers use expressive timing to bring about a desired structural organization for a particular tempo, different perceptions might result for the same relative expressive timing pattern played at a different tempo. Repp (1995b) independently manipulated the amount of expressive timing (incremented in terms of a power function) and the global tempo (incremented in terms of total piece duration) of performances. Listeners gave higher ratings of aesthetic quality to the reduced expression at fast tempo and to the augmented expression at slow tempo for the same musical pieces, which suggests that listeners preferred the amount of expressive timing to change with tempo (Repp 1995b). Although these perceptual findings do not indicate the mechanisms controlling performance timing, they suggest that a perceptual analogue exists for the tempo effects on expressive timing documented in performance.

Kinematic Models

The view that rhythm generates movement is reflected in the notion that music performance and perception have their origins in the kinematic and dynamic characteristics of typical motor actions. For example, regularities observed in a sequence of foot movements during walking or running are similar to regularities observed in sequences of beats or note values when a musical performance changes tempo. A rhythmic framework may be transmitted from performers to listeners through sound (Shove & Repp 1995), as suggested by computational models of music performance in which the auditory system interacts directly with the motor system (Todd 1995). The kinematics of movement allow a common origin for performance and perceptual phenomena, based on similar kinematic properties applying across individuals. Consequently, aesthetically satisfying performances should be those that satisfy kinematic constraints of biological motion (Shove & Repp 1995).

Kinematic models were first applied to the large decelerations in performance tempo that commonly occur at the ends of pieces, called the final ritard. Pianists' final ritards were modeled in two parts—a variable timing curve followed by a systematic, constant decrease in tempo (called linear tempo) (Sundberg & Verrillo 1980). The "motor music" used in the studies, which contains a regular sequence of events with short durations, may create associations for listeners with experiences of physical motion (Kronman & Sundberg 1987). Feldman et al (1992) modeled both ritards and positive accelerations that occurred throughout performances. Based on modeling fits to the timing of a few ensemble performances, cubic polynomial models were chosen to minimize the jerk or jumpiness in connecting points of tempo changes (ritards) to the constant tempo that preceded them. Repp (1992b) modeled the expressive timing of a short melodic gesture in piano performances of a Schumann piece, finding a best-fitting quadratic polynomial. The three parameters represented a positive constant that corresponded to overall tempo, a negative linear coefficient that corresponded to vertical and horizontal displacement of the parabola, and a positive quadratic coefficient that corresponded to degree of curvature. Synthesized performances for the same melodic segment based on altered parameter values were played for listeners, who preferred timing profiles that fit the original parabolic functions (Repp 1992a).

Although most models of motion in performance address timing, some apply to dynamic (intensity) changes as well. Some measurements of performance suggest a coupling between expressive timing and dynamics in singing (Gjerdingen 1988, Seashore 1938) and piano performance (Gabrielsson 1987a, Palmer 1996a), in which tempo and intensity increase and decrease together over a musical section such as a phrase. Todd (1992) proposed an underlying kinetic energy model for performance expression, in which intensity is proportional to the square of musical velocity (number of events per unit time). Contrasting the fit of different parabolic models to intensity and timing patterns in piano performances, Todd settled on a model with constant acceleration (linear tempo). Like Sundberg & Verrillo, Todd (1992) proposed that musical expression induces a percept of self-motion in listeners.

The notion that performance expression has its origins in the kinematic and dynamic properties of motor actions was extended in a general framework of perception and performance (Todd 1995). A linear tempo model equivalent to Kronman & Sundberg's (1987) was fit to the expressive timing of piano performance segments, which were identified by changes in the sign of acceleration. Todd (1995) proposed an auditory model of rhythm performance and perception, based on a time-domain process that computes temporal segmentation of onsets (low-pass filters) and a frequency-domain process that computes a periodicity analysis (bandpass filters). In addition, a sensory-motor feedback filter has two periodic components: the tactus (a filter centered at 600 ms), modeling beats, and body sway (a filter centered at 5 sec), modeling large-scale body movements. Performers' body and limb movements can specify some aspects of music performance, as evidenced in observers' ratings of performances based on visual information only from point-light displays (Davidson 1993, 1994). Todd's (1995) model requires further testing to eliminate potential overfitting of data, and its identification of line segments can be problematic. The model's advantage is that it is a purely bottom-up segmentation method that requires no input structural markers, as are required by several of the kinematic models discussed above.

Arguments against kinematic models suggest that physical notions of energy cannot be equated with psychological concepts of musical energy (Desain & Honing 1992). An alternative explanation suggests that tempo changes in performance are guided by perceptual rather than kinematic properties. For instance, large tempo changes cannot occur too quickly, because the rhythmic categories that occur within the region of tempo change will not be perceived intact (Desain & Honing 1992). Rhythm identification and discrimination tests suggest that categorical distinctions underlie the perception of rhythmic structure, and performers use expressive timing to separate durational categories of note events even more when the events' absolute durations are converging at fast tempi (Clarke 1985). Thus, tempo changes in performance may operate in a noncontinuous, stepwise fashion across absolute durations to retain the perception of intended rhythmic categories (Desain & Honing 1992), which is another explanation for why relational invariance may not hold across tempo changes. Although this explication is not yet fully developed, it incorporates perceptual constraints and sensitivity to musical structure in explaining the control of movement in music performance.

CONCLUDING COMMENTS

Scientific study of music performance has witnessed tremendous growth in the past ten years, due to both technological advances and theoretical interest from the related fields of psychoacoustics, biomechanics, artificial intelligence, computer music, music theory, and music education. Performance studies now draw on concepts from music theory, and structural parallels from psycholinguistics are often fruitful. Distinctions between the psychological mechanisms proposed for music perception and performance are becoming blurred. For example, listeners' (and performers') abilities to track the beat and recover categorical information in continuously varying performances are now active issues for researchers in both perception and performance. Music performance offers a well-defined domain in which to study basic psychological constructs underlying sequence production, skill acquisition, individual differences, and emotional response, all of which will be the focus of future research directions. Finally, interdisciplinary approaches to this domain are growing, in part because current findings document music performance as a seemingly unique human ability that is not unique in its underlying cognitive mechanisms.

ACKNOWLEDGMENTS

Preparation of this chapter was supported in part by NIMH grant R29-MH45764. I gratefully acknowledge the comments of Eric Clarke, Peter Desain, Carolyn Drake, Henkjan Honing, Richard Jagacinski, Mari Riess Jones, Bruno Repp, and John Sloboda, and the aid of Peter Knapp, Rosalee Meyer, Brent Stansfield, and Timothy Walker in preparing this manuscript.

Literature Cited

Askenfelt A. 1986. Measurement of bow motion and bow force in violin playing. *J. Acoust. Soc. Am.* 80:1007–15

Bengtsson I, Gabrielsson A. 1977. Rhythm research in Uppsala. In *Music, Room, and Acoustics,* 17:19–56. Stockholm: R. Swed. Acad. Music

Bengtsson I, Gabrielsson A. 1983. Analysis

and synthesis of musical rhythm. See Sundberg 1983, pp. 27–60

Bernstein N. 1967. *The Co-ordination and Regulation of Movements.* New York: Pergamon

Bregman AS, Pinker S. 1978. Auditory streaming and the building of timbre. *Can. J. Psychol.* 32:19–31

Clarke EF. 1982. Timing in the performance of Erik Satie's 'Vexations'. *Acta Psychol.* 30: 1–19

Clarke EF. 1985. Structure and expression in rhythmic performance. In *Musical Structure and Cognition,* ed. P Howell, I Cross, R West, pp. 209–36. London: Academic

Clarke EF. 1987. Levels of structure in the organization of musical time. *Contemp. Music Rev.* 2:211–38

Clarke EF. 1988. Generative principles in music performance. In *Generative Processes in Music: The Psychology of Performance, Improvisation, and Composition,* ed. JA Sloboda, pp. 1-26. New York: Oxford Univ. Press

Clarke EF. 1993. Imitating and evaluating real and transformed musical performances. *Music Percept.* 10:317–41

Clarke EF. 1995. Expression in performance: generativity, perception and semiosis. See Rink 1995, pp. 21–54

Clarke EF. 1997. Rhythm and timing in music. See Deutsch 1997. In press

Clarke EF, Baker-Short C. 1987. The imitation of perceived rubato: a preliminary study. *Psychol. Music* 15:58–75

Clynes M. 1977. *Sentics: The Touch of Emotions.* New York: Doubleday

Clynes M. 1983. Expressive microstructure in music, linked to living qualities. See Sundberg 1983, pp. 76–181

Clynes M. 1986. When time is music. In *Rhythm in Psychological, Linguistic and Musical Processes,* ed. JR Evans, M Clynes, pp. 169–224. Springfield, IL: Thomas

Clynes M. 1995. Microstructural musical linguistics: composers' pulses are liked most by the best musicians. *Cognition* 55: 269–310

Clynes M, Walker J. 1986. Music as time's measure. *Music Percept.* 4:85–120

Cone ET. 1968. *Musical Form and Musical Performance.* New York: Norton

Cooper G, Meyer LB. 1960. *The Rhythmic Structure of Music.* Chicago: Univ. Chicago Press

Cuddy LL, Lunney CA. 1995. Expectancies generated by melodic intervals: perceptual judgments of melodic continuity. *Percept. Psychophys.* 57:451–62

Davidson JW. 1993. Visual perception of performance manner in the movements of solo musicians. *Psychol. Music* 21:103–13

Davidson JW. 1994. Which areas of a pianist's body convey information about expressive intention to an audience? *J. Hum. Mov. Stud.* 26:279–301

Desain P, Honing H. 1991. Towards a calculus for expressive timing in music. *Comput. Music Res.* 3:43–94

Desain P, Honing H. 1992. *Music, Mind, and Machine: Studies in Computer Music, Music Cognition, and Artificial Intelligence.* Amsterdam: Thesis

Desain P, Honing H. 1994. Does expressive timing in music performance scale proportionally with tempo? *Psychol. Res.* 56: 285–92

Deutsch D, ed. 1997. *The Psychology of Music,* Vol. 2. New York: Academic. In press

Drake C. 1993. Perceptual and performed accents in musical sequences. *Bull. Psychon. Soc.* 31:107–10

Drake C, Dowling WJ, Palmer C. 1991. Accent structures in the reproduction of simple tunes by children and adult pianists. *Music Percept.* 8:315–34

Drake C, Palmer C. 1993. Accent structures in music performance. *Music Percept.* 10: 343–78

Dunsby J. 1989. Guest editorial: performance and analysis of music. *Music Anal.* 8: 5–20

Epstein D. 1995. *Shaping Time: Music, the Brain, and Performance.* New York: Macmillan

Ericsson KA, Krampe R, Tesch-Romer C. 1993. The role of deliberate practice in the acquisition of expert performance. *Psychol. Rev.* 100:363–406

Ericsson KA, Lehmann AC. 1996. Expert and exceptional performance: evidence of maximal adaptation to task constraints. *Annu. Rev. Psychol.* 47:273–305

Essens PJ. 1986. Hierarchical organization of temporal patterns. *Percept. Psychophys.* 40:69–73

Essens PJ, Povel D-J. 1985. Metrical and nonmetrical representations of temporal patterns. *Percept. Psychophys.* 37:1–7

Feldman J, Epstein D, Richards W. 1992. Force dynamics of tempo change in music. *Music Percept.* 10:185–204

Fraisse P. 1982. Rhythm and tempo. In *The Psychology of Music,* ed. D Deutsch, pp. 149–80. New York: Academic

Gabrielsson A. 1973a. Similarity ratings and dimension analyses of auditory rhythm patterns. I. *Scand. J. Psychol.* 14:138–60

Gabrielsson A. 1973b. Similarity ratings and dimension analyses of auditory rhythm patterns. II. *Scand. J. Psychol.* 14:161–76

Gabrielsson A. 1974. Performance of rhythm patterns. *Scand. J. Psychol.* 15:63–72

Gabrielsson A. 1982. Perception and performance of musical rhythm. In *Music, Mind, and Brain: The Neuropsychology of Music,* ed. M Clynes, pp. 159–69. New York: Plenum

Gabrielsson A. 1987a. Once again: the theme from Mozart's piano Sonata in A Major (k.331). See Gabrielsson 1987b, pp. 81–104

Gabrielsson A, ed. 1987b. *Action and Perception in Rhythm and Music.* Stockholm: R. Swed. Acad. Music

Gabrielsson A. 1995. Expressive intention and performance. In *Music and the Mind Machine,* ed. R Steinberg, pp. 35–47. Berlin: Springer-Verlag

Gabrielsson A. 1997. Music performance. See Deutsch 1997. In press

Gabrielsson A, Juslin PN. 1996. Emotional expression in music performance: between the performer's intention and the listener's experience. *Psychol. Music* 24:68–91

Garcia-Albea JE, del Viso S, Igoa JM. 1989. Movement errors and levels of processing in sentence production. *J. Psycholinguist. Res.* 18:145–61

Garrett MF. 1980. Levels of processing in sentence production. In *Language Production. Speech and Talk,* ed. B Butterworth, 1: 177–220. London: Academic

Gentner DR. 1987. Timing of skilled motor performance: tests of the proportional duration model. *Psychol. Rev.* 94:255–76

Geringer JM, Madsen CK. 1987. Programmatic research in music: perception and performance of intonation. In *Applications of Research in Music Behavior,* ed. CK Madsen, CA Prickett, pp. 244–53. Tuscaloosa: Univ. Ala. Press

Gjerdingen RO. 1988. Shape and motion in the microstructure of song. *Music Percept.* 6: 35–64

Handel S, Lawson GR. 1983. The contextual nature of rhythmic interpretation. *Percept. Psychophys.* 34:103–20

Henderson MT. 1936. Rhythmic organization in artistic piano performance. See CE Seashore 1936, pp. 281–305

Hirsh IJ. 1959. Auditory perception of temporal order. *J. Acoust. Soc. Am.* 31: 759–67

Jagacinski RJ, Marshburn E, Klapp ST, Jones MR. 1988. Tests of parallel versus integrated structure in polyrhythmic tapping. *J. Mot. Behav.* 20:416–42

Johnson C. 1996. An empirical investigation of musicians' and nonmusicians' assessment of perceived rubato in musical performance. *J. Res. Music Educ.* 44:84–96

Jones MR. 1987. Perspectives on musical time. See Gabrielsson 1987b, pp. 153–75

Jones MR. 1990. Musical events and models of musical time. In *Cognitive Models of Psychological Time,* ed. RA Block, pp. 207–40. Hillsdale, NJ: Erlbaum

Keele SW. 1968. Movement control in skilled motor performance. *Psychol. Bull.* 70:387–403

Keele SW, Summers JJ. 1976. The structure of motor programs. In *Motor Control: Issues and Trends,* ed. GE Stelmach, pp. 109–42. New York: Academic

Kendall RA, Carterette EC. 1990. The communication of musical expression. *Music Percept.* 8:129–64

Kronman U, Sundberg J. 1987. Is the musical ritard an allusion to physical motion? See Gabrielsson 1987b, pp. 57–68

Krumhansl CL. 1995. Music psychology and music theory: problems and prospects. *Music Theory Spect.* 17:53–80

Krumhansl CL. 1996. A perceptual analysis of Mozart's Piano Sonata, K. 282: segmentation, tension, and musical ideas. *Music Percept.* 13:401–32

Krumhansl CL, Kessler EJ. 1982. Tracing the dynamic changes in perceived tonal organization in a spatial representation of musical keys. *Psychol. Rev.* 89:334–68

Kurakata K, Kuwano S, Namba S. 1993. Factors determining the impression of the equality of intensity in piano performances. *J. Acoust. Soc. Jpn.* E 14:441–47

Langer S. 1953. *Feeling and Form: A Theory of Art.* New York: Scribner

Large EW, Palmer C, Pollack JB. 1995. Reduced memory representations for music. *Cogn. Sci.* 19:53–96

Lashley K. 1951. The problem of serial order in behavior. In *Cerebral Mechanisms in Behavior: The Hixon Symposium,* ed. LA Jeffress, pp. 112–36. New York: Wiley

Lehmann AC, Ericsson KA. 1993. Sight-reading ability of expert pianists in the context of piano accompanying. *Psychomusicology* 12:182–95

Lerdahl F. 1996. Calculating tonal tension. *Music Percept.* 13:319–64

Lerdahl F, Jackendoff R. 1983. *A Generative Theory of Tonal Music.* Cambridge, MA: MIT Press

Levitin DJ, Cook PR. 1996. Memory for musical tempo: additional evidence that auditory memory is absolute. *Percept. Psychophys.* 58:928–36

Levy JM. 1995. Beginning-ending ambiguity: consequences of performance choices. See Rink 1995, pp. 150–69

MacKenzie CL, Van Eerd DL. 1990. Rhythmic precision in the performance of piano scales: motor psychophysics and motor programming. In *Attention and Performance: Motor Representation and Control,* ed. M Jeannerod, 13:375–408. Hillsdale, N.J.: Erlbaum

McPherson GE. 1995. The assessment of musical performance: development and validation of five new measures. *Psychol. Music* 23:142–61

Meyer LB. 1956. *Emotion and Meaning in Music.* Chicago: Univ. Chicago Press

Meyer LB. 1973. *Explaining Music: Essays and Explorations.* Chicago: Univ. Chicago Press

Moore RS. 1994. Effects of age, sex, and melodic/harmonic patterns on vocal pitch-matching skills of talented 8-11–year olds. *J. Res. Music Educ.* 42:5–13

Nakamura T. 1987. The communication of dynamics between musicians and listeners through musical performance. *Percept. Psychophys.* 41:525–33

Narmour E. 1990. *The Analysis and Cognition of Basic Melodic Structures: The Implication-Realization Model.* Chicago: Univ. Chicago Press

Narmour E. 1996. Analyzing form and measuring perceptual content in Mozart's Sonata K. 282: a new theory of parametric analogues. *Music Percept.* 13:265–318

Nilsson J, Thorstensson A. 1989. Ground reaction forces at different speeds of human walking and running. *Acta Physiol. Scand.* 136:217–27

Nuki M. 1984. Memorization of piano music. *Psychologia* 27:157–63

Palmer C. 1988. *Timing in skilled piano performance.* PhD thesis. Cornell Univ., Ithaca, NY

Palmer C. 1989. Mapping musical thought to musical performance. *J. Exp. Psychol.: Hum. Percept. Perform.* 15:331–46

Palmer C. 1992. The role of interpretive preferences in music performance. In *Cognitive Bases of Musical Communication,* ed. MR Jones, S Holleran, pp. 249–62. Washington, DC: Am. Psychol. Assoc.

Palmer C. 1996a. Anatomy of a performance: sources of musical expression. *Music Percept.* 13:433–54

Palmer C. 1996b. On the assignment of structure in music performance. *Music Percept.* 14:21–54

Palmer C, Kelly MH. 1992. Linguistic prosody and musical meter in song. *J. Mem. Lang.* 31:525–42

Palmer C, van de Sande C. 1993. Units of knowledge in music performance. *J. Exp. Psychol.: Learn. Mem. Cogn.* 19:457–70

Palmer C, van de Sande C. 1995. Range of planning in skilled music performance. *J. Exp. Psychol.: Hum. Percept. Perform.* 21: 947–62

Parncutt R. 1994. A perceptual model of pulse salience and metrical accent in musical rhythms. *Music Percept.* 11:409–64

Povel D-J. 1981. Internal representation of simple temporal patterns. *J. Exp. Psychol.: Hum. Percept. Perform.* 7:3–18

Povel D-J, Essens P. 1985. Perception of temporal patterns. *Music Percept.* 2:411–40

Rasch RA. 1979. Synchronization in performed ensemble music. *Acustica* 43: 121–31

Repp BH. 1989. Expressive microstructure in music: a preliminary perceptual assessment of four composers' "pulses." *Music Percept.* 6:243–74

Repp BH. 1990. Patterns of expressive timing in performances of a Beethoven minuet by nineteen famous pianists. *J. Acoust. Soc. Am.* 88:622–41

Repp BH. 1992a. A constraint on the expressive timing of a melodic gesture: evidence from performance and aesthetic judgment. *Music Percept.* 10:221-42

Repp BH. 1992b. Diversity and commonality in music performance: an analysis of timing microstructure in Schumann's "Traumerei." *J. Acoust. Soc. Am.* 92: 2546–68

Repp BH. 1992c. Probing the cognitive representation of musical time: structural constraints on the perception of timing perturbations. *Cognition* 44:241–81

Repp BH. 1994. Relational invariance of expressive microstructure across global tempo changes in music performance: an exploratory study. *Psychol. Res.* 56:269–84

Repp BH. 1995a. Detectability of duration and intensity increments in melody tones: a partial connection between music perception and performance. *Percept. Psychophys.* 57:1217–32

Repp BH. 1995b. Quantitative effects of global tempo on expressive timing in music performance: some perceptual evidence. *Music Percept.* 13:39–57

Rink J, ed. 1995. *The Practice of Performance: Studies in Musical Interpretation.* Cambridge: Cambridge Univ. Press

Rosenbaum DA, Weber RJ, Hazelett WM, Hindorff V. 1986. The parameter remapping effect in human performance: evidence from tongue twisters and finger fumblers. *J. Mem. Lang.* 25:710–25

Schenker H. 1969. *Five Graphic Music Analyses.* New York: Dover

Schmalfeldt J. 1985. On the relation of analysis to performance: Beethoven's Bagatelles Op. 126, Nos. 2 and 5. *J. Music Theory* 29:1–31

Schmidt RA. 1975. A schema theory of discrete motor skill learning. *Psychol. Rev.* 82: 225–60

Schmuckler MA. 1989. Expectation in music: investigation of melodic and harmonic processes. *Music Percept.* 7:109–50

Schmuckler MA. 1990. The performance of global expectations. *Psychomusicology* 9: 122–47

Seashore CE, ed. 1936. *Objective Analysis of Musical Performance,* Vol. 4. Iowa City: Univ. Iowa Press

Seashore CE. 1938. *Psychology of Music*. New York: McGraw-Hill

Seashore HG. 1936. An objective analysis of artistic singing. See CE Seashore 1936, pp. 12–157

Shaffer LH. 1980. Analyzing piano performance: a study of concert pianists. In *Tutorials in Motor Behavior,* ed. GE Telmach, J Requin, pp. 443-45. Amsterdam: North-Holland

Shaffer LH. 1981. Performances of Chopin, Bach, and Bartok: studies in motor programming. *Cogn. Psychol.* 13:326–76

Shaffer LH. 1982. Rhythm and timing in skill. *Psychol. Rev.* 89:109-22

Shaffer LH. 1984. Timing in solo and duet piano performances. *Q. J. Exp. Psychol.* 36A:577–95

Shaffer LH. 1995. Musical performance as interpretation. *Psychol. Music* 23:17–38

Shaffer LH, Clarke EF, Todd NP. 1985. Metre and rhythm in piano playing. *Cognition* 20: 61–77

Shaffer LH, Todd NP. 1987. The interpretive component in musical performance. See Gabrielsson 1987b, pp. 139–52

Shove P, Repp BH. 1995. Musical motion and performance: theoretical and empirical perspectives. See Rink 1995, pp. 55–83

Sloboda JA. 1974. The eye-hand span: an approach to the study of sight reading. *Psychol. Music* 2:4–10

Sloboda JA. 1976. The effect of item position on the likelihood of identification by inference in prose reading and music reading. *Can. J. Psychol.* 30:228–37

Sloboda JA. 1977. Phrase units as determinants of visual processing in music reading. *Br. J. Psychol.* 68:117–24

Sloboda JA. 1983. The communication of musical metre in piano performance. *Q. J. Exp. Psychol.* A 35:377–96

Sloboda JA. 1985a. Expressive skill in two pianists: metrical communication in real and simulated performances. *Can. J. Psychol.* 39:273–93

Sloboda JA. 1985b. *The Musical Mind: The Cognitive Psychology of Music.* Oxford: Clarendon

Sloboda JA, Davidson JW, Howe MJA, Moore DG. 1996. The role of practice in the development of performing musicians. *Br. J. Psychol.*

Sundberg J, ed. 1983. *Studies of Music Performance.* Stockholm: R. Swed. Acad. Music

Sundberg J, Askenfelt A, Fryden L. 1983a. Musical performance: a synthesis-by-rule approach. *Comput. Music J.* 7:37–43

Sundberg J, Friberg A, Fryden L. 1991. Common secrets of musicians and listeners: an analysis-by-synthesis study of musical performance. In *Representing Musical Structure,* ed. P Howell, R West, I Cross, pp. 161–97. London: Academic

Sundberg J, Friberg A, Fryden L. 1993. *Music and locomotion—perception of tones with envelopes replicating force patterns of walking.* Presented at Stockholm Music Acoust. Conf., Stockholm

Sundberg J, Fryden L, Askenfelt A. 1983b. What tells you the player is musical? An analysis-by-synthesis study of music performance. See Sundberg 1983, pp. 61–75

Sundberg J, Verrillo V. 1980. On the anatomy of the retard: a study of timing in music. *J. Acoust. Soc. Am.* 68:772–79

Sundin N-G. 1984. Musical interpretation in performance: music theory, musicology, and musical consciousness. *J. Music Res.* 5:93–129

Thompson WF. 1989. Composer-specific aspects of musical performance: an evaluation of Clyne's theory of pulse for performances of Mozart and Beethoven. *Music Percept.* 7:15–42

Thompson WF, Sundberg J, Friberg A, Fryden L. 1989. The use of rules for expression in the performance of melodies. *Psychol. Music* 17:63–82

Todd NPM. 1985. A model of expressive timing in tonal music. *Music Percept.* 3:33–58

Todd NPM. 1989. A computational model of rubato. *Contemp. Music Rev.* 3:69–88

Todd NPM. 1992. The dynamics of dynamics: a model of musical expression. *J. Acoust. Soc. Am.* 91:3540–50

Todd NPM. 1995. The kinematics of musical expression. *J. Acoust. Soc. Am.* 97: 1940–49

van Galen G, Wing AM. 1984. The sequencing of movements. In *The Psychology of Human Movement,* ed. M Smyth, AM Wing, pp. 153-82. London: Academic

Vernon LN. 1936. Synchronization of chords in artistic piano music. See CE Seashore 1936, pp. 306–45

Vorberg D, Hambuch R. 1978. On the temporal control of rhythmic performance. In *Attention and Performance,* ed. J Requin, 7: 535–55. Hillsdale, NJ: Erlbaum

Vorberg D, Hambuch R. 1984. Timing of two-handed rhythmic performance. *Ann. NY Acad. Sci.* 423:390-406

Wing AM, Kristofferson AB. 1973a. Response delays and the timing of discrete motor responses. *Percept. Psychophys.* 14:5–12

Wing AM, Kristofferson AB. 1973b. The timing of interresponse intervals. *Percept. Psychophys.* 13:455–60

Annu. Rev. Psychol. 1997. 48:139–62

GENDER, RACIAL, ETHNIC, SEXUAL, AND CLASS IDENTITIES

Deborrah E. S. Frable

Women's Studies Program, University of Michigan, 234 West Engineering, Ann Arbor, Michigan 48109

KEY WORDS: gender, race, ethnicity, sexuality, class, multiple social identities

ABSTRACT

Identity is the individual's psychological relationship to particular social category systems. This chapter summarizes how people create and negotiate their gender, racial, ethnic, sexual, and class identities. Theories, methods, and priorities in each of these content areas differ. However, each systematically excludes particular research participants and thus ignores the complexity of people's multiple social identities. Research suggests that gender, racial, ethnic, sexual, and class identities are fluid, multidimensional, personalized social constructions that reflect the individual's current context and sociohistorical cohort. However, far too little empirical work captures the richly textured, theoretical conceptions of identity development, maintenance, and change. Innovative methods for assessing the content and structure of people's identities now exist. Future research should include groups other than young children or college students; should explore functions of identity other than just self-esteem, adjustment, or well-being; and should implement methodologies that are longitudinal and that assess people's many social identities.

CONTENTS

0084-6570/97/0201-0139$08.00

INTRODUCTION

This chapter summarizes how people create and negotiate their gender, racial, ethnic, sexual, and class identities. Identity is the individual's psychological relationship to these social category systems (Sherif 1982). Identity is a unified, purposeful aspect of self and hence is only part of the self-concept (McAdams 1995). Identity is also the term most often invoked by those who struggle to create meaning and purpose when culturally significant, ideologically powerful social category systems clash with personal and collective group member experiences (Tajfel 1978).

New in the study of identity is an emerging willingness by psychologists to emphasize in their empirical work the cultural categories that matter, i.e. the ones that we all pay attention to in our daily lives (e.g. Deaux et al 1995). Also new is a concomitant willingness to attend to the personal meanings of these culturally weighted categories, to understand how these meanings reflect historical events and cultural codes, and to study how these meanings interact with specific situations for individuals (e.g. Hurtado et al 1994, Kitzinger & Wilkinson 1995, Stewart & Ostrove 1993, Waters 1994). Also new is the empowerment of disenfranchised category members; by writing about the diverse experiences of being "Other," they translate these experiences into a new inclusive paradigm (Trickett et al 1994).

By putting the gender, racial, ethnic, sexual, and class identity literatures together in a single review, I hope that the theories, methods, and priorities of each area might inform the others. The review is necessarily eclectic. Previous *Annual Review of Psychology* chapters supplement the material presented here (Banaji & Prentice 1994, Porter & Washington 1993, Shweder & Sullivan 1993, Waters & Eschbach 1995).

GENDER IDENTITIES

While gender identity always involves an individual's relationship to gender as a social category, it carries a different spin in each of psychology's subspeciality literatures. Traditionally, gender identity fell into the domain of medicine; it referred to the individual's psychological sense of being male or female (exact definitions vary; see Fagot & Leinbach 1985, Money 1994). This particular construct is useful for studying the origin of gender identity. Research assesses the psychological gender of children who are born with inconsistent biological sex markers and then assigned to the male or female category. Early work suggested that the child's sex of assignment or rearing environment is the most potent predictor of gender identity and that this gender identity cannot be easily changed after the age of two and a half (Money & Ehrhardt 1972). Two observations challenged this conclusion. The well-known MZ twin—a biological male with a masculine pattern of prenatal hormones who was accidentally castrated at birth, was assigned the female gender role, and exhibited "perfect" childhood femininity—began to question her gender identity during adolescence (Diamond 1982). In the Dominican Republic, 16 of 18 genetic males—assigned the female gender role at birth because of their feminine-appearing external genitalia—adopted a male gender identity at puberty when testosterone masculinized their external genitalia (Imperato-McGinley et al 1979). Theorists and researchers now acknowledge that biology does influence the gender identity process (minimally, by making a particular body for which cultures have expectations), and they attribute more plasticity to people's gender identities (Bem 1993, Herdt 1990).

In the modern psychiatric and clinical psychology literature, gender identity first appeared with the publication of the third *Diagnostic and Statistical Manual* in 1980. Today, gender identity disorders are characterized by "strong and persistent cross-gender identification accompanied by persistent discomfort with one's assigned sex" (American Psychiatric Association 1994, p. 493). Three diagnoses are possible: gender identity disorder in children, gender identity disorder in adolescents or adults, and gender identity disorder not otherwise specified. People with inconsistent biological sex markers (e.g. androgen insensitivity syndrome, congenital adrenal hyperplasia) are limited to the last diagnosis. The first two differ only by the age of the individual. Boys are more likely than girls to be referred for psychiatric help (5:1), and most children with a childhood diagnosis do not carry it to adulthood. Although the *DSM-IV* manual states that no gender identity disorder test exists (pp. 537–38 for diagnostic criteria), the literature does offer a 12-item gender identity interview for children (Zucker et al 1993a), the Feminine Gender Identity Scale for adult men (Freund et al 1974), and the Masculine Gender Identity Scale for adult women (Blanchard & Freund 1983). Reviews of sex reassignment surgery outcomes are available (Green & Fleming 1990), as are social critiques of the medical establishment's insistence on the gender dichotomy (Eichler 1983). Behavior change programs for diagnosed children may relieve a child's personal distress from social ostracism (Green 1987), but they also enforce gender conformity (Bem 1993). Boys with a childhood diagnosis are more likely to report a homosexual or bisexual orientation in adulthood than controls (Bailey & Zucker 1995, Green 1987), they may be more physically attractive (Green et al 1985, Zucker et al 1993b), and they may have more male siblings and a later birth order (Blanchard et al 1995). In all this work, diagnostic and assessment advances far exceed those in research etiology and treatment outcome studies.

In the developmental literature, psychologists focus on the usual path by which children become psychological males and females. With respect to gender identity, Lawrence Kohlberg remains the most influential theorist (Maccoby 1990). He defines gender identity as the "cognitive self-categorization as 'boy' or 'girl'" (Kohlberg 1966, p. 88) and proposes a three-step acquisition process: First, the child learns to label the self and others accurately (gender identity); second, the child learns that boys become men and girls become women (gender stability); and finally, the child learns that being male or female is permanent and not changed by cultural gender cues (gender constancy). Unfortunately, his use of the term gender identity is ambiguous (Fagot & Leinbach 1985). Others suggest that children's gender understanding includes four tasks: identifying the self and others correctly (labeling), then understanding that identity continues over time (stability) and that identity is not changed by wishes (motive), and finally recognizing identity's permanence despite hairstyle or clothing changes (constancy) (Eaton & Von Bargen 1981). Considerable research supports either developmental sequence, although reported age ranges vary enormously (Huston 1983). Critiques of constancy measures exist: The interview questions are open to multiple interpretations; the child's ability to conserve is not always tested (i.e. they never see a perceptual transformation); the pictorial stimuli are often schematic drawings and hence artificial; and, perhaps most importantly, biological knowledge (presumably, the essence on which constancy is based) is simply not assessed (Bem 1989, Martin & Halverson 1983). Sandra Bem (1989) proposed a new measure that uses photographs of real children to pit biological sex against cultural gender, and she found that much younger children (40% of three-, four-, and five-year-olds) are gender constant, but only if they know that genitalia are the defining attributes of male and female. Although gender inference tasks differentially challenge children's competence (Gelman et al 1986), children are also more competent than typical constancy procedures suggest.

Gender constancy, while only one component of gender identity, is a focus in the literature because Kohlberg (1966) proposes that children use gender to organize their behaviors only when they are "categorically certain of its unchangeability" (p. 95). In contrast, Huston (1983) found gender constancy to be remarkably independent of other components of gender-related behaviors, and recent research concurs. Gender constancy is unrelated to sex-typed toy choice (Carter & Levy 1988, Downs & Langlois 1988, Emmerich & Shepard 1984, Levy & Carter 1989, Lobel & Menashri 1993; for exceptions, see Stangor & Ruble 1989), to the imitation of same gender models (Bussey & Bandura 1984), to the correct attributions of stereotypes to male and female figures (Levy & Carter 1989), to measures of gender schematic processing (Levy & Carter 1989), to attitudes toward boys and girls (Yee & Brown 1994), and to gender discrimination in reward allocation (Yee & Brown 1994). Perhaps constancy measures are faulty (Bem 1989). Perhaps a weaker version of

Kohlberg's hypothesis is more appropriate (Maccoby 1990, Stangor & Ruble 1987) and in line with gender schema theories. Or perhaps gender is a multidimensional construct in children's development, and gender-related cognitions and behaviors do not always go together (Downs & Langlois 1988, Hort et al 1991, Huston 1983). The latter view is supported by the work of Beverly Fagot and Mary Leinbach, who focus on gender labeling rather than on gender constancy (Leinbach & Fagot 1986). Boys and girls who pass their gender labeling test are more likely to play with same-sex peers; girls who use the labels accurately are less aggressive than girls who had not yet mastered the labels (Fagot et al 1986). Labelers are more knowledgeable about sex stereotypes; they exhibit more sex-typed behavior at 27 months; their parents give them more positive and negative feedback to sex-typed toy play; and their parents have more traditional attitudes toward women, sexuality, and family roles (Fagot & Leinbach 1989, Fagot et al 1992). These results suggest a certain coherence among environmental inputs (parents), gender labeling, gender knowledge, and gender behaviors, but longitudinal and cross-sectional studies also underscore the multidimensional nature of gender and a complex pattern in development.

After early childhood, gender identity development almost disappears from the developmental literature, with two exceptions. Phyllis Katz (1986) proposed a model of gender identity development with four milestone events: gender labeling, gender constancy, sexual gender (puberty), and reproductive gender (adulthood). Here, gender identity is the individual's "internal awareness and experience of gender" (p. 25). No one has tested the model, but Katz's suggestion that milestone events require elaborations and changes of the individual's gender identity is worth pursuing. Researchers also examine the influence of gender on identity within Erik Erikson's developmental theory (1968) as operationalized by John Marcia (1980). Few gender differences exist with respect to ego identity status, identity formation (e.g. timing or salient domains), or identity meaning, but women are less likely than men to exhibit a sequential identity-intimacy pattern, and women may be more mature in interpersonal domains (Marcia et al 1993). Related work considers the importance of identity statuses during women's adulthood (Josselson 1987) and demonstrates how sociohistorical events mediate the relation between ego identity and outcomes for women (Helson et al 1995).

The literature in social and personality psychology is heavily influenced by the failure of the gender differences and the gender-as-a-personality-variable paradigms to explain all gender-related phenomena. Gender is now understood as a social category (Deaux & Major 1987), and gender identity has finally emerged as a construct of interest. Janet Spence (1985) defines gender identity as a "fundamental existential sense of one's maleness or femaleness" and a "primitive, unarticulated concept of self, initially laid down at an essentially preverbal stage of development and maintained at an unverbalized level" (pp. 79–80). Gender identity guides the early acquisition of gender-congruent behaviors, but once established, it is simply protected by doing enough of your own sex's stuff. Thus, gendered traits, attributes, values, interests, preferences, and behaviors hang together with the weakest of glues (Spence 1993). Spence's model is consistent with the litter of BSRI and PAQ studies (for an alternative perspective, see Frable 1989). It may also be consistent with the developmental literature's hint that very young children are of particular interest in studying gender acquisition. What is less clear is how to measure this primitive, unarticulated sense of self and what hypotheses should then be tested.

A second definition of gender identity also suggests that the self-system is an essential construct for studying individual gender psychology (Sherif 1982). Richard Ashmore (1990) defines gender identity as "the structured set of gendered personal identities that results when the individual takes the social construction of gender and the biological 'facts' of sex and incorporates them into an overall self-concept" (p. 512). Gender identity includes personal and social attributes, social relationships, interests and abilities, symbolic and stylistic behaviors, and biological/physical/material attributes. An individual's gender identity is separate from his or her sex stereotypes and gender attitudes. Ashmore's model is particularly useful in delineating all possible components of the individual's gender psychology. Moreover, relations among many components can be studied via currently existing measures of traits, behaviors, and ideology. New measures need to be created, and relations among components must be assessed. The model does not clearly specify which components should be related and why. The usefulness of the gender multiplicity model is seen easily in the empirical work of Richard Koestner and Jennifer Aube (1995).

Three other notions of gender identity exist in social psychology. First, for social identity theorists (Tajfel & Turner 1979, Turner et al 1987), gender identity is men's and women's awareness of and feelings for their gender category. Gurin & Townsend (1986) measured three properties of women's gender identity and showed that each property has a different relation to gender ideology (Gurin & Markus 1989). Other researchers focus on how context makes gender categories salient, increases gender identification, and may lead to traditional attitudes and behaviors (Abrams et al 1985, 1990). Second, for symbolic interactionists (McCall & Simmons 1966; Stryker 1980, 1987), gender identity refers to people's self-conceptions that are based on the particular gender roles they play. Recent work suggests few differences with respect to these gender identities (Thoits 1995; for another view, see Simon

1992). Other work proposes an innovative methodology for assessing gender identity (Burke & Tully 1977). Finally, for social constructionists, gender identity is created from structured, social constraints. Robin Leidner (1991) showed how distinct gender identities are created in two interactive service jobs that require the exact same skills but have different training emphases. Robin Ely (1995) demonstrated how the number of "allowable" gender identities for junior women in law firms varies with the number of senior female partners present.

In all of psychology's subspeciality literatures (e.g. clinical, developmental, social-personality), the acquisition of gender identity is relatively free of personal conflict (for an exception, see Frey & Ruble 1992). Some individuals, however, reject the existing social category system of gender, choose to revise their relationship to it, and in essence redefine their gender identity. Two models of this revision process exist: One describes the development of a feminist identity (Downing & Roush 1985; for measures, see Bargad & Hyde 1991, Rickard 1987; for validity, see Henderson-King & Stewart 1994, Rickard 1990), the other describes moving from external gender standards to internal ones (Ossana et al 1992).

RACIAL AND ETHNIC IDENTITIES

The racial and ethnic demographics of the United States are shifting rapidly. According to the US Bureau of the Census (1996), by 2050, the US population will be 53% European American, 25% Hispanic or Latino American (Mexican, Puerto Rican, Cuban, Central and South American), 14% African American (African-Caribbean, African immigrant), 8% Asian American (Chinese, Japanese, Korean, Vietnamese, Cambodian, Thai, Filipino), and 1% Native American (Cherokee, Navajo, Sioux, Chippewa, Aleuts, Inuit). Current values are 74, 10, 12, 3, and 1, respectively (US Bureau of the Census 1996). In addition, although not evident in the Census, a growing portion of the population classify themselves as biracial or biethnic (Root 1992). The assimilation or melting pot metaphor of US immigration is passé, replaced by the image of a multicultural "salad bowl" in which people are at least biculturally competent (Cross 1991, Harrison et al 1990, LaFromboise, Coleman & Gerton 1993, Phinney & Rotheram 1987, Ramirez 1983). In this new emphasis on human diversity, one of the unifying concepts is that of identity (Sampson 1993, Trickett et al 1994).

Race is used by social scientists to refer to distinctions drawn from physical appearance (skin color, eye shape, physiognomy), and ethnicity is used to refer to distinctions based on national origin, language, religion, food, and other cultural markers. Race has a quasi-biological status (Zuckerman 1990), and among psychologists, the use of race terminology is hotly debated (Betancourt

& Lopez 1993, Yee et al 1993). In the United States, race is also a socially defined, politically oppressive categorization scheme that individuals must negotiate while creating their identities (Helms 1994). National perception, however incorrect, is that four distinguishable racial groups exist: Asian, black, white, and Native American; Latino is often treated as a fifth racial group, although it exhibits all "racial" characteristics of the other four (Helms 1994). The racial and ethnic identity terms are often used inappropriately in psychology. While black immigrants to the United States may have a racial identity as black, their ethnic identity reflects their country of origin; racial identity is much more likely to be problematic in the United States than ethnic identity. Whether a researcher assesses racial identity, ethnic identity, or some combination may only be clear after reading the Methods section of their report. The identity studies I reference here are those in which researchers assess participants' subjective perceptions or internal representations of their racial or ethnic groups; I exclude studies that use racial or ethnic group merely as a nominal classification scheme.

In the developmental literature, some conceptual clarity exists about how racial and ethnic identities are measured in children and how the data may be interpreted (Aboud 1987, Katz 1987, Spencer & Markstrom-Adams 1990). Two lines of work stand out as particularly scholarly. First, William Cross's book *Shades of Black: Diversity in African-American Identity* (1991) summarizes the results of 181 empirical studies on black identity. Of the 45 studies (most based on children) that assess both reference group orientation (e.g. race awareness, race esteem, race ideology) and personal identity self-concept (e.g. self-esteem, self-worth, self-confidence), 37 found no relation between the two constructs. Furthermore, the reference group orientation studies suggest that whereas black children's preferences have changed from white (1939–1960) to black (1968–1980), they actually exhibit a bicultural appreciation pattern (Cross 1991). Second, Martha Bernal, George Knight, and their colleagues (Bernal et al 1990) creatively but systematically measured the multiple components of ethnic identity (ethnic self-identification, ethnic constancy, ethnic role behaviors, ethnic knowledge, and ethnic preferences) among Mexican-American children. In contrast with previous research, they assess self-identification by means of many measures, and their measures intercorrelate. Children's performance on each ethnic identity component is positively related to age and to the use of Spanish in the home. Other studies link family socialization practices (teaching about Mexican culture, teaching about ethnic pride, having Mexican objects in the home) to the child's development of a Mexican-American identity; this identity predicts the child's display of a cooperative and culturally specific behavioral style (Knight et al 1993a,b). The child development literature is now characterized by an insistence that the racial and ethnic identities of nonwhite children be understood in their own terms. Within-group differences are particularly important; when measured, white children's responses are no longer treated as the standard from which responses of others deviate.

With respect to adolescents and adults, Jean Phinney reviewed 70 empirical articles in the literature from 1972 to 1989 in a *Psychological Bulletin* paper (1990; see also Spencer & Markstrom-Adams 1990). Phinney noted the inconsistent use of the ethnic identity term: Some authors mean self-identification (self-definition, self-labeling), others emphasize attitudes and feelings (group belonging, commitment, and pride), and yet others stress cultural aspects (knowledge of ethnic language, behavior, and values; involvement with group members and practices). Results from the 70 studies are inconsistent with respect to relations among ethnic identity components and whether ethnic identity relates to self-esteem and adjustment. Phinney concluded that the most pressing issues are the lack of reliable and valid measures of ethnic identity (especially those that can be used for all ethnic groups), experimental and longitudinal studies (most are descriptive or correlational), accurate measurement of ethnic heritage, and inclusion of contextual variables (particularly socioeconomic status). These issues remain current concerns.

Three theoretical frameworks dominate the adolescent and adult literature: identity development (Erikson 1968), social identity theory (Tajfel & Turner 1979), and acculturation theory (Park 1928, Stonequist 1937). Within identity development, the most richly textured, influential description of racial identity continues to be Cross's (1971) black identity model (1991; see also Helms 1990, 1994; Parham 1989), which was created to explain particular identity changes among African Americans within the Black Social Movement from 1968 to 1975. Models exist for Asian Americans (Kim 1981), Latinos (Keefe & Padilla 1987), European or white ethnic groups (Helms 1990, Ponterotto 1988), biracial people (Poston 1990), and ethnic minorities in general (Atkinson et al 1989, Phinney 1989). Individuals usually begin with an unexamined racial or ethnic identity (this identity may be devalued, denied, or simply not salient). The individual is then challenged by experiences that make race or ethnicity personally problematic. To resolve the conflict, the individuals initiate an exploration of their racial or ethnic identity, immersing themselves in a culture specific to their race or ethnicity. This search leads individuals to value their racial, ethnic, or minority group membership and integrate it with other identities (e.g. ethnicity may become the most important identity or one of several salient identities). Theory suggests that this developmental cycle reoccurs during the lifespan (Parham 1989), and "stages" may be better understood as ego statuses that, once differentiated, are world views for handling racial and ethnic information (Helms 1994). Critiques exist: Some models reflect a particular sociohistorical framework, treat individuals as passively reacting to environmental events, or assume Eurocentricity; other models are not systematically developed or empirically tested (Sue 1994). Only one model accounts for multiple group memberships (Myers et al 1991).

Research within this identity development theory has two dominant lines. First, empirical work based on Cross's black identity model suggests that nigrescence (i.e. the process of becoming black) changes reference group orientation variables (e.g. racial self-image, attitudes toward other blacks, types of organizational memberships, and racial frames of reference) from low to high salience, apolitical to political, and Eurocentric to Afrocentric (Cross 1991, Cross et al 1996). Unfortunately, researchers also continue to correlate reference group orientation (racial identity attitudes) with "personal identity self concept" (self-esteem, well-being, and adjustment), documenting negative to positive shifts (Carter 1991, Munford 1994, Pyant & Yanico 1991; for an explanation, see Cross 1991). Other empirical work reflects narrowly focused dependent variables of interest primarily to counseling psychologists (e.g. attitudes toward counseling, preference for counselor's race). Suggestions do exist for expanding the focus, method, and measurement of this research area (Helms 1989, Ponterotto 1989, Ponterotto & Wise 1987). Examples include white racial identity development (Rowe et al 1994) and the relation between family ethnic socialization and children's racial identity attitudes (Sanders 1994).

The second body of research is based on Phinney's model of ethnic identity development, which purports to capture identity development for all ethnic groups (1989). Her 14-item Multigroup Ethnic Identity questionnaire assesses three common components of ethnic identity: positive ethnic attitudes and a sense of belonging, ethnic identity achievement, and ethnic behaviors and practices (Phinney 1992). Phinney's inclusion of adolescents is noteworthy. Her data suggest that blacks, Hispanics, and Asian Americans perceive ethnic identity as more important than whites do (Phinney 1989, Phinney & Alipuria 1990; see also Crocker et al 1994). Cross-sectional and longitudinal interview and questionnaire studies support a developmental progression (Phinney 1989, 1992; Phinney & Chavira 1992; Phinney & Tarver 1988). Ethnic identity achievement is associated with self-esteem and adjustment. However, the role of self-esteem as an outcome or precursor variable and its relation to other ethnic identity components remains unclear (Phinney 1989, 1991; Phinney & Alipuria 1990; Phinney & Chavira 1992).

With respect to social identity theory, identity studies that assess individuals' group perceptions are sparse (particularly those with American racial and ethnic groups), but several are exemplary. Taking a sociohistorical perspective, Hurtado et al (1994) showed that Chicanos (second or later generation) have a more differentiated identity structure than Mexicanos (first generation immigrants). The identity content for Chicanos reflects a cultural adaptation to the United States; content for Mexicanos reflects a homeward focus or Latin American consciousness. Retainment of Mexican culture among Chicanos is positively related to a Raza political identity and negatively associated with a US middle-class identity; cultural retainment among Mexicanos is only predicted by a working-class identity. The paper makes multiple points: Ethnicity as a social identity is multidimensional; social histories influence identity structure and content; and these complexities need to be included in empirical work. The method of measuring identity structure and the lack of concern with self-esteem variables are admirable. Using a longitudinal design (much needed in this literature), Ethier & Deaux (1994) examined how Hispanic students maintain their ethnic group identification during their first year at Anglo universities. Students' ethnic identities are initially associated with the strength of their cultural background; over time that link weakens, and students support or "remoor" their ethnic identity with culturally relevant activities at school. Students from strong cultural backgrounds become involved in activities that strengthen their ethnic group identification; students without such backgrounds perceive college as more threatening, which then predicts less favorable ethnic group perceptions and, ultimately, lower group identification. In sum, ethnic identity is supported by environmental structures (cultural background); its fluidity is visible across changing contexts (home to school); and identity negotiation takes multiple forms (varying with the importance of the identity to the individual).

Within the acculturation theory literature, two identity models exist. The linear model suggests that as individuals strengthen their identity in the new culture, they weaken their identity in the original culture (the melting pot). The two-dimensional model suggests that the individual's ties to the original culture and to the new culture are independent dimensions (the salad bowl). One option here is to have strong ties to both cultures, and such biculturalism is the current zeitgeist (Ramirez 1984, Szapocznik & Kurtines 1980). Components of bicultural competence are proposed (LaFromboise et al 1993), and by using identity and behavior as separate dimensions, various bicultural styles can be described (Birman 1994). Some research asks participants to choose reference group labels (e.g. ethnically identified, bicultural, mainstream identified) and then finds logical relations between label choice and acculturation attitudes (Rotheram-Borus 1990). Other work asks participants to complete acculturation measures in which identity and ethnic pride constitute one component. Some studies show that ethnic identity and pride remain high across generations, whereas ethnic knowledge and cultural practices decrease (Keefe & Padilla 1987). Others show that acculturation is associated with positive attitudes toward mental health services (Atkinson & Gim 1989). Empirical work lags behind theory.

In sum, racial and ethnic identities are fluid and multidimensional (Nagel 1994, Padilla 1993). Similarities emerge in how these identities "work," but their structure and content differ for each group as do their behavioral implications (Hurtado et al 1994, Jones 1994, Keefe 1992). New methods for measuring these identities exist (Apollon & Waters 1990, Deaux 1993, Hurtado et al 1994, Luhtanen & Crocker 1992, Phinney 1989), and researchers must be sensitive to assessment issues (Okazaki & Sue 1995). More research is needed with respect to Asian Americans, Native Americans, and those of mixed heritages; longitudinal research designs are essential.

SEXUAL IDENTITIES

In the nineteenth century, the idea appeared that homosexual behavior made a particular kind of person; homosexuality, in essence, defined an individual's identity, and this identity was labeled as a sickness (D'Emilio & Freedman 1988, Faderman 1981, Foucault 1979). Today, political movements offer alternatives to this rigid, negative construct. The gay rights movement, the feminist movement, and the bisexual movement support many identities: oppressed minority member, gay rights activist, woman-identified-woman, gay community member, bisexual feminist, etc (D'Emilio 1983, Herdt 1989, Radicalesbians 1973, Weise 1992). This historical background suggests that sexual identity is fluid (Garnets & Kimmel 1993) and is created by individuals (Brown 1989), communities (Bayer 1987, Krieger 1983), and sociohistorical events (D'Emilio 1983, Golden 1994).

The most affirmative descriptions of gay identity are developmental stage models (Cass 1979, 1984; Chapman & Brannock 1987; Troiden 1989; for a review of biological and psychodynamic models, see Brown 1995). Two models are theoretically grounded, empirically tested, and reasonably detailed. First, working within interpersonal congruency theory, Vivenne Cass (1979, 1984) proposed six progressive stages of positive gay identity development: identity confusion, identity comparison, identity tolerance, identity acceptance, identity pride, and identity synthesis. Cass (1984) created a self-report questionnaire to measure the characteristic emotions, cognitions, and behaviors of both men and women for each stage. Discriminant analysis distinguishes among her six hypothesized groups, and profile analyses provide validity for the questionnaire. Working with Cass's model, Brady & Busse (1994) created the Gay Identity Questionnaire to measure the six stages more easily. Their results suggest a sharp distinction in psychological well-being between subjects in the identity tolerance stage and those in the identity acceptance, pride, and synthesis stages. The identity acceptance group was also less likely to have "come out" than the identity pride and synthesis groups. With the caveat that women subjects were not included, these results are consistent with Cass's model (1979, 1984).

In the second model, working within symbolic interactionist theory, Richard Troiden (1989) synthesized various identity models (including Cass's) into four stages: sensitization, identity confusion, identity assumption, and commitment. Sensitization ("generalized feelings of marginality and perceptions of being different from same-sex peers") occurs before adolescence (Troiden 1989, p. 50). Identity confusion occurs in adolescence when individuals realize that their feelings, thoughts, and behaviors might be labeled homosexual. Identity assumption means that the individual believes that he or she is gay and begins to present the self as gay. Finally, commitment means the individual has accepted being gay as a way of life and is happy with that identity and role. Empirical support for this model comes from comparisons between homosexuals and heterosexuals (Bell et al 1981). For example, with respect to sensitization, 72% of homosexual males and 72% of lesbians said they felt "very much or somewhat" different from same-sex peers in grade school compared with only 39% of heterosexual males and 54% of heterosexual females (Bell et al 1981). Similarly, with respect to identity confusion, empirical data suggest that gay men and women are more likely than their heterosexual peers to experience both heterosexual and homosexual arousal (Bell et al 1981). Other support for the model comes from the modal ages for "milestone events" (Garnets & Kimmel 1993). Gay men and lesbians appear to require several years to move from same-gender feelings (identity confusion) to gay self-identification (identity assumption) to positive gay identity (commitment).

The stage models can be critiqued. First, most models are atheoretical; they describe ideal types averaged from the narratives of gay men, lesbians, and bisexual people. Gay affirmative research needed such descriptions because the heterosexist bias in psychology is well documented (Morin 1977, Morin & Rothblum 1991). Now that the descriptions exist, the work can be integrated into mainstream personality, self, and identity theory (Coyle 1992, Gonsiorek & Rudolph 1990). Second, most models make questionable assumptions: People progress linearly through stages (Rust 1993, Sophie 1985/1986), people are discovering their true selves (Chapman & Brannock 1987, Kitzinger & Wilkinson 1995), or people should self-disclose to ever-widening audiences (Cain 1991). The models may describe one route to positive gay identity (e.g. that of a gay male activist), but they neither describe all routes (Faderman 1984) nor capture the fluidity of sexual identity (Golden 1987). Third, most models are based on gay male respondents. Sexual identity development in women is different (Brown 1995, Gonsiorek 1995, Risman & Schwartz 1988): Women self-identify as gay or bisexual later than men do (Garnets & Kimmel

1993), women more often self-identify in the context of emotional-romantic relationships (Sears 1989), and women less often subscribe to the essentialist perspective about sexual orientation (Chapman & Brannock 1987). Alternative models for women are available (McCarn & Fassinger 1996), but they are often hidden in unpublished doctoral dissertations. Fourth, the models focus on adolescence and early adulthood (Patterson 1995); they miss identity changes that occur later in life (Kitzinger & Wilkinson 1995) and "repeating spiral patterns" of identity development (Garnets & Kimmel 1993, p. 15). Fifth, these models classify people as gay, lesbian, bisexual, or heterosexual according to self-identification, and this procedure does not include some people (Bem 1992). Reliance on self-identification also masks the multiple components of sexual orientation (Coleman 1987, Klein et al 1985) and with concealable populations may produce contradictory results based on participant selection procedures (e.g. self-identification vs sexual behavior vs community participation) (Rothblum 1994). Sixth, these models are based on cross-sectional studies that use retrospective self-report data. Such data overestimate consistencies (within and across individuals) and do not establish causal connections; prospective, longitudinal data are needed.

Taken together, developmental stage models propose testable links among positive gay identity, personal visibility, cultural stigma, gay community networks, and mental health. Positive gay identity is the critical construct, and it is typically measured by asking people how good they feel about their homosexuality and how willing they are to change it (Bell et al 1981). As expected, having a positive gay identity is associated with better mental health (e.g. McDonald 1982, Miranda & Storms 1989, Schmitt & Kurdek 1987, Walters & Simoni 1993). The stage models also suggest and empirical research supports the view that increased gay community participation (Bell & Weinberg 1978, McDonald 1982), increased personal visibility or self-disclosure (Bell & Weinberg 1978, Bradford & Ryan 1987, McDonald 1982, Miranda & Storms 1989), and fewer cultural stigma experiences (Hetrick & Martin 1987) are associated with having a positive gay identity. Some research also suggests that increased community participation (Harry & DeVall 1978, Kurdek 1988), increased personal visibility (Friend 1980, Schmitt & Kurdek 1987), and fewer cultural stigma experiences (Ross 1990) are associated with better mental health. Studies often have limited sample sizes or restricted age ranges, most report only frequency counts or simple correlations, most do not assess the direct relation between variables while controlling for the other aspects of daily gay life, and none calculate the total effect of one variable on another. Getting large sample sizes, measuring all aspects of daily gay life, and using sophisticated analyses are critical for creating viable, empirical models of positive gay identity (Frable et al 1996).

The stage models also include a rich description of strategies that people use to negotiate the social category scheme of sexuality. At the identity confusion stage, people may deny, repair, avoid, redefine, or accept their homosexual behavior (Cass 1979, Troiden 1989). At the identity assumption stage, people may evade social stigma by capitulation (avoiding homosexuality), minstrelization (playing stereotypes), passing (concealing homosexual status), or group alignment (immersion in the gay community) (Troiden 1989). At the identity commitment stage, people may manage social stigma by covering, blending, or conversion (Troiden 1989). However, empirical research associating identity stages with management strategies is not substantial, the evaluative connotations implicit in the discussion of these strategies is problematic, the list of strategies is incomplete, and alternative conceptualizations of this identity negotiation process exist. For example, de Monteflores (1986) conceptualizes the issue as acceptance/rejection of the dominant culture; she proposes that gay individuals manage difference using assimilation, confrontation, ghettoization, and specialization. Wood (1992) found that strategies vary with an individual's work context; the choice of gay male professionals to counterfeit a heterosexual identity, avoid sexual identity questions, or integrate their gay identity in the work place is predicted by economic vulnerability, role models, and workplace homophobia. How gay men, lesbians, and bisexual people manage information about their gay identity, how they negotiate social interactions once their identity is known, and what the precursors and consequences of various strategies are all need systematic empirical attention. To distinguish the effects between sexual orientation and cultural stigma, cohort differences should also be explored.

Many of the first critiques of the stage models cited above are made by authors describing lesbian identity development (Faderman 1984, Sophie 1985/1986). The second wave of critiques comes from those describing bisexual identity development (Fox 1995). In contrast with the "in transition" or "denial" stereotypes (Ochs 1996), Cass (1990) suggested that bisexuality is a viable sexual identity with its own developmental pathway. Empirical data agree: Bisexuals self-identify later than lesbians and gay men (Rust 1993, Weinberg et al 1994), bisexuals have less stable identity histories (Rust 1993, Weinberg et al 1994), and bisexuality is less likely than homosexuality to be tied to preadult sexual feelings (Bell et al 1981). A bisexual identity is increasingly visible and carries social acknowledgment and community support (Garber 1995, Hutchins & Kaahumananu 1991); it challenges the premise that sexual feelings and behaviors revolve around the dimension of gender of partner. A third wave of critiques comes from the experiences of African Americans (Loiacano 1989), Asian Americans (Chan 1995), Native Americans (Williams 1986), and Latino Americans (Espin 1995). Investigators question whether

Western models of sexual identity are applicable to members of non-Western cultures (Greene 1994), and alternative models are proposed (Morales 1989).

Throughout the sexual identities literature, sexual identity is a political statement and not just information about self-perception. "Homosexual identity" evolved into "gay and lesbian identity," creating group cohesion and identity politics (Phelan 1993, Sampson 1993). Sexual identity theory is now on the cutting edge of understanding the intersection of identity, sociohistorical forces, cultural diversity, and individual lives.

CLASS IDENTITIES

Psychologists use class two ways: to describe research participants (often with the ubiquitous phrase "most subjects were white and middle class") and as an independent variable (to control uninteresting variation or to show that class does not interact with "more important" constructs). With few exceptions, class as a meaningful identity is simply absent from the psychological literature.

Among the exceptions, class identity often becomes salient when the individual moves from one context to another. Students from working-class backgrounds negotiate their marginal status at elite academic institutions (Stewart & Ostrove 1993). Downwardly mobile divorced women must reconcile a lower-class economic reality with their past middle-class lives (Grella 1990). Second- and third-generation immigrants are more likely than their first-generation peers to have class identities reflecting US cultural conceptions (Hurtado et al 1994). Poor women who clean wealthy women's houses don the masks of deference as they cross neighborhoods (Collins 1991). These works focus on handling stigma, reconciling contradictions, and resisting, capitulating, or accommodating to class-based norms.

Quantitative reports are rare. Hurtado et al (1994) found that Chicanos (second and third generation) have more class identities (reflecting their dual US and Mexican heritages) than Mexicanos (first generation). Stewart & Ostrove (1993) found that women from working-class backgrounds who graduated from Radcliffe in 1964 were less likely than their middle- and upper-class classmates to be homemakers and have children in 1979; these women's narratives indicate that their class identities allowed them to resist middle-class norms.

MULTIPLE IDENTITIES—SEEING PEOPLE AS WHOLE

This chapter reflects the current identity literature in psychology with respect to gender, race, ethnicity, sexuality, and class. Research focuses on the personal meanings of these social categories one at a time. This practice fragments the literature and systematically excludes particular populations. Gender identity research excludes racial and ethnic minorities and those who are not middle class. Racial and ethnic identity research often avoids gender and sexuality. Sexual identity research focuses on white middle-class gay men and lesbians. Class identity research attends to the wealthy (usually white) or the poor (usually women and ethnic minorities). Critiques of these practices exist, but even when new research with previously excluded social groups contradicts traditional theory, it rarely leads to new theoretical conceptions. Even more unusual is the actual testing of any new theoretical conceptions that reflect dual or multiple social group memberships.

Currently, longitudinal research is rare; such designs are essential to test developmental theories, to follow identity paths, and to demonstrate fluidity. In addition, self-esteem, adjustment, and other well-being indices are overworked dependent variables; identity has other functions needing exploration. Innovative methods for assessing the content and structure of people's identities now exist; they were designed or can be adapted to assess the many personally meaningful social categories on which people base their identities. The empirical work that stands out in this literature acknowledges that the personal meanings of social group memberships change over time, and these meanings are best understood in the context of sociohistorical events. Work that is produced without taking this context into account can be nonsensical, trite, or harmful; such work usually applies as normative a white, middle-class standard.

A powerful vision of what empirical work on identity could look like exists in the narrative writings of feminists, particularly those who are women of color (Collins 1991, Comas-Diaz & Greene 1994, Heath & McLaughlin 1993, Hurtado 1989, King 1988, MacPherson & Fine 1995, Reid 1994). These accounts capture excluded groups, excluded dimensions, and excluded relationships. They attend to sociohistorical contexts, family niches, and on-going milieus. They see identity as a continuously re-created, personalized social construction that includes multiple social categories and that functions to keep people whole.

These narratives are focused, detailed, and individualized; they come from people traditionally labeled as "Other" on multiple dimensions. Thus, they are first-hand accounts of how the important social category systems actually work together. Integrating the insights of these narratives into carefully designed empirical studies may lead to an identity literature that sees people as whole.

ACKNOWLEDGMENTS

I thank Janet Spence, Abigail Stewart, and John Seidel for making this chapter possible and Jose Soto, Lisa Vagge, and Christie Gilbert for relentlessly pursuing references. Financial assistance was provided by the Women's Studies Program at the University of Michigan and the Psychology Department at Harvard University.

Literature Cited

Aboud F. 1987. The development of ethnic self-identification. See Phinney & Rotheram 1987, pp. 32–55

Abrams D, Sparkes K, Hogg M. 1985. Gender salience and social identity: the impact of sex of siblings on educational and occupational aspirations. *Br. J. Educ. Psychol.* 55: 224–32

Abrams D, Thomas J, Hogg M. 1990. Numerical distinctiveness, social identity and gender salience. *Br. J. Soc. Psychol.* 29:87–92

American Psychiatric Association. 1994. *Diagnostic and Statistical Manual*, Vol. 4. Washington, DC: Am. Psychiatr. Assoc.

Apollon K, Waters M. 1990. *Haitian Americans and Black Americans: an analysis of race and ethnic identities.* Presented at Meet. Soc. Study Soc. Probl., Washington, DC

Ashmore R. 1990. Sex, gender and the individual. In *Handbook of Personality: Theory and Research,* ed. L Pervin, pp. 486–526. New York: Guilford

Atkinson D, Gim R. 1989. Asian-American cultural identity and attitudes toward mental health services. *J. Couns. Psychol.* 36:209– 12

Atkinson D, Morten G, Sue D. 1989. *Counseling American Minorities: A Cross Cultural Perspective.* Dubuque: Brown

Bailey M, Zucker K. 1995. Childhood sex-typed behavior and sexual orientation: a conceptual analysis and quantitative review. *Dev. Psychol.* 31:43–55

Banaji M, Prentice D. 1994. The self in social contexts. *Annu. Rev. Psychol.* 45:297–332

Bargad A, Hyde J. 1991. A study of feminist identity development in women. *Psychol. Women Q.* 15:181–201

Bayer R. 1987. *Homosexuality and American Psychiatry: The Politics of Diagnosis.* Princeton: Princeton Univ. Press

Bell A, Weinberg M. 1978. *Homosexualities: A Study of Diversity among Men and Women.* New York: Simon & Schuster

Bell A, Weinberg M, Hammersmith S. 1981. *Sexual Preference: Its Development in Men and Women.* New York: Simon & Schuster

Bem S. 1989. Genital knowledge and gender constancy in preschool children. *Child Dev.* 60:649–62

Bem S. 1992. On the inadequacy of our sexual categories: a personal perspective. *Fem. Psychol.* 2:435–37

Bem S. 1993. *The Lenses of Gender: Transforming the Debate on Sexual Inequality.* New Haven, CT: Yale Univ. Press

Bernal M, Knight G, Garza C, Ocampo C, Cota M. 1990. The development of ethnic identity in Mexican-American children. *Hisp. J. Behav. Sci.* 12:3–24

Betancourt H, Lopez S. 1993. The study of culture, ethnicity, and race in American psychology. *Am. Psychol.* 48:629–37

Birman D. 1994. Acculturation and human diversity in a multicultural society. See Trickett et al 1994, pp. 261–84

Blanchard R, Freund K. 1983. Measuring masculine gender identity in females. *J. Consult. Clin. Psychol.* 51:205–14

Blanchard R, Zucker K, Bradley S, Hume C. 1995. Birth order and sibling sex ratio in homosexual male adolescents and probably prehomosexual feminine boys. *Dev. Psychol.* 31:22–30

Bradford J, Ryan C. 1987. *National Lesbian Health Care Survey. Mental Health Implications.* Washington, DC: Natl. Lesbian Gay Health Found.

Brady S, Busse W. 1994. The gay identity questionnaire: a brief measure of homosexual identity formation. *J. Homosex.* 26:1–22

Brown L. 1989. New voices, new visions: toward a lesbian/gay paradigm for psychology. *Psychol. Women* 13:445–58

Brown L. 1995. Lesbian identities: concepts and issues. See D'Augelli & Patterson 1995, pp. 3–23

Burke P, Tully J. 1977. The measurement of role identity. *Soc. Forces* 55:881–97

Bussey K, Bandura A. 1984. Influence of gender constancy and social power on sex-linked modeling. *J. Pers. Soc. Psychol.* 47: 1292–302

Cain R. 1991. Stigma management and gay identity development. *Soc. Work* 36:67– 73

Carter D, Levy G. 1988. Cognitive aspects of children's early sex-role development: the influences of gender schemas on preschoolers' memories and preferences for sex-typed toys and activities. *Child Dev.* 59:782–93

Carter R. 1991. Racial identity attitudes and

psychological functioning. *J. Multicult. Couns. Dev.* 19:105–14

Cass V. 1979. Homosexual identity formation: a theoretical model. *J. Homosex.* 4:219–35

Cass V. 1984. Homosexual identity formation: testing a theoretical model. *J. Sex Res.* 20: 143–67

Cass V. 1990. The implications of homosexual identity formation for the Kinsey model and scale of sexual preference. In *Homosexuality/Heterosexuality: Concepts of Sexual Orientation,* ed. D McWhirter, S Sanders, J Reinisch, pp. 239–66. New York: Oxford Univ. Press

Chan C. 1995. Issues of sexual identity in an ethnic minority: the case of Chinese American lesbians, gay men, and bisexual people. See D'Augelli & Patterson 1995, pp. 87–101

Chapman B, Brannock J. 1987. A proposed model of lesbian identity development: an empirical investigation. *J. Homosex.* 14: 69–80

Coleman E. 1987. Assessment of sexual orientation. *J. Homosex.* 14:9–24

Collins P. 1991. *Black Feminist Thought: Knowledge, Consciousness, and the Politics of Empowerment.* New York: Routledge

Comas-Diaz L, Greene B, eds. 1994. *Women of Color: Integrating Ethnic and Gender Identities in Psychotherapy.* New York: Guilford

Coyle A. 1992. "My own special creation?" The construction of gay identity. In *Social Psychology of Identity and the Self Concept,* ed. G Breakwell, pp. 187–220. London: Surrey Univ. Press

Crocker J, Luhtanen R, Blaine B, Broadnax S. 1994. Collective self-esteem and psychological well-being among white, black, and Asian college students. *Pers. Soc. Psychol. Bull.* 20:503–13

Cross W. 1971. Negro-to-Black conversion experience. *Black World* 20:13–27

Cross W. 1991. *Shades of Black: Diversity in African-American Identity.* Philadelphia: Temple Univ. Press

Cross W, Parham T, Helms J. 1996. Nigrescence revisited: theory and research. In *Advances in Black Psychology,* ed. R Jones. Los Angeles: Cobb & Henry. In press

D'Augelli A, Patterson C, ed. 1995. *Lesbian, Gay, and Bisexual Identities Over the Lifespan.* New York: Oxford

Deaux K. 1993. Reconstructing social identity. *Pers. Soc. Psychol. Bull.* 19:4–12

Deaux K, Major B. 1987. Putting gender into context: an interactive model of gender-related behavior. *Psychol. Rev.* 94:369–89

Deaux K, Reid A, Mizrahi K, Ethier E. 1995. Parameters of social identity. *J. Pers. Soc. Psychol.* 68:280–91

D'Emilio J. 1983. *Sexual Politics, Sexual Communities: The Making of a Homosexual Minority in the United States,* 1940–1970. Chicago: Univ. Chicago Press

D'Emilio J, Freedman E. 1988. *Intimate Matters: A History of Sexuality in America.* New York: Harper & Row

de Monteflores C. 1986. Notes on the management of difference. In *Contemporary Perspectives on Psychotherapy with Lesbians and Gay Men,* ed. T Stein, C Cohen, pp. 73–101. New York: Plenum

Diamond M. 1982. Sexual identity, monozygotic twins reared in discordant sex roles and a BBC follow-up. *Arch. Sex. Behav.* 11: 181–86

Downing N, Roush K. 1985. From passive acceptance to active commitment: a model of feminist identity development for women. *Couns. Psychol.* 13:695–709

Downs A, Langlois J. 1988. Sex typing: construct and measurement issues. *Sex Roles* 18:87–100

Eaton W, Von Bargen D. 1981. Asynchronous development of gender understanding in preschool children. *Child Dev.* 52:1020–27

Eichler M. 1983. Sex change operations: the last bulwark of the double standard. In *Feminist Frontiers,* ed. L Richardson, V Taylor, pp. 106–15. Reading, MA: Addison-Wesley

Ely R. 1995. The power of demography: women's social constructions of gender identity at work. *Acad. Manage. J.* 38:589–634

Emmerich W, Shepard K. 1984. Cognitive factors in the development of sex-typed preferences. *Sex Roles* 11:997–1007

Erikson E. 1968. *Identity: Youth and Crisis.* New York: Norton

Espin O. 1995. "Race," racism, and sexuality in the life narratives of immigrant women. *Fem. Psychol.* 5:223–38

Ethier K, Deaux K. 1994. Negotiating social identity when contexts change: maintaining identification and responding to threat. *J. Pers. Soc. Psychol.* 67:243–51

Faderman L. 1981. *Surpassing the Love of Men: Romantic Friendship and Love Between Women from the Renaissance to the Present.* New York: Morrow

Faderman L. 1984. The "new gay" lesbians. *J. Homosex.* 10:85–95

Fagot B, Leinbach M. 1985. Gender identity: some thoughts on an old concept. *J. Am. Acad. Child Psychiatry* 24:684–88

Fagot B, Leinbach M. 1989. The young child's gender schema: environmental input, internal organization. *Child Dev.* 60:663–72

Fagot B, Leinbach M, Hagan R. 1986. Gender labeling and the adoption of sex-typed behaviors. *Dev. Psychol.* 22:440–43

Fagot B, Leinbach M, O'Boyle C. 1992. Gender labeling, gender stereotyping, and parenting behaviors. *Dev. Psychol.* 28: 225–30

Foucault M. 1979. *The History of Sexuality.* London: Allen Lane

Fox R. 1995. Bisexual identities. See D'Augelli & Patterson 1995, pp. 48–86

Frable D. 1989. Sex typing and gender ideology: two facets of the individual's gender psychology that go together. *J. Pers. Soc. Psychol.* 56:95–108

Frable D, Wortman C, Joseph J. 1996. Predicting self-esteem, well-being, and distress in a cohort of gay men: the importance of cultural stigma, personal visibility, community networks, and positive identity. *J. Pers.* In press

Freund K, Nagler E, Langevin R, Zajac A, Steiner B. 1974. Measuring feminine gender identity in homosexual males. *Arch. Sex. Behav.* 3:249–60

Frey K, Ruble D. 1992. Gender constancy and the "cost" of sex-typed behavior: a conflict hypothesis. *Dev. Psychol.* 28:714–21

Friend R. 1980. Gayging: adjustment and the older gay male. *Altern. Lifestyles* 3:231–48

Garber M. 1995. *Vice Versa: Bisexuality and the Eroticism of Everyday Life.* New York: Simon & Schuster

Garnets L, Kimmel D, eds. 1993. *Psychological Perspectives on Lesbian and Gay Male Experiences.* New York: Columbia Univ. Press

Gelman S, Collman P, Maccoby E. 1986. Inferring properties from categories versus inferring categories from properties: the case of gender. *Child Dev.* 57:394–404

Golden C. 1987. Diversity and variability in women's sexual identities. In *Lesbian Psychologies,* ed. Boston Lesbian Psychol. Collect., pp. 18–34. Chicago: Univ. Ill. Press

Golden C. 1994. Our politics and choices: the feminist movement and sexual orientation. In *Lesbian and Gay Psychology: Theory, Research and Clinical Applications,* ed. B Greene, G Herek, pp. 54–70

Gonsiorek J. 1995. Gay male identities: concepts and issues. See D'Augelli & Patterson 1995, pp. 24–47

Gonsiorek J, Rudolph J. 1990. Homosexual identity: coming out and other developmental events. In *Homosexuality: Research Implications for Public Policy,* ed. J Gonsiorek, J Weinrich, pp. 161–76. Newbury Park, CA: Sage

Green R. 1987. *The "Sissy Boy Syndrome" and the Development of Homosexuality.* New Haven, CT: Yale Univ. Press

Green R, Fleming D. 1990. Transsexual surgery follow-up: status in the 1990s. *Annu. Rev. Sex Res.* 1:163–74

Green R, Williams K, Goodman M. 1985. Masculine or feminine gender identity in boys: developmental differences between two diverse family groups. *Sex Roles* 12: 1155–62

Greene B. 1994. Lesbian women of color: triple jeopardy. See Comas-Diaz & Greene 1994, pp. 389–427

Grella C. 1990. Irreconcilable differences: women defining class after divorce and downward mobility. *Gender Soc.* 4:41–55

Gurin P, Markus H. 1989. Cognitive consequences of gender identity. In *The Social Identity of Women,* ed. S Skevington, D Baker, pp. 152–72. London: Sage

Gurin P, Townsend A. 1986. Properties of gender identity and their implications for gender consciousness. *Br. J. Soc. Psychol.* 25: 139–48

Harrison A, Wilson M, Pine C, Chan S, Buriel R. 1990. Family ecologies of ethnic minority children. *Child Dev.* 61:347–62

Harry J, DeVall W. 1978. *The Social Organization of Gay Males.* New York: Praeger

Heath S, McLaughlin M, eds. 1993. *Identity and Inner-City Youth: Beyond Ethnicity and Gender.* New York: Teach. Coll. Press

Helms J. 1989. Considering some methodological issues in racial identity counseling research. *Couns. Psychol.* 17:227–52

Helms J. 1990. *Black and White Racial Identity: Theory, Research, and Practice.* Westport, CT: Greenwood

Helms J. 1994. The conceptualization of racial identity and other "racial" constructs. See Trickett et al 1994, pp. 285–311

Helson R, Stewart A, Ostrove J. 1995. Identity in three cohorts of midlife women. *J. Pers. Soc. Psychol.* 69:544–57

Henderson-King D, Stewart A. 1994. Women or feminists? Assessing women's group consciousness. *Sex Roles* 31:505–16

Herdt G. 1989. Gay and lesbian youth, emergent identities, and cultural scenes at home and abroad. *J. Homosex.* 10:39–52

Herdt G. 1990. Mistaken gender: 5-alpha reductase hermaphroditism and biological reductionism in sexual identity reconsidered. *Am. Anthropol.* 92:433–46

Hetrik E, Martin A. 1987. Developmental issues and their resolution for gay and lesbian adolescents. *J. Homosex.* 14:25–44

Hort B, Leinbach M, Fagot B. 1991. Is there coherence among the cognitive components of gender acquisition? *Sex Roles* 24: 195–207

Hurtado A. 1989. Relating to privilege: seduction and rejection in the subordination of White women and women of Color. *Signs* 14:833–55

Hurtado A, Gurin P, Peng T. 1994. Social identities: a framework for studying the adaptations of immigrants and ethnics: the adap-

tations of Mexicans in the United States. *Soc. Probl.* 41:129–51
Huston A. 1983. Sex-typing. In *Handbook of Child Psychology,* ed. EM Hetherington, P Mussen, pp. 387–467. New York: Wiley
Hutchins L, Kaahumananu L, eds. 1991. *Bi Any Other Name: Bisexuals Speak Out.* Boston: Alyson
Imperato-McGinley J, Peterson R, Gautier T, Sturla E. 1979. Androgens and the evolution of male gender identity among male pseudohermaphrodites with 5-alpha-reductase deficiency. *N. Engl. J. Med.* 300: 1233–37
Jones J. 1994. Our similarities are different: toward a psychology of affirmative diversity. See Trickett et al 1994, pp. 27–45
Josselson R. 1987. *Finding Herself: Pathways to Identity Development in Women.* San Francisco: Jossey-Bass
Katz P. 1986. Gender identity: development and consequences. In *The Social Psychology of Female-Male Relations,* ed. R Ashmore, F Del Boca, pp. 21–67. New York: Academic
Katz P. 1987. Developmental and social processes in ethnic attitudes and self-identification. See Phinney & Rotheram 1987, pp. 92–99
Keefe S. 1992. Ethnic identity: the domain of perceptions of and attachment to ethnic groups and cultures. *Hum. Organ.* 51:35–43
Keefe S, Padilla A. 1987. *Chicano Ethnicity.* Albuquerque: Univ. NM Press
Kim J. 1981. *Processes of Asian American identity development: a study of Japanese American women's perceptions of their struggles to achieve positive identities.* PhD thesis. Univ. Mass., Amherst. 204 pp.
King D. 1988. Multiple jeopardy, multiple consciousness: the context of a Black feminist ideology. *Signs* 14:42–72
Kitzinger C, Wilkinson S. 1995. Transitions from heterosexuality to lesbianism: the discursive production of lesbian identities. *Dev. Psychol.* 31:95–104
Klein F, Sepekoff B, Wolf T. 1985. Sexual orientation: a multi-variable dynamic process. *J. Homosex.* 11:35–49
Knight G, Bernal M, Garza C, Cota M, Ocampo K. 1993a. Family socialization and the ethnic identity of Mexican-American children. *J. Cross-Cult. Psychol.* 24:99–114
Knight G, Cota M, Bernal M. 1993b. The socialization of cooperative, competitive, and individualistic preferences among Mexican American children: the mediating role of ethnic identity. *Hisp. J. Behav. Sci.* 15: 291–309
Koestner R, Aube J. 1995. A multifactorial approach to the study of gender characteristics. *J. Pers.* 63:681–710
Kohlberg L. 1966. A cognitive-developmental analysis of children's sex-role concepts and attitudes. In *The Development of Sex Differences,* ed. E Maccoby, pp. 82–172. Stanford, CA: Stanford Univ. Press
Krieger S. 1983. *The Mirror Dance: Identity in a Women's Community.* Philadelphia: Temple Univ. Press
Kurdek L. 1988. Perceived social support in gays and lesbians in cohabiting relationships. *J. Pers. Soc. Psychol.* 51:365–70
LaFromboise T, Coleman H, Gerton J. 1993. Psychological impact of biculturalism: evidence and theory. *Psychol. Bull.* 114:395–412
Leidner R. 1991. Serving hamburgers and selling insurance: gender, work, and identity in interactive service jobs. *Gender Soc.* 5: 154–77
Leinbach M, Fagot B. 1986. Acquisition of gender labels: a test for toddlers. *Sex Roles* 15:655–66
Levy G, Carter D. 1989. Gender schema, gender constancy, and gender-role knowledge: the roles of cognitive factors in preschoolers' gender-role stereotype attributions. *Dev. Psychol.* 25:444–49
Lobel R, Menashri J. 1993. Relations of conceptions of gender-role transgressions and gender constancy to gender-typed toy preferences. *Dev. Psychol.* 29:150–55
Loiacano D. 1989. Gay identity issues among Black Americans: racism, homophobia and the need for validation. *J. Couns. Dev.* 68: 21–25
Luhtanen R, Crocker J. 1992. A collective self-esteem scale: self-evaluation of one's social identity. *Pers. Soc. Psychol. Bull.* 18: 302–18
Maccoby E. 1990. The role of gender identity and gender constancy in sex-differentiated development. *New Dir. Child Dev.* 47:5–20
MacPherson P, Fine M. 1995. Hungry for an Us: adolescent girls and adult women negotiating territories of race, gender, class and difference. *Fem. Psychol.* 5:181–200
Marcia J. 1980. Identity in adolescence. In *Handbook of Adolescent Psychology,* ed. J Adelson, pp. 159–87. New York: Wiley
Marcia J, Waterman A, Matteson D, Archer S, Orlofsky J. 1993. *Ego Identity: A Handbook for Psychosocial Research.* New York: Springer-Verlag
Martin C, Halverson C. 1983. Gender constancy: a methodological and theoretical analysis. *Sex Roles* 9:775–90
McAdams D. 1995. What do we know when we know a person? *J. Pers.* 63:365–96
McCall G, Simmons J. 1966. *Identities and Interactions.* New York: Free Press
McCarn S, Fassinger R. 1996. Re-visioning

sexual minority identity formation: a new model of lesbian identity and its implications for counseling and research. *Couns. Psychol.* 24:508–34
McDonald G. 1982. Individual differences in the coming out process for gay men: implications for theoretical models. *J. Homosex.* 8:47–60
Miranda J, Storms M. 1989. Psychological adjustment of lesbians and gay men. *J. Couns. Dev.* 68:41–45
Money J. 1994. The concept of gender identity disorder in childhood and adolescence after 39 years. *J. Sex Marital Ther.* 20:163– 77
Money J, Ehrhardt A. 1972. *Man and Woman, Boy and Girl: The Differentiation and Dimorphism of Gender Identity from Development to Maturity.* Baltimore, MD: John Hopkins Press
Morales E. 1989. Ethnic minority families and minority gays and lesbians. *Marriage Fam. Rev.* 14:217–39
Morin S. 1977. Heterosexual bias in psychological research on lesbianism and male homosexuality. *Am. Psychol.* 32:629–37
Morin S, Rothblum E. 1991. Removing the stigma: fifteen years of progress. *Am. Psychol.* 46:947–49
Munford M. 1994. Relationship of gender, self-esteem, social class, and racial identity to depression in Blacks. *J. Black Psychol.* 20:157–74
Myers L, Speight S, Highlen P, Cox C, Reynolds A, et al. 1991. Identity development and worldview: toward an optimal conceptualization. *J. Couns. Dev.* 70:54–63
Nagel J. 1994. Constructing ethnicity: creating and recreating ethnic identity and culture. *Soc. Probl.* 41:152–76
Ochs R. 1996. Biphobia: it goes more than two ways. In *The Psychology and Politics of an Invisible Minority,* ed. B Firestein. In press
Okazaki S, Sue S. 1995. Methodological issues in assessment research with ethnic minorities. *Psychol. Assess.* 7:367–75
Ossana S, Helms J, Leonard M. 1992. Do "womanist" identity attitudes influence college women's self-esteem and perceptions of environmental bias? *J. Couns. Dev.* 70: 402–8
Padilla F. 1993. On Hispanic identity. In *Handbook of Hispanic Cultures in the United States,* ed. F Padilla, pp. 292–303. Houston: Arte Publico Press
Parham T. 1989. Cycles of psychological nigrescence. *Couns. Psychol.* 17:187–226
Park R. 1928. Human migration and the marginal man. *Am. J. Sociol.* 6:881–93
Patterson C. 1995. Sexual orientation and human development: an overview. *Dev. Psychol.* 31:3–11
Phelan S. 1993. (Be)coming out: lesbian identity and politics. *Signs* 18:765–90
Phinney J. 1989. Stages of ethnic identity in minority group adolescents. *J. Early Adolesc.* 9:34–49
Phinney J. 1990. Ethnic identity in adolescents and adults: review of research. *Psychol. Bull.* 108:499–514
Phinney J. 1991. Ethnic identity and self-esteem: a review and integration. *Hisp. J. Behav. Sci.* 13:193–208
Phinney J. 1992. The multigroup ethnic identity measure: a new scale for use with diverse groups. *J. Adolesc. Res.* 7:156–76
Phinney J, Alipuria L. 1990. Ethnic identity in college students from four ethnic groups. *J. Adolesc.* 13:171–83
Phinney J, Chavira V. 1992. Ethnic identity and self-esteem: an exploratory longitudinal study. *J. Adolesc.* 15:271–81
Phinney J, Rotheram M, eds. 1987. *Children's Ethnic Socialization.* Newbury Park, CA: Sage
Phinney J, Tarver S. 1988. Ethnic identity search and commitment in Black and White eighth graders. *J. Early Adolesc.* 8: 265–77
Ponterotto J. 1988. Racial consciousness development among White counselor trainees. *J. Multicult. Couns. Dev.* 16:146–56
Ponterotto J. 1989. Expanding directions for racial identity research. *Couns. Psychol.* 17:264–72
Ponterotto J, Wise S. 1987. Construct validity study of the racial identity attitude scale. *J. Couns. Psychol.* 34:218–23
Porter J, Washington R. 1993. Minority identity and self-esteem. *Annu. Rev. Sociol.* 19: 139–61
Poston W. 1990. The biracial identity development model: a needed addition. *J. Couns. Dev.* 69:152–55
Pyant C, Yanico B. 1991. Relationship of racial identity and gender-role attitudes to black women's psychological well-being. *J. Couns. Psychol.* 38:315–22
Radicalesbians. 1973. Women-identified women. In *Radical Feminism,* ed. A Koedt, W Levine, A Rapone, pp. 240–45. New York: Quadrangle Books
Ramirez M. 1983. *Psychology of the Americas: Mestizo Perspectives on Personality and Mental Health.* New York: Pergamon
Ramirez M. 1984. Assessing and understanding biculturalism—Multiculturalism in Mexican- American adults. In *Chicano Psychology,* ed. J Martinez, R Mendoza, pp. 77–94. San Diego: Academic
Reid P. 1994. *Development of gender and class identities: African Americans in context.* Presented at Annu. Meet. Am. Psychol. Assoc., 102nd, Los Angeles
Rickard K. 1987. *Feminist identity develop-*

ment: scale development and initial validation studies. Presented at Annu. Meet. Assoc. Women Psychol., 12th, Denver

Rickard K. 1990. The effect of feminist identity level on gender prejudice toward artists' illustrations. *J. Res. Pers.* 24:145–62

Risman B, Schwartz P. 1988. Sociological research on male and female homosexuality. *Annu. Rev. Sociol.* 14:125–47

Root M. 1992. *Racially Mixed People in America.* Newbury Park, CA: Sage

Ross M. 1990. The relationship between life events and mental health in homosexual men. *J. Clin. Psychol.* 46:402–11

Rothblum E. 1994. "I only read about myself on bathroom walls": the need for research on the mental health of lesbians and gay men. *J. Consult. Clin. Psychol.* 62: 213–20

Rotheram-Borus M. 1990. Adolescents' reference-group choices, self-esteem, and adjustment. *J. Pers. Soc. Psychol.* 59:1075–81

Rowe W, Bennett S, Atkinson D. 1994. White racial identity models: a critique and alternative proposal. *Couns. Psychol.* 22:129–46

Rust P. 1993. "Coming out" in the age of social constructionism: sexual identity formation among lesbian and bisexual women. *Gender Soc.* 7:50–77

Sampson E. 1993. Identity politics: challenges to psychology's understanding. *Am. Psychol.* 48:1219–30

Sanders Thompson V. 1994. Socialization to race and its relationship to racial identification among African Americans. *J. Black Psychol.* 20:175–88

Schmitt J, Kurdek L. 1987. Personality correlates of positive identity and relationship involvement in gay men. *J. Homosex.* 13: 101–9

Sears J. 1989. The impact of gender and race on growing up lesbian and gay in the South. *Natl. Women's Stud. Assoc. J.* 1:422–57

Sherif C. 1982. Needed concepts in the study of gender identity. *Psychol. Women Q.* 6:375– 98

Shweder R, Sullivan M. 1993. Cultural psychology: Who needs it? *Annu. Rev. Psychol.* 44:497–523

Simon R. 1992. Parental role strains, salience of parental identity and gender differences in psychological distress. *J. Health Soc. Behav.* 33:25–35

Sophie J. 1985/1986. A critical examination of stage theories of lesbian identity development. *J. Homosex.* 12:39–51

Spence J. 1985. Gender identity and its implications for the concepts of masculinity and femininity. In *Psychology and Gender, Nebraska Symposium on Motivation,* ed. T Sonderegger, 32:59–95. Lincoln: Univ. Nebr. Press

Spence J. 1993. Gender-related traits and gender ideology: evidence for a multifactorial theory. *J. Pers. Soc. Psychol.* 64:624–35

Spencer M, Markstrom-Adams C. 1990. Identity processes among racial and ethnic minority children in America. *Child Dev.* 61: 290–310

Stangor C, Ruble D. 1987. Development of gender rule knowledge and gender constancy. In *Children's Gender Schemata,* ed. L Liben, M Signorella, pp. 5–22. San Fransisco: Jossey-Bass

Stangor C, Ruble D. 1989. Effects of gender schemas and gender constancy on children's information processing and behavior. *Soc. Cogn.* 7:353–72

Stewart A, Ostrove J. 1993. Social class, social change, and gender: working class women at Radcliffe and after. *Psychol. Women Q.* 17:475–97

Stonequist E. 1937. *The Marginal Man: A Study in Personality and Culture Conflict.* New York: Scribner's Sons

Stryker S. 1980. *Symbolic Interactionism: A Social Structural Version.* Palo Alto, CA: Benjamin/Cummings

Stryker S. 1987. Identity theory: developments and extensions. In *Self and Identity: Psychosocial Perspectives,* ed. K Yardley, T Honess, pp. 83–103. New York: Wiley

Sue D. 1994. Racial/cultural identity development models: future directions. *Focus* 8: 4–5. Off. Publ. Div. 45, Am. Psychol. Assoc.

Szapocznik J, Kurtines W. 1980. Acculturation, biculturalism and adjustment among Cuban Americans. In *Psychological Dimensions on the Acculturation Process: Theory, Models, and Some New Findings,* ed. A Padilla, pp. 139–59. Boulder, CO: Westview

Tajfel H. 1978. The social psychology of minorities. *Rep. 38,* pp. 1–20. London: Minority Rights Group

Tajfel H, Turner J. 1979. An integrative theory of intergroup conflict. In *The Social Psychology of Intergroup Relations,* ed. W Austin, S Worchel, pp. 33–47. Monterey, CA: Brooks/Cole

Thoits P. 1995. Identity-relevant events and psychological symptoms: a cautionary tale. *J. Health Soc. Behav.* 36:72–82

Trickett E, Watts R, Birman D, eds. 1994. *Human Diversity: Perspectives on People in Context.* San Francisco: Jossey-Bass

Troiden R. 1989. The formation of homosexual identities. *J. Homosex.* 17:43–73

Turner J, Hogg M, Oakes P, Reicher S, Wetherell M. 1987. *Rediscovering the Social Group: A Self-Categorization Theory.* Oxford: Blackwell

US Bureau of the Census. 1996. *Population Projections of the United States by Age, Sex, Race and Hispanic Origin: 1995 to 2050.* (Popul. Char. Ser. P-25 No. 1130). Washington, DC: US Gov. Print. Off.

Walters K, Simoni J. 1993. Lesbian and gay male group identity attitudes and self-esteem: implications for counseling. *J. Couns. Psychol.* 40:94–99

Waters M. 1994. Ethnic and racial identities of second-generation Black immigrants in New York City. *Int. Migr. Rev.* 28: 795–820

Waters M, Eschbach K. 1995. Immigration and ethnic and racial inequality in the United States. *Annu. Rev. Sociol.* 21:419–46

Weinberg M, Williams C, Pryor D. 1994. *Dual Attraction: Understanding Bisexuality.* New York: Oxford Univ. Press

Weise E, ed. 1992. *Closer to Home: Bisexuality & Feminism.* Seattle: Seal

Williams W. 1986. Persistence and change in the Berdache traditional among contemporary Lakota Indians. *J. Homosex.* 11:191–200

Woods J. 1992. *The corporate closet: managing gay identity on the job.* PhD thesis. Univ. Pa. 379 pp.

Yee A, Fairchild H, Weizmann F, Wyatt G. 1993. Addressing psychology's problems with race. *Am. Psychol.* 48:1132–40

Yee M, Brown R. 1994. The development of gender differentiation in young children. *Br. J. Soc. Psychol.* 33:183–96

Zucker K, Bradley S, Sullivan C, Kuksis M, Birkenfeld-Adams A, Mitchell J. 1993a. A gender identity interview for children. *J. Pers. Assess.* 61:443–56

Zucker K, Wild J, Bradley S, Lowry C. 1993b. Physical attractiveness of boys with gender identity disorders. *Arch. Sex. Behav.* 22: 23–36

Zuckerman M. 1990. Some dubious premises in research and theory on racial differences: scientific, social and ethical issues. *Am. Psychol.* 45:1297–303

Annu. Rev. Psychol. 1997. 48:163–89

DISCOURSE COMPREHENSION

Arthur C. Graesser

Department of Psychology, The University of Memphis, Memphis, Tennessee 38152

Keith K. Millis

Department of Psychology, Northern Illinois University, DeKalb, Illinois 60115

Rolf A. Zwaan

Department of Psychology, Florida State University, Tallahassee, Florida 32306

KEY WORDS: discourse processing, inferences, reading, text comprehension

ABSTRACT

The field of discourse processing has dissected many of the levels of representation that are constructed when individuals read or listen to connected discourse. These levels include the surface code, the propositional textbase, the referential situation model, the communication context, and the discourse genre. Discourse psychologists have developed models that specify how these levels are mentally represented and how they are dynamically built during comprehension. This chapter focuses on the meaning representations that are constructed when adults read written text, such as literary stories, technical expository text, and experimenter-generated "textoids." Recent psychological models have attempted to account for the identification of referents of referring expressions (e.g. which person in the text does *she* refer to), the connection of explicit text segments, the establishment of local and global coherence, and the encoding of knowledge-based inferences.

CONTENTS

0084-6570/97/0201-0163$08.00

INTRODUCTION

A distinguished experimental psychologist approached one of us at a conference and grumbled "Why do you waste your time studying discourse? Why don't you study something fundamental, like perception, learning, memory, or eyelid conditioning in rabbits?" Shocked and bewildered, a witty insightful response was never delivered to the elderly gentleman. However, we have periodically imagined the perfect response over the years. A flip answer would be "Because it's there." This answer would be entirely correct, of course. Adults in this culture do spend most of their conscious life speaking, hearing, writing, and reading various forms of connected discourse. A more confrontational response would be "Because discourse *is* fundamental." This response would reflect what we believe. Discourse is what makes us human, what allows us to communicate ideas, facts, and feelings across time and space. Introductory texts in cognitive psychology should have a chapter on discourse, just as there are chapters on perception, memory, learning, problem solving, and language. The practical response would be "Because it's useful." The currency of psychology rises to the extent that discourse psychologists can improve reading, text design, complex learning, and social interaction.

There are more insightful reasons for investigating discourse processing as a primary object of inquiry. First, discourse processing has some unique properties that cannot be reduced to other subareas of psychology, such as psycho linguistics and memory. Connected discourse is more than language per se, and much more than a sequence of individual sentences. Comprehension cannot be reduced to problems of accessing and constructing memory representations. Second, discourse spans enough context to constrain the interpretation of input in a systematic fashion. As one colleague put it, a sentence out of context is always ambiguous, whereas a sentence in a discourse context is rarely ambiguous. Third, some genres of discourse, such as stories, are microcosms of events and experiences in the real world. Both stories and everyday experiences include people performing actions in pursuit of goals, events that present obstacles to these goals, conflicts between people, and emotional reactions. Experimenters can test psychological theories of human cognition, behavior, and emotion by systematically creating story microworlds, controlling several variables, and observing the comprehenders' responses. Fourth, discourse contains multiple levels of representation, such as phonemes, words, syntax, propositions, and global messages. The fact that comprehenders are able to coordinate these multiple levels very quickly is a major achievement that is worthy of scrutiny. And fifth, discourse processing is intertwined with virtually all cognitive functions and processes, including memory, perception, problem solving, and reasoning. When a person is asked to solve a problem, for example, the problem is frequently presented as discourse, and a successful solution presupposes an adequate comprehension of the problem.

The field of discourse processing has grown tremendously during the past decade, which has resulted in several new journals, societies, and conferences. It is beyond the scope of this chapter to provide a comprehensive coverage of the exciting new empirical findings and theoretical developments. We focus here on the comprehension of written text. The scenario to imagine is a college student reading a literary short story for enjoyment, or studying a technical text for an examination. Thus, the emphasis is on written text rather than oral conversation, and on comprehension rather than the production of discourse. We also focus on the representation of meaning, which includes semantics, pragmatics, and the body of knowledge conveyed in the text. The more shallow levels of code (such as phonology, intonation, syntax, and the lexicon of word meanings) are addressed only to the extent that they help clarify how meaning representations are constructed. We recommend Gernsbacher's (1994) *Handbook of Psycholinguistics* for readers who desire a comprehensive coverage of psycholinguistics and all levels of discourse processing. An excellent coverage of oral discourse is provided in books by Clark (1993), Levelt (1989), and Rubin (1995).

Discourse psychologists have investigated a broad array of written texts. At one extreme, researchers investigate naturalistic texts that are written by professional writers for the general public (van Oostendorp & Zwaan 1994). In the narrative genre, the texts have ranged from simple well-formed folktales to literary short stories (Dixon et al 1993, Gerrig 1993, Kreuz & MacNealy 1996, Miall & Kuiken 1994). Texts in the expository genre have frequently covered topics in history (Perfetti et al 1995, Voss & Silfies 1996) and science (Chi et al 1994, Kintsch 1994). These investigations of naturalistic text uncover a representative set of discourse features, patterns, devices, meanings, and comprehension processes that are prevalent in a culture. However, the advantage of ecological validity comes at the cost of losing precise control over the texts' stimulus properties. Consequently, at the other extreme, experimenters carefully craft texts to manipulate independent variables, control for extraneous variables, and satisfy counterbalancing constraints. We call these experimenter-generated materials "textoids" because they are not naturalistic discourse segments that are written to convey an informative or interesting message to a comprehender. Indeed, the texts in far too many experiments are meandering, choppy, pointless, and uninteresting; such texts may impose control over shallow levels of code (such as word frequency, word meanings, and syntactic composition) but fail miserably in providing control over global coherence and information value. There is the risk that the study of textoids unveils unnatural representations and processing strategies. Discourse psychologists are on solid footing when a hypothesis is confirmed in a sample of naturalistic texts in addition to properly controlled textoids.

The methods of investigating text comprehension are quite diverse (Haberlandt 1994). Sometimes the objective is to study the meaning representations that are established after comprehension is completed. Claims about these mental representations are tested by collecting recall protocols, summary protocols, answers to questions, and various judgments on test statements (e.g. new/old recognition judgments, true/false verification judgments, importance ratings). However, these "off-line" measures are not well suited to capturing the processes and representations that are constructed "on-line" during comprehension. What measures and tasks uncover on-line comprehension processes? This question has been debated at length and is far from settled. One straightforward approach is to collect reading times as readers normally read the text. In eye tracking experiments, the researcher records gaze durations on individual words and patterns of eye movements across the words (Garrod et al 1994, Just & Carpenter 1992, Rayner et al 1994). Self-paced reading times are collected by having the reader press a response key after reading individual text segments, such as words, clauses, sentences, or paragraphs (Haberlandt & Graesser 1985). Although these reading times are natural, the times can sometimes be ambiguous with respect to the contents and types of processes they index. Additional clarity is provided in tasks that periodically interrupt the reader and collect data during comprehension. For example, in a "think aloud" task, the reader expresses ideas that come to mind as each clause in the text is comprehended. The content extracted from think aloud protocols is a very rich source of data for discovering possible comprehension strategies and for testing detailed claims about the representations that enter the reader's consciousness. Researchers have also demonstrated that think aloud protocols are somewhat valid reflections of normal comprehension activities (Chi et al 1994, Ericsson & Simon 1993, Trabasso & Magliano 1996, Zwaan & Brown 1996). However, the protocols do not reliably tap unconscious comprehension processes. Both conscious and unconscious comprehension processes can be tapped in a word-naming task in which readers are periodically interrupted during comprehension and asked to name a test word as quickly as possible. The word-naming latency should be quick if the features of the word closely match a representation that is active in the reader's mind. As an alternative to the word-naming latencies, researchers frequently collect lexical decision latencies on test strings (i.e. whether a sequence of letters forms a word or a nonword), or word recognition latencies (i.e. whether a test word appeared earlier in the text). Unfortunately, there is a drawback to these tasks that interrupt the reader for data collection: The reader might suffer from "comprehension interruptus" and resort to constructing an unnatural, choppy, shallow representation. Therefore, the rigorous discourse psychologist insists on converging evidence from multiple methods before accepting an empirical claim as valid. Some researchers have advocated a "three-pronged method" that coordinates (*a*) predictions generated by theories, models, and hypotheses; (*b*) data from think aloud protocols; and (*c*) behavioral measures that assess processing time (Graesser et al 1994, Magliano & Graesser 1991, Millis & Graesser 1994, Suh & Trabasso 1993, Zwaan & Brown 1996).

MULTIPLE LEVELS OF DISCOURSE REPRESENTATION

Several levels of discourse representation have been identified by scholars in text linguistics, computational linguistics, sociolinguistics, and literary studies. However, some of these levels have not been embraced by discourse psychologists because they are esoteric or are applicable to a very narrow set of discourse contexts. Most discourse psychologists adopt van Dijk & Kintsch's (1983) distinctions among the *surface code,* the *textbase,* and the referential *situation model.* The surface code preserves the exact wording and syntax of clauses. Comprehenders normally retain the surface code of only the most recent clause unless aspects of this surface code have important repercussions on meaning. The textbase contains explicit text propositions in a stripped-down form that preserves meaning, but not the exact wording and syntax. The textbase also includes a small number of inferences that are needed to establish local text coherence. The situation model is the content or the microworld that the text is about. The situation model for a story refers to the people, spatial setting, actions, and events in the mental microworld. This microworld is constructed inferentially through interactions between the explicit text and background world knowledge.

In addition to these three levels of representation, psychologists normally acknowledge representations and processes at two other levels, which we call the *communication* level and the *text genre* level. The communication level refers to the pragmatic communicative context within which the text is embedded. Thus, the writer prepares the text to communicate ideas to readers (Nystrand 1986), and story narrators communicate episodes to narratees. Regarding text genre, discourse analysts have identified many categories and subcategories of text genre (Biber 1988), such as narration, exposition, description, persuasion, jokes, and so on. A newspaper article, for example, involves quite different structural components, features, and pragmatic ground rules than a joke. All five of these levels contribute to the meaning representations that readers build during comprehension. Moreover, it is a profound understatement to say that these various levels interact with one another in complex ways that are not well understood.

To illustrate the five levels of representation, consider the excerpt below that was extracted from the novel *Einstein's Dreams* by Alan Lightman (1993, p. 102):

> A mushy, brown peach is lifted from the garbage and placed on the table to pinken. It pinkens, it turns hard, it is carried in a shopping sack to the grocer's, put on a shelf, removed and crated, returned to the tree with pink blossoms. In this world, time flows backward.

The *text genre* is literary narrative. The excerpt is extracted from the beginning of a chapter, somewhere in the middle of the book. The novel has a series of chapters that describe different fictitious villages in Switzerland in 1905. Each village directly challenges our normal concept of time by transforming a basic assumption in our TIME schema. For example, the citizens in one village know about the future but not the past, which is opposite to one assumption in our TIME schema. In the village described above, time flows backward, which clearly violates the normal forward flow of time, from past to present to future. At the pragmatic *communication* level, the writer or narrator is attempting to unveil fresh insights about time, reality, and life to the reader by violating the normal assumptions about time. The writer has used a well-known literary device called defamiliarization (Miall & Kuiken 1994). That is, prototypical concepts are transformed in an unfamiliar way by stylistic devices, which forces the reader to reinterpret referents and view them in a new perspective. The events in the first two sentences are very difficult to comprehend as they are being read on-line because there are no obvious causal connections between successive events. The sequence of events in this *situation model* is incoherent. Then the third sentence reveals that time flows backward; consequently, the order of events in the explicit text is opposite to the normal flow of events in a generic FRUIT DISTRIBUTION schema. A diligent reader would have to reinterpret the situation model that was constructed from the first two sentences. It is uncertain at this point exactly what deep messages the author wants to communicate by crafting a text with discrepancies among (*a*) the presentation order of events in the text, (*b*) the order of events in a generic FRUIT DISTRIBUTION schema, and (*c*) the chronological order of events in the situation model for that village in Switzerland.

The *textbase* is normally represented as a structured set of *propositions*. A proposition refers to a state, event, or action and may have a truth value with respect to a real or imaginary world. Each proposition contains a *predicate* (e.g. main verb, adjective, connective) and one or more *arguments* (e.g. nouns, embedded propositions). Each argument has a functional role, such as agent, patient, object, or location. The textbase of propositions is presented below for the first sentence in the example excerpt.

PROP 1: lift (AGENT = X, OBJECT = peach, SOURCE = from garbage)
PROP 2: brown (OBJECT = peach)
PROP 3: mushy (OBJECT = peach)
PROP 4: place (AGENT = X, OBJECT = peach, LOCATION = on table)
PROP 5: pinken (OBJECT = peach)
PROP 6: [in order] to (PROP 4, PROP 5)
PROP 7: and (PROP 1, PROP 4)

The seven propositions have predicates that are verbs (lift, place, pinken), adjectives (brown, mushy), and connectives (in order to, and). The arguments include objects (peach, garbage, table), an unidentified agent (X), and embedded propositions (e.g. PROP 4 and PROP 5 are embedded in PROP 6). Note that the propositional textbase does not capture several features of the *surface code,* such as tense, aspect, voice, and the determinacy of the nouns. For example, the textbase does not capture the fact that the sentence syntax is in the passive voice rather than the active voice. It does not indicate that peach has an indeterminate referring expression (i.e. a peach) whereas table is determinate (i.e. the table).

Separation and Interaction of Levels

Most researchers believe that the five levels of representation exist and are sufficiently distinct for researchers to isolate. However, these beliefs have been challenged. For example, there is not a perfect consensus that there is a separate textbase. Instead, the syntactic composition and lexical items may directly serve as cues or processing instructions on how to construct the situation model, without there being any intermediate textbase of propositions (Gernsbacher 1990, Givón 1992, Perfetti & Britt 1995). Similarly, the reader of a novel may not construct an invisible, virtual writer or storyteller that communicates with the reader, unless there are explicit features in the text that signal that communication level. Instead, the reader may merely become absorbed in the microworld as a voyeur or side participant (Duchan et al 1995, Gerrig 1993). A persistent challenge has been to devise experimental tasks that isolate the separate levels of representation.

Discourse psychologists have collected sentence recognition judgments in an effort to tease apart the surface code, the textbase, and the situation model (Kintsch et al 1990, Schmalhofer & Glavanov 1986, Zwaan 1994). After reading a text, the participants are given a recognition test on the following classes of test sentences: (*a*) the original sentence verbatim, (*b*) a paraphrase of the original sentence, (*c*) a plausible inference with respect to the situation model, and (*d*) a false statement. A subtraction procedure is used to define the surface code (*a* minus *b*), the textbase (*b* minus *c*), and the situation model (*c* minus *d*). This approach to measuring the three discourse levels has produced theoretically sensible results. For example, there was a rapid decay of the surface code as a function of retention interval and a very slow decay of the situation model, with the textbase in between. When readers believe they are reading literature, the surface code is enhanced, and the situation model is reduced compared with when readers believe they are reading newspaper articles (Zwaan 1994). Therefore, readers are concerned about what is true about the world when they read newspaper articles, whereas they attend to more of the wording and stylistic devices when they read literature. Results such as these suggest that there are natural demarcations among the surface code, the textbase, and the situation model.

Kintsch and his associates have also explored individual differences among readers in an effort to segregate differences between the textbase and the situation model (Kintsch 1994, Mannes 1994, McNamara et al 1995). In McNamara et al, a technical text on the functioning of the heart was studied by students who varied in their background knowledge about the heart (low versus high knowledge). The coherence of the textbase was manipulated by having different versions of the text. Text coherence was enhanced by linking clauses with appropriate connectives and/or by inserting topic sentences, headings, and subheadings at appropriate locations. After studying the texts, the students were tested with tasks that tap the textbase (such as recall for the text) and tasks that tap the situation model (such as difficult questions that require reasoning and problem solving). The results for the low-knowledge readers were compatible with virtually all theories of comprehension. That is, a coherent textbase enhanced performance on measures of both the textbase and the situation model. For high-knowledge readers, however, the pattern of results was more interesting. A coherent textbase slightly enhanced recall but actually lowered performance on tasks that tap the situation model. This cross-over interaction supports the claim that the textbase can be separated from the situation model. Moreover, these results have intriguing implications for education and the writing of textbooks. A coherent textbook improves learning for readers with low knowledge, no matter how the learning is measured. However, readers with an adequate background knowledge may actually benefit from a text with coherence gaps and other obstacles that prevent superficial processing. A coherent text that explicitly lays out the material may give readers with comparatively high knowledge an illusory feeling that they have understood all of the explicit text and its implications, when in fact their representations are imperfect at the deeper situation model.

There have been some lively debates about the interaction of and the time course of constructing the discourse levels. One debate addresses whether the processing of the surface code (which is known to be very quick) is initially influenced by the other four levels of discourse. According to modularity theory (Fodor 1983), there is an autonomous module for processing syntax, and this module is executed much more quickly than the other discourse levels. The other discourse levels may subsequently override the initial product of the syntax module, but it is syntax that reigns supreme early in the processing stream. According to an interactive theory (Just & Carpenter 1992, MacDonald et al 1994, McClelland & Rumelhart 1986, Whitney et al 1995), the semantic and discourse context can exert its influence early in syntactic parsing. There appears to be some support for modularity theory in analyses of eye tracking data and other measures of on-line processing (Rayner et al 1992), but occasionally a highly constraining semantic or discourse context can have an early influence on parsing (MacDonald 1994, Perfetti & Britt 1995). A similar debate has been pitched at lexical processing. According to modularity theory, the different senses of a word are quickly activated autonomously. In the first sentence of the example text by Lightman (above), the word *table* has at least two senses (e.g. furniture versus organized information on a page), but only the furniture sense is compatible with the situation model. Are both senses automatically activated, or does discourse somehow alter the activation of the two senses? Early research supported modularity theory, but more recent studies have demonstrated that discourse does quickly affect word sense activation (Hess et al 1995, Morris 1994, Rayner et al 1994).

Another debate is pitched at deeper levels of discourse analysis. Sometimes there is a discrepancy between the literal meaning of a sentence (which corresponds to the textbase level) and the meaning that the writer intends to convey (which corresponds to the communication level). A discrepancy between the literal and intended meanings occurs in the case of metaphor (e.g. "All jobs are jails"), irony (e.g. "What lovely weather!" being expressed in a rainstorm), and indirect requests (e.g. "Could you pass the salt?"). It technically is not true that all jobs are jails, so the reader infers that the statement must be metaphorical and that the writer is making some illuminating point. The exclamation "What lovely weather!" directly contradicts the rainy state of the world, so the comprehender infers that the statement is ironical or sarcastic. "Could you pass the salt?" would be an insincere question if the addressee were perfectly capable of passing the salt, so the addressee infers that the speech act is intended as an indirect request for the addressee to perform an action. Early research suggested that there is a two-stage model in which (*a*) the literal meaning was constructed before the intended meaning and (*b*) the intended meaning was constructed only if the literal meaning was implausible in the discourse context (Clark & Lucy 1975). However, subsequent research revealed that intended meanings can be constructed as quickly as literal meanings and do not depend on an implausible literal meaning (Gibbs 1994, Glucksberg et al 1982). In fact,

Gibbs has directly challenged the concept of literal meaning and the claim that a literal meaning is constructed in a discourse context.

Pragmatics and Agents of Communication

It is sometimes claimed that multiple agents, dialogues, and channels of communication are implicitly constructed when texts are comprehended (Bakhtin 1981, Chafe 1994, Clark 1993, Graesser et al 1996, Moffett & McElheny 1995). The agents are capable of speaking, perceiving, knowing, wanting, acting, and experiencing emotions. *Character* agents comprise one ensemble of agents in novels and short stories. These character agents communicate with each other in stories through direct speech (e.g. June told Henry, "I'm pregnant") and indirect speech (June told Henry she was pregnant). *Pragmatic* agents participate in the communicative exchange between the narrator and narratee, or between the writer and reader. It is possible to amalgamate the character agents with the pragmatic agents. In first-person narration, the narrator agent is amalgamated with a character agent (e.g. I woke up one morning and discovered I was pregnant). In second-person narration, there may be an amalgamation of the narrator, the narratee, the reader, and a character in an effort to engage the reader (e.g. You wake up one morning and discover you are pregnant). In third-person narration, there may be a detached, omniscient, all-knowing agent that oversees the storyworld and reports it to the reader (e.g. She woke up one morning and discovered that she was pregnant). The omniscient third-person narrator is invisible to most readers who are not trained in literary studies (Duchan et al 1995, Graesser et al 1996). Discourse psychologists have recently explored how much comprehenders keep track of the knowledge and points of view of the various agents in these multiagent systems (Duchan et al 1995; Graesser et al 1996; Keysar 1994, 1996; Schober 1995, Stein & Liwag 1996). For example, Graesser et al (1996) reported that college students are quite good at keeping track of *who said what* and *who knows what* in literary short stories, except in the case of the third-person narrators. Keysar (1996) reported that readers are better able to keep track of the intentions and knowledge of the speakers than the addressees in embedded dialogues.

Pragmatic principles facilitate communication between agents when messages are composed (Clark 1993, Givón 1992, Grice 1975). Agents that both send and receive messages must mutually agree that these ground rules are operating. When the principles are violated, comprehension time increases or misunderstandings occur.

1. *Monitor common ground and mutual knowledge.* The writer should keep track of words, ideas, and entities that the reader already knows. If some-

thing new is being introduced, it should be signaled syntactically and embellished with adjectives, phrases, or examples.

2. *Use discourse cues to distinguish "given" versus "new" information.* For example, the given information is typically included in the subject noun-phrase of a clause and the first clause of multiclause sentences, whereas the new information is in the verb-phrase and additional clauses.
3. *Use discourse cues to signal important information.* For example, the first sentence in a paragraph should convey a main point and serve as an umbrella for subsequent sentences in the paragraph.
4. *Make true claims about the situation model under consideration.* In expository text, claims should be true about the world in general. In narrative fiction, the claims should be true about the fictitious microworld.
5. *The incoming sentence should be relevant to the previous discourse context.* New topics, subtopics, and episodes need to be flagged with discourse cues, such as subtitles and transitional phrases (e.g. Another point is that…, The next morning…).
6. *The order of mentioning events should correspond to the chronological order of events in the situation model.* This principle is violated in the first two sentences of the Lightman excerpt, but then the third sentence explicitly declares that time flows backwards.
7. *Statements should not contradict one another.*

These pragmatic principles are automatized and unconscious in the minds of most readers, at least those who do not work in a communication profession. Indeed, the principles are so entrenched that some readers never regard it as an option that a writer would express ideas that are false, contradictory, or irrelevant; they faithfully accept pretty much whatever the writer expresses. Beck et al (1996) has implemented a year-long program in the classroom (called Questioning the Author) that trains students to question the rationale and evidence behind particular statements expressed by authors. The students imagine a real flesh-and-blood writer and ask questions such as "What is the author trying to say?" and "What did the author mean by that?" This inquisitive strategy produces a more elaborate representation at the communication and situation model levels. Without this mindset, most readers assume that the writer is faithfully following the pragmatic principles.

Studies have shown that it is difficult for readers to detect anomalous statements (i.e. those that are false, irrelevant, or contradictory) in expository texts on unfamiliar topics (Graesser & McMahen 1993, Otero & Kintsch 1992). Readers miss these anomalies and assume that they understand the text in the absence of such problematic textual features (Glenberg & Epstein 1987). It apparently takes a large amount of background knowledge for a reader to detect anomalous information. However, anomalies are well remembered when they are detected (Albrecht & O'Brien 1993, Davidson 1994, Graesser et al 1979).

PSYCHOLOGICAL MECHANISMS IN THEORIES OF COMPREHENSION

Psychological models of discourse processing have specified in rich detail how the multilevel meaning representations are built during comprehension. Discourse psychologists have consistently recognized the need to ground these complex models in general theories of cognition. This section briefly enumerates the key cognitive components, processes, and factors that have frequently been adopted by discourse psychologists.

Cognitive Components

1. *Knowledge structures.* The knowledge in texts and in packages of world knowledge are represented as a network of *nodes* (i.e. concepts, referents, propositions) that are interconnected by relational *arcs* (Graesser & Clark 1985, van Dijk & Kintsch 1983). One source of comprehension difficulty lies in the amount of background knowledge of the reader.
2. *Spreading activation of nodes in knowledge networks.* When a node in a network is activated, activation spreads to neighboring nodes, then neighbors of neighbors, and so on. The activation level of a node decreases as a function of the number of arcs between the originally activated node and another node in the network (Anderson 1983).
3. *Memory stores.* There are three memory stores in most discourse models: short-term memory (STM), working memory (WM), and long-term memory (LTM). As a gross approximation, STM holds the most recent clause being comprehended and WM holds about two sentences. Important information is actively recycled in WM (Fletcher & Bloom 1988, Kintsch & van Dijk 1978, Trabasso & Magliano 1996).
4. *Discourse focus.* Consciousness and focal attention is concentrated on one or two nodes in the discourse representation (Chafe 1994, Givón 1992, Grosz & Sidner 1986, Sanford & Garrod 1981). In the situation model for a narrative text, the discourse focus is analogous to a mental camera that zooms in on particular characters, objects, actions, events, and spatial regions (Bower 1989).
5. *Resonance.* The content (i.e. cues, features, nodes) that resides in the discourse focus, STM, and WM may match highly with content that was presented earlier in the text or with other content in LTM. If so, there is resonance with the content in LTM, and the information in LTM gets activated (Albrecht & O'Brien 1993, McKoon & Ratcliff 1992, McKoon et al 1996, Myers et al 1994, O'Brien et al 1995). The content of WM on p.

124 in a novel could quickly activate the content on p. 14 via resonance, without activating any of the content between pp. 15 and 123.

6. *Activation, inhibition, and suppression of nodes.* As sentences are comprehended, nodes in the discourse structure and LTM are activated, strengthened, inhibited, and suppressed (Gernsbacher 1990, Kintsch 1988). The primary goal of some discourse models is to explain the fluctuations in activation values of discourse nodes during the dynamic processes of comprehension.
7. *Convergence and constraint satisfaction.* Discourse nodes receive more strength of encoding to the extent that they are activated by several information sources and to the extent that they mesh with the constraints of other information sources (Graesser & Clark 1985, Kintsch 1988, MacDonald et al 1994).
8. *Repetition and automaticity.* Repetition increases the speed of accessing a knowledge structure and the nodes within the structure. Thus, familiar words are processed faster than unfamiliar words. The nodes in an automatized package of world knowledge are holistically accessed and used at little cost to the resources in WM.
9. *Explanations.* Memory for information is enhanced when the reader constructs causal explanations of why events in the situation model occur and why the writer expresses information (Chi et al 1994, Graesser et al 1994, Pressley et al 1988, Trabasso & Magliano 1996, Zwaan & Brown 1996). Readers actively seek these explanations during reading (Graesser at al 1994).
10. *Reader goals.* The goals of the reader influence text comprehension and memory (Graesser et al 1994, Lorch et al 1995, Zwaan et al 1995b). Reading a novel for enjoyment is rather different from reading it to take a university exam.

Cognitive Models and Architectures

Discourse psychologists have developed some sophisticated quantitative and computational models of text comprehension (Britton & Graesser 1996, Golden & Rumelhart 1993, Just & Carpenter 1992, Kintsch 1988, St. John 1992). These models specify the representations, processes, and interactive mechanisms in sufficient detail to simulate complex patterns of comprehension data. The most fine-grained models simulate the creation, activation, inhibition, and suppression of each node in the discourse representation, as text is dynamically comprehended, word-by-word or clause-by-clause. Consider the activation strength of a word node at a particular point in a text. That strength value should predict latencies in such tasks as word naming, word recognition, and lexical decision. Word reading times and the gaze durations on words should correlate with the number of processing cycles that the model takes to interpret the word. Memory for text propositions should correlate with the cumulative strength of activation for the proposition across the entire text. In fact, these complex models have had some success in simulating such data.

Two cognitive models have dominated most of the efforts in simulating discourse data: the CAPS/READER model developed by Just & Carpenter (1992) and the construction-integration model developed by Kintsch (1988). Goldman et al (1996) developed a hybrid model that combines these two models. The CAPS/READER model adopts a production system architecture (Anderson 1983) for creating, updating, and removing nodes in WM and LTM. The production system contains a set of production rules with an "IF<condition C>,THEN<action A>" format; if the content of WM matches condition C, then the cognitive or physical action A is performed. Condition C may consist of an arbitrarily complex set of substates. There also is a threshold criterion for a condition, such that the condition is satisfied if the aggregate activation value of all its substates meets the threshold. Therefore, the production rules in CAPS are hardly brittle, discrete, and simple. The set of production rules are evaluated in parallel in each cycle of processing. Those rules that meet the threshold of activation end up executing various actions, such as scanning explicit input, modifying activation values of nodes in WM, changing the load on WM, strengthening nodes in LTM, and producing output.

Kintsch's (1988) construction-integration model adopts a connectionist (neural network) architecture of cognition (McClelland & Rumelhart 1986). During the construction phase, an incoming clause very quickly adds to WM a set of nodes that corresponds to words, referents, textbase propositions, and the situation model. These new nodes are combined with the previous content of WM. Suppose, for illustration, that WM has a total of N nodes when the incoming clause is comprehended. In the spirit of connectionism, there is a set of weights $[N \times (N - 1)]$ that designates how much each node (M) would activate or inhibit each of the other nodes if node M were in fact activated. There is a separate weight space for the surface code, the textbase, and the situation model, along with weights that connect nodes between levels. Whereas the construction phase is accomplished quickly and automatically, the integration phase is more time consuming and spans several processing cycles. The integration phase begins as soon as one or more of the N nodes becomes activated. An activated node spreads activation or inhibition to the other nodes according to the weights in the weight space. The spreading activation continues over several processing cycles until the connectionist network settles on a stable set of activation values for the entire set of discourse nodes. The activation strength of a particular node is modified dynamically over time and over sentences in the text.

REFERRING EXPRESSIONS

Referring expressions are nouns, pronouns, and noun-phrases that refer to an entity or proposition in the textbase, situation model, or world. An *anaphoric* referring expression refers to a node that was mentioned previously in the text, whereas *cataphoric* expressions refer to future text nodes, and *deictic* expressions point to the world. Anaphoric expressions have received the most attention by discourse psychologists (Garrod et al 1994, Gernsbacher 1990, Greene et al 1992, Marslen-Wilson et al 1993, McKoon et al 1996, Sanford & Garrod 1981), but recently some serious attention has turned to cataphoric expressions (Gernsbacher & Jescheniak 1995) and deictic expressions (Duchan et al 1995, Mauner et al 1995). A concrete example of anaphora is when a reader encounters the pronoun *he* in the middle of a novel. Who does *he* refer to? The process of resolving the referent for *he* consults all levels of discourse.

The selection of referring expressions normally conforms to a small set of simple rules (Chafe 1994, Gernsbacher 1990, Givón 1992, Sanford & Garrod 1981). When a new entity is first introduced in a text, the referring expression contains (*a*) the indefinite determiner *a* or *an,* (*b*) a richly specified noun, and (*c*) a descriptive set of adjectives and prepositional phrases (e.g. *A big bad wolf with brown fur*). A pronoun is appropriate when the entity has already been mentioned in the text and is also in the discourse focus. When the entity has already been introduced, but is not in the discourse focus, an appropriate referring expression contains a definite determiner (e.g. *the, that, this*) and the noun (*the wolf*); the noun is sometimes at a more abstract level of specification (*the animal* instead of *the wolf*). If two discourse entities are similar, the referring expression needs to be sufficiently rich to distinguish them. Thus, fewer words and less specificity are needed to the extent that the entity is in the reader's working memory, and fewer yet when the entity is in the reader's focal attention. More explicit cues are needed in referring expressions when information needs to be created from scratch, to be dredged from LTM, or to distinguish entities. When these simple rules are violated, it takes longer to compute the referent of a referring expression, and comprehension may break down (Gernsbacher 1990, Gordon & Chan 1995).

Gernsbacher's (1990) *structure building framework* accounts for much of the experimental data on the processing of anaphoric references. Three subprocesses occur when discourse representations are constructed on-line. Readers first "lay a foundation" by constructing memory nodes when a new topic is introduced. The foundation gets elaborated by "mapping on information" from subsequent text that is relevant to the topic. However, the incoming text may not be relevant, so the reader shifts attention to "initiate a new substructure" or to lay an entirely new foundation. The first two subprocesses explain why the discourse focus is on the first character in sentences such as *Tina beat Lisa in the state tennis match. Tina* is the discourse focus, so *Tina* should have a higher level of activation and be accessed faster than *Lisa;* if the next word were *she,* the reader would bind the pronoun to *Tina* rather than *Lisa.* Gernsbacher's experiments have supported this prediction, dubbed the "advantage of first mention." Her experiments also support a phenomenon called "the advantage of clause recency," which predicts that information from the most recent clause in a sentence is more accessible than information from an earlier clause. The word *oil* is more accessible immediately after comprehending the sentence *Now that artists are working fewer hours,* oil *prints are rare* than the sentence *Now that artists are working in* oil, *prints are rare.* Comprehenders represent each clause in these two-clause sentences in its own mental substructure. When a new clause arrives, the old substructure from clause 1 is abandoned and attention shifts to the new substructure associated with clause 2.

Our discussion of anaphora presents a simple sketch of the processing and appropriate composition of the referring expressions. However, there are times when matters are far more complex (Clark 1993, Garrod et al 1994, Greene et al 1992, Marslen-Wilson et al 1993, McKoon et al 1996). In some cases, for example, readers do not bother fetching a referent for an anaphor because the referent is vague, indeterminate, difficult to compute, or nonexistent (such as the pronoun *it* in technical documents).

CONNECTING STATEMENTS IN DISCOURSE

The explicit statements in a text need to be connected conceptually if the text is to be regarded as coherent. Local coherence is achieved if the reader can connect the incoming statement to information in the previous sentence or WM. Global coherence is achieved if the incoming statement can be connected to a text macrostructure or to information much earlier in the text that no longer resides in WM. Readers normally attempt to achieve coherence at both the local and global levels (Albrecht & O'Brien 1993, Graesser et al 1994, Hakala & O'Brien 1995, Hess et al 1995, Long et al 1996, Myers et al 1994, O'Brien & Albrecht 1992, Sanford & Garrod 1981, Singer et al 1994, Trabasso & Magliano 1996). Suppose, for example, that a character is described as a vegetarian early in the text and that much later the text states that the character ate a hamburger. The contradiction could only be detected if the reader were attempting to achieve global coherence. Reading times have been found to increase for such contradictory statements under conditions in which the statement *X is a vegetarian* has no local connections to *X ate a hamburger* (Albrecht & O'Brien 1993, Hakala & O'Brien 1995, Myers et al 1994). This increase in reading time would not occur if text comprehension was driven entirely by local connections. However, it is important to acknowledge that attempts at achieving global coherence will diminish and local coherence will dominate if the text is incoherent, if the reader is unmotivated, or if the reader has a low WM span (Graesser et al 1994, Hess et al 1995, Whitney et al 1991). Comprehension suffers substantially when neither local nor global coherence can be achieved, as in the case of the first two sentences of the Lightman excerpt. As a general underlying principle, readers attempt to achieve the most global level of understanding that can be achieved given the text composition, the reader's knowledge base, and the reading goals.

Several dimensions of conceptual continuity link an incoming statement to the previous discourse context (Chafe 1994, Graesser & Clark 1985, Grimes 1975, Halliday & Hasan 1976, Mann & Thompson 1986, Sanders et al 1992). The reading time for a sentence increases when there are breaks in continuity on one or more of these dimensions. One dimension of continuity is *argument overlap* (Kintsch & van Dijk 1978). Continuity is achieved if there is a noun-phrase argument in the incoming statement that overlaps an argument within any textbase proposition in WM. In the Lightman example, the pronoun *it* in sentence 2 refers to the argument *peach* in sentence 1; therefore the two sentences are connected by argument overlap. Discourse psychologists have sometimes regarded argument overlap as the primary dimension for establishing text coherence (Kintsch & van Dijk 1978, McKoon & Ratcliff 1992). The reading time for a sentence in text does normally increase if it fails to share an argument with any textbase proposition in WM (Kintsch & van Dijk 1978). However, argument overlap is sometimes not a major dimension if the text is in the narrative genre or is fortified by rich background knowledge (Zwaan et al 1995a,b).

Zwaan proposed an *event indexing model* to account for the reader's construction of a multithreaded situation model while reading simple stories and literary short stories (Zwaan et al 1995a,b). According to this model, the reader monitors five conceptual dimensions during reading: the protagonist, temporality, spatiality, causality, and intentionality (i.e. character goals). A break in continuity may occur on any of these dimensions when an incoming statement is read.

1. *Spatial discontinuity.* The incoming event occurs in a spatial setting that is different from the prior event. Sometimes this is manifested by a transitional phrase (e.g. *Back at the ranch,...*).
2. *Temporal discontinuity.* The incoming event occurs much later in time (e.g. *The next day...*) or is part of a flashback.
3. *Causal discontinuity.* The incoming event is not causally related to the prior text (as in the Lightman example).
4. *Intentional discontinuity.* The incoming event is embedded in a character's plan that is different from the local discourse context.

5. *Protagonist discontinuity.* The incoming event has a character that is different from the characters in the previous event.

An incoming event in the story may have discontinuities on more than one of these five dimensions. Zwaan et al (1995a) reported that the reading time for an explicit event in a literary story increased as a function of the number of dimensions with discontinuities and that each dimension had its own unique impact on reading time. The event indexing model is also compatible with a large body of research that has examined each of these dimensions one at a time. That is, researchers have confirmed that readers construct a situation model that monitors spatiality (Glenberg et al 1987, Haenggi et al 1995, Morrow et al 1987, O'Brien & Albrecht 1992, Rinck et al 1996), temporality (Bestgen & Vonk 1995, Ohtsuka & Brewer 1992, Zwaan 1996), causality (Fletcher & Bloom 1988, Keenan et al 1984, Klin & Myers 1993, Magliano et al 1993, Millis & Graesser 1994, Singer et al 1992, Trabasso & van den Broek 1985, Trabasso & Magliano 1996, van den Broek & Lorch 1993), intentionality (Dopkins 1996, Long et al 1992, Suh & Trabasso 1993), and properties of the protagonist (Albrecht & O'Brien 1993, Hakala & O'Brien 1995, Myers et al 1994).

The surface code delivers critical cues to the reader, who is actively monitoring the dimensions of conceptual continuity. As suggested above, transitional phrases are quite important signals for spatial and temporal discontinuity (e.g. *Back at the ranch,... The next morning.*). Verb tense and aspect are also important cues for situating events on a chronological time line. One very important class of cues for the dimensions of temporality, causality, and intentionality is that of connectives, such as *before, after, during, and, then, because, in order to,* and *so that.* Discourse researchers have investigated reading times and recall for successive text statements that are explicitly linked by causal connectives (such as *because*) and temporal connectives (such as *and*), versus no connective (Caron et al 1988, Deaton & Gernsbacher 1996, Millis et al 1993, Millis & Just 1994, Murray 1995). Compared with temporal connectives and no connective, the causal connectives facilitate reading time and later recall for the statements. However, these effects apparently do not always occur. Memory is not facilitated if the events linked by a causal connective already have a very strong causal relationship or no causal relationship. Thus, a writer cannot simply slap in a causal connective and expect it to work its magic. The causal connective needs to mesh with the pragmatic levels of the discourse context in an incisive way. For example, according to Ford's (1994) analysis of causal connectives in speech and writing, the connective *because* (in an expression *X because Y*) is appropriate when (*a*) event *X* violates a norm or deviates from shared expectations and (*b*) *Y* explains the anomaly (e.g. *The boss was absent because he was accused of sexism*).

Discourse psychologists have only a rudimentary understanding of how the various strands of the situation model are constructed during comprehension. Additional research needs to examine interactions among temporality, spatiality, causality, intentionality, and the protagonists. There needs to be a more detailed understanding of how these strands of conceptual continuity are furnished by the surface code, assumptions about communication, and text genre. Hopefully, future researchers will explore these conceptual jungles with the same care and detail with which they have investigated the lexicon, syntax, and semantics during the past three decades.

KNOWLEDGE-BASED INFERENCES

Discourse psychologists have developed and tested models that predict what inferences are generated on-line during comprehension (Graesser & Bower 1990, Graesser et al 1994, McKoon & Ratcliff 1992). When an adult reads a novel, for example, the following classes of knowledge-based inferences are potentially generated: The goals and plans that motivate characters' actions, character traits, characters' knowledge and beliefs, character emotions, causes of events, the consequences of events and actions, properties of objects, spatial contexts, spatial relationships among entities, the global theme or point of the text, the referents of nouns and pronouns, the attitudes of the writer, and the appropriate emotional reaction of the reader. It is conceivable that readers generate all these inferences on-line. In essence, the mind would construct a high-resolution mental videotape of the situation model, along with details about the mental states of characters and the communicative exchange between the writer and reader. However, discourse psychologists are convinced that only a subset of these inferences are generated on-line. Why? Because the generation of all these inferences would create a computational explosion problem, because WM has limited resources, and because reading is accomplished too quickly for some time-consuming inferences to be generated. Which of these classes of inferences are constructed on-line? That is the central question.

Suppose an adult read a simple fairy tale that contained two successive actions in the middle of the text: "The dragon was dragging off the girl. A hero came and fought the dragon." There are five classes of inferences that might be encoded when the second sentence is read:

1. *Superordinate goal (motive).* The hero wanted to rescue the girl.
2. *Subordinate goal or action.* The hero threw a spear.
3. *Causal antecedent.* The girl was frightened.
4. *Causal consequence.* The hero married the girl.
5. *Static property.* The dragon has scales.

Experiments can be designed to assess which of these inferences are encoded. For example, after reading the second sentence, the reader would quickly complete a word-naming task (or alternatively a lexical decision task) and receive a test word extracted from one of these inferences (i.e. rescue, throw, fright, marry, and scales). The same words would also be tested in an unrelated context to obtain a measure of inference encoding from the word-naming latencies: [latency (unrelated context)—latency (inference context)]. The inference encoding score should be above zero to the extent that the inference is generated on-line. In a properly designed study, the words in these inference classes would be equilibrated on several variables, such as number of letters, number of syllables, word frequency, syntactic class, free association norms with words in the text, and the proportion of readers in a normative group who articulate the inference in a think aloud task (Graesser et al 1994, Kintsch 1988, Long et al 1992, Magliano et al 1993, Millis & Graesser 1994). All things being equal, which classes of inference should have the strongest encoding during comprehension?

Existing models make quite different predictions about which of the five classes of inferences are encoded on-line. At one extreme, there is a *promiscuous inference generation* position that predicts that all five classes are encoded. This is a strawperson position, however, for reasons discussed above. At the other extreme, there is a textbase position that predicts that none of the inferences are encoded (Kintsch & van Dijk 1978). Local text coherence could be established at the textbase level by virtue of argument overlap (i.e. *dragon* appears in both sentences) so there would be no need to construct a situation model. According to McKoon & Ratcliff's (1992) *minimalist hypothesis,* the causal antecedents would be the only class of inferences among the five that might be encoded with any consistency. The other four classes are elaborative inferences that are encoded only if the reader has a special comprehension goal that is tuned to such levels. The minimalist hypothesis assumes that the reader generates only those inferences that are needed to establish local text coherence (i.e. either causal antecedents or none at all) and that are readily available in memory (i.e. in WM or highly active in LTM).

Graesser et al (1994) has argued that the available research on inference generation supports a *constructionist theory* rather than the above three positions (as well as others that will not be addressed here). The constructionist theory assumes that readers encode three sets of inferences, namely (*a*) inferences that address the readers' comprehension goals, (*b*) inferences that explain *why* events, actions, and states occur, and (*c*) inferences that establish coherence in the situation model at local and global levels. From the standpoint of the five classes of inferences in the above example, it is the explanation assumption that offers distinctive predictions. The explanation-based inferences include superordinate goals and causal antecedents, but not subordinate goals/actions, causal consequences, and static properties. It is the superordinate goals and the causal antecedents that answer *why* an action or event occurs (Graesser et al 1991). For example, when asked "Why did the hero fight the dragon?" a reasonable answer would include the superordinate goal (in order to rescue the girl) and the causal antecedent (because the girl was frightened), but not the other three classes (i.e. in order to throw the spears, in order to marry the girl, because the dragon has scales). The subordinate goals/actions and static properties are minor ornaments that merely embellish the core plot and explanations of the plot. Regarding the causal consequences, it is too difficult for readers to forecast multiple hypothetical plots with new plans of characters and long event chains into the future. Most of the forecasts that readers generate to "What happens next?" questions end up being wrong (Graesser & Clark 1985), so the readers would be uselessly spinning their wheels if they did generate many causal consequences. According to the constructionist model, the only causal consequences that are generated on-line are the achieved superordinate goals of character actions (i.e. the hero in fact did rescue the girl), emotional reactions of characters to actions and events, and consequences that are highly activated and constrained by prior context (see Keefe & McDaniel 1993, van den Broek 1990). Analyses of think aloud protocols in fact confirm that most readers (and good comprehenders in particular) generate more explanation-based inferences than predictions and associative elaborations in simple stories (Trabasso & Magliano 1996), in literary short stories (Zwaan & Brown 1996), and in technical expository texts (Chi et al 1994). Experiments that have collected word-naming and lexical decision latencies confirm the constructionist theory's predictions that readers generate superordinate goals much more than subordinate goals/actions (Long et al 1992), and causal antecedents much more than causal consequences (Magliano et al 1993, Millis & Graesser 1994, Potts et al 1988).

We suspect that each of the above models is correct in certain conditions. The textbase position and minimalist hypotheses are probably correct when the reader is very quickly reading the text, when the text lacks global coherence, and when the reader has very little background knowledge. The constructionist theory is on the mark when the reader is attempting to comprehend the text for enjoyment or mastery at a more leisurely pace, when the text has global coherence, and when the reader has some background knowledge. The promiscuous inference generation model may even be valid when a literary scholar is savoring a good short story at a very slow cruise.

There are many gaps in our understanding of the generation of knowledge-based inferences. We need to analyze the precise time course of constructing, maintaining, and modifying particular classes of inferences (Keefe &

McDaniel 1993, Kintsch 1988, Magliano et al 1993). Some inferences may slowly emerge as text is received rather than discretely popping in when a particular statement is comprehended. Very little research has examined global inferences, such as themes, points, morals, and attitudes of the writer (Long et al 1996, Seifert et al 1986). Global inferences have tentacles to many elements in the text and span large stretches of text. These global inferences are more difficult to study than inference classes that discretely pop in at a particular locus in the text. There also needs to be much more work on how inference generation is influenced by readers who differ in comprehension skill, working memory span, and other psychological attributes (Dixon et al 1993, Haenggi et al 1995, Perfetti et al 1996, Singer & Ritchot 1996, Whitney et al 1991).

SUMMARY AND CONCLUSIONS

Discourse psychologists have developed sophisticated models of text comprehension during the short 25-year history of the field. These models have specified the cognitive representations and processes that participate in the construction of meaning. Five levels of representation are important in the construction of these meaning representations: the surface code, the propositional textbase, the referential situation model, the communication between writer and reader, and the text genre. Discourse psychologists have explained the processing of these five levels by grounding the research in general cognitive theories. For example, discourse processing theories have postulated the existence of multiple memory stores (STM, WM, LTM), the process of spreading activation in knowledge networks, production systems with if-then rules, connectionist neural networks, and constraint satisfaction. However, the models developed by discourse psychologists furnish distinctive predictions that cannot simply be reduced to other areas of psychology.

This chapter has examined three phenomena that have been extensively investigated by discourse psychologists: The processing of referring expressions, the connection of statements in text, and the encoding of knowledge-based inferences. Readers execute these processes in an effort to achieve coherence at local and global levels and to explain why information is mentioned in the text. Discourse psychologists have tested models of these phenomena by collecting eye-tracking data, self-paced reading times, word-naming latencies on test words that are interspersed in text, recall and recognition memory measures, think aloud protocols, and data from dozens of other experimental tasks. There have been some attempts to assess differences among readers concerning background knowledge about the text topics, working memory span, and general comprehension skill. Some researchers have tested their models on naturalistic texts, whereas others have focused on experimenter-generated textoids that impose some control over particular variables. In some cases, complex patterns of data have been simulated by sophisticated mathematical and computational models.

The empirical and theoretical progress in discourse processing has had some straightforward applications for improving reading, education, text design, and social interaction. For example, Britton & Gulgoz (1991) used Kintsch & van Dijk's 1978 model to guide the revision of technical expository texts. The original texts were naturalistic samples of texts that periodically had problematic referring expressions and coherence gaps. The Kintsch & van Dijk model identified points in the text where these problems occurred. The texts were revised by clarifying referents of referring expressions (with definitions and/or examples) and by making explicit some important connections between different parts of the text and some critical bridging inferences in the original text. These theory-based revisions dramatically improved memory for the texts when adults were given a delayed-recall test. Moreover, these theory-guided revisions improved memory much more than revisions by writers for *Time* magazine. It was theory that prevailed in improving the memorability of the texts. This is a heart-warming confirmation of one of our favorite quotes from Kurt Lewin (1951, p. 169): "There is nothing so practical as a good theory."

Literature Cited

Albrecht JE, O'Brien EJ. 1993. Updating a mental model: maintaining both local and global coherence. *J. Exp. Psychol. Learn. Mem. Cogn.* 19:1061–70

Anderson JR. 1983. *The Architecture of Cognition.* Cambridge, MA: Harvard Univ. Press

Bakhtin MM. 1981. *The Dialogic Imagination.* Ed./Transl. C Emerson, M Holquist. Texas: Texas Univ. Press

Beck IL, McKeown MG, Worthy J, Sandora CA, Kucan L. 1996. Questioning the author: a year-long classroom implementation to engage students with text. *Elem. Sch. J.* In press

Bestgen Y, Vonk W. 1995. The role of temporal segmentation markers in discourse processing. *Discourse Process.* 19:385–406

Biber D. 1988. *Variation Across Speech and Writing.* Cambridge: Cambridge Univ. Press

Bower GH. 1989. Mental models in text understanding. In *Cognition in Individual and Social Contexts,* ed. AF Bennett, KM McConkey, pp. 129–44. Amsterdam: Elsevier

Britton BK, Graesser AC, eds. 1996. *Models of Understanding Text.* Mahwah, NJ: Erlbaum

Britton BK, Gulgoz S. 1991. Using Kintsch's computational model to improve instructional text: effects of repairing inference calls on recall and cognitive structures. *J. Educ. Psychol.* 83:329–45

Caron J, Micko HC, Thuring M. 1988. Conjunctions and recall of composite sentences. *J. Mem. Lang.* 27:309–23

Chafe W. 1994. *Discourse, Consciousness, and Time.* Chicago: Univ. Chicago Press

Chi MTH, de Leeuw N, Chiu M, LaVancher C. 1994. Eliciting self-explanations improves understanding. *Cogn. Sci.* 18:439–77

Clark HH. 1993. *Arenas of Language Use.* Chicago: Univ. Chicago Press

Clark HH, Lucy P. 1975. Understanding what is meant from what is said: a study in conversationally conveyed requests. *J. Verbal Learn. Verbal Behav.* 14:56–72

Davidson D. 1994. Recognition and recall of irrelevant and interruptive atypical actions in script-based stories. *J. Mem. Lang.* 33:757–75

Deaton JA, Gernsbacher MA. 1996. Causal conjunctions and implicit causality cue

mapping in sentence comprehension. *J. Mem. Lang.* In press
Dixon P, Bortolussi M, Twilley LC, Leung A. 1993. Literary processing and interpretation: towards empirical foundations. *Poetics* 22:5–34
Dopkins S. 1996. Representation of superordinate goal inferences in memory. *Discourse Process.* 21:85–104
Duchan JF, Bruder GA, Hewitt LE, eds. 1995. *Deixis in Narrative: A Cognitive Science Perspective.* Hillsdale, NJ: Erlbaum
Ericsson KA, Simon HA. 1993. *Protocol Analysis: Verbal Reports as Data.* Cambridge, MA: MIT Press. 2nd ed.
Fletcher CR, Bloom CP. 1988. Causal reasoning in the comprehension of simple narrative texts. *J. Mem. Lang.* 19:70–80
Fodor JD. 1983. *Modularity of Mind.* Cambridge, MA: MIT Press
Ford CE. 1994. Dialogic aspects of talk and writing: *because* on the interactive-edited continuum. *Text* 14:531–54
Garrod S, Freudenthal D, Boyle E. 1994. The role of different types of anaphor in the on-line resolution of sentences in a discourse. *J. Mem. Lang.* 33:39–68
Gernsbacher MA. 1990. *Language Comprehension as Structure Building.* Hillsdale, NJ: Erlbaum
Gernsbacher MA, ed. 1994. *Handbook of Psycholinguistics.* New York: Academic
Gernsbacher MA, Jescheniak JD. 1995. Cataphoric devices in spoken discourse. *Cogn. Psychol.* 29:24–58
Gerrig RJ. 1993. *Experiencing Narrative Worlds.* New Haven, CT: Yale Univ. Press
Gibbs RW. 1994. *The Poetics of Mind.* Cambridge: Cambridge Univ. Press
Givón T. 1992. The grammar of referential coherence as mental processing instructions. *Linguistics* 30:5–55
Glenberg AM, Epstein W. 1987. Inexpert calibration of comprehension. *Mem. Cogn.* 15: 84–93
Glenberg AM, Meyer M, Lindem K. 1987. Mental models contribute to foregrounding during text comprehension. *J. Mem. Lang.* 26:69–83
Glucksberg S, Gildea P, Bookin HB. 1982. On understanding nonliteral speech. Can people ignore metaphor? *J. Verbal Learn. Verbal Behav.* 21:85–98
Golden RM, Rumelhart DE. 1993. A parallel distributed processing model of story comprehension and recall. *Discourse Process.* 16:203–37
Goldman SR, Varma S, Cote N. 1996. Extending capacity-constrained construction integration: toward "smarter" and flexible models of text comprehension. See Britton & Graesser 1996, pp. 73–114
Gordon PC, Chan D. 1995. Pronouns, passives, and discourse coherence. *J. Mem. Lang.* 34:216–31
Graesser AC, Bower GH, eds. 1990. *The Psychology of Learning and Motivation: Inferences and Text Comprehension.* San Diego, CA: Academic
Graesser AC, Bowers CA, Bayen UJ, Hu X. 1996. Who said what? Who knows what? Tracking speakers and knowledge in narrative. In *Narrative Perspective: Cognition and Emotion,* ed. W van Peer, E Andriga, D Schram, E Tan. In press
Graesser AC, Clark LF. 1985. *Structures and Procedures of Implicit Knowledge.* Norwood, NJ: Ablex
Graesser AC, Gordon SE, Sawyer JD. 1979. Memory for typical and atypical actions in scripted activities: test of a script + tag hypothesis. *J. Verbal Learn. Verbal Behav.* 18:319–32
Graesser AC, Lang KL, Roberts RM. 1991. Question answering in the context of stories. *J. Exp. Psychol. Gen.* 120:254–77
Graesser AC, McMahen CL. 1993. Anomalous information triggers questions when adults solve problems and comprehend stories. *J. Educ. Psychol.* 85:136–51
Graesser AC, Singer M, Trabasso T. 1994. Constructing inferences during narrative text comprehension. *Psychol. Rev.* 101: 371–95
Greene SB, McKoon G, Ratcliff R. 1992. Pronoun resolution and discourse models. *J. Exp. Psychol. Learn. Mem. Cogn.* 18: 266–83
Grice HP. 1975. Logic and conversation. In *Syntax and Semantics: Speech Acts,* ed. P Cole, JL Morgan, pp. 3:41–58. San Diego, CA: Academic
Grimes J. 1975. *The Thread of Discourse.* The Hague: Mouton
Grosz BJ, Sidner CL. 1986. Attention, intentions, and the structure of discourse. *Comput. Linguist.* 12:175–204
Haberlandt K. 1994. Methods in reading research. See Gernsbacher 1994, pp. 1–31
Haberlandt K, Graesser AC. 1985. Component processes in text comprehension and some of their interactions. *J. Exp. Psychol. Gen.* 114:357–74
Haenggi D, Kintsch W, Gernsbacher MA. 1995. Spatial situation models and text comprehension. *Discourse Process.* 19: 173–99
Hakala CM, O'Brien EJ. 1995. Strategies for resolving coherence breaks in reading. *Discourse Process.* 20:167–86
Halliday MAK, Hasan R. 1976. *Cohesion in English.* London: Longmans
Hess DJ, Foss DJ, Carroll P. 1995. Effects of global and local context on lexical process-

ing during language comprehension. *J. Exp. Psychol. Gen.* 124:62–82
Just MA, Carpenter PA. 1992. A capacity theory of comprehension: individual differences in working memory. *Psychol. Rev.* 99:122–49
Keefe DE, McDaniel M. 1993. The time course and durability of predictive inferences. *J. Mem. Lang.* 32:446–63
Keenan JM, Baillet SD, Brown P. 1984. The effects of causal cohesion on comprehension and memory. *J. Verbal Learn. Verbal Behav.* 23:115–26
Keysar B. 1994. The illusory transparency of intention: linguistic perspective taking in text. *Cogn. Psychol.* 26:165–208
Keysar B. 1996. Language users as problem solvers. Just what ambiguity problem do they solve? In *Social and Cognitive Psychological Approaches to Interpersonal Communication,* ed. SR Fussell, RJ Kreuz. Mahwah, NJ: Erlbaum. In press
Kintsch W. 1988. The role of knowledge in discourse comprehension: a constructive-integration model. *Psychol. Rev.* 95:163–82
Kintsch W. 1994. Text comprehension, memory, and learning. *Am. Psychol.* 49:294–303
Kintsch W, van Dijk TA. 1978. Toward a model of text comprehension and production. *Psychol. Rev.* 85:363–94
Kintsch W, Welsch D, Schmalhofer F, Zimny S. 1990. Sentence memory: a theoretical analysis. *J. Mem. Lang.* 29:133–59
Klin CM, Myers JL. 1993. Reinstatement of causal information during reading. *J. Exp. Psychol. Learn. Mem. Cogn.* 19:554–60
Kreuz RJ, MacNealy MS. 1996. *Empirical Approaches to Literature and Aesthetics.* Norwood, NJ: Ablex
Levelt WJM. 1989. *Speaking: From Attention to Articulation.* Cambridge, MA: MIT Press
Lewin K. 1951. *Field Theory in Social Science.* New York: Harper & Row
Lightman A. 1993. *Einstein's Dreams.* New York: Warner
Long DL, Golding JM, Graesser AC. 1992. The generation of goal-related inferences during narrative comprehension. *J. Mem. Lang.* 5:634–47
Long DL, Oppy BJ, Seely MR. 1996. Individual differences in sentence- and text-level representations. *J. Mem. Lang.* In press
Lorch RF, Klusewitz MA, Lorch EP. 1995. Distinctions among reading situations. See Lorch & O'Brien 1995, pp. 375–98
Lorch RF, O'Brien JD, eds. 1995. *Sources of Coherence in Reading.* Mahwah, NJ: Erlbaum
MacDonald MC, Pearlmutter NJ, Seidenberg MS. 1994. The lexical nature of syntactic ambiguity resolution. *Psychol. Rev.* 101: 676–703
Magliano JP, Baggett WB, Johnson BK, Graesser AC. 1993. The time course of generating causal antecedent and causal consequence inferences. *Discourse Process.* 16:35–53
Magliano JP, Graesser AC. 1991. A three-pronged method for studying inference generation in literary text. *Poetics* 20:193–232
Mann WC, Thompson SA. 1986. Relational propositions in discourse. *Discourse Process.* 9:57–90
Mannes S. 1994. Strategic processing of text. *J. Educ. Psychol.* 86:577–88
Marslen-Wilson WD, Tyler LK, Koster C. 1993. Integrative processes in utterance resolution. *J. Mem. Lang.* 32:647–66
Mauner G, Tanenhaus MK, Carlson GN. 1995. Implicit arguments in sentence processing. *J. Mem. Lang.* 34:357–82
McClelland JL, Rumelhart DE, eds. 1986. *Parallel Distributed Processing: Explorations in the Microstructure of Cognition.* Cambridge, MA: MIT Press
McKoon G, Gerrig RJ, Greene SB. 1996. Pronoun resolution without pronouns: some consequences of memory-based text processing. *J. Exp. Psychol. Learn. Mem. Cogn.* In press
McKoon G, Ratcliff R. 1992. Inference during reading. *Psychol. Rev.* 99:440–66
McNamara DS, Kintsch E, Songer NB, Kintsch W. 1995. Text coherence, background knowledge and levels of understanding in learning from text. *Cogn. Instr.* In press
Miall DS, Kuiken D. 1994. Beyond text theory: understanding literary response. *Discourse Process.* 17:337–52
Millis KK, Graesser AC. 1994. The time-course of constructing knowledge-based inferences for scientific texts. *J. Mem. Lang.* 33:583–99
Millis KK, Graesser AC, Haberlandt K. 1993. The impact of connectives on the memory for expository texts. *Appl. Cogn. Psychol.* 7:317–39
Millis KK, Just MA. 1994. The influence of connectives on sentence comprehension. *J. Mem. Lang.* 33:128–47
Moffett J, McElheny KR. 1995. *Points of View: An Anthology of Short Stories.* New York: Penguin
Morris RK. 1994. Lexical and message-level sentence context effects on fixation times in reading. *J. Exp. Psychol. Learn. Mem. Cogn.* 20:92–103
Morrow DG, Greenspan SL, Bower GH. 1987. Accessibility and situation models in narra-

tive comprehension. *J. Mem. Lang.* 26: 165–87

Murray JD. 1995. Logical connectives and local coherence. See Lorch & O'Brien 1995, pp. 107–25

Myers JL, O'Brien EJ, Albrecht JE, Mason RA. 1994. Maintaining global coherence during reading. *J. Exp. Psychol. Learn. Mem. Cogn.* 20:876–86

Nystrand M. 1986. *The Structure of Written Communication: Studies in Reciprocity Between Readers and Writers.* Norwood, NJ: Ablex

O'Brien EJ, Albrecht JE. 1992. Comprehension strategies in the development of a mental model. *J. Exp. Psychol. Learn. Mem. Cogn.* 18:777–84

O'Brien EJ, Albrecht JE, Hakala CM, Rizzella ML. 1995. Activation and suppression of antecedents during reinstatement. *J. Exp. Psychol. Learn. Mem. Cogn.* 21:626–34

Ohtsuka K, Brewer WF. 1992. Discourse organization in the comprehension of temporal order. *Discourse Process.* 15:317–36

Otero J, Kintsch W. 1992. Failures to detect contradictions in a text: what readers believe versus what they read. *Psychol. Sci.* 3:229–35

Perfetti CA, Britt MA. 1995. Where do propositions come from? In *Discourse Comprehension: Essays in Honor of Walter Kintsch,* ed. CA Weaver, S Mannes, CR Fletcher, pp. 11–34. Hillsdale, NJ: Erlbaum

Perfetti CA, Britt MA, Georgi MA. 1995. *Text-Based Learning and Reasoning: Studies in History.* Hillsdale, NJ: Erlbaum

Perfetti CA, Marron MA, Foltz PW. 1996. Sources of comprehension failure: theoretical perspectives and case studies. In *Reading Comprehension Disabilities,* ed. C Cornoldi, J Oakhill. Hillsdale, NJ: Erlbaum. In press

Potts GR, Keenan JM, Golding JM. 1988. Assessing the occurrence of elaborative inferences: lexical decision versus naming. *J. Mem. Lang.* 27:399–415

Pressley M, Symons S, McDaniel MA, Snyder BL, Turnure JE. 1988. Elaborative interrogation facilitates acquisition of confusing facts. *J. Educ. Psychol.* 80:268–78

Rayner K, Garrod S, Perfetti CA. 1992. Discourse inferences during parsing are delayed. *Cognition* 45:109–39

Rayner K, Pacht JM, Duffy SA. 1994. Effects of prior encounter and global discourse bias on the processing of lexically ambiguous words: evidence from eye fixations. *J. Mem. Lang.* 33:527–44

Rinck M, Williams P, Bower GH, Becker ES. 1996. Spatial situation models and narrative understanding: some generalizations and extensions. *Discourse Process.* 21:23–56

Rubin DC. 1995. *Memory in Oral Traditions: The Cognitive Psychology of Epic, Ballads, and Counting-Out Rhymes.* New York: Oxford Univ. Press

Sanders TJM, Spooren WPM, Noordman LGM. 1992. Toward a taxonomy of coherence relations. *Discourse Process.* 15:1–36

Sanford AJ, Garrod SC. 1981. *Understanding Written Language: Explorations in Comprehension Beyond the Sentence.* New York: Wiley

Schmalhofer F, Glavanov D. 1986. Three components of understanding a programmer's manual: verbatim, propositional, and situational representations. *J. Mem. Lang.* 25: 279–94

Schober MF. 1995. Speakers, addressees, and frames of reference: whose is minimized in conversations about locations? *Discourse Process.* 20:219–47

Seifert CM, McKoon G, Abelson RP, Ratcliff R. 1986. Memory connections between thematically similar episodes. *J. Exp. Psychol. Learn. Mem. Cogn.* 12:220–31

Singer M, Graesser AC, Trabasso T. 1994. Minimal or global inference during reading. *J. Mem. Lang.* 33:421–41

Singer M, Halldorson M, Lear JC, Andrusiak P. 1992. Validation of causal bridging inferences in discourse understanding. *J. Mem. Lang.* 31:507–24

Singer M, Ritchot K. 1996. The role of working memory capacity and knowledge access in text inference processing. *Mem. Cogn.* In press

St. John MF. 1992. The story Gestalt: a model of knowledge-intensive process in text comprehension. *Cogn. Sci.* 16:271–306

Stein NL, Liwag MD. 1996. Children's understanding, evaluation, and memory for emotional events. In *Developmental Spans in Event Comprehension and Representation,* ed. P van den Broek, P Bauer, T Bourg. Hillsdale, NJ: Erlbaum. In press

Suh SY, Trabasso T. 1993. Inferences during reading: converging evidence from discourse analysis, talk-aloud protocols, and recognition priming. *J. Mem. Lang.* 32: 279–300

Trabasso T, Magliano JP. 1996. Conscious understanding during comprehension. *Discourse Process.* In press

Trabasso T, van den Broek P. 1985. Causal thinking and the representation of narrative events. *J. Mem. Lang.* 24:612–30

van den Broek P. 1990. Causal inferences and the comprehension of narrative texts. See Graesser & Bower, pp. 25:175–94

van den Broek P, Lorch RF. 1993. Network representations of causal relations in memory for narrative texts: evidence from primed recognition. *Discourse Process.* 17: 75–98 van Dijk TA, Kintsch W. 1983. *Strategies of Discourse Comprehension.* New York: Academic

van Oostendorp H, Zwaan RA, eds. 1994. *Naturalistic Text Comprehension.* Norwood, NJ: Ablex

Voss JF, Silfies LN. 1996. Learning from history text: the interaction of knowledge and comprehension skill with text structure. *Cogn. Instr.* In press

Whitney P, Budd D, Bramucci RS, Crane RS. 1995. On babies, bathwater, and schemata: a reconsideration of top-down processes in comprehension. *Discourse Process.* 20: 135–66

Whitney P, Ritchie BG, Clark MB. 1991. Working memory capacity and the use of elaborative inferences in text comprehension. *Discourse Process.* 14:133–45

Zwaan RA. 1994. Effects of genre expectations on text comprehension. *J. Exp. Psychol. Learn. Mem. Cogn.* 20:920–33

Zwaan RA. 1996. Processing narrative time shifts. *J. Exp. Psychol. Learn. Mem. Cogn.* In press

Zwaan RA, Brown CM. 1996. The influence of language proficiency and comprehension skill on situation model construction. *Discourse Process.* In press

Zwaan RA, Langston MC, Graesser AC. 1995a. The construction of situation models in narrative comprehension: an event-indexing model. *Psychol. Sci.* 6:292–97

Zwaan RA, Magliano JP, Graesser AC. 1995b. Dimensions of situation model construction in narrative comprehension. *J. Exp. Psychol. Learn. Mem. Cogn.* 21:386–97

Annu. Rev. Psychol. 1997. 48:191–214

THE EFFECTS OF STRESSFUL LIFE EVENTS ON DEPRESSION

Ronald C. Kessler

Department of Health Care Policy, Harvard Medical School, Boston, Massachusetts 02115

KEY WORDS: life events, stress

ABSTRACT

This chapter reviews recent research on the relationship between stressful life experiences and depression. A distinction is made between aggregate studies of overall stress effects and focused studies of particular events and difficulties. A distinction is also made between effects of life stress on first onset of depression and on the subsequent course of depression. Although the available evidence suggests that acute stressful life events can lead to the recurrence of episodes of major depression, a series of methodological problems compromise our ability to make clear causal inferences about the effects of life events on first onset of major depression or about the effects of chronic stress on either onset or recurrence of depression. The main problems of this sort are discussed, and recommendations made for ways of addressing these problems in future studies.

CONTENT

INTRODUCTION

Despite ample theories of psychopathology and many associated empirical studies, it is uncertain whether stressful life events promote psychiatric disorders. This chapter reviews contemporary theorizing and research about mental health in the context of stress. Although I focus on major depression, the most commonly investigated outcome, effects of stress on other psychiatric disorders are also considered (e.g. Blazer et al 1987, Dohrenwend et al 1995, Falsetti et al 1995, Kessler et al 1995).

The fundamental question—Does stress cause depression?—can only be evaluated rigorously in an experiment. Two different experimental literatures have developed to address this question. One addresses the effects of stress on what appear to be episodes of depression in animals (Soumi 1991a,b), and one addresses the effects of experimentally manipulated presumed mediating or modifying variables in field experiments of people facing serious stressors (Mrazek & Haggerty 1994). Both paradigms are limited in the evidence they provide about the effects of stress on major depression. It is unclear whether the results of animal studies generalize to human beings. Intervention experiments, which provide more direct evidence about major stress effects on human beings, are limited in that they manipulate stress mediators or modifiers rather than stress itself. In such work, the range within which stress effects can be changed is evaluated rather than the magnitude of these effects.

Because of these limitations, most evidence for a depressogenic effect of stressful life events comes from nonexperimental research. Inferences about the effects of stress in nonexperimental research are based on attempts to approximate the conditions of experimental random exposure by some combination of matching and use of control variables. Several methodological problems exist in most of these studies that make it difficult to estimate the effects of life events on depression and make it even more difficult to address complex questions about the importance of refining life event measures, distinguishing the effects of life events on onset and course of depression, and investigating stress-modifying effects. The review discusses these questions in sections. Each section begins with a review of the literature and then discusses theoretical and methodological problems. Sections end with suggestions to resolve these problems and advance the substantive research agenda.

ESTIMATING THE SHORT-TERM EFFECTS OF STRESS ON DEPRESSION

Aggregate Life Event Studies

The most common study estimating the effects of life events on depression focuses on short-term effects, typically a recall period of no more than one year. These studies compare scores on aggregated stressful life event scales between persons who did and did not report the recent onset of an episode of major depression. Community surveys (e.g. Brown & Harris 1978) and case-control studies of depressed patients and matched nondepressed controls (Dohrenwend et al 1995) have been used to make these comparisons. The comparisons have generally been, of necessity, retrospective in the sense that information about stress exposure was gathered after onset of depression. Retrospective life event assessment is the norm even in prospective studies, where information about intercurrent events and depressive episodes between waves of data collection is collected in the later wave (e.g. Lewinsohn et al 1988).

Many such studies have been conducted in the past two decades (Bidzinska 1984, Billings et al 1983, Brown et al 1987, Hammen et al 1985, Holahan & Moos 1991, Kendler et al 1995a, Lloyd 1980, Patrick et al 1978, Paykel 1979, Shrout et al 1989, Williamson et al 1995) and mainly show the following: 1. There is a consistently documented association between exposure to stressful life events and subsequent onset of episodes of major depression. 2. However, the magnitude of this association varies across studies depending on how life events are measured, with associations generally stronger when "contextual" measures are used rather than simple life event checklists. 3. There is consistent evidence for a dose-response relationship between stressful events and depression, with severe events more strongly associated with depression than nonsevere events. 4. Stressful life events are highly prevalent in these studies. Although the majority of depressed people report the occurrence of a stressful event shortly before the onset of their depression, only a minority of those people exposed to such events become depressed.

Two main methodological problems compromise our ability to make causal inferences about stress effects from these studies. First, most of the studies failed to consider that accuracy in reporting life events is associated with depression. These studies failed to adjust for the bias introduced by this possibility. For example, many studies failed to confirm whether events occurred before depression. Because depression can cause some events (Hammen 1991) and because people with a history of depression have more events than others even when not in episodes of depression (Kessler & Magee 1993), there may be a bias toward finding specious associations between life events and depression. A number of researchers have found, consistent with this concern, that the relationship between "dependent" events and depression is stronger than the relationship between "independent" events and depression (Williamson et al 1995), where a dependent event was defined as one that could plausibly be a consequence of the respondent's own actions (e.g. being fired from a job) while an independent event could not be defined so (e.g. losing a job due to a plant closing).

The fact that independent events were generally significant predictors of depression in those studies that distinguished independent and dependent events has been considered evidence that life events do cause depression (e.g. Brown & Harris 1978). However, another type of confounding could have led to the association between independent events and depression. Retrospective reports about event exposure might have been biased in these studies by differential recall accuracy or differential willingness to disclose and discuss stressful experiences among currently (at the time of interview) depressed versus non-depressed respondents in such a way that created the appearance that life events cause depression. Consistent with this possibility, experimental research has shown that induction of depressed mood can lead to a significant increase in reports of past stressful events (Cohen et al 1988). Furthermore, recent research with twins has documented a significant heritable component in reports about the occurrence of both independent and dependent life events, which could be due to a stable difference in reporting styles that is associated with liability to depression (Kendler et al 1993).

The problems of accuracy of life event reporting and dating can be partially overcome by obtaining independent reports about life events from informants or archival records. However, this is seldom practiced, and even when it is, these procedures can only provide a partial solution because it is impossible to find informants for all study respondents, many important events will not be known to informants even when they exist, informants will not be perfectly accurate even when they are aware of all relevant events, and archival records exist for only a small fraction of all relevant events.

A second methodological problem compromising our ability to make causal inferences about stress effects involves the logic of causal analysis used in nonexperimental studies of aggregate stress effects. As noted above, these studies interpret the associations between life events and depression as indicating a causal effect of the former on the latter. The assumption implicit in this interpretation is that exposure to life events occurs randomly with respect to other causes of depression. However, this assumption is generally incorrect. Some researchers have attempted to adjust for this problem statistically by introducing controls for confounding variables in multivariate causal models. The recent statistical literature shows quite clearly, though, that efforts of this sort are doomed to failure in the absence of highly unrealistic assumptions about completeness of controls and linearity-additivity of multivariate influences (Holland 1986, Sobel 1990).

It is important to emphasize in this regard that misspecification can invalidate the control variable approach even when confounding variables are correctly measured. The most obvious example involves the case where the researcher assumes that confounding variables have additive effects. Given what we know about stress-modifying effects, it is almost certain that this is not the case in most applications. Common causes of event exposure and depression, such as a genetic liability or various aspects of personality or access to supportive social relationships, are likely to modify the impact of stressful life events on depression and lead to a biased estimate of the magnitude of this impact in the absence of a correct specification of interactions between the events and the controls.

Focused Studies of Individual Events

Because of the methodological problems enumerated above, the studies cited above cannot be interpreted as providing unequivocal support for the view that aggregated stressful life events cause depression. However, other studies do provide support. Such studies exploit the fact that the relationship between a stressful life event and a health outcome can be interpreted as if it were based on an experiment when exposure to the event occurred for reasons that are random with respect to the outcome. There are cases where this situation occurs, but these are almost entirely limited to single events such as job loss due to economic conditions, exposure to an unanticipated natural disaster, or involvement in a fatal automobile accident where the other driver was at fault. These "natural experiments," each focusing on a single fairly common event such as job loss (e.g. Dew et al 1987), widowhood (e.g. Umberson et al 1992), and divorce (e.g. Aseltine & Kessler 1993), provide the strongest evidence about the effects of stressful life events on depression. This evidence is especially strong when the sample of people exposed to these events is obtained from archival data so that there is no risk of selective recall bias. All these studies show that serious stressful events are associated with a substantial increase in depressive episodes.

A New Emphasis on Chronic Stress

Although early research on life stress and depression was almost exclusively concerned with life events, the past decade has seen a new interest in chronic stress. This interest draws on a long-standing epidemiological research tradition that has studied the health-damaging effects of chronic work stress (e.g. House & Cottington 1986, Karasak & Theorell 1990, Kasl 1978) and a growing body of literature on the relationship between chronic marital difficulties and depression (e.g. Beach et al 1990, Gotlib & McCabe 1990). We know from these studies that chronic role-related stresses are significantly associated with chronically depressed mood (Mirowsky & Ross 1989, Pearlin 1989). We also know from the handful of life event studies that have included assessments of them that chronic stresses are often associated with an exacerbation of the effects of life events on episodes of major depression, especially when the life domains affected by the events are the same as the domains affected by the chronic stresses (Brown et al 1987, McGonagle & Kessler 1990).

Recent research has also begun to focus on chronic stresses as mediators of the effects of life events on depression. These studies suggest that enduring stressful sequelae of stressful events account for most of the effects of life events on major depression. For example, the adverse effects of unemployment on depression are partly mediated by resultant financial stresses (Kessler et al 1987), while the relationship between loss of spouse and depression is partly mediated by social isolation (Umberson et al 1992). As discussed below, an exciting opportunity for increasing our understanding of the processes linking life events to depression involves the disaggregation of life event effects through these mediating chronic stresses.

Future Directions

AGGREGATE LIFE EVENT STUDIES It is important for researchers to grapple more seriously with the complex methodological problems involved in conducting naturalistic studies of aggregate stress effects in community samples. Focused studies of individual randomly occurring events are limited because few life events occur for reasons that are entirely random with respect to the outcome of interest. This means that reliance on those few opportunities where natural experiments present themselves or the somewhat larger set of opportunities where design enhancements can be used to develop the functional equivalents of natural experiments (Kessler et al 1996b), while providing clear documentation that life events lead to depression, provide no insights into the dynamics of the much more common situations in which potentially dependent events occur before the onset of depression. Yet we need to study these complex situations because they are most commonly associated with depression. It is a challenge for future research to develop procedures to do this. These procedures will presumably require innovations in research design and analysis (Kessler et al 1996b).

FOCUSED STUDIES OF INDIVIDUAL EVENTS In addition, life events researchers need to begin working more seriously with studies of individual events to better understand causal relationships. Many focused studies already exist on the stress and coping processes associated with such important stressors as unemployment (Feather 1990), bypass surgery (Kulik & Mahler 1993), and rape (Von et al 1991). However, the vast majority of these studies are by clinicians interested in treatment effects rather than life event effects. As a result, the studies generally lack control groups and usually focus on people in treatment rather than on representative community samples of those who have been exposed to the event under investigation. Consequently, it is impossible to draw any inferences about stress effects (Burgess & Holstrom 1979). Despite such limitations, the results from these studies provide a rich source of information about the meanings of stressful events in the lives of the people who experience them, the coping challenges these events elicit, and the resources and vulnerabilities associated with successful and unsuccessful coping efforts. These results could be invaluable to future researchers who attempt to apply the logic of nonexperimental causal analysis to new investigations of the effects of these events on depression. Such studies should include prospective designs and use carefully constructed control groups in an effort to estimate the magnitude of life event effects, the pathways through which these effects operate, and the modifying factors that lead these events to vary in their effects across respondents.

CHRONIC STRESS STUDIES The methodological issues are a good deal more complex in research on the relationship between chronic stress and chronic depression. The possibility that chronic role-related stress is an important determinant of chronic depression is certainly consistent with the observation that people who have chronic major depression or dysthymia often report ongoing problems in one or more of their central life roles. However, a major problem in interpreting this fact is that both the chronic role-related stresses and the chronic depression by definition have occurred for so long that deciding unambiguously which came first is difficult. No serious efforts address this problem of causal order. The researcher, however, may focus on stresses that can be assumed to have occurred randomly with respect to other risk factors of depression and to be inescapable, in which case matched comparison can be used to make causal inferences about long-term stress effects. A good example is the matched comparison of the parents of children having cancer, diabetes, or some other serious childhood physical disorder with the parents of healthy children. Disorders of this sort are quite common and occur, in most cases, for reasons that are unrelated to other risk factors for parental psychiatric disorder (Pless 1994). The small amount of research shows that these childhood physical disorders have significant psychiatric effects on the family (Jessop et al 1988, Krosnick 1970).

The more usual case, however, is one in which nonrandom exposure to the chronic stress cannot be ruled out, as in studies of the relationship between chronic marital difficulties and chronic depression. Frequently an added complication is systematic selection out of exposure (e.g. differential likelihood of seeking a less stressful job based on individual differences in the depressogenic effects of job stress). Standard longitudinal data collection methods have limited potential for studying chronic stress situations because these situations, by their very nature, are quite stable. These problems make it much more difficult to assess the long-term effects of chronic stress on chronic depression than the short-term effects of life events on episodic depression. Nevertheless, there are some opportunities for making provisional assessments of this sort when exposure is nonrandom. For example, prospective research can be carried out to investigate role entry (e.g. the first few years of marriage or of employment) in an effort to study selection processes into and out of stressful situations in light of the prior existence of both depression and risk factors for depression (Orbuch et al 1993, Veroff et al 1993). Another opportunity for making provisional assessment of causal effects is to focus on microprocesses of chronic stress effects using daily diaries or other fine-grained time-series methods (Csikszentmihalyi & Larson 1987, Eckenrode & Bolger 1995).

REFINING LIFE EVENT MEASURES

Checklists versus Contextual Measures

As noted above, there is considerable variation in the estimated effects of life events, depending on whether scores are based on checklists or contextual measures. The intellectual origin of the checklist approach is usually traced to Adolf Meyer's use of a "life chart" to summarize information provided by patients at intake (Lief 1948), the subsequent use of the life chart method by Wolff and his colleagues (1950) to study the relationship between life change and illness onset, and the eventual refinement of this method by Holmes & Rahe (1967) in the Social Readjustment Rating Scale (SRRS). The SRRS was a checklist of 43 stressful experiences generated on the basis of clinical research to characterize the events that most often occurred to patients before seeking treatment. Separate life change unit (LCU) weights were generated by a panel of raters for each event in the SRRS and used to construct a summary LCU score from this checklist.

The publication of the SRRS led to an enormous amount of research on the relationship between life events and various types of illness onset, with over 1000 papers using the SRRS published in the first decade after its development (Holmes 1979). Subsequent research with mental health outcomes (typically screening scales of nonspecific psychological distress) led to refinements and proliferation of life event checklists (Turner & Wheaton 1995). Refinements included the following: 1. At least three of the events in the SRRS were thought by many critics to be better conceptualized as early symptoms of illness (change in sleeping habits, change in eating habits, sexual difficulties) than life events. Subsequent checklists eliminated these events. 2. Many of the events in the SRRS were actually vaguely defined categories of events (e.g. business readjustment, change in financial state). Subsequent checklists replaced these with a longer set of more concretely defined events within each of these categories. 3. The SRRS was a fairly short checklist that omitted a great many stressful events (e.g. rape, criminal victimization, witnessing a traumatic event). Subsequent checklists added these events and sometimes customized event lists to special populations (e.g. Kessler et al 1992).

In addition, methodological studies of the SRRS and the various checklists based on it were carried out. The main results of these studies were as follows: 1. Negative events are much more powerful predictors of mental health outcomes than positive events (Zautra & Reich 1983), which led to the conclusion that life change is not the central dimension linking stressful life events to psychological disorder and that the LCU weighting approach in the SRRS leads to an underestimation of life event effects. 2. Within the set of fairly serious events typically included in life event checklists like the SRRS, the use of differential weights does not markedly increase the association between negative life event scales and measures of psychological distress (Zimmerman 1983). 3. However, distinctions along a number of other dimensions (e.g. amount of loss, amount of threat, degree of controllability of consequences of the event) do lead to substantial increases in the association between negative life event scales and measures of distress (Thoits 1983).

A key feature of the checklist approach is that all life events of a given type are treated as equivalent. Death of a spouse, for example, was assigned a 100 point LCU score on the SRRS irrespective of the suddenness of the death, the quality of the marriage, or any circumstances surrounding the death that might have made it more stressful (e.g. the death occurred in an automobile accident in which the respondent was driving) or less stressful (e.g. the death occurred peacefully after the spouse had spent many years suffering from a degenerative illness). There is clear evidence from focused studies of individual events that the strength of the relationship between life events and depression increases substantially when these sorts of distinctions are made. Based on this observation, a number of researchers have attempted to modify the checklist approach in such a way as to consider these distinctions.

Two strategies have been used to make these adjustments. One is to allow each respondent to assign a subjective weight to his or her own events (Sarason et al 1978). The other is to use objective information about the person and his life situation to construct an independent judgment of how stressful the event would be for a typical person in that same situation. The first of these strategies has been rejected as confounding measurement of the event with emotional reaction to the event (Turner & Wheaton 1995, Zimmerman 1983) and has consequently been abandoned. The second strategy has evolved into what has been termed the "contextual" approach to rating life events.

The intellectual origins of the contextual approach can be traced to the work of Brown & Harris (1978), who developed a method of using a rating panel to assign scores on a variety of dimensions to stressful life events. According to this rating scheme, the death of a neighbor would be rated as more severe than otherwise if the respondent who reported it was a rural elderly person who lived alone and was a housebound invalid whose main source of social contact was the weekly visit of the neighbor for lunch. To obtain adequate contextual information for rating events, the Brown & Harris method requires intensive personal interviews and qualitative probes to specify precisely the characteristics of the events believed to be relevant to contextual ratings. Detailed probing is also used to establish the timing of the event in relation to the onset of the depression. Precise dating is also used to identify the aspects of the event that are thought to affect depression onset.

Methodological studies suggest that such intensive interviewing is much more effective than the comparatively mechanical procedures used in the administration of checklists in avoiding misdating of events (McQuaid et al 1992), communicating to the respondent the importance of accurate recall (Cannell et al 1981), and facilitating the use of memory aids to improve recall of events and accurate dating of event occurrence (e.g. calendars, visual representations, reminders of personally salient events reported previously in the interview). Such aids have been shown to significantly improve accuracy of life event reports (Sobell et al 1990). Furthermore, the use of contextual ratings has been shown to substantially reduce the response errors in checklist measures due to individual differences, such as checking off the occurrence of a "serious physical illness" that, in fact, was only a cold, or otherwise giving reports that are inconsistent with the implied severity thresholds in the checklist events (Kessler & Wethington 1991, Raphael et al 1991).

There are two practical problems with the contextual rating approach to life events measurement. The first is that great care is needed to make sure information about the occurrence of depression after the event does not contaminate the ratings of context, possibly by highlighting to the interviewer an aspect of the respondent's life situation that would not have been known were it not for the fact that the respondent became depressed. Concerns have been raised that some users of the Brown & Harris method are not sufficiently attentive to this possibility, which can result in confounding of stress ratings with outcomes (Bebbington 1986). The second practical problem is that the intensive interviews used to make contextual life event ratings are very labor intensive. Interviewers must be highly trained. Interviews can take as much as five hours to complete. A complicated rating scheme typically requiring several additional hours to complete is needed to review interview audiotapes. Weekly panel meetings sometimes last an entire day to review these ratings (Brown

1989). Several attempts have been made to evaluate whether a short-cut can be devised to approximate the Brown & Harris method (Cooke 1985, Dohrenwend et al 1993, Kessler & Wethington 1991, Miller & Salter 1984). The most promising of these is a structured version of the method, still being pilot tested, that appears to generate information similar to the original in a shorter interview period and with fewer demands for complex postprocessing (Wethington et al 1995).

There is also a conceptual problem with the contextual rating method. As described below, life events researchers are greatly interested in stress-modifying factors: aspects of the personal and situational environments of people exposed to stressful events that are associated with variation in the impact of these events on their probability of becoming depressed. The contextual rating method subverts this investigation by absorbing information about stress modifiers into the ratings of life event severity. Indeed, the information used by the Brown & Harris ratings panel can be seen as hypotheses concerning stress modifiers that never have a chance to be investigated because they are assumed in rating event severity. A clearly preferable approach would be to subject these hypotheses to empirical test. The difficulty of doing so until now, though, has been that studies of the sort using the Brown & Harris method have all had quite small sample sizes due to the labor-intensive nature of the method. This has meant that the number of subjects has been too small to test specific hypotheses about the modifying effects of particular aspects of context.

Unpacking Events in Focused Studies of Individual Events

The confounding of measures of life event severity with stress modifiers can work in the opposite way as well, by suggesting that there are individual differences in emotional reactivity to an event when, in fact, the event is not the same for all people who experience it. A good illustration is found in research on the relationship between widowhood and depression, which consistently shows that death of a spouse is more strongly associated with depression among men than women (Stroebe & Stroebe 1983). Does this mean that men are less capable of coping with emotional losses than women? Or, alternatively, is widowhood a different stress for men than women? One way to distinguish these two possibilities is to carry out focused studies in which the researcher attempts to disaggregate widowhood in such a way as to unpack its stress components and study how these components explain the effect of the event on depression.

Several recent studies of this sort have been carried out, each focused on a single major event such as divorce (Aseltine & Kessler 1993), unemployment (Turner et al 1991), and widowhood (Umberson et al 1992). The basic approach in each study has been to start with a conceptual model of the dimensions that lead to the effects of the event on depression and then measure these dimensions longitudinally in a sample of people who were exposed to the event and in an appropriate comparison sample of people not exposed to it. Standard multivariate procedures have then been used to study the mediating effects of the stress dimensions on the overall relationship between the event and depression. Umberson et al (1992), for example, examined how much the observed gender difference in the impact of widowhood on depression in a national sample was due to male-female differences in the impact of widowhood on stress dimensions versus differences in the impact of these dimensions on depression. The analysis documented that the greater depressogenic effect of widowhood on men than women is, at least in part, because the death of a spouse leads to a number of secondary stresses for men that do not exist for women. For example, death of a spouse leads to a significant decrease in contact and emotional closeness between the surviving parent and adult children among widowed men but not widowed women.

A consistent result in these studies has been that most of the association between some stressful events and depression is due to a mediating effect on role-related stresses. Caution is needed in interpreting this result, however, in light of the fact that only one of the three studies (Aseltine & Kessler 1993) was truly prospective (i.e. assessed both depression and the mediators before the onset of the stressful event) and none of them controlled for other possible confounding effects. Future work on unpacking life event effects needs to be based on prospective designs that use carefully matched control groups and use intensive interview methods and contextual ratings to define the intervening chronic stress dimensions.

DISTINGUISHING THE EFFECTS OF STRESS ON ONSET AND COURSE ON DEPRESSION

The Effects of Traumatic Stress on Lifetime Depression

The results discussed so far have focused on the short-term effects of recent stressful life events on episodes of depression. Another area of stress research is concerned with the long-term effects of previous stresses (usually either childhood or lifetime traumatic stresses) on lifetime depression. The only programmatic research of this sort we know of is that of Kessler & Magee (1993, 1994a), who analyzed lifetime retrospective data on the relationship between childhood adversities and lifetime depression in a nationally representative general population sample of adults. They concluded that most severe childhood adversities have significant effects on early-onset depression (defined as an onset before age 20) but not on later-onset depression, which indicates that there is some risk period for the impact of childhood adversities beyond which they lose their depressogenic effects. Subsequent work by the same investigators in two other large-scale community surveys yielded similar results (Kessler et al 1996a).

This investigation has the potential to yield important information about life course variations in the effects of traumatic events. By studying differential effects as a function of time since occurrence of the event, it might be possible to document variation in both initial impact and in the length of the risk period associated with the event. We would expect these effects to vary depending on the event and the age of exposure. An investigation of the association between childhood parental loss and clinical depression, for example, would probably look for fairly rapid onset of the disorder after the traumatic event, while an investigation of the association between childhood sexual abuse and lifetime depression might be interested in the possibility of more long-term delayed reactions. By investigating the possibility of variation in the long-term effects of traumas as a function of the respondent's age at occurrence, in comparison, the researcher can investigate the hypothesis that some traumas have their most powerful health-damaging effects during certain critical developmental phases of the life course.

The Long-Term Effects of Traumatic Stress on Current Depression

Related research considers the long-term effects of traumatic stress on current adult depression. A number of studies have been carried out in both psychiatric patient samples and general population samples. These studies have all been based on retrospective data and comparative analyses of persons who are depressed with those who are not. The studies consistently find that depressed adults report the occurrence of more childhood adversities such as separation from a parent, family turmoil, parental psychopathology, and physical/sexual abuse than those who are not depressed (e.g. Birtchnell et al 1988, Brown & Anderson 1991, Bryer et al 1987, Earls et al 1988, Faravelli et al 1986, Fendrich et al 1990, Holmes & Robins 1988, McLeod 1991, Rutter 1989, Tennant 1988, West & Prinz 1987, Stein et al 1988, Yama et al 1993).

The use of long-term retrospective recall to assess these relationships raises concerns about confounding based on selective recall as a function of current depression even though there is evidence that fairly objective adversities such as parental death or divorce are recalled with good reliability (Brewin et al 1993). It is important, in light of these concerns, that researchers who work with retrospective data maximize accuracy of assessment, perhaps by using follow-back designs based on archival records or relying on evaluation of the effects of self-reports about fairly objective and major childhood stressors. In addition, it is important that methodological research be conducted to refine methods of collecting retrospective data to improve the accuracy of respondent reports (Kessler et al 1997).

Disaggregating Long-Term Stress Effects on Onset and Course

History of depression might explain, either in whole or in part, the relationship between childhood adversities and current depression. The plausibility of this hypothesis is supported by research showing that many forms of childhood adversity are associated with increased risk of depression in adolescence and early adulthood (Fleming & Offord 1990, Goodyear 1990) and that early-onset depression is associated with high recurrence risk (Lewinsohn et al 1988). Recent research, in fact, suggests that there is specificity in the continuation of depression between childhood and adulthood (Harrington et al 1990). Because of this observation, it is important for research on the long-term effects of childhood adversities on current depression to control for history and distinguish effects on first onset, recurrence, and speed of episode recovery.

Analyses of this type could shed light on the pathways involved in the long-term effects of early adversities. What little is known about these pathways suggests that childhood adversities are associated with difficulties in making successful role transitions into early adulthood, which in turn are associated with depression during the adult years (McLeod 1991, Quinton et al 1984). Childhood adversities have also been linked to intrapsychic factors that predict adult depression, such as helplessness, low self-esteem, and interpersonal dependency (Brown et al 1987). However, an important limitation in this research is that prior history of depression has not been considered a potential confounding variable. This makes it much more difficult to interpret the true effects of other mediating variables than it would be otherwise.

A good illustration of this problem is provided by Parker & Hadzi-Pavlovic's (1984) investigation of women whose mothers died during the women's childhoods. Retrospective reports about lack of care from fathers and stepmothers after the death of the mothers were significantly associated with high adult scores on screening scales of both state depression and trait depression. These associations were attenuated among respondents with supportive spouses, which led the authors to conclude that success in forming intimate relationships "largely corrected any diathesis to greater depression created by uncaring parenting." However, this conclusion ignores the alternative hypothesis that lack of success in forming a supportive marriage and current depression were both due to a history of depression that began after the death of the mother but before marriage. If this is true, there might be no causal effect of success in forming a supportive marriage on subsequent depression even though there is a significant association between these two variables.

As noted above, Kessler and his associates (Kessler & Magee 1993, 1994b; Kessler et al 1996a) examined these issues and found that a wide variety of retrospectively reported childhood adversities are associated with lifetime onset of depression before age 20 and that few of these adversities continue to be associated with later risk of either first onset or episode recurrence. Their studies have not examined the relationships between childhood adversities and speed of episode recovery. Replications and extensions of these studies are needed in more focused samples.

Controlling History in Studying the Determinants of Episode Onset

An understanding of history of depression could be important in evaluating the short-term effects of stressful life events on episode onset. The literature on sex differences in depression provides an interesting illustration of this situation. Point prevalence of depression is much higher among women than men (Blazer et al 1994, Weissman et al 1988). However, there is no sex difference in recurrence of depression (Coryell et al 1991), nor in speed of episode recovery of depression (Kessler et al 1993), which means that the higher rate of current depression typically found among women is presumably due to a relationship between sex and lifetime depression (Eaton et al 1989, Weissman et al 1988). We know that the average age of onset of depression for both men and women is in the early twenties (Sorenson et al 1991). However, the sex difference in prevalence of depression is more pronounced in mid-life because the density of recurrent episodes of depression is greatest in this period of the life cycle. This mid-life bulge in the sex difference in depression has been considered by many commentators as evidence that chronic life stresses associated with sex roles explain the sex difference in depression (e.g. Ensel 1982). However, a consideration of sex differences in first onset and in recurrence shows that the mid-life increase in the sex difference is largely because of a sex difference in lifetime onset of depression that occurs by the early twenties. The implications of this observation for current ideas about the relationship between the chronic stresses associated with adult sex roles and depression are profound.

An informative illustration of the importance of controlling for depression history in studying the short-term effects of stressful life events comes from reanalysis of date collected in the Epidemiologic Catchment Area (ECA) study, a major five-site collaborative study of the epidemiology of adult psychiatric disorders (Robins & Regier 1991). Data from the ECA public-use file shows that 91% of the respondents who reported an episode of depression in the 12 months before the baseline ECA interview had a previous history of depression. An obvious question is whether prior depression should be considered a predictor in studies of the short-term effects of stressful life events on episodes of depression. It is clear that such a variable would be a powerful predictor of subsequent episode onset. In the ECA data, history of depression had an odds-ratio close to 40.0 in predicting an episode onset in the 12 months before the baseline ECA interview, an association that dwarfs the effects of any other risk factor in the literature on depression.

Much evidence is consistent with the possibility that history might be an important predictor of current stress, in which case failure to control history could lead to serious bias in estimation of short-term stress effects. History of depression, for example, is thought to influence interpersonal style in ways that provoke other people to act toward depressed people in ways that are nonsupportive and that could lead to increased exposure to interpersonal loss events (Coyne 1976, Monroe & Steiner 1986). This possibility implies that a risk-factor analysis that includes history of depression as a control variable might find that social support and interpersonal loss are less powerful predictors of episode onset than an analysis that failed to control for history.

There is only one published report that investigated this possibility empirically. Kessler & Magee (1994b) introduced a control for history of depression into a risk-factor model for episode onset of recent depression and found that a number of previously significant predictors became insignificant. As discussed below, they also found that history significantly modified the relationships between most other risk factors, which suggests that future work on risk factors for depressive episodes needs to look separately at the predictors of onset and recurrence. As a practical matter, given that the vast majority of episode onsets in adulthood are recurrences, this injunction implies that studies of the relationship between stressful life events and depression in adult samples should explicitly recognize that they are, in effect, studying recurrence of depression. Therefore, the appropriate comparison group is the subsample of respondents with a lifetime history of depression who have not had a recent recurrence and where controls or matching should be used to adjust for variation in age of onset and course of depression before the onset of events as well as for the possibility of selection into dependent events on the basis of prior course of the disorder.

Stress Effects on Speed of Episode Recovery

A number of studies have examined the relationship between stressful life experiences that occurred before the onset of depressive episodes and speed of recovery of these episodes. Most were carried out in patient samples (Brugha et al 1990, Huxley et al 1979, Karp et al 1993, Keller et al 1986, Krantz & Moos 1988, Mann et al 1981, Monroe et al 1992, Parker et al 1988, Weissman et al 1978), although a few were carried out in community samples (Beiser 1976, McLeod et al 1992, Sargeant et al 1990). In these studies, stressful life events and chronic difficulties were generally found to predict slow speed of recovery. A smaller number of studies examined the relationship between intercurrent life events and speed of episode recovery (Brown & Moran 1994, Brown et al 1995, Tennant 1988). These studies found that events arising in the midst of a depressive episode impede recovery if they exacerbate the stressful situations that triggered the episode (e.g. foreclosure in the wake of a job loss). However, events that reverse or resolve an earlier stress are associated with more rapid recovery (e.g. reemployment after a job loss). An especially interesting result is that otherwise negative events can sometimes lead to episode recovery either because they resolve an ongoing difficulty (e.g. separation from an abusive spouse) or because they put the event that triggered the episode into perspective (e.g. a near-death experience in an automobile accident leading to the realization that a recent job loss was not really life-shattering).

STRESS-MODIFYING EFFECTS

Substantive Modifiers

I have focused until now on investigations that document the existence of aggregate effects of stress on depression. However, contemporary research on stress and depression typically accepts this association as a given and focuses more on the consistent finding that the majority of people exposed to all but the most extreme stressful life experiences do not become depressed. An attempt is made to explain this finding and, more generally, individual differences in stress reactivity by searching for characteristics of the individual or the environment in which the individual is embedded that modify stress effects. These modifying factors are sometimes referred to as stress-buffering factors, vulnerability factors, or stress-diathesis factors.

It is beyond the scope of this review to provide an overview of the enormous literature that has accumulated over the past decade to study this diverse array of modifying factors. Instead, see reviews by Gotlib & Hammen (1992), Mrazek & Haggerty (1994), and Taylor & Aspinwall (1996). Several factors have been repeatedly shown to predict an attenuation of the relationship between subsequent events and episode onset of depression, including access to social support, various aspects of personality, appraisal processes, intellectual capabilities such as cognitive flexibility and effective problem-solving skills, interpersonal skills such as social competence and communication ability, and various coping strategies.

History of Depression as a Modifier

There is a problem with interpreting these substantive results in causal terms because virtually none of the studies distinguished modifiers of the stress-depression relationship for first onset of depression from the modifiers of the stress-depression relationship for recurrence of depression, nor did they control for the possible confounding effect of history of depression. As noted above, Kessler & Magee (1994b) found that a number of previously significant stress-modifying factors became statistically insignificant, and the effects of others were substantially attenuated, when they controlled for history of depression and considered that history operates as a stress modifier. Failure to introduce similar controls seriously compromises our ability to draw any inferences from the larger literature on stress-modifying factors in depression.

It is important to reemphasize two earlier points in making this criticism of the literature on stress-modifying effects. First, recurrent major depression can profoundly affect most of the individual-level and environmental factors that have been studied in the modifier literature. Consistent with this observation, Kessler & Magee (1994b) found strong relationships between retrospective reports of a lifetime history of depression and current scores on most of the variables that are normally considered to be stress modifiers in their nationally representative survey. Second, history of depression is itself a stress modifier. That is, the relationship between stressful life events and first onset of depression in the subsample of adult respondents who report no prior history of depression is much weaker than the relationship between stressful life events and recurrence of depression in the subsample of adult respondents who report having a prior history (Kessler & Magee 1994b). The conjunction of these two observations implies that many of the variables currently thought to be stress modifiers will appear to have modifying effects even if they do not. This will occur because they are related to history of depression.

Number of Prior Episodes of Depression as a Modifier

In addition to the distinction between people who have and have not previously been depressed, recent research has shown that number of episodes in the subsample of people with a history is also significantly related to stress reactivity. Post et al (1986) were the first to report this phenomenon and noted that even though stressful life events often precipitate early episodes of depression, as the number of episodes increases "the illness appears to evolve with its own rhythmicity and spontaneity, independent of life events." A subsequent review of epidemiologic studies supported this clinical observation (Post 1992), which led Post to postulate that "sensitization to stressors and episode sensitization occur and become encoded at the level of gene expression" in such a way that responsivity to stress is permanently altered.

Genetic Predisposition as a Modifier

A related line of research has examined the possibility that genetic factors influence stress reactivity. The plausibility of this possibility is suggested by a variety of twin and adoption studies that document genetic influences on major depression (Kendler et al 1992, Tsaung & Farone 1990). However, these genetic effects could occur either independent of environmental stress effects or in interaction with stress by affecting emotional vulnerability to the effects of stress. A recent study by Kendler et al (1995a) in a general population sample of adult female twins investigated this issue by using information on zygosity and co-twin history of depression to define a gradient of genetic vulnerability to depression. The results showed that genetic liability is associated with a threefold increase in the stress-depression relationship.

It is also important to recognize that genetic influences can account for what appears to be an effect of a substantive stress-modifying variable. Kessler et al (1992) found in a study of the stress-buffering effect of social support on the relationship between life events and depression that it was not support itself but the genetically determined component of social support that became more strongly associated with depression in the presence of stressful life events. Future research on stress modifiers should use genetically informative designs, such as twin or adoption studies, to investigate related possibilities in more detail.

OVERVIEW

The evidence reviewed above clearly shows that inventories of stressful events predict subsequent depression. A smaller number of controlled comparative studies of people exposed to single major life events provide strong evidence that at least part of this association is due to events causing depression. It is also clear from other studies that this relationship can be reciprocal and that depression can elicit or exacerbate certain stressful events and difficulties.

In addition, much evidence from prospective studies shows that the association between stressful life events and depression varies considerably depending on prior characteristics of the people exposed to the events and the environments in which these people are embedded. However, this evidence cannot be interpreted unequivocally as demonstrating that these factors are stress modifiers. The reason for this is that unmeasured variables such as prior history of depression or genetic vulnerability could be confounding factors that explain the associations between the presumed stress modifiers and depression.

The results of experimental interventions aimed at preventing depression among people exposed to particular life events offer great promise for reducing this uncertainty about stress modifiers. A number of such interventions have been shown to reduce the depressogenic effects of certain otherwise stressful events by manipulating either stress modifiers and/or the secondary stresses created by the events (Bloom et al 1985, Heaney 1992, Price et al 1992), which shows that some aspects of the stress process can be modified. However, it has not been possible to use this information to make informed judgments about the significance of individual stress modifiers.

There are two reasons for this. First, all the interventions had multiple components. Further nonexperimental process evaluation of their outcome results would consequently be needed to make informed judgments about the effects of separate intervention components. Second, none of these interventions included carefully matched control groups of people who were not exposed to the events, which made it impossible to distinguish stress-modifying effects from the effects of presumed modifiers operating in exactly the same way among people who were not exposed to the events used to define the intervention subjects.

It is unclear why there has not been more collaboration between interventionists and nonexperimental stress researchers. It is conceivable that disciplinary differences in orientation are involved. Preventive interventions are typically carried out by clinical or community psychologists, while naturalistic stress studies are typically conducted by personality/social psychologists, epidemiologists, and sociologists. Future advances in our understanding of the relationship between life events and depression, in my view, will require a collaboration between both perspectives.

The above review has repeatedly implied why such a collaboration would be useful to naturalistic researchers but has also emphasized that these researchers must work harder at approximating the conditions of experiments to clarify the meanings of their results. One unique way of doing this is to work with interventionists to construct control groups of people who were not exposed to the events under investigation and to use the manipulation of intervention exposure with parallel measurement in the control group to facilitate analysis of stress-modifying effects. It is also important to recognize, though, that there is another side of the exchange: Nonexperimental studies are equally important for intervention specialists. Such studies are needed to select intervention targets and to interpret the pathways involved in the effects of successful interventions. Once reliable data on pathways are obtained, nonexperimental studies should search for factors that might effectively block these pathways. This kind of iterative cross-fertilization is our best hope for advancing research on stressful events and depression in the future.

Literature Cited

Aseltine RH Jr, Kessler RC. 1993. Marital disruption and depression in a community sample. *J. Health Soc. Behav.* 34:237–51

Beach SRH, Sandeen EE, O'Leary KD. 1990. *Depression in Marriage: A Model for Etiology and Treatment.* New York: Guilford

Bebbington P. 1986. Establishing causal links: recent controversies. In *Life Events and Psychiatric Disorder: Controversial Issues,* ed. H Katchnig, pp. 188–200. Cambridge: Cambridge Univ. Press

Beiser M. 1976. Personal and social factors associated with the remission of psychiatric symptoms. *Arch. Gen. Psychiatry* 33:941–45

Bidzinska E. 1984. Stress factors in affective diseases. *Br. J. Psychiatry* 144:161–66

Billings A, Cronkite R, Moos R. 1983. Social-environmental factors in unipolar depression: comparisons of depressed patients and nondepressed controls. *J. Abnorm. Psychol.* 93:119–33

Birtchnell J, Evans C, Kennard J. 1988. Life history factors associated with neurotic symptomatology in a rural community sample of 40–49 year old women. *J. Affect. Disord.* 3:271–85

Blazer D, Hughes D, George LK. 1987. Stressful life events and the onset of a generalized anxiety syndrome. *Am. J. Psychiatry* 144:1178–83

Blazer DG, Kessler RC, McGonagle KA, Swartz MS. 1994. The prevalence and distribution of major depression in a national community sample: the National Comorbidity Survey. *Am. J. Psychiatry* 151: 979–86

Bloom BL, Hodges WF, Kerns MB, McFadden SC. 1985. A preventive intervention program for the newly separated. *Am. J. Orthopsychiatry* 55:9–26

Brewin CR, Andrews B, Gotlib IH. 1993. Psychopathology and early experience: a reappraisal of retrospective reports. *Psychol. Bull.* 113:82–98

Brown GR, Anderson B. 1991. Psychiatric morbidity in adult inpatients with childhood histories of sexual and physical abuse. *Am. J. Psychiatry* 148:55–61

Brown GW. 1989. Life events and measurement. In *Life Events and Illness,* ed. GW Brown, TO Harris, pp. 3–45. New York: Guilford

Brown GW, Bifulco A, Harris TO. 1987. Life events, vulnerability and onset of depression: some refinements. *Br. J. Psychiatry* 150:30–42

Brown GW, Harris TO. 1978. *Social Origins of Depression: A Study of Psychiatric Disorder in Women.* New York: Free Press

Brown GW, Harris TO, Hepworth C. 1995. Loss, humiliation and entrapment among women developing depression: a patient and nonpatient comparison. *Psychol. Med.* 25:7–21

Brown GW, Moran P. 1994. Clinical and psychosocial origins of chronic depressive episodes. I. A community survey. *Br. J. Psychiatry* 165:447–56

Brugha TS, Bebbington PE, MacCarthy B, Sturt S, Wykes T, Potter J. 1990. Gender, social support and recovery from depressive disorders: a prospective clinical study. *Psychol. Med.* 20:147–56

Bryer JB, Nelson BA, Miller JB, Krol PA. 1987. Childhood sexual and physical abuse as factors in adult psychiatric illness. *Am. J. Psychol.* 144:1426–30

Burgess AW, Holmstrom LL. 1979. Adaptive strategies and recovery from rape. *Am. J. Psychol.* 136:1278–82

Cannell CF, Miller PV, Oksenberg L. 1981. Research on interviewing techniques. In *Sociological Methodology* 1981, ed. S Leinlandt, pp. 389–437. San Francisco: Jossey-Bass

Cohen LH, Towbes LC, Flocco R. 1988. Effects of induced mood on self-reported life events and perceived and received social support. *J. Pers. Soc. Psychol.* 55:669–74

Cooke DJ. 1985. The reliability of a brief life event interview. *J. Psychosom. Res.* 29: 361–65

Coryell W, Endicott J, Keller MB. 1991. Predictors of relapse into major depressive disorder in a nonclinical population. *Am. J. Psychol.* 148:1353–58

Coyne JC. 1976. Depression and the response of others. *J. Abnorm. Psychol.* 85:186–93

Csikszentmihalyi M, Larson R. 1987. Validity and reliability of experience sampling method. *J. Nerv. Ment. Dis.* 175:526–36

Dew MA, Bromet EH, Schulberg HC. 1987. A comparative analysis of two community stressors' long-term mental health effects. *Am. J. Community Psychol.* 15:167–84

Dohrenwend BP, Raphael KG, Schwartz S, Stueve A, Skoldol A. 1993. The structured event probe and narrative rating method for measuring stressful life events. See Mazure 1995, pp. 174–99

Dohrenwend BP, Shrout PE, Link BG, Skodol AE, Stueve A. 1995. Life events and other possible psychosocial risk factors for episodes of schizophrenia and major depression: a case-control study. See Mazure 1995, pp. 43–66

Earls F, Reich W, Jung KG, Cloninger CR. 1988. Psychopathology in children of alcoholic and antisocial parents. *Alcohol Clin. Exp. Res.* 12:481–87

Eaton WW, Kramer M, Anthony JC, Dryman A, Shapiro S, Locke BZ. 1989. The incidence of specific DIS/DSM-III mental disorders: data from the NIMH epidemiologic catchment area program. *Acta Psychiatr. Scand.* 79:163–78

Eckenrode J, Bolger N. 1995. Daily and within-day event measurement. See Cohen et al 1995, pp. 80–101

Ensel WM. 1982. The role of age in the relationship of gender and marital status to depression. *J. Nerv. Ment. Dis.* 170:536–43

Falsetti SA, Resnick HS, Dansky BS, Lydiard RB, Kilpatrick DG. 1995. The relationship of stress to panic disorder: cause or effect? See Mazure 1995, pp. 111–48

Faravelli C, Sacchetti E, Ambonetti A, Conte G, Pallanti S, Vita A. 1986. Early life events and affective disorder revisited. *Br. J. Psychiatry* 148:288–95

Feather NT. 1990. *The Psychological Impact of Unemployment.* New York: Springer-Verlag

Fendrich M, Warner V, Weissman MM. 1990. Family risk factors, parental depression, and psychopathology in offspring. *Dev. Psychol.* 26:40–50

Fleming JE, Offord DR. 1990. Epidemiology of childhood depressive disorders: a critical review. *J. Am. Acad. Child Adolesc. Psychiatry* 29:571–80

Goodyear IM. 1990. Family relationships, life events and childhood psychopathology. *J. Child Psychol. Psychiatry* 31:161–92

Gotlib IH, Hammen C. 1992. *Psychological Aspects of Depression: Toward a Cognitive-Interpersonal Integration.* New York: Wiley

Gotlib IH, McCabe SB. 1990. Marriage and

psychopathology. In *The Psychology of Marriage: Basic Issues and Applications,* ed. F Fincham, T Bradbury, pp. 226–55. New York: Guilford

Hammen C. 1991. The generation of stress in the course of unipolar depression. *J. Abnorm. Psychol.* 100:555–61

Hammen C, Marks T, Mayol A, Deayo R. 1985. Depressive self-schemas, life stress, and vulnerability to depression. *J. Abnorm. Psychol.* 94:308–19

Harrington R, Fudge H, Rutter M, Pickles A, Hill J. 1990. Adult outcomes of childhood and adolescent depression. *Arch. Gen. Psychiatry* 47:465–73

Heaney CA. 1992. Enhancing social support at the workplace: assessing the effects of the Caregiver Support Program. *Health Ed. Q.* 18:477–94

Holahan C, Moos R. 1991. Life stressors, personal and social resources, and depression: a 4-year structural model. *J. Abnorm. Psychol.* 100:31–38

Holland PW. 1986. Statistics and causal inference (with discussion). *J. Am. Stat. Assoc.* 81:945–70

Holmes SJ, Robins LN. 1988. The role of parental disciplinary practices in the development of depression and alcoholism. *Psychiatry* 51:24–36

Holmes TH. 1979. Development and application of a quantitative measure of life change magnitude. In *Stress and Mental Disorder,* ed. JE Barrett, RM Rose, GL Klerman, pp. 37–54. New York: Raven

Holmes TH, Rahe RH. 1967. The social adjustment rating scale. *J. Psychosom. Res.* 11: 213–18

House JS, Cottington E. 1986. Health and the workplace. In *Applications of Social Science to Clinical Medicine and Health Policy,* ed. LH Aiken, D Mechanic, pp. 382–415. New Brunswick, NJ: Rutgers Univ. Press

Huxley PJ, Goldberg DP, Maguire GP, Kincey VA. 1979. The prediction of the course of minor psychiatric disorders. *Br. J. Psychiatry* 135:535–43

Jessop DJ, Riessman CK, Stein RE. 1988. Chronic childhood illness and maternal mental health. *J. Dev. Behav. Pediatr.* 9: 147–56

Karasek RA, Theorell T. 1990. *Healthy Work.* New York. Basic Books

Karp JF, Frank E, Anderson B, George CG, Reynolds CF, et al. 1993. Time to remission in late-life depression: analysis of effects of demographic, treatment, and life-events measures. *Depression* 1:250–56

Kasl SV. 1978. Epidemiological contributions to the study of work stress. In *Stress at Work,* ed. C Cooper, R Payne, pp. 3–48. New York: Wiley

Keller MB, Lavori PW, Rice J, Coryell W, Hirschfeld RWA. 1986. The persistent risk of chronicity in recurrent episodes of nonbipolar major depressive disorder: a prospective follow-up. *Am. J. Psychiatry* 143: 24–28

Kendler KS, Kessler RC, Walters EE, MacLean C, Neale MC, et al. 1995a. Stressful life events, genetic liability, and onset of an episode of major depression in women. *Am. J. Psychiatry* 152:833–42

Kendler KS, Neale MC, Kessler RC, Heath AC, Eaves LJ. 1992. A population-based twin study of major depression in women: the impact of varying definitions of illness. *Arch. Gen. Psychiatry* 49:257–66

Kendler KS, Neale MC, Kessler RC, Heath AC, Eaves LJ. 1993. A twin study of recent life events and difficulties. *Arch. Gen. Psychiatry* 50:789–96

Kendler KS, Walters EE, Neale MC, Kessler RC, Heath AC, Eaves LJ. 1995b. The structure of the genetic and environmental risk factors for six major psychiatric disorders in women. *Arch. Gen. Psychiatry* 52: 374–83

Kessler RC, Gillis-Light J, Magee WJ, Kendler KS, Eaves LJ. 1996a. Childhood adversity and adult psychopathology. In *Trajectories and Turning Points: Stress and Adversity Over the Life Course,* ed. IH Gotlib, B Wheaton. New York: Cambridge Univ. Press. In press

Kessler RC, Kendler KS, Heath A, Neale MC, Eaves LJ. 1992. Social support, depressed mood, and adjustment to stress: a genetic epidemiologic investigation. *J. Pers. Soc. Psychol.* 62:257–72

Kessler RC, Magee WJ. 1993. Childhood adversities and adult depression: basic patterns of association in a U.S. National Survey. *Psychol. Med.* 23:679–90

Kessler RC, Magee WJ. 1994a. Childhood family violence and adult recurrent depression. *J. Health Soc. Behav.* 35:13–27

Kessler RC, Magee WJ. 1994b. The disaggregation of vulnerability to depression as a function of the determinants of onset and recurrence. In *Stress and Mental Health: Contemporary Issues and Prospects for the Future,* ed. WR Avison, IH Gotlib, pp. 239–58. New York: Plenum

Kessler RC, Magee WJ, Nelson CB. 1996b. Analysis of psychosocial stress. In *Psychosocial Stress: Perspective on Structure, Theory, Life Course and Methods,* ed. H Kaplan, pp. 333–66. Academic

Kessler RC, McGonagle KA, Swartz M, Blazer DG, Nelson CB. 1993. Sex and depression in the National Comorbidity Survey I. Lifetime prevalence, chronicity, and recurrence. *J. Affect. Disord.* 29:85–96

Kessler RC, Mroczek DK, Belli RF. 1997. Ret-

rospective adult assessment of childhood psychopathology. In *Assessment in Child Psychopathology,* ed. D Shaffer, J Richeters. New York: Guilford. In press
Kessler RC, Sonnega A, Bromet E, Hughes M, Nelson CB. 1995. Posttraumatic stress disorder in the National Comorbidity Survey. *Arch. Gen. Psychiatry* 52:1048–60
Kessler RC, Turner JB, House JS. 1987. Intervening processes in the relationship between unemployment and health. *Psychol. Med.* 17:949–61
Kessler RC, Wethington E. 1991. The reliability of life event reports in a community survey. *Psychol. Med.* 21:723–38
Krantz SE, Moos RH. 1988. Risk factors at intake predict nonremission among depressed patients. *J. Consult. Clin. Psychol.* 56:863–69
Krosnick A. 1970. Psychiatric aspects of diabetes. In *Diabetes Mellitus: Theory and Practice,* ed. M Ellenberg, H Rifkin, pp. 920–33. New York: McGraw-Hill
Kulik JA, Mahler HIM. 1993. Emotional support as a moderator of adjustment and compliance after coronary artery bypass surgery: a longitudinal study. *J. Behav. Med.* 16:45–64
Lewinsohn PM, Hoberman HM, Rosenbaum M. 1988. A prospective study of risk factors for unipolar depression. *J. Abnorm. Psychol.* 97:251–64
Lief A. 1948. *The Commonsense Psychiatry of Dr. Adolf Meyer.* New York: McGraw-Hill
Lloyd C. 1980. Life events and depressive disorders reviewed. II. Events as precipitating factors. *Arch. Gen. Psychiatry* 37:541–48
Mann AH, Jenkins R, Belsey E. 1981. The twelve-month outcome of patients with neurotic illness in general practice. *Psychol. Med.* 11:535–50
Mazure C, ed. 1995. *Does Stress Cause Psychiatric Illness?* Washington, DC: Am. Psychiatr. Press
McGonagle KA, Kessler RC. 1990. Chronic stress, acute stress, and depressive symptoms. *Am. J. Community Psychol.* 18:681–705
McLeod JD. 1991. Childhood parental loss and adult depression. *J. Health Soc. Behav.* 35: 205–20
McLeod JD, Kessler RC, Landis KR. 1992. Speed of recovery from major depressive episodes in a community sample of married men and women. *J. Abnorm. Psychol.* 101: 277–86
McQuaid J, Monroe SM, Roberts JR, Johnson SL, Garamoni GL, et al. 1992. Toward the standardization of life stress assessment: definitional discrepancies and inconsistencies in method. *Stress Med.* 8:47–56
Miller P, Salter DP. 1984. Is there a short-cut? An investigation into the life event interview. *Acta Psychiatr. Scand.* 70:417–27
Mirowsky J, Ross C. 1989. *Social Causes of Psychological Distress.* New York: Aldine de Gruyter
Monroe SM, Kupfer DJ, Frank E. 1992. Life stress and treatment outcome of recurrent depression. I. Response during index episode. *J Consult. Clin. Psychol.* 60:718–24
Monroe SM, Steiner SC. 1986. Social support and psychopathology: interrelations with preexisting disorder, stress, and personality. *J. Abnorm. Psychol.* 95:29–39
Mrazek PB, Haggerty RJ. 1994. *Reducing Risks for Mental Disorders: Frontiers for Preventive Intervention Research.* Washington, DC: Natl. Acad. Press
Orbuch TL, Veroff J, Holmberg D. 1993. Becoming a married couple: the emergence of meaning in the first years of marriage. *J. Marriage Fam.* 55:815–26
Parker G, Bliguault I, Manicavasagar V. 1988. Neurotic depression: delineation of symptom profiles and their relation to outcome. *Br. J. Psychiatry* 152:15–23
Parker G, Hadzi-Pavlovic D. 1984. Modification of levels of depression in mother-bereaved women by parental and marital relationships. *Psychol. Med.* 14:125–35
Patrick V, Dunner D, Fieve R. 1978. Life events and primary affective illness. *Acta Psychiatr. Scand.* 58:48–55
Paykel E. 1979. Recent life events in the development of the depressive disorders. In *The Psychobiology of the Depressive Disorders: Implications for the Effects of Stress,* ed. R Depue, pp. 245–62. New York: Academic
Pearlin LI. 1989. The sociological study of stress. *J. Health Soc. Behav.* 30:241–56
Pless IB. 1994. *The Epidemiology of Childhood Disorders.* New York: Oxford Univ. Press
Post RM. 1992. Transduction of psychosocial stress into the neurobiology of recurrent affective disorder. *Am. J. Psychiatry* 149: 999–1010
Post RM, Rubinow DR, Ballenger JC. 1986. Conditioning and sensitisation in the longitudinal course of affective illness. *Br. J. Psychiatry* 149:191–201
Price RH, Van Ryn N, Vinokur A. 1992. Impact of a preventive job search intervention on the likelihood of depression among the unemployed. *J. Health Soc. Behav.* 33: 158–67
Quinton D, Rutter M, Liddle C. 1984. Institutional rearing, parenting, difficulties and marital support. *Psychol. Med.* 14:107–24
Raphael KG, Cloitre N, Dohrenwend BP. 1991. Problems with recall and misclassification with checklist methods of measuring stressful life events. *Health Psychol.* 10: 62–74

Robins LN, Regier DA. 1991. *Psychiatric Disorders in America: The Epidemiologic Catchment Area Study.* New York: Free Press
Rutter M. 1989. Pathways from childhood to adult life. *J. Child Psychol. Psychiatry* 30: 23–51
Sarason IG, Johnson JH, Siegel JM. 1978. Assessing the impact of life change: development of the Life Experiences Survey. *J. Consult. Clin. Psychol.* 46:32–46
Sargeant JK, Bruce ML, Florio LP, Weissman MM. 1990. Factors associated with 1-year outcome of major depression in the community. *Arch. Gen. Psychiatry* 47:519–26
Shrout PE, Link B, Dohrenwend B, Skodol AE. 1989. Characterizing life events as risk factors for depression: the role of fateful loss events. *J. Abnorm. Psychol.* 98:460–67
Sobel ME. 1990. Effect analysis of causation in linear structural equation models. *Psychometrika* 55:495–515
Sobell LG, Toneatto T, Sobell MB, Schuller R, Maxwell M. 1990. A procedure for reducing error in reports of life events. *J. Psychosom. Res.* 2:163–70
Sorenson SB, Rutter CM, Aneshensel CS. 1991. Depression in the community: an investigation into age of onset. *J. Consult. Clin. Psychol.* 59:541–46
Soumi SJ. 1991a. Adolescent depression and depressive symptoms: insights from longitudinal studies with rhesus monkeys. *J. Youth Adolesc.* 20:272–87
Soumi SJ. 1991b. Primate separation models of affective disorders. In *Neurobiology of Learning, Emotion and Affect,* ed. J Madden IV, pp. 195–214. New York: Raven
Stein JA, Golding JM, Siegel JM, Burnam MA, Sorenson SB. 1988. Long-term psychological sequelae of child sexual abuse: the Los Angeles Epidemiologic Catchment Areas Study. In *Lasting Effects of Child Sexual Abuse,* ed. GE Wyatt, GJ Powell, pp. 135–54. Newbury Park, CA: Sage
Stroebe MS, Stroebe W. 1983. Who suffers most? Sex differences in health risks of the widowed. *Psychol. Bull.* 93:279–301
Taylor SE, Aspinwall LG. 1996. Mediating and moderating processes in psychosocial stress: appraisal, coping, resistance, and vulnerability. In *Psychosocial Stress, Perspective on Structure, Theory, Life-Course, and Methods,* ed. H Kaplan, pp. 71–110. San Diego: Academic
Tennant C. 1988. Parental loss in childhood: its effect in adult life. *Arch. Gen. Psychiatry* 45:1045–50
Thoits PA. 1983. Dimensions of life events that influence psychological distress: an evaluation and synthesis of the literature. In *Psychosocial Stress: Trends in Theory and Research,* ed. HB Kaplan, pp. 33–103. New York: Academic
Tsaung MT, Farone SV. 1990. *The Genetics of Mood Disorders.* Baltimore: Johns Hopkins Univ. Press
Turner JB, Kessler RC, House JS. 1991. Factors facilitating adjustment to unemployment: implications for intervention. *Am. J. Community Psychol.* 19:521–42
Turner RJ, Wheaton B. 1995. Checklist Measurement of Stressful Life Events. See Cohen et al 1995, pp. 29–53
Umberson D, Wortman CB, Kessler RC. 1992. Widowhood and depression: explaining long-term gender differences in vulnerability. *J. Health Soc. Behav.* 33:10–24
Veroff J, Douvan E, Hatchett S. 1993. Marital interaction and marital quality in the first year of marriage. In *Advances in Personal Relationships,* ed. W Jones, D Pearlman, 4:103–37. Greenwich, CT: JAI
Von JM, Kilpatrick DG, Burgess AW, Hartman CR. 1991. Rape and sexual assault, In *Violence in America: A Public Health Approach,* ed. ML Rosenberg, MA Finley, pp. 95–122. New York: Oxford Univ. Press
Weissman MM, Leaf PJ, Tischler GL, Blazer DG, Karno M, et al. 1988. Affective disorders in five United States communities. *Psychol. Med.* 18:141–53
Weissman MM, Prusoff BA, Klerman GL. 1978. Personality and the prediction of long-term outcome of depression. *Am. J. Psychiatry* 135:797–800
West MO, Prinz RJ. 1987. Parental alcoholism and childhood psychopathology. *Psychol. Bull.* 102:204–18
Wethington E, Brown GW, Kessler RC. 1995. Interview measurement of stressful life events. See Cohen et al 1995, pp. 59–79
Williamson DE, Birmaher B, Anderson BP, Al-Shabbout M, Ryan ND. 1995. Stressful life events in depressed adolescents: the role of dependent events during the depressive episode. *J. Acad. Child Adolesc. Psychiatry* 34:591–98
Wolff HG, Wolf S, Hare CC. 1950. *Life Stress and Bodily Disease.* Baltimore: Williams & Wilkins
Yama MF, Tovey SL, Fogas BS. 1993. Childhood family environment and sexual abuse as predictors of anxiety and depression in adult women. *Am. J. Orthopsychiatry* 63: 136–41
Zautra AJ, Reich JW. 1983. Life events and perceptions of life quality: developments in a two-factor approach. *J. Community Psychol.* 1:121–32
Zimmerman M. 1983. Methodological issues in the assessment of life events: a review of issues and research. *Clin. Psychol. Rev.* 3: 339–70

Annu. Rev. Psychol. 1997. 48:215–41

LANGUAGE ACQUISITION: The Acquisition of Linguistic Structure in Normal and Special Populations

Janet L. McDonald

Department of Psychology, Louisiana State University, Baton Rouge, Louisiana 70803

KEY WORDS: prosody and phonology, function words, morphological decomposition, special populations, age of acquisition

ABSTRACT

This review examines how language learners master the formal structure of their language. Three possible routes to the acquisition and mastery of linguistic structure are investigated: (*a*) the use of prosodic and phonological information, which is imperfectly correlated with syntactic units and linguistic classes; (*b*) the use of function words to syntactically classify co-occurring words and phrases, and the effect of location of function-word processing on structural mastery; and (*c*) the use of morphology internal to lexical items to determine language structure, and the productive recombination of these subunits in new items. Evidence supporting these three routes comes from normal language acquirers and from several special populations, including learners given impoverished input, learners with Williams syndrome, specific language-impaired learners, learners with Down syndrome, and late learners of first and second languages. Further evidence for the three routes comes from artificial language acquisition experiments and computer simulations.

CONTENTS

0084-6570/97/0201-0215$08.00

INTRODUCTION

Given the linguistic input that children receive, how are they able to learn and master the structure (i.e. morphology and syntax) of language? Some theorists have proposed that learners use semantic information to bootstrap into syntax. That is, meaning and meaning commonalities are used as a basis for initial linguistic categories and serve learners in gaining access into language structure. This viewpoint has been well documented elsewhere (Pinker 1984). This review considers alternatives to the semantic route, including the use of prosodic and/or phonological information (Gleitman et al 1988), and the analysis of the distributional and co-occurrence patterns of linguistic elements (Maratsos & Chalkley 1980). The latter possibility will be further distinguished by whether the linguistic elements are at or below the word level. Gaining structural information from elements at the word level involves using function words to classify co-occurring words or phrases. Gaining structural information from elements below the word level involves performing a morphological analysis on lexical items, extracting meaningful units, and looking for patterns in the occurrence of these units across items.

This review examines evidence that learners use the above routes of prosodic and phonological information, function words, and morphological decomposition to master the structure of their language. Evidence from normal young native-language learners is presented first, followed by evidence from two classes of special populations of language learners—one class that succeeds at mastering linguistic structure despite impediments, and one class that fails. Finally, data supporting a causal link between the three routes and the acquisition of linguistic structure are presented from artificial language learning experiments and computer simulations.

ACQUISITION IN NORMAL POPULATIONS

Prosodic and Phonological Information

Use of prosodic and phonological information to figure out language structure is known as phonological bootstrapping (Morgan & Demuth 1996a). This approach examines whether infants can exploit a variety of prosodic and phonological cues in the input that are imperfectly correlated with syntactic units. Prosodic and phonological information is readily available in the input stream and is exploitable at an early age. The results of research on phonological bootstrapping, detailed below, show that infants younger than one year already know a great deal about the prosodic and phonological characteristics of their native language and are capable of using this information to help segment the input into smaller units. These smaller units often, but not always, correspond to syntactically meaningful units. In addition to providing segmentation information, prosody and phonology also provide information about individual lexical items. This information can be used to classify lexical items into distinct categories that mirror syntactic classes, such as content and function words. Over the past decade, research on the use of prosody and phonology in segmentation and categorization has yielded substantial results.

SEGMENTATION As infants progress through their first year of life, they appear to be able to use prosodic and/or phonological information to detect smaller and smaller units in a continuous speech stream. Seven-month-old infants prefer speech interrupted at clause boundaries to speech interrupted elsewhere (Hirsh-Pasek et al 1987; see also Fernald & McRoberts 1996). Nine-month-olds (but not six-month-olds) prefer speech interrupted at major syntactic phrase boundaries to that interrupted at minor boundaries; prosodic cues correlated to these major boundaries include pitch and durational changes (Jusczyk et al 1992). If prosodic cues to syntactic boundaries are not present, this preference for pauses between syntactic units does not occur (Gerken et al 1994). Eleven-month-olds (but not nine-month-olds) prefer connected speech interrupted between word boundaries rather than within a word (research cited in Hirsh-Pasek & Golinkoff 1993). This preference for word boundary interruption is probably not based on prosody but on sensitivity to more specific phonological information in the speech stream. Such information could include allophonic variations (differences in the way phonemes are pronounced within vs across word boundaries) and phonotactic rules (the legality of phoneme sequences that can occur within vs across word boundaries). Infants do show sensitivity to these phonological cues in word-list form: Two-month-olds are sensitive to allophonic differences that mark word boundaries (Hohne & Jusczyk 1994), and nine-month-olds (but not six-month-olds) are sensitive to the phonotactic properties and constraints of their native language (Jusczyk et al 1993b,1994).

While sensitivity, in connected speech, to units as small as words does not appear to develop until near the end of the first year, research on short isolated strings shows that very young infants can detect units on both the word and syllable level. Infants as young as three days old can detect the difference between isolated bisyllables that contain word boundaries and those that do not; correlated cues to word boundaries include differences in duration and energy characteristics of the phonemes on either side of the boundary (Christophe et al 1994). Three- and four-day-old infants can also detect the difference between bi- and trisyllabic isolated strings; this performance may be based on discrimination of vowel nuclei (Bijeljac-Babic et al 1993).

The ability to segment the speech stream using prosodic and phonological cues may be only one example of a general segmentation ability. For example, four-and-a-half-month-old infants prefer music with pauses inserted at musical phrase boundaries over pauses inserted elsewhere. These boundaries are marked by specific acoustic cues such as a drop in pitch height and an increase in duration before the boundary (Jusczyk & Krumhansl 1993).

Some researchers have proposed a general device for segmenting language input into subunits based on the rhythmic cues present in prosody (Cutler & Mehler 1993, Petitto 1993). These theories propose that infants are born with a bias or sensitivity to periodic or rhythmically alternating subunits and that this bias enables them to segment linguistic input (see also Morgan 1994). Because different languages have different periodic units (e.g. English has stress units and French has syllabic units), infants use this bias to segment their language appropriately. This bias is not specific to speech input. Young sign-language learners also segment their input into syllable-like units, and they use these units in their manual babbling (Petitto & Marentette 1991).

CATEGORIZATION OF UNITS Even if infants can segment the speech stream into structurally meaningful units, they still are far from having learned the grammar. After segmentation is achieved, learners must be able to classify these units into syntactically meaningful categories. That is, it is not enough to know where one phrase or word ends and another one starts; a further prerequisite for grammatical mastery is the classification of units occurring in different utterances as members of a common syntactic category (e.g. noun phrase, verb phrase, etc for phrases; determiner, noun, adjective, etc for words). Once units are classified into syntactic categories, patterns in their occurrences can be detected. Although there are semantic correlates to syntactic categories, recent research has shown that there are also phonological and prosodic correlates (for some of these correlates, see Kelly 1992, Morgan et al 1996). Below I examine whether such correlates could be used by infants to form word-class categories.

One distinction particularly important to the acquisition of grammar is that between closed-class words (function words such as determiners and prepositions) and open-class words (content words such as nouns and verbs). Since function words serve as markers of syntactic structure, the ability to distinguish this class of items should greatly enhance the acquisition of syntax. Perhaps due to their status as structural markers, function words do tend to have prosodic and phonological properties different from content words. An analysis of function words and content words in child-directed speech across two languages shows significant differences between these two word classes on such properties as number of syllables, syllable complexity, and vowel duration (Morgan et al 1996). However, there is a high degree of overlap between function and content words on any one of these properties. When one tries to classify individual words on the basis of one of these properties, classification is correct only about 65% of the time. However, if information from all cues is considered jointly, classification performance jumps to as high as 91%. This high level of performance also occurs if all the cues are fed into a neural network, which is able to classify words without any prior knowledge of category membership (Morgan et al 1996). Thus, information from multiple cues, each weakly correlated to the class distinction, may allow for good discrimination between classes.

In addition to distinguishing between function words and content words, a language learner also has to distinguish between content word classes such as nouns and verbs. Besides the obvious semantic differences between these two form classes, Kelly (1992) has shown there are multiple partially correlated phonological cues to these classes. These cues include stress patterns, number of syllables, duration, and types of vowels and consonants used. There is good evidence that young infants are sensitive to at least some of these cues. For example, nine-month-old infants can discriminate bisyllables with strong-weak stress from those with weak-strong stress. They also prefer the former dominant English pattern if English is their native language (Jusczyk et al 1993a). As already noted, four-day-old infants can distinguish between bi- and trisyllabic strings (Bijeljac-Babic et al 1993). Thus, it is possible that learners could distinguish members of noun and verb form classes on a phonological as well as a semantic basis.

In summary, recent research on prosodic and phonological cues to structure has supported the possibility that these surface features may be a route into syntax. Infants appear to be sensitive to a variety of these cues and could use them to aid in segmenting the speech stream and in determining form class. It is important to note that the correspondence between these types of cues and syntactic structure is imperfect. That is, any individual cue may be only weakly correlated with the syntactic unit. However, there are usually multiple possible cues, and these cues tend to be intercorrelated. Learning is actually easier in such an intercorrelated system than in a single cue system, whether the correspondence is perfect or imperfect (Billman 1989).

Function Words

Another access route into the structure of language is the use of function words to help classify clauses, phrases, and words into grammatical categories. Of course, the learner must first know which words are function words in order to use them to help with structural acquisition. As outlined above, however, function and content words may be distinguished early in acquisition using prosodic and phonological cues.

Evidence from language production indicates that function words are produced later than content words. Function words tend to be omitted from early utterances, which results in the telegraphic speech characteristic of early learners. New function words are less acceptable to children than new content words. For example, three-to-five-year-old children are less likely to correctly repeat a sentence containing a nonsense word if the word serves in a function-word capacity than if it serves in a content-word capacity (Chafetz 1994).

Although the evidence from production seems to indicate that children do not have strong control over function words, there is evidence that they can use these words to aid comprehension from an early age. For example, two-year-olds more accurately pick out a picture of an item if it is requested in a sentence frame where the noun is preceded by a structurally appropriate article rather than by an inappropriate auxiliary (Gerken & McIntosh 1993). Thus, even at the young age of two, children have some awareness of co-occurrence restrictions between specific function and content words and thus may be able to use function-word information to make assignments of form class to following words.

While children's awareness and use of function words may develop early, their ability to process these types of words in the rapid automatic way manifested by adults does not develop until much later. Adults appear to process function words largely in the left-hemisphere anterior temporal regions, and they process content words more bilaterally and in the posterior regions (Mohr et al 1994, Neville et al 1992). Adults also show more rapid processing of function words than of content words; and although processing of function words is impervious to semantic context, that of content words is not (Friederici 1985).

Children do not show the above adult distinctions in processing closed- and open-class items. Young learners appear to process function and content words in the posterior regions, similar to the way adults process content words. With development, this posterior response to function words diminishes, and a left-hemisphere anterior response emerges that reaches adult levels at around 15 to 16 years of age (research cited in Neville 1995). Children with better grammatical knowledge show earlier emergence of the left-hemisphere anterior response, as do children with less superior cortical gray matter volume (Neville 1995). This latter result implies that mastery of function-word processing occurs around the same time that the excessive synaptic connections in a child's brain undergo pruning, a potential correlate of automatization.

Children also do not show the quick and automatic processing of function words seen in adults. Young children actually process function words more slowly than content words and show semantic context effects to function words as well as content words. With development, function-word processing speed catches up with that of content words, but it is not until the ages of nine to eleven years that the adult reaction-time patterns (i.e. more rapid processing of function words than of content words, and lack of semantic context effects on latencies to function words) are seen (Friederici 1983). However, the error rates of these children still do not show the same pattern as adults, which indicates that eleven-year-olds still have not totally achieved adultlike processing.

In summary, while children may be able to use function words early on to help figure out language structure, specialized processing of function words is not present from birth. Rather, it develops slowly with time, not reaching adult levels until the teenage years.

Morphological Decomposition

Some cues to language structure occur within a lexical unit. For example, in English, morphological markers of a verb's person and number (-s for third person singular), or tense (-ed for past), are directly attached to the verb. To master these word internal markers, learners must be able to decompose items into their subunits and then notice commonalities across items.

Young learners can decompose words into morphological subunits. Classic evidence for such morpheme extraction ability is seen in the overregularization of irregular past-tense forms (e.g. eated) that occurs when learners apply the regular past-tense morpheme to irregular verbs. Although there is not a specific developmental period where all irregular verbs are overregularized (Marcus et al 1992), overregularization on a microlevel appears to occur when learners have acquired a critical mass of verbs and, importantly, when a significant proportion of these verbs are regular (Marchman & Bates 1994; but see Marcus 1996).

A very striking case of morphological analysis is seen in deaf children exposed to a standard sign language [e.g. American Sign Language (ASL)] by native signers from birth. ASL signs typically consist of multiple morphemes simultaneously articulated. Individual morphemes correspond to grammatical units, such as verb agreement and aspect, or meaning units such as the classification of an object as human, animate nonhuman, or as belonging to other such classes. The child learners of this language show a typical developmental trend in which signs are first produced correctly as unanalyzed wholes. They then appear to regress and produce signs that only contain one or two morphemes; the rest are omitted. Next they may produce all the morphemes present in the target sign, but one after another, rather than simultaneously. At this point, they are showing knowledge but not yet full mastery of the componential nature of the signs. Full mastery of the morphological structure of signs does not occur until four to five years of age (Newport 1988).

In summary, initially words may be acquired as unanalyzed wholes. Subsequently learners do decompose words into morphological subcomponents.

The emergence of morphological analysis may depend on vocabulary size and composition.

ACQUISITION IN SPECIAL POPULATIONS

I now turn to language-acquisition characteristics for two classes of special populations of language learners. The first class includes two groups of learners who largely succeed in mastering the structure of language despite strong limitations. This class includes deaf children receiving impoverished language input and people with Williams syndrome who have diminished cognitive capacity. In the second class are learners who largely fail to master linguistic structure. This class includes children with specific language impairment, people with Down syndrome, and late learners of first or second languages. After the findings for all these groups are reviewed, explanations for their success or failure are considered according to the three routes to structural mastery outlined for normal learners.

Successful Learners

LEARNERS GIVEN IMPOVERISHED INPUT Impoverished, low-structure input is received naturalistically by some deaf children of hearing parents. These parents have chosen not to expose their child to a formal sign language. Rather, they communicate with their child orally with accompanying gestures. In this situation, deaf children develop a method of gestural communication known as home sign.

The gestural input of the parents tends to be primarily single gestures, and the strings that are produced do not show many ordering regularities (Goldin-Meadow & Mylander 1984). There also appears to be little consistent internal morphology in the parental gestures. Hand shape and movement components of parental gestures frequently cannot be assigned consistent meaning, and the components occur in limited combination. Particular combinations also refer to a particular object or action, not to a class (Goldin-Meadow & Mylander 1990, Goldin-Meadow et al 1995).

In contrast to this impoverished parental input, the home sign systems of the children contain structure on both the sentence and single gesture level. Gestural strings contain ordering and deletion regularities, as well as recursion (Goldin-Meadow & Mylander 1984). Internal morphology is consistent, with individual gestures consisting of a limited set of hand shapes and motion components. These individual shape and motion components can be tied to particular meanings, and these components are combined in far more ways than in the parental input. In addition, particular combinations refer to classes of events rather than to just a single event (Goldin-Meadow & Mylander 1990, Goldin-Meadow et al 1995).

This morphological system is not present from the beginning of signing but develops with time. A developmental analysis of the morphological nature of one home signer's gestures showed that initially signs were treated holistically, with individual signs referring to a particular object or action. However, around the age of 3;3–3;5 signs were extended to classes of events, and more importantly, components of signs were used in new combinations to refer to appropriate objects/events (Goldin-Meadow & Mylander 1990, Mylander & Goldin-Meadow 1991). The home signer had apparently decomposed his holistic signs into components and was able to productively recombine the components to convey new information. At around the time of this morphological analysis, the home signer began to treat a sign differently depending on its syntactic class. Earlier the signer had used different signs for nouns and verbs. However, at 3;3 the same sign was used in both a noun and a verb sense, but the way the sign was produced differed according to syntactic class in terms of completeness of the gesture, place where the gesture was made, and/or position in the output string (Goldin-Meadow et al 1994). Again, there was no basis for this distinction in the parental input.

Thus, although the input received by the home signer was greatly impoverished—i.e. it contained little word order regularity, inconsistent mapping between sign components and meanings, and no marking of form class—the learner manifested some control of all these levels of linguistic structure. Moreover, the young learner was able to perform morphological decomposition and recombination of his own signs and was able to distinguish in formal ways between two types of content words. Although what the home signer did was truly remarkable, it should be pointed out that he did not totally reinvent all aspects of language structure. For example, syntactic regularity was limited, and no evidence was found for invention or use of function words.

The ability to create morphological regularity also has been found when deaf infants are exposed to a standard sign language by nonnative signers. In this case, the input to the learner is not as impoverished as that given to the home signer, but the nonnative signers do make errors in their production. This results in an imperfect correspondence between morphological components and meaning. Just as in the case of the home signer, the learner in this situation is able to go beyond the input given and form a system that has high morphological consistency (Newport 1988, Singleton 1989).

Thus, it appears that even when given impoverished or errorful input, children are capable of obtaining some degree of structural sophistication. When learning from nonsigners or nonnative signers, children go beyond the input they are given and form a consistent morphological system.

WILLIAMS SYNDROME People with Williams syndrome show mental retardation coupled with linguistic skills above their mental ages. Adolescent and adult

Williams syndrome subjects have good vocabularies and good grammatical command (Bellugi et al 1994). It is interesting to note that this linguistic advancement is not apparent at young ages. For example, two Williams syndrome subjects studied by Thal et al (1989), one at 5;6 and the other at 1;11, were only at the one-word stage.

People with Williams syndrome manifest some unusual auditory processing properties. For example, event-related brain potential (ERP) studies of tone processing show that Williams syndrome subjects process auditory stimuli in the same area of the brain as normals, but their responses display less refraction. That is, at short intervals (200 ms), Williams syndrome subjects show more excitation to tones than normals, who are still in the refractory period. This effect is specific to auditory stimuli; it does not occur in the visual domain (Neville et al 1994). In addition, auditorily presented words elicit different ERP profiles from Williams syndrome subjects than normals. However, the two groups show similar patterns for visually presented words. Williams syndrome subjects also show a larger differential ERP response to congruent versus anomalous sentence completions than normal subjects. Parallel to previous results, this larger effect is only true in the auditory and not the visual modality (Neville et al 1994). Thus, research has consistently found processing differences between Williams syndrome subjects and normals in the auditory domain and failed to find them in the visual domain. Williams syndrome subjects appear to be using a different system than normals to process auditory information, including language.

Young Williams syndrome children tend to do well on gesturing tasks when given good contextual support, but they do poorly when abstract or analytic processing must occur (Thal et al 1989). This suggests that Williams syndrome subjects may be using holistic or rote strategies. Some researchers have speculated that use of such strategies may allow for the high-level language development shown by older Williams syndrome subjects (Thal et al 1989). This possibility contrasts with findings in the visuospatial domain that indicate that Williams syndrome subjects do not do holistic processing. If they are asked to reproduce a large figure made up of smaller components (e.g. a large letter "D" formed by arranging "Y"s in a D shape), Williams syndrome adolescents produce the smaller components but miss the larger configuration (Bihrle et al 1989). This result parallels that found for right hemisphere damage patients who also show attention to local detail and not to global configuration and who have relatively intact language capabilities (Bihrle et al 1989).

Unsuccessful Learners

LANGUAGE-IMPAIRED LEARNERS Specific language impairment (SLI) is a classification applied to people (usually children) who have significant delays in language abilities but who do not have other cognitive, neurological, or perceptual (particularly hearing) deficits (for overviews, see Bishop 1992, Fletcher & Ingham 1995). English-speaking SLI subjects may have impaired syntax and vocabulary and may have particular difficulty with grammatical morphemes such as third-person singular, regular past tense, determiners, and the auxiliary 'be' (Leonard et al 1992; for a summary table of studies, see Fletcher & Ingham 1995). Cross-linguistic research on SLI children has shown, however, that these particular morphemes are not difficult to acquire in general. Italian SLI children show little difficulty with third-person singular morphology (Leonard et al 1992), and Hebrew SLI children show little difficulty with past-tense morphology (Dromi et al 1993). Leonard (1989) has proposed that rather than grammatical status, it is the low phonetic content of certain grammatical morphemes that contributes to the difficulties SLI children have. Across languages, the grammatical morphemes that do give SLI children trouble appear to have in common a relative short duration and a lack of perceptual salience. This includes the above-mentioned morphemes in English, unstressed articles and clitics in Italian (Leonard et al 1992), and unstressed accusative case markers in Hebrew (Dromi et al 1993). In German, SLI children have difficulties with articles, auxiliaries, case morphology, and subject-verb agreement inflections (Clahsen 1989). While many of these have low phonetic substance, they also involve agreement between disparate elements. This factor may also impact SLI learners (Clahsen 1989, Rice & Oetting 1993), although cross-linguistic results do not always support this theory (Leonard et al 1992).

Other researchers have also found problems with phonological encoding or storage in SLI learners. This is reflected in their poorer performance than age-matched controls on tests of short-term memory that require a verbal response and that emphasize sequential ordering. For example, young SLI children aged three to five have significantly smaller word spans than age-matched controls (Kushnir & Blake 1996). Ten- and eleven-year-old SLI children show a similar result, verbally recalling fewer items than age-matched controls on a pictorially presented list. Language-impaired children have difficulty with item ordering and make semantically related intrusion errors, which indicates that they may have lost the phonological form of the items (Kirchner & Klatzky 1985).

Gathercole & Baddeley (1990) have proposed that language-impaired children have deficits specifically in phonological storage. For example, language-impaired children are significantly worse than normal children (even younger children matched for language level) at a nonword repetition task (Gathercole & Baddeley 1990, Montgomery 1995a,b). It is not the case that SLI children cannot encode information phonologically—they show the standard phonological encoding effects of word length and phonological similarity in word-list recall on short lists (Gathercole & Baddeley 1990, Montgomery 1995b).

However, for SLI children these effects diminish or disappear on longer lists, whereas they do not for age- and language-matched controls. Thus, at these longer list lengths, the language-impaired children may have reached the limit of their phonological store and switched to another encoding strategy, while normal children continued using their phonological store (Gathercole & Baddeley 1990). While the ability to repeat a nonword may seem remote from real language processing, it has been shown that this ability is positively correlated with measures of sentence comprehension (Montgomery 1995a) and with later vocabulary level in normal children (Gathercole & Baddeley 1989).

The above theories and results focus on difficulties SLI children have with phonological encoding and storage. However, the problems SLI learners have are not limited to the linguistic domain. Whether the stimuli are linguistic or nonlinguistic in nature, SLI children generally appear to have difficulty processing rapid sequential information. For example, language-impaired children perform significantly worse than age-matched controls in rapidly supplying words in response to a sequence of pictures. They also are similarly impaired if asked to respond with gestures in the same task. They also tend to have more difficulty than normals in oral (e.g. rapid word repetition) and manual (e.g. finger touching) rapid sequenced motor behavior (Katz et al 1992).

Tallal and colleagues have proposed that the difficulty SLI learners have with processing rapid sequential information, and their phonological difficulties, are due to a general deficit in temporal processing. Deficits in temporal processing would cause sequential information to be difficult to encode and maintain. Such a deficit would also impact the processing of phonological information, because to identify certain phonemes listeners must be able to analyze rapid transitions in particular formants. SLI learners do indeed show difficulty in detecting brief formant transitions (Tallal & Piercy 1973, 1975). This difficulty in detecting formant transitions would especially impair the processing of short unstressed morphemes where formant transitions would be of shortest duration, and thus may help explain the difficulty SLI learners have with these low-phonetic-substance morphemes.

In contrast to specific deficits in phonological encoding and storage or in a temporal processing mechanism, some researchers have proposed that the difficulties experienced by SLI learners are due to a more general processing limitation (Bishop 1992, Ellis Weismer & Hesketh 1996, Leonard 1996). Under this view, children will be slower acquirers but will develop along the same paths as normal children (Curtiss et al 1992).

There is also evidence that SLI children who have particular difficulties with grammar do not process function words in the same manner as normal children. ERP responses to function words are stronger in the left than in the right hemisphere for normal children and for SLI children with a relatively good command of grammar. In contrast, responses to function words are stronger in the right hemisphere than in the left for SLI children with low grammar ability. These group differences are only found for function words. ERP responses to content words are similar for normal and SLI children (Neville et al 1993).

The diagnosis of SLI covers a heterogeneous class of people. Thus, across the population of SLI subjects more than one reason for their impairment may exist. The overview above has shown that possible reasons include difficulty with phonological encoding or storage, difficulty processing rapid sequential information, limited processing capacity, and abnormal processing of function words.

DOWN SYNDROME People with Down syndrome have mental retardation and limited language development. They show delayed onset of speech (around two-and-a-half to four years old), have slow phonological development, and low morpho-syntactic development (Chapman 1995, Rondal 1993). Down syndrome subjects tend to reach their maximum mental age of four or five in their early adolescence, and their language development may cease at that time, although some investigators have found that language continues to develop in Down syndrome subjects beyond puberty (Chapman 1995, Rondal 1993). Regardless of whether development continues beyond adolescence, the language mastery of Down syndrome subjects remains limited, especially in the morpho-syntactic domain.

Down syndrome subjects may suffer from an auditory processing disadvantage that is above and beyond any hearing impairments they may have (Chapman 1995). Down syndrome subjects perform more poorly than mental-age matched normals and retarded controls on auditory short-term memory tasks, whereas the three groups perform similarly on visual STM tasks (Marcell et al 1988). Down syndrome subjects also fail to show the standard superiority of auditory over visual presentation in STM tasks (Marcell et al 1988, Pueschel et al 1987).

People with Down syndrome may also have trouble decomposing items into their constituent parts. For example, if asked to draw a large figure composed of smaller components, Down syndrome adolescents produce the large figure but ignore the smaller components (Bihrle et al 1989). This inability to break down a whole into its parts (although here demonstrated in the spatial domain) could contribute to problems Down syndrome individuals have with structural elements in language. Indeed, left-hemisphere–damage patients also show this pattern of global processing in the spatial domain and poor language ability (Bihrle et al 1989).

LATE LEARNERS OF A FIRST LANGUAGE Another population that has problems mastering language is late learners, that is, people who do not begin their language exposure until late childhood or beyond. While typically this happens more frequently with second-language exposure, it also occurs naturalistically with first-language exposure.

Perhaps the most familiar examples of late exposure to a first language occur in the cases of so-called wild children. Owing to unusual circumstances, including abuse and neglect, these children are not exposed to normal language input in their early years. The most famous of these cases, Genie, was not discovered until her early teen years and never did gain mastery of syntax and morphology (Curtiss 1977). Language mastery by other language-deprived children varies, with at least some children catching up to age peers over time (Skuse 1993). It is not clear from this limited number of case studies what factors dictate whether language mastery will occur, although possibilities include degree of malnutrition during deprivation, cognitive level (including mental retardation and autism), ability to form social bonds, and the age when the child was discovered.

A less familiar instance of late first-language exposure occurs in the case of deaf children born to parents who do not know or learn a signed language. Late exposure to a signed language occurs for these children usually when they are placed in a school with other deaf children. The research reviewed below shows that late learners, even those with many years of language exposure, do perform significantly differently than native signers on on-line language tasks.

Late learners have difficulty decoding the surface form of signs and gaining rapid access to the lexicon. For example, if signers are presented with increasingly long samples of a sign in a gating paradigm, late learners need larger time slices than native signers to correctly guess the sign (Emmorey & Corina 1990). Late learners appear not to be qualitatively different from native signers but appear to be slower in identifying surface phonological features and thus in identifying signs.

This difficulty in rapidly identifying signs causes late learners problems in real-time tasks. For example, although both late learners and native signers make errors in shadowing and recalling sign-language sentences, native learners substitute signs that are similar in meaning, whereas late learners substitute signs that have similar surface form (Mayberry & Fischer 1989). This pattern indicates that early learners have accessed the meaning of the signs, while late learners have not; they were still decoding surface form. This problem with surface-form decoding increases linearly with age of acquisition, with the oldest acquirers tested—adolescents—showing the most phonological substitutions and the least semantic substitutions (Mayberry & Eichen 1991, Mayberry & Fischer 1989).

This slow-down in the ability to decode and recognize signs may increase the working memory load on late signers and consequently may cause other problems in language understanding. For example, late learners who have the most difficulty decoding the surface form of signs, as witnessed by their high number of surface form substitution errors in a memory task, also show the greatest problems in discourse comprehension in general (Mayberry 1995). The high memory load involved in surface decoding appears to prevent late learners from doing specific high-memory-demanding comprehension tasks. For example, late learners have trouble giving the previous referents for pronouns if there are multiple (e.g. three) pronouns in a string; early learners, however, are able to do this (Mayberry 1995).

Late signers also appear to have problems in recognizing and making rapid use of certain types of morphological information. Late learners are more likely than native signers to simply leave off bound morphemes in a recall task (Mayberry & Eichen 1991). Nonnative signers perform more poorly than native signers on the production and comprehension of grammatical morphemes, and this decline is linear with age of acquisition (Newport 1990). Even if late signers have conscious knowledge of ASL morphology, they may not be able to use it in on-line tasks. For example, nonnative signers are just as able as native signers to detect violations of verb-agreement morphology in an off-line grammatical judgment task. However, when they are asked to monitor a sentence for a particular sign, nonnative signers do not show disruption in performance if the sign occurs after a verb-agreement error. Native speakers, however, do show disruption after agreement errors (Emmorey et al 1995). Thus, even though they have knowledge of the correct form, late signers do have trouble detecting and using certain morphemes in on-line tasks. Late learners do not show this difficulty detecting errors on-line for all grammatical morphemes. For example, late signers are just as disrupted as native signers by aspect morphology errors in a sign monitoring task (Emmorey et al 1995).

While the above research shows that late learners are slow at decoding surface form and recognizing and using certain morphological information, it just indicates a delay in use, which is especially noticeable in on-line tasks. The late learner does appear to have knowledge of the morphological structure of sign language. However, other research has indicated that late learners may not have completely analyzed the morphological structure of their language. For example, late learners appear to use some multimorphemic signs as frozen units and do not adjust the internal morphology of these signs to correspond to changes in the situation being described. Native signers, however, do make the appropriate changes in internal morphology (Newport 1988).

Another example of lack of complete morphological analysis in late learners involves the classifier handshape component of signs. This component indicates the type of entity—human, animate nonhuman, vehicle, etc, that is involved in an action. Late (adolescent) learners are not disrupted by violations in classifier handshape in a sign monitoring task, whereas younger (early childhood) learners and natives are. In addition to not being able to use classifier information in an on-line task, late learners also have some difficulty with classifiers in an off-line grammatical judgment task; this indicates weak knowledge of this component (Emmorey 1993).

LATE LEARNERS OF A SECOND LANGUAGE More common than late exposure to a first language is late exposure to a second language. Late learners are often distinguishable from native speakers in casual conversations through their accents and through their grammatical errors or use of unusual linguistic structures.

Late second-language learners perform consistently worse than native speakers and early second-language learners on tests of syntax and morphology; their performance on grammatical judgment tests does not even overlap that of native speakers (Coppieters 1987, Johnson 1992, Johnson & Newport 1989). Even in some cases where native speakers and late learners give the same grammaticality judgment for a sentence, their linguistic intuitions or reasons that they give for their answers still differ (Coppieters 1987). Certain types of grammatical constructions give late learners more trouble than others. For example, late learners of English from Chinese- or Korean-speaking backgrounds have a great deal of difficulty with determiners, plurals, and subcategorization information but have less difficulty with the present progressive and word order (Johnson & Newport 1989).

One study has failed to find a difference between late learners and native speakers on a test of grammar (Birdsong 1992). In this study there was a high amount of overlap between the level of performance of adult second-language learners and natives. It should be pointed out, however, that this was due to the variability of the native group being high rather than to the variability of the late learners being low.

While late (adult) second-language learners perform more poorly than native speakers on grammatical tests, childhood and early adolescent second-language acquirers also have problems. Learners acquiring their second language after the age of seven are significantly worse at grammatical judgments than native speakers (Johnson & Newport 1989). Grammatical competency appears to decrease linearly with age: There is a significant linear decrease in performance for learners acquiring a second language between the ages of 3 and 15 (Johnson & Newport 1989). This linear decreasing trend may disappear for postpuberty learners (Johnson & Newport 1989). However, at least one study found a significant linear decrease with age of acquisition for adult learners (Birdsong 1992). The effect of age of acquisition holds even if years of exposure and use are partialed out or held constant.

Late second-language learners may have some trouble decoding phonological information in on-line tasks. A comparison of a grammatical judgment task that was given auditorily to an identical test given in a written format found an effect of age of acquisition for both versions (Johnson 1992). However, while some grammatical markers (e.g. determiners and plurals) were difficult in both versions of the test, others (e.g. pronouns and past tense) were easier for nonnative speakers to process in the written than in the auditory mode. This suggests that nonnative speakers may have had trouble detecting some phonological information quickly enough in the auditory presentation to allow them to apply the grammatical knowledge they displayed in the written mode (Johnson 1992).

A body of research using ERPs has found differences between native speakers and late second-language learners in the location and timing of grammatical information processing. For example, native English speakers have a reaction in the left frontal and anterior temporal regions to closed-class words and in the temporal and posterior regions in both hemispheres to open-class words (Neville et al 1992). Late second-language learners of English, in this case deaf native ASL signers who learned English after enrolling in a deaf school, do not show a reaction specific to the left hemisphere to the closed-class words. They do, however, demonstrate the same pattern of response as native speakers to open-class words (Neville et al 1992). This particular group of late learners scored poorly on objective grammar tests. A group of deaf late learners of English who performed well (at native levels) on tests of English grammar, however, did show the nativelike left hemisphere response to closed-class words (Neville 1991).

In another study, the second-language learners of English were native speakers of Chinese who had learned English at various ages, ranging from before three to after sixteen. While these second-language learners showed the nativelike left hemisphere response to closed-class words and bilateral reaction to open-class words, if their age of acquisition was over seven the reaction to closed-class words was delayed (Weber-Fox 1994). A further test was run on the detection of grammatical violations. Native English speakers as well as the young second-language learners manifested a reaction in the left hemisphere to these violations. Older second-language learners, however, manifested a more symmetrical pattern (Weber-Fox 1994).

One interesting study exists in which age of late acquisition was held constant, and the acquisition of a language was compared for those learners who were acquiring it as a first language and those who were acquiring it as a second language (Mayberry 1993). Both subject groups had massive exposure (about 50 years) to ASL, the language in question. The first–language acquisition group consisted of congenitally deaf people who had learned ASL as a first language at around age nine. The second–language acquisition group consisted of native English speakers who had lost their hearing in late childhood, around the age of nine, and then adopted ASL as their primary means of communication. A group of native ASL signers was also included for comparison. Late first-language learners showed the typical patterns detailed in the prior section. Compared to native ASL speakers, they tended to have less accurate recall of base signs and to make a higher proportion of phonological errors and a lower proportion of semantic errors in a sentence recall task. They also gave fewer grammatical and meaning preserving answers. The late second-language group, while still having less accurate recall of base signs, was otherwise basically closer to the native ASL group than to the late first-language learners. Late second-language learners had the low phonological/high semantic error pattern of native speakers and gave better grammatical and meaning preserving answers than the late first-language learners (although they were still distinct from native speakers on the latter measure). Thus, although the late second-language learners had difficulty identifying signs, they were better able to cope with this problem than late first-language learners. Perhaps late second-language learners were able to use knowledge about their first language to aid in processing their second. The focus of their advantage may be in memory; late second-language learners have larger STM sign spans than late first-language learners. This larger span may indicate they have more capacity for processing linguistic information than late first-language learners (Mayberry 1993).

Summary of Data from Special Populations

Evidence from the special populations described above provides support for all three of the routes to structural mastery reviewed in the first section.

PROSODIC AND PHONOLOGICAL INFORMATION To succeed in acquiring linguistic structure, learners may need to have access to information from the surface form of language. This would require adequate auditory processing for spoken language and visual processing for signed language. Any difficulties with sensory perception, processing, or storage could lead to problems with grammatical mastery.

There are no problems with surface form processing for either of the populations of successful learners. No problems in visual/spatial processing occur for home signers. In addition, while auditory processing actually appears to be different from normals in Williams syndrome subjects, their increased auditory sensitivity seems to give them a processing advantage for this type of information.

All of the populations of unsuccessful learners manifest some problem with processing surface form information. SLI learners have difficulty detecting certain phonological information (Tallal & Piercy 1973, 1975), have trouble with low phonetic substance grammatical morphemes (Dromi et al 1993, Leonard 1989, Leonard et al 1992), and may also have inadequate phonological stores (Gathercole & Baddeley 1990, Kirchner & Klatzky 1985, Montgomery 1995a,b). Down syndrome subjects have a processing deficit specific to the auditory modality (Marcell et al 1988). Late learners, while not having a sensory deficit per se, have trouble rapidly using surface form information (Emmorey & Corina 1990), and they thus show differences and deficits in many real-time tasks (Emmorey et al 1995, Mayberry & Eichen 1991, Mayberry & Fischer 1989).

FUNCTION WORDS Information about the processing of function words was not available for all the special populations. However, two of the unsuccessful learner groups do manifest difficulty with function words, including SLI learners, who have difficulty with determiners and some auxiliaries in English (Leonard et al 1992) and later learners of a second language, who have difficulty, for example, with determiners (Johnson 1992, Johnson & Newport 1989).

While use of function words may help learners break into syntax, the achievement of native-like grammatical mastery may require rapid, automatic processing of those words. This automatization seems to correspond to a shift to left hemisphere anterior temporal processing of function words that occurs in the teen-age years (Neville et al 1992). Learners who have trouble on grammatical tests generally do not show the same hemispheric specialization of processing of function words and grammatical information as normal adults. This is true for SLI children (Neville et al 1993) and late second-language learners (Neville et al 1992, Weber-Fox 1994). Those few SLI and late learners who do show good grammatical performance also show the left hemisphere processing set-up of natives (Neville 1991, Neville et al 1993).

MORPHOLOGICAL DECOMPOSITION The ability to decompose lexical items into component morphemes is a hallmark of the first group of successful learners, young children exposed to impoverished (Goldin-Meadow & Mylander 1990, Mylander & Goldin-Meadow 1991) or flawed input (Newport 1988, Singleton 1989). The second class of successful learners, Williams syndrome subjects, also manifests the ability to break wholes down into their parts in a visual spatial task (Bihrle et al 1989).

At least two groups of unsuccessful learners show problems with decomposing units into their component parts. Down syndrome subjects are not able to draw the smaller components making up a larger spatial configuration (Bihrle et al 1989). Late learners of ASL often fail to analyze their signs into their component parts and inappropriately use these frozen wholes in contexts that demand internal adjustment (Newport 1988).

ACQUISITION OF ARTIFICIAL LANGUAGES AND COMPUTER MODELS

While the above evidence supports the possibility that the three routes of prosody and phonology, function words, and morphological decomposition could help learners break into the structure of their language, it does not establish a direct causal link. That is, it remains to be shown that the use of any of the three routes will allow mastery of language structure, or that problems in any of the routes will lead to a failure in mastery. Below, such causal evidence is presented from studies of artificial language learning in adults and in computer models.

Artificial Languages

Researchers have used artificial languages to examine the cues adults can use to acquire linguistic structure. An artificial language consists of legal grammatical strings generated by an underlying phrase structure grammar. Vocabulary consists of nonce words assigned to particular syntactic classes. Learners are exposed to a subset of grammatical strings of words and later are asked to form new strings or judge new strings for grammaticality. Mastery of various structural rules is tested by varying the type of new strings tested.

Results of research using artificial languages have yielded evidence that each of the three routes outlined here do allow adults to master the grammatical structure of an artificial language. First, there is evidence that adults can use prosodic grouping cues to master the phrase structure grammar underlying an artificial language. Adults perform better on tests of grammatical knowledge if training strings have pauses inserted at syntactic boundaries than if the pauses are inserted arbitrarily or if no pauses occur (Morgan et al 1987). Second, adults use lexical items that act as function words to help master the grammatical structure. Adults show better structural mastery if either words and/or phrases are systematically marked by function words than when no such markers are present (Green 1979, Morgan et al 1987, Valian & Coulson 1988). Further, these function words are best utilized if the stress pattern of function and content words in the artificial language follows that of the native language (Cutler 1993). Third, learners also use morphological components internal to lexical items to master linguistic structure. Adults show better mastery of linguistic structure when lexical items in syntactically meaningful phrases are marked by common morphological elements than when arbitrary marking or no such marking is present (Meier & Bower 1986, Morgan et al 1987). Learners can also use word internal commonalities to learn and generalize membership in linguistic categories (Brooks et al 1993).

Computer Models

Computer simulations of language acquisition also provide evidence for causal links between some of the proposed access routes and mastery of linguistic structure. The first simulation reported below shows how a weakened phonological representation causes problems in the mastery of morphology. The remaining simulations illustrate how a limited working memory capacity may aid in the morphological decomposition process and may improve mastery of linguistic structure.

Hoeffner & McClelland (1993) have examined how the strength of the phonological representation in a computer model affects its subsequent mastery of verb morphology. In the simulation, they exposed a neural network to 385 monosyllabic English verbs in their base form, as well as four inflected forms: past tense, third-person singular, progressive, and past participle. One version of the simulation was presented with normal phonological input, and another was presented with systematically weakened phonological input. In general, the phonologically impaired model exhibited slower acquisition and was more error prone than the standard model. It is interesting to note that the pattern of errors that the impaired model made was not uniform across the different verb forms. Rather, this model showed selective impairment on regular past tense, third-person singular, and past participle forms. The base, irregular past tense, and progressive forms were only minimally impacted. Thus, the effect of a weakened phonological input had specific consequences for mastery of morphology. Most importantly, the pattern of disruption manifested by the phonologically impaired model—problems with regular past tense, third-person singular, and past participle forms—is the same pattern shown by SLI learners. The model therefore supports the theory that the difficulties SLI learners have mastering morphology are due to problems with phonological processing.

Other simulations have explored the role of limited memory capacity in mastering linguistic structure. It has been proposed that the ability of young children to perform morphological decomposition is actually a consequence of their limited working memory capacity (Newport 1988, 1990, 1991). This "Less Is More" hypothesis states that the limited memory capacity of young children may actually aid them in the acquisition of language in that they may only be able to perceive and encode small pieces of input. In effect, this automatically decomposes the language for them. Older learners, however, with their larger memory capacity, may be able to encode large stretches of linguistic input, memorize these as wholes, and consequently never gain mastery over their component parts.

In a computer simulation test of the "Less Is More" hypothesis, Goldowsky & Newport (1992) tested how a full model and a capacity-limited model learned the mapping between morphology and meaning. Models were exposed to pairs of items, the first one consisting of three morphological components and the second of three meaning components. There was a one-to-one correspondence between individual morphological and meaning components. In attempting to learn this correspondence, the full model considered all possible combinations of individual, pairs, and triples of morphemes, and individual, pairs, and triples of meaning units. While the full model did find the correspondence between individual morphemes and their meaning, it was also filled with spurious noise—correspondences on higher levels that were supported by the data but that did not reflect the true mapping of a single morpheme to a single meaning. These false correspondences capture inappropriate generalizations of the kind seen in late learners. In contrast to the full model, the capacity-limited model only considered one or two morphological components and one or two meaning components for any pair of items; these components were chosen at random. The limited-capacity model also found the correct form-meaning correspondences but contained far less noise than the full model. Thus, considering only a random subset of the input actually made it easier to discover the correct form-meaning correspondences.

Although Newport has proposed that a limited working memory capacity aids a child by filtering the input and breaking down the language into subcomponents, others have proposed that a limited working memory capacity may amplify relationships present in the input (Kareev 1995). For example, in attempting to map morphemes to meanings, learners must examine the correlations between form and meaning in the input. However, learners must base their estimate of this correlation on limited samples of the input—whatever they can consider at one time in their limited-capacity system. The distribution of the correlation coefficients obtained from limited samples, however, do not represent the true correlation. In fact, they tend to be skewed toward the extremes, and more so for smaller sample sizes. Thus, if a small sample size is used to compute a correlation, it is likely that the correlation will appear to be stronger than it truly is (Kareev 1995). A child, with a more limited working memory capacity than an adult, would be basing correlation estimates on smaller sample sizes. Thus, the child may actually be better able to detect a correlation in the environment than an adult, due to this exaggeration effect of smaller sample sizes. Thus, it is perhaps not so surprising that young children can outperform their inaccurate adult language models in making the mapping between morphology and meaning (Goldin-Meadow & Mylander 1990, Mylander & Goldin-Meadow 1991, Newport 1988, Singleton 1989). For the young learner, the correlation between the two appears to be higher than it actually is.

Although not investigating the effect of morphological decomposition per se, another simulation has directly tested the effect of limited memory capacity on mastery of linguistic structure. In this simulation of language acquisition, Elman (1993) trained a neural network on a fairly complex artificial language. A full network exposed to the entire corpus of sentences in this language could not learn the structure of the language. Elman then created a network that had a working memory limitation in the form of reduced memory for prior elements in the sentence; the severity of this limitation gradually decreased during exposure to the entire corpus of sentences. This memory-limited system, which had the equivalent exposure as the full network, was able to achieve structural mastery of the language.

Exploration of the properties of neural networks help explain the inferiority of the unlimited system. Unlimited systems are easily influenced early on in learning, and depending on the type of input first encountered, may be doing initial learning on a nonrepresentative set. Unlimited systems also easily fall into and cannot get out of local minima—that is, solutions that are consonant with the early input but that are incorrect for the entire learning set. Limited systems, however, have more noise in their input because of their memory limitation. This noise slows down learning and allows a larger set of input to impact initial learning, thus decreasing the chance of becoming trapped in a local minimum.

The models of Newport, Kareev, and Elman all focus on how a limited memory capacity aids learning; however, each offers a somewhat different explanation. Newport claims that a limited capacity system helps break down language into its component parts, i.e. performing de facto morphological decomposition. Kareev suggests that a limited capacity exaggerates relationships present in the input. This could make it easier to acquire form-function mappings imperfectly represented in the input. Elman notes that a limited capacity system delays early learning and that this helps the learner avoid incorrect solutions.

CLOSING REMARKS

Given the information reviewed above, what can we conclude about the routes a learner can use to gain access to language structure, and what properties may be necessary for the learner to achieve native-like mastery? Prosodic and phonological information is imperfectly correlated with syntactic structure. Young children are sensitive to this information, and adults in artificial language experiments are able to use it to master syntactic structure. People who have trouble with processing of this type of information, whether it be due to deficient encoding or storage (e.g. SLI learners, Down syndrome learners), or due to a simple inability to use the information rapidly (e.g. late learners), do not achieve native mastery of language structure.

Function words mark syntactically meaningful units. Despite delays in production, young children are sensitive to function words in comprehension, and adults in artificial language experiments can successfully use function words to master linguistic structure. Learners (e.g. SLI learners, late learners) who do not achieve the native adult pattern of processing function words in the left anterior temporal region also do not demonstrate native mastery of linguistic structure.

Morphology internal to lexical items also carries structural information. Young learners, even those with impoverished input, appear able to decompose words into their morphological units and then to recombine them to form new, appropriate items. Adults are able to use word internal morphology to master the syntactic structure of an artificial language. Learners (e.g. late learners) who have not succeeded in doing a complete morphological analysis of their language make nonnative-like structural errors.

In summary, there is substantial evidence that all three of the routes considered here can help a learner to master the structure of language. However, that does not mean that other routes are not effective. Solving the riddle of how learners master language structure will involve examining how various routes combine or interact with one another.

ACKNOWLEDGMENTS

I thank Claudius Kessler and Janna Oetting for helpful comments on an earlier draft of this review.

Literature Cited

Bellugi U, Wang PP, Jernigan TL. 1994. Williams syndrome: an unusual neuropsychological profile. See Broman & Grafman 1994, pp. 23–56

Bihrle AM, Bellugi U, Delis D, Marks S. 1989. Seeing either the forest or the trees: dissociation in visuospatial processing. *Brain Cogn.* 11:37–49

Bijeljac-Babic R, Bertoncini J, Mehler J. 1993. How do 4-day-old infants categorize multisyllabic utterances? *Dev. Psychol.* 29:711–21

Billman D. 1989. Systems of correlations in rule and category learning: use of structured input in learning syntactic categories. *Lang. Cogn. Process.* 4:127–55

Birdsong D. 1992. Ultimate attainment in second language acquisition. *Language* 68: 706–55

Bishop D. 1992. The underlying nature of specific language impairment. *J. Child Psychol. Psychiatry* 33:3–66

Bishop D, Mogford K, eds. 1993. *Language Development in Exceptional Circumstances.* Hillsdale, NJ: Erlbaum

Broman SH, Grafman J, eds. 1994. *Atypical Cognitive Deficits in Developmental Disorders.* Hillsdale, NJ: Erlbaum

Brooks PJ, Braine MDS, Catalano L, Brody RE, Sudhalter V. 1993. Acquisition of gender-like noun subclasses in an artificial language: the contribution of phonological markers to learning. *J. Mem. Lang.* 32:76–95

Chafetz J. 1994. The closed-class vocabulary as a closed set. *Appl. Psycholinguist.* 15: 273–87

Chapman RS. 1995. Language development in children and adolescents with Down syndrome. See Fletcher & MacWhinney 1995, pp. 641–63

Christophe A, Dupoux E, Bertoncini J, Mehler

J. 1994. Do infants perceive word boundaries? An empirical study of the bootstrapping of lexical acquisition. *J. Acoust. Soc. Am.* 95:1570–80

Clahsen H. 1989. The grammatical characterization of developmental dysphasia. *Linguistics* 27:897–920

Coppieters R. 1987. Competence differences between native and near-native speakers. *Language* 63:544–73

Curtiss S. 1977. *Genie: A Psycholinguistic Study of a Modern Day "wild child."* New York: Academic

Curtiss S, Katz W, Tallal P. 1992. Delay versus deviance in the language acquisition of language impaired children. *J. Speech Hear. Res.* 35:373–83

Cutler A. 1993. Phonological cues to open- and closed-class words in the processing of spoken sentences. *J. Psycholinguist. Res.* 22:109–31

Cutler A, Mehler J. 1993. The periodicity bias. *J. Phonet.* 21:103–8

Dromi E, Leonard LB, Shteiman M. 1993. The grammatical morphology of Hebrew-speaking children with specific language impairment: some competing hypotheses. *J. Speech Hear. Res.* 36:760–71

Ellis Weismer S, Hesketh LJ. 1996. Lexical learning by children with specific language impairment: effects of linguistic input presented at varying speaking rates. *J. Speech Hear. Res.* 39:177–90

Elman JL. 1993. Learning and development in neural networks: the importance of starting small. *Cognition* 48:71–99

Emmorey K. 1993. Processing a dynamic visual-spatial language: psycholinguistic studies of American Sign Language. *J. Psycholinguist. Res.* 22:153–87

Emmorey K, Bellugi U, Friederici A, Horn P. 1995. Effects of age of acquisition on grammatical sensitivity: evidence from on-line and off-line tasks. *Appl. Psycholinguist.* 16:1–23

Emmorey K, Corina D. 1990. Lexical recognition in sign language: effects of phonetic structure and morphology. *Percept. Mot. Skills* 71:1227–52

Fernald A, McRoberts G. 1996. Prosodic bootstrapping: a critical analysis of the argument and the evidence. See Morgan & Demuth 1996b, pp. 365–88

Fletcher P, Ingham R. 1995. Grammatical impairment. See Fletcher & MacWhinney 1995, pp. 603–22

Fletcher P, MacWhinney B, eds. 1995. *The Handbook of Child Language.* Cambridge, MA: Blackwell

Friederici AD. 1983. Children's sensitivity to function words during sentence comprehension. *Linguistics* 21:717–39

Friederici AD. 1985. Levels of processing and vocabulary types: evidence from on-line comprehension in normals and agrammatics. *Cognition* 19:133–66

Gathercole SE, Baddeley AD. 1989. Evaluation of the role of phonological STM in the development of vocabulary in children: a longitudinal study. *J. Mem. Lang.* 28: 200–13

Gathercole SE, Baddeley AD. 1990. Phonological memory deficits in language disordered children: is there a causal connection? *J. Mem. Lang.* 29:336–60

Gerken L, Jusczyk PW, Mandel DR. 1994. When prosody fails to cue syntactic structure: 9-month-olds' sensitivity to phonological versus syntactic phrases. *Cognition* 51:237–65

Gerken L, McIntosh BJ. 1993. Interplay of function morphemes and prosody in early language. *Dev. Psychol.* 29:448–57

Gleitman LR, Gleitman H, Landau B, Wanner E. 1988. Where learning begins: initial representations for language learning. In *Linguistics: The Cambridge Survey. Language: Psychological and Biological Aspects,* ed. FJ Newmeyer, 3:150–93. Cambridge: Cambridge Univ. Press

Goldin-Meadow S, Butcher C, Mylander C, Dodge M. 1994. Nouns and verbs in a self-styled gesture system: What's in a name? *Cogn. Psychol.* 27:259–319

Goldin-Meadow S, Mylander C. 1984. Gestural communication in deaf children: the effects and noneffects of parental input on early language development. *Monogr. Soc. Res. Child Dev.* 49:1–121

Goldin-Meadow S, Mylander C. 1990. The role of parental input in the development of a morphological system. *J. Child Lang.* 17: 527–63

Goldin-Meadow S, Mylander C, Butcher C. 1995. The resilience of combinatorial structure at the word level: morphology in self-styled gesture systems. *Cognition* 56: 195–262

Goldowsky BN, Newport EL. 1992. Modeling the effects of processing limitations on the acquisition of morphology: the Less is More hypothesis. *Child Lang. Res. Forum* 24:124–38

Green TRG. 1979. The necessity of syntax markers: two experiments with artificial languages. *J. Verbal Learn. Verbal Behav.* 18:481–96

Hirsh-Pasek K, Golinkoff RM. 1993. Skeletal supports for grammatical learning: what infants bring to the language learning task. In *Advances in Infancy Research,* ed. C Rovee-Collier, LP Lipsitt, 8:299–338. Norwood, NJ: Ablex

Hirsh-Pasek K, Kemler Nelson DG, Jusczyk PW, Cassidy KW, Druss B, Kennedy L. 1987. Clauses are perceptual units for young infants. *Cognition* 26:269–86

Hoeffner JH, McClelland JL. 1993. Can a perceptual processing deficit explain the impairment of inflectional morphology in development dysphasia? A computational investigation. *Child Lang. Res. Forum* 25: 38–49

Hohne EA, Jusczyk PW. 1994. Two-month-old infants' sensitivity to allophonic differences. *Percept. Psychophys.* 56:613–23

Johnson JS. 1992. Critical period effects in second language acquisition: the effect of written versus auditory materials on the assessment of grammatical competence. *Lang. Learn.* 42:217–48

Johnson JS, Newport EL. 1989. Critical period effects in second language learning: the influence of maturational state on the acquisition of English as a second language. *Cogn. Psychol.* 21:60–99

Jusczyk PW, Cutler A, Redanz NJ. 1993a. Infants' preference for the predominant stress patterns of English words. *Child Dev.* 64: 675–87

Jusczyk PW, Friederici AD, Wessels JM, Svenkerud VY, Jusczyk AM. 1993b. Infants' sensitivity to the sound patterns of native language words. *J. Mem. Lang.* 32: 402–20

Jusczyk PW, Hirsh-Pasek K, Kemler Nelson DG, Kennedy LR, Woodward A, Piwoz J. 1992. Perception of acoustic correlates of major phrasal units by young infants. *Cogn. Psychol.* 24:252–93

Jusczyk PW, Krumhansl CL. 1993. Pitch and rhythmic patterns affecting infants' sensitivity to musical phrase structure. *J. Exp. Psychol.: Human Percept. Perform.* 19: 627–40

Jusczyk PW, Luce PA, Charles-Luce J. 1994. Infants' sensitivity to phonotactic patterns in the native language. *J. Mem. Lang.* 33: 630–45

Kareev Y. 1995. Through a narrow window: working memory capacity and the detection of covariation. *Cognition* 56:263–69

Katz WF, Curtiss S, Tallal P. 1992. Rapid automatized naming and gesture by normal and language-impaired children. *Brain Lang.* 43:623–41

Kelly MH. 1992. Using sound to solve syntactic problems: the role of phonology in grammatical category assignments. *Psychol. Rev.* 99:349–64

Kirchner DM, Klatzky RL. 1985. Verbal rehearsal and memory in language-disordered children. *J. Speech Hear. Res.* 28: 556–65

Kushnir CC, Blake J. 1996. The nature of the cognitive deficit in specific language impairment. *First Lang.* 16:21–40

Leonard LB. 1989. Language learnability and specific language impairment in children. *Appl. Psycholinguist.* 10:179–202

Leonard LB. 1996. Characterizing specific language impairment: a cross-linguistic perspective. In *Toward a Genetics of Language,* ed. ML Rice, pp. 243–56. Mahwah, NJ: Erlbaum

Leonard LB, Bortolini U, Caselli MC, McGregor KK, Sabbadini L. 1992. Morphological deficits in children with specific language impairment: the status of features in the underlying grammar. *Lang. Acquis.* 2:151–79

Maratsos M, Chalkley MA. 1980. The internal language of children's syntax: the nature and ontogenesis of syntactic categories. In *Children's Language,* ed. K Nelson, 2: 127–213. New York: Gardner

Marcell MM, Harvey CF, Cothran LP. 1988. An attempt to improve auditory short-term memory in Down's syndrome individuals through reducing distractions. *Res. Dev. Disabil.* 9:405–17

Marchman VA, Bates E. 1994. Continuity in lexical and morphological development: a test of the critical mass hypothesis. *J. Child Lang.* 21:339–66

Marcus GF. 1996. Why do children say "breaked"? *Curr. Dir. Psychol. Sci.* 5:81–85

Marcus GF, Ullman M, Pinker S, Hollander M, Rosen TJ, Xu F. 1992. Overgeneralization in language acquisition. *Monogr. Soc. Res. Child Dev.* 57:1–182

Mayberry RI. 1993. First-language acquisition after childhood differs from second-language acquisition: the case of American Sign Language. *J. Speech Hear. Res.* 36: 1258–70

Mayberry RI. 1995. Mental phonology and language comprehension, or what does that sign mistake mean? In *Language, Gesture and Space,* ed. K Emmorey, JS Reilly, pp. 355–70. Hillsdale, NJ: Erlbaum

Mayberry RI, Eichen EB. 1991. The long-lasting advantage of learning sign language in childhood: another look at the critical period for language acquisition. *J. Mem. Lang.* 30:486–512

Mayberry RI, Fischer SD. 1989. Looking through phonological shape to lexical meaning: the bottleneck of nonnative sign language processing. *Mem. Cogn.* 17:740–54

Meier RP, Bower GH. 1986. Semantic reference and phrasal grouping in the acquisition of a miniature phrase structure language. *J. Mem. Lang.* 25:492–505

Mohr B, Pulvermüller F, Zaidel E. 1994. Lexical decision after left, right and bilateral presentation of function words, content words and nonwords: evidence for interhemispheric interaction. *Neuropsychologia* 32:105–24

Montgomery JW. 1995a. Sentence comprehension in children with specific language impairment: the role of phonological working memory. *J. Speech Hear. Res.* 38:187–99

Montgomery JW. 1995b. Examination of phonological working memory in specifically language-impaired children. *Appl. Psycholinguist.* 16:355–78

Morgan JL. 1994. Converging measures of speech segmentation in preverbal infants. *Infant Behav. Dev.* 17:389–403

Morgan JL, Demuth K. 1996a. Signal to syntax: an overview. See Morgan & Demuth 1996b, pp. 1–22

Morgan JL, Demuth K, eds. 1996b. *Signal to Syntax: Bootstrapping from Speech to Grammar in Early Acquisition.* Mahwah, NJ: Erlbaum

Morgan JL, Meier RP, Newport EL. 1987. Structural packaging in the input to language learning: contributions of prosodic and morphological marking of phrases to the acquisition of language. *Cogn. Psychol.* 19:498–550

Morgan JL, Shi R, Allopenna P. 1996. Perceptual bases of rudimentary grammatical categories: toward a broader conceptualization of bootstrapping. See Morgan & Demuth 1996b, pp. 263–83

Mylander C, Goldin-Meadow S. 1991. Home sign systems in deaf children: the development of morphology without a conventional language model. In *Theoretical Issues in Sign Language Research,* ed. P Siple, SD Fischer, 2:41–63. Chicago: Univ. Chicago Press

Neville HJ. 1991. Neurobiology of cognitive and language processing: effect of early experience. In *Brain Maturation and Cognitive Development,* ed. KR Gibson, AC Petersen, pp. 355–80. New York: Aldine de Gruyter

Neville HJ. 1995. Developmental specificity in neurocognitive development in humans. In *The Cognitive Neurosciences,* ed. MS Gazzaniga, pp. 219–31. Cambridge, MA: MIT Press

Neville HJ, Coffey SA, Holcomb PJ, Tallal P. 1993. The neurobiology of sensory and language processing in language-impaired children. *J. Cogn. Neurosci.* 5:235–53

Neville HJ, Mills DL, Bellugi U. 1994. Effects of altered auditory sensitivity and age of language acquisition on the development of language-relevant neural systems: preliminary studies of Williams syndrome. See Broman & Grafman 1994, pp. 67–83

Neville HJ, Mills DL, Lawson DS. 1992. Fractionating language: different neural subsystems with different sensitive periods. *Cereb. Cortex* 2:244–58

Newport EL. 1988. Constraints on learning and their role in language acquisition: studies of the acquisition of American Sign Language. *Lang. Sci.* 10:147–72

Newport EL. 1990. Maturational constraints on language learning. *Cogn. Sci.* 14:11–28

Newport EL. 1991. Contrasting conceptions of the critical period for language. In *The Epigenesis of Mind,* ed. S Carey, R Gelman, pp. 111–30. Hillsdale, NJ: Erlbaum

Petitto LA. 1993. On the ontogenetic requirements for early language acquisition. In *Developmental Neurocognition: Speech and Face Processing in the First Year of Life,* ed. B de Boysson-Bardies, S de Schonen, P Jusczyk, P McNeilage, J Morton, pp. 365–83. Dordrecht: Kluwer

Petitto LA, Marentette PF. 1991. Babbling in the manual mode: evidence for the ontogeny of language. *Science* 251:1493–96

Pinker S. 1984. *Language Learnability and Language Development.* Cambridge, MA: Harvard Univ. Press

Pueschel SM, Gallagher PL, Zartler AS, Pezzullo JC. 1987. Cognitive and learning processes in children with Down syndrome. *Res. Dev. Disabil.* 8:21–37

Rice ML, Oetting JB. 1993. Morphological deficits of children with SLI: evaluation of number marking and agreement. *J. Speech Hear. Res.* 36:1249–57

Rondal JA. 1993. Down's syndrome. See Bishop & Mogford 1993, pp. 165–76

Singleton JL. 1989. *Restructuring of language from impoverished input: Evidence for linguistic compensation.* PhD thesis. Univ. Ill., Champaign. 188 pp.

Skuse DH. 1993. Extreme deprivation in early childhood. See Bishop & Mogford 1993, pp. 29–46

Tallal P, Piercy M. 1973. Developmental aphasia: impaired rate of nonverbal processing as a function of sensory modality. *Neuropsychologia* 11:389–98

Tallal P, Piercy M. 1975. Developmental aphasia: the perception of brief vowels and extended stop consonants. *Neuropsychologia* 13:69–74

Thal D, Bates E, Bellugi U. 1989. Language and cognition in two children with Williams syndrome. *J. Speech Hear. Res.* 32: 489–500

Valian V, Coulson S. 1988. Anchor points in language learning: the role of marker frequency. *J. Mem. Lang.* 27:71–86

Weber-Fox C. 1994. *Maturational constraints on cerebral specializations for language processing: ERP and behavioral evidence in bilingual speakers.* Presented at Louisiana State Univ., Baton Rouge

Annu. Rev. Psychol. 1997. 48:243–67

FAMILIES AS SYSTEMS

Martha J. Cox and Blair Paley

Frank Porter Graham Child Development Center, University of North Carolina at Chapel Hill, CB# 8180, 105 Smith Level Road, Chapel Hill, North Carolina 27599-8180

KEY WORDS: family systems, family processes, developmental theory

ABSTRACT

In this chapter, we discuss theoretical and conceptual models that use an organismic or systems metaphor for understanding families. We suggest that such theories are important for stimulating new research and organizing existing data, and that advances in these theories over the past few decades have expanded the potential for understanding child development, as well as adult adaptation and the development of close relationships. These paradigms follow from models that view development as resulting from the transactional regulatory processes of dynamic systems. Such models are helpful for considering multiple influences on development and adaptation and have implications for the design of effective interventions. We focus on the specifics of systems theories as applied to families, and the research generated by or consistent with these views. Our review is not exhaustive; rather, we intend to give a sense of the direction of this work and its importance for the understanding of development and adaptation.

CONTENTS

INTRODUCTION

We discuss theoretical and conceptual models that use an organismic or systems metaphor to understand families. We suggest that such theories are important for stimulating new research and organizing existing data, and that advances in these theories over the past few decades have expanded the potential for understanding child development, as well as adult adaptation and the development of close relationships. These paradigms follow from models that view development as resulting from the transactional regulatory processes of dynamic systems. Such models are helpful for considering multiple influences on development and adaptation and have implications for the design of effective interventions. We focus on the specifics of systems theories as applied to families, and the research generated by or consistent with these views. Our review is not exhaustive; rather, we intend to give a sense of the direction of this work and its importance for the understanding of development and adaptation.

It has been noted (Cairns 1983, Sameroff 1983) that advances in embryology provided the empirical demonstrations for a view of development now known as organismic theory or systems theory. Each cell has it own inner controls, but during differentiation each must respond to external controls because each is part of a larger whole. "It is in the balance between individual and collection, part and whole, that the organismic model derives its metaphor. By examining embryological development in detail, it is possible to see how a wholistic emphasis is necessary to understand living systems" (Sameroff 1983, p. 252). Cairns (1983) made a similar point and further observed that (p. 80):

> It required only a modest conceptual leap to consider behavior to be an essential component of the organismic system, and behavioral development to be understood in terms of biological and social features of the system. Hence the "system" in which the organism developed was not merely under the skin. The concept of "organization" would be broadened to include feedback from other organisms and from the social network in which development occurred.

So the metaphor of the system has usefulness in considering environments as systems, yet as Sameroff (1983) noted, although "it is no longer a revolutionary idea for developmental psychologists to see the organism as having psychological structure (thanks primarily to Piaget), few current theories credit the environment with the same property" (p. 242).

The influence of systemic thinking can be seen in work by sociologists such as Cottrell and among early family therapists, including Nathan Ackerman's application of psychoanalytic formulations to family systems, Bowen's notion of the multigenerational transmission of pathology, the Bateson group's (including Jackson, Haley, and Weakland) emphasis on communication patterns within the family, Haley and the Palo Alto group's development of strategic family therapy, the Milan group's systemic family therapy, and Minuchin's structural approach, which emphasizes family organization and regulation of boundaries (for reviews, see Combrinck-Graham 1990, Goldenberg & Goldenberg 1991, Hoffman 1981). However, this literature has existed generally outside of the child development literature and has not had a developmental focus (Kreppner 1989). The recognition that individuals and families are embedded in a larger network of social systems also can be seen in life-span theories (Baltes 1987, Lerner 1989, Parke 1988), ecological theories (Bronfenbrenner 1979), and Lewin's psychological field theory (Cairns 1983). Over the past two decades, the family as a relational environment with systems qualities has received more and more attention from both developmental psychologists and ethologists (e.g. Cowan et al 1991, Hinde 1989, Kreppner & Lerner 1989a, Wagner & Reiss 1995) and is proving useful in guiding and interpreting research.

Sameroff (1983) noted that because the organismic model is really only a metaphor, a more rigorous theory is required that incorporates the principles of an organismic model placed in a more generalized concept. General systems theory, attributed primarily to Bertalanffy (1968), represents such an effort. Although a detailed discussion of Bertalanffy's ideas, developed primarily in the 1930s, is beyond the scope of this review, such discussions can be found elsewhere (Sameroff 1983). We consider here some of the principles of a general systems theory as applied to understanding the family as an organized system. These include properties of (*a*) wholeness and order, referring to the idea that a whole is greater than the sum of its parts and has properties that cannot be understood simply from the combined characteristics of each part; (*b*) hierarchical structure, wherein systems are composed of subsystems that are really systems of their own; (*c*) adaptive self-stabilization, which refers to homeostatic features of systems that compensate for changing conditions in the environment by making coordinated changes in the internal workings of the system; and (*d*) adaptive self-organization, complementary to the notion of self-stabilization, referring to the ability of open, living systems to adapt to change in or challenge to the existing system.

FAMILY AS AN ORGANIZED WHOLE, WITH INTERDEPENDENT COMPONENTS AND HIERARCHICAL STRUCTURE

In emphasizing the importance of understanding properties of the whole, Bertalanffy was responding to the effort in classical science to isolate the elements of the observed universe with the expectation that by putting these elements together again, the whole would be intelligible. Bertalanffy argued that one needs to understand not only the elements of a system but, more importantly, their interrelations (Sameroff 1983). Using the perspective of the family as a system highlights the idea that the family is a "complex, integrated whole" (Minuchin 1988, p. 8), wherein individual family members are necessarily interdependent, exerting a continuous and reciprocal influence on one another. Thus, any individual family member is inextricably embedded in the larger family system and can never be fully understood independent of the context of that system (Kreppner & Lerner 1989b, Minuchin 1985, Sameroff 1994).

Families also show hierarchical structure. Hinde (1989) has noted the importance of recognizing the family as characterized by "successive levels of complexity...[and that] each level is to be considered not as an entity but as a process in continuous creation through the agency of the dialectics" (p. 151). That is, the family is viewed as a hierarchically organized system, comprised of smaller subsystems (e.g. parental, marital, and sibling) but also embedded within larger systems (e.g. the community), and interactions occur within and across these various levels. Subsystems are defined by boundaries, and family members learn rules for relating to one another within and across these boundaries in the context of repeated family interactions. Boundaries between subsystems allow for differentiation in the system. For effective family functioning, boundaries must be clear but flexible. That is, while family members must be allowed to function within subsystems without interference from other members, they also must be able to access resources from the larger family unit as well (Minuchin 1974). Thus, siblings must learn how to negotiate conflict without constant interference from their parents, but they also must be able to seek support or mediation from their parents at times. An important implication of the notion of hierarchical organizations is that "systems at each level do not have unidirectional control functions over those of lower levels" (Sameroff 1983, p. 270). Thus, for example, problematic parent-child relationships may make it more difficult for the young child to develop good self-regulation, but poor regulation in the child can further exacerbate problematic parent-child relationships.

Much of family research has focused on the patterns of interaction within and across family subsystems (e.g. marital and parent-child, parent-child and sibling, parent-child and individual). Less research has focused on the impact of larger units in the family (triadic and whole family), perhaps because conceptualizing and measuring characteristics of the whole system has been difficult. In the next sections, research on the interrelations of family subsystems is considered, followed by a discussion of the limited research on the way in which characteristics of the whole influence the parts.

Individual Functioning and Parent-Child Relationships

Much research considers links between a wide variety of indices of child and adolescent functioning and the quality of parent-child relationships in the family (e.g. Blatt & Homann 1992, Chase-Lansdale et al 1995, Cummings & Davies 1995, Dishion et al 1995, Hauser et al 1991, Radke-Yarrow et al 1995). This research cannot be adequately considered in its entirety here. This body of work, however, provides strong support for the notion that "any understanding of individual behavior divorced from relationship aspects will be seriously incomplete—both because of the influences of relationships and relationship histories on behavior and because of the prominent role of social relations in evaluating individual adaptation" (Sroufe 1989, p. 104). In addition, although much of the focus has been on the role of the mother-child relationship in child development, researchers have increasingly given greater consideration to the importance of other family relationships in both normative development as well as maladaptive trajectories, including father-child (see Belsky 1981, Cox et al 1989, Lamb 1976, Parke 1990, Phares & Compas 1992) and sibling (see Boer & Dunn 1992) relationships. The addition of the father into research on the development of children in families has been particularly important in that relationships with fathers seem to provide experiences for the child that are not simply duplicates of the child's relationship with the mother (Parke 1990).

Individual Functioning, Parent-Child Relationships, and Marital Relationships

A growing body of literature also has documented an association between marital dissatisfaction or conflict and problematic outcomes for children and adolescents (see Cummings 1994, Emery 1982, Grych & Fincham 1990) and disturbances in parent-child relationships (e.g. Cox & Owen 1993, Easterbrooks & Emde 1988, Katz & Gottman 1995), and it suggests that it is through disruption of parenting that marital discord is particularly detrimental for children's development (e.g. Fauber et al 1990, Gottman & Katz 1989). Given the interdependence of family relationships, conflict in the marital dyad is likely to extend to other parts of the family system (Gano-Phillips & Fincham 1995). Minuchin (1974) emphasized the importance of maintaining a clear but permeable boundary between the marital and parent-child subsystems: "the spouse subsystem in an intact family must...differentiate to perform the tasks of socializing a child without losing the mutual support that should characterize the spouse subsystem. A boundary must be drawn which allows the child access to both parents while excluding him from spouse functions" (p. 57). Cummings (1994) has noted that in families with high levels of parental conflict this boundary is likely to be dissolved, as children attempt to mediate, comfort, or distract their parents during disputes.

Emery and colleagues (1992), however, have highlighted the importance of also considering the direct impact of marital conflict on children, as well as children's impact on their parents' marriage. Parents likely serve as models of adult relationships and, in particular, of male-female relationships for their children, providing them with examples of how emotions are communicated and how problems are resolved (or not resolved) between adults (Minuchin 1988). Further, we are reminded that the linkages between these subsystems are likely to be complex. Several investigators have noted that different patterns of marital conflict seem to compromise children in different ways (Fincham & Osborne 1993; Katz & Gottman 1993, 1994; Margolin 1988). Other researchers suggest that exposure to some forms of marital disagreement may actually be beneficial for children, if disagreements are effectively resolved and parents model adaptive problem-solving skills (Cummings & Wilson 1997). Children influence their parents' marriages, as well as being influenced by them. For example, a large body of literature documents that the birth of a child is a significant source of stress on the marital relationship (e.g. Belsky & Pensky 1988, Cowan et al 1991, Cox 1995). Thus, the linkages between marriage, parenting, and child functioning are complex. The findings of studies investigating these linkages attest to the importance of considering the multiple levels of the family system and the mutual impact of these levels in research on child development (Emery et al 1992).

Parent-Child Relationships, Marital Relationships, and Sibling Relationships

Research on siblings provides further evidence that patterns of functioning within one family subsystem are related in systematic ways to functioning within other subsystems. Positive parent-child relationships, for example, are related to more harmonious sibling relationships (e.g. Hetherington 1988, Teti & Ablard 1989, Volling & Belsky 1992), although parental "favoritism" of one child is associated with increased sibling conflict (e.g. Brody et al 1992, Bryant & Crockenberg 1980). Other studies suggest that frequent interventions by parents in sibling conflict also may be problematic (e.g. Brody & Stoneman 1987, Kendrick & Dunn 1983), perhaps because constant intrusions prevent siblings from negotiating the rules that regulate interactions within their relationships. Discordant marital relationships also have been linked to less positive sibling relationships (Hetherington 1988, Jenkins 1992). Again, the integrity of the sibling subsystem may be weakened if siblings are being drawn away from their roles as siblings and into their parents' marital disputes.

Larger Units in the Family System and Dyadic and Individual Functioning

Family therapists have long recognized the importance of expanding their focus to units beyond the dyad in understanding family processes and disturbances. Both Bateson and Bowen, for example, originally viewed schizophrenic behavior in the context of dyadic interactions (usually between parent and child), but they broadened their perspectives to include triadic interactions and the larger family system (see Hoffman 1981). They suggested that individual symptoms indicated the organization of the larger family system and served to maintain that organization. Observations of triadic and whole family interactions may be particularly informative with regard to patterns of family interaction not discernible in dyadic interactions, such as coalitions within the family (i.e. two family members are aligned against a third member), or difficulties regulating boundaries between subsystems (Minuchin 1985). Recent investigations suggest that families with symptomatic children are characterized by weak marital alliances and cross-generational coalitions (Christensen & Margolin 1988, Gilbert et al 1984) or parental coalitions in which "problem" children are scapegoated (Christensen et al 1983, Vuchinich et al 1994). Observing parents functioning as both spouses and parents in the same context may provide much more informative data about the processes by which conflicted marital interactions compromise parent-child relationships.

These ideas suggest the importance of the extension of the unit of analysis in family research to triadic and whole family interactions. However, few studies, using either clinical or normative samples, investigate family units beyond the dyad (Parke 1988). There has been general acceptance that by studying the dyad, one is studying the family. However, the notion of family relationships as dyadic is, at least in part, an artificial construction of researchers. The majority of this dyadic research has focused on the mother-child relationship. Minuchin (1985) has noted that "most of our ideas about child rearing and its effects are based on data drawn from one parent, who has been treated either as the representative of parenting in the family or as the primary source" (p. 296). Many studies suggest that such a limited perspective will be "inadequate for understanding the impact of social interaction patterns in families" (Parke 1988, p. 166). For example, numerous studies indicate that interactions between parent and child are affected by the presence of the other parent (Belsky & Volling 1987, Buhrmester et al 1992, Clarke-Stewart 1978).

A significant amount of parenting occurs in the presence of both parents, yet there have been relatively few studies examining the process of "co-parenting" (Floyd & Zmich 1991, Gable et al 1995, Maccoby et al 1990). Marital conflicts regarding parenting issues may arise in front of children, and conflicts of this nature appear to be particularly distressing for children (see Cummings 1994). In addition, a number of studies have shown that the arrival of a new sibling impacts parents' relationships with their first-born child (e.g. Dunn & Kendrick 1980, Kreppner 1988), while other studies have examined children's involvement in conflicts between their mothers and siblings (Dunn & Munn 1985) and family discussions of sibling problems (Brody et al 1992).

One area of research especially ripe for greater consideration of the larger family unit concerns the study of attachment relationships. While the study of child-caregiver attachment has traditionally been considered in the context of a dyadic (usually mother-child) relationship and has focused on the implications of this relationship for individual child development, a systems perspective underscores the importance of considering not only how dynamics within the larger family system may shape the quality of child-caregiver attachment, but also the consequences of such attachments for the larger family system (Marvin & Stewart 1990).

FAMILIES AND ADAPTIVE SELF-STABILIZATION AND SELF-ORGANIZATION

Adaptive self-stabilization refers to the features of systems that compensate for changing conditions in the environment by making coordinated changes in the internal workings of the system. This buffering capacity reduces the effects of the outside environment on the system (Sameroff 1983). No living system could survive without pattern and structure (Hoffman 1981). Applied to the family, this notion leads to a consideration of the regularities, rules, and structures that organize the family system and maintain its features through negative feedback when significant deviations occur, as when members violate shared family rules or values. Sameroff (1989) referred to the family codes that regulate development to produce members that fulfill a role within the family. Minuchin (1985) noted that these processes form part of the family's self-regulation and for most families are adaptive. However, when patterns involve self-defeating cycles, stereotyped solutions, rigidly applied rules, and intolerance for change, they may set the stage for dysfunction (Sroufe 1989). In dysfunctional families, the processes of regulation may incorporate symptoms and maladaptive behaviors as necessary aspects that maintain the family system (Minuchin 1985), such as in systems in which the generational boundaries are unclear and children are repeatedly called upon to meet the emotional, or even sexual, needs of a parent (Sroufe 1989). This notion of homeostatic features is commonly seen in writings of family therapists and is considered critical to the family therapist's understanding of how a family functions (Minuchin 1985). While various therapeutic approaches may emphasize different aspects of family interaction, they nonetheless share a common focus in regarding individual symptoms as reflective of the functioning of the larger family system in which individuals are embedded, and in emphasizing "the role played by symptomatic behaviors in helping to balance or unbalance that system" (Hoffman 1981, p. 17). Such approaches have been applied to a variety of psychiatric disorders, including schizophrenia (e.g. Bateson et al 1956, Bowen 1959) and eating disorders (Minuchin et al 1978), and they have continued to stimulate family systems conceptualizations of substance abuse (e.g. Stanton et al 1982), depression (e.g. Coyne et al 1992), and antisocial behavior (e.g. Patterson 1982).

Complementary to the property of adaptive self-stabilization, natural systems are seen as having a property called "adaptive self-organization," which refers to the capacity of systems to reorganize in response to changes from external forces acting on internal constraints. The term "adaptive" suggests that the direction of change is one in which the existing system can best continue to function in the face of the new circumstances (Sameroff 1983). Using this property as metaphor with regard to the family, it suggests that there will be challenges to existing patterns at all levels of the family system at certain normative transition times (i.e. birth of a child, transition to school) and at some less normative transition times (i.e. departure of a partner or spouse or entrance of a new partner, death of a family member). Because these challenges will affect the family at multiple levels, consideration must be given to how change in activity at each level influences other levels requiring change again in a feedback loop. Thus, we must look at how individuals in the family respond to transitions, but it also is important to understand the developmental trajectories of larger units in the family (i.e. husband-wife dyad or parent-child dyad) as well as the family unit itself and the dialectics between levels (Parke 1988). These inputs will disrupt ongoing patterns in the system, and eventually new patterns will emerge as an adaptation to the family's changed circumstances. Frequently, these new patterns are more complex and differentiated (Minuchin 1985). Sameroff (1983) noted that "adaptively reorganized systems are not necessarily more stable systems. They may deal well with forces that elicit the process of self-organization, but they may not be more resistant to all factors in the general environment. To the extent that self-organization results in a greater complexity of structure, the system becomes thermodynamically more 'improbable' and potentially unstable" (p. 267). Thus, reorganizations of the family as a system, though they may be responsive to the challenges to the system, may create new vulnerabilities. These notions as applied to the family suggest the importance of looking at transition points in the family life cycle and have implications for our understanding of continuity and discontinuity in adult adaptation, child development, and family functioning. Transition points may be particularly important in stimulating disruptions and challenges at each level of family systems. They may be times of greatest risk for family dysfunction.

In line with the view that systems are dynamic and changing through time, transitions do not occur at a discrete point in time but rather are best understood in process terms: Reorganization of a system during a transition unfolds over time (Cowan 1991). Several transition processes have been studied. Because of limited space, we discuss here how a systems model helps organize findings from two specific areas of study of transitions: research on the transition to parenthood and the transition in family structure associated with divorce or remarriage. Following this we consider how the properties of self-stabilization and self-organization can help us understand processes of continuity and discontinuity at all levels of family systems.

Transition to Parenthood

Much research now exists on the transition to parenthood. Many of the studies capture the systemic quality of the family and consider the mutual and interactive impact of family subsystems. It is clear from this research that the birth of a child and the need for the couple to reorganize around the caregiving of the infant impacts both the individual adults and the marital relationship, and that the changes at these levels feed back into the family system. New parents are at greater risk for psychosis, depression, and the "blues" (Campbell et al 1992, Cowan et al 1991). In addition, Cowan et al (1991) have detailed how new parents in middle-class European-American families typically change attitudes and roles in accommodating to the care of an infant. Gender roles become more traditional, with women taking over more household tasks and care of the child. Men and women show diverging attitudes about their sense of selves as "parents" and "workers," the relative importance of parental versus outside child care, and shifting relationships with kin networks and friends. These new patterns may be more appropriate to the provision of child care, but as Sameroff suggests, they may not be more resistant to all factors in the general environment. In fact, the Cowans find, consistent with the findings of others (Belsky et al 1986), that these increased differences between the roles and attitudes of spouses in response to the task of rearing a child set the stage for greater vulnerability in the marital dyad for dissatisfaction and disruption.

It is common for each partner's satisfaction with the marriage to decrease over time after the birth of the first child and for the amount of negative interaction between partners to increase (Belsky & Pensky 1988, Cox 1995, Cowan et al 1991). In most family systems, this is followed by recovery at about two years after the birth such that marital satisfaction returns to prebirth levels and the amount of negative interaction decreases to prebirth levels. Yet, in other couples the recovery does not occur. Lack of recovery can be seen more often in couples in which the individual spouses have more depressive symptoms, the pregnancy was unplanned, and the couple showed less competent problem-solving skills before the birth of the child (Cox 1995).

Moreover, there is good evidence that there is a mutual impact between the quality of the adaptation in the marital subsystem and the development of the parent-child dyadic relationship (e.g. Cowan et al 1991; Cox et al 1989, 1996; Isabella & Belsky 1985), as well as between the quality of the infant's development and the quality of the parent-child relationship (Belsky et al 1991, van den Boom 1991). Emde (1989) has noted that the infant truly cannot survive and develop without the care of a parenting figure and that appropriate care involves satisfaction of emotional and physical needs. Thus, we almost cannot think about the infant individually without considering the caregiving relationships in that infant behavior is so much a product of the mutual regulatory processes in that relationship. The ability of parents to provide the regulation that infants require seems mutually conditioned by the support derived from the marital relationship (Cox et al 1989). Qualities of the infant's early regulation also seem to feed into the caregiving system. van den Boom (1991) found that when mother-child dyads with first-borns selected for extreme irritability from observations in the first few days of life were compared with those with infants not classified as irritable, the mothers with irritable infants showed increasing maternal noninvolvement over the first 6 months of life. Infants with less regulation in the first few days of life, by their aversive behavior, seem to stimulate fewer attempts at regulation by their caregivers, and thus they may become less regulated over time. This mutual regulation between mother and child also can be seen in work by Belsky et al (1984), who found that maternal behavior at 1 month was associated with infant fussiness at 3 months, which in turn was associated with the qualities of the infant-mother attachment relationship at 9 months. Similarly, Engfer (1986) found that early maternal insensitivity made babies look more difficult to the mother at 4 and 18 months, and later the babies actually showed more difficult behaviors that supported the mother's perceptions and stabilized the mother's view that the babies were difficult. This evidence for the importance of these transactional regulatory processes in understanding mother or baby behavior at any one point in time points to the limitations of static notions of "difficult temperaments" or "insensitive mothers" where the label is assumed to refer to a more permanent quality of the individual. The transition to parenthood research demonstrates the importance of considering change at multiple levels of the family and the mutual regulation between levels to understand the developmental trajectory of family members and their relationships. The research on divorce demonstrates similar phenomena.

Divorce and Remarriage

Much of the early research on divorce contrasted the adjustment of family members in divorced and not divorced homes at a single point in time. Important contributions to our understanding of this family transition have come from recent research that focuses on divorce and remarriage not as single events but as processes occurring over time and involving reorganization at all levels of the family system with change at each level affecting other levels and back again in a network of feedback loops (Hetherington 1992a). Indeed, the challenge to the family may come from many different sources. Not only are changes in family structure, roles, and relationships involved, but frequently changes in residence, income, and kin relationships (Elder 1991).

To understand the process of adaptation of any one individual or relationship in the family, it is necessary to look at change that occurs at all levels of the family system and the mutual influences between levels. In the case of divorce, although some couples continue to support each other as parents and the relationship between parent and child remains positive, many custodial mothers are preoccupied and distressed in the months following separation or divorce and become temporarily erratic, uncommunicative, nonsupportive, and more punitive in their interactions with their children as they face the challenge of single parenthood and often continuing conflict with their ex-spouse (Ahrons 1981, Hetherington 1992b). The behavior of children during this period is complex and seems to differ depending on the age and gender of the child, the quality of the relationships in which the child participated before the transition, and whether the child has been functioning for some time within a conflicted and hostile marital and family environment (Emery 1988, Gano-Phillips & Fincham 1995). More difficult behavior in the child often coincides with a mother less able to respond in a nonpunitive fashion, so that in the early period after divorce, mutually negative cycles of interaction between mothers and their children, especially sons, are common (Hetherington 1989). In divorced mothers with young children, recovery over the two years after divorce often occurs such that individuals and relationships become more positive and less distressed. However, in some families, particularly those with more stress, the mutually negative cycles continue (Hetherington 1981, Shaw & Emery 1987). With adolescents, the more negative interactions are likely to lead to a pattern of disengagement between the parent and child, which accelerates the pattern of increasing disengagement and autonomy that normally occurs between adolescents and their parents (Hetherington & Clingempeel 1992).

Thus, there is good evidence that these processes involve circular causality between different levels of the family system and that the behavior of any one individual in the family is best understood according to their functioning within the network of interpersonal relationships in which the individual is embedded, rather than according to individual behavior considered alone. Maccoby (1992) noted that the failure of the parent in some divorced families to effectively guide the adolescent may stem as much from the adolescent's resistance to being socialized as from the parent's competence in socializing. The dynamics of families in the period after divorce often involve a weakening of clear generational boundaries (e.g. parents relying on children as confidants and other role reversals). This adaptation, though it may be an effective response to some of the challenges of transition (e.g. the loneliness and isolation of the parent), may be less adaptive in terms of the parent providing effective control and monitoring of the child's behavior. Sibling relationships also show change in divorcing families and are mutually influenced by the quality of each sibling's adjustment and the other relationships in the family including adult-child (Brody et al 1987, Hetherington & Clingempeel 1992) and adult-adult relationships both before and after divorce (MacKinnon 1989).

The transition to a stepparent family also illustrates the importance of considering changes at multiple levels of the family system and the mutual influences between levels. Remarriage is associated with the mother feeling happier, increased income for the family, and often higher rates of marital satisfaction, at least initially, than those in never-divorced couples. Although positive marital relationships are linked with more positive parent-child relationships in never-divorced families, in the initial stages of remarriage positive marital relationships can be associated with increased behavior problems in children and difficulties in parent-child interaction (Bray 1988, Hetherington 1988). This may occur because of the different meanings of relationships in stepparent families as compared with families with biological parents only. It also illustrates the importance of understanding different linkages within different family contexts.

For most families with young children, the challenges of establishing new roles and relationships in the remarried family seem to be met eventually with children accepting the reorganization of parental authority, especially when the stepfather is warm and accepting (Hetherington 1989) and the previous experience of divorce has not left a legacy of negative relationships and behavior problems in the children (Furstenberg 1988). For families with adolescents, in contrast, the reorganization of roles and relationships appears much more difficult. Adolescents are more likely than younger children to respond negatively to the stepfather in the parental role, and disengagement by both parents from the adolescent over time is not uncommon (Hetherington & Clingempeel 1992).

Continuity and Discontinuity

The metaphor of the system provides a different perspective on the notion of continuity and discontinuity in individual child development, an issue of concern to developmental psychologists. It suggests that continuity cannot be explained as a characteristic of the child because if the child is viewed as a part of an ongoing, dynamic system, then continuity can only be located in the relation between the child and the family or caregiving environment. Thus, Caspi & Moffit (1995) concluded from a review of the literature that continuities in antisocial behavior over time are better explained in the interaction of the person and the environment than by manifestation of an intrapersonal disposition. Egeland et al (1993) provided data demonstrating that resilience, rather than being a quality of the child, is best considered as a transactional process between the child and the environment. Rutter (1987) noted that strong continuities found in dyadic relationships in families (such as between siblings) may actually be more of a function of the continuity in qualities of the broader family system and the reciprocal effects of those different levels of the family system over time.

This perspective also suggests that there may be lawful reasons why some individuals depart from particular developmental trajectories. Researchers find that positive changes in the child's adaptive behavior can be linked to earlier positive changes in the family caregiving (Vaughn et al 1979). Discontinuity can arise at any level of the family system, and the change at that level can stimulate change in the individual and his or her relationships and in the whole family system. The property of adaptive self-organization, the capacity of systems to reorganize in response to changes, suggests that discontinuity would be expected. Discontinuity may arise particularly at transition times when new contexts stimulate reorganization (Pianta & Walsh 1996). The very nature of the developmental process may carry with it the necessary expectation of a degree of discontinuity (Rutter 1987). In a follow-up study of adult life of institution-reared girls, Quinton et al (1984) found continuity from the early disadvantage of the institution-reared girls to increased rates of poor psychosocial functioning and serious parenting difficulties in adult life. This continuity seemed to be mediated by the influence of the institutional upbringing on poor spouse choice, in that most of these women chose deviant spouses. Conversely, discontinuity (such that the women were functioning better than expected) seemed to arise when the transition to marriage involved a harmonious union with a nondeviant man. Although this analysis surely oversimplifies the numerous transactions through the life course that led these women to their level of functioning in young adulthood, still the continuities and discontinuities in their life courses seemed to be associated with variation in responses to new opportunities at crucial transitions.

It is important to note that although a systemic model suggests that continuity cannot be explained simply as a characteristic of the individual child, the model does not neglect the importance of the individual. Each individual within the family is a system of its own as well as a subsystem within the hierarchy of systems; carries forward its own organization; and like any system, is dynamic, open to constant revision, and constantly influenced by and influencing the other systems in which it is embedded. The current adaptation or organization of an individual is best thought of as a product of current circumstances and past history (Egeland et al 1993, Sroufe et al 1990). The child as part of the family system will be an active participant in the creation of relationships over time (Rutter 1987). Competence at one point may make the child more broadly adapted to the environment and its challenges at future points, and continuity may be seen at the level of organization of behavior, such as in the way that the child coordinates social, emotional, and cognitive systems, rather than in identical behaviors at different points in time (Egeland et al 1993). Thus, for example, the 12-month-old infant may cry at a brief separation from mother but settle rapidly when she returns. Yet months later the same infant might not show particular distress at a brief separation but still show joyous greeting and active initiation of interaction when the mother returns, where the two sets of behaviors show a similar underlying organization (Sroufe 1979).

EXTENDED FAMILY AND FAMILIES AS SYSTEMS

Several researchers have highlighted the importance of considering the role that extended family may play in family functioning (e.g. Bengtston & Harootyan 1994, Burton & Dilworth-Anderson 1991). In discussing research on the transition to parenthood, Minuchin (1988) observed that "the current relationship between the [adult children] and their parents (now grandparents) is a major neglected factor" (p. 11). The quality of the current relationship between parent and grandparent may be a source of support or stress that impacts the parent's functioning with their spouse and children. Many grandparents also are likely to directly participate in some family interactions, and in a small but growing number of families, grandparents may assume primary caregiving responsibilities, either temporarily or on a more permanent basis (Burton 1992, Wilson 1989). The emphasis on the continuing role of grandparents in their adult children's lives also highlights the importance of examining the development of adults in context as well. Much of the work of early family therapists was inspired by observations of adult patients with their families of origin (Bateson et al 1956, Bowen 1959), and such research has continued in clinical samples, demonstrating that certain dimensions of family interactions may predict relapse in adults diagnosed with schizophrenia (see Kavanagh 1992), depression (e.g. Hooley et al 1986), and bipolar disorder (Miklowitz et al 1988). Despite such evidence that parents and siblings may continue to play an important role in adult life, there is a dearth of research in normative samples examining adults' interactions with their families of origin (Minuchin 1988).

FAMILIES AS SYSTEMS IN THE BROADER SOCIAL CONTEXT

The influence of family relationships not only extends across generations but also to systems outside the family. For example, there is a considerable body of research suggesting that disturbances in marital, parent-child, and sibling relationships may all portend poor peer relationships for children (for reviews, see Dunn & McGuire 1992, Ladd 1992, Parke et al 1989). Family members' transactions with the outside environment also may impact functioning within the family. Previous research suggests, for example, that social support promotes more positive parent-child interactions (e.g. Belsky 1993, Crockenberg 1981), while other studies have demonstrated that economic stress negatively impacts parenting and marital relationships (e.g. Brody et al 1995; Conger et al 1990, 1993; McLoyd 1990a). It is important to view the family system's relationship with the environment as reciprocal, wherein the family may be impacted by external forces but also shapes and selects its environment. Thus, for example, although children may learn social skills in the context of family interactions, children's peer relationships also may be influenced by the family's choice of neighborhood, schools, and utilization of community resources (Ladd et al 1993). Similarly, Belsky (1993) has proposed that although maltreating parents receive less social support, this may be due in part to these parents actively contributing, albeit inadvertently, to their isolation from the larger community. A major task for the family system is to regulate transactions with the environment while also preserving the integrity of family boundaries (Broderick 1993). In this regard, Reiss (1981) has explored the concept of family paradigms, or family members' shared assumptions about the safety and stability of their social environment. Reiss & Oliveri (1983) suggested that these family paradigms shape interactions both within the family and between the family and their social contexts, and that families may select environments that are consistent with their paradigms.

The emphasis on families as existing within a larger social context (e.g. neighborhoods, communities) highlights the importance of exploring the diversity that characterizes families, particularly concerning ethnicity, and the cultural and social contexts in which minority families are embedded. Although the study of minority families has been a relatively neglected area of family research, a growing number of investigators have underscored the need for a better understanding of the adaptations that families make with regard to family structure, organization, and life trajectories in response to environmental challenges (Dilworth-Anderson et al 1993; Harrison et al 1990; McLoyd 1990a,b; Wilson 1989). Such research highlights the point that what is adaptive in one context may not be adaptive in another.

One line of research has examined the different patterns of life-course development that may characterize minority families and children (e.g. Burton 1990, Burton et al 1995, Burton & Dilworth-Anderson 1991). These authors note that expectations about the timing and sequences of family transitions reflect the family culture, and consequently "for some families, these norms may not be synonymous with the schedules of family life course events inferred from patterns assumed to exist in larger society" (Stack & Burton 1993, p. 162). In her study of multigenerational black families, Burton (1990) has suggested, for example, that teenage childbearing may reflect, in part, that individuals have "a truncated view of the length of the life course given the life expectancies of black men and women" (p. 125). These alternate life trajectories, rather than viewed as deviant, are understood as viable and legitimate in their cultural and historical contexts.

The work on alternate life-courses is particularly illuminating as it challenges some of the traditional notions of family therapists (e.g. Minuchin 1974) regarding what are appropriate boundaries within the family system. Burton et al (1995) have noted that the worlds of adolescents and their parents may overlap to a greater extent in economically disadvantaged minority families than in more mainstream cultures. An example of this can be seen in some African-American adolescent males and their fathers who, due to high unemployment rates, are often competing for the same jobs. Another example can be seen in Stack & Burton's (1993) observation in two communities of low-income blacks that grandmothers are often the primary caregivers for their grandchildren, while their daughters care for their own grandmothers. Consequently, mothers' relationships with their children are more like sibling relationships than parent-child relationships. Rather than viewing such families as pathological because they do not maintain what might be considered appropriately clear boundaries between parent and child subsystems, the ability to be more flexible in social roles may be seen as an adaptive strategy for minority families (Harrison et al 1990).

FURTHER ISSUES

Methodological Considerations

A systemic model suggests that progress in understanding the development of individuals or relationships in families will come from investigations of circular causal processes reflecting the reciprocal influences of various levels of the family system, rather than from investigations that look for linear causality. However, our common statistical procedures are not well suited to detect circular causality (Rutter 1987), and investigators do not often look for circular processes (Emery et al 1992). In addition, although a number of researchers (e.g. Emde 1988, Hinde & Stevenson-Hinde 1988, Parke 1988) have emphasized the importance of data collected at multiple levels (e.g. individual, dyadic, whole family), it is rare for research on the family to include measurement that reflects all the levels of the family system. Even when researchers purport to have done so, the measurement often is not faithful to the level of analysis that is intended. Minuchin (1988) has noted that in an attempt to capture family-level phenomena, researchers sometimes "statistically construct" a system. Broderick (1993), for example, cited studies in which spouses' individual marital happiness scores are averaged to arrive at a "more accurate estimate" of marital satisfaction. Broderick noted that "the average of two discrepant marital satisfaction scores represents an opinion that is held by neither participant and which is attributed to a social system that—like all social systems—is intrinsically incapable of any opinion at all.... To make any sense at all, qualities attributed to social systems must pertain to the system as systems" (p. 49). Self-report measures or other indices of "individual" perception are not in and of themselves problematic; rather, it is when they are interpreted as reflecting properties of a larger system, or in essence treated as proxy for data on family interactions, that the use of such measures is subject to criticism.

Although the measurement of multiple levels of the family system clearly creates a challenge for family researchers who have to find the resources necessary for such ambitious undertakings, the data provided are likely to significantly advance our understanding of how individuals and families shape and are shaped by the larger contexts in which they are embedded (Hinde 1989).

Implications for Intervention Approaches

Systemic approaches also have implications for intervention strategies, especially in terms of the timing and the focus of interventions. Regarding timing, the most effective interventions may occur at points of transition for family members and family systems. Transitions are times of challenge when there is more fluidity in systems and reorganizations are occurring. Because transition periods offer opportunity for change, targeting prevention and intervention efforts at these periods may be effective (Cicchetti & Toth 1992). Transitions also are periods when difficulties may be more likely to arise and interventions are most needed.

Regarding the target of interventions, Pianta & Walsh (1996), in considering effective interventions in school contexts, noted that a systemic view highlights the fact that challenges that children face in transitions are not faced by the child alone but by the child in relationship with parents, peers, and teachers. Thus, they make the case that effective interventions to facilitate these transitions must be aimed at this network of relationships. In general, a systems model suggests that interventions aimed at the individual alone will not be as effective as interventions that address the relationship systems in which the individual's behavior is regulated. Several researchers have demonstrated the effectiveness of interventions when interventions are aimed at multiple levels of systems during transitions (e.g. Cowan & Cowan 1995) or at important relationships rather than individual behavior (e.g. Erickson et al 1992, Lieberman 1992).

IN CLOSING

We have tried to suggest the value of a systemic approach to understanding family relationships and individual development. Such an approach points to the multiple levels of influence within families, the circular causality of levels of the system, and the dynamic qualities of families. We assert that research and intervention efforts will be improved by viewing a changing individual in a changing network of family relationships. Yet, the question arises: Do these systemic models offer insights that researchers would be unlikely to generate without them? The recognition that family relationships are interdependent can be seen in the thoughtful writing of several scholars who do not specifically refer to systems theories (e.g. Belsky 1981, Hinde & Stevenson-Hinde 1988). However, dynamic models suggest much more than the interdependencies of subsystems and can point researchers in new and important directions. One good example of this is the recent work by Gottman (1991) in which he uses a specific dynamic systems theory, chaos theory, to explore a "cascade" model of divorce. Gottman's use of chaos theory shows the potential for describing how events can push couples or families beyond critical thresholds and set them on a new course (Ward 1995). Gottman (1993) maintained that in stable marriages, positive behaviors exceed negative ones, but once a critical threshold of the ratio of positive to negative behaviors is crossed, the couple's perception of the relationship can shift from positive to negative, which can lead to a cascade of negative attributions, a recasting of the history of the marriage, and eventual divorce. Ward (1995), alluding primarily to the work of Patterson (1982, 1993), suggested that such a model may help explain the "cascade" effect in the development of antisocial behavior in boys. The "cascade," Ward suggested, begins with an escalating cycle of inadequate parenting and childhood aggression and opposition. This leads, in turn, to poor social and academic skills such that the child is rejected by peers, experiences academic failure, and becomes depressed. This increasingly marginal position, Ward suggested further, tends to move the child into an antisocial peer group that encourages delinquent behavior. Such delinquency is further supported by a failure in parental monitoring. In general, complex dynamic systems theories, like chaos theory, can be important for understanding families, particularly in situations where families are pushed farther and farther from steady states by internal and environmental changes such that major discontinuities can occur and small effects may lead to disproportionately large consequences (Ward 1995). We assert that these models have the potential to stimulate new and productive directions in family research.

ACKNOWLEDGMENTS

We thank the following reviewers for their helpful comments on drafts of this chapter: Jay Belsky, Phil Cowan, John Darley, Gilbert Gottlieb, Stuart Hauser, and Margaret Tresch Owen. Partial support for Martha Cox for the preparation of this review was provided by the following grants: NIMH-R01-MH49694 (Research Consortium on Family Risk and Resilience) and US Department of Education Office of Educational Research Institute R307A60004 (National Center for Early Development and Learning). Support for Blair Paley was provided by the following grant: NIMH MH19734 (Multisite Research Training in Family Risk and Resilience).

Literature Cited

Ahrons CR. 1981. The continuing coparental relationship between divorced spouses. *Am. J. Orthopsychiatry* 51:415–28

Baltes PB. 1987. Theoretical propositions of life-span developmental psychology: on the dynamics between growth and decline. *Dev. Psychol.* 23:611–26

Bateson G, Jackson D, Haley J, Weakland J. 1956. Toward a theory of schizophrenia. *Behav. Sci.* 1:1–264

Belsky J. 1981. Early human experience: a family perspective. *Dev. Psychol.* 17:3–23

Belsky J. 1993. Etiology of child maltreatment: a developmental-ecological analysis. *Psychol. Bull.* 114:413–34

Belsky J, Fish M, Isabella R. 1991. Continuity and discontinuity in infant negative and positive emotionality: family antecedents and attachment consequences. *Dev. Psychol.* 27:421–31

Belsky J, Lang M, Huston TL. 1986. Sex typing and division of labor as determinants of marital change across the transition to parenthood. *J. Pers. Soc. Psychol.* 50:517–22

Belsky J, Pensky E. 1988. Developmental history, personality, and family relationships: toward an emergent family system. See Hinde & Stevenson-Hinde 1988, pp. 193–217

Belsky J, Rovine M, Taylor DG. 1984. The Pennsylvania Infant and Family Development Project. III. The origins of individual differences in infant-mother attachment: maternal and infant contributions. *Child Dev.* 55:718–28

Belsky J, Volling B. 1987. Mothering, fathering and marital interaction in the family triad: exploring family systems processes. In *Men's Transitions to Parenthood: Longitudinal Studies of Early Family Experience,* ed. P Berman, F Pederson, pp. 37–63. Hillsdale, NJ: Erlbaum

Bengtson VL, Harootyan RA. 1994. *Intergen-*

erational Linkages: Hidden Connections in American Society. New York: Springer-Verlag

Bertalanffy L von. 1968. *General Systems Theory*. New York: Braziller

Blatt SJ, Homann E. 1992. Parent-child interaction in the etiology of dependent and self-critical depression. *Child Psychol. Rev.* 12:47–91

Boer F, Dunn J, eds. 1992. *Children's Sibling Relationships: Developmental and Clinical Issues*. Hillsdale, NJ: Erlbaum

Bowen M. 1959. Family relationship in schizophrenia. In *Schizophrenia: An Integrated Approach,* ed. A Auerbach, pp. 147–78. New York: Ronald

Bray JH. 1988. Children's development during early remarriage. See Hetherington & Arasteh 1988, pp. 279–98

Broderick CB. 1993. *Understanding Family Process: Basics of Family Systems Theory*. Newbury Park, CA: Sage

Brody GH, Stoneman Z. 1987. Sibling conflict: contributions of the siblings themselves, the parent-sibling relationship, and the broader family system. *J. Child. Contemp. Soc.* 19:39–53

Brody GH, Stoneman Z, Burke M. 1987. Family system and individual child correlates of sibling behavior. *Am. J. Orthopsychiatry* 57:561–69

Brody GH, Stoneman Z, Flor D. 1995. Linking family processes and academic competence among rural African-American youth. *J. Marriage Fam.* 57:567–79

Brody GH, Stoneman Z, McCoy JK, Forehand R. 1992. Contemporaneous and longitudinal associations of sibling conflict with family relationship assessments and family discussion about sibling problems. *Child Dev.* 63:391-400

Bronfenbrenner U. 1979. *The Ecology of Human Development.* Cambridge, MA: Harvard Univ. Press

Brooks-Gunn J, Cox M, eds. 1997. *Conflict and Closeness: The Formation, Functioning, and Stability of Families.* Hillsdale, NJ: Erlbaum. In press

Bryant BK, Crockenberg SB. 1980. Correlates and dimensions of prosocial behavior: a study of female siblings with their mothers. *Child Dev.* 51:529–44

Buhrmester D, Camparo L, Christensen A, Gonzalez LS, Hinshaw SP. 1992. Mothers and fathers interacting in dyads and triads with normal and hyperactive sons. *Dev. Psychol.* 28:500–9

Burton LM. 1992. Black grandparents rearing children of drug-addicted parents: stressors, outcomes, and social service needs. *Gerontologist* 32:744–51

Burton LM. 1990. Teenage childbearing as an alternative life-course strategy in multigenerational black families. *Hum. Nat.* 1: 123–43

Burton LM, Allison K, Obeidallah D. 1995. Social context and adolescence: perspectives on development among inner-city African-American teens. In *Pathways Through Adolescence: Individual Development in Relation to Social Context,* ed. L Crockett, A Crouter, pp. 119-38. Hillsdale, NJ: Erlbaum

Burton LM, Dilworth-Anderson P. 1991. The intergenerational family roles of aged black Americans. *Marriage Fam. Rev.* 16:311–30

Cairns RB. 1983. The emergence of developmental psychology. See Mussen & Kessen 1983, pp. 41–102

Campbell SB, Cohn JF, Meyers TA, Ross S, Flanagan C. 1992. Course and correlates of postpartum depression during the transition to parenthood. *Dev. Psychopathol.* 4:29–47

Caspi A, Moffitt TE. 1995. The continuity of maladaptive behavior: from description to understanding in the study of antisocial behavior. In *Developmental Psychopathology: Risk, Disorder, and Adaptation,* ed. D Cicchetti, D Cohen, 2:472–511. New York: Wiley

Chase-Lansdale PL, Wakschlag LS, Brooks-Gunn J. 1995. A psychological perspective on the development of caring in children and youth: the role of the family. *J. Adolesc.* 18:515–56

Christensen A, Margolin G. 1988. Conflict and alliance in distressed and nondistressed families. See Hinde & Stevenson-Hinde 1988, pp. 263–82

Christensen A, Phillips S, Glasgow RE, Johnson SM. 1983. Parental characteristics and interactional dysfunction in families with child behavior problems: a preliminary investigation. *J. Abnorm. Child Psychol.* 11:153–66

Cicchetti D, Toth SL. 1992. The role of developmental theory in prevention and intervention. *Dev. Psychopathol.* 4:489–93

Clarke-Stewart A. 1978. And daddy makes 3: the father's impact on mothers and young children. *Child Dev.* 49:466–78

Combrinck-Graham L. 1990. Developments in family systems theory and research. *J. Am. Acad. Child Adolesc. Psychiatry* 29:501–12

Conger RD, Conger KJ, Elder GH Jr, Lorenz FO, Simons RL, Whitbeck LB. 1993. Family economic stress and adjustment of early adolescent girls. *Dev. Psychol.* 29:206–19

Conger RD, Elder GH Jr, Lorenz FO, Conger KJ, Simons RL, et al. 1990. Linking economic hardship to marital quality and instability. *J. Marriage Fam.* 52:643–56

Cowan CP, Cowan PA. 1995. Interventions to ease the transition to parenthood: Why are they needed and what they can do. *Fam. Relat.* 44:412–23

Cowan CP, Cowan PA, Herring G, Miller NB. 1991. Becoming a family: marriage, parenting, and child development. See Cowan & Hetherington 1991, pp. 79–109

Cowan PA. 1991. Individual and family life transitions: a proposal for a new definition. See Cowan & Hetherington 1991, pp. 3–30

Cowan PA, Hetherington EM, eds. 1991. *Family Transitions.* Hillsdale, NJ: Erlbaum

Cox MJ. 1995. *Developmental changes in relationships: marriage across the transition to parenthood.* Presented at Intimacy Conf., Inst. Soc. Res., Univ. Mich.

Cox MJ, Owen MT. 1993. *Marital conflict and conflict negotiation: effects on infant-mother and infant-father relationships.* Presented at Bienn. Meet. Soc. Res. Child Dev., New Orleans

Cox MJ, Owen MT, Lewis JL, Henderson VK. 1989. Marriage, adult adjustment, and early parenting. *Child Dev.* 60:1015–24

Cox MJ, Paley B, Payne CC, Burchinal P. 1996. Marital conflict and closeness in families and the formation of parent-child relationships. See Brooks-Gunn & Cox 1997. In press

Coyne JC, Downey G, Boergers J. 1992. Depression in families: a systems perspective. In *Rochester Symposium on Developmental Psychology: Developmental Perspectives on Depression,* ed. D Cicchetti, SL Toth, 4:211–49. Rochester: Univ. Rochester Press

Crockenberg S. 1981. Infant irritability, mother responsiveness, and social support influences on the security of infant-mother attachment. *Child Dev.* 52:857–65

Cummings EM. 1994. Marital conflict and children's functioning. *Soc. Dev.* 3:16–59

Cummings EM, Davies PT. 1995. The impact of parents on their children: an emotional security hypothesis. *Ann. Child Dev.* 10: 167-208

Cummings EM, Wilson A. 1997. Contexts of marital conflict and children's emotional security: exploring the distinction between constructive and destructive conflict from the children's perspective. See Brooks-Gunn & Cox 1997. In press

Dilworth-Anderson P, Burton LM, Johnson LB. 1993. Reframing theories for understanding race, ethnicity, and families. In *Sourcebook of Family Theories and Methods: A Contextual Approach,* ed. P Boss, WJ Doherty, R LaRossa, WR Schumm, SK Steinmetz, pp. 627–46. New York: Plenum

Dishion TJ, French GR, Patterson GR. 1995. The development and ecology of antisocial behavior. In *Developmental Psychopathology: Risk, Disorder, and Adaptation,* ed. D Cicchetti, D Cohen, 2:421–71. New York: Wiley

Dunn J, Kendrick C. 1980. The arrival of a sibling: changes in patterns of interaction between mother and first-born child. *J. Child Psychol. Psychiatry* 21:119–32

Dunn J, McGuire S. 1992. Sibling and peer relationships in childhood. *J. Child Psychol. Psychiatry* 33:67–105

Dunn J, Munn P. 1985. Becoming a family member: family conflict and the development of social understanding in the second year. *Child Dev.* 56:480–92

Easterbrooks MA, Emde RN. 1988. Marital and parent-child relationships: the role of affect in the family system. See Hinde & Stevenson-Hinde 1988, pp. 83–103

Egeland B, Carlson E, Sroufe LA. 1993. Resilience as process. *Dev. Psychopathol.* 5: 517–28

Elder GH. 1991. Family transitions, cycles, and social change. See Cowan & Hetherington 1991, pp. 31–57

Emde RN. 1988. The effect of relationships on relationships: a developmental approach to clinical intervention. See Hinde & Stevenson-Hinde 1988, pp. 354–64

Emde RN. 1989. The infant's relationship experience: developmental and affective aspects. See Sameroff & Emde 1989, pp. 33–51

Emery RE. 1982. Interparental conflict and the children of discord and divorce. *Psychol. Bull.* 92:310–30

Emery RE. 1988. *Marriage, Divorce, and Children's Adjustment.* Newbury Park, CA: Sage

Emery RE, Fincham FD, Cummings EM. 1992. Parenting in context: systemic thinking about parental conflict and its influence on children. *J. Consult. Clin. Psychol.* 60: 909–12

Engfer A. 1986. *Stability and change in perceived characteristics of children 4 to 43 months of age.* Presented at Eur. Conf. Dev. Biol., 2nd, Rome

Erickson MF, Korfmacher J, Egeland BR. 1992. Attachments past and present: implications for therapeutic intervention with mother-infant dyads. *Dev. Psychopathol.* 4: 495–508

Fauber R, Forehand R, Thomas AM, Wierson M. 1990. A mediational model of the impact of marital conflict on adolescent adjustment in intact and divorced families: the role of disrupted parenting. *Child Dev.* 61:1112–23

Fincham FD, Osborne LN. 1993. Marital conflict and children: retrospect and prospect. *Clin. Psychol. Rev.* 13:75–88

Floyd FJ, Zmich DE. 1991. Marriage and the parenting partnership: perceptions and interactions of parents with mentally retarded

and typically developing children. *Child Dev.* 6:1434–48
Furstenberg FF. 1988. Child care after divorce and remarriage. See Hetherington & Arasteh 1988, pp. 245–61
Gable S, Belsky J, Crnic K. 1995. Coparenting during the child's 2nd year: a descriptive account. *J. Marriage Fam.* 57:609–16
Gano-Phillips S, Fincham FD. 1995. Family conflict, divorce, and children's adjustment. In *Explaining Family Interactions,* ed. MA Fitzpatrick, AL Vangelisti, pp. 206-31. Thousand Oaks, CA: Sage
Gilbert R, Christensen A, Margolin G. 1984. Patterns of alliance in nondistressed and multiproblem families. *Fam. Process* 23: 75–87
Goldenberg I, Goldenberg H. 1991. *Family Therapy: An Overview.* Pacific Grove, CA: Brooks/Cole. 3rd ed.
Gottman JM. 1991. Chaos and regulated change in families: a metaphor for the study of transitions. See Cowan & Hetherington 1991, pp. 247–72
Gottman JM. 1993. A theory of marital dissolution and stability. *J. Fam. Psychol.* 7:57–75
Gottman JM, Katz LF. 1989. Effects of marital discord on young children's peer interaction and health. *Dev. Psychol.* 25:373–81
Grych JH, Fincham FD. 1990. Marital conflict and children's adjustment: a cognitive-contextual framework. *Psychol. Bull.* 108: 267–90
Harrison AO, Wilson MN, Pine CJ, Chan SQ, Buriel R. 1990. Family ecologies of ethnic minority children. *Child Dev.* 61:347–62
Hauser ST, Houlihan J, Powers SI, Jacobson AM, Noam GG, et al. 1991. Adolescent ego development within the family: family styles and family sequences. *Int. J. Behav. Dev.* 14:165–93
Hetherington EM. 1981. Divorce: a child's perspective. *Am. Psychol.* 34:851–58
Hetherington EM. 1988. Parents, children and siblings six years after divorce. See Hinde & Stevenson-Hinde 1988, pp. 311–31
Hetherington EM. 1989. Coping with family transitions: winners, losers, and survivors. *Child Dev.* 60:1–14
Hetherington EM. 1992a. Coping with marital transitions: a family systems perspective. See Hetherington & Clingempeel 1992, pp. 1–14
Hetherington EM. 1992b. Summary and discussion. See Hetherington & Clingempeel 1992, pp. 200–6
Hetherington EM, Arasteh JD, eds. 1988. *Impact of Divorce, Single Parenting and Stepparenting on Children.* Hillsdale, NJ: Erlbaum
Hetherington EM, Clingempeel WG, eds. 1992. *Coping with marital transitions. Monogr. Soc. Res. Child Dev.* 57(2–3, Ser. No. 227). Chicago: Univ. Chicago Press
Hinde RA. 1989. Reconciling the family systems and relationships approaches to child development. See Hinde & Stevenson-Hinde 1988, pp. 149–63
Hinde RA, Stevenson-Hinde J. 1988. Epilogue. See Hinde & Stevenson-Hinde 1988, pp. 365–85
Hinde RA, Stevenson-Hinde J, eds. 1988. *Relationships Within Families: Mutual Influences.* Oxford: Clarendon
Hoffman L. 1981. *Foundations of Family Therapy: A Conceptual Framework for Systems Change.* New York: Basic Books
Hooley JM, Orley J, Teasdale JD. 1986. Levels of expressed emotion and relapse in depressed patients. *Br. J. Psychiatry* 148: 642–47
Isabella R, Belsky J. 1985. Marital change across the transition to parenthood and the security of infant-parent attachment. *J. Fam. Issues* 6:505–22
Jenkins J. 1992. Sibling relationships in disharmonious homes: potential difficulties and protective effects. See Boer & Dunn 1992, pp. 125–38
Katz LF, Gottman JM. 1993. Patterns of marital conflict predict children's internalizing and externalizing behaviors. *Dev. Psychol.* 29:940–50
Katz LF, Gottman JM. 1994. Patterns of marital interaction and children's emotional development. See Parke & Kellam 1994, pp. 49–74
Katz LF, Gottman JM. 1995. Marital interaction and child outcomes: a longitudinal study of mediating and moderating processes. In *Rochester Symposium on Developmental Psychopathology: Emotion, Cognition, and Representation,* ed. D Cicchetti, SL Toth, 6:301-42. Univ. Rochester Press
Kavanagh DJ. 1992. Recent developments in expressed emotion and schizophrenia. *Br. J. Psychiatry* 160:601–20
Kendrick C, Dunn J. 1983. Sibling quarrels and maternal responses. *Dev. Psychol.* 19:62–70
Kreppner K. 1988. Changes in dyadic relationships within a family after the arrival of a second child. See Hinde & Stevenson-Hinde 1988, pp. 143–67
Kreppner K. 1989. Linking infant development-in-context research to the investigation of life-span family development. See Kreppner & Lerner 1989a, pp. 33–64
Kreppner K, Lerner RM, eds. 1989a. *Family Systems and Life-Span Development.* Hillsdale, NJ: Erlbaum
Kreppner K, Lerner RM. 1989b. Family systems and life-span development: issues and perspectives. See Kreppner & Lerner 1989a, pp. 1–33

Ladd GW. 1992. Themes and theories: perspectives on processes in family-peer relationships. In *Family-Peer Relationships: Modes of Linkages,* ed. RD Parke, GW Ladd, pp. 3–34. Hillsdale, NJ: Erlbaum

Ladd GW, Le Sieur KD, Profilet SM. 1993. Direct parental influences on young children's peer relations. In *Understanding Relationship Processes: Learning About Relationships,* ed. S Duck, 2:152–83. Newbury Park, CA: Sage

Lamb ME. 1976. *The Role of the Father in Child Development.* New York: Wiley

Lerner RM. 1989. Developmental contextualism and the life-span view of person-context interaction. In *Interaction in Human Development,* ed. MH Bornstein, JS Bruner, pp. 217–39. Hillsdale, NJ: Erlbaum

Lieberman AF. 1992. Infant-parent psychotherapy with toddlers. *Dev. Psychopathol.* 4:559–74

Maccoby EE. 1992. Family structure and children's adjustment: Is quality of parenting the major mediator? See Hetherington & Clingempeel 1992, pp. 230–38

Maccoby EE, Depner CE, Mnookin RH. 1990. Coparenting in the second year after divorce. *J. Marriage Fam.* 52:141–55

MacKinnon CE. 1989. An observational investigation of sibling interactions in married and divorced families. *Dev. Psychol.* 25: 36–44

Margolin G. 1988. Marital conflict is not marital conflict is not marital conflict. In *Social Learning and Systems Approaches to Marriage and the Family,* ed. R DeV Peters, RJ MacMahon, pp. 193–216. New York: Brunner/Mazel

Marvin RS, Stewart RB. 1990. A family systems framework for the study of attachment. In *Attachment in the Preschool Years,* ed. MT Greenberg, D Cicchetti, EM Cummings, pp. 51-86. Chicago: Univ. Chicago Press

McLoyd VC. 1990a. The impact of economic hardship on black families and children: psychological distress, parenting, and socioemotional development. *Child Dev.* 61: 311–46

McLoyd VC. 1990b. Minority children: introduction to the special issue. *Child Dev.* 61: 263–66

Miklowitz DJ, Goldstein MJ, Nuechterlein KH, Snyder KS, Mintz J. 1988. Family factors and the course of bipolar affective disorder. *Arch. Gen. Psychiatry* 45:225–31

Minuchin P. 1985. Families and individual development: provocations from the field of family therapy. *Child Dev.* 56:289–302

Minuchin P. 1988. Relationships within the family: a systems perspective on development. See Hinde & Stevenson-Hinde 1988, pp. 7–26

Minuchin S. 1974. *Families and Family Therapy.* Cambridge, MA: Harvard Univ. Press

Minuchin S, Rosman BL, Baker L. 1978. *Psychosomatic Families: Anorexia Nervosa in Context.* Cambridge, MA: Harvard Univ. Press

Mussen PH, Kessen W, eds. 1983. *Handbook of Child Psychology: History, Theory, and Methods,* Vol. 1. New York: Wiley. 4th ed.

Parke RD. 1988. Families in life-span perspective: a multilevel developmental approach. In *Child Development in Life-Span Perspective,* ed. EM Hetherington, RM Lerner, M Perlmutter, pp. 159–90

Parke RD. 1990. In search of fathers. In *Methods of Family Research: Normal Families,* ed. IE Sigel, GH Brody, 1:153–88. Hillsdale, NJ: Erlbaum

Parke RD, Kellam SG, eds. 1994. *Exploring Family Relationships with Other Social Contexts.* Hillsdale, NJ: Erlbaum

Parke RD, MacDonald KB, Burks VM, Carson J, Bhavnagri N. 1989. Family and peer systems: in search of the linkages. See Kreppner & Lerner 1989a, pp. 65–92. Hillsdale, NJ: Erlbaum

Patterson GR. 1982. *A Social Learning Approach. III. Coercive Family Processes.* Eugene, OR: Castalia

Patterson GR. 1993. Orderly change in a stable world: the antisocial trait as a chimera. *J. Consult. Clin. Psychol.* 61:911–19

Phares V, Compas BE. 1992. The role of fathers in child and adolescent psychopathology: make room for daddy. *Psychol. Bull.* 111:387–412

Pianta RC, Walsh DJ. 1996. *High-Risk Children in Schools: Constructing Sustaining Relationships.* New York: Routledge & Kegan-Paul

Quinton D, Rutter M, Liddle C. 1984. Institutional rearing, parenting difficulties, and marital support. *Psychol. Med.* 14:107–24

Radke-Yarrow M, McCann K, DeMulder E, Belmont B, Martinez P, Richardson DT. 1995. Attachment in the context of high-risk conditions. *Dev. Psychopathol.* 7:247–65

Reiss D. 1981. *The Family's Construction of Reality.* Cambridge, MA: Harvard Univ. Press

Reiss D, Oliveri ME. 1983. The family's construction of social reality and its ties to its kin network: an exploration of causal direction. *J. Marriage Fam.* 45:81–91

Rutter M. 1987. Continuities and discontinuities from infancy. In *Handbook of Infant Development,* ed. J Osofsky, pp. 1256–96. New York: Wiley. 2nd ed.

Sameroff AJ. 1983. Developmental systems: context and evolution. See Mussen & Kessen 1983, pp. 237–94

Sameroff AJ. 1989. General systems and the

regulation of development. In *Systems and Development. The Minnesota Symposium on Child Psychology,* ed. M Gunnar, E Thelen, 22:219–35. Hillsdale, NJ: Erlbaum

Sameroff AJ. 1994. Developmental systems and family functioning. See Parke & Kellam 1994, pp. 199–214

Sameroff AJ, Emde RN, eds. 1989. *Relationship Disturbances in Early Childhood: A Developmental Approach.* New York: Basic Books

Shaw DS, Emery RE. 1987. Parental conflict and other correlates of the adjustment of school-aged children whose parents have separated. *J. Abnorm. Child Psychol.* 15: 269–81

Sroufe LA. 1979. The coherence of individual development: early care, attachment, and subsequent developmental issues. *Am. Psychol.* 34:834–41

Sroufe LA. 1989. Relationships and relationship disturbances. See Sameroff & Emde 1989, pp. 97–124

Sroufe LA, Egeland B, Kreutzer T. 1990. The fate of early experience following developmental change: longitudinal approaches to individual adaptation in childhood. *Child Dev.* 61:1363–73

Stack CB, Burton L. 1993. Kinscripts. *J. Comp. Fam. Stud.* 24:157–70

Stanton MD, Todd TC, eds. 1982. *The Family Therapy of Drug Abuse and Addiction.* New York: Guilford

Teti DM, Ablard KE. 1989. Security of attachment and infant-sibling relationships: a laboratory study. *Child Dev.* 60:1519–28

van den Boom DC. 1991. The influence of infant irritability on the development of the mother-infant relationship in the first six months of life. In *The Cultural Context of Infancy,* ed. JK Nugent, BM Lester, TB Brazelton, 2:63–89. Norwood, NJ: Ablex

Vaughn B, Egeland B, Waters E, Sroufe LA. 1979. Individual differences in infant-mother attachment at 12 and 18 months: stability and change in families under stress. *Child Dev.* 50:971–75

Volling BL, Belsky J. 1992. The contribution of mother-child and father-child relationships to the quality of sibling interaction: a longitudinal study. *Child Dev.* 62:1209–22

von Bertalanffy L. 1968. *General Systems Theory.* New York: Braziller

Vuchinich S, Wood B, Vuchinich R. 1994. Coalitions and family problem-solving with preadolescents in referred, at-risk, and comparison families. *Fam. Process* 33: 409–24

Wagner BM, Reiss D. 1995. Family systems and developmental psychopathology: courtship, marriage, or divorce. In *Developmental Psychopathology,* ed. D Cicchetti, DJ Cohen, 1:696–730. New York: Wiley

Ward M. 1995. Butterflies and bifurcations: can chaos theory contribute to our understanding of family systems? *J. Marriage Fam.* 57:629–38

Wilson MN. 1989. Child development in the context of the black extended family. *Am. Psychol.* 44:380–85

Annu. Rev. Psychol. 1997. 48:269–97

VISUAL ATTENTION: Control, Representation, and Time Course

Howard E. Egeth and Steven Yantis

Department of Psychology, The Johns Hopkins University, Baltimore, Maryland 21218

KEY WORDS: attention, cognition, human subjects, perception, psychophysics, reaction time, vision, visual search

ABSTRACT

Three central problems in the recent literature on visual attention are reviewed. The first concerns the control of attention by top-down (or goal-directed) and bottom-up (or stimulus-driven) processes. The second concerns the representational basis for visual selection, including how much attention can be said to be location- or object-based. Finally, we consider the time course of attention as it is directed to one stimulus after another.

CONTENTS

INTRODUCTION

We review the literature on three fundamental aspects of attention that have been the focus of much recent research. The first concerns attentional control, or the extent to which the deployment of attention is a result of the observer's deliberate state of attentional readiness (called top-down or goal-directed control), or whether attention is captured by certain aspects of the image independently of current perceptual goals (called bottom-up or stimulus-driven control). We emphasize stimulus-driven control and the interaction between the two attentional control modes. The second topic concerns the representational basis for visual selection. In particular, we examine the conditions under which attention may be said to be directed to regions of space, as space-based theories assert, or to preattentively defined perceptual objects, as suggested by object-based theories of attention. Finally, we examine recent evidence concerning the time course of attention, both as it moves through space and as events occurring sequentially in time are selected. In this section, several different estimates of the time scale on which attentional events occur are reviewed.

A single chapter cannot completely cover the broad and active field of attention. Readers interested in pursuing these and other aspects of attention may consult three recent tutorial volumes (Dagenbach & Carr 1994, Kramer et al 1996, Pashler 1996a) or several recent monographs (LaBerge 1995, Pashler 1996b, van der Heijden 1992). In addition, there are several recent *Annual Review* chapters on attention (Desimone & Duncan 1995, Johnston & Dark 1986, Kinchla 1992).

STIMULUS-DRIVEN AND GOAL-DIRECTED CONTROL OF ATTENTION

When William James (1890) first delineated the varieties of attention over a century ago, one major categorical boundary was the distinction between *passive* and *active* attention. The modern terms are usually *bottom-up* and *top-down* or the less metaphorical *stimulus-driven* and *goal-directed.* The idea is that the deployment of attention may sometimes depend on the properties of the image almost exclusively (e.g. sudden movement in the periphery); other times it may be under strict supervision according to the observer's goals. Mounting evidence has revealed that these two domains of attentional control almost invariably interact. With a few possible exceptions, both the properties of the image and the expectations and goals of the observer determine the attentional consequences of a given perceptual episode. (We consider the time course of attentional control in the last section of this chapter.)

The past 25 years have yielded ample evidence that the distribution of attention can be controlled by the intentions of the observer. Helmholtz (1925, p. 455) first noted this ability in the past century, but it was not until the 1950s that the perceptual consequences of the deliberate deployment of attention were first studied systematically by Mertens (1956). Much of the modern evidence for top-down control has been reviewed previously (e.g. Johnston &

Dark 1986). Significant advances in our understanding of the top-down deployment of attention began with a seminal series of studies by Eriksen and his colleagues (e.g. Eriksen & Hoffman 1972, 1973). Subjects identified a letter indicated by a bar marker and attempted to ignore other letters in the display. The amount of interference caused by the to-be-ignored letters provided a measure of the efficiency and time course of attentional deployment. Studies by Posner and colleagues (e.g. Posner 1980, Posner et al 1980) further examined top-down attentional control.

The evidence concerning the capture of attention (i.e. bottom-up control), unlike that for top-down control, is more recent and is the focus of this section. Two major categories of stimulus properties that could in principle capture attention can be distinguished: stimuli that differ substantially in one or more simple visual attributes (e.g. color, orientation, or motion) from their backgrounds—hereafter called *feature singletons* or simply *singletons*—and abrupt visual onsets. We consider the evidence about each of these categories in turn, and we return to this topic in the section entitled "The Time Course of Attention."

Feature Singletons and Attentional Capture

In considering what stimulus properties might capture attention regardless of (or in spite of) the observer's state of attentional readiness, feature singletons appear to be likely candidates. Feature singletons are judged as subjectively salient, and there is ample evidence that such stimuli can be found efficiently in visual search. For example, Neisser (1967) observed that curved letters could be found easily among straight letters, and using a somewhat different paradigm, Egeth et al (1972) drew a similar conclusion. Treisman & Gelade (1980) also showed, using a visual search paradigm like that of Egeth et al (1972), that various feature singletons could be efficiently detected in visual search. Many examples have been catalogued by Treisman & Gormican (1988; see also Bravo & Nakayama 1992).

These demonstrations provide no direct evidence, however, about whether feature singletons capture attention, because in all the cited cases the stimulus in question was itself the target of search and therefore presumably elicited top-down, deliberate deployment of attention. Therefore, one must design experiments that explicitly dissociate the observer's attentional set from the properties of the stimulus array. Several such studies have been reported, but they have yielded different conclusions. We first review papers that might lead one to conclude that feature singletons do capture attention. We next consider studies that suggest otherwise and end the section with discussion of a paper that provides a possible reconciliation.

SINGLETONS CAPTURE ATTENTION Pashler (1988, Experiment 7) had subjects search for a slash (/) in an array of many *O*s or for an *O* among /s. The identity of the target was not known in advance. On some trials, two of the items in the array were uniquely colored. These were always irrelevant to the task, and subjects were told to ignore them. Pashler found that reaction time (RT) to locate the target shape was prolonged on those trials in which the color singletons appeared despite subjects' intentions to the contrary. Because of these results, one might tentatively conclude that feature singletons do capture attention.

Theeuwes (1991a, 1992) further explored the conditions under which feature singletons controlled the deployment of attention. In his tasks, subjects typically searched for an easy-to-detect target (e.g. a diamond) in an array of distractors (e.g. circles). Each stimulus had inscribed in it a line segment, either horizontal or vertical (in the target) or oblique (in the distractors). To demonstrate successful target acquisition, the subject had to indicate whether the line in the target was horizontal or vertical. Subjects were told that the critical line would always be contained within the shape singleton. On half the trials, all the stimuli had the same color (e.g. red), and on the remaining trials, one of the stimuli—never the target shape—was unique in color (e.g. green). Subjects were instructed to ignore the color variation. Additionally, the total number of elements in the display varied (5, 7, or 9). Reaction time was independent of display size, which suggests parallel processing. With respect to the issue of attentional capture, this experiment is similar in many ways to that of Pashler (1988, Experiment 7). Results were similar as well: RTs were prolonged on those trials containing a color singleton compared with the trials without a color singleton. Theeuwes (1991a) concluded that when subjects search for a target in parallel, which is possible when the target is a feature singleton, then top-down control is not possible and attention is captured even by singletons known to be irrelevant to the task.

Another example of stimulus-driven capture was reported recently by Joseph & Optican (1996). Subjects were required to search for an *L* embedded in an array of *T* stimuli; this target array was flashed briefly and then masked. Subjects were required to report the location (one of four quadrants) in which the *L* appeared. Immediately preceding the target array, a cue array was presented briefly. The cue array consisted of vertical line segments in which a single horizontal segment was embedded. Subjects were correctly informed that the location of the orientation singleton in the cue array was uncorrelated with the location of the upcoming target. (To call an uninformative stimulus a cue may seem problematic; we accede here to what appears to be common usage in the field.) Nevertheless, responses were more accurate when the cue appeared in the location subsequently occupied by the target, which suggested that attention was drawn to the cue even though it was known to be irrelevant to the task.

SINGLETONS DO NOT CAPTURE ATTENTION These preceding studies all suggest that feature singletons, even ones that are known to be task irrelevant, do capture visual attention. However, there is also evidence for the opposite conclusion. Jonides & Yantis (1988) reported that color and brightness singletons do not capture attention. Observers were required to search for a letter in an array of multiple letters. On each trial one letter differed from all the rest in color for some subjects and in brightness for others. Subjects were told that the target would occasionally be the unique element, but only on randomly selected trials. That is, the feature singleton provided no help in solving the primary task, which was to find the target letter. At issue was whether RT to find the target differed when the target did and did not happen to be the unique element. Yantis & Jonides found that it made no difference: Responses were no faster when the target was the singleton than when it was not. This result was subsequently corroborated by Theeuwes (1990).

Hillstrom & Yantis (1994) reported that not even visual motion captures attention under all circumstances. They had subjects search for a rotated T among rotated Ls. One of the stimuli on each trial exhibited one of five different types of visual motion. In all cases, the position of the target element was uncorrelated with the position of the moving element. At issue was whether RT differed according to whether the target happened to correspond to the moving element. If motion captures attention, then one would expect more rapid RTs to moving targets than to stationary ones. Hillstrom & Yantis found, however, that RT did not differ for the two conditions.

ATTENTIONAL CONTROL Thus, several studies suggest that singletons do capture attention, whereas several others suggest that they do not. Bacon & Egeth (1994) proposed a reconciliation by suggesting that these conflicting results are manifestations of two different attentional strategies adopted by subjects. Under some circumstances, subjects enter *singleton detection mode,* in which attention is directed to the location in the array exhibiting the largest local feature contrast (for further evidence, see Bravo & Nakayama 1992; Nothdurft 1992, 1993). In singleton detection mode, the location of the greatest contrast can be accessed, but not the identity of the dimension(s) on which the stimuli differ. Thus, when one is searching for, say, a shape singleton, an irrelevant color singleton may "win out" because of its greater local feature contrast. Other stimulus conditions might lead subjects to adopt *feature search mode,* in which attention is directed to locations that match some task-defined visual feature (e.g. "red" or "vertical"). Bacon & Egeth (1994) supported this proposal by showing that capture by a to-be-ignored feature singleton only occurred when the task could be carried out in singleton detection mode. When that strategy was made ineffective, then capture by irrelevant feature singletons did not occur. In one experiment, singleton detection mode was made ineffective by including several identical target shapes, thus ensuring that no one of them could serve as a singleton target. In another experiment, several unique stimuli were present that were nontargets, again ensuring that the target could not be found efficiently simply by looking for a singleton.

Abrupt Visual Onsets and Attentional Capture

A category of stimuli that behaves somewhat differently than most feature singletons is abrupt visual onset. Early studies of whether abrupt onsets capture attention were motivated by the cuing technique introduced by Eriksen and his colleagues (e.g. Eriksen & Hoffman 1972). Jonides (1981) showed that a peripheral attentional cue (i.e. a bar marker presented near the location subsequently occupied by a to-be-identified letter) draws attention "automatically," whereas a central arrowhead cue requires a deliberate shift of attention. The automaticity of the peripheral cue was demonstrated in his Experiment 2 by showing that peripheral cues drew attention whether they were informative about the location of the target or not, while central cues only controlled the deployment of attention when they were informative. Remington et al (1992) found that a peripheral cue captures attention even when it is known *never* to indicate the target location.

Yantis & Jonides (1984) proposed that peripheral cues like the ones employed by Jonides (1981) might capture attention because they have abrupt onsets. The magnocellular visual pathway is known to be quite sensitive to high temporal frequency, and one of its functions might be to signal the location to which attention should be directed (Breitmeyer & Ganz 1976 originally proposed this idea). Yantis & Jonides (1984) pursued this idea with a visual search task in which observers searched for a prespecified target letter embedded in an array of nontarget letters. The letters were formed by illuminating a subset of the segments of a figure eight as on a digital alarm clock (borrowing a technique devised by Todd & Van Gelder 1979). Each trial began with an array of complete figure-eight placeholders. These were actually letters that were "camouflaged" with irrelevant line segments. The figure eights remained on the screen for 1 s. The camouflaging line segments were then removed from the figure eights to reveal letters (these were designated "no-onset" letters), and simultaneously a single letter appeared in a previously blank location (the "onset" letter). The target letter was present on half the trials. On the target-present trials, the target was the onset letter on $1/n$ of the trials (where n is the total number of letters in the display). Because the target had an abrupt onset only rarely, there was no incentive to deliberately attend to it.

Even though there was no incentive to attend to the abrupt onset letter, Yantis & Jonides (1984) found that RT to find the target when it happened to be the onset letter was fast and did not vary with the number of elements to be searched, whereas RT to find the target when it was one of the no-onset letters was slower and increased linearly with the number of elements to be searched. They concluded that the onset letter captured attention on each trial. If the target happened to be the onset letter, a response was made immediately and no further searching was required, but if the onset letter was not the target, then an attentionally demanding search had to be initiated. Yantis & Jonides (1990) found that this capture, which occurs in the absence of any relevant attentional set, is prevented when subjects are induced to focus attention on a different spatial location in advance of each trial. This finding was corroborated using different approaches by Theeuwes (1991b) and by Koshino et al (1992) and Juola et al (1995).

At least two potential mechanisms could account for attentional capture by abrupt onsets (Yantis & Hillstrom 1994). One, mentioned above, is that the luminance increment activates visual pathways that respond to high temporal frequency, which in turn direct attention to the eliciting object. A second possibility is that the appearance of a perceptual object, which requires the creation of an episodic perceptual representation, elicits a shift of attention. This second possibility might be a "hard-wired" response to the need to rapidly identify new objects entering the visual field. Yantis & Hillstrom (1994) performed a series of experiments that permitted them to determine which of these accounts was correct. They used stimuli that were equiluminant with their backgrounds (e.g. random-dot stereograms in which the letters were composed of dots exhibiting binocular disparity against a zero-disparity background). These displays thus exhibited no change in mean luminance, but they did include the appearance of a new perceptual object. The experiment provided clear support for the new-object account: Attention was captured by new perceptual objects even though they did not exhibit a luminance increment. Hillstrom & Yantis (1994) corroborated this finding by showing that while motion per se does not capture attention when it is task irrelevant (as noted above), when motion segments an object from its background (as when the motion of a moth's camouflaging wings segment it from a tree's bark), attention is captured. For a recent debate about the new-objects account, see Gibson (1996a,b) and Yantis & Jonides (1996).

Interaction of Goal-Driven and Stimulus-Driven Capture

The studies reviewed so far in this section provide evidence that under certain circumstances attention is drawn to objects (e.g. feature singletons or abrupt onsets) without a deliberate intent to direct attention there. However, in each case, top-down control plays a role. One example of top-down control is that irrelevant feature singletons capture attention only when subjects enter singleton detection mode, where feature contrast gradients control the distribution of attention. Another example is that attentional capture by abrupt onsets can be prevented or at least modulated by focused attention elsewhere in the display.

Folk et al (1992) proposed a theoretical framework for the interaction between goal-driven attentional control and stimulus-driven attentional capture. They argued that any given perceptual act entails an "attentional control setting," which is part of the explicit or implicit set of perceptual goals held by the observer at that moment. These goals might be a result of instructions provided by an experimenter (e.g. "search for the red vertical bar"), or, more often, by the individual's current plan of action in everyday life (e.g. searching for the car keys). The visual features that are of current interest (e.g. "red" or "vertical") will control the distribution of attention.

They provided evidence for this idea by showing that the deployment of attention depends critically on what the subject is set for. In one experiment, each trial consisted of a fixation display, followed in rapid succession by a cue display and a target display. Each element shown in the target display was either an **x** or an =. Two types of target displays were used. Color target displays consisted of three white elements and one red element, and the task was to identify the red element as quickly as possible as either an **x** or an =. Onset target displays consisted of only one element, and so the target was characterized as being the only element with an abrupt onset. Again, the task was to identify the target as being an **x** or an =. Immediately preceding the target display, a cue display appeared; this could consist of either color cues (in which one location was surrounded by red dots and the other three locations were surrounded by white dots) or onset cues (in which one location was surrounded by suddenly onset white dots and the remaining locations remained blank). Each type of target display was combined with each type of cue display. Cue validity was manipulated between blocks; in one condition the cue was 100% valid (It always indicated the location of the to-be-identified target element), and in another condition it was 100% invalid (It always indicated a nontarget element). Folk et al (1992) found that when the cue and target were of the same type, i.e. both color or both onset, cue validity had a large effect. In particular, subjects could not ignore invalid cues. However, when the cue and target were of different types (e.g. a color cue and an onset target), then the cue had little or no influence on response times. This result is consistent with the idea that the state of attentional readiness adopted by the observer determines what sorts of feature singletons will capture attention.

A similar idea motivated Wolfe's (1994) Guided Search model (see also Cave & Wolfe 1990, Wolfe et al 1989). According to Guided Search, attention is directed to objects serially in order of priority. Attentional priority is determined jointly by two things. One is top-down activation, that is, how closely an object matches the current attentional set. For example, if the subject is searching for a red vertical bar, then all red things and all vertical things will receive higher priority than things that are neither red nor vertical. Things that are both red and vertical will, of course, receive the most activation. The other determinant is bottom-up activation, that is, how much a given object differs from neighboring objects within any given perceptual dimension. For example, a red object surrounded by green objects will have greater bottom-up activation than will a red object surrounded by orange objects. These two sources of activation are combined to produce an "attention map" that determines the order in which objects are visited during visual search.

Both these theories incorporate a principle that William James recognized: The deployment of attention depends jointly on properties of the image and the goals and expectations of the observer.

THE REPRESENTATIONAL BASIS OF VISUAL SELECTION

In an important 1981 paper, Kahneman & Henik asked, "If attention selects a stimulus, what is the stimulus that it selects?" (p. 183). Until that point—with some notable exceptions—attention was viewed (implicitly or explicitly) as similar to a spotlight directed to regions of space, "illuminating" the objects located there (e.g. Eriksen & Hoffman 1972, Hoffman & Nelson 1981, Posner et al 1980). The evidence consisted primarily of demonstrations that the spatial separation between elements significantly modulated attentional effects. For example, Hoffman & Nelson (1981) required subjects to identify a target letter that appeared in one of four locations in the visual field, and then to identify a secondary shape that was either near the target letter or elsewhere in the display. They found that identification accuracy was much better when the two stimuli were adjacent to each other, which suggested a spatial limitation in dividing attention. Downing & Pinker (1985) cued subjects to attend to one of ten boxes arranged in a horizontal row (five on either side of fixation) in anticipation of a luminance increment in one of the boxes, most often in the cued box. Detection RT was fastest when the target event occurred within the cued box, and it slowed monotonically as the distance between the target and the attended location increased. This strongly suggested a spatial gradient of selective attention.

Kahneman & Henik (1981) urged readers, however, to consider the possibility that attention might be directed not only to spatial locations but also to perceptual objects. The idea is that the raw retinal image provides only a fragmented representation of the scene because of occlusion, yet perceptual experience is coherent and "smooth." Therefore, some early visual mechanism is required to construct representations of objects. Discovering the principles by which object representations are constructed was a major goal of the Gestalt psychologists. Kahneman & Henik suggested that often the object representations resulting from perceptual organization serve as the representational basis for visual selection.

Because objects occupy locations, experiments designed to provide evidence for object-based accounts must demonstrate that a given finding is due to allocation of attention to a locationally invariant object representation and not to a spatial location. Several strategies have been adopted that accomplish this. Evidence for object-based theories of attention fall into two broad categories. Locations or features in an image can be probed that differ according to their relationship to object structure, but that do not differ in spatial location or separation. Attention may also be directed to moving objects, which by definition involves continuously changing spatial locations. Within each of these two categories, many specific techniques have been devised.

Overlap and Grouping

One of the earliest demonstrations of object-specific attentional benefits was reported by Rock & Guttman (1981) in an experiment showing that subjects can selectively attend to one of two objects appearing in the same spatial location. Observers viewed a sequence of 10 pictures. Each picture consisted of two superimposed outline drawings of novel shapes, one drawn in red ink and one in green. The subject was asked to make an aesthetic judgment of the object drawn in red ink (or, for half the subjects, green ink) and to ignore the object drawn in the other color. The judgment task was merely a cover to induce subjects to process the items selectively. After viewing all the drawings, subjects were given a surprise recognition test. One third of the test items had been attended during the judgment task, one third had been unattended, and one third were new. Subjects were much more likely to report attended items as old than unattended or new items. Their judgments for unattended and new items did not differ. This result shows that attention need not be purely location-based, but that it is possible to selectively attend to one of two spatially coincident perceptual objects.

Duncan (1984) laid out explicitly the distinction between space-based theories and object-based theories of attention and explored the distinction empirically with a perceptual version of the memory task employed by Rock & Guttman. Subjects viewed a display consisting of a rectangle with a tilted line drawn through the middle. Each object could take on two values for each of two attributes: The line could be tilted right or left, and it could be dotted or dashed in texture. The rectangle could be tall or short, and it had a small gap in its contour on the right or left side. The display was flashed briefly and was followed by a mask. Subjects were asked to report two attributes on each trial. On some trials, the two attributes belonged to the same object (e.g. the tilt and texture of the line), while on other trials they belonged to different objects (e.g. the height of the rectangle and the tilt of the line). Responses were more accurate when the attributes belonged to the same object. This was taken as evidence that observers attend to objects as a whole: When judgments had to be made about both objects, a cost was incurred because of the need to shift attention from one object to the other.

Vecera & Farah (1994) verified that Duncan's results reflected an object-based effect (rather than what they termed a spatial "grouped array" effect). They noted that a spatial account predicts that the magnitude of the object-specific benefit should be larger when the two objects are spatially separated than when they are spatially superimposed. They found no evidence of such a pattern. However, when the task required judgments that did not involve accessing the shapes of the objects but required only the detection of a small dot at various locations on the object contours, then only space-based effects were observed. They concluded that simple detection tasks may access a strictly spatial level of representation, while shape discrimination tasks require object-based representations and therefore yield object-based attentional effects.

The studies just reviewed employing two overlapping objects revealed that one can selectively attend to an object occupying the same spatial location as another object, as object-based theories predict. A related technique is to show that when attention is directed to one part of an object, other parts of the object enjoy an attentional benefit, whereas equally distant locations in other objects do not. Several examples of this approach have been reported. Baylis & Driver (1993) showed that judging the relative locations of two "corners" of a complex stimulus was more difficult when they belonged to two objects rather than one. This was the case even when the one-object and two-object displays were physically identical, with instructions determining how many objects were seen in the display. Baylis & Driver found, like Duncan, that judgments about two parts of a single object were made faster than those about parts of two different objects (for further discussion of this procedure, see Baylis 1994, Gibson 1994).

M Behrmann, RS Zemel & MC Mozer (unpublished manuscript) documented a similar object-specific benefit using a perceptual matching task. Subjects were shown a display in which two rectangles, one oriented at +45° and the other at −45°, overlapped such that one rectangle was seen as being in front of the other. Two of the rectangle ends had either two or three "bumps" on them, and subjects were required to report whether the number of bumps was the same or different on the two ends (the other two ends were straight). Of greatest interest was whether the ends to be judged were part of the same perceptual object. For example, the rectangle ends to be judged could be at either end of the partly occluded rectangle, or one could be at one end of the occluding rectangle, and the other could be at one end of the partly occluded rectangle. The main result was that judgments made about two parts of the same object were faster than judgments made about parts of two different objects, even when the object in question was partly occluded. This finding is related in many ways to the result reported by Duncan (1984). In this case, however, the partly occluded objects were fragmented in the image. Perceptual organization mechanisms were required to put the object fragments together into coherent object representations.

Egly et al (1994) had subjects view a display containing two vertically (or, on other trials, horizontally) oriented rectangles presented side by side. One end of one of the rectangles was cued (its local contour was briefly brightened), and after a short delay one end of one of the rectangles was filled in (this was the "target"). Subjects were to press a button when the target appeared (a simple detection task). They were told that the target would appear at the cued location on 80% of the trials (the valid condition), at the other end of the cued object on 10% of the trials (the same-object condition), and at the same end of the uncued object on 10% of the trials (the different-object condition). The latter two locations were equally distant from the cued location, but they differed in their relation to the cued object. The authors found that mean RT in the valid condition was faster than the other two conditions. More revealing was the presence of an object-specific benefit: RTs in the same-object condition were faster than in the different-object condition. This outcome is consistent with an object-based account.

A related study was carried out by Yantis & Moore (1995). They used rectangle pairs like those used by Egly et al, but in some conditions they placed an occluding surface in front of the rectangles. At issue was whether the object-specific benefits documented by Egly et al persisted when the objects containing the target events were partly occluded and required perceptual organization to be completed [as in the Behrmann and colleagues (unpublished manuscript) study]. The results revealed a robust object-specific benefit. Yantis & Moore (1995) went on to show that when the perceptual task required of subjects was a temporal-order judgment, no object-specific benefit was observed; instead only location-based effects were observed. This latter result parallels the similar finding by Vecera & Farah (1994) noted earlier.

Several studies have shown that the attentional effects of image features can vary as a function of how they are perceptually grouped, rather than where they are located in the image. Such results support object-based theories of attention, on the assumption that the function of perceptual grouping is to create object representations. For example, Driver & Baylis (1989; Baylis & Driver 1992) asked whether interference from to-be-ignored stimuli during target identification depended only on relative spatial location or on more complex grouping principles. They employed the flankers task developed by Eriksen & Eriksen (1974) in which subjects are required to report the identity of a centrally located target letter and ignore adjacent noise letters. Eriksen & Eriksen found that when the noise letters were assigned to a response that conflicted with the response associated with the target letter, responses were significantly slowed, which suggests that attention could not be completely focused on the target letters.

Baylis & Driver (1992) constructed displays in which the stimuli were colored letters. For example, in their Experiment 2, five letters were arranged in a row. The first, third, and fifth letters were one color (e.g. red), and the second and fourth letters were another color (e.g. green). The letters X and Y were assigned to one response (e.g. press the right button), and C and S were assigned to another response (e.g. press the left button). H and T were neutral letters not assigned to a response; they never served as target letters. Subjects were supposed to press the button assigned to the identity of the middle (third) letter in the string. Baylis & Driver (1992) found that the identity of the letters that matched the target in color, and not the letters that were spatially closest to the target, had the greatest influence (facilitation and inhibition of RT). For example, the string X^r H^g S^r H^g X^r (where the superscript indicates that letter's color) produced longer RTs than did the string H^r X^g S^r X^g H^r, even though the response-incompatible Xs are closer to the target in the second string than in the first string. Driver & Baylis (1989) obtained qualitatively identical results using grouping via common motion.

These results have been corroborated by Kramer & Jacobson (1991), who found that the extent to which flanking elements interfered with the identification of a target depended on whether the flankers were joined via connecting line segments to the target (producing large interference effects) or to other objects (producing smaller effects).

Motion

A second approach to exploring the representational basis of visual selection is to separate objects from their location via motion. Kahneman et al (1992) introduced a priming technique that produces what they term an object-specific "re-viewing" effect. We here describe a simplified version of their Experiment 4. Each trial began with the appearance of a square and a triangle on opposite sides of the display (e.g. above and below fixation) for 500 ms. A capital letter then appeared within each shape for 1 s and then disappeared; this initial display constituted the "preview field." The empty shapes smoothly moved to new positions to the left and right of fixation over a period of 590 ms, at which time they stopped and a target letter appeared within one of the shapes. The subjects were required to name the target letter vocally as quickly as possible after it appeared. The target letter could either be one of the two in the preview field, or it could be new. When it was one of the preview letters, it either appeared within the same object as it did in the preview field, or in the other object. This led to three possible trial types. For example, if the preview field consisted of an S in the square and a P in the triangle, then a *same-object trial* would consist of an S in the square during the target display, a *different-object trial* would consist of an S in the triangle during the target display, and a *no-match* trial would consist of a V in either shape.

Kahneman et al (1992) found that naming latencies were much slower for no-match trials than for the other conditions. More importantly, however, RTs were significantly faster for the same object condition than for the different object condition. They interpreted this finding as follows. When a visual object appears in the visual field, an object file is created for it. An object file is a temporary episodic representation of a visual object, containing a record of its location, its various attributes (including, perhaps, its name), and its recent history (Kahneman & Treisman 1984). In the case of the experiment described above, object files for the square (and the letter appearing with it in the preview display) and for the triangle (and its preview letter) are created at the start of the trial. When the target letter appears after the shapes move to their new locations, then the object file is reaccessed, and if the object file corresponding to the shape in which the target appears contains a trace of the target letter (as it would in the same-object condition) then naming latency is speeded relative to the no-match condition. This is a form of object-specific perceptual priming.

Another study in which motion was used to separate objects from their locations was reported by Yantis (1992), who used a multi-element visual tracking procedure devised by Pylyshyn & Storm (1988). On each trial, ten elements (small plus signs) appeared on the screen, usually in random locations. A subset of these (n = 1 to 5) was flashed several times. This constituted the *target set.* The targets stopped flashing, and all 10 elements began to move about the screen independently, changing direction at random times and bouncing off one another and the edges of the screen. After 7 s, the elements stopped moving, and one was flashed. Subjects were to report whether this probe element was a member of the target set or not. Pylyshyn & Storm (1988) had shown that this task could be carried out with reasonably good accuracy, and to explain this they invoked a theory of visual indexing (Pylyshyn 1989) according to which each target element is independently indexed at the start of the trial. When the probe appears, it is queried to determine whether it is among the indexed set.

Yantis (1992) suggested instead that this task was carried out by grouping the target elements into a "virtual polygon," an object representation that is analogous to an object file (Kahneman & Treisman 1984, Kahneman et al 1992). Evidence for selective attention to the target elements supports an object-based representation for selection, because the target and nontarget elements could not be distinguished on the basis of spatial location (They were spatially intermixed as they moved so that no convex spatial region contained all and only targets). The experiments were designed to show that task performance was modulated by factors that influenced how easily perceptual groups could be created and maintained. In Experiment 4, for example, the configuration of target elements was either unconstrained or was constrained to remain convex during motion. The convexity constraint ensured that the virtual polygon would remain coherent throughout motion (i.e. the ordering of vertices along the perimeter remained constant), and this permitted observers to use a single object representation throughout motion. Performance in the constrained condition was significantly better than in the unconstrained condition.

Several studies have attempted to dissociate objects and locations in an *inhibition of return* (IOR) paradigm. Summoning covert attention to a spatial location with a task-irrelevant peripheral cue can either speed or slow detection of a subsequent target. When the target follows the onset of the cue by 150 ms or less, RTs are usually faster when targets are displayed in the cued location than in an uncued location (e.g. Maylor 1985, Posner & Cohen 1984). This facilitation has been thought to reflect one consequence of attending to a location. When the target follows the cue by more than 300 ms, however, time to detect a target is often faster for targets presented at previously uncued locations than at previously cued locations. It is this effect that Posner et al (1985) called inhibition of return. We consider here just one aspect of inhibition of return, namely whether it is associated with a spatial location or a perceptual object. (For discussions of other aspects of this phenomenon, see e.g. Abrams & Dobkins 1994, Klein & Taylor 1994, Kwak & Egeth 1992, Rafal et al 1989.)

Early experiments suggested that IOR was associated with spatial locations, specifically spatial locations defined in fixed environmental coordinates (Maylor & Hockey 1985, Posner & Cohen 1984). However, these locations often happened to coincide with objects. For example, in Posner & Cohen's (1984) study, displays consisted of squares. When brightened or dimmed, these squares served as cues. A target could then appear in a cued or an uncued square. However, the squares appeared in fixed locations on a screen, and thus it was not possible to say whether the resulting IOR was associated with a particular location, a particular square, or both.

In an effort to distinguish among these possibilities, Tipper et al (1991) set the squares into motion. Subjects fixated a central location around which two diametrically opposed squares revolved in a clockwise direction along the circumference of an imaginary circle. At a certain time during this circular motion one square was briefly cued (brightened). Both squares continued to revolve for a variable time until the target (a dot) was shown inside either the cued or the uncued square. Consider the case in which a square was cued as it reached the leftmost point of the circle, and the target dot was presented after the pair of squares had completed an additional half-turn (i.e. 180°) around fixation. If RT were slower when the target appeared at the left location, which is the same location in environmental coordinates as the original cue, than when it appeared at the right location, a location-based account would be supported. The pattern of results observed by Tipper et al (1991) clearly favored the opposite outcome. RT was slower when the target appeared within the previously cued object, which suggested that IOR is object-based under these conditions. In a subsequent study Tipper et al (1994) found evidence for both location-based and object-based IOR.

We have so far distinguished between object-based and location-based representations. This simple distinction might lead us to think that when attention is paid to an object, then the entire object benefits (or, in the case of IOR, suffers) equally. We conclude with a brief description of one additional study that suggests representations may be more complex than that. Gibson & Egeth (1994) argued that the conception of an object as *independent* of location should not be understood to imply that an object is *devoid* of location. (See also Baylis & Driver 1993, Farah et al 1990.)

An outcome of visual object processing appears to be a structural description that includes an explicit specification of relative locations of parts or surfaces within an object (e.g. Hummel & Biederman 1992). Thus, although objects are distinct from the spatial locations that they occupy, there exist other intraobject locations that may be fixed with respect to the overall object. That is, an object can be construed as a "microenvironment" within which specific locations may be tagged by the mechanisms that produce IOR or attentional facilitation. To test these notions, Gibson & Egeth (1994) employed a computer-generated depiction of a "brick" that rotated in depth in the time between the presentation of a cue and a subsequent target. The results of a series of four experiments showed that IOR was associated both with locations on the brick that remained fixed with respect to the brick as well as with locations that were fixed in reference to the unmoving environment.

THE TIME COURSE OF ATTENTION

The deployment of attention from one stimulus to another is by no means instantaneous. A substantial body of research has explored the temporal characteristics of attentional deployment. In this section we examine (*a*) how quickly attention can be directed to a particular stimulus, (*b*) how long attention remains directed at a particular stimulus (the dwell time of attention), and (*c*) how attention moves from location to location.

Directing Attention

There is a substantial literature concerning how attention may be covertly directed to a particular stimulus or to a location in the visual field, which was covered in a recent *Annual Review of Psychology* article (Kinchla 1992). Only basic findings are recounted here. In studies by Eriksen and his colleagues (e.g. Eriksen & Collins 1969, Eriksen & Rohrbaugh 1970) stimuli were briefly displayed letters on the circumference of an imaginary circle. A cue indicating the location of the to-be-reported letter could be shown in advance of the letter display. Accuracy of report increased with increasing stimulus-onset asynchrony (SOA) between the cue and the target letter. There was substantial improvement with just a 50-ms SOA, and the effect of the precue was asymptotic by about 200 ms. However, the story is not quite as simple as that description might suggest. As discussed in the section on attentional control, apparently two different mechanisms can direct attention to a stimulus or stimulus location—one that is stimulus-driven and another that is goal directed. We review here studies that reveal the time course of these mechanisms.

In a study by Müller & Rabbitt (1989), subjects fixated the center of a display while four boxes were present in the periphery of the display at the corners of a larger imaginary square. Subjects had to discriminate the orientation of a T presented in one of the boxes; the remaining three boxes contained plus signs. Before the presentation of these characters, subjects received a cue that was either the brief brightening of one of the four boxes (a peripheral cue) or the presentation of an arrow at the center of the display that pointed at one of the boxes (a central cue). These cues were partially valid. Half of the time they indicated the box that contained the critical T-shape, and half of the time they indicated one of the boxes that contained a plus sign. Performance was examined as a function of the SOA between the cue and the characters. The results showed that the peripheral cue had a fast-acting effect on performance. For example, with a valid peripheral cue, performance was quite good even at the shortest SOA (100 ms). It improved as SOA increased to 175 ms and then declined somewhat to a stable level for SOAs beyond 400 ms. In contrast, a valid central cue was virtually ineffective at 100 ms; performance increased steadily until, at 400 ms, it reached approximately the same stable level as that achieved by the peripheral cue. Thus, the peripheral cue was characterized as having a fast, transient response, and the central cue was characterized as having a slow, sustained response. More specifically, central cues elicit a deliberate shift of attention that is characterized by a monotonic rise to an asymptote, while peripheral cues produce a quick rise and then fall to a lower asymptotic level (and, perhaps, inhibition of return at still longer intervals). Similar findings have been reported by Kröse & Julesz (1989), Nakayama & Mackeben (1989), and Cheal & Lyon (1991).

The Dwell Time of Attention

VISUAL SEARCH In much of the recent research on attention the visual search paradigm has been used to probe the mechanisms of attention. Among other things, this paradigm has been used to estimate the amount of time spent per item in the visual display. Let us take as a starting point search for a T in any orientation in a background of Ls in any orientation (see e.g. Bergen & Julesz 1983, Egeth & Dagenbach 1991, Wolfe et al 1989). This task is demanding and may well require serial processing (a requirement for any straightforward estimate of time per item). If one plots mean RT against display size, the resulting target-absent and target-present functions are nearly linear and have substantial slopes that stand in roughly a 2:1 ratio. For example, in the study by Wolfe et al (1989, Experiment 4) the present and absent slopes for one set of conditions were 19.2 and 41.6 ms per item, respectively, and for another set of conditions were 24.9 and 60.9 ms per item, respectively. Taken together, these two data sets suggest a serial search that inspects nontargets at the rate of approximately 50 ms per item until the target is found, with the shallower slope of the target-present function due to the subject terminating the search upon finding the target after half of the stimuli (on average) have been inspected. The slope of the target-absent function can be construed as the time that attention dwells on an item before moving to the next item. Obviously this dwell time will depend on many factors, such as the difficulty of the discrimination between targets and nontargets (see e.g. Cheal & Lyon 1992, Palmer 1994).

Use of the slope of a search function as an estimate of how long attention dwells on a stimulus has substantial face-validity, but it is not without interpretive problems (e.g. Palmer & McLean 1995; Townsend 1971, 1990). Perhaps the biggest problem is that the underlying serial model may be inappropriate. Suppose, for example, that nontargets were rejected in parallel by a limited-capacity process (such that it takes longer to work the more elements there are in the display). One could still compute a slope, but it would not accurately reflect the time course of attention across discrete items in the display. For examples of models with varying degrees and kinds of parallelism, see Duncan

& Humphreys (1989), Grossberg et al (1994), Hoffman (1979), Palmer & McLean (1995), and Wolfe (1994).

RAPID SERIAL VISUAL PRESENTATION (RSVP): WHOLE REPORT If we move beyond the search task, we find other paradigms that cast light on the time course of attention. Several involve the sequential display of stimuli as opposed to the simultaneous display of the visual search task. (For some early applications of such displays to the issue of whether processing is parallel or serial, see e.g. Eriksen & Spencer 1969, Shiffrin & Gardner 1972, Travers 1973.) Some of the sequential display procedures have yielded estimates of dwell time that are shorter than the roughly 50 ms estimates we get from visual search studies, while others have provided substantially longer estimates.

Saarinen & Julesz (1991) presented two, three, or four numerals in random positions on a ring surrounding fixation. Each numeral was followed by a mask in the same location. Each numeral and each mask was presented for 33 ms, and there was a blank interval of variable duration (0, 33, or 67 ms) between each numeral and its following mask. Each mask appeared simultaneously with the appearance on screen of the next numeral. Thus, SOAs in this experiment were 33, 67, or 100 ms. At the end of the stimulus presentation the subject was to type in all the numerals in the sequence in the correct order. Not surprisingly, as the number of numerals in the sequence increased, the proportion of trials on which the subject could correctly identify all of them decreased. The authors emphasized, however, that performance was above chance even when there were four numerals in the sequence and the SOA was 33 ms. They concluded that the speed of focal visual attention can be quite fast (at least 50 ms per item), with performance still respectable at 33 ms per item.

In a subsequent experiment, exposure durations as short as 16.7 ms were used, in addition to a condition in which stimuli were presented simultaneously (Hung et al 1995). Again performance was better than chance even with four-numeral sequences presented at the shortest SOA (i.e. 16.7 ms). Accuracy of report in the correct order in that condition was approximately 0.2%; their estimate of chance in that condition was 0.02%.

There is a problem, however, with basing this argument on the fact that performance was above chance. Suppose subjects always saw the first numeral clearly but, because of capacity limitations, saw none of the following items, which they would have to guess randomly. Even such minimal information would lead to above-chance performance, but such performance could not then be converted into a meaningful estimate of dwell time per item. By our own calculations, performance in the Saarinen & Julesz study appears to be too good to be accounted for in terms of subjects seeing one item and guessing three. If anything, it is more like seeing three clearly and guessing one. Thus, the work of Julesz and his colleagues strongly suggests a high speed for focal attention, but it is not clear whether a precise estimate of that speed is possible based on this technique.

The research of Saarinen & Julesz (1991) and Hung et al (1995) attempted to estimate dwell time by presenting stimuli sequentially and determining how quickly they can be presented while still maintaining above-chance performance. A different approach to estimating dwell time asks instead how slowly stimuli need to be presented to keep report accuracy at a high level. Some early research using RSVP was concerned with reading and so used letter sequences that formed words. Kolers & Katzman (1966) presented six letters one after the other in the same spatial location; they found that it took an SOA of 375 ms for accurate report (over 90% correct) of the letters in a sequence. Haber & Nathanson (1969) used a similar display format and presented words that varied in length from four to eight letters. They found that the SOA required for asymptotic performance increased with word length. For four-letter words they estimated the critical SOA to be 65 ms, and for eight-letter words 110 ms. Haber & Nathanson gave several reasons for believing that the relationship they found between word length and SOA may be artifactual. For example, there was no mask before the first letter or after the last letter. Thus two of the four letters in a four-item list are particularly easy, but only two of the eight items in an eight-item list were particularly easy. Thus, the 65 ms estimate of required processing time is probably too short. It is possible that the 110 ms estimate is also too short, at least if we consider the results of Travers (1973). In a condition in which the letters of a word were presented sequentially in the same spatial location (with the string preceded and followed by a mask) an exposure duration of 375 ms yielded between 80 and 85% of words (not letters) correctly identified.

RAPID SERIAL VISUAL PRESENTATION: PARTIAL REPORT One problem with interpreting the aforementioned studies is that the use of words creates opportunities for all sorts of guessing strategies to occur. To avoid these problems, one might present random letter strings (e.g. Kolers & Katzman 1966, Travers 1973). However, this creates problems of its own. In particular, memory requirements come to dominate task performance. One solution to this problem is to eliminate the need for whole report (Sperling 1960). A variety of interesting designs have adopted this approach. They have in common the requirement that subjects report the status of just one or two items, called target items, that are differentiated from the other items in the stream in some way.

In a series of four experiments, Broadbent & Broadbent (1987) distinguished targets from nontargets in several different ways. In one task, subjects had to report two uppercase target words presented in an RSVP stream of otherwise all lowercase words. Subjects were unable to report both targets if they were presented in temporally adjacent positions. Moreover, this deficit persisted even when words were separated by one, two, or three intervening nontargets. (At the exposure duration of 80 ms, three intervening items translates into an SOA of 320 ms between successive targets.) In another experiment using a somewhat more difficult discrimination (targets were designated by the presence of a hyphen on either side), the deficit in reporting both words was present for temporal separations of up to 480 ms. The difficulty of reporting both targets was not limited to situations in which target and foil were distinguished by a simple physical feature. Similar results were obtained in another task in which all items were lowercase and subjects had to report animal names. This lengthy refractory period is consistent with Duncan's (1980) claim that it is difficult to process two targets at the same time.

The RSVP studies supply an appreciation of what the phrase "at the same time" means. Roughly speaking, poor performance on the second target may be viewed as reflecting the duration of processing of the first target. However, this is a simplification. When items follow one another rapidly, subjects often process them in the "wrong" order. For example, in the Broadbent & Broadbent (1987) experiment using uppercase targets, when the two targets were temporally adjacent the probabilities of reporting the first and second targets were 0.46 and 0.35 respectively, but the probability of reporting both correctly was only 0.075. Thus, apparently on many trials subjects were able to report the second but not the first target. In contrast, when the targets were separated by three intervening items, the corresponding probabilities were 0.45, 0.14, and 0.075. Here the deficit would appear to be mostly, but not entirely, due to prolonged processing of the first target. Reeves & Sperling (1986) and Weichselgartner & Sperling (1987) provided detailed temporal analyses of responses in multitarget tasks.

The RSVP studies we have reviewed suggest that the allocation of attention to a target in a stimulus stream produces a fairly protracted deficit. It is not clear what the nature of this deficit is. In studies that required word identification the deficit may be in word identification, or it may be in some lower-level visual process. Similarly, in the Weichselgartner & Sperling (1987) study the deficit may be in memory mechanisms, or it may be in perceptual or attentional processes. Raymond et al (1992) suggested that what we are seeing in these studies is a suppression of visual processing. They wrote that "these data suggest that the mechanisms involved in target identification are temporarily shut down after use. It is as if the perceptual and attentional mechanisms blink" (p. 851).

Raymond et al (1992) designed a dual-task RSVP experiment in which response requirements were somewhat simpler than in preceding studies. Letters were presented one at a time at a rate of 11 per second. One letter was white; all the rest were black. Subjects had to identify the white letter. On half of the trials there was an "X" somewhere in the stream (but never prior to the white letter). On the other half of the trials there was no *X*. After reporting the identity of the white letter, the subject was to indicate whether the stream had contained an *X*. (Note that on some trials the white letter was an *X*.) Both responses were unspeeded, and the memory load was minimal. The focus of this study was on the consequences associated with paying attention to a target; for this reason, the white letter was referred to as the *target*, while the *X* was referred to as the *probe*. In the control condition, the subject was instructed to ignore the white letter and just indicate whether the probe was present or not. Note that the stimuli were identical in the experimental and control conditions. This allows one to determine whether posttarget performance deficits are due to sensory factors such as masking of the probe by the target or to the attentional demands of identifying the target letter.

The relevant data are the percentages of correct detections of the probe as a function of the position of the probe in the series. When the subject did not have to identify the white letter, probe detection was very good, averaging about 90% correct, and did not vary as a function of probe position. However, when subjects did have to identify the white letter, probe detection probability was similar to control performance at position 0, i.e. when the probe and target coincided, and declined steadily until, at position 3, probe detection was less than 50%. Performance then recovered gradually until, by position 6, it once again did not differ from control performance. This substantial and extended dip in performance of the experimental condition was referred to by Raymond et al (1992) as the *attentional blink*. In that study, it was statistically significant in the posttarget interval from 180 to 450 ms. We are concerned here chiefly with documenting the existence and extent of the attentional blink. Several attempts to provide theoretical accounts of the phenomenon have been proposed recently (e.g. Chun & Potter 1995, Grandison et al 1996, Raymond et al 1995, Seiffert & DiLollo 1996).

RAPID SERIAL VISUAL PRESENTATION: MINIMAL SEQUENCES The partial report procedure is clearly a simplification of the whole report method. However, RSVP with a multi-item sequence is a daunting task nevertheless, requiring selection of stimuli presented at high speed. One further simplification has been introduced. Duncan et al (1994; see also Ward et al 1996) presented just two stimuli sequentially and had subjects identify both. The stimuli were presented in two different locations and were both postmasked. When the stimuli were presented close together in time, the first stimulus interfered with the second. The investigators measured the interval over which the interference persisted. They took this to be an index of the time course of the first object's attentional demand (or, as they put it, of the dwell time of attention). The result is consistent with other estimates from the RSVP literature. Dwell times were several hundred milliseconds. A summary estimate of 500 ms would not be far off the mark.

The simplicity of the experimental paradigm makes this perhaps the strongest piece of evidence that search cannot shift between objects fast enough to account for the reaction times that are obtained in typical visual search tasks.

WHY THE DISCREPANT RESULTS? We take the high speed (17–33 ms) estimates of dwell time derived from the studies of Saarinen & Julesz (1991) and Hung et al (1995) to be provocative but, for the reasons stated above, not yet sufficiently secure to serve as the basis for further theoretical speculation. What remains, then, is to consider why the results from search tasks (50 ms per item) and a wide variety of RSVP tasks (500 ms per item) yield such different results. This section must be considered speculative because little work has addressed this question.

Moore et al (1996) noted that the experiments by Duncan et al (1994) and Ward et al (1996) used masked stimuli. Typically, masked stimuli are not used in visual search tasks. If dwell time depends on the specific stimuli and tasks used, then perhaps the discrepancy is more apparent than real. More specifically, attention may remain focused longer for a difficult discrimination than for an easy discrimination, and it is reasonable to think that masking may have made the discrimination difficult and thus led to an unusually long dwell time.

The Moore et al (1996) experiment was very similar in design to the experiments by Duncan and his colleagues. The one crucial difference is that in one condition both the first and second stimulus were postmasked immediately after their exposure (as in Duncan et al), while in another condition the first and second stimuli were masked at the same time (immediately after the exposure of the second stimulus). The critical question was whether the change in masking status of the first stimulus would affect the dwell time of attention on that stimulus. It did. Dwell time was reduced to about 200 ms. Although still longer than the times derived from visual search tasks, this time is less than half of the estimate in Duncan et al (1994). It seems possible that other differences between the methods might reduce the time still further.

Bennett & Wolfe (1996) have made a further effort to bridge the methodological gap between visual search and RSVP procedures. Subjects searched for a rotated T among rotated Ls, a task that would seem likely to elicit serial search. Stimuli were presented one at a time at random locations in a large field. SOAs varied across trials: 26, 52, 78, or 104 ms. Once presented, a stimulus remained in view until the end of the trial. Reaction time was measured from the onset of the trial until the subject pressed a key. What was of interest was how well subjects could "keep up" with the sequential presentation of items. If subjects could move attention from stimulus to stimulus at the same rate that they were being shown, then the slope of the function relating mean RT to the time in the sequence when the target was found should be 1.0. The seven subjects kept up with stimulus presentation at SOAs of 104, 78, and 52 ms, and fell behind only at 26 ms. This suggests that subjects can discriminate rotated Ts and Ls at a rate of about 50 ms per item.

With this interesting paradigm and result we have come full circle. Although presentation was sequential, the estimate of dwell time was as short as those from simultaneous presentations in classical studies of visual search. It is by no means clear just what it is about these various paradigms that leads to such differing results; this remains a problem for further research. Nevertheless, it seems reasonable to conclude, following MM Chun, JM Wolfe & MC Potter (unpublished manuscript) that "while it is *possible* to tie up attention for several hundred ms after a target has been detected, such commitment by no means represents a *mandatory* minimum dwell time for successful processing."

The Movement of Attention

It is widely accepted that attention can be shifted from one location to another in the visual field without any concomitant movement of the eyes. However, the nature of the shift is less clear. Does attention move in an analog, continuous fashion, or is the shift of attention accomplished abruptly, without any actual movement?

Several investigators have obtained results that they took to support the idea that, like a spotlight, attention moves continuously through space (e.g. Shulman et al 1979) and thus requires more time to move a greater distance (e.g. Tsal 1983). For example, Tsal (1983) had subjects rapidly discriminate an "X" from an "O". Stimulus presentations were 4°, 8°, or 12° to the left or right of fixation. At a variable time before the letter was presented, a cue was briefly flashed at the location in which the letter was to appear. Tsal reasoned that the cue should be beneficial. On the basis of the assumption that attention takes time to move, he reasoned further that the maximum benefit of the cue should occur progressively later in time the further away from fixation the stimulus appeared. This was the pattern he observed.

This research suggesting that attention moves in an analog fashion has been criticized in some detail by Eriksen & Murphy (1987) and Yantis (1988). For example, one problem with the study by Tsal is that it did not include a control for general arousal or alertness. Yantis (1988, p. 205) concluded that both the Tsal (1983) and Shulman et al (1979) experiments "are simply inconclusive about whether attention shifts have continuous or discrete dynamics." However, there are some other approaches that avoid the problems of the aforementioned studies.

Sagi & Julesz (1985) showed evidence for an abrupt relocation of attention. Subjects had to decide whether two simultaneously presented stimuli were the same or different. The stimuli—rotated Ts and Ls—were presented at varying separations and were followed by a mask to limit processing time. The finding of chief interest was that at any given stimulus-mask onset asynchrony, discrimination accuracy was independent of distance, which they took as evidence for "fast, noninertial shifts of attention" (p. 141).

Converging evidence of distance-independent relocation of attention was provided by Kwak et al (1991). Subjects made same-different judgments about pairs of Ts and Ls that varied in separation. In their experiments, stimuli appeared at varying separations on an imaginary circle, to control acuity. The dependent variable of chief interest was reaction time. As in the Sagi & Julesz study, performance was independent of separation. This was true for both upright Ts and Ls (Experiment 1) and rotated Ts and Ls (Experiments 2, 3). Remington & Pierce (1984) reported a similar result.

In both the Sagi & Julesz (1985) and Kwak et al (1991) experiments, it is important to establish that the tasks actually required attention. If the tasks were accomplished preattentively, there would be little reason to speak of reallocation of attention. We focus here on the analysis provided by Kwak et al (1991, Experiment 3). To establish that the two stimuli were examined one after the other, they used a diagnostic based on the additivity of a within-display visual quality manipulation (Egeth & Dagenbach 1991). This diagnostic applies to situations in which processing of stimuli must be exhaustive. This is the case in a same-different matching task because both stimuli must be examined to make a correct response.

The two letters in the display were, independently, either high or low in contrast. If the letters are processed sequentially, then the slowing caused by presenting low-contrast characters should be additive. That is, if making one character low in contrast increases mean RT by 20 ms, then making both characters low in contrast should increase mean RT by 40 ms. However, if processing is parallel, then the 20 ms slowing produced by one low-contrast letter should not be exacerbated by making the other letter low in contrast. That is, the effects of reducing the contrasts of the two letters should be subadditive. The results showed a clear pattern of additivity for the rotated Ts and Ls. Thus, attention presumably had to move serially from one item to the other. Sagi & Julesz (1985) used some very different experimental diagnostics that also pointed to serial processing. Thus, it seems reasonable to suggest that it is appropriate to speak of the (null) results of the distance manipulation in these studies as indicating that it does not take longer for attention to move greater distances.

Sperling & Weichselgartner (1995) have independently reported evidence that longer movements of attention do not require more time. They further showed that attention can skip over an intervening obstacle without any time cost. Together these results suggest that the movement of attention is "quantal" rather than analog.

Concluding Remarks

Our review reveals significant recent advances in the understanding of attention. Of course, many of the issues and some of the mechanisms that occupy journal pages today were anticipated to some degree as long as a century ago by William James and others. Nevertheless, many empirical details have been clarified, richer theoretical frameworks have evolved, and important new ideas, such as the distinction between object-based and location-based selection, have been advanced and developed. There is no reason to believe that this recent progress will subside any time soon; behavioral studies of attention, augmented by neuroimaging studies of the functioning brain and neuropsychological studies of brain-damaged patients, promise new insights into the mechanisms of visual attention.

Literature Cited

Abrams RA, Dobkins RS. 1994. Inhibition of return: effects of attentional cueing on eye movement latencies. *J. Exp. Psychol.: Hum. Percept. Perform.* 20:467–77

Bacon WF, Egeth HE. 1994. Overriding stimulus-driven attentional capture. *Percept. Psychophys.* 55:485–96

Baylis GC. 1994. Visual attention and objects: two-object cost with equal convexity. *J. Exp. Psychol.: Hum. Percept. Perform.* 20: 208–12

Baylis GC, Driver JS. 1992. Visual parsing and response competition: the effect of grouping factors. *Percept. Psychophys.* 51:145–62

Baylis GC, Driver JS. 1993. Visual attention and objects: evidence for hierarchical coding of locations. *J. Exp. Psychol.: Hum. Percept. Perform.* 19:451–70

Bennett SC, Wolfe JM. 1996. Serial visual search can proceed at 50 msec per item. *Invest. Ophthalmol. Vis. Sci.* 37:298 (Abstr.)

Bergen JR, Julesz B. 1983. Parallel versus serial processing rapid pattern discrimination. *Nature* 303:696–98

Bravo MJ, Nakayama K. 1992. The role of attention in different visual-search tasks. *Percept. Psychophys.* 51:465–72

Breitmeyer BG, Ganz L. 1976. Implications of sustained and transient channels for theories of visual pattern masking, saccadic suppression, and information processing. *Psychol. Rev.* 83:1–36

Broadbent DE, Broadbent MHP. 1987. From detection to identification: response to multiple targets in rapid serial visual presentation. *Percept. Psychophys.* 42:105–13

Cave KR, Wolfe JM. 1990. Modeling the role of parallel processing in visual search. *Cogn. Psychol.* 22:225–71

Cheal ML, Lyon DR. 1991. Central and peripheral precuing of forced-choice discrimination. *Q. J. Exp. Psychol.* 43A: 859–80

Cheal ML, Lyon DR. 1992. Attention in visual search: multiple search classes. *Percept. Psychophys.* 52:113–38

Chun MM, Potter MC. 1995. A two-stage model for multiple target detection in rapid serial visual presentation. *J. Exp. Psychol.: Hum. Percept. Perform.* 21:109–27

Dagenbach D, Carr TH, eds. 1994. *Inhibitory Processes in Attention, Memory, and Language.* San Diego: Academic. 461 pp.

Desimone R, Duncan J. 1995. Neural mechanisms of selective visual attention. *Annu. Rev. Neurosci.* 18:193–222

Downing CJ, Pinker S. 1985. The spatial structure of visual attention. See Posner & Marin 1985, pp. 171–87

Driver JS, Baylis GC. 1989. Movement and visual attention: the spotlight metaphor breaks down. *J. Exp. Psychol.: Hum. Percept. Perform.* 15:448–56

Duncan J. 1980. The locus of interference in the perception of simultaneous stimuli. *Psychol. Rev.* 87:272–300

Duncan J. 1984. Selective attention and the organization of visual information. *J. Exp. Psychol.: Gen.* 113:501–17

Duncan J, Humphreys G. 1989. Visual search

and stimulus similarity. *Psychol. Rev.* 96: 433–58

Duncan J, Ward R, Shapiro K. 1994. Direct measurement of attentional dwell time in human vision. *Nature* 369:313–15

Egeth H, Jonides J, Wall S. 1972. Parallel processing of multidimensional displays. *Cogn. Psychol.* 3:674–98

Egeth HE, Dagenbach D. 1991. Parallel versus serial processing in visual search: further evidence from subadditive effects of visual quality. *J. Exp. Psychol.: Hum. Percept. Perform.* 17:551–60

Egly R, Driver J, Rafal RD. 1994. Shifting visual attention between objects and locations: evidence from normal and parietal lesion subjects. *J. Exp. Psychol.: Gen.* 123:161–77

Eriksen BA, Eriksen CW. 1974. Effects of noise letters upon the identification of a target letter in a nonsearch task. *Percept. Psychophys.* 16:143–49

Eriksen CW, Collins JF. 1969. Temporal course of selective attention. *J. Exp. Psychol.* 80:264–61

Eriksen CW, Hoffman JE. 1972. Temporal and spatial characteristics of selective encoding from visual displays. *Percept. Psychophys.* 12:201–4

Eriksen CW, Hoffman JE. 1973. The extent of processing noise elements during selective encoding from visual displays. *Percept. Psychophys.* 14:155–60

Eriksen CW, Murphy TD. 1987. Movement of attentional focus across the visual field: a critical look at the evidence. *Percept. Psychophys.* 42:299–305

Eriksen CW, Rohrbaugh JW. 1970. Some factors determining efficiency of selective attention. *Am. J. Psychol.* 83:330–42

Eriksen CW, Spencer T. 1969. Rate of information processing in visual perception: some results and methodological considerations. *J. Exp. Psychol.* 79:1–16

Farah MJ, Brunn JL, Wong AB, Wallace MA, Carpenter PA. 1990. Frames of reference for allocating attention to space: evidence from the neglect syndrome. *Neuropsychologia* 28:335–47

Folk CL, Remington RW, Johnston JC. 1992. Involuntary covert orienting is contingent on attentional control settings. *J. Exp. Psychol.: Hum. Percept. Perform.* 18:1030–44

Gibson BS. 1994. Visual attention and objects: one versus two or convex versus concave? *J. Exp. Psychol: Hum. Percept. Perform.* 20:203–7

Gibson BS. 1996a. Visual quality and attentional capture: a challenge to the special role of abrupt onsets. *J. Exp. Psychol.: Hum. Percept. Perform.* 22:1496–1504

Gibson BS. 1996b. The masking account of attentional capture: a reply to Yantis and Jonides (1996). *J. Exp. Psychol.: Hum. Percept. Perform.* 22:1514–20

Gibson BS, Egeth H. 1994. Inhibition of return to object-based and environment-based locations. *Percept. Psychophys.* 55:323–39

Grandison TD, Ghirardelli TG, Egeth HE. 1996. Masking of the target is sufficient to cause the attentional blink. *Percept. Psychophys.* In press

Grossberg S, Mingolla E, Ross WD. 1994. A neural theory of attentive visual search: interactions of boundary, surface, spatial, and object representations. *Psychol. Rev.* 101: 470–89

Haber RN, Nathanson LS. 1969. Processing of sequentially presented letters. *Percept. Psychophys.* 5:359–61

Helmholtz H von. 1925. (1866). *Treatise on Physiological Optics,* Vol. 3, ed./transl. JPC Southhall. Washington, DC: Opt. Soc. Am. 3rd ed.

Hillstrom AP, Yantis S. 1994. Visual motion and attentional capture. *Percept. Psychophys.* 55:399–411

Hoffman JE. 1979. A two-stage model of visual search. *Percept. Psychophys.* 25:319–27

Hoffman JE, Nelson B. 1981. Spatial selectivity in visual search. *Percept. Psychophys.* 30:283–90

Hummel JE, Biederman I. 1992. Dynamic binding in a neural network for shape recognition. *Psychol. Rev.* 99:480–517

Hung GK, Wilder J, Curry R, Julesz B. 1995. Simultaneous better than sequential for brief presentations. *J. Opt. Soc. Am. A* 12: 441–49

James W. 1890. *The Principles of Psychology.* New York: Holt

Johnston WA, Dark VJ. 1986. Selective attention. *Annu. Rev. Psychol.* 37:43–75

Jonides J. 1981. Voluntary versus automatic control over the mind's eye's movement. In *Attention and Performance,* ed. JB Long, AD Baddeley, pp. 187–203. Hillsdale, NJ: Erlbaum. 9th ed.

Jonides J, Yantis S. 1988. Uniqueness of abrupt visual onset in capturing attention. *Percept. Psychophys.* 43:346–54

Joseph JS, Optican LM. 1996. Involuntary attentional shifts due to orientation differences. *Percept. Psychophys.* 58:651–65

Juola JF, Koshino H, Warner CB. 1995. Tradeoffs between attentional effects of spatial cues and abrupt onsets. *Percept. Psychophys.* 57:333–42

Kahneman D, Henik A. 1981. Perceptual organization and attention. In *Perceptual Organization,* ed. M Kubovy, JR Pomerantz, pp. 181–211. Hillsdale, NJ: Erlbaum

Kahneman D, Treisman A. 1984. Changing views of attention and automaticity. In *Va-*

rieties of Attention, ed. R Parasuraman, DA Davies, pp. 29–61. New York: Academic

Kahneman D, Treisman A, Gibbs BJ. 1992. The reviewing of object files: object-specific integration of information. *Cogn. Psychol.* 24:175–219

Kinchla RA. 1992. Attention. *Annu. Rev. Psychol.* 43:711–43

Klein RM, Taylor TL. 1994. Categories of cognitive inhibition with reference to attention. See Dagenbach & Carr 1994, pp. 113–50

Kolers PA, Katzman MT. 1966. Naming sequentially presented letters and words. *Lang. Speech* 9:84–95

Koshino H, Warner CB, Juola JF. 1992. Relative effectiveness of central, peripheral, and abrupt-onset cues in visual search. *Q. J. Exp. Psychol.* 45A:609–31

Kramer AF, Coles MGH, Logan GD. 1996. *Converging Operations in the Study of Visual Selective Attention.* Washington, DC: Am. Psychol. Assoc.

Kramer AF, Jacobson A. 1991. Perceptual organization and focused attention: the role of objects and proximity in visual processing. *Percept. Psychophys.* 50:267–84

Kröse J, Julesz B. 1989. The control and speed of shifts of attention. *Vis. Res.* 23:1607–19

Kwak HW, Dagenbach D, Egeth H. 1991. Further evidence for a time-independent shift of the focus of attention. *Percept. Psychophys.* 49:473–80

Kwak HW, Egeth H. 1992. Consequences of allocating attention to locations and to other attributes. *Percept. Psychophys.* 51: 455–64

LaBerge D. 1995. *Attentional Processing: The Brain's Art of Mindfulness.* Cambridge, MA: Harvard Univ. 262 pp.

Maylor E. 1985. Facilitory and inhibitory components of orienting in visual space. See Posner & Marin 1985, pp. 189–204

Maylor E, Hockey R. 1985. Inhibitory components of externally controlled covert orienting in visual space. *J. Exp. Psychol.: Hum. Percept. Perform.* 11:777–87

Mertens JJ. 1956. Influences of knowledge of target location upon the probability of observation of peripherally observable test flashes. *J. Opt. Soc. Am.* 46:1069–70

Moore CM, Egeth H, Berglan L, Luck S. 1996. Are attentional dwell items inconsistent with serial visual search? *Psychon. Bull. Rev.* 3:360–65

Müller HJ, Rabbitt PMA. 1989. Reflexive and voluntary orienting of visual attention: time course of activation and resistance to interruption. *J. Exp. Psychol.: Hum. Percept. Perform.* 15:315–30

Nakayama K, Mackeben M. 1989. Sustained and transient components of focal visual attention. *Vis. Res.* 29:1631–47

Neisser U. 1967. *Cognitive Psychology.* New York: Appleton-Century-Crofts. 351 pp.

Nothdurft HC. 1992. Feature analysis and the role of similarity in preattentive vision. *Percept. Psychophys.* 52:355–75

Nothdurft HC. 1993. Saliency effects across dimensions in visual search. *Vis. Res.* 33: 839–44

Palmer J. 1994. Set-size effects in visual search: The effect of attention is independent of the stimulus for simple tasks. *Vis. Res.* 34:1703–21

Palmer J, McLean J. 1995. *Imperfect, unlimited-capacity parallel search yields large set-size effects.* Presented at Soc. Math. Psychol., 28th, Irvine, CA

Pashler H. 1988. Cross-dimensional interaction and texture segregation. *Percept. Psychophys.* 43:307–18

Pashler H, ed. 1996a. *Attention.* London: Univ. Coll. London Press

Pashler H. 1996b. *The Psychology of Attention.* Camgridge, MA: MIT Press

Posner MI. 1980. Orienting of attention. *Q. J. Exp. Psychol.* 32:3–25

Posner MI, Cohen Y. 1984. Components of visual orienting. In *Attention and Performance,* ed. H Bouma, DG Bouwhuis, pp. 531–55. Hillsdale, NJ: Erlbaum. 10th ed.

Posner MI, Marin O, eds. 1985. *Attention and Performance.* Hillsdale, NJ: Erlbaum. 11th ed.

Posner MI, Rafal RD, Choate L, Vaughan J. 1985. Inhibition of return: neural basis and function. *Cogn. Neuropsychol.* 2:211–28

Posner MI, Snyder CRR, Davidson BJ. 1980. Attention and the detection of signals. *J. Exp. Psychol.: Gen.* 109:160–74

Pylyshyn ZW. 1989. The role of location indexes in spatial perception: a sketch of the FINST spatial-index model. *Cognition* 32: 65–97

Pylyshyn ZW, Storm RW. 1988. Tracking multiple independent targets: evidence for a parallel tracking mechanism. *Spat. Vis.* 3:179–97

Rafal RD, Calabresi PA, Brennan CW, Sciolto TK. 1989. Saccade preparation inhibits reorienting to recently attended locations. *J. Exp. Psychol.: Hum. Percept. Perform.* 15: 673–85

Raymond JE, Shapiro KL, Arnell KM. 1992. Temporary suppression of visual processing in an RSVP task: an attentional blink? *J. Exp. Psychol.: Hum. Percept. Perform.* 18:849–60

Raymond JE, Shapiro KL, Arnell KM. 1995. Similarity determines the attentional blink. *J. Exp. Psychol.: Hum. Percept. Perform.* 21:653–62

Reeves A, Sperling G. 1986. Attention gating in short-term visual memory. *Psychol. Rev.* 93:180–206

Remington RW, Johnston JC, Yantis S. 1992. Involuntary attentional capture by abrupt onsets. *Percept. Psychophys.* 51:279–90
Remington RW, Pierce L. 1984. Moving attention: evidence for time-invariant shifts of visual selective attention. *Percept. Psychophys.* 35:393–99
Rock I, Guttman D. 1981. The effect of inattention on form perception. *J. Exp. Psychol.: Hum. Percept. Perform.* 7:275–85
Saarinen J, Julesz B. 1991. The speed of attentional shifts in the visual field. *Proc. Natl. Acad. Sci. USA* 88:1812–14
Sagi D, Julesz B. 1985. Fast noninertial shifts of attention. *Spat. Vis.* 2:141–49
Seiffert AE, DiLollo V. 1996. Low-level masking in the attentional blink. *J. Exp. Psychol.: Hum. Percept. Perform.* In press
Shiffrin RM, Gardner GT. 1972. Visual processing capacity and attentional control. *J. Exp. Psychol.* 93:72–82
Shulman GL, Remington RW, McLean JP. 1979. Moving attention through visual space. *J. Exp. Psychol.: Hum. Percept. Perform.* 5:522–26
Sperling G. 1960. *The information available in brief visual presentations.* Psychol. Monogr. 74 (Whole No. 498)
Sperling G, Weichselgartner E. 1995. Episodic theory of the dynamics of spatial attention. *Psychol. Rev.* 102:503–32
Theeuwes J. 1990. Perceptual selectivity is task-dependent: evidence from selective search. *Acta Psychol.* 74:81–99
Theeuwes J. 1991a. Cross-dimensional perceptual selectivity. *Percept. Psychophys.* 50: 184–93
Theeuwes J. 1991b. Exogenous and endogenous control of attention: the effect of visual onsets and offsets. *Percept. Psychophys.* 49:83–90
Theeuwes J. 1992. Perceptual selectivity for color and form. *Percept. Psychophys.* 51: 599–606
Tipper SP, Driver JS, Weaver B. 1991. Object-centered inhibition of return of visual attention. *Q. J. Exp. Psychol.* 43A:289–98
Tipper SP, Weaver B, Jerreat LM, Burak AL. 1994. Object- and environment-based inhibition of return of visual attention. *J. Exp. Psychol.: Hum. Percept. Perform.* 20: 478–99
Todd JT, Van Gelder P. 1979. Implications of a transient-sustained dichotomy for the measurement of human performance. *J. Exp. Psychol.: Hum. Percept. Perform.* 5: 625–38
Townsend JT. 1971. A note on the identifiability of parallel and serial processes. *Percept. Perform.* 10:161–63
Townsend JT. 1990. Serial vs. parallel processing: Sometimes they look like Tweedledum and Tweedledee but they can (and should) be distinguished. *Psychol. Sci.* 1:46–54
Travers JR. 1973. The effects of forced serial processing on identification of words and random letter strings. *Cogn. Psychol.* 5: 109–37
Treisman AM, Gelade G. 1980. A feature-integration theory of attention. *Cogn. Psychol.* 12:97–136
Treisman AM, Gormican S. 1988. Feature analysis in early vision: evidence from search asymmetries. *Psychol. Rev.* 95: 15–48
Tsal Y. 1983. Movements of attention across the visual field. *J. Exp. Psychol.: Hum. Percept. Perform.* 9:523–30
van der Heijden AHC. 1992. *Selective Attention in Vision.* New York: Routledge, Chapman & Hall. 310 pp.
Vecera SP, Farah MJ. 1994. Does visual attention selection objects or locations? *J. Exp. Psychol.: Gen.* 123:146–60
Ward R, Duncan J, Shapiro K. 1996. The slow time-course of visual attention. *Cogn. Psychol.* 10:79–109
Weichselgartner E, Sperling G. 1987. Dynamics of controlled visual attention. *Science* 238:778–80
Wolfe JM. 1994. Guided search 2.0: a revised model of visual search. *Psychon. Bull. Rev.* 1:202–38
Wolfe JM, Cave KR, Franzel SL. 1989. Guided search: an alternative to the feature integration model for visual search. *J. Exp. Psychol.: Hum. Percept. Perform.* 15:419–33
Yantis S. 1988. On analog movements of visual attention. *Percept. Psychophys.* 43: 203–6
Yantis S. 1992. Multi-element visual tracking: attention and perceptual organization. *Cogn. Psychol.* 24:295–340
Yantis S, Hillstrom AP. 1994. Stimulus-driven attentional capture: evidence from equiluminant visual objects. *J. Exp. Psychol.: Hum. Percept. Perform.* 20:95–107
Yantis S, Jonides J. 1984. Abrupt visual onsets and selective attention: evidence from visual search. *J. Exp. Psychol.: Hum. Percept. Perform.* 10:601–21
Yantis S, Jonides J. 1990. Abrupt visual onsets and selective attention: voluntary versus automatic allocation. *J. Exp. Psychol.: Hum. Percept. Perform.* 16:121–34
Yantis S, Jonides J. 1996. Attentional capture by abrupt visual onsets: new perceptual objects or visual masking? *J. Exp. Psychol.: Hum. Percept. Perform.* 22:1505–13
Yantis S, Moore C. 1995. *Spread of visual attention behind an occluding surface.* Presented at Annu. Meet. Psychon. Soc., 36th, Los Angeles

Annu. Rev. Psychol. 1997. 48:299–337

PERSONNEL SELECTION

Walter C. Borman

Department of Psychology, BEH339, University of South Florida, Tampa, Florida 33620, and Personnel Decisions Research Institutes, Inc., 100 South Ashley Dr., Ste. 1230, Tampa, Florida 33602

Mary Ann Hanson and Jerry W. Hedge

Personnel Decisions Research Institutes Inc., 100 South Ashley Dr., Ste. 1230, Tampa, Florida 33602

KEYWORDS: performance, validity, industrial/organizational psychology

ABSTRACT

This chapter reviews literature from approximately mid-1993 through early 1996 in the areas of performance and criteria, validity, statistical and equal opportunity issues, selection for work groups, person-organization fit, applicant reactions to selection procedures, and research on predictors, including ability, personality, assessment centers, interviews, and biodata. The review revolves around three themes: (*a*) attention toward criteria and models of performance, (*b*) interest in personality measures as predictors of job performance, and (*c*) work on the person-organization fit selection model. In our judgment, these themes merge when it is recognized that development of performance models that differentiate criterion constructs reveal highly interpretable relationships between the predictor domain (i.e. ability, personality, and job knowledge) and the criterion domain (i.e. technical proficiency, extra-technical proficiency constructs such as prosocial organizational behavior, and overall job performance). These and related developments are advancing the science of personnel selection and should enhance selection practices in the future.

CONTENTS

0084-6570/97/0201-0299$08.00

INTRODUCTION

Our critical review covers roughly the period of mid-1993 through early 1996. Computerized and manual literature searches, as well as invitations to more than 100 active researchers in the field to submit relevant materials, have resulted in a wide range of published and unpublished literature to review. The chapter is necessarily selective, emphasizing what we believe are the most important and interesting developments in the area of personnel selection.

Three major themes are especially critical for selection research and practice. First, increased attention is being focused on criteria and models of performance. This attention is very important because enhanced knowledge about criterion constructs will lead to better understanding of predictor-criterion linkages, and accordingly, to advances in the science of personnel selection.

The second theme involves the burgeoning interest in personality measures as predictors of job performance. It is becoming increasingly apparent that job performance is a function of both ability and motivational or dispositional factors, and that the latter elements of performance have links to personality. In our view, these two themes merge when it is recognized that development of performance models that differentiate criterion constructs reveal highly interpretable relationships between ability, personality, job knowledge, technical proficiency, and work performance.

The third theme relates to increased activity in person-organization (P-O) fit research, in part, we believe, as a reaction to emerging organizational realities including: 1. Organizations increasingly employ task-force teams whose members rotate from activity to activity rather than staying in one job. 2. In a related manner, as globalization and downsizing of many organizations continue apace, they are compelled to require more of employees, including "continuous improvement" in acquisition of new skills and flexibility in work focus as the external business environment changes. These realities argue for greater reliance on selecting people according to their general fit to the organization rather than for a particular job. In addition to expanding on these themes, we cover recent literature on performance measures, abilities, personality, interviews, biodata, computerized testing, selection for teams, applicant reactions, validity, psychometrics, equal employment opportunity (EEO) issues, and P-O fit.

PERFORMANCE AND CRITERIA

Job analysis continues to be an important first step in selection research and practice. A recent major development in this area is a Department of Labor initiative to analyze virtually all jobs in the US economy in order to build a database of occupational information (O*Net). This database may be used by organizations and individuals to help match people with jobs (Peterson et al 1995). O*Net has as its basis a content model of occupational characteristics and person requirements. This content model consists of hierarchically organized taxonomies (e.g. skills, generalized work activities) so that users can enter the database at different levels of specificity according to their needs. Several occupations have been mapped using the content model, and the ultimate goal is to get close to complete coverage for the US economy. The person-job fit feature of the O*Net will enable comparisons between content-model person attributes and targeted occupational requirements. There is also an organizational-characteristics component in the content model that may facilitate P-O matches. The hope is that O*Net will help unemployed workers and students entering the workforce to find more appropriate jobs and careers, and employers to identify more highly qualified employees. These matches should be realized more systematically and with more precision than has been possible heretofore. An additional hope is that this initiative will encourage research that further advances the effectiveness of person-job matching, person-organization fit, and the science of personnel selection.

In a *Fortune* article, Bridges (1994) wrote about the "end of the job," how increasingly work will not be packaged in familiar envelopes we call jobs. Organizations that used to have a structure of jobs now have "fields of work." As mentioned above, people are increasingly on project teams that exist only as long as the project lasts, at which time they move to another project (Bridges 1994). Selection in such a context is still necessary. The task is to match knowledges, skills, abilities, and other personal characteristics (KSAOs) to requirements of the work. Lawler's (1994) essay on competency-based organizations is instructive on this topic. He believes that selection in this type of organization will require identifying persons who fit the "learning environment" and are likely to be capable of developing the skills necessary to do the organization's work. In a related manner, Sparrow (1994) discussed the effect on selection practices of flatter organizations, with a task force, team approach to getting work done. Selecting for adaptability, interactional skills, a willingness to learn, and a repertoire of multiple skills predicted to be important to future organizational functioning will be increasingly important. More research on this topic appears in the section on "Person-Organization Fit."

As mentioned, job performance models are beginning to foster more scientific understanding of criteria. These models have at least two different forms. One type attempts to explicate the central latent variables that can best characterize all performance requirements in work. A second type examines relations between elements of performance (e.g. job knowledge and proficiency) toward learning more about the criterion space. Regarding the first type, Campbell et al (1993) posited eight latent criterion factors that summarize the performance requirements for all jobs. Several of these latent constructs emerged consistently in the Project A research [a large-scale selection and classification study conducted in the US Army (Campbell 1990)], across the many jobs studied in that program. Accordingly, there is some impressive empirical support for at least part of this performance taxonomy. The importance of this research direction is considerable. The criterion domain should be carefully mapped, just as various predictor areas have already been (e.g. abilities and personality). This specification of criterion content should importantly shape the way selection research gets done (Campbell et al 1993). Consistent with one theme of this review, a criterion taxonomy will help to organize accumulating research findings by addressing questions about links between predictors and individual criteria rather than predictors and overall performance. Research by McCloy et al (1994) supports this view of predictor-criterion relations. These authors divided the criterion space into declarative knowledge, procedural knowledge and skill, and motivational components. Using data from eight jobs in Project A, they demonstrated that declarative knowledge is predicted primarily by cognitive ability, whereas the motivational element of performance (indexed by ratings) is linked to personality.

The second type of job performance model first emerged in Hunter (1983), in which path analysis results suggested that ability has primarily a direct effect on individuals' acquisition of job knowledge which, in turn, influences job holders' technical proficiency. Supervisory performance ratings were a function of both ratee job knowledge and technical proficiency. Subsequent research focused more on antecedents of performance ratings. A recent paper (Borman et al 1995) concluded that ratee technical performance and dependability were equally influential on supervisory ratings. This finding confirms results from Motowidlo & Van Scotter (1994) that technical and contextual performance (Borman & Motowidlo 1993)—the latter similar to prosocial organizational behavior—are roughly equally weighted by supervisors in making overall performance ratings. Other studies have reported similar results (e.g. Dunn et al 1995, Ferris et al 1994, Werner 1994), although McIntyre & James (1995) demonstrated that dimension weights differ for different ratees. We believe this work on job performance models is important in that, like Campbell's effort, it differentiates criterion constructs, and attempts to increase understanding of each, as well as of relationships among them. To underscore this point, Campbell et al (1996) urged that in structural models such as Hunter's (1983) and Borman et al's (1995), we move beyond studying overall performance ratings as the dependent, endogenous variable to examining individual dimensions of performance from the substantive models referred to previously (e.g. Campbell et al 1993). These thrusts to differentiate criterion constructs conceptually and, most importantly, in measuring them are prerequisites toward systematically studying links between individual predictor and criterion variables.

In fact, such links have been explored. Project A validation results show that ability best predicts performance on the technical proficiency criteria, and personality, especially dependability, best predicts performance on the contextual dimension, personal discipline. Motowidlo & Van Scotter (1994) and Van Scotter & Motowidlo (1996) found that personality predictors generally correlated higher with contextual performance than with task performance. DuBois et al (1993) also demonstrated that when the criterion space is divided up and separate elements are correlated with predictor scores, a coherent pattern of relationships emerges. In a sample of supermarket checkers, these authors found that general cognitive ability correlated higher with a maximal performance measure than with typical performance. Organ & Ryan (1995) reported substantial correlations between conscientiousness and organizational citizenship behavior. If more research can be accomplished to precisely identify predictor links with individual dimensions of job behavior, the science of personnel selection will be enhanced enormously.

In the last Annual Review chapter on selection, Landy et al (1994) predicted that organizational citizenship, prosocial organizational behavior, and contextual performance would get increased attention as criterion issues. This has occurred. Beyond the studies discussed above, a special issue of the *Employee Responsibilities and Rights Journal* has several articles about citizenship behavior and its relationship with, especially, procedural justice and organizational commitment. Finally, and more broadly, we see an important contribution to thinking about expanded criterion domains in Ilgen (1994). Ilgen and colleagues construe jobs in the context of roles that evolve for job holders. These authors' job-role differentiation framework recognizes the importance of social factors in defining "the job." These social factors are likely to introduce contextual-like performance elements into the criterion domain.

We now consider laboratory and field studies that address issues in rater training and the performance judgment process. Regarding rater training, Woehr & Huffcut (1994) conducted a meta-analysis and found that frame-of-reference (FOR) training is overall the most effective rater training treatment. Sulsky & Day (1994) found that FOR training promoted accuracy in performance ratings. However, their results for ratings occurring two days after training suggested that subjects did not recall specific behaviors but instead previously formed impressions of ratees. This in turn suggests that FOR training might not be so useful in helping raters give behavioral feedback to ratees. Lab studies are moving beyond whether FOR and other training treatments "work" to evaluate the information processing mechanisms important for success or failure of rater training programs.

Regarding halo in ratings (i.e. larger than warranted correlations between dimensions), Lance et al (1994) conducted an innovative study comparing causal models representing three different conceptualizations of halo in ratings: 1. General Impression: Overall impression influences ratings on individual dimensions. 2. Salient Dimension: A rating on a single salient dimension influences other dimensional ratings. 3. Inadequate Discrimination: A failure to discriminate between relatively independent dimensions. The first model explained the rating data best, even in situations where the other two types of halo were explicitly encouraged.

Hartel (1993) returned to rating format issues by studying an interaction between rater characteristics and format type. In a lab study, she found that field-independent raters were more accurate than field-dependent raters when a holistic format was employed. Harris (1994) presented a model of supervisory rater motivation in the performance appraisal process. His view is that motivation in this process is a function of both situational (e.g. accountability) and personal (e.g. self-efficacy) factors. Elsewhere, Sanchez & De La Torre (1996) found that observation and evaluation accuracy were related only immediately after viewing performance and only for the components of accuracy involving identification of ratee strengths and weaknesses (i.e. stereotype and differential accuracy). In addition, Ganzach (1995) found evidence of nonlinearity in performance ratings in three field data sets. In particular, the ratings were conjunctive, with negative information influencing the overall performance judgments more than positive information. In a meta-analysis, Viswesvaran et al (1996) estimated the 1-rater interrater reliability of supervisor and peer ratings on 10 dimensions of performance, each at about the same level of specificity as the Campbell et al (1993) taxonomy discussed above. Highlights of the results are: 1. Overall performance interrater reliabilities for supervisors average .52; .42 for peer ratings. 2. Interrater reliabilities for individual dimensions are at about the same level. The latter result is at odds with findings from personality psychology (e.g. Funder 1995) that hypothesize and demonstrate empirically that some traits are more observable and more salient than others, which results in higher interobserver agreement in ratings.

Computerized performance monitoring (CPM) is becoming more common in the communications, banking, insurance, and other industries (e.g. Hedge & Borman 1995). In general, I/O psychologists have used little of their expertise in performance measurement and appraisal to help guide the development, implementation, and evaluation of CPM systems. Exceptions are Kulik & Ambrose (1993), who found in a lab study that raters paid more attention to secretarial performance they actually viewed than CPM information on the same secretaries, and Aiello & Kolb (1995), who found that for high-skill data-entry workers CPM improved performance and that for low-skill workers CPM led to lower performance. In other developments, Pritchard's Productivity Measurement System (ProMES) has now been used in many settings. An edited book (Pritchard 1995) described successful applications of this method in several manufacturing, service, and other settings. Finally, Quinones et al (1995) showed that work experience is not a unitary concept by demonstrating with meta-analysis that although the overall correlation of experience and job performance is .27, this relationship is significantly higher when experience is defined at the task (rather than the job or organizational) level and as amount (e.g. number of times performed).

PREDICTORS: CONTENT

Abilities and Achievement

COGNITIVE ABILITIES A recently published book, *The Bell Curve* (Herrnstein & Murray 1994), brought a great deal of public attention and debate to the issues surrounding the meaning of intelligence test scores and the nature of general intelligence. The central premise of this book is that individual differences in intelligence have implications for life outcomes and for society as a whole. In an attempt to clarify the issues involved in this debate, the American Psychological Association (APA) assembled a task force to develop an authoritative report on the current status of the relevant scientific findings. The product of this task force was an article in the *American Psychologist* (Neisser et al 1996) reflecting a consensus among many of the leading researchers in the area concerning the nature of general intelligence, subgroup differences, the heritability of intelligence, environmental effects on intelligence, and a variety of related topics. This article is important because discussion generated by *The Bell Curve* seems to "have gone well beyond the scientific findings, making explicit recommendations on various aspects of public policy" (Neisser et al 1996, p. 78).

In the personnel selection arena, the debate concerning the ubiquitousness of the role of general mental ability or *g* in the prediction of training and job performance continues to simmer. Several recent studies have again demonstrated that psychometric *g*, which is generally operationalized as the common variance in a battery of cognitive ability tests (e.g. the first principal component), accounts for the majority of the predictive power in the test battery, and that the remaining variance (often referred to in this research as "specific abilities") accounts for little or no additional variance in the criterion (e.g. Larson & Wolfe 1995, Ree et al 1994b). This line of research also suggests that specific ability components account for somewhat more variance when the criterion is job performance than when it is training performance (e.g. Olea & Ree 1994, Ree et al 1994b), which highlights the importance of the selection of criteria in validation research. Defining *g* statistically using a principal components model is not without its critics. Specific abilities will, by definition, be correlated with the general factor. Thus, it could be argued that it is just as valid to enter specific abilities first and then say that *g* doesn't contribute beyond the prediction found with specific abilities alone (e.g. Murphy 1996b). In fact, Muchinsky (1993) found this to be the case for a sample of manufacturing jobs, where mechanical ability was the single best predictor of performance, and an intelligence test had no incremental validity beyond the mechanical test alone.

While there is a growing consensus concerning the predictive efficiency of *g*, there is less agreement about what this means, especially as it relates to personnel selection practices and research. Some have concluded that "refinements in the measurement of abilities and aptitudes are unlikely to contribute nontrivial increments to validity beyond that which is produced by good measures of general mental ability" (Schmidt 1994, p. 348). Others suggest a variety of scientific and pragmatic reasons why the measurement of specific abilities may still be important and potentially useful. On the scientific side, possibly the most important note of caution is the fact that our understanding of the basic cognitive processes that underlie intelligent behavior and the reasons some people are more able than others is still quite limited (e.g. Murphy 1996b). In addition, an understanding of the processes by which abilities affect performance and the latent structure of the ability-performance relationships is needed to advance the science of personnel selection (e.g. Bobko 1994).

Specific abilities are likely to be more useful (in addition to or in place of *g*) when our goal is understanding, rather than just predictive efficiency (e.g. Alderton & Larson 1994, Murphy 1996b). For example, several recent studies have demonstrated meaningful patterns of relationships between specific abilities and criteria. Carretta & Ree (1995) found that different subtests of the Air

Force Officer Qualifying Test (AFOQT) were most valid during different phases of pilot training, and for different training criterion measures. Silva & White (1993) found that a language aptitude battery had significant incremental validity beyond general mental ability for predicting success in a language training course. Dror et al (1993) examined differences in spatial ability between pilots and nonpilots and found that pilots were superior in very specific aspects of spatial ability (e.g. mental rotation) rather than in general spatial ability. In addition to the potential for promoting understanding, improved measures of specific abilities and expanded test batteries have also been found to improve the measurement of *g* (e.g. Larson & Wolfe 1995) which, in turn, may improve validities.

Cognitive psychologists have been studying the nature of intelligence for years, and although their models are just beginning to see application in personnel-related contexts, this sort of theory-based approach clearly has potential for, again, improving our understanding of cognitive ability and of ability-performance relationships. For example, the Air Force is conducting a programmatic research effort to develop and evaluate an ability test battery based on a "consensus information processing model" (Kyllonen 1994). Information is not yet available concerning prediction of training or job performance with these tests, but preliminary results are promising. The internal structure of the test battery is consistent with the information processing model. It has been shown to predict laboratory learning tasks somewhat better than more traditional ability measures, and at least one of these elementary cognitive tasks (working memory) is strongly related to general mental ability. Cognitive psychologists have also identified what appear to be "new" abilities (e.g. time sharing, dynamic spatial ability) that could eventually find selection applications as well (e.g. Jackson et al 1993). One potential concern is that practice and coaching may be more of a problem for the relatively novel tasks included on many of these tests when they are used for selection purposes. Regarding computerized testing more generally, test design issues are discussed by McHenry & Schmitt (1994). In addition, Bennett (1994) provided a review of "constructed" response (i.e. free response) tests that are administered and scored by computer.

Conclusions about the predictive efficiency of specific abilities are very different when the goal is classification rather than simply selection. Zeidner & Johnson (1994) and Scholarios et al (1994) have shown that specific abilities substantially improve classification efficiency, beyond the use of general cognitive ability alone. Using somewhat different procedures, other researchers have confirmed and extended these findings (Abrahams et al 1994, Rosse et al 1995). The amount of gain possible from classification versus selection is negatively related to the intercorrelations among the specific ability tests or composites of tests and positively related to the number of jobs or job families into which applicants are to be classified. However, substantial gains have been found even with predictors (e.g. composites) that are quite highly correlated. These findings are also relevant for vocational/occupational counselors and others concerned with placement (e.g. in the new O*Net), because their decisions are similar to classification decisions in this context.

ACHIEVEMENT We know very little about the nature of specific abilities when they are defined as the variance remaining once a general factor is extracted statistically. It is interesting to note that what little information is available suggests that these "specific ability" components tend to be most strongly related to cognitive ability tests that have a large knowledge component [e.g. aviation information (Olea & Ree 1994)]. This is consistent with previous research showing that job knowledge tests tend to be slightly more valid than ability tests (Hunter & Hunter 1984), and also with research demonstrating that job knowledge appears to mediate the relationship between abilities and job performance (e.g. Borman et al 1993). In a recent meta-analysis, Dye et al (1993) demonstrated the generality of job knowledge tests as predictors of job performance. In addition, they found that the validity of job knowledge tests was moderated by job complexity and by job-test similarity, with validities significantly higher for studies involving high-complexity jobs and those with high job-test similarity. The average corrected validity for job knowledge tests with high job-test similarity was .62 for job performance and .76 for training performance, and this is somewhat higher than the average corrected validity typically found for cognitive ability tests [e.g. .53 (Hunter & Hunter 1984)]. Cognitive task analysis—employing protocol analysis to create an elaborated definition of job expertise—may be especially useful for developing job knowledge tests (e.g. DuBois et al 1995).

It might be helpful to discuss research in this area in the context of the distinction between aptitudes and achievement. Briefly, aptitude tests typically draw their items from a wide range of human experience or involve content that is not learned (e.g. reaction time). Achievement tests, however, consist of material that is necessarily more circumscribed. Scores can increase rapidly because of exposure to information from the relevant content area. It is likely that tests of aptitudes and achievement actually fall on a continuum, and these definitions represent the extremes of this continuum. Job knowledge tests are clearly measures of achievement, whereas most cognitive ability tests are near the aptitude extreme of the continuum. Thus, when the content of achievement tests is closely related to the criteria they are used to predict, these tests show greater validity than aptitude measures.

In this context, these results are consistent with research on "tacit knowledge" (i.e. action-oriented knowledge acquired without direct help from others). Tacit-knowledge measures ask respondents to place themselves in a series of job-related situations and then to report what they would or should do. Sternberg and his colleagues have repeatedly found significant validities and some incremental value (over general intelligence) for measures of tacit knowledge in predicting job performance or success (Sternberg et al 1995). Tacit knowledge has been shown to be at least somewhat trainable and to differ according to relevant expertise, which argues for it being placed closer to the achievement end of the aptitude-achievement continuum than more traditional ability tests. Thus, tacit knowledge measures could be viewed as achievement tests with high job-test similarity (and thus high validity). And yet, these measures target knowledge that can arguably be acquired without formal training or job experience (e.g. knowledge related to interpersonal effectiveness). Sternberg characterizes the measured construct as practical intelligence or "street smarts," which is more in concert with the aptitude end of this continuum. It is currently unclear what underlying construct(s) is (are) being measured by these tests. We note that tacit-knowledge measures are very similar to situational judgment tests, described in more detail in the section on "Assessment Centers".

In this same vein, behavioral consistency measures (Wernimont & Campbell 1968) might be viewed as the extreme case of achievement measures with criterion-related content (though there is arguably a motivational component in these measures as well). Hanisch & Hulin (1994) found that a measure of behavioral consistency (operationalized as training performance) significantly increased validity beyond that provided by general ability measures alone for predicting performance on an air traffic control task; however, including ability did not increase validity beyond training performance alone. Using data from the Army's Project A, Campbell et al (1994) demonstrated that both measured abilities and training performance added unique variance to the prediction of future performance. It is not clear why abilities provided incremental validity in the latter research and not in the former, but it is apparent that training performance can increase the validity of ability measures alone in predicting later job performance.

PHYSICAL ABILITIES Although physical ability tests are reported to be used more widely for selection now than ever before (Hogan & Quigley 1994), not much new information has been published in this area since Landy et al's review. In one recent study, Blakley et al (1994) provided additional evidence that isometric strength tests are valid predictors across a variety of different physically demanding jobs, and also that the prediction of work simulation performance was better than the prediction of supervisory ratings of physical ability. Blakley et al also found, in a large applicant sample, that females scored substantially lower than males on these isometric strength tests. In light of these findings, there is a recent and growing interest in reducing adverse impact through pretest preparation. Hogan & Quigley (1994) demonstrated that participation in a physical training program can improve females' upper body strength and muscular endurance, and that participation in a pretest physical training program was significantly related to the likelihood of passing a firefighter physical ability test.

Personality

Research on personality predictors of job performance continues apace. Evidence mounts that personality predicts job performance (e.g. Barrick & Mount 1991, Hogan et al 1996). One possible reason for the generally positive validity findings can be derived from the results discussed above showing that personality predicts contextual performance (e.g. Motowidlo & Van Scotter 1994). Many of the criteria used in the Barrick & Mount (1991) meta-analysis, for example, were overall job performance ratings, and we have learned that these ratings weight both technical and contextual performance (e.g. Borman et al 1995). Accordingly, the personality measures may be picking up on the contextual component of the criteria. This implies that where the contextual elements of performance can be measured separately, these validities might be higher. A related issue has emerged about whether we learn more about personality-performance links if we use relatively broad traits or narrow traits and if we use general or specific performance constructs. Hough & Schneider (1996) and Schneider & Hough (1995) argued that the Big 5 personality taxonomy (five summary dimensions often identified in factor analyses of personality ratings or self-reports) may be at too coarse a level for use in personnel selection. A nine-factor system was proposed. As evidence that a more fine-grained representation of personality may be useful in prediction, they showed that achievement, which is a more narrow construct than are the Big 5 factors, correlated more highly than did conscientiousness (previously found to correlate the highest of the Big 5 with job performance) with the criteria of overall job performance, job proficiency, training success, educational success, sales effectiveness, and effort. What Hough & Schneider (1996) called compound traits—constructs that don't line up precisely with the Big 5 but which have clear alignment to criterion constructs—are also likely to be useful for selection.

However, Ones & Viswesvaran (1996) argued that broader, rather than narrower, fine-grained personality measures are preferable for use in personnel selection. This is because global measures are likely to be more reliable and job performance criteria are usually complex. They also noted that integrity tests (often a composite of several Big 5 constructs) appear to have higher validity on average than any of the Big 5 traits by themselves (Ones et al 1993). Schneider et al (1996) disputed the Ones & Viswesvaran (1996) conclusion regarding "broader is better." They contended that when strong hypotheses about specific trait-specific criterion links can be made, narrower trait constructs will show better prediction. Hogan & Roberts (1996) provided several examples of narrower personality trait measures predicting specific criteria better than broader such measures. Also, Blake et al (1993) found that some specific scales of the California Psychological Inventory (CPI) predicted overall performance of military academy students (a broad criterion) as well as or better than the more global structural scales, and Powell et al (1995) found that the Big 5 predicted global measures of performance and that more specific facets of these measures predicted more specific dimensions of customer service. Finally, Crant (1995) demonstrated that a relatively specific personality scale predicted real estate sales performance incrementally over measures of the Big 5. As far back as Dunnette (1963), we have believed that the science of personnel selection is best served by studying links between specific predictor and criterion constructs, so this issue is a very important one. The updated arguments by Campbell (Campbell et al 1993, 1996) are compelling to us. If we are interested in learning more about predictor-performance relations, we need to examine linkages between predictor constructs and different facets of job performance.

There has been considerable recent activity around integrity or honesty testing for selection. PR Sackett & JE Wanek (unpublished manuscript) provide a comprehensive review of issues regarding integrity testing. Of special interest are links between both overt (i.e. direct questions about honesty, integrity, etc) and personality-based integrity tests and the Big 5 personality factors. In an especially useful table, these authors summarize data from Barrick & Mount (1993) and Ones et al (1993) that reveal correlations corrected for attenuation between overt and personality-based integrity tests, the Big 5, and job performance. Meta-analysis results show that on average, overt integrity tests correlate .45 with one another; personality-based tests intercorrelate more highly ($r = .70$ on average). The mean correlation between the two types of integrity tests is .39 (Ones et al 1993). Correlations between overt and personality-based tests and the conscientiousness Big 5 factor are substantial, but so are correlations with the agreeableness and emotional stability factors. Both types of integrity tests correlate .41 with job performance (Ones et al 1993). Conscientiousness and integrity measures, taken together, are likely to produce higher correlations with performance than either one on its own (PR Sackett & JE Wanek, unpublished manuscript). Finally, Murphy (1993) contributed a thorough treatment of honesty in the workplace, including a chapter on integrity testing for personnel selection. In addition, Collins & Schmidt (1993) administered personality, personality-based integrity, and biodata scales to prison inmates incarcerated for white-collar crimes and individuals employed in upper-level positions of authority. Cross-validated discriminant function analysis showed large differences between these two groups, especially on the integrity test, and suggested that "social conscientiousness" best differentiated these groups. Importantly, the criteria used to examine the validity of integrity tests has broadened from theft to a range of counterproductive behaviors including disciplinary actions, accidents, unexcused absences, terminations, drug or alcohol abuse, admissions of wrongdoing, and violence.

The issue of faking or impression management in responding to personality items is of course important in the personnel selection context. Several recent papers confirm that, while slanting of responses occurs in selection settings, validity does not seem to suffer. Barrick & Mount (1996) demonstrated that although self-deception and impression management response distortion of personality items occurred in their sample, validity of the responses was not adversely affected. Christiansen et al (1994) used the 16PF fake good and fake bad scales to correct the scores of assessment center candidates and found that criterion-related validity was unaffected.

Although response distortion does not appear to have a major impact on personality inventory validity in a selection context (e.g. Barrick & Mount 1996), it is still of some concern because these measures are definitely fakeable. One approach to detecting faking when using computerized administration of personality tests is to measure response latencies. Holden & Hibbs (1995) have refined this strategy; the trick is to first correct latencies for both person effects (e.g. slow vs fast readers) and item effects (e.g. longer vs shorter to read). Holden & Hibbs find that these adjusted latency scores can correctly classify about 82% of the test-takers instructed to respond honestly and those told to try to maximize their chances of getting the job. This method deserves more attention. Relatedly, Siem (1996) demonstrated incremental validity in predicting Air Force pilot performance for some MMPI scales when response latencies were incorporated in the scoring system.

Worthwhile for I/O psychologists to be aware of in the personality literature are possible moderators of personality-performance correlations. These include specific personal moderators (e.g. the centrality of a given trait may vary across individuals), general personal moderators (e.g. low self-monitors are more predictable), situational moderators (e.g. high-autonomy jobs have lower situational strength and thus personality predicts performance better in them), and aptitude by treatment interactions (e.g. the validity of achievement via conformance and independence may be different in high- and low-structure workplaces). Schneider & Hough (1995) provide a nice discussion of these issues for I/O psychologists.

There were several other interesting papers on the topic of personality. Although conscientiousness has been viewed as a consistent predictor of job performance (Barrick & Mount 1991), Hogan & Hogan (1993) demonstrated that this relationship may vary across occupational type, with artistic jobs showing a negative correlation, for example. Schmit et al (1995), in a study with college students found that providing an "at work" context for personality test items improved the predictive validity of their conscientiousness scale against a criterion of GPA and did not alter the factor structure of the inventory scores. McDaniel & Frei (1994) conducted a meta-analysis of customer service predictor validities and found a corrected mean validity of .49 based on 49 correlations and an N of 6441. Virtually every study of personality in a selection context has used self-reports to measure personality constructs. However, Mount et al (1994) found that observer ratings (i.e. supervisor, peer, and customer) of Big 5 personality constructs added to the prediction of job performance beyond self-reports alone. Finally, Hogan & Blake (1996) argued that vocational interests are meaningfully related to personality and urged that vocational psychology's taxonomic schemes be considered in studying links between individual differences in personality and work outcomes, including performance (but see Schmidt 1994).

PREDICTORS: PROCESS

Assessment Centers

The assessment center (AC) continues to be popular in US organizations and elsewhere. For example, Payne et al (1992) report a threefold increase (1985–1990) in the use of ACs for managerial selection in the United Kingdom. However, published literature on ACs has dropped off. We believe this is because: (*a*) the predictive validity of ACs is now largely assumed, and (*b*) there is less hope and enthusiasm for finding a way to establish their internal construct validity. Regarding the latter point, the consistent finding has been that exercise rather than trait factors emerge from factor analyses of AC ratings. This is important if we are using ACs for developmental purposes. Feedback to participants on dimensions that are not rated reliably across exercises cannot be easily justified.

At any rate, there have been a few interesting studies on ACs. Henderson et al (1995) developed an AC in the United Kingdom focused on tapping competencies likely to be important in future business settings. Ryan et al (1995) had college students view performance in an AC exercise either in vivo, videotaped, or videotaped with an opportunity to pause and rewind. Observation accuracy was somewhat better in the latter condition, but no significant differences were found for evaluation accuracy.

An important trend in organizations using or interested in using assessment for selection or promotion is to streamline those assessments. Employing fewer exercises or assessors, reducing exercise length, reinventing the consensus meeting process, etc, are given increasingly serious consideration as companies struggle to reduce costs in human resources practices and elsewhere. "Low fidelity" assessment or situational judgment tests (SJTs) can be viewed as a rather extreme attempt to streamline ACs. As mentioned above, SJTs generally present difficult but realistic situations job incumbents might face and ask what the testee would or should do in each situation. Often SJTs have a multiple-choice format, and testee responses are scored against expert judgments of each response option's level of effectiveness (e.g. Motowidlo & Tippins 1993).

These tests are not new (e.g. File 1945), but they have recently become more popular. Further, SJTs have been successful in predicting job performance (e.g. Motowidlo & Tippins 1993) and attrition (e.g. Dalessio 1994). An obvious inherent limitation of SJTs is that they probably do not measure can-do or will-do performance but should-do performance and are thus more similar to achievement or job knowledge tests (see the section on "Abilities and Achievement"). Nonetheless, Kerr (1995) and Sternberg et al (1995) reported correlations of about .30 and .60, respectively, between business tacit knowledge test scores and AC ratings. In addition, video-based SJTs (e.g. Drasgow, unpublished working paper 1993) may reduce the fidelity deficit somewhat. Our view is that more research is needed on what SJTs are actually measuring, similar to what has been called for regarding ACs (e.g. Klimoski & Brickner 1987).

Interviews

Much continues to be written about the interview and its validity. Most notable are reviews that supplement previous meta-analytic work, and discussions surrounding the interaction between structure in the interview and the interview's purpose. We group relevant research into five major thematic areas.

First, additional quantitative and qualitative reviews of interview reliability and validity have been conducted. Huffcutt & Arthur (1994) revisited the Hunter & Hunter (1984) meta-analysis to assess interview validity compared with that of ability tests. By recategorizing interview studies according to level of structure, the authors found that interview validities increased as structure increased, with the top two levels of structure comparable to validities found by Hunter & Hunter for ability tests. A meta-analysis of interview reliabilities (Conway et al 1995) showed that interrater reliability levels are higher when interviews incorporate multiple ratings, interviewer training, and standardization of questions and response evaluation. Such reviews continue to supply optimism for, and guidance concerning, use of the interview as a selection tool.

A second area of research encompasses what Dipboye & Gaugler (1993) referred to as the cognitive and behavioral processes in the interview. Most of these studies isolate a particular variable or two in the interview process and attempt to determine the impact on the outcome of the interview. For example, Williams et al (1993) found that preinterview impressions had their greatest effect when applicants' interview performance was average; high performers' ratings were slightly affected by negative preimpressions, while low performers were rated low regardless of the preimpressions. Stevens & Kristof (1995) found that applicants' impression management tactics significantly predicted interviewers' evaluations, and applicants seemed to use more self-promotion tactics than ingratiation tactics. Dalessio & Silverhart (1994) suggested that interviewers may not give much weight to candidate performance in the interview if they are aware of high biographical test score data, but they will place more credence on interview performance if biodata information is less supportive of a decision to hire. In an intriguing study, Motowidlo & Burnett (1995) demonstrated that raters who watched videotaped interviews with no sound provided reasonably valid ratings, that interviewers do rely on visual cues even when aural cues are present, and that aural and visual cues are somewhat redundant. Pulakos et al (1996) examined individual differences in interviewer ratings and found no support for the hypothesis that systematic interviewer errors will attenuate interview validity when data are aggregated across interviewers. In addition, consensus ratings were shown to have slightly higher validities than averaged ratings. Howard & Ferris (1996) examined the social and situational context of employment interview decisions using structural equation modeling. They found that high levels of appropriate nonverbal behavior (i.e. smiling, nodding, eye contact) by applicants increased interviewers' ratings of their competence. In addition, more highly trained interviewers perceived self-promoting applicants as less competent than did interviewers with less training. More expansive, model-based studies like this one will help to advance current knowledge about the interview process.

A third major area involves comparison of interview techniques, primarily future-oriented (e.g. situational) and past-oriented (e.g. behavior description) interviews. Campion et al (1994) reported higher validities for past-oriented (.51) than future-oriented interviews (.39). In addition, when ratings from both types of questions were regressed against job performance, past questions showed incremental validity over future questions, but not vice versa. Pulakos & Schmitt (1995), using professional government employees as subjects, compared situational versus past behavior questions in a structured interview and found that only the past behavior questions were valid in predicting supervisor ratings. Using a group of French- and English-speaking Canadian managers, Latham & Skarlicki (1996) demonstrated that both the situational and behavior description interviews were resistant to same-race bias (e.g. in-group favoritism, out-group discrimination), while the conventional interview was not. It seems well established now that structured interviews are more valid than their unstructured counterparts for predicting job performance. About the question of what kind of structured interview is more valid, the advantage presently goes to the behavior description procedure. We are likely to see more comparison studies in the future.

A fourth area involves a broad examination of constructs underlying the interview. Sue-Chan et al (1995) administered the Wonderlic Personnel Test, a tacit knowledge test, a measure of self-efficacy, and an interview to undergraduate nursing students. Neither the situational nor patterned interview correlated significantly with the cognitive or tacit knowledge tests but both did so with the self-efficacy measure. In addition, the situational interview showed incremental validity beyond the cognitive test, using grade-point average as the criterion. Campion et al (1994) investigated the notion that a structured interview has incremental validity over a battery of cognitive ability tests and found that the interview correlated .60 with the battery of tests, but showed incremental validity when regressed against job performance ratings. We echo Landy et al's (1994) endorsement of continued emphasis on examining the nomological network around interview judgments.

The fifth and final area involves a debate, sometimes heated, about what the true purpose of the interview should be. Herriot (1993) proposed that the interview's focus should reflect a dynamic interpersonal process, rather than the prevalent psychometric perspective. Herriot characterizes the latter as academic, while the former is seen as more practitioner oriented, and therefore more useful to organizations. In related work, Adams et al (1994) emphasized the importance of the interview from something other than a "prediction-of-performance" view, stressing its usefulness for assessing applicant-organization fit. A similar theme was sounded earlier by Anderson (1992), who reviewed and categorized eight decades of interview research into objectivist-psychometric and subjectivist-social perception perspectives. Howard & Ferris (1996) stressed this theme when they suggested interviewer training that considers the context of the organization might help interviewers better gauge whether applicants will be successful in the organization. This notion of organizational fit was also discussed by Latham & Skarlicki (1995), who investigated the criterion-related validity of the situational and patterned interview using organizational citizenship behavior as the criterion. They found that the situational interview predicted citizenship behavior and concluded that extra-role behavior can indeed be predicted with an interview format.

Finally, in an excellent review of the interview literature, Dipboye (1994) cited reasons why structured procedures show greater validities than unstructured procedures. He also discussed why unstructured interviews continue to be used, including: 1. Recruitment (in addition to selection) is often a concern.

2. More interviewer autonomy and self-expression is possible. 3. Chances for a good fit between hires and the context of the job are improved. Dipboye (1994) argued that we need more dynamic models of employee selection in which the interview maintains structure in the assessment of applicants while fulfilling other functions such as evaluating fit to the organization. Such an approach suggests broadening the attributes that are assessed to include personality characteristics, personal values, and the like, attributes relatively neglected in the current structured interview approaches.

Biodata

In the two preceding Annual Reviews of personnel selection (Landy et al 1994, Schmidt et al 1992), the authors emphasized the importance of increased attention to theory and to the constructs being measured in biodata research, development, and application. Three documents published in the period covered by this review suggest movement in that direction. First, publication of the *Biodata Handbook* by Stokes et al (1994) provides coverage of job analysis, item development, scoring, validation, legal issues, theories, and applications. As Dunnette (1994) noted in his foreword, "publication of the *Biodata Handbook* marks a juncture, serving not only to outline current knowledge of the practical and scientific bases of biographical information, but also to provide a framework for extending our knowledge substantially in the years to come" (p. xi).

A second source for biodata information can be found in Trent & Laurence (1993), a monograph for the Department of Defense examining adaptability screening for the Armed Forces. The monograph provides a good overview of the social, political, and technical issues surrounding use of biodata in the military. In a third volume, edited by Rumsey et al (1994), Mael (1994) discussed approaches to biographical data, especially related to how they are viewed from a legal perspective. In the same volume, Schmidt (1994) provided insightful comments about biodata theory and practice. These three edited pieces portend an increasing emphasis on biodata in the years ahead. Elsewhere, Brown & Campion (1994) found that recruiters perceive both cognitive and noncognitive information in biodata, and each can be interpreted quite reliably. In addition, Mael & Ashforth (1995) suggested that biodata may capture dispositional elements associated with person-organization fit, internal cultural socialization, preference for group attachments, and achievement-oriented pursuits.

Applicant Reactions

Landy et al (1994) referred to the history of personnel selection as pre-Copernican in that the center of the universe with respect to selection has been the needs and goals of the user (i.e. the employer). This is changing, with continued interest in applicant reactions to selection procedures, the "social side" of selection. First, why might applicant reactions to selection procedures be important to study? Smither et al (1993) and Rynes (1993) provided good responses to this question. Beyond what some would see as a moral imperative to become involved with applicants' concerns: 1. Organizational attractiveness to applicants is growing in importance because organizations increasingly see them as customers to be satisfied in the applicant-employer relationship. 2. There is increased potential for unpopular or controversial selection procedures to lead to lawsuits against the organization. 3. Negative applicant reactions may indirectly affect the validity of a selection procedure.

The most straightforward way to study this topic is to ask applicants essentially how they feel about each type of selection test or procedure. For example, Rynes & Connerley (1993) surveyed job seekers about their general reactions to 13 different selection procedures. Most popular were simulations and tests with business-related content. Least popular were personality, honesty, and drug testing. Kluger & Rothstein (1993) found that business student subjects were more comfortable with a biographical inventory than with an ability test in that they viewed themselves as having more control over their performance, thought it was fairer and less difficult, and believed the test better captured "who they were." Rosse et al (1994) found that, in general, relatively concrete and more obviously job-related predictors are seen as fairer in a selection setting. However, Tepper (1994) demonstrated the danger of using lab research to study attitudes toward selection procedures. Subjects in a lab setting rated favorably drug testing for safety-sensitive occupations, whereas individuals actually tested for drugs in these occupations had more negative attitudes.

Rynes (1993) provided an excellent overview of the early research on applicant reactions. She focused on how applicant attitudes toward organizations are influenced by selection practices and how those attitudes may affect applicant behaviors, job-choice decisions, and early expectations as a job incumbent. Her position is that this area of study will become more important as drug and integrity testing, background checks, and personality assessment become more popular. Rynes calls for more qualitative research (e.g. protocol analysis and other direct process-oriented methods) to better frame the process of responding to selection practices.

A path to get beyond individual studies of best- and least-liked selection procedures is to develop a framework related to social issues involved in the selection process. Two kinds of models have recently emerged. Schuler (1993) and Arvey & Sackett (1993) provided listings of possible determinants of fairness perceptions. Gilliland (1993) presented a model of reactions that depicts the situational and personal conditions that influence how procedural and distributive justice rules are judged to be satisfied (or violated). Conditions include job relatedness and consistency of the selection procedures, opportunity for two-way communication with company representatives and to be reconsidered if rejected, feedback about test performance, and the propriety/invasiveness of questions.

Macan et al (1994) and Smither et al (1993) found, somewhat counterintuitively, that applicant reactions to selection procedures are unrelated to how well they do in the process. Macan et al also showed that although perceptions of the tests (an ability test and assessment center) were important in influencing job acceptance intentions, overall impressions of the work and organization were even more important. Applicant reactions to selection procedures should continue to be an important area of study. Research will be most useful when rooted in organizational justice theories (e.g. Gilliland 1994).

VALIDITY AND UTILITY

Models of Validity

As we go to press, a distinguished panel of psychologists and educational experts is finishing a draft of the Standards for Psychological and Educational Testing. This document is being prepared with support from (and under the scrutiny of) the American Psychological Association, the American Educational Research Association, and the National Council on Measurement and Evaluation. A very important element of the Standards will be their treatment of the concept of validity. In the literature, validity has been increasingly discussed as a unified concept (e.g. Messick 1995) rather than as composed of various categories (e.g. content validity, criterion-related validity). A key but controversial aspect of Messick's definition of construct validity is the incorporation of consequences. Messick argues convincingly that the meaning of test scores can only be interpreted in the context in which they are used. Others (e.g. Brown 1994; Tenopyr, unpublished working paper) have expressed concern that endorsement of "consequential validity," especially in the new Standards, is likely to be abused and misinterpreted by those opposed to testing, most notably in the education arena where the multiple-choice test is currently in disfavor. Smith (1994) has proposed a theory that attempts to explain relationships between the content of selection measures and their relationships with job performance. He distinguishes between universals (characteristics required for success in virtually all jobs) and occupationals (characteristics required for a subset of jobs or a single job). The third aspect of test content, "relationals," is focused on characteristics required for person-organization fit (discussed elsewhere).

Meta-Analysis and Validity Generalization

Numerous meta-analyses addressing a variety of important questions have been published during the period covered by this review. Allen & Preiss (1993) discussed the "necessary and symbiotic relationship between meta-analysis and replication research" (p. 9), with replication providing the input to meta-analysis and meta-analysis providing the direction for future research. In related work, Murphy (1994a) discussed the importance of the quality of the research that is included in meta-analyses. For example, the average size of the individual samples included in meta-analyses and the quality of the criterion measures used are directly related to the power of meta-analyses to detect moderator effects. Sagie & Koslowsky (1993) demonstrated that meta-analytic techniques have limited power to detect moderators, especially if the moderator effects are relatively small. Since individual studies lack power to detect moderators as well (see section on "Statistical and Measurement Issues"), this is particularly disheartening.

There have been a number of methodological advances in meta-analysis, and some of these advances have implications for conclusions drawn based on past meta-analyses. Law et al (1994) demonstrated that recent refinements in the Hunter et al (1982) procedures do, in fact, increase the accuracy of results. Vevea et al (1993) developed procedures for identifying and assessing bias in the selection of studies to be included in meta-analyses and used these procedures to demonstrate that selection bias does not appear to affect conclusions drawn in previous meta-analyses of GATB validities. Using a Monte Carlo approach, Koslowsky & Sagie (1994) provided information about the relative proportions of true and artifactual variance in meta-analyses under a variety of conditions. In general, sampling error (not unexpectedly) accounted for most artifactual variance, and commonly used corrections for range restriction decreased the proportion of artifactual variance more than corrections for measurement error. Huffcutt & Arthur (1995) developed a statistic appropriate for detecting outliers in meta-analyses and demonstrated that, in their meta-analysis, the removal of outliers helped clarify what had been a confusing meta-analytic result.

In perhaps the most exciting potential methodological advance in this area, Viswesvaran & Ones (1995) discussed procedures for using meta-analytically derived matrices of estimated true score correlations as the input for structural modeling. This allows for large-scale theory testing, even when all of the relevant variables and relationships have not been included in each study. Variations on this approach have already been used in a handful of studies, but a great deal of work is needed on the assumptions and calculations involved before widespread application is prudent. For example, the use of correlations as opposed to covariance matrices in these analyses may be problematic.

Selection Utility

Utility researchers continue to battle with the problems involved in estimating key parameters included in traditional utility models, most notably the standard deviation of performance in dollars (SD*y*). While additional approaches have been proposed, there is little consensus concerning the proper measurement methods (e.g. Cesare et al 1994, Raju et al 1993). Another problem that continues to plague this area is the lack of interest managers and other decision makers have in the results of utility analyses. In fact, Latham & Whyte (1994) found that managers expressed less support for implementing a valid selection procedure when they were presented with utility information than they did when they were presented with validity information only. Because the primary purpose of utility analysis is to communicate the value of human resource management systems to managers, these troubling results have stimulated a good deal of discussion. Some have suggested that research is needed regarding how managers actually make selection decisions and what types of information they might find useful (e.g. Boudreau et al 1994).

Another approach to this problem has been to expand the concept of utility to make the results more relevant to managers' and decision makers' needs. Some simplifying assumptions made in traditional utility analyses have been called into question, and models have been proposed that attempt to more accurately reflect organizational realities. Boudreau et al (1994) suggested that utility models should consider: (*a*) the fact that performance is multidimensional, (*b*) that predictors are typically added to existing selections systems rather than replacing them, and (*c*) that organizations often do not use optimal top-down selection. Boudreau et al also pointed out that individuals' value to the organization may go beyond their current performance in a particular job, which suggests that utility analyses may be improved by incorporating considerations of person-organization fit. Russell et al (1993) further suggested that utility analyses need to reflect the strategic context faced by managerial decision makers, where profit maximization may be only one of many strategic objectives, and maximizing performance is only one of several possible goals in selection. Russell et al also suggested that many of the variables relevant to utility estimation can change over time (e.g. strategic needs, predictor-criterion relationships), and thus it is likely that utility will need to be periodically reassessed. Costs not traditionally included in utility analyses have also been incorporated, such as recruitment costs (Law & Myors 1993) and legal exposure (Roth 1994).

STATISTICAL AND MEASUREMENT ISSUES

There has been increasing endorsement of the notion that validation is an estimation problem, and we see commensurate interest in improving the available procedures for providing more accurate estimates. Regarding corrections for restriction in range, Held & Foley (1994) provided an assessment of the relative accuracy of univariate and multivariate corrections in a variety of situations. Abrahams et al (1993) demonstrated that validities are severely underestimated when criterion data are unavailable for the lower performing portion of the sample due to failure, resignation, or dismissal; and they demonstrated the effectiveness of a new procedure for more accurately estimating validities in these cases.

Unfortunately, a relatively small proportion (4%) of validity studies actually employ range restriction corrections (Ree et al 1994a). One major obstacle to the use of range restriction corrections in applied settings is the fact that estimates of predictor variance in the unrestricted (i.e. applicant) sample are often not available. Hoffman (1995) provided some support for using published norms to make these corrections, by demonstrating their consistency with empirical results. However, Sackett & Ostgard (1994) used a large sample of data (but only a single test, the Wonderlic Personnel Test) to demonstrate that job-specific applicant pools have smaller standard deviations than the national norms, especially for complex jobs. They recommend considering these differences when using published norms to make corrections.

The detection of variables that moderate validity and the psychometric issues involved have received much recent research attention. One important finding in this area is the alarming lack of power most statistical procedures have for detecting existing moderators. Aguinis (1995) provided a summary of the issues and recent progress in this area. Research has generally shown that moderated multiple regression (MMR) is the most powerful procedure for the detection of moderators. Factors influencing the power of MMR include the distributions of variables (e.g. restriction in range), measurement error, "coarseness" of the variables, the true effect size, and (obviously) sample size. Worse yet, many of these effects are actually interactive, which results in very low power in many common situations. This literature suggests that conclusions concerning the absence of a significant moderator variable should be drawn cautiously, and power to assess moderators should be assessed whenever possible. Suggestions for addressing these problems in future research include basing the search for moderator variables on sound substantive theories, paying more attention to the dependent variables (Bobko & Russell 1994), and using structural modeling to address measurement error problems (for an example, see Jaccard & Wan 1995).

There has been somewhat of an explosion in the use of structural modeling analyses in a variety of areas of psychology, including personnel psychology (Stone-Romero et al 1995). Uses have included assessing the effects of method variance (Schmitt et al 1995, Williams & Anderson 1994), exploring the relative accuracy of different response scales (Chang 1994), and modeling the structure of performance (Hanson et al 1993). These studies illustrate the potential of structural modeling to untangle error and true score variance to more directly assess underlying relationships.

Computer programs for fitting structural equation models to the data and estimating model fit are becoming more readily available and user friendly. There have also been many improvements in the available measures of model fit, as well as improvements in model testing procedures. Medsker et al (1994) provided an excellent summary of this rapidly progressing area. These authors also reviewed applications of structural equation modeling in recent studies and noted that while there have been some improvements in the procedures used, current practices have not kept up with methodological advances. It is worth noting that some are critical of structural modeling techniques and the potential of this approach for advancing our field (e.g. Brannick 1995), but others argue that many of the identified shortcomings reflect deficiencies in applications of structural modeling and not the approach itself (e.g. Williams 1995).

A few miscellaneous statistical and measurement developments also deserve mention. Sidick et al (1994) found that a three-alternative multiple-choice test had psychometric properties similar to those of five-alternative tests, confirming and extending similar work in the education arena. Three-alternative tests take less time to develop and to administer, so this finding could enhance efficiency a great deal. White et al (1993) reviewed recent advances in log-linear modeling and described how these procedures can be used to obtain more information concerning categorical and nominal variables than is provided by more traditional approaches (e.g. chi-square tests).

There have been several recent attacks on traditional significance testing, highlighting the deficiencies of null hypothesis testing (Cohen 1994, Schmidt 1996). Although some of the criticisms are not new, the pervasiveness of reliance on significance testing indicates that they may still be warranted. A particularly serious problem occurs when exclusive reliance is placed on significance testing in studies with low power. Recommended alternatives are point estimates and confidence intervals, with results across studies combined using meta-analytic procedures. However, confidence intervals for even relatively simple statistical estimates can be fairly complex (for some very useful examples, see Olkin & Finn 1995), with confidence intervals for more complex multivariate procedures difficult or impossible to conceptualize or calculate. While Schmidt's proposal to abandon significance testing may be controversial, the merits of reducing the role of significance testing are more widely accepted.

One somewhat unfortunate theme emerging in this literature is that there are many improvements in statistical procedures available for use in selection research, but researchers are slow to adopt these improvements. This could be because statistical procedures are becoming unwieldy in their complexity. Keeping up with the state of the art in the wide variety of multivariate procedures that have become so integral to our field (e.g. meta-analysis, structural modeling) is rapidly becoming a full-time job. Perhaps future research will more often require collaboration with statistical or measurement specialists who can provide the insight needed to use these powerful procedures appropriately and with maximum benefit.

EQUAL EMPLOYMENT OPPORTUNITY AND LEGAL ISSUES

Recent activities on the legal and legislative fronts provide clear focal points for research and, especially, practice activities. Within the past several years, the National Academy of Science's (NAS's) report on *Fairness in Employment Testing,* the Civil Rights Act (CRA) of 1991, and the 1990 Americans with Disabilities Act (ADA), have fueled renewed and increased scrutiny of industrial/organizational psychology science and practice.

Sackett & Wilk (1994) provided an excellent in-depth discussion of score adjustment (e.g. according to race or gender) in preemployment testing, reviewing the legal environment for personnel selection surrounding passage of the CRA of 1991, as well as the background, rationale, and consequences of score adjustment. These authors also provide a review of group differences and their relationships to job performance for cognitive ability, personality and physical ability tests, biodata, and interest inventories. A second article in the same issue of the *American Psychologist,* by Gottfredson (1994), discusses within-group norming in the context of what she calls "politically selective science." She calls for the addition of noncognitive tests to cognitive test batteries to help reduce adverse impact but notes that this strategy is most likely to provide little help with cognitively complex jobs. Kehoe & Tenopyr (1994) summarized the literature on group differences, types of adjustment strategies, and evaluation of these adjustment strategies. Finally, Varca & Pattison (1993) reviewed recent employment discrimination litigation to examine changing interpretations of evidentiary standards (i.e. causation, burden of proof, and business necessity) and concluded that currently only the burden of proof standard is clear cut (it rests with the defendant); and Ledvinka (1995) discussed the CRA of 1991, the ADA, and recent antitesting initiatives (e.g. Soroka *v.* Dayton-Hudson Corporation) within the context of government regulatory activity.

A more specialized debate has evolved concerning the use of banding as a method of score adjustment. Banding involves defining a range of scores that will be treated as if they were equivalent; the width of this range is determined by the reliability and standard error of measurement. In fact, Murphy (1994b) suggested that when tests of moderate to low reliability are used, banding may lead to treatment of many applicants as statistically indistinguishable. Essentially, tests with high reliability work against achieving diversity with a banding approach! In 1994, the Scientific Affairs Committee of the Society for Industrial and Organizational Psychology released a report on banding, examining the rationale, methods, and implications of banding procedures. The committee concluded that general research on banding systems highlights a number of issues that must be considered in evaluating specific strategies, but it does not necessarily resolve policy debates that surround banding. The decision to use or reject banding in specific circumstances requires a careful evaluation of its costs and benefits.

Murphy et al (1995) examined separate and joint effects of several selection system characteristics (e.g. selection ratio, reliability, preferential hiring) and applicant pool characteristics (e.g. proportion with lower scores, mean differences between subgroups) on selection outcomes under banding. They suggest that the single best strategy for increasing the proportion hired from a lower scoring group is to change the applicant pool, rather than modify the selection system. Schmidt & Hunter (1995) argued that the statistical rationale for banding, and the operational banding procedure itself, are inconsistent and that the latter is used by advocates to mask minority preference rules. Siskin (1995) presented a mathematical model that includes the expected difference in performance between the top-ranked and bottom-ranked person in the band, and the likelihood that the top-ranked person will actually outperform the bottom-ranked person. Siskin argues that the results support the use of banding, and he suggests that the social gains of banding may be greater than the economic cost. In a chapter on personnel selection in *The Changing Nature of Work* (Howard 1995), Landy et al (1995) discussed the sliding band approach and pointed out that the best estimate of a candidate's true score on a test is still the observed score, regardless of the standard error; the rebuttal is that some modest precision might be sacrificed to realize the social goal of workforce diversity. The use of banding as a viable score adjustment approach is sure to be debated further in the literature and in the courts.

The ADA of 1990 generated much discussion about the disabilities covered and what constitutes a "medical test." Working definitions should continue to evolve based on administrative guidelines and relevant case law. Klimoski & Palmer (1993) reviewed the ADA with regard to the recruitment and assessment of job applicants and provided a discussion of issues and concerns from both the applicant and employer perspective. Fischer (1994) and Pati & Bailey (1995) summarized the ADA and discussed its practical implications related to measurement issues and organizational practices.

Although previous studies have shown age to be a poor predictor of performance, age stereotypes continue to prevail in the workforce. Finklestein et al (1995) reviewed the existing studies of age discrimination in simulated employment settings, identified situational characteristics that might contribute to this type of discrimination in employment-related decisions, and developed a conceptual framework for studying age discrimination. They also conducted a meta-analysis of lab study findings and found that older workers were rated as less favorable when research participants were younger workers and when no job-relevant information was provided.

Regarding practice issues, Pulakos & Schmitt (1996) examined two strategies for reducing adverse impact in a federal investigative job and found increases in criterion-related validity and decreases in subgroup differences when a paper-and-pencil verbal ability measure was supplemented with a situational judgment test, a biodata measure, and a structured interview. Lefkowitz (1994) found a significant pattern of assigning new clerical employees at a large commercial bank to supervisors of the same ethnic group; likewise, later reassignment increased the percentage of organizational "ethnic drift" toward same-race supervisor-subordinate dyads. Finally, Gutman (1993) published a book on EEO law covering current employment issues such as Title VII of the CRA of 1964, the CRA of 1991, the ADEA, and the ADA, with an emphasis on the pragmatic implications of such issues for human resources practitioners. The current litigious nature of our society suggests that legal issues will continue to play an important role in selection research and practice in the years ahead; few topics in our field provide such polarized points of view.

SELECTION FOR WORK GROUPS

The use of groups to accomplish work tasks is enormously popular in a wide variety of organizations. Research concerning the nature of work groups and work group effectiveness continues to accumulate at an accelerating pace (e.g. Guzzo & Salas 1995, Salas et al 1995). Work groups serve a variety of purposes and take on a variety of different forms, and Klimoski & Jones (1995) make a strong case that different types of work groups have different knowledge, skill, and ability (KSA) requirements. One type of work group that has received a good deal of research attention, mostly in the military, is the "team," which has been defined as including, at a minimum, two people, a common goal, specific role assignments, and interdependence of members. Important themes in the research on teams include uncovering the behavioral correlates of effective teamwork and developing measures of team performance (Salas et al 1995). Results of this research provide a great deal of information regarding characteristics needed in effective team members.

Stevens & Campion (1994) reviewed the literature on work groups and provided a discussion of the potential KSA requirements for teamwork and the implications of these teamwork KSAs for selecting group members. Not surprisingly, interpersonal skills consistently emerge as important for working in groups. These include conflict management and resolution, collaborative problem solving, and communication. Hogan & Lock (1995) pointed to the current lack of empirical information concerning the interpersonal skills needed in the workplace and developed a taxonomy of these skills using the critical incident technique. Stevens & Campion suggest that interviews, assessment centers, and biodata might be appropriate for tapping such KSAs, and they demonstrate that a situational judgment type measure can also be useful in selecting work group members. In addition, work group members are often required to have broader skill sets than individuals who work more independently. Frequently work group members are expected or required to know aspects of one anothers' jobs in order to facilitate coordination and communication or to provide backup for other group members (Salas et al 1995).

The issues involved in staffing work groups take on another level of complexity when we consider the mix of people within each work group. Past research has yielded equivocal results concerning the effects of work group heterogeneity on performance. A model recently developed by Jackson et al (1995) attempts to describe how work group diversity impacts on performance and to integrate research findings in this area. One important point in this regard is that the type of diversity is very important, not just its presence or absence. Work group diversity has been discussed in the past as if it were a unitary concept, when in fact groups can be diverse in terms of member abilities, skills, knowledge, demographics, personality, and so on. Klimoski & Jones (1995) discussed the importance of having the correct mix of people in work groups, and suggested taking group norms into account when selecting people to join an existing team. Research in this area is still a long way from realizing the potential payoff Landy et al (1994) suggested was possible, but there has been a great deal of progress made toward understanding work groups and some preliminary attempts to apply this understanding to selection and staffing issues.

PERSON-ORGANIZATION FIT

The past few years have seen a surge of interest in person-organization (P-O) fit research and thinking. The basic notion here is that a fit between personal attributes and characteristics of the target organization contributes to important individual and organizational outcomes. Kristof (1996) noted, however, that there is considerable confusion about what P-O fit is. For example, P-O congruence is sometimes equated with person-environment fit, where the latter also encompasses person-vocation and person-job fit. In addition, researchers have studied direct judgments of perceived fit (e.g. interviewers' perceptions of applicant fit) and indirect measures of actual fit (e.g. the fit between independent judgments of individual and organizational characteristics). Kristof provided a very useful overview of current progress and problems in P-O congruence research. Overall, Schneider's work on the attraction-selection-attrition (ASA) model is perhaps most noteworthy in this area. Schneider et al (1996) provided an update of ASA research. The ASA framework suggests a different way of viewing personnel selection, at the organizational rather than individual effectiveness level. This approach has evolved over the years, and Schneider et al now argue that homogeneity in organizations (e.g. in personality, attitudes, and values) is probably good early in the life of organizations because it contributes to enhanced cooperation and communication; however, such homogeneity may later lead to inflexibility and difficulty adapting to changing external environments. Related to this view, Ostroff (1993) found that high schools where there was an overall good fit between organizational climate and teachers' personalities tended to be more effective as organizations, though the N was quite small (N = 29). In addition, the relationship was reversed for the climate dimensions of structure and hierarchy, which suggests that lack of congruence in some areas might be important for organizational effectiveness.

One aspect of the ASA argument is the "gravitational hypothesis" that persons in the work force will over time sort themselves into jobs that are compatible with their interests, values, etc. Wilk et al (1995) tested this hypothesis and found that general cognitive ability predicted whether workers moved to higher or lower complexity jobs over a five-year period, and that longer-term employees in jobs are somewhat more homogenous in ability compared with shorter-tenured employees. Lancaster et al (1994) found that, in an employment agency setting, persons with similar abilities and vocational interests tended to apply for similar jobs, but this was not true for personality. The authors speculate that ability and vocational interest requirements are relatively homogenous for *jobs,* whereas personality may be more of a P-O fit variable.

Two studies used a forced-choice test format to select for fit. Villanova et al (1994) developed a job compatibility test for selecting motion-picture theater workers. With a predictive validity design, they found significant correlations with job performance and turnover. Barrett (1995) reported research on an instrument that has as items performance requirements for the target job that applicants rate according to importance. Supervisors provide Q-sort ratings of each one's "actual" importance and applicant-supervisor fit is evaluated. Concurrent and predictive validities are mostly in the 30s and higher.

Adkins et al (1994) found that recruiters' assessments of P-O fit in work values are somewhat idiosyncratic and better aligned with the fit between *recruiter* and interviewee work values. Further, recruiter judgments of P-O fit did not predict their ratings of employability. In an interesting study, Gustafson & Mumford (1995) found that patterns of personality scores used to form homogenous groups were related to job satisfaction and performance, but importantly, the influence of personality type on these outcomes was enhanced when type of work situation was taken into account, supporting a P-O fit interpretation. Cable & Judge (1994) showed that characteristics of compensation systems had a main effect on pay preferences but that fit between individuals' personality and pay system characteristics enhanced the prediction of pay preferences and job attractiveness. In a lab study, Bretz & Judge (1994) studied the impact of various organizational characteristics such as group-based reward systems and procedural justice policies on the dependent variable of whether students would accept a job offer from each of the hypothetical organizations. Most important, interactions were found demonstrating support for the hypothesis that human resource system characteristics may be most influential regarding job choice when considered in the context of P-O fit. Edwards (1994) provided a major methodological criticism of congruence indices that most P-O fit research employs. A polynomial regression approach is proposed to overcome these problems.

In other studies, Spector et al (1995) found in a sample of civil service employees that two personality traits—anxiety and optimism—correlated significantly with several job characteristics (e.g. autonomy, variety) describing these persons' job. Finally, Day & Bedeian (1995) found that similarity between the personality of individuals and others in the organization predicted job performance. These authors call for a test of the predictive power of the traditional selection model matching applicant attributes with job performance requirements to this congruence model matching applicant attributes with the attributes of organizations or their members. Designing a fair test of these models will not be easy, but it is reasonable to ask the question of how well the P-O congruence model predicts performance and perhaps other important outcome variables compared with the person-job requirement fit model that has been our standard methodology. Importantly, the end-of-jobs (e.g. Bridges 1994) and competency-based-organizations (e.g. Lawler 1994) view of the future argues for increased use of the P-O model for selection. As organizational flexibility in effectively utilizing employees increasingly becomes an issue (e.g. workers are more often moved from job to job in the organization), the P-O model may be more relevant in comparison with the traditional person-job match approach (e.g. Kristof 1996). Our view is that both models will be useful and may productively be employed in concert.

SUMMARY OF MAJOR TRENDS

In the introduction, we described three themes that provide a way of characterizing recent progress in the area of personnel selection. First, increased attention to criteria and models of performance is a promising development. For years, work on criteria lagged behind work already accomplished in several predictor domains. It is encouraging to see renewed energy applied toward development of taxonomies and models of performance. We expect this trend to continue for the foreseeable future. The reemergence of personality and related volitional constructs as predictors is also a positive sign, in that this trend should result in a more complete mapping of the KSAO requirements for jobs and organizations, beyond general cognitive ability, for example. What is even more exciting, however, is how these two themes come together to reveal interpretable relationships between individual predictors and criterion constructs. Much more work is needed to clarify these linkages, but it now appears, for example, that ability best predicts technical proficiency–related criteria and personality best predicts such criterion domains as teamwork, interpersonal effectiveness, and contextual performance. We strongly encourage continued research to discover and confirm relationships between ability, personality, experience, job knowledge, technical proficiency, extra-technical proficiency domains, and overall job performance. This work continues to help us raise personnel selection from a technology to a science.

The third theme, person-organization (P-O) fit research, is gaining in popularity. As mentioned earlier, we would like to see more clarity in how P-O fit is defined and measured. In addition, we need to gain more understanding of how effective the P-O congruence model is for personnel selection applications compared with the more traditional model of person-job matching. Conceptually, it seems that P-O congruence becomes a more appropriate model for selection where "the job" is not as relevant a concept. We look forward to further developments in P-O fit research that evaluate the usefulness of this model for selection.

More broadly, we are optimistic for the future regarding the science and practice of personnel selection. Beyond our central themes, meta-analyses suggest that many of our predictor measures are encouragingly valid for predicting job performance. Methods available for studying predictor-criterion links are increasingly powerful. In addition, new areas of research, such as applicant reactions, team selection, and computerized testing, are emerging and progressing. As public and private sector organizations reconfigure and reposition themselves to remain competitive in an expanding global environment, we believe that personnel selection research will play an important role in the process. We are enthusiastic about participating in the personnel selection research and practice enterprise of the future.

ACKNOWLEDGMENTS

The authors thank Patti Haas, Victoria Cole, Daren Easterling, Martha Sutton, Marguerite Nee, and Karen Oberne for providing clerical and other technical support. Thanks also to Norm Abrahams, Steve Motowidlo, Phil Bobko, and Frank Schmidt for commenting on an earlier version of the manuscript. Please contact Walter Borman for an extended bibliography that includes material we could not cite due to space limitations.

Literature Cited

Abrahams NM, Alf EF, Kieckhaefer WF, Pass JJ, Cole DR, Walton-Paxton E. 1994. *Classification utility of test composites from the ASVAB, CAT-ASVAB, and ECAT batteries* (Contract N66001-90-D-9502, Delivery Order 7J16). San Diego: Navy Pers. Res. Dev. Cent.

Abrahams NM, Alf EF, Neumann I. 1993. The treatment of failures in validation research. *Mil. Psychol.* 5(4):235–49

Adams GA, Elacqua TC, Colarelli SM. 1994. The employment interview as a sociometric selection technique. *J. Group Psychother. Psychodrama Sociom.* Fall:99–113

Adkins CL, Russell CJ, Werbel JD. 1994. Judgments of fit in the selection process: the role of work value congruence. *Pers. Psychol.* 47:605–23

Aguinis H. 1995. Statistical power problems with moderated multiple regression in management research. *J. Manage.* 21(6): 1141–58

Aiello JR, Kolb KJ. 1995. Electronic performance monitoring and social context: impact on productivity and stress. *J. Appl. Psychol.* 80(3):339–53

Alderton DL, Larson GE. 1994. Dimensions of ability: diminishing returns? See Rumsey et al 1994, pp. 137–44

Allen M, Preiss R. 1993. Replication and meta-analysis: a necessary connection. *J. Soc. Behav. Pers.* 8(6):9–20

Anderson NR. 1992. Eight decades of employment interview research: a retrospective meta-review and prospective commentary. *Eur. Work Organ. Psychol.* 2(1):1–32

Anderson N, Herriot P, eds. 1994. *Assessment and Selection in Organizations.* London: Wiley

Arvey RD, Sackett PR. 1993. Fairness in selection: current developments and perspectives. See Schmitt & Borman 1993, pp. 171–202

Barrett RS. 1995. Employee selection with the performance priority survey. *Pers. Psychol.* 48:653–62

Barrick MR, Mount MK. 1991. The big five personality dimensions and job performance: a meta-analysis. *Pers. Psychol.* 44:1–26

Barrick MR, Mount MK. 1993. Autonomy as a moderator of the relationships between the big five personality dimensions and job performance. *J. Appl. Psychol.* 78:111–18

Barrick MR, Mount MK. 1996. Effects of impression management and self-deception on the predictive validity of personality constructs. *J. Appl. Psychol.* 81(3):261–72

Bennett RE. 1994. Environments for presenting and automatically scoring complex constructed-response items. See Rumsey et al 1994, pp. 173–92

Blake RJ, Potter EH III, Sliwak RE. 1993. Validation of the structural scales of the CPI for predicting the performance of junior officers in the US Coast Guard. *J. Bus. Psychol.* 7(4):431–48

Blakley BR, Quinones MA, Crawford MS, Jago IA. 1994. The validity of isometric strength tests. *Pers. Psychol.* 47:247–74

Bobko P. 1994. Issues in operational selection and classification systems: comments and commonalities. See Rumsey et al 1994, pp. 443–56

Bobko P, Russell CJ. 1994. On theory, statistics, and the search for interactions in the organizational sciences. *J. Manage.* 20(1): 193–200

Borman WC, Hanson MA, Oppler SH, Pulakos ED, White LA. 1993. Role of early supervisory experience in supervisor performance. *J. Appl. Psychol.* 78(3):443–49

Borman WC, Motowidlo SJ. 1993. Expanding the criterion domain to include elements of contextual performance. See Schmitt & Borman 1993, pp. 71–98

Borman WC, White LA, Dorsey DW. 1995. Effects of ratee task performance and interpersonal factors on supervisor and peer performance ratings. *J. Appl. Psychol.* 80(1):168–77

Boudreau JW, Sturman MC, Judge TA. 1994.

Utility analysis: what are the black boxes, and do they affect decisions? See Anderson & Herriot 1994, pp. 77–96

Brannick MT. 1995. Critical comments on applying covariance structure modeling. *J. Organ. Behav.* 16:201–13

Bretz RD, Judge TA. 1994. The role of human resource systems in job applicant decision process. *J. Manage* 20:531–51

Bridges W. 1994. The end of the job. *Fortune* 130(6):62–74

Brown BK, Campion MA. 1994. Biodata phenomenology: recruiters' perceptions and use of biographical information in resume screening. *J. Appl. Psychol.* 79(6):897–908

Brown DC. 1994. What's new for the 1990's standards? *Indus.-Organ. Psychol.* 31(3): 97–98

Cable DM, Judge TA. 1994. Pay preferences and job search decisions: a person-organization fit perspective. *Pers. Psychol.* 47: 317–48

Campbell JP. 1990. An overview of the army selection and classification project (Project A). *Pers. Psychol.* 43:231–39

Campbell JP, Gasser MB, Oswald FL. 1996. The substantive nature of performance variability. See Murphy 1996a, pp. 258–99

Campbell JP, McCloy RA, Oppler SH, Sager CE. 1993. A theory of performance. See Schmitt & Borman 1993, pp. 35–70

Campbell JP, Peterson NG, Johnson J. 1994. The prediction of future performance from current performance and from training performance. In *Building and Retaining the Career Force: New Procedures for Accessing and Assigning Army Enlisted Personnel. Annu. Rep. 1993 Fisc. Year,* ed. J Campbell, L Zook. Alexandria, VA: US Army Res. Inst. Behav. Soc. Sci.

Campion MA, Campion JE, Hudson JP. 1994. Structured interviewing: a note on incremental validity and alternative question types. *J. Appl. Psychol.* 79(6):998–1002

Carretta TR, Ree MJ. 1995. Air Force officer qualifying test validity for predicting pilot training performance. *J. Bus. Technol.* 9(4):379–88

Cesare SJ, Blankenship MH, Giannetto PW. 1994. A dual focus of SD*y* estimations: a test of linearity assumption and multivariate application. *Hum. Perform.* 7(4): 235–55

Chang L. 1994. A psychometric evaluation of 4-point and 6-point Likert-type scales in relation to reliability and validity. *Appl. Psychol. Meas.* 18(3):205–15

Christiansen ND, Goffin RD, Johnston NG, Rothstein MG. 1994. Correcting the 16PF for faking: effects on criterion-related validity and individual hiring decisions. *Pers. Psychol.* 47:847–60

Cohen J. 1994. The earth is round ($p < .05$). *Am. Psychol.* 49:997–1003

Collins JM, Schmidt FL. 1993. Personality, integrity, and white collar crime: a construct validity study. *Pers. Psychol.* 46:295–311

Conway JM, Jako RA, Goodman DF. 1995. A meta-analysis of interrater and internal consistency reliability of selection interviews. *J. Appl. Psychol.* 80(5):565–79

Crant JM. 1995. The proactive personality scale and objective job performance among real estate agents. *J. Appl. Psychol.* 80(4): 532–37

Dalessio AT. 1994. Predicting insurance agent turnover using a video-based situational judgment test. *J. Bus. Psychol.* 9:23–32

Dalessio AT, Silverhart TA. 1994. Combining biodata test and interview information: predicting decisions and performance criteria. *Pers. Psychol.* 47:303–15

Day DV, Bedeian AG. 1995. Personality similarity and work-related outcomes among African-American nursing personnel: a test of the supplementary model of person-environment congruence. *J. Vocat. Behav.* 46:55–70

Dipboye RL. 1994. Structured and unstructured selection interviews: beyond the job-fit model. *Res. Pers. Hum. Res. Manage.* 12:79–123

Dipboye RL, Gaugler BB. 1993. Cognitive and behavioral processes in the selection interview. See Schmitt & Borman 1993, pp. 135–70

Dror IE, Kosslyn SM, Waag WL. 1993. Visual-spatial abilities of pilots. *J. Appl. Psychol.* 78(5):763–73

DuBois CLZ, Sackett PR, Zedeck S, Fogli L. 1993. Further exploration of typical and maximal performance criteria: definitional issues, prediction, and white-black differences. *J. Appl. Psychol.* 78:205–11

DuBois D, Shalin VL, Levi KR, Borman WC. 1995. *A cognitively-oriented approach to task analysis and test development.* Off. Naval Res. Tech. Rep.

Dunn WS, Mount MK, Barrick MR, Ones DS. 1995. Relative importance of personality and general mental ability in managers' judgments of applicant qualifications. *J. Appl. Psychol.* 80:500–9

Dunnette MD. 1963. A note on the criterion. *J. Appl. Psychol.* 47:251–54

Dunnette MD. 1994. Forward. See Stokes et al 1994, pp. xi–xii

Dye DA, Reck M, Murphy MA. 1993. The validity of job knowledge measures. *Int. J. Sel. Assess.* 1(3):153–57

Edwards JR. 1994. The study of congruence in organizational behavior research: critique and a proposed alternative. *Organ. Behav. Hum. Decis. Process.* 58:51–100

Ferris GR, Judge TA, Rowland KM, Fitzgibbons DE. 1994. Subordinate influence and the performance evaluation process: test of a model. *Organ. Behav. Hum. Decis. Process.* 58:101–35
File QW. 1945. The measurement of supervisory quality in industry. *J. Appl. Psychol.* 30:323–37
Finklestein LM, Burke MJ, Raju NS. 1995. Age discrimination in simulated employment contexts: an integrative analysis. *J. Appl. Psychol.* 80(6):652–63
Fischer RJ. 1994. The Americans With Disabilities Act: implications for measurement. *Educ. Measure.: Issues Pract.* Fall: 17–26
Funder DC. 1995. On the accuracy of personality judgment: a realistic approach. *Psychol. Rev.* 102(4):652–70
Ganzach Y. 1995. Negativity (and positivity) in performance evaluation: three field studies. *J. Appl. Psychol.* 80:491–99
Gilliland SW. 1993. The perceived fairness of selection systems: an organizational justice perspective. *Acad. Manage. Rev.* 18:694–734
Gilliland SW. 1994. Effects of procedural and distributive justice on reactions to a selection system. *J. Appl. Psychol.* 79:691–701
Gottfredson LS. 1994. The science and politics of race-norming. *Am. Psychol.* 49(11): 955–63
Gustafson SB, Mumford MD. 1995. Personal style and person-environment fit: a pattern approach. *J. Vocat. Behav.* 46:163–88
Gutman A. 1993. *EEO Law and Personnel Practices.* Newbury Park, CA: Sage
Guzzo R, Salas E, eds. 1995. *Team Effectiveness and Decision Making in Organizations.* San Francisco: Jossey-Bass
Hanisch KA, Hulin CL. 1994. Two-stage sequential selection procedures using ability and training performance: incremental validity of behavioral consistency measures. *Pers. Psychol.* 47:767–85
Hanson MA, Campbell JP, McKee AS. 1993. Development of the longitudinal validation sample second-tour performance model. In *Building and Retaining the Career Force: New Procedures for Accessing and Assigning Enlisted Personnel. Annu. Rep. 1993 Fisc. Year,* (ARI Res. Note 94–27), ed. J Campbell, L Zook. Alexandria, VA: US Army Res. Inst. Behav. Soc. Sci.
Harris MM. 1994. Rater motivation in the performance appraisal context: a theoretical framework. *J. Manage.* 20:737–56
Hartel CEJ. 1993. Rating format research revisited: format effectiveness and acceptability depend on rater characteristics. *J. Appl. Psychol.* 78:212–17
Hedge JW, Borman WC. 1995. Changing conceptions and practices in performance appraisal. See Howard 1995, pp. 451–81
Held JD, Foley PP. 1994. Explanations for accuracy of the general multivariate formulas in correcting for range restriction. *Appl. Psychol. Meas.* 18(4):355–67
Henderson F, Anderson N, Rick S. 1995. Future competency profiling. *Pers. Rev.* 24: 19–31
Herriot P. 1993. A paradigm bursting at the seams. *J. Organ. Behav.* 14:371–75
Herrnstein RJ, Murray C. 1994. *The Bell Curve: Intelligence and Class Structure in American Life.* New York: Free Press
Hoffman CC. 1995. Applying range restriction corrections using published norms: three case studies. *Pers. Psychol.* 48:913–23
Hogan J, Hogan RT. 1993. *Ambiguities of conscientiousness.* Presented at Annu. Meet. Soc. Ind. Organ. Psychol., 8th, San Francisco
Hogan J, Lock J. 1995. *A taxonomy of interpersonal skills for business interactions.* Presented at Annu. Meet. Soc. Ind. Organ. Psychol., 10th, Orlando, FL
Hogan J, Quigley A. 1994. Effects of preparing for physical ability tests. *Public Pers. Manage.* 23(1):85–104
Hogan J, Roberts BW. 1996. Issues and nonissues in the fidelity/bandwidth tradeoff. *J. Organ. Behav.* In press
Hogan R, Blake R. 1996. Vocational interest measurement: the compatibility of individual self-concept with the work environment. See Murphy 1996a, pp. 89–144
Hogan RT, Hogan J, Roberts BW. 1996. Personality measurement and employment decisions: questions and answers. *Am. Psychol.* 51:469–77
Holden RR, Hibbs N. 1995. Incremental validity of response latencies for detecting fakers on a personality test. *J. Res. Pers.* 29(3):362–72
Hough LM, Schneider RJ. 1996. Personality traits, taxonomies, and applications in organizations. See Murphy 1996a, pp. 31–88
Howard A, ed. 1995. *The Changing Nature of Work.* San Francisco: Jossey-Bass
Howard JL, Ferris GR. 1996. The employment interview context: social and situational influences on interviewer decisions. *J. Appl. Soc. Psychol.* In press
Huffcutt AI, Arthur W. 1994. Hunter and Hunter (1984) revisited: interview validity for entry-level jobs. *J. Appl. Psychol.* 79(2):184–90
Huffcutt AI, Arthur W. 1995. Development of a new outlier statistic for meta-analytic data. *J. Appl. Psychol.* 80(2):327–34
Hunter JE. 1983. A causal analysis of cognitive ability, job knowledge, job performance and supervisory ratings. In *Performance*

Measurement and Theory, ed. F Landy, S Zedeck, J Cleveland, pp. 257–66. Hillsdale, NJ: Erlbaum

Hunter JE, Hunter RF. 1984. Validity and utility of alternative predictors across studies. *Psychol. Bull.* 96:72–98

Hunter JE, Schmidt FL, Jackson GB. 1982. *Meta-analysis: Cumulating Findings Across Research.* Beverly Hills, CA: Sage

Ilgen DR. 1994. Jobs and roles: accepting and coping with the changing structure of organizations. See Rumsey et al 1994, pp. 13–32

Jaccard J, Wan CK. 1995. Measurement error in the analysis of interaction effects between continuous predictors using multiple regression: multiple indicator and structural equation approaches. *Psychol. Bull.* 117(2): 348–57

Jackson DN, Vernon PA, Jackson DN. 1993. Dynamic spatial performance and general intelligence. *Intelligence* 17:451–60

Jackson SE, May KE, Whitney K. 1995. Understanding the dynamics of diversity in decision-making teams. See Guzzo & Salas 1995, pp. 204–61

Kehoe JF, Tenopyr ML. 1994. Adjustment in assessment scores and their usage: a taxonomy and evaluation of methods. *Psychol. Assess.* 6(4):291–303

Kerr MR. 1995. Tacit knowledge as a predictor of managerial success: a field study. *Can. J. Behav. Sci.* 27:36–51

Klimoski R, Jones RG. 1995. Staffing for effective group decision making: key issues in matching people and teams. See Guzzo & Salas 1995, pp. 291–332

Klimoski R, Palmer S. 1993. The ADA and the hiring process in organizations. *Consult. Psychol. J.* 45(2):10–36

Klimoski RJ, Brickner M. 1987. Why do assessment centers work? The puzzle of assessment center validity. *Pers. Psychol.* 40: 243–60

Kluger AN, Rothstein HR. 1993. The influence of selection test type on applicant reactions to employment testing. *J. Bus. Psychol.* 8: 3–25

Koslowsky M, Sagie A. 1994. Components of artifactual variance in meta-analytic research. *Pers. Psychol.* 47:561–74

Kristof AL. 1996. Person-organization fit: an integrative review of its conceptualizations, measurement, and implications. *Pers. Psychol.* 49:1–49

Kulik CT, Ambrose ML. 1993. Category-based and feature-based processes in performance appraisal: integrating visual and computerized sources of performance data. *J. Appl. Psychol.* 78:821–30

Kyllonen PC. 1994. Cognitive abilities testing: an agenda for the 1990s. See Rumsey et al 1994, pp. 103–25

Lancaster SJ, Colarelli SM, King DW, Beehr TA. 1994. Job applicant similarity on cognitive ability, vocational interests, and personality characteristics: Do similar persons choose similar jobs? *Educ. Psychol. Meas.* 54(2):299–316

Lance CE, LaPointe JA, Fisicaro SA. 1994. A test of the context dependency of three causal models of halo rater error. *J. Appl. Psychol.* 79:332–40

Landy FJ, Shankster LJ, Kohler SS. 1994. Personnel selection and placement. *Annu. Rev. Psychol.* 45:261–96

Landy FJ, Shankster-Cawley L, Moran SK. 1995. Advancing personnel selection and placement methods. See Howard 1995, pp. 252–89

Larson GE, Wolfe JH. 1995. Validity results for g from an expanded test base. *Intelligence* 20:15–25

Latham GP, Skarlicki DP. 1995. Criterion-related validity of the situational and patterned behavior description interviews with organizational citizenship behavior. *Hum. Perform.* 8:67–80

Latham GP, Skarlicki DP. 1996. The effectiveness of the situational, patterned behavior and conventional structured interviews in minimizing in-group favoritism of Canadian Francophone managers. *Appl. Psychol.: Int. Rev.* 45(2):177–84

Latham GP, Whyte G. 1994. The futility of utility analysis. *Pers. Psychol.* 47:31–46

Law KS, Myors B. 1993. Cutoff scores that maximize the total utility of a selection program: comment on Martin and Raju's (1992) procedure. *J. Appl. Psychol.* 78(5) 736–40

Law KS, Schmidt FL, Hunter JE. 1994. Nonlinearity of range corrections in meta-analysis: test of an improved procedure. *J. Appl. Psychol.* 79(3):425–38

Lawler EE. 1994. From job-based to competency-based organizations. *J. Organ. Behav.* 15:3–15

Ledvinka J. 1995. Government regulation of human resources. See Howard 1995, pp. 67–86

Lefkowitz J. 1994. Race as a factor in job placement: serendipitous findings of "Ethnic Drift." *Pers. Psychol.* 47:497–513

Macan TH, Avedon MJ, Paese M, Smith DE. 1994. The effects of applicants' reactions to cognitive ability tests and an assessment center. *Pers. Psychol.* 47:715–38

Mael FA. 1994. If past behavior really predicts future, so should biodata's. See Rumsey et al 1994, pp. 273–92

Mael FA, Ashforth BE. 1995. Loyal from day one: biodata, organizational identification, and turnover among newcomers. *Pers. Psychol.* 48:309–33

McCloy RA, Campbell JP, Cudeck R. 1994. A

confirmatory test of a model of performance determinants. *J. Appl. Psychol.* 79: 493–505

McDaniel MA, Frei RL. 1994. *Validity of customer service measures in personnel selection: a meta-analysis.* Presented at Annu. Meet. Soc. Ind. Organ. Psychol., 9th, Nashville

McHenry JJ, Schmitt N. 1994. Multimedia testing. See Rumsey et al 1994, pp. 193–232

McIntyre MD, James LR. 1995. The inconsistency with which raters rate and combine information across targets. *Hum. Perform.* 8:95–111

Medsker GJ, Williams LJ, Holahan PJ. 1994. A review of current practices for evaluating causal models in organizational behavior and human resources management research. *J. Manage.* 20(2):439–64

Messick S. 1995. Validity of psychological assessment. *Am. Psychol.* 50(9):741–49

Motowidlo SJ, Burnett JR. 1995. Aural and visual sources of validity in structured employment interviews. *Organ. Behav. Hum. Decis. Process.* 61(3):239–49

Motowidlo SJ, Tippins N. 1993. Further studies of the low-fidelity simulation in the form of a situational judgment inventory. *J. Occup. Organ. Psychol.* 66:337–44

Motowidlo SJ, Van Scotter JR. 1994. Evidence that task performance should be distinguished from contextual performance. *J. Appl. Psychol.* 79:475–80

Mount MK, Barrick MR, Strauss JP. 1994. Validity of observer ratings of the Big Five personality factors. *J. Appl. Psychol.* 79: 272–80

Muchinsky PM. 1993. Validation of intelligence and mechanical aptitude tests in selecting employees for manufacturing jobs. *J. Bus. Psychol.* 7(4):373–82

Murphy KR. 1993. *Honesty in the Workplace.* Belmont, CA: Brooks/Cole

Murphy KR. 1994a. Meta-analysis and validity generalization. See Anderson & Herriot 1994, pp. 57–76

Murphy KR. 1994b. Potential effects of banding as a function of test reliability. *Pers. Psychol.* 47:477–95

Murphy KR, ed. 1996a. *Individual Differences and Behavior in Organizations.* San Francisco: Jossey-Bass

Murphy KR. 1996b. Individual differences and behavior in organizations: much more than "g". See Murphy 1996a, pp. 3–30

Murphy KR, Osten K, Myors B. 1995. Modeling the effects of banding in personnel selection. *Pers. Psychol.* 48:61–84

Neisser U, Boodoo G, Bouchard TJ, Boykin AW, Brody N, et al. 1996. Intelligence: knowns and unknowns. *Am. Psychol.* 51(2):77–101

Olea MM, Ree MJ. 1994. Predicting pilot and navigator criteria: not much more than g. *J. Appl. Psychol.* 79(6):845–51

Olkin I, Finn JD. 1995. Correlations redux. *Psychol. Bull.* 118(1):155–64

Ones DS, Viswesvaran C. 1996. Bandwidth-fidelity dilemma in personality measurement for personnel selection. *J. Organ. Behav.* In press

Ones DS, Viswesvaran C, Schmidt FL. 1993. Comprehensive meta-analysis of integrity test validities: findings and implications for personnel selection and theories of job performance. *J. Appl. Psychol.* 78(4):679–703

Organ DW, Ryan K. 1995. A meta-analytic review of attitudinal and dispositional predictors of organizational citizenship behavior. *Pers. Psychol.* 48:775–802

Ostroff C. 1993. Relationships between person-environment congruence and organizational effectiveness. *Group Organ. Manage.* 18(1):103–22

Pati GC, Bailey EK. 1995. Empowering people with disabilities: strategy and human resource issues in implementing the ADA. *Organ. Dyn.* 23(3):52–69

Payne T, Anderson N, Smith T. 1992. Assessment centres, selection systems, and cost effectiveness: an evaluative case study. *Pers. Rev.* 21:48–56

Peterson NG, Mumford MD, Borman WC, Jeanneret PR, Fleishman EA. 1995. *Development of Prototype Occupational Information Network (O*NET) Content Model,* Vols. 1, 2. Salt Lake City: Utah Dep. Empl. Secur.

Powell AB, Fritzsche BA, Hoffman R. 1995. *Predicting customer service job performance with the five-factor model.* Presented at APA Conf., 103rd, New York

Pritchard RD, ed. 1995. *Productivity Measurement and Improvement: Organizational Case Studies.* New York: Praeger. 380 pp.

Pulakos ED, Schmitt N. 1995. Experience-based and situational interview questions: studies of validity. *Pers. Psychol.* 48: 289–308

Pulakos ED, Schmitt N. 1996. An evaluation of two strategies for reducing adverse impact and their effects on criterion related validity. *Hum. Perform.* 9(3):241–58

Pulakos ED, Schmitt N, Whitney D. 1996. Individual differences in interviewer ratings: the impact of standardization, consensus discussion, and sampling error on the validity of a structured interview. *Pers. Psychol.* 49:85–102

Quinones MA, Ford JK, Teachout MS. 1995. The relationship between work experience and job performance: a conceptual and meta-analytic review. *Pers. Psychol.* 48: 887–910

Raju NS, Burke MJ, Normand J, Lezotte DV.

1993. What would be if what is wasn't? Rejoinder to Judiesch, Schmidt, and Hunter (1993). *J. Appl. Psychol.* 78(6):912–16

Ree MJ, Carretta TR, Earles JA, Albert W. 1994a. Sign changes when correcting for range restriction: a note on Pearson's and Lawley's selection formulas. *J. Appl. Psychol.* 79(2):298–301

Ree MJ, Earles JA, Teachout MS. 1994b. Predicting job performance: not much more than g. *J. Appl. Psychol.* 79(4):518–24

Rosse JG, Miller JL, Stecher MD. 1994. A field study of job applicants' reactions to personality and cognitive ability testing. *J. Appl. Psychol.* 79:987–92

Rosse RL, Peterson NG, Whetzel D. 1995. Estimating classification gains: development of a new analytic method. In *Building and Retaining the Career Force: New Procedures for Accessing and Assigning Army Enlisted Personnel. Final Report,* ed. J Campbell, L Zook. Alexandria, VA: US Army Res. Inst. Behav. Soc. Sci.

Roth PL. 1994. Multi-attribute utility analysis using the ProMES approach. *J. Bus. Psychol.* 9(1):69–80

Rumsey M, Walker C, Harris J, eds. 1994. *Personnel Selection and Classification.* Hillsdale, NJ: Erlbaum

Russell CJ, Colella A, Bobko P. 1993. Expanding the context of utility: the strategic impact of personnel selection. *Pers. Psychol.* 46:781–801

Ryan AM, Daum D, Bauman T, Grisez M, Mattimore K, et al. 1995. Direct, indirect, and controlled observation and rating accuracy. *J. Appl. Psychol.* 80(6):664–70

Rynes SL. 1993. Who's selecting whom? Effects of selection practices on applicant attitudes and behavior. See Schmitt & Borman 1993, pp. 240–74

Rynes SL, Connerley ML. 1993. Applicant reactions to alternative selection procedures. *J. Bus. Psychol.* 4:261–77

Sackett PR, Ostgard DJ. 1994. Job-specific applicant pools and national norms for cognitive ability tests: implications for range restriction corrections in validation research. *J. Appl. Psychol.* 79(5):680–84

Sackett PR, Wilk SL. 1994. Within-group norming and other forms of score adjustment in preemployment testing. *Am. Psychol.* 49(11):929–54

Sagie A, Koslowsky M. 1993. Detecting moderators with meta-analysis: an evaluation and comparison of techniques. *Pers. Psychol.* 46:629–40

Salas S, Bowers C, CannonBowers J, eds. 1995. Special issue: team processes, training, and performance. *Mil. Psychol.* 7(2): 53–139

Sanchez JI, De La Torre P. 1996. A second look at the relationship between rating and behavioral accuracy in performance appraisal. *J. Appl. Psychol.* 81:3–10

Schmidt FL. 1994. The future of personnel selection in the U.S. Army. See Rumsey et al 1994, pp. 333–50

Schmidt FL. 1996. Statistical significance testing and cumulative knowledge in psychology: implications for the training of researchers. *Psychol. Methods.* In press

Schmidt FL, Ones DS, Hunter JE. 1992. Personnel selection. *Annu. Rev. Psychol.* 43: 627–70

Schmidt FL, Hunter JE. 1995. The fatal internal contradiction in banding: its statistical rationale is logically inconsistent with its operational procedures. *Hum. Perform.* 8(3):203–14

Schmit MJ, Ryan AM, Stierwalt SL, Powell AB. 1995. Frame-of-reference effects on personality scale scores and criterion-related validity. *J. Appl. Psychol.* 80(5): 607–20

Schmitt N, Borman WC, eds. 1993. *Personnel Selection in Organizations.* San Francisco: Jossey-Bass

Schmitt N, Nason E, Whitney DJ, Pulakos ED. 1995. The impact of method effects on structural parameters in validation research. *J. Manage.* 21(1):159–74

Schneider BS, Goldstein HW, Smith DB. 1996. The ASA framework: an update. *Pers. Psychol.* 48:747–73

Schneider RJ, Hough LM. 1995. Personality and industrial/organizational psychology. In *International Review of Industrial and Organizational Psychology,* ed. C Cooper, I Robertson, pp. 75–129. Chichester, Engl: Wiley

Schneider RJ, Hough LM, Dunnette M. 1996. Broadsided by broad traits, or how to sink science in five dimensions or less. *J. Organ. Behav.* In press

Scholarios DM, Johnson CD, Zeidner J. 1994. Selecting predictors for maximizing the classification efficiency of a battery. *J. Appl. Psychol.* 79(3):412–24

Schuler H. 1993. Social validity of selection situations: a concept and some empirical results. In *Personnel Selection and Assessment: Individual and Organizational Perspectives,* ed. H Schuler, J Farr, M Smith, pp. 11–26. Hillsdale, NJ: Erlbaum

Sidick JT, Barrett GV, Doverspike D. 1994. Three-alternative multiple choice tests: an attractive option. *Pers. Psychol.* 47: 829–35

Siem FM. 1996. The use of response latencies to enhance self-report personality measures. *Mil. Psychol.* 8:15–29

Silva JM, White LA. 1993. Relation of cognitive aptitudes to success in foreign language training. *Mil. Psychol.* 5(2):79–93

Siskin BR. 1995. Relation between performance and banding. *Hum. Perform.* 8(3): 215–26

Smith M. 1994. A theory of the validity of predictors in selection. *J. Occup. Organ. Psychol.* 67:13–31

Smither JW, Reilly RR, Millsap RE, Pearlman K, Stoffey RW. 1993. Applicant reactions to selection procedures. *Pers. Psychol.* 46: 49–76

Sparrow PR. 1994. Organizational competencies: creating a strategic behavioural framework for selection and assessment. See Anderson & Herriot 1994, pp. 1–26

Spector PE, Jex SM, Chen PY. 1995. Relations of incumbent affect-related personality traits with incumbent and objective measures of characteristics of jobs. *J. Organ. Behav.* 16:59–65

Sternberg RJ, Wagner RK, Williams WM, Horvath JA. 1995. Testing common sense. *Am. Psychol.* 50(11):912–27

Stevens CK, Kristof AL. 1995. Making the right impression: a field study of applicant impression management during job interviews. *J. Appl. Psychol.* 80(5):587–606

Stevens MJ, Campion MA. 1994. The knowledge, skill, and ability requirements for teamwork: implications for human resource management. *J. Manage.* 20: 503–30

Stokes G, Mumford M, Owens W, eds. 1994. *Biodata Handbook: Theory, Research, and Use of Biographical Information in Selection and Performance Predication.* Palo Alto, CA: Consult. Psychol. Press

Stone-Romero EF, Weaver AE, Glenar JL. 1995. Trends in research designs and data analytic strategies in organizational research. *J. Manage.* 21:141–57

Sue-Chan C, Latham GP, Evans MG. 1995. *The construct validity of the situational and patterned behavior description interviews: Cognitive ability, tacit knowledge, and self-efficacy as correlates.* Presented at Annu. Conf. CPA, Prince Edward Island, Canada

Sulsky LM, Day DV. 1994. Effects of frame-of-reference training on rater accuracy under alternative time delays. *J. Appl. Psychol.* 78:535–43

Tepper BJ. 1994. Investigation of general and program-specific attitudes toward drug-testing policies. *J. Appl. Psychol.* 79:392–401

Trent T, Laurence J, eds. 1993. *Adaptability Screening for the Armed Forces.* Washington, DC: Off. Assist. Secr. Def. (Force Manage. Pers.)

Van Scotter JR, Motowidlo SJ. 1996. Evidence for two factors of contextual performance: job dedication and interpersonal facilitation. *J. Appl. Psychol.* In press

Varca PE, Pattison P. 1993. Evidentiary standards in employment discrimination: a view toward the future. *Pers. Psychol.* 46: 239–58

Vevea JL, Clements NC, Hedges LV. 1993. Assessing the effects of selection bias on validity data for the general aptitude test battery. *J. Appl. Psychol.* 78(6):981–87

Villanova P, Bernardin HJ, Johnson DL, Dahmus SA. 1994. The validity of a measure of job compatibility in the prediction of job performance and turnover of motion picture theater personnel. *Pers. Psychol.* 47:73–90

Viswesvaran C, Ones DS. 1995. Theory testing: combining psychometric meta-analysis and structural equations modeling. *Pers. Psychol.* 48:865–85

Viswesvaran C, Ones DS, Schmidt FL. 1996. A comparative analysis of the reliability of job performance ratings. *J. Appl. Psychol.* In press

Werner JM. 1994. Dimensions that make a difference: examining the impact of in-role and extra-role behaviors on supervisory ratings. *J. Appl. Psychol.* 79:98–107

Wernimont PF, Campbell JP. 1968. Signs, samples, and criteria. *J. Appl. Psychol.* 52: 372–76

White M, Tansey R, Smith M, Barnett T. 1993. Log-linear modeling in personnel research. *Pers. Psychol.* 46:667–86

Wilk SL, Desmarais LB, Sackett PR. 1995. Gravitation to jobs commensurate with ability: longitudinal and cross-sectional tests. *J. Appl. Psychol.* 80(1):79–85

Williams KB, Binning JF, Foster LA. 1993. *Effects of preinterview impressions and interviewee response quality on interviewers' evaluations.* Presented at Annu. Meet. Soc. Ind. Organ. Psychol., 8th, San Francisco

Williams LJ. 1995. Covariance structure modeling in organizational research: problems with the method versus applications of the method. *J. Organ. Behav.* 16:225–33

Williams LJ, Anderson SE. 1994. An alternative approach to method effects by using latent-variable models: applications in organizational behavior research. *J. Appl. Psychol.* 79(3):323–31

Woehr DJ, Huffcutt AI. 1994. Rater training for performance appraisal: a quantitative review. *J. Occup. Organ. Psychol.* 67: 189–205

Zeidner J, Johnson CD. 1994. Is personnel classification a concept whose time has passed? See Rumsey et al 1994, pp. 377–410

Annu. Rev. Psychol. 1997. 48:339–70

THE USE OF ANIMAL MODELS TO STUDY THE EFFECTS OF AGING ON COGNITION

Michela Gallagher

Department of Psychology, University of North Carolina at Chapel Hill, Chapel Hill, North Carolina 27599

Peter R. Rapp

Center for Behavioral Neuroscience, State University of New York at Stony Brook, Stony Brook, New York 11794

KEY WORDS: memory, hippocampus, medial temporal lobe, frontal lobe, attention

ABSTRACT

This review addresses the importance of animal models for understanding the effects of normal aging on the brain and cognitive functions. First, studies of laboratory animals can help to distinguish between healthy aging and pathological conditions that may contribute to cognitive decline late in life. Second, research on individual differences in aging, a theme of interest in studies of elderly human beings, can be advanced by the experimental control afforded in the use of animal models. The review offers a neuropsychological framework to compare the effects of aging in human beings, monkeys, and rodents. We consider aging in relation to the role of the medial temporal lobe in memory, the information processing functions of the prefrontal cortex in the strategic use of memory, and the regulation of attention by distributed neural circuitry. We also provide an overview of the neurobiological effects of aging that may account for alterations in psychological functions.

CONTENTS

0084-6570/97/0201-0339$08.00

INTRODUCTION

From a life-span perspective, the study of aging seeks to understand the changing capacities of the elderly as a normal developmental process. Within this framework, the biology of aging is an important determinant. Just as functions and adaptive capacities depend on the biological development of the young child or adolescent, later life provides a distinctive biological setting in which familiar tasks are performed and new challenges are met. In addition, environmental factors late in life combine with many decades of a person's history to influence the capacities of an individual. We offer the view that important insights into aging as a developmental process can be provided by the study of animal models. The review covers areas of research that illustrate and support this premise.

NORMAL AGING AND ANIMAL MODELS

A major challenge in the study of aging is to define the boundaries of normal change as distinct from pathological conditions. Such boundaries are recognized for development in early life. For example, landmarks are defined for physical growth and cognitive functions; departure from the norm is identified by a failure to manifest certain changes that are expected in the usual course of development. The boundaries of normal aging, as distinct from pathological conditions, are less clearly defined because certain expected changes in cognition during aging do not differ from the earliest manifestations of age-related pathological conditions. For example, the incidence of Alzheimer's disease (AD) increases with advancing age. Although the occurrence of AD is relatively rare before the age of 60, it becomes increasingly prevalent in the decades that follow. Impaired memory, which is the hallmark symptom of AD in its earliest stages, is also one of the most common cognitive features of nondemented elderly individuals (Craik & Jennings 1992, Crook et al 1986). Currently no definitive test can diagnose AD in its earliest stages so that memory impairment associated with this pathological condition can be separated from memory decline that might be attributable to nonpathological aging.

Age-related neurodegenerative diseases such as Alzheimer's have a slow progressive course. If such diseases remain undetected for many years before a clinically significant phase of decline, relatively subtle changes in presumably healthy older individuals that are ascribed to normal aging might, at least in part, be due to occult pathological processes. Effects of Alzheimer's disease on the brain, such as plaques and neurofibrillary tangles, that meet neuropathological criteria for diagnosis have been detected in autopsy material from individuals not judged to have been impaired by clinical assessment before death (Crystal et al 1988, Morris et al 1991). On this basis, it is likely that studies of elderly human subjects will include some individuals with unrecognized neurological disease.

Additional findings from neurological assessments combined with functional testing support this conjecture. Elderly individuals who have radiological evidence of medial temporal lobe atrophy in the brain along with mild cognitive impairment determined by clinical screening were found to be at high risk for developing dementia (de Leon et al 1993). At follow-up four years after the original assessment, 25 of 86 such subjects had received a diagnosis of AD. Brain atrophic changes are also found in some elderly individuals who show no evidence of cognitive impairment in clinical assessments. In a sample of approximately 150 elderly subjects (ages 55–88 years, mean 70.0 years) who were presumed to be healthy, Golomb et al (1993) found atrophy of the medial temporal lobe in certain individuals. Although no participants in this study showed evidence of cognitive impairment in clinical assessments, differences between the subjects with and without medial temporal lobe atrophy were evident in more sensitive tests of cognitive function. Subjects with atrophy performed more poorly on tests of recent memory than the neurologically normal individuals. Much current interest is also focused on a biological marker, the e4 allele of apolipoprotein E, associated with higher risk for dementia (Corder et al 1993). Recent reports indicate that presumably healthy individuals bearing this marker perform less well on assessments of memory than their aged cohorts (Bondi et al 1995, Helkala et al 1996). Such findings raise the question of whether even mild memory impairment might represent a very early indicator of a pathological process.

Notwithstanding the findings discussed above, other evidence indicates that cognitive alterations in aging occur apart from degenerative neurological disease. Age-associated memory impairment (AAMI) was defined a decade ago (Crook et al 1986) to identify elderly individuals who complain of memory impairment by self-report and have memory test performance at least one standard deviation below the mean established for young adults. According to these criteria it is estimated that the occurrence of AAMI substantially exceeds what would be expected based on the prevalence and incidence of probable Alzheimer's disease (prevalence and incidence of AAMI about 35% and 6.6% per year compared with 13% and 3% per year for probable AD) (Lane & Snowdon 1989). Furthermore, Youngjohn & Crook (1993) reported that AAMI is stable in elderly individuals based on follow-up assessment four years later. These investigators concluded that AAMI is a relatively benign condition that does not follow a progressive course. Several limitations of this study, however, are worth noting. First, a considerable number of participants that did not return for follow-up testing might have had greater decline than those that did, a phenomenon that is problematic for research of this type. Second, the subjects in this study, who were on average in their early sixties at the first assessment, were followed for a relatively brief interval of four years when the incidence of Alzheimer's disease continues to be low. Further examination of such individuals into later decades might be needed to provide a better indication of the course of AAMI.

A related issue in the definition of normal aging concerns the observation of individual differences in the elderly population. As indicated above, cognitive decline is evident in some individuals in the elderly population (e.g. AAMI), whereas function is better preserved in other aged individuals. In contrast with the usual individual differences that exist at earlier points in development, variability is often described as markedly increased with advancing age. In accordance with this description, a recent survey of published data found greater variability (coefficients of variation) among the elderly compared with young adults on a number of measures widely reported to be sensitive to aging, e.g. reaction time, memory, and fluid intelligence (Morse 1993). Although this phenomenon is often observed, the origin of increased variability in aging is not well defined. Perhaps variability in aging reflects differences that are expressed only in the later decades of life. Alternatively, individual differences might become magnified late in life because of the cumulative impact of different biological and experiential backgrounds over many decades. More information about factors underlying individual differences will be important for understanding normal aging.

The discussion above provides a background for considering the usefulness of animal models in the study of aging. The likelihood that the same pathological processes in human disease occur and are manifest in identical ways across several species could be considered quite low. Many progressive neurological diseases such as Alzheimer's do not afflict species commonly used in laboratory research on aging, e.g. rats, mice, monkeys. However, it is reasonable to expect that at least some features that characterize biological aging of the mammalian brain would be evident in different species. Thus, commonalities across species might help to identify normal neurobiological aging, as distinct from pathological conditions, and those psychological functions most affected by aging.

The use of laboratory animals can address other aspects of human aging that have proven difficult to study in a systematic way. If normal aging is characterized by increased variability, this phenomenon of individual differences might be evident in other species. Because cohorts of laboratory animals can be maintained under relatively controlled conditions it should also be possible to isolate factors contributing to such individual differences.

The relevance of research with laboratory animals for an understanding of human aging, however, depends on whether the specific functions and biological systems targeted for study are appropriate models for human aging. Scientific advances over the past few decades have provided a foundation for developing useful animal models of aging. We outline a framework currently employed for investigating the neurobiological basis of functional changes in aging. The approach is built on a background of research in neuropsychology, cognitive psychology, and neuroscience.

The field of neuropsychology originally led to clinical descriptions and psychometric profiles for certain types of brain damage as an aid to diagnosis. Because the consequences of certain forms of damage were remarkably selective, neuropsychological studies also came to serve as a basis for making inferences about the normal function of specific brain regions. Alongside developments that came from neuropsychological research, cognitive psychology has greatly contributed to our understanding of psychological processes. Cognitive psychology studies the components and organization of functions such as memory within the framework of information processing and representation. As a related burgeoning field, cognitive neuroscience is building on advances in psychology using new technologies, such as functional neuroimaging and methods for recording the ensemble encoding of information by neurons, to study information processing in the brain. Research derived from these traditions of neuropsychology and cognitive neuroscience has contributed to the development of animal models in the study of aging, as exemplified by the areas covered in the following sections.

MEDIAL TEMPORAL LOBE SYSTEM

Psychological Functions of the Medial Temporal Lobe

Patients with medial temporal lobe damage have circumscribed deficits in memory; the syndrome includes an anterograde amnesia and spares remote memory and general intellectual capacities (Corkin 1984, Scoville & Milner 1957). Anterograde amnesia refers to the inability to remember new information and episodes of life that occur after medial temporal lobe damage. The anterograde memory impairment is considered to represent a defect in mechanisms that allow long-term retention of new material. In support of this concept many domains of information processing and immediate memory (e.g. digit span) are preserved in these amnesic patients. Moreover, the recognition that patients with such amnesia have areas of preserved memory, e.g. priming and skill learning, advanced the concept that the brain possesses multiple memory systems (Cohen & Squire 1980). The domain of memory in medial temporal lobe amnesia is variously described as declarative or explicit memory, referring to representations in memory that provide a basis for the conscious recollection of facts and events.

Research using animal models has sought to define the components of the medial temporal lobe that contribute to the amnesic syndrome. Considerable evidence for deficits in declarative memory has been obtained in other species, but agreement has not yet been achieved about the underlying structures subserving memory within the medial temporal system. The most widely used animal model under study in this area of research is a recognition memory task performed by rhesus (or cynomolgous) monkeys (Squire & Zola-Morgan 1991). In this delayed nonmatch-to-sample task, monkeys are presented with an object on an information trial. After a variable delay, the original object is presented with a novel object, and selection of the novel object is rewarded. Considerable consensus surrounds the observation that damage to cortical regions of the medial temporal lobe (perirhinal, entorhinal, parahippocampal cortex) produces a significant delay-dependent deficit in this object-recognition task (Meunier et al 1993, Suzuki et al 1993). Less consensus has been achieved concerning the effects of damage confined to the hippocampus (Murray 1996). However, it is clear that damage to the hippocampus alone produces less severe impairment than damage restricted to the cortical regions of the medial temporal lobe. It is interesting to note that relatively similar findings have been reported in studies of rodents designed to parallel the delayed nonmatch-to-sample task used with monkeys. Damage to cortical structures associated with the hippocampal formation produces delay-dependent impairments that are not observed after selective damage to the hippocampus (Otto & Eichenbaum 1992, Wilner et al 1993).

Different perspectives are offered to account for findings in this line of research. By one view, a common function in memory is served by the component medial temporal lobe cortical regions and the hippocampus, with more severe impairment resulting from more extensive damage to this system (Squire & Zola-Morgan 1991). Another view is that the components of this system may serve somewhat different functions in declarative memory. For example, the relative insensitivity of delayed nonmatch-to-sample tasks to damage of the hippocampus alone may indicate that the medial temporal cortical regions can subserve memory representation for individual items independent of the hippocampus, while the hippocampus is essential for the formation of more complex representations in memory (Eichenbaum et al 1994). In agreement with this distinction, certain representations that provide a basis for the flexible use of information in memory appear to be highly sensitive to selective hippocampal damage in laboratory animals. For example, it has been argued that spatial information is an exemplar of this type of representation, and it is well documented that severe deficits in spatial tasks are observed after lesions of the hippocampus. Another instance of memory representation sensitive to disruption of the hippocampus comes from a study using probes for memory after animals were trained on a set of nonspatial stimulus-stimulus associations. Normal rats demonstrated two forms of flexible memory that were not shown by rats with selective hippocampal lesions, i.e. transitivity, reflected in the ability to compare across stimulus pairs that share a common element, and symmetry, referring to the ability to associate paired elements presented in the reverse of the training order (Bunsey & Eichenbaum 1996).

Additional research is needed to establish more firmly whether the brain regions that comprise the medial temporal lobe are functionally heterogeneous with respect to their roles in declarative memory. Further advances in this area of cognitive neuroscience will continue to provide an important background for understanding the neurobiological basis of altered memory processes in the elderly.

Psychological Functions of the Medial Temporal Lobe in Normal Aging: Human Beings

The characteristics of memory impairment in presumably healthy elderly adults appear to parallel the general features of medial temporal lobe amnesia (Craik & Jennings 1992). Remote memory and immediate memory (e.g. digit span) are spared. Elderly subjects, however, perform more poorly on typical tests of declarative memory (e.g. paired associates, delayed paragraph recall). Such deficits point to involvement of medial temporal lobe structures. Evidence that alterations in the medial temporal lobe may underlie age-associated memory impairment is noted above; Golomb et al (1993) found that elderly individuals with hippocampal atrophy performed less well on tests of delayed recall.

Functional neuroimaging studies are now providing new information about the relative activation of this system in young and elderly individuals during performance of memory tasks. Grady et al (1995) measured cerebral blood flow during encoding and recognition of faces. They reported that poorer memory performance in healthy elderly individuals relative to young individuals was associated with a reduction in hippocampal and prefrontal cortical activation during encoding. In the context of this observation, it is noteworthy that hypoactivity in the medial temporal lobe is not invariably observed in the brains of elderly subjects. In contrast with the results of Grady et al, another recent study found comparable medial temporal lobe activation in young and elderly subjects during successful recall (Schacter et al 1996). In that experiment, a word-stem completion task was administered to produce either high or low recall of study words. When neuroimaging was done during retrieval tests, equivalent hippocampal activation in young and aged groups was observed during successful recollection (high recall versus either low recall or baseline), which indicates that an age-related deficiency localized to the medial temporal lobe does not occur in all conditions where hippocampal activation is observed. These results also suggest that memory deficits in the elderly are not due to deficient medial temporal function during the retrieval of information. Rather, deficits may be attributable, at least in part, to a functional impairment in medial temporal lobe processing of new information, i.e. encoding, that serves as a basis for later recognition or recall.

Before turning to the examination of memory performance in aged laboratory animals, we reiterate that age-associated memory impairment is not evident in all individuals in the elderly human population. Thus, it is of interest in studies of laboratory animals to assess whether similarities can be found in the effects of aging on memory that resemble those features encountered in human beings and to determine whether individual differences also exist in other species over the course of aging.

Psychological Functions of the Medial Temporal Lobe in Normal Aging: Animal Models

The delayed nonmatching-to-sample task used to assess recognition memory in young monkeys with medial temporal lobe damage has also been used to test aged monkeys (Moss et al 1988, Presty et al 1987, Rapp & Amaral 1989). Although aged monkeys have difficulty in learning this task with a very brief retention interval, given sufficient training virtually all older subjects are able to reach a criterion equivalent to young monkeys. When the memory demands are then manipulated by increasing delays, monkeys approximately 25 years or older are impaired. Individual differences in recognition memory among aged monkeys are also observed, with an impairment in a subset of aged monkeys that qualitatively resembles the effect of medial temporal lobe damage in young monkeys (Rapp & Amaral 1991). Furthermore, aged monkeys with such deficits also perform more poorly on rapidly learned two-choice object discrimination problems, another assessment that is sensitive to medial temporal lobe damage (Rapp 1993). An additional parallel in the pattern of impairment across aged monkeys and young monkeys with medial temporal lobe damage is found in a task that increases the load of information in memory.

Subjects are tested for identification of each new item added to an array of previously presented items (Killiany et al 1995). Thus, studies of nonhuman primates have demonstrated memory impairments on tests sensitive to the integrity of the medial temporal lobe. Moreover, the presence and/or severity of such deficits varies considerably in the aged population. Because the neural substrate within the medial temporal lobe system for the most commonly used task in this research, delayed nonmatching-to-sample, is not clearly defined, age-related impairment on this assessment might reflect alterations in medial temporal lobe cortical systems either alone or together with alterations in the hippocampus.

Other evidence for alterations in the hippocampus in aged monkeys comes from a report of impairment in the flexible use of information in memory. As noted in the prior section, a test for the use of information in memory that is sensitive to selective damage of the hippocampus has recently been demonstrated by probes for transitive inference in rodents. After learning a set of stimulus-stimulus associations, young intact rats infer relations among the items, an ability that is lacking in rats with lesions confined to the hippocampus (Bunsey & Eichenbaum 1996). In a recent study, monkeys that learned a hierarchy of object-object discriminations were tested for their use of information in memory. The performance of aged monkeys during probes failed to show response latency effects that are taken to reflect the relational processing of information that underlies transitive inference (Rapp et al 1996).

Deficits that are widely studied in aged rodents in spatial tasks may also reflect a declarative memory impairment. Aged rats, like young rats with damage to the hippocampus, have deficits in a variety of spatial tasks (for an overview, see Gallagher et al 1995). Moreover, impaired spatial learning in aged rats or in young rats with hippocampal damage can be demonstrated to occur independent of decline in sensorimotor/motivational functions and in learning that is guided by a stimulus or object used as a local cue (Gage et al 1989, Gallagher et al 1993). In addition, individual differences have been particularly well documented in this line of research. Among certain strains of rats, a proportion of aged animals exhibit highly preserved performance on such tasks, while other aged cohorts perform entirely outside the range of young rats (Gallagher et al 1993).

With respect to the neurological basis for impairments of aged rodents on spatial tasks, note that these tests do not provide an entirely selective assessment of the function of the hippocampus (Gage et al 1984). For example, young rats with lesions of cortical systems interconnected with hippocampus, e.g. entorhinal/perirhinal cortex, also exhibit deficits in spatial tasks (Nagahara et al 1995). Thus additional assessment is needed to distinguish between impairment that may have a basis in the altered status of the hippocampus versus these cortical regions. As noted earlier, a version of delayed nonmatch-to-sample developed for studies of rodents has revealed a sensitivity to entorhinal/perirhinal cortex damage that was not seen after selective damage to the hippocampus in young rats (Otto & Eichenbaum 1992). A recent study reported that aged rats that learned this task at short retention intervals performed no differently than young rats when increasing delays were introduced (Zyzak et al 1995). The same rats used in this assessment were also evaluated in a spatial task where an age-related deficit was observed. Thus, aged rats that are impaired in a spatial task that is sensitive to the integrity of the hippocampus can display intact performance on an assessment that is more selectively sensitive to the integrity of related cortical regions in the temporal lobe. Such results support the concept that impairment in spatial tasks reflects an effect of aging on the hippocampus.

Behavioral studies demonstrating a decline in functions associated with medial temporal lobe structures in laboratory animals provide evidence for age-associated memory impairment independent of pathological conditions that affect the elderly human population. Moreover, individual differences in aging are often documented in studies of nonhuman primates and rodents, which provides an additional parallel with observations in human beings.

Neurobiology of Aging in the Medial Temporal Lobe

Much current research in laboratory animals is directed at the neurobiological basis of decline in cognitive functions associated with the medial temporal lobe. Two concepts about the basis for this decline in aging, which have prevailed for several decades, have recently come under new scrutiny. In the first case, neurodegeneration within the hippocampus had been thought to play a significant role (Meaney et al 1988). A second influential concept held that degeneration in the basal forebrain cholinergic system, a component of which innervates the hippocampus and related cortical structures, provides a basis for memory deficits in aging (Bartus et al 1982). In each case, recent studies indicate that these long-standing concepts may be incorrect. After discussing the research dealing with those topics, we consider other potential substrates for age-related loss of function in the medial temporal lobe system.

The conclusion that neuron loss occurs in the aged hippocampus was reached in earlier studies of human, nonhuman primate, and rodent brains (Brizzee et al 1980, Dam 1979, Issa et al 1990, Meaney et al 1988). In some of these reports, the concept that neurodegeneration causes age-related cognitive decline was further bolstered by evidence that the presence and severity of behavioral impairment were correlated with loss of principal neurons in the hippocampus (Issa et al 1990). It is important to note, however, that studies of neurodegeneration were originally based on methods for estimating neuron density. Neurodegeneration is now being studied using new methods that are unbiased for many factors that could influence measures of neuron density, such as the size of neurons and the size or composition of nonneural cells, and so forth. Recent results using these new methods for measuring the total number of neurons in a brain structure indicate that no neuron loss appears to occur in the hippocampus during normal aging across a variety of species.

Studies of aging in human, nonhuman primate, and rat brain have now shown equivalent numbers of the principal neurons (Figure 1) in the hippocampus (Rapp & Gallagher 1996, Rasmussen et al 1996, West 1993, West et al 1993). Moreover, the recent anatomical studies of rats showed that even aged animals with substantial deficits indicating hippocampal dysfunction exhibited no loss of neurons in this structure. For example, Rapp & Gallagher (1996) observed a wide range of spatial ability in the aged rats included in their study but relatively little variability in numbers of hippocampal neurons and no suggestion of a decline in neuron number associated with age or behavioral impairment.

Additional evidence indicates that neuron number is preserved in the hippocampal formation of aged nonhuman primates, including those monkeys with identified memory impairment (West et al 1993). In addition to comparable numbers of principal neurons in the hippocampus proper, this study found no significant loss of neurons in cortical regions associated with the hippocampal formation (e.g. entorhinal cortex and subiculum). This finding is particularly noteworthy because a subset of the aged monkeys had deficits in recognition memory assessed in delayed nonmatch-to-sample, a task that is sensitive to the integrity of cortical areas in the medial temporal lobe.

Neurodegeneration in the hippocampus was formerly viewed as an inevitable consequence of normal aging. Reports that the principal neurons of the hippocampus are preserved across a variety of species, even in the presence of substantial behavioral impairment, may prompt a shift in the view that neuronal loss in this structure serves as a basis for age-related cognitive decline. Neurodegeneration in the hippocampus also appears to distinguish certain pathological conditions from normal aging. In contrast with normal aging, stereological methods detect significant reductions in the number of principal neurons in the hippocampus in individuals with diagnosed Alzheimer's disease (West et al 1994).

A second long-standing concept about the neurobiological basis of cognitive decline in aging has focused on the basal forebrain cholinergic system (Bartus et al 1982). Cholinergic neurons within this system that are located in the medial septum and vertical limb of the diagonal band (MS/vDB) provide innervation of the hippocampus and related medial temporal cortex (Koliatsos et al 1990). Atrophy and degeneration of these neurons is detected in aged brains (Fischer et al 1989, Smith & Booze 1995, Stroessner-Johnson et al 1992), and marked pathology affects this system in Alzheimer's disease

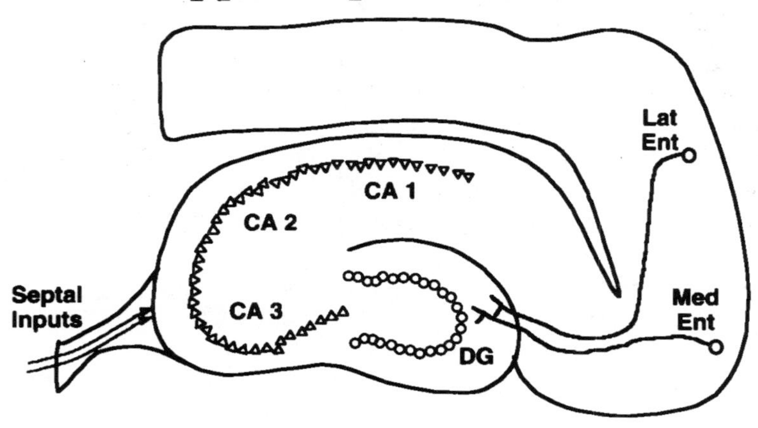

Figure 1 The schematic shows the principal neurons of the hippocampal formation, the granule cells of the dentate gyrus (DG), and the pyramidal neurons of the hippocampus proper (areas CA1–CA3). Two major input pathways to the hippocampal formation are illustrated. Input from the lateral and medial entorhinal cortex (Lat Ent and Med Ent) provides highly processed information and terminates primarily on the dendrites of the granule cells in the dentate gyrus. A subcortical pathway (Septal Inputs) enters through another route and provides widespread innervation of the hippocampal formation. This latter input includes the cholinergic innervation of the hippocampal formation. A trisynaptic circuit through the hippocampus (not shown) begins with the synapses formed by the entorhinal cortex projection onto the dentate granule cells. Those cells in turn project to the CA3 area. The CA3 pyramidal neurons form a third set of synapses within this structure, projecting onto the pyramidal cells in the CA1 area.

(Coyle et al 1983, Davies & Maloney 1976). It is further noteworthy that the number and size of these neurons are affected by age across a variety of species, including rats, monkeys, and human beings. The possibility that neurodegeneration within this population of neurons contributes to functional impairment has found support in numerous studies showing that the amount of cholinergic neuron deterioration is related to the severity of behavioral deficit in aged subjects (for an overview, see Gallagher et al 1995). Note that the vast majority of these correlational studies have used rat performance on spatial tasks as the behavioral assessment. Recent evidence, however, challenges the conclusion that deterioration of cholinergic neurons can account for age-related impairments in spatial tasks (Gallagher & Colombo 1995). At issue in this line of research is not whether degeneration occurs within the basal forebrain cholinergic system, but whether that effect of aging causes behavioral decline.

One way to assess the contribution of the septohippocampal cholinergic system to age-related impairments is to examine whether removing these neurons in young animals reproduces the deficits observed in aging. A newly developed immunotoxin 192 IgG-saporin can be used to target selectively basal forebrain cholinergic neurons. After injection of the immunotoxin into the MS/vDB, a nearly complete removal of the cholinergic innervation of the hippocampus can be achieved. It has come as a surprise, given the cholinergic hypothesis of age-related impairment, that immunotoxin-induced lesions of the septohippocampal cholinergic system fail to produce reliable spatial learning deficits (Baxter et al 1995a, 1996; Berger-Sweeney et al 1994, Torres et al 1994). Young rats with over 90% depletion of the cholinergic-specific enzyme choline acetyltransferase (ChAT) in hippocampus perform normally on a spatial learning protocol that is highly sensitive to deficits in aged rats (Baxter et al 1995a), and no impairment is even detected after removal of the entire basal forebrain cholinergic system, including the input to the hippocampal formation and the widespread innervation of the cerebral cortex (Baxter et al 1996). Moreover, comparable cholinergic lesions in aged rats do not appear to exacerbate or induce impairment in spatial tasks (Baxter & Gallagher 1996). Thus it is unlikely that deterioration in the septohippocampal cholinergic system by itself provides a sufficient basis for age-related deficits that are commonly observed in spatial tasks. We return in a later section of this review to the function of the cholinergic innervation of the hippocampus and its possible contribution to behavioral deficits in aging.

A current theme in research on normal aging is that a reduction in the number of synaptic connections, rather than frank neurodegeneration, provides a basis for age-related alterations in cognition. For example, atrophy and degeneration in the basal forebrain cholinergic system is likely to result in some loss of hippocampal innervation by these neurons. In agreement with this expectation, the cholinergic response mediated by stimulation of the septohippocampal input is reduced in all areas of the aged rat hippocampal formation (Shen & Barnes 1996). However, the failure of specific cholinergic lesions to reproduce memory deficits that have been well documented in aged rodents makes it unlikely that this alteration, by itself, serves a broad basis for impairments in aged rats.

Apart from the subcortical input to the hippocampus that originates in the septal region, an additional loss of synaptic input from another source is well documented to occur in aging. That input, which provides the primary route for transfer of highly processed cortical information to the hippocampus, derives from neurons in the entorhinal cortex (refer to Figure 1). Ultrastructural studies of rat brain have demonstrated a significant loss of synaptic connections in the hippocampal formation that are formed by entorhinal cortex input (Geinisman et al 1992). In addition, individual differences in cognitive decline among aged rats are reported to coincide with differences in the loss of this innervation (Geinisman et al 1986). Reduced numbers of synaptic connections may also occur in other areas of the hippocampal formation (Barnes et al 1994).

It might be reasonable to expect that reduced numbers of synaptic connections in the hippocampal formation could provide a basis for behavioral deficits that depend on the integrity of this system. However, it should be recognized that a number of factors might argue against that outcome. Neurobiological systems possess a number of mechanisms that are geared to maintain function. Considerable evidence indicates that such mechanisms are recruited in the aged brain. For example, although fewer synaptic connections are made in the dentate gyrus of the hippocampal formation in aged rats, the response to input at the remaining synapses is greatly increased (Foster et al 1991). In addition, a loss of synapses from cortical input induces a sprouting response in which new connections are formed by inputs from other sources. Evidence for such sprouting in the hippocampal dentate gyrus has come from studies of aged brains and is also observed in Alzheimer's disease (Geddes et al 1992, Nicolle et al 1996). This type of sprouting may be compensatory in nature, as new connections are made to replace those that are lost. However, such reactive growth may not always be beneficial. New connections might add to the adverse effects of aging because they come from a different source than the original input. Studies of aging often lack the functional analysis necessary to distinguish between these possibilities. Recent studies using behavioral assessment along with neurobiological analysis are being conducted to evaluate whether such alterations in the brain provide protection or impose further adverse effects on outcome (Nicolle et al 1996, Stack et al 1995, Stenvers et al 1996). If a neurobiological response in the aged brain is compensatory, then the degree to which this response occurs should predict a better outcome, i.e. less behavioral impairment. However, if a reactive process only adds to dysfunction then the presence of such a change in the brain might be associated with greater impairment. Research of this type should lead to a better understanding of the consequences of reactive and reorganizational processes that occur in the aged brain.

Studies of neurodegeneration and synaptic connectivity provide important information about structural features of the brain during aging. Apart from such structural features, effects of aging are evident in the functional integrity of existing neurons and connections. Such changes may be important factors in diminishing the overall performance of the medial temporal lobe system during aging.

Neurons in the hippocampal system possess a complex array of biological mechanisms for information processing. In addition to specialized receptors for specific inputs, receptors are coupled to a variety of transduction systems that are necessary to produce physiological responses to those inputs (refer to Figure 2). Furthermore, transduction mechanisms are not only used for the processing of information transmitted between neurons but also play a role in altering the functional properties of synaptic connections. Long-term potentiation (LTP), referring to the long-lasting increase in the effectiveness of synaptic connections that can be readily induced in the hippocampal system, has attracted widespread interest as a possible physiological mechanism for the storage of information in the mammalian brain.

Studies on transduction mechanisms may provide insight into the basis for changes in information processing and information storage during aging. The findings from such research are especially informative in a system where neurodegeneration is not a prominent feature of aging. In such a setting, measurable decreases in components of transduction systems, including receptors, coupling mechanisms, and second and third messengers, do not merely reflect a loss of neurons but indicate a change in the functional integrity of existing neurons. For this reason, recent evidence for preserved numbers of

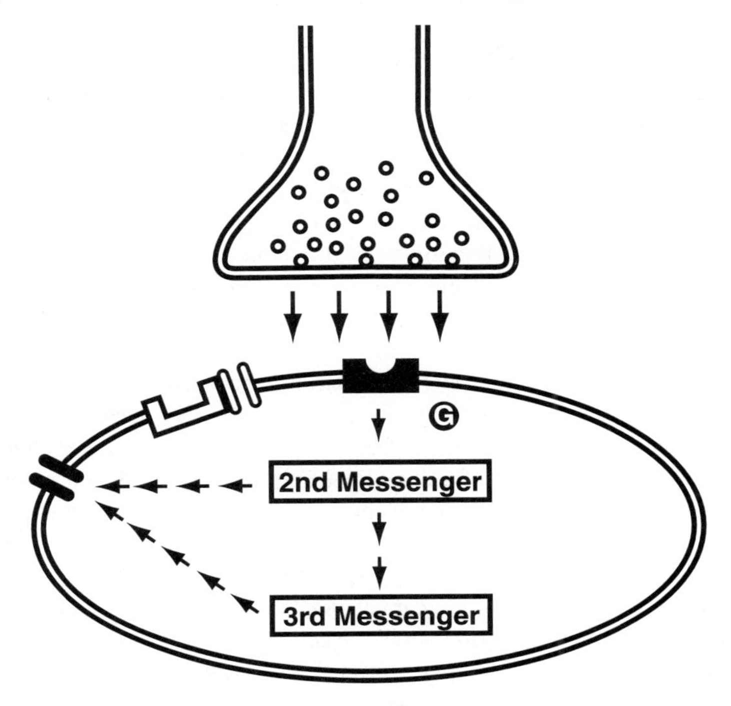

Figure 2 Schematic illustrates interneuron communication. Transmission from an input produces a postsynaptic response through a variety of transduction mechanisms. The components of this communication system include receptors that either directly regulate a neuron's excitability or work through biochemical cascades (2nd and 3rd messenger systems).

neurons in the hippocampus is important for interpreting the effects of aging on other neurobiological measures.

In addition to an absence of frank neurodegeneration within the hippocampus during aging, at least some types of receptors that serve as targets for neurotransmitters are also relatively unaffected by aging in this structure. For example, substantial preservation of postsynaptic receptors for acetylcholine is reported in a number of studies (Chouinard et al 1995, Quirion et al 1995, Smith et al 1995). To the extent that postsynaptic targets are preserved, then strategies to address the effects of aging might be developed to increase function at these sites. Such a rationale has served as a basis for developing drugs to compensate for age-related deterioration of the basal forebrain cholinergic neurons. Acetylcholinesterase inhibitors (e.g. Tacrine) are intended to augment the action of acetylcholine at its receptors in the forebrain by preventing the degradation of this transmitter (Davis et al 1992, Thal et al 1989). Because such drug treatments can improve cognitive function in young rats, some benefit might be achieved in aged animals even if the basis for impairment is not solely due to a cholinergic defect (Gallagher & Colombo 1995). The effectiveness of augmenting cholinergic function would depend, however, on an intact physiological response at cholinergic receptors. In the case of those receptors, however, a blunted response to cholinergic stimulation has recently been documented in the aged rodent hippocampus (Chouinard et al 1995, Undie et al 1995). In one of these studies, a greater reduction in the postsynaptic response to cholinergic stimulation was seen in aged rats that were found to have more pronounced cognitive impairment (Chouinard et al 1995). Moreover, the neurobiological defect in this case appeared to reside at a point in the biochemical machinery that would potentially affect the physiological response to other transmitter/receptor inputs that use the same transduction pathway.

In addition to the role that transduction mechanisms serve in information processing, long-lasting changes in the properties of synapses depend on the functional integrity of neurons. It has long been recognized that alterations in the mechanisms required for neural plasticity could provide a basis for cognitive decline during aging. One of the earliest studies of individual differences in spatial learning in aged rats showed that this impairment correlated with a deficiency in neural plasticity in hippocampus (Barnes 1979). In those experiments an in vivo study of LTP at perforant/dentate synapses was conducted in the same rats that were behaviorally tested in a spatial learning task. Although asymptotic (saturated) LTP did not differ between the age groups, this LTP was achieved less readily and decayed more rapidly in the aged rats than in young rats. Furthermore, the impairment in behavioral learning was significantly correlated with the effect of aging on LTP. Additional studies continue to document that LTP is adversely affected during the aging process (Barnes &

McNaughton 1985, Moore et al 1993). A modest loss of the receptors required for induction of LTP may occur in the aged hippocampus in both primates and rodents (Clark et al 1992, Gazzaley et al 1996, Nicolle et al 1996, Wang et al 1996). A highly active area of research aimed at defining the mechanisms underlying LTP in adult animals will provide a route for better understanding the basis of the deterioration seen in aging.

Consistent with a variety of evidence for functional alterations in the aged hippocampal formation, recording the activity of hippocampal neurons while animals perform certain tasks has provided evidence that the representation of information in this system is altered in older animals. Such studies have shown less reliability and specificity of the information encoded by hippocampal neurons (Barnes et al 1983, Mizumori et al 1996; but see Markus et al 1994). In a recent study of aged rats, individual differences were also evident. In aged rats that were impaired in a cognitive assessment of spatial learning, representations of relationships among stimuli in a spatial environment were relatively impoverished and inflexible compared with either young rats or aged cohorts with preserved behavioral functions (Tanila et al 1996). Further research of this type will help to elucidate the computational cost of the neurobiological effects of aging within this brain system. Identification of mechanisms underlying diminished function within that circuitry will undoubtedly provide an impetus to the development of new therapeutic strategies to treat age-related impairment.

In conclusion, cognitive impairments that resemble those seen in elderly human beings can be observed in the study of aged laboratory animals. Individual differences in the effects of aging on tasks sensitive to the integrity of the medial temporal lobe are also mirrored in the presence and severity of some neurobiological changes found in this system. Beyond the effort to construct a description of normal aging, research using animal models promises to provide a setting for productive research on mechanisms of brain aging. This may include a better understanding of how the rate or severity of aging provides a basis for individual differences in cognitive abilities late in life.

FRONTAL LOBE SYSTEMS

Psychological Functions of Frontal Lobe Systems

In contrast with amnesia resulting from medial temporal lobe damage, human beings with frontal lobe lesions perform accurately on many standard tests of declarative memory (reviewed in Moscovitch & Ulmita 1991). Current perspectives instead emphasize that the prefrontal cortex supports a variety of organizational processes that importantly influence the strategic use of memory. In addition, compelling evidence has revealed functional heterogeneity across the regions comprising the prefrontal cortex. A popular view is that these areas function in a "central executive" capacity, mediating the on-line manipulation of memory, particularly under circumstances emphasizing the spatial, temporal, or other contextual attributes of acquired information (reviewed in Moscovitch & Ulmita 1991). Recent evidence consistent with this view comes from neuroimaging studies in normal human subjects. Cerebral blood flow is selectively increased in a region of the dorsolateral prefrontal cortex when memory for temporal order is necessary for successful performance relative to conditions involving the same sensory and motor demands but lacking a temporal order component (Petrides et al 1993a,b). A slightly more posterior prefrontal region (area 8), by comparison, is activated during a conditional discrimination procedure placing relatively greater emphasis on the environmental contingencies governing ongoing behavior (Petrides et al 1993a). Such data support the concept that the prefrontal cortex comprises a variety of functionally distinct subsystems. In addition, this background of information helps to account for the pattern of impairments observed following frontal lobe damage, which includes prominent deficits in memory for temporal order, impaired recall for the source of acquired information (i.e. source amnesia), and difficulties modifying behavior appropriately in response to changing environmental contingencies (i.e. perseveration) (Janowsky et al 1989a,b; Shimamura et al 1990).

Another feature of specialization within the prefrontal cortex is suggested by studies focusing on the component processes of declarative memory, e.g. encoding, retrieval, and so forth. As noted previously, encoding processes and the successful conscious recollection of events are associated with hippocampal activation (Grady et al 1995, Schacter et al 1996). Lateralized prefrontal cortical activation is particularly associated with effortful retrieval of information from memory (Schacter et al 1996). This observation supports the concept that the activity of prefrontal cortex is engaged by specific retrieval strategies in support of declarative memory (Buckner & Petersen 1996). By this account, successful performance on tests of declarative memory in patients with frontal damage presumably reflects the utilization of alternate retrieval mechanisms mediated by intact structures. Findings from studies of normal human aging, reviewed in the next section, are consistent with this proposal.

Psychological Functions of Frontal Lobe Systems in Normal Aging: Human Beings

Although deficits in declarative memory are frequently observed in the elderly, older subjects exhibit a variety of impairments that would not be anticipated as a consequence of dysfunction restricted to the medial temporal lobe. Many of the most prominent and consistent signs of age-related cognitive decline instead occur in the information-processing capacities traditionally associated with the prefrontal cortex (for recent reviews, see Rapp & Heindel 1994, Shimamura 1994). For example, normal elderly individuals have difficulty remembering the source of acquired information (Janowsky et al 1989b, McIntyre & Craik 1987, Naveh-Benjamin & Craik 1995), even under circumstances where explicit recollection of target items is relatively intact (Dywan et al 1994, Glisky et al 1995). Source memory deficits can also predict performance on other tests of frontal lobe function, which suggests that a common neurobiological basis may underlie these impairments (Craik et al 1990, Glisky et al 1995; but see Spencer & Raz 1994). A further parallel with the effects of frank frontal lobe damage is that memory for temporal order appears particularly susceptible to decline as human beings age (Daigneault & Braun 1993, Parkin et al 1995).

It is noteworthy that certain impairments associated with the function of prefrontal cortex emerge relatively early in the life span, during middle-age, and are unrelated to the status of encoding and retrieval processes that support normal declarative memory. Moreover, when age-related impairments that resemble both medial temporal and prefrontal dysfunction coexist in the same persons, these cognitive deficits may be somewhat dissociable. A particularly interesting report relevant to this point studied healthy aged individuals between the ages of 65 and 87 years (Glisky et al 1995). Two factors were obtained in a factor analysis of the neuropsychological test data. Tests traditionally viewed as assessing the status of prefrontal cortex (e.g. Wisconsin Card Sorting) loaded onto one factor, whereas assessments of declarative memory sensitive to medial temporal lobe status (e.g. paired associates, delayed cued recall) loaded strongly onto a second factor. A subsequent study of item and source memory showed a double dissociation among these elderly individuals that corresponded with their relative functioning on medial temporal lobe and prefrontal assessments, respectively. In addition to suggesting that there is not necessarily an obligatory relationship in the effects of aging across different information processing domains, these data suggest that the underlying biological alterations that cause decline in medial temporal lobe- and prefrontal cortex–dependent functions may occur somewhat independently.

In agreement with the neuropsychological assessments of aged human beings noted above, assessment of the neurobiological status of the prefrontal cortex indicates its susceptibility to age-related decline. Cortical atrophy during normal human aging is especially pronounced in the frontal lobe, progressing at a rate greatly exceeding atrophy observed in the cerebral hemispheres as a whole (Coffey et al 1992). Measurements of regional cerebral blood flow under a variety of testing conditions also provide an indication of diminished function. One of the principal findings to emerge from this approach is that task demands sufficient to produce prefrontal cortical activation in young subjects fail to increase activity in this same region in older adults (Grady et al 1995). Neuroimaging has also localized different patterns of activation coincident with efforts to retrieve information, relative to activity induced by the conscious recollection of target items (Schacter et al 1996). In young subjects, retrieval efforts are accompanied by significant activation in anterior aspects of the frontal lobe, but a more posterior frontal region is activated in aged subjects under the same testing conditions. No age difference, in contrast, was observed during the successful recollection of target information, which predominantly engages medial temporal lobe structures. The interesting implication of these results is that when recollection is not readily achieved, young and aged subjects may use different retrieval strategies, mediated by distinct prefrontal processing systems. Independent of the validity of this particular hypothesis, it is evident that abnormalities in the activation of prefrontal cortex occur in relation to cognitive aging.

Psychological Functions of Frontal Lobe Systems in Normal Aging: Animal Models

The development of a nonhuman primate model of normal cognitive aging has revealed a number of interesting parallels with findings in human beings. Deficits on delayed response tests of short-term memory are among the most conspicuous and well characterized signs of behavioral decline in the aged monkey (Bartus et al 1978, Dean & Bartus 1988). In the standard delayed response task, a reward, placed in one of two locations, is retrieved by the monkey after a varying delay. There is compelling evidence, however, that the delayed response deficit is not necessarily symptomatic of a general memory impairment of the type that results from damage to the medial temporal lobe. For example, aged monkeys with pronounced delayed response deficits often perform normally on standard tests of recognition memory (i.e. delayed nonmatch-to-sample) and on a variety of other procedures that are sensitive to medial temporal lobe lesions (Bachevalier et al 1991, Rapp & Amaral 1989). In addition, delayed response impairments emerge relatively early in the life span, preceding the decline in memory abilities that require the functional integrity of the medial temporal lobe (Bachevalier et al 1991). Consistent with conclusions from human research discussed in the prior section (Glisky et al 1995), these findings emphasize that age effects are not uniform across different information-processing domains, and that medial temporal lobe dysfunction alone may fail to account for certain key features of cognitive aging in nonhuman primates (for recent reviews, see Dean & Bartus 1988, Rapp 1995).

A number of the behavioral impairments observed in aged monkeys appear to reflect a decline in memory-related processes mediated by the prefrontal cortex (Dean & Bartus 1988, Rapp 1995). In this context, a noteworthy aspect of standard delayed response testing is that it makes substantial demands on memory for temporal order. This is a consequence of the procedural arrangement in which a reward is hidden randomly, across trials, among a relatively small number of possible locations. Accurate performance therefore requires memory for the location baited most recently, and the ability to discriminate the current trial from information presented earlier in testing. Standard delayed response testing also incorporates an explicit spatial component that is thought to specifically engage processing functions of the dorsolateral prefrontal cortex (Wilson et al 1993). Consistent with the view that delayed response deficits reflect prefrontal cortical decline, aged monkeys exhibit deficits on other tasks as a function of demands on temporal ordering (Rapp & Amaral 1989). Increased perseveration is also observed in aged nonhuman primates (Anderson et al 1993, Bartus et al 1979), similar to effects seen in aged human beings (Janowsky et al 1989b), and qualitatively resembling the difficulties young subjects with frontal lobe damage display in modifying behavior under conditions of shifting task contingencies (Janowsky et al 1989a).

A unified perspective on the functional organization of the prefrontal cortex that accommodates results from both rats and primates has yet to be achieved. Nonetheless, studies of aged rats have noted a number of qualitative similarities with the behavioral effects of frontal lobe damage in young adult rats. In a direct comparison of this type, Winocur (1992) evaluated delayed nonmatch-to-sample performance in young and aged groups, and in young rats with lesions of either the prefrontal cortex or dorsal hippocampus. The sample stimulus in this operant procedure consisted of a panel light that was illuminated at one of two intensities. During the recognition phase of each trial, reward was contingent on the rat's committing or withholding a lever response (i.e. "go," "no-go") depending on whether a matching or nonmatching light intensity was presented. Similar to delayed response testing in monkeys, the opportunity for intertrial interference is substantial in this procedure, and successful performance requires animals to distinguish between the current sample and the same items presented in earlier trials. Aged rats, and young rats with prefrontal cortical lesions, displayed substantial acquisition deficits under conditions where no delay was imposed between the sample presentation and recognition test. In contrast, young rats with hippocampal lesions acquired the task at a normal rate. These findings broadly parallel results in monkeys and human beings, consistent with the view that the temporal organization of memory is significantly disrupted in the aged rat. Qualitative similarities in the effects of aging and direct prefrontal cortical damage have also been noted in studies using other behavioral testing procedures (Winocur 1991, Zyzak et al 1995).

Neurobiology of Aging in Frontal Lobe Systems

Compared with the research on the medial temporal lobe system reviewed above, only limited experimental attention has focused on defining the neurobiological consequences of prefrontal cortical aging. Recent neuroimaging, however, has revealed that metabolic activity in the monkey prefrontal cortex declines with age, and interestingly, that variability among aged subjects is substantially greater than among young animals (Eberling et al 1995). On this basis, it is tempting to speculate that individual differences in metabolic activity might predict the status of cognitive processes mediated by the prefrontal cortex. Preliminary findings from a study combining functional neuroimaging and delayed response assessment in the same subjects suggest that this may be the case (Roberts et al 1996).

Changes in the structural integrity of the prefrontal cortex are currently under examination as a possible basis for age-related cognitive decline. Consistent with a growing body of evidence indicating that neuron number is generally preserved during normal aging in the medial temporal lobe cortical structures (Rapp & Gallagher 1996, Rasmussen et al 1996, West 1993, West et al 1993; and see section on "Neurobiology of Aging in the Medial-Temporal Lobe"), Peters et al (1994) failed to observe any age-related decline in neuron density in the dorsolateral prefrontal cortex. A subjective scoring of white matter pathology in the same subjects, however, revealed prominent age effects, with the greatest degree of change apparently observed among aged monkeys that were most impaired on standard tests of learning and memory. Subtle age-related alterations in other morphological parameters have also been noted, including a decline in the dendritic arborization of prefrontal cortical neurons (Cupp & Uemura 1980). Providing an additional parallel with studies of the medial temporal lobe, structural features in the prefrontal cortex are relatively intact, with possibly greater alterations in neuropil and connectivity as opposed to frank neurodegeneration of cortical neurons.

Compared with the relatively preserved structural features of prefrontal cortex, considerable evidence points to a substantial impact of age on subcortical systems that project to cortex. In addition to the cholinergic neurons in the basal forebrain system, several collections of monoamine neurons in the brainstem appear to undergo significant degeneration and/or atrophy during aging (DeKeyser et al 1990, Irwin et al 1994). In young subjects, systemic pharmacological manipulations of noradrenergic and dopaminergic function significantly influence spatial and temporal aspects of memory, and at least some of these effects appear to be mediated at the level of cortical projection targets in the frontal lobe (Murphy et al 1996). These normative findings, then, lead to the expectation that age-related alterations in neurochemically defined subcortical projection systems might significantly disrupt information processing functions dependent on the prefrontal cortex.

Concerning the function of prefrontal cortex, considerable evidence indicates that age-related alterations in its dopaminergic innervation may be particularly important. This interpretation is consistent with electrophysiological results demonstrating that application of dopamine receptor antagonists can modulate the memory-related firing properties of single prefrontal cortical neurons (Williams & Goldman-Rakic 1995). Research addressing the neurochemistry of aging in the monkey indicates that endogenous dopamine concentrations are markedly reduced in the prefrontal cortex and that this decline is substantially greater than that observed in other cortical regions (Goldman-Rakic & Brown 1981, Wenk et al 1989). In addition, Luine et al (1990) observed that during aging in the rat, a dopamine deficiency in the frontal cortex was significantly correlated with impaired working memory performance on a radial maze. Although dopamine agonist administration in young subjects can affect a variety of behavioral domains including motor function, effects of dopaminergic agents in aged monkeys are selectively attenuated on tasks that require the functional integrity of the prefrontal cortex, such as the standard delayed response task (Arnsten et al 1995). Combined with a substantial body of earlier research (reviewed in Arnsten 1993), these findings raise the possibility that alterations in subcortical systems, such as the mesocortical dopaminergic neurons, might contribute to certain aspects of cognitive aging by disrupting the information processing functions of cortical target regions in the frontal lobe. This area of research also supports the broader theme, developed throughout this review, that cortical and subcortical brain systems are differentially sensitive to the neurobiological consequences of normal aging. The neurodegeneration often associated with brain aging appears to be more characteristic of certain subcortical systems that innervate forebrain structures than of cortical neurons themselves.

AGING AND ATTENTION IN HUMAN BEINGS AND ANIMAL MODELS

As noted in the preceding sections, certain effects of aging on cognition resemble, in mild form, damage to systems in the forebrain, including the medial temporal lobe and prefrontal cortex, for which a substantial background of neuropsychological research exists. Furthermore, neurobiological studies are beginning to provide an understanding of alterations in the brain that are most likely to serve as a basis for cognitive decline in functions associated with those systems. Alongside these areas of research, interest in the study of attention in aging has grown in recent years.

Attention refers to multiple component functions that are important in the selection and processing of information. The study of attention in aging is currently benefiting from advances in cognitive neuroscience that are providing a better definition of the neural systems that are critical for the normal regulation of attention. For example, these include systems that regulate overall levels of sustained attention (arousal or vigilance) and systems that are important for the selective processing of information among competing inputs. Sustained attention can be assessed in settings that require performance of a simple task without the subject losing track of the task objective, a function that appears to be little affected by aging (Albert & Moss 1996). In contrast, other evidence points to an effect of aging on the selective processing of information, particularly under conditions of competition among many items for processing resources (Greenwood et al 1993, Mouloua & Parasuraman 1995).

As recounted in the chapter in this volume on "Central Cholinergic Systems and Cognition" (Everitt & Robbins 1997), a role in the regulation of attention may represent the primary function of the basal forebrain cholinergic neurons that innervate cortex. Furthermore, a growing consensus now views the neurodegeneration within this system that occurs in aging, and to a more severe degree in Alzheimer's disease, as providing a basis for deficits in attention rather than underlying a decline in memory processes (Parasuraman & Haxby 1993).

The cholinergic neurons in the basal forebrain that provide widespread innervation of the cortex in rats, monkeys, and human beings are located posterior to the cholinergic neurons in the basal forebrain that target the hippocampal formation (Koliatsos et al 1990). Previous studies have revealed deficits in attention as a consequence of lesioning the area of the basal forebrain that supplies cortical cholinergic innervation. In one well-studied paradigm, such lesions interfere with the ability of rats to detect and respond to a briefly presented target stimulus that can appear in any of several locations (five-choice reaction time task) (Muir et al 1994, Robbins et al 1989). Those lesions decrease the accuracy of performance, an effect that can be overcome by increasing the target duration, which suggests that the impairment is attentional in nature. Impairments in the ability of aged rats to detect targets in the five-choice reaction time task that resemble the effects of basal forebrain lesions in young rats have recently been reported (Jones et al 1995). Another paradigm, a spatial cueing task originally designed for studies of attention in human beings, has also shown sensitivity to lesions of the basal forebrain in monkeys (Voytko et al 1994). Although the lesion methods used in this line of research with laboratory animals, until recently, have been relatively nonselective, removing both cholinergic and noncholinergic neurons in the basal forebrain, studies using a selective immunotoxin for cholinergic neurons have successfully produced deficits in attention when the cortical cholinergic projections are removed (Chiba et al 1995a,b).

The role of the basal forebrain cholinergic system in attention may extend to the component of this system that provides innervation of the hippocampal formation. As noted in an earlier section of this review, removal of those neurons with the selective immunotoxin fails to reproduce deficits in spatial tasks that are readily observed in aged rats (Baxter et al 1995a). In the chapter by Everitt & Robbins, the effects of less selective lesions are cited as evidence that the septohippocampal cholinergic system plays a role in memory. However, whether any substantial deficit in memory is observed with selective removal of these cholinergic neurons has yet to be demonstrated. In contrast, young rats with selective immunotoxic lesions of the cholinergic neurons that project to the hippocampal formation do have a marked impairment in a task in which attentional processing is modified in intact young rats (Baxter et al 1995b). The task involves repeated exposure to a cue that is subsequently used as a conditioned stimulus in associative learning. Preexposure to the cue usually retards subsequent learning, a phenomenon referred to as latent inhibition. Although more than one psychological explanation of latent inhibition has been offered, a number of explanations converge on the concept that decrements in attention to, or processing of, the preexposed cue serve as a basis for latent inhibition. In this context it is notable that either selective damage to the hippocampus (Han et al 1995) or selective removal of the cholinergic projection to the hippocampus impairs latent inhibition in rats (Baxter et al 1995b). The concept that a latent inhibition deficit might exist in aged rats because of diminished function of the cholinergic projection to the hippocampus has not yet been tested directly. It is interesting to note, however, that a recent study showed that information encoding of neurons in hippocampus in young rats will become unresponsive to cues that are not reliable features of a spatial environment, an effect not seen to the same extent in aged rats (Tanila et al 1996). Thus, apparently the selection of information that is subject to processing and encoding by hippocampal neurons is altered during aging in a manner that might be predicted from the effects of removing cholinergic neurons in young rats.

CONCLUSION

As information accumulates about the alterations that occur during aging in the brain, it becomes increasingly clear that a number of different types of changes can be identified in different neural systems. Moreover, the severity of age-related changes in particular brain systems often coincides with the extent of decline in cognitive functions associated with those systems. Certain evidence has also indicated that heterogeneity in the effects of aging may exist in different cognitive domains and neurobiological systems. All these lines of evidence suggest that aging is not a global process, a conclusion that can be applied to the information derived from animal models as well as human studies.

In those cases where comparisons can be made across studies of human beings and laboratory animals, an important insight into the neurobiology of aging is emerging. Research using advanced stereological methods indicates that neuron loss is not characteristic of cortical systems, including the hippocampus, but that neurodegeneration does affect distinct populations of subcortical neurons that provide cortical innervation. Apart from such structural features of the brain, other aspects of functional integrity are also affected during aging. Although many of the detailed analyses available from studies of animal models have yet to be extended to studies of human brains, neuroimaging research provides support for the concept that processing within the existing circuits of the brain can be compromised during aging.

The comparison of functional analyses across species, including neuroimaging research with human beings, highlights the need to advance new models for understanding the neurobiological basis of cognitive alterations that occur late in life. Aging differs from many conditions involving brain damage, which neuropsychological studies were originally intended to address. Animal models for those conditions frequently entail the virtual destruction of a brain system to test hypotheses about the underlying substrate for cognitive functions of interest, e.g. the medial temporal lobe and declarative memory. During normal aging, in contrast, substantial structural integrity is preserved over the entire life span, and neurons that do exhibit appreciable neurodegeneration, such as those in the basal forebrain cholinergic system, are by no means eliminated. For this reason, lesion models may have limited utility for capturing the performance of neural systems in the aged brain, in which considerable remodeling occurs and a variety of functional alterations within the existing systems can be detected (Gallagher et al 1994).

Finally, the theme of individual differences in aging is well supported by studies of laboratory animals, including behavioral models developed for their sensitivity to memory functions subserved by the medial temporal lobe. Moreover, individual differences in behavioral capacities within these models often correlate with the severity of neurobiological alterations in the relevant brain systems. These lines of research give credence to the concept that age-associated memory decline in human beings can reflect a normal aging process, as distinct from a preclinical condition that heralds dementia. An understanding of the basis for individual differences in the effects of aging is likely to be advanced by further studies on the neurobiology of aging using animal models as an important adjunct to the study of human beings. In this endeavor, it will be particularly important to determine the factors that distinguish those aged individuals that maintain preserved function from those that experience decline, an undertaking that will benefit from the bridges that can be formed between human beings and the study of aging in well-developed animal models.

ACKNOWLEDGMENTS

The authors wish to acknowledge Lisa Brooks for preparation of the figures, and grants AG09973 and KO5 MH 01149 to MG, and AG10606 to PR for support of the work.

Literature Cited

Albert MS, Moss MB. 1996. Neuropsychology of aging: findings in humans and monkeys. In *Handbook of the Biology of Aging,* ed. E Scheider, J Rowe, 4:217–30. San Diego: Academic

Anderson JR, Anthouard M, de Monte M, Kempf J. 1993. Differences in performance of young and old monkeys on a visuospatial memory task. *Q. J. Exp. Psychol.* 46B: 391–98

Arnsten AF. 1993. Catecholamine mechanisms in age-related cognitive decline. *Neurobiol. Aging* 14:639–41

Arnsten AF, Cai JX, Steere JC, Goldman-Rakic PS. 1995. Dopamine D2 receptor mechanisms contribute to age-related cognitive decline: the effects of quinpirole on memory and motor performance in monkeys. *J. Neurosci.* 15:3429–39

Bachevalier J, Landis LS, Walker LC, Brickson M, Mishkin M, et al. 1991. Aged monkeys exhibit deficits indicative of widespread cerebral dysfunction. *Neurobiol. Aging* 12:99–111

Barnes CA. 1979. Memory deficits associated with senescence: neurophysiological and behavioral study in the rat. *J. Comp. Physiol. Psychol.* 93:74–104

Barnes CA, McNaughton BL. 1985. An age-comparison of the rates of acquisition and forgetting of spatial information in relation to long-term enhancement of hippocampal synapses. *Behav. Neurosci.* 99:1040–48

Barnes CA, McNaughton BL, O'Keefe J. 1983. Loss of place specificity in hippocampal complex spike cells of senescent rat. *Neurobiol. Aging* 8:521–45

Barnes CA, Treves A, Rao G, Shen J. 1994. Electrophysiological markers of cognitive aging: region specificity and computational consequences. *Semin. Neurosci.* 6:359–67

Bartus RT, Dean RL, Beer B, Lippa AS. 1982. The cholinergic hypothesis of geriatric memory dysfunction. *Science* 217:408–18

Bartus RT, Dean RL, Fleming DL. 1979. Aging in the rhesus monkey: effects on visual discrimination learning and reversal learning. *J. Gerontol.* 34:209–19

Bartus RT, Fleming D, Johnson HR. 1978. Aging in the rhesus monkey: debilitating effects on short-term memory. *J. Gerontol.* 33:858–71

Baxter MG, Bucci DJ, Gorman LK, Wiley R, Gallagher M. 1995a. Selective immunotoxic lesions of basal forebrain cholinergic cells: effects on learning and memory in rats. *Behav. Neurosci.* 109:714–22

Baxter MG, Bucci DJ, Sobel TJ, Williams MJ, Gorman LK, Gallagher M. 1996. Intact spatial learning following lesions of basal forebrain cholinergic neurons. *NeuroReport* 7:1417–20

Baxter MG, Gallagher M. 1996. Intact spatial learning in both young and aged rats following selective removal of hippocampal cholinergic input. *Behav. Neurosci.* 110: 460–67

Baxter MG, Gallagher M, Holland PC. 1995b. Disruption of decremental attentional processing by selective removal of hippocampal cholinergic input. *Soc. Neurosci. Abstr.* 21:935

Berger-Sweeney J, Heckers S, Mesulam M-M, Wiley RG, Lappi DA, Sharma M. 1994. Differential effects on spatial navigation of immunotoxin-induced cholinergic lesions of the medial septal area and nucleus basalis magnocellularis. *J. Neurosci.* 14: 4507–19

Bondi MW, Salmon DP, Monsch AU, Galasko D, Butters N, et al. 1995. Episodic memory changes are associated with the APOE-4 allele in nondemented older adults. *Neurology* 45:2203–6

Brizzee KR, Ordy JM, Bartus RT. 1980. Localization of cellular changes within multimodal sensory regions in aged monkey brain: implications for age-related cognitive loss. *Neurobiol. Aging* 1:45–52

Buckner RL, Petersen SE. 1996. What does neuroimaging tell us about the role of prefrontal cortex in memory retrieval? *Semin. Neurosci.* 8:47–55

Bunsey M, Eichenbaum H. 1996. Conservation of hippocampal memory function in rats and humans. *Nature* 379:255–57

Chiba AA, Bucci DJ, Holland PC, Gallagher M. 1995b. Basal forebrain cholinergic lesions disrupt increments but not decrements in conditioned stimulus processing. *J. Neurosci.* 15:7315–22

Chiba AA, Bushnell PJ, Oshiro WM, Gallagher M. 1995a. Altered selective attention in rats with cholinergic lesions of the substantia innominata. *Soc. Neurosci. Abstr.* 21:936

Chouinard ML, Gallagher M, Yasuda RP, Wolfe BB, McKinney M. 1995. Hippocampal muscarinic receptor function in spatial learning-impaired aged rats. *Neurobiol. Aging* 16:955–63

Clark AS, Magnusson KR, Cotman CW. 1992. In vitro autoradiography of hippocampal excitatory amino acid binding in aged Fischer 344 rats: relationship to performance on the Morris water maze. *Behav. Neurosci.* 106:324–35

Coffey CE, Wilkinson WE, Parashos IA, Soady SAR, Sullivan RJ, et al. 1992. Quantitative cerebral anatomy of the aging human brain: a cross-sectional study using magnetic resonance imaging. *Neurology* 42:527–36

Cohen NJ, Squire LR. 1980. Preserved learning and retention of pattern-analyzing skill in amnesia: dissociation of "knowing how" and "knowing that." *Science* 210:207–9

Corder EH, Saunders AM, Strittmatter WJ, Schmechel DE, Gaskell PC, et al. 1993. Gene dose of apolipoprotein E type 4 allele and the risk of Alzheimer's disease in late onset families. *Science* 261:921–23

Corkin S. 1984. Lasting consequences of bilateral medial temporal lobectomy: clinical course and experimental findings in H. M. *J. Neurosci.* 2:1214–29

Coyle JT, Price DL, DeLong MR. 1983. Alzheimer's disease: a disorder of cortical cholinergic innervation. *Science* 219:1184–90

Craik FIM, Jennings JM. 1992. Human memory. In *Handbook of Aging and Cognition,* ed. FIM Craik, TA Salthouse, pp. 51–83. Hillsdale, NJ: Erlbaum

Craik FIM, Morris LW, Morris RG, Loewen ER. 1990. Relations between source amnesia and frontal lobe functioning in older adults. *Psychol. Aging* 5:148–51

Crook T, Bartus RT, Ferris SH, Whitehouse P, Cohen GD, Gershon S. 1986. Age-associated memory impairment: proposed diagnostic criteria and measures of clinical change: report of a NIMH work group. *Dev. Neuropsychol.* 2:261–76

Crystal H, Dickson D, Fuld P, Masur D, Scott R, et al. 1988. Clinico-pathologic studies in dementia: nondemented subjects with pathologically confirmed Alzheimer's disease. *Neurology* 38:1682–87

Cupp CJ, Uemura E. 1980. Age-related changes in prefrontal cortex *of Macaca mulatta:* quantitative analysis of dendritic branching patterns. *Exp. Neurol.* 69: 143–69

Daigneault S, Braun CM. 1993. Working memory and the self-ordered pointing task: further evidence of early prefrontal decline in normal aging. *J. Clin. Exp. Neuropsychol.* 15:881–95

Dam AM. 1979. The density of neurons in the human hippocampus. *Neuropathol. Appl. Neurobiol.* 5:249–64

Davies P, Maloney AJF. 1976. Selective loss of central cholinergic neurons in Alzheimer's disease. *Lancet* 2:1403

Davis KL, Thal LJ, Gamzu ER, Davis CS, Woolson RF, et al. 1992. A double-blind, placebo-controlled multicenter study of tacrine for Alzheimer's disease. *New Engl. J. Med.* 327:1253–59

Dean RL, Bartus RT. 1988. Behavioral models of aging in nonhuman primates. In *Handbook of Psychopharmacology,* ed. LL Iversen, SD Iversen, SH Snyder, 20: 325–92. New York: Plenum

DeKeyser J, Ebinger G, Vanquelin G. 1990. Age-related changes in the human nigrostriatal dopaminergic system. *Ann. Neurol.* 27:157–61

de Leon MJ, Golomb J, George AE, Convit A, Tarshish CY, et al. 1993. The radiologic prediction of Alzheimer Disease: the atrophic hippocampal formation. *Am. J. Neuroradiol.* 14:897–906

Dywan J, Segalowitz SJ, Williamson L. 1994. Source monitoring during name recognition in older adults: psychometric and electrophysiological correlates. *Psychol. Aging* 9:568–77

Eberling JL, Roberts JA, De Manincor DJ, Brennan KM, Hanrahan SM, et al. 1995. PET studies of cerebral glucose metabolism in conscious rhesus macaques. *Neurobiol. Aging* 16:825–32

Eichenbaum H, Otto T, Cohen NJ. 1994. Two functional components of the hippocampal memory system. *Behav. Brain Sci.* 17: 449–518

Everitt BJ, Robbins TW. 1997. Central cholin-

ergic systems and cognition. *Annu. Rev. Psychol.* 48:649–84
Fischer W, Gage F, Björklund A. 1989. Degenerative changes in forebrain cholinergic nuclei correlate with cognitive impairments in aged rats. *Eur. J. Neurosci.* 1:34–45
Foster TC, Barnes CA, Rao G, McNaughton BL. 1991. Increase in perforant path quantal size in aged F-344 rats. *Neurobiol. Aging* 12:441–48
Gage FH, Dunnett SB, Björklund A. 1989. Age-related impairments in spatial memory are independent of those in sensorimotor skills. *Neurobiol. Aging* 10:347–52
Gage FH, Kelly P, Björklund A. 1984. Regional changes in brain glucose metabolism reflect cognitive impairments in aged rats. *J. Neurosci.* 4:2856–65
Gallagher M, Burwell R, Burchinal M. 1993. Severity of spatial learning impairment in aging: development of a learning index for performance in the Morris water maze. *Behav. Neurosci.* 107:618–26
Gallagher M, Colombo PJ. 1995. Aging: the cholinergic hypothesis of cognitive decline. *Curr. Opin. Neurobiol.* 5:161–68
Gallagher M, Gill TM, Baxter MG, Bucci DJ. 1994. The development of neurobiological models for cognitive decline in aging. *Semin. Neurosci.* 6:351–58
Gallagher M, Nagahara AH, Burwell RD. 1995. Cognition and hippocampal systems in aging: animal models. In *Brain and Memory: Modulation and Mediation of Neuroplasticity,* ed. JL McGaugh, N Weinberger, G Lynch, pp. 103–26. New York: Oxford Univ. Press
Gazzaley AH, Siegel SJ, Kordower JH, Mufson EJ, Morrison JH. 1996. Circuit-specific alterations of *N*-methyl-D-aspartate receptor subunit 1 in the dentate gyrus of aged monkeys. *Proc. Natl. Acad. Sci. USA* 93: 3121–25
Geddes JW, Monaghan DR, Cotman CW, Lott IT, Kim RC, Chui HC. 1992. Plasticity of hippocampal circuitry in Alzheimer's disease. *Science* 230:1179–81
Geinisman Y, de Toledo-Morrell L, Morrell F. 1986. Loss of perforated synapses in the dentate gyrus: morphological substrate of memory deficit in aged rats. *Proc. Natl. Acad. Sci. USA* 83:3027–31
Geinisman Y, de Toledo-Morrell L, Morrell F, Persina IS, Rossi M. 1992. Age-related loss of axcospinous synapses formed by two afferent systems in the rat dentate gyrus as revealed by the unbiased stereological dissector technique. *Hippocampus* 2:437–44
Glisky EL, Polster MR, Routhieaux BC. 1995. Double dissociation between item and source memory. *Neuropsychology* 9:229–35
Goldman-Rakic PS, Brown RM. 1981. Regional changes of monoamines in cerebral cortex and subcortical structures of aging rhesus monkeys. *Neuroscience* 6:177–87
Golomb J, de Leon MJ, Kluger A, George AE, Tarshish C, Ferris SH. 1993. Hippocampal atrophy in normal aging: an association with recent memory impairment. *Arch. Neurol.* 50:967–73
Grady CL, McIntosh AR, Horwitz B, Maisog J, Ungerleider L, et al. 1995. Age-related reductions in human recognition memory due to impaired encoding. *Science* 269: 218–21
Greenwood P, Parasuraman R, Haxby JV. 1993. Visuospatial attention across the adult life span. *Neuropsychologia* 31:471–85
Han J-S, Gallagher M, Holland PC. 1995. Hippocampal lesions disrupt decrements but not increments in conditioned stimulus processing. *J. Neurosci.* 15:7323–29
Helkala EL, Koivisto K, Hänninen T, Vanhanen M, Kervinen K, et al. 1996. Memory functions in human subjects with different apolipoprotein E phenotypes during a 3-year population-based follow-up study. *Neurosci. Lett.* 204:177–80
Irwin I, DeLanney LE, McNeill T, Chan P, Forno LS, et al. 1994. Aging and the nigrostriatal dopamine system: a nonhuman primate study. *Neurodegeneration* 3:251–65
Issa AM, Rowe W, Gauthier S, Meaney MJ. 1990. Hypothalamic-pituitary-adrenal activity in aged, cognitively impaired and cognitively unimpaired rats. *J. Neurosci.* 10:3247–54
Janowsky JS, Shimamura AP, Kritchevsky M, Squire LR. 1989a. Cognitive impairment following frontal lobe damage and its relevance to human amnesia. *Behav. Neurosci.* 103:548–60
Janowsky JS, Shimamura AP, Squire LR. 1989b. Source memory impairment in patients with frontal lobe lesions. *Neuropsychologia* 27:1043–56
Jones DNC, Barnes JC, Kirkby DL, Higgins GA. 1995. Age-associated impairments in a test of attention: evidence for involvement of cholinergic systems. *J. Neurosci.* 15:7282–92
Killiany RJ, Moss MB, Rosene DL, Herndon J, Lai ZC. 1995. Age-related changes in the rhesus monkey: memory executive function and "IQ" in a nonhuman primate model of normal human aging. *Soc. Neurosci. Abstr.* 21:1564
Koliatsos VE, Martin LJ, Price DL. 1990. Efferent organization of the mammalian basal forebrain. In *Brain Cholinergic Systems,* ed. SM Biesold, pp. 120–52. New York: Oxford Univ. Press
Lane F, Snowden J. 1989. Memory and de-

mentia: a longitudinal survey of suburban elderly. In *Clinical and Abnormal Psychology,* ed. P Lovibond, P Wilson, pp. 365–76. New York: Elsevier

Luine V, Bowling D, Hearns M. 1990. Spatial memory deficits in aged rats: contributions of monoaminergic systems. *Brain Res.* 537:271–78

Markus EJ, Barnes CA, McNaughton BL, Gladden VL, Skaggs WE. 1994. Spatial information content and reliability of hippocampal CA1 neurons: effects of visual input. *Hippocampus* 4:410–21

McIntyre JS, Craik FIM. 1987. Age difference in memory for item and source information. *Can. J. Psychol.* 41:175–92

Meaney MJ, Aitken DH, van Berkel C, Bhatnagar S, Sapolsky RM. 1988. Effect of neonatal handling on age-related impairments associated with the hippocampus. *Science* 239:766–68

Meunier M, Bachevalier J, Mishkin M, Murray EA. 1993. Effects on visual recognition of combined and separate ablations of the entorhinal and perirhinal cortex in rhesus monkeys. *J. Neurosci.* 13:5418–32

Mizumori SJY, Lavoie AM, Kalyani A. 1996. Redistribution of spatial representation in the hippocampus of aged rats performing a spatial memory task. *Behav. Neurosci.* 110: 1006–16

Moore CI, Browning MD, Rose GM. 1993. Hippocampal plasticity induced by primed burst, but not long-term potentiation, stimulation in area CA1 of aged Fisher 344 rats. *Hippocampus* 3:57–66

Morris JC, McKeel DW, Storandt M, Rubin EH, Price JL, et al. 1991. Very mild Alzheimer's disease: informant-based clinical, psychometric and pathological distinction from normal aging. *Neurology* 41:469–78

Morse CK. 1993. Does variability increase with age? An archival study of cognitive measures. *Psychol. Aging* 8:156–64

Moscovitch M, Ulmita C. 1991. Conscious and nonconscious aspects of memory: a neuropsychological framework of modules and central systems. In *Perspectives on Cognitive Neuroscience,* ed. RG Lister, HJ Weingartner, pp. 229–66. New York: Oxford Univ. Press

Moss MB, Rosene DL, Peters A. 1988. Effects of aging on visual recognition memory in the rhesus monkey. *Neurobiol. Aging* 9: 495–502

Mouloua M, Parasuraman R. 1995. Aging and cognitive vigilance: effects of spatial uncertainty and event rate. *Exp. Aging Res.* 21:17–32

Muir JL, Everitt BJ, Robbins TW. 1994. AMPA-induced excitotoxic lesions of the basal forebrain: a significant role for the cortical cholinergic system in attentional function. *J. Neurosci.* 14:2313–26

Murphy BL, Arnsten AF, Goldman-Rakic PS, Roth RH. 1996. Increased dopamine turnover in the prefrontal cortex impairs spatial working memory performance in rats and monkeys. *Proc. Natl. Acad. Sci. USA* 93: 1325–29

Murray EA. 1996. What have ablation studies told us about the neural substrates of stimulus memory? *Semin. Neurosci.* 8:13–22

Nagahara AH, Otto T, Gallagher M. 1995. Entorhinal/Perirhinal cortex lesions impair performance on two versions of place learning in the Morris water maze. *Behav. Neurosci.* 109:3–9

Naveh-Benjamin M, Craik FIM. 1995. Memory for context and its use in item memory: comparisons of younger and older persons. *Psychol. Aging* 10:284–93

Nicolle MM, Bizon J, Gallagher M. 1996. Ionotropic glutamate receptors in the hippocampus and striatum of aged rats: relationship to cognitive decline. *Neuroscience.* In press

Otto T, Eichenbaum H. 1992. Complementary roles of the orbital prefrontal cortex and the perirhinal-entorhinal cortices in an odor-guided delayed-nonmatching-to-sample task. *Behav. Neurosci.* 106:762–75

Parasuraman R, Haxby JV. 1993. Attention and brain function in Alzheimer's Disease: a review. *Neuropsychology* 7:242–72

Parkin AJ, Walter BM, Hunkin NM. 1995. Relationships between normal aging, frontal lobe function, and memory for temporal and spatial information. *Neuropsychology* 9:304–12

Peters A, Leahu D, Moss MB, McNally J. 1994. The effects of aging on area 46 of the frontal cortex of the rhesus monkey. *Cereb. Cortex* 6:621–35

Petrides M, Alivisatos B, Evans AC, Meyer E. 1993a. Dissociation of human mid-dorsolateral from posterior dorsolateral frontal cortex in memory processing. *Proc. Natl. Acad. Sci. USA* 90:873–77

Petrides M, Alivisatos B, Meyer E, Evans AC. 1993b. Functional activation of the human frontal cortex during the performance of verbal working memory tasks. *Proc. Natl. Acad. Sci. USA* 90:878–82

Presty SK, Bachevalier J, Walker LC, Struble RG, Price DL, et al. 1987. Age differences in recognition memory of the rhesus monkey (*Macaca mulatta*). *Neurobiol. Aging* 8: 435–40

Quirion R, Wilson A, Rowe W, Aubert I, Richard J, et al. 1995. Facilitation of acetylcholine release and cognitive performance by an M2-Muscarinic receptor antagonist in aged memory-impaired rats. *J. Neurosci.* 15:1455–62

Rapp PR. 1993. Neuropsychological analysis of learning and memory in the aged nonhuman primate. *Neurobiol. Aging* 14:627–29

Rapp PR. 1995. Cognitive neuroscience perspectives on aging in nonhuman primates. In *Emotion, Memory and Behavior,* ed. T Nakajima, T Ono, pp. 197–211. Tokyo: Jpn. Sci. Soc.

Rapp PR, Amaral DG. 1989. Evidence for task-dependent memory dysfunction in the aged monkey. *J. Neurosci.* 9:3568–76

Rapp PR, Amaral DG. 1991. Recognition memory deficits in a subpopulation of aged monkeys resemble the effects of medial temporal lobe damage. *Neurobiol. Aging* 12:481–86

Rapp PR, Gallagher M. 1996. Preserved neuron number in the hippocampus of aged rats with spatial learning deficits. *Proc. Natl. Acad. Sci. USA.* 93:9926–30

Rapp PR, Heindel WC. 1994. Memory systems in normal and pathological aging. *Curr. Opin. Neurol.* 7:294–98

Rapp PR, Kansky MT, Eichenbaum H. 1996. Learning and memory for hierarchical relationships in the monkey: effects of aging. *Behav. Neurosci.* 110:887–97

Rasmussen T, Schliemann T, Sørensen JC, Zimmer J, West M. 1996. Memory impaired aged rats: no loss of principal hippocampal and subicular neurons. *Neurobiol. Aging* 17:143–47

Robbins TW, Everitt BJ, Marston HM, Wilkinson J, Jones GH, Pagae KJ. 1989. Comparative effects of ibotenic acid and quisqualic acid-induced lesions of the substantia innominata on attentional function in the rat: further implications for the role of the cholinergic neurons of the nucleus basalis in cognitive processes. *Behav. Brain Res.* 35:221–40

Roberts JA, Eberling JL, Rapp PR, Tuszynski MH, Jagust WJ. 1996. Reductions in cerebral glucose metabolism are associated with memory deficits in aged rhesus macaques. *Soc. Neurosci. Abstr.* In press

Schacter DL, Savage CR, Alpert NM, Rauch SL, Albert MS. 1996. The role of the hippocampus and frontal cortex in age-related memory changes: a PET study. *NeuroReport.* In press

Scoville WB, Milner B. 1957. Loss of recent memory after bilateral hippocampal lesions. *J. Neurol. Neurosurg. Psychiatry* 20: 11–21

Shen J, Barnes CA. 1996. Age-related decrease in cholinergic synaptic transmission in three hippocampal subfields. *Neurobiol. Aging* 17:439–51

Shimamura AP. 1994. Neuropsychological perspectives on memory and cognitive decline in normal human aging. *Semin. Neurosci.* 6:387–94

Shimamura AP, Janowsky JS, Squire LR. 1990. Memory for the temporal order of events in patients with frontal lobe lesions and amnesic patients. *Neuropsychologia* 28:803–13

Smith ML, Booze RM. 1995. Cholinergic and gabaergic neurons in the nucleus basalis region of young and aged rats. *Neuroscience* 67:679–88

Smith TD, Gallagher M, Leslie FM. 1995. Cholinergic binding sites in rat brain: analysis by age and cognitive status. *Neurobiol. Aging* 16:161–73

Spencer WD, Raz N. 1994. Memory for facts, source, and context: can frontal lobe dysfunction explain age-related differences? *Psychol. Aging* 9:149–59

Squire L, Zola-Morgan S. 1991. The medial temporal lobe memory system. *Science* 253:1380–86

Stack EC, Gallagher M, Rapp PR. 1995. Reorganization of hippocampal circuitry in the aged rat. *Soc. Neurosci. Abstr.* 21:472

Stenvers KL, Lund PK, Gallagher M. 1996. Increased hippocampal expression of type 1 insulin-like growth factor (IGF) receptor messenger RNA is associated with cognitive decline in aged rats. *Neuroscience* 72: 505–18

Stroessner-Johnson HM, Rapp PR, Amaral DG. 1992. Cholinergic cell loss and hypertrophy in the medial septal nucleus of the behaviorally characterized aged rhesus monkey. *J. Neurosci.* 12:1936–44

Suzuki WA, Zola-Morgan S, Squire LR, Amaral DG. 1993. Lesions of the perirhinal and parahippocampal cortices in the monkey produce long-lasting memory impairment in the visual and tactual modalities. *J. Neurosci.* 13:2430–51

Tanila H, Shapiro M, Eichenbaum H. 1996. Hippocampal place fields in aged rats with spatial memory deficit. *Soc. Neurosci. Abstr.* 21:943

Thal LJ, Masur DM, Blau AD, Fuld PA, Klauber MR. 1989. Chronic oral physostigmine without lecithin improves memory in Alzheimer's disease. *J. Am. Geriat. Soc.* 37:42–48

Torres EM, Perry TA, Blokland A, Wilkinson LS, Wiley RG, et al. 1994. Behavioural, histochemical and biochemical consequences of selective immunolesions in discrete regions of the basal forebrain cholinergic system. *Neuroscience* 63:95–122

Undie AS, Wang H-Y, Friedman E. 1995. Decreased phospholipase C-β immunoreactivity, phosphoinositide metabolism, and protein kinase C activation in senescent F-344 rat brain. *Neurobiol. Aging* 16:19–28

Voytko ML, Olton DS, Richardson RT, Gorman LK, Tobin JR, Price DL. 1994. Basal forebrain lesions in monkeys disrupt atten-

tion but not learning and memory. *J. Neurosci.* 14:167–86
Wang YH, Luo JH, Yasuda RP, Gallagher M, Kellar KJ, Wolfe BB. 1996. Age-related changes in NMDA receptor subunits, NR1, NR2A, and NR2B in rat striatum and hippocampus. *Soc. Neurosci. Abstr.* 22
Wenk GL, Pierce DJ, Struble RG, Price DL, Cork LC. 1989. Age-related changes in multiple neurotransmitter systems in the monkey brain. *Neurobiol. Aging* 10:11–19
West MJ. 1993. Regionally specific loss of neurons in the aging human hippocampus. *Neurobiol. Aging* 14:287–93
West MJ, Amaral DG, Rapp PR. 1993. Preserved hippocampal cell number in aged monkeys with recognition memory deficits. *Soc. Neurosci. Abstr.* 19:599
West MJ, Coleman PD, Flood DG, Troncoso JC. 1994. Differences in the pattern of hippocampal neuronal loss in normal aging and Alzheimer's disease. *Lancet* 344:769–72
Williams GV, Goldman-Rakic PS. 1995. Modulation of memory fields by dopamine D1 receptors in prefrontal cortex. *Nature* 376:572–75
Wilner J, Otto T, Gallagher M, Eichenbaum H. 1993. Hippocampal lesions that impair place learning facilitate delayed nonmatching performance in rats. *Soc. Neurosci. Abstr.* 19:358
Wilson FAW, Scalaidhe SP, Goldman-Rakic PS. 1993. Dissociation of object and spatial processing domains in primate prefrontal cortex. *Science* 260:1955–58
Winocur G. 1991. Conditional learning in aged rats: evidence of hippocampal and prefrontal cortex impairment. *Neurobiol. Aging* 13:131–35
Winocur G. 1992. A comparison of normal old rats and young adult rats with lesions to the hippocampus or prefrontal cortex on a test of matching-to-sample. *Neuropsychologia* 30:769–81
Youngjohn JR, Crook TH. 1993. Stability of everyday memory in age-associated memory impairment: a longitudinal study. *Neuropsychology* 7:406–16
Zyzak DR, Otto T, Eichenbaum H, Gallagher M. 1995. Cognitive decline associated with normal aging in rats: a neuropsychological approach. *Learn. Mem.* 2:1–16

Annu. Rev. Psychol. 1997. 48:371–410

KEY ISSUES IN THE DEVELOPMENT OF AGGRESSION AND VIOLENCE FROM CHILDHOOD TO EARLY ADULTHOOD

Rolf Loeber

Western Psychiatric Institute and Clinic, School of Medicine, University of Pittsburgh, Pittsburgh, Pennsylvania 15213

Dale Hay

Faculty of Social and Political Sciences, Cambridge University, Cambridge, England CB5 8BA

KEY WORDS: gender differences, prediction

ABSTRACT

Different manifestations of aggression from childhood to early adulthood are reviewed to establish how early manifestations are related to later manifestations. Similarities and differences in manifestations of aggression between the two genders are noted. Developmental sequences and pathways from minor aggression to violence are highlighted. Long-term escalation is contrasted with short-term escalation at older ages. Although studies have emphasized high stability of aggression over time, data show that a substantial proportion of aggressive youth desist over time. Temperamental, emotional, and cognitive aspects of aggression are reviewed, either as precursors or co-occurring conditions to aggression. Selected processes in the realms of the family, peers, and neighborhoods are highlighted that are known to be associated with juvenile aggression. Cumulative, long-term causes are contrasted with short-term causes, and causes associated with desistance in aggression are reviewed.

0084-6570/967/0201-0371$08.00

CONTENTS

INTRODUCTION

The enormity of the problem of juvenile aggression and violence is difficult to grasp. Violence statistics (e.g. Lowry et al 1995, Snyder & Sickmund 1995) are usually poor approximations of how much violence affects a nation. The level of violence in the United States is far higher than in other industrialized countries (Rosenberg 1991). The level of juvenile violence has dramatically increased in the past decade, particularly in terms of homicide in the 14- to 17-year-old age group. After vehicle accidents, it is the leading cause of fatal injuries. Since the mid-1980s the homicide victimization rate for this age group has nearly doubled. The increase in juvenile homicides has been concentrated in the African-American subpopulation (Snyder & Sickmund 1995).

The volume of publications on aggression and violence is large (e.g. Weiler 1995), and there are several excellent surveys on juvenile aggression (e.g. Berkowitz 1993, Coie & Dodge 1997, Eron et al 1994, Pepler & Rubin 1991, Reiss & Roth 1993). Most longitudinal studies in the United States on violence have been based on official delinquency records of violent offenses (Hamparian et al 1978, Miller et al 1982, Shannon 1988, Wolfgang et al 1987), but these studies do not link predelinquent forms of aggression to delinquent forms of violence and so do not address the early development of aggression. In addition, relatively few reviews address key developmental issues, which is the aim of this paper (but see Farrington 1993, his anonymous appendix in Reiss & Roth 1993, and Pepler & Slaby 1994).

A developmental approach to juvenile deviant behavior, including aggression and violence, can open many avenues to knowledge (Loeber & Le Blanc 1990). We address the following key developmental issues: 1. The manifestations of aggression change dramatically throughout childhood, adolescence, and early adulthood, and the changes are not exactly the same for each gender. The concept of development implies both change and continuity, and both the differentiation of behavior and the consolidation of preexisting tendencies. 2. Whereas some degree of aggression is age-normative, at least in boys, some variations in normal development eventually produce highly aggressive individuals. Understanding the developmental course from less serious to more serious forms of aggression and violence requires knowledge about the onset of the behaviors, changes in their prevalence with age, and their continuity over time. 3. Violent individuals do not necessarily share the same behavioral history. Whereas most violent individuals have undergone a development characterized by escalation in the severity of aggression over several years, a minority of violent individuals experience a late onset of violence without such a history. 4. Clearly violence has both cognitive and emotional antecedents and components. Among the earliest manifestations of violence antecedents are difficult temperament and poor emotional regulation. General cognitive antecedents are low intelligence, reading problems, and attention problems (including hyperactivity). In addition, several cognitive factors are more specific to aggression, including social cognitive deficiencies, mental scripts, attitudes favorable to aggression, rejection sensitivity, and inflated self-esteem. 5. We review selected long-term and short-term social processes relevant to the etiology of aggression and violence. We focus especially on processes within the family, peer groups, and neighborhoods. We do not review the extensive literature on the biological bases of aggression and violence, but see, for example, Coie & Dodge (1997), Lahey et al (1995), Moffitt (1990a, 1993), Pennington & Ozonoff (1996), Plomin et al (1990), Raine (1993), Quay (1993), Reiss & Roth (1993).

Although the term aggression may be familiar to many, its interpretation varies. We focus here on aggression as a category of behavior that causes or threatens physical harm to others. We define aggression with regard to harm because the effect is objectively verifiable (because of blood drawn or the infliction of injuries upon a person). Note, however, that some authors (e.g. Coie & Dodge 1997) include the qualification that the perpetrator had the intent to inflict harm (excluding accidental harm) in their definition of aggression. We believe that for the purposes of most studies the qualification of intent encumbers the definition of aggression because intent is not observable by others and because many perpetrators are known to deny intent.

All too often authors have defined aggression very loosely (Tremblay 1991). Therefore, we exclude from our review otherwise excellent studies based on self-reported personality questionnaires, assessments of antisocial behavior, and conduct problems that usually include nonaggressive disruptive behaviors as well (e.g. Eron & Huesmann 1990, Kazdin 1987, Patterson et al 1991); studies on aggression against property (such as fire setting and vandalism); and studies that include aggression against self (e.g. Lochman & Dodge 1994). We almost always exclude studies based on aggression scores derived from factor analyses that often include other problem behaviors as well (e.g. Achenbach & Edelbrock 1987).

The term aggression covers a whole range of acts that vary according to age-typical manifestations, severity, and choice of opponents or victims. Thus, aggression is not a unitary term but consists of different manifestations, including verbal aggression, bullying, physical fighting, and different forms of violence, such as robbery, rape, and homicide. Studies show that different forms of aggression tend to be intercorrelated to different degrees (e.g. Choy nowski 1995, Frick et al 1993, Loeber & Schmaling 1985). Although differing distinctions between various types of aggression have been made (Coie & Dodge 1997, Reiss & Roth 1993), we concentrate on developmental distinctions. Therefore, we focus on both observations and adults' reports of aggression in children, juveniles' self-reports of aggression and violence, and official records of juveniles' contact with the police and/or the courts for violent acts. Although aggression is often accompanied by several other problems, including internalizing problems (anxiety and withdrawal, depression and suicide), property offenses, and substance-related problems (substance use and drug dealing), we do not review these aspects. We do include studies from different ethnic populations, but do not focus on differences between ethnic groups.

MANIFESTATIONS OF AGGRESSION FROM INFANCY TO EARLY ADULTHOOD

Infancy

The earliest manifestations of aggression occur in the infant's earliest encounters with the social world. Most infants show signs of frustration and rage, and there is no marked disparity between young females and young males. Particular facial configurations associated with the experience of anger in adults can already be identified by three months of age (Izard et al 1995). The expression of anger emerges in tandem with the cognitive changes occurring in the second half of the first year of life, when infants begin to understand cause-and-effect relations. By twelve months, actions that lead to conflict among older individuals provoke either protest or retaliation (Caplan et al 1991).

Although there is virtually no evidence for gender differences in possible precursors to aggression in infancy, there are some signs of difference between the sexes in emotional expressiveness and self-control that may predate later gender-differentiated problems. Weinberg & Tronick (1997) have identified gender-typical patterns of interaction with the mother in the earliest months of life. Boys are more emotionally labile than girls and express both positive and negative emotions at higher rates. Infant girls can better regulate their own emotional states, whereas boys depend more on input from their mothers. Infant boys are more likely than girls to show anger (Weinberg & Tronick 1997).

Toddlerhood

During the second and third years of life, behavioral signs of temper tantrums and aggression toward adults and peers can be observed, and a few gender differences are noted, although the overall picture is one of similarity between girls and boys. In early childhood, conflict is inevitable but not often shown at high rates, to the exclusion of other social activities (for reviews, see Hay 1984, Shantz 1987).

Studies of peer interaction suggest that personal as opposed to instrumental aggression is infrequent and rarely shown at the very beginning of a conflict, as opposed to later stages of a dispute (Caplan et al 1991, Hay & Ross 1982). Few gender differences in peer-directed aggression have been noted in laboratory studies. In observations of small groups of one- and two-year-olds, groups with a majority of females were more likely than groups with a majority of males to come into conflict and to use personal force (Caplan et al 1991). Similarly, in laboratory studies of sibling interaction, no main effects of sex of child are observed, though same-sex dyads are more likely than mixed-sex ones to enter into conflict (Hay et al 1993, Vespo et al 1995).

Interview studies show that mothers and fathers report gender differences that are not necessarily backed up by direct observation. Parents, especially fathers, reported boys as showing more negative behaviors than girls. In contrast, teachers and observers noted no main effect of gender and rated girls who experienced an insecure attachment relationship with their mothers as more difficult than boys and secure girls (Fagot & Kavanagh 1990). In a British sample, mothers saw girls as more aggressive than boys (Hay et al 1995).

The Early School Years

Gender differences in levels of aggression become marked in the years between the third and sixth birthdays, when in many societies children first participate in organized peer groups for educational or day-care purposes. Males show higher rates of physical aggression (both instrumental grabs of objects and personal force) than girls (for reviews, see Coie & Dodge 1997, Hay 1984). Several investigators have argued that females tend to use more verbal and indirect aggression rather than physical aggression, such as alienation, ostracism, and character defamation (Bjorkqvist et al 1992, Cairns et al 1989). Girls also often display relational aggression (Crick 1995, Crick & Grotpeter 1995), through peer exclusion, gossip, and collusion directed at the relational bonds between "friends."

There is some suggestion from observational studies that girls use physical aggression against their peers but hide such activities from watching adults, including teachers and playground observers. Pepler and her colleagues (Pepler & Craig 1995) revealed incidents of female aggression by using remote audiovisual recording in which children on a playground were fitted with wireless microphones. This technique revealed that bullying by girls occurred at the same rates as bullying by boys, although in interviews the girls were much less likely to admit to bullying (Pepler & Craig 1995).

The pattern in peer relations shown by most girls and many boys from early to middle childhood is one of a decrease in aggression and a rise in interpersonal skills, with only a particular subgroup of boys failing to control their aggression. However, marked gender differences in aggression are less apparent with siblings than with peers: Both girls and boys report fairly high rates of physical aggression with their siblings (Dunn 1993). Extensive quarreling between siblings is not, therefore, necessarily seen as a form of maladjustment. However, analyses of children at high risk for disruptive behavior showed that a highly conflictual sibling relationship increased the likelihood of aggression at school (Storashak et al 1996).

Finally, in the early school years cruelty to other children and cruelty to animals, which are symptoms of conduct disorder, may emerge in a proportion of children (American Psychiatric Association 1994). Each can be seen as advanced symptoms of aggression, which have implications for the development of other forms of aggression (e.g. Ascione 1993).

Adolescence and Early Adulthood

Several major changes in the level and pattern of aggression occur during adolescence and early adulthood. First, aggressive acts increase in impact to the extent that they cause injury or death, partly because of an increase with age in juveniles' physical strength, and partly because of the use of weapons (Berkowitz 1994, Reiss & Roth 1993) and an increase in the lethality of weapons with age (Arria et al 1995). Cross-sectional data from the National Household Education Survey of 1993 indicate that the proportion of students carrying weapons in American schools rapidly increases between the 6th grade (24%) and 9th grade (48%) and levels off after that (Snyder et al 1996).

The dramatic increase in juvenile homicide in the past decade in the United States resulted largely from an increase in gun-related killings. National data from 1991 show that more than half the juvenile homicide victims have been killed with a firearm (Snyder & Sickmund 1995). In one metropolitan study of males, almost six times as many youth were wounded by guns as opposed to killed by guns (R Loeber, MM Smalley, G Tita, J Cohen & WB Van Kammen, unpublished manuscript). Not surprisingly, male juvenile offenders and inner-city high-school males are among those most likely to carry guns, and drug dealers are particularly more likely to carry guns (Sheley & Wight 1993, cited in O'Donnell 1995). In one longitudinal sample, half the boys under age 16 reported owning a firearm compared with 5% of the girls. The boys in this sample reported that firearms were available in 81% of their households (Cairns & Cairns 1994). However, Lizotte et al (1994) have shown that juveniles' ownership of guns for protection rather than for sportsmen's use is related to delinquent offending.

A second change in adolescence is that peer groups in schools more commonly engage in collective forms of violence, such as pressing younger children into doing things against their will (e.g. telling on others or giving up possessions). Members of social networks in secondary schools are often similar to one another in levels of aggression and in other antisocial tendencies (Cairns & Cairns 1994). Group relations may promote aggression and other forms of delinquency to such an extent that these activities may be seen as almost normative during adolescence (DiLalla & Gottesman 1989, Moffitt 1993).

More organized gangs emerge in early adolescence. They are characterized by particular forms of dress, insignia, or hand symbols and often engage in violence (Howell 1995, Klein 1995). Gangs often operate in their own defined neighborhoods, but also in schools. A national United States survey shows that the percentage of students reporting gangs operating in schools increased from 19% in sixth grade to about 40% from ninth grade onward. The presence of gangs in schools is associated with a doubling of reports of weapons in schools (Snyder et al 1996), and youths who join a gang are more heavily involved in violent crime than those who do not (Fagin 1990). Furthermore, gangs in schools are often associated with gang presence in the community. Group fights, compared with individual fights, are more likely to produce injuries (Farrington et al 1982). The presence of gangs is associated with increased availability of guns and high levels of delinquency and violence (Bjerregaard & Lizotte 1995, Howell 1995).

Third, as juveniles increase in physical strength, a minority of them eventually strike out or hit a parent (usually the mother) or a teacher (Callahan & Rivara 1992, Johnston et al 1993). Rates of parent-child conflict typically increase during the adolescent years (Hill 1987, Smetana 1989).

Fourth, there is an increase in cross-gender aggression. During middle-childhood and continuing into early adolescence, girls and boys spend much of their time in gender-segregated groups (Cairns & Kroll 1994, Maccoby 1988), and most instances of conflict with peers occur between members of the same sex. In middle childhood, direct physical aggression is shown in the conflicts of girls with girls as well as those of boys with boys. Over the years of adolescence, girls' conflicts tend to become less violent, whereas boys' disputes continue to show aggression and other forms of direct confrontation (Cairns & Cairns 1994, Olweus 1991). In adolescence, cross-gender conflict increases, though girls report more conflicts with boys than boys report with girls (Cairns & Cairns 1994). As dating begins, violence between the sexes becomes more common. Different degrees of coercion may occur that culminate in date rape (Vicary et al 1995). Also during this period, adolescent males begin to rape strangers.

Fifth, with the onset of sexual maturity, juveniles may become parents and may begin to abuse their children. Abuse of a partner may also become a feature of their lives (O'Leary et al 1989). Some researchers suggest that highly aggressive individuals who appear to desist from crime in young adulthood have actually turned their aggressive impulses toward family members (Moffitt 1993).

PREDICTION AND PATHWAYS FROM CHILDHOOD TO EARLY ADULTHOOD

Our review of different manifestations of aggression does not reveal how much the manifestations at one age are related to those at another. In addition, it does not reveal whether the behavioral histories of violent individuals are the same or whether there is a need to distinguish between subgroups of violent people, each with a distinctive behavioral history.

To address these issues we first summarize age trends in the onset and prevalence of aggression. The findings that we want to reconcile are those from childhood to early adulthood: (*a*) the cumulative onset of aggression (in boys) gradually increases, (*b*) the prevalence of physical fighting tends to decrease, (*c*) but the prevalence of serious violence tends to increase, (*d*) while the stability of aggression tends to increase.

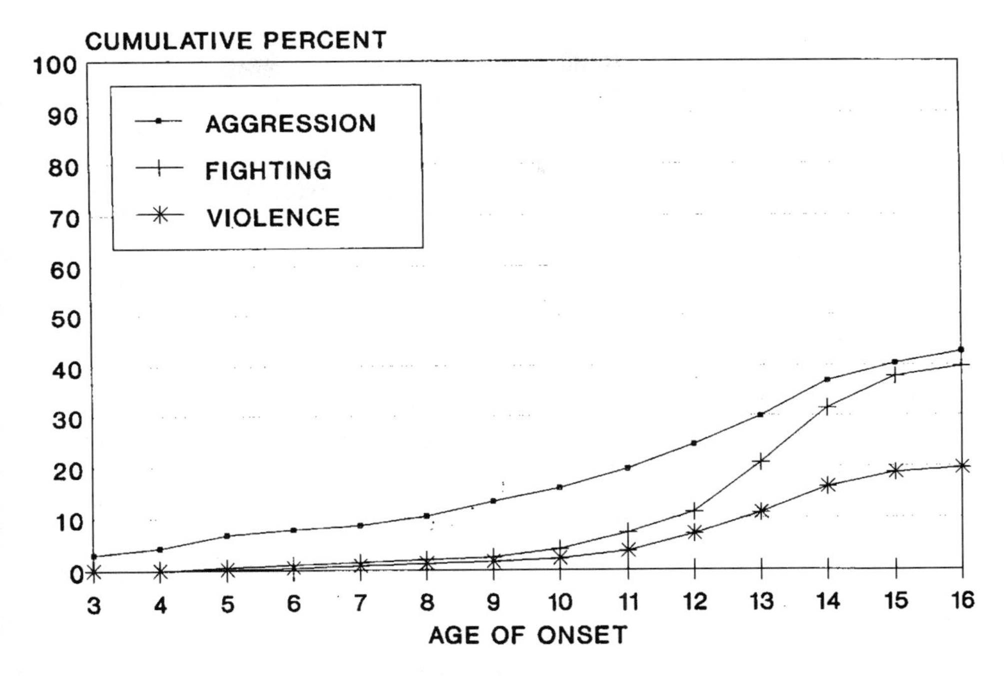

Figure 1 Cumulative onset curves for minor aggression, physical fighting, and violence in the oldest sample of the Pittsburgh Youth Study (Loeber et al 1997a,b).

Onset

Several issues are important concerning the onset of aggression. First, to what extent is the onset of less serious aggression occurring before the onset of more serious forms of aggression? Second, at what ages do the onsets of different levels of severity of aggression accelerate?

Loeber and associates (Loeber et al 1993, 1997a,b) created age-of-onset graphs of different forms of aggression using prospective and retrospective information from parents, and where possible, from their sons. Onset curves were very similar for annoying others and bullying and so were merged under minor aggression. Similarly, the onset curves for physical fighting and gang fighting were merged in a single onset curve labeled physical fighting. Moreover, the onset curves for strongarming, attacking someone, and forced sex were very similar and were also merged into a curve of violence. The resulting three onset curves for the youngest sample (N = 503) of the Pittsburgh Youth

Study are shown in Figure 1 (Loeber et al 1997a,b) and show (*a*) that the age of onset of aggression gradually increases for each level of severity of aggression and (*b*) that there is a developmental ordering of the seriousness of aggression with age. Minor aggression emerged first almost linearly from about age 3 to age 16, followed by physical fighting, which accelerated from age 10 onward. Fighting, in turn, was followed by the onset of violence, which accelerated from age 11 onward. The graphs illustrate that the onset of boys' aggression is not only concentrated in the preschool period but also that throughout childhood and into adolescence more boys experience the onset of aggression (see also Haapasalo & Tremblay 1994).

The results shown in Figure 1 constitute a replication of previous results from the middle and the oldest samples in the Pittsburgh Youth Study (Loeber et al 1993). In addition, retrospective information collected from a sample of clinic-referred girls and their parents showed a highly similar ordering of minor aggression, physical fighting, and violence (SM Green, R Loeber, K Keenan & J Navratil, unpublished manuscript). Similar graphs are needed, however, for different forms of aggression by girls.

Some researchers have postulated that distinctions should be made between early-onset and late-onset antisocial behavior (Moffitt 1993, Patterson et al 1992). Moffitt (1993) postulated that there is a group of life course–persistent antisocial individuals who experience an early onset, contrasted with an ado-

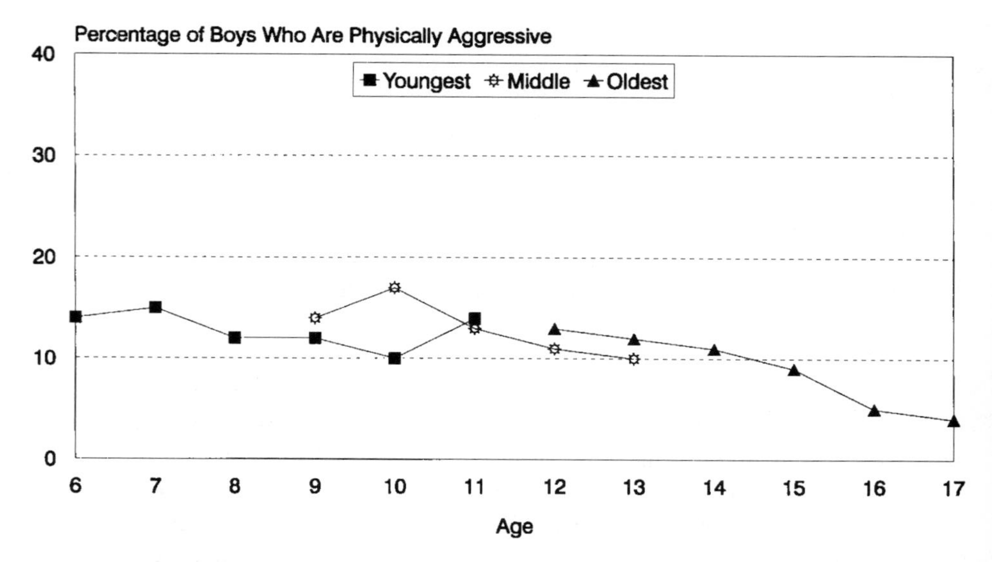

Figure 2 The prevalence of boys' physical aggression from ages 6 to 17 based on parents' reports of the youngest, middle, and oldest samples in the Pittsburgh Youth Study (Loeber & Smith 1996; data are weighted to correct for initial screening of sample).

lescent-limited group whose deviance flares up in adolescence but does not persist over years.

Although the early- and late-onset distinction is plausible, there are several caveats. First, different measures of aggression or antisocial behavior may generate different indexes of stability or discontinuity. For example, official records of delinquency are notorious in failing to identify all serious delinquents, and this failing also applies to violent offenders (Elliott 1994). Second, most studies have not had sufficient follow-ups to demonstrate that the adolescent-limited group does, indeed, completely discontinue deviance. A test of Moffitt's model on conviction data from England showed that desistance of the purported adolescence-limited males was incomplete, and that they continued to get into fights and commit criminal acts at age 32 (Nagin et al 1995). Third, the conceptualization is based on data from males; females usually have a later onset than males, and a proportion of these late-onset cases become persistent offenders (e.g. Elliott 1994, Wikström 1990). Fourth, the early-late onset division ignores the fact that a proportion of serious violence in adulthood is committed by individuals who were not necessarily highly aggressive earlier in life (e.g. Windle & Windle 1995, and see below). Finally, the cumulative graphs for aggression in boys shown in Figure 1 indicate that there is no bimodal distribution of onset that would justify a simple early- vs late-onset distinction.

Prevalence

Survey studies have shown that, on average, the prevalence of physical aggression is highest early in life and decreases subsequently during adolescence (Cairns et al 1989, Loeber 1982). This is shown in prevalence data from the youngest, middle, and oldest samples in the Pittsburgh Youth Study (Figure 2) based on parental reports of their sons' physical aggression (Loeber & Smith 1996). The results show that the prevalence of physical fighting decreased from early adolescence onward, and this decrease accelerated between ages 14 and 16.

More serious violence, however, tends to increase with age, especially during adolescence. Studies (e.g. Farrington 1986) show that the prevalence of violence tends to follow the well-known age-crime curve, peaking in late adolescence or early adulthood and then decreases with age. With some variations, this applies to official records and self-reports of violence. For example, in a Dutch cross-sectional study, the prevalence of violence directed at persons was 26.3% at ages 14–15 and 16–17 but then dropped to 19.9% at ages 18–19 and 16.7% at ages 20–21 (Terlouw & Bruinsma 1994). However, the hazard rate of self-reported serious violence and the prevalence of aggression appear to peak slightly earlier for females than males (about age 14 vs 16, respectively) (Elliott 1994, Kann et al 1995, White et al 1993). In addition, official records show that a relatively high proportion of assaults occurs in the 10–14 year age group for females. However, the peak crime arrest rates for criminal violence vary little by gender (Kruttschnitt 1994).

We argue that prevalence rates of aggression and violence between toddlerhood and early adulthood represent diverse groups of youth that need to be disaggregated: (*a*) youth who desist in aggression, (*b*) youth whose aggression is stable and who continue their aggression either unabatedly or intermittently at the same level, (*c*) youth who escalate in the severity of their aggression and make the transition to violence, and (*d*) youth who experience the onset of aggression.

Stability

Olweus (1979) showed that on average the correlation between early aggression in childhood or adolescence and later aggression was .63 (.79 when corrected for attenuation), which is as high as the stability of intelligence over time. His findings have since been replicated in many subsequent longitudinal studies based on different forms of aggression, including severe, emotional temper tantrums (e.g. Caspi et al 1987; Farrington 1991, 1994; Haapasalo & Tremblay 1994; Loeber et al 1989b; Pulkkinen 1992; Tremblay et al 1991). Early aggression clearly is predictive of different manifestations of later violence, including frequent fighting by age 18, assault on wife or cohabitee, and conviction for violent offenses by age 32 (Farrington 1994, Stattin & Magnusson 1989).

How early in life does aggression become stable? Toddlers' proactive but not retaliative aggression is stable over six months for both girls and boys (Hay 1995). Aggression in infancy predicted boys' externalizing problems at age three (Shaw et al 1994). Longer-term stability is apparently more evident for boys than for girls, with high levels of aggression in laboratory observations at two years of age predicting high rates in a similar situation three years later (Cummings et al 1989). In contrast, girls' levels of aggression in the toddler period did not predict aggression at age five.

The fact that the prevalence of typical forms of aggression is lower among females than males does not necessarily imply that the stability of aggression is higher for males than for females. Several studies show that the stability for aggression tends to be as high or higher for females than males (Cairns & Cairns 1984, Elliott 1994, Verhulst & Vander Ende 1991), but not all studies are in agreement, with the findings partly depending on mode of measurement (Olweus 1981, Pulkkinen & Pitkänen 1993, Stattin & Magnusson 1989).

Given that personality features tend to become more stable with age, it is plausible that aggression may also become more stable with age. A comparison of stability coefficients across different studies (Loeber 1982) suggests that the magnitude of the coefficients increases by early adolescence. The

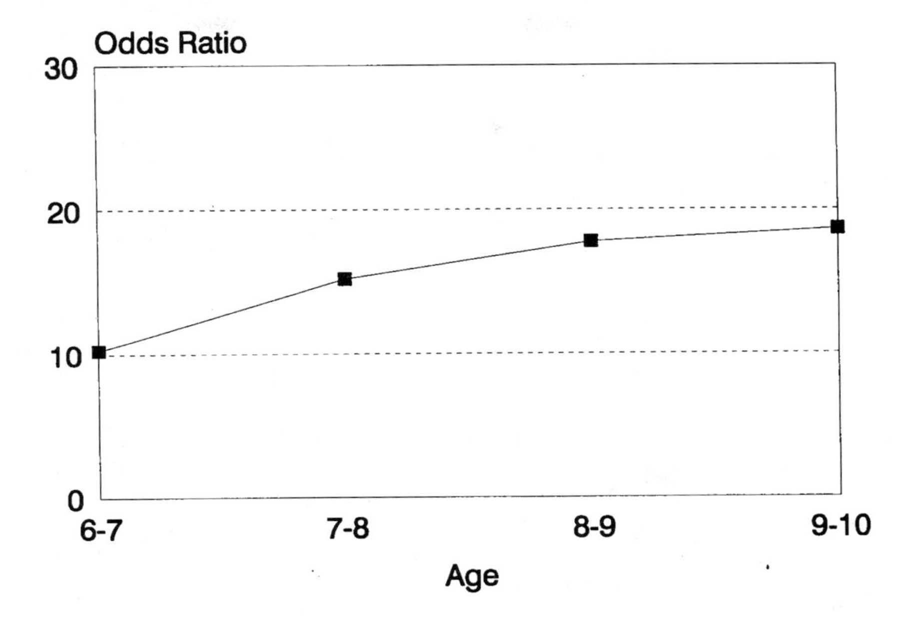

Figure 3 The yearly stability of boys' physical aggression in the youngest sample of the Pittsburgh Youth Study, based on parents' reports, expressed in odds ratios (Loeber & Smith 1996).

implication of this finding is that more change in aggression is apparent early in life, but that from early adolescence on, aggression becomes more stable over time. Longitudinal results from the Pittsburgh Youth Study (Figure 3) show that the year-to-year stability of physical fighting (based on parent report) in the youngest sample tended to increase from age 6 (odds ratio = 10.3) to 9 (odds ratio = 18.6) (Loeber & Smith 1996).

Reported correlation coefficients between early and late aggression (for either gender) should be accepted with some reservations. First, as Loeber (1982) has shown, there are large individual differences in the stability of aggression. The most stable individuals are those who initially are either the least aggressive or the most aggressive. That is, populations of youths are heterogeneous according to the stability of aggression of their members (see e.g. Le Blanc et al 1991). Second, measurement error has not been considered in most studies. For example, the stability of conduct and oppositional defiant behavior/antisocial behavior is substantially higher when based on latent Markov analysis compared with traditional continuity indexes that do not consider measurement error (Fergusson et al 1995, Zoccolillo et al 1992).

Presumably, this also applies to the stability of aggression, but we have not found studies to that effect. Second, it is not uncommon that some juveniles are highly aggressive or violent during one period, less aggressive in the next period, and highly aggressive or violent at a later stage (Thornberry et al 1995). This periodicity of aggression is rarely considered in measurements, and therefore stability coefficients of Time 1 and Time 2 are probably an underestimate of the true stability of aggression over time.

Finally, what does a high correlation between aggression early and later in life actually mean? Correlation coefficients indicate the degree to which subjects' ranking on an aggression score at Time 1 stays the same as their ranking at Time 2. Thus, a high correlation means that those who scored high at Time 1 also tend to score high at Time 2. However, a correlation does not consider population changes in the severity levels of aggression from childhood and adolescence. As shown above, the prevalence of physical fighting tends to decrease in that period, but prevalence of violence tends to increase with age. Knowledge of a high correlation does not reveal changes in the severity level of aggression with age. Specifically, correlations do not reveal what proportion of juveniles show decreases in the severity aggression, what proportion of juveniles display stable aggression, nor the proportion of juveniles whose aggression increases in severity with age.

Long-Term Escalation

We distinguish between two types of escalation toward violence that are dramatically different in antecedents. Long-term escalation refers to the gradual development of violence that can occur over many years and has as a precursor in earlier patterns of less serious forms of aggression. Short-term escalation in violence refers to violence in the absence of a history of aggression.

Most violence appears to erupt in youths who have been aggressive earlier in life. Several longitudinal studies show that aggression in early adolescence predicts later spouse or partner abuse and conviction for violent offenses (Farrington 1978, 1994; Magnusson et al 1983; Pulkkinen 1983) often better than property crimes (Loeber & Dishion 1983, Loeber & Stouthamer-Loeber 1987). Although frequent playing with toy guns may be related to later use of weapons, including guns, empirical studies are wanting (Berkowitz 1994). Forward prediction over time is often imperfect, with a proportion of individuals showing aggression early in life who do not commit violence later, and a proportion of nonaggressive youth who become violent later (Loeber & Stouthamer-Loeber 1987). Postdiction, that is, tracing back the earlier behavior of known violent adults, shows that most violent offenders were highly aggressive when young. For example, Farrington (1978) showed that approximately 7 out 10 men charged with violent crime by age 21 had been rated as highly aggressive between age 12 and 14. This finding is replicated in several studies, but the proportion varies depending on when aggression was measured in childhood and when the lifetime measure of violence was taken (see e.g. Loney et al 1983, Magnusson et al 1983, Mulligan et al 1963, Pulkkinen & Hurme 1984). We conclude that aggression early in life predicts later violence, but the prediction is far from perfect, both in terms of false-positive errors (youth who are at risk for violence but who are not violent) and false-negative errors (individuals who were not highly aggressive early in life who become violent).

DEVELOPMENTAL PATHWAYS In recent years, the emphasis on prediction has shifted somewhat toward understanding the processes leading to violence. There is a need to document within-individual changes in the patterns of aggression that occur during the developmental years and to establish whether individuals' development toward violence occurs in an orderly fashion. This aspect of development is denoted as a developmental pathway, in which individuals

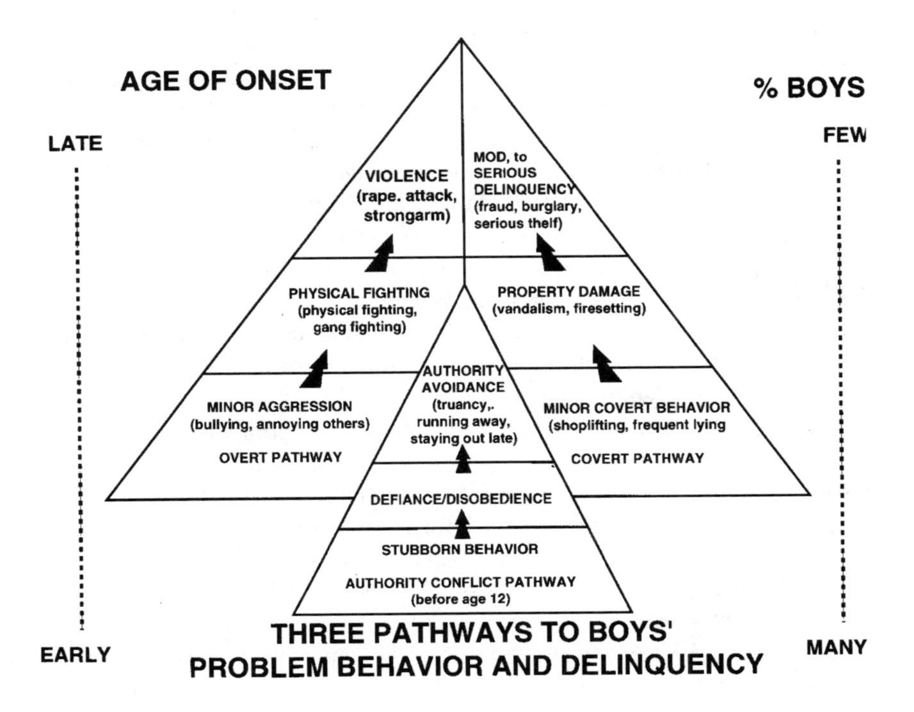

Figure 4 Three developmental pathways in boys' disruptive behavior, including the Overt Pathway leading to violence (Loeber & Hay 1994).

progress through an orderly sequence of aggressive acts of increasing severity over time. Since the onset curves in Figure 1 represent the onset of different individuals, the graphs do not show whether a given individual who becomes violent over time has experienced the onset of minor aggression first and then the onset of physical fighting.

Loeber and associates (Loeber et al 1993, 1997a,b) found evidence for three developmental pathways for males during childhood and adolescence (Figure 4). The Overt Pathway has aggression (annoying others, bullying) as the first stage, physical fighting (fighting, gang fighting) as the next stage, and violence (attacking someone, strongarming, forced sex) as the third stage. The other two pathways, the Covert Pathway (consisting of an escalation in covert, concealing problem behaviors), and an Authority Conflict Pathway (which concerns conflict with and avoidance of authority figures).

Results in these studies show that the majority of boys who showed some form of aggression fit the Overt Pathway in that their sequence of development fits the postulated developmental sequence in aggression. The findings held across the three samples, with the fit (defined as following the sequence or showing concurrent onsets) being better for younger than for older boys (96.2%, 89.5%, and 80.9%, in the youngest, middle, and oldest samples, respectively), but this could be a function of reliance on retrospective recall before their first age of assessment. The fit was equally good for African-American and Caucasian boys in the youngest and middle samples, and worse for African-American boys in the oldest sample. Moreover, most persistently aggressive boys entered the Overt Pathway at the first stage rather than at a later stage, and most boys who had engaged in violence were shown to have engaged first in behaviors comprising the earlier stages of the Overt Pathway. Thus, a temporal model of escalation in aggression and violence best applied (this is also supported by other studies, e.g. Elliott 1994).

A potential problem in the identification of pathways is that some juvenile problem behavior and aggression may be of a very temporary nature or may be in response to transitory provocation by peers. Therefore, it is important to distinguish between these "experimenters" and those youths whose aggression tends to persist over time. A recent refinement of the pathway model found that the developmental pathways model applied even better to "persisters" than experimenters, that is, those whose problem behavior did not persist over a period of six months (Loeber et al 1997a,b).

It remains to be seen whether especially the impulsive, aggressive youth in the Overt Pathway arm themselves with one or more weapons and become responsible for most criminal acts of violence. For some children, arming appears to escalate to the use of lethal weapons. A follow-up study of a school population in an urban setting (Arria et al 1995) showed that the carrying of a stick or a knife in one year was significantly associated with the subsequent carrying of a gun in later years.

Short-Term Escalation at Late Onset

Evidence from longitudinal studies (Farrington 1978, 1994; Magnusson et al 1983) and from analyses of developmental pathways (Loeber et al 1993, 1997a,b) shows that a minority of adult violent offenders do not have an antecedent patterns of aggressiveness early in life. Robins & Ratcliff (1980) noted that a proportion of the eventual violent African-American offenders in their study did not qualify as having conduct disorder earlier in life, which would suggest that "the violent offender was 'more normal' as a child than the property offender" (p. 258).

A study by Windle & Windle (1995) lends further support to the existence of late-onset violent offenders. The study, which consists of retrospective reports by Vietnam veterans (N = 4462) in their mid-30s about their life-course changes in aggression, provides provocative findings that can be tested in future prospective studies. However, we must be cautious about the generality of the findings because the sample concerned only selected males, was based only on self-reports, and may have biased results because of the limitations of retrospective recall. The authors distinguished between aggression in childhood only (to age 15), aggression in adulthood only (defined as 18 onward), and aggression in childhood and adulthood (aggression in the late teens was not included by the authors in this classification).

Of the entire sample, 19.4% recalled an onset of aggression in childhood (child-only aggression), 6.5% showed continuity of aggression from childhood to adulthood (continuity group), and 6.2% showed onset of aggression in adulthood (adult-onset group), with the remainder consisting of nonaggressive controls. If we take all the aggressive males as a base, almost two thirds (62.2%) were child-only aggressors, and the remainder was about equally divided into the continuity and the adult-onset groups. Thus, a substantial proportion of males had an onset of aggression in adulthood only, thereby showing a considerable discontinuity in their behavior over time and supporting the existence of short-term escalation of aggression at late onset.

A plausible explanation of late-onset violence without antecedent patterns of aggression rests on the concept of overcontrolled offenders that Megargee (1966) proposed. As Blackburn (1993) summarized, "overcontrolled offenders...have strong inhibitions, and aggress only when instigation (anger arousal) is sufficiently intense to overcome inhibitions" (p. 238). Whether individuals in this group are truly problem free earlier in life is unknown. For example, Pulkkinen (1982) found highly submissive girls had a risk of developing conduct problems. In addition, findings reported by Windle & Windle

(1995) showed that adult-only aggressors scored significantly higher on nonaggressive problems in childhood than boys in the control group. The adult-only group, compared with the child-only group, was also significantly more exposed to stressors and tended to suffer from psychiatric conditions.

Desistance

High stability coefficients for aggression may give the impression of high continuity and little change. However, there is substantial evidence that a proportion of juveniles desist in aggressive behavior over time. The age of desistance is defined here as the age at which an individual displays a particular behavior for the last time (e.g. Sampson & Laub 1993).

Population changes in the rate of desistance of aggression with age have been poorly studied (Fagan 1989) but appear concentrated during the transition from preschool to elementary school and during late adolescence. Several studies document a decrease in the prevalence of aggression in preschool to elementary school children (Goodenough 1931, Haapasalo & Tremblay 1994, Kingston & Prior 1995, Loeber et al 1989a), accompanied by decreases in the frequency and duration of aggressive acts during that period (Cummings et al 1989). For example, Haapasalo & Tremblay (1994) found a decrease in physical fighting, with 12.4% of boys in a community sample becoming desisting fighters, i.e. they fought at kindergarten age but desisted by ages 10 through 12 (in comparison, 8.3% were stable high fighters during the period). In addition, desistance in physical aggression occurs during adolescence, as can be inferred from the decrease in the prevalence of physical aggression during that period (Figure 2; see also McCord 1983, McCord et al 1963).

Gender differences in desistance of aggression have been little studied. It seems probable that girls during the preschool period outgrow aggression more speedily than boys. Moreover, serious violence peaks somewhat earlier for females compared with males, and this may mean that the subsequent desistance rate is steeper for females (Elliott 1994).

In all studies that concern desistance, it is unclear whether desistance is complete, not temporary. Moreover, does desistance in one form of violence mean desistance in other forms of serious aggression as well? To what extent is desistance in violence accompanied by a desistance in minor forms of aggression?

Researchers disagree about the developmental course of desistance. For example, Le Blanc & Fréchette (1989) found that the age of termination for delinquency was related to the age of onset, with the behaviors that started first terminating first, and those that started last terminating last. The probability of desistance in males is negatively related to the age of onset of early disruptive behavior and the degree to which they have escalated to serious disruptive behavior (Loeber 1988a), but it is unclear whether this applies specifically to aggression and violence.

TEMPERAMENTAL, EMOTIONAL, AND COGNITIVE CONTRIBUTORS TO AGGRESSION

Temperament and Emotional Regulation

Classic theories of aggression have long pointed to its emotional dimensions, including the association between frustration and aggression and the contribution of anger and rage to aggressive actions (for a review, see Cairns 1979). The control of anger and tolerance of frustrating circumstances are a major achievement in early socialization and not one that comes automatically. Temper tantrums and disruptive reactions to frustration are a common feature in toddlers. By middle childhood, however, most children have acquired self-control strategies that permit them to manage anger and tolerate frustrating circumstances. Girls in particular acquire ways of masking their anger, especially with adults (Underwood et al 1992). Some children, however, still have great difficulty in regulating their emotions and controlling their impulses.

Systematic individual differences in temperament emerge very early. Even in infancy, some babies are less easy to soothe and have problems adapting to the rhythms of social life, a persisting cluster of problems termed "difficult temperament" (Thomas et al 1968) that, in the toddler years, is associated with high rates of mother-child conflict (Lee & Bates 1985). Particular infants' reactions to frustration are stable over time (Fox 1989). Some of these early dimensions of temperament may be inborn. A longitudinal study of infant twins showed that parental reports of infants' irritability and expression of negative emotions, including anger, indicated significant genetic influence. The infants' reactions to frustration, however, did not, which suggests that early reactions to the social world may also be affected by early social experiences (Emde et al 1992). As mentioned above, early problems in regulating emotion in infancy are more frequently shown by boys than by girls (Weinberg & Tronick 1997), which may antedate later gender differences in self-control of impulses. Mothers' discipline techniques are partly influenced by their infants' temperament, so some children may find it particularly difficult to progress toward successful socialization (Kochanska 1993).

Difficult temperament, as reported by parents, is associated with a greater likelihood of behavioral problems and aggression (Kingston & Prior 1995, Sanson et al 1993), although it may interact with other risk factors such as the quality of the mother-child attachment relationship (Bates et al 1985), the home environment (Earls & Jung 1987), and the child's preterm birth (Goldberg et al 1990). Uncontrolled, impulsive behavior later in childhood is associated with some aspects of conduct problems; impulsivity in childhood predicts delinquency (White et al 1994). More explicit attention needs to be given to the links between early difficult temperament and aggression in particular.

Cognitive Factors

With age, children acquire cognitive skills and social understanding that help them avoid conflict or resolve their disputes with others (Dunn 1988, Shantz 1987). However, some children have both general and specific cognitive problems that promote aggression and make self-regulation more difficult.

LOW INTELLIGENCE Antisocial behavior is often accompanied by academic problems (Hinshaw 1992, Maguin & Loeber 1996, Maughan 1994), and so it is plausible that persistent aggression is at least partly a product of general intellectual deficits. However, the relationship applies more to males than females. In childhood, boys' aggression scores are negatively related to cognitive ability (Sharp et al 1995), but girls' conduct problems are positively associated with intelligence (Sonuga-Barke et al 1994). Whether this gender difference translates to different relationships between intelligence and violence in each gender is not clear.

A recent meta-analysis (Maguin & Loeber 1996) showed that low intelligence and attention problems rather than poor educational performance predicts later delinquency, but few studies have examined the relationship for violence. For instance, Farrington (1989) found that boys' low verbal intelligence between ages 8 and 10 was one of the best predictors of convictions for violence up to age 32. However, Stattin & Magnusson (1989) showed that both early aggression and intelligence predicted later delinquency and that in regression analyses early aggression predicted later delinquency independent of intelligence. These results suggest that aggressive youth, irrespective of their intelligence, tend to become delinquent but that low intelligence also forecasts delinquency. It is important to know whether this applies specifically to juvenile violence.

ATTENTION PROBLEMS The onset of attention problems [as evident in attention-deficit hyperactivity disorder (ADHD)] mostly occurs during the preschool period, the time when aggression also appears in a proportion of children. Several prospective longitudinal studies have shown that children with attention problems exhibit increased levels of antisocial behavior and aggression during childhood, adolescence, and adulthood (Campbell 1990, Hechtman et al 1984, Loney et al 1982, Sanson et al 1993, Satterfield et al 1982). The evidence that early attention problems without concurrent aggression are related to later aggression is weak (Loeber 1988b, Magnusson & Bergman 1990), but some studies claimed support for this hypothesis (Gittelman et al 1985, Mannuzza et al 1991, Mannuzza et al 1993). Actually, several studies show that early aggression alone rather than attention problems alone is associated with later aggression. For example, Cadoret & Stewart (1991) reported that a childhood history of ADHD was not directly related to antisocial personality disorder, "but indirectly through a set of aggressive behaviors" (p. 79). However, hyperactivity rather than inattention could be the factor that best predicts aggression. In that context, Gagnon et al (1995) found in a logistic regression that teacher-rated hyperactivity, rather than inattention, predicted stable aggression between the ages of 10 and 12.

Loney & Milich (1982) have shown that, according to teacher ratings, aggressive and hyperactive boys showed more severe symptoms than boys who were either aggressive only or hyperactive only. One longitudinal study (Sanson et al 1993) measured persistent aggression and hyperactivity at 5–6 and 7–8 years of age and then examined the children's prior history of problem behaviors. The results showed that "even at 4 to 8 months, the groups who later displayed aggressive behavior were more irritable and less cooperative-manageable" than the hyperactive only or nonaggressive children (p. 1214). At 32 to 36 months, the hyperactive-aggressive children were clearly the most difficult to handle, and according to the mothers, they were more inflexible than hyperactive only children. At the next assessments (to ages 7–8), the hyperactive-aggressive group continued to display the most difficult temperament and behavior in the home and the school.

Follow-up studies consistently show that boys with attention problems and conduct problems had a much earlier age of onset of conduct problems than boys with conduct problem and no attention problems (Loeber et al 1995, Moffitt 1990b, Offord et al 1979). For example, Loeber et al (1995) followed up 177 clinic-referred boys for six years and found that ADHD was associated with a 3.5 years earlier age of onset of conduct problems, while the combination of physical aggression and oppositional behavior best predicted the onset of conduct problems at any age.

In summary, attention problems appear to be important aspects of juvenile aggression that may help to predict the onset and perhaps the persistence of later aggression. However, given that attention problems often include hyperactive and impulsive behaviors as well, it remains to be seen which of these components is most relevant for the etiology of aggression.

Specific Aggression-Related Cognitive Factors

SOCIAL COGNITIVE DEFICIENCIES AND SENSITIVITIES Much work on the cognitive underpinnings of aggression focuses on specific social cognitive factors that make aggression more likely. Dodge and his colleagues (Dodge 1991, Dodge et al 1986) have argued that aggression derives from basic social cognitive deficiencies that make it difficult for some children to find nonaggressive solutions to interpersonal dilemmas. Aggressive children often cannot generate diverse solutions to problems and also frequently misunderstand others' intentions. According to Dodge, aggressive children tend to think that their companions have aggressive intent, and react accordingly, which increases the likelihood that the other child will be aggressive. Often the aggressive child misinterprets prosocial overtures as aggressive (Dodge et al 1984). These self-fulfilling prophecies lead to conflict with and then eventual rejection by peers (Dodge et al 1990).

Negative attributions promote conflict between mothers and children as well as between peers (MacKinnon-Lewis et al 1992). The social cognitive deficiencies shown by aggressive children are themselves associated with a history of maltreatment (Dodge et al 1990, Weiss et al 1992). Research by Downey and colleagues (G Downey, A Lebolt & C Rincón, unpublished manuscript; Feldman & Downey 1994) indicates that children's sensitivity to rejection places them at risk for behavioral and emotional problems. The sensitivity is linked to early experiences of overt rejection (e.g. child physical abuse) or covert rejection (e.g. emotional neglect) that are internalized by children. The sensitivity later becomes anticipatory and is accompanied by emotional arousal. Rejection sensitivity often is accompanied by either anger or anxiety, depending on situations and individuals' predispositions. Sometimes juveniles' sensitivity to rejection by their peers probably is a continuation of sensitivity to rejection by parents, which often is exacerbated by the parents' physical maltreatment or emotional neglect (Feldman & Downey 1994).

Other studies indicate, however, that social problem-solving difficulties may be related to family adversity but need not be. Sometimes a child's ability to solve social problems can compensate for adverse family circumstances (Downey & Walker 1989). Some children of psychiatrically ill parents have particularly acute social problem–solving abilities (Beardslee et al 1987). A proportion of children may use their social cognitive abilities to avoid conflict; others may learn to engage in conflict without violence and pursue their own self-interest in socially acceptable ways. This depends on knowledge of manners and other social conventions that prevent conflicts from arising and on being able to justify one's own aims and actions. Even in the toddler and preschool years, some children resolve conflicts with their peers by sharing objects or expressing affection (Caplan et al 1991, Sackin & Thelen 1984). However, these social cognitive skills are finely honed in the family circle, and children with older siblings are more advanced in their social cognitive ability than other children, acquiring a mature "theory of mind" sooner than firstborns or only children (Perner et al 1994). Just as Patterson (1986) has described the sibling relationship as a training ground for aggression, so Dunn (1988, 1993) has emphasized its importance for the development of negotiation skills and self-justification. Parents' reactions to siblings' conflicts over toys and use of space teach children about general principles of justice that can be used to prevent or resolve future conflicts (Ross et al 1990). To the extent that family conflicts are dealt with verbally and are satisfactorily resolved, children's social cognitive abilities may be fostered. To the extent that sibling conflict and conflict between parents and children is frequent and intense, opportunities for the acquisition of these social cognitive skills may be lacking. However, even in middle childhood and adolescence social problem–solving ability continues to develop and becomes more likely to be shown by females than males (Vuchinich et al 1988).

It is important to note, however, that social cognitive abilities may be necessary but not sufficient to control or prevent aggression. Treatment procedures may improve social cognitive abilities but not reduce observed aggression (Minde 1992). Cairns & Cairns (1994) noted that although adolescent girls, as opposed to adolescent boys, have acquired skills to express anger in less overtly aggressive ways, "some adolescent girls…are fully capable of a Rambo-like attack" (p. 59).

ATTITUDES TOWARD AGGRESSION AND MENTAL SCRIPTS The observations that maltreated children are likely to show misattributions of other people's intentions (Dodge et al 1990) and heightened sensitivity to rejection (G Downey, A Lebolt & C Rincón, unpublished manuscript) is consonant with the notion that children construct a general world view based on their own interpretation of their experiences. Children's gradual acquisition of gender identity and sex-typed behavior may be seen in terms of the construction of a general cognitive sense of self and world view. Sex-typing begins in the preschool years, at about the same time that gender differences in aggression first appear, but it continues to consolidate over the years of middle childhood. In middle childhood, fighting is seen as a masculine trait (Serbin et al 1993). The decline in girls' overt aggression and the development of other ways of expressing anger may partly be influenced by the cognitive aspects of the sex-typing process (Cairns & Cairns 1994).

It is also important to think about how much children's exposure to intense levels of violence and conflict creates a preoccupation with aggression that enhances their own aggressive tendencies. Exposure to conflict and violence creates immediate emotional reactions (e.g. Cummings et al 1989) but may also have more long-standing effects on a child's world view. For example, inner-city children who were directly exposed to the Los Angeles riots were more likely than children in other inner-city communities to tell stories filled with references to aggression and destruction (Farmer & Frosch 1996). Thus, theorists who emphasize the importance of children's exposure to conflict and aggression (e.g. Cummings et al 1991, Richters & Martinez 1993) must examine children's cognitive interpretations of such experiences as well as their immediate emotional reactions.

Children, like adults, differ in their attitudes toward aggression, with some showing a more favorable, approving attitude than others. The association between attitudes and delinquency is somewhat conflicting (e.g. Agnew 1991, Thornberry et al 1994). Zhang et al (1997) examined the association between favorable attitudes toward minor aggression and serious violent offenses and actual minor aggression and violent acts in three samples of preadolescent and adolescent boys. They found that attitudes favorable to minor aggression and violence increased with age and that the association between favorable attitudes to aggression and violence and aggressive/violent behavior tended to become stronger with age. In addition, the stability of attitudes favorable toward aggression or violence increased with age and was higher for favorable attitude toward violence than for favorable attitude toward minor aggression. Furthermore, their results showed mutual predictability between attitudes and behavior. However, during childhood there was a trend for favorable attitudes to predict minor aggression and violence better than for the aggressive and violent behavior to predict the favorable attitude. At later ages, the predictive power for both directions was roughly the same magnitude. Much needs to be learned about how attitudes favorable to aggression are formed (although much is known about the unfavorable influence of children's watching repeated violence on television, Huesmann & Eron 1986).

INFLATED SELF-ESTEEM Several authors have assumed that poor self-esteem is germane to aggressive individuals and that it plays an etiological role in the genesis of aggression (e.g. Anderson 1994, Schoenfield 1988). However, the empirical basis for this is weak (Baumeister et al 1996). Instead, a recent review (Baumeister et al 1996) highlights that aggressive individuals often have an inflated self-esteem, and "the more favorable one's view of oneself, the greater the range of external feedback that will be perceived as unacceptably low" (p. 9). Thus, these individuals are more prone to boast about themselves and to show aggression in response to a perceived threat to their ego (such as slights, disrespect, and negative feedback). The childhood precursors for inflated self-esteem are far from clear.

SOCIAL PROCESSES AND CAUSES It is likely that pathways to violence are partly driven by biological predispositions (e.g. Raine 1993). However, it seems clear that in some social settings children are at heightened risk for violent careers. Families, peers, and neighborhoods all may foster violence and aggression.

Family Factors

A large body of literature on familial correlates of aggression and violence exists (e.g. see reviews by Coie & Dodge 1997, Loeber & Stouthamer-Loeber 1986, Perry et al 1990). We examine the family's role in promoting aggression at different developmental periods.

MOTHER-INFANT RELATIONSHIPS Insecure attachment relationships in infancy predict later behavioral problems, and in boys these take the form of aggressive noncompliance. Insecure girls may be either aggressive or especially compliant in the preschool setting (Fagot & Kavanagh 1990, Greenberg et al 1992, Turner 1991). Insecure attachment is sometimes associated with maternal depression (DeMulder & Radke-Yarrow 1991), which promotes externalizing problems (Sharp et al 1995) and an aggressive stance toward interpersonal conflict, especially in boys (Hay et al 1992). Depression in the first year is associated with scores on an "aggression" factor rated by mothers and fathers; boys' aggression scores were, however, accounted for by considerable cognitive deficits associated with the mother's illness (Sharp et al 1995). In a sample of depressed mothers and their two-year-old children, it was noted that age-normative struggles over objects did not predict subsequent externalizing problems. In contrast, dysregulated, "out-of-control" aggression reliably predicted mothers' ratings of externalizing problems and children's self-reported personal difficulties at five years of age (Zahn-Waxler et al 1990). This suggests that "maladjusted" as opposed to age-normative aggression may be distinguished on empirical grounds and may be associated with maternal mood.

DISCIPLINARY PRACTICES During the preschool and school years, many family interactions involve discipline and parent-child conflict, which escalates in some families. Patterson's (1982) influential model focuses on both perpetrators and victims in family life, each of whom are engaged in repeated aggressive interchanges. Several child-rearing practices by parents are associated with the child's later aggression and violence, including coercive interactions (Patterson 1982), physical punishment or punitive discipline (Farrington 1978; SM Green, R Loeber, K Keenan & J Navratil, unpublished manuscript) and child physical abuse (Manly et al 1994). However, it is not always clear whether harsh disciplinary practices were used a priori or were evoked by the children's high levels of aggression or transgressions. However, parental psychopathology, including depression and antisocial personality disorder, can disrupt child-rearing practices and thus directly affect the formation of deviant behavior in the offspring (Frick et al 1992, Loeber & Stouthamer-Loeber 1986).

The consistency of parental discipline, as well as its harshness, and in particular children's perceptions of favoritism toward other siblings, may promote behavioral problems. An excessive degree of control of older compared with younger siblings explained 27% of the variance in the older siblings' externalizing behavior (Dunn et al 1990).

FAMILY STRUCTURE Several studies have found that aggressive children are often reared by single parents (Gagnon et al 1995, Kupersmidt et al 1995, Loeber et al 1989b, Tremblay et al 1997). For example, children characterized as stable fighters early in life were more likely to come from single-parent families (75%), compared with variable fighters (46%) and fighters who have desisted over time (17%). Single parenthood, however, is associated with type of neighborhood, and the interaction between these factors helps explain some of the variance in juvenile aggression (Kupersmidt et al 1995). Divorced families that have achieved stability may show less conflict than married families (Smetana et al 1991), and authoritative parenting in single-parent families may outweigh the effects of family structure (Hetherington et al 1992).

MULTIPLE RISKS The prediction of aggression is best achieved by considering multiple risk factors in family life. For example, Farrington (1989) found that the best independent familial childhood predictors of violence up to age 32 were low parental interest in the boys' education, authoritarian parents, a convicted parent, and harsh parental discipline. These multiple risks and the other factors reviewed here can account for the long-term development of aggression and violence over childhood. For example, mothers' mood in infancy predicts the child's later criminality, even when controlling for socioeconomic factors (Stattin & Klackenberg-Larsson 1990). A major question remains about the family process associated with the short-term escalation of late-onset violence that can occur in previously over-controlled individuals. Some theorists have focused more attention on peers and adult experiences in explaining late-onset aggression (e.g. Moffitt 1993), which in turn underscores the importance of nonfamilial influences throughout the life-course.

Peer Influences

As children grow older, the form of their play with peers changes. Bouts of rough play occur less often than more structured games with rules and formal sports, and physical aggression declines in frequency, especially for girls (Cairns & Cairns 1994). Friends are as likely as acquaintances to have disputes (Berndt et al 1986, Hartup et al 1988), but as children grow older and physical aggression becomes less usual, children who have frequent disagreements do not become friends (Hartup 1992). Highly aggressive children are rejected by their peers, partially as a function of the social cognitive deficiencies and biases that accompany their aggression (Parker & Asher 1987, Pope et al 1989). Rejection is evident as early as age 6 and predicts later negative outcomes (Kupersmidt & Coie 1990, Tremblay et al 1988). Apparently it is not just the presence of aggression but also the absence of more positive features that leads to children's rejection by their peers. Sociometric studies always identify some children who are controversial, that is, liked by some and disliked by others. Controversial children may show some aggression, but they also share and cooperate with others (Volling et al 1993). Furthermore, aggressive children who are rejected, compared with those who are not, show more diverse and severe conduct problems (Bierman et al 1993).

Peer rejection promotes the rejected child's aggressive stance against the world, and thus a vicious circle of effects is in place (e.g. Dodge et al 1986). However, in a multiple regression, Kupersmidt & Coie (1990) found that aggression and not peer rejection predicted later police contacts for delinquency. Thus, it remains to be seen whether aggressive forms of delinquency can be best explained by peer rejection, beyond the association with children's own preexisting levels of aggression that got them rejected. However, apparently peer rejection at age 10 promotes association with antisocial peers two years later (Dishion et al 1991), and association with antisocial peers promotes overt as well as covert forms of delinquency (Keenan et al 1995).

During middle childhood, as the highly aggressive child becomes rejected by the majority of the peer group, dyadic relationships form and become the arenas for most peer-directed aggression (Perry et al 1992). Some are asymmetrical, with one child a bully directing aggression consistently to a particular victim. Victims often lack social skills, are rejected by their peers, and are sometimes aggressive themselves (Perry et al 1988). Repeatedly victimized juveniles are prone to become aggressors as well (Hotaling et al 1989, Olweus 1978).

Because of the effects of repeated victimization, some dyadic aggressive relationships become more symmetrical, featuring a high level of conflict with each member of the dyad aggressing against the other (Perry et al 1992). Conflictual peer relationships may eventually promote alliances among aggressive youngsters who can work together to harass and bully others, forming coalitions that foster the emergence of aggressive peer groups and gangs. Gang membership promotes violence; longitudinal data show that, following entry into a gang, an individual's rate of violence usually increases and only drops when leaving the gang (Thornberry et al 1993).

By the onset of adolescence, most aggressive youths are not friendless; rather they have formed social networks with other deviant peers (Cairns et al 1988). These networks often prove attractive to other adolescents who were not aggressive nor rejected earlier in childhood, and the glamour associated with groups of delinquent peers may contribute to the late onset of aggression in adolescents with no prior history of serious problems (Moffitt 1993). This process, however, may be heightened in some communities more than others.

Neighborhood Factors

Neighborhoods vary much in the level of aggression and violence displayed individually or collectively by their inhabitants. The stability of these differences among neighborhoods is often high over time (see e.g. Farrington et al 1993, Sampson & Lauritsen 1994, Shaw & McKay 1942).

There is increasing evidence that neighborhoods not only have an impact on violence in adults but also on aggression in children (Attar et al 1994, Kupersmidt et al 1995, Loeber & Wikström 1993). For example, physical aggression in boys and girls is often concentrated in large urban areas (e.g. Tremblay et al 1997).

Stressful life events are associated with heightened aggression in children. Attar et al (1994) found that children living in the most disadvantaged neighborhoods experienced more stressful life events than children in other neighborhoods. The authors also found that stressful life events predicted increases in a teacher-rated aggression factor over a one-year period. Neighborhoods may also affect age of onset: Loeber & Wikström (1993) found that the worse the neighborhood the higher degree that 10- to 12-year-old boys had progressed to physical fighting or violence in the Overt Pathway. The finding did not apply to 13- to 15-year-old boys, for whom the progression to physical fighting and violence was more evenly distributed across different neighborhoods. Early onset of juvenile aggression and violence occurred mostly in the worst neighborhoods (supported by Sommers & Baskin's 1994 findings for females), but with age, juvenile aggression and violence also becomes evident in more advantaged neighborhoods. The association between juvenile aggression and neighborhood quality need to be seen within the context of a variety of causes that foster aggression.

Causes

Given the wide age range of onset of aggression and violence during childhood and adolescence, it would be implausible to conceptualize the causes of aggression and violence to be the same for any age of onset and subsequent ages of development. In addition, intermittency of aggression and violence (Thornberry et al 1995) needs to be explained and is difficult to sustain in a model of constant risk factors that do not covary with aggression. Several authors have commented on the heterogeneity of risk and causal factors underlying delinquency, including violence (Huizinga et al 1991, Loeber 1990). We use the term cause with considerable caution because research on the causal status of risk factors is often wanting. We see a distinction between causes whose cumulative effects can only be discerned over long periods, and causes with more immediate effects.

CUMULATIVE, LONG-TERM CAUSES Although precise data are wanting, children's escalation from minor aggression to violence in either the home or the school may take years. Repeated practice of aggressive acts is thought to be the basis for the formation of violence (Patterson 1982). Examples of cumulative, long-term causes are poor parenting practices (Loeber & Stouthamer-Loeber 1986) and children's often repeated exposure to violence on television (Huesmann & Eron 1986).

SHORT-TERM CAUSES Several conditions may enhance the short-term probability of subsequent aggression, and this may especially apply to certain categories of youth. For example, alcohol consumption may facilitate aggression, and this may specifically apply to individuals with prior high levels of aggressive behavior (Lang 1993). The heightened level of individuals' violence after their introduction into a gang may largely result from gangs' attracting already aggressive youngsters equipped with weapons (Bjerregaard & Lizotte 1995). Likewise, after the onset of drug dealing, an acceleration in individuals' rates of violent acts has been found (Blumstein 1995, Van Kammen & Loeber 1994).

Note that short-term causes are not always easy to distinguish from selection effects, i.e. individuals selecting peers, settings, and activities that match their own preferences for violent experiences. This selection process can directly influence the individual's rate of violence.

SHORT-TERM CAUSES FOR LATE-ONSET VIOLENCE We emphasized above that not all violent individuals have a background of childhood aggression, but that some of these individuals may have displayed nonaggressive disruptive behavior early in life. Much needs to be learned about short-term antecedents that trigger violence in otherwise nonaggressive individuals. For example, the retrospective research by Windle & Windle (1995) indicated that adult-onset aggression was associated with several stressors: high-school drop-out and marital instability. In addition, the adult-onset aggressive group showed a relatively high prevalence of psychiatric disorders such as major depressive disorder and generalized anxiety disorder. Thus, late-onset violence is possibly more common among those individuals exposed to high levels of life stressors, or those with certain psychiatric disorders.

ARE THE CAUSES FOR MINOR AGGRESSION THE SAME AS THOSE FOR VIOLENCE? We postulate that the causes of minor aggression only partly overlap with the causes of violence. For example, individuals who display minor aggression and individuals who display violence each may have been reared in households characterized by a high rate of coercive interchanges. Although a high rate of coercive interchanges may be important to the etiology of minor aggression, the emergence of violence may rest on the accumulation of additional risk factors. Given that the prevalence of aggression is much higher than that of violence, we postulate that the causes of violence may be less common and more proximal to the act than the causes of aggression.

CAUSES AND SETTINGS Children differ greatly in their fighting across different settings. Some fight in the home only, others fight at school, and still others fight in both settings (Loeber & Dishion 1984). That aggression by juveniles can generalize from one setting to another setting is well known. There is more evidence that aggression in the home generalizes to aggression in the school than vice versa. Causes located in the home setting are relevant for the emergence of aggression in other settings such as schools (see review by Loeber & Stouthamer-Loeber 1997). For example, physical abuse of children in the home setting alters their relationships with other adults outside the home. Boney-McCoy & Finkelhor (1995) found that in a national sample of children aged 10–16, being victimized by parental violence increased the risk of the children having trouble with a teacher, but the effect was only found for girls. In addition, abuse is associated with later violence. For instance, Smith & Thornberry (1995) found that child maltreatment by a parent (physical or sexual) was associated with the later prevalence and frequency of violent offending in the community. Much less is known about causal factors in the school or in the community that might influence children's aggression at home.

CAUSES OF DESISTANCE A much neglected area of investigation involves the circumstances that foster desistance in aggression and violence. Most studies and theorizing about desistance concern delinquency rather than aggression or violence. For example, Sampson & Laub (1993) developed an age-grade theory of informal social control to explain crime and deviance from childhood to adulthood. They theorized that desistance resulted from strong social ties to adult institutions (e.g. family, community, and work). Our conceptualization builds on this and extends it back to adolescence. We consider that the probability of desistance varies with the severity of the delinquent acts and is a function of the perpetrator's perception of the yield of the acts and of the likelihood of social sanction. This reflects a shift away from external sanctions for transgressions (e.g. by parental discipline) to internal control of behavior, which is a central theme in development from childhood to adulthood. It is likely that cognitive factors and the ability to regulate one's anger and impatience may play a role in the cessation of aggression and violence.

Desistance in violence presumably is facilitated by individuals' adoption of antiviolent values and standards of conduct. This clearly needs to be investigated, especially in samples of males during early adulthood when desistance becomes more common (Farrington 1986), and when young males settle down to have families, experience job success, and form positive ties with their community. However, for some previous violent offenders, violence may become directed to spouses and children rather than to others outside the family.

PATHOLOGY OR UNFAVORABLE CIRCUMSTANCES? Another aspect of causation concerns whether aggression is a focus of psychopathology or an adaptive response to disadvantaged circumstances. Adults do not universally agree about the need to reduce aggression in children. Some argue that antisocial behavior (and implicitly, aggression) is not necessarily a form of pathology but rather a necessary and inevitable response by children to survive in settings or communities where threats to their well-being are common (e.g. Richters & Cicchetti 1993). Children going to schools in which fighting is common or who live in high-crime neighborhoods fall into this category. According to this view, without the skills to aggress or fight, the child would likely be repeatedly victimized by other children's aggression.

The fight-or-suffer justification for children's aggression is not shared by others, who instead believe that aggression in some children constitutes a form of maladjustment, especially when it is frequently directed at the parents themselves or at other siblings in the home. Proponents of this viewpoint see aggression as slowly emerging over time, increasing in severity, and generalizing to different settings outside the home. They may see much of the child's initiation of aggression as either occurring unprovoked or easily triggered by events that rarely provoke others. In particular, some children display aggressive behavior without obvious provocation, such as using force to dominate, getting others to gang up on peers, and initiation of threats or bullying of others (Dodge & Coie 1987). Children themselves condemn unprovoked aggression (Hay et al 1992).

We agree that maladaptive aggression, in contrast with aggression in response to unfavorable circumstances, is relatively insensitive to variations of settings and individuals. Such children often show their aggression in multiple settings (e.g. the home, the school, and the community) and multiple victims (e.g. siblings, parents, peers, strangers). It is this possible subpopulation of children—yet to be characterized as a homogenous group through stringent empirical verification—that may most profit from early identification and intervention.

ACKNOWLEDGMENTS

The authors are indebted to several of their collaborators and others for their inspiration and advice, including David P Farrington, David Fergusson, Dan Olweus, and Debra Pepler. We are grateful to Sandy Smith and Laura Schmidt for their assistance with analyses based on the data from the Pittsburgh Youth Study, to Alaina Winters and Stephanie M Green for reading and commenting on an early draft, and to JoAnn Fraser for compiling the reference list. The paper was written with the financial support of Grants MH 48890 and MH 42529 of the National Institute of Mental Health, and Grant No. 86-JN-CX-0009 of the Office of Juvenile Justice and Delinquency Prevention. Points of view or opinions in this document are those of the authors and do not necessarily represent the official position of either agency.

Literature Cited

Achenbach TM, Edelbrock CS. 1987. *Manual for the Youth Self-Report and Profile.* Burlington, VT: Univ. Vt. Dep. Psychiatry

Agnew R. 1991. A longitudinal test of social control theory and delinquency. *J. Quant. Crim.* 28:126–56

American Psychiatric Association. 1994. *Diagnostic and Statistical Manual of Mental Disorders.* Washington, DC: Am. Psychiatr. Assoc. 4th ed.

Anderson E. 1994. The code of the streets. *Atl. Mon.* 5:81–94

Arria AM, Wood NP, Anthony JC. 1995. Prevalence of carrying a weapon and related behaviors in urban schoolchildren 1989 to 1993. *Arch. Pediatr. Adolesc. Med.* 149:1345–50

Ascione FR. 1993. Children who are cruel to animals: a review of research and implications for developmental psychopathology. *Anthrozoös* 6:226–46

Attar BK, Guerra NG, Tolan PH. 1994. Neighborhood disadvantage, stressful life events, and adjustment in urban elementary-school children. *J. Clin. Child Psychol.* 23:391–400

Bates JE, Maslin CA, Frankel KA. 1985. Attachment security, mother-child interaction, and temperament as predictors of behavior problem ratings at age three years. *Monogr. Soc. Res. Child Dev.* 50:209

Baumeister RF, Smart L, Boden JM. 1996. Relation of threatened egotism to violence and aggression: the dark side of high self-esteem. *Psychol. Bull.* 103:5–33

Beardslee WR, Schultz LH, Selman RL. 1987. Level of social-cognitive development, adaptive functioning and DSM-III diagnoses in adolescent offspring of parents with affective disorders: implications of the development of the capacity for mutuality. *Dev. Psychol.* 23:807–15

Berkowitz L. 1993. *Aggression: It's Causes, Consequences and Control.* Philadelphia: Temple Univ. Press

Berkowitz L. 1994. Guns and youth. See Eron et al 1994, pp. 251–79

Berndt TJ, Hawkins JA, Hoyle SG. 1986. Changes in friendship during a school year: effects on children's and adolescents' impressions of friendship and sharing with friends. *Child Dev.* 57:1284–97

Bierman KL, Smoot DL, Aumiller K. 1993. Characteristics of aggressive-rejected, aggressive (nonrejected), and rejected (nonaggressive) boys. *Child Dev.* 64: 139–51

Bjerregaard B, Lizotte AJ. 1995. Gun ownership and gang membership. *J. Crim. Law Criminol.* 86:37–58

Bjorkqvist K, Lagerspetz KMJ, Kaukiainen A. 1992. Do girls manipulate and boys fight? Developmental trends in regard to direct and indirect aggression. *Aggress. Behav.* 18:117–27

Blackburn R. 1993. *The Psychology of Criminal Conduct.* Chichester: Wiley

Blumstein A. 1995. Young people and why the deadly nexus? *Natl. Inst. Justice J.* 229:2–9

Boney-McCoy S, Finkelhor D. 1995. Psychosocial sequelae of violent victimization in a national youth sample. *J. Consult. Clin. Psychol.* 63:726–36

Cadoret RJ, Stewart MA. 1991. An adoption study of attention deficit hyperactivity, aggression and their relationships to adult antisocial personality. *Compr. Psychiatry* 32: 73–82

Cairns RB. 1979. *Social Development: The Origins and Plasticity of Interactions.* San Francisco: Freeman

Cairns RB, Cairns BD. 1984. Predicting aggressive patterns in girls and boys: a developmental study. *Aggress. Behav.* 10:227–42

Cairns RB, Cairns BD. 1994. *Lifelines and Risks: Pathways of Youth in Our Time.* Cambridge: Univ. Cambridge Press

Cairns RB, Cairns BD, Neckerman HJ, Gariépy J-L, Ferguson LL. 1989. Growth and aggression. I. Childhood to early adolescence. *Dev. Psychol.* 25:320–30

Cairns RB, Cairns BD, Neckerman HJ, Gest SD, Gariépy J-L. 1988. Social networks and aggressive behavior: peer support or peer rejection? *Dev. Psychol.* 24:815–23

Cairns RB, Kroll AB. 1994. Developmental perspective on gender differences and similarities. See Rutter & Hay 1994, pp. 350–72

Callahan CM, Rivara FP. 1992. Urban high school youth and handguns. *J. Am. Med. Assoc.* 267:3038–42

Campbell SB. 1990. Longitudinal studies of active and aggressive preschoolers: individual differences in early behavior and in outcome. In *Internalizing and Externalizing Expressions of Dysfunction,* ed. D Cicchetti, SL Toth, pp. 57–90. Hillsdale, NJ: Earlbaum

Caplan M, Vespo JE, Pedersen J, Hay DF. 1991. Conflict and its resolution in small groups of one- and two-year-olds. *Child Dev.* 62:1513–24

Caspi A, Elder GH, Bem DJ. 1987. Moving against the world: life-course patterns of explosive children. *Dev. Psychol.* 23:308–13

Choynowski M. 1995. Does aggressiveness have a factorial structure? *Pers. Individ. Differ.* 18:167–87

Coie JD, Dodge KA. 1997. Aggression and antisocial behavior. In *Handbook of Child Psychology,* Vol. 3: *Social, Emotional and Personality Development,* ed. W Damon, N Eisenberg. 5th ed. In press

Crick NR. 1995. Relational aggression: the role of intent attributions, feelings of distress, and provocation type. *Dev. Psychopathol.* 7:313–22

Crick NR, Grotpeter JK. 1995. Relational aggression, gender, and social-psychological adjustment. *Child Dev.* 66:710–22

Cummings EM, Ballard M, El-Sheikh M, Lake M. 1991. Resolution and children's responses to interadult anger. *Dev. Psychol.* 27:462–70

Cummings EM, Iannotti RJ, Zahn-Waxler C. 1989. Aggression between peers in early childhood: individual continuity and developmental change. *Child Dev.* 60:887–95

DeMulder EK, Radke-Yarrow M. 1991. Attachment and affectively ill and well mothers: concurrent behavioral correlates. *Dev. Psychopathol.* 3:227–42

DiLalla LF, Gottesman I. 1989. Heterogeneity of causes for delinquency and criminality: life span perspectives. *Dev. Psychopathol.* 1:339–49

Dishion TJ, Patterson GR, Stoolmiller M, Skinner ML. 1991. Family, school, and behavioral antecedents to early adolescent involvement with antisocial peers. *Dev. Psychol.* 27:172–80

Dodge KA. 1991. The structure and function of reactive and protective aggression. See Pepler & Rubin 1991, pp. 201–18

Dodge KA, Bates JE, Pettit GS. 1990. Mechanisms in the cycle of violence. *Science* 250: 1678–83

Dodge KA, Coie JD. 1987. Social information processing factors in reactive and proactive aggression in children's peer groups. *J. Pers. Soc. Psychol.* 53:1146–58

Dodge KA, Murphy RR, Buchsbaum K. 1984. The assessment of intention-cue detection skills in children: implications for developmental psychopathology. *Child Dev.* 55: 163–73

Dodge KA, Pettit GS, McClaskey CL, Brown MM. 1986. Social competence in children. *Monogr. Soc. Res. Child Dev.* 51:Ser. No. 213

Downey G, Walker E. 1989. Social cognition and adjustment in children at risk for psychopathology. *Dev. Psychol.* 25:835–45

Dunn J. 1988. *The Beginnings of Social Understanding.* Cambridge, MA: Harvard

Dunn J. 1993. *From preschool to adolescence: a ten-year follow-up of siblings in Cambridge.* Presented to Cent. Fam. Res., Cambridge

Dunn J, Stocker C, Plomin R. 1990. Nonshared experiences within the family: correlates of behavioral problems in middle childhood. *Dev. Psychopathol.* 2:113–26

Earls FE, Jung KG. 1987. Temperament and home environment characteristics as causal factors in the early development of childhood psychopathology. *J. Am. Acad. Child Adolesc. Psychiatry* 36:491–98

Elliott DS. 1994. Serious violent offenders: onset, developmental course, and termination. The American Society of Criminology 1993 presidential address. *Criminology* 32: 1–21

Emde RN, Plomin R, Robinson J, Corley R, DeFries J, et al. 1992. Temperament, emotion, and cognition at fourteen months: the MacArthur Longitudinal Twin Study. *Child Dev.* 63:1437–55

Eron LD, Gentry JH, Schlegel P, eds. 1994. *Reason to Hope: A Psychosocial Perspective on Violence and Youth.* Washington, DC: Am. Psychol. Assoc.

Eron LD, Huesmann LR. 1990. The stability of aggressive behavior: even unto the third generation. See Lewis & Miller 1990, pp. 147–56

Fagan J. 1989. Cessation of family violence: deterrence and dissuasion. See Ohlin & Tonry 1989, pp. 377–425

Fagin J. 1990. The social organization of drug use and drug dealing among urban gangs. *Criminology* 27:633–69

Fagot B, Kavanagh K. 1990. The prediction of antisocial behavior from avoidant attachment classification. *Child Dev.* 61:864–73

Farmer JAM, Frosch DL. 1996. L. A. stories: aggression in preschoolers' narratives after the riots of 1992. *Child Dev.* 67:19–32

Farrington DP. 1978. The family background of aggressive youths. In *Aggression and Antisocial Behavior in Childhood and Adolescence,* ed. LA Hersov, M Berger, D Schaffer, pp. 73–93. Oxford: Pergamon

Farrington DP. 1986. Age and crime. See Tonry & Morris 1986, 7:29–90

Farrington DP. 1989. Early predictors of adolescent aggression and adult violence. *Violence Vict.* 4:79–100

Farrington DP. 1991. Childhood aggression and adult violence: early precursors and later life outcomes. See Pepler & Rubin 1991, pp. 8–30

Farrington DP. 1993. Understanding and preventing bullying. See Tonry & Morris 1986, 17:381–458

Farrington DP. 1994. Childhood, adolescent, and adult features of violent males. In *Aggressive Behavior: Current Perspectives,* ed. LR Huesmann, pp. 215–40. New York: Plenum

Farrington DP, Berkowitz L, West DJ. 1982. Differences between individual and group fights. *Br. J. Soc. Psychol.* 21:323–33

Farrington DP, Sampson RJ, Wikström P-OH, eds. 1993. *Integrating Individual and Ecological Aspects of Crime.* Stockholm: Liber-Verlag

Feldman S, Downey G. 1994. Refection sensitivity as a mediator of the impact of childhood exposure to family violence on adult attachment behavior. *Dev. Psychopathol.* 6:231–47

Fergusson DM, Horwood LJ, Lynskey MT. 1995. The stability of disruptive childhood behaviors. *J. Abnorm. Child Psychol.* 23: 379–96

Fox N. 1989. The psychophysiological correlates of emotional reactivity during the first year of life. *Dev. Psychol.* 25:364–72

Frick PJ, Lahey BB, Loeber R, Stouthamer-Loeber M, Christ MAG, Hanson K. 1992. Familial risk factors to Oppositional Defiant Disorder and Conduct Disorder: parental psychopathology and maternal parenting. *J. Consult. Clin. Psychol.* 60:49–55

Frick PJ, Lahey BB, Loeber R, Tannenbaum L, Van Horn Y, et al. 1993. Oppositional defiant disorder and conduct disorder: a meta-analytic review of factor analyses and cross-validation in a clinic sample. *Clin. Psychol. Rev.* 13:319–40

Gagnon C, Craig WM, Tremblay RE, Zhou RM, Vitaro F. 1995. Kindergarten predictors of boys' stable behavior problems at the end of elementary school. *J. Abnorm. Child Psychol.* 23:751–66

Gittelman R, Mannuzza S, Shenker R, Bonagura N. 1985. Hyperactive boys almost grown up. *Arch. Gen. Psychiatry* 42: 937–47

Goldberg S, Corter C, Lojkasek M, Minde K. 1990. Prediction of behavior problems in 4-year olds born prematurely. *Dev. Psychopathol.* 2:15–30

Goodenough F. 1931. *Anger in Young Children.* Minneapolis: Univ. Minn. Press

Greenberg M, Speltz ML, DeKlyen M, Endniga M. 1992. Attachment security in preschoolers with and without externalizing behavior problems: a replication. *Dev. Psychopathol.* 3:413–30

Haapasalo J, Tremblay RE. 1994. Physically aggressive boys from ages 6 to 12: family background, parenting behavior, and prediction of delinquency. *J. Consult. Clin. Psychol.* 62:1044–52

Hamparian DM, Schuster R, Dinitz S, Conrad JP. 1978. *Violent Few: A Study of Dangerous Juvenile Offenders.* Lexington, MA: Heath Lexington

Hartup WW. 1992. Conflict and friendship relations. See Shantz & Hartup 1992, pp. 186–215

Hartup WW, Laursen B, Stewart MI, Eastenson A. 1988. Conflict and the friendship relations of young children. *Child Dev.* 59: 1590–600

Hay DF. 1984. Social conflict in early childhood. *Ann. Child Dev.* 1:1–44

Hay DF. 1995. *Continuities and change in aggression in very early childhood.* Presented at Meet. Life Hist. Soc., Chatham, MA

Hay DF, Castle J, Stimson CA, Davies L. 1995. The social construction of character in toddlerhood. In *Mortality in Everyday Life: Developmental Perspectives,* ed. M Killen, D Hart, pp. 23–51. Cambridge: Cambridge Univ. Press

Hay DF, Ross HS. 1982. The social nature of early conflict. *Child Dev.* 53:105–11

Hay DF, Vespo JE, Zahn-Waxler C, Radke-Yarrow M. 1993. *Patterns of family conflict when the mother is depressed.* Presented at Eur. Conf. Dev. Psychol., 6th, Bonn

Hay DF, Zahn-Waxler C, Cummings EM, Iannotti RJ. 1992. Young children's views about conflict with peers: a comparison of the daughters and sons of depressed and well women. *J. Child Psychol. Psychiatry* 33:669–83

Hechtman L, Weiss G, Perlman T, Amsel R. 1984. Hyperactives as young adults: initial predictors of adult outcome. *J. Am. Acad. Child Psychiatry* 23:250–60

Hetherington EM, Clingempeel WG, Anderson ER, Deal JE, Hagan MS, et al. 1992. Coping with marital transitions: a family systems perspective. *Monogr. Soc. Res. Child Dev.* 57:Ser. No. 227

Hill JP. 1987. Research on adolescents and their families: past and prospect. In *New Directions for Child Development: Adoles-*

cent Social Behavior and Health, ed. C Irwin, pp. 13–32. San Francisco: Jossey-Bass

Hinshaw SP. 1992. Externalizing behavior problems and academic underachievement in childhood and adolescence: causal relationships and underlying mechanisms. *Psychol. Bull.* 111:127–55

Hotaling GT, Straus MA, Lincoln AJ. 1989. Intrafamily violence, and crime and violence outside of the family. See Ohlin & Tonry 1989, pp. 315–75

Howell JC. 1995. Gangs and youth violence. In *A Sourcebook: Serious, Violent, and Chronic Juvenile Offenders,* ed. JC Howell, B Krisberg, JD Hawkins, JJ Wilson, pp. 261–74. Thousand Oaks, CA: Sage

Huesmann LR, Eron LD, eds. 1986. *Television and the Aggressive Child: A Cross-National Comparison.* Hillsdale, NJ: Erlbaum

Huizinga D, Esbensen F-A, Weiher AW. 1991. Are there multiple paths to delinquency? *J. Crim. Law Criminol.* 82:83–118

Izard CE, Fantauzzo CA, Castle JM, Haynes OM, Rayias MR, Putnam PH. 1995. The ontogeny of infants' facial expressions in the first nine months of life. *Dev. Psychol.* 31:997–1013

Johnston LD, O'Malley PM, Bachman JG. 1993. *Monitoring the Future Study for Goal 6 of the National Education Goals: A Special Report for the National Education Goals Panel.* Ann Arbor: Univ. Mich. Inst. Soc. Res.

Kann L, Warren CW, Harris WA, Collins JL, Douglas KA, et al. 1995. Youth Risk Behavior Surveillance: United States 1993. *Morbid Mortal. Wkly. Rep.* 1995 44 (No. SS-1), CDC Surveill. Summer

Kazdin AE. 1987. *Conduct Disorders in Childhood and Adolescence.* New York: Sage

Keenan K, Loeber R, Zhang Q, Stouthamer-Loeber M, Van Kammen WB. 1995. The influence of deviant peers on the development of boys' disruptive and delinquent behavior: a temporal analysis. *Dev. Psychopathol.* 7:715–26

Kingston L, Prior M. 1995. The development of patterns of stable, transient, and school-age aggressive behavior in young children. *J. Am. Acad. Child Adolesc. Psychiatry* 34: 348–58

Klein MW. 1995. *The American Street Gang.* New York: Oxford Univ. Press

Kochanska G. 1993. Toward a synthesis of parental socialization and child temperament in early development of conscience. *Child Dev.* 64:325–47

Kruttschnitt C. 1993. Gender and interpersonal violence. See Reiss & Roth 1993, 3:293–376

Kupersmidt JB, Coie JD. 1990. Preadolescent peer status, aggression, and school adjustment as predictors of externalizing problems in adolescence. *Child Dev.* 61: 1350–62

Kupersmidt JB, Griesler PC, DeRosier ME, Patterson CJ, Davis PW. 1995. Childhood aggression and peer relations in the context of family and neighborhood factors. *Child Dev.* 66:360–75

Lahey BB, McBurnett K, Loeber R, Hart EL. 1995. Psychobiology of conduct disorder. In *Conduct Disorders in Children and Adolescents: Assessments and Interventions,* ed. GP Sholevar, pp. 27–44. Washington, DC: Am. Psychiatr. Press

Lang R. 1993. Alcohol related violence: psychological perspectives. In *Alcohol and Interpersonal Violence: Fostering Interdisciplinary Perspectives,* ed. S Martin. NIAAA Res. Monogr. Ser. 24:121–48. Washington, DC: Dep. Health Hum. Serv.

Le Blanc M, Côté G, Loeber R. 1991. Temporal paths in delinquency: stability, regression and progression analyzed with panel data from an adolescent and a delinquent sample. *Can. J. Criminol.* 33:23–44

Le Blanc M, Fréchette M. 1989. *Male Offending from Latency to Adulthood.* New York: Springer-Verlag

Lee CL, Bates JE. 1985. Mother-child interaction at age two years and perceived difficult temperament. *Child Dev.* 56:1314–25

Lewis M, Miller SM, eds. 1990. *Handbook of Developmental Psychopathology.* New York: Plenum

Lizotte AJ, Tesoriero JM, Thornberry TP, Krohn M. 1994. Patterns of adolescent firearms ownership and use. *Justice Q.* 11:51–74

Lochman JE, Dodge KA. 1994. Social-cognitive processes to severely violent, moderately aggressive, and nonaggressive boys. *J. Consult. Clin. Psychol.* 62:366–74

Loeber R. 1982. The stability of antisocial and delinquent child behavior. *Child Dev.* 53: 1431–46

Loeber R. 1988a. Natural histories of conduct problems, delinquency, and associated substance use. In *Advances in Clinical Child Psychology,* ed. BB Lahey, AE Kazdin, 11: 73–124. New York: Plenum

Loeber R. 1988b. Behavioral precursors and accelerators of delinquency. In *Explaining Delinquency,* ed. W Buikhuisen, SA Mednick, pp. 51–67. Leiden, Holl: Brill

Loeber R. 1990. Development and risk factors of juvenile antisocial behavior and delinquency. *Clin. Psychol. Rev.* 10:1–41

Loeber R, Dishion TJ. 1983. Early predictors of male delinquency: a review. *Psychol. Bull.* 94:68–99

Loeber R, Dishion TJ. 1984. Boys who fight at home and in school: family conditions influencing cross-setting consistency and discontinuity. *J. Consult. Clin. Psychol.* 52: 759–68

Loeber R, Green SM, Keenan K, Lahey BB. 1995. Which boys will fare worse? Early predictors of the onset of conduct disorder in a six-year longitudinal study. *J. Am. Acad. Child. Adolesc. Psychiatry* 34:499–509

Loeber R, Green SM, Lahey BB, Stouthamer-Loeber M. 1989a. Optimal informants on childhood disruptive behaviors. *Dev. Psychopathol.* 1:317–37

Loeber R, Hay DF. 1994. Developmental approaches to aggression and conduct problems. See Rutter & Hay 1994, pp. 488–516

Loeber R, Keenan K, Zhang Q. 1997a. Boys' experimentation and persistence in developmental pathways toward serious delinquency. *J. Child Fam. Stud.* In press

Loeber R, Le Blanc M. 1990. Toward a developmental criminology. See Tonry & Morris 1986, 12:375–473

Loeber R, Schmaling K. 1985. Empirical evidence for overt and covert patterns of antisocial conduct problems. *J. Abnorm. Child Psychol.* 13:337–52

Loeber R, Smalley MM, Keenan K, Zhang Q. 1997b. A prospective replication of developmental pathways in disruptive and delinquent behavior. In *The Individual as a Focus in Developmental Research,* ed. RB Cairns. Thousand Oaks, CA: Sage. In press

Loeber R, Smith S. 1996. *Unpublished aggression data from the Pittsburgh Youth Study.* West. Psychiatr. Inst. Clinic, Sch. Med., Univ. Pittsburgh, PA

Loeber R, Stouthamer-Loeber M. 1986. Family factors as correlates and predictors of juvenile conduct problems and delinquency. See Tonry & Morris 1986, 7:29–149

Loeber R, Stouthamer-Loeber M. 1987. Prediction. In *Handbook of Juvenile Delinquency,* ed. HC Quay, pp. 325–82. New York: Wiley

Loeber R, Stouthamer-Loeber M. 1997. Developmental aspects of violence in the home and at school. In *Schools and Violence,* ed. DS Elliott, K Williams, B Hamburg. New York: Cambridge Univ. Press. In press

Loeber R, Tremblay RE, Gagnon C, Charlebois P. 1989b. Continuity and desistance in disruptive boys' early fighting in school. *Dev. Psychopathol.* 1:39–50

Loeber R, Wikström P-OH. 1993. Individual pathways to crime in different types of neighborhood. See Farrington et al 1993, pp. 169–204

Loeber R, Wung P, Keenan K, Giroux B, Stouthamer-Loeber M, Van Kammen WB. 1993. Developmental pathways in disruptive child behavior. *Dev. Psychopathol.* 5: 101–32

Loney J, Kramer J, Milich RS. 1982. The hyperactive child grows up: predictors of symptoms, delinquency, and achievement at follow-up. In *Psychosocial Aspects of Drug Treatment for Hyperactivity,* ed. KD Gadow, J Loney, pp. 381–415. Boulder, CO: Westview

Loney J, Milich R. 1982. Hyperactivity inattention, and aggression in clinical practice. In *Advances in Behavioral Pediatrics,* ed. M Wolraich, DK Routh, 3:33–147. Greenwich, CT: JAI

Loney J, Whaley-Klahn MA, Kosier T, Conboy J. 1983. Hyperactive boys and their brothers at 21: predictors of aggressive and antisocial outcomes. See Van Dusen & Mednick 1983, pp. 181–208

Lowry R, Sleet D, Duncan C, Powell K, Kolbe L. 1995. Adolescents at risk for violence. *Educ. Psychol. Rev.* 7:7–39

Maccoby EE. 1988. Gender as a social category. *Dev. Psychol.* 24:735–65

MacKinnon-Lewis C, Lamb ME, Arbuckle B, Baradaran LP, Volling BL. 1992. The relationship between biased maternal and filial attributions and the aggressiveness of their interactions. *Dev. Psychopathol.* 4: 403–15

Magnusson D, Bergman LR. 1990. A pattern approach to the study of pathways from childhood to adulthood. In *Straight and Devious Pathways from Childhood to Adulthood,* ed. L Robins, M Rutter, pp. 101–15. Cambridge: Univ. Cambridge Press

Magnusson D, Stattin H, Dunér A. 1983. Aggression and criminality in a longitudinal perspective. See Van Dusen & Mednick 1983, pp. 277–302

Maguin E, Loeber R. 1996. Academic performance and delinquency. See Tonry & Morris 1986, 20:145–264

Manly JT, Cicchetti D, Barnett D. 1994. The impact of subtype, frequency, chronicity, and severity of child maltreatment on social competence and behavior problems. *Dev. Psychopathol.* 7:121–43

Mannuzza S, Klein RG, Bessler A, Malloy P, LaPadula M. 1993. Adult outcome of hyperactive boys. Educational achievement, occupational rank, and psychiatric status. *Arch. Gen. Psychiatry* 50:565–76

Mannuzza S, Klein RG, Bonagura N, Malloy P, Giampino TL, Addalli DA. 1991. Hyperactive boys almost grown up. 5. Replications of psychiatric status. *Arch. Gen. Psychiatry* 48:77–84

Maughan B. 1994. School influences. See Rutter & Hay 1994, pp. 134–58

Minde K. 1992. Aggression in preschoolers: its

relation to socialization. *J. Am. Acad. Child Adolesc. Psychiatry* 31:853–62

McCord J. 1983. A longitudinal study of aggression and antisocial behavior. See Van Dusen & Mednick 1983, pp. 269–75

McCord J, McCord W, Howard A. 1963. Family interactions as antecedent to the direction of male aggressiveness. *J. Abnorm. Soc. Psychol.* 66:239–42

Megargee EI. 1966. Undercontrolled and overcontrolled personality types in extreme antisocial aggression. *Psychol. Monogr.* 80: Whole No. 611

Miller SJ, Dinitz S, Conrad JP. 1982. *Careers of the Violent: The Dangerous Offender and Criminal Justice.* Lexington, MA: Heath Lexington

Moffitt TE. 1990a. The neuropsychology of juvenile delinquency: a critical review. See Tonry & Morris 1986, 12:99–169

Moffitt TE. 1990b. Juvenile delinquency and attention deficit disorder: boys' developmental trajectories from age 13 to age 15. *Child Dev.* 61:893–910

Moffitt TE. 1993. Adolescence-limited and life-cycle-persistent antisocial behavior: a developmental taxonomy. *Psychol. Rev.* 100:674–701

Mulligan G, Douglas JWB, Hammond WH, Tizard J. 1963. Delinquency and symptoms of maladjustment. *Proc. R. Soc. Med.* 56: 1083–86

Nagin DS, Farrington DP, Moffitt TE. 1995. Life-course trajectories of different types of offenders. *Criminology* 33:111–39

O'Donnell CR. 1995. Firearm deaths among children and youth. *Am. Psychol.* 50:771–76

Offord DR, Sullivan K, Allen N, Abrams N. 1979. Delinquency and hyperactivity. *J. Nerv. Ment. Disord.* 167:734–41

Ohlin L, Tonry M, eds. 1989. *Family Violence.* Chicago: Univ. Chicago Press

O'Leary KD, Barling J, Arias I, Rosenbaum A, Malone J, Tyree A. 1989. Prevalence and stability of physical aggression between spouses: a longitudinal analysis. *J. Consult. Clin. Psychol.* 57:263–68

Olweus D. 1978. *Aggression in Schools.* New York: Wiley

Olweus D. 1979. Stability of aggressive reaction patterns in males: a review. *Psychol. Bull.* 86:852–57

Olweus D. 1981. Bullying among school-boys. In *Children and Violence,* ed. N Cantwell, pp. 97–131. Stockholm: Akademilitteratur

Olweus D. 1991. Bully/victim problems among school children: basic facts and effects of a school-based intervention program. See Pepler & Rubin 1991, pp. 411–48

Parker JG, Asher SR. 1987. Peer relations and later adjustment: Are low-accepted children at risk? *Psychol. Bull.* 102:357–89

Patterson GR. 1982. *Coercive Family Interactions.* Eugene, OR: Castalia

Patterson GR. 1986. The contribution of siblings to training for fighting: a microsocial analysis. In *Development of Antisocial and Prosocial Behavior: Research, Theories, and Issues,* ed. D Olweus, J Block, M Radke-Yarrow, pp. 235–61. New York: Academic

Patterson GR, Capaldi D, Banks L. 1991. An early starter model for predicting delinquency. See Pepler & Rubin 1991, pp. 139–68

Patterson GR, Crosby L, Vuchinich S. 1992. Predicting risk for early police arrest. *J. Quant. Crim.* 8:335–55

Pennington BF, Ozonoff S. 1996. Executive functions and development of psychopathology. *J. Child Psychol. Psychiatry* 37: 51–87

Pepler DJ, Craig WM. 1995. A peek behind the fence: naturalistic observations of aggressive children with remote audiovisual recording. *Dev. Psychol.* 31:548–53

Pepler DJ, Rubin KH, eds. 1991. *The Development and Treatment of Childhood Aggression.* Hillsdale, NJ: Erlbaum

Pepler DJ, Slaby RG. 1994. Theoretical and developmental perspective on youth and violence. See Eron et al 1994, pp. 27–58

Perner J, Ruffman T, Leekam SR. 1994. Theory of mind is contagious: you catch it from your sibs. *Child Dev.* 65:1228–38

Perry DG, Kusel SJ, Perry LC. 1988. Victims of peer aggression. *Dev. Psychol.* 24:807–14

Perry DG, Perry LC, Boldizar JP. 1990. Learning of aggression. See Lewis & Miller 1990

Perry DG, Perry LC, Kennedy E. 1992. Conflict and the development of antisocial behavior. See Shantz & Hartup 1992, pp. 301–29

Plomin R, Nitz K, Rowe DC. 1990. Behavioral genetics and aggressive behavior in childhood. See Lewis & Miller 1990, pp. 119–33

Pope AW, Bierman KL, Mumma GH. 1989. Relations between hyperactive and aggressive behaviors and peer relations at three elementary grade levels. *J. Abnorm. Child Psychol.* 17:253–67

Pulkkinen L. 1982. Self-control and continuity from childhood to late adolescence. In *Life-Span Development and Behavior,* ed. PB Baltes, OG Brim, 4:63–105. New York: Academic

Pulkkinen L. 1983. Predictability of criminal behavior. *Psykologia* 18:3–10

Pulkkinen L. 1992. The path to adulthood for

aggressively inclined girls. In *Of Mice and Women: Aspects of Female Aggression,* ed. K Bjorkqvist, P Niemela, pp. 113–21. New York: Academic

Pulkkinen L, Hurme H. 1984. Aggression as a predictor of weak self-control. In *Human Action and Personality,* ed. L Pulkkinen, P Lyytinen, pp. 172–89. Jyvaskyla, Finl.: Univ. Jyvaskyla

Pulkkinen L, Pitkänen T. 1993. Continuities in aggressive behavior from childhood to adulthood. *Aggress. Behav.* 19:249–63

Quay HC. 1993. The psychobiology of undersocialized aggressive conduct disorder: a theoretical perspective. *Dev. Psychopathol.* 5:165–80

Raine A. 1993. *The Psychopathology of Crime.* San Diego, CA: Academic

Reiss AJ, Roth JA, eds. 1993. *Understanding and Preventing Violence.* Washington, DC: Natl. Acad. Press

Richters JE, Cicchetti D. 1993. Mark Twain meets DSM-III-r: conduct disorder, development, and the concept of harmful dysfunction. *Dev. Psychopathol.* 5:5–29

Richters JE, Martinez PE. 1993. The NIMH Community Violence Project. I. Children as victims of and witnesses to violence. *Psychiatry* 56:7–21

Robins LN, Ratcliff KS. 1980. Childhood conduct disorders and later arrest. In *The Social Consequences of Psychiatric Illnes,* ed. LN Robins, PJ Clayton, JK Wing, pp. 1–12. New York: Brunner/Mazel

Rosenberg ML. 1991. *Violence in America.* New York: Oxford Univ. Press

Ross HS, Tesla C, Kenyon B, Lollis SP. 1990. Maternal intervention in toddler peer conflict: the socialization of principles of justice. *Dev. Psychol.* 26:994–1003

Rutter M, Hay DF, eds. 1994. *Development Through Life: A Handbook for Clinicians.* Oxford: Blackwell

Sackin S, Thelen E. 1984. An ethological study of peaceful associative outcomes to conflict in preschool children. *Child Dev.* 55: 1098–102

Sampson RJ, Laub JH. 1993. *Crime in the making: Pathways and Turning Points Through Life.* Cambridge, MA: Harvard Univ. Press

Sampson RJ, Lauritsen JL. 1993. Violent victimization and offending: individual-, situational-, and community-level risk factors. See Reiss & Roth 1993, pp. 1–114

Sanson A, Smart D, Prior M, Oberklaid F. 1993. Precursors of hyperactivity and aggression. *J. Am. Acad. Child Adolesc. Psychiatry* 32:1207–16

Satterfield JM, Hoppe CM, Schell AM. 1982. A prospective study of delinquency in 110 adolescent boys with attention deficit disorder and 88 normal adolescent boys. *Am. J. Psychiatry* 139:795–98

Schoenfield CG. 1988. Blacks and violent crime: a psychoanalytical oriented analysis. *J. Psychiatry Law* 16:269–301

Serbin LA, Powlishta KK, Gulko J. 1993. The development of sex typing in middle childhood. *Monogr. Soc. Res. Child Dev.* 58: Ser. No. 232

Shannon LW. 1988. *Criminal Career Continuity: Its Social Context.* New York: Hum. Sci. Press

Shantz CU. 1987. Conflicts between children. *Child Dev.* 58:282–305

Shantz CU, Hartup WW, eds. 1992. *Conflict in Child and Adolescent Development.* Cambridge: Cambrdige Univ. Press

Sharp D, Hay DF, Pawlby S, Schmucker G, Allen H, Kumar R. 1995. The impact of postnatal depression on boys' intellectual development. *J. Child. Psychol. Psychiatry* 36:1315–36

Shaw CR, McKay HD. 1942. *Juvenile Delinquency and Urban Areas: A Study of Rates of Delinquency in Relation to Differential Characteristics of Local Communities in American Cities.* Chicago: Univ. Chicago Press

Shaw DS, Keenan K, Vondra JI. 1994. Developmental precursors of externalizing behavior: ages 1 to 3. *Dev. Psychol.* 30:355–64

Sheley JF, Wight JH. 1993. *Gun Acquisition and Possession in Selected Juvenile Samples.* NCJ #145326. Washington, DC: Off. Juv. Justice Delinq. Prev.

Smetana JG. 1989. Adolescents' and parents' reasoning about actual family conflict. *Child Dev.* 60:1052–67

Smetana JG, Yau J, Restrepo A, Braeges JL. 1991. Adolescent-parent conflict in married and divorced families. *Dev. Psychol.* 27:1000–10

Smith C, Thornberry TP. 1995. The relationship between childhood maltreatment and adolescent involvement in delinquency. *Criminology* 33(4):451–77

Snyder HN, Sickmund M. 1995. *Juvenile Offenders and Victims: a National Report. Doc. #NCJ-153569.* Washington, DC: Off. Juv. Justice Delinq. Prev.

Snyder HN, Sickmund M, Poe-Yamagata E. 1996. *Juvenile Offenders and Victims:1996 Update on Violence. Doc. #NCJ-159107.* Washington, DC: Off. Juv. Justice Delinq. Prev.

Sommers I, Baskin DR. 1994. Factors related to female adolescent initiation into violent street crime. *Youth Soc.* 25:468–89

Sonuga-Barke EJS, Lamparelli M, Stevenson J, Thompson M, Henry A. 1994. Behavioral problems and pre-school intellectual attainment: the associations of hyperactivity and conduct problems. *J. Child Psychol. Psychiatry* 35:949–60

Stattin H, Klackenberg-Larsson I. 1990. The relationship between maternal attributes in the early life of the child and the child's future criminal behavior. *Dev. Psychopathol.* 2:99–111

Stattin H, Magnusson D. 1989. The role of early aggressive behavior in the frequency, seriousness, and types of later crime. *J. Consult. Clin. Psychol.* 57:710–18

Storashak EA, Bellanti CJ, Bierman KL. 1996. The quality of sibling relationships and the development of social competence and behavior control in aggressive children. *Dev. Psychol.* 32:79–89

Terlouw G-J, Bruinsma JN. 1994. Self-reported delinquency in the Netherlands. In *Delinquent Behavior among Young People in the Western World,* ed. J Junger-Tas, G-J Terlouw, MW Klein, pp. 102–30. Amsterdam: Kluger

Thomas A, Chess S, Birch HG. 1968. *Temperament and Behavior Disorders in Children.* New York: NY Univ. Press

Thornberry TP, Huizinga D, Loeber R. 1995. The prevention of serious delinquency and violence: implications from the Program of Research on the Causes and Correlates of Delinquency. In *Sourcebook on Serious, Violent and Chronic Juvenile Offenders,* ed. J Howell, B Krisberg, D Hawkins, JD Wilson, pp. 213–37. Thousand Oaks, CA: Sage

Thornberry TP, Krohn MD, Lizotte AJ, Chard-Wierschem D. 1993. The role of juvenile gangs in facilitating delinquent behavior. *J. Res. Crime Delinq.* 30:55–87

Thornberry TP, Lizotte AJ, Krohn MD, Farnworth M, Jang SJ. 1994. Delinquent peers, beliefs, and delinquent behavior: a longitudinal test of interactional theory. *Criminology* 32:47–83

Tonry M, Morris N, eds. 1986. *Crime and Justice.* Chicago: Univ. Chicago Press

Tremblay RE. 1991. Aggression, prosocial behavior, and gender: three magic words but no magic wand. See Pepler & Rubin 1991, pp. 71–78

Tremblay RE, Le Blanc M, Schwartzman AE. 1988. The predictive power of first grade peer and teacher ratings of behavior and personality at adolescence. *J. Abnorm. Psychol.* 16:571–84

Tremblay RE, Loeber R, Gagnon C, Charlebois P, Larivée S, Le Blanc M. 1991. Disruptive boys with stable and unstable high fighting behavior patterns during junior and elementary school. *J. Abnorm. Psychol.* 19: 285–300

Tremblay RE, Mâsse LC, Kurtz L, Vitaro F. 1997. From childhood physical aggression to adolescent maladjustment: the Montréal Prevention Experiment. In *Childhood Disorders, Substance Abuse & Delinquency: Prevention and Early Intervention Approaches,* ed. RD Peters, RJ McMahon, pp. 1–62. Thousand Oaks, CA: Sage. In press

Turner PJ. 1991. Relations between attachment, gender and behavior with peers in preschool. *Child Dev.* 62:1475–88

Underwood MK, Coie JD, Herbsman CR. 1992. Display rules for anger and aggression in school-age children. *Child Dev.* 63: 366–80

Van Dusen KT, Mednick SA, eds. 1983. *Prospective Studies of Crime and Delinquency.* Boston: Kluwer-Nijhoff

Van Kammen WB, Loeber R. 1994. Are fluctuations in delinquent activities related to the onset and offset of juvenile illegal drug use and drug dealing? *J. Drug Issues* 24:9–24

Verhulst FC, Vander Ende J. 1991. Four year follow-up of teacher-reported problem behaviours. *Psychol. Med.* 21:965–77

Vespo JE, Pedersen J, Hay DF. 1995. Young children's conflicts with peers and siblings: gender effects. *Child Stud. J.* 25:189–212

Vicary JR, Klingaman LR, Harkness WL. 1995. Risk factors associated with date rape and sexual assault of adolescent girls. *J. Adolesc.* 18:289–306

Volling BL, MacKinnonLewis C, Rabiner D, Baradaran LP. 1993. Children's social competence and sociometric status: further exploration of aggression, social withdrawal, and peer rejection. *Dev. Psychopathol.* 5:459–83

Vuchinich S, Emery RE, Cassidy J. 1988. Family members as third parties in dyadic family conflict: strategies, alliances, and outcomes. *Child Dev.* 59:1293–302

Weiler RM. 1995. Violence: an annotated bibliography of selected publications and resources. *Educ. Psychol. Rev.* 7:125–34

Weinberg KM, Tronick EZ. 1997. Maternal depression and infant maladjustment: a failure of mutual regulation. In *The Handbook of Child and Adolescent Psychiatry,* ed. J Noshpitz. New York: Wiley. In press

Weiss B, Dodge KA, Bates JE, Pettit GS. 1992. Some consequences of early harsh discipline: child aggression and a maladaptive social information processing style. *Child Dev.* 63:1321–35

White HR, Hansell S, Brick J. 1993. Alcohol use and aggression among youth. *Alcohol Health Res. World* 17:144–50

White J, Moffitt TE, Caspi A, Bartusch DJ, Needles DJ, Stouthamer-Loeber M. 1994. Measuring impulsivity and examining its relation to delinquency. *J. Abnorm. Psychol.* 103:192–205

Wikström P-OH. 1990. Age and crime in a Stockholm cohort. *J. Quant. Criminol.* 6: 61–84

Windle RC, Windle M. 1995. Longitudinal patterns of physical aggression: associations with adult social, psychiatric, and personality functioning and testosterone levels. *Dev. Psychopathol.* 7:563–85

Wolfgang ME, Thornberry TP, Figlio RM. 1987. *From Boy to Man, From Delinquency to Crime.* Chicago: Univ. Chicago Press

Zahn-Waxler C, Iannotti RJ, Cummings EM, Denham S. 1990. Antecedents of problem behaviors in children of depressed mothers. *Dev. Psychopathol.* 2:271–91

Zhang Q, Loeber R, Stouthamer-Loeber M. 1997. Developmental trends of delinquency attitudes and delinquency: replication and synthesis across time and samples. *J. Quant. Criminol.* In press

Zoccolillo M, Pickles A, Quinton D, Rutter M. 1992. The outcome of Conduct Disorder: implications for defining adult personality disorder and Conduct Disorder. *Psychol. Med.* 22:1–161

Annu. Rev. Psychol. 1997. 48:411–47

HEALTH PSYCHOLOGY: What is an Unhealthy Environment and How Does It Get Under the Skin?

Shelley E. Taylor and Rena L. Repetti

Department of Psychology, 1283 Franz Hall, University of California, Los Angeles, Los Angeles, California 90095-1563; e-mail: taylor@psych.sscnet.ucla.edu

Teresa Seeman

Andrus Gerontology Center, University of Southern California, Los Angeles, California 90089-0191

KEY WORDS: family, social support, SES, community, work

ABSTRACT

This review explores the role of environments in creating chronic and acute health disorders. A general framework for studying the nesting of social environments and the multiple pathways by which environmental factors may adversely affect health is offered. Treating socioeconomic status (SES) and race as contextual factors, we examine characteristics of the environments of community, work, family, and peer interaction for predictors of positive and adverse health outcomes across the lifespan. We consider chronic stress/allostatic load, mental distress, coping skills and resources, and health habits and behaviors as classes of mechanisms that address how unhealthy environments get "under the skin," to create health disorders. Across multiple environments, unhealthy environments are those that threaten safety, that undermine the creation of social ties, and that are conflictual, abusive, or violent. A healthy environment, in contrast, provides safety, opportunities for social integration, and the ability to predict and/or control aspects of that environment.

0084-6570/97/0201-0411$08.00

CONTENTS

HEALTH PSYCHOLOGY: WHAT IS AN UNHEALTHY ENVIRONMENT AND HOW DOES IT GET UNDER THE SKIN?

The role of the environment in health and illness has been known since the time of Hippocrates. With the discovery that infectious agents produce disease, physicians and public health researchers directed their attention to the environmental conditions that give rise to these agents and permit them to breed. Following breakthroughs in water treatment, sewage control, food storage, and waste disposal, the incidence of many infectious diseases declined substantially, soon to be replaced by the slower-developing chronic illnesses of heart disease, cancer, and diabetes, among others. These diseases have come to be known as diseases of lifestyle, because behavioral risk factors are clearly involved in their etiology and progression. An unintended consequence of the focus on lifestyle has been to divert attention away from the role of the environment in producing disease in favor of an emphasis on behavior. As health psychologists have increasingly identified what risk factors people incur and how they incur them, the focus of health prevention has moved from environmental interventions to individual behavior. Some scientists have argued that this focus has led to a culture of blame, whereby individuals are held responsible for good health and blamed or discredited for their illnesses (Becker 1993).

The role of the environment in producing chronic as well as acute disease merits renewed attention in the context of the current concerns addressed by health psychology. Specifically, as research has identified the individual difference predictors of chronic illness, including health behaviors, use of health services, social factors such as social support, and psychological factors such as hostility and depression, it has become clear that these predictors are nested within geographic, developmental, occupational, and social environments. In this review, we focus attention on these environments and the ways environmental characteristics may influence health and also influence individual characteristics or behaviors that pose risks for health.

In so doing, our analysis gives primary status neither to environmental characteristics nor to their concomitant effects on individuals. Not all individuals in the same environment are affected by that environment in the same way, nor will all individuals in a given environment sustain health risks. Thus, we explicitly reject the notion that the health effects of environments can be reduced to or explained by individual-level factors. Rather, we maintain that individual characteristics are nested within social environments (see Figure 1), with each level of analysis revealing information about the causes of health and illness that consideration of one level alone cannot provide.

As we note below, social class and race provide a context for understanding the effects of environment. These characteristics are well-established predictors of all-cause mortality and a variety of specific diseases, and they are also reliably associated with individual differences in exposure to stress, the practice of health behaviors, coping strategies, and other factors of interest to psychologists (Adler & Matthews 1994, Williams & Collins 1995). With SES and race as background, we then examine community, family, work, and peer groups as specific environments that have a contributing role in health and illness (see Figure 1). Within each environment, we ask the question, "How do the health-relevant characteristics of this environment get under the skin?" For example, some children live in conflict-ridden families and others do not, and the health risks sustained differ between the two groups. We ask how that environmental characteristic may translate into risks that have the identified health consequences. In so doing, we consider several general pathways in

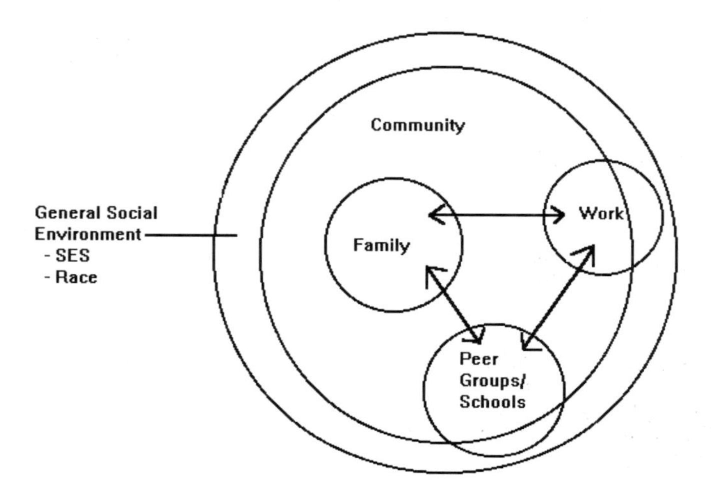

Figure 1 Diagrammatic representation of social environments that have health-relevant implications. This representation assumes that the proximal environments of family, work, and peer groups are nested or partially nested within neighborhood and fully nested within a larger social environment in which such factors as socioeconomic status (SES) and race have health implications.

each of the environments. These general pathways, as well as more complex combinations of them, are illustrated in Figure 2.

Environments exert direct effects on health (Figure 2, Segment a) that may be largely unmediated or unmoderated by psychological and social processes, except insofar as they lay the initial groundwork for their occurrence. For example, the poor and African-Americans are disproportionately likely to contract certain kinds of cancers because of differential exposure to toxins at work or in their neighborhoods. At present, research has not progressed to the point of identifying whether there are social or psychological factors that contribute to these adverse effects.

Because this is a psychological review, the routes on which we focus most of our attention are psychosocial pathways for the development of health risks. A first route whereby environments may get under the skin is by differentially exposing people to chronic stress (Segments fk). That chronic stress may have a cumulative effect on the body was first observed by Hans Selye (1956) in his articulation of the General Adaptation Syndrome. Selye maintained that individuals respond to stressful events with nonspecific reactions that, over time, produce wear and tear on the system. Repeated cycling through the three-phase syndrome of alarm, resistance, and exhaustion, Selye argued, leads to cumula-

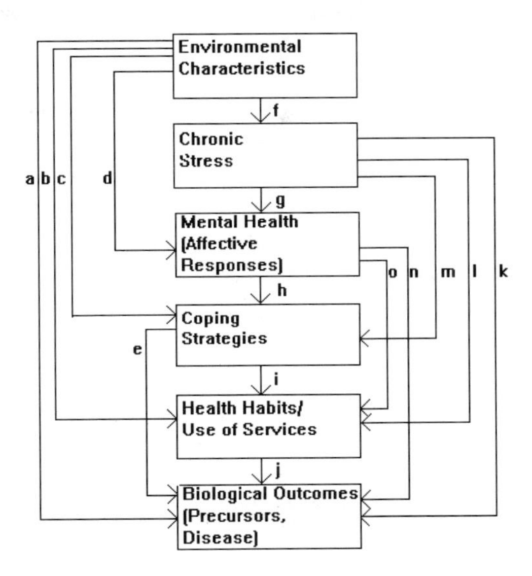

Figure 2 A range of models by which environmental characteristics may come to exert adverse biological outcomes on individuals. Segments b–o represent partial pathways that may concatenate to form more complex pathways.

tive damage to the organism. Building on these ideas, McEwen & Stellar (1993) proposed that, beginning early in life, there are cascading relationships between environmental factors and genetic predispositions that lead to large individual differences in susceptibility to stress and, in some cases, to disease. Physiological systems within the body fluctuate to meet demands from external forces, a state termed allostasis. Over time, the allostatic load builds up, which is defined as the physiological costs of chronic exposure to fluctuating or heightened neural or neuroendocrine responses that result from repeated or chronic environmental challenges that an individual reacts to as stressful. For example, the hypothesized links between recurrent changes in autonomic reactivity produced by stress and the subsequent development of chronic hypertension (Anderson et al 1991) may be thought of as an allostatic load model. The allostatic load formulation, then, explicitly argues that stress produces cumulative identifiable damage that results in increased pathology (Seeman et al 1996).

A second route by which environments may have adverse health effects is via an impact on mental health or mental distress (Melamed 1995) (Segments dn). Negative emotions, such as depression, anxiety, and hostility, appear to play a significant role in health risks, including all-cause mortality (Martin et al 1995) and especially coronary heart disease risk (Booth-Kewley & Friedman 1987). These relations are apparently not due to behavior changes associated with affective disorders, such as increased smoking or alcohol consumption. Major depression, depressive symptoms, history of depression, and anxiety have all been related to the likelihood of cardiac events (Frasure-Smith et al 1995), and depression is a risk factor for mortality following myocardial infarction, independent of cardiac disease severity (Frasure-Smith et al 1995). State depression and clinical depression have both been related to sustained suppressed immunity (Herbert & Cohen 1993). Anger appears to be significant in the development of coronary artery disease and hypertension, at least among some individuals (Frasure-Smith et al 1995). These health effects of negative emotions may result from the activation of both the sympathetic-adrenal-medullary (SAM) system and the hypothalamic-pituitary-adrenocortical (HPA) axis. The former is manifested in increased blood pressure, heart rate, circulating levels of epinephrine and norepinephrine, and constriction of peripheral blood vessels. SAM activation is believed to contribute to the development of coronary artery disease (Manuck et al 1995), essential hypertension (Krantz & Manuck 1984), and susceptibility to infectious disease (Cohen & Herbert 1996). The activation of HPA leads to high circulating levels of corticotrophin-releasing hormone, adrenocorticotropic hormone, and cortisol. HPA activation has been linked to atherosclerosis (Troxler et al 1977) and chronic inflammatory responses, as are found in rheumatoid arthritis and reactivity of the airways in people with asthma (McNeil 1987). Although biologically based predispositions appear to play some role in the relation of affective diseases to physical state changes, environmental factors are also reliably related to sustained depression, anxiety, and anger. As such, mental health/distress constitutes a second important route by which environments may get under the skin.

Coping strategies constitute a third explanatory route that may clarify how unhealthy environments adversely affect health (Segments ce). Individuals who find constructive ways of coping with stress, such as taking direct action or finding meaning in their experience, may be better able to withstand the potential adverse effects of stressful circumstances. In addition, there may be stressor-specific coping styles, such as expressing hostility or suppressing anger, that have health implications both generally and for specific disorders, such as cardiovascular disease and hypertension. In addition, environments influence the development of coping strategies, especially those involved in managing conflict and stress, and the ability to develop social ties.

Health habits are heavily implicated in the development of illness, especially chronic illness, as numerous reviews have documented (e.g. Adler &

Matthews 1994) (Segments bj). They include smoking, alcohol and drug abuse, diet, exercise, the use of preventive and secondary health services, and adherence to treatment recommendations. Environments constitute the contexts in which health habits are learned, encouraged, and practiced. The family is an important context for the acquisition of health habits, and it lays the groundwork for a broad array of healthy and unhealthy behaviors (Taylor 1995). The peer group, first in adolescence and then in adulthood, is an important context within which many health-compromising behaviors are acquired and enacted, including smoking, alcohol, and drug abuse.

These, then, are the routes we consider in each of the environments analyzed. These routes are not independent or even discrete pathways by which unhealthy environments affect health; all represent routes in potential causal chains involving two or more of these processes. Thus, for example, a chronically stressful family environment may prevent the development of effective coping strategies (Segments fm), compromise the learning of health habits (Segments fl), and produce chronic anxiety and/or depression (Segments fg), all of which feed into enhanced health risks (Segments e, j, and n). In most areas, research has not progressed to the point where these complex pathways can be identified or tested in the context of particular health problems or disorders. Thus, Figure 2 is offered largely as a representation of potential routes, rather than established routes, by which pernicious environments exact adverse health effects.

SOCIOECONOMIC STATUS AND RACE

We begin our consideration of the question "What is an unhealthy environment?" by examining SES and race differences in health. Because SES and race heavily determine the more proximal environments in which people live, such as neighborhood and work, they provide important contexts for understanding the features of these more proximal environments that may compromise health (Williams & Collins 1995).

SES is traditionally measured by education, income, and occupation. Using these criteria, an extensive, highly consistent literature documents the negative health outcomes that result as one moves lower on the SES gradient (for reviews, see Adler et al 1993, Williams & Collins 1995). Analyses of potential measurement artifacts or natural or social selection suggest that these inequalities are real and affected little by selection factors (see Macintyre 1997). SES is related to higher prevalence and incidence of most chronic and infectious disorders and to higher rates of nearly all major causes of morbidity and mortality across populations and across time (Adler et al 1993, Macintyre 1997, Williams & Collins 1995). Moreover, SES differentials in morbidity and mortality appear to be widening rather than narrowing (e.g. Marmot 1994, Wagener & Schatzkin 1994).

The association of SES with morbidity and mortality is, for the most part, linear, with increasingly better health outcomes as one ascends the SES continuum. As such, the relation of SES to health and mortality involves more than the obvious role of inadequate financial resources or poor and dangerous living conditions associated with poverty. While SES differentials may be found among children (Durkin et al 1994) and among the elderly (e.g. Seeman et al 1994), the largest social inequalities in health and mortality are seen most frequently for those aged 40 to 65.

Substantial race differences also exist in health. On virtually every major index of health status, African-Americans look worse than whites, and these differences in health occur across the lifespan (Williams & Collins 1995). With the exception of race-specific disorders such as sickle-cell anemia, these black-white differences are apparently not due primarily to genetic or biological factors that differentiate blacks from whites (for discussion, see Anderson et al 1991, Williams & Collins 1995). Socioeconomic differences account substantially for these health status differences, inasmuch as approximately one third of the African-American population lives in poverty, compared with 11% of the white population. Nonetheless, poverty does not fully account for black-white differences in health (e.g. Rushing et al 1992). Within every level of SES, African-Americans typically have worse health than whites (Williams & Collins 1995).

Although SES and race are not themselves environments, they provide an important and often overlooked context for understanding the more immediate environments within which people live, namely communities, work, family, and social life. As such, they provide the environmental backdrop against which more specific environmental encounters occur.

COMMUNITY

Certain characteristics of the communities in which people live have been shown to have adverse effects on health. Many of these arise because of the social class and racial composition of those communities. Consequently, they act as the proximal manifestation of these characteristics. For example, low-SES neighborhoods have higher rates of cancer, hypertension, heart disease, and upper-respiratory disorders, including asthma, bronchitis, and emphysema (Adler et al 1993). Other health-enhancing or health-compromising characteristics of environment are less dependent upon community social class or racial composition.

Chronic Stress

The degree of chronic stress experienced by individuals is heavily influenced by the characteristics of their communities. Residents of middle- and upper-income communities typically have access to high-quality housing, an abundance of shops, banks, health-care services and transportation. In poor neighborhoods, these resources are less likely to be available (Troutt 1993). Consequently, the lower one is on the SES continuum, the greater the amount of hassle and time needed to address basic tasks of living. Further contributing to the chronic stress of lower SES communities are characteristics such as police-documented higher crime rates (Macintyre et al 1993), greater perceived threat of crime and more local problems (Sooman & Macintyre 1995), more refused services (e.g. taxi, credit, ambulance; Sooman & Macintyre 1995), and poorer transportation and recreational facilities (Macintyre et al 1993). Lower SES neighborhoods also have been linked to greater exposure to physical hazards such as air and water pollutants, hazardous wastes, pesticides, and industrial chemicals (Calnan & Johnson 1985) and to greater crowding and exposure to noise (Evans 1997).

Lack of available housing typically leads to overcrowding, both in the form of high density within the neighborhood and crowding within the home (defined as 1.5 persons or more per room). High density is associated with higher all-cause mortality (Levy & Herzog 1974) and with higher rates of mortality due to cancer and stroke, but not heart disease (Levy & Herzog 1978). High-density living is also associated with death due to homicide, but negatively associated with death due to suicide, which appears to be tied to isolation and loss of family ties (Levy & Herzog 1978). A potential mediating pathway for these effects is suggested by the fact that high-density living is associated with both higher reports of chronic stress and with biochemical indices of stress, such as urinary excretion of norepinephrine and epinephrine (Fleming et al 1987). Crowding in the home has been related to increased likelihood of infections and to higher death rates from heart disease, to respiratory disorders, and to all-cause mortality (Levy & Herzog 1978). In addition to its association with crowding, substandard housing may affect health in other ways. Older buildings with poorly lit hallways and debris pose risks to safety and to health by attracting rodents and insects that may spread infection, for example.

Community studies of the effects of noise on physical health have identified few clear-cut relations to disease morbidity in the adult population. Acute noise produces short-lived elevations in cardiovascular and neuroendocrine functioning, but many adults appear to habituate to chronic noise. However, some studies suggest a relation of chronic noise to the development of hypertension, links that necessitate further investigation (Evans 1997). Recent evidence suggesting a relation of noise exposure to abnormal fetal development also merits continued consideration (Evans 1997). As noted below, noise may adversely affect health habits as well.

High rates of crime and delinquency are associated with a variety of adverse health characteristics, including a high rate of infant mortality, low birth rate, tuberculosis, and child abuse (Sampson 1992). Women living in high-violence neighborhoods are significantly more likely to experience pregnancy complications than women living in neighborhoods with little violence (Zapata et al 1992).

Because a number of the adverse characteristics of neighborhoods are intercorrelated, investigators have attempted to operationalize the concept of high-stress neighborhood. Harburg et al (1973) defined areas characterized by low socioeconomic status, high population density, high geographic mobility, high rates of marital breakup, and high crime as high stress; low-stress areas had more favorable ratings on all these variables. Harburg found higher rates of hypertension in the high-stress than low-stress locales, especially among dark-skinned black men. Others (e.g. Troutt 1993) have argued that in such neighborhoods there are low levels of economic opportunity, poor marriage pools, and poor transportation, which erodes the ability of residents, especially single mothers, to seek employment in the neighborhood, to marry, or to move to a better neighborhood. As noted below, such characteristics may have adverse effects on parenting, which affects the health of children.

Mental Health/Distress

Little research has addressed the impact of community characteristics on mental health, and still less has tied such effects to physical health outcomes. To date, the only community characteristic to receive systematic study is exposure to violence, especially for children. Osofsky (1995) argued that exposure to chronic community violence directly and adversely affects children's mental health. Children's reports of psychological distress are significantly related to their reports of witnessing acts of violence (Richters & Martinez 1993). Children who live in violent neighborhoods show signs of posttraumatic stress disorder, including disrupted patterns of eating and sleeping, difficulties in controlling attention and relating to others, anxiety responses and fear, and reexperiences of the violent episodes they have witnessed (for a review, see Osofsky 1995). Among adults, sleep disturbances, nightmares, and manifestations of anxiety are common (Pynoos 1993). Exposure to violence may also adversely affect the mental health of children and adults because of the need to deal with losses and to cope with grieving for family members, neighbors, and friends who have been killed. Such grieving may compromise immune functioning (Kiecolt-Glaser et al 1994).

Coping Skills and Resources

Community characteristics may affect coping skills and resources in several ways that have health implications. Repeated arousal of intense negative emotions due to exposure to chronic violence, for example, may lead to difficulty in the effective regulation of emotions among children (Osofsky 1993). The adverse effects of chronic exposure to violence may be partially offset if an individual has at least one supportive person in the neighborhood, a protective place to go, or certain personal resources such as an adaptable temperament or a high level of intelligence (Osofsky 1993). Low-SES neighborhoods may also compromise the development of coping skills relating to the recruitment and effective use of social contacts. Parents who are concerned about exposing their children to drugs and crime may keep their children inside and otherwise restrict social behavior. Thus, the ability to develop or utilize a supportive network may be somewhat compromised (Sampson 1992). Whether these disruptions in the formation of social ties have negative effects on health in childhood or cumulative effects on adult health is unknown.

The inherently social nature of communities affects coping and health at both the community level and the individual level. In particular, characteristics of communities influence the degree to which social capital may be created (Coleman 1990). Social capital exists when the relations among people make possible individual or joint achievements that otherwise would not be possible (Coleman 1990). Social capital involves parents and children in friendship networks and community organizations, both formal and informal, which are characterized by a set of obligations, expectations, and social ties that connect the adults, and that help to bring about the control and supervision of children. Through such a process, it is argued, information is exchanged, norms are established, and informal systems of social control are laid down. As such, a child is raised in a neighborhood environment with norms and sanctions that are not or cannot be brought about by one adult in isolation. The creation of social capital is virtually impossible to develop in unstable communities, and mere density of a community is insufficient to establish it. Social capital, then, constitutes a community-level coping variable.

"Social impoverishment," the absence of social capital, has been tied to several health-related outcomes. Such indicators predict high rates of child abuse (Garbarino & Sherman 1980), which is important as a cause of morbidity and mortality and also as a predictor of violence in adulthood (Widom 1989). Indicators of social capital are inversely related to levels of adolescent aggression and delinquency which, in turn, are predictors of homicide and suicide. Low levels of social organization are associated with high levels of adult crime as well. Social disorganization also predicts whether young girls will become pregnant (Osofsky 1990); whether they will be supported by a network in limiting high-risk maternal behavior such as smoking, drinking, and drug abuse (Wallace 1990); and whether they will abuse their children after birth (Sampson 1992). Overall, the more formal and informal ties exist in a community, the more dense and multiplex the networks and the greater the constraints on deviant, often health-compromising behavior, both for adolescents and adults (Sampson 1992).

On the individual level, the lack of social capital may erode the quality of social support available to an individual. Rapid mobility in and out of an area reduces the marriage pool initially, and the likelihood of remarriage following divorce. Fear of crime fosters a distrust of others that can contribute to social isolation (Krause 1992). Social isolation has, in turn, been related to an array of adverse health outcomes (House et al 1988a), and it is known to compromise immunologic functioning (Kiecolt-Glaser et al 1994). In contrast, social opportunities provided via information networks, intergenerational networks, churches, and other community organizations may foster the creation of individual social ties that have a health-protective effect (Sampson 1992).

Health Habits and Behaviors

Community characteristics influence the degree to which certain health habits may be practiced. Because poorer neighborhoods have fewer facilities and resources, the adoption of public health recommendations such as obtaining a healthy diet and obtaining regular exercise sometimes cannot be met. High-stress neighborhoods, characterized by high density, high crime, and high mobility, may also lead to the development of health-compromising behaviors that act as efforts to cope with stress, such as smoking, alcohol consumption, and drug abuse. Noise appears to increase rates of smoking and the use of some drugs (Evans 1997).

Health habits are also affected by the social capital generated within communities. For example, pregnant women, especially young, single pregnant women, show higher levels of prenatal care in neighborhoods with strong social networks, perhaps because these networks put pressure on them to avoid compromising the health of their fetus and also provide them with more information about what constitutes effective prenatal care (Sampson 1992). Other health habits may be similarly affected.

The availability of health care varies substantially by neighborhood. Consistently poor health services are found in low-income, minority, and transient areas (Macintyre et al 1993, Williams 1990, Wyke et al 1992). Especially for children, the combination of rapid population loss coupled with inadequate health services is devastating. Communities experiencing poverty, overcrowding, and rapid population change show rises in infant mortality and low birth weight (Wallace & Wallace 1990). In contrast, the information networks that develop in stable communities transmit knowledge of and linkages to clinic services (Sampson 1992), including prenatal services, child health services, and general child care.

Conclusion

Documenting the effects of community characteristics on health is difficult. Studies that control for demographic characteristics, such as SES and race, on the one hand, and more proximal family characteristics, such as family income, on the other hand, may statistically underestimate the contribution of community to health by virtue of drawing off variance into these more distal and proximal predictors (G Duncan, J Connell & P Klebanov, unpublished observations). Moreover, estimating the independent contribution of highly correlated community characteristics, such as population density, population mobility, and community SES level creates problems of data analysis and interpretation. In addition, community characteristics do not have uniformly positive or negative effects that consistently translate into health outcomes. For example, the presence of middle-SES neighbors appears to have a protective effect in reducing aggression and delinquency among low-SES youngsters, especially black males from low-income, single-parent homes, but it may simultaneously adversely affect the ability to develop social relationships with their peers (Kupersmidt et al 1995).

Despite the difficulties with drawing inferences from community studies, the evidence suggests several community characteristics that have adverse effects on health, including crowding, air pollution, exposure to violence, and the absence of social networks and social ties. In addition, the protective effects of informal and formal social ties and networks appear to be robust. Exactly how community and neighborhood characteristics affect health is still largely unknown (Jencks & Mayer 1990); the evidence is strongest for chronic stress, the erosion of social ties, and development of poor health behaviors, although the links to physiology have yet to be established. The role of mental distress and coping skills other than those relating to social capital are less well studied.

THE FAMILY SOCIAL ENVIRONMENT

The family environment clearly influences children's health. The link can be direct, as when a parent's behavior exposes a fetus to drugs in the womb (Neuspiel et al 1989). We focus on indirect links and highlight four characteristics of the family social environment that appear to influence child and adolescent health: (*a*) the quality of parenting, especially emotional aspects of the parent-child relationship; (*b*) the family's social climate, especially the amount of conflict and violence in the home; (*c*) the parents' mental health and other behavioral characteristics of the parents; and (*d*) variables associated with social-economic conditions of the household, such as whether the child lives with one or both parents and the educational level of parents.

Chronic Stress

Characteristics of a family environment that appear to be associated with health problems in children include a lack of warmth and emotional support from parents and a high level of conflict and violence. A cold and unresponsive parenting style has been associated with retarded infant growth and increased rates of illness in childhood (Bradley 1993, Gottman & Katz 1989). A stressful family environment can even influence prenatal development (Collins et al 1993). Quarreling and fighting at home have been linked to psychosomatic symptoms such as headaches and stomachaches in adolescents (Mechanic & Hansell 1989). When family dysfunction and conflict escalate to the point of abuse, the direct and indirect effects on child health can be lethal. Children with histories of physical abuse and neglect have an elevated mortality risk for all causes of death, including homicide, transportation injury, other unintentional injury, and disease (Sorenson & Peterson 1994). A history of sexual abuse can have health consequences years later, leading to increased rates of psychological distress, headache, asthma, diabetes, arthritis, HIV infection, gynecological problems, and various somatic symptoms (Braaten 1996). Some of the effects of sexual abuse on health may be mediated by poor health habits. Women with a history of childhood sexual abuse are more likely to smoke, abuse drugs, and engage in risky sexual behavior, and they are less likely to use medical care (Springs & Friedrich 1992). Other indirect effects of abuse may be mediated by conditions in the family. For example, the instability and social isolation that is often found in abusive families appear to mediate the effects of maltreatment on children's poor academic performance (Eckenrode et al 1995) and may influence health as well (House et al 1988b).

Repeated interference with homeostatic processes may be one physiologic pathway through which a chronically stressful family environment causes health problems in children. Experimental manipulations resembling two of the family characteristics considered, namely the presence of anger and conflict and the absence of emotional warmth and responsiveness, can disrupt patterns of cardiovascular and neuroendocrine regulation in children. For example, preschoolers respond to videotapes of angry adult interactions with increases in heart rate and blood pressure (El-Sheikh et al 1989), and separations from mothers lead to increased heart rates as well as elevations in norepinephrine and cortisol, particularly among socially shy children (Kagan et al 1987, 1988). However, a secure infant-mother attachment predicts lower stress response (as indexed by salivary cortisol) to new or strange situations (Hertsgaard et al 1995). Cortisol responses to separation are also attenuated in the presence of a responsive caregiver (Gunnar et al 1992). A buildup in allostatic load experienced by a child who is responding physiologically to repeated social challenges at home may help to explain the poor development and high rates of illness observed in children from stressful family environments.

Mental Health/Distress

Depression is clearly associated with deleterious health outcomes among children and adolescents, such as increased acute illness and physical symptoms and unhealthy behaviors such as smoking and substance abuse (Gore et al 1992, Lewinsohn et al 1994). Household economic conditions influence both the risk of childhood depression and its link to health. Risk factors for childhood depression include living in a single parent household, parental unemployment, and parents' poor educational background (Gore et al 1992, Kaslow et al 1994, Lewinsohn et al 1994). Depression is more strongly linked to poor health among adolescents with a lower standard of living (Gore et al 1992).

More depressed children are also found among families whose members provide one another with little or no support, families that do not experience a sense of cohesiveness, and families characterized by high levels conflict, especially marital conflict (Kaslow et al 1994, Lewinsohn et al 1994). Characteristics of the parent-child relationship that are associated with depression include low levels of behavioral and emotional involvement, high levels of conflict and hostility, and a parenting style that is more autocratic, dominant, and controlling (Kaslow et al 1994, Lewinsohn et al 1994). Children of depressed mothers appear to be at increased risk for both depression and suicidal behavior, as well as a variety of other psychiatric diagnoses (Kaslow et al 1994). The behavior of depressed parents may contribute to this risk. Most studies find depressed mothers to be less responsive, more critical, negative, and irritable, and more controlling and intrusive with their children (Downey & Coyne 1990, Nolen-Hoeksema et al 1995).

Abuse within the family is also associated with depression and suicide (Malinosky-Rummell & Hansen 1993). Evidence suggests that the connection between a childhood history of family violence and recurrent depressions in adulthood is mediated by chronic interpersonal problems in the adult's life (Kessler & Magee 1994).

In summary, the links between family and parenting characteristics and depression in children and adolescents are clear. There is also evidence for negative short-term health effects in the form of increased rates of acute illness and suicide. Chronic or intermittent depression in childhood and adolescence may be associated with patterns of coping and/or physiologic responses to stress that contribute to long-term adverse health outcomes as well.

Coping Skills and Resources

Davies & Cummings (1994) suggested that emotionally secure children are better able to regulate their emotions in the face of stress and therefore cope more effectively with daily problems. According to their model, emotional security is threatened by destructive forms of family conflict, such as conflicts between parents that involve physical aggression, and by parent-child relationships marked by instability and a lack of parental warmth and responsiveness. Family social environments with features such as these, including abuse, discord, and parental psychopathology, are associated with maladaptive coping in children, in particular difficulty with anger regulation (Crittenden 1992, Cummings & El-Sheikh 1991, Zahn-Waxler et al 1984). Because anger and its regulation have been tied to the development of heart disease and hypertension, there may be health risks associated with growing up in homes that have these characteristics.

Family experiences also influence how children learn to negotiate interpersonal situations involving frustration and anger. Violent boys are more likely to live in mother-headed households, or to have fathers who use spanking for discipline and rarely express affection for their sons (Sheline et al 1994). Prospective research indicates that the development of hostile attitudes and behaviors in male adolescents is associated with family interactions that are nonsupportive and have a negative affective tone (Matthews et al 1996). Parent-child conflict and ineffective parenting practices foster problems in social information processing and social skill deficits in children that, in turn, lead to poor coping in school, in particular during interactions with peers (Patterson et al 1989). Children from families in which there is greater organization and consistency in the home use fewer aggressive coping strategies in response to everyday stress (Hardy et al 1993).

Dysfunctional coping strategies in children and adolescents may persist into adulthood. Thus, maladaptive coping styles that are first acquired in response to a stressful family environment in childhood may be associated with greater autonomic reactivity and poorer health outcomes throughout the lifespan. For example, hostility measured in adolescence is linked to coronary risk factors (such as high lipid ratios, larger body mass, smoking, and caffeine consumption) assessed more than 20 years later (Siegler et al 1992).

Health Habits and Behaviors

The abuse of substances, such as alcohol, cigarettes, and illicit drugs, and risky sexual behavior are two health-threatening classes of behavior that are usually first observed during adolescence. In addition to their direct effects on health, these behaviors are linked with patterns of sleep, diet, and physical activity that indicate an unhealthy adolescent lifestyle (Donovan et al 1991).

The use of drugs by family members, both parents and siblings, is a reliable risk factor for adolescent drug usage (Denton & Kampfe 1994). Although genetics may play a role in cigarette smoking (Rowe & Linver 1995), the family's influence on adolescents' use of other drugs may be mediated by social environment factors. In addition to the imitation of behaviors observed at home, teens whose parents abuse substances appear to be more vulnerable to stress (Barrera et al 1995) and to acquire attitudes and coping styles that lead to increased affiliation with substance-using peers (Wills et al 1994). The experience of maltreatment in the home is also a risk factor for adolescent drug use (Malinosky-Rummell & Hansen 1993). In contrast, supportive and cohesive families help protect adolescents with problem-drinking fathers (Farrell et al 1995).

Drug-abusing teens are more likely to live in single-parent homes and homes from which they feel alienated (Denton & Kampfe 1994). A lack of support and sense of rejection and detachment from parents has been associated with adolescent substance use (Barrera et al 1993, Turner et al 1993). Deficits in parental support partially mediate the association between low parental education and increased substance use among teens (Wills et al 1995b). Prospective longitudinal data suggest that fathers' difficulty controlling anger predicts sons' future alcohol and drug usage (D'Angelo et al 1995). Maternal behavior rated as cold, unresponsive, and underprotective when children were five years old has been associated with frequent drug usage during adolescence (Shedler & Block 1990). Findings like these do not rule out the possibility that the same stable personality traits in a child that undermine the development of supportive family relationships may also increase the child's propensity to abuse substances (Wills et al 1995a).

There are conflicting findings regarding the role that parental control, supervision, and monitoring play in adolescent drug use. On the one hand, studies suggest that the homes of some abusing adolescents are overly controlling and that the children experience a lack of autonomy (Denton & Kampfe 1994, Webb et al 1991). On the other hand, longitudinal evidence relates abuse of drugs and smoking by teens to homes with less consistent enforcement of rules, less parental monitoring of the child's behavior, fewer parental demands of the child, and less imposition of structure and organization (Biglan et al 1995, Stice & Barrera 1995). In addition, some parents respond to their teen's use of drugs with fewer attempts at control and less support, which may signal the parents' acquiescence or sense of helplessness (Stice & Barrera 1995).

Many of the characteristics of families that are linked to substance abuse are also linked to adolescent sexual behavior. Teens growing up in single-parent households and those with histories of physical or sexual abuse show an increased probability of engaging in risky sexual behavior (Cunningham et al 1994, Jemmott & Jemmott 1992). Teens engage in more frequent sexual activity and more risky sexual behaviors when there is less parental monitoring and more permissiveness at home (Jemmott & Jemmott 1992, Metzler et al 1994). However, there is also evidence of increased sexual activity among adolescents whose parents overprotect them and fail to help them to learn to function independently (Turner et al 1993).

Conclusion

Research findings consistently point to three characteristics of family environments that can undermine the health of children and adolescents: (*a*) a social climate that is conflictual and angry or, worse, one that is violent and abusive; (*b*) relationships, particularly parent-child relationships, that are unresponsive and lacking in cohesiveness, warmth, and emotional support; and (*c*) parenting that is either overly controlling and dominating on the one hand or uninvolved with little monitoring of the child and little imposition of rules and structure on the other hand. These dimensions of a family environment are stressful for children, and they are associated with depression, maladaptive ways of coping with negative affect, and health-threatening behaviors in adolescence. The family characteristics identified as contributors to poor health outcomes in childhood are often embedded within households characterized by economic strain and few resources. Evidence suggests that parenting behavior may mediate some of the effects of economic strain (Huston et al 1994); however, economic strain may mediate the effects of other family characteristics, such as the number of parents in the home (Gore et al 1992).

THE PEER SOCIAL ENVIRONMENT

Chronic Stress and Mental Health/Distress

Characteristics similar to the factors identified in stressful communities and families predict chronic stress in the peer and school environments: less adult attention and stability at school, and more conflict with and less acceptance by peers. For example, children who show greater cardiovascular reactivity are more prone to develop respiratory illnesses when they are enrolled in preschools that are unstable and unable to provide individual adult attention (e.g. those with high teacher-child ratios, high staff turnover, more part-time teachers, etc) (Boyce et al 1995). As highly reactive children in less stable and less attentive preschools repeatedly respond to social stressors in the environment, they may build up high allostatic load, which may result in more illnesses.

Adolescents spontaneously mention interpersonal stressors involving peers—such as conflicts with friends, feeling lonely or left out of peer groups, and boyfriend/girlfriend problems—as among the most common and most distressing problems that they face in daily life (Repetti et al 1996). Being neglected or rejected by peers has been associated in longitudinal studies with both increased aggression and depression (Kupersmidt & Patterson 1991). The complex interactions between the family and peer social environments are illustrated by research indicating that poor parenting practices often result in child behavior problems that can, in turn, lead to peer rejection (Patterson et al 1989).

Coping Skills and Resources

As youngsters move from childhood into their teenage years they spend less time with their families and (especially for girls) more time with peers (Larson & Richards 1991). Not surprisingly, then, adolescents often turn to their friends for support, especially when there is turmoil at home (Aseltine et al 1994). The presence of supportive peer relationships is usually associated with better mental health among children and adolescents, although that association partly reflects the impact of psychological functioning on the development of supportive friendships (Hirsch & DuBois 1992). The peer group may facilitate children's coping by enhancing self-esteem, perceptions of control, and the perceived security of social relations (Sandler et al 1989b). Empirical evidence for the stress-buffering role of peer social support has been mixed. Some studies suggest that support from friends can provide protection from the negative impact of stress on children's psychological adjustment (Dubow & Tisak 1989), but others do not find evidence of a moderating role of peer support (Cumsille & Epstein 1994). The effectiveness of peer support is likely to vary as a function of the stressor with which the adolescent is coping (Gore & Aseltine 1995).

Health Habits and Behaviors

Adolescents' beliefs about the prevalence and acceptance of alcohol and drug use by peers are risk factors for alcohol and drug use, with peer influence increasing as children age (Bailey & Hubbard 1990, Donaldson 1995). In addition to passive social pressures exerted by the perceived behavior and attitudes of peers, social contact with certain individuals may increase the availability of these substances (Dolcini & Adler 1994). For example, residence in a fraternity or sorority and the adoption of a party-centered lifestyle are reliable predictors of binge drinking among college students (Wechsler et al 1995).

Peer social influence affects other behaviors that pose significant threats to adolescent health. For example, high school students are more likely to engage in risky sexual behavior if their friends are sexually active or if they believe that a majority of their peers have had intercourse (Walter et al 1992). Consistent with data on other risky behaviors, one of the best-known predictors of adolescent smoking is association with peers who smoke (Biglan et al 1995). The appeal of smoking may derive, in part, from its function as a social signal suggesting adult role status and independence from parents (Rowe & Linver 1995).

The influence exerted by peers may be at least partially shaped by the family social environment. On the one hand, children are more likely to affiliate with substance-abusing peers if their parents abuse substances or inadequately supervise their activities (Biglan et al 1995, Wills et al 1994). On the other hand, the effect of peer drug use is much weaker when parenting is authoritative (i.e. parents are involved, make demands, and supervise while demonstrating acceptance and warmth) (Mounts & Steinberg 1995).

Conclusion

The social environments provided at school and by peers affect child and adolescent health at each point in Figure 2. There is particularly strong evidence for the stressfulness of conflicts and rejection by peers and for the social influence of peers over several categories of health-threatening behavior. An important finding is that the effects of the peer social environment must be understood within the context of the family environment.

ADULT SOCIAL ENVIRONMENT

A broad range of social ties has been examined concerning adult health. These ties include not only immediate family and other close relatives and friends but also ties to larger formal and informal groups. An extensive literature documents the range of negative health outcomes that accrue to those whose social environment is either structurally impoverished (i.e. characterized by fewer social ties) or functionally impoverished (i.e. characterized by a dearth of socially supportive interactions with others) (Berkman 1995, Broadhead et al 1983).

Although social ties have generally been seen as serving a health-promoting role, the social environment can also be a source of increased and potentially chronic stress, which contributes to increased rather than decreased health risks; that is, social relationships are characterized by costs as well as benefits. Such costs can take the form of requests/demands for assistance, criticism, or other forms of interpersonal conflict (Averill 1982). When such characteristics predominate in the social environment, they can result in increased risks for poor mental and physical health (for discussion and review, see Burg & Seeman 1994, Seeman et al 1996).

Chronic Stress

The health-promoting effects of the social environment are generally hypothesized to result from the stress-reducing effects of social integration within a nurturant, supportive milieu (Cohen 1992). Evidence linking social environment characteristics to physiologic stress responses supports this view, pointing to the potential importance of the social environment in the accumulation of allostatic load.

Although being married has been generally associated with better immune responses as measured by various parameters of immune reaction (Kiecolt-Glaser et al 1994), spousal interaction characterized by greater hostility and conflict has been associated with greater cardiovascular and neuroendocrine reactivity and lower immune function (Kiecolt-Glaser et al 1994). The stress-inducing combination of emotional and physical demands of caring for a sick spouse has also been related to lowered immune function (e.g. among those with a spouse with cancer or those who are caring for a spouse with Alzheimer's disease) as well as elevated lipids and increased endocrine reactivity (for a review, see Kiecolt-Glaser et al 1994). Ambulatory monitoring of blood pressure at work and at home indicates that men show a reduction in blood pressure in the home environment whereas women do not (Unden et al 1991), which may be due to the greater demands of home and child care frequently assumed by women. Beyond the marital relationship, individuals reporting lower levels of support from close friends and family also exhibit higher heart rate and systolic blood pressure (Dressler et al 1986, Unden et al 1991), higher serum cholesterol and lower immune function (Thomas et al 1985), and higher levels of neuroendocrine activity (Seeman et al 1994).

Experimental studies also demonstrate the physiologic impacts of social interactions. Interpersonal challenge or hostility have been shown to elicit increased neuroendocrine and cardiovascular activity (Brown & Smith 1992, Krantz et al 1986). The presence of a friend or supportive confederate, however, generally attenuates cardiovascular reactivity in subjects confronted with challenging laboratory tasks (for a review, see Seeman & McEwen 1996). By contrast, the presence of a stranger observing the testing session produces increased reactivity (Snydersmith & Cacioppo 1992) as does the presence of others (friends or strangers) who disagree with the subject about some aspect of the session (Back & Bogdonoff 1964, Gerin et al 1992). Reactivity appears to be reduced by the presence of even one other person who agrees with the subject (Back & Bogdonoff 1964, Gerin et al 1992).

Mental Health/Distress

The positive and negative effects of the social environment on mental health have been extensively documented (for a review, see George 1989). Greater social integration, particularly as reflected in the presence of primary ties with spouse, children, and other kinds of supportive significant others are associated with lower risk of depression (George 1989), while marital disruption—either through bereavement, marriage dissolution, or the cognitive impairment of one's spouse—is associated with increased risks for psychological distress (Aseltine & Kessler 1993, Bloom et al 1978, Moritz et al 1989). The quality of existing relationships, however, appears equally important in predicting mental health outcomes. Relationships that are characterized by criticism, unwelcome advice or conflict, or demands for caregiving have been associated with increased psychological distress (Kessler et al 1985). Depression and/or negative affect in significant others is also associated with increased depression and psychological distress (Joiner 1994). Even in the absence of overtly negative social interactions, failure of the family or friends to provide anticipated or expected support can result in increased psychological distress (Brown & Harris 1989).

Women may be especially vulnerable to the psychological consequences of nonsupportive interactions with family or friends. Although men and women both report more supportive than negative social interactions, women report relatively more negative interactions with nondiscretionary family or kin ties (Lefler et al 1986, Schuster et al 1990) and appear to be more emotionally distressed by such negative interactions (Lefler et al 1986, Wethington et al 1987). Men benefit more consistently from greater social integration (House et al 1988a).

Coping Skills and Resources

Throughout life, one's family and friends serve as the social context within which events are appraised and coping strategies are evaluated and initiated (Cohen 1992). Family and/or friends can affect coping efforts through provision of actual instrumental and/or informational support and can serve as sources of emotional support (Cohen 1992). Such social resources may be particularly important in coping with lower-SES environmental demands: The relationship between lower occupational status and greater psychological vulnerability to life events disappears for lower-status women reporting high social support (Turner & Noh 1983).

The influence of the family or friends on coping, however, may not always be health promoting. The assistance provided by family and friends in coping with illness and/or disability can result in increased dependency and disability (for reviews, see Seeman et al 1996, Thompson & Sobolew-Shubin 1993) or poorer disease control. Diabetic men with larger support networks exhibit poorer control of their diabetes (e.g. significant increases in glycosylated hemoglobin, cholesterol and triglycerides, glucose and weight; Kaplan & Hartwell 1987) as do teenagers reporting greater satisfaction with their social-support systems (Kaplan et al 1985), possibly because members of the support network undermine diabetes-related diet behaviors. Studies also document limits to the effectiveness of social support in promoting better coping. In the face of severe stressors such as life-threatening disease, even the presence of close and apparently supportive relationships is not always associated with reductions in psychological distress or greater physical recovery (Bolger et al 1997, Coyne & Fiske 1992).

Health Habits and Behaviors

The social environment also serves as a source of learning and reinforcement for attitudes and behaviors that affect health. People who are more socially integrated exhibit greater preventive health behavior, including less smoking and drinking (Broman 1992) and more cancer screening (for a review, see Berkman 1995) and more successful risk reduction efforts such as reducing dietary fat, exercising, and stopping smoking (Bovbjerg et al 1995, Sallis et al 1989). Supportive family environments have also been related to better adherence in hemodialysis treatment (Christensen et al 1992). However, the social environments provided by family and friends also carry the potential for encouraging more detrimental health behaviors such as problem drinking (Seeman et al 1988), less successful efforts to quit smoking (Cohen 1992), and as indicated above, poorer control of diabetes. Family environments can also present more direct health threats in the form, for example, of second-hand smoke exposure from living with a smoker (Sandler et al 1989a) and physical abuse (Mercy & Saltzman 1989).

Evidence linking social environment characteristics to health-care utilization is neither extensive nor consistent. Consultations with family and friends can result in increased or decreased utilization, depending on the degree to which their attitudes and behaviors favor such utilization as well as their ability to provide assistance to facilitate utilization (Geertsen et al 1975, Penning 1995, Sampson 1992).

Conclusion

The characteristics of the social environment that relate most strongly to adult health outcomes—lack of social integration and poor quality of social relationships—also exhibit links with postulated pathways for these health effects. Specifically, social relationships characterized by conflict and hostility are associated not only with increased mental distress but also with increased physiologic arousal and lowered immune function, profiles of physiologic activity with known links to disease pathology (McEwen & Stellar 1993). In contrast with these health-damaging effects of impoverished social environments, environments characterized by supportive relationships appear to serve a stress-reducing, health-promoting function, enhancing psychological functioning and reducing physiologic arousal. In addition, the social environment can impact directly and importantly on health behaviors and health-care utilization.

WORK

The work environment represents an important life arena for adults that contributes to life satisfaction. Controlling for SES and health, those who work report a higher quality of life than those who do not (Ruchlin & Morris 1991). Moreover, full-time employment predicts slower declines in perceived health and in physical functioning for both men and women (Ross & Mirowsky 1995). Nonetheless, adverse characteristics of the work environment have long been suspected to contribute to ill health. Work stressors are among the most common and upsetting stressors that people report, and because the majority of adults work full-time, they may be exposed to the health-compromising effects of these conditions over the long term.

The work environment may directly affect illness precursors or illness, including injuries, cancers, and respiratory and cardiovascular disease, by exposing workers to physical, chemical, and biological hazards (House & Smith 1985). Because this voluminous literature has not yet implicated psychosocial mechanisms in disease pathology, apart from the fact that such adverse exposure is strongly linked to SES and race, we do not review it here.

Chronic Stress

Chronic stress is the mechanism most commonly offered to explain the adverse effects of the work environment on health. Work overload is one of the chief factors studied. Workers who feel required to work too long and too hard at too many tasks report more stress (e.g. Caplan & Jones 1975), practice poorer health habits (Sorensen et al 1985), and report more health complaints than do workers not suffering from overload (Repetti 1993). Work overload appears to trigger neuroendocrine and cardiovascular reactions that, over time, can increase the likelihood of cardiovascular disease. Working 40 or more hours a week is a risk factor for producing babies of low birth weight among employed women (Peoples-Sheps et al 1991). Work pressure also predicts ill health. Men reporting high job pressure or demands sought medical attention more and showed more documented signs of pathology; a follow-up investigation revealed these men were more likely to die in the following decade

(House et al 1986). Consistently, however, research demonstrates a stronger relationship between reported work overload and physical health complaints than between number of hours worked and poor health (e.g. Herzog et al 1991), which raises the possibility that psychological distress or negative affectivity is implicated in this relation.

Role conflict and role ambiguity have also been tied to illness precursors and illness (Caplan & Jones 1975). Role conflict occurs when an individual receives conflicting information about work tasks or standards. Chronically high blood pressure and elevated pulse have been tied to role conflict and role ambiguity (French & Caplan 1973).

Responsibility for others may contribute to ill health. For example, a study comparing illness rates of air-traffic controllers and second-class airmen found that hypertension was four times more common and diabetes and peptic ulcers twice as common among the air-traffic controllers than among the airmen, who did not have responsibility for the fates of others. Moreover, all three diseases were diagnosed at a younger age among the air-traffic controllers. Hypertension and ulcers were more common among controllers at busier airports (Cobb 1976).

The perception that one's career or job development has been inadequate may also contribute to ill health. People who feel they have been promoted too quickly or too slowly, who feel insecure about their jobs, and who feel that their ambitions are thwarted are more likely to report stress, to seek help for psychological distress, and to show higher rates of illness, especially cardiovascular disease (Catalano et al 1986).

Research has especially focused on the effects of a high-strain work environment defined as one with a high level of demands and a low level of decision latitude (Karasek & Theorell 1990). Considerable research has supported the hypothesized relation of high work strain to poor health (e.g. Landsbergis et al 1992). Work strain is significantly negatively associated with health-related quality of life, including physical functioning, role functioning related to physical health, vitality, social functioning, and mental health (Lerner et al 1994). Job strain has been linked to higher fibrinogen levels among working middle-aged women (Davis et al 1995) and to low birth weight (Woo 1994). Frankenhaeuser (1991) found that the catecholamine/cortisol balance is different in high- versus low-control situations, with cortisol levels lower in high-control situations. Not all studies find adverse effects of high levels of job demands and strain, however (Albright et al 1992), and studies relating job demands and decision latitude to coronary heart disease risk factors (cholesterol, smoking, and systolic and diastolic blood pressure) are inconsistent (Alterman et al 1994, Pieper et al 1989). Nonetheless, research suggests that the risk that role overload will lead to heart disease may be reduced when people are given a high degree of control in the work environment (Karasek & Theorell 1990).

Job uncertainty and unemployment have been associated with a variety of adverse mental and physical health outcomes, including depression, physical symptoms, physical illness (Hamilton et al 1990), alcohol abuse (Catalano et al 1993), and a heightened mortality rate (Sorlie & Rogot 1990). The negative effects of unemployment appear to be generated partly by the financial strain produced by unemployment and by the fact that unemployment creates vulnerability to other life events. Being unstably employed is also related to poor health (Pavalko et al 1993, Rushing et al 1992).

Research has focused increasingly not only on work stress but on its interactive effects with the stress induced by other roles, especially into the family. Much of this work has focused on married women with young children who are employed and who are chiefly responsible for household and child-care tasks. Overall, combining marital, parental, and occupational roles does not appear to significantly affect mortality (Kotler & Wingard 1989). However, attempting to juggle heavy responsibilities at both work and home reduces the enjoyment of all tasks (Williams et al 1991). On the other hand, employment can also be beneficial for women's well-being (Repetti et al 1989). Whether the effects of multiple roles are positive or negative appears to depend heavily on resources available. Having control and flexibility over one's work, having a good income, and having someone to help with the housework or child care all reduce the likelihood that combining multiple roles will produce psychological costs (Lennon & Rosenfield 1992, Rosenfield 1992). Although less research has been conducted on men, what evidence there is suggests that for men, multiple roles are protective (Adelmann 1994).

Mental Health/Psychological Distress

Mental health or psychological distress has typically not been examined as a pathway to poor health in the work environment but has been treated as an outcome in its own right. This is because psychological distress often translates into outcomes of importance to employers, specifically job dissatisfaction, absenteeism, disability claims, and high rates of turnover. Overall research suggests that the factors that compromise physical health also compromise mental health (for a review, see Taylor 1995). Whether anxiety and depression generated by job stress constitute a route by which the chronic stress of the work environment translates into poor health outcomes is unknown.

Coping Skills and Resources

The role of coping strategies in moderating the relation between chronic work stress and adverse health outcomes is an understudied area. This may be true partly because objective work demands are often so powerful that individual coping strategies have little room in which to operate. In addition, understanding how people cope with job stress may necessitate the examination of coping strategies specific to a particular job (Dewe & Guest 1990). Nonetheless, active coping strategies have been associated with more effective coping in a variety of situations (for a review, see Haidt & Rodin 1995), and the Karasek model of work strain is consistent with such an argument in positing that the degree to which individuals have decision latitude reduces work strain. Nonetheless, under conditions of high psychological demands, decision latitude may have negative effects.

Social support has been extensively studied in the work environment, and its effects are generally beneficial. Social support can have both direct (e.g. Ganster et al 1986, Loscocco & Spitze 1990) and moderating effects (e.g. Repetti et al 1989) on reported stress and health problems in the workplace. Those who report being unable to develop satisfying relationships report more negative affect at work (Buunk et al 1993) and poorer physical and mental health (Repetti 1993). Poor social relations at work have been tied directly to heightened catecholamine levels (Cooper & Marshall 1976), to risk for coronary heart disease (Repetti 1993), and to heightened fibrinogen levels in working women (Davis et al 1995). A study of government workers found that high workload was related to high blood pressure, but this relationship was attenuated among employees who had supportive relationships with their supervisors (House 1981). Adverse effects of unemployment also appear to be moderated by the seeking of social support (Turner et al 1991). Social support may be especially important for buffering work stress for minority group members (Gutierres et al 1996).

Health Habits and Behaviors

As noted, health habits are adversely affected by job stress and as such, may also play a moderating role in the relation between work stress and adverse health outcomes. People who feel they have more control over work are less likely to engage in risky health behaviors (Wickrama et al 1995). Substance abuse in the work environment has been extensively studied. Muntaner et al (1995) found that after adjusting for SES, alcoholism, and certain work conditions, drug abuse was higher in individuals with high-strain jobs. Job strain may not lead people to start smoking, but it does appear to lead to heavier smoking (Green & Johnson 1990). High job dissatisfaction is associated with heavy drinking, and negative consequences of drinking are associated with the job characteristics of low autonomy, little use of capacities, and lack of participation in decision making (Greenberg & Grunberg 1995). However, some research suggests that such abuse may be more related to general feelings of powerlessness, alienation, and lack of commitment than to specific job characteristics (Seeman et al 1988). Problem drinking in response to job characteristics may also depend on the degree to which alcohol consumption is perceived to be a useful means of coping (Greenberg & Grunberg 1995). Most studies relating job characteristics to health habits are cross-sectional, so it is difficult to determine whether job strain and health habits may be due to some third factor, such as emotional distress.

Conclusion

Research links work stress to a broad array of acute diseases, and evidence that it contributes to chronic disease such as cardiovascular disease, is mounting (Repetti 1993). The main psychosocial pathway from the work environment to poor health that has been studied involves chronic stress. Other potential routes, such as mental health or emotional distress, coping strategies, and health habits, have been studied not as pathways but as outcomes in their own right. The research on occupational stress could clearly profit from a consideration of more complex and multiple causal routes in relating chronic stress to adverse health outcomes.

CONCLUSIONS

Individual experiences and behaviors predictive of health outcomes are nested within geographic, social, developmental, and economic environments. The initial context for this observation is the recognition that social class and race are related to all-cause mortality and morbidity associated with a wide range of disorders. Those in the lower ends of the social class distribution and African-Americans disproportionately live in high-stress communities, occupy jobs characterized by high demands and low control, and live in family and social environments where they are disproportionately exposed to violence, conflict, and abuse. The type of community in which one lives and the demands of the work environment feed into the family environment and the kinds of social ties external to the family that may be developed. Thus, social environments influence health in a complex and interactive fashion.

The health effects of individual characteristics such as hostility, or the health effects of a family environment characteristic such as a high level of conflict, must be understood within the larger environments in which these behaviors are learned and expressed. At the very least, such an analysis should alert the psychologist to the potential risks of "psychologizing" or "biologizing" health-predictive variables without considering the contexts in which they occur. For example, recent empirical studies identifying a genetic component to the perception of social support (Kendler et al 1991) and suggesting that social support is partly a function of individual dispositions in personality

(Cohen et al 1986) must be balanced by the recognition that environments play an important role in fostering or undermining the ability to create social ties. Psychosocial predictors of health outcomes do not occur and should not be studied in an economic, racial, developmental, and social vacuum. With respect to interventions, the implications of such a viewpoint are complex. On the one hand, considering multiple levels of analysis simultaneously suggests multiple intervention points ranging from the individual through the family to the community. On the other hand, any intervention focus must acknowledge the interrelatedness of these environments and the fact that change induced at one level may have modest long-term effects, if corresponding changes do not occur at other levels.

Substantial evidence relates characteristics of environments to health-relevant outcomes, including all-cause mortality and a wide range of chronic diseases. Manifold pathways, reviewed above, have been implicated, including the exposure of individuals to chronic stress and the increased allostatic load that may result, the creation of chronic or intermittent emotional distress, the development or use of ineffective coping strategies and the inability to form and make use of social ties, and the acquisition and practice of health habits that are dependent upon environmental factors that limit personal and social resources. Empirically, the links from environmental characteristics to chronic stress to identifiable biological endpoints have most commonly been made. Pathways involving the other routes are less well studied, and more complex concatenations of these pathways, as suggested by Figure 2, have barely been studied at all. Each of the environments studied provides suggestive evidence about likely pathways that may guide research in the future.

At the outset, we asked "What is an unhealthy environment and how does it get under the skin?" Answering such a question definitively is currently beyond the scope of any review, because much of the research one would like to see has not yet been conducted. Nonetheless, despite the gaps in the literature, the beginning of an answer is emerging. Consistently across the environments examined—community, family, work, and peers—those that threaten personal safety; that limit the ability to develop social ties; or that are characterized by conflictual, violent, or abusive interpersonal relationships are related to a broad array of adverse health outcomes. These effects appear to occur across the lifespan, beginning prenatally and carrying through into old age. Likewise, a picture of the healthy environment is coming into view. Environments are healthy to the degree that they provide safety and opportunities for social integration. In addition, the ability to experience a sense of personal control may be important, within certain parameters.

People have evolved as social animals and as such appear to be sensitively "tuned in" to others in the social world. Therefore, it should not be surprising that the social environment has such potential to affect physiology, both positively and negatively. Evidence continues to accumulate that throughout the lifespan, the structure and quality of social interactions have profound effects on psychological, behavioral, and physiologic functioning, and ultimately on our health and well-being.

ACKNOWLEDGMENTS

Funds for this review were provided in part by the MacArthur Foundation's SES Planning Initiative on Health. Preparation of this manuscript was also supported by MH 42152 from the National Institute of Mental Health to the first author and by FIRST Award R29-48593 from the National Institute of Mental Health to the second author. The third author was supported, in part, by a grant from the MacArthur Research Network on Successful Aging and by NIA-SERCA grant AG-00586. The authors gratefully acknowledge the helpful comments of Sheldon Cohen on a prior draft.

Literature Cited

Adelmann PK. 1994. Multiple roles and psychological well-being in a national sample of older adults. *J. Gerontol.: Soc. Sci.* 49: S277–85

Adler NE, Boyce WT, Chesney MA, Folkman S, Syme SL. 1993. Socioeconomic inequalities in health: no easy solution. *J. Am. Med. Assoc.* 269:3140–45

Adler NE, Matthews KA. 1994. Health and psychology: Why do some people get sick and some stay well? *Annu. Rev. Psychol.* 45:229–59

Albright CL, Winkleby MA, Ragland DR, Fisher J, Syme SL. 1992. Job strain and prevalence of hypertension in a biracial population of urban bus drivers. *Am. J. Public Health* 82:984–89

Alterman T, Shekelle RB, Vernon SW, Burau KD. 1994. Decision latitude, psychologic demand, job strain, and coronary heart disease in the Western Electric study. *Am. J. Epidemiol.* 139:620–27

Anderson NB, McNeilly M, Myers H. 1991. Autonomic reactivity and hypertension in blacks: a review and proposed model. *Ethn. Dis.* 1:163–70

Aseltine RG, Kessler RC. 1993. Marital disruption and depression in a community sample. *J. Health Soc. Behav.* 34:237–51

Aseltine RH Jr, Gore S, Colten ME. 1994. Depression and the social developmental context of adolescence. *J. Pers. Soc. Psychol.* 67:252–63

Averill JR. 1982. *Anger and Agression: An Essay on Emotion.* New York: Springer-Verlag

Back KW, Bogdonoff MD. 1964. Plasma lipid responses to leadership, conformity, and deviation. In *Psychobiological Approaches to Social Behavior,* ed. HP Leiderman, D Shapiro, pp. 24–42. Stanford, CA: Stanford Univ. Press

Bailey SL, Hubbard RL. 1990. Developmental variation in the context of marijuana initiation among adolescents. *J. Health Soc. Behav.* 31:58–70

Barrera M, Chassin L, Rogosch F. 1993. Effects of social support and conflict on adolescent children of alcoholic and nonalcoholic fathers. *J. Pers. Soc. Psychol.* 64: 602–12

Barrera M, Li SA, Chassin L. 1995. Effects of parental alcoholism and life stress on Hispanic and non-Hispanic Caucasian adolescents: a prospective study. *Am. J. Commmunity Psychol.* 23:479–507

Becker MH. 1993. A medical sociologist looks at health promotion. *J. Health Soc. Behav.* 34:1–6

Berkman LF. 1995. The role of social relations in health promotion. *Psychosom. Med.* 57: 245–54

Biglan A, Duncan TE, Ary DV, Smolkowski K. 1995. Peer and parental influences on adolescent tobacco use. *J. Behav. Med.* 18:315

Bloom BL, Asher SJ, White SW. 1978. Marital disruption as a stressor: a review and analysis. *Psychol. Bull.* 85:867–94

Bolger N, Foster M, Vinokur AD, Ng R. 1997. Close relationships and adjustment to a life crisis: the case of breast cancer. *J. Pers. Soc. Psychol.* In press

Booth-Kewley S, Friedman HS. 1987. Psychological predictors of heart disease: a quantitative review. *Psychol. Bull.* 101:343–62

Bovbjerg VE, McCann BS, Brief DJ, Follette WC, Retzlaff BM, et al. 1995. Spouse support and long-term adherence to lipid-lowering diets. *Am. J. Epidemiol.* 141:451–60

Boyce WT, Chesney M, Alkon A, Tschann JM, Adams S, et al. 1995. Psychobiologic reactivity to stress and childhood respiratory illness: results of two prospective studies. *Psychosom. Med.* 57:411–22

Braaten LS. 1996. Sexual dysfunction in sexually traumatized women. *Health Psychol.* 18:6

Bradley RH. 1993. Children's home environments, health, behavior, and intervention efforts: a review using the home inventory as a marker measure. *Genet. Soc. Gen. Psychol. Monogr.* 119:437–90

Broadhead EW, Kaplan BH, James SA, Wagner EH, Schoenbach VJ, et al. 1983. The epidemiologic evidence for a relationship between social support and health. *Am. J. Epidemiol.* 117:521–37

Broman C. 1992. Social relationships and health-related behavior. *J. Behav. Med.* 16: 335–50

Brown GW, Harris TO, eds. 1989. *Life Events and Illness.* New York: Guilford

Brown PC, Smith TW. 1992. Social influence, marriage, and the heart: cardiovascular consequences of interpersonal control in husbands and wives. *Health Psychol.* 11: 88–96

Burg MM, Seeman TE. 1994. Families and Health: the negative side of social ties. *Ann. Behav. Med.* 16:109–15

Buunk BP, Doosje BJ, Jans LGJM, Hopstaken LEM. 1993. Perceived reciprocity, social support, and stress at work: the role of exchange and communal orientation. *J. Pers. Soc. Psychol.* 65:801–11

Calnan M, Johnson B. 1985. Health, health risks, and inequalities: an exploratory study of women's perceptions. *Sociol. Health Ill.* 7:55–75

Caplan RD, Jones KW. 1975. Effects of work load, role ambiguity, and Type A personality on anxiety, depression, and heart rate. *J. Appl. Psychol.* 60:713–19

Catalano R, Dooley D, Wilson G, Hough R. 1993. Job loss and alcohol abuse: a test using data from the epidemiological catchment area. *J. Health Soc. Behav.* 34: 215–25

Catalano RA, Rook K, Dooley D. 1986. Labor markets and help-seeking: a test of the employment security hypothesis. *J. Health Soc. Behav.* 27:277–87

Christensen AJ, Smith TW, Turner CW, Holman JM Jr, Gregory MC, Rich MA. 1992. Family support, physical impairment, and adherence in hemodialysis: an investigation of main and buffering effects. *J. Behav. Med.* 15:313–25

Cobb S. 1976. Social support as a moderator of life stress. *Psychosom. Med.* 38:300–14

Cohen S. 1992. Stress, social support, and disorder. In *The Meaning and Measurement of Social Support,* ed. HOF Veiel, U Baumann, pp. 109–24. New York: Hemisphere

Cohen S, Herbert TB. 1996. Health psychology: psychological factors and physical disease from the perspective of human psychoneuroimmunology. *Annu. Rev. Psychol.* 47:113–42

Cohen S, Sherrod DR, Clark MS. 1986. Social skills and the stress-protective role of social support. *J. Pers. Soc. Psychol.* 50:963–73

Coleman JS. 1990. *Foundations of Social Theory.* Cambridge, MA: Harvard Univ. Press

Collins NL, Dunkel-Schetter C, Lobel M, Scrimshaw SCM. 1993. Social support in pregnancy: psychosocial correlates of birth outcomes and postpartum depression. *J. Pers. Soc. Psychol.* 65:1243–58

Cooper CJ, Marshall J. 1976. Occupational sources of stress: a review of the literature relating to coronary heart disease and mental ill health. *J. Occup. Psychol.* 49:11–28

Coyne JC, Fiske V. 1992. Couples coping with chronic and catastrophic illness. In *Family Health Psychology,* ed. TJ Akamatsu, SC Crowther, SE Hobfoll, MAP Stevens, pp. 129–49. Washington, DC: Hemisphere

Crittenden PM. 1992. Children's strategies for coping with adverse home environments: an interpretation using attachment theory. *Child Abuse Negl.* 16:329–43

Cummings EM, El-Sheikh M. 1991. Children's coping with angry environments: a process-oriented approach. In *Life-Span Developmental Psychology: Perspectives on Stress and Coping,* ed. EM Cummings, AL Greene, KH Karraker, pp. 131–50. Hillsdale, NJ: Erlbaum

Cumsille PE, Epstein N. 1994. Family cohesion, family adaptability, social support, and adolescent depressive symptoms in outpatient clinic families. *J. Fam. Psychol.* 8:202–14

Cunningham RM, Stiffman AR, Dore P, Earls F. 1994. The association of physical and sexual abuse with HIV risk behaviors in adolescence and young adulthood: implications for public health. *Child Abuse Negl.* 18:233–45

D'Angelo LL, Weinberger DA, Feldman SS. 1995. Like father, like son? Predicting male adolescents' adjustment from parents' distress and self-restraint. *Dev. Psychol.* 31:883–96

Davies PT, Cummings EM. 1994. Marital conflict and child adjustment: an emotional security hypothesis. *Psychol. Bull.* 116: 387–411

Davis MC, Matthews KA, Meilahn EN, Kiss JE. 1995. Are job characteristics related to fibrinogen levels in middle-aged women? *Health Psychol.* 14:310–18

Denton RE, Kampfe CM. 1994. The relationship between family variables and adolescent substance abuse: a literature review. *Adolescence* 29:475–95

Dewe PJ, Guest DE. 1990. Methods of coping with stress at work: a conceptual analysis and empirical study of measurement issues. *J. Organ. Behav.* 11:135–50

Dolcini MM, Adler NE. 1994. Perceived competencies, peer group affiliation, and risk behavior among early adolescents. *Health Psychol.* 13:496–506

Donaldson SI. 1995. Peer influence on adolescent drug use: a perspective from the trenches of experimental evaluation research. *Am. Psychol.* 50:801–2

Donovan JE, Jessor R, Costa FM. 1991. Adolescent health behavior and conventionality-unconventionality: an extension of problem-behavior theory. *Health Psychol.* 10:52–61

Downey G, Coyne JC. 1990. Children of depressed parents: an integrative review. *Psychol. Bull.* 108:50–76

Dressler WW, Dos Santos EJ, Viteri FE. 1986. Blood pressure, ethnicity, and psychosocial resources. *Psychosom. Med.* 48:509–19

Dubow EF, Tisak J. 1989. The relation between stressful life events and adjustment in elementary school children: the role of social support and social problem-solving skills. *Child Dev.* 60:1412–23

Durkin MS, Davidson LL, Kuhn L, O'Connor P, Barlow B. 1994. Low-income neighborhoods and the risk of severe pediatric injury: a small-area analysis in northern Manhattan. *Am. J. Public Health* 84: 587–92

Eckenrode J, Rowe E, Laird M, Brathwaite J. 1995. Mobility as a mediator of the effects of child maltreatment of academic performance. *Child Dev.* 66:1130–42

El-Sheikh M, Cummings EM, Goetsch V. 1989. Coping with adults' angry behavior: behavioral, physiological, and self-report responding in preschoolers. *Dev. Psychol.* 25:490–98

Evans GW. 1997. Environmental stress and health. In *Handbook of Health Psychology,* ed. A Baum, T Revenson, JE Singer. Hillsdale, NJ: Erlbaum

Farrell MP, Barnes GM, Banerjee S. 1995. Family cohesion as a buffer against the effects of problem-drinking fathers on psychological distress, deviant behavior, and heavy drinking in adolescents. *J. Health Soc. Behav.* 36:377–85

Fleming I, Baum A, Davidson LM, Rectanus E, McArdle S. 1987. Chronic stress as a factor in physiologic reactivity to challenge. *Health Psychol.* 6:221–37

Frankenhaeuser M. 1991. The psychophysiology of workload, stress, and health: comparison between the sexes. *Ann. Behav. Med.* 13:197–204

Frasure-Smith N, Lesperance F, Talajic M. 1995. The impact of negative emotions on prognosis following myocardial infarction: is it more than depression? *Health Psychol.* 14:388–98

French JRP Jr, Caplan RD. 1973. Organizational stress and the individual strain. In *The Failure of Success,* ed. AJ Marrow. New York: AMACON

Ganster DC, Fusilier MR, Mayes BT. 1986. Role of social support in the experience of stress at work. *J. Appl. Psychol.* 71:102–10

Garbarino J, Sherman D. 1980. High-risk neighborhoods and high-risk families: the human ecology of child maltreatment. *Child Dev.* 51:188–98

Geertsen R, Klauber MR, Rindflesh M, Kane R, Gray R. 1975. A re-examination of Suchman's view on social factors in health care utilization. *J. Health Soc. Behav.* 16: 226–37

George LK. 1989. Stress, social support, and depression over the life-course. In *Aging, Stress, Social Support, and Health,* ed. K Markides, C Cooper, pp. 241–67. London: Wiley

Gerin W, Pieper C, Levy R, Pickering TG. 1992. Social support in social interaction: a moderator of cardiovascular reactivity. *Psychosom. Med.* 54:324–36

Gore S, Aseltine RH Jr. 1995. Protective processes in adolescence: matching stressors with social resources. *Am. J. Community Psychol.* 23:301–27

Gore S, Aseltine RH Jr, Colten ME. 1992. Social structure, life stress and depressive symptoms in a high school-aged population. *J. Health Soc. Behav.* 33:97–113

Gottman JM, Katz LF. 1989. Effects of marital discord on young children's peer interaction and health. *Dev. Psychol.* 25:373–81

Green KL, Johnson JV. 1990. The effects of psychosocial work organization on patterns of cigarette smoking among male chemical plant employees. *Am. J. Public Health* 80: 1368–71

Greenberg ES, Grunberg L. 1995. Work alienation and problem alcohol behavior. *J. Health Soc. Behav.* 36:83–102

Gunnar MR, Larson MC, Hertsgaard L, Harris ML, Brodersen L. 1992. The stressfulness of separation among nine-month-old infants: effects of social context variables and infant temperament. *Child Dev.* 63: 290–303
Gutierres SE, Saenz DS, Green BL. 1996. Job stress and health outcomes among Anglo and Hispanic employees: a test of the person-environment fit model. In *Stress in the 90's,* ed. G Keita, S Sauter. Washington, DC: Am. Psychol. Assoc. In press
Haidt J, Rodin J. 1995. *Control and Efficacy: An Integrative Review.* Rep. John D and Catherine T MacArthur Found. Prog. Ment. Health Hum. Dev. Univ. Michigan, Ann Arbor
Hamilton VL, Broman CL, Hoffman WS, Renner DS. 1990. Hard times and vulnerable people: initial effects of plant closing on autoworkers' mental health. *J. Health Soc. Behav.* 31:123–40
Harburg E, Erfurt JC, Havenstein LS, Chape S, Schull WJ, Schork MA. 1993. Socioecological stress, suppressed hostility, skin color, and black-white male blood pressure: Detroit. *Psychosom. Med.* 35:176–96
Hardy DF, Power TG, Jaedicke S. 1973. Examining the relation of parenting to children's coping with everyday stress. *Child Dev.* 64:1829–41
Herbert TB, Cohen S. 1993. Depression and immunity: a meta-analytic review. *Psychol. Bull.* 113:472–86
Hertsgaard L, Gunnar M, Erickson FM, Nachmias M. 1995. Adrenocortical responses to the strange situation in infants with disorganized/disoriented attachment relationships. *Child Dev.* 66:1100–6
Herzog AR, House JS, Morgan JN. 1991. Relation of work and retirement to health and well-being in older age. *Psychol. Aging* 6: 202–11
Hirsch BJ, DuBois DL. 1992. The relation of peer social support and psychological symptomatology during the transition to junior high school: a two-year longitudinal analysis. *Am. J. Community Psychol.* 20:333–47
House JS. 1981. *Work Stress and Social Support.* Reading, MA: Addison-Wesley
House JS, Landis KR, Umberson D. 1988a. Social relationships and health. *Science* 241:540–45
House JS, Smith DA. 1985. Evaluating the health effects of demanding work on and off the job. In *Assessing Physical Fitness and Physical Activity in Population-Base Surveys,* ed. TF Drury, pp. 481–508. Hyattsville, MD: Natl. Cent. Health Stat.
House JS, Strecher V, Meltzner HL, Robbins CA. 1986. Occupational stress and health among men and women in the Tecumseh Community health study. *J. Health Soc. Behav.* 27:62–77
House JS, Umberson D, Landis KR. 1988b. Structures and processes of social support. *Annu. Rev. Sociol* 14:293–318
Huston AC, McLoyd VC, Coll CG. 1994. Children and poverty: issues in contemporary research. *Child Dev.* 65:275–82
Jemmott LS, Jemmott JB III. 1992. Family structure, parental strictness, and sexual behavior among inner-city black male adolescents. *J. Adolesc. Res* 7:192–207
Jencks C, Mayer S. 1990. The social consequences of growing up in a poor neighborhood. In *Inner-City Poverty in the United States,* ed. L Lynn, M McGeary, pp. 111–86. Washington, DC: Natl. Acad.
Joiner TE Jr. 1994. Contagious depression: existence, specificity to depressed symptoms, and the role of reassurance seeking. *J. Pers. Soc. Psychol.* 67:287–96
Kagan J, Reznick JS, Snidman N. 1987. The physiology and psychology of behavioral inhibition in young children. *Child Dev.* 58: 1359–473
Kagan J, Reznick JS, Snidman N. 1988. Biological bases of childhood shyness. *Science* 240:167–71
Kaplan M, Chadwick MW, Schimmel LE. 1985. Social learning intervention to promote metabolic control in Type I diabetes mellitus: pilot experiment results. *Diabetes Care* 8:152–55
Kaplan RM, Hartwell SL. 1987. Differential effects of social support and social network on physiological and social outcomes in men and women with Type II diabetes mellitus. *Health Psychol.* 6:387–98
Karasek R, Theorell T. 1990. *Healthy Work: Stress, Productivity, and the Reconstruction of Working Life.* New York: Basic Books
Kaslow NJ, Deering CG, Racusin GR. 1994. Depressed children and their families. *Clin. Psychol. Rev.* 14:39–59
Kendler KS, Kessler RC, Heath AC, Neale MC, Eaves LJ. 1991. Coping: a genetic epidemiological investigation. *Psychol. Med.* 21:337–46
Kessler RC, MacLeod JD, Wethington E. 1985. The costs of caring: a perspective on the relationship between sex and psychological distress. In *Social Support: Theory, Research and Applications,* ed. IG Sarason, BR Sarason, pp. 491–506. Dordrecht: Martinus Nijhoff
Kessler RC, Magee WJ. 1994. Childhood family violence and adult recurrent depression. *J. Health Soc. Behav.* 35:13–27
Kiecolt-Glaser JK, Malarkey WB, Cacioppo JT, Glaser R. 1994. Stressful personal rela-

tionships: immune and endocrine function. In *Handbook of Human Stress and Immunity,* ed. R Glaser, J Kiecolt-Glaser, pp. 321–39. San Diego: Academic

Kotler P, Wingard DL. 1989. The effect of occupational, marital, and parental roles on mortality: the Alameda County study. *Am. J. Public Health* 79:607–12

Krantz DS, Manuck SB. 1984. Acute psychophysiologic reactivity and risk of cardiovascular disease: a review and methodologic critique. *Psychol. Bull.* 96:435–64

Krantz DS, Manuck SB, Wing RR. 1986. Psychological stressors and task variables on elicitors of reactivity. In *Handbook of Stress, Reactivity, and Cardiovascular Disease,* ed. KA Matthews, SM Weiss, T Detre, TM Dembroski, B Falkner, et al, pp. 85–107. New York: Wiley

Krause N. 1992. Stress and isolation form close ties in later life. *J. Gerontol.* 46: S183–94

Kupersmidt JB, Griesler PC, DeRosier ME, Patterson CJ, Davis PW. 1995. Childhood aggression and peer relations in the context of family and neighborhood factors. *Child Dev.* 66:360–75

Kupersmidt JB, Patterson CJ. 1991. Childhood peer rejection, aggression, withdrawal, and perceived competence as predictors of self-reported behavior problems in preadolescence. *J. Abnorm. Child Psychol.* 19: 427–49

Landsbergis PA, Schnall PL, Deitz D, Friedman R, Pickering T. 1992. The patterning of psychological attributes and distress by "job strain" and social support in a sample of working men. *J. Behav. Med.* 15: 379–414

Larson R, Richards MH. 1991. Daily companionship in late childhood and early adolescence: changing developmental contexts. *Child Dev.* 62:284–300

Lefler A, Krannich RS, Gillespie DL. 1986. Contact, support and friction: three faces of networks in community life. *Sociol. Perspect.* 29:337–55

Lennon MC, Rosenfeld S. 1992. Women and mental health: the interaction of job and family conditions. *J. Health Soc. Behav.* 33:316–27

Lerner DJ, Levine S, Malspeis S, D'Agostino RB. 1994. Job strain and health-related quality of life in a national sample. *Am. J. Public Health* 84:1580–85

Levy L, Herzog A. 1974. Effects of population density and crowding on health and social adaptation in The Netherlands. *J. Health Soc. Behav.* 15:228–40

Levy L, Herzog A. 1978. Effects of crowding on health and social adaptation in the city of Chicago. *Hum. Ecol.* 3:327–54

Lewinsohn PM, Roberts RE, Seeley JR, Rohde P, Gotlib IH, Hops H. 1994. Adolescent psychopathy. II. Psychosocial risk factors for depression. *J. Abnorm. Psychol.* 103: 302–15

Loscocco KA, Spitze G. 1990. Working conditions, social support, and the well-being of female and male factory workers. *J. Health Soc. Behav.* 31:313–27

Macintyre S. 1997. The black report and beyond: What are the issues? *Soc. Sci. Med.* In press

Macintyre S, Maciver S, Solomon A. 1993. Area, class and health: Should we be focusing on places or people? *Int. Soc. Policy* 22:213–34

Malinosky-Rummell R, Hansen DJ. 1993. Long-term consequences of childhood physical abuse. *Psychol. Bull.* 114:68–79

Manuck SB, Marsland AL, Kaplan JR, Williams JK. 1995. The pathogenicity of behavior and its neuroendocrine mediation: an example from coronary artery disease. *Psychosom. Med.* 57:275–83

Marmot MG. 1994. Social differentials in health within and between populations. *Health Wealth: J. Am. Acad. Arts Sci.* 123: 197–216

Martin LR, Friedman HS, Tucker JS, Schwartz JE, Criqui MH, et al. 1995. An archival prospective study of mental health and longevity. *Health Psychol.* 14:381–87

Matthews KA, Woodall KL, Jacob T, Kenyon K. 1996. Negative family environment as a predictor of boys' future status on measures of hostile attitudes, interview behavior, and anger expression. *Health Psychol.* 15:30–37

McEwen BS, Stellar E. 1993. Stress and the individual: mechanisms leading to disease. *Arch. Intern. Med.* 153:2093–101

McNeil GN. 1987. Depression. In *Handbook of Psychiatric Differential Diagnosis,* ed. SM Soreff, GN McNeil, pp. 57–126. Littleton, MA: PSG

Mechanic D, Hansell S. 1989. Divorce, family conflict, and adolescents' well-being. *J. Health Soc. Behav.* 30:105–16

Melamed BG, ed. 1995. Special section: the interface of mental and physical health. *Health Psychol.* 14:371–426

Mercy JA, Saltzman LE. 1989. Fatal violence among spouses in the United States 1976-85. *Am. J. Public Health* 79:595–99

Metzler CW, Noell J, Biglan A, Ary D, Smolkowski K. 1994. The social context for risky sexual behavior among adolescents. *J. Behav. Med.* 17:419–38

Moritz DJ, Kasl SV, Berkman LF. 1989. The health impact of living with a cognitively impaired elderly spouse: depressive symptoms and social functioning. *J. Gerontol: Soc. Sci.* 44:S17–27

Mounts NS, Steinberg L. 1995. An ecological

analysis of peer influence on adolescent grade point average and drug use. *Dev. Psychol.* 31:915–22

Muntaner C, Anthony JC, Crum RM, Eaton WW. 1995. Psychosocial dimensions of work and the risk of drug dependence among adults. *Am. J. Epidemiol.* 142:183–90

Neuspiel DR, Rush D, Butler NR, Golding J, Buur PE, Kurzon M. 1989. Parental smoking and post-infancy wheezing in children: a prospective cohort study. *Am. J. Public Health* 79:168–71

Nolen-Hoeksema S, Wolfson A, Mumme D, Guskin K. 1995. Helplessness in children of depressed and nondepressed mothers. *Dev. Psychol.* 31:377–87

Osofsky JD. 1990. *Gender issues in the development of deviant behavior: the case for teenage pregnancy.* Presented at the Prog. Hum. Dev. Crim. Behav., Radcliffe Coll.

Osofsky JD. 1993. Applied psychoanalysis: how research with infants and adolescents at high psychosocial risk informs psychoanalysis. *J. Am. Acad. Psychoanal.* 41: 193–207

Osofsky JD. 1995. The effects of exposure to violence on young children. *Am. Psychol.* 50:782–88

Patterson GR, DeBaryshe BD, Ramsey E. 1989. A developmental perspective on antisocial behavior. *Am. Psychol.* 44:329–35

Pavalko EK, Elder GH Jr, Clipp EC. 1993. Worklives and longevity: insights from a life course perspective. *J. Health Soc. Behav.* 34:363–80

Penning MJ. 1995. Health, social support, and the utilization of health services among older adults. *J. Gerontol.* 50B:S330–39

Peoples-Sheps MD, Siegel E, Suchindran CM, Origasa H, Ware A, Barakat A. 1991. Characteristics of maternal employment during pregnancy: effects on low birthweight. *Am. J. Public Health* 81:1007–12

Pieper C, LaCroix AZ, Karasek RA. 1989. The relation of psychosocial dimensions of work with coronary heart disease risk factors: a meta-analysis of five United States data bases. *Am. J. Epidemiol.* 129:483–94

Pynoos RS. 1993. Traumatic stress and developmental psychopathology in children and adolescents. In *American Psychiatric Press Review of Psychiatry,* ed. JM Oldham, MB Riba, A Tasman, Vol. 12. Washington, DC: Am. Psychiatric Assoc.

Repetti RL. 1993. The effects of workload and the social environment at work on health. In *Handbook of Stress,* ed. L Goldberger, S Bresnitz, pp. 368–85. New York: Free Press

Repetti RL, Matthews KA, Waldrun I. 1989. Employment and women's health. *Am. Psychol.* 44:1394–401

Repetti RL, McGrath EP, Ishikawa SS. 1996. Daily stress and coping in childhood and adolescence. In *Handbook of Pediatric and Adolescent Health Psychology,* ed. AJ Goreczny, M Hersen. Allyn & Bacon. In press

Richters JE, Martinez P. 1993. The NIMH community violence project: Vol. 1: children as victims of and witnessses to violence. *Psychiatry* 56:7–21

Rosenfield S. 1992. The costs of sharing: wives' employment and husbands' mental health. *J. Health Soc. Behav.* 33:213–25

Ross CE, Mirowsky J. 1995. Does employment affect health? *J. Health Soc. Behav.* 36:230–43

Rowe DC, Linver MR. 1995. Smoking and addictive behaviors: epidemiological, individual, and family factors. In *Behavior Genetic Approaches in Behavioral Medicine,* ed. JR Turner, LR Cardon, JK Hewitt, pp. 67–84. New York: Plenum

Rushing B, Ritter C, Burton RPD. 1992. Race differences in the effects of multiple roles on health: longitudinal evidence from a national sample of older men. *J. Health Soc. Behav.* 33:126–39

Ruchlin HS, Morris JN. 1991. Impact of work on the quality of life in community-residing young elderly. *Am. J. Public Health* 81: 498–500

Sallis JF, Hovell MF, Hofstetter CR, Faucher P, Elder JP, et al. 1989. A multivariate study of determinants of vigorous exercise in a community sample. *Prev. Med.* 18:20–34

Sampson RJ. 1992. Family management and child development: insights from social disorganization theory. In *Facts, Frameworks, and Forecasts: Advances in Criminological Theory,* ed. J McCord, 3:63–93. New Brunswick, NJ: Transaction

Sandler DP, Helsing KJ, Comstock GW, Shore DL. 1989a. Factors associated with past household exposure to tobacco smoke. *Am. J. Epidemiol.* 129:380–87

Sandler IN, Miller P, Short J, Wolchik SA. 1989b. Social support as a protective factor for children in stress. In *Children's Social Networks and Social Support,* ed. D Belle, pp. 277–304. New York: Wiley

Schuster TL, Kessler RC, Aseltine RH Jr. 1990. Supportive interactions, negative interactions, and depressed mood. *Am. J. Community Psychol.* 18:423–38

Seeman M, Seeman AZ, Budros A. 1988. Powerlessness, work, and community: a longitudinal study of alienation and alcohol use. *J. Health Soc. Behav.* 29:185–98

Seeman TE, Berkman LF, Blazer D, Rowe J. 1994. Social ties and support and neuroendocrine function: MacArthur Studies of Succesful Aging. *Ann. Behav. Med.* 16:95–106

Seeman TE, Bruce ML, McAvay G. 1996. Social network characteristics and onset of ADL disability. *J. Gerontol.: Soc. Sci.* In press

Seeman TE, McEwen BS. 1996. Social environment characteristics and neuroendocrine function: the impact of social ties and support on neuroendocrine regulation. *Psychosom. Med.* In press

Selye H. 1956. *The Stress of Life.* New York: McGraw-Hill

Shedler J, Block J. 1990. Adolescent drug use and psychological health: a longitudinal inquiry. *Am. Psychol.* 45:612–30

Sheline JL, Skipper BJ, Broadhead WE. 1994. Risk factors for violent behavior in elementary school boys: Have you hugged your child today? *Am. J. Public Health* 84:661–63

Siegler IC, Peterson BL, Barefoot JC, Williams RB. 1992. Hostility during late adolescence predicts coronary risk factors at mid-life. *Am. J. Epidemiol.* 136:146–54

Snydersmith MA, Cacioppo JT. 1992. Parsing complex social factors to determine component effects. I. Autonomic activity and reactivity as a function of human association. *J. Soc. Clin. Psychol.* 11:263–78

Sooman A, Macintyre S. 1995. Health and perceptions of the local environment in socially contrasting neighborhoods in Glasgow. *J. Health Place.* 1:15–26

Sorensen G, Pirie P, Folsom A, Luepker R, Jacobs D, Gillum R. 1985. Sex differences in the relationship between work and health: the Minnesota heart survey. *J. Health Soc. Behav.* 26:379–94

Sorenson SB, Peterson JG. 1994. Traumatic child death and documented maltreatment history, Los Angeles. *Am. J. Public Health* 84:623–27

Sorlie PD, Rogot E. 1990. Mortality by employment status in the national longitudinal mortality study. *Am. J. Epidemiol.* 132:983–92

Springs FE, Friedrich WN. 1992. Health risk behaviors and medical sequelae of childhood sexual abuse. *Mayo Clin.* 67:527– 32

Stice E, Barrera M Jr. 1995. A longitudinal examination of the reciprocal relations between perceived parenting and adolescents' substance use and externalizing behaviors. *Dev. Psychol.* 31:322–34

Taylor SE. 1995. *Health Psychology.* New York: McGraw-Hill. 3rd ed.

Thomas PD, Goodwin JM, Goodwin JS. 1985. Effect of social support on stress-related changes in cholesterol level, uric acid level, and immune function in an elderly sample. *Am. J. Psychiatry* 142:735–37

Thompson SC, Sobolew-Shubin A. 1993. Perceptions of overprotection in ill adults. *J. Appl. Soc. Psychol.* 23:85–97

Troutt DD. 1993. *The Thin Red Line: How the Poor Still Pay More.* San Francisco: Consum. Union US West Coast Reg. Off.

Troxler RG, Sprague EA, Albanese RA, Fuchs R, Thompson AJ. 1977. The association of elevated plasma cortisol and early atherosclerosis as demonstrated by coronary angiography. *Atheroscleroses* 26:151–62

Turner JB, Kessler RC, House JS. 1991. Factors facilitating adjustment to unemployment: implications for intervention. *Am. J. Community Psychol.* 19:521–42

Turner RA, Irwin CE Jr, Tschann JM, Millstein SG. 1993. Autonomy, relatedness, and the initiation of health risk behaviors in early adolescence. *Health Psychol.* 12:200–8

Turner RJ, Noh S. 1983. Class and psychological vulnerability among women: the significance of social support and personal control. *J. Health Soc. Behav.* 24:2–15

Unden AL, Orth-Gomer K, Elofsson S. 1991. Cardiovascular effects of social support in the work place: twenty-four-hour ECG monitoring of men and women. *Psychosom. Med.* 53:50–60

Wagener DK, Schatzkin A. 1994. Temporal trends in the socioeconomic gradient for breast cancer mortality among US women. *Am. J. Public Health* 84:1003–6

Wallace R. 1990. Urban desertification, public health and public order: "planned shrinkage," violent death, substance abuse and AIDS in the Bronx. *Soc. Sci. Med.* 31:801–13

Wallace R, Wallace D. 1990. Origins of public health collapse in New York City: the dynamics of planned shrinkage, contagious urban decay and social disintegration. *Bull. NY Acad. Med.* 66:391–434

Walter HJ, Vaughan RD, Gladis MM, Ragin DF, Kasen S, Cohall ST. 1992. Factors associated with AIDS risk behaviors among high school students in an AIDS epicenter. *Am. J. Public Health* 82:528–32

Webb JA, Baer PE, McLaughlin RJ, McKelvey RS, Caid CD. 1991. Risk factors and their relation to initiation of alcohol use among early adolescents. *J. Am. Acad. Child Adolesc. Psychiatry* 30:563–68

Wechsler H, Dowdall GW, Davenport A, Castillo S. 1995. Correlates of college student binge drinking. *Am. J. Public Health* 85:921–26

Wethington E, McLeod JD, Kessler RC. 1987. The importance of life events in explaining sex differences in psychological distress. In *Gender and Stress,* ed. RC Barnett, LB Biener, GK Baruch, pp. 144–56. New York: Basic Books

Wickrama K, Conger RD, Lorenz FO. 1995.

Work, marriage, lifestyle, and changes in men's physical health. *J. Behav. Med.* 18: 97–112
Widom C. 1989. The cycle of violence. *Science* 244:160–66
Williams DR. 1990. Socioeconomic differentials in health: a review and redirection. *Soc. Psychol. Q.* 53:81–99
Williams DR, Collins C. 1995. US socioeconomic and racial differences in health: patterns and explanations. *Annu. Rev. Sociol.* 21:349–86
Williams KJ, Suls J, Alliger GM, Learner SM, Wan CK. 1991. Multiple role juggling and daily mood states in working mothers: an experience sampling study. *J. Appl. Psychol.* 76:664–74
Wills TA, DuHamel K, Vaccaro D. 1995a. Activity and mood temperament as predictors of adolescent substance use: test of a self-regulation mediational model. *J. Pers. Soc. Psychol.* 68:901–16
Wills TA, McNamara G, Vaccaro D. 1995b. Parental education related to adolescent stress-coping and substance use: development of a mediational model. *Health Psychol.* 14:464–78
Wills TA, Schreibman D, Benson G, Vaccaro D. 1994. Impact of parental substance use on adolescents: a test of a mediation model. *J. Pediatr. Psychol.* 19:537–56
Woo G. 1994. *Strain in daily activities during pregnancy: associations of physical exertion, psychological demand, and personal control with birth outcomes.* PhD thesis. Univ. Calif., Los Angeles
Wyke S, Campbell G, MacIver S. 1992. Comparison of the provision of, and patient satisfaction with, primary care services in a relatively affluent and a relatively deprived area of Glasgow. *Br. J. Gen. Pract.* 42: 271–75
Zahn-Waxler C, Cummings EM, McKnew DH, Radke-Yarrow M. 1984. Altruism, aggression, and social interactions in young children with a manic-depressive parent. *Child Dev.* 55:112–22
Zapata BC, Rebolledo C, Atalah E, Newman B, King M-C. 1992. The influence of social and political violence on the risk of pregnancy complications. *Am. J. Public Health* 82:685–90

Annu. Rev. Psychol. 1997. 48:449–80

PSYCHOSOCIAL TREATMENTS FOR POSTTRAUMATIC STRESS DISORDER: A Critical Review

E. B. Foa and E. A. Meadows

Allegheny University of the Health Sciences, East Falls Campus, 3200 Henry Avenue, Philadelphia, Pennsylvania 19129

KEY WORDS: PTSD, psychosocial treatments

ABSTRACT

Posttraumatic stress disorder (PTSD) has been the subject of growing recognition since its inception in 1980. Owing in part to the relatively recent inclusion of PTSD in the psychiatric nomenclature, research is only beginning to address its treatment in methodologically rigorous studies. In this review, we discuss issues such as prevalence of trauma and of PTSD, and gold standards for treatment outcome research. We then critically review the extant literature on the treatment of PTSD. Finally, we include a discussion of issues specific to various trauma populations and factors that may influence treatment efficacy across types of trauma.

CONTENTS

0084-6570/97/0201-0449$08.00

INTRODUCTION

The concept of trauma-related emotional disturbance has existed for over a century, having names such as shell shock, war neurosis, and rape trauma syndrome. However, its official categorization in the diagnostic nomenclature as posttraumatic stress disorder (PTSD) is quite recent. It was first introduced in the third edition of the *Diagnostic and Statistical Manual of Mental Disorders* (*DSM-III*) (American Psychiatric Association 1980). Because of the recent recognition of PTSD as a formal disorder, critical issues such as predictors of failure to recover from a trauma and the development and evaluation of effective treatments have just begun to be addressed in research using rigorous methodology.

In this review, we first discuss the diagnostic criteria for PTSD and consider prevalence of chronic PTSD associated with various stressors. We then critically review the current treatment outcome literature, using a model of an ideal treatment outcome study for PTSD. Finally, after exploring issues specific to particular groups of trauma victims, we discuss factors that may influence differences in treatment efficacy across types of trauma.

DIAGNOSTIC CRITERIA OF PTSD

The *DSM-IV* diagnosis of PTSD includes six criteria. The first is the qualifying trauma. A traumatic event is defined as one in which: (*a*) the person experienced, witnessed, or was confronted with an event that involved actual or perceived threat to life or physical integrity; and (*b*) the person's emotional response to this event included horror, helplessness, or intense fear.

Psychological symptoms of PTSD are categorized into three clusters: reexperiencing, avoidance/numbing, and increased arousal. The reexperiencing symptoms (e.g. nightmares, flashbacks) have been considered the hallmark of PTSD (e.g. Foa & Rothbaum 1992). The second cluster consists of symptoms of effortful avoidance (i.e. deliberately avoiding trauma-related stimuli) and symptoms of emotional numbing (Foa et al 1995b, Litz 1993); the latter are considered distinguishing features of PTSD. The third symptom cluster, increased arousal, includes symptoms such as difficulty sleeping, hypervigilance, and irritability.

PREVALENCE OF PTSD IN VARIOUS TRAUMA POPULATIONS

According to epidemiological data reported by Helzer et al (1987), approximately 1–2% of the general US population meets criteria for PTSD, but it has been argued (e.g. Davidson et al 1991; EB Foa & C Molnar, unpublished manuscript; Keane et al 1994) that Helzer et al underestimated the prevalence of the disorder. Retrospective epidemiological studies of specific trauma populations place the prevalence of PTSD at higher rates. For example, Resnick et al (1993) found that of women victims of rape, 32% met criteria for lifetime and 12.4% for current PTSD. The National Vietnam Veterans Readjustment Study (NVVRS) (Kulka et al 1988) found a lifetime PTSD prevalence rate of 30% in Vietnam veterans, with a current rate of 15%. Similarly high PTSD prevalence rates have been found in studies of natural disasters (e.g. Green 1993, McFarlane 1989, Shore et al 1986) and motor vehicle accidents (e.g. Taylor & Koch 1995).

Given the high rates of both traumatic events and of resulting PTSD, combined with the ever growing population of those with PTSD because of the chronicity of the disorder, it is imperative to be able to identify immediately following a trauma those who are likely to develop chronic PTSD and to develop efficacious and cost-effective treatments for these individuals. This is especially warranted given that prospective studies of trauma victims typically reveal higher rates of PTSD (Foa 1995b, Rothbaum et al 1992).

It may also be useful to conceptualize the reactions of victims to other highly stressful events, such as the death of a loved one following a lingering illness, as a PTSD-like syndrome. Researchers have found that after death of a partner, 50% of participants met PTSD symptom criteria at some point during the following two years, and 9% met criteria at each of four assessment points (Schut et al 1991). Moreover, treatments developed for PTSD seem to help bereaved patients (e.g. Marmar et al 1988). With this consideration in mind, studies of treatment outcome for symptoms following such events are also discussed.

MEASURES

A number of measures have been used in PTSD outcome studies, in both interview and self-report formats. These measures vary widely according to symptoms assessed, time to administer, and psychometric properties, among other dimensions. Because the choice of measures is so important in evaluating treatment outcome studies, we review briefly the most commonly used instruments in PTSD research.

Interviews

The Structured Clinical Interview for *DSM* (SCID) (Spitzer et al 1987) is probably the most widely used diagnostic interview measure (Weiss 1993), and it is generally considered the so-called gold standard against which other measures are compared. Although useful as an indicator of diagnostic status before and after treatment, the SCID cannot be used to determine symptom severity. Two other interviews, the PTSD Interview (PTSD-I) (Watson et al 1991) and the Structured Interview for PTSD (SI-PTSD) (Davidson et al 1989), have adequate psychometric properties but have not been validated with victims of a wide range of traumas. Two interviews are becoming quite widely used in PTSD treatment outcome studies. The Clinician-Administered PTSD Scale (CAPS) (Blake et al 1990) permits a diagnosis and severity measure of PTSD, but its administration requires about 45–60 min. More importantly, its psychometric properties were determined exclusively in a veteran population. The second interview, the PTSD Symptom Scale Interview (PSS-I) (Foa et al 1993), includes a combined frequency/severity rating of each of the 17 PTSD symptoms and thus yields both a diagnosis and a continuous severity rating. Unlike the CAPS, the PSS-I takes only about 15–20 min to administer, which saves valuable clinician time. The PSS-I is the only interview mentioned here that was studied with female assault victims, and it is currently being studied with victims of various other traumas as well. However, as a relatively new measure, the PSS-I has not yet been as widely used as the CAPS.

Self-Report Measures

The first measure of trauma-related symptoms was the Revised Impact of Events Scale (RIES) (Horowitz et al 1979), a self-report measure that yields two factors: intrusion and avoidance. Although the RIES has demonstrated high test-retest reliability and internal consistency, it does not assess all PTSD symptoms and thus cannot indicate diagnostic status. A revised version of the RIES (DS Weiss & CR Marmar, unpublished manuscript) includes hyperarousal items,but it has shown mixed results in reliability studies and still does not correspond fully to the *DSM* PTSD symptoms.

Two scales that have excellent psychometric properties, but that do not correspond fully to the *DSM* symptoms, are the Mississippi Scale (Keane et al 1988) and the Penn Inventory (Hammarberg 1992). The former was originally developed for combat-related PTSD, but a civilian counterpart exists (Vreven et al 1995). Because both the Penn Inventory and Mississippi Scale were validated with veteran populations, their validity in other trauma populations is not yet known.

The PTSD Symptom Scale–Self Report (PSS-SR) (Foa et al 1993) and its descendent, the PTSD Diagnostic Scale (PDS) (Foa 1995a), were developed as self-report instruments that would provide information about each of the 17 *DSM-IV* symptoms. Therefore, they yield both diagnostic and severity information. The PSS-SR demonstrated good reliability and validity in a sample of female assault victims. The PDS aims at assessing all *DSM-IV* criteria, and thus it includes information about the nature of the traumatic event and the level of functional interference. It was validated in a sample of victims of a wide range of traumas, and thus it can be confidently employed in outcome studies of various trauma populations. The PDS has demonstrated satisfactory test-retest reliability, internal consistency, and convergent and concurrent validity (Foa 1995a).

"GOLD STANDARDS" FOR TREATMENT OUTCOME STUDY

Methodology of outcome studies has advanced considerably over the years so that assessment and treatment strategies acceptable, or even common, in early studies are no longer considered sufficiently rigorous today. In this section we review some of the parameters of a methodologically sound outcome study.

1. Clearly Defined Target Symptoms

Major researchers now concur that, in the absence of psychiatric disturbances, the experiencing of a trauma does not constitute sufficient basis for receiving treatment. Significant trauma-related psychopathology, such as the presence of PTSD or other common reactions to trauma (e.g. depression), should be present to justify treatment. Whatever the target symptom or syndrome, it should be defined clearly so that appropriate measures can be employed to assess improvement.

In addition to ascertaining diagnostic status, it is also important to specify a threshold of symptom severity as an inclusion criterion for entering treatment. Including individuals with mild symptoms of PTSD may muddle treatment findings for two reasons. First, it is more difficult to detect improvement in such individuals. Second, they are likely to exhibit very mild symptoms following treatment simply because of their relatively low initial psychopathology. These two scenarios may lead to opposite biases, the first minimizing treatment efficacy and the second inflating its effects.

An issue related to target symptoms is the importance of delineating inclusion and exclusion criteria. Studies that accept, for example, all rape victims with a PTSD diagnosis regardless of other psychopathology are likely to yield different results than studies that exclude patients with certain comorbid diagnoses. Delineation of inclusion and exclusion criteria can be of assistance in examining predictors of outcome as well. In addition, if a treatment is effective regardless of sample differences, it proves more robust and therefore more useful.

2. Reliable and Valid Measures

Once target symptoms have been identified and the population defined, measures with good psychometric properties should be employed (see above discussion on measures). For studies targeting a particular diagnosis, assessment should include instruments designed to yield diagnoses as well as instruments that assess symptom severity.

3. Use of Blind Evaluators

Early studies of treatment of trauma victims relied primarily on therapist and patient reports to evaluate treatment efficacy. This introduces expectancy and demand biases into the evaluation. The use of blind evaluators is a current requirement for a credible treatment outcome study. Two procedures are involved in keeping an evaluator blind. First, the evaluator should not be the same person conducting the treatment. Second, patients should be trained not to reveal their treatment condition during the evaluation. For example, patients who have flashbacks during trauma reliving practices required in exposure therapy should be trained to report only those that occur spontaneously.

4. Assessor Training

The reliability and validity of an assessment depends largely on the skill of the evaluator, and thus training of assessors is critical, and a minimum criterion should be specified. This includes demonstrating interrater reliability and calibrating assessment procedures during the study to prevent evaluator drift.

5. Manualized, Replicable, Specific Treatment Programs

It is also important that the treatment chosen is designed to address the target problem defined by inclusion criteria. For example, if PTSD is the disorder targeted for treatment, employing a treatment developed for depression, such as Beck's Cognitive Therapy (Beck 1976), may not be appropriate despite the high prevalence of depression in patients with PTSD.

Detailed treatment manuals are justifiably a requirement for conducting treatment outcome research. They help to ensure consistent treatment delivery across patients and across therapists and afford replicability of the treatment to determine generalizability.

6. Unbiased Assignment to Treatment

Patients should be assigned randomly to treatment condition, or assigned via a stratified sampling approach. This helps to ensure that observed differences or similarities among treatments are due to the techniques employed rather than to extraneous factors. To separate the effects of treatment from therapists, each treatment should be delivered by at least two therapists, and patients should be randomly assigned to therapists within each condition.

7. Treatment Adherence

The final component of the "ideal" study is the use of treatment adherence ratings. These ratings inform about whether the treatments were carried out as planned, and whether components of one treatment condition drifted into another. This may be especially important when one treatment excludes a technique that is part of a competing treatment and the aim of the study is to evaluate the importance of that technique. A similar problem arises when a study compares treatments offering different rationales for similar techniques (such as the exposure component in behavioral and psychodynamic treatments). In these studies, the effect of the rationale provides the comparison of interest, and including bits of the competing rationale in both conditions effectively renders the two treatments identical.

Having outlined the components of an ideal treatment outcome study, we now review the treatment outcome literature with an eye toward comparisons with our ideal.

CRISIS INTERVENTION AND ACUTE POSTTRAUMA STRESS

The importance of immediate intervention following a trauma to prevent chronic posttrauma problems has often been emphasized (cf Bell 1995). Many such interventions follow the debriefing model proposed by Mitchell & Bray (1990), which includes seven phases conducted in small groups within three days of the traumatic event. The first phase consists of establishing the purpose of the debriefing and the ground rules, typically including emphasis on confidentiality and suspension of rank. Other phases include activities such as "recreating" the event by having all participants give their perspective on what occurred, discuss their thoughts at the time of the event (phase three), describe the worst part of the event for them (phase four), and discuss reactions to the event. The final phases include a teaching component, where common reactions to trauma are described by group leaders to normalize participants' responses, and a wrap-up in which participants provide comments or closing statements and may stay to meet informally with one another and the team leaders.

Interventions such as the one described here have been applied to survivors of a variety of traumatic situations. However, as noted by Raphael et al (1995), randomized well-controlled studies of such programs have not yet been conducted, and thus the efficacy of such interventions is still unknown. Raphael et al noted that the existing uncontrolled studies suggest that the debriefing had either no effect or a deleterious effect. The results notwithstanding, in each case the participants and/or the authors felt the debriefing was helpful and valuable.

Crisis intervention has also been employed in women's centers and rape crisis clinics (e.g. Burgess & Holmstrom 1974). Kilpatrick (1984) studied a brief behavioral program for reducing postrape symptoms, but methodological flaws precluded interpretation of the findings. However, given the utility of behavioral interventions in the treatment of posttraumatic reactions, as described below, such methods might prove efficacious in acute posttrauma reactions as well. To address this issue, Foa et al (1995a) conducted a study of a brief prevention (BP) program for female assault survivors. BP included a number of techniques helpful in treating chronic PTSD, such as exposure, relaxation training, and cognitive restructuring. In this study, 10 patients participated in the BP program and were compared with 10 matched control participants who were repeatedly assessed in an assessment control (AC) condition. Participants were not randomly assigned because of the pilot nature of this study. Both programs were conducted over four weekly two-hour sessions, which began within one month of the assault. Patients were assessed via standardized interview and self-report measures, administered by blind evaluators. All patients met symptom criteria for PTSD, although because of the one-month duration criterion none could receive a diagnosis of PTSD at their entry into the study. Treatment was manualized, with supervision to ensure adherence.

Following the program, 7 of 10 women in the BP condition no longer met PTSD symptom criteria, compared with only one in the AC condition. Furthermore, the BP group showed a mean 72% reduction in severity of PTSD symptoms versus a mean 33% reduction in the AC group. Although the small sample size precludes drawing definitive conclusions about the efficacy of the BP, the results are encouraging.

In summary, there is no evidence to date that the commonly used crisis interventions are effective, but they have not yet been rigorously tested. With female assault victims, short-term behavioral interventions may help in preventing chronic posttrauma problems. One difference between the crisis intervention programs and the Foa et al (1995a) study is that the former are usually instituted within days of the trauma, whereas the BP program in the latter study was instituted about two weeks posttrauma. Perhaps trauma victims are better able to benefit from interventions that aim at enhancing trauma processing if they are not begun immediately following the trauma, when victims may still be in a state of shock.

PSYCHOSOCIAL TREATMENT FOR CHRONIC PTSD

Hypnotherapy

The use of hypnosis in the treatment of trauma-related distress can be traced at least to the time of Freud (for a review, see Spiegel 1989), who used the technique to encourage the abreaction and catharsis he felt were necessary to resolve conflict. Hypnosis has continued to be used in treating trauma victims, with a variety of theoretical underpinnings (Spiegel 1989).

A number of case reports (e.g. Jiranek 1993; Kingsbury 1988; Leung 1994; MacHovec 1983; Peebles 1989; Spiegel 1988, 1989), involving a wide range of traumas from the common to the idiosyncratic, have testified to the usefulness of hypnosis in treating PTSD. Most, however, lack methodological rigor and thus cannot provide a basis for assessing the efficacy of hypnosis for PTSD and related pathology. None specifies the symptoms targeted for treatment, other than noting that the patient underwent some type of trauma. In several of the reports (Jiranek 1993, Leung 1994, Peebles 1989), patients were said to have PTSD, but no information was provided about how the diagnosis was ascertained. Only two of the above reports (Leung 1994, MacHovec 1983) detailed how hypnotherapy was conducted, and none employed the controls suggested in our gold standard criteria.

In one controlled study (Brom et al 1989) of 112 trauma victims, hypnosis was compared with desensitization and psychodynamic psychotherapy versus a wait-list control group. Patients in this sample suffered from a variety of traumas, although the majority did not directly experience the trauma but, rather, had lost a loved one. All patients met symptom criteria for PTSD, although the assessment method was not explicitly described. Assessment included two pretreatment, but no posttreatment, interviews, thus precluding independent evaluations of outcome. Outcome was based solely on standardized self-report measures, introducing possible expectancy bias into all active treatment conditions.

Treatments were carried out by trained and supervised therapists, but adherence ratings were not obtained. Therapists provided the type of treatment in which they specialized, which thus increased their faith and competence in the treatment but introduced a possible confound of therapist effects that cannot be teased apart from treatment differences. Several other potential biases occurred: Patients in the wait-list condition received unspecified treatment outside the research setting, and number of sessions varied across treatments. In sum, the Brom et al study meets some of our gold standard criteria, such as random assignment and standardized measurements, and falls short in such areas as blind evaluation.

All three conditions produced superior improvement to the wait-list condition, but no differences across the three treatments were observed. Psychodynamic therapy decreased avoidance more than intrusion symptoms, and desensitization and hypnosis revealed the reverse pattern. Inspection of the means indicated improvement on the RIES was 29% for psychodynamic therapy, 34% for hypnotherapy, and 41% for desensitization. Noting the limitations discussed earlier, this study suggests that hypnotherapy, as well as desensitization and psychodynamic therapy, may somewhat alleviate posttrauma suffering.

Psychodynamic Treatments

In an attempt to account for posttrauma reactions, psychodynamic theorists (e.g. Horowitz 1976) emphasize concepts such as denial, abreaction, catharsis, and stages of recovery from trauma in developing treatment for posttrauma difficulties. Although deriving from a different theoretical viewpoint, such treatments include components similar to those seen in the cognitive-behavioral treatments discussed below. For example, Horowitz's concept of "dosing" of the traumatic experience and of "encouraging expression" are quite similar to exposure techniques.

Other psychodynamic theorists focus largely on group process (e.g. Yalom 1995). Although the psychodynamic therapies were derived from interesting theories of trauma and its sequelae, they have not been widely tested in controlled outcome studies, and those studies that exist have suffered from numerous methodological difficulties. Nevertheless, several studies have suggested that psychodynamic treatments may be useful in the treatment of PTSD.

In a study with survivors of the Beverly Hills Supper Club fire, Lindy et al (1983) examined the use of brief psychodynamic therapy. Survivors, defined as those who were present at the scene, rescue workers, relatives of the deceased, and those who identified the bodies, were assessed for trauma-related diagnoses using *DSM-III* criteria, although the method of assessment was not described. Of the 30 participants in this study, only 9 met criteria for PTSD. The others received various trauma-related diagnoses (e.g. adjustment disorder), and two participants did not have trauma-related diagnoses.

Three measures were used to assess treatment outcome: a self-report symptom checklist (SCL-90-R) (Derogatis 1983), a therapist-rated target symptoms measure, and an independent global rating of impairment severity. Treatment was manualized and therapists trained and regularly supervised. Although no control groups or random assignment were used, survivors who did not request psychotherapy but agreed to participate in the research study served as an untreated comparison group. Patients revealed only subclinical symptoms two years after the trauma. The nontreated comparison group failed to improve at the same rate.

Because this study hardly meets any of our standard criteria, the results are uninterpretable. At best they may suggest the usefulness of the psychodynamic treatment employed here with trauma victims who do not evidence significant trauma-related pathology.

Roth et al (1988) treated 13 female sexual assault victims in group therapy based on Horowitz's model of responses to trauma. The only inclusion criterion was having been raped. There was a control condition, but participants were not randomly assigned to these two groups. Owing to high attrition, only 7 women were included in the final analyses. The majority of women in the therapy group were also in ongoing individual counseling before beginning the group, and others began such counseling during the group therapy, which added additional variance in the experimental condition. Among other problems in design, blind evaluations were not used, and the IES was not used as originally validated.

Due to the attrition of control participants, noted above, only a subset of analyses included comparisons with the control group. Of these, the majority did not show differences between the two groups, and one showed a greater decrease in symptoms (the Intrusions subscale of the IES) in the control group relative to the therapy group. This absence of group differences may have been due to the small sample and thus lack of sufficient power to detect differences. Results over a longer period generally showed greater improvement in the therapy participants. Although these results appear promising, they cannot be attributed to treatment only, because of the methodological problems discussed above and because, due to attrition in the control group, data for this group were available for only the first few months.

As discussed in the previous section on hypnotherapy, Brom et al (1989) conducted a controlled study of Horowitz's brief psychodynamic therapy, comparing this treatment with hypnosis, desensitization, and a wait-list control group. Although the authors found no differences among the three active treatment conditions, inspection of the means on the IES suggested that psychodynamic therapy in this study yielded inferior outcome compared with desensitization (29% vs 41% mean pre-post reduction).

In a study of psychodynamic treatment for conjugal bereavement, Marmar et al (1988) randomly assigned 61 women to 12 weekly sessions either of brief dynamic therapy or of a mutual help group treatment led by a nonclinician. Although death of a husband does not necessarily meet the trauma criterion, many of the women in this study reported symptoms of PTSD. *DSM-III* diagnoses were derived by two of the authors on the basis of clinical records and were broken down as follows: adjustment disorder, 29 patients; PTSD, 17; major depressive disorder (MDD), 10; PTSD and MDD, 5. Although no inclusion criteria were noted other than seeking treatment for bereavement, a number of exclusion criteria were delineated. Follow-up evaluations were conducted by independent evaluators using an unstandardized semi-structured interview and several standardized self-report measures. Treatment was manualized for the mutual help group condition but not for the dynamic treatment condition, which was based upon the Horowitz (1976) model of brief dynamic therapy for stress response syndromes. No measures of adherence to treatment were noted.

Results indicated that on both interview and self-report ratings of PTSD symptoms, patients in both conditions improved slightly, but there were no differences between groups. On one of many measures, the total score of the SCL-90, the dynamic therapy condition showed greater reduction in symptoms at follow-up. However, the group treatment evidenced a much higher attrition rate than did the dynamic condition, which rendered these results ambiguous. Analyses of just those patients who had participated in at least two thirds of the treatment sessions, however, did not change the results.

The findings from this study suggest that both brief dynamic therapy and peer-led mutual help groups may be slightly effective in treating symptoms arising from conjugal bereavement. Because no results were reported on differences in treatment response across diagnostic groups, this study cannot speak to the issue of treatment efficacy for PTSD.

Preliminary results from another psychodynamically oriented treatment offer more promise. Using a quasi-experimental design, Scarvalone et al (1995) compared interpersonal process group therapy (IPGT) with a naturally occurring wait-list control in a sample of 43 female childhood sexual abuse survivors. History of abuse was the only specified inclusion criterion, reminiscent of the early studies on rape victims where victimization itself was taken as indication for treatment. Exclusion criteria included both psychopathology variables (i.e. psychosis, suicidality) and history variables (i.e. adulthood assault). Diagnoses were made via the SCID, with additional information obtained through the Child Maltreatment Interview Schedule (Briere & Runtz 1990). At posttreatment, only some of the patients were assessed by independent evaluators. Self-report measures included several psychometrically sound instruments that assessed PTSD symptoms, depression, and other associated features. Treatment was conducted by clinicians trained to use the IPGT protocol developed for this study, which was based on the treatment guidelines established by Courtois (1988) and Yalom (1995), and were supervised regularly by the senior clinician.

Results indicated that IPGT patients improved on a number of measures. At posttreatment, only 39% of the IPGT group versus 83% of the control group met criteria for PTSD. On some measures (e.g. self-report measure of intrusion) the IPGT group showed greater symptom reduction than did the control group, whereas on others (e.g. depression, dissociation) both groups evidenced symptom reduction. Because of the lack of blind evaluators, the extent to which expectancy for improvement was responsible for these positive findings cannot be ascertained.

In summary, early studies of psychodynamic psychotherapy were inflicted with methodological flaws, including lack of controls, lack of adequate assessment of outcome, and vaguely described treatments. More recent studies, however, have employed more rigorous standards. With more studies using such standards, we will be able to evaluate the efficacy of these therapies for the amelioration of PTSD.

Cognitive-Behavioral Treatments

The most studied psychosocial treatments for PTSD are the cognitive-behavioral interventions. These include a variety of treatment programs, including exposure procedures, cognitive restructuring procedures, anxiety management programs, and their combinations.

EXPOSURE PROCEDURES Exposure treatments, all involving the common feature of having patients confront their fears, vary on the dimensions of exposure medium (imaginal vs in vivo), exposure length (short vs long), and arousal level during exposure (low vs high). Systematic desensitization (SD), for example, is at the extreme of imaginal, brief, and minimally arousing exposure, and in vivo at the other extreme on each dimension. (For more details, see Foa et al 1989.)

Systematic desensitization Some of the earliest studies of behavioral treatments for PTSD adopted the systematic desensitization (SD) technique pioneered by Wolpe (1958) (e.g. Frank et al 1988, Schindler 1980, Wolff 1977). This technique pairs imaginal exposure to feared stimuli with relaxation in a graded, hierarchical fashion. Although participants in these studies showed improvement in posttrauma symptoms, methodological problems plagued each of these studies, rendering the results inconclusive. An exception was the Brom et al (1989) study described above. In this study, patients in the desensitization condition showed a mean improvement of 41% on the IES, which was higher than the other treatments examined, although the difference did not reach statistical significance.

In most of the SD studies, neither standardized measurements of PTSD nor blind independent evaluations were used; nor were manualized treatment protocols and adherence ratings reported. In addition, some of the patients included were recent assault victims, at least some of whom would be expected to recover naturally via the passage of time alone (Foa et al 1995a), which thus inflated treatment effects.

Prolonged imaginal and in vivo exposure Following promising results from a number of uncontrolled studies (e.g. Johnson et al 1982, Keane & Kaloupek 1982, Schindler 1980), several controlled studies have suggested that imaginal and in vivo exposure are effective for PTSD. As with the SD studies, participants in these studies were primarily veterans and assault victims, although exposure treatments are increasingly being used with other populations as well.

Both imaginal and in vivo exposure treatments emerged from conditioning theory that invoked the concepts of classical and operant conditioning for acquisition of fear, and the concept of extinction (or habituation) for fear reduction. In more recent conceptualizations of mechanisms underlying exposure therapy, Foa & Kozak (1986) invoked the concept of emotional processing to explain fear reduction during exposure. This conceptualization draws from Lang's bioinformation theory of emotion (Lang 1979) in which fear is viewed as a cognitive structure that includes representations of stimuli, responses, and their meaning. It also adopts Rescorla's (1988) conception of conditioning as a change in meaning. Specifically, Foa & Kozak suggested that exposure corrects erroneous associations (i.e. deconditioning) and evaluations. This process of correction, which is the essence of emotional processing, requires the activation of the fear structure via introduction of feared stimuli, and the presentation of corrective information that is incompatible with the pathological elements of the fear structure. Thus, exposure promotes symptom reduction by allowing patients to realize that contrary to their mistaken ideas: (*a*) being in objectively safe situations that remind one of the trauma is not dangerous; (*b*) remembering the trauma is not equivalent to experiencing it again; (*c*) anxiety does not remain indefinitely in the presence of feared situations or memories, but rather it decreases even without avoidance or escape; and (*d*) experiencing anxiety/PTSD symptoms does not lead to loss of control (Foa & Jaycox 1996).

Several controlled studies evaluated the efficacy of exposure therapy relative to other treatments or to a wait-list condition. Other studies have examined either the efficacy of a given exposure program itself or compared the efficacy of specific exposure procedures. Cooper & Clum (1989) studied imaginal flooding (IF) as an adjunct to standard psychosocial and pharmacological treatment in veterans with combat-related PTSD. In this study, 26 veterans who met PTSD criteria via two independent diagnostic evaluations and who did not meet exclusion criteria such as psychosis or prisoner-of-war history were invited to participate. Sixteen participants completed treatment (two of whom were excluded from analyses because of continuing treatment beyond the allotted sessions). In addition to diagnostic interviews, other measures included self-monitoring of reexperiencing and of sleep, symptom questionnaires, and a behavioral avoidance test (BAT). Although no blind evaluations were conducted, the BAT does provide some objective measure of improvement. Patients were randomly assigned to either Standard Treatment (ST) or ST plus imaginal flooding (IF). Groups were counterbalanced on medication and race, and yoking was used to match the experimental and the control groups on time between assessments. The IF treatment adjunct was flexible regarding number and timing of sessions (between 6 and 14 sessions, up to 9 of which included flooding), but otherwise was fairly well standardized. The ST consisted of individual and group treatments that were also described well. There was no description of treatment adherence ratings.

Results of this study indicated that the addition of IF to ST led to increased improvement of some symptoms such as nightmares (96% reduction in IF vs 15% in ST) and anxiety during the BAT (33% reduction in IF and 18% increase in ST). Again, while none of these measures were conducted by an independent evaluator, these results do suggest that adding an exposure component to standard VA hospital outpatient treatment leads to greater reduction in PTSD and associated symptoms.

Keane et al (1989) studied implosive therapy, or flooding, for Vietnam veterans. In this study, 24 patients were randomly assigned either to a 14–16 session treatment program or to a wait-list control group. Patients underwent a multimethod assessment, and PTSD diagnosis was confirmed by trained clinicians during a consensus meeting based on the above assessment. Treatment included relaxation training, practice in nontraumatic imagery, and flooding (imaginal exposure) to the traumatic memories.

Many of our gold standard criteria were met in this study. PTSD symptoms were the treatment targets, adequately assessed in several ways. Concomitant symptoms such as depression and general anxiety were also assessed via psychometrically sound self-report instruments. Patients were randomly assigned to treatment versus wait list, and treatment content and process were manualized. Using our framework, the major pitfall of the Keane et al study was the lack of blind evaluators. Treatment appeared to reduce fear (40% reduction in the flooding group vs 33% increase in controls) and depression (39% and 0% reduction, respectively) as well as some PTSD symptoms (35% reduction for reexperiencing symptoms but leaving the numbing/avoidance symptoms unaffected). However, it cannot be determined conclusively whether this improvement represented a true treatment effect or was due to therapist and patient expectancies. Another omission in this study, albeit a less significant one, is the lack of adherence ratings. Finally, patients in the wait-list group continued to receive other treatments during the waiting time, which was variable in duration. Despite these limitations, the Keane et al study does support the use of imaginal exposure in treating at least the reexperiencing of symptoms of PTSD.

In another test of exposure treatment in veterans with PTSD, Boudewyns and colleagues (Boudewyns & Hyer 1990, Boudewyns et al 1990) published two reports on studies conducted with Vietnam veterans in a special inpatient unit of a VA hospital. Patients who were participating in a large ongoing study were randomly assigned for this study to either direct therapeutic exposure (DTE) or a control condition of traditional individual counseling. DTE consisted of 10–12 50-min sessions of implosive therapy (either imaginal or in vivo) over a 10-week period. Both groups also participated in the standard inpatient milieu program in the special PTSD unit at the hospital.

A number of the gold standard criteria outlined earlier were again met in this study. For example, inclusion and exclusion were clearly delineated, as were the target symptoms (total PTSD severity and physiological arousal in response to trauma-related stimuli), and diagnosis was determined by structured interviews conducted by trained evaluators. Although no minimum threshold of symptom severity was required, all patients in the study were also participating in an inpatient program at the time and thus were likely to have had severe psychopathology. Manualized treatment was conducted by trained therapists.

However, the Boudewyns et al (1990) study did not meet several of our other criteria. There was no indication of treatment adherence ratings, which is particularly problematic given the design of this study. Whereas the treatment condition was clearly defined, as just noted, the control condition appears very flexible, and therapists were not given specific instructions regarding what to include in these sessions. Although therapists were instructed not to use specific behavioral or cognitive techniques,it is possible that some control patients received informally some components of the DTE. Another drawback is that all patients were participating in the standard milieu program of the special PTSD unit, and these activities included elements of DTE as well, introducing an additional confound. No blind assessments were conducted. In one of the Boudewyns reports (Boudewyns et al 1990), results were determined by comparing "successes" with "failures" based on responses to a self-report measure, the Vets Adjustment Scale administered at three months posttreatment. The other report (Boudewyns & Hyer 1990) compared groups on a number of measures of physiological and self-report instruments, also conducted at least three months posttreatment.

Both studies found that DTE evidenced some superiority over the control condition on self-reported psychological functioning, although not on physiological responding. The positive outcome thus may have reflected expectancy effects of patients, rather than specific efficacy of DTE. Moreover, improvement was defined by change on general measures of psychological functioning rather than on a specific measure of PTSD, the targeted syndrome. Thus the efficacy of DTE for PTSD cannot be ascertained from these reports.

In another comparison of exposure with other treatments, Foa et al (1991) randomly assigned women victims of sexual or nonsexual assault to one of three treatment conditions:prolonged exposure (PE) (including both imaginal and in vivo exposure), stress inoculation training (SIT), or supportive counseling. These were compared with a wait-list control condition. Treatment targets were symptoms of PTSD, and a PTSD diagnosis was required, although there was no minimum threshold of symptom severity. Symptoms were assessed at pre- and posttreatment and at follow-up evaluations using psychometrically sound interviews and self-report measures, with the interviews conducted by trained clinicians who were blind to treatment condition. All treatments included nine 90-min sessions conducted over five weeks following detailed manuals. The same therapists conducted all three treatments to avoid therapist confound, and they were supervised throughout the study. Thus, with the exception of the absence of a required minimum severity threshold and details about ongoing interrater reliability assessments, this study fulfills all our gold standard criteria.

Immediately following treatment, both SIT and PE patients improved on all three clusters of PTSD symptoms. Patients receiving supportive counseling or wait list improved on the arousal symptoms of PTSD but not on the avoidance or reexperiencing symptoms. At follow-up, PE appeared the most successful on all measures of psychopathology. In addition, 55% of women in the PE treatment no longer met the diagnosis of PTSD, relative to 50% for SIT and 45% for supportive counseling.

A second study compared PE, SIT, the combination of SIT and PE, and a wait-list control group. This study was similar to the previous Foa et al (1991) study with regard to meeting our gold standard criteria. All three active treatments showed significant improvement in PTSD symptoms and depressive symptoms at posttest, and the wait list did not improve. These treatment effects were maintained at six-month follow-up. An examination of patients who achieved good end-state functioning (defined by criterion scores on PTSD symptoms and measures of depression and anxiety) showed that 21% of patients in SIT, 46% of patients in PE, and 32% of patients in SIT/PE achieved this goal at posttreatment (Foa 1995a). At six-month follow-up, 75% of patients in PE, 68% of patients in SIT, and 50% of patients in SIT/PE lost the PTSD diagnosis, whereas all wait-list patients retained the diagnosis. The differences between the three active treatment groups were not statistically significant.

Two additional studies also provided support for the efficacy of exposure treatment for PTSD, in samples heterogeneous with regard to their traumas. Richards et al (1994) treated 14 patients either with four sessions of imaginal exposure followed by four sessions of in vivo exposure or with in vivo followed by imaginal exposure. This study included a number of standardized self-report measures as well as several process measures such as Subjective Units of Distress (SUDS) ratings during exposure practices. Treatment protocols were clearly defined, although no measures of treatment adherence were reported, and the target of PTSD symptoms and general health and functioning were adequately measured, with all patients meeting PTSD criteria at pretreatment. Overall, patients in both treatment conditions improved considerably. The authors noted that the symptom reduction of 65–80% in this study is much higher than that of most treatment studies for other anxiety disorders. In addition, at posttreatment and at one-year follow-up, no patients met criteria for PTSD. The only notable difference between the two exposure types was in the area of phobic avoidance, on which in vivo exposure appeared to be more effective regardless of the order in which it was presented.

While the Richards et al study does not include a control group with which to compare the exposure conditions, nor blind evaluations with which to judge outcome, it does further support the use of exposure and provides information about the separate effects of the two exposure modalities, imaginal and in vivo.

Thompson et al (1995) conducted an open trial of eight weekly sessions of imaginal and in vivo exposure treatment with 23 patients who had experienced various traumas. Patients met *DSM-III-R* criteria for PTSD based on the CAPS as well as a minimum threshold of symptom severity on several measures. Although the study was well designed in many respects, no blind evaluation was conducted, and there was no control group. Patients improved significantly on a variety of measures at posttreatment, with reductions of 42% on the IES, 61% on a measure of general health (General Health Questionnaire), 38% on a general symptom checklist (SCL-90), and 35% on the CAPS. However, the influence of expectancy effects, along with other threats to validity such as history and maturation, cannot be ruled out.

The results from the studies reviewed above consistently support the efficacy of imaginal and in vivo exposure for the treatment of PTSD. There was some suggestion that the efficacy of these treatments is stronger in nonveteran populations than in veterans. Possible explanations for these differences are discussed below.

Eye Movement Desensitization and Reprocessing A new technique, Eye Movement Desensitization and Reprocessing (EMDR) (Shapiro 1995), is a form of exposure (desensitization) accompanied by saccadic eye movements. EMDR consists of a patient focusing on a disturbing image or memory (including related emotions and cognitions) while the therapist waves a finger across the patient's visual field with the patient tracking the finger. After each sequence, patients indicate their SUDS level and their degree of belief in a positive cognition [Validity of Cognition (VOC)].

EMDR has been the focus of considerable controversy for a number of reasons, including claims by its originator about its remarkable success in only a single session (Shapiro 1989). For a review of this controversy, see Tolin et al 1996. A number of case studies have reported positive findings (for a comprehensive review, see Lohr et al 1996). These reports suffer from the lack of control typical of most case reports, as well as from the use of inappropriate statistical analyses and lack of standardized measures or blind evaluations.

Several studies have compared EMDR either with alternative treatments or with variations of the technique for PTSD in either controlled or semicontrolled designs. Shapiro (1989) randomly assigned trauma victims to either one session of EMDR or an exposure control condition (i.e. EMDR without the eye movements). This study did not meet most of our gold standard criteria; it lacked inclusion and exclusion criteria, diagnostic assessment, standardized measures or blind evaluations, clearly defined target of treatment, and ratings of treatment adherence. Although results showed that EMDR patients reported lower SUDS ratings after the one session of EMDR than did the exposure control patients, the relationship of this finding to PTSD improvement is unknown.

Boudewyns et al (1993) compared two 90-min EMDR sessions to an exposure control (EC)—EMDR without the eye movements—as an adjunct to standard milieu treatment for veterans with PTSD. A third group of patients were treated with standard milieu treatment alone. The target of treatment was PTSD, which was assessed via CAPS as well as by standardized self-report measures and physiological data. Patients were randomly assigned to the three conditions, which were delineated clearly. Several adequate measures were used for initial inclusion, but blind evaluations of outcome were not conducted.

SUDS ratings to traumatic stimuli were lower in the EMDR group, and therapists rated more patients as responders in the EMDR vs EC group. However, the three groups did not differ on standardized self-report measures, CAPS, or physiological responses; none improved. These negative results, even for the exposure condition, contrast with the proven efficacy of exposure treatments discussed above. As noted by Boudewyns et al, these negative results may be due to an insufficient number of sessions or to the difficulties in treating service-connected veterans.

Jensen (1994) randomly assigned 74 veterans with PTSD to either three sessions of EMDR conducted within 10 days or to a control condition of standard VA services. Patients were assessed through structured interview, standardized self-report measures, the SUDS ratings, and the VOC measure said to be integral to EMDR. Treatment was manualized, with measures taken to ensure therapist training and adherence to treatment procedures. On the PTSD severity measure, the groups did not differ from one another; neither improved. Despite the negative outcome, SUDS ratings decreased in the EMDR group and not in controls.

To examine the role of specific components of EMDR, Renfrey & Spates (1994) treated 23 trauma victims with standard EMDR or one of two variations: an EMDR analog in which eye movements were induced by a flashing light rather than a waving finger [automated eye movement (AEM)], and an analog in which a light blinked only in the center of the visual field [visual attention (VA)]. Assessment included standardized PTSD and related measures, SUDS ratings, and physiological data. Blind evaluations were not conducted. After treatment, only five of the patients met criteria for PTSD, but these were not confined to any one treatment condition. No analyses were reported on the standardized PTSD measures. Groups did not differ on physiological measures, SUDS, or the VOC.

Using a sample of 36 victims of heterogenous traumas, Vaughan et al (1994) conducted a more rigorous test of EMDR. They compared the procedure with Imagery Habituation Training (IHT), which involves repeated presentation of traumatic stimuli in the form of an oral scenario, and Applied Muscle Relaxation Training (AMT) (Ost 1987), an anxiety management procedure. Treatments consisted of three to five sessions conducted over two to three weeks. Assessment included several standardized measures, including two independent interviews. Patients were randomly assigned to treatment conditions. The authors concluded that all three groups were equally improved on the independent assessors' rating of PTSD.

Silver et al (1995) compared standard milieu treatment with milieu treatment plus EMDR, biofeedback, or group relaxation training in a sample of 100 veterans with PTSD. No standardized measures were used, and it is not clear how the diagnosis of PTSD was derived. Patients were not randomly assigned to treatment conditions, and no blind evaluations were conducted. EMDR led to greater reduction of symptoms relative to the control and the biofeedback groups in five of eight areas assessed by a measure of general symptoms. However, the nature of the measures was obscure and the study had many methodological flaws. Thus, these results cannot be interpreted.

Wilson et al (1995) compared EMDR to a delayed-treatment condition in a mixed sample of "traumatized" individuals (only 30% of the target events met the *DSM-IV* definition of a trauma), about half of whom were said to have PTSD. Outcome was assessed via self-report measures. Independent standardized evaluations could not be analyzed because changes in the instrument rendered it invalid at posttreatment. Treatment was manualized, with considerable measures taken to ensure adherence. Patients were randomly assigned to the two conditions after meeting specific exclusion criteria. Therefore, this study meets some of our gold standard criteria. However, because neither a PTSD diagnosis nor a minimum threshold of PTSD symptoms was required, how much patients suffered from trauma-related symptoms is unclear.

Overall, patients in the EMDR group reported decreases in presenting complaints and in anxiety, and increases in positive cognitions at posttreatment, whereas the wait-list group reported no improvement. Because the results are based solely on self-report data, they may reflect effects of patients' expectancy for improvement rather than effects of EMDR. Moreover, the generalizability of these results to individuals with PTSD is unknown.

A well-controlled study on the efficacy of EMDR was conducted by Rothbaum (1995), who randomly assigned 21 female victims of rape to either EMDR or a wait-list control group. Measures consisted of standardized self-report and interview instruments, with the interviews conducted by a blind evaluator. Treatment consisted of four weekly sessions conducted by a well-trained clinician, and treatment adherence was monitored and deemed acceptable by an independent evaluator designated by EMDR's originator. EMDR led to improvement on PTSD symptoms on both interview (57% reduction in symptom severity) and RIES (74% reduction), and gains were maintained at a three-month follow-up. Thus, this study suggests that a brief course of EMDR can effectively reduce symptoms of PTSD.

In another methodologically sound study, Pitman et al (1996) compared EMDR with and without the eye movement component in a crossover design with 17 male veterans diagnosed with PTSD. Patients met specific inclusion and exclusion criteria and were randomly assigned to the two conditions. Measures included standardized self-report and independent interviews. Treatment was manualized and provided by therapists who completed advanced training in seminars developed by the originator of EMDR. Adherence to treatment was rated to be adequate by an independent assessor.

Both treatments effected modest improvement in symptoms as measured by the RIES, but not on the independent assessment. Contrary to expectations, on the RIES, there was slightly more improvement in the eyes-fixed condition than in EMDR. Thus, this study suggests that the eye movements, which constitute the primary component of EMDR other than exposure and nonspecific factors, do not explain the outcome.

In summary, the picture emerging from the studies reviewed here is mixed. Many studies failed to demonstrate efficacy of EMDR. Some found improvement, but methodological flaws rendered most though not all of these findings uninterpretable. The test of the efficacy of this much-discussed treatment awaits adequately controlled studies.

ANXIETY MANAGEMENT PROGRAMS Anxiety management treatments (AMT) (e.g. Suinn 1974) take the view that pathological anxiety stems from skills deficits and that AMT provide patients with a repertoire of strategies to handle anxiety. Strategies include relaxation training, positive self-statements, breathing retraining, biofeedback, social skills training, and distraction techniques. Unlike exposure therapy (Foa & Kozak 1986) and cognitive therapy (Beck et al 1985), which are designed to correct the mechanisms underlying pathological anxiety, AMT aim to provide ways to manage anxiety when it occurs. Foa et al (1995a) noted that one of the most commonly used anxiety management treatments for PTSD is stress inoculation training (SIT). This program, originally developed by Meichenbaum (1975) for anxious individuals, incorporates a number of educational and skills components such as relaxation, thought stopping, and guided self-dialog. Although other anxiety management techniques have been suggested for use with trauma victims, for example biofeedback (e.g. Blanchard & Abel 1976, Hickling et al 1986), we focus in this section on SIT because it was more widely studied with trauma victims.

The efficacy of SIT with female rape victims was examined in two uncontrolled studies (Kilpatrick et al 1982, Veronen & Kilpatrick 1982) with encouraging results. These studies did not include the controls called for in our gold standards but are among the first attempts to systematically evaluate treatment efficacy in rape victims and are notable for their pioneering efforts. In the Kilpatrick et al (1982) study, patients were allowed to choose among three treatments offered: SIT, SD, and a peer counseling condition. No patients chose the SD treatment; 70% chose SIT and 30% chose peer counseling. One goal of the study was to assess which treatments rape victims preferred.

Both these reports focused on postrape sequelae of fear, intrusions, and avoidance, rather than on the full syndrome of PTSD, which was quite new at that time. Standardized measures were used to assess some PTSD symptoms (i.e. the IES) and general fear and anxiety rather than the entire range of the PTSD symptoms. In addition, personalized target fears and situations were developed collaboratively by the patient and therapist, and ratings of these targets served as outcome measures. Inclusion criteria included the presence of fear, anxiety, and avoidance related to the rape, although no minimum threshold for this distress was noted. Women with other conditions that might interfere with treatment were excluded. The SIT treatment was spelled out in considerable detail and was delivered by peer counselors (as opposed to professional clinicians) who had experience in counseling rape victims and who received specific training in SIT.

The Veronen & Kilpatrick (1982) study suggested that SIT was effective in reducing rape-related fear and anxiety, and avoidance, general tension, and depressions. Most of these gains were maintained at three-month follow-up. Although the lack of a control group precludes definitive conclusions about the efficacy of SIT in this study, it suggests that SIT can effectively reduce rape-related psychopathology.

The first controlled study examining the efficacy of SIT in ameliorating postrape psychological problems was conducted by Resick et al (1988). Rape victims were assigned to four conditions: SIT, assertion training, supportive psychotherapy, and a naturally occurring wait list. Assignment to treatment condition was determined upon openings in the next available treatment. This study uses a quasi-experimental design, which is less than ideal relative to the criteria outlined earlier but still useful relative to the uncontrolled studies that assessed SIT alone. Target symptoms were rather vague, and the specific psychological difficulties required to enter the study were not detailed. Inclusion criteria were described only as having been raped at least three months before study participation, absence of incest history, absence of severe competing psychopathology, and problems with rape-related fear and anxiety. Several self-report measures were included, incorporating a range of psychometric adequacy, including the RIES. A structured interview, not explicitly described, was also used at the initial evaluation.

At posttreatment, all three treatments produced improvement in fear and anxiety, whereas patients on the wait list did not show such improvement. Improvement was modest, the best occurring on the RIES: SIT produced 27% reduction compared with an increase of 14% in the wait-list controls. Because of the problems in the study design, it is difficult to draw strong conclusions about these data.

Other studies examining the efficacy of SIT, in comparison and in combination with other treatments and control groups, were reviewed in detail in the previous section, and thus they are summarized only briefly here. In a study of female assault victims, Foa et al (1991) found that in comparison with wait-list controls, SIT and PE patients improved on all three clusters of PTSD symptoms. At follow-up, however, PE appeared to show a somewhat superior outcome. On independent assessment of total PTSD severity, PE evidenced 60% mean reduction vs 49% for SIT and 36% for supportive counseling. A second study (Foa 1995b) compared PE, SIT, the combination of SIT and PE, and a wait-list control group. At posttreatment, mean PTSD severity as judged by an independent evaluation was decreased by 66% in PE and 52% in SIT. At follow-up (mean of 10 months), PE showed a mean of 66% reduction and SIT showed a mean of 48% reduction.

In summary, the available studies support the efficacy of SIT in the treatment of PTSD. However, all these studies were conducted with female assault victims; therefore, the efficacy of SIT for other trauma populations is still unknown. Compared with PE, there are only two well-controlled studies on SIT, both from the same research group. Thus, a firm conclusion about the efficacy of SIT awaits further studies by other groups.

COMBINED TREATMENT PROGRAMS Because of positive results seen in the PE and SIT studies, it would seem that combining such approaches might enhance the treatment benefit by providing ways to manage stress and anxiety while confronting the feared memories and cues. Two such programs have been studied in women with assault-related PTSD.

The first of these studies (Foa 1995b) has been discussed in previous sections, but we mention it again briefly. Although it was hypothesized that the combination therapy would be superior to either SIT or PE alone, all three groups produced similar improvement on overall PTSD severity. At both posttreatment and at follow-up, the combined treatment produced a mean reduction of 53% in PTSD symptom severity. Because the combined treatment was delivered in the same number and length of sessions, patients in this condition did not receive as much imaginal exposure as the PE group, nor as much SIT as the SIT group. This might explain the failure of the combined approach to outperform the single procedure treatments.

The second combined treatment approach, Cognitive Processing Therapy (CPT), was developed by Resick & Schnicke (1992b). Drawing from cognitive and information processing models, CPT was designed specifically for rape victims. CPT includes exposure and cognitive components, but these differ somewhat from those described in previous sections. In CPT, exposure consists of describing the rape in writing and then reading this account. Cognitive restructuring was based on the procedure in cognitive therapies for other disorders. Earlier accounts of cognitive therapy for rape victims also used a variation of Beck's cognitive therapy (e.g. Frank et al 1988). What distinguishes CPT from traditional cognitive therapy is the focus on five primary themes identified a priori in CPT. These themes include safety, trust, power, esteem, and intimacy, which are believed by McCann & Pearlman (1990) to comprise the core difficulties in female rape victims.

In a quasi-experimental study, Resick & Schnicke (1992a) treated 19 rape victims with group CPT and compared their results with a naturally occurring wait-list control group. The focus of treatment was PTSD. Patients were assessed with the SCID and a number of standardized self-report measures, including the SCL-90-R, PSS-SR, and RIES. However, because of changes in measures over the duration of the study, not all participants completed the same assessment. Thus, the authors report comparison findings only on the SCL-90-R, the one measure completed by all patients.

Treatment itself was conducted by clinicians trained in this manualized approach and supervised by the originator of the therapy. No information was provided about adherence to protocol. Posttreatment and follow-up assessments were sometimes, but not always, conducted by blind evaluators. Because the blind and nonblind ratings did not differ significantly from one another, Resick & Schnicke (1992a) asserted that the assessments on the whole were not biased.

Overall, women who received CPT improved significantly compared with those in the wait-list group. On the SCL-90-R PTSD scale, the mean symptom reduction for CPT was 40% vs 1.5% for the wait-list controls. Thus, despite the methodological problems described above, the results suggest that CPT may be an effective treatment for PTSD in rape victims. Since CPT was not compared with other treatments, nor dismantled, it is unclear which components were active, and whether these components act differently within CPT than they do on their own.

In an updated report of this study, Resick & Schnicke (1992b) examined a larger sample of 54 female rape victims. Patients in this study included the sample reported upon in the previous study plus additional patients. Initially, 96% of the patients met criteria for PTSD. Following CPT, about 88% lost their diagnosis. Decrease in depressive symptoms was noted as well.

A modified version of Foa et al's (1995a) SIT/PE program was adopted by EB Blanchard & EJ Hickling (personal communication) to treat 10 motor vehicle accident (MVA) victims. The modification consisted of the addition of pleasurable activity scheduling and discussion of existential issues. The study was intended to provide pilot data for a future controlled study and therefore did not include a comparison group, random assignment, or blind evaluations. It did, however, include thorough assessments conducted with psychometrically sound instruments and a detailed and replicable treatment program. Like Thompson et al (1995), the Blanchard & Hickling study used a minimum threshold of PTSD symptom severity. This advantage is negated somewhat by the inclusion of patients with subsyndromal PTSD (i.e. those who did not meet full symptom criteria for the diagnosis) because the threshold of CAPS score required for entrance was rather low. These preliminary data suggest that the 9–12 sessions of combined treatment reduced PTSD symptoms by 68% on the CAPS. Thus, treatment was effective in reducing symptoms of PTSD in MVA victims, but it is unclear which aspect of treatment is most active.

In summary, the studies to date have not supported the use of combination treatments over PE or SIT alone. However, taking into account the possible explanations for these findings noted above (i.e. the reduced time allotted to each treatment component in multicomponent programs), Foa and her colleagues are testing a simplified version of their PE/SIT treatment, comparing PE alone with a treatment that combines PE with cognitive restructuring (PE/CR). In addition, Resick and her colleagues are comparing PE and CPT to a wait-list control condition. It remains to be seen which programs will improve on the quite satisfactory, but far from perfect, outcomes of SIT and PE.

SUMMARY AND CONCLUSIONS

We have offered a critical review of the literature concerning treatment outcome for PTSD. We have done so by first delineating a set of methodological standards that need to be employed in outcome studies to allow results to reflect the effects of the treatment under study rather than extraneous or nonspecific factors. Our list of standards is by no means exhaustive. The statistics employed and the sample size are also important considerations in evaluating outcome studies. And yet, even with the limited standards we have outlined, it is readily apparent that research on the efficacy of psychosocial treatments for PTSD has only recently begun to approach these standards. This is somewhat to be expected, given that PTSD has only recently entered the *DSM* and thus captured the attention of clinical researchers. However, enough research has accumulated to allow at least some preliminary conclusions about efficacy of treatment for PTSD.

Overall, cognitive-behavioral treatments enjoy the greatest number of controlled outcome studies, and have been the most rigorously tested. These studies converge to demonstrate that both prolonged exposure procedures and stress inoculation training are effective in reducing symptoms of PTSD. CPT has shown promising initial findings, but it awaits the results of more rigorously controlled studies before its efficacy can be determined. Resick and her colleagues are currently conducting such a study, but the efficacy of this treatment needs to be investigated in other settings as well. The vast majority of the studies examining EMDR are inundated with methodological flaws, and the results are mixed. The efficacy of this treatment cannot yet be estimated.

Contrary to clinical intuition, there is no evidence indicating the superiority of programs that combine different cognitive behavioral techniques. Perhaps the combination programs that have been examined have not been the most suitable and shortchanged the individual components by limited time allotted for each. In addition, SIT includes several techniques, some of which (e.g. thought stopping) are not effective with other anxiety disorders such as obsessive-compulsive disorder (Stern & Marks 1973). Although it will be prohibitive to dismantle all the components of SIT, one of SIT's components, cognitive restructuring, is a promising candidate for enhancing the efficacy of prolonged exposure. Such a combination has been found to be superior to either component alone for other anxiety disorders (Butler et al 1991, Mattick et al 1989). As mentioned above, a study to test this hypothesis is being conducted by Foa and her colleagues.

Given the state of the art where SIT alone and PE alone perform as well as combined programs, PE might be considered the treatment of choice for PTSD. PE enjoys more studies attesting to its efficacy in a variety of trauma populations than SIT and CPT. In addition, PE is fairly simple to implement and therefore can be more readily disseminated to clinicians who practice at outside specialty centers. SIT and CPT include more components and more complex techniques and thus require more training. However, note that PE might not be suitable for all trauma victims, and that in some cases the technique might need to be modified to be effective. For a review of such indications, see Jaycox & Foa (1996). In particular, PTSD sufferers whose traumatic memories are about being perpetrators rather than victims may not benefit from PE and perhaps will even deteriorate from such treatment (Pitman et al 1991).

Nonbehavioral treatments have not been the subject of well-controlled studies to the extent that cognitive-behavioral treatments have. However, this is not to say that they cannot prove effective as well. Hopefully, the recently emerging literature on these treatments may clarify their efficacy for treating PTSD.

CONSIDERATIONS FOR SPECIFIC TRAUMA POPULATIONS

Veterans

A number of issues arise in the treatment of veterans. One of the most obvious is that almost all veterans studies are conducted through the VA system, which includes significant secondary gains for its patients to remain ill. In addition, many veterans may never enter studies that are based in military systems, as those with more resources have access to private treatment.

A clear difference between veterans and most other trauma survivors is the level of perpetration as well as victimization exhibited by the patient. Although guilt and shame are common reactions among many trauma survivors (e.g. rape victims frequently blame themselves for not having done more to deter the rapist, or for "allowing" the penetration), the triggers for guilt and shame in veterans are frequently quite rational. Thus, while challenging the guilt associated with being raped is clearly appropriate, the veteran who killed innocent civilians might rightly resist attempts to challenge the justification for his guilt. F Weathers (personal communication) noted alternative strategies for dealing with such issues, including exploring ways of making reparations and bearing witness, such as volunteer work with veterans' families. Kubany

(1994) also addresses the issue of guilt in combat-related PTSD and has developed a model of different guilt types that are associated with different errors in logic. He suggests that cognitive therapy can be used to address these logical errors and thus ameliorate such combat-related guilt.

Sexual Assault Victims

Unlike veterans who have returned to peace zones, assault victims must face the reality that their traumas could reoccur without warning. Issues of daily safety thus become very important in treating assault victims, and therapists might need to specifically train some patients in discriminating safe from unsafe situations. In exposure therapy, therapists have the opportunity to discover areas of possible poor risk recognition as the patient recounts her story, and they may use such examples in training patients to recognize potential danger early on. Another related issue arises in developing in vivo exposure exercises. To do this, the therapist and patient generate a list of situations the patient avoids, with assignments to confront these situations. However, in some cases, a woman might be fearful of situations that remind her of the trauma but that are in fact unsafe (such as walking alone at night in deserted areas). Such situations should obviously not be included in exposure practices, and training focusing on delineating PTSD-related avoidance versus realistic precautions is particularly salient in this population.

Childhood Abuse Victims

One of the essential features of PTSD is that the symptoms represent a change from pretrauma functioning. In childhood abuse victims, such a change might not be possible to ascertain: Many such children have never known a life without trauma. The therapist must, in this case, make inferences about the degree to which these symptoms represent PTSD before implementing treatments designed to alleviate PTSD. An additional complication is that in child-abuse victims, the trauma and subsequent recovery overlap with normal developmental processes, which further complicates the picture. Adjunct techniques, such as education about "normal" interpersonal interactions, might prove helpful in such cases.

Literature Cited

American Psychiatric Association. 1980. *Diagnostic and Statistical Manual of Mental Disorders.* Washington, DC: Am. Psychiatr. Assoc. 3rd ed.

American Psychiatric Association. 1987. *Diagnostic and Statistical Manual of Mental Disorders.* Washington, DC: Am. Psychiatr. Assoc. 3rd ed. (Revis.)

American Psychiatric Association. 1994. *Diagnostic and Statistical Manual of Mental Disorders.* Washington, DC: Am. Psychiatr. Assoc. 4th ed.

Beck AT. 1976. *Cognitive Therapy and the Emotional Disorders.* New York: Int. Univ. Press

Beck AT, Emery G, Greenberg RL. 1985. *Anxiety Disorders and Phobias: A Cognitive Perspective.* New York: Basic Books

Bell JL. 1995. Traumatic event debriefing: service delivery designs and the role of social work. *Soc. Work* 40:36–43

Blake DD, Weathers FW, Nagy LM, Kaloupek DG, Klauminzer G, et al. 1990. A clinician rating scale for assessing current and lifetime PTSD: the CAPS-1. *Behav. Ther.* 18: 187–88

Blanchard EB, Abel GG. 1976. An experimental case study of the biofeedback treatment of a rape induced psychophysiological cardiovascular disorder. *Behav. Ther.* 7:113–19

Boudewyns PA, Hyer L. 1990. Physiological response to combat memories and preliminary treatment outcome in Vietnam veterans: PTSD patients treated with direct therapeutic exposure. *Behav. Ther.* 21:63–87

Boudewyns PA, Hyer L, Woods MG, Harrison WR, McCranie E. 1990. PTSD among Vietnam veterans: an early look at treatment outcome using direct therapeutic exposure. *J. Trauma. Stress* 3:359–68

Boudewyns PA, Stwertka S, Hyer L, Albrecht W, Sperr E. 1993. Eye movement desensitization for PTSD of combat: a treatment outcome pilot study. *Behav. Ther.* 16:29–33

Briere J, Runtz N. 1990. Augmenting Hopkins SCL scales to measure dissociative symptoms: data from two nonclinical samples. *J. Pers. Assess.* 55:376–79

Brom D, Kleber RJ, Defres PB. 1989. Brief psychotherapy for posttraumatic stress disorders. *J. Consult. Clin. Psychol.* 57:607–12

Burgess AW, Holmstrom LL. 1974. The rape trauma syndrome. *Am. J. Psychol.* 131: 981–86

Butler G, Fennell M, Robson P, Gelder M. 1991. Comparison of behavior therapy and cognitive behavior therapy in the treatment of generalized anxiety disorder. *J. Consult. Clin. Psychol.* 59:167–75

Cooper NA, Clum GA. 1989. Imaginal flooding as a supplementary treatment for PTSD in combat veterans: a controlled study. *Behav. Ther.* 3:381–91

Courtois C. 1988. *Healing the Incest Wound: Adult Survivors in Therapy.* New York: Norton. 396 pp.

Davidson JRT, Hughes D, Blazer DG, George LK. 1991. Post-traumatic stress disorder in the community: an epidemiological study. *Psychol. Med.* 21:713–21

Davidson JRT, Smith R, Kudler H. 1989. Validity and reliability of the DSM-III criteria for posttraumatic stress disorder: experience with a structured interview. *J. Nerv. Ment. Dis.* 177:336–41

Derogatis LR. 1983. *SCL-90: Administration, Scoring and Procedures Manual for the Revised Version.* Baltimore: Clin. Psychom. Res.

Foa EB. 1995a. *PDS (Posttraumatic Stress Diagnostic Scale) Manual.* Minneapolis: Natl. Comput. Syst.

Foa EB. 1995b. *Failure of emotional processing: post trauma psychopathology.* Presented at World Congr. Behav. Cogn. Ther., Copenhagen

Foa EB, Hearst-Ikeda DE, Perry KJ. 1995a. Evaluation of a brief cognitive-behavioral program for the prevention of chronic PTSD in recent assault victims. *J. Consult. Clin. Psychol.* 63:948–55

Foa EB, Jaycox LH. 1996. Cognitive-behavioral treatment of post-traumatic stress disorder. In *The Practice of Psychotherapy,* ed. D Spiegel. Washington, DC: Am. Psychiatr. Press. In press

Foa EB, Kozak MJ. 1986. Emotional processing of fear: exposure to corrective information. *Psychol. Bull.* 99:20–35

Foa EB, Riggs DS, Dancu CV, Rothbaum BO. 1993. Reliability and validity of a brief instrument for assessing post-traumatic stress disorder. *J. Trauma. Stress* 6:459–73

Foa EB, Riggs DS, Gershuny BS. 1995b. Arousal, numbing and intrusion: symptom structure of post traumatic stress disorder following assault. *Am. J. Psychol.* 152: 116–20

Foa EB, Rothbaum BO. 1992. Post-traumatic stress disorder: clinical features and treatment. In *Aggression and Violence Throughout the Life Span,* ed. RD Peters, RJ McMahon, VL Quinsey, pp. 155–70. Newbury Park, CA: Sage

Foa EB, Rothbaum BO, Kozak MJ. 1989. Behavioral treatments of anxiety and depression. In *Anxiety and Depression: Distinctive and Overlapping Features,* ed. P Kendall, D Watson, pp. 413–54. New York: Academic

Foa EB, Rothbaum BO, Riggs D, Murdock T. 1991. Treatment of post-traumatic stress disorder in rape victims: a comparison between cognitive-behavioral procedures and counseling. *J. Consult. Clin. Psychol.* 59: 715–23

Frank E, Anderson B, Stewart BD, Dancu C, Hughes C, West D. 1988. Efficacy of cognitive behavior therapy and systematic desensitization in the treatment of rape trauma. *Behav. Ther.* 19:403–20

Green B. 1993. *Disasters and PTSD.* Prepared for the *DSM-IV.* In *Posttraumatic Stress Disorder: DSM-IV and Beyond,* ed. JRT Davidson, EB Foa, pp. 75–97. Washington, DC: Am. Psychiatr. Press

Hammarberg M. 1992. Penn Inventory for Posttraumatic Stress Disorder: psychometric properties. *Psychol. Assess.* 4:67–76

Helzer JE, Robins L, McEvoy L. 1987. Post-

traumatic stress disorder in the general population. *N. Engl. J. Med.* 317:1630–34
Hickling EJ, Sison GFP, Vanderploeg RD. 1986. Treatment of posttraumatic stress disorder with relaxation and biofeedback training. *Behav. Ther.* 16:406–16
Horowitz MJ. 1976. *Stress-Response Syndromes.* Northvale, NJ: Aronson
Horowitz MJ, Wilner N, Alvarez W. 1979. Impact of Event Scale: a measure of subjective distress. *Psychosom. Med.* 41:207–18
Jaycox LH, Foa EB. 1996. Obstacles in implementing exposure therapy for PTSD: case discussions and practical solutions. *Clin. Psychother. Int. J. Theory Pract.* In press
Jensen JA. 1994. An investigation of Eye Movement Desensitization and Reprocessing (EMD/R) as a treatment for posttraumatic stress disorder (PTSD) symptoms of Vietnam combat veterans. *Behav. Ther.* 25: 311–25
Jiranek D. 1993. Use of hypnosis in pain management and post-traumatic stress disorder. *Aust. J. Clin. Exp. Hypn.* 21:75–84
Johnson CH, Gilmore JD, Shenoy RZ. 1982. Use of a feeding procedure in the treatment of a stress-related anxiety disorder. *J. Behav. Ther. Exp. Psychiatry* 13:235–37
Keane TM, Caddell JM, Taylor K. 1988. Mississippi Scale for Combat-Related Post-Traumatic Stress Disorder: three studies in reliability and validity. *J. Consult. Clin. Psychol.* 56:85–90
Keane TM, Fairbank JA, Caddell JM, Zimering RT. 1989. Implosive (flooding) therapy reduces symptoms of PTSD in Vietnam combat veterans. *Behav. Ther.* 20:245–60
Keane TM, Fisher LM, Krinsley KE, Niles BL. 1994. Posttraumatic stress disorder. In *Handbook of Prescriptive Treatments for Adults,* ed. M Hersen, RT Ammerman, pp. 237–60. New York: Plenum
Keane TM, Kaloupek DG. 1982. Imaginal flooding in the treatment of post-traumatic stress disorder. *J. Consult. Clin. Psychol.* 50:138–40
Kilpatrick DG. 1984. *Treatment of fear and anxiety in victims of rape.* Termin. Progr. Rep. Grant #MH29602. Rockville, MD: Natl. Inst. Ment. Health
Kilpatrick DG, Veronen LJ, Resick PA. 1982. Psychological sequelae to rape: assessment and treatment strategies. In *Behavioral Medicine: Assessment and Treatment Strategies,* ed. DM Dolays, RL Meredith, pp. 473–97. New York: Plenum
Kingsbury SJ. 1988. Hypnosis in the treatment of posttraumatic stress disorder: an isomorphic intervention. *Am. J. Clin. Hypn.* 31:81–90
Kubany ES. 1994. A cognitive model of guilt typology in combat-related PTSD. *J. Trauma. Stress* 7:3–19
Kulka RA, Schlenger WE, Fairbank JA, Hough RL, Jordan BK, et al. 1988. *Contractual report of findings from the National Vietnam veterans readjustment study.* Research Triangle Park, NC: Research Triangle Inst.
Lang PJ. 1979. A bio-informational theory of emotional imagery. *Psychophysiology* 6: 495–511
Leung J. 1994. Treatment of post-traumatic stress disorder with hypnosis. *Aust. J. Clin. Exp. Hypn.* 22:87–96
Lindy JD, Green BL, Grace M, Titchener J. 1983. Psychotherapy with survivors of the Beverly Hills Supper Club fire. *Am. J. Psychother.* 4:593–610
Litz BT. 1993. Emotional numbing in combat-related post-traumatic stress disorder: a critical review and reformulation. *Clin. Psychol. Rev.* 12:417–32
Lohr JM, Kleinknecht RA, Tolin DF, Barrett RH. 1996. The empirical status of the clinical application of Eye Movement Desensitization and Reprocessing. *J. Behav. Ther. Exp. Psychiatry* 26:285–302
MacHovec FJ. 1983. Treatment variables and the use of hypnosis in the brief therapy of post-traumatic stress disorders. *Int. J. Clin. Exp. Hypn.* 1:6–14
Marmar CR, Horowitz MJ, Weiss DS, Wilner NR, Kaltreider NB. 1988. A controlled trial of brief psychotherapy and mutual-help group treatment of conjugal bereavement. *Am. J. Psychiatry* 145:203–9
Mattick RP, Peters L, Clarke JC. 1989. Exposure and cognitive restructuring for social phobia: a controlled study. *Behav. Ther.* 20:3–23
McCann IL, Pearlman LA. 1990. *Psychological Trauma and the Adult Survivor: Theory, Therapy, and Transformation.* New York: Brunner/Mazel
McFarlane AC. 1989. The aetiology of post-traumatic morbidity: predisposing, precipitating and perpetuating factors. *Br. J. Psychol.* 154:221–28
Meichenbaum D. 1975. Self-instructional methods. In *Helping People Change,* ed. FH Kanfer, AP Goldstein, pp. 357–91. New York: Pergamon
Mitchell JT, Bray G. 1990. *Emergency Services Stress: Guidelines for Preserving the Health and Careers of Emergency Services Personnel.* Englewood Cliffs, NJ: Prentice Hall
Mowrer OA. 1960. *Learning Theory and Behavior.* New York: Wiley
Ost LG. 1987. Applied relaxation: description of a coping technique and review of controlled studies. *Behav. Res. Ther.* 25: 397–409
Peebles MJ. 1989. Through a glass darkly: the psychoanalytic use of hypnosis with post-

traumatic stress disorder. *Int. J. Clin. Exp. Hypn.* 37:192–206

Pitman RK, Altman B, Greenwald E, Longpre RE, Macklin ML, et al. 1991. Psychiatric complications during flooding therapy for posttraumatic stress disorder. *J. Clin. Psychol.* 52:17–20

Pitman RK, Orr SP, Altman B, Longpre RE, Poire RE, Macklin ML. 1996. Emotional processing during eye-movement desensitization and reprocessing therapy of Vietnam veterans with chronic post-traumatic stress disorder. *Compr. Psychiatry.* In press

Raphael B, Meldrum L, McFarlane A. 1995. Does debriefing after psychological trauma work? *Br. Med. J.* 310:1479–80

Renfrey G, Spates CR. 1994. Eye movement desensitization: a partial dismantling study. *J. Behav. Ther. Exp. Psychiatry* 25:231–39

Rescorla RA. 1988. Pavlovian conditioning: It's not what you think it is. *Am. Psychol.* 43:151–60

Resick PA, Jordan CG, Girelli SA, Hutter CK, Marhoefer-Dvorak S. 1988. A comparative victim study of behavioral group therapy for sexual assault victims. *Behav. Ther.* 19: 385–401

Resick PA, Schnicke MK. 1992a. Cognitive processing therapy for sexual assault victims. *J. Consult. Clin. Psychol.* 60:748–56

Resick PA, Schnicke MK. 1992b. *Cognitive processing therapy for sexual assault victims.* Presented at Annu. Meet. Int. Soc. Trauma. Stress Stud., 8th, Los Angeles

Resnick HS, Kilpatrick DG, Dansky BS, Saunders BE, Best CL. 1993. Prevalence of civilian trauma and posttraumatic stress disorder in a representative national sample of women. *J. Consult. Clin. Psychol.* 61:984–91

Richards DA, Lovell K, Marks IM. 1994. Post-traumatic stress disorder: evaluation of a behavioral treatment program. *J. Trauma. Stress* 7:669–80

Roth S, Dye E, Lebowitz L. 1988. Group therapy for sexual-assault victims. *Psychotherapy* 25:82–93

Rothbaum BO. 1995. *A controlled study of EMDR for PTSD.* Presented at Assoc. Adv. Behav. Ther., Washington, DC

Rothbaum BO, Foa EB, Murdock T, Riggs D, Walsh W. 1992. A prospective examination of post-traumatic stress disorder in rape victims. *J. Trauma. Stress* 5:455–75

Saunders BE, Arata CM, Kilpatrick DG. 1990. Development of a Crime-Related Post-Traumatic Stress Disorder scale for women within the Symptom Checklist-90–Revised. *J. Trauma. Stress* 3:439–48

Scarvalone P, Cloitre M, Difede J. 1995. *Interpersonal process therapy for incest survivors: preliminary outcome data.* Presented at Soc. Psychother. Res., Vancouver

Schindler FE. 1980. Treatment by systematic desensitization of a recurring nightmare of a real life trauma. *J. Behav. Ther. Exp. Psychiatry* 11:53–54

Schut HA, de Keijser J, Van den Bout J, Dijkhuis JH. 1991. Post-traumatic stress symptoms in the first years of conjugal bereavement. *Anx. Res.* 4:225–34

Shapiro F. 1989. Eye movement desensitization: a new treatment for post-traumatic stress disorder. *J. Behav. Ther. Exp. Psychiatry* 20:211–17

Shapiro F. 1995. *Eye Movement Desensitization and Reprocessing: Basic Principles, Protocols, and Procedures.* New York: Guilford

Shore JH, Tatum E, Vollmer WM. 1986. Psychiatric reactions to disaster: the Mt. St. Helen's experience. *Am. J. Psychol.* 143: 590–95

Silver SM, Brooks A, Obenchain J. 1995. Treatment of Vietnam war veterans with PTSD: a comparison of Eye Movement Desensitization and Reprocessing, biofeedback, and relaxation training. *J. Trauma. Stress* 8:337–42

Spiegel D. 1988. Dissociation and hypnosis in post-traumatic stress disorders. *J. Trauma. Stress* 1:17–33

Spiegel D. 1989. Hypnosis in the treatment of victims of sexual abuse. *Psychiatr. Clin. N. Am.* 12:295–305

Spitzer RL, Williams JBW, Gibbon M. 1987. *Structured Clinical Interview for DSM-III-R (SCID).* New York: Biomedical Res. Dept., NY State Psychiatr. Inst.

Stern RS, Marks IM. 1973. Brief and prolonged flooding: a comparison in agoraphobic patients. *Arch. Gen. Psychol.* 28: 270–76

Suinn R. 1974. Anxiety management training for general anxiety. In *The Innovative Therapy: Critical and Creative Contributions,* ed. R Suinn, R Weigel, pp. 66–70. New York: Harper & Row

Taylor S, Koch WJ. 1995. Anxiety disorders due to motor vehicle accidents: nature and treatment. *Clin. Psychol. Rev.* 15:721–38

Thompson JA, Charlton PFC, Kerry R, Lee D, Turner SW. 1995. An open trial of exposure therapy based on deconditioning for post-traumatic stress disorder. *Br. J. Clin. Psychiatry* 34:407–16

Tolin DF, Montgomery RW, Kleinknecht RA, Lohr JM. 1996. An evaluation of Eye Movement Desensitization and Reprocessing (EMDR). In *Innovations in Clinical Practice,* 14:423–37. Sarasota, FL: Prof. Resour. Press

Vaughan K, Armstrong MS, Gold R, O'Connor N, Jenneke W, et al. 1994. A trial of eye movement desensitization compared to image habituation training and applied

muscle relaxation in post-traumatic stress disorder. *J. Behav. Ther. Exp. Psychiatry* 25:283–91
Veronen LJ, Kilpatrick DG. 1982. *Stress inoculation training for victims of rape: efficacy and differential findings.* Presented at the Annu. Conv. Assoc. Adv. Behav. Ther., 16th, Los Angeles
Vreven DL, Gudanowski DM, King LA, King DW. 1995. The civilian version of the Mississippi PTSD scale: a psychometric evaluation. *J. Trauma. Stress* 8:91–109
Watson CG, Juba MP, Manifold V, Kucala T, et al. 1991. The PTSD interview: Rationale, description, reliability, and concurrent validity of a DSM-III based technique. *J. Clin. Psy.* 47:179–88
Weiss DS. 1993. Structured clinical interview techniques. In *International Handbook of Traumatic Stress Syndromes,* ed. JP Wilson, B Raphael, pp. 179–87. New York: Plenum
Wilson SA, Becker LA, Tinker RH. 1995. Eye Movement Desensitization and Reprocessing (EMDR) treatment for psychologically traumatized individuals. *J. Consult. Clin. Psychol.* 63:928–37
Wolff R. 1977. Systematic desensitization and negative practice to alter the aftereffects of a rape attempt. *J. Behav. Ther. Exp. Psychiatry* 8:423–25
Wolpe J. 1958. *Psychotherapy by Reciprocal Inhibition.* Stanford, CA: Stanford Univ. Press
Yalom I. 1995. *The Theory and Practice of Group Psychotherapy.* New York: Basic Books. 602 pp. 4th ed.

Annu. Rev. Psychol. 1997. 48:481–514

PSYCHOBIOLOGICAL MODELS OF HIPPOCAMPAL FUNCTION IN LEARNING AND MEMORY

Mark A. Gluck and Catherine E. Myers

Center for Molecular and Behavioral Neuroscience, Rutgers University, 197 University Avenue, Newark, New Jersey; e-mail: gluck@pavlov.rutgers.edu

KEY WORDS: hippocampus, computation, neural networks

ABSTRACT

We review current computational models of hippocampal function in learning and memory, concentrating on those that make strongest contact with psychological issues and behavioral data. Some models build upon Marr's early theories for modeling hippocampal field CA3's putative role in the fast, temporary storage of episodic memories. Other models focus on hippocampal involvement in incrementally learned associations, such as classical conditioning. More recent efforts have attempted to bring functional interpretations of the hippocampal region in closer contact with underlying anatomy and physiology. In reviewing these psychobiological models, three major themes emerge. First, computational models provide the conceptual glue to bind together data from multiple levels of analysis. Second, models serve as important tools to integrate data from both animal and human studies. Third, previous psychological models that capture important behavioral principles of memory provide an important top-down constraint for developing computational models of the neural bases of these behaviors.

CONTENTS

0084-6570/97/0201-0481$08.00

INTRODUCTION

Many models and theories have been proposed over the past few decades that attempt to characterize the role of the hippocampal region in learning and memory. Most of these theories are qualitative, consisting of a central concept or metaphor that attempts to capture the essence of hippocampal-region function. We focus here on more formal computational network models of hippocampal function in learning and memory. Such models have an advantage in that they can be rigorously tested with computer simulations and, occasionally, formal mathematical analysis.

Given the breadth and diversity of current hippocampal models, we concentrate on just that subset of hippocampal theories that make strongest contact with psychological issues and data from behavioral studies of learning and memory. Given this psychobiological perspective, we omit more physiological models that make less contact with behavioral aspects of learning and memory. Among the theories that do address observable memory behaviors, we emphasize those that relate most strongly to traditional theories and models within the literature.

Our purpose in the first part of the review is to provide a general understanding of the aims, successes, and limitations of the computational approach to understanding hippocampal function in learning and memory behavior. The emphasis is on describing the spirit and behavior of the models, rather than on their exact mathematical underpinnings. A few mathematical equations are given where critical to this description. For a full exposition on implementation details, see the original journal articles.

The remainder of the review is organized as follows. We present a brief summary of the major points of hippocampal anatomy and a review of the empirical data on memory deficits produced by hippocampal damage in animals and human beings. We then provide some important historical background, discussing David Marr's early theories of the hippocampus as an autoassociative memory storage device. In the section entitled "Autoassociative Models of CA3 and Episodic Memory" we show how Marr's earlier theories have influenced current computational models of hippocampal region CA3 and its role in episodic memory. Next we turn to more incremental forms of associative learning, reviewing models of conditioning and hippocampus. The next two sections illustrate how some of these models, at different levels of analysis, are beginning to converge into integrated theories incorporating a wider range of behavioral and biological detail.

THE HIPPOCAMPAL REGION IS CRITICAL FOR LEARNING AND MEMORY

The hippocampal region (Figure 1) is comprised of a group of brain structures located deep inside the brain that form part of what (in human beings) is often called the *medial-temporal lobe.* The region includes the *hippocampus* and the nearby *dentate gyrus, subiculum,* and *entorhinal cortex.* The outermost of these structures—the entorhinal cortex—receives highly processed information from the entire spectrum of sensory modalities as well as from multimodal association areas. Information flows in a roughly unidirectional fashion from the entorhinal cortex to the dentate gyrus, to the hippocampus, to the subiculum, and back to the entorhinal cortex before returning to the same sensory areas where it originally arose. In addition to this basic pathway of information flow, there are many direct connections between the structures of the region. The hippocampus also has another input and output pathway through the *fornix,* a fiber bundle connecting it with subcortical structures that provide modulation.

Hippocampal Damage Produces Amnesia in Human Beings

Damage to the hippocampal region in human beings produces a characteristic *anterograde amnesia* syndrome, which strongly impairs the acquisition of new information (Squire 1987). Human hippocampal damage can result from a variety of causes, including aneurysms to the arteries that vascularize the hippocampus, anoxia, and epileptic seizures (Zola-Morgan & Squire 1993). The hippocampal region is also among the first structures to be damaged in the course of Alzheimer's disease and normal aging (de Leon et al 1993). Damage to other related structures, such as the basal forebrain, can also cause amnesic syndromes that share features with hippocampal amnesia, presumably because such damage indirectly interferes with normal hippocampal-region processing (Volpe & Hirst 1983).

The anterograde amnesia that follows human hippocampal-region damage is most saliently characterized by an inability to acquire new *episodic* information, the kind of information about individual events and experiences that is

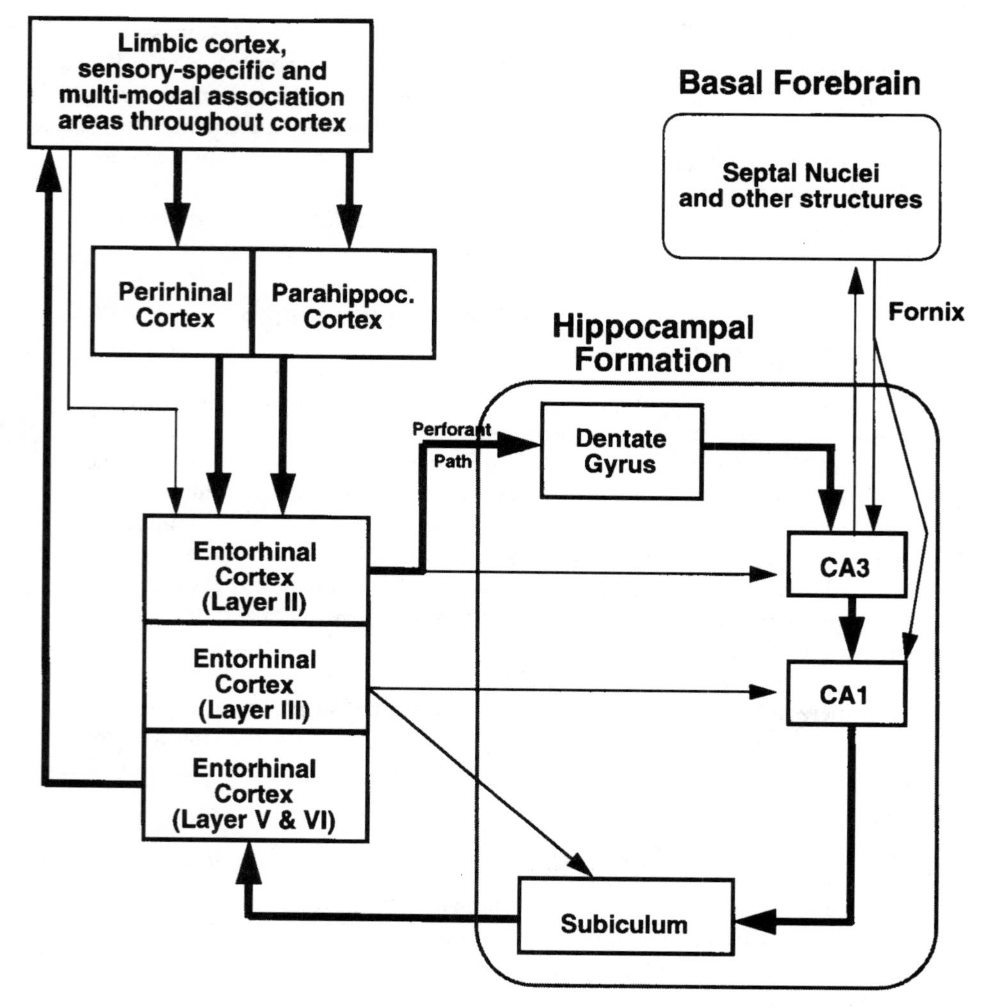

Figure 1 The structures of the hippocampal region. CA3, hippocampal field CA3; CA1, hippocampal field CA1. [Adapted from Myers et al (1996).]

accessible to conscious control. Patients with this debilitation may also show some degree of retrograde amnesia—disruption of previously acquired information—but this is usually limited to information acquired shortly before the trauma and tends to lessen in a time-graded fashion for information acquired longer ago (Squire 1987). This relationship between hippocampal damage and anterograde amnesia led to the idea that the hippocampus is a specialized memory processor needed to lay down new episodic memories.

Hippocampal Damage Produces Varied Memory Deficits in Animals

Animal models of hippocampal amnesia have had an obvious difficulty in addressing this loss of episodic information in nonverbal subjects; animals are unable to tell the experimenter directly what they can remember. However, by using indirect memory tests in which the animal is challenged to use memory of specific events, hippocampal-region damage in animals has been shown to cause learning deficits broadly similar to the episodic memory loss in human hippocampal amnesics (Eichenbaum 1992). Animal studies have also documented that certain kinds of learning capabilities do survive hippocampal-region damage. For example, the acquisition of learned responses in elementary associative conditioning tasks is largely unimpaired (Gabrieli et al 1995). Human hippocampal amnesics show similar residual learning abilities in motor-reflex conditioning, cognitive skill learning, and simple categorization tasks (Cohen 1984). All these tasks are learnable over many trials and do not require the formation of single episodic memories.

However, even the simple iterative tasks such as conditioning are disrupted in hippocampal-damaged animals if they involve additional complexities, such as requiring comparisons or configurations of multiple stimulus cues, or if attention to the experimental context is important (see section entitled "Stimulus Representation in Associative Learning"; Hirsh 1974; Rudy & Sutherland 1989, 1995).

MARR'S AUTOASSOCIATIVE MEMORY STORE

One of the earliest and most influential models of hippocampal-region processing was proposed by David Marr (1971). Starting with what was known then about hippocampal anatomy and physiology, Marr sought to infer an emergent information-processing capability. His ideas gave rise to a broad class of models, often termed *Hebb-Marr* models because they incorporate Hebb's (1949) ideas on how associations are acquired between groups of cells in the brain (McNaughton & Nadel 1990). Since Marr's original publication, new empirical data have shown that some aspects of his model are incomplete or incorrect (see e.g. Willshaw & Buckingham 1990). Nonetheless, many of the basic ideas in the Hebb-Marr model of hippocampus have withstood continuing empirical and theoretical tests and remain the basis for many current models and theories. This section reviews a generalized version of the Hebb-Marr model. Later sections describe several more current models that build on Marr's original specification.

Marr's basic idea was to distinguish separable roles in memory for the archicortex, including hippocampus, and for the neocortex. He assumed that the chief role of neocortex was to store large complex *event memories*—broadly equivalent to what today are usually called *episodic memories*—composed of several integrated associations. For example, the event memory of a meal might include associations about the food eaten, the meal's location and time, and the company sharing it. In Marr's model, an event memory is defined as a pattern E of activities over a large number of neocortical cells, evoked by a particular set of sensory inputs (Figure 2*A*). Such a pattern is stored by associating its elements so that activation of some of the

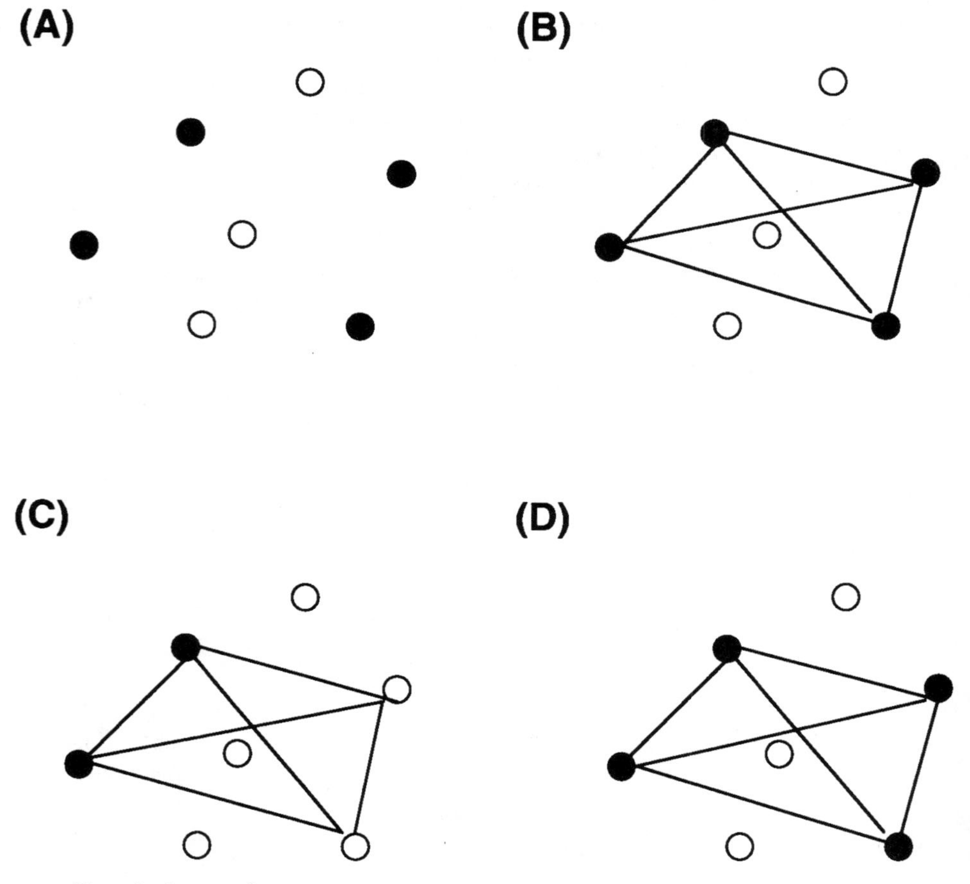

Figure 2 Storage of an event memory as a pattern of cell activations in neocortex, according to Marr's (1971) model. (*A*) Initially, the event memory simply evokes a pattern of activations (*darkened circles*) across a group of unrelated cells. (*B*) As the pattern is stored, various elements of the pattern are associated by weighted connections (*lines*). (*C*) Later, if a partial version of the original pattern is presented (*darkened circles*), activation spreads along the associations to activate the complete pattern (*D*).

cells representing elements in *E* can activate other elements in turn (Figure 2*B*). Later, if a subset of *E* is presented to the neocortex, the neocortex should be able to retrieve the full pattern *E* (Figure 2*C*). This ability is *pattern completion.* One difficulty in implementing this function in the neocortex is that a large number of very precise connections is required to associate each element in *E* with every other element in *E*. Further, the associations required to store *E* may well disrupt preexisting associations created to store other patterns with common elements. Worse, if another stored pattern *F* shares common elements with *E*, then *F* may interfere with attempted retrieval of *E:* If a subset of *E* is presented, activation will spread to these common elements, which will then begin to retrieve *F* as well as *E*. At the extreme, if many overlapping patterns are stored, an attempt to retrieve any stored pattern will result in a pattern of activation that shares elements with all stored patterns but is identical to none. This situation is called *catastrophic interference* (Hetherington 1990).

Because of this potential for interference in recall, Marr suggested that it would be useful to have a separate processor—such as the hippocampus—that could rapidly store event memories, and then allow gradual transfer of this pattern to neocortex, which would reorganize and classify this information, incorporating it with existing knowledge to reduce interference. More specifically, Marr proposed that the hippocampus is able to rapidly store new patterns, holding them in a temporary memory store, but is not able to integrate them with the larger body of existing knowledge.

Marr imagined the hippocampus as functionally consisting of two layers or groups of cells (Figure 3*A*). Inputs cause activity on the first A layer of cells, which project onto the second B layer of cells. The B cells in turn project back to the A cells. All synapses between cells are modifiable, but they are simplified to allow only binary on or off values. Similarly, cell activity is assumed to be either on or off. This network is essentially the same as that shown in Figure 2, except that cells are differentiated according to whether they directly receive external input (A cells) or not (B cells). A stored pattern can be retrieved if, when part is presented to the A cells, the evoked activity on the B cells feeds back to complete the original firing pattern on the A cells. As shown in the next section, Marr's pattern associator model forms the basis for many subsequent—and more detailed—models of hippocampal physiology and function.

AUTOASSOCIATIVE MODELS OF CA3 AND EPISODIC MEMORY

The network described by Marr is a form of *autoassociator.* An autoassociator network learns to associate an input pattern with an identical output pattern

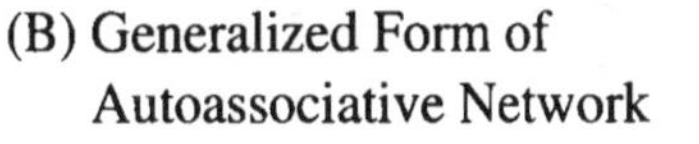
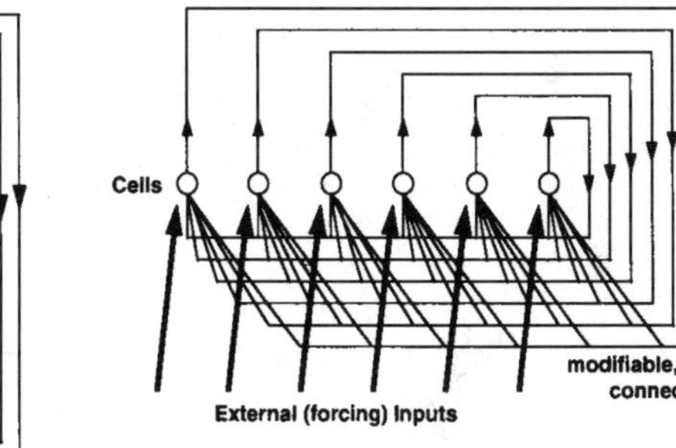

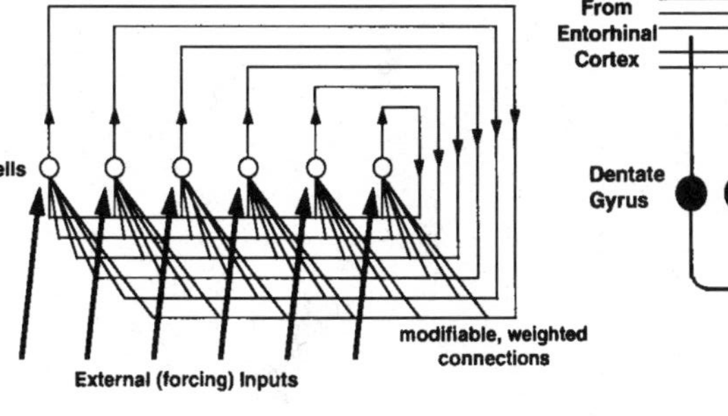

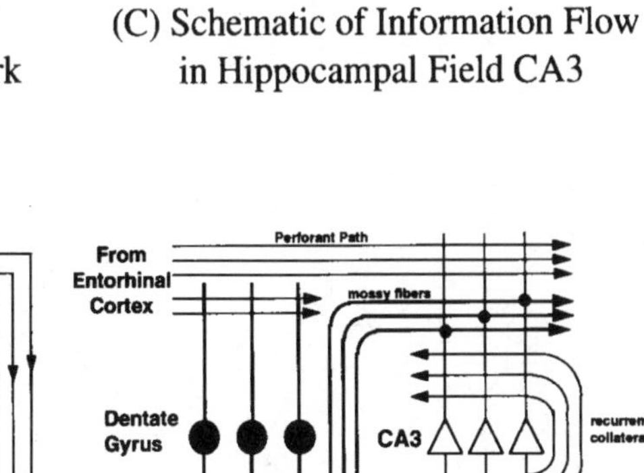

Figure 3 (*A*) Simplified schematic of Marr's (1971) model of hippocampus. Cells are either A cells, which receive direct activation from the external input (*heavy lines*), or B cells, which are driven only by A cells and afferent them in turn. Learning consists of strengthening connections between B cells and the A cells that activate them. Later, if a partial version of a stored pattern is presented to the A cells, the B cells feed back and activate the remaining A cells required to complete the stored pattern. (*B*) A generalized form of autoassociative network. There is a single layer of cells with outputs that ramify to provide feedback input to the cell layer. These synapses are weighted, and cells become active if the total weighted synaptic input exceeds a threshold (Equation 1). Patterns are stored by presenting external (forcing) input to the cells; learning then consists of weighting the synapses between all pairs of co-active cells (Equation 2). Later, if a partial version of a stored pattern is presented on the external inputs, activity spreads iteratively through the recurrent feedback connections, which activates additional cells until the entire pattern is reconstructed. (*C*) A schematic representation of information flow in hippocampal field CA3. Inputs to the pyramidal cells arrive directly from entorhinal cortex as well as indirectly via the mossy fibers from dentate gyrus. The mossy fiber afferents make sparse, presumably strong, synapses onto CA3 dendrites, and so they are putative forcing inputs to the network. CA3 pyramidal cell outputs ramify to become feedback afferents to CA3, and also exit to hippocampal field CA1 and through the fornix to other, extrahippocampal targets.

(Anderson 1977, Hinton 1989, Kohonen 1984). A general form of autoassociator is shown in Figure 2*B* and consists of a single layer of nodes receiving excitatory connections from external sources as well as from each other. Nodes are assumed to have binary states: either active or firing (represented by an output value of 1), or quiescent (represented by an output value of 0). Node j becomes active if the sum of inputs exceeds some firing threshold (cf Grossberg 1976, Kohonen 1984, McCulloch & Pitts 1943, Rosenblatt 1962):

$$y_j = 1 \quad \text{iff} \quad \sum_i w_{ij} y_j > \theta_j, \qquad 1.$$

$$else = 0.$$

In Equation 1, y_j is the output or activation of cell j, w_{ij} is the weight of the synapse on j from another cell i, and θ_j is cell j's threshold. This threshold, θ_j, is then set so that j will become active if the weighted sum of its inputs exceeds some proportion of the total inputs active in the original pattern. Additional inhibitory processes, not shown in Figure 2*B*, may be required to determine the threshold. More complex networks may also allow continuous (real-valued) inputs and outputs, but the central ideas are the same.

A binary pattern E is stored in this network by presenting E as external input. The nth element of E is presented to the nth node in the network and forces that node to output the same value as that element. For this reason, the external inputs are often termed *forcing inputs,* and the one synapse each node receives from the forcing input is often called a *forcing synapse.* The network then undergoes synaptic plasticity at the feedback connections, so that synapses from active presynaptic cells have excitatory effects on other active postsynaptic cells. This can be accomplished by a Hebbian learning rule of the form:

$$w_{ij} = \alpha\left(y_i y_j\right). \qquad 2.$$

where y_i and y_j are the activities of presynaptic cell i and postsynaptic cell j, α is a constant term, and w_{ij} is the weight of the synapse between i and j. Note that synaptic mechanisms of long-term potentiation and depression (LTP and LTD) are Hebbian in nature (Levy et al 1983, McNaughton & Morris 1987). Later, if some subset of E is presented to the network, activity in the recurrent collaterals will iterate through the network and activate the cells needed to complete the missing parts of E. Thus, this network performs pattern completion.

Three Common Features of Autoassociators and Field CA3

Marr's important contribution was to conceptualize the hippocampus as an autoassociator network that performs pattern storage and retrieval. Many subsequent models have elaborated on this idea (Hasselmo 1995, Hasselmo et al

1996, McNaughton & Morris 1987, McNaughton & Nadel 1990, Rolls 1989, Treves & Rolls 1992). An autoassociator such as the one shown in Figure 3*B* has three basic requirements: (*a*) a high degree of internal recurrency among the principal cells; (*b*) strong, sparse synapses from external afferents, which could function as forcing synapses; and (*c*) plasticity at the synapses between co-active cells.

These requirements suffice to allow the functions of pattern storage, completion, and retrieval. Hippocampal field CA3 satisfies all three requirements (Figure 3*C*). First, the principal neurons of CA3—pyramidal cells—are perhaps unique in the brain for their high degree of internal recurrency: Each CA3 pyramidal may receive contact from about 4% of other pyramidals in the field, a high enough contact probability to allow autoassociation (Rolls 1989). Second, in addition to recurrent collaterals and sparse entorhinal afferents, CA3 pyramidals receive a small number of inputs from mossy fibers, containing entorhinal information that reaches CA3 via the dentate gyrus. While each CA3 pyramidal in rat may receive 12,000 synapses from recurrent collaterals and 4000 synapses from direct entorhinal afferents, it may only receive about 50 mossy fiber synapses (Treves & Rolls 1992). However, the mossy fiber synapses are very large and presumably also very strong, so that coincident activity on a relatively small number of mossy fiber synapses could activate a CA3 pyramidal (Rolls 1989). The mossy fiber synapses are thus good candidates for forcing synapses in an autoassociator (Marr 1971, McNaughton 1991, McNaughton & Morris 1987). Third, plasticity in the form of LTP has been demonstrated at the synapses of recurrent collaterals in CA3 (Bliss & Lomo 1973, Kelso et al 1986). LTP involves strengthening of synapses between coactive pre- and postsynaptic cells; this could implement Hebbian learning as defined in Equation 2 above.

In summary, CA3 seems to be a likely candidate to implement autoassociative memory in the brain. Patterns would be stored by presentation over the mossy fibers, which would force CA3 pyramidal output. Recurrent collateral synapses between coactive pyramidals would then undergo LTP to store the pattern. Later, if a partial version of that pattern is presented along the weaker entorhinal afferents, some CA3 pyramidals would become active. After several iterations of activity through the recurrent collaterals, more CA3 pyramidals would be activated until the entire stored pattern is retrieved. Additional inhibitory units are also generally assumed to allow implementation of the firing thresholds.

Autoassociative Networks Implement Hippocampal-Dependent Memory Behaviors

This type of autoassociative network can be used to implement various forms of memory, many of which are much like those that appear to be impaired following hippocampal damage in animals and human beings. For example, autoassociative memories can create unified memories from several component features and then retrieve the entire memory from a partial input.

SEQUENCE LEARNING Many models of hippocampal function have drawn on the details of its anatomy and physiology to argue that it has the capacity for learning sequences of input patterns. These models are often generally based on the recurrent architectures of autoassociative networks: Given a partial input consisting of the present state, an autoassociative network can perform pattern completion and retrieve the predicted next state. Levy (1996) presented a model of hippocampal region CA3 as a sequence predictor and argues that this general sequence prediction paradigm can provide a computational unification of a variety of putative hippocampal-dependent functions, including contextual sensitivity, configuration, and cognitive mapping (see also Levy et al 1995, Prepscius & Levy 1994). Granger et al (1996) presented a model of field CA1 incorporating an LTP learning rule in which the amount of potentiation depends on the order of arrival of afferent activity to a target neuron. They show that with this temporally dependent LTP learning, the CA1 network model can learn to store brief simulated temporal sequences of inputs. Liaw & Berger (1996) also described a model of hippocampal neurons in which they argued that the dynamic interplay of hippocampal synaptic mechanisms for facilitative and inhibitory processes results in an emergent "temporal chunking" mechanism for sequential pattern recognition. In this model, each dynamic synapse learns to respond to a small sub-pattern of inputs, and the postsynaptic neuron learns how to properly combine these subpatterns.

SPATIAL MEMORY AND NAVIGATION This aspect of autoassociative memory systems seems ideal for implementing a spatial processor, in which the broad memory of a place should be evoked by any of several views of the area, even if some of the usual cues are missing. In fact, spatial memory is extremely hippocampal dependent in rats (e.g. O'Keefe & Nadel 1978), and many connectionist models of hippocampal-processing in spatial learning have been based on autoassociative models of the hippocampal region (Burgess et al 1994, Levy 1989, McNaughton & Morris 1987, McNaughton & Nadel 1990, Muller et al 1987, Muller & Stead 1996, Recce & Harris 1996, Sharp 1991, Sharp et al 1996). One possibility is to define spatial maps as composed of sets of complex configural associations representing places (McNaughton 1989, McNaughton & Nadel 1990). In one place, there may be many views, depending on which way the animal is facing, the location of landmarks, etc. The hippocampal autoassociator would be able to map from one of these views to the full representation of the current place. With this interpretation, place learning need not be fundamentally different from any other kind of representational learning. However, because of the need for such complex representations in spatial tasks, these behaviors might be especially sensitive to hippocampal damage.

EPISODIC MEMORY AND CONSOLIDATION Perhaps most pervasive is the idea that the fast, temporary storage in an autoassociator is an important component of an episodic or declarative memory system, in which arbitrary patterns are stored (Alvarez & Squire 1994, Hasselmo et al 1996, McClelland & Goddard 1996, Murre 1996, O'Reilly & McClelland 1994, Treves & Rolls 1992). It is generally assumed in these models that a relatively small temporary store in the hippocampus interacts with a relatively large neocortical system (Figure 4). Such an assumption was made by Marr (1971), and many connectionist models of amnesia center on similar assumptions (e.g. Alvarez & Squire 1994, Lynch & Granger 1992, McClelland et al 1994, Murre 1996, O'Reilly & McClelland 1994, Treves & Rolls 1992). Many preconnectionist models assume this general organization as well (e.g. Mishkin 1982, Teyler & DiScenna 1986, Wickelgren 1979).

In these models, the central assumption is that a stimulus enters the neocortex via the sensory system and subsequently activates cells in the hippocampus. The hippocampus in turn feeds back to the neocortex and initiates activation patterns there. It may activate new cell populations, which are then added to the representation, or it may allow connections to form between

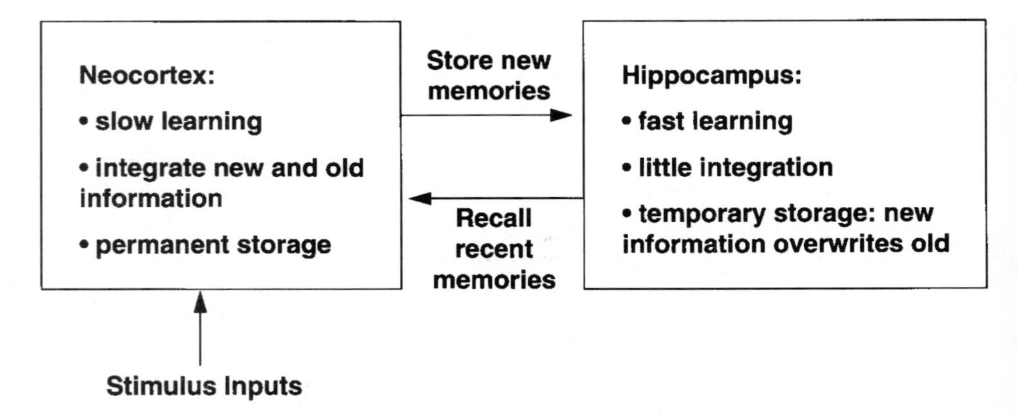

Figure 4 General format of many connectionist models of amnesia. The neocortex is assumed to be a large-capacity, permanent store for memory associations, and to be able to integrate new information with old associations. However, learning is assumed to be slow and possibly require several iterated presentations. The hippocampus is assumed to be capable of storing memory within as little as a single exposure, but older memories are liable to be overwritten by newer ones. The hippocampus therefore captures episodic memories and iteratively allows the neocortex to integrate these memories with existing associations.

active cells in the neocortex. The hippocampus may be required to present memories to the neocortex repeatedly, over some period, to allow the neocortex to integrate new knowledge without overwriting the old (McClelland et al 1994). This process is termed memory *consolidation.* Over time, as this consolidation occurs, the sensory input is able to activate these cells directly, without hippocampal intervention. At this point, the hippocampus has completed its function of helping to bind together disparate cortical activities into a coherent pattern, and memories are safe from subsequent hippocampal damage. However, a more recent memory, which is not yet fully consolidated, may be disrupted. The probability of such disruption is higher for more recent memories, which have had less time to be consolidated, than older ones. This is consistent with data showing that while hippocampal damage leads to severe anterograde amnesia, there is only temporally gradated retrograde amnesia (Squire & Alvarez 1995). This inverse relationship between memory age and hippocampal independence is known as the *Ribot gradient* of retrograde amnesia (Ribot 1882; see also Alvarez & Squire 1994). Examples from animal and human experiments are shown in Figures 5*A* and 5*B* (Kim & Fanselow 1992, Squire & Cohen 1979).

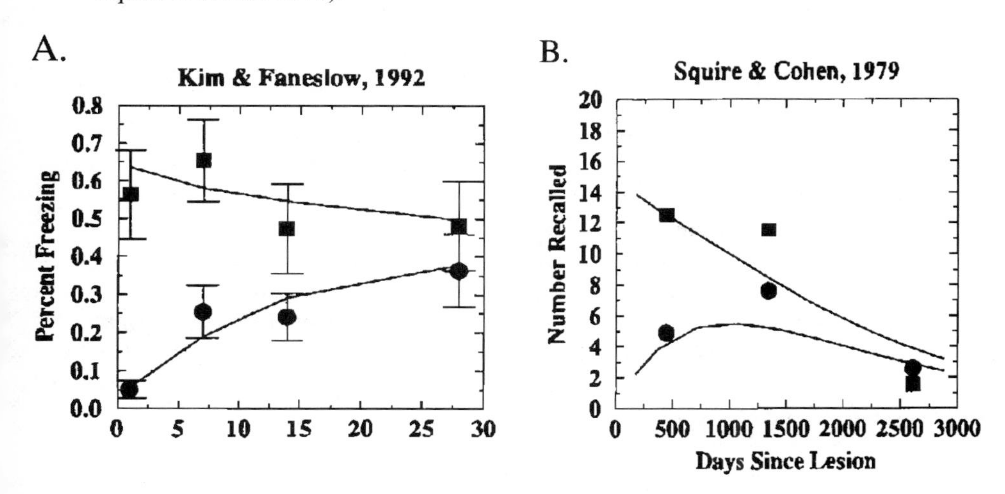

Figure 5 Examples of Ribot gradients, which illustrate how older memories are less likely to be disrupted by hippocampal damage than are newer memories. (*A*) Ribot gradient in animal data. Behavioral responses of animals receiving extensive hippocampal system lesions (*circles*) or control lesions (*squares*) as a function of the number of days elapsing between exposure to the relevant experiences and the occurrence of the lesion. Fear response (freezing) behavior shown by rats when returned to an environment in which they had experienced paired presentations of tones with foot shock. Bars surrounding each datapoint indicate the standard error (from Kim & Faneslow 1992). (*B*) Ribot gradient in human data. Recall by depressed human subjects of details of television shows aired different numbers of years before the time of test, after electroconvulsive treatment (*circles*) or just before treatment (*squares*) (from Squire & Cohen 1979).

Note that a model consisting of an autoassociator alone would predict the opposite effect: namely, that older memories would be increasingly susceptible to interference from newer memories. The addition of a "remote" neocortical storage site allows the models of hippocampal-cortical interaction to account for both the anterograde and retrograde aspects of hippocampal amnesia. Further elaborations may be assumed on this general model scheme, such as nonspecific modulatory influences that determine the storage rates in CA3 (Grossberg 1976, Hasselmo et al 1995, Murre 1996, Treves & Rolls 1992), or additional preprocessing in dentate gyrus and postprocessing in CA1 (Hasselmo & Schnell 1994, Levy 1989, McNaughton 1991, Treves & Rolls 1992).

Open Issue: How and When Does Consolidation Take Place?

A major challenge confronting these models of anterograde amnesia is to specify in detail just how consolidation of memories from hippocampus to neocortex might take place. One small-scale implementation is provided by Alvarez & Squire (1994), who suggested that most memory consolidation may occur during sleep (see also Buzsaki 1989, Crick & Mitchison 1983, McClelland et al 1994). This is consistent with recent data showing that hippocampal activity during slow-wave sleep echoes specific patterns recorded earlier while the animal was exploring its environment (Wilson & McNaughton 1994). Alvarez & Squire suggested that this activity reflects a process during which the hippocampus reinstates patterns it stored earlier and presents them to neocortex for consolidation. The electrical activity in the hippocampus is markedly different during waking exploration and slow-wave sleep, which further suggests that the hippocampus is operating in two different modes (information storage and information reinstatement) during these two behavioral states (Buzsaki 1989). Other possible mechanisms of consolidation may include conscious and unconscious rehearsal (Murre 1996). All these hypotheses await thorough verification through combined neurophysiological and neuropsychological studies.

Open Issue: The Problem of Interference in Memory Networks

Another issue concerns the problem of interference. One constraint on the utility of an autoassociative network is that it has very limited capacity. A network of n nodes is able to store only about $0.15n$ random patterns before they begin to interfere with one another (Hopfield 1982). Interference refers to the likelihood that patterns overlap sufficiently such that retrieval of one will activate retrieval of part or all of additional patterns, and the resulting network output will contain elements of multiple stored patterns. In the extreme, in a net that is filled to capacity, addition of a single new pattern can disrupt the ability to correctly retrieve any previously stored pattern. As described above, this phenomenon is called catastrophic interference (Hetherington 1990), and it is a general feature of all connectionist networks that perform fast storage, as the hippocampal auto-associative network is assumed to do (McClelland et al 1994). One way to increase capacity and avoid catastrophic interference is to explicitly decrease the overlap between patterns. It has been suggested that this is one effect of the sparse connections from dentate gyrus to CA3: Since any one mossy fiber contacts only about 14 of the 3×10^5 CA3 cells in rat, there is very little probability that two patterns of mossy fiber activity will activate the same pattern of CA3 activity (Rolls 1989). In addition, plasticity in the dentate gyrus may further help to sparsify CA3 inputs (Hasselmo 1995, O'Reilly & McClelland 1994, Treves & Rolls 1992). Even with such *pattern separation,* a pattern stored in the hippocampus will only remain intact for a limited period before it is overwritten by storage of newer memories. This implies that memories stored in the hippocampus must be transferred elsewhere to survive for long periods.

STIMULUS REPRESENTATION IN ASSOCIATIVE LEARNING

The models described above focus on the ability of the hippocampal region to perform fast, temporary storage, and they suggest that this underlies the hippocampal region's role in episodic memory formation. This is consistent with the basic idea that episodic memory impairments are the most obvious behavioral effects in human amnesia following hippocampal region damage. Nondeclarative learning (including procedural or implicit learning) often survives such damage. For example, animals with hippocampal-region damage can often show normal acquisition of classically conditioned responding (e.g. Solomon & Moore 1975) or discrimination of successively presented odors (Eichenbaum et al 1988). Similarly, human hippocampal-damaged amnesics are not impaired at acquiring conditioned motor reflex responses (Daum et al 1989, Gabrieli et al 1995, Woodruff-Pak 1993), learning simple classification tasks (Knowlton et al 1994), or learning new motor skills such as mirror drawing (Cohen 1984). All these tasks can be solved by incremental formation of habits or tendencies, without requiring episodic memories of any individual learning session.

However, there are other tasks that seem superficially to be just as nondeclarative but that are impaired after hippocampal-region damage. For example, although the simplest acquisition of a classically conditioned response is not impaired by hippocampal-region damage, there may be severe impairments in classical conditioning tasks that require learning about unreinforced stimuli

(Kaye & Pearce 1987, Solomon & Moore 1975), configurations of stimuli (Rudy & Sutherland 1989), contextual information (Hirsh 1974), or relationships that span short delays (Moyer et al 1990, Port et al 1986). These findings imply that the hippocampal region does participate in information processing during procedural tasks, although this participation may not necessarily be evident in the simplest kinds of learning. These findings also indicate that a conception of the hippocampal region as a purely passive store for episodic memories is insufficient.

Several recent qualitative theories and computational models have focused on possible information processing roles for the hippocampal region, especially in incrementally acquired (nondeclarative) learning (e.g. Eichenbaum et al 1992b; Gluck & Myers 1993, 1995; Hirsh 1974; Moore & Stickney 1980; Myers et al 1995, 1996; Schmajuk & DiCarlo 1992; Sutherland & Rudy 1989). In turn, these models are less concerned with the issues that motivate the above-described models of consolidation. A full account of hippocampal-region function would, of course, address its role in both information processing and the consolidation of declarative memories.

Most of these associative theories of incremental learning assume that while the hippocampus is required for some complicated forms of stimulus association, the neocortex is sufficient for simpler stimulus-response associations such as those that underlie classical conditioning (e.g. Gluck & Myers 1993; Myers et al 1995; Schmajuk & DiCarlo 1990, 1992). Here we focus on one representative computational model, which incorporates some of the earlier ideas regarding hippocampal autoassociation (Gluck & Myers 1993).

Hippocampal Function and Stimulus Representations

Gluck & Myers (1993) presented a computational theory of hippocampal-region function in associative learning, which argued that the hippocampal region is critical during learning for recoding neural representation to reflect environmental regularities. Central to this theory is the definition of a stimulus representation as a pattern of activities over a set of elements (neuron groups in a brain or nodes in a connectionist network) evoked by the stimulus. Learning to make a response to that stimulus involves mapping from that representation to appropriate behavioral outputs. Learning about one stimulus will transfer—or generalize—to other stimuli as a function of how similar their representations are. Therefore, the particular representations can have a great impact on how hard a task is to learn.

The key idea of Gluck and Myers's (1993) cortico-hippocampal model is that the hippocampal region is able to facilitate learning by adapting representations in two ways. First, it is assumed to compress, or make more similar, representations of stimuli that co-occur; second, it is assumed to differentiate, or make less similar, representations of stimuli that are to be mapped to different responses. This kind of function can be implemented in a connectionist model that is related to the autoassociators described above but that includes a middle (often termed hidden) layer of nodes. Such a network, termed an autoencoder (Hinton 1989), is shown on the left in Figure 6. It maps input activations representing stimulus inputs through weighted connections to activate the middle layer of nodes that in turn feed through weighted connections to activate the output layer of nodes. The network is trained to produce outputs that reconstruct the inputs as well as predict the behavioral response. Because the autoencoder has a narrow hidden layer of nodes, this task can only be accomplished by compressing redundant information, while preserving and differentiating enough predictive information to allow reconstruction at the output layer. Although the details of the model are not biologically realistic (especially the use of backpropagation error-correction for updating the autoencoder weights), the model nevertheless is a useful tool for exploring the

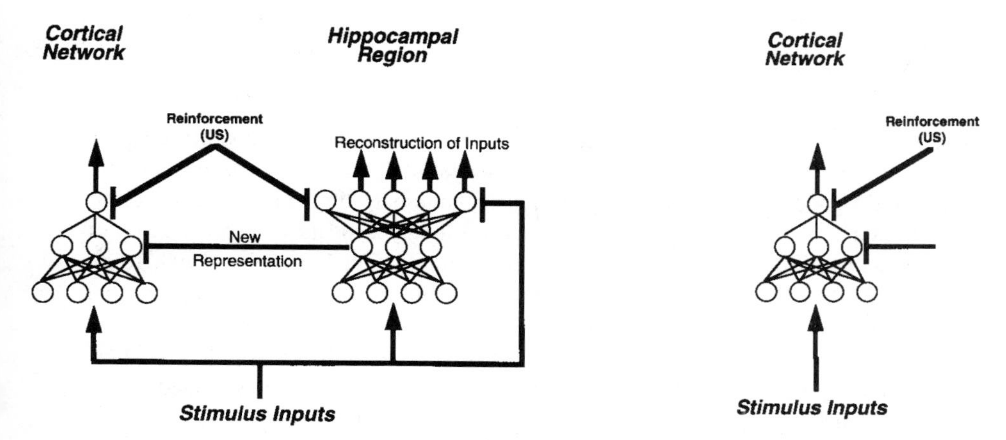

Figure 6 The cortico-hippocampal model (Gluck & Myers 1993). (*A*) The intact system is assumed to include a predictive autoencoder, representing hippocampal-region processing that constructs new stimulus representations in its internal layer that are biased to compress redundancies while differentiating predictive information. These stimulus representations are acquired by long-term storage sites in the cortex, represented as a multilayer network that learns to predict US arrival. The cortical network uses the Rescorla-Wagner rule to map from inputs to the hippocampal-mediated internal representations, and again to map from the internal layer to output activations. (*B*) Hippocampal-region lesion is assumed to disable the hippocampal network, in which case the cortical network can no longer acquire new internal representations but can acquire new behavioral responses based on its preexisting (and now fixed) internal representations. (Reprinted from Myers & Gluck 1995.)

kinds of representations that might evolve under the constraints of the two biases described above (for a more biological instantiation of these same ideas, see section on "Dissociating Parahippocampal and Hippocampal Contributions" and Myers et al 1995).

This network is incorporated into the full cortico-hippocampal model shown in Figure 6 (Gluck & Myers 1993). A cortical network is shown on the left, which is assumed to map from stimulus inputs to outputs that determine the behavioral response. However, this network is assumed to be unable to construct hidden layer representations on its own. Instead, it can adopt those representations formed in the hidden layer of the hippocampal region network. It can then learn to map from these to the correct responses. Hippocampal lesion is simulated in this model by disabling the hippocampal network, and assuming that the hidden layer representations in the cortical network are now fixed. Those already acquired are maintained, so little retrograde amnesia is expected after hippocampal-region damage (although the model does not rule out the idea of an indefinitely long consolidation period during which information is transferred, as suggested by the models of McClelland, Murre, and others reviewed above). Further, the cortical network can still learn to map from the existing representations to new behavioral responses. All that is lost is the hippocampal-dependent ability to modify those representations.

Application to Behavioral Data

Gluck & Myers's (1993) model can be applied to classical conditioning by assuming that the inputs are conditioned stimuli, and that the output is a conditioned response that is expected to anticipate the reinforcing unconditioned stimulus. The model then captures many aspects of the behavior of intact and hippocampal-region–damaged animals (Gluck & Myers 1993, 1996; Myers & Gluck 1994, 1996). For example, the model correctly expects that hippocampal-region damage causes no particular impairment—or even a slight facilitation—in learning a conditioned response. For such a simple task, new adaptive representations are probably not needed, and even the lesioned model can learn to map from its existing representations to the correct response. In fact, because the intact model is slowed by constructing new representations, it may often be slower than the lesioned model. This is consistent with similar effects often seen in animals (e.g. Eichenbaum et al 1988, Schmaltz & Theos 1972, etc).

However, latent inhibition—the slower learning after unreinforced exposure to the to-be-conditioned stimulus (Lubow 1973)—is disrupted by broad hippocampal-region damage (Figure 7*A*) (Kaye & Pearce 1987, Solomon & Moore 1975). The model correctly shows these effects (Myers & Gluck 1994). During the exposure phase, the stimulus is partially redundant with the back-

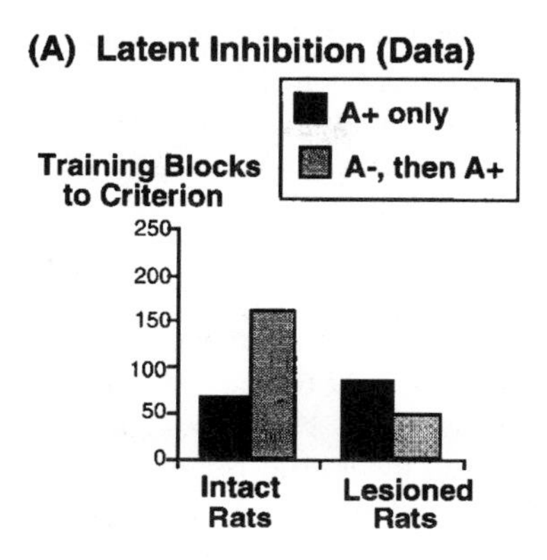

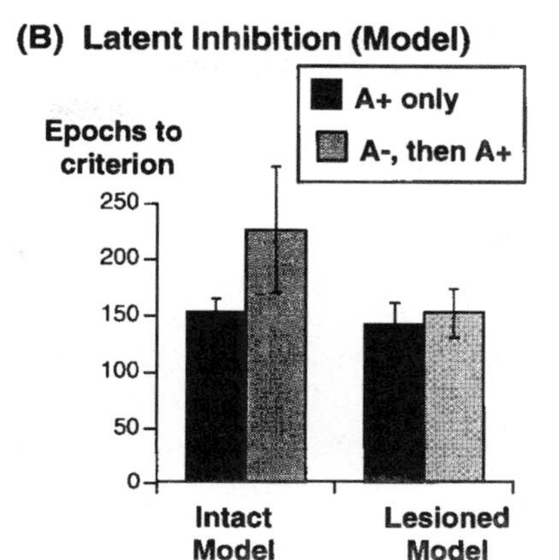

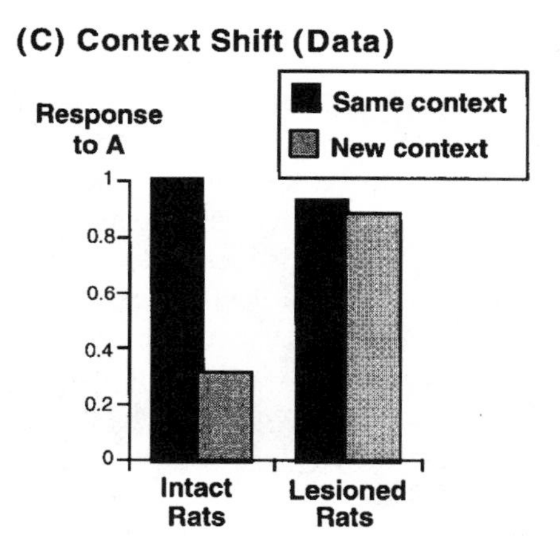

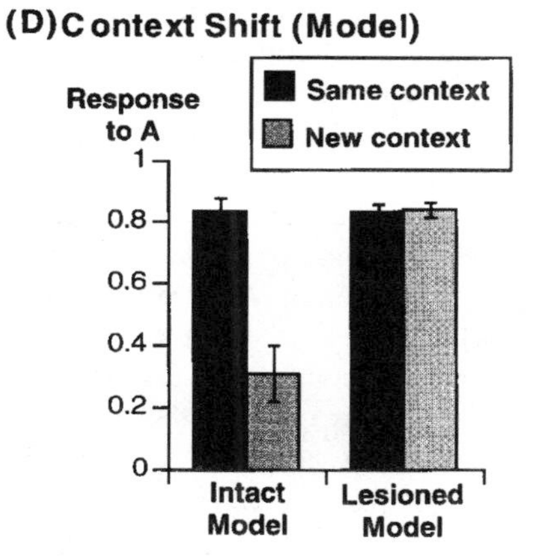

Figure 7 Behavioral results from intact and hippocampal-lesioned animals compared with simulation results from intact and lesioned cortico-hippocampal model. (*A*) Latent inhibition. In intact animals, unreinforced preexposure to a cue A slows later acquisition of conditioned responding to A (Lubow 1973). This is reflected in longer training times until criterion is reached on responding to A. Broad hippocampal-region lesion eliminates this effect (Kaye & Pearce 1987, Solomon & Moore 1975). (Figure plotted from data presented in Solomon & Moore 1975.) (*B*) The intact model correctly shows latent inhibition, whereas the lesioned model does not. (Figure reprinted from Myers et al 1995.) (*C*) In normal animals, a conditioned response to A may show a decrement if A is then presented in a new context (Hall & Honey 1989). Hippocampal-lesioned animals do not show this response decrement after a context shift (Honey & Good 1993, Penick & Solomon 1991). (Figure replotted from data presented in Penick & Solomon 1991.) (*D*) The intact but not lesioned model correctly shows this response decrement with context shift (Myers & Gluck 1994). (Figure reprinted from Myers et al 1995.)

ground context. Neither predicts any reinforcing event, so the hippocampal-region network compresses their representations. Later, when the task is to respond to the stimulus but not the context alone, this compression must be undone, which results in slowed learning in the intact model (Figure 7*B*). In contrast, the lesioned model has no compression during the exposure phase, so learning is not retarded in the subsequent learning phase (Figure 7*B*).

Many of the learning deficits associated with hippocampal damage can be described as context effects (Hirsh 1974). For example, human hippocampal-damaged amnesics may be able to remember an experience but not where or when that information was acquired—and they may even be unaware they know the information itself until indirectly prompted for it (Haist et al 1991, Weiskrantz & Warrington 1979). Animals show related effects. For example, under some conditions, an animal trained to respond to a stimulus in one environment gives a decremented response when that stimulus is presented in another environment (Figure 7*C*) (Hall & Honey 1989). A hippocampal-lesioned animal does not show this decrement but responds just as strongly in the new environment (Honey & Good 1993, Penick & Solomon 1991). The cortico-hippocampal model implies a similar effect (Figure 7*D*) (Myers & Gluck 1994) because the hippocampal-region autoencoder is assumed to reconstruct not only the conditioned stimuli but also any background or context cues that are present during learning. Thus, as the autoencoder learns to represent a conditioned stimulus, information about the context is included in that representation. As a result, if the stimulus is presented in a new context, the representation of that stimulus will be less weakly activated than usual, and in turn the conditioned response will be decremented, just as observed in intact animals. In contrast, the lesioned model does not form new, compressed representations, and so responding does not drop in a new context.

In the same way that the cortico-hippocampal model can account for latent inhibition and context shift phenomena, it can similarly address results from a range of conditioning studies (Gluck & Myers 1993, 1996; Myers & Gluck 1994, 1996). It provides a computational instantiation of several prior qualitative theories that posited hippocampal region roles in context learning (Hirsh 1974), configural learning (Sutherland & Rudy 1989), and representational learning (Eichenbaum & Bunsey 1995).

Open Issues and Alternative Approaches

The most obvious limitation of the cortico-hippocampal model, like others in the same domain, is that it does not make any particular attempt to address the episodic memory deficits that are the most obvious feature of human hippocampal amnesia. This is the converse of the limitation of models that address episodic memory but not information processing in the hippocampal region.

Eventually, a complete model of hippocampal-region function will have to account for both these aspects of hippocampal-region damage. For now, though, these models should be judged on the basis of how well they account for the circumscribed set of data they attempt to address.

There are also several limitations of Gluck & Myers's cortico-hippocampal model. As a trial-level model, it cannot capture any of the intricacies of timing within a trial—such as the effects of varying stimulus scheduling, the latency of onset of the conditioned response, and so on. Other models (e.g. Schmajuk & DiCarlo 1990, 1992) do include real-time effects in their models, and they capture these aspects of animal learning. In the next section we consider in more detail another model of Schmajuk and colleagues that addresses a similar body of behavioral conditioning data.

A more general limitation of this entire class of models is the restricted degree of physiological realism they involve. The network architectures and learning algorithms are determined more by functional (behavioral) considerations than by biological properties. In fact, most of these models include properties that are clearly unrealistic, e.g. full or near-full connectivity between sets of nodes. Some attempts have been made to address this limitation. These are reviewed in the next section, which considers more recent attempts to take abstract theories of hippocampal region function and clarify more precisely the functional role of the different anatomical components of this region.

DISSOCIATING PARAHIPPOCAMPAL AND HIPPOCAMPAL CONTRIBUTIONS

Recent refinements in lesion techniques indicate that the extent of memory impairment often depends critically on exact lesion extent. This suggests that the different substructures of the hippocampal region have differentiable contributions to the processing of the region as a whole. However, the precise assignment of function to substructure, and the ways in which they interact, are as yet poorly understood. One example is the latent inhibition effect described earlier, in which prior unreinforced exposure to a stimulus retards later learning to respond to that stimulus (Lubow 1973). Latent inhibition is attenuated by broad hippocampal-region damage (Kaye & Pearce 1987, Solomon & Moore 1975) but not by damage strictly limited to the hippocampus and sparing entorhinal cortex (Honey & Good 1993, Reilly et al 1993). Similarly, odor discrimination reversal is impaired by hippocampal lesion but actually facilitated after entorhinal lesion (Otto et al 1991).

Although the representational theory of hippocampal function proposed by Gluck & Myers (1993) treated the hippocampal region as a single processing system, subsequent work by these researchers have suggested how their basic representational processes might be subdivided, and the subfunctions localized in different anatomical sites around the region (Myers et al 1995). In particular, Myers et al (1995) proposed that stimulus-stimulus redundancy compression could emerge from the anatomy and physiology of superficial entorhinal cortex.

Parahippocampal Function in Stimulus Compression and Clustering

The Myers et al model of entorhinal (and parahippocampal) function in learning is derived from an earlier physiologically realistic model of superficial piriform (olfactory) cortex by Ambros-Ingerson et al (1990), which argued that the anatomy and physiology of this cortical structure are sufficient to implement hierarchical clustering of odor inputs. In brief, Ambros-Ingerson et al proposed a competitive network model in which local recurrent inhibition silences all but the most strongly responding pyramidal cells. These so-called winning cells come to respond to a family or cluster of inputs with similar features. Recurrent feedback from the piriform cortex to olfactory bulb is also assumed to allow iterative responses to odors, from which successively finer-grained (hierarchical) classifications can be constructed. One aspect of this model is that, since similar inputs tend to be clustered to similar output responses, the network performs redundancy compression of exactly the sort previously proposed by Gluck & Myers (1993) to occur in the hippocampal region (Myers et al 1995). In particular, if two inputs co-occur, they will be treated as a single compound input. Later, if one of the inputs occurs alone, the network will tend to treat this as a degraded version of the compound input and assign it to the same cluster as the compound.

The piriform cortex and entorhinal cortex elide in rat, and their superficial layers are closely related anatomically and physiologically, suggesting the possibility of related functionality (Price 1973, van Hoesen & Pandya 1975, Woodhams et al 1993). Specifically, superficial entorhinal cortex contains pyramidal cells with sparse nontopographic connections with afferents in layer I (van Hoesen & Pandya 1975) with denser feedback connections to local inhibitory cells (Kohler 1986), and shows NMDA-dependent, theta-induced long-term potentiation (LTP) (de Curtis & Llinas 1993). Noting this similarity, Gluck & Granger (1993) suggested that entorhinal cortex could perform a similarity-based clustering operation similar to that proposed to occur in piriform cortex.

In sum, then, Myers et al (1995) have proposed that the entorhinal cortex would be sufficient to implement the redundancy compression aspect of the representational changes that Gluck & Myers (1993) ascribe to the hippocampal region as a whole (Myers et al 1995). A model implementing these proposed processes, and based on the physiologically and anatomically motivated model of Ambros-Ingerson et al (1990), is shown in Figure 8*A*. One difference between the piriform and entorhinal models is that the piriform model assumes repetitive sampling and input masking, based on recurrent connections from piriform cortex to olfactory bulb. Myers et al (1995) have not assumed this in the entorhinal model, and so it only performs a single-stage, similarity-based clustering or compression of its inputs. The resulting network is similar to the unsupervised, competitive-learning systems developed by Kohonen (1984), Rumelhart & Zipser (1985), Grossberg (1976), and others. A second important difference between the piriform and entorhinal cortices is that, while the piriform cortex is primarily an olfactory area, the entorhinal cortex receives input from a broad spectrum of polymodal cortices, as well as from the piriform cortex. Thus, Myers et al (1995) have suggested that while the piriform cortex might be sufficient to implement redundancy compression within the olfactory domain, the entorhinal cortex might be required to implement redundancy compression between stimuli from different modalities, or across the polymodal features of a single stimulus (Myers et al 1995).

This model can be compared with a lesion that selectively damages the hippocampus and dentate gyrus but that leaves intact the entorhinal cortex. As noted above, such lesions often produce different results from lesions of the entire hippocampal region. For example, such a restricted lesion does not disrupt latent inhibition, although as described above a larger lesion does (Honey & Good 1993, Reilly et al 1993). The selectively lesioned model produces the same effect (Figure 8*B*). The redundancy compression in the entorhinal network is sufficient to mediate latent inhibition. The model accounts for several other selective-lesion effects (Myers et al 1995), as well as makes specific novel predictions that other behaviors, which are interpreted as reflecting stimulus compression, are likely to depend more on the entorhinal cortex than on hippocampus proper, and so should survive such a localized lesion.

The idea that the entorhinal cortex is involved in stimulus compression also relates to a suggestion by Eichenbaum & Bunsey (1995) that the entorhinal cortex performs "fusion" of coincident or nearly coincident stimuli, based on the tendency of animals with selective hippocampal (but not entorhinal) damage to overcompress stimulus information.

This hypothesis regarding the selective contribution of entorhinal processing to hippocampal-region function assumes that the remaining subfunction of predictive differentiation could be implemented elsewhere in the hippocampal region. One possibility is that the dentate gyrus or hippocampus proper could perform this subfunction. This idea is consistent with several suggestions that the hippocampus is involved in predicting future events (such as US arrival) given current inputs (e.g. Gray 1985, Levy 1985, Lynch & Granger 1992, McNaughton & Nadel 1990, Treves & Rolls 1992).

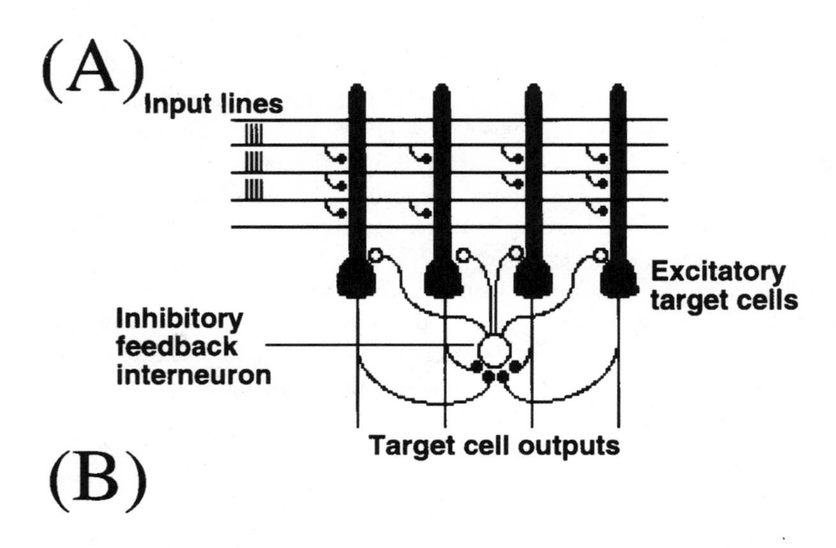

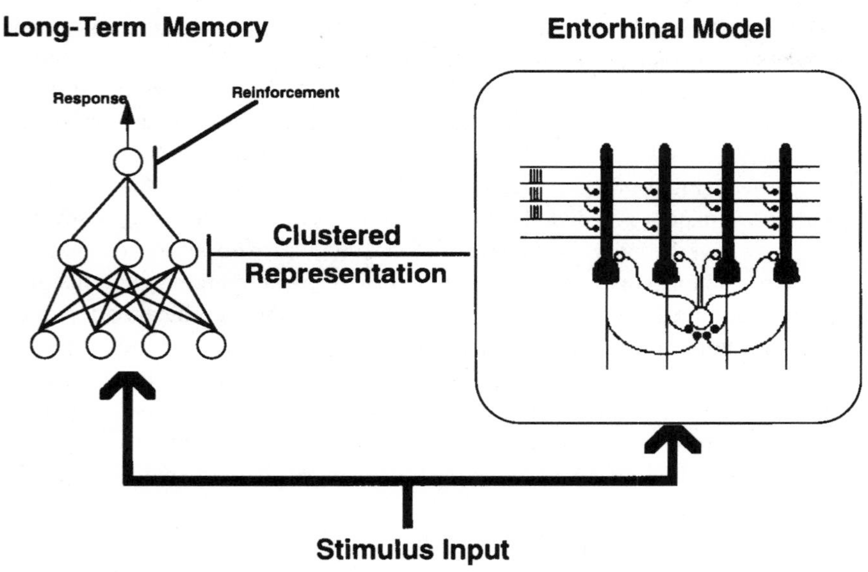

Figure 8 (*A*) In the entorhinal model, target cells are excited by sparse afferents, and in turn activate local inhibitory feedback interneurons. Feedback silences all but the most strongly activated target cells. Synaptic plasticity makes these "winning" target cells more likely to "win" in response to similar inputs in the future. The resulting network activity is constrained by stimulus-stimulus redundancy compression. (*B*) The H-lesioned model, in which an entorhinal cortex network provides new compressed representations to the internal layer of a long-term memory network. (Adapted from Myers et al 1995.)

Parahippocampal Function in Configural Associations

In an alternative approach to modeling entorhinal function, Schmajuk and Blair (Schmajuk 1994, Schmajuk & Blair 1993) have suggested the particular contribution of the entorhinal cortex to the Schmajuk-DiCarlo (Schmajuk & DiCarlo 1992) model of hippocampal-region function is stimulus competition, while the hippocampus proper is responsible for configural association. They therefore predict that localized hippocampal lesion, which does not otherwise damage entorhinal cortex, should eliminate the configural but not the stimulus competition function. Empirical data are somewhat consistent with this idea (see Schmajuk 1994), although further empirical studies are certainly indicated, as mentioned above in the context of testing our own model of entorhinal function. The stimulus competition function proposed by Schmajuk & Blair is quite distinct from the stimulus-stimulus clustering we have proposed as an entorhinal function. In fact, our entorhinal stimulus-stimulus clustering is probably more closely related to the configural function that Schmajuk & Blair assign not to the entorhinal cortex but to the hippocampus proper. Until such time as more empirical data become available, it may be difficult to provide a definitive discrimination between these two accounts. However, future experiments that address the selective role of the entorhinal cortex in stimulus competition and in stimulus-stimulus clustering are required to properly evaluate these two models.

In a more recent paper, Buhusi & Schmajuk (1996) presented a different model of hippocampal function in conditioning that attributes both attentional and configural mechanisms to specific components of the hippocampal region. Buhusi & Schmajuk proposed that the entorhinal and parahippocampal cortices have a unique role in error-correction in which expected reinforcement is compared with actual reinforcement. In contrast, we have argued that these same overlying cortices are essential for stimulus-stimulus redundancy compression. This is consistent with studies showing that latent inhibition, a result Myers et al (1995) have interpreted as being mediated by stimulus compression, is spared after hippocampal lesions that do not extend to entorhinal cortex (Honey & Good 1993, Reilly et al 1993).

INCORPORATING SUBCORTICAL CHOLINERGIC MODULATION

The models of episodic memory and consolidation reviewed in the section on "Autoassociative Models of CA3 and Episodic Memory" are fairly abstract in that there is no particular mapping of nodes and connections to neurons and synapses. As Hasselmo and colleagues have shown, however, it is possible to construct autoassociative models that are much more physiologically realistic.

In this vein, Hasselmo & Schnell (1994; see also Hasselmo et al 1995) have developed a model of laminar connections in the hippocampus to study the possible function of the strong cholinergic input from the medial septum. These authors have suggested that the function of this cholinergic input is to allow the hippocampus to switch between pattern storage and pattern retrieval states. When a new pattern is presented to an autoassociative network as a forcing input, it will activate some of the nodes in the network. Activation from these nodes will travel through the recurrent feedback connections to activate other nodes, and after several iterations, this runaway excitation may result in the entire network becoming active, rather than just those nodes associated with the pattern to be stored. To avoid this runaway excitation, an autoassociative network is usually assumed to operate in two modes, a storage mode during which forcing inputs are present but feedback collaterals are suppressed, and a recall mode, during which there is no forcing input, and recurrent collaterals are allowed to activate nodes. In the context of a network model, it is easy to define two such disparate states.

If hippocampal field CA3 is assumed to operate as an autoassociative network, with mossy fiber afferents providing the forcing inputs, there must be a physiological mechanism to suppress activity on the recurrent collaterals during storage. Hasselmo (Hasselmo 1995, Hasselmo & Schnell 1994) proposed that the septal cholinergic input can provide this switch. Briefly, he suggested that cholinergic input suppresses the recurrent collaterals to allow storage of the new pattern without runaway excitation. When cholinergic input is absent, and entorhinal inputs activate a few CA3 cells, feedback connections recruit more cells to activity, until a stored pattern is recalled and instated on the CA3 nodes. Hasselmo (Hasselmo 1995, Hasselmo & Schnell 1994) further proposed a scheme whereby CA3 can self-regulate this cholinergic input, allowing the hippocampus to recognize when a new pattern should be stored, and signal the septum to send the cholinergic input that allows storage to proceed. In model simulations, such self-regulated suppression of recurrent collaterals does suffice to allow switching between storage and recall states in an autoassociative network (Hasselmo & Schnell 1994). In empirical support of this hypothesis, Hasselmo et al (1995) have shown that a cholinergic agonist carbachol does suppress activity of CA3 cells in slice more in the stratum radiatum, where the recurrent collaterals afferent CA3 dendrites, than in the stratum lucidum, where the mossy fibers afferent CA3 dendrites. Further support comes from findings of anterograde amnesia after medial septal lesion (Berry & Thompson 1979) or pharmacological disruption through anticholinergic drugs such as scopolamine (Solomon et al 1983), consistent with Hasselmo's prediction that cholinergic input is necessary for storage of new information in the hippocampus (Hasselmo 1995, Hasselmo & Schnell 1994).

In the next subsection, we discuss how this cholinergic model of Hasselmo can be related to independently developed models of hippocampal function in classical conditioning (Myers et al 1996) reviewed above.

Septohippocampal Cholinergic Modulation in Conditioning

Myers and Gluck, in collaboration with Hasselmo and Solomon, have recently shown how a simplified version of Hasselmo's cholinergic hypothesis can be instantiated within the Gluck & Myers model, to provide an interpretation of Solomon's data on the behavioral consequences of anticholinergic drugs on classical conditioning. In brief, the integrated model assumes that the tendency of the hippocampal-region network to store new information, as opposed to simply processing it and recalling old information, is determined by the hippocampal-region network's learning rate (Myers et al 1996). Disrupting septal input can therefore be approximated within the Gluck & Myers model by lowering this learning rate—although not the rate at which this information is transferred to the cortical network, nor the rate at which cortical associations develop. The consequence of this depressed hippocampal learning rate is to prolong the initial nonresponding phase before onset of the initial conditioned responses (Figure 8*B*), much as is seen in the experimental data (Figure 8*A*). This computational model of cholinergic function in conditioning is broadly consistent with an earlier suggestion by Thompson & Berry (1979), who argued that the medial-septum is involved primarily in early attentional stages of learning rather than subsequent associational processes.

With this interpretation of cholinergic function, Myers et al (1996) showed that the Gluck & Myers model correctly expects that hippocampal disruption retards conditioning even though outright hippocampal lesion does not. This apparent paradox has previously been noted in the animal literature (Solomon et al 1983), and the model provides insight into why it might be so. Further, the model predicts that if lowering hippocampal learning rates retards learning, increasing learning rates may speed it (Myers et al 1996). This is consistent with data showing that cholinergic agonists can improve learning in subjects with abnormally reduced levels of brain acetylcholine (for a review, see Myers et al 1996). However, in the model, increasing hippocampal learning rates beyond some optimal level actually results in degraded learning, as the network becomes unstable (Myers et al 1996). Therefore, the model predicts that cholinergic therapy should only be transiently effective in normal subjects. In fact, this is the case: While cholinergic agonists at moderate doses tend to improve learning, higher doses may either result in no facilitation or actually impair learning (for a review, see Myers et al 1996). The model therefore provides an account for this empirical phenomenon, which has been problematic in the clinical pharmacology literature.

An alternative approach to modeling septohippocampal cholinergic pathways is the model of Buhusi & Schmajuk (1996). These authors interpret the septohippocampal cholinergic pathways as providing an error-signal that drives learning. In contrast, Myers et al (1996) argued that these pathways can be functionally interpreted as providing modulation of learning rates, which builds upon similar arguments by Hasselmo (see Hasselmo et al 1996). Despite different functional interpretations of the medial septal inputs, both the Buhusi & Schmajuk (1996) and the Myers et al (1996) models correctly expect that cholinergic antagonists (such as scopolamine) should impair acquisition, but not latent inhibition. Buhusi & Schmajuk have not, however, addressed the detailed aspects of learning curves that are analyzed by Myers et al (1996).

SUMMARY AND GENERAL DISCUSSION

We have reviewed several computational models of hippocampal function in learning and memory, concentrating on those that make strongest contact with psychological issues and data from behavioral experiments. Many of these models can be traced to the influential early model of Marr (1971) that, in turn, built upon Hebb's (1949) ideas on how associations are acquired between groups of cell assemblies in the brain. The basic network architecture described by Marr's theory is known as an autoassociator that learns to associate all components of an input pattern with all other components of the same pattern.

Many subsequent researchers have used Marr's basic framework for modeling episodic or event memories in the hippocampus, especially within hippocampal field CA3 that shares many of the basic connectivity requirements for an autoassociator (Hasselmo et al 1996, McNaughton & Nadel 1990, McNaughton & Morris 1987, Rolls 1989). These models focus on the ability of the hippocampal region to perform fast, temporary storage, which suggests that this underlies the hippocampal region's role in episodic memory formation. This is consistent with the neuropsychological data showing that episodic memory impairments are the most obvious behavioral effects in human amnesia following hippocampal region damage. Variations on the hippocampal autoassociator model have been developed to explain sequential learning (for reviews, see Granger et al 1996, Levy 1996, Liaw & Berger 1996), spatial navigation (Burgess et al 1994, Levy 1989, McNaughton & Morris 1987, McNaughton & Nadel 1990, Muller 1987, Muller & Stead 1996, Recce & Harris 1996, Sharp et al 1996, Sharp 1991), and the consolidation of episodic memories (Alvarez & Squire 1994, McClelland & Goddard 1996, Murre 1996, O'Reilly & McClelland 1994, Treves & Rolls 1992).

Another class of hippocampal models have focused on hippocampal involvement in incrementally learned associative habits, such as classical condi-

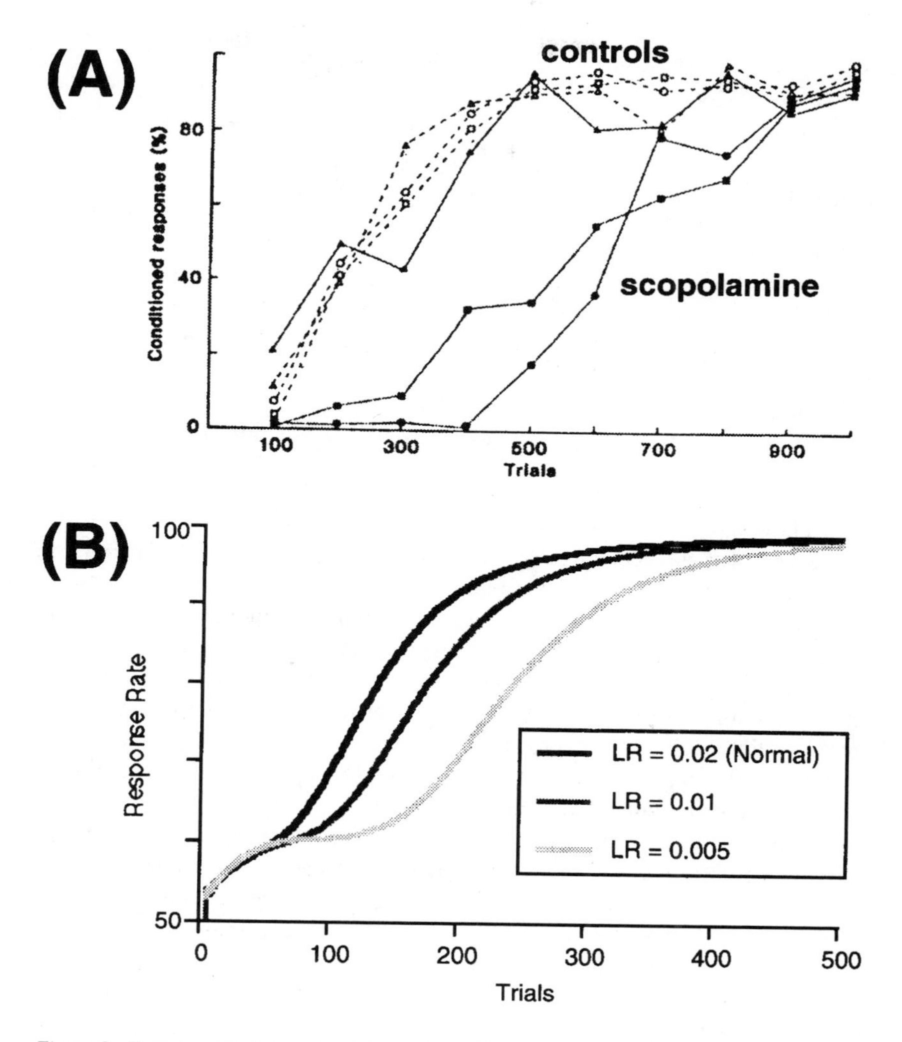

Figure 9 Experimental data and modeling of the effects of the anticholinergic drug scopolamine on acquisition of a conditioned eyeblink response. (*A*) Systemic application of scopolamine (Solomon et al 1983) in which it is shown that the effect of scopolamine is to delay the onset of conditioning, rather than preventing it. (*B*) Learning curves for three different hippocampal learning rates in the Myers et al (1996) model showing how lowered learning rates shift the acquisition curve to the right, delaying the onset of learning, much as seen in Figure 9*A*.

tioning or probabilistic pattern classification. Many recent qualitative theories and several computational models have focused on possible information processing roles for the hippocampal region that are most evident from studying complex training procedure in incrementally acquired learning (Buhusi & Schmajuk 1996; Eichenbaum et al 1992b; Gluck & Myers 1993, 1995, 1996; Hirsh 1974; Moore & Stickney 1980; Schmajuk & DiCarlo 1992; Sutherland & Rudy 1989). More recent modeling efforts have attempted to make closer contact with the underlying anatomy and physiology. This includes models of parahippocampal function (Myers et al 1995, Schmajuk & Blair 1993) and models of the subcortical influences of cholinergic modulation (Buhusi & Schmajuk 1996, Myers et al 1996).

In reviewing these psychobiological models of hippocampal function in learning and memory, three major themes have emerged. First, we have seen how computational models can provide the "glue" to bind together analysis and data at multiple levels of analysis including cellular, physiological, anatomical, and behavioral levels. In particular, we noted how some models are developed in a top-down fashion, beginning with detailed behavioral analyses and then seeking a mapping to underlying biological substrates. Other models are developed in a more bottom-up fashion, beginning with biological details and, via computational simulations, seeking to identify emergent functional properties of these substrates (for further discussion of these distinctions in learning models, see Gluck & Granger 1993).

A second theme that emerged was the importance of models as tools to integrate data from both animal and human studies of hippocampal function in learning and memory. Although these two bodies of research have often been quite separate and disconnected, it seems clear that ultimately they must converge so that each body of literature and theory can inform the other, which will hopefully lead to a more general and broadly applicable understanding of the hippocampal region in all species.

Finally, a third theme that emerged from reviewing these models is the importance of relating current computational models to earlier traditions in memory research, especially the many earlier psychological models that capture important behavioral principles of memory. In drawing these connections between current models, and earlier qualitative theories in psychology and neurobiology, one can see to what extent the models represent cumulative progress.

All the models reviewed here represent preliminary attempts to incorporate both biological data and behavioral analysis within formal computationally defined theories. Crude approximations at best, the value of these models will become most clearly apparent if they lead to important new empirical studies that will inform and constrain future generations of models and theories.

ACKNOWLEDGMENTS

For their helpful comments and suggestions on early drafts of this manuscript, we are grateful to Gyorgy Buzsaki, Michael Hasselmo, Brandon Ermita, Kari

Hoffman, and Todd Allen. This research was supported by grants to MAG from the Office of Naval Research through the Young Investigator program and by grant N00014-88-K-0112, as well as a grant from the McDonnell-Pew Program in Cognitive Neuroscience.

Literature Cited

Alvarez P, Squire L. 1994. Memory consolidation and the medial temporal lobe: a simple network model. *Proc. Natl. Acad. Sci. USA* 91:7041–45

Ambros-Ingerson J, Granger R, Lynch G. 1990. Simulation of paleocortex performs hierarchical clustering. *Science* 247:1344–48

Anderson J. 1977. Neural models with cognitive implications. In *Basic Processes in Reading: Perception and Comprehension,* ed. D LaBerge, S Samuels, pp. 27–90. Hillsdale, NJ: Erlbaum

Berry S, Thompson R. 1979. Medial septal lesions retard classical conditioning of the nictitating membrane response in rabbits. *Science* 205:209–11

Bliss T, Lomo T. 1973. Long-lasting potentiation of synaptic transmission in the dentate area of the anaesthetized rabbit following stimulation of the perforant path. *J. Physiol.* 232:331–56

Buhusi C, Schmajuk N. 1996. Attention, configuration, and hippocampal function. *Hippocampus.* In press

Burgess N, Recce M, O'Keefe J. 1994. A model of hippocampal function. *Neural Networks* 17:1065–81

Buzsaki G. 1989. Two-stage model of memory-trace formation: a role for "noisy" brain states. *Neuroscience* 31(3):551–70

Cohen N. 1984. Preserved learning capacity in amnesia: evidence for multiple learning systems. See Squire & Butters 1984, pp. 83–103

Crick F, Mitchison G. 1983. The function of dream sleep. *Nature* 304:111–14

Daum I, Channon S, Canavan A. 1989. Classical conditioning in patients with severe memory problems. *J. Neurol. Neurosurg. Psychiatry* 52:47–51

de Curtis M, Llinas R. 1993. Entorhinal cortex long-term potentiation evoked by theta-patterned stimulation of associative fibers in the isolated in vitro guinea pig brain. *Brain Res.* 600:327–30

de Leon M, Golomb J, George A, Convit A, Rusinek H, et al. 1993. Hippocampal formation atrophy: prognostic significance for Alzheimer's disease. In *Alzheimer's Disease: Advances in Clinical and Brain Research,* ed. B Corain, K lqbal, M Nicolini, B Winblad, H Wisniewski, P Zatta, pp. 35–46. New York: Wiley

Eichenbaum H. 1992. The hippocampal system and declarative memory in animals. *J. Cogn. Neurosci.* 4(3):217–31

Eichenbaum H, Bunsey M. 1995. On the binding of associations in memory: clues from studies on the role of the hippocampal region in paired associate learning. *Curr. Dir. Psychol. Sci.* 4:19–23

Eichenbaum H, Cohen NJ, Otto T, Wible C. 1992. Memory representation in the hippocampus: functional domain and functional organization. In *Memory Organization and Locus of Change,* ed. LR Squire, G Lynch, NM Weinberger, JL McGaugh, pp. 163–204. Oxford: Oxford Univ. Press

Eichenbaum H, Fagan A, Mathews P, Cohen NJ. 1988. Hippocampal system dysfunction and odor discrimination learning in rats: impairment or facilitation depending on representational demands. *Behav. Neurosci.* 102(3):331–39

Gabrieli J, McGlinchey-Berroth R, Carrillo M, Gluck M, Cermack L, Disterhoft J. 1995. Intact delay-eyeblink classical conditioning in amnesia. *Behav. Neurosci.* 109(5): 819–27

Gluck MA, Granger R. 1993. Computational models of the neural bases of learning and memory. *Annu. Rev. Neurosci.* 16:667–706

Gluck MA, Myers C. 1993. Hippocampal mediation of stimulus representation: a computational theory. *Hippocampus* 3:491–516

Gluck M, Myers C. 1995. Representation and association in memory: a neurocomputational view of hippocampal function. *Curr. Dir. Psychol. Sci.* 4(1):23–29

Gluck MA, Myers CE. 1996. Integrating behavioral and physiological models of hippocampal function. *Hippocampus.* (Special Issue on Hippocampal Computation & Memory; M Gluck, Guest Editor)

Granger R, Wiebe S, Taketani M, Lynch G. 1996. Distinct memory circuits comprising the hippocampal region. *Hippocampus.* In press

Gray JA. 1985. Memory buffer and comparator can share the same circuitry. *Behav. Brain Sci.* 8(3):501

Grossberg S. 1976. Adaptive pattern classification and recoding: part I. *Biol. Cybern.* 23: 121–34

Haist F, Musen G, Squire LR. 1991. Intact priming of words and nonwords in amnesia. *Psychobiology* 19(4):275–85

Hall G, Honey RC. 1989. Contextual effects in conditioning, latent inhibition, and habituation: associative and retrieval functions of contextual cues. *J. Exp. Psychol.: Anim. Behav. Process.* 15(3):232–41

Hasselmo ME. 1995. Neuromodulation and cortical function: modeling the physiological basis of behavior. *Behav. Brain Res.* 67:1–27

Hasselmo ME, Schnell E. 1994. Laminar selectivity of the cholinergic suppression of synaptic transmission in rat hippocampal region CAl: computational modeling and brain slice physiology. *J. Neurosci.* 14: 3898–914

Hasselmo ME, Schnell E, Barkai E. 1995. Dynamics of learning and recall at excitatory recurrent synapses and cholinergic modulation in rat hippocampal region CA3. *J. Neurosci.* 15:5249–62

Hasselmo ME, Wyble B, Wallenstein G. 1996. Encoding and retrieval of episodic memories: role of cholinergic and GABAergic modulation in the hippocampus. *Hippocampus.* In press

Hebb DO. 1949. *The Organization of Behavior.* New York: Wiley

Hetherington P. 1990. *The sequential learning problem in connectionist networks.* MS thesis. McGill Univ.

Hinton G. 1989. Connectionist learning procedures. *Artif. Intell.* 40:185–234

Hirsh R. 1974. The hippocampus and contextual retrieval of information from memory: a theory. *Behav. Biol.* 12:421–44

Honey RC, Good M. 1993. Selective hippocampal lesions abolish the contextual specificity of latent inhibition and conditioning. *Behav. Neurosci.* 107(1):23–33

Hopfield JJ. 1982. Neural networks and physical systems with emergent collective computational abilities. *Proc. Natl. Acad. Sci. USA* 79:2554–58

Kaye H, Pearce J. 1987. Hippocampal lesions attenuate latent inhibition and the decline of the orienting response in rats. *Q. J. Exp. Psychol.* 39:107–25

Kelso SR, Ganong AH, Brown TH. 1986. Hebbian synapses in hippocampus. *Proc. Natl. Acad. Sci. USA* 83:5326–30

Kim JJ, Fanselow MS. 1992. Modality-specific retrograde amnesia of fear. *Science* 256: 676

Knowlton B, Squire L, Gluck M. 1994. Probabilistic classification learning in amnesia. *Learn. Mem.* 1:106–20

Kohler C. 1986. Intrinsic connections of the retrohippocampal region in the rat brain. II. The medial entorhinal area. *J. Comp. Neurol.* 246:149–69

Kohonen T. 1984. *Self-Organization and Associative Memory.* New York: Springer-Verlag

Levy W. 1985. An information/computation theory of hippocampal function. *Soc. Neurosci. Abstr.* 11:493

Levy WB. 1989. A computational approach to hippocampal function. In *Psychology of Learning and Motivation,* R Hawkins, G Bower, pp. 243–304. London: Academic

Levy WB. 1996. A sequence predicting CA3 is a flexible associator that learns and uses context to solve hippocampal-like tasks. *Hippocampus.* In press

Levy WB, Brassel SE, Moore SD. 1983. Partial quantification of the associative synaptic learning rule of the dentate gyrus. *Neuroscience* 8(4):799–808

Levy W, Wu X, Baxter R. 1995. Unifications of hippocampal function via computational/encoding considerations. *Int. J. Neur. Syst.* 6(Suppl.): 71–80

Liaw J, Berger TW. 1996. Dynamic synapses: dancing to the neural tune. *Hippocampus.* In press

Lubow R. 1973. Latent inhibition. *Psychol. Bull.* 79:398–407

Lynch G, Granger R. 1992. Variations in synaptic plasticity and types of memory in corticohippocampal networks. *J. Cogn. Neurosci.* 4(3):189–99

Marr D. 1971. Simple memory: a theory for archicortex. *Proc. R. Soc. London Ser. B* 841:262;23–81

McClelland J, Goddard N. 1996. Considerations arising from a complementary learning systems perspective on hippocampus and neocortex. *Hippocampus.* In press

McClelland J, McNaughton B, O'Reilly R. 1994. *Why we have complementary learning systems in the hippocampus and neocortex: Insights from the successes and failures of connectionist models of learning and memory.* No. Tech. Rep. PDP.CNS.94.1. Carnegie Mellon Univ., Pittsburgh

McCulloch WS, Pitts W. 1943. A logical calculus of the ideas immanent in neural nets. *Bull. Math. Biographys.* 5:115–37

McNaughton B. 1989. Neuronal mechanisms for spatial computation and information storage. *Neural Connections, Mental Computations,* ed. L Nadel, L Cover, P Culicover, R Harnish, pp. 285–350. Cambridge, MA: MIT Press

McNaughton BL. 1991. Associative pattern completion in hippocampal circuits: new evidence and new questions. *Brain Res. Rev.* 16:202–4

McNaughton BL, Morris RGM. 1987. Hippocampal synaptic enhancement and information storage. *Trends Neurosci.* 10(10): 408–15

McNaughton BL, Nadel L. 1990. Hebb-Marr networks and the neurobiological representation of action in space. *Neuroscience and Connectionist Theory,* ed. M Gluck, D Rumelhart, pp. 1–63. Hillsdale, NJ: Erlbaum

Mishkin M. 1982. A memory system in the monkey. *Philos. Trans. R. Soc. London* 298:85–92

Moore J, Stickney K. 1980. Formation of attentional-associative networks in real time: role of the hippocampus and implications for conditioning. *Physiol. Psychol.* 8(2): 207–17

Moyer JR, Deyo RA, Disterhoft JF. 1990. Hippocampectomy disrupts trace eye-blink conditioning in rabbits. *Behav. Neurosci.* 104(2):243–52

Muller RU, Kubie JL, Ranck JB. 1987. Spatial firing patterns of hippocampal complex-spike cells in a fixed environment. *J. Neurosci.* 7(7):1935–50

Muller R, Stead M. 1996. Hippocampal place cells connected by hebbian synapses can solve spatial problems. *Hippocampus.* In press

Murre J. 1996. Models of amnesia. *Hippocampus.* In press

Myers C, Gluck M. 1994. Context, conditioning and hippocampal re-representation. *Behav. Neurosci.* 108(5):835–47

Myers CE, Gluck MA. 1996. Cortico-hippocampal representations in simultaneous odor discrimination: a computational interpretation of Eichenbaum, Mathews, and Cohen (1989). *Behav. Neurosci.* 110(4): 1–22

Myers CE, Gluck MA, Granger R. 1995. Dissociation of hippocampal and entorhinal function in associative learning: a computational approach. *Psychobiology* 23(2): 116–38

Myers CM, Ermita BR, Harris K, Hasselmo M, Solomon P, Gluck MA. 1996. A computational model of cholinergic disruption of septo-hippocampal activity in classical eyeblink conditioning. *Neurobiol. Learn. Mem.* 66:51–66

O'Keefe J, Nadel L. 1978. *The Hippocampus as a Cognitive Map.* Oxford: Clarendon

O'Reilly R, McClelland J. 1994. Hippocampal conjunctive encoding, storage, and recall: avoiding a tradeoff. *Hippocampus* 4:661–82

Otto T, Schottler F, Staubli U, Eichenbaum H, Lynch G. 1991. Hippocampus and olfactory discrimination learning: effects of entorhinal cortex lesions on olfactory learning and memory in a successive-cue, go-no-go task. *Behav. Neurosci.* 105(1):111–19

Penick S, Solomon R. 1991. Hippocampus context and conditioning. *Behav. Neurosci.* 105(5):611–17

Port R, Romano A, Patterson M. 1986. Stimulus duration discrimination in the rabbit: effects of hippocampectomy on discrimination and reversal learning. *Physiol. Psychol.* 4(3–4):124–29

Prepscius C, Levy W. 1994. Sequence prediction and cognitive mapping by a biologically plausible neural network. In *Proc. World Congr. Neur. Netw.* 4:164, 5:169. San Diego: INNS Press

Price J. 1973. An autoradiographic study of complementary laminar patterns of termination of afferent fiber to the olfactory cortex. *J. Compar. Neurol.* 150:87–108

Recce M, Harris K. 1996. Memory for places: a navigation model in support of Marr's theory of hippocampal function. *Hippocampus.* In press

Reilly S, Harley C, Revusky S. 1993. Ibotenate lesions of the hippocampus enhance latent inhibition in conditioned taste aversion and increase resistance to extinction in conditioned taste preference. *Behav. Neurosci.* 107(6):996–1004

Ribot T. 1882. *The Diseases of Memory.* New York: Appleton

Rolls E. 1989. The representation and storage of information in neural networks in the primate cerebral cortex and hippocampus. In *The Computing Neuron,* ed. R Durbin, C Miall, G Mitchison, pp. 125–59. Wokingham, UK: Addison-Wesley

Rosenblatt F. 1962. *Principles of Neurodynamics.* New York: Spartan

Rudy JW, Sutherland RJ. 1989. The hippocampal formation is necessary for rats to learn and remember configural discriminations. *Behav. Brain Res.* 34:97–109

Rudy JW, Sutherland RJ. 1995. Configural association theory and the hippocampal formation: an appraisal and reconfiguration. *Hippocampus* 5:375–89

Rumelhart D, Zipser D. 1985. Feature discovery by competitive learning. *Cogn. Sci.* 9: 75–112

Schmajuk NA. 1994. Stimulus configuration, classical conditioning, and spatial learning: role of the hippocampus. In *Proc. World Congr. Neur. Netw.* 2:723-28. San Diego: INNS

Schmajuk NA, Blair HT. 1993. Stimulus configuration, spatial learning and hippocampal function. *Behav. Brain Res.* 59: 103–17

Schmajuk NA, DiCarlo JJ. 1990. *Backpropagation, classical conditioning and hippocampal function.* Tech. Rep., Northwestern Univ.

Schmajuk NA, DiCarlo JJ. 1991. A neural network approach to hippocampal function in classical conditioning. *Behav. Neurosci.* 105:82–110

Schmajuk NA, DiCarlo JJ. 1992. Stimulus configuration, classical conditioning and hippocampal function. *Psychol. Rev.* 99: 268–305

Schmaltz LW, Theios J. 1972. Acquisition and extinction of a classically conditioned response in hippocampectomized rabbits (*Oryctolagus cuniculus*). *J. Comp. Physiol. Psychol.* 79:328–33

Sharp P. 1991. Computer simulation of hippocampal place cells. *Psychobiology* 19(2): 103–15

Sharp P, Blair H, Brown M. 1996. Neural network modeling of the hippocampal formation spatial signals, and their possible role in navigation: a modular approach. *Hippocampus.* In press

Solomon PR, Moore J. 1975. Latent inhibition and stimulus generalization of the classically conditioned nictitating membrane response in rabbits (*Oryctolagus cuniculus*) following dorsal hippocampal ablation. *J. Comp. Physiol. Psychol.* 89:1192–203

Solomon PR, Solomon SD, Van der Schaaf E, Perry HE. 1983. Altered activity in the hippocampus is more detrimental to classical conditioning than removing the structure. *Science* 220:329–31

Squire L. 1987. *Memory and Brain.* New York: Oxford Univ. Press

Squire L, Butters N, eds. 1984. *Neuropsychol. Mem.* New York: Guilford

Squire LR, Alvarez P. 1995. Retrograde amnesia and memory consolidation: a neurobiological perspective. *Curr. Opin. Neurobiol.* 5:169–77

Squire LR, Cohen N. 1979. Memory and amnesia: resistance to disruption develops for years after learning. *Behav. Neur. Biol.* 25: 118

Sutherland R, Rudy J. 1989. Configural association theory: the role of the hippocampal formation in learning, memory and amnesia. *Psychobiology* 17(2):129–44

Teyler T, DiScenna P. 1986. The hippocampal memory indexing theory. *Behav. Neurosci.* 100(2):147–54

Treves A, Rolls E. 1992. Computational constraints suggest the need for two distinct input systems to the hippocampal CA3 network. *Hippocampus* 2(2):189–200

van Hoesen G, Pandya D. 1975. Some connections of the entorhinal (area 28) and perirhinal (area 35) cortices of the rhesus monkey. I. Temporal lobe afferents. *Brain Res.* 95:1–24

Volpe BT, Hirst W. 1983. Amnesia following the rupture and repair of an anterior communicating artery aneurysm. *J. Neurol. Neurosurg. Psychiatry.* 46:704–9

Weiskrantz L, Warrington EK. 1979. Conditioning in amnesic patients. *Neuropsychologia* 17:187–94

Wickelgren W. 1979. Chunking and consolidation: a theoretical synthesis of semantic networks, configuring in conditioning, S-R versus cognitive learning, normal forgetting, the amnesic syndrome, and the hippocampal arousal system. *Psychol. Rev.* 86(1):44–60

Willshaw D, Buckingham J. 1990. An assessment of Marr's theory of the hippocampus as a temporary memory store. *Philos. Trans. R. Soc. London Ser. B* 329:205–15

Wilson MA, McNaughton BA. 1994. Reactivation of hippocampal ensemble memories during sleep. *Science* 265:676–79

Woodhams PLL, Celio MR, Ulfig N, Witter MP. 1993. Morphological and functional correlates of borders in the entorhinal cortex and hippocampus. *Hippocampus* 3: 313–11

Woodruff-Pak D. 1993. Eyeblink classical conditioning in HM: delay and trace paradigms. *Behav. Neurosci.* 107(6):911–25

Zola-Morgan, Squire LR. 1993. Neuroanatomy of memory. *Annu. Rev. Neurosci.* 16:547–63

Annu. Rev. Psychol. 1997. 48:515–46

ORGANIZATIONAL BEHAVIOR IN THE NEW ORGANIZATIONAL ERA

Denise M. Rousseau

Heinz School of Public Policy and Management and Graduate School of Industrial Administration, Carnegie Mellon University, Pittsburgh, Pennsylvania 15213

KEY WORDS: employment relations, performance paradox, organizational change, organizational learning, organizing, self-management

ABSTRACT

Changes in contemporary firms and their competitive environments translate into a new focus in organizational research. This chapter reviews organizational behavior research reflecting the shift from corporatist organizations to organizing. Key research themes include emerging employment relations, managing the performance paradox, goal setting and self-management, discontinuous information processing, organization learning, organizational change and individual transitions, and the implications of change for work-nonwork relations. Research into organizing is building upon and extending many of the field's traditional concepts. This chapter suggests that some assumptions of organizational behavior research are being superseded by those more responsive to the new organizational era.

This chapter is dedicated to Herbert Simon on the occasion of his eightieth birthday.

CONTENTS

0084-6570/97/0201-0515$08.00

INTRODUCTION

Contemporary organizations are changing, and the field of organizational behavior is changing with them. This chapter describes the shifts organizational research manifests as firms transition to a new era of flexible, lateral forms of organizing (Davis 1987, Miles & Creed 1995). It seeks answers to two questions. First, how are core features of organizational research influenced by the changes contemporary organizations are undergoing? Second, what new dynamics and features are emerging as important organizational research issues?

The central problems in organizational behavior are influenced by changes in organizations themselves (Barley & Kunda 1992, Goodman & Whetten 1995). Although *Annual Review of Psychology* (*ARP*) authors often have reported the durability of such traditional categories as work motivation and performance, absenteeism and turnover, climate and culture, and groups and leadership (e.g. O'Reilly 1991), other recent commentaries report more substantial shifts. The time frame used to review a body of research is probably the greatest determinant of whether we observe change or stability. For example, Barley & Kunda's (1992) investigation of trends in managerial thought ranged from the 1870s to the present and reported alternating cycles of rational (e.g. scientific management) and normative (e.g. human relations) thinking among managers and scholars predicated on the degree of expansion or contraction in the economy of the time. From their starting point in the 1950s, Goodman & Whetten (1995) noted an adaptive quality in the field's work that shifts attention toward particular applied problems firms face within a given decade: Organizational development was a theme in the 1950s and 1960s, and organizational decline and interorganizational relations were themes in the 1980s and 1990s. In the *ARP,* the historic reach of chapters typically centers around the intervening years since a subject's last review, a practice that can highlight stability and mask trends.

Several previous *ARP* reviewers have characterized the field as "moribund" (O'Reilly 1991) or "fallow" (Mowday & Sutton 1993), concluding pessimistically that neither innovation nor progress was evident. However, both the time frame of a review and the categories reviewers focus on shape how dynamic or stable the field appears. I conducted a content analysis of *ARP* chapters (described in the Appendix of this chapter) to determine the field's key content areas and their stability over time. That analysis provides evidence of both change and stability in the field's major topics. It suggests that though a stable core of topics reappear—focusing on organizational and individual performance, motivation, and worker responses—the correlation of categories over time is moderate, with issues emerging and receding with the field's advances and shifts in the problems organizations face. A trend toward increased specialization is evident, which may make overall progress in the field difficult to gauge. With this in mind, the present chapter focuses on research particularly responsive to contemporary organizational changes. In contrast with the conclusions of earlier reviewers, I show that there is cause for optimism about the progress being made in organizational research.

A NEW ERA IN ORGANIZATIONAL RESEARCH

This review is predicated on the premise that the meaning of organization is changing. The term organization has two principal definitions. "The act or process of organizing" is the longest established meaning. The second refers to "a body of persons organized for some end or work," or alternatively "the administrative personnel or apparatus of a business" (Merriam-Webster Inc. 1989). As Drucker (1994) noted, the second definition—"the" organization as an entity—has been widely used only since the 1950s, which is concurrent with the era of the industrial state. This second definition has been operative in organizational research. Now, however, there is evidence that organizational behavior researchers are reconnecting with the more traditional meaning of organization as process, given the increasing attention to group-level—particularly team-level—phenomena, social networks, managerial cognition and information processing, and entrepreneurship (e.g. Arthur & Rousseau 1996, Drazin & Sandelands 1992, Snow et al 1992, Weick 1996). In his *ARP* chapter, Wilpert (1995) described the related "social construction of organizations" perspective as a respected tradition in European research. However, more is going on here than just a shift in epistemological assumptions.

Increasing interest in social construction occurs at a time when firms and work roles themselves have an emergent quality in response to an era of upheaval and transition. Changes in several institutional sectors are influencing firms (Davis 1987, Handy 1989): The Reagan Era's conservative approach to antitrust laws opened up a set of previously illegal interorganizational relationships; global competition has heightened; information technology has exploded in the manufacturing and service sectors; distressed educational institutions are struggling to meet new skill demands; and escalating pressures coupled with lagging resources stress families and other social institutions caught in the transition. These institutional forces often operate quite differently across societies and can yield distinct local variations in firms (Rousseau & Tinsley 1996). In most industrialized societies, institutional forces are manifesting themselves in several related organizational changes: the movement to small-firm employment in the United States (Small Business Association

1992), the United Kingdom (Storey 1994), and elsewhere (Castells 1992); reliance on interfirm networks to substitute for corporate expansion, one product of which is outsourcing work among firms (Bettis et al 1992); new and more differentiated employment relations [e.g. core and peripheral part-time workers and independent contractors, guest workers such as technical-support people employed by a vendor but working inside a client firm (Handy 1989)]; and new forms of interdependence among workers and work groups, which in turn link rising performance standards with the concurrent assertion of the interests of many stakeholders, such as customers, workers, and stockholders (Davis 1987). Inevitably, transition costs occur, for people, firms, and society (Mirvis & Hall 1994, Perrow 1996).

The shift from organization to organizing translates into activities that were once predominately repetitive becoming predominately novel, networks formerly based on roles now forming around knowledge, careers once firm-based now depending more on personal resources, and work structures once rule-centered now constructed by the people doing the work (cf Drazin & Sandelands 1992, Manz 1992). The disappearance of old work structures along with expansion of small-firm employment and the demise of hierarchical advancement—particularly the decline in middle-management posts and the concomitant rise of professional and technical jobs—removes cues provided to people from traditional internal labor markets and career paths. The shift from managerial prerogatives to self-management removes a good deal of formal control over work. With the erosion of traditional external guides for behavior, internally generated guides are needed to operate within and around the more fluid boundaries of firms, interfirm networks, and work groups. With fewer external guides for work, greater value is placed on improvisation and learning (Weick 1996).

RESEARCH THEMES REGARDING ORGANIZING

Shifting to more flexible ways of organizing work and employment introduces new elements to established organizational research topics and, more significantly, gives new meanings to existing concepts. We can observe the most significant changes in those areas where the effects of organizing are greatest.[1]

New Employment Relations

Since 1987, 7 million Americans have lost their jobs (Cascio 1995), and several industrial sectors have expanded their hiring concomitantly. This evi-

[1] The present chapter omits areas relevant to organizing that are already treated in contemporary reviews: teams (Guzzo & Dickson 1996), personnel selection, and other human resource practices (Borman et al 1997, Cascio 1995).

dent mobility is tied to the formation of new and more varied employment relationships across industries as well as within specific firms. Worldwide shifts in personnel management practices are evident, including decline of seniority-based wages in Japan (Mroczkowski & Hanaoka 1989), decline in job security coupled with higher performance demands in England (Herriot & Pemberton 1995), and higher unemployment prolonging postsecondary school education and apprenticeships in Germany (Roberts et al 1994). In addition, Eastern Europe has undergone a strategic reorientation from placement via centralized workforce planning to recruitment through labor markets (Roe 1995).

Research on the employment relationship reflects both new employment arrangements and the by-products of transition. The shift to organizing is evident in the weaker role of hierarchy and greater decentralization of personnel practices, the role of strategic and environmental factors in shaping incentives for workers and work groups, and generally increased turbulence and uncertainty in employment. Central themes include rewards available from labor force participation and performance, how workers understand new psychological contracts, and the impact of these contracts on equity, worker attachment, and other responses.

ACCESSING REWARDS The rewards that motivate workforce participation and performance—such as compensation and benefits, career opportunities, and fulfilling work—are central to research on motivation. Accessing rewards entails issues of who distributes rewards, how they are allocated, and what the parties understand the exchange to mean. Reward distribution is a major theme in organizational research, particularly regarding the locus of decision making about incentives and personnel actions. Control over hiring, firing, and pay levels appears to be increasingly decentralized to permit responsiveness to local market conditions (Cappelli 1996). Wages are now more sensitive to the influence of local labor markets (Katz & Kruger 1991), while rewards based on seniority have declined (Chauvin 1992). Decentralizing personnel decisions means relations with immediate superiors and coworkers are important in the accessing of rewards. Impression management—particularly with superiors—has been found to impact performance ratings and the ability to access rewards beyond an individual or group's actual level of performance (Ancona 1990, Tsui et al 1995). Most reward distribution remains mediated by managers, even as their roles shift under self-management (Manz & Sims 1987).

Delayering coupled with broader spans of control complicates the role leaders play in distributing rewards and motivating employees. High-quality leader-member exchanges (LMX) have been found to increase the opportunities both parties have to perform well and access rewards (Graen & Scandura 1987). However, LMX has historically depended upon two conditions—a long-term supervisor-subordinate relationship and demographic similarity (Graen & Scandura 1987)—that are increasingly unlikely in a mobile, heterogeneous workforce. The meaning of quality LMX under conditions of organizing is unclear. Nonetheless, trust-based relations between workers and managers appear to be increasingly critical as workers are held accountable for their performance across more dimensions (e.g. internal and external customers) (Miles & Creed 1995). The problem of how to distribute rewards appropriately with fewer managers increases the relevance of "substitutes for leadership" (Kerr & Jermier 1978, Podsakoff et al 1993) such as member socialization, computer-based performance monitoring, and client/customer feedback (Podsakoff et al 1993). Gainsharing has been found to increase peer monitoring of coworker behavior (Welbourne et al 1995), which suggests that social comparisons and peer pressure increase when an individual's rewards are tied to peer performance. Rearranged jobs and a rising proportion of pay that is performance-contingent combine to make individual and team performance more observable, as occurs in organizing around projects. Contingent pay and peer pressure generated by teams are emerging as substitutes for both managerial influence and internalized member commitment, in effect creating short-term contracts that are heavily leveraged on individual or team performance.

The rewards themselves are changing. Promotions and formal status gains are being reduced and replaced by lateral moves presented as "career-building" assignments (Arthur 1994, Kanter 1989). In particular, autonomous work groups and job rotation tend to break down narrow job descriptions and reduce the number of job titles, a process referred to as "broad banding" (Katz 1985). Employability, the ability to access alternative work on the external labor market (Kanter 1989), is replacing job security in some segments. High-involvement work systems have been found to offer job security to valued, highly skilled workers in whom the firm has considerable investments (Handy 1989). These shifts are evidence that external labor-market factors drive employee experiences within the firm.

Workers often perceive training as a reward, providing self-actualization and the motivation to learn; career development with increased responsibility, autonomy, and likelihood of advancement; and personal psychosocial benefits, including increased confidence, new friendships, and better functioning in nonwork life (Noe & Wilk 1993, Nordhaug 1989). However, employer-provided training varies widely with market forces. Bartel & Sicherman (1994) reported that training is more frequent where unemployment rates are low, which suggests that employers provide skills through training where labor markets are tight but that they are less likely to do so when they can buy skills on the outside market. Hicks & Klimoski (1987) provided evidence that reactions to development opportunities can be enhanced when employees receive realistic information about the benefits of training; yet environmental uncertainty can make it difficult to forecast accurately the benefits of training. In any case, as the context of training is altered, the meaning workers attach to it is likely to change as well.

Traditional organizational research has viewed rewards as discrete exchanges (e.g. pay for performance). Increasingly, rewards and other conditions of employment are viewed as compensation "bundles" (Gerhart & Milkovich 1992). Koys (1991) found that employees' attitudes toward the firm are influenced by their perceptions of the motives that underlie reward systems and other human resource practices. Though increasingly threatened by cost cutting and shifts to peripheral employment (contractors, temporaries), the availability of benefits and employee perceptions of their importance contribute jointly to employee commitment and their perception of organizational support (Eisenberger et al 1986, Greenberger et al 1989, Sinclair et al 1995).

Although rewards are traditionally thought of as static and discrete, with workers having similar understandings of the firm's, management's, or supervisor's intentions in reward distribution, the concept of a psychological contract suggests otherwise. Psychological contracts are beliefs individuals hold about the exchange relationship between themselves and an employer, in essence, what people understand the employment relationship to mean [e.g. a high-involvement relationship or limited transactional employment (Rousseau 1995)]. Introducing the concept of a psychological contract distinguishes traditional notions of discrete rewards from the meaning ascribed to the whole exchange relationship. They have been characterized as schemas or mental models that capture how employees interpret bundles of rewards. The same reward (e.g. training or development) can signal distinct kinds of relationships (e.g. short-term incentive or long-term benefit) depending on the employment context in which it occurs. Contracts are dynamic, with time playing two important roles: First, employment duration can alter the rewards accrued. Second, psychological contracts can undergo unannounced changes in terms and meaning giving rise to idiosyncratic work roles (Miner 1990) and employment relationships (Rousseau 1995). Trusted senior workers who have more flexibility in responsibilities and work hours than do their junior colleagues are likely to perceive themselves party to a more relationally oriented contract with their employer. As mental models of the employment relationship, psychological contracts are formed typically at certain points in time (e.g. at hiring or when undergoing socialization for new assignments) and resist revision except when circumstances signal the need to revise an old schema or create a new one (Rousseau 1995). Those who had the strongest attachment to their employers have been found to react more adversely to contract violations (Robinson & Rousseau 1994), and these violations of promised contractual commitments engender more adverse reactions than do unmet expectations (Robinson 1995). When psychological contracts are congruent with changes in work practices, workers have been found to more fully implement change (Rousseau & Tijoriwala 1996).

INEQUALITY AND SHIFTING REWARD ALLOCATIONS Polls of public opinion in the United States observe that the optimistic attitudes of the 1960s toward one's economic success have given way in the 1990s to fear of losing affluence (Yankelovich 1993). Workplace justice, a long-standing topic in organizational research, is an increasing concern with the often uneven consequences of transitions. Critics of organizational restructurings have raised concern that short-term shareholder value is being increased by appropriating valued employment conditions, such as job security, for which workers have contracted (Smolowe 1996). Compensation research has focused on specific distributive issues, including the disparity between "haves and have nots" across organizational hierarchies (Cowherd & Levine 1992), particularly the high salaries and bonuses of corporate executives in comparison to those of rank-and-file employees. Cowherd & Levine reported higher product quality in firms with less disparity in compensation between executives and the rank and file. Redistributing rewards among workers with different employment relations raises issues of employee equity and of appropriate management practices for firms not used to dealing simultaneously with distinct types of workers. Firms most likely to have internal labor markets, that is, firms with more than 1000 employees, demonstrate the greatest expansion in use of temporary help (Magnum et al 1985). This means that firms with the most extensive commitments to some employees are also using workers to whom they make few commitments, and that these firms are still learning how to manage each type of employee simultaneously. Full-time employees often benefit from the presence of temporaries. Although firms requiring greater amounts of technical skills were less likely to use temporaries (Davis-Blake & Uzzi 1993), even a limited presence of temporary workers can enhance the quality of work life for full-time core employees because promotion opportunities are typically limited to core workers. Pearce (1993) found that managers are more likely to assign temporary workers tasks that require little knowledge and to shift complex assignments involving teamwork to full-timers. Although wages are about the same for part-time and temporary workers as for full-time employees (from a 1988 Bureau of National Affairs survey cited by Cappelli 1996, p. 19), benefits were perhaps half as likely. This rise in dual (or even multiple) labor markets within the same organization raises issues of social comparison and equity, as well as broader issues of employment relations (e.g. social questions such as whether temporary or noncore workers should be invited to holiday parties or participate in company orientations). Legal issues surrounding the contingent workforce are still being sorted out (Feldman & Klaas 1996).

NEW EMPLOYMENT RELATIONS BRING NEW MEANINGS TO OLD DEPENDENT VARIABLES New distinctions among core, peripheral, temporary, and contingent workers raise issues for microorganizational behavior's typical measures of individual-level responses. Traditionally, commitment has been viewed as an individual outcome, largely motivated by individual differences (Mathieu & Zajac 1990). Commitment—particularly its behavioral component, the intention to remain—has recently been examined as a two-way street (Eisenberger et al 1986, Shore & Wayne 1993), the product of an interaction between individual and employer. Measures of employee-firm attachment, such as commitment, are problematic for new employment relations. Quite commonly, employees of temporary-help agencies work for more than one agency (National Association of Temporary Staffing Services 1994). Where the employment relationship takes on the form of an organized open market, a hiring hall, people may stay within the same occupation but not necessarily with the same employer for any length of time. Thus, occupational commitment may be a better indicator of attachment than organizational commitment. Increasingly, workers are "participants," if not necessarily "employees," in several firms (e.g. the technician paid by Xerox to work out of an office at Motorola headquarters exclusively servicing the Xerox equipment Motorola uses). However, it is also possible that outsourcing has merely shifted loyalties such that outsourced information systems staff who once were committed to a multifunctional corporation (e.g. AT&T) are now similarly committed to the specialty firm for which they work (e.g. EDS).

Research on dual commitments has focused on union and organizational commitment (e.g. Gordon & Ladd 1990), but we know very little about multiple commitment to several employers or multiple clients or customers. Hunt & Morgan (1994) tested competing models contrasting organizational commitment as one of many distinct commitments (e.g. commitments to work group, supervisor) with organizational commitment as a mediating construct in the relations between constituency-specific commitments and outcomes, such as citizenship and intention to quit. Their analysis supported the role of organizational commitment as a mediator between attachment to different constituencies and outcomes. Finding no evidence of conflict among different commitments, they concluded that employee commitments to different parties within the organization either promote global organizational commitment or are not significantly related to it. More research can be expected regarding multiple commitments, that is, commitments to occupation, employer, client, internal customers, team, union, and others.

Trust, particularly between labor and management, has long been considered important to organizational success (for an extensive historical review, see Miles & Creed 1995). Its base rate may have declined in recent years even while its value has risen (Barney & Hansen 1994). Trust for the general manager in a chain of restaurants has been found to be significantly related to sales, profits, and employee turnover (Davis et al 1995). Davis et al (1995) argued that trust fulfills Barney's (1986) requirements for competitive advantage: Trust adds value by reducing transaction costs, it is rare between employees and management, and it is not easily copied. Mayer et al (1995) offer an integrative framework defining organizational trust as "the willingness to be vulnerable" to another. Under conditions of organizing, the parties associated with organizational trust include but are not limited to coworkers, immediate superiors, senior managers and executives, and the organization in general. Organizing can, however, signal a shift in the dynamics of trust. Traditionally, trust derived from long-term experiences of reciprocity (Creed & Miles 1996); however, the rise of temporary work systems such as product design teams, film crews, and campaign organizations requires what has been termed "swift trust" (Meyerson et al 1996) supported by social networks and vulnerability to social reputation. In organizing, trust plays a fluid role as both cause and result.

Organizational citizenship is a correlate and possible outcome of trust (Organ 1990). It has been found to be influenced by perceptions of procedural though not distributive fairness (Ball et al 1994, Moorman 1991). As competitive pressure increases performance demands, the meaning of citizenship may shift as "performance beyond expectations" becomes expected. Perhaps due to organizational transitions, there has been a shift in the types of citizenship behaviors investigated, with increasing focus on more negative citizenship, or retributive behaviors (such as sabotage or theft) that directly work against the interests of the organization. Using multidimensional scaling, Robinson & Bennett (1995) developed a typology of deviant workplace behavior that varies along two dimensions: minor vs serious, and interpersonal vs organizational. Consistent with distinctions made by Hollinger & Clark (1982), organizationally relevant behaviors fall into two types: production deviance (e.g. leaving early, taking excessive breaks), assessed as relatively minor; and property deviance (e.g. sabotaging equipment, stealing from the company), assessed as serious. In their framework for research on organizationally motivated aggression, O'Leary-Kelly et al (1996) proposed that organizational insiders (e.g. members) are primarily responsible for violence in the workplace (as opposed to outsiders), but that poor treatment by the organization and hierarchical or control-oriented organizational norms influence both the incidence and targets of violence. Surveying human resource management executives in public corporations, Griffin (R Griffin, unpublished manuscript) respondents reported that violence in the form of threats, verbal attacks, and racial and sexual harassment is increasing in their organizations. Human resource (HR) managers attributed these changes to the effects of downsizing, reengineering, and increased employee workload.

In conclusion, research on the employment relationship in the new organizational era has two overarching themes: the greater complexity of the worker-firm relationship than appreciated previously and the often-negative consequences that have resulted in the shift from organization to organizing. Awareness has increased regarding the importance of trust in the employment relationship as well as how misleading it can be to atomistically study that relationship's terms in isolation.

Performance: Measurement and Management

Performance issues have long been a central theme in organizational research. Escalating competition and expanded performance-measurement capabilities have made greater scrutiny of organizational performance evident in all sectors of the economy. This attention has led to the recognition of a phenomenon referred to as the "performance paradox" (Meyer & Gupta 1994, National Research Council 1994). This paradox has two features: First, measures of performance often are observed to be only loosely interrelated. Second, performance improvements in subunits do not necessarily translate into productivity gains for the firm. An example of the first feature is that organizational success in obtaining market share often bears little relationship to other performance indicators: Those organizations good in some areas may be poor in others. Although this pattern was observed in early studies of organizational performance (e.g. Seashore et al 1960), it largely went unnoted. An example of the second would be a division whose successful innovations do not lead to firm-wide innovation (e.g. the Saturn division of General Motors). As competitive pressures and performance expectations have increased, both researchers and managers are becoming more aware of the two features of this paradox, calling attention to the need for enhanced coordination within firms (Goodman et al 1994) as well as performance monitoring, reconciling diverse sources of performance information (client, peer, subordinate, task/technical), customer responsiveness, organizational learning, and more systematic performance management (Pritchard 1994, Sink & Smith 1994).[2]

---

[2] In this section, we focus primarily upon research pertinent to the first feature of the paradox. The second is addressed in the later section on within-firm organizational learning. Research into high-reliability organizations indicates that major—and sometimes catastrophic—errors can occur, while other performance indicators are positive (Perrow 1984, Sagan 1993). Organizational factors contributing to high performance in indicators such as customer satisfaction are likely to be different from those contributing to safety or cost containment. Firms may also have limited focus of attention, which can constrain their ability to gather information and provide support for performance in more than a few areas.

So what does organizational research say for firms seeking to be good at several things at once? More mature firms have been found to be most successful in their efforts to perform well on several indicators concurrently, which suggests that it takes time to learn how to do several things well at once (Meyer & Gupta 1994). A meta-analysis of management by objectives (an amalgam of participative management, goal setting, and performance feedback) and its impact on organizational productivity indicate the critical role of top management commitment [56% average gain under high commitment vs 6% under low commitment (Rodgers & Hunter 1991)]. Absence of top management commitment was reported also to give rise to local innovations that go unused by the larger firm and to coordination problems for units seeking to obtain a high-priority objective that conflicts with the goals of another unit with which it is interdependent. It is a truism that top management commitment promotes productivity improvement. As firms become smaller and less hierarchical, the critical processes for productivity improvement may change. Research is needed on the effects of concurrent feedback from a multiplicity of performance indicators for groups, individuals, and organizations, in decentralized as well as hierarchical settings. Effects might range anywhere from responsiveness and high performance to vigilance and overload.

The goal of high-performance work teams is to perform well on multiple dimensions (financial, customer satisfaction, employee well-being). Huselid's (1995) study of 968 firms in major industries indicates that human resource management practices associated with high-performance work systems (bundling training, participative decision making, incentive systems, and open communications) impact both employee outcomes (turnover and productivity) and corporate financial results. Findings suggest that firms that have top managers focused on a set of clearly defined goals supported by integrated HR practices are less likely to manifest the suboptimal performance paradox.

ProMES (Productivity Measurement and Enhancement System), a methodology for measuring and managing organizational performance developed by Robert Pritchard (1990), is designed to address some of the difficulties related to the performance paradox. Using consensus-building among stakeholders, ProMES combines the integration of multiple conflicting goals and performance feedback that can be readily understood and acted upon, with incentives and other managerial support for performance improvement. As the demand for high performance escalates, successful new performance-management methodologies are likely to find ways of increasing the firm's capacity to focus its attention broadly enough to reflect major constituents and interests, while being sufficiently selective to provide feedback useful in directing and coordinating efforts to improve performance.

Goal Setting Becomes Self-Management

Goal setting has been essential to organizational research on motivation and performance at many levels: individual, group, and organization. Its centrality makes it a bellwether for issues in the new organizational era. Goal setting's stylized fact has been that moderately difficult goals motivate high performance (Locke & Latham 1990). However, researchers in this area acknowledge that it largely has focused on repetitive tasks (see Locke et al 1981), often in the context of assignment of performance objectives by a hierarchical superior. There is a striking shift toward studying goal setting as it relates to more complex tasks and social arrangements (e.g. Smith et al 1990). In field settings, research investigates the role of goal setting to a firm's (as well as an individual's or group's) planning processes, strategy, and performance (Rodgers & Hunter 1991) and has shown significant effects of goal setting on firm productivity.

Perhaps the most significant shift is a new (or perhaps renewed) focus on self-management in goal setting (Gist et al 1990, Latham & Locke 1991). Self-regulation has long been implicit in goal-setting theory, because setting goals and translating them into action is a volitional process (Latham & Locke 1991), where acceptance of goals, when they are not self-set, is critical to their achievement. Frederick Kanfer (1975) focused attention on self-control mechanisms as a basis in clinical practice to modify addictive behavior, training people to stop smoking or overeating. Self-management teaches people to assess their problems, set specific hard goals to address these problems, self-monitor the effects of the environment on goal attainment, and appropriately administer rewards or penalties while working toward the goals. Although goal setting and self-management have been linked theoretically for many years, "classic" goal-setting research emphasized goal setting alone, while self-management focused attention on the learning and orchestration of cognitive processes for acquiring skills, self-monitoring progress, and providing self-reinforcement (Gist et al 1990). Gist et al found that goal setting per se is less effective in novel, complex tasks than is self-management, a process in which more skills are learned and actively displayed, even when the effects of goal level are controlled. Goal setting and the cognitive and behavioral processes surrounding goal achievement remain at the core of self-management practices, but the latter focus attention on learning, adaptation, knowledge transfer, and the flexibility to adapt to changing circumstances.

Organizational delayering and the rise of smaller, often entrepreneur-based, firms give self-management new meaning [including self-leading teams, (Manz 1992)]. This new meaning gives rise to debates over the distinction between the personal autonomy of self-management and the interdependent forms of shared governance, where the self in "self-managed" can mean person (Gist et al 1991), work group (Manz 1992), or broader institution (Welch 1994). At the heart of this shift in meanings is a debate over who sets the strategic goals for the firm, coupled with questions about the legitimacy and competence of stakeholders involved in these strategic choices (Manz 1992). Case analysis of W.L. Gore and Associates, the firm that developed the product Gore-tex, provides evidence that self-management practices where learning is emphasized can yield a fluid ad hoc work system, reflecting organizing processes rather than formal structure and resulting in innovation, high performance, and collaborative shaping of the firm's goals (Shipper & Manz 1992). In Brazil, similar self-management practices—based on a combination of profit sharing, collaborative decision making, and shared financial information—are reported to be successful (Semler 1989).

Self-management in the achievement of personal and organizational goals introduces a new twist to research on organizational leadership, both stretching and challenging how leadership is conceptualized. Podsakoff et al (1993) conducted an empirical investigation of Kerr & Jermier's (1978) model of Substitutes for Leadership. Originally developed to account for the often-limited effect of managers and supervisors on subordinate performance, this model identified factors that might neutralize the effects of (or minimize the need for) leaders. Podsakoff et al reported that contingent rewards, professional orientation, nonroutine work, organizational formalization, and spatial distance from others contribute to employee criterion variables while reducing the impact of leader behaviors. However, leader support appears to aid employees experiencing role ambiguity. Under conditions of organizing, self-management practices coupled with appropriate rewards and developments appear to enhance performance in the absence of formal leaders. In a highly turbulent business environment, Howell & Avolio (1993) found that transformational leadership positively predicted business-unit performance over a one-year interval, while transactional leadership, including contingent rewards, was negatively related to business-unit performance. They suggest it may be counterproductive for leaders to spend too much time focusing on meeting goals as opposed to promoting freedom of action in dynamic environments.

The concept of stretch goals (Sherman 1996) is predicated on the idea that seemingly impossible goals can motivate high performance by mandating creativity and assumption-breaking thinking that takes the performer "out of the box." On the surface, stretch goals appear to violate an essential premise of goal theory, that workers cannot accept a goal that does not seem feasible. Related to the concepts of transformational leadership, where performance expectations are elevated well beyond the limits of past experience (Bass 1985), and double-loop learning (Argyris & Schoen 1996), where previously successful frameworks are questioned, revised, or discarded, the fact that prior experience is often a poor guide for stretch-goal achievement shifts the performers' attention away from old routines and assumptions toward novel and creative approaches. Wood et al (1987) reported that "do-your-best" goals worked better than difficult, specific goals when the task was novel and highly complex. Plausibly, both worker self-efficacy and the credibility of the people setting the stretch goal contribute to the resulting performance. Kelly & McGrath (1985) have suggested dysfunctional consequences for groups working on especially difficult tasks, such as stringent time deadlines, where they spend less time discussing task ideas (e.g. agreements or modifications) that might affect product quality or interpersonal issues (e.g. conflicts, needs) that can affect member support and well-being. Further, they reported that these negative interaction processes carry over even to later trials for which time limits have changed.

Employers that reward only extreme performance have been found to foster some unexpected consequences. In a study of high-technology firms, Zenger (1992) reported that performance-based compensation that aggressively rewards extreme performance while largely ignoring performance distinctions at moderate levels yields retention of extremely high and moderately low performers. In contrast, moderately high and extremely low performers were likely to depart. New issues arise as organizations and goal-setting researchers turn their attention to more complex circumstances and ever more challenging levels of performance.

Information Processing: Discontinuous and Multiphased

Turbulent competitive environments, technological sophistication, and flexible organizing give rise to greater novelty and complexity in work, which contributes to an expanding interest in individual and managerial cognition (Kiesler & Sproull 1992) and the broader domain of information processing by firms and individuals (Fiol 1994, Louis & Sutton 1991). Evidence that people process information differently in novel vs routine situations has led to the development of the concept of "discontinuous information processing" (Sims & Gioia 1986). Organizing promotes use of controlled information processing, where information is actively sought and carefully processed to make a quality decision when there is little experience on which to rely. This phenomenon has been used to characterize the vigilance and flexibility required to operate American aircraft carriers as "high-reliability organizations" (Weick & Roberts 1993), where even hierarchy must be adaptable. Models of rational decision making such as expectancy theory (Vroom 1964) tend to work well in accounting for behavior in nonroutine decisions such as choosing a career (Wanous et al 1983) but do less well in explaining routine behaviors. In routine situations such as sustained performance in a stable situation over time, controlled processes give way to reliance on automatic processes using established mental models and routines (Bartunek & Moch 1987, Fiol 1994, Sims & Gioia 1986).

An individual's capacity to switch back and forth between routine and nonroutine information processing ["shifting the gears" (Louis & Sutton 1991)] is postulated to be influenced by personality characteristics (e.g. locus of control) as is an individual's capacity to enact the "weak situations" characteristic of work settings where organizing is required (Weick 1996). Research is needed on the impact of personality and cognitive styles on both discontinuous information processing and enactment of weak situations. Cascio (1995) has suggested that personality tests offer important predictive power for successful performance in new forms of work.

"Shifting the gears" in cognitive processes is evident in research on training (Hesketh et al 1989), socialization (Louis & Sutton 1991), and organizational learning (Argyris 1991, Nicolini & Meznar 1995). In training, unpredictability and variation tend to cause difficulties for the learner. Yet these factors also enhance the ability to apply training in the future, when diverse circumstances arise that are not necessarily anticipated at the time of training (Neal et al 1995). In socialization, individuals may be open to learning about the organization only at certain points in time (Guzzo & Noonan 1994, Louis & Sutton 1991). Organizational learning based on active thinking has been advocated (Fiol & Lyles 1985), while strategic failings have been traced to overreliance upon automatic processing (Starbuck & Milliken 1988).

Organizational Learning

Although organizational learning has played a role in the organizational literature for decades (e.g. Congelosi & Dill 1965), until recently there was little empirical research on the subject. Rising competitive pressures have fueled interest in organizational learning as a major determinant of sustainable organizational performance, which suggests that to survive and thrive firms will need to learn at an increasingly rapid rate. Competition has been observed to promote organizational learning in single-unit firms, typically small, frequently entrepreneurial enterprises, while larger multiunit firms tend to manifest less learning in response to competition, instead levering their market position to obtain competitive advantage (Barnett et al 1994). Learning necessitates a facility for discontinuous information processing on the part of both firms and individuals, the capability to deploy knowledge and demonstrable skills in novel ways and flexible combinations (Argyris & Schoen 1996). Organizational learning can occur within a firm when it involves diffusion of knowledge between members and across units (e.g. Epple et al 1996) or between firms, with dissemination and implementation of new knowledge obtained through external monitoring or benchmarking and interpersonal contact (Miner & Robinson 1994).

WITHIN-FIRM: MEMORY AND SHARED UNDERSTANDING To a point, organizational learning displays several features of individual learning, particularly in its need for memory and the transfer of learning to new settings and problems. The major distinction is organizational learning's requirement that members convey their learning to one another, develop shared understandings or common cognitive structures regarding application of shared knowledge, and otherwise externalize what they learn (Lyles & Schwenk 1992; Goodman & Darr 1996). The prevalence of the second feature of the performance paradox (above), where innovations in a subunit do not necessarily translate into innovations for the firm as a whole, suggests that within-firm learning is difficult. Nonetheless, it does occur. In an empirical study of a large financial firm, Fiol (1994) observed that gradual consensus building with interactions among different subgroups played a critical role in overcoming resistance to change and led to a collective understanding that acknowledged both differences and agreement regarding a new venture. In pizza franchises, unit cost declined significantly as stores gained experience in production (Darr et al 1994). Knowledge transferred across stores owned by the same franchisee but not across stores owned by different franchisees. Employee turnover contributed to "forgetting," or knowledge depreciation, in this high-turnover industry.

The repeated finding that turnover leads to organizational "forgetting" raises questions about whether organizational learning has really occurred when performance gains are manifest. It can be difficult to distinguish between gains due to individual learning among many members as opposed to organizational learning embedded in new processes and procedures. In a laboratory simulation, paired subjects developed interlocked task-performance patterns that displayed characteristics of organizational routines (Cohen & Bacdayan 1994). Procedural memory explains how such routines arise, stabilize, and change. Procedures can become enduring properties of organizations. But unless they are externalized (e.g. written down or incorporated into training programs), they may not be effectively retained when knowledgeable individuals leave.

Internal organizational barriers often inhibit within-firm learning. Goodman & Darr (1996) report that even a multiunit firm ostensibly committed to learning may find it difficult to disseminate information and create shared understandings about new processes and capabilities. If shared cognitive structures are critical for organizational learning, these may be easier to achieve in smaller, single-unit firms. Embedding knowledge in technology has been found to facilitate transfer across shifts (Epple et al 1996). This research suggests useful directions for research into transfer mechanisms (e.g. representations, flow diagrams, and procedures) that inhibit forgetting induced by employee turnover. These transfer mechanisms themselves may distinguish organizational learning from that of individuals.

LEARNING BETWEEN FIRMS: CAREERS AND SOCIAL NETWORKS New organizational forms such as joint ventures, outsourcing among organizational networks, research consortia, and other forms of organizing (Aldrich & Sasaki 1995) provide evidence that organizational learning will occur across increasingly blurry boundaries. While outsourcing has been linked to declines in organizational learning in outsourced functions (Bettis et al 1992), networked organizations with flexible memberships can promote it (Snow et al 1992). These "boundaryless" organizations, defined here as organizations whose membership, departmental identity, and job responsibilities are flexible (Kanter 1989, Miner & Robinson 1994), yield a pattern of more flexibly structured careers. Career patterns are found to contribute to organizational learning by generating diverse frames of reference for problem solving, redirecting old routines in new ways, and harvesting organizational memory (Miner & Robinson 1994). Job transitions (loss, rehire, rotation, transfers, international assignments, horizontal moves, demotions) become commonplace and can promote organizational and individual learning (Miner & Robinson 1994). Transitions out of firms complicate retention but create opportunities for learning in new firms, particularly given the movement of employees from large to smaller firms where routinization is often lower. Nonhierarchical careers recombine personal and organizational learning in novel ways and themselves can become repositories of knowledge (Bird 1994).

Social networks outside corporations and other firms have become sources of career advantage (DeFilippi & Arthur 1994) and expertise (Miner & Robinson 1994), functioning in ways similar to occupational communities that influence career decisions and transitions of members (Van Maannen & Barley 1984). Firms that cultivate relationships with educational institutions such as high schools improve their access to appropriately skilled workers (Rosenbaum et al 1990). The impact social networks outside the firm have on career advancement may be particularly important to the career development of women and minorities. Evidence suggests that within-firm social networks can work to the advantage of white men over women (Ibarra 1992) and over African-Americans (Thomas & Higgins 1996).

In sum, organizing—with its flexible work arrangements, personnel movements, reliance upon personal expertise, and systematic information processing—places a premium on experimentation and collective learning. As boundaries between firms blur, we can expect more rapid organizational learning and possibly a similar rate of forgetting, along with greater attention to mechanisms for retaining knowledge with or without a stable membership. The shift toward network organizations (Snow et al 1992) suggests that knowing who is becoming as important as knowing how (DeFillippi & Arthur 1994).

Managing Organizational Change and Individual Transitions

Transitions abound in the new organizational era both for firms and for the workforce. Managing organizational change and individual transitions is an overarching research theme.

ORGANIZATIONAL CHANGE Change management focuses on the implementation and ultimately the successful institutionalization of new technology, culture, strategy, and related employment arrangements. Organizational Development (OD), the traditional practice side of organizational research, has long had a shaky reputation among organizational scientists for its lack of rigor and "pop" style. However, the boundary between OD and organizational science has become blurred as more researchers tackle the problems of implementing change (e.g. Kiesler & Sproull 1992, Novelli et al 1995).

Organizing is typically a radical departure from the traditional ways people think and act in firms. Stable and enduring mental models or schemas have been found to contribute to reactions to change (e.g. Bartunek & Moch 1987). Lau & Woodman (1995) identify three features of schemas pertinent for change: causality (attributions used to understand causes of change), valence (meaning and significance), and inferences (predictions of future outcomes). They reported that organizational commitment is related to these features of change schemas, consistent with the argument that a fundamental realignment in how people understand the firm is needed to foster organizational change.

Organizational change also has become a justice issue (Novelli et al 1995). Distributive justice, the perceived fairness of the outcomes, is a particular focus because the departures from the status quo that constitute change are commonly experienced as losses, and gains from change may take time to realize, particularly when mastery of a radical new organizational form is required. Offsetting losses from work system changes has been found to improve distributive fairness by helping people gain the skills needed to be successful and gain rewards under the new system (Kirkman et al 1994).

Interactional justice pertains to the communication process in managing change. Presenting bad news with politeness and respect (Folger 1985) and providing credible explanations or social accounts foster more positive reactions (Bies & Moag 1986). In labor disputes, the general public was found to react with stronger perceptions of unfairness, more sympathy, and more support for grievances based on interactional justice rather than procedural justice, which in turn generated more intense reactions than grievances based on distributive injustice (Leung et al 1993). For victims of change, when outcomes are particularly severe, explanations high on specificity were judged to be more adequate and led to more positive reactions than did explanations emphasizing interpersonal sensitivity. Effects are enhanced when the explanation is delivered orally rather than via memo or letter (Shapiro et al 1994).

Procedural justice in change refers to the processes whereby implementation decisions were made. Voice mechanisms that allow affected people to participate in deciding upon the change or planning its implementation enhance procedural justice, as do procedures to correct for biases or inaccuracy of information used in the process (Sheppard et al 1992). In a study of new technology implementation, employee strain increased during the implementation phase and was highest among those individuals who were not included in the implementation process (Korunka et al 1993). However, voice had no effect in reactions to seven facility relocations (Daly & Geyer 1994), although the researchers speculate that employees may not have expected to have a voice in relocation decisions. The timing and phases of change may also play a role in effective implementation (Jick 1993), but these have received less systematic attention.

INDIVIDUAL TRANSITIONS Employment displacements are occurring at faster rates than in the past and are predicted to continue (Handy 1989). Job loss has been associated with lower self-esteem (Cohn 1978), increased anxiety, and psychological distress (Winefield et al 1991). Moreover, workers who are pressured to leave but opt to stay report unusually high levels of psychological distress (Price & Hooijberg 1992). Reemployment can mean settling for unsatisfactory new jobs (Liem 1992), which can engender long-term adverse consequences. In a longitudinal study of laid-off industrial workers, Leana & Feldman (1996) found that financial pressures, levels of optimism and self-blame, and the amount of problem-focused and symptom-focused coping individuals engage in were significant predictors of reemployment, which supports previous research on the importance of individual differences in successful searches (Kanfer & Hulin 1985). Jobs programs coupled with interpersonal support have been found to play a role in successful reemployment (Vinocur et al 1991).

Forecasting repeated cycles of employment and unemployment for skilled as well as unskilled workers, several organizational researchers predict that transitions will become less disruptive as people develop skills for adapting to change (Weick 1995) and as personal expectations and definitions of psychological success recast "unemployment" as an opportunity for personal development or family benefit (Mirvis & Hall 1994). A major factor in worker adaptation is likely to be the broader societal supports—educational, cultural, and economic—for workers and nonworkers alike.

Leisure, Nonwork, and Community: Personal and Institutional Supports

Escalating pressures on the workforce due to restructuring manifest in the attention paid to work-nonwork relations (Mirvis & Hall 1994). Decline of corporatist firms and their traditional benefits raises concerns about the infrastructure needed to support both new forms of employment and organizing and individual workers and their families—evident in an emerging area of scholarship on social capital (Etzioni 1993, Perrow 1996).

Social capital refers to civic life and public trust, the societal infrastructure from which workers and organizations receive support. Social institutions such as family and schools are reported to have difficulty responding to the prevailing economic pressures (Etzioni 1993), a fact suggesting that more active individual involvement in community life may be required to sustain these institutions. Greater involvement in off-the-job activities has been associated with reduced role interference and psychological strain (Gutek et al 1991, O'Driscoll et al 1992). Kirchmeyer (1995) found that employee commitment is enhanced when organizations provide resources to help employees fulfill family and other nonwork responsibilities. She further reported that workers prefer benefits that let them manage their responsibilities themselves (e.g. flexible scheduling) rather than have the firm do it for them (e.g. on-site child care).

Kanter (1977) suggested that early in the twentieth century, corporations tried to "swallow the family and take over its functions." Subsequently, firms moved to separate work and family in order to exclude competing loyalties. Demographic changes, particularly working mothers and dual income-career families, have increased the interdependence of work and family and intensified conflicts, particularly regarding time allocation. Recent studies support the significance of institutional factors, including societal beliefs about the role of women and work-family relations, in expanded organizational emphasis on work-nonwork relations (Goodstein 1994, Ingram & Simons 1995). Consistent with institutional arguments, larger (i.e. more publicly visible) firms seek legitimacy by adopting child-care benefits and work flexibility (Goodstein 1994). However, Ingram & Simons (1995) reported that institutional pressures explain late adoption of "family friendly" HR practices, while early adopters are likely to do so instead to gain strategic advantage (e.g. professional firms coping with labor shortages by filling positions with qualified women and dual-career spouses). Early adoption is linked to significant numbers of women in a firm's workforce, while late adoptions are less affected by firm-specific demographics (Galinsky & Stein 1990, Goodstein 1994).

Traditional corporate firms have been implicated in an erosion of community and civic life (Etzioni 1993, Perrow 1996). If corporations did in fact erode social capital, the shift to organizing does not reverse such effects. Organizing may require more social capital than did organizations with huge internal infrastructures, particularly in respect to education (Handy 1989), portable retirement and health-care benefits (Lucero & Allen 1994), and family support (Mirvis & Hall 1994). As a result, organizational researchers are likely to expand their consideration of work-nonwork relations to include a broader array of support systems and community institutions.

CONCLUSION

The evolution from organization to organizing changes both the phenomena traditionally studied by organizational research and the meaning of some traditional concepts. The answer to the opening questions of this review are apparent. Core features of organizational research, including its focus on performance and worker-firm relations, endure, but they do so with new dimensions. Performance now involves a multiplicity of results pursued concurrently and with an expanded focus on adaptive and sustained learning. Goal setting and leadership may converge into self-management. However, new dynamics are evident in the shift toward an interactive view of the employment relationship, reoriented from a focus on what managers offer workers to how workers across all ranks access rewards contingent upon the firm's strategic concerns. We see an increasingly complex view of information processing, reflecting a more rapid cycling from novel to routine and back again, characteristic of a more dynamic environment. There is also a broader concern for the personal and societal impact of the way work is organized.

This chapter has focused on topics particularly sensitive to the dynamics of organizing. Assuming the shift from organization to organizing will not be quickly undone, what are its implications for organizational research as a whole? Barley & Kunda (1992) maintain that periods of economic contraction lead to more emphasis on relationship building, organizational support, and strengthening of employee-firm commitment (witness Elton Mayo's Human Relations movement during the depression of the 1930s). Formerly, firms displaced workers only when the economy was shrinking. The recent coupling of massive terminations with economic expansion fragments the managerial ideologies that both justify and guide organizational actions. They may do the same for research ideologies. As a result, we might expect to find more researchers investigating competing hypotheses from more distinct and often divergent frameworks. A central theme may be the drive to increase shareholder value coupled with concern about the costs of displacement and transition for the workforce which creates that value. Clearly, organizational research needs to dig into the messy problems of serving multiple constituencies.

This chapter is not an attempt to create a "short" list of research topics; no prescriptions are intended for future researchers about topics to "buy" or to "sell." Several key research themes, including customer service (Schneider & Bowen 1995), quality (Dean & Bowen 1994), and the adoption of new technology (Leonard-Barton & Sinha 1993) were omitted because of space limitations. Rather, this chapter highlights broad areas where the effects of organizing are more visible, where our learning progresses even as further research needs appear. If the past is a prologue, we can expect that relevant organizational changes will manifest themselves in other areas, too. However, while new topics such as the performance paradox appear, established ones keep their labels but shift their focus. Perhaps it is for this reason that in the many years of *ARP*s reviewed in preparation for this chapter, certain core themes have endured. Yet, at some point, we might need to acknowledge that changes in firms are profound enough to alter further basic assumptions on which the field is based. In any case, a new era in organizational behavior appears to be in the making.

APPENDIX

In preparing this chapter, a content analysis was conducted on the 23 *ARP* chapters since 1979 dealing with organizational research (organizational behavior, industrial/organizational psychology, personnel and human resource management, training and development, and organizational development and change). Substantive topics covered were categorized by having two raters read each chapter and identify their central concepts. Raters generated a set of categories and then coded chapters according to their content (rate of agreement was 85%). In the case of the 1979 *ARP*, for example, Mitchell's (1979) chapter on organizational behavior was coded as including personality, job attitudes, commitment, motivation, and leadership. That volume contained a second organizationally relevant chapter, Dunnette & Borman's (1979) "Personnel Selection and Classification Systems," which was coded as including categories of validity, job analysis, performance ratings, equal opportunity, and selection practices. Content coding identified 94 discrete categories altogether.

Correlations computed between category matrices for each time period assess the degree of stability in category patterns over time. Using the QAP correlation technique (Krackhart 1987), correlations were computed between entries in two matrices, and the observed correlations were compared to the frequency of random correlations to provide a test of statistical significance (based on 500 permutations). This analysis, using normalized data (Table 1), indicates moderate stability in *ARP* categories with slightly greater convergence in categories in *ARP* chapters across periods 1 and 3. It also suggests a fair degree of variety over time in the issues addressed.

Table 1 *Annual Review of Psychology*: summary information

Time period	*ARP* # of articles	*ARP* # of categories	Times	*ARP*[a]
Time 1: 1979–1984	9	47	1 × 2	.23
Time 2: 1985–1990	8	57	2 × 3	.24
Time 3: 1991–1995	6	44	1 × 3	.34
Total[b]	23	94		

[a]Correlations are significantly different from .00, the average correlation across all cells in matrix.

[b]Represents total number of total distinct categories where many categories may appear in several time periods.

Examination of frequently cited categories across the three periods (Table 2) suggests that categories related to the general topics of performance (e.g. predictors of individual performance, measurement, organizational performance, ineffectiveness, and failure), motivation (e.g. effort resulting from goal setting or rewards offered), and employee responses (e.g. stress, satisfaction, and commitment) form a stable core. These categories comprise what apparently are the central dependent variables or outcomes operationalized in organizational behavior research. Other durable categories with basically consistent levels of research/citation throughout this extended period include the personnel-related areas of job analysis and performance appraisal. Topics where reports of research activities are increasing over time include individual cognition, organizational change, and organizational performance. A multidimensional scaling (MDS) of the *ARP* categories within each time period (Krackhardt et al 1994) suggests that the field has moved from three core areas (Change, Personnel, and Micro OB) of earlier years to a more highly differentiated set of category clusters (Personnel, Micro OB, Context Power and Influence, Organization environment). Figures 1 and 2 display MDS for the first and third periods. Categories in ellipses bridge two or more areas, thus Pers (Personality) bridges Personnel and Micro-OB in both periods while Operf (Organizational Performance) emerges as a bridge among Micro OB, Personnel, and Context in period 3. Bridging categories provide an opportunity for integration across disciplines and paradigms. Nonetheless, from 1979 to 1995, a trend toward specialization is evident. Further information about this analysis is available from the author.

ACKNOWLEDGMENTS

I wish to thank Colin Housing for his help with the literature review, Tiziana Casciaro for her work with the quantitative review, and both Tiziana and

Table 2 Frequent categories

	ARP
TIME 1	Performance predictors = 5
	Stress = 5
	Job analysis = 4
	EEO = 4
	Motivation = 4
	Personnel selection = 3
	Satisfaction = 3
	Equity = 3
	Performance appraisal = 3
	Job design = 2
	Methodology = 2
	Fairness = 2
	Organizational performance = 2
	Personality = 2
	Individual difference = 2
	Personnel training = 2
TIME 2	Job analysis = 6
	Leadership = 6
	Motivation = 5
	Performance predictors = 3
	Affect = 2
	Organizational culture = 2
	Organizational change = 2
	Performance appraisal = 2
	Personnel selection = 2
	Personnel layoffs = 2
TIME 3	Organization context/cross level effects = 3
	Motivation = 2
	Stress = 2
	Performance predictors = 2
	Organizational technology = 2
	Organizational performance = 2
	Performance appraisal = 2
	Personality = 2
	Job analysis =2
	Legal issues = 2
	Organizational demography = 2

Kristina Dahlin for their assistance in coding the data. David Krackhardt merits special thanks for help with the multidimensional scaling analysis and the figures. Michael Arthur, Kathleen Carley, Paul Goodman, and Laurie Weingart provided useful input at various points in this chapter's preparation. Thanks also to Catherine Senderling for her editorial work and to Carole McCoy for wordprocessing.

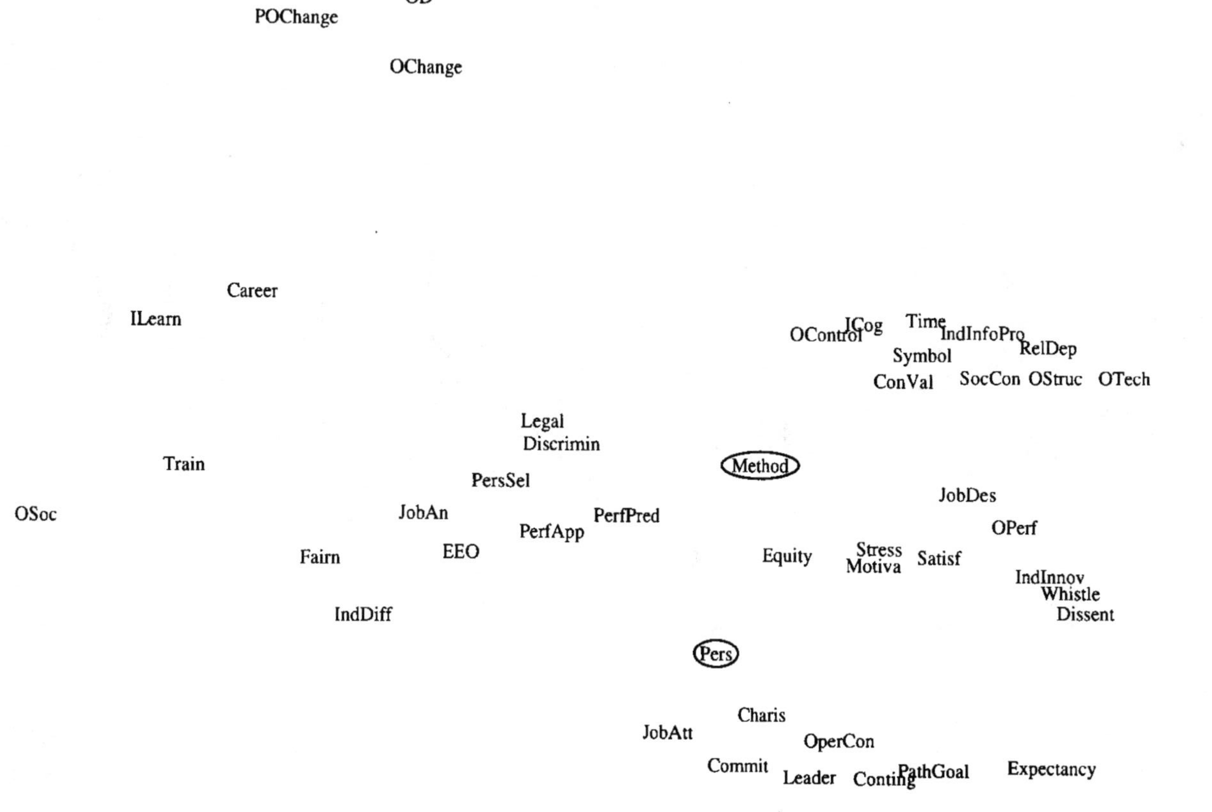

Figure 1 MDS on *ARP* for Period 1.

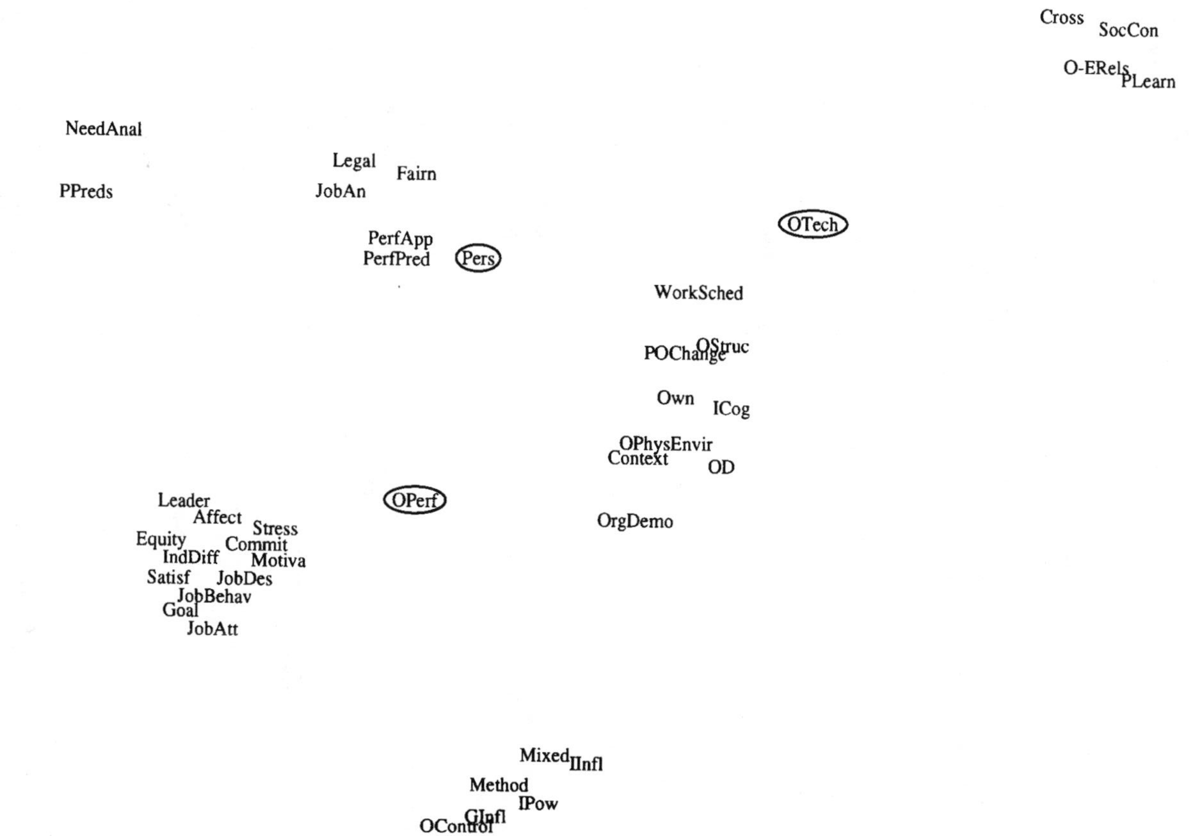

Figure 2 MDS of *ARP* for Period 3.

Literature Cited

Aldrich HE, Sasaki T. 1995. R&D consortia in the United States and Japan. *Res. Policy* 24:301–16

Ancona DG. 1990. Outward bound: strategies for team survival in an organization. *Acad. Manage. J.* 33:334–65

Argyris C. 1991. Teaching smart people how to learn. *Harvard Bus. Rev.* 69:99–109

Argyris C, Schoen DA. 1996. *Organizational Learning II.* Reading, MA: Addison-Wesley

Arthur MB. 1994. The boundaryless career: a new perspective for organizational inquiry. *J. Organ. Behav.* 15:295–306

Arthur M, Rousseau DM, eds. 1996. *The Boundaryless Career: A New Employment Principle for a New Organizational Era.* New York: Oxford Univ. Press

Ball GA, Trevino LK, Sims HP Jr. 1994. Just and unjust punishment: influences on subordinate performance and citizenship. *Acad. Manage. J.* 37:299–322

Barley S, Kunda G. 1992. Design and devotion: surges of rational and normative ideologies of control in managerial discourse. *Adm. Sci. Q.* 37:463–99

Barnett WP, Greve HR, Park DY. 1994. An evolutionary model of organizational performance. *Strateg. Manage. J.* 15:11–28

Barney JB. 1986. Organizational culture: Can it be a source of sustained competitive advantage? *Acad. Manage. Rev.* 11:656–65

Barney JB, Hansen MH. 1994. Trustworthiness as a source of competitive advantage. *Strateg. Manage. J.* 15:175–90

Bartunek JM, Moch MK. 1987. First-order, second-order, and third-order change and organizational development interventions: a cognitive approach. *J. Appl. Behav. Sci.* 23:483–500

Bass BM. 1985. *Leadership and Performance Beyond Expectations.* New York: Free Press

Bettis RA, Bradley SP, Hamel G. 1992. Outsourcing and industrial decline. *Acad. Manage. Exec.* 6:7–22

Bies RJ, Moag JS. 1986. Interactional justice: communication criteria of fairness. In *Research on Negotiations in Organizations,* ed. MH Bazerman, R Lewicki, B Sheppard, pp. 1:43–55. Greenwich, CT: JAI

Bird A. 1994. Careers as repositories of knowledge: a new perspective on boundaryless careers. *J. Organ. Behav.* 15:325–44

Borman W, Hanson M, Hedge J. 1997. Personnel selection. *Annu. Rev. Psychol.* 48:299–337

Cappelli P. 1996. Rethinking employment. *Br. J. Ind. Relat.* In press

Cascio WF. 1995. Whither industrial and organizational psychology in a changing world of work? *Am. Psychol.* 50:928–39

Castells M. 1992. Four Asian tigers with a dragon head: a comparative analysis of the state, economy and society in the Asian Pacific Rim. In *States and Development in the Asian Pacific Rim,* ed. RP Applebaum, J Henderson, pp. 33–70. Newbury Park, CA: Sage

Chauvin K. 1992. Declining returns to tenure for managerial jobs. *Manage. Econ.*

Cohen MD, Bacdayan P. 1994. Organizational routines are stored as procedural memory: evidence from a laboratory study. *Organ. Sci.* 5:554–68

Cohn R. 1978. The effects of employment status change on self-attitudes. *Soc. Psychol.* 41:81–93

Congelosi VE, Dill WR. 1965. Organizational learning: observations toward a theory. *Adm. Sci. Q.* 10:175–203

Cowherd DM, Levine DI. 1992. Product quality and pay equity between lower-level employees and top management: an investigation of distributive justice theory. *Adm. Sci. Q.* 37:302–20

Creed WED, Miles RE. 1996. Trust in organizations: a conceptual framework linking organizational forms, managerial philosophies, and the opportunity costs of controls. See Kramer & Tyler 1996, pp. 16–38

Daly JP, Geyer PD. 1994. The role of fairness in implementing large-scale change: employee evaluations of process and outcome in seven facility relocations. *J. Organ. Behav.* 15:623–38

Darr E, Argote L, Epple D. 1994. The acquisition transfer, and depreciation of knowledge in service organizations. *Manage. Sci.* 41:1750–62

Davis JH, Mayer RC, Schoorman FD. 1995. *The trusted general manager and firm performance: empirical evidence of a strategic advantage.* Presented at Strateg. Manage. Soc. Meet., Oct., Mexico City

Davis S. 1987. *Future Perfect.* Reading, MA: Addison-Wesley

Davis-Blake A, Uzzi B. 1993. Determinants of employment externationalization: the case of temporary workers and independent contractors. *Adm. Sci. Q.* 29:195–223

Dean JW Jr, Bowen DE. 1994. Management theory and total quality: improving research and practice through theory development. *Acad. Manage. Rev.* 19:392– 418

DeFillippi RJ, Arthur MB. 1994. The boundaryless career: a competency-based perspective. *J. Organ. Behav.* 15:307–24

Drazin R, Sandelands L. 1992. Autogenesis: a perspective on the process of organizing. *Organ. Sci.* 3:230–49

Drucker PF. 1994. The age of social transformation. *Atl. Mon.* 275:53–80

Dunnette MD, Borman WC. 1979. Personnel selection and classification systems. *Annu. Rev. Psychol.* 30:477–526

Eisenberger R, Huntington R, Hutchinson S, Sowa D. 1986. Perceived organizational support. *J. Appl. Psychol.* 71:500–7

Epple D, Argote L, Murphy K. 1996. An empirical investigation of the micro structure of knowledge acquisition and transfer through learning by doing. *Manage. Sci.* In press

Etzioni A. 1993. *The Spirit of Community: Rights, Responsibilities, and the Communitarian Agenda.* New York: Crown

Feldman DC, Klaas BS. 1996. Temporary workers: employee rights and employer responsibilities. *Empl. Responsib. Rights J.* 9:1–21

Fiol M. 1994. Consensus, diversity, and learning in organizations. *Organ. Sci.* 5:403–20

Fiol MC, Lyles MA. 1985. Organizational learning. *Acad. Manage. Rev.* 10:803–13

Folger R. 1985. *The Churchill Effect.* A. B. Freeman Sch. Bus., Tulane Univ., New Orleans

Galinsky E, Stein PJ. 1990. The impact of human resource policies: balancing work and family issues. *J. Fam. Issues* 11:368–83

Gerhart B, Milkovich GT. 1992. Employee compensation: research and practice. In *Handbook of Industrial and Organizational Psychology,* ed. MD Dunnette, LM Hough, pp. 481–569. Palo Alto, CA: Consult. Psychol. Press. 2nd ed.

Gist ME, Bavetta AG, Stevens CK. 1990. Transfer training method: its influence on skill generalization, skill repetition, and performance level. *Pers. Psychol.* 43: 501–23

Gist ME, Stevens CK, Bavetta AG. 1991. Effects of self-efficacy and post-training intervention on the acquisition and maintenance of complex interpersonal skills. *Pers. Psychol.* 44:837–61

Goodman PS, Darr E. 1996. Exchanging best practices through computer-aided systems. *Acad. Manage. Exec.* 10(2):7–19

Goodman PS, Lerch J, Mukhopadhyay T. 1994. Linkages and performance improvements. See National Research Council 1994, pp. 54–80

Goodman PS, Whetten DA. 1997. Fifty years of organizational behavior from multiple perspectives. In *A Half Century of Challenge and Change in Employment Relations,* ed. M Neufeld, J McKelvey. Ithaca, NY: ILR Press. In press

Goodstein JD. 1994. Institutional pressures and strategic responsiveness: employer involvement in work-family issues. *Acad. Manage. J.* 37:350–82

Gordon ME, Ladd RT. 1990. Dual allegiance: renewal, reconsideration, and recantation. *Pers. Psychol.* 43:37–69

Graen GB, Scandura TA. 1987. Toward a psychology of dynamic organizing. In *Research in Organizational Behavior,* ed. LL Cummings, BM Staw, 9:175–208. Greenwich, CT: JAI

Greenberger E, Goldberg WA, Hamill S, O'Neill R, Payne CK. 1989. Contributions of a supportive work environment to parents' well-being and orientation to work. *Am. J. Commun. Psychol.* 17:755–83

Griffin R. 1995. *Stress, aggression, and violence in the new workplace.* Cent. Hum. Resour. Manage., Tex. A&M Univ., College Station

Gutek B, Searle S, Klepa L. 1991. Rational versus gender role explanations for work-family conflict. *J. Appl. Psychol.* 76:560–68

Guzzo RA, Dickson MW. 1996. Teams in organizations: recent research on performance and effectiveness. *Annu. Rev. Psychol.* 47:307–38

Guzzo RA, Noonan KA. 1994. Human resource practices as communications and the psychological contract. *Hum. Res. Manage.* 33:447–62

Handy C. 1989. *The Age of Unreason.* Cambridge: Harvard Bus. Sch. Press

Herriot P, Pemberton C. 1995. *New Deals: The Revolution in Managerial Careers.* Chichester: Wiley

Hesketh B, Andrews S, Chandler P. 1989. Training for transferable skills: the role of examples and schema. *Educ. Train. Technol. Int.* 26:156–65

Hicks WD, Klimoski RJ. 1987. Entry into training programs and its effects on training outcomes. *Acad. Manage. J.* 30:542– 52

Hollinger RC, Clark JP. 1982. Formal and informal social controls of employee deviance. *Sociol. Q.* 23:333–43

Howell JM, Avolio B. 1993. Transformational leadership, transactional leadership, locus of control, and support for innovation. *J. Appl. Psychol.* 78:891–902

Hunt SD, Morgan RM. 1994. Organizational commitment: one of many commitments or key mediating construct? *Acad. Manage. J.* 37:1568–87

Huselid MA. 1995. The impact of human resource management practices on turnover, productivity, and corporate financial performance. *Acad. Manage. Rev.* 3:635–72

Ibarra H. 1992. Homophily and differential returns: sex differences in network structure and access in an advertising firm. *Adm. Sci. Q.* 37:422–47

Ingram P, Simons T. 1995. Institutional and resource dependence determinants of responses to work-family issues. *Acad. Manage. J.* 38:1466–82

Jick TD. 1993. *Managing Change: Cases and Concepts.* Burr Ridge, IL: Irwin

Kanfer FH. 1975. Self-management methods. In *Helping People Change,* ed. FH Kanfer, pp. 309–55. New York: Wiley

Kanfer R, Hulin CL. 1985. Individual differences in successful job searches following layoff. *Pers. Psychol.* 38:835–47
Kanter RM. 1977. *Work and Family in the United States: A Critical Review and Agenda for Research and Policy.* New York: Russell Sage Found.
Kanter RM. 1989. *When Giants Learn to Dance.* New York: Simon & Schuster
Katz HC. 1985. *Shifting Gears: Changing Labor Relations in the U.S. Automobile Industry.* Cambridge, MA: MIT Press
Katz LF, Kruger AB. 1991. Changes in the structure of wages in the public and private sectors. In *Research in Labor Economics,* ed. RG Ehrenberg, 12. Greenwich, CT: JAI
Kelly JR, McGrath J. 1985. Effects of time limits and task types on task performance and interaction of four-person groups. *J. Pers. Soc. Psychol.* 49:395–407
Kerr S, Jermier JM. 1978. Substitutes for leadership: their meaning and measurement. *Organ. Behav. Hum. Perform.* 22:375–403
Kiesler S, Sproull L. 1992. Managerial response to changing environments: perspectives on problem sensing from social cognition. *Adm. Sci. Q.* 27:548–70
Kirchmeyer C. 1995. Managing the work-nonwork boundary: an assessment of organizational responses. *Hum. Relat.* 48:515– 36
Kirkman BL, Shapiro DL, Novelli L Jr. 1994. *Employee resistance to work teams: a justice perspective.* Presented at Acad. Manage. Meet., Aug., Dallas
Korunka C, Weiss A, Karetta B. 1993. Effects of new technologies with special regard for the implementation process per se. *J. Organ. Behav.* 14:331–48
Koys DJ. 1991. Fairness, legal compliance, and organizational commitment. *Empl. Responsib. Rights* 4:283–91
Krackhardt D. 1987. QAP partialling as a test of spuriousness. *Soc. Netw.* 9:171–86
Krackhardt D, Blythe J, McGrath C. 1994. KrackPlot 3.0: an improved network drawing program. *Connections* 17:53–55
Kramer RM, Tyler TR, eds. 1996. *Trust in Organizations: Frontiers of Theory and Research.* Thousand Oaks, CA: Sage
Latham GP, Locke EA. 1991. Self-regulation through goal setting. *Organ. Behav. Hum. Decis. Process.* 50:212–47
Lau C, Woodman R. 1995. Understanding organizational change: a schematic perspective. *Acad. Manage. J.* 38:537–54
Leana CR, Feldman DC. 1996. Finding new jobs after a plant closing: antecedents and outcomes of the occurrence and quality of reemployment. *Hum. Relat.* In press
Leonard-Barton D, Sinha DK. 1993. Developer-user interaction and user satisfaction in internal technology transfer. *Acad. Manage. J.* 36:1125–39
Leung K, Chiu W, Au Y. 1993. Sympathy and support for industrial actions. *J. Appl. Psychol.* 78:781–87
Liem R. 1992. Unemployed workers and their families: social victims or social critics? In *Families and Economic Distress,* ed. P Voydanoff, LC Majka, pp. 135–51. Beverly Hills, CA: Sage
Locke EA, Latham GP. 1990. *A Theory of Goal Setting and Task Performance.* Englewood Cliffs, NJ: Prentice-Hall
Locke EA, Shaw KN, Saari LM, Latham GP. 1981. Goal setting and task performance: 1969–1980. *Psychol. Bull.* 90:125–52
Louis MR, Sutton RI. 1991. Switching cognitive gears: from habits of mind to active thinking. *Hum. Relat.* 44:55–76
Lucero MA, Allen RE. 1994. Employee benefits: a growing source of psychological contract violations. *Hum. Res. Manage.* 33:425–46
Lyles MA, Schwenk CR. 1992. Top management, strategy, and organizational knowledge structures. *J. Manage. Stud.* 29:155–74
Magnum G, Mayhall D, Nelson K. 1985. The temporary help industry: a response to the dual internal labor market. *Ind. Labor Relat. Rev.* 38:599–611
Manz CC. 1992. Self-leading work teams: moving beyond self-management myths. *Hum. Relat.* 45:1119–40
Manz CC, Sims HP Jr. 1987. Leading workers to lead themselves: the external leadership of self-managing work teams. *Adm. Sci. Q.* 32:106–28
Mathieu JE, Zajac DM. 1990. A review and meta-analysis of the antecedents, correlates, and consequences of organizational commitment. *Psychol. Bull.* 98:224–53
Mayer RC, Davis JH, Schoorman FD. 1995. An integrative model of organizational trust. *Acad. Manage. Rev.* 20:709–34
Merriam-Webster Inc. 1985. *Webster's Third International Dictionary.* Springfield, MA: Merriam-Webster
Meyer M, Gupta V. 1994. The performance paradox. In *Research in Organizational Behavior,* ed. B Staw, LL Cummings, 16: 309–69. Greenwich, CT: JAI
Meyerson D, Weick KE, Kramer RM. 1996. Swift trust and temporary groups. See Kramer & Tyler 1996, pp. 166–95
Miles RE, Creed WED. 1995. Organizational forms and managerial philosophies. In *Research in Organizational Behavior,* ed. LL Cummings, BM Staw, 17:333–72. Greenwich, CT: JAI
Miner AS. 1990. Structural evolution through idiosyncratic jobs: the potential for unplanned learning. *Organ. Sci.* 1:195–210
Miner AS, Robinson DF. 1994. Organization and population level learning as engines for career transitions. *J. Organ. Behav.* 15:345–64
Mirvis PH, Hall DT. 1994. Psychological suc-

cess and the boundaryless career. *J. Organ. Behav.* 15:365–80

Mitchell TR. 1979. Organizational behavior. *Annu. Rev. Psychol.* 30:243–82

Moorman RH. 1991. Relationship between organizational justice and organizational citizenship behaviors: do fairness perceptions influence employee citizenship. *J. Appl. Psychol.* 76:845–55

Mowday R, Sutton RI. 1993. Organizational behavior: linking individuals and groups to organization contexts. *Annu. Rev. Psychol.* 44:195–229

Mroczkowski T, Hanaoka M. 1989. Continuity and change in Japanese management. *Calif. Manage. Rev.* 31:39–53

National Association of Temporary and Staffing Services. 1994. *Temporary Help/Staffing Services Industry Continues to Create Employment Opportunities.* Alexandria, VA: Natl. Assoc. Temp. Staff. Serv.

National Research Council, ed. 1994. *Organizational Linkages: Understanding the Productivity Paradox.* Washington, DC: Natl. Acad. Press

Neal A, Hesketh B, Andrews S. 1995. Instance-based categorization: intentional versus automatic forms of retrieval. *Mem. Cogn.* 23:227–42

Nicolini D, Meznar MB. 1995. The social construction of organizational learning: conceptual and practical issues in the field. *Hum. Relat.* 48:727–46

Noe RA, Wilk SL. 1993. Investigation of the factors that influence employees' participation in development activities. *J. Appl. Psychol.* 78:291–302

Nordhaug O. 1989. Reward functions of personnel training. *Hum. Relat.* 42:373–88

Novelli L, Kirkman BL, Shapiro DL. 1995. Effective implementation of organizational change: an organizational justice perspective. In *Trends in Organizational Behavior,* ed. CL Cooper, DM Rousseau, pp. 2:15–36. Chichester: Wiley

O'Driscoll MP, Ilgen DR, Hildreth K. 1992. Time devoted to job and off-job activities, interrole conflict, and affective experiences. *J. Appl. Psychol.* 77:272–79

O'Leary-Kelly AM, Griffin RW, Glew DJ. 1996. Organization-motivated aggression: a research framework. *Acad. Manage. Rev.* 21:225–53

O'Reilly CA. 1991. Organizational behavior: where we've been, where we're going. *Annu. Rev. Psychol.* 42:427–58

Organ DW. 1990. The motivational basis of citizenship behavior. In *Research in Organizational Behavior*, ed. LL Cummings, BM Staw, 12:43–72. Greenwich, CT: JAI

Pearce JL. 1993. Toward an organizational behavior of contract laborers: their psychological involvement and effects on employee co-workers. *Acad. Manage. J.* 36: 1082–96

Perrow C. 1984. *Normal Accidents: Living with High-risk Technologies.* New York: Basic Books

Perrow C. 1996. The bounded career and the demise of civil society. See Arthur & Rousseau 1996, pp. 297–313

Podsakoff PM, Niehoff BP, MacKenzie SB, Williams ML. 1993. Do substitutes for leadership really substitute for leadership? An empirical examination of Kerr and Jermier's situational leadership model. *Organ. Behav. Hum. Decis. Process.* 54:1–44

Price RH, Hooijberg R. 1992. Organizational exit pressures and role stress: impact on mental health. *J. Organ. Behav.* 13:641–52

Pritchard RD. 1990. *Measuring and Improving Organizational Productivity.* New York: Praeger

Pritchard RD. 1994. Decomposing the productivity linkages paradox. See National Research Council 1994, pp. 161–92

Roberts K, Clark SC, Wallace C. 1994. Flexibility and individualisation: a comparison of transitions into employment in England and Germany. *Soc.* 28:31–54

Robinson SL. 1995. Violation of psychological contracts: impact on employee attitudes. See Tetrick & Barling 1995, pp. 91–108

Robinson SL, Bennett RJ. 1995. A typology of deviant workplace behaviors: a multidimensional scaling study. *Acad. Manage. J.* 38:555–72

Robinson SL, Rousseau DM. 1994. Violating the psychological contract: not the exception but the norm. *J. Organ. Behav.* 15: 245–59

Rodgers R, Hunter JE. 1991. Impact of management by objectives on organizational productivity. *J. Appl. Psychol.* 76:322–36

Roe RA. 1995. Developments in Eastern Europe and work and organizational psychology. In *International Review of Industrial and Organizational Psychology,* ed. CL Cooper, IT Robertson. Chichester: Wiley

Rosenbaum JE, Kariya T, Settersten R, Maier T. 1990. Market and network theories of the transition from high school to work. *Annu. Rev. Soc.* 16:263–99

Rousseau DM. 1995. *Psychological Contracts in Organizations: Understanding Written and Unwritten Agreements.* Newbury Park, CA: Sage

Rousseau DM, Tijoriwala S. 1996. *It takes a good reason to change a psychological contract.* Presented at Soc. Ind./Organ. Psychol., April, San Diego

Rousseau DM, Tinsley K. 1996. Human resources are local: society and social contracts in a global economy. In *Handbook of Selection and Appraisal,* ed. N Anderson, P Herriot. London: Wiley. In press

Sagan S. 1993. *The Limits of Safety: Organizations, Accidents, and Nuclear Weapons.* Princeton, NJ: Princeton Univ. Press

Schneider B, Bowen DE. 1995. *Winning the Service Game.* Boston: Harvard Bus. Sch. Press

Seashore SE, Indik BP, Georgopolous BS. 1960. Relationships among criteria of job performance. *J. Appl. Psychol.* 44:195–202

Semler R. 1989. Managing without managers. *Harv. Bus. Rev.* 67(5):76–84

Shapiro DL, Buttner EH, Barry B. 1994. Explanations: What factors enhance their perceived adequacy? *Organ. Hum. Decis. Process.* 58:346–68

Sheppard BH, Lewicki RJ, Minton JW. 1992. *Organizational Justice: The Search for Fairness in the Workplace.* New York: Lexington Books

Sherman S. 1995. Stretch goals: the dark side of asking for miracles. *Fortune,* Nov. 13. pp. 231–32

Shipper F, Manz CC. 1992. Employee self-management without formally designated teams: an alternative road to empowerment. *Organ. Dyn.* 20:48–61

Shore LM, Wayne SJ. 1993. Commitment and employee behavior: comparison of affective commitment and continuance commitment with perceived organizational support. *J. Appl. Psychol.* 78:774–80

Sims HP, Gioia DA, eds. 1986. *The Thinking Organization: The Dynamics of Organizational Social Cognition.* San Francisco: Jossey-Bass

Sinclair RR, Hannigan MA, Tetrick LE. 1995. Benefit coverage and employee attitudes: a social exchange perspective. See Tetrick & Barling 1995, pp. 163–85

Sink DS, Smith GL. 1994. The influence of organizational linkages and measurement practices on productivity and management. See National Research Council 1994, pp. 131–60

Small Business Administration. 1992. *The State of Small Business.* Washington, DC: US Gov. Print. Off.

Smith KG, Locke EA, Barry D. 1990. Goal setting, planning, and organizational performance: an experimental simulation. *Organ. Behav. Hum. Decis. Process.* 46:118–34

Smolowe J. 1996. *Reap as ye shall sow: pay-for-performance standards are a jackpot this year for executives but not for workers. Time,* Feb. 5, p. 45

Snow CC, Miles RE, Coleman HJ. 1992. Managing 21st century network organizations. *Organ. Dyn.* 20:5–20

Starbuck WH, Milliken FJ. 1988. Executives' perceptual filters: what they notice and how they make sense. In *The Executive Effect: Concepts and Methods for Studying Top Managers,* ed. D Hambrick. Greenwich, CT: JAI

Storey DJ. 1994. *Understanding the Small Business Sector.* London: Routledge

Tetrick LE, Barling J, eds. 1995. *Changing Employment Relations: Behavior and Social Perspectives.* Washington, DC: Am. Psychol. Assoc.

Thomas D, Higgins M. 1996. Mentoring and the boundaryless career: lessons from the minority experience. See Arthur & Rousseau 1996. In press

Tsui AS, Ashford SJ, St. Clair L, Xin KR. 1995. Dealing with discrepant expectations: response strategies and managerial effectiveness. *Acad. Manage. J.* 38: 1515–43

Van Maannen J, Barley SR. 1984. Occupational communities: culture and control in organizations. In *Research in Organizational Behavior,* ed. BM Staw, 8:287–364. Greenwich, CT: JAI

Vinocur AD, van Ryn M, Gramlich EM, Price RH. 1991. Long-term follow-up and benefit-cost analysis of the jobs program: a preventive intervention for the unemployed. *J. Appl. Psychol.* 76:213–19

Vroom V. 1964. *Work and Motivation.* New York: Wiley

Wanous JP, Keon TL, Latack JC. 1983. Expectancy theory and occupational organizational choices: a review and test. *Organ. Behav. Hum. Perform.* 32:66–85

Weick KE. 1995. *Sensemaking in Organizations.* Thousand Oaks, CA: Sage

Weick KE. 1996. Enactment and the boundaryless career: organizing as we work. See Arthur & Rousseau 1996, pp. 40–57

Weick KE, Roberts KH. 1993. Collective mind in organizations. *Adm. Sci. Q.* 38:357–81

Welbourne TM, Balkin DB, Gomez-Mejia LR. 1995. Gainsharing and mutual monitoring: a combined agency–organizational justice interpretation. *Acad. Manage. J.* 38:881–99

Welch R. 1994. European works councils and their implications: the potential impact on employer practices and trade unions. *Empl. Relat.* 16:48–61

Wilpert B. 1995. Organizational behavior. *Annu. Rev. Psychol.* 46:59–90

Winefield A, Winefield H, Tiggeman M, Goldney R. 1991. A longitudinal study of the psychological effects of unemployment and unsatisfactory employment on young adults. *J. Appl. Psychol.* 76:424–31

Wood R, Mento A, Locke E. 1987. Task complexity as a moderator of goal effects: a meta-analysis. *J. Appl. Psychol.* 72:416–25

Yankelovich D. 1993. How changes in the economy are reshaping American values. In *Values and Public Policy,* ed. HJ Aaron, TE Mann, T Taylor. Washington, DC: Brookings Inst.

Zenger TR. 1992. Why do employers only reward extreme performance? Examining the relationships among performance, pay, and turnover. *Adm. Sci. Q.* 37:198–220

Annu. Rev. Psychol. 1997. 48:547–72

DECLARATIVE MEMORY: Insights from Cognitive Neurobiology

Howard Eichenbaum

Department of Psychology, Boston University, Boston, Massachusetts 02215

KEY WORDS: amnesia, learning, cognitive neuroscience, hippocampus, natural memory, single neurons

ABSTRACT

The discovery of declarative memory as distinct from other forms of memory is a major recent acheivement in cognitive science. Basic issues about the nature of declarative memory are considered in this review from the perspective of studies on its underlying brain mechanisms. These studies have shown that declarative memory is mediated by a specific brain system including areas of the cerebral cortex and hippocampal region that make distinct functional contributions to memory processing. These processing mechanisms mediate the organization of memories in ways that can support the special properties of declarative or explicit memory expression. Furthermore, the basic properties of declarative memory in human beings can be viewed as evolving from a capacity for organized memory representation and flexible memory expression in animals.

CONTENTS

INTRODUCTION

Declarative memory involves representations of facts and events that are subject to conscious recollection, verbal reflection, and explicit expression. Conscious and explicit memory can be dissociated from other types of memory expression both in normal human subjects (Richardson-Klavehn & Bjork 1988; for a review, see Metcalfe et al 1994) and in amnesia (e.g. Butters & Delis 1995, Squire et al 1993), which has led several investigators to propose that declarative memory is a distinct form of memory. However, despite these major breakthroughs in identifying declarative memory, our understanding of its mechanisms is really quite superficial. We don't know whether declarative memory is mediated by a distinct "memory system" or is more appropriately characterized as a "kind of knowledge" or a particular "level of processing." We know little about the fundamental associational structure of declarative memory, or about the cognitive mechanisms that underlie conscious recollection and explicit memory expression. In addition, we poorly understand how or why declarative memory evolved and became so important in everyday life. In this review I briefly introduce the history and state of our knowledge about declarative memory as a distinct form of memory and then address these outstanding questions.

My focus is on the contributions of cognitive neurobiology, the area of psychological research that seeks to understand cognition by describing its underlying brain substrates. The potential advantages of the cognitive neurobiology approach are numerous, particularly as applied in studies on animals. In these studies the scope and amount of learning are under direct experimental control. Basic memory processes can be examined separately from potentially overwhelming influences of linguistic competence. Anatomical and behavioral manipulations can be pursued at a level of selectivity and resolution not possible in human subjects. Neural coding mechanisms and measures of neural plasticity can be characterized directly. And explorations of animal memory can provide insights about how particular memory mechanisms evolved.

At the same time, and particularly regarding declarative memory, there are special challenges associated with this approach. Obviously animals do not express their memories by verbal declaration, and whether they have a capacity for conscious recollection is a matter of scientific and philosophical debate. In addition, it is not clear what "explicit" expression means in the context of animal testing paradigms. How these challenges are being met is addressed below. The following sections are divided according to specific questions about declarative memory and how the cognitive neurobiology approach might succeed in answering them.

IS DECLARATIVE MEMORY A "MEMORY SYSTEM"?

From Tolman (1932) to Tulving (1985), the suggestion that there are different kinds of learning and memory or multiple memory systems has received considerable support. Categorizations of learning and memory have been proposed in several formats and at different times in the study of memory, even well before the beginning of experimentalism in psychology. Comprehensive reviews of this history are available elsewhere (Eichenbaum 1994, Polster et al 1991, Schacter 1987, Schacter & Tulving 1994b). I focus here on how previous accounts have provided specific insights about declarative memory that inspire or contribute to neurobiological explorations.

All previous accounts have distinguished a complex form of memory, with the properties of declarative memory, from simpler ones that lack these properties. In recent years the most prominent dichotomy of this sort has focused on the specific distinction between "declarative" or "explicit" memory versus "procedural," "implicit," or "nondeclarative" memory. The defining features of declarative memory, as introduced above, are found in its mode of expression—the ability to bring facts and experiences to mind, that is, to consciously recall items in memory—and then to express the recalled memory in a variety of ways, most prominently by verbal reflection on a learned fact or past experience. In contrast, procedural memory is characterized by its inaccessibility to conscious recall and by expression only through implicit measures of performance, typically an increase in speed or a shift in choice bias during repetition of a mental procedure (Cohen & Eichenbaum 1993). Although several dichotomies of human memory have been proposed (cf Squire 1987), most are consensual in these properties that distinguish a conscious, declarative memory from forms of unconscious memory.

Neuropsychological Dissociations of Declarative and Procedural Memory in Human Amnesia

Our understanding of declarative memory from a neuropsychological perspective began with studies on the patient HM, who, after removal of most of the hippocampal formation and its associated medial temporal-lobe structures, suffered a profound impairment in new learning that was remarkable in its severity, pervasiveness, and selectivity (Scoville & Milner 1957, Corkin 1984). HM's memory was severely impaired regardless of the form of the learning materials or modality of their presentation. Yet, even the early observations on HM indicated that the hippocampal region was important to only some aspects of memory. He showed normal retention of most memories he had acquired years before the surgery, i.e. of his childhood. In addition, he demonstrated intact primary- or immediate-memory capacity. These observations of preserved remote and immediate memory capacities permitted investigators to conclude that it was his memory, and not his perceptual, cognitive, linguistic, and motor capacities, that was impaired. These observations showed that different kinds of memory can be distinguished in amnesia.

In addition, even within new learning, HM has a broad set of distinctly preserved learning capacities. His acquisition of motor skills (Corkin 1968, Milner 1962) and perceptual "priming" (Warrington & Weiskrantz 1968) remained intact. These findings were first viewed as exceptions to an otherwise global long-term memory impairment but, following recent studies, are now viewed as merely examples of a large domain of preserved learning capacities observed in amnesic patients, including HM (see Cohen 1984, Cohen & Eichenbaum 1993, Corkin 1984, Schacter 1987, Shimamura 1986, Squire 1987, Squire et al 1993, Tulving & Schacter 1990). The range of intact learning capacities in amnesia includes motor, perceptual, and cognitive skills, sensory adaptations, and priming of perceptual and lexical stimuli (for an extended review, see Cohen & Eichenbaum 1993). Even learning involving the identical materials may be either severely impaired or fully spared in amnesic subjects, depending on whether they were asked to use conscious recollection to recall or recognize the study phase, as is typical in most memory tasks, or whether memory was assessed by more subtle measures such as changes in response bias or speed after exposure to the test materials (e.g. Graf et al 1984).

What Can Cognitive Neurobiology Add to This Story?

These findings have led many investigators to view declarative memory as a separate so-called memory system. For example, in their recent review, Schacter & Tulving (1994a) distinguished several memory systems by each one's ability to support performance on a set of tasks that share particular features and properties, and by our ability to dissociate these performances by multiple approaches. Declarative memory was distinguished from procedural and perceptual memory systems, and it was recognized that many different kinds of memory could exist within a single system. In their categorization, memory subsystems were differentiated by the domain of information involved, e.g. visual memory, olfactory memory. From their point of view, a memory system is defined by the generic memory processing operations it performs and not by the materials that are remembered. Schacter & Tulving's distinctions went beyond having a single declarative system; they listed semantic, primary, and episodic memory systems, all of which are declarative. In addition, they considered the neuropsychological approach as only one way to dissociate memory systems. Thus, in Schacter & Tulving's view, memory systems and brain circuits are not isomorphic; that is, one can have one brain circuit mediate multiple memory systems, or conversely many brain circuits might combine to mediate a particular memory system. The notion of a memory system as a psychological rather than structural entity is a useful heuristic. But, as will be argued here, this is not the only way, and perhaps not the most fruitful perspective, for understanding mechanisms of memory.

At the other extreme is the position taken here that memory is not an entity at all, but rather a reflection of the plasticity properties that characterize each functional circuit of the brain. The consequences of this view are important for how we think about multiple memory systems, especially how they came about and how to pursue describing them. I offer two examples that show the utility of this neurobiological perspective. First, within their framework described above, Schacter & Tulving 1994a (Schacter 1992, Tulving & Schacter 1990) distinguished a set of modality-specific perceptual memory subsystems and grouped them as a perceptual recognition system for categorization and priming. Without contesting the utility of comparing types of memory, the underlying differences between their modality-specific subsystems are viewed here as a natural consequence of the anatomical separation of sensory pathways in the brain. Similarly, Schacter & Tulving's grouping of subsystems into a single "perceptual recognition system" is entirely attributable to commonalities across cortical processing units in the computational circuitry for stimulus categorization and in the inherent plasticity mechanisms by which these codings can be tuned and biased to more strongly represent frequently experienced and important stimuli throughout life (Merznich et al 1991, Weinberger et al 1990).

My second example involves comparing philosophical arguments and neurobiological evidence for multiple memory systems. In 1804 the philosopher Maine de Biran (1929) suggested three separate kinds of memory with different properties. He argued that "mechanical memory" supports the unconscious acquisition of motor and verbal habits, "sensitive memory" supports the unconscious acquisition of feelings associated with specific images and events, and "representative memory" supports conscious recollection of ideas and events. Nearly 200 years later, a virtually identical set of distinctions surfaced in a triple dissociation between memory functions supported by the dorsal striatum, the amygdala, and the hippocampus (McDonald & White 1993). These distinctions were demonstrated in an experiment where rats were trained on a radial maze (a maze with a central platform with eight arms radiating outward) to find food rewards. By carefully manipulating the task demands McDonald & White created three different versions of the task for which performance on each required only one of these structures. The dorsal striatum was critical for associating specific stimuli with an approach response, the amygdala for associating stimuli with reinforcers, and the hippocampus for learning spatial relationships. Based on these findings, Maine de Biran's propositions can now be interpreted as reflections of the different types of associations supported by separate anatomical pathways: the convergence of sensory inputs and motor system connections in the dorsal striatum supporting mechanical memory, the convergence of sensory and affective inputs in the amygdala supporting sensitive memory, and the convergence of higher-order sensory inputs in the hippocampus mediating representative memory.

These considerations have three general implications for our understanding of declarative memory. First, we should continue to refer to a declarative memory system, but we must keep in mind that the underlying basis for its functional properties is to be found in understanding the circuitry and plasticity of a particular brain circuit. Second, although based on a neurobiological perspective, this view is entirely consistent with the perspective of cognitive psychologists who have argued that dissociations between declarative and nondeclarative memory may reflect differences in the level or type of cognitive processing demanded by the task (Graf 1994, Jacoby 1991, Roediger 1990). In my view, transfer between performances on task variations will emerge when and only when distinct brain circuits that mediate distinctive types of processing are called into play by the different tests. Third, the emphasis on processing functions, rather than on memory per se, obligates us to identify the circuitry and computational functions of the hippocampus. In the next section, I consider what information processing is accomplished by the hippocampus and associated structures.

UNCOVERING BASIC MECHANISMS OF DECLARATIVE MEMORY

Conscious recollection and explicit memory expression are relatively easily operationalized for studies on human subjects. In contrast, as mentioned above, it is not obvious how to assess these forms of memory expression directly in animals. Moreover, beyond recognizing and manipulating the demand for conscious or explicit expression, the underlying cognitive or associational mechanisms that support these phenomena, even in human beings, are not obvious. However, there are good hints about the fundamental cognitive mechanisms in both early and modern accounts of memory, and these can be explored in animals as well as human beings.

Early Notions about Multiple Memory Systems that Suggest Mechanisms of Declarative Memory

At the origins of modern experimental psychology, William James's (1890) writings reflected the widely followed separation of conscious memories, what we today would call declarative memories, from the acquisition of unconscious habits (see also Mishkin & Petri 1984). Memories were viewed as mediated by a systematic organization of associations based on various relationships between items, and James argued that our ability for conscious recollection is related to the number and diversity of associative connections within the network organization. In contrast, habits were viewed as simple, inflexible, and automatic mechanisms that could be concatenated to guide even very complex actions, such as playing well-practiced tunes on the piano. In one contrast, articulated in practical terms, James suggested that one could not optimize memory performance by simply attempting to strengthen traces, but could by increasing the number of divergent associations: "[A]ll improvement of the memory lies in the line of elaborating the associates of each of the several things to be remembered" (James 1890, p. 663). In the converse admonition, James advised students not to cram for exams, arguing that, "Things learned thus in a few hours, on one occasion, for one purpose, cannot possibly have formed many associations with other things in the mind." Such a strategy would produce only the kind of serial chain that characterized habits.

Additional historical insights can be found in accounts of memory offered by other early experimentalists. Bartlett (1932) examined the recall of mythical and surreal narrative stories. He observed that people omitted or made more realistic those details that were inconsistent with the conventional social structure and experiences of his subjects. He proposed that remembering is guided by a systematic mental representation of experiences or "an active organization of past reactions," what he called schemas. Modern investigations on the active nature of schema-based processing emphasize the application of inferential organization of material to fit the schematic representation (Koriat & Goldsmith 1996, Schacter 1989). Tolman (1932, 1948, 1949) provided complementary insights from studies of maze learning in rats in which he distinguished different types of learning and focused on the representation of spatial environments by "cognitive maps." He distinguished cognitive maps from the acquisition of habits by both the contents of the representation and the flexibility with which memories could be expressed. He argued that organisms learn to anticipate not only particular stimuli, but also that the interconnected elements of the cognitive map make possible the ability to take appropriate short-cuts and roundabout routes in maze solution, that is, to make navigational inferences. Based on evidence from early neurophysiological studies, Hebb (1949) offered a circuit level theory for associational networks and inferential memory expression. He suggested that groups of neighboring neurons called cell assemblies process specific percepts and can be activated in an ordered fashion—a "phase sequence"—such that "two concepts may acquire a latent 'association' without ever having occurred together in the subject's past experience" (p. 132).

In sum, the collective work of James, Bartlett, Tolman, and Hebb addressed the issues of conscious recollection, and suggested cognitive and neural mechanisms behind recollective experiences. These accounts focused on conscious memory as an elaborate network of associations that can be used with great flexibility for comparing items not previously experienced together during learning, and for guiding behavior in various situations, including explicit memory expression. In contrast, nondeclarative memories may be able to guide both simple and complex behavioral sequences but are characterized by their rigidity and applicability within the confined context of repeating specific sensory and motor processing events.

What Can Cognitive Neurobiology Add to This Story?

Based on these previous accounts, and on the more recent discoveries about human amnesia (Cohen & Squire 1980), Neal Cohen and I developed the hypothesis that declarative memory is supported by a relational representation, that is, an encoding of memories according to relevant relationships among the items (Eichenbaum et al 1992a,b; Cohen & Eichenbaum 1993). Furthermore, a central property of this type of memory is its representational flexibility, a quality that permits inferential use of memories in novel situations. Conversely, nondeclarative memories involve individual representations; such memories are isolated in that they are encoded only within the brain modules in which perceptual or motor processing is engaged during learning. These individual representations are inflexible in that they can be revealed only through reactivation of those modules within the restrictive range of stimuli and situations in which the original learning occurred.

We tested these hypotheses within the general framework that damage to the same structures known to be critical for declarative memory in HM should be essential for these properties of memory representation in animals. Most of our investigations exploited the excellent learning and memory capacities of rats in odor discrimination learning. In our initial studies we found that rats with hippocampal damage were selectively impaired in tasks that encourage the learning of relationships among stimuli (Eichenbaum et al 1988, 1989; see also Alvarado & Rudy 1995, Sutherland et al 1989). Conversely, intact learning was observed in tasks that encouraged separate representations for the items to be remembered. In addition, we found that, even when learned performance was indistinguishable from normal performance, animals with hippocampal system damage were impaired when challenged to choose between familiar discriminative stimuli presented in novel configurations, that is, to use their memories flexibly.

Recently, we have more directly asked whether rats can make inferential judgments about indirectly related odors and whether the hippocampus itself plays a role in such performance (Bunsey & Eichenbaum 1996). To address these questions we developed an odor-guided version of the paired associate task for rats, and we extended the learning requirement to include multiple stimulus-stimulus associations with overlapping stimulus elements. Exploiting rodents' natural foraging strategies that employ olfactory cues, animals were trained with stimuli that consisted of distinctive odors added to a mixture of ground rat chow and sand through which they dug to obtain buried cereal rewards (Figure 1*A*). On each paired associate trial one of two sample odors initially presented was followed by two choice odors, each assigned as the "associate" of one of the samples and baited only when preceded by that sample. Following training on two sets of overlapping odor-odor associations, subsequent probe tests were used to characterize the extent to which learned representations supported two forms of flexible memory expression, transitivity, the ability to judge inferentially across stimulus pairs that share a common element, and symmetry, the ability to associate paired elements presented in the reverse of training order (Figure 1*B*).

Intact rats learned paired associates rapidly, and hippocampal damage did not affect acquisition rate on either of the two training sets (Figure 1*C*), which is consistent with recent reports on stimulus-stimulus association learning in rats and monkeys (Murray et al 1993, Saunders & Weiskrantz 1989). Intact rats also showed strong transitivity across the sets reflected in a preference for items indirectly associated with the presented sample (Figure 1*D*). In contrast, rats with selective hippocampal lesions were severely impaired in that they showed no evidence of transitivity. In the symmetry test, intact rats again showed the appropriate preference in the direction of the symmetrical association (Figure 1*E*). In contrast, rats with hippocampal lesions again were severely impaired, showing no significant capacity for symmetry.

These results provide compelling evidence that normal rats have the capacity for inferential memory expression. These findings provide an extension to animals of classic views on human memory, including William James's (1890) description of (declarative) memory as involving an elaborated network of associations that can be applied across a broad range of situations, Tolman's characterization of inference in cognitive mapping, and Hebb's proposal that conscious memory supports inferences about indirect relations between stimuli not previously experienced together. These observations also provide a bridge to present-day characterizations of human declarative memory, such as Cohen's (Cohen & Eichenbaum 1993) description of declarative memory as promiscuous in its accessibility by novel routes of expression, as well as Dickinson's (1980) views about inferential capacities as evidence for declarative processing in animal memory. The results of this study also show that some form of stimulus-stimulus representations can be acquired independent of the hippocampus itself in animals, as is the case in human amnesic pateients as well (Moscovitch et al 1994, Musen & Squire 1993). How this might have been accomplished is discussed at length below. However, only a hippocampally mediated representation can support the flexible expression of associations among items within a larger organization.

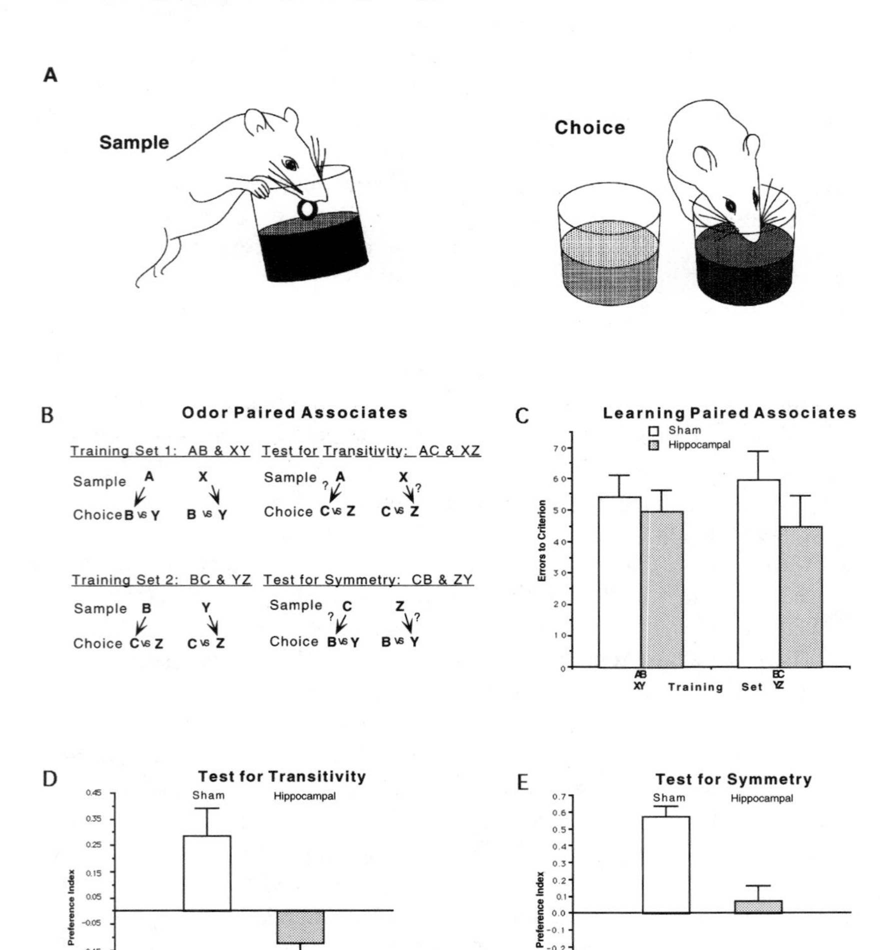

The Encoding of Relations Between Stimuli by Hippocampal Neurons

Precisely what aspects of events are represented within hippocampal circuitry? Corresponding to my argument that the hippocampus supports a relational representation, the activity of single hippocampal neurons should reflect specific relationships among stimuli relevant to the behavioral task at hand. Evidence supporting this expectation is derived from experiments in which the activity of single hippocampal neurons was recorded while rats performed in a variety of learning and memory tasks (reviewed in Eichenbaum 1996; Eichenbaum et al 1992a, 1994). For example, in our own research involving some of the same odor-guided learning and memory paradigms described above, we found hippocampal cells that increased firing dependent on the conjunction or combination of multiple odors presented either in different spatial configurations or temporal sequences (Eichenbaum et al 1986, Otto & Eichenbaum 1992a, Wiener et al 1989). Others have found hippocampal neuronal activity corresponding to spatial and temporal configurations of visual, auditory, and spatial discrimination and matching tasks in rats (Deadwyler et al 1995, Foster et al 1987, Sakurai 1990, Wible et al 1986) and to conjunctions of two-dimensional patterns and their spatial or temporal positions in visual recognition, conditional discrimination, or delayed-response tasks in monkeys (Eifuku et al 1995, Riches et al 1991, Rolls et al 1989, Watanabe & Niki 1985).

Other prominent examples of functional correlates of hippocampal neural activity are derived from studies of rats performing open field exploration or spatial memory tasks. The major finding of these studies is that many hippocampal output neurons fire when the rat is in a particular place in the environ-

◀

Figure 1 Odor paired associate learning and inferential expression of odor-odor associations. (*A*) Training on odor-odor paired associates. Each training trial consisted of two phases. In the sample phase, the subject was presented with a cup containing a scented mixture of sand and ground rat chow with a buried reward. In the subsequent choice phase, two scented choices were presented. Both choice items involved odors that were different from the sample odor, and which item was baited depended on the identity of the sample. (*B*) Schematic diagram of paired associate training and probe testing. Letters represent odor stimulus items; arrows without question marks indicate trained pairings, whereas arrows with question marks indicate expected transitive and symmetrical choices. Rats are first trained on two overlapping sets of paired associates (*left*). Then (*right*) they are tested for inferential expression in two ways. In the test for transitivity, they are presented with one of two sample cues from the first training set and are required to select between the choice cues from the second set, based on the shared associates of these items. In the test for symmetry or reversibility of the associations, they are presented with one of two choice cues from the second set and required to select the appropriate sample cue from that set. (*C*) Errors to criterion on acquisition of the two sets of paired associates for sham operated and hippocampal subjects. (*D*) Preferences on the test for transitive inference. For these probe trials a preference score was calculated as $(X - Y)/(X + Y)$, where X and Y were the digging times in the transitive and alternate choices, respectively. (*E*) Preferences on the test for symmetrical expression.

ment as the animal explores a large open field (cf O'Keefe 1976, 1979). It is widely accepted that the "place cell" phenomenon reflects the representation of relevant positional relations among distal stimuli that determine the spatial layout of the environment. This suggestion is supported by the finding that place fields move in concert with rotations of salient visual cues (Miller & Best 1980, Muller et al 1987, O'Keefe & Conway 1978, O'Keefe & Speakman 1987) and that the place fields of some cells scale with enlargement of all features of the environment (Muller & Kubie 1987). Notably, cells that have spatial firing properties in some tasks also have other nonspatial firing correlates when the task demands change (see Eichenbaum 1996, Eichenbaum & Cohen 1988). Furthermore, in recent studies using a radial maze task where both spatial and nonspatial cues were prominent, we found that hippocampal cells encoded both types of information, and that the overall hippocampal representation reflected both spatial and nonspatial relations among cues and associated behavioral actions (Young et al 1994). So, spatial and nonspatial relations are both prominently represented in the hippocampus. If there is a common property across the variety of observations on hippocampal neural activity in behaving animals, one reasonable candidate is that hippocampal representations involve all manner of relations among cues and actions relevant to the task at hand. This characterization of hippocampal coding is entirely consistent with findings from lesion studies discussed above.

A Cortical-Hippocampal Circuit for Declarative Memory

Additional insights about the processing mechanisms that underlie declarative memory are found by considering the distinct roles and nature of information coding at successive processing stages in the circuit of cortical structures in which the hippocampus participates (Amaral & Witter 1989, Burwell et al 1995, Witter et al 1989). This research is guided by a simple conception of cortical-hippocampal pathways in which there are three main serially and bidirectionally connected components: the cortex, the parahippocampal region, and the hippocampus itself (Figure 2*A*). The beginning and end point of this circuit involves several tertiary or association cortical areas whose outputs converge on the parahippocampal region. This region, composed of the interconnected perirhinal, parahippocampal (or postrhinal), and entorhinal cortices, surround the hippocampus in both rats and monkeys and merge different sources of cortical input bound for the hippocampus. Within the hippocampus itself there are several stages of serial and parallel processing, and the outcome of this integration is sent back to the parahippocampal region, which in turn sends its main outputs to the same tertiary cortical areas that provided the source of input.

A commonly held view about how these structures interact is that organized memory representations are established in the cortex, and that the parahippo-

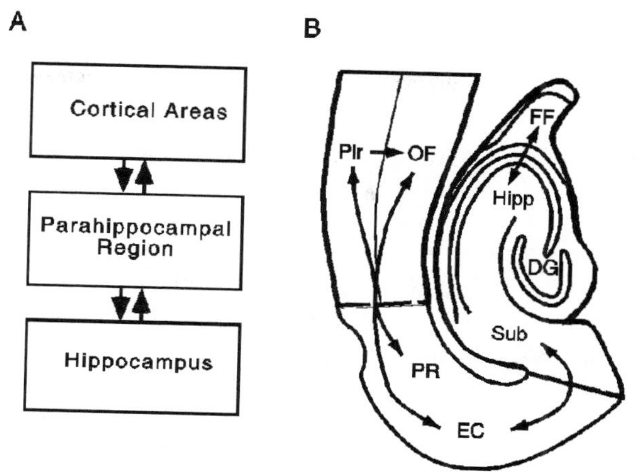

Figure 2 (*A*) Simple schematic diagram of cortical-hippocampal connections.(*B*) Outline of a horizontal rat brain section illustrating the locations and flow of information between components of the hippocampus, parahippocampal region, and adjacent cortical areas. DG, dentate gyrus; EC, entorhinal cortex; FF, fimbria-fornix; Hipp, hippocampus proper; OF, orbitofrontal cortex; Pir, piriform cortex; PR, perirhinal cortex; Sub, subiculum.

campal region and the hippocampus contribute to memory processing by modifying the persistence and organization of those cortical representations. Our own explorations of this working hypothesis have focused on the set of interconnected olfactory-cortical and hippocampal structures that are fully evolved in rodents and that provide a model in which to examine the contributions of each component of the circuit (Figure 2*B;* Burwell et al 1995, Deacon et al 1983, Price et al 1991).

OLFACTORY CORTEX The piriform and orbitofrontal cortex are critical to olfactory learning in rodents (e.g. Eichenbaum et al 1983). To uncover the nature of organized odor representations in olfactory cortex that might depend on hippocampal processing we explored a simple kind of learned stimulus organization that might be found in sensory cortex, namely an acquired association between two odors such that presentation of one of them predicts the subsequent occurrence of the other (Schoenbaum & Eichenbaum 1995a,b). We were able to show that rats can learn a predictable relationship between sequentially presented odor stimuli, and we found neural traces of the association in the firing properties of olfactory cortical neurons. Some cells fired differently in response to an odor depending on whether the preceding odor predicted its occurrence. Other cells fired in anticipation of a predicted odor as well as more strongly during the presentation of the predicted odor, similar to findings on another part of association cortex in monkeys (Miyashita 1993). These results indicate that learned stimulus associations are indeed established within the olfactory cortex. Whether their development or persistence depends on hippocampal function remains to be confirmed.

THE PARAHIPPOCAMPAL REGION The earliest reports of amnesia in human beings following damage to the hippocampal region emphasized the critical role of the hippocampus in bridging between immediate memory and permanent memory formation (Milner 1962, Scoville & Milner 1957). In amnesic patients and animals with hippocampal region damage, deficits in memory persistence are characteristically observed as a dissociation between intact immediate memory versus subsequent abnormally rapid forgetting. Initially it was thought that the hippocampus itself played the primary role in extending retention beyond immediate memory. However, recent data have brought this view into question and have turned attention specifically to the parahippocampal region (Brown et al 1987, Murray 1990).

Efforts to delineate the anatomical structures involved in maintaining a memory trace have focused on the delayed nonmatch to sample (DNMS) task first developed for monkeys using three-dimensional junk objects that provide rich and salient cues for this species (Gaffan 1974, Mishkin & Delacour 1975; see also Mishkin 1978, Zola-Morgan & Squire 1985). In our own work on rats we developed a variant of the DNMS task that used odor cues (Otto & Eichenbaum 1992b). In this task a sequence of odor cues is presented, and subjects are rewarded for responding to a stimulus that is different from (a nonmatch with) the preceding cue, but they are not rewarded for responding to a stimulus that is the same as (a match with) the preceding odor. We compared the effects of selective ablation of the parahippocampal region versus that of damage to the hippocampus (fornix transection) and found that neither lesion affected the acquisition rate. In subsequent tests with longer memory delays, intact rats showed a gradual performance decline, but rats with damage to the parahippocampal region had an abnormally rapid memory decay, showing a severe deficit within several seconds. In contrast, rats with hippocampal damage were unimpaired across delays, showing the same gradual memory decay as intact rats. These results indicate that neither hippocampal component is critical to odor perception, acquisition of the nonmatch rule, or immediate memory. However, the parahippocampal region is critical to extending the persistence of cortical representations beyond immediate memory in rats (Jarrard 1993, Mumby & Pinel 1994), as it is in monkeys (Murray & Mishkin 1986, Zola-Morgan et al 1989) and human beings. Furthermore, through its direct and reciprocal connections with the cortex, the parahippocampal region is sufficient to mediate this memory function independent of hippocampal processing.

In complementary electrophysiological studies, we have also examined the response properties of neurons in the parahippocampal region and the hippocampus in rats performing the odor-guided DNMS task (Otto & Eichenbaum 1992a, Young et al 1995). Cells in the parahippocampal region showed selective or coarse tuning to odor stimuli, which indicates that this area encodes specific odor representations. In addition, odor representations in the parahippocampal region were observed to persist through the memory delay. In the hippocampus, cells were also selectively active during stimulus sampling, and the activity of some reflected the match or nonmatch relationship critical to performance in this task. However, unlike cells in the parahippocampal region, hippocampal cells did not fire associated with particular odors that composed specific comparisons. Rather, hippocampal cellular activity reflected all comparisons with the same outcome. We interpreted this finding as entirely consistent with the results of our lesion studies: Apparently the parahippocampal region, but not the hippocampus, maintains specific and persistent representations sufficient to support recognition performance. In contrast, the hippocampus itself encodes abstract relations among cues in DNMS, as in many other situations (see above).

We also have begun to investigate the role of the parahippocampal region in learning stimulus-stimulus associations. Above, I considered one example of paired associate learning and notably found that hippocampal lesions did not affect the initial acquisition of stimulus-stimulus association, but only the flexible, inferential use of them. For our studies on the role of the parahippocampal region in paired associate learning, we developed a version of the task that involved a list of four odor-paired associates that had to be distinguished from many different foils, some composed of the same odor elements in different pairings (Bunsey & Eichenbaum 1993). On each trial two odors were presented in rapid sequence, separated by a brief blank period, much as in conventional verbal paired associate tasks for human subjects. Subjects had to perform a discriminative response to obtain a reward when a paired associate sequence was presented and learned to withhold the response for other stimulus sequences not associated with reward. We found that normal rats gradually learned to distinguish paired associates from mispairings of the same odor elements. In contrast, rats with parahippocampal lesions could not learn to distinguish paired associates from mispairings, even when given nearly twice as many training trials as normal rats. Similar findings indicating the parahippocampal region plays a critical role in stimulus-stimulus association have been made in monkeys (Murray et al 1993).

HIPPOCAMPUS To directly compare the role of the hippocampus and parahippocampal region in stimulus-stimulus association, we (Eichenbaum & Bunsey 1995) tested the effects of selective hippocampal damage on the identical paired associate task described just above. In contrast with the severe impairment observed after parahippocampal region damage, hippocampal lesions did not result in an impairment in distinguishing paired associates from mispairings, similar to the findings of no-deficit in acquisition of stimulus-stimulus associations in the first described version of paired associate learning (Bunsey & Eichenbaum 1996). However, the experiment described above indicated that the hippocampus did play a role in flexible expression of these associations, as it does in paired associate recall in human beings (Zola-Morgan et al 1986). To account for different roles of the hippocampus and parahippocampal region we speculated that stimulus representations that support paired associate learning could be encoded in two fundamentally different ways, one subserved by the parahippocampal region in the absence of a hippocampal influence and another when the hippocampus is intact.

What could be the nature of these two forms of associative encoding? We turned again to William James (1890). In his classic considerations of the binding problem in perception and memory, James suggested that stimulus elements may be conceived of either as not distinct from one another and consequently bound by a conceptual fusion or, alternatively, as separate and then bound by association in memory. Extending our results on DNMS showing that the parahippocampal region can maintain persistent stimulus representations, we have suggested this area can mediate the encoding of the elements of paired associates as fused representations, even when the hippocampus is removed (Eichenbaum et al 1994). Alternatively, in the intact system, we suggest the hippocampus can prevent this fusion and instead mediate the separate codings of stimulus elements and their association according to the relevant relationships between the items. This account is supported by observations that hippocampal lesions that spare the parahippocampal region do not prevent stimulus-stimulus learning; rather, the putative fused representations are marked by the absence of representational flexibility [e.g. transitivity and symmetry (Bunsey & Eichenbaum 1996)]. Notably, studies of amnesia have also provided evidence of fused representations in human beings following hippocampal damage. Amnesics are indeed profoundly impaired in learning, but when they do succeed, their performance has been characterized as hyper-specific, based on a unitized structure that can be expressed only in highly constrained conditions that imitate the conditions of original learning (Schacter 1985; see also Eichenbaum et al 1992c, Moscovitch et al 1994, Musen & Squire 1993).

THE HIPPOCAMPAL SYSTEM AND "REAL-LIFE" MEMORY

To obtain a comprehensive understanding of declarative memory, the notions of relational representation and representational flexibility should offer insights into two domains outside conventional laboratory memory research: how declarative memory is used in everyday "real life," and how it evolved as an adaptive cognitive mechanism in the real lives of animals as well as human beings.

Everyday, Real-Life Memory in Human Beings and Animals

Recent research using naturalistic or ecological approaches to human memory highlights the need for greater consideration of the organization of memory representation beyond that traditionally done in most laboratory research. Koriat & Goldsmith (1996) elegantly contrasted laboratory research on human memory as primarily focused on the quantity of information that is stored and maintained in memory, and its evaluation according to the number of items recovered, versus naturalistic approaches that have shifted the focus toward considerations of the content of memory, and its evaluation according to the correspondence between experience and memory. Thus interest in naturalistic studies of memory has grown, at least in part, out of the limitations of the traditional testing methods and focuses on characterizing the organization of memory in real-life situations, including autobiographical memory, eyewitness testimony, and flashbulb memory. Studies on each of these types of memory incorporate the rich context in which everyday learning and memory performance occurs and reflect the relevant social, motivational, and functional factors at least as much as when and how much information is stored.

Analyses of everyday memory in human beings provide important elaborations of the features of memory I have used above to characterize declarative memory. Thus, extending Bartlett's (1932) views, Neisser (1967) characterized natural memory as an "active" and "reconstructive" effort at making sense of new experiences within an existing organization of memory, as constrasted with passive priming or entrenching of perceptions that characterizes nondeclarative representations. Consistent with my emphasis on processing systems, Lockhart & Craik (1990) suggested that memory should be thought of "not as the result of a specialized memory encoding process, but rather as a by product or record of normal cognitive processes such as comprehension, categorization, and discrimination" (p. 89). Similarly, in the recall phase, the naturalistic approach emphasizes active reconstructive processes in memory search and recall. For example, Kelly & Jacoby (1990) have emphasized the notion that "the conscious experience of remembering is not to be found in a memory trace. Rather, remembering is an inference based on internal and situational cues" (p. 49). Within this framework it might be concluded that the main role of memory in everyday real life is to create and express a coherent structural organization of our knowledge base using the kind of network memory processes described by early memory researchers.

Concerns about the limitations of laboratory studies on learning have also been voiced by those whose work is directed at real-life learning in animals (Gould & Marler 1994, Rozin 1976, Sherry & Schacter 1987, Shettleworth 1993). Against the mainstream of most traditional laboratory research on animal learning and memory, students of natural animal learning long ago proposed the existence of multiple forms of memory, suggesting that distinct memory systems evolved as specialized adaptations to address specific, ecologically relevant problems (Rozin & Kalat 1971, Sherry & Schacter 1987, Shettleworth 1972). Sherry & Schacter (1987) most clearly articulated this view in their proposal that different memory systems might come about because of functional incompatabilities between the requirements of different learning tasks; for example, song learning and food storing in birds. However, consistent with my emphasis on processing systems, Gould & Marler (1994) proposed that each type of learning is to be understood as plasticity within instinctive or prewired response patterns.

What Can Cognitive Neurobiology Add to This Story?

These considerations heighten the importance of identifying the role of the hippocampal memory system in real-life learning in animals, both to draw out parallels with the human literature on everyday memory and to shed light on how and why declarative memory evolved. A central question within these considerations is whether the origins of declarative memory are to be found in a specialized system or whether it emerges as a general capacity for access to memory across separate specialized systems (Rozin 1976). Inspired by evidence indicating an important role for the hippocampus in spatial maze learning (O'Keefe & Nadel 1978), research exploring the functional evolution of the hippocampus has focused on natural spatial behaviors in birds and mammals. Krebs (1990) showed, for example, that the avian homologue of the hippocampus is larger in birds species that store food and must remember cache locations than in related nonstoring species. Other work has demonstrated a similar correlation between hippocampal size and ecological demands on spatial behavior in voles (Sherry et al 1992). These findings provide impressive evidence suggesting adaptive advantages for spatial memory might have driven the evolution of the hippocampal system.

In our own work we sought to broaden the focus on spatial learning by exploring how the relational memory functions of the hippocampus, discovered in experiments on odor-guided learning, could underlie spatial learning performance that depends on hippocampal function (Eichenbaum et al 1990). We studied the effects of hippocampal damage on spatial learning using the Morris water maze task, which replicates some of the demands of natural spatial navigation (Morris et al 1982). The apparatus used in these studies is a large circular swimming pool filled with an opaque water solution and containing an escape platform slightly submerged at a fixed location relative to salient extra-maze visual cues. In the standard version of this task, rats are released into the water at different starting points on successive trials, a manipulation that strongly encourages rats to develop a representation of spatial relations among cues. Under this condition, intact animals rapidly learned the place of the platform, as demonstrated by their escaping with progressively shorter latencies. In contrast, rats with hippocampal damage failed to learn the escape locus.

When we eliminated the demand for learning spatial relations by releasing the rat from a constant start position on each trial, rats with hippocampal damage learned to escape nearly as rapidly as normal animals. We ascertained that the representation of hippocampal rats was based on the distal cues, as was the case for normal rats. Then, to assess the flexibility of the spatial memory representation supporting accurate performance on this version of the water maze task, we presented rats with different types of probe trials. In one of our probes we required animals to navigate using the same cues, but beginning each swim from a novel start location. Normal rats swam directly to the platform regardless of the starting position, but rats with hippocampal damage swam in various directions and sometimes never located the platform. Thus, as in olfactory learning, the hippocampus is critical when learning relations among cues is emphasized; when this demand is eliminated, rats with hippocampal damage can succeed in place learning (see also Whishaw et al 1995). Moreover, spatial memory expression in normal rats is flexible; that is, it can support navigation based on inference as described by Tolman (1948), whereas the spatial representation of rats with hippocampal damage is inflexible; that is, limited to repetition of the training path.

One interpretation of these findings is that the hippocampus initially evolved specifically to mediate spatial learning and memory, and only later was this function co-opted for application to other stimulus modalities (Bingman 1992, Nadel 1991, O'Keefe & Nadel 1978). Alternatively, it is possible that the hippocampus evolved as a general mechanism for relational representation, and spatial learning is a very good example of the adaptive advantage it provides. Evidence favoring such a broader role of hippocampal function requires demonstrating how the generic properties of hippocampal-dependent learning I have described come into play in adaptive nonspatial behaviors.

In an effort to investigate the range of hippocampal involvement in natural learning and memory, we assessed the role of the hippocampal region in a type of social olfactory learning and memory, the social transmission of food preferences (Galef & Wigmore 1983, Strupp & Levitsky 1984). Social transmission of food preferences involves alterations in food selection patterns consequent to experience with a conspecific that has recently eaten a particular food. When a so-called observer rat encounters another (demonstrator) rat that has recently eaten a distinctively scented food, the probability that the observer will later select that same food over other foods increases (Figure 3*A;* Galef & Wigmore 1983, Strupp & Levitsky 1984). This form of social learning is interpreted within the heuristic that a food recently consumed by a conspecific is safe, and that transmitting this information is adaptive in rat society.

In a series of studies Galef et al (1988) have shown that the mechanism underlying this learning involves an association between two odors present in the observer rat's breath, the odor of the recently eaten food and an odorous constituent of rat's breath, carbon disulfide. It is of particular importance that exposing the observer to the distinctive food odor alone or to carbon disulfide alone has no effect on later food preference. Thus, the shift in food choice cannot be attributed to mere familiarity with the food odor. In contrast, exposure to the scented food mixed with carbon disulfide, even without the social context in which this association is usually experienced, increased later consumption of food with the same odor. The clear conclusion from these studies is that the formation of a specific stimulus-stimulus association, in the absence of any primary reinforcement, is both necessary and sufficient to support the shift in food selection.

Memory for the social transmission of food preference is decidedly nonspatial, and hence would not be expected to depend on hippocampal function according to the view that the hippocampus evolved as part of a specialized spatial memory system. However, social transmission of food preferences involves the formation of a specific stimulus-stimulus association in a single training episode, plus expression of the memory in a situation different from the learning event, consistent with the general relational properties of declarative memory. Following a previous observation that this type of learning is dependent on the hippocampal region (Winocur 1990), we investigated the role of the hippocampus itself in this task, assessing both immediate memory and delayed (1 day) memory for social exposure to the odor of a novel food (Bunsey & Eichenbaum 1995). Normal rats showed strong memory in both tests (Figure 3*B*). In contrast, rats with damage selective to the hippocampus itself showed intact short-term memory but completely forgot the association within 24 hours. These findings, similar to the pattern of sparing and impairment in human amnesics, indicate that the hippocampus is not required for perceptual or motivational components of learning or for the ability to express a learned food selection. However, the hippocampus itself is required for long-term expression of this natural and nonspatial stimulus assocation.

Other lines of evidence are also currently demonstrating the generality of hippocampal involvement in naturalistic memory in monkeys and rats. In a

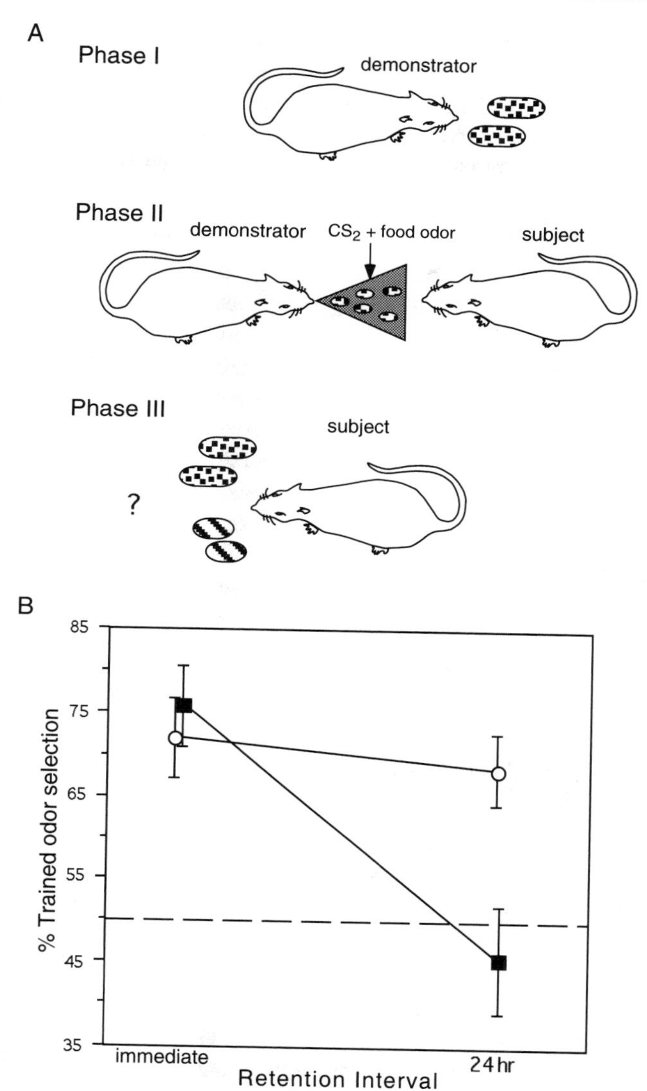

Figure 3 (*A*) Training and testing on a natural odor-odor association task. In Phase I a demonstrator rat is given a distinctively scented food. In Phase II the demonstrator is presented to an experimental subject for a brief period of social interaction during which subjects associate the distinctive food odor and carbon disulfide (CS_2). In Phase III, to test memory for the food odor–CS_2 association, subjects are presented with the same food and another distinctively scented food, either immediately or after a 24-h delay. (*B*) Mean (+ s.e.) selection of trained food odor in intact rats (*open circles*) and rats with selective hippocampal lesions (*closed squares*) at different retention intervals.

recent study of DNMS performance in monkeys, intact monkeys showed a natural inclination to select and manipulate novel objects (that is, they tended to nonmatch) for the first block of trials, whereas monkeys with selective hippocampal damage did not (Zola-Morgan et al 1994). In addition, while not typically impaired in simple pattern discriminations, monkeys with fornix lesions are impaired when the stimuli involve complex, varying backgrounds (Gaffan 1994). The test situations in both of these experiments more closely approximate visual problems monkeys face in the real world than traditional experimental tests in which a simple shape is repeatedly presented in precisely the same background context from trial to trial.

Readdressing the issue of how declarative memory evolved, the collective findings presented above are consistent with Rozin's (1976) proposal about the evolution of conscious memory. He speculated that initially several distinct and specialized information processing (and memory) systems evolved to serve particular adaptive purposes, and that these could not be accessed by any general behavioral or cognitive system. He suggested that conscious memory emerged with evolution of accessibility to those specialized representations. The present account extends this notion and suggests that the hippocampal system mediates the proposed access to specialized representations throughout the brain. In doing so, the hippocampal circuit plays its critical role in conscious recollection in animals as well as in human beings.

CONCLUDING COMMENTS

Studies on the cognitive neurobiology of memory have informed us about the fundamental mechanisms of declarative memory, which can be characterized according to the following tentative conclusions: Declarative memory is mediated by a brain circuit composed of functionally distinct components in the cerebral cortex, parahippocampal region, and hippocampus. The fundamental processing mechanisms that underlie conscious recollection and explicit memory expression include the extended persistence of memory traces for single episodes, the organization of memories according to relevant relations among them, and the capacity for flexible, inferential access to memory representations. Finally, the declarative memory system evolved as a general processing pathway that supports these mechanisms across a broad variety of circumstances in the everyday life of animals and human beings.

ACKNOWLEDGMENTS

Supported by grants from HFSP, NIMH, NIA, and ONR.

Literature Cited

Alvarado MC, Rudy JW. 1995. Rats with damage to the hippocampal formation are impaired on the transverse patterning problem but not on elemental discriminations. *Behav. Neurosci.* 109:204–11

Amaral DG, Witter MP. 1989. The three-dimensional organization of the hippocampal formation: a review of anatomical data. *Neuroscience* 31:571–91

Bartlett FC. 1932. *Remembering.* London: Cambridge Univ. Press

Bingman VP. 1992. The importance of comparative studies and ecological validity for understanding hippocampal structure and cognitive function. *Hippocampus* 2:213–20

Brown MW, Wilson FAW, Riches IP. 1987. Neuronal evidence that inferomedial temporal cortex is more important than hippocampus in certain processes underlying recognition memory. *Brain Res.* 409:158–62

Bunsey M, Eichenbaum H. 1993. Paired associate learning in rats: critical involvement of the parahippocampal region. *Behav. Neurosci.* 107:740–47

Bunsey M, Eichenbaum H. 1995. Selective damage to the hippocampal region blocks long term retention of a natural and nonspatial stimulus-stimulus association. *Hippocampus* 5:546–56

Bunsey M, Eichenbaum H. 1996. Conservation of hippocampal memory function in rats and humans. *Nature* 379:255–57

Burwell RD, Witter MP, Amaral DG. 1995. Perirhinal and postrhinal cortices in the rat: a review of the neuroanatomical literature and comparison with findings from the monkey brain. *Hippocampus* 5:390–408

Butters N, Delis DC. 1995. Clinical assessment of memory disorders in amnesia and dementia. *Annu. Rev. Psychol.* 46:493–523

Butters N, Squire LR, eds. 1984. *Neuropsychology of Memory.* New York: Guilford

Cohen NJ. 1984. Preserved learning capacity in amnesia: evidence for multiple memory systems. See Butters & Squire 1984, pp. 83–103

Cohen NJ, Eichenbaum H. 1993. *Memory, Amnesia, and the Hippocampal System.* Cambridge, MA: MIT Press

Cohen NJ, Squire LR. 1980. Preserved learning and retention of a pattern-analyzing skill in amnesia: dissociation of knowing how and knowing that. *Science* 210:207–10

Corkin S. 1968. Acquisition of a motor skill after bilateral medial temporal lobe excision. *Neuropsychologia* 6:225–65

Corkin S. 1984. Lasting consequences of bilateral medial temporal lobectomy: clinical course and experimental findings in H.M. *Semin. Neurol.* 4:249–59

Deacon TW, Eichenbaum H, Rosenberg P, Eckmann KW. 1983. Afferent connections of the perirhinal cortex in the rat. *J. Comp. Neurol.* 220:168–90

Deadwyler SA, Bunn T, Hampson RE. 1995. Hippocampal ensemble activity during spatial delayed-nonmatch-to-sample performance in rats. *J. Neurosci.* 16:354–72

Dickinson A. 1980. *Contemporary Animal Learning Theory.* Cambridge: Cambridge Univ. Press

Eichenbaum H. 1994. The hippocampal system and declarative memory in humans and animals: experimental analysis and historical origins. See Schacter & Tulving 1994b, pp. 147–202

Eichenbaum H. 1996. Is the rodent hippocampus just for "place"? *Curr. Opin. Neurobiol.* 6:187–95

Eichenbaum H, Bunsey M. 1995. On the binding of associations in memory: clues from studies on the role of the hippocampal region in paired-associate learning. *Curr. Dir. Psychol. Sci.* 4:19–23

Eichenbaum H, Clegg RA, Feeley A. 1983. A re-examination of functional subdivisions of the rodent prefrontal cortex. *Exp. Neurol.* 79:434–51

Eichenbaum H, Cohen NJ. 1988. Representation in the hippocampus: What do the neurons code? *Trends Neurosci.* 11:244–48

Eichenbaum H, Cohen NJ, Otto T, Wible CG. 1992a. Memory representation in the hippocampus: functional domain and functional organization. In *Memory: Organization and Locus of Change,* ed. LR Squire, G Lynch, NM Weinberger, JL McGaugh, pp. 163–204. Oxford: Oxford Univ. Press

Eichenbaum H, Cohen NJ, Otto T, Wible CG. 1992c. A snapshot without the album. *Brain Res. Rev.* 16:209–15

Eichenbaum H, Fagan A, Mathews P, Cohen NJ. 1988. Hippocampal system dysfunction and odor discrimination learning in rats: impairment or facilitation depending on representational demands. *Behav. Neurosci.* 102:3531–42

Eichenbaum H, Kuperstein M, Fagan A, Nagode J. 1986. Cue-sampling and goal-approach correlates of hippocampal unit activity in rats performing an odor discrimination task. *J. Neurosci.* 7:716–32

Eichenbaum H, Mathews P, Cohen NJ. 1989. Further studies of hippocampal representation during odor discrimination learning. *Behav. Neurosci.* 103:1207–16

Eichenbaum H, Otto T, Cohen NJ. 1992b. The

hippocampus: What does it do? *Behav. Neural Biol.* 57:2–36

Eichenbaum H, Otto T, Cohen NJ. 1994. Two functional components of the hippocampal memory system. *Brain Behav. Sci.* 17:449–518

Eichenbaum H, Stewart C, Morris RGM. 1990. Hippocampal representation in spatial learning. *J. Neurosci.* 10:331–39

Eifuku S, Nishijo H, Kita T, Ono T. 1995. Neuronal activity in the primate hippocampal formation during a conditional association task based on the subject's location. *J. Neurosci.* 15:4952–69

Foster TC, Christian EP, Hampson RE, Campbell KA, Deadwyler SA. 1987. Sequential dependencies regulate sensory evoked responses of single units in the rat hippocampus. *Brain Res.* 40:86–96

Gaffan D. 1974. Recognition impaired and association intact in the memory of monkeys after transection of the fornix. *J. Comp. Physiol. Psychol.* 86:1100–9

Gaffan D. 1994. Scene-specific memory for objects: a model of episodic memory impairment in monkeys with fornix transection. *J. Cogn. Neurosci.* 6:305–20

Galef BG Jr, Mason JR, Preti G, Bean NJ. 1988. Carbon disulfide: a semiochemical mediating socially-induced diet choice in rats. *Physiol. Behav.* 42:119–24

Galef BG Jr, Wigmore SR. 1983. Transfer of information concerning distant foods: a laboratory investigation of the "information-centre" hypothesis. *Ann. Behav.* 31: 748–58

Gould JL, Marler P. 1994. Learning by instinct. *Sci. Am.* 256:74–85

Graf P. 1994. Explicit and implicit memory: A decade of research. In *Attention and Performance XV*, eds. C Ulmita, M Moscovitch, pp. 681–96. Cambridge, MA: MIT Press

Graf P, Squire LR, Mandler G. 1984. Amnesic patients perform normally on one kind of memory test for previously presented words. *J. Exp. Psychol.: Learn. Mem. Cogn.* 10:164–78

Hebb DO. 1949. *The Organization of Behavior.* New York: Wiley

Jacoby LL. 1991. A process dissociation framework: Separating automatic from intentional uses of memory. *J. Mem. Lang.* 30:513–41

James W. 1890. (1918). *The Principles of Psychology.* New York: Holt

Jarrard LE. 1993. Review: on the role of the hippocampus in learning and memory in the rat. *Behav. Neural Biol.* 60:9–26

Kelly CM, Jacoby LL. 1990. The construction of subjective experience: memory attributions. *Mind Lang.* 5:49–68

Koriat A, Goldsmith M. 1996. Memory metaphors and the real-life/laboratory controversy: correspondence versus storehouse conceptions of memory. *Brain Behav. Sci.* In press

Krebs JR. 1990. Food storing in birds: adaptive specialization in brain and behavior? *Philos. Trans. R. Soc. B* 329:153–60

Lockhart RS, Craik FIM. 1990. Levels of processing: a retrospective commentary on a framework for memory research. *Can. J. Psychol.* 44:87–112

McDonald RJ, White NM. 1993. A triple dissociation of memory systems: hippocampus, amygdala, and dorsal striatum. *Behav. Neurosci.* 107:3–22

Maine de Biran. 1929. (1804). *The Influence of Habit on the Faculty of Thinking.* Baltimore: Williams & Wilkins

Merznich MM, Recanzone GH, Jenkins WM, Grajski KA. 1991. Adaptive mechanisms in cortical networks underlying cortical contributions to learning and nondeclarative memory. In *The Brain,* pp. 873–87. Cold Spring Harbor, NY: Cold Spring Harbor Symp.

Metcalfe J, Mencl WE, Cottrell GW. 1994. Cognitive binding. See Schacter & Tulving 1994b, pp. 369–94

Mishkin M. 1978. Memory in monkeys severely impaired by combined but not separate removal of the amygdala and hippocampus. *Nature* 273:297–98

Miller VM, Best PJ. 1980. Spatial correlates of hippocampal unit activity are altered by lesions of the fornix and entorhinal cortex. *Brain Res.* 194:311–23

Milner B. 1962. Les troubles de la memoire accompagnant des lesions hippocampiques bilaterales. In *Physiologie de Hippocampe,* ed. P Passquant, pp. 257–72. Paris: Cent. Natl. Rech. Sci.

Mishkin M, Delacour J. 1975. An analysis of short-term visual memory in the monkey. *J. Exp. Psychol.: Anim. Behav. Proc.* 1: 326–34

Mishkin M, Petri HL. 1984. Memories and habits: some implications for the analysis of learning and retention. See Butters & Squire 1984, pp. 287–96

Miyashita Y. 1993. Inferior temporal cortex: where visual perception meets memory. *Annu. Rev. Neurosci.* 16:245–63

Morris RGM, Garrud P, Rawlins JNP, O'Keefe J. 1982. Place navigation impaired in rats with hippocampal lesions. *Nature* 297: 681–83

Moscovitch M, Goshen-Gottstein Y, Vriezen E. 1994. Memory without conscious recollection: a tutorial review from a neuropsychological perspective. See Graf 1994, pp. 619–60

Muller RU, Kubie JL. 1987. The effects of changes in the environment on the spatial firing of hippocampal complex-spike cells. *J. Neurosci.* 7:1951–68

Muller RU, Kubie JL, Ranck JB Jr. 1987. Spatial firing patterns of hippocampal complex spike cells in a fixed environment. *J. Neurosci.* 7:1935–50

Mumby DG, Pinel PJ. 1994. Rhinal cortex lesions and object recognition in rats. *Behav. Neurosci.* 108:11–18

Murray EA. 1990. Representational memory in nonhuman primates. In *Neurobiology of Comparative Cognition,* ed. RP Kesner, DS Olton, pp. 127–55. Hillsdale, NJ: Erlbaum

Murray EA, Gaffan D, Mishkin M. 1993. Neural substrates of visual stimulus-stimulus association in rhesus monkeys. *J. Neurosci.* 13:4549–61

Murray EA, Mishkin M. 1986. Visual recognition in monkeys following rhinal cortical ablations combined with either amygdalectomy or hippocampectomy. *J. Neurosci.* 6: 1991–2003

Musen G, Squire LR. 1993. On implicit learning of novel associations by amnesic patients and normal subjects. *Neuropsychology* 7:119–35

Nadel L. 1991. The hippocampus and space revisited. *Hippocampus* 1:221–29

Neisser U. 1967. *Cognitive Psychology.* New York: Appleton-Century-Crofts

O'Keefe JA. 1976. Place units in the hippocampus of the freely moving rat. *Exp. Neurol.* 51:78–109

O'Keefe JA. 1979. A review of hippocampal place cells. *Prog. Neurobiol.* 13:419–39

O'Keefe JA, Conway DH. 1978. Hippocampal place units in the freely moving rat: why they fire when they fire. *Exp. Brain Res.* 31:573–90

O'Keefe JA, Nadel L. 1978. *The Hippocampus as a Cognitive Map.* New York: Oxford Univ. Press

O'Keefe JA, Speakman A. 1987. Single unit activity in the rat hippocampus during a spatial memory task. *Exp. Brain Res.* 68: 1–27

Otto T, Eichenbaum H. 1992a. Neuronal activity in the hippocampus during delayed nonmatch to sample performance in rats: evidence for hippocampal processing in recognition memory. *Hippocampus* 2:323–34

Otto T, Eichenbaum H. 1992b. Complementary roles of orbital prefrontal cortex and the perirhinal-entorhinal cortices in an odor-guided delayed nonmatching to sample task. *Behav. Neurosci.* 106:763–76

Polster MR, Nadel L, Schacter DL. 1991. Cognitive neuroscience analyses of memory: a historical perspective. *J. Cogn. Neurosci.* 3:95–116

Price JL, Carmichael ST, Carnes K, Clugnet M-C, Kuroda M, Ray JP. 1991. Olfactory input to the prefrontal cortex. In *Olfaction: A Model System for Computational Neuroscience,* ed. JL Davis, H Eichenbaum, pp. 101–20. Cambridge, MA: MIT Press

Richardson-Klavehn A, Bjork RA. 1988. Measures of memory. *Annu. Rev. Psychol.* 39:475–543

Riches IP, Wilson FAW, Brown MW. 1991. The effects of visual stimulation and memory on neurons of the hippocampal formation and the neighboring parahippocampal gyrus and inferior temporal cortex of the primate. *J. Neurosci.* 11:1763–79

Roediger HL. 1990. Implicit memory: Retention without remembering. *Am. Psychol.* 45:1043–56

Rolls ET, Miyashita Y, Cahusac PMB, Kesner RP, Niki H, et al. 1989. Hippocampal neurons in the monkey with activity related to the place where a stimulus is shown. *J. Neurosci.* 9:1835–45

Rozin P. 1976. The evolution of intelligence and access to the cognitive unconscious. *Prog. Psychobiol. Physiol. Psychol.* 6: 245–80

Rozin P, Kalat JW. 1971. Specific hungers and poison avoidance as adaptive specializations of learning. *Psychol. Rev.* 78:459–86

Sakurai Y. 1990. Hippocampal cells have behavioral correlates during performance of an auditory working memory task in the rat. *Behav. Neurosci.* 104:253–63

Saunders RC, Weiskrantz L. 1989. The effects of fornix transection and combined fornix transection, mammillary body lesions and hippocampal ablations on object pair association memory in the rhesus monkey. *Behav. Brain Res.* 35:85–94

Schacter DL. 1985. Multiple forms of memory in humans and animals. In *Memory Systems of the Brain,* ed. NM Weinberger, JL McGaugh, G Lynch, pp. 351–80. New York: Guilford

Schacter DL. 1987. Implicit memory: history and current status. *J. Exp. Psychol.: Learn. Mem. Cogn.* 13:501–18

Schacter DL. 1989. *Memory.* In *Foundations of Cognitive Science,* ed. MI Posner, pp. 683–726. Cambridge, MA: MIT Press

Schacter DL. 1992. Priming and multiple memory systems: perceptual mechanisms of implicit memory. *J. Cogn. Neurosci.* 4: 232–43

Schacter DL, Tulving E. 1994a. What are the memory systems of 1994? See Schacter & Tulving 1994b, pp. 1–38

Schacter DL, Tulving E, eds. 1994b. *Memory Systems 1994.* Cambridge, MA: MIT Press

Schoenbaum G, Eichenbaum H. 1995a. Information coding in the rodent prefrontal cortex. I. Single neuron activity in the orbitofrontal cortex compared with that in the piriform cortex. *J. Neurophysiol.* 74: 733–50

Schoenbaum G, Eichenbaum H. 1995b. Information coding in the rodent prefrontal cortex. II. Ensemble activity in the orbitofrontal cortex. *J. Neurophysiol.* 74:751–62

Scoville WB, Milner B. 1957. Loss of recent memory after bilateral hippocampal lesions. *J. Neurol. Neurosurg. Psychiatry* 20: 11–12

Sherry DF, Jacobs LF, Gaulin SJC. 1992. Adaptive specialization of the hippocampus. *Trends Neurosci.* 15:298–303

Sherry DF, Schacter DL. 1987. The evolution of multiple memory systems. *Psychol. Rev.* 94:439–54

Shettleworth SJ. 1972. Constraints on learning. *Adv. Study Behav.* 4:1–68

Shettleworth SJ. 1993. Varieties of learning and memory in animals. *J. Exp. Psychol.: Anim. Behav. Proc.* 19:5–14

Shimamura AP. 1986. Priming effects in amnesia: evidence for a dissociable memory function. *Q. J. Exp. Psychol. A* 38:619–44

Squire LR, Knowlton B, Musen G. 1993. The structure and organization of memory. *Annu. Rev. Psychol.* 44:453–95

Squire LR. 1987. *Memory and Brain.* New York: Oxford Univ. Press

Strupp BJ, Levitsky DA. 1984. Social transmission of food preferences in adult hooded rats (Rattus Norvegicus). *J. Comp. Psychol.* 98:257–66

Sutherland RJ, Macdonald RJ, Hill CR, Rudy JW. 1989. Damage to the hippocampal formation in rats selectively impairs the ability to learn cue relationships. *Behav. Neur. Biol.* 52:331–56

Tolman EC. 1932. (1951). *Purposive Behavior in Animals and Men.* Berkeley: Univ. Calif. Press

Tolman EC. 1948. Cognitive maps in rats and men. *Psychol. Rev.* 55:189–208

Tolman EC. 1949. There is more than one kind of learning. *Psychol. Rev.* 56:144–55

Tulving E. 1985. How many memory systems are there? *Am. Psychol.* 40:385–98

Tulving E, Schacter DL. 1990. Priming and human memory systems. *Science* 247: 301–6

Warrington EK, Weiskrantz L. 1968. New method for testing long-term retention with special reference to amnesic patients. *Nature* 217:972–74

Watanabe T, Niki H. 1985. Hippocampal unit activity and delayed response in the monkey. *Brain Res.* 325:241–54

Weinberger NM, Ashe JH, Metherate R, McKenna TM, Diamond D, Bakin J. 1990. Retuning auditory cortex by learning: a preliminary model of receptive field plasticity. *Concepts Neurosci.* 1:91–132

Whishaw IQ, Cassel J-C, Jarrard LE. 1995. Rats with fimbria-fornix lesions display a place response in a swimming pool: a dissociation between getting there and knowing where. *J. Neurosci.* 15:5779–88

Wible CG, Findling R, Shapiro M, Lang EJ, Crane S, Olton DS. 1986. Mnemonic correlates of unit activity in the hippocampus. *Brain Res.* 399:97–110

Wiener SI, Paul CA, Eichenbaum H. 1989. Spatial and behavioral correlates of hippocampal neuronal activity. *J. Neurosci.* 9: 2737–63

Winocur G. 1990. Anterograde and retrograde amnesia in rats with dorsal hippocampal or dorsomedial thalamic lesions. *Behav. Brain Res.* 38:145–54

Witter MP, Groenewegen HJ, da Silva FHL, Lohman AHM. 1989. Functional organization of the extrinsic and intrinsic circuitry of the parahippocampal region. *Prog. Neurobiol.* 33:161–253

Young BJ, Fox GD, Eichenbaum H. 1994. Correlates of hippocampal complex spike cell activity in rats performing a nonspatial radial arm maze task. *J. Neurosci.* 14: 6553–63

Young BJ, Otto T, Fox GD, Eichenbaum H. 1995. Neuronal activity in the parahippocampal region of rats performing a delayed nonmatch to sample task. *Soc. Neurosci. Abstr.* 21:943

Zola-Morgan S, Squire LR. 1985. Medial temporal lesions in monkeys impair memory on a variety of tasks sensitive to human amnesia. *Behav. Neurosci.* 99:22–34

Zola-Morgan S, Squire LR, Alvarez P. 1994. Abnormal performance during the first 10 trials of learning the trial-unique delayed nonmatching to sample task by monkeys with lesions limited to the hippocampal region. *Soc. Neurosci. Abstr.* 20:1074

Zola-Morgan S, Squire LR, Amaral DG. 1986. Human amnesia and the medial temporal lobe region: enduring memory impairment following a bilateral lesion limited to the filed CA1 of the hippocampus. *J. Neurosci.* 9:897–912

Zola-Morgan S, Squire LR, Amaral DG, Suzuki WA. 1989. Lesions of perirhinal and parahippocampal cortex that spare the amygdala and hippocampal formation produce severe memory impairment. *J. Neurosci.* 9:4355–70

Annu. Rev. Psychol. 1997. 48:573–607

WHAT'S ELEMENTARY ABOUT ASSOCIATIVE LEARNING?

Edward A. Wasserman

Department of Psychology, University of Iowa, Iowa City, Iowa 52242-1407

Ralph R. Miller

Department of Psychology, Binghamton University, Binghamton, New York 13902-6000

KEY WORDS: Pavlovian conditioning, Thorndikean conditioning, association formation, learned behavior, conditioned responding

ABSTRACT

The scientific study of associative learning began nearly 100 years ago with the pioneering studies of Thorndike and Pavlov, and it continues today as an active area of research and theory. Associative learning should be the foundation for our understanding of other forms of behavior and cognition in human and nonhuman animals. The laws of associative learning are complex, and many modern theorists posit the involvement of attention, memory, and information processing in such basic conditioning phenomena as overshadowing and blocking, and the effects of stimulus preexposure on later conditioning. An unresolved problem for learning theory is distinguishing the formation of associations from their behavioral expression. This and other problems will occupy future generations of behavioral scientists interested in the experimental investigation of associative learning. Neuroscientists and cognitive scientists will both contribute to and benefit from that effort in the next 100 years of inquiry.

CONTENTS

0084-6570/97/0201-0573$08.00

INTRODUCTION AND BROAD OVERVIEW

Nearly every student who has taken an introductory psychology course has heard of Pavlov and Thorndike and learned a bit about their pioneering studies of classical and instrumental conditioning. However, students' textbooks seldom inform them that associative learning is key to understanding both human and animal behavior or that the field is an active and controversial one. Unresolved issues have been revisited and new phenomena discovered for experimental study and theoretical explication. In addition, contributors from neuroscience and cognitive science are making the study of associative learning interdisciplinary.

We hope to convey the challenge and vitality of the field by reviewing the literature of the past dozen years. The last two *Annual Review of Psychology* articles on associative learning appeared in 1978 (Dickinson & Mackintosh) and 1982 (Rescorla & Holland). Because these articles were narrow in focus, we also cover some earlier research.

What Is the Domain of Elementary Associative Learning?

As the final notes fade at the close of the symphony's tranquil third movement, a listener's body tenses as she eagerly anticipates the boisterous opening of the final movement. When he nears the breakfast table, a small boy pushes aside the chair that stands between his seat and the television, thereby permitting him an unobstructed view of his favorite cartoon show. These examples illustrate the operation of associative learning, in which one event comes to be linked with another because of an individual's past experiences.

The first example, in which the associated events do not include the individual's behavior illustrates Pavlovian, classical, or respondent conditioning, whereas the second, in which the individual's behavior is one of the associated events, is one of Thorndikean, instrumental, or operant conditioning. Although the events in Pavlovian and Thorndikean conditioning are decidedly different, the rules that govern these cases of learning are strikingly similar (Dickinson 1980). Largely for convenience, in this review we focus more heavily on Pavlovian conditioning.

What is the History of Associative Learning?

Associative learning has been appreciated since the time of the ancient Greeks and has long been the subject of philosophical speculation (Warren 1921). Yet it was not until the end of the nineteenth century that a true experimental science of associative learning was born. In the United States, Thorndike (1911) arranged a response-outcome contingency that permitted an animal to receive a reward when it performed a prescribed or instrumental behavior. That behavior increased in likelihood when the animal was again placed in the experimental setting. In Russia, Pavlov (1927, 1928) paired two stimuli with each other independently of the organism's behavior. After repeated pairings, conditioned stimuli (CSs) came to elicit conditioned responses (CRs) similar to the unconditioned responses (URs) that had initially been elicited only by unconditioned stimuli (USs).

Since those discoveries, scientists around the world have been assiduously studying the principles of instrumental and classical conditioning, primarily in nonhuman animals. This work peaked in the 1930s, 1940s, and 1950s, when the research and theories of Hull, Skinner, Spence, and Tolman dominated experimental psychology (Bower & Hilgard 1981). Since the 1960s, the study of associative learning has declined in popularity, replaced by research in other aspects of cognition such as attention, memory, and information processing in human beings and animals (Wasserman 1993).

What Is the Current State of the Field?

Although no longer dominant in experimental psychology, associative learning remains a highly active area of research and theory. Work here still focuses on the behavior of animals, but the study of associative learning in human beings is growing in interest and importance (Shanks 1994). Most noteworthy is recent research in causal perception and the success that has been achieved there by associative theories (Allan 1993, Young 1995). Researchers in neuroscience and cognitive science have also become interested in associative learning.

What Is the Promise of the Field?

This objective approach to the study of associative learning has ambitious goals. To Pavlov, "along this path will be found the final triumph of the human mind over its uttermost and supreme problem—the knowledge of the mechanism and laws of human nature" (1928, p. 41). Thorndike further hoped to understand the origin and development of the human mental faculty because "out of...associative processes have arisen human consciousnesses with their sciences and arts and religions" (1911, p. 22). Far from being merely the laboratory study of learning in animals, the field still hopes to elucidate human and animal cognition by detailing the laws of associative learning.

BASIC RESEARCH PHENOMENA

Since the work of Thorndike and Pavlov, many research phenomena have been discovered and investigated. Those phenomena are central to the empirical corpus of the field and have inspired many theories of associative learning. Here we review some of those key phenomena.

Simple Acquisition with a Single Cue or Response

CONTIGUITY AND SIMILARITY Temporal contiguity between events has been one of the most important and well-researched factors in associative learning. In Pavlovian conditioning, temporal contiguity is defined by the CS-US interval; in Thorndikean conditioning, temporal contiguity is defined by the response-outcome delay.

Most authors who have surveyed the effects of the interstimulus interval (ISI) in Pavlovian conditioning have concluded that simultaneity of CS and US is not optimal for promoting CRs; rather, there is an advantage to the CS preceding the US by a relatively short time, with that advantage being a nonmonotonic function of the CS-US interval (Mackintosh 1983, Rescorla 1988; cf Matzel et al 1988c). The best ISI for promoting CRs is not a fixed point in time; it differs with the response, the intensity and nature of CS and US, and the temporal distribution of CS-US pairings (Atkins et al 1994, Berk & Miller 1978, Lennartz & Weinberger 1992, Schneiderman 1972). Moreover, lengthening the intertrial interval (ITI) raises the optimal ISI (Gibbon et al 1977, Levinthal et al 1985), which suggests that the key variable is the ISI/ITI ratio.

The customary interpretation of ISI effects is that the CS-US interval directly affects the acquisition of a CS-US association. However, other variables may participate. For example, limited prior training at ineffective ISIs nonetheless facilitates later CRs at an effective ISI; indeed, this facilitation is as great after pretraining at many ineffective ISIs as it is after pretraining at effective ones (Ross & Scavio 1983). In addition, reducing the number of trials per session increases the efficacy of longer ISIs (Kehoe et al 1991). These and other results are best interpreted by admitting performance variables into the behavioral equation (DeCola & Fanselow 1995, Yin et al 1994).

The low level of CRs that is often seen after simultaneous presentations of CS and US is usually attributed to a failure of acquisition. However, Rescorla (1980) argued that simultaneous events actually yield maximal learning, unless the US distracts the subject from the CS. He showed that robust acquisition occurs when the simultaneously paired events are not biologically significant and hence do not distract from one another. Suggestive of an alternative explanation, Matzel et al (1988c) and Barnet et al (1991) found that the CR deficit is at least in part due to a failure of the organism to express an association that it had actually acquired.

In Thorndikean conditioning, increasing the delay between response and outcome reduces the efficacy of a reinforcer (for a review, see Tarpy & Sawabini 1974; for data, see Dickinson et al 1992, Wilkenfield et al 1992) or a punisher (for a review, see Azrin & Holz 1966; for data, see Baron et al 1969, Cohen 1968) in controlling learned behavior.

Spatial contiguity and interevent similarity also affect associative learning and performance. Locating CSs and USs spatially near to one another aids Pavlovian conditioning (Ellins & von Kluge 1990, Testa 1975; see also Marshall et al 1979, Rescorla & Cunningham 1979). So, too, does using CSs and USs with similar attributes (Testa 1975; see also Rescorla & Furrow 1977, Rescorla & Gillan 1980). Thorndikean discrimination learning is aided by the instrumental response spatially coinciding with the discriminative stimulus (Harrison et al 1977, Ramey & Goulet 1971; cf Rumbaugh et al 1989) and by the discriminative and reinforcing stimuli sharing similar patterns of stimulation (for a review, see JD Miller & Bowe 1982; for data, see Bowe et al 1987; cf Neill & Harrison 1987).

NECESSITY AND SUFFICIENCY Within the Pavlovian paradigm, sufficiency refers to the likelihood of the US occurring given the presence of the CS and can be expressed in probabilistic notation as $P(US|CS)$, which depends on the frequencies with which the CS and US occur together and the CS occurs alone. Consistent reinforcement constitutes a sufficiency of 1.0, and extinction treatment constitutes a sufficiency of 0.0. Trials on which both the CS and US occur enhance CRs to the CS, whereas trials on which only the CS occurs impair CRs (Van Hamme & Wasserman 1994, Young 1995). Necessity refers to the US not occurring in the absence of the CS and can be expressed as $1 - P(US|No\ CS)$, which depends on the frequencies with which the US occurs alone and times when neither the US nor the CS occurs. Occasions on which only the US occurs weaken CRs, whereas occasions lacking both the CS and the US strengthen CRs, as when the ITI is lengthened (Young 1995). Within the Thorndikean paradigm, similar relations hold (Wasserman et al 1993). The concepts of sufficiency and necessity are jointly captured by the notion of contingency (discussed below).

Complex Phenomena with a Single Cue or Response

EXPERIMENTAL EXTINCTION Operationally, experimental extinction refers to the occurrence of the antecedent event (CS or instrumental response) without the reinforcer that followed it during acquisition. Empirically, extinction is the decrease in CRs that occurs because of this treatment. To explain extinction, Pavlov (1927) posited an inhibitory CS-US association that countered the excitatory association that was formed during acquisition; extinction was thus a form of further learning rather than an eradication of earlier learning. Subsequently, many other explanations of extinction were proposed (for a review, see Kimble 1961), which were similar only in that they (*a*) rarely subscribed to unlearning and (*b*) could explain why inconsistent reinforcement during training generally yields greater resistance to extinction than does consistent reinforcement.

More recently, the widely cited model of Rescorla & Wagner (1972) has treated extinction as unlearning. Rescorla & Wagner made this proposal to retain the simplicity of their model, but the earlier reasons for rejecting unlearning are still valid. For instance, presentation of a strong novel stimulus before presentation of an extinguished CS temporarily restores CRs to the extinguished CS ("external inhibition"), and extinguished CRs frequently undergo partial "spontaneous" recovery with increasing retention intervals (Pavlov 1927). Contemporary research suggests that an extinguished CS has all the properties of a conditioned inhibitor (Calton et al 1996, Hart et al 1995), which brings us back almost to Pavlov's view of extinction.

A notable addition to our knowledge about extinction is that it is context specific. Bouton and his colleagues have shown that when training occurs in one context and extinction occurs in another, CRs are still obtained if testing occurs in the first context (Bouton & Bolles 1979, Bouton & King 1983). If testing occurs in a third context, then CRs are also observed. These results suggest that, rather than responding being specific to the acquisition context, nonresponding is specific to the extinction context. Bouton (1993) and Brooks & Bouton (1994) interpreted these results in terms of the context serving as a salient retrieval cue, with the context used for acquisition training having a broader stimulus generalization gradient than the context used for extinction training. Bouton has supported this account by showing that even when acquisition and extinction occur in the same context, so that there are no CRs in that context at the end of extinction, CRs are again observed when testing occurs in another context (Bouton & Ricker 1994). This modulatory role of the context underscores the increasing attention paid to the contextual control of acquired behavior (Balsam & Tomie 1985, Swartzentruber 1995).

US-PREEXPOSURE EFFECT Repeated exposure to a reinforcer may retard the acquisition of behavioral control during later training (Randich & LoLordo 1979). Although nonassociative habituation may reduce the efficacy of the US, the prime factor responsible for the US-preexposure effect appears to be the excitatory status of the training context. During US preexposure, a context-US association may be formed that blocks the CS-US association during later training. Consistent with this interpretation, either extinction of the context or a change in context between US-preexposure and CS-US training attenuates the effect (Randich 1981). Matzel et al (1988b) further found that a conditioned release of endorphins elicited by the context at the time of CS-US training is necessary to obtain the US-preexposure effect with aversive USs.

Although the US-preexposure effect is commonly thought to reflect a failure for the subject to acquire a CS-US association, Matzel et al (1987) found that extinguishing the training context after CS-US pairings attenuated the effect. Moreover, JS Miller et al (1993) have observed spontaneous recovery from the deficit. Thus, the US-preexposure effect is not entirely due to a deficit in acquisition. If blocking by the context is responsible for the effect, then it is blocking of expression rather than acquisition of the CS-US association.

CS-PREEXPOSURE EFFECT When subjects are extensively exposed to a CS before CS-US pairings, acquisition of behavioral control by the CS is retarded (Lubow & Moore 1959). This effect is called "latent inhibition"; however, this is a misnomer because a preexposed CS does not pass the summation test for conditioned inhibition (Reiss & Wagner 1972, Rescorla 1971). The most popular account of the CS-preexposure effect is that, during preexposure, subjects reduce their perceptual attention to the CS (Lubow et al 1976). Implicit here is the assumption that attention is necessary for acquisition. However, despite its popularity, this type of attentional theory has many problems. For example, it cannot easily explain the retardation of behavioral control found when a CS is paired with a strong US after the CS has been paired with a weaker version of the same US (Hall & Pearce 1979). Because pairings of the CS with the weak US result in behavioral control by the CS, it is unlikely that subjects have decreased their perceptual attention to the CS and hence that this decrease is the basis for the later retardation in learning when the CS is paired with the strong US. This Hall-Pearce negative transfer effect is also a problem for some attentional models that focus on associability rather than on perceptual attention (Mackintosh 1975), but not for others (Pearce & Hall 1980).

The main competitors to attentional explanations are models that focus on context-CS associations that are formed during CS preexposure. Wagner (1981) posited a context-CS association that interferes with acquisition of the CS-US association. Miller & Matzel (1988) and Grahame et al (1994) also focus on the context-CS association, but they posit that this association impairs the expression of the CS-US association. Consistent with both views, a context shift between CS preexposure and CS-US pairings (Hall & Minor 1984) or extinction of the context between CS-preexposure and CS-US pairings (Baker & Mercier 1982, Wagner 1979; cf Hall & Minor 1984) attenuates the effect. Distinguishing between these views, Grahame et al (1994) found that extinction of the context after CS-US pairings restores CRs to the CS, Kraemer et al (1991) found spontaneous recovery from the CS-preexposure deficit, and Kasprow et al (1984) found that a posttraining "reminder" can restore CRs. If acquisition were impaired, as Wagner's account suggests, then no posttraining treatment other than retraining should restore CRs to the CS. Thus, the CS-preexposure effect appears to be largely a failure to express, not to acquire information. If one adheres to a perceptual-attentional view, then this evidence implies that attention during training may not be necessary for acquisition, although it may well facilitate it; rather, attention during training may facilitate later expression of the acquired information, perhaps by creating more effective links to modulate information retrieval.

Operationally, CS preexposure and habituation are identical. Both effects involve the CS losing its potential to control behavior. Thus, one might suspect that they arise from a common process. However, habituation wanes rapidly with increases in the retention interval (Thompson & Spencer 1966), whereas the CS-preexposure effect does not (Hall & Schachtman 1987). In addition, habituation survives a context shift (Marlin & Miller 1981), whereas CS-preexposure does not (Hall & Honey 1989). Thus, different processes evidently underlie the CS-preexposure effect and habituation.

LEARNED IRRELEVANCE Random presentations of CSs and USs proactively interfere with associative learning. Mackintosh (1973) found that randomly presented CSs and USs produced more proactive interference than did either CSs alone or USs alone, a result he took to mean that animals can learn the irrelevance of the CS for predicting the US. Mackintosh argued that "learned irrelevance" makes it more difficult for the animal later to learn either an excitatory or an inhibitory interstimulus association (Baker 1977, Baker & Mackintosh 1977).

There is an obvious rival account of the learned irrelevance effect: namely, that it is simply the sum of the effects of CS alone and US alone preexposure. Early efforts to distinguish learned irrelevance from the summation of CS- and US-preexposure effects (Baker & Mackintosh 1979, Matzel et al 1988d, Tomie et al 1980) supported the existence of learned irrelevance by showing that manipulations that eliminate the CS- and US-preexposure effects do not eliminate the learned irrelevance effect. Providing more support, Bennett et al (1995) found that daily intermixture of CSs and USs more adversely affected later conditioning than did giving the same number of CSs and USs in different blocks of sessions. However, Bonardi & Hall (1996) have shown that this effect depends on USs serving as part of the conditioning context. Thus, the reality of learned irrelevance is still uncertain.

Complex Phenomena with Multiple Cues or Responses

SENSORY PRECONDITIONING A common criticism of associative learning is that learning may only occur when biologically significant stimuli are the reinforcers. Yet learning often takes place without the obvious involvement of biologically significant stimuli. If this criticism were valid, then very real limits would apply to the generality of associative principles. There is strong evidence that associative learning does occur in the absence of biologically significant stimuli. The best known case is "sensory preconditioning," an effect first named by Brogden (1939) but first studied in 1932 by Podkopaev in Pavlov's laboratory (Kimmel 1977). Initially, Podkopaev paired a whistle with a light (CSB-CSA). Next he paired the light with footshock (CSA-US). Finally, he tested the dog with the whistle. Despite the fact that the whistle had never been paired with footshock, it elicited leg flexion. When appropriate controls are included, this procedure provides compelling evidence of learning with biologically insignificant stimuli.

Later research has attested to the robustness of sensory preconditioning and has explored several variables that influence it (Razran 1971, Thompson 1972). Many of the variables that affect associative learning when the outcome is biologically significant affect sensory preconditioning in a similar way, which leads some authors to conclude that the same associative mechanisms are at work in both cases. Responding to CSB is an increasing function of the number of CSB-CSA pairings (Prewitt 1967), the percentage of trials on which CSB is followed by CSA (Tait et al 1971, 1972), and the intensity of CSB (Rogers 1973, Tait & Suboski 1972). Responding to CSB is reduced by presenting both CSB and CSA alone before CSB-CSA pairings (Parks 1968), by increasing the time between CSB and CSA (Lavin 1976, Spiker & Ferraro 1977), by presenting CSB alone after CSB-CSA pairings (Tait et al 1969), and by presenting CSA alone after CSA-US pairings (Rizley & Rescorla 1972). All the above research employed Pavlovian contingencies. An analogous case of "response preconditioning" with Thorndikean contingencies was reported by St. Claire-Smith & MacLaren (1983).

Sensory preconditioning has historically involved a three-step paradigm for investigating the association of biologically insignificant stimuli. Other research in Pavlov's laboratory by Narbutovich (Kimmel 1977) entailed only a single training period. Here, a scuffling sound at one spatial site regularly preceded the spinning of a disk at another. After these pairings, the dog not only oriented toward the scuffling sound, it also turned toward the site where the disk was about to spin. The dog's receptor orienting acts provided direct evidence of the association between the auditory and visual stimuli; no additional training was needed to prove the point. Another way to directly assay the association between neutral stimuli is to record electrical brain activity during CSB and CSA. When a visual stimulus, but not an auditory stimulus, is presented, alpha activity is blocked. After tone-light pairings, human beings show alpha blocking to the tone, which suggests the formation of a tone-light association (Smith & Putney 1979).

HIGHER-ORDER CONDITIONING Another well-known case in which associative learning occurs in the absence of stimuli of inherent biological significance is "higher-order" conditioning, discovered by Pavlov. Here, the same phases of training are administered as in sensory preconditioning, but in the reverse order. Initially, CSA is paired with a biologically significant US (CSA-US). Then, CSB is paired with CSA (CSB-CSA). The result is that CSB now produces a CR, even though it was never paired with the US. Control groups prove that both phases of training are necessary for the resultant CR to CSB (Rescorla 1973).

Second-order conditioning has been found with numerous responses in many species, including proboscis extension in honeybees (Bitterman et al 1983), target striking in goldfish (Amiro & Bitterman 1980), sexual activity in quail (Crawford & Domjan 1995), and keypecking in chicks (Deich et al, in Wasserman 1981). Stronger responding to CSB has been reported when CSA was paired with larger USs than with smaller ones (O'Connell & Rashotte 1982) and when CSB was consistently followed by CSA than when it was inconsistently followed by CSA (Colwill & Rescorla 1985, Rashotte et al 1981). In addition, increasing the CSB-CSA interval lowers responding to CSB (Gibbs et al 1991; cf Popik et al 1979). Second-order conditioning is even demonstrable with a single CSA-US pairing followed by a single CSB-CSA pairing (Bond & DiGuisto 1976).

Much research in second-order conditioning sprang from Rizley & Rescorla's (1972) finding that performance of the second-order CR might be independent of the ability of the first-order CS to elicit a CR. So, after CSA-US and CSB-CSA training, CSA alone presentations might weaken the CR to CSA, but not affect the CR to CSB (cf Rizley & Rescorla's 1972 results of the same manipulation on sensory preconditioning). Insensitivity of CSA extinction on CSB responding was found by later workers (e.g. Barnet et al 1991, Robertson et al 1984), but that result has not been general. Extinction of CSA can produce reliable drops in responding to CSB (e.g. Colwill & Rescorla 1985, Hittesdorf & Richards 1982). Efforts to reconcile these conflicting findings according to the species of organism and the nature of the CSs and USs (Nairne & Rescorla 1981) were not successful. Had it been generally true that extinction of responding to CSA left responding to CSB intact, one could have concluded that second-order associations never depend on a representation of CSA. Moreover, Rescorla (1973) devalued the US representation without impairing second-order conditioning, which argues against the US representation being essential to second-order conditioning. Evidence against reinforcer-specific second-order associations also comes from Stanhope (1992), who successfully trained topographically different CRs to two different CSAs: one paired with water and the other with food. Topographically different CRs were not formed, however, to two different CSBs, each of which was specifically paired with previously food- or water-paired CSAs.

Another glimpse into the associations involved in higher-order conditioning was provided by Stefurak et al (1990). Rats exhibit a preference for places paired with morphine, but an aversion for tastes paired with morphine. However, if a place CSB is paired with a taste CSA, then rats exhibit a place aversion, and if a taste CSB is paired with a place CSA, then rats exhibit a taste preference. Clearly, the first-order stimulus conditioned to morphine represents in memory only the single motivational effect of morphine to which it is preferentially associated.

SERIAL CONDITIONING Another situation in which associations may be formed between events lacking obvious biological significance is serial conditioning. In Pavlovian conditioning, serial conditioning might involve a succession of stimuli before reinforcement: CSB-CSA-US. In addition to the individual associations between CSB and the US and between CSA and the US, CSB and CSA may be associated with each other. Although this proposal is reasonable enough, empirical documentation has been slow in coming. One tactic has been to compare responding to CSB after serial conditioning with that obtained when the same two stimuli have been separately presented the same number of times in the same individual temporal relations to reinforcement. Should responding to CSB in the former case exceed that in the latter, it would be tempting to conclude that the superiority is due to the association between CSB and CSA. Just such a difference in responding has been reported (Schreurs et al 1993), but it has not been easy to eliminate other explanations for the result; the mere presence of CSA may help to "bridge" the temporal delay between CSB and the US or to "mark" the occurrence of CSB making it more distinctive, quite apart from any direct association between CSB and CSA (e.g. Hall & Honey 1993, Lieberman et al 1985, Rescorla 1982).

A different, more direct tactic was used by Wasserman et al (1978). In an autoshaping situation, pigeons were given two serial keylight compounds that were each followed by food: CSB1-CSA1-US and CSB2-CSA2-US. CSB1 involved two response keys lit with one color, and CSB2 involved the same two keys lit with a different color. CSA1 entailed only the left key lighted with a third stimulus, and CSA2 entailed only the right key lighted with the same third stimulus. The pigeons pecked the left key during CSB1 and the right key during CSB2, consistent with their forming highly specific associations between the CSBs and the CSAs.

Later work has used matching-to-sample procedures. The discriminative response in those Thorndikean tasks depended on the pigeon discriminating and remembering the temporal order in which two earlier key colors (C1 and C2) had occurred. Different reinforcement contingencies were in place after

C1-C2 and C2-C1 sequences. To control for the first or the second stimulus alone cueing the discriminative response, C1-C1 and C2-C2 sequences were also given. Pigeons showed clear control by the temporal order of two biologically insignificant stimuli (MacDonald 1993, Wasserman et al 1984, Weisman et al 1980). This ability to discriminate and remember the temporal order of two nonidentical stimuli implies a far richer representation of stimulus events than is usually granted to animals, and it lends support to the idea that the temporal relationship between events is encoded as part of an interevent association (Matzel et al 1988c).

COMPOUND STIMULUS CONTROL Is the whole more than the sum of its parts? This question was central to Gestalt psychology, a school that more strongly stressed perceptual than associative principles. Still, there has been much interest in this question in the field of associative learning.

One situation that has been extensively explored involves simultaneous compound stimuli that are paired with reinforcement without the presentation of the compound's elemental stimuli. After training, the subject is given the compound and its elements to see if the former more effectively produces behavior than the latter; if so, then there is reason to suggest that "configural" conditioning has occurred. The evidence might be even stronger if increases in the amount of compound stimulus training led to increases in compound responding and to decreases in element responding. Most theories of associative learning do not expect the compound to gain behavioral control at the expense of its elements, but this result might nonetheless occur if it takes a long time for the individual stimulus elements to "fuse" into an effective compound (Razran 1971). Greater responding to the compound than to its elements has been reported in both Pavlovian (e.g. Bellingham & Gillette 1981a, Kamin & Idrobo 1978) and Thorndikean (e.g. Bellingham & Gillette 1981b, Rescorla 1972) conditioning. However, in none of these reports were increases in compound training clearly accompanied by increases in compound responding and decreases in element responding. To observe this result seems to require the "positive patterning" procedure, which provides reinforcement on compound trials and withholds it on element trials: AB+, A–, B–. Pavlov (1927) was the first to investigate the effects of such training; he found greater responding to the compound stimulus than to its components.

Later research has confirmed the efficacy of the positive patterning procedure. TW Baker (1969) and Wickens et al (1970) not only found more responding to the compound than to its elements, they also found increases in compound responding and decreases in element responding with increases in discrimination training. Wickens et al (1970) further reported that the compound-element discrimination was a direct function of the CS-US interval, perhaps because the increasing duration of the compound stimulus and its elements that accompanied increases in the ISI helped to fuse the elements into a configured stimulus. Consistent with this interpretation, Kehoe & Schreurs (1986) replicated the ISI result and also showed that, with the CS-US interval held constant, the compound-element discrimination was a direct function of CS duration.

Although positive patterning is often interpreted as indicating configuring, the result can also be explained by the conditioning of the individual elements and the summation of their response strengths when the elements are jointly presented. Consequently, most theorists argue that the best case for configural conditioning comes from the "negative patterning" procedure, which provides reinforcement on element trials and withholds it on compound trials: AB–, A+, B+. Robust responding on element trials but not on compound trials cannot be explained by summation. Here, too, Pavlov (1927) was the first to investigate negative patterning; he found less responding to the compound stimulus than to its components.

Later research has confirmed the efficacy of the negative patterning procedure (e.g. Redhead & Pearce 1995b, Rescorla et al 1985). Whitlow & Wagner (1972) further found that less responding to AB than to A or B cannot be attributed to some general properties of compound stimuli, like their greater intensity, numerosity, or complexity. Related results were reported by Rescorla (1972; see also Davidson et al 1993), who, along with Whitlow & Wagner, argued that the simultaneous presentation of two stimuli might involve three functional stimuli: A, B, and a unique configural cue AB. This configural cue presumably provides the critical stimulus allowing the organism to respond discriminatively in positive and negative patterning situations. The slow speed of learning positive and negative patterning discriminations suggests that the configural cue is of low salience. Hypothesizing a unique configural cue also helps us understand how biconditional discriminations such as AC+, BD+, AD–, BC– are learned (Saavedra 1975). Control by the elements would be expected to decrease because of their equivalent association with reinforcement and nonreinforcement, to be replaced by control by the unique configural cues associated with reinforcement (AC and BD) and nonreinforcement (AD and BC).

Other details of negative patterning are that discrimination learning is a direct function of the percentage of compound trials (Bellingham et al 1985, Kehoe & Graham 1988) and the CS-US interval (Kehoe & Graham 1988). In addition, prior positive patterning impairs negative patterning but not vice versa (Bellingham et al 1985). Furthermore, adding a common cue to both compound and element trials slows the speed of negative patterning (Pearce & Redhead 1993, Rescorla 1972; also see Redhead & Pearce 1995a), presumably because this addition makes the task more difficult. Finally, and controversially, given the animal data attesting to the specificity of configural stimulus control (Davidson et al 1993, Rescorla 1972, Whitlow & Wagner 1972), human beings may learn a general compound stimulus rule on both negative and positive patterning discriminations. They may respond less to the novel CD compound than to the novel elements C and D after AB–, A+, B+ training, whereas they may respond more to the novel CD compound than to the novel elements C and D after AB+, A–, B– training (Kleinschmidt & Lachnit 1993, Lachnit & Kimmel 1993).

CUE COMPETITION Cue competition refers to a retardation in behavioral control by a target CS due to its being trained in the presence of another CS that is more salient or a better predictor of the US. Examples include overshadowing (Pavlov 1927), blocking (Kamin 1968), and the relative validity effect (Wagner et al 1968), each of which occurs in both Thorndikean and Pavlovian conditioning (Pearce & Hall 1978, Williams 1975). Overshadowing (Mackintosh & Reese 1979) and blocking (Balaz et al 1982b) can be obtained with a single compound trial, but each effect is more robust with several compound trials. However, overshadowing (Bellingham & Gillette 1981a) and blocking (Azorlosa & Cicala 1986) can be eliminated by a sufficiently large number of compound trials. The latter findings are problematic for many contemporary theories of learning, as are the results of several posttraining manipulations that yield a partial if not complete restoration of responding to target CSs after cue competition has occurred, including (*a*) extinction of the successfully competing CS (Cole et al 1995, Kaufman & Bolles 1981, Matzel et al 1985), (*b*) "reminder" treatments with a component of training like the CS or US (Balaz 1982a, Cole et al 1996, Kasprow et al 1982), and (*c*) spontaneous recovery (Kraemer et al 1988, JS Miller et al 1990). This reversibility without further CS-US training suggests that cue competition is due, at least in part, to a failure of the organism to express a CS-US association that it had in fact acquired.

Although overshadowing is quite general, the opposite outcome is sometimes found; the presence of a second CS may actually enhance CRs to the less salient CS (Clarke et al 1979, Palmerino et al 1980). Such potentiation is usually (but not exclusively) observed when the more salient CS is a gustatory cue. Potentiation has most commonly been observed when the less salient CS is olfactory, but it has also been obtained with CSs in other modalities (Best et al 1985). Durlach & Rescorla (1980) argued that potentiation may be due to within-compound associations, with the indirect (second-order) association between the target CS and the US that is mediated by the CS of greater salience more than compensating for the reduction in CRs due to overshadowing of the direct (first-order) association between the target CS and the US.

One widely held view of blocking is that "surprise" may be necessary for learning about X (Kamin 1968), and that forward blocking is due to the absence of surprise when the US occurs in Phase 2 (AX-US). Presumably, Phase 1 training (A-US) establishes an expectation of the US based on A. In this view, a change in the US between Phases 1 and 2 should attenuate blocking. Consistent with this prediction, Dickinson et al (1976) and Mackintosh et al (1977) found that omission of a second US after Phase 1 training with two successive USs on each trial (A-US-US) produced "unblocking" (i.e. less blocking). However, several more recent studies have failed to obtain unblocking with notable, albeit different, changes in the US between Phases 1 and 2 (Ganesan & Pearce 1988, Williams 1994). The basis for this disparity is not yet clear (cf Holland 1988).

One variant in the conventional blocking procedure is "backward blocking," in which AX-US trials precede A-US trials. Backward blocking has received recent attention because it is often obtained with human subjects in causal judgment tasks (Chapman 1991, Shanks 1985), but not with animals in Pavlovian tasks (RR Miller et al 1990). In addition, various models of learning make different predictions about backward blocking. Rescorla & Wagner (1972) predicted forward, but not backward, blocking, whereas Miller & Matzel (1988) predicted both forward and backward blocking. Van Hamme & Wasserman's (1994) Revised Rescorla-Wagner model more accurately predicts backward blocking in some situations but not others. Empirically, Miller & Matute (1996) and Denniston et al (1996) have found that the observed discrepancies in backward blocking do not arise from potential differences between causal judgment tasks and Pavlovian tasks nor from differences between human and nonhuman subjects; rather, the critical factor appears to be whether the to-be-blocked stimulus has ever been able to elicit robust responding. Robust responding can be elicited by either effective USs or effective CSs. Hall et al (1977) and Miller & Matute (1996) also found that such effective cues are protected against forward blocking.

CONDITIONED INHIBITION Prior discussion considered circumstances under which a CS comes to elicit a CR. One way to view this general result is to regard the CS as activating an expectation of the US, which in turn evokes the CR. Under other training circumstances, a CS can come to reduce the incidence of the CR; such a CS is called a conditioned inhibitor, and it is often viewed as activating an expectation of the nonoccurrence of the US (Wagner & Rescorla 1972).

The earliest measure of conditioned inhibition was developed by Pavlov (1927), who proposed that a stimulus be called a conditioned inhibitor if it passed a "summation" test, which consists of presenting the target stimulus in compound with a previously established conditioned excitor to see whether the target decreases CRs to the excitor. However, if the conditioned excitor used in the summation test had been presented together with the target stimulus during the putative inhibitory training, then the reduced CRs could reflect a discrimination between the excitor alone (reinforced in training) and the compound of the excitor and the target stimulus (not reinforced in training). To eliminate this possibility, Pavlov also did summation tests using conditioned excitors that had no prior history with the target stimulus. If the target stimulus reduces CRs to such a "transfer" excitor, then discrimination explanations become implausible. Still, increased attention to the target stimulus at the cost of attention to the transfer excitor and/or stimulus generalization decrement from the transfer excitor alone to the compound of the transfer excitor plus the target stimulus could account for a summation effect.

To preclude both attentional and generalization decrement accounts, Rescorla (1969) and Hearst (1972) advocated a second test for inhibition: namely, that the target stimulus should be paired with the US to see if CRs to the target stimulus would require more pairings to emerge than would be the case without prior inhibitory training. This "retardation" test is itself subject to an attentional explanation: Inhibitory training could decrease attention to the target CS, so that less is learned about it during its pairings with the US. However, Rescorla and Hearst argued that inhibition training could not both increase and decrease attention. Therefore, if a target stimulus passes both summation and retardation tests, then one might reject attentional accounts (see also Papini & Bitterman 1993, Williams et al 1992). This conclusion hinges on the possibly incorrect assumption that the same type of attention is involved in the two tests.

A third assay of inhibition is the approach/withdrawal test of Wasserman et al (1974), who proposed that subjects will approach a CS with an excitatory relationship to an appetitive US and will withdraw from a CS with an inhibitory relationship to an appetitive US. These predictions are reversed for aversive USs. The approach/withdrawal test avoids the attentional, configurational, and generalization decrement accounts of summation and retardation tests. This test assumes that excitation and inhibition are mutually exclusive, but some data argue against this assumption (Droungas & LoLordo 1994, Matzel et al 1988a). Agreement over the assessment of conditioned inhibition lies in the future.

Generally, a stimulus becomes an inhibitor when it is presented in compound with another stimulus that predicts the occurrence of a US, but the US fails to occur. Moreover, Pavlov (1927) found that the inhibitory value of a stimulus increased with the magnitude of the omitted US. The first method reported to produce conditioned inhibition used reinforced presentations of an excitatory CS (A-US) interspersed with nonreinforced presentations of a compound stimulus comprising the reinforced CS and the target cue (AX-No US) (Pavlov 1927). A second technique (the method of negative contingency) for producing conditioned inhibition consists of presenting the target stimulus and the US in an explicitly unpaired fashion (Rescorla 1968). However, if one regards the context as becoming a conditioned excitor because of the unsignaled USs administered in this procedure, then this method is really the same as Pavlov's, with the context playing the role of the excitor. There are other procedures for producing conditioned inhibition, but they are often less effective than the above two methods (for a review, see LoLordo & Fairless 1985).

OCCASION SETTING When a stimulus is presented with a partially reinforced target CS and reinforcement depends on the presence or absence of that stimulus, we call the stimulus a positive feature in the former case and a negative feature in the latter case. When the feature is simultaneous with the target CS, subjects often learn the feature-positive (-negative) problem by treating the feature like an excitatory (inhibitory) CS. However, when it precedes the CS, the feature often acts by modulating the associative potential of the target CS; in this capacity, the feature is called a positive or negative occasion setter (Holland 1983, 1992).

Some factors that favor a stimulus becoming an occasion setter rather than a simple CS include: (*a*) inserting a temporal gap (5–15 s) between feature offset and CS onset, (*b*) having the CS (rather than the feature) occur at the optimal CS-US interval, (*c*) using a feature from a different modality than the CS, and (*d*) using a feature that is less salient than the CS (Holland 1985, 1986). Notably, the occasion-setting properties of a stimulus and its properties as a Pavlovian CS are largely independent. Thus, training a negative occasion setter to be a Pavlovian excitor does not degrade its occasion-setting potential, nor does experimental extinction degrade the occasion-setting potential of a stimulus (Holland 1989). A stimulus can even be an occasion setter and a Pavlovian CS simultaneously without appreciable interaction (Holland 1989).

The notion of occasion setting was introduced by Skinner (1938), who proposed that discriminative stimuli set the occasion for operant behavior to be reinforced. Recently, the concept has been applied primarily to Pavlovian conditioning, where it is now attracting considerable attention because occasion setting is seen as one way in which associative theory might explain complex patterns of behaviors, such as biconditional discriminations, that previously appeared to be refractory to simple associative analysis. One problem that could undermine the interpretive value of occasion setting is that substantial training is required before animals master serial feature discriminations. However, research has shown that entire contexts can serve as occasion setters and that contextual stimuli more rapidly acquire occasion-setting properties than discrete stimuli (Bouton & Swartzentruber 1986). Contextual control of associative behavior has long been recognized and occasion setting is one likely means by which contextual control occurs.

THEORETICAL PERSPECTIVES AND CONTROVERSIES

To explain the rich empirical literature of associative learning, some of which we have just reviewed, many theories have been advanced. In this section, we highlight and evaluate some of the most prominent of the recent theories. We also examine the interrelation between learning and expressed behavior.

Contiguity Models

Pavlov (1927) believed that close temporal contiguity was critical for associative learning; the CS and US had to occur near in time for the CS to come to evoke a CR. Long delays between CS and US did not support conditioning, although they could maintain CRs that had been established with more contiguous stimulation (Lucas et al 1981, Ross et al 1979). Thorndike also emphasized temporal contiguity. When a response is shortly followed by a consequence, a reward makes it more likely and a punisher makes it less likely that the situation will again elicit that response. Later work has led theorists to reconsider these ideas. The notion of absolute temporal contiguity has yielded to a relativistic alternative.

Gibbon & Balsam (1981) theorized that the CS-US interval contributes to the strength of CRs relative to the time between USs. In the autoshaping situation "the association between the signal and food depends on an appreciation of the improvement in the average delay to reinforcement in the signal compared with the average delay overall or in the background" (p. 248). Jenkins et al (1981) reached a similar conclusion, that "the effectiveness of a reference trial depends on the waiting time in the reference trial relative to the overall waiting time between feedings within the experimental setting" (p. 276). These two theories are very similar, but they do have distinguishable behavioral implications (Lucas & Wasserman 1982). Although these theories describe acquisition well, they have limitations; for example, they cannot explain US intensity effects (Lucas & Wasserman 1982), and they do not address cue competition.

The idea of relative contiguity can be extended to Thorndikean conditioning. Wasserman & Neunaber (1986) have restated relative contiguity in operant conditioning as "the extent to which the delay of reinforcement after occurrences of the...operant response differs from that after [any of the organism's other] responses" (p. 31) (see also Fantino & Abarca 1985). Through this temporal discrimination, organisms may be able to detect cases in which one of their responses hastens or delays the occurrence of outcomes. They may also be able to discriminate cases in which their responses have no effect at all on the occurrence of outcomes. The notion of relative contiguity is closely aligned with contingency formulations of learning (Peterson et al 1993).

Contingency and Rule-Based Models

A different analysis of Pavlovian and Thorndikean experiments is traceable to Tolman (1932), who argued that learning was basically a matter of discovering "what leads to what." The concept of "contingency" provides one means of tightening and operationalizing Tolman's informal approach. In Pavlovian conditioning, the contingency between CS and US can be formalized as the difference between the probability of the US given the occurrence of the CS and the probability of the US given the nonoccurrence of the CS: $\Delta P = P(US|CS) - P(US|No\ CS)$. Emphasis on CS-US contingency broadens the scope of the Pavlovian procedure because it emphasizes that events may be either positively or negatively correlated with one another. Positive CS-US contingencies involve signaled increases in US likelihood, whereas negative CS-US contingencies involve signaled decreases in US likelihood (as in conditioned inhibition). Thanks largely to the efforts of Rescorla (1968), we now know that animals learn about negative CS-US contingencies as well as about positive ones. Thus, nonpairings of CS and US influence behavior as do pairings of CS and US. Tolman's suggestion that animals learn "what leads to what" is also applicable to Thorndikean conditioning. Here, contingency can be defined by the difference between the probability of an outcome given the occurrence of a response and the probability of an outcome given the nonoccurrence of the response: $\Delta P = P(O|R) - P(O|No\ R)$.

Modern interest in the role of contingency in learning was rekindled by observations that presenting the US without the CS during training decreased CRs to the CS (Rescorla 1968). This finding challenged the view that acquired behavior depended only on CS-US contiguity (cf Papini & Bitterman 1990). Early contingency theories were intended to replace contiguity as the explanation of acquisition. However, the observation that extinction of the training context can enhance CRs to the CS (Hallam et al 1992) suggests that contingency may affect the expression, rather than the acquisition of acquired behavior. Thus, Hallam et al proposed that acquisition of information is governed by contiguity, whereas behavioral expression of that information is governed by contingency. Consistent with this view, Miller & Matzel (1988) have noted that the calculation of contingency requires the subject to know the frequency with which the CS and US have occurred together; but registering a CS-US pairing requires learning an association between CS and US. Hence, learning must occur before contingency can be calculated, and contingency cannot be the basis of learning.

Many important research results in recent years were stimulated by contingency theories. One of these results is that the four types of interevent combinations (e.g. CS and US present) do not contribute equally to acquired behavior. Despite having equal normative weights, they have different psychological weights. Wasserman et al (1990) and Kao & Wasserman (1993) have found that CS-US trials have more impact on behavior than CS only trials and US only trials, both of which in turn have more impact than No CS–No US trials. Various associative (Van Hamme & Wasserman 1994) and rule-based (Busemeyer 1991) models have been designed to incorporate these interevent biases. A second important result is that USs that are not signaled by the target CS (US only trials) apparently do not enter into a subject's estimation of contingency if the US is signaled by another "cover" CS (Cooper 1991, Durlach 1983; cf Jenkins & Lambos 1983). The protective effect of cover stimuli was problematic for early forms of contingency theory, but it can be readily reconciled with more recent versions (Cheng 1993).

An important application of contingency theory was provided by Seligman et al (1971), who argued that a history of uncontrollable aversive events may render organisms "helpless." When later given control over those events, organisms with such prior training may be retarded in learning escape or avoidance responses. "Learned helplessness" has not only had great influence on laboratory research but on clinical psychology as well (Peterson et al 1993). A prior history of uncontrollable appetitive events may also render organisms "lazy" when they are later given control over those events (Engberg et al 1972; cf Beatty & Maki 1979, Schwartz et al 1974).

Associative Models

Over the past 25 years, associative models designed primarily to explain cue competition have dominated the field of elementary learning. We briefly review five of them here. We selected these models because each proposes something different from the others, but all of them posit associative links between representations of events.

RESCORLA-WAGNER The Rescorla-Wagner (1972) model is a direct descendant of the Bush-Mosteller (1951) linear operator model, in which the strength of an association between stimulus X and a US is constrained by limiting the increase in associative strength to a multiplicative factor of $\lambda - V_X$, where λ is the maximum amount of associative strength that can be supported by the US on that trial and V_X is the current associative strength of the stimulus. This model predicts no interaction between the associative status of one stimulus and the change in associative status of another simultaneously presented stimulus; thus, it cannot explain cue competition. The Rescorla-Wagner model surmounts this difficulty by limiting the increase in associative strength to a multiplicative factor of $\lambda - V_\Sigma$, where V_Σ is the total associative strength (with respect to the US) of all CSs present on that trial. The difference $\lambda - V_\Sigma$ represents the disparity between what the subject expected on that trial and what actually occurred, in accord with Kamin's (1968) contention that learning depends on the "surprisingness" of the US.

More specifically, the Rescorla-Wagner model states that conditioned responding is based on the current associative strength of all stimuli present on a given trial, and that after the trial, the associative value (V) of each stimulus (X) is adjusted according to the formula: $V_X(\text{new}) = V_X(\text{old}) + \Delta V_X$, where ΔV_X (the change in associative strength because of the last trial) $= \alpha\beta(\lambda - V_\Sigma)$, with α and β being the associabilities of CS and US, respectively. Extinction is treated like acquisition, except that λ for US absent is zero and β for US absent is nonzero, but smaller than for US present. Conditioned excitation corresponds to positive values of V_X, whereas conditioned inhibition corresponds to negative values of V_X.

The Rescorla-Wagner model explains most cases of cue competition including forward blocking, overshadowing, and the relative validity effect. It also accounts for many conditioning phenomena like acquisition, extinction, discrimination, conditioned inhibition, contingency effects, and the US-preexposure effect. Still, the model suffers from important failures. It does not predict the CS-preexposure effect or one-trial overshadowing (James & Wagner 1980, Mackintosh & Reese 1979); it treats extinction as unlearning, which makes it unable to explain external inhibition, spontaneous recovery, or reminder-induced recovery from extinction (Rescorla & Heth 1975); it wrongly predicts that nonreinforced presentations of a conditioned inhibitor will reduce inhibition (Zimmer-Hart & Rescorla 1974); and it attributes cue competition and the US-preexposure effect to acquisition failure, whereas recovery from these deficits occurs without further training (Balaz et al 1982a, Cole et al 1995, Kaufman & Bolles 1981, Kraemer et al 1988, Matzel et al 1987). Miller et al (1995) reviewed the many successes and failures of the model.

The Rescorla-Wagner model has been the dominant theory of associative learning in the last quarter of the twentieth century. Its success is to be seen more in the research that it stimulated than in the accuracy of its predictions. Our empirical knowledge of learning has been greatly increased because of the many tests of the model's predictions. Moreover, considerable attention has been given to the model because it is a form of the Widrow-Hoff (1960) delta rule, which is frequently used to correct the weights of connections between units in connectionist models (Quinlan 1991).

The Rescorla-Wagner model assumes that a CS that is absent on a given trial will undergo no change in associative status because $\alpha = 0$. This zero value of α contrasts with the nonzero value of β when a US is absent. Van Hamme & Wasserman (1994) proposed that α may take a nonzero value on trials in which the CS is absent, if that trial is in some way related to CS training. Their Revised Rescorla-Wagner model treats CS and US more symmetrically (although at the cost of adding a parameter), and it is able to predict several phenomena that were highly problematic for the original model such as backward blocking, which can be observed with both human (Chapman 1991, Shanks 1985) and nonhuman subjects (Denniston et al 1996, Miller & Matute 1996).

MACKINTOSH Unlike the Rescorla-Wagner model, which assumes that CS processing does not change (α is constant), Mackintosh's (1975) model posits changes in CS processing as a result of experience (α is variable). It states that on each trial, the associative strength of a stimulus changes according to the rule: $\Delta V_X = \alpha\theta(\lambda - V_X)$, where θ is a growth parameter. After this change in V_X, the associability (α) of the cue that best predicted the outcome on that trial will increase and the associabilities of all other cues present on that trial will decrease. The change in α does not affect the present trial, but it will affect learning on the next trial on which the cue occurs. Moreover, the magnitude of changes in α will be inversely related to the accuracy of a cue's predictions about the US.

To appreciate the model, consider its account of overshadowing (AX-US). On Trial 1, A and X each gain associative value as if the other were not present. Assuming that A is more salient than X ($\alpha_A > \alpha_X$), ΔV_A will be larger than ΔV_X. On Trial 2, A and X again gain associative value as if the other were not present; but, at the beginning of Trial 2, there is now a difference in their predictive values for the US (A is a better predictor than X). As a result, after Trial 2, α_A increases and α_X decreases. So, on Trial 3, learning about X will be impaired relative to what would have happened if A had not accompanied X on Trials 1 and 2. Mackintosh's model can explain multitrial but not one-trial overshadowing (James & Wagner 1980, Mackintosh & Reese 1979). It can also explain the relative validity effect and multitrial blocking but not one-trial blocking (Balaz et al 1982b). In addition, unlike the Rescorla-Wagner model, Mackintosh's model does not predict reciprocal overshadowing between A and X; the data on this issue are mixed (Mackintosh 1971, 1976). Although the model is often described as predicting the CS-preexposure effect, it does so only by making a special supposition explicitly to accommodate the result. The model has stimulated rather little research.

PEARCE-HALL The Pearce-Hall (1980) model assumes that growth in associative strength is limited entirely by changes in CS processing. It states that after a trial, $V_X(\text{new}) = V_X(\text{old}) + \Delta V_X$, and $\Delta V_X = S_X\alpha_X\lambda$, with α_X representing the associability of X, S_X the salience of X (a parameter that is largely a function of CS intensity), and λ the maximum amount of associative strength that the US can support. The rule for modifying CS associability is $\alpha_X = |\lambda - V_\Sigma|$, where V_Σ

is the sum of the strengths of all cues presented on the last trial on which X occurred and λ is based on the US presented on that trial. In essence, the model says that the associability of a CS reflects the degree to which the US on the last presentation of the CS was surprising.

The model has enjoyed success in explaining select phenomena that are unexplained by other theories. For example, both the CS-preexposure effect (Lubow & Moore 1959) and the Hall-Pearce (1979) negative transfer effect can be understood in terms of the consistent outcomes of Phase 1 training decreasing the associability of the CS. The model also successfully predicts that the Hall-Pearce effect will be attenuated by a single nonreinforced trial between Phases 1 and 2 because the absence of a US on that trial is surprising and it consequently increases the associability of the CS (Hall & Pearce 1982).

Given the model's reliance on CS associability to explain learning, an independent measure of associability would be desirable. Toward this end, data have been reported that suggest that the orienting response to a stimulus is a valid measure of its associability (Kaye & Pearce 1984).

PEARCE In Rescorla & Wagner's model, associative strength is largely allocated to the high-salience elements of compound stimuli and little to the presumably low-salience configural cues involving some or all of the presented elements. This model has had moderate success in accounting for research in compound stimulus control.

Pearce (1987, 1994) has proposed an alternative account of the acquisition of control by compound stimuli that even more explicitly and heavily weights configural cues. According to Pearce, any compound conditioning trial results in a single configural representation of all the stimuli that are present; that representation then enters into association with the outcome of the trial. Pearce's theory predicts that AB+ training will result in the AB compound receiving all the direct reinforcement available, with responding to A and B alone occurring only insofar as they resemble the AB compound. It further predicts that AB+, A–, B– training will produce positive patterning and that AB–, A+, B+ training will produce negative patterning because all three stimulus conditions in these two tasks differ discriminably from one another. Pearce's theory also correctly predicts that adding a common element to both positive and negative CSs of the negative patterning problem will slow learning (Pearce & Redhead 1993, Rescorla 1972; see also Redhead & Pearce 1995a), a prediction not made by the Rescorla-Wagner model. Finally, Pearce's theory outperforms the Rescorla-Wagner model in predicting the correct ordering of responding to the seven stimulus patterns of the following discrimination: (A+, B+, C+) > (AB+, AC+, BC+) > (ABC–) (Redhead & Pearce 1995a). Pearce's model is an interesting and important theory that merits further experimental examination.

WAGNER Wagner's (1981) SOP (sometimes opponent process) model is a real-time theory of learning that borrows much of its architecture from Atkinson & Shiffrin (1968) and embellishes it with features of Wagner's (1976, 1978) priming theory. The model is too complex to detail here. Suffice it to say that the model avoids directly hypothesizing a role for the surprise value of the US, but it achieves the same end through rules about how event representations are distributed among three different memory states and how learning and the expression of memory differentially depend on the contents of these states. The model explains the attenuated UR observed to a US that is given immediately after an initial US or an established CS for that US (Terry 1976). Albert et al (1993) and Ayres & Albert (1990) have also used SOP to explain some of the effects of different ISIs with CSs of different lengths, but the model failed on other counts.

Wagner & Brandon (1989) proposed AESOP (affective extension of SOP) to explain (*a*) divergences among multiple behavioral indices of a single CS-US association, (*b*) occasion-setting phenomena, and (*c*) CRs sometimes resembling URs and sometimes appearing diametrically opposed to URs. AESOP differs from SOP by hypothesizing a dual representation of each CS-US association: one for the emotive qualities of the US (which support general preparatory behavior) and the other for the remaining sensory qualities of the US [which support more focused consummatory behavior (Konorski 1967)]. These representations have different parameters in the equations describing their processing; sensory information is subject to more rapid decay. This difference results in emotive conditioning (e.g. conditioned suppression) being acquired at longer ISIs than sensory conditioning (e.g. eyelid conditioning). AESOP explains occasion setting by the occasion setter eliciting emotive responding that modulates the CR later made to the CS (Bombace et al 1991, Brandon & Wagner 1991, Brandon et al 1991). Given the explanatory successes of SOP and AESOP, it is perhaps surprising that these models have not received more attention; however, they may be too complex to afford unambiguous predictions.

Learning Versus Expression

The very name of the field—associative learning—connotes the acquisition of information. However, the true concern of the field is *acquired behavior,* which involves not only acquisition but also retrieval from long-term memory, decision making, and response generation. The error in the field's recent narrow focus on acquisition is becoming increasingly clear. There is a growing trend for workers to view many behavioral deficits as failures to express information that had actually been acquired (Bouton 1993, Miller et al 1986, Miller & Matzel 1988, Spear 1973). An earlier generation of theorists better appreciated the importance of performance or expression variables (Hull 1952, Spence 1956, Tolman 1932; for a review, see Wasserman 1981).

It is important to note the asymmetry in documenting failures of expression and learning: Expression failures can be demonstrated by recovery from the deficit without further training, but acquisition failures defy definitive demonstration. Any failure to demonstrate recovery from a behavioral deficit might reflect a true acquisition failure or an inadequate recovery treatment.

From an expression-failure viewpoint, acquisition might very well be explained by a simple associative rule such as contiguity because phenomena like cue competition can now be explained by performance factors. We next describe two models, each of which focuses on factors that appear to independently modulate the behavioral expression of an association.

COMPARATOR THEORY Miller & Matzel's (1988) comparator hypothesis posits that CRs result from a comparison between a US representation that is directly activated by the CS and a US representation that is indirectly activated by the CS through a "comparator" stimulus. Comparator stimuli are background or other discrete cues that were prominent during CS training. Excitatory responding to the CS is anticipated to the degree that the CS better predicts the US than does the comparator. Behavior indicating inhibition is anticipated to the degree that the comparator better predicts the US than does the CS. This view is much like ΔP in contingency theory; however, the comparator hypothesis assumes that the critical comparison between these expectations occurs during testing, rather than exclusively during training, as is assumed by contingency theory. Thus, the comparator hypothesis is a model of performance rather than acquisition.

The comparator hypothesis predicts that posttraining changes in the associative value of the comparator stimulus should modify CRs to the CS. Specifically, deflating the associative status of the comparator should attenuate behavioral inhibition and enhance behavioral excitation, and vice versa for inflating the associative status of the comparator. Consistent with this view, Grahame et al (1994) found that posttraining extinction of the experimental context attenuates the CS-preexposure effect, and Matzel et al (1987) found that the same treatment attenuates the US-preexposure effect. Cole et al (1995), Kaufman & Bolles (1981), and Matzel et al (1985) found that posttraining extinction of a competing cue attenuates different forms of cue competition. Hallam et al (1992), Kaplan (1985), and Kasprow et al (1987) found decreases in conditioned inhibition due to posttraining extinction of the excitatory CS or context that was present during inhibition training. Until recently, the comparator hypothesis had little success with its predictions about posttraining inflation of comparator stimuli (RR Miller et al 1990; cf Denniston et al 1996, Miller & Matute 1996). The hypothesis also predicts one-trial overshadowing (Mackintosh & Reese 1979) and is unique in correctly predicting enhanced inhibition after nonreinforcement of the inhibitor (Zimmer-Hart & Rescorla 1974).

TEMPORAL CODING HYPOTHESIS The weak CRs that are often seen after simultaneous conditioning pose a serious problem for contiguity theory. Barnet et al (1991) and Matzel et al (1988c) explained this result with their temporal coding hypothesis, which states that (*a*) learning depends on temporal contiguity, (*b*) the temporal relationship between events is encoded as part of the association, and (*c*) the temporal relationship between events is a determinant of the nature of the CR. These researchers showed that simultaneous associations may be formed, but may not be expressed because most measures of conditioning involve anticipatory behavior, which would be inappropriate here. In line with this account, Barnet et al (1993) found that one simultaneously trained CS will block control by another simultaneously trained CS, but not by a serially trained CS, and vice versa. Barnet & Miller (1996) also found that, in conditioned inhibition training, subjects encode when an omitted US should have occurred. Holland et al (1996) have extended the idea of temporal encoding to serial occasion setting. They found that features best modulate responding when they precede the testing CS by the same interval that had separated the feature and the training CS.

CONCLUDING COMMENTS

What's elementary about associative learning? In accord with Thorndike's and Pavlov's early speculations, elementary associative learning still seems able to serve as the foundation for our understanding of many complex forms of behavior and cognition. However, our review reveals a rich body of knowledge about associations that surely causes us to question the simplicity of even this basic brand of mentation. Other cognitive processes such as attention, memory, and information processing are now being invoked to help explain the facts of associative learning. The next several years of research will be exciting ones, as neuroscientists and cognitive scientists join experimental psychologists in an interdisciplinary attack on the challenging problems of associative learning and behavior change.

ACKNOWLEDGMENTS

We thank the National Institute of Mental Health for supporting the research of EAW (MH47313 and MH51562) and RRM (MH33881).

Literature Cited

Albert M, Ricker S, Bevins RA, Ayres JJB. 1993. Extending continuous versus discontinuous conditioned stimuli before versus after unconditioned stimuli. *J. Exp. Psychol. Anim. Behav. Process.* 19:255–64

Allan LG. 1993. Human contingency judgments: rule based or associative? *Psychol. Bull.* 114:435–48

Amiro TW, Bitterman ME. 1980. Second-order appetitive conditioning in goldfish. *J. Exp. Psychol. Anim. Behav. Process.* 6: 41–48

Atkins CK, Domjan M, Gutierrez G. 1994. Topology of sexually conditioned behavior in male Japanese quail (*Coturnix japonica*) depends on the CS-US interval. *J. Exp. Psychol. Anim. Behav. Process.* 20:199–209

Atkinson RC, Shiffrin RM. 1968. Human memory: a proposed system and its control processes. In *The Psychology of Learning and Motivation,* ed. KW Spence, JT Spence, 2:89–195. New York: Academic

Ayres JJB, Albert M. 1990. Extending conditioned stimuli before versus after unconditioned stimuli: implications for real-time models of conditioning. *Learn. Motiv.* 21: 399–414

Azorlosa JL, Cicala GA. 1986. Blocking of conditioned suppression with 1 or 10 compound trials. *Anim. Learn. Behav.* 14: 163–67

Azrin NH, Holz WC. 1966. Punishment. In *Operant Behavior: Areas of Research and Application,* ed. WK Honig, pp. 380–447. New York: Appleton-Century-Crofts

Baker AG. 1977. Conditioned inhibition arising from a between-sessions negative correlation. *J. Exp. Psychol. Anim. Behav. Process.* 3:144–55

Baker AG, Mackintosh NJ. 1977. Excitatory and inhibitory conditioning following uncorrelated presentations of the CS and UCS. *Anim. Learn. Behav.* 5:315–19

Baker AG, Mackintosh NJ. 1979. Preexposure to the CS alone, US alone, or CS and US uncorrelated: latent inhibition, blocking by context, or learned irrelevance? *Learn. Motiv.* 10:278–94

Baker AG, Mercier P. 1982. Extinction of the context and latent inhibition. *Learn. Motiv.* 13:391–416

Baker TW. 1969. Component strength in a compound CS as a function of number of acquisition trials. *J. Exp. Psychol.* 79: 347–52

Balaz MA, Gutsin P, Cacheiro H, Miller RR. 1982a. Blocking as a retrieval failure: reactivation of associations to a blocked stimulus. *Q. J. Exp. Psychol.* 34B:99–113

Balaz MA, Kasprow WJ, Miller RR. 1982b. Blocking with a single compound trial. *Anim. Learn. Behav.* 10:271–76

Balsam PD, Tomie A, eds. 1985. *Context and Learning.* Hillsdale, NJ: Erlbaum

Barnet RC, Arnold HM, Miller RR. 1991. Simultaneous conditioning demonstrated in second-order conditioning: evidence for similar associative structure in forward and simultaneous conditioning. *Learn. Motiv.* 22:253–68

Barnet RC, Grahame NJ, Miller RR. 1993. Temporal encoding as a determinant of blocking. *J. Exp. Psychol. Anim. Behav. Process.* 19:327–41

Barnet RC, Miller RR. 1996. Temporal encoding as a determinant of inhibitory control. *Learn. Motiv.* 27:73–91

Baron A, Kaufman A, Fazzini D. 1969. Density and delay of punishment of free-operant avoidance. *J. Exp. Anal. Behav.* 12: 1029–37

Beatty WW, Maki WS. 1979. Acquisition of instrumental responding following noncontingent reinforcement: failure to observe "learned laziness" in rats. *Bull. Psychon. Soc.* 13:268–71

Bellingham WP, Gillette K. 1981a. Attenuation of overshadowing as a function of nondifferential compound conditioning trials. *Bull. Psychon. Soc.* 18:218–20

Bellingham WP, Gillette K. 1981b. Spontaneous configuring to a tone-light compound using appetitive training. *Learn. Motiv.* 12: 420–34

Bellingham WP, Gillette-Bellingham K, Kehoe EJ. 1985. Summation and configuration in patterning schedules with the rat and rabbit. *Anim. Learn. Behav.* 13:152–64

Bennett CH, Maldonado A, Mackintosh NJ. 1995. Learned irrelevance is not the sum of exposure to CS and US. *Q. J. Exp. Psychol.* 48B:117–28

Berk AM, Miller RR. 1978. LiCl-induced aversions to audiovisual cues as a function of response measure and CS-US interval. *Behav. Biol.* 24:184–208

Best MR, Batson JD, Meachum CL, Brown ER, Ringer M. 1985. Characteristics of taste-mediated environmental potentiation in rats. *Learn. Motiv.* 16:190–209

Bitterman ME, Menzel R, Fietz A, Schafer S. 1983. Classical conditioning of proboscis extension in honeybees (*Apis mellifera*). *J. Comp. Psychol.* 97:107–19

Black AH, Prokasy WF, eds. 1972. *Classical Conditioning II: Current Research and Theory.* New York: Appleton-Century-Crofts

Bombace JC, Brandon SE, Wagner AR. 1991.

Modulation of a conditioned eyeblink response by a putative emotive stimulus conditioned with hindleg shock. *J. Exp. Psychol. Anim. Behav. Process.* 17:323–33

Bonardi C, Hall G. 1996. Learned irrelevance: no more than the sum of CS and US preexposure effects? *J. Exp. Psychol. Anim. Behav. Process.* 22:183–91

Bond NW, DiGuisto EL. 1976. One trial higher-order conditioning of a taste aversion. *Aust. J. Psychol.* 28:53–55

Bouton ME. 1993. Context, time, and memory retrieval in the interference paradigms of Pavlovian learning. *Psychol. Bull.* 114: 80–99

Bouton ME, Bolles RC. 1979. Contextual control of the extinction of conditioned fear. *Learn. Motiv.* 10:445–66

Bouton ME, King DA. 1983. Contextual control of the extinction of conditioned fear: tests for associative value of the context. *J. Exp. Psychol. Anim. Behav. Process.* 9: 248–65

Bouton ME, Ricker ST. 1994. Renewal of extinguished responding in a second context. *Anim. Learn. Behav.* 22:317–24

Bouton ME, Swartzentruber DE. 1986. Analysis of the associative and occasion-setting properties of contexts participating in a Pavlovian discrimination. *J. Exp. Psychol. Anim. Behav. Process.* 12:333–50

Bowe CA, Green L, Miller JD. 1987. Differential acquisition of discriminated autoshaping as a function of stimulus qualities and locations. *Anim. Learn. Behav.* 15:285–92

Bower GH, Hilgard ER. 1981. *Theories of Learning.* Englewood Cliffs, NJ: Prentice-Hall. 5th ed.

Brandon SE, Bombace JC, Falls WA, Wagner AR. 1991. Modulation of unconditioned defensive reflexes by a putative emotive Pavlovian conditioned stimulus. *J. Exp. Psychol. Anim. Behav. Process.* 17:312–22

Brandon SE, Wagner AR. 1991. Modulation of a discrete Pavlovian conditioned reflex by a putative emotive Pavlovian conditioned stimulus. *J. Exp. Psychol. Anim. Behav. Process.* 17:299–311

Brogden WJ. 1939. Sensory pre-conditioning. *J. Exp. Psychol.* 25:323–32

Brooks DC, Bouton ME. 1994. A retrieval cue for extinction attenuates response recovery (renewal) caused by a return to the conditioning context. *J. Exp. Psychol. Anim. Behav. Process.* 20:366–79

Busemeyer JR. 1991. Intuitive statistical estimation. In *Contributions to Information Integration Theory: Cognition,* ed. NH Anderson, 1:187–215. Hillsdale, NJ: Erlbaum

Bush RR, Mosteller F. 1951. A mathematical model for simple learning. *Psychol. Rev.* 58:313–23

Calton JL, Mitchell KG, Schachtman TR. 1996. Conditioned inhibition produced by an extinction of a conditioned stimulus. *Learn. Motiv.* In press

Chapman GB. 1991. Trial order affects cue interaction in contingency judgment. *J. Exp. Psychol. Learn. Mem. Cogn.* 17:837–54

Cheng PW. 1993. Separating causal laws from causal facts: pressing the limits of statistical relevance. In *The Psychology of Learning and Motivation,* ed. DL Medin, 30: 215–64. San Diego, CA: Academic

Clarke JC, Westbrook RF, Irwin J. 1979. Potentiation instead of overshadowing in the pigeon. *Behav. Neural. Biol.* 25:18–29

Cohen PS. 1968. Punishment: the interactive effects of delay and intensity of shock. *J. Exp. Anal. Behav.* 11:789–99

Cole RP, Barnet RC, Miller RR. 1995. Effect of relative stimulus validity: learning or performance deficit? *J. Exp. Psychol. Anim. Behav. Process.* 21:293–303

Cole RP, Denniston JC, Miller RR. 1996. Reminder-induced attenuation of the effect of relative stimulus validity. *Anim. Learn. Behav.* In press

Colwill RM, Rescorla RA. 1985. Postconditioning devaluation of a reinforcer affects instrumental responding. *J. Exp. Psychol. Anim. Behav. Process.* 11:120–32

Commons ML, Herrnstein RJ, Wagner AR, eds. 1982. *Quantitative Analyses of Behavior,* Vol. 3, *Acquisition.* Cambridge, MA: Ballinger

Commons ML, Herrnstein RJ, Wagner AR, eds. 1983. *Quantitative Analyses of Behavior,* Vol. 4, *Discrimination Processes.* Cambridge, MA: Ballinger

Cooper LD. 1991. Temporal factors in classical conditioning. *Learn. Motiv.* 22:129–52

Crawford LL, Domjan M. 1995. Second-order conditioning in male Japanese quail (*Coturnix japonica*). *Anim. Learn. Behav.* 23: 327–34

Davidson TL, McKernan MG, Jarrard LE. 1993. Hippocampal lesions do not impair negative patterning: a challenge to configural association theory. *Behav. Neurosci.* 107:227–34

DeCola JP, Fanselow MS. 1995. Differential inflation with short and long CS-US intervals: evidence of a nonassociative process in long-delay taste avoidance. *Anim. Learn. Behav.* 23:154–63

Denniston JC, Miller RR, Matute H. 1996. Biological significance as a determinant of cue competition. *Psychol. Sci.* In press

Dickinson A. 1980. *Contemporary Animal Learning Theory.* Cambridge: Cambridge Univ. Press

Dickinson A, Mackintosh NJ. 1978. Classical conditioning in animals. *Annu. Rev. Psychol.* 29:587–612

Dickinson A, Hall G, Mackintosh NJ. 1976.

Surprise and the attenuation of blocking. *J. Exp. Psychol. Anim. Behav. Process.* 2: 313–22

Dickinson A, Watt A, Griffiths WJ. 1992. Free-operant acquisition with delayed reinforcement. *Q. J. Exp. Psychol.* 45B:241–58

Droungas A, LoLordo VM. 1994. Evidence for simultaneous excitatory and inhibitory associations in the explicitly unpaired procedure. *Learn. Motiv.* 25:1–25

Durlach PJ. 1983. The effect of signaling intertrial USs in autoshaping. *J. Exp. Psychol. Anim. Behav. Process.* 9:374–89

Durlach PJ, Rescorla RA. 1980. Potentiation rather than overshadowing in flavor-aversion learning: an analysis in terms of within-compound associations. *J. Exp. Psychol. Anim. Behav. Process.* 6:175–87

Ellins SR, von Kluge S. 1990. Auditory food cue conditioning: effects of spatial contiguity and taste quality. *Q. J. Exp. Psychol.* 42B:73–86

Engberg LA, Hansen G, Welker RL, Thomas DR. 1972. Acquisition of key-pecking via autoshaping as a function of prior experience: "learned laziness?" *Science* 178: 1002–4

Fantino E, Abarca N. 1985. Choice, optimal foraging, and the delay-reduction hypothesis. *Behav. Brain Sci.* 8:315–62

Ganesan R, Pearce JM. 1988. Effect of changing the unconditioned stimulus on appetitive blocking. *J. Exp. Psychol. Anim. Behav. Process.* 14:280–91

Gibbon J, Balsam P. 1981. Spreading association in time. See Locurto et al 1981, pp. 219–53

Gibbon J, Baldock MD, Locurto C, Gold L, Terrace HS. 1977. Trial and intertrial durations in autoshaping. *J. Exp. Psychol. Anim. Behav. Process.* 3:264–84

Gibbs CM, Cool V, Land T, Kehoe EJ, Gormezano I. 1991. Second-order conditioning of the rabbit's nictitating membrane response: interstimulus interval and frequency of CS-CS pairings. *Integ. Physiol. Behav. Sci.* 26: 282–95

Grahame NJ, Barnet RC, Gunther LM, Miller RR. 1994. Latent inhibition as a performance deficit resulting from CS-context associations. *Anim. Learn. Behav.* 22:395–408

Hall G, Honey RC. 1989. Contextual effects in conditioning, latent inhibition, and habituation: associative and retrieval functions of contextual cues. *J. Exp. Psychol. Anim. Behav. Process.* 15:232–41

Hall G, Honey RC. 1993. Poststimulus events in discrimination learning with delayed reinforcement: role of distraction and implications for "marking." *Learn. Motiv.* 24: 242–54

Hall G, Mackintosh NJ, Goodall G, Dal Martello M. 1977. Loss of control by a less valid or by a less salient stimulus compounded with a better predictor of reinforcement. *Learn. Motiv.* 8:145–58

Hall G, Minor H. 1984. A search for context-stimulus associations in latent inhibition. *Q. J. Exp. Psychol.* 36B:145–69

Hall G, Pearce JM. 1979. Latent inhibition of a CS during CS-US pairings. *J. Exp. Psychol. Anim. Behav. Process.* 5:31–42

Hall G, Pearce JM. 1982. Changes in stimulus associability during conditioning: implications for theories of acquisition. See Commons et al 1982, 3:221–39

Hall G, Schachtman TR. 1987. Differential effects of a retention interval on latent inhibition and the habituation of an orienting response. *Anim. Learn. Behav.* 15:76–82

Hallam SC, Grahame NJ, Harris K, Miller RR. 1992. Associative structures underlying enhanced negative summation following operational extinction of a Pavlovian inhibitor. *Learn. Motiv.* 23:43–62

Harrison JM, Iversen SD, Pratt SR. 1977. Control of responding by location of auditory stimuli. *J. Exp. Anal. Behav.* 28:243–51

Hart JA, Bourne MA, Schachtman TR. 1995. Slow reacquisition of a conditioned taste aversion. *Anim. Learn. Behav.* 23:297–303

Hearst E. 1972. Some persistent problems in the analysis of conditioned inhibition. In *Inhibition and Learning,* ed. RA Boakes, MS Halliday, pp. 5–39. London: Academic

Hittesdorf M, Richards RW. 1982. Aversive second-order conditioning in the pigeon: elimination of conditioning to CS1 and effects on established second-order conditioning. *Can. J. Psychol.* 36:462–77

Holland PC. 1983. Occasion setting in Pavlovian feature positive discriminations. See Commons et al 1983, 4:183–206

Holland PC. 1985. The nature of conditioned inhibition in serial and simultaneous feature negative discriminations. In *Information Processing in Animals: Conditioned Inhibition,* ed. RR Miller, NE Spear, pp. 267–97. Hillsdale, NJ: Erlbaum

Holland PC. 1986. Temporal determinants of occasion setting in feature positive discriminations. *Anim. Learn. Behav.* 14: 111–20

Holland PC. 1988. Excitation and inhibition in unblocking. *J. Exp. Psychol. Anim. Behav. Process.* 14:261–79

Holland PC. 1989. Feature extinction enhances transfer of occasion setting. *Anim. Learn. Behav.* 17:269–79

Holland PC. 1992. Occasion setting in Pavlovian conditioning. In *The Psychology of Learning and Motivation,* ed. DL Medin, 28:69–125. San Diego, CA: Academic

Holland PC, Hamlin PA, Parsons JP. 1996.

Temporal specificity in serial feature positive discrimination learning. *J. Exp. Psychol. Anim. Behav. Process.* In press

Hull CL. 1952. *A Behavior System.* New Haven, CT: Yale Univ. Press

James JH, Wagner AR. 1980. One-trial overshadowing: evidence of distributed processing. *J. Exp. Psychol. Anim. Behav. Process.* 6:188–205

Jenkins HM, Barnes RA, Barrera FJ. 1981. Why autoshaping depends on trial spacing. See Locurto et al 1981, pp. 255–84

Jenkins HM, Lambos WA. 1983. Tests of two explanations of response elimination by noncontingent reinforcement. *Anim. Learn. Behav.* 11:302–8

Kamin LJ. 1968. "Attention-like" processes in classical conditioning. In *Miami Symposium on the Prediction of Behavior: Aversive Stimulation,* ed. MR Jones, pp. 9–31. Miami, FL: Univ. Miami Press

Kamin LJ, Idrobo F. 1978. Configural conditioning in the CER: a possible artifact. *Anim. Learn. Behav.* 6:290–93

Kao SF, Wasserman EA. 1993. Assessment of an information integration account of contingency judgment with examination of subjective cell importance and method of information presentation. *J. Exp. Psychol. Learn. Mem. Cogn.* 19:1363–86

Kaplan PS. 1985. Explaining the effects of relative time in trace conditioning: a preliminary test of a comparator hypothesis. *Anim. Learn. Behav.* 13:233–38

Kasprow WJ, Cacheiro H, Balaz MA, Miller RR. 1982. Reminder-induced recovery of associations to an overshadowed stimulus. *Learn. Motiv.* 13:155–66

Kasprow WJ, Catterson D, Schachtman TR, Miller RR. 1984. Attenuation of latent inhibition by postacquisition reminder. *Q. J. Exp. Psychol.* 36B:53–63

Kasprow WJ, Schachtman TR, Miller RR. 1987. The comparator hypothesis of conditioned response generation: manifest conditioned excitation and inhibition as a function of relative excitatory associative strengths of CS and conditioning context at the time of testing. *J. Exp. Psychol. Anim. Behav. Process.* 13:395–406

Kaufman MA, Bolles RC. 1981. A nonassociative aspect of overshadowing. *Bull. Psychon. Soc.* 18:318–20

Kaye H, Pearce JM. 1984. The strength of the orienting response during Pavlovian conditioning. *J. Exp. Psychol. Anim. Behav. Process.* 10:90–109

Kehoe EJ, Cool V, Gormezano I. 1991. Trace conditioning of the rabbit's nictitating membrane response as a function of CS-US interstimulus interval and trials per session. *Learn. Motiv.* 22:269–90

Kehoe EJ, Graham P. 1988. Summation and configuration: stimulus compounding and negative patterning in the rabbit. *J. Exp. Psychol. Anim. Behav. Process.* 14:320–33

Kehoe EJ, Schreurs BG. 1986. Compound-component differentiation as a function of CS-US interval and CS duration in rabbit's nictitating membrane response. *Anim. Learn. Behav.* 14:144–54

Kimble GA. 1961. *Hilgard and Marquis' Conditioning and Learning.* New York: Appleton-Century-Crofts

Kimmel HD. 1977. Notes from "Pavlov's Wednesdays:" sensory preconditioning. *Am. J. Psychol.* 90:319–21

Kleinschmidt H, Lachnit H. 1993. Pavlovian conditioning and rule learning. *Integ. Physiol. Behav. Sci.* 28:158–62

Konorski J. 1967. *Integrative Activity of the Brain: An Interdisciplinary Approach.* Chicago: Univ. Chicago Press

Kraemer PJ, Lariviere NA, Spear NE. 1988. Expression of a taste aversion conditioned with an odor-taste compound: Overshadowing is relatively weak in weanlings and decreases over a retention interval in adults. *Anim. Learn. Behav.* 16:164–68

Kraemer PJ, Randall CK, Carbary TJ. 1991. Release from latent inhibition with delayed testing. *Anim. Learn. Behav.* 19:139–45

Lachnit H, Kimmel HD. 1993. Positive and negative patterning in human classical skin conductance response conditioning. *Anim. Learn. Behav.* 21:314–26

Lavin MJ. 1976. The establishment of flavor-flavor associations using a sensory preconditioning training procedure. *Learn. Motiv.* 7:173–83

Lennartz RC, Weinberger NM. 1992. Analysis of response systems in Pavlovian conditioning reveals rapidly versus slowly acquired conditioned responses: support for two factors, implications for behavior and neurobiology. *Psychobiology* 20:93–119

Levinthal CF, Tartell RH, Margolin CM, Fishman H. 1985. The CS-US interval ISI function in rabbit nictitating membrane response conditioning with very long intertrial intervals. *Anim. Learn. Behav.* 13: 228–32

Lieberman DA, Davidson FH, Thomas GV. 1985. Marking in pigeons: the role of memory in delayed reinforcement. *J. Exp. Psychol. Anim. Behav. Process.* 11:611–24

Locurto CM, Terrace HS, Gibbon J, eds. 1981. *Autoshaping and Conditioning Theory.* New York: Academic

LoLordo VM, Fairless JL. 1985. Pavlovian conditioned inhibition: the literature since 1969. In *Information Processing in Animals: Conditioned Inhibition,* ed. RR Miller, NE Spear, pp. 1–49. Hillsdale, NJ: Erlbaum

Lubow RE, Moore AV. 1959. Latent inhibition: the effect of nonreinforced exposure to the conditioned stimulus. *J. Comp. Physiol. Psychol.* 52:415–19

Lubow RE, Schnur P, Rifkin B. 1976. Latent inhibition and conditioned attention theory. *J. Exp. Psychol. Anim. Behav. Process.* 2: 163–74

Lucas GA, Deich JD, Wasserman EA. 1981. Trace autoshaping: acquisition, maintenance, and path dependence at long trace intervals. *J. Exp. Anal. Behav.* 36:61–74

Lucas GA, Wasserman EA. 1982. US duration and local trial spacing affect autoshaped responding. *Anim. Learn. Behav.* 10:490–98

MacDonald SE. 1993. Delayed matching-to-successive-samples in pigeons: short-term memory for item and order information. *Anim. Learn. Behav.* 21:59–67

Mackintosh NJ. 1971. An analysis of overshadowing and blocking. *Q. J. Exp. Psychol.* 23:118–25

Mackintosh NJ. 1973. Stimulus selection: learning to ignore stimuli that predict no change in reinforcement. In *Constraints on Learning: Limitations and Predispositions,* ed. RA Hinde, J Stevenson-Hinde, pp. 75–96. London: Academic

Mackintosh NJ. 1975. A theory of attention: variations in the associability of stimuli with reinforcement. *Psychol. Rev.* 82: 276–98

Mackintosh NJ. 1976. Overshadowing and stimulus intensity. *Anim. Learn. Behav.* 4: 186–92

Mackintosh NJ. 1983. *Conditioning and Associative Learning.* Oxford: Oxford Univ. Press

Mackintosh NJ, Bygrave DJ, Picton BMB. 1977. Locus of the effect of a surprising reinforcer in the attenuation of blocking. *Q. J. Exp. Psychol.* 29:327–36

Mackintosh NJ, Reese B. 1979. One-trial overshadowing. *Q. J. Exp. Psychol.* 31:519–26

Marlin NA, Miller RR. 1981. Associations to contextual stimuli as a determinant of long-term habituation. *J. Exp. Psychol. Anim. Behav. Process.* 7:313–33

Marshall BS, Gokey DS, Green PL, Rashotte ME. 1979. Spatial location of first- and second-order visual conditioned stimuli in second-order conditioning of the pigeon's keypeck. *Bull. Psychon. Soc.* 13:133–36

Matzel LD, Brown AM, Miller RR. 1987. Associative effects of US preexposure: modulation of conditioned responding by an excitatory training context. *J. Exp. Psychol. Anim. Behav. Process.* 13:65–72

Matzel LD, Gladstein L, Miller RR. 1988a. Conditioned excitation and conditioned inhibition are not mutually exclusive. *Learn. Motiv.* 19:99–121

Matzel LD, Hallam SC, Miller RR. 1988b. Contribution of conditioned opioid analgesia to the shock-induced associative US-preexposure deficit. *Anim. Learn. Behav.* 16:486–92

Matzel LD, Held FP, Miller RR. 1988c. Information and expression of simultaneous and backward associations: implications for contiguity theory. *Learn. Motiv.* 19:317–44

Matzel LD, Schachtman TR, Miller RR. 1985. Recovery of an overshadowed association achieved by extinction of the overshadowing stimulus. *Learn. Motiv.* 16:398–412

Matzel LD, Schachtman TR, Miller RR. 1988d. Learned irrelevance exceeds the sum of the CS-preexposure and US-preexposure deficits. *J. Exp. Psychol. Anim. Behav. Process.* 14:311–19

Miller JD, Bowe CA. 1982. Roles of the qualities and locations of stimuli and responses in simple associative learning: the quality-location hypothesis. *Pavlov. J. Biol. Sci.* 17:129–39

Miller JS, Jagielo JA, Spear NE. 1990. Changes in the retrievability of associations to elements of the compound CS determine the expression of overshadowing. *Anim. Learn. Behav.* 18:157–61

Miller JS, Jagielo JA, Spear NE. 1993. The influence of retention interval on the US preexposure effect: changes in contextual blocking over time. *Learn. Motiv.* 24: 376–94

Miller RR, Barnet RC, Grahame NJ. 1995. Assessment of the Rescorla-Wagner model. *Psychol. Bull.* 117:363–86

Miller RR, Hallam SC, Grahame NJ. 1990. Inflation of comparator stimuli following CS training. *Anim. Learn. Behav.* 19:434–43

Miller RR, Kasprow WJ, Schachtman TR. 1986. Retrieval variability: sources and consequences. *Am. J. Psychol.* 99:145–218

Miller RR, Matute H. 1996. Biological significance in forward and backward blocking: toward a resolution of a discrepancy between animals and humans in contingency judgments. *J. Exp. Psychol. General.* In press

Miller RR, Matzel LD. 1988. The comparator hypothesis: a response rule for the expression of associations. In *The Psychology of Learning and Motivation,* ed. GH Bower, 22:51–92. San Diego, CA: Academic

Nairne JS, Rescorla RA. 1981. Second-order conditioning with diffuse auditory reinforcers in the pigeon. *Learn. Motiv.* 12:65–91

Neill JC, Harrison JM. 1987. Auditory discrimination: the Konorski quality-location effect. *J. Exp. Anal. Behav.* 48:81–95

O'Connell JM, Rashotte ME. 1982. Reinforcement effects in first- and second-order conditioning of directed action. *Learn. Motiv.* 13:1–25

Palmerino CC, Rusiniak DW, Garcia J. 1980. Flavor-illness aversions: the peculiar roles of odor and taste in memory for poisons. *Science* 208:753–55

Papini MR, Bitterman ME. 1990. The role of contingency in classical conditioning. *Psychol. Rev.* 97:396–403

Papini MR, Bitterman ME. 1993. The two-test strategy in the study of inhibitory conditioning. *J. Exp. Psychol. Anim. Behav. Process.* 19:342–52

Parks ER. 1968. The orienting reaction as a mediator of sensory preconditioning. *Psychon. Sci.* 11:11–12

Pavlov IP. 1927. *Conditioned Reflexes.* London: Oxford Univ. Press

Pavlov IP. 1928. *Lectures on Conditioned Reflexes.* New York: International

Pearce JM. 1987. A model for stimulus generalization in Pavlovian conditioning. *Psychol. Rev.* 94:61–73

Pearce JM. 1994. Similarity and discrimination: a selective review and a connectionist model. *Psychol. Rev.* 101:587–607

Pearce JM, Hall G. 1978. Overshadowing the instrumental conditioning of a lever press response by a more valid predictor of reinforcement. *J. Exp. Psychol. Anim. Behav. Process.* 4:356–67

Pearce JM, Hall G. 1980. A model for Pavlovian conditioning: variations in the effectiveness of conditioned but not unconditioned stimuli. *Psychol. Rev.* 87:332–52

Pearce JM, Redhead ES. 1993. The influence of an irrelevant stimulus on two discriminations. *J. Exp. Psychol. Anim. Behav. Process.* 19:180–90

Peterson C, Maier SF, Seligman MEP. 1993. *Learned Helplessness: A Theory of Personal Control.* New York: Oxford Univ. Press

Popik RS, Stern SD, Frey PW. 1979. Second-order conditioning: different outcomes in fear and eyelid conditioning. *Anim. Learn. Behav.* 7:355–59

Prewitt EP. 1967. Number of preconditioning trials in sensory preconditioning using CER training. *J. Comp. Physiol. Psychol.* 64:360–62

Quinlan P. 1991. *Connectionism and Psychology.* Chicago: Univ. Chicago Press

Ramey CT, Goulet LR. 1971. Effects of spatial separation of stimulus, response, and reward in discrimination learning by children. *Child Dev.* 42:978–82

Randich A. 1981. The US preexposure phenomenon in the conditioned suppression paradigm: a role for conditioned situational stimuli. *Learn. Motiv.* 12:321–41

Randich A, LoLordo VM. 1979. Preconditioning exposure to the unconditioned stimulus affects the acquisition of a conditioned emotional response. *Learn. Motiv.* 10: 245–77

Rashotte ME, Marshall BS, O'Connell JM. 1981. Signaling functions of the second-order CS: partial reinforcement during second-order conditioning of the pigeon's keypeck. *Anim. Learn. Behav.* 9:253–60

Razran G. 1971. *Mind in Evolution: An East-West Synthesis of Learned Behavior and Cognition.* Boston: Houghton-Mifflin

Redhead ES, Pearce JM. 1995a. Similarity and discrimination learning. *Q. J. Exp. Psychol.* 48B:46–66

Redhead ES, Pearce JM. 1995b. Stimulus salience and negative patterning. *Q. J. Exp. Psychol.* 48B:67–83

Reiss S, Wagner AR. 1972. CS habituation produces a "latent inhibition effect" but no active "conditioned inhibition." *Learn. Motiv.* 3:237–45

Rescorla RA. 1968. Probability of shock in the presence and absence of CS in fear conditioning. *J. Comp. Physiol. Psychol.* 66:1–5

Rescorla RA. 1969. Pavlovian conditioned inhibition. *Psychol. Bull.* 72:77–94

Rescorla RA. 1971. Summation and retardation tests of latent inhibition. *J. Comp. Physiol. Psychol.* 75:77–81

Rescorla RA. 1972. "Configural" conditioning in discrete-trial bar pressing. *J. Comp. Physiol. Psychol.* 79:307–17

Rescorla RA. 1973. Second-order conditioning: implications for theories of learning. In *Contemporary Approaches to Conditioning and Learning,* ed. FJ McGuigan, DB Lumsden, pp. 127–50. Washington, DC: Winston

Rescorla RA. 1980. Simultaneous and successive associations in sensory preconditioning. *J. Exp. Psychol. Anim. Behav. Process.* 6:207–16

Rescorla RA. 1982. Effect of a stimulus intervening between CS and US in autoshaping. *J. Exp. Psychol. Anim. Behav. Process.* 8: 131–41

Rescorla RA. 1988. Behavioral studies of Pavlovian conditioning. *Annu. Rev. Neurosci.* 11:329–52

Rescorla RA, Cunningham CL. 1979. Spatial contiguity facilitates Pavlovian second-order conditioning. *J. Exp. Psychol. Anim. Behav. Process.* 5:152–61

Rescorla RA, Furrow DR. 1977. Stimulus similarity as a determinant of Pavlovian conditioning. *J. Exp. Psychol. Anim. Behav. Process.* 3:203–15

Rescorla RA, Gillan DJ. 1980. An analysis of the facilitative effect of similarity on second-order conditioning. *J. Exp. Psychol. Anim. Behav. Process.* 6:339–51

Rescorla RA, Grau JW, Durlach PJ. 1985. Analysis of the unique cue in configural discriminations. *J. Exp. Psychol. Anim. Behav. Process.* 11:356–66

Rescorla RA, Heth CD. 1975. Reinstatement of fear to an extinguished conditioned stimulus. *J. Exp. Psychol. Anim. Behav. Process.* 1:88–96

Rescorla RA, Holland PC. 1982. Behavioral studies of associative learning in animals. *Annu. Rev. Psychol.* 33:265–308

Rescorla RA, Wagner AR. 1972. A theory of Pavlovian conditioning: variations in the effectiveness of reinforcement and nonreinforcement. See Black & Prokasy 1972, pp. 64–99

Rizley RC, Rescorla RA. 1972. Associations in second-order conditioning and sensory preconditioning. *J. Comp. Physiol. Psychol.* 81:1–11

Robertson D, Krane RV, Garrud P. 1984. Second-order conditioned taste aversion in the rat: shared modality is not sufficient to promote an association between S1 and S2. *Anim. Learn. Behav.* 12:316–22

Rogers JD. 1973. Stimulus intensity and trace intervals in sensory preconditioning using the CER. *Bull. Psychon. Soc.* 1:107–9

Ross RT, Scavio MJ. 1983. Perseveration of associative strength in rabbit nictitating membrane response conditioning following ISI shifts. *Anim. Learn. Behav.* 11:435–38

Ross RT, Scavio MJ, Erikson K, Gormezano I. 1979. Performance of the nictitating membrane CR following CS-US interval shifts. *Bull. Psychon. Soc.* 14:189–92

Rumbaugh DM, Richardson WK, Washburn DA, Savage-Rumbaugh ES. 1989. Rhesus monkeys (*Macaca mulatta*), video tasks, and implications for stimulus-response spatial contiguity. *J. Comp. Psychol.* 103: 32–38

Saavedra MA. 1975. Pavlovian compound conditioning in the rabbit. *Learn. Motiv.* 6: 314–26

Schneiderman N. 1972. Response system divergencies in aversive classical conditioning. See Black & Prokasy 1972, pp. 341–76

Schreurs BG, Kehoe EJ, Gormezano I. 1993. Concurrent associative transfer and competition in serial conditioning of the rabbit's nictitating membrane response. *Learn. Motiv.* 24:395–412

Schwartz B, Reisberg D, Vollmecke T. 1974. Effects of treadle training on autoshaped keypecking: learned laziness and learned industriousness or response competition? *Bull. Psychon. Soc.* 3:369–72

Seligman MEP, Maier SF, Solomon RL. 1971. Unpredictable and uncontrollable aversive events. In *Aversive Conditioning and Learning,* ed. FR Brush, pp. 347–400. New York: Academic

Shanks DR. 1985. Forward and backward blocking in human contingency judgement. *Q. J. Exp. Psychol.* 37B:1–21

Shanks DR. 1994. Human associative learning. In *Animal Learning and Cognition,* ed. NJ Mackintosh, pp. 335–74. San Diego, CA: Academic

Skinner BF. 1938. *The Behavior of Organisms.* New York: Appleton-Century-Crofts

Smith ST, Putney RT. 1979. Temporal factors in the sensitivity of the alpha rhythm to habituation and conditioning. *Physiol. Psychol.* 7:381–86

Spear NE. 1973. Retrieval of memories in animals. *Psychol. Rev.* 80:163–94

Spence KW. 1956. *Behavior Theory and Conditioning.* New Haven, CT: Yale Univ. Press

Spiker VA, Ferraro DP. 1977. Within-subject analysis of the CS1-CS2 interval in sensory preconditioning with rats. *Psychol. Rec.* 27: 771–78

St. Claire-Smith R, MacLaren D. 1983. Response preconditioning effects. *J. Exp. Psychol. Anim. Behav. Process.* 9:41–48

Stanhope KJ. 1992. The representation of the reinforcer and the force of the pigeon's keypeck in first- and second-order conditioning. *Q. J. Exp. Psychol.* 44B:137–58

Stefurak TL, Martin G, van der Kooy D. 1990. The representation in memory of morphine's unconditioned motivational effects depends on the nature of the conditioned stimulus. *Psychobiology* 18:435–42

Swartzentruber D. 1995. Modulatory mechanisms in Pavlovian conditioning. *Anim. Learn. Behav.* 23:123–43

Tait RW, Black M, Katz M, Suboski MD. 1972. Discriminative sensory preconditioning. *Can. J. Psychol.* 26:201–5

Tait RW, Marquis HA, Williams R, Weinstein L, Suboski MD. 1969. Extinction of sensory preconditioning using CER training. *J. Comp. Physiol. Psychol.* 69:170–72

Tait RW, Simon E, Suboski MD. 1971. "Partial reinforcement" in sensory preconditioning with rats. *Can. J. Psychol.* 25: 427–35

Tait RW, Suboski MD. 1972. Stimulus intensity in sensory preconditioning of rats. *Can. J. Psychol.* 26:374–81

Tarpy RM, Sawabini FL. 1974. Reinforcement delay: a selective review of the last decade. *Psychol. Bull.* 81:984–97

Terry WS. 1976. The effects of priming US representation in short-term memory on Pavlovian conditioning. *J. Exp. Psychol. Anim. Behav. Process.* 2:354–70

Testa TJ. 1975. Effects of similarity of location and temporal intensity pattern of conditioned and unconditioned stimuli on the acquisition of conditioned suppression in rats. *J. Exp. Psychol. Anim. Behav. Process.* 1: 114–21

Thompson RF. 1972. Sensory preconditioning. In *Topics in Learning and Performance,* ed. RF Thompson, JF Voss, pp. 105–29. New York: Academic

Thompson RF, Spencer WA. 1966. Habituation: a model phenomenon for the study of neuronal substrates of behavior. *Psychol. Rev.* 73:16–43

Thorndike EL. 1911. *Animal Intelligence: Experimental Studies.* New York: Macmillan

Tolman EC. 1932. *Purposive Behavior in Animals and Men.* New York: Century

Tomie A, Murphy AL, Fath S, Jackson RL. 1980. Retardation of autoshaping following pretraining with unpredictable food: effects of changing the context between training and testing. *Learn. Motiv.* 11:117–34

Van Hamme LJ, Wasserman EA. 1994. Cue competition in causality judgments: the role of nonpresentation of compound stimulus elements. *Learn. Motiv.* 25: 127–51

Wagner AR. 1976. Priming in STM: an information-processing mechanism for self-generated or retrieval-generated depression in performance. In *Habituation: Perspectives from Child Development, Animal Behavior, and Neurophysiology,* ed. TJ Tighe, RN Leaton, pp. 95–128. Hillsdale, NJ: Erlbaum

Wagner AR. 1978. Expectancies and priming in STM. In *Cognitive Processes in Animal Behavior,* ed. SH Hulse, H Fowler, WK Honig, pp. 177–209. Hillsdale, NJ: Erlbaum

Wagner AR. 1979. Habituation and memory. In *Mechanisms of Learning and Motivation: A Memorial Volume to Jerzy Konorski,* ed. A Dickinson, RA Boakes, pp. 53–82. Hillsdale, NJ: Erlbaum

Wagner AR. 1981. SOP: a model of automatic memory processing in animal behavior. In *Information Processing in Animals: Memory Mechanisms,* ed. NE Spear, RR Miller, pp. 5–47. Hillsdale, NJ: Erlbaum

Wagner AR, Brandon SE. 1989. Evolution of a structured connectionist model of Pavlovian conditioning. AESOP. In *Contemporary Learning Theories: Pavlovian Conditioning and the Status of Traditional Learning Theory,* ed. SB Klein, RR Mowrer, pp. 149–89. Hillsdale, NJ: Erlbaum

Wagner AR, Logan FA, Haberlandt K, Price T. 1968. Stimulus selection in animal discrimination learning. *J. Comp. Physiol. Psychol.* 76:171–80

Wagner AR, Rescorla RA. 1972. Inhibition in Pavlovian conditioning: application of a theory. In *Inhibition and Learning,* ed. RA Boakes, MS Halliday, pp. 301–36. London: Academic

Warren HC. 1921. *A History of the Association Psychology.* New York: Scribner's

Wasserman EA. 1981. Response evocation in autoshaping: contributions of cognitive and comparative-evolutionary analyses to an understanding of directed action. See Locurto et al 1981, pp. 21–54

Wasserman EA. 1993. Comparative cognition: beginning the second century of the study of animal intelligence. *Psychol. Bull.* 113: 211–28

Wasserman EA, Carr DL, Deich JD. 1978. Association of conditioned stimuli during serial conditioning by pigeons. *Anim. Learn. Behav.* 6:52–56

Wasserman EA, DeLong RE, Larew MB. 1984. Temporal order and duration: their discrimination and retention by pigeons. *Ann. NY Acad. Sci.* 423:103–15

Wasserman EA, Dorner WW, Kao SF. 1990. Contributions of specific cell information to judgments of interevent contingency. *J. Exp. Psychol. Learn. Mem. Cogn.* 16: 509–21

Wasserman EA, Elek SM, Chatlosh DL, Baker AG. 1993. Rating causal relations: the role of probability in judgments of response-outcome contingency. *J. Exp. Psychol. Learn. Mem. Cogn.* 19:174–88

Wasserman EA, Franklin SR, Hearst E. 1974. Pavlovian appetitive contingencies and approach vs. withdrawal to conditioned stimuli in pigeons. *J. Comp. Physiol. Psychol.* 86:616–27

Wasserman EA, Neunaber DJ. 1986. College students' responding to and rating of contingency relations: the role of temporal contiguity. *J. Exp. Anal. Behav.* 46:15–35

Weisman RG, Wasserman EA, Dodd PWD, Larew MB. 1980. Representation and retention of two-event sequences in pigeons. *J. Exp. Psychol. Anim. Behav. Process.* 6: 312–25

Whitlow JW Jr, Wagner AR. 1972. Negative patterning in classical conditioning: summation of response tendencies to isolable and configural components. *Psychon. Sci.* 27:299–301

Wickens DD, Nield AF, Tuber DS, Wickens C. 1970. Classically conditioned compound-element discrimination as a function of length of training, amount of testing, and CS-UCS interval. *Learn. Motiv.* 1:95–109

Widrow G, Hoff ME. 1960. Adaptive switching circuits. *Inst. Radio Eng., West. Electr. Show Conv., Conv. Rec.* 4:96–104

Wilkenfield J, Nickel M, Blakely E, Poling A. 1992. Acquisition of lever-press responding in rats with delayed reinforcement: a comparison of three procedures. *J. Exp. Anal. Behav.* 58:431–43

Williams BA. 1975. The blocking of reinforcement control. *J. Exp. Anal. Behav.* 24: 215–25

Williams BA. 1994. Blocking despite changes in reinforcer identity. *Anim. Learn. Behav.* 22:442–57

Williams DA, Overmier JB, LoLordo VM. 1992. A reevaluation of Rescorla's early dictums about Pavlovian conditioned inhibition. *Psychol. Bull.* 111:275–90
Yin H, Barnet RC, Miller RR. 1994. Trial spacing and trial distribution effects in Pavlovian conditioning: contributions of a comparator mechanism. *J. Exp. Psychol. Anim. Behav. Process.* 20:123–34
Young ME. 1995. On the origin of personal causal theories. *Psychon. Bull. Rev.* 2:83–104
Zimmer-Hart CL, Rescorla RA. 1974. Extinction of a Pavlovian conditioned inhibitor. *J. Comp. Physiol. Psychol.* 86:837–451

Annu. Rev. Psychol. 1997. 48:609–47

ATTITUDES AND ATTITUDE CHANGE

Richard E. Petty

Department of Psychology, Ohio State University, Columbus, Ohio 43210

Duane T. Wegener

Department of Psychology, Yale University, New Haven, Connecticut 06520

Leandre R. Fabrigar

Department of Psychology, Queen's University, Kingston, Ontario, Canada K7L 3N6

KEY WORDS: persuasion, evaluation, bias, attitude structure, affect

ABSTRACT

We review empirical and conceptual developments over the past four years (1992–1995) on attitudes and persuasion. A voluminous amount of material was produced concerning attitude structure, attitude change, and the consequences of holding attitudes. In the structure area, particular attention is paid to work on attitude accessiblity, ambivalence, and the affective versus cognitive bases of attitudes. In persuasion, our review examines research that has focused on high effort cognitive processes (central route), low effort processes (peripheral route), and the multiple roles by which variables can have an impact on attitudes. Special emphasis is given to work on cognitive dissonance and other biases in message processing, and on the multiple processes by which mood influences evaluations. Work on the consequences of attitudes focuses on the impact of attitudes on behavior and social judgments.

CONTENTS

0084-6570/97/0201-0609$08.00

INTRODUCTION

Because of the sheer amount of published research from 1992 to 1995, Allport's (1935) statement that "attitude" is the single most indispensable construct in social psychology may again be true. In addition, a plethora of new books (e.g. Eagly & Chaiken 1993, Perloff 1993, Petty & Krosnick 1995, Shavitt & Brock 1994, Stiff 1994) provided further testament to the vitality of the field.

Because of space limitations, many interesting applications of attitude change theory, especially in the areas of counseling and consumer psychology (e.g. Heesacker et al 1995), cannot be included in this review. We note that interest in attitude measurement remains strong. In recent years, a small cottage industry has developed around studying the best ways to ask questions in attitude surveys (e.g. Schwarz & Sudman 1996, Tanur 1992). Notable developments in attitude measurement included Roese & Jamieson's (1993) review of 20 years of research on the bogus pipeline procedure, and continuing work to develop an actual pipeline for assessing controversial attitudes. For example, Fazio et al (1995) developed an unobtrusive measure of racial prejudice based on the automatic attitude activation effect (Fazio et al 1986). Cacioppo et al (1994) developed a procedure in which the amplitude of late positive brain potentials is used to detect the extent of evaluative consistency between a target and prior stimuli. These late positive potentials were present regardless of the accuracy of participants' attitude reports (Crites et al 1995).

Two interesting new research areas emerged. One is the dynamical systems approach to attitudes (e.g. Eiser 1994). For example, Latané & Nowak (1994) derived from catastrophe theory the notion that attitudes should become more categorical with increases in involvement (see also Sherif & Sherif 1967). Another addressed implicit theories of persuasion. One study, for instance, found that although people have beliefs consistent with classical conditioning theory, they do not show a general belief in cognitive dissonance effects (Snell et al 1995). Although there was some past work on this topic (e.g. Rule & Bisanz 1987), there now appears to be a critical mass of researchers interested in this issue (e.g. Broniarczyk & Alba 1994, Friestad & Wright 1994, Kover 1995, Trafimow & Davis 1993).

Of course, most of the work during our review period continued themes that were dominant in earlier periods, falling into three traditional areas: the structure and bases of attitudes, attitude change, and the consequences of attitudes.

ATTITUDE BASES AND STRUCTURE

Attitudes have been defined in a variety of ways, but at the core is the notion of evaluation. Thus, attitudes are commonly viewed as summary evaluations of objects (e.g. oneself, other people, issues, etc) along a dimension ranging from positive to negative (e.g. Petty et al 1994). One traditional theme in attitude research is the investigation of the underlying bases and structure of these evaluations. Much work on the bases and structure of attitudes was carried out under the label of *attitude strength* because differences in the underlying structure of attitudes is thought to produce differences in strength. A recent edited book (Petty & Krosnick 1995) contains reviews of the many variables thought to make attitudes strong (i.e. persist over time, resist counterpersuasion, and have an impact on judgments and behavior) (Krosnick & Petty 1995).

Structural and Functional Bases of Attitudes

ACCESSIBILITY Research suggests that the strength of object-evaluation associations (i.e. the accessibility of attitudes) has important implications for understanding the functioning of attitudes (for a review, see Fazio 1995). One recent controversy has centered around the automatic attitude activation effect. Fazio et al (1986) argued that attitudes can sometimes be automatically activated from memory upon merely encountering an attitude object. They found that the strength of this effect increased as the accessibility of people's attitudes toward the attitude-object increased. Bargh et al (1992) challenged this conceptualization. First, they presented evidence that automatic activation of attitudes occurred for relatively inaccessible attitudes. Second, contrary to the model proposed by Fazio et al, they reported results suggesting that normative accessibility (i.e. differences across objects) rather than idiosyncratic accessibility (i.e. differences across individuals) determined the strength of the automatic activation effect. However, Fazio (1993, 1995) noted that although Bargh et al (1992) obtained consistent evidence for automatic activation even at low levels of accessibility, whereas his original studies did not, the strength of the automatic activation effect in Bargh et al (1992) was still moderated by attitude accessibility. Fazio (1993, 1995) also criticized evidence supporting the superiority of normative measures of accessibility by arguing that these analyses failed to adequately control for individual differences in baseline speed of responding. He noted that reanalyses of the Bargh et al (1992) data found that idiosyncratic measures of accessibility were superior to normative measures when stronger controls for individual differences in baseline responding were included. More recently, Chaiken & Bargh (1993) have suggested that although accessibility moderates automatic activation using Fazio's traditional paradigm, it does not do so under certain procedural conditions or when the task is made nonevaluative (Bargh et al 1996). Thus, accessibility moderates automatic activation in Fazio's traditional paradigm, but perhaps not in other paradigms. Future research must clarify the psychological mechanisms responsible for regulating when accessibility does or does not moderate the automatic activation of attitudes.

Another relevant topic concerns the use of repeated attitude expressions as a manipulation of the strength of the object-evaluation association. Manipulating how often a person expresses his or her attitude has generally been thought to influence the accessibility of the attitude without changing other properties of the attitude (e.g. Powell & Fazio 1984). However, Judd and colleagues found that repeated expression manipulations also influenced the extremity of attitudes (Brauer et al 1995, Downing et al 1992; see also Judd & Brauer 1995). This effect was also obtained for nonevaluative judgments (Downing et al 1992; cf Mandler et al 1987). However, the exact mechanisms underlying these effects and their generality remain a matter of considerable speculation (Fazio 1995, Judd & Brauer 1995).

Research also examined the conditions under which repeated expression leads to enhanced attitude accessibility. Breckler & Fried (1993) investigated the moderating role of object representation. They found that responses were faster when preceded by previous ratings of objects in the same representational format (i.e. odor-odor or verbal label of the odor-verbal label of the odor) but not when preceded by previous ratings in a different representational format (i.e. odor-verbal label or verbal label-odor). In addition, Maio & Olson (1995a) found that both truthful and untruthful repeated attitude expression led to enhanced attitude accessibility as long as the untruthful responses required subjects to consciously recall their true attitude.

Although the importance of an attitude issue is determined largely by its perceived self-relevance (Boninger et al 1995a, Petty et al 1992), evidence that the importance of an attitude increases as the mere number of times a person expresses an attitude increases was obtained by Roese & Olson (1994). Mediational analyses suggested that the impact of repeated expression on importance was mediated by its influence on the accessibility of the attitude. Roese & Olson suggested that the association between accessibility and importance might occur because people use ease of retrieval as a cue for inferring importance.

AMBIVALENCE Another structural property of attitudes that has been the focus of recent attention is the extent to which attitudes are ambivalent (i.e. based on evaluatively inconsistent information). An interesting development in this literature is Cacioppo & Berntson's (1994) Bivariate Evaluative Space Model. Cacioppo & Berntson suggested that researchers have often assumed that positive and negative evaluative reactions are reciprocally activated (i.e. increases in one will be associated with decreases in the other), but that findings from research literatures as diverse as attitude research and animal learning suggest this assumption is often not tenable. Although explicit adoption of this assumption in the attitude literature may be rare, it is possible that some researchers improperly interpreted the ubiquitous negative correlation between positive and negative evaluative responses as implying reciprocal activation. Cacioppo & Berntson argued that the relation between positive and negative responses should be viewed as a bivariate evaluative plane in which reciprocal or coactive activation can occur. They noted the inability of traditional bipolar attitude scales to fully differentiate among these possibilities and suggested that future research use separate measures of the positive and negative bases of attitudes (perhaps in addition to the traditional bipolar assessment of attitudes; see also Kaplan 1972, Thompson et al 1995).

It is important to recognize that any measure of attitudes, be it bipolar or otherwise, will fail to capture fully the multitude of potentially important differences in the structure and bases of attitudes. Even measures that assess positivity and negativity separately will be unable to distinguish among attitudes that differ in other meaningful ways (e.g. accessibility, affective/cognitive bases, etc). Thus, although there are benefits of examining the positive and negative bases of attitudes, it is unclear whether failure to do so should be considered a fundamental measurement flaw any more than failure to assess other bases and structural properties of attitudes.

Other ambivalence research focused on a variety of empirical issues. Some research examined the validity of different formulas for combining positive and negative responses to arrive at an overall index of attitudinal ambivalence (Breckler 1994, Thompson et al 1995). Thompson & Zanna (1995) examined the role of personality dispositions (i.e. need for cognition, personal fear of invalidity) and domain-specific factors (i.e. issue involvement) as antecedents of ambivalence. Leippe & Eisenstadt (1994) found that compliance with a counterattitudinal request in a dissonance paradigm increased as attitudinal ambivalence increased. Finally, Vallacher et al (1994) used a measure that assessed moment-to-moment shifts in evaluation to demonstrate that increased ambivalence was associated with lower attitude stability.

AFFECTIVE/COGNITIVE BASES OF ATTITUDES Conceptualizing attitudes as having affective (emotional) and cognitive (belief) bases has been one of the most popular means of classifying the different types of information upon which attitudes are based. One theme that has emerged recently is an increased concern with appropriate measurement of attitude-relevant affect and cognition. Eagly et al (1994) criticized past research for relying on close-ended measures of affect and cognition (e.g. rating scales, checklists), which they suggested suffered from methodological limitations. To correct these problems, Eagly et al (1994) used open-ended measures in which participants were asked to list their emotions and beliefs separately and found that these measures of affect and cognition often contributed unique explanatory power to the prediction of attitudes. Unfortunately, no empirical comparisons were made between the open-ended measures and traditional close-ended measures, so it was impossible to confirm that the new measures were an improvement over past measures.

A different approach was reported by Crites et al (1994). In an initial study, evidence was obtained suggesting that many measures used in past affect/cognition research lacked important psychometric properties (e.g. reliability, convergent validity, and discriminant validity). Two subsequent studies showed that new scales designed to assess the affective and cognitive bases of attitudes had high levels of reliability across attitude objects as diverse as social issues, academic subjects, and animals. Factor analyses of the scales also suggested that the scales had good convergent and discriminant validity. Finally, the scales could detect an experimental manipulation of the affective and cognitive bases of attitudes.

Research also continued to explore the extent to which attitudes are based on affect and cognition in various domains. Haddock et al (1993) found that, for people high in authoritarianism, attitudes toward homosexuals were driven primarily by symbolic beliefs and past experiences. In contrast, among people low in authoritarianism, attitudes were determined primarily by stereotype beliefs and affect. Rosselli et al (1995) found that postmessage attitudes were based on affective and cognitive responses when the message was emotional in nature but only on cognitive responses when the message was fact based. These results only occurred when participants were in a neutral mood. In positive moods, cognitive and affective responses had no impact on postmessage attitudes.

VALUES AND ATTITUDE FUNCTIONS AS BASES OF ATTITUDES Researchers continued to explore the extent to which values and attitude functions influence attitudes. Feather (1995) found that the importance people placed in specific values influenced their attitudes toward behavioral choices designed to reflect different value orientations (see also Stern et al 1995). Gastil (1992) found that the level of support for democracy was related to the extent to which democracy was seen as fulfilling a value-expressive function and an ego-defensive function. Other research examined the extent to which the functional basis of an attitude moderated the relation between values and attitudes. For instance, Mellema & Bassili (1995) found that values were more predictive of attitudes for people low in self-monitoring than for people high in self-monitoring. Similarly, Maio

& Olson demonstrated by measuring (Maio & Olson 1994) and by manipulating attitude functions (Maio & Olson 1995b) that the impact of values on attitudes and behavior increased as the extent to which attitudes served a value-expressive function increased.

Individual Differences as a Basis of Attitudes

One interesting recent development has been the recognition among psychologists that attitudes can have some genetic basis (e.g. Lykken et al 1993) and the implications of this. For instance, Tesser (1993) argued that attitudes that have a substantial genetic basis will tend to be stronger than attitudes with little genetic basis. To support this assertion, he conducted a series of studies comparing attitudes that past research indicated varied in their genetic basis. Tesser found that as the amount of variance in attitudes attributable to genetic factors increased, so did the accessibility of attitudes in memory, the resistance of attitudes to conformity pressures, and the impact of the attitudes on interpersonal attraction.

Research on the genetic basis of attitudes challenges traditional attitude theories that have stressed the role of experience as the basis of attitudes (e.g. McGuire 1969). However, there are important limitations to this research. First, methodological challenges make exact estimates of the genetic versus environmental basis of attitudes controversial (e.g. Bouchard et al 1992, Olson & Zanna 1993, see Cropanzano & James 1990). A second limitation is a lack of clearly articulated or empirically verified mediating processes. Discussions of the possible mechanisms by which genetic factors might influence attitudes have been brief and speculative, though highly interesting (e.g. Tesser 1993).

ATTITUDE CHANGE

In the 1950s, researchers assigned a critical role for memory of message arguments as a mediator of persuasion (e.g. Hovland et al 1953). Following Greenwald et al's (1968) comparison of message memory versus cognitive responses as mediators of attitude change, however, research on memory and persuasion waned. Over the past decade, however, a limited but important role for message memory has been established. Specifically, as might be anticipated from Hastie & Park's (1986) research, current work indicates that message memory is most important in predicting attitudes when elaboration of message arguments at the time of exposure is unlikely, an unexpected judgment is requested sometime after message exposure, and simple cues to message validity are relatively unavailable at the time of judgment (Frey & Eagly 1993, Haugtvedt & Petty 1992, Haugtvedt & Wegener 1994, Mackie & Asuncion 1990; for a discussion, see Petty et al 1994). In such circumstances, people apparently judge the advocacy by retrieving whatever message substance they can, and then either evaluating these recalled arguments or making an inference of validity based on the number of arguments remembered.

Much persuasion work continues to be guided by the elaboration likelihood model (ELM) (Petty & Cacioppo 1986) and the heuristic-systematic model (HSM) (Chaiken et al 1989). These models have likely maintained their popularity over the past five review periods in part because these theories encompass the effects of a multitude of persuasion variables, processes, and outcomes. Although differences between these frameworks have been noted that could be important in certain circumstances, the theories are generally more similar than different, and typically they can accommodate the same empirical results, though the explanatory language and sometimes the assumed mediating processes vary (see Eagly & Chaiken 1993, Petty 1994, Petty & Wegener 1997). In the ELM, the central route (high-effort scrutiny of attitude-relevant information) and peripheral route (less effortful shortcuts to evaluating attitude objects) anchor opposite ends of an elaboration likelihood continuum. Even though "central" processes increase in impact as elaboration increases across the continuum and "peripheral" processes decrease in impact as elaboration increases, attitude change is often determined by both central and peripheral processes (though much early research attempted to capture one or the other by examining the endpoints of the continuum; see Petty et al 1993b). The HSM also accommodates the joint impact of systematic and heuristic processing on attitudes. We organize our review of the attitude change literature by focusing first on central route (systematic) processes and then on peripheral processes, including the use of heuristics. Following this, we focus on work that has revealed the multiple roles that many source, message, and recipient variables play in persuasion processes.

High-Elaboration Processes: Focus on Biased Information Processing

OBJECTIVE VERSUS BIASED INFORMATION PROCESSING To account for both objective and biased information processing, the HSM makes a distinction between accuracy, defense, and impression motives, with the latter two motivations producing bias (Chaiken et al 1989, 1996a). In the ELM, whether message processing is relatively objective or biased is determined by both motivational and ability factors (Petty & Cacioppo 1986, Petty et al 1994, Petty & Wegener 1997). Thus, people can engage in biased processing (an outcome) for a variety of motivational (e.g. consistency motivation, reactance, self-esteem maintenance) and ability (e.g. one-sided knowledge on a topic, mood primes favorable thoughts) reasons. Furthermore, a biased processing outcome can be produced by unbiased motivation but biased ability, or by unbiased ability but biased motivation.

For biased elaborative (i.e. central route/systematic) processing to occur, people must be both motivated and able to think (Chaiken et al 1989, Petty & Cacioppo 1986). Thus, although increased personal relevance provides a motivation to process and understand a message in a relatively objective manner when no other biasing factors are present, such as when people have no vested interest in the position taken or have little knowledge on the topic (Petty & Cacioppo 1979b, 1990), when personal relevance is combined with a vested interest or biased knowledge, then the intensive processing induced by the relevance is likely to be biased (cf Petty & Cacioppo 1979a). In a demonstration of the importance of motivational and ability variables in biased processing, Chen et al (1992) found that a forewarning of message content on a counterattitudinal issue led people to resist the message and generate unfavorable thoughts primarily when the issue was personally involving and they were not distracted. That is, a forewarning produced biased processing only when the recipients were both motivated (i.e. high relevance) and able (low distraction) to process the message. In another study, Liberman & Chaiken (1992) found that women who were personally vulnerable to a threatening message engaged in more biased processing of it than women who were not personally vulnerable to the threat. Similarly, Hutton & Baumeister (1992) found that placing message recipients in front of a mirror (enhancing self-awareness) increased their thoughtful resistance to a message that was counterattitudinal and personally important, but not to a message that was not.

One of the most well-known studies of biased processing was reported by Lord et al (1979), and it has generated considerable recent interest. Lord et al demonstrated that after examining evidence on both sides of an issue, people believed that the evidence on their side was more compelling than the evidence on the other side ("biased assimilation"), and they came to believe that their own attitudes toward the issue had polarized. In a conceptual replication of this study, Schuette & Fazio (1995) found that the biased assimilation effect was strongest when attitudes toward the topic were made highly accessible, and recipients were not made apprehensive about the accuracy of their judgments. Miller et al (1993) noted that the Lord et al study did not demonstrate any actual attitude change resulting from biased assimilation (only perceived polarization was assessed). Thus, Miller et al conducted conceptual replications of the Lord et al research and included measures of participants' attitudes toward the topic. Although they replicated the biased assimilation effect and self-reports of polarization, no evidence was obtained for actual attitude polarization. In another pertinent study using the Lord et al paradigm, Pomerantz et al (1995) examined the relations among attitude strength, biased assimilation, and attitude polarization. Several common measures of attitude strength were assessed (see Wegener et al 1995). In contrast with the inconsistent factor structures observed in some prior research (e.g. Krosnick et al 1993), factor analyses of their measures produced a consistent two-factor structure over three samples and five attitude issues. One factor (called commitment) was associated with biased processing and attitude polarization, but the other factor (called embeddedness) was associated with more open-minded processing. In sum, current research suggests that polarization is not a necessary outcome of scrutiny of both sides of an issue. Rather, factors related to attitude strength will likely determine whether the information processing is relatively objective or biased and thus whether polarization, no change, or depolarization will occur.

In the related primacy/recency paradigm, two sides of an issue are presented as in Lord et al, but one group receives the messages in one order (e.g. pro-con) and the other group receives the messages in the reverse order. This paradigm allows one to examine whether the first or the second message has greater impact. Previous research had provided evidence for both primacy and recency effects in persuasion. On the basis of the ELM, Haugtvedt & Wegener (1994) hypothesized and found that if recipients engage in careful processing of the messages (because of high personal relevance), the strong attitudes formed after the first message bias processing of the second message, and thus relative primacy occurs (see also, Haugtvedt & Petty 1992). However, if the messages receive little scrutiny, then recency is more likely because recipients' attitudes are more influenced by their most recent message exposure.

In a surprising prediction, Lammers & Becker (1992) hypothesized that although distraction should disrupt the difficult processing involved in discerning whether the arguments in a message are strong or weak (Petty et al 1976), it might enhance the operation of simple motivated biases that can be applied independently of the actual evidence in a message. In support of this reasoning, distraction increased biased processing when people were simply instructed to pro- or counterargue a message (Lammers 1982), and it enhanced the operation of bias motivated by cognitive dissonance (Lammers & Becker 1992).

Finally, individual differences in biased processing received some attention. In one study, people who scored high in dogmatism held on to the opinions that they initially formed in the light of new information more so than nondogmatics (Davies 1993). Similarly, individuals high in need for closure whether induced situationally or assessed via individual differences (Webster & Kruglanski 1994) were more likely to hold on to their opinions when challenged if the initial opinions had an informational basis, but they were more likely to succumb to influence than those low in need for closure if they did not (Kruglanski et al 1993). Having an informational base may provide both motivation and ability to defend one's view.

DISSONANCE THEORY For over 30 years, dissonance theory has captivated the imagination of social psychologists as virtually no other, and it has continued to generate interesting new research in the period of our review. Four versions of dissonance phenomena are currently generating research. The first, of course, is Festinger's (1957) original proposition that inconsistency among elements in one's cognitive system produces dissonance. In support of Festinger's view, Cialdini et al (1995) developed a scale to assess individual differences in "preference for consistency" (PFC) and found that the attitudes of those high in PFC were influenced by whether their counterattitudinal behavior was performed under high- or low-choice conditions (a classic dissonance finding), but the attitudes of low-PFC people were not.

A second viewpoint on dissonance is Cooper & Fazio's (1984; Cooper 1992) "new look" approach, which holds that dissonance results from individuals feeling personally responsible for bringing about an aversive or unwanted event. In this view, inconsistency per se is not necessary for dissonance. Thus, even if a person engages in a proattitudinal action that brings about potentially foreseeable negative consequences, dissonance could occur (but see Johnson et al 1995b). Of course, one could argue that it is inconsistent with one's view of oneself as an intelligent human being to engage in any action (pro- or counterattitudinal) that results in potentially foreseeable aversive consequences (Aronson 1992). Thus, inconsistency of sorts might still be involved in the aversive consequences approach.

During our review period, additional evidence supported the view that dissonant behavior induces a general discomfort in people, and that attitude change can eliminate this discomfort (Elliot & Devine 1994). This finding is consistent with Cooper & Fazio's (1984) claim that attitude change is motivated by the uncomfortable feelings that result once individuals have attributed their arousal to a dissonant action. This view appears to assume that the more one recognizes one's discomfort because of dissonant behavior, the greater is the motivation to do something, such as changing one's attitudes. However, Pyszcynski et al (1993) suggested the opposite. They reasoned that if one function of motivated cognitive biases is to protect people from painful emotions, then perhaps acknowledging one's distress would eliminate the need to distort cognitions. In support of this view, Pyszcynski et al showed that people who were encouraged to express their emotions showed no dissonance effect, but people who were encouraged to suppress their emotions did. Unfortunately, the instructions given to the express emotions group in this research could have made subjects feel good about their discomfort (i.e. they were told their emotions were healthy), whereas the instructions to suppress emotions were not likely to do this (i.e. they were told their emotions were a sign of poor adjustment). The former instruction could attenuate the dissonance effect, whereas the latter could enhance it if dissonance-induced attitude change is in the service of reducing a consciously experienced negative state.

A third view of dissonance is Aronson's (1968) self-concept analysis (Aronson 1992, Thibodeau & Aronson 1992), which holds that inconsistency is critical, but that the inconsistency is between some aspect of the self-concept and one's behavior. In an attempt to demonstrate this, Stone et al (1994) produced behavior change by making people aware of their past (hypocritical) behavior that was inconsistent with a proattitudinal advocacy (see also Dickerson et al 1992). Fried & Aronson (1995) showed that the hypocrisy effect could be eliminated when a plausible misattribution opportunity was presented, evidence that this hypocrisy induction works by a dissonance mechanism. Because the advocacy in hypocrisy studies is proattitudinal and would likely produce beneficial rather than harmful effects, Aronson (1992) argued that no dissonance should be produced according to the aversive consequences view. However, if one considers that in this research people are reminded that they freely chose to engage in hypocritical behavior, they could feel responsible for bringing about this unwanted and aversive state of affairs, and this would induce dissonance according to an aversive consequences (for self) approach (Petty 1995).

A fourth explanation for dissonance phenomena is Steele's (1988) self-affirmation theory, which holds that people desire to maintain a perception of global integrity and that when this perception is threatened, people attempt to restore it. According to this view, the more positive one's self-concept, the easier it is to recruit ideas that affirm one's overall self-adequacy and thus the less need there is for dissonance reduction. Others (e.g. Aronson 1968) have made the opposite argument. That is, a dissonance-provoking act is more discrepant with one's self-concept for a person of high than low self-esteem, so greater consistency restoring attitude change should occur among high self-esteem individuals. In one study (Steele et al 1993), when participants were reminded of their self-esteem just before a choice among alternatives task, low self-esteem individuals engaged in greater spreading of the alternatives than did high self-esteem individuals. When not focused on their self-evaluative resources, no differences for self-esteem emerged. Although these results appear to support the self-affirmational view, this study leaves open the question of why earlier research using a similar paradigm found that it was high self-esteem individuals who showed greater dissonance effects (e.g. Gerard et al 1964).

Just as self-affirmation theory provides an alternative account for some dissonance effects, Simon et al (1995) proposed a dissonance explanation for a typical self-affirmation finding. Simon et al noted that most dissonance research has focused on attitude change as the dominant means of dissonance reduction but that other modes are possible. For example, Festinger (1957) noted that dissonance could be reduced by decreasing the importance of the elements involved in a dissonant relationship. To examine this, Simon et al (1995) had participants engage in a dissonant act and allowed some of them to rate the importance of the dissonant elements after the act but before the attitude measure, whereas others did the reverse. Dissonance subjects showed change on whichever measure came first. Thus, providing the opportunity to trivialize the dissonant elements eliminated the typical attitude change effect. Simon et al argued that this trivialization effect might be what is happening in the typical self-affirmation study. That is, in self-affirmation work, an important aspect of the self is made salient, and when this occurs, the dissonant elements involved could seem trivial in comparison (a contrast effect).

In another challenge to self-affirmation theory, Aronson et al (1995) found that individuals were selective in their self-affirmation strategies in a manner consistent with dissonance theory. In one study, after being induced to write an uncompassionate essay, participants selectively avoided positive personality feedback about their own compassion but not other irrelevant positive feedback because the former information would presumably be inconsistent with their essay-writing behavior. If, however, attitude change on the topic was assessed before the feedback measure, no selective avoidance was present. In a second study, people also were induced to write an uncompassionate essay but were then asked to rate the importance of various dimensions of personality. These individuals trivialized the trait of compassion (but not irrelevant traits) but only when an attitude measure was not included before the trait-rating task. This result is quite compatible with the research by Simon et al (1995). In sum, recent work on trivialization effects provides an intriguing challenge to strict self-affirmation views of dissonance effects.

Other papers on dissonance examined the utility of dissonance principles in modifying attitudes toward important social and health issues (e.g. Aitken et al 1994, Eiser et al 1995, Leippe & Eisenstadt 1994). Research also demonstrated that dissonance effects (i.e. reevaluation of a chosen alternative) are greater when an obtained object results from an act of commission (trading a current prize for another one) rather than omission (keeping one's current prize) (Gilovich et al 1995) and that increasing choice in the decision to engage in some dissonant behavior increases attitude change, but that increasing choice in the specific dissonant behavior in which to engage reduces attitude change (Beauvois et al 1995). In choosing a specific compliant behavior, people can reduce dissonance by reasoning that the other counterattitudinal acts would have been worse. Note that self-perception theory (Bem 1967), an earlier nemesis of dissonance, would have predicted that choosing the specific essay to write would have enhanced attitude change because people would infer their attitude from their behavior.

Peripheral Processes

According to the dual process models of attitude change, when motivation or ability to scrutinize attitude-relevant information is lacking, one or more peripheral processes are likely to determine persuasion outcomes. Within the ELM framework, peripheral processes include use of simple decision rules (either generated on-line or stored as heuristics), conditioning processes, mere-exposure processes, and other processes that do not involve scrutiny of the central merits of the attitude object (Petty & Cacioppo 1986). Recent research has investigated a variety of peripheral processes, and it has shown that many of those processes are more likely to operate when motivation or ability to scrutinize attitude-relevant information are relatively low.

Recent research has further developed our general knowledge of peripheral cues that have been studied a great deal in past work [e.g. communicator credibility (Hurwitz et al 1992, Tripp et al 1994), attractiveness (Shavitt et al 1994)]. Other research, especially in the consumer psychology area, has identified additional aspects of communicators or settings that act as peripheral cues to influence attitudes [and behaviors such as purchase decisions (Miniard et al 1992)]. It is important to note that many of these cues have been shown to have a greater impact when motivation and/or ability to scrutinize the central merits of the products are low [e.g. when the consumers are not knowledgeable about the product category (Maheswaran 1994) or when the purchase choice is unimportant (Darke et al 1995, Maheswaran et al 1992)]. In some recent research, motivation has been shown to moderate the impact of peripheral cues by increasing scrutiny of the central merits of the products, thereby decreasing the direct (non–thought-mediated) impact of peripheral cues (MacKenzie & Spreng 1992; see also Haugtvedt et al 1992). In addition, peripheral cues have been shown to be used more when attitudes cannot be based on central merits of the target, either because the stimuli are quite difficult to assess (e.g. Pelham & Neter 1995) or the targets are equally attractive (Heath et al 1994). As Pelham & Neter (1995) put it, "if the only tool at a person's disposal is a hammer, convincing the person to work harder only leads to more vigorous hammering" (p. 583). For similar suggestions, see Petty & Cacioppo (1986) and Chaiken et al (1989).

Although much of the work on peripheral cues has focused on variables that might operate by simple decision rules or stored heuristics [e.g. source characteristics such as credibility, attractiveness, or power (for a review, see Chaiken et al 1996b, Petty & Wegener 1997)], other peripheral processes such as classical conditioning and mere exposure have received renewed attention.

Work demonstrating that conditioning and mere exposure can occur when stimuli are presented subliminally (noted below) provides a strong challenge to those who imply that all attitude changes occur through presumably conscious belief (expectancy X value) change mechanisms (Fishbein & Middlestadt 1995).

CONDITIONING AND AFFECTIVE PRIMING PROCESSES Over the years, researchers have found that a number of procedures associating novel targets with actions or stimuli already associated with approach (positive feelings) or avoidance (negative feelings) can influence attitudes toward the novel targets. Cacioppo et al (1993) showed that arm flexion (typically associated with gathering in desired items) led to more favorable attitudes toward novel stimuli than arm extension [(typically associated with pushing away undesirable stimuli (Solarz 1960)]. Consistent with the view that conditioning effects can be obtained by nonthoughtful means, De Houwer et al (1994) reported evidence of evaluative conditioning even when the unconditioned stimuli were presented subliminally, ruling out a contingency awareness problem. Also consistent with the notion that conditioning processes largely act as a peripheral means to establish or change attitudes, Cacioppo et al (1992) showed that classical conditioning using electric shock had a greater impact on initially neutral nonwords (which, of course, were not associated with any preexisting meaning or knowledge) than on initially neutral words.

In a variant on conditioning procedures ("backward conditioning" or "affective priming"), research participants encounter either positively or negatively valenced stimuli immediately before encountering each target stimulus. In a variety of studies, novel targets (e.g. Chinese ideographs or unfamiliar people) encountered after positive stimuli were evaluated more positively than when the targets were encountered after negative stimuli (Krosnick et al 1992, Murphy & Zajonc 1993). This effect only occurs when the conditioning stimuli are presented "suboptimally," with very brief exposure duration (Murphy & Zajonc 1993, Murphy et al 1995).

MERE EXPOSURE Another procedure that can implicitly influence attitudes (Greenwald & Banaji 1995) is mere exposure to the attitude object (Zajonc 1965). That is, the more often a person encounters a novel (usually neutral) attitude object, the more favorable he or she is likely to evaluate that object; this effect is stronger when exposure to the object is subliminal rather than supraliminal (Bornstein & D'Agostino 1992, Janiszewski 1993; cf Murphy et al 1995). In addition, the mere exposure effect is stronger if the perceptual fluency for the attitude object is not attributed to the experimental procedure [and it is weaker if people believe that the object seems familiar because of the exposure procedure (Bornstein & D'Agostino 1994)]. Mere exposure effects have also been found for the number of times a target person attends a college class (Moreland & Beach 1992), a situation in which exposure to the target is incidental to the (presumably) focal task of class attendance and attention (see also Janiszewski 1993).

Multiple Roles for Persuasion Variables: Focus on Effects of Mood on Persuasion

One of the hallmarks of the ELM perspective is that a given variable can impact persuasion via different processes at different levels of elaboration likelihood. That is, a given variable might act as a peripheral cue (when elaboration likelihood is quite low), might act as an argument or bias processing of information (when elaboration likelihood is quite high), or might influence the amount of message processing that occurs (when elaboration likelihood is not constrained to be particularly high or low, and especially if message recipients are not sure if the message warrants scrutiny) (Petty & Cacioppo 1986, Petty et al 1993b). Several variables have been shown to influence persuasion through different processes across different levels of elaboration likelihood, but the most discussed variable in this regard is a person's mood state. Thus, we focus on the multiple roles for mood here (for detailed discussion of mood, see Wegener & Petty 1996). In one examination of multiple roles for mood, Petty et al (1993a) found that the mood state of message recipients (induced by a television program or music) directly influenced attitudes toward a product or advocacy when elaboration likelihood was low (when the product was low in personal relevance or the message recipients were low in need for cognition). However, the same differences in mood influenced attitudes only through mood-based biases in the thoughts that were generated in response to the message when elaboration likelihood was high (when the product was high in relevance or message recipients were high in need for cognition).

Several other studies investigated the overall judgmental effects of moods, but the process producing these effects was not always clear. Many mood studies show some form of positive/negative mood congruency in evaluations (e.g. Mayer et al 1992, Mayer & Hanson 1995), although some differences among specific negative emotions have been found (e.g. Hansen & Shantz 1995), and some negative feelings, such as fear, have at times led to more favorable perceptions of message advocacies (Struckman-Johnson et al 1994), perhaps through mood-specific changes in perceptions of the arguments in the message (see Petty & Wegener 1991). Many of these overall demonstrations of effects of mood could be attributable to either direct (peripheral) effects of mood, or to mood-based biases in scrutiny of relevant information.

Although mood-based biases in processing often bring about mood-congruent persuasion outcomes, they need not. Most persuasive arguments state that good things will happen if the advocacy is adopted—a positive frame. If mood influences processing of persuasive messages in part through changes in the perceived desirability and likelihood of consequences of advocacy adoption (e.g. the good things might seem better and more likely in a good rather than neutral mood), then different forms of the message might lead to different mood-based outcomes, at least when people are engaged in enough scrutiny of the message to assess and combine these likelihood and desirability components (Petty & Wegener 1991). Consistent with this notion, Wegener et al (1994) found different mood-effects across different message frames, but only for people high in need for cognition (who were intrinsically motivated to scrutinize the messages). For those people, positively framed messages were more persuasive when message recipients were in a happy rather than sad mood. However, negatively framed messages (lack of advocacy adoption will lead to bad things) were more persuasive when people were in a sad rather than happy mood (because the bad things seemed more likely to follow from lack of advocacy adoption in the sad rather than the happy mood).

In addition to studies of cue or biased processing effects of mood, recent research has investigated effects of mood on the amount of scrutiny given to persuasive message arguments (which, according to the ELM, should be most likely to emerge when nonmood factors do not constrain elaboration likelihood to be particularly high or low). The conclusion of several researchers has been that people in sad or neutral moods spontaneously process information more effortfully than people in happy states (e.g. Bless et al 1992, Bohner et al 1992; see also Bohner et al 1994) unless attention is drawn to the nonmessage source of the mood (Sinclair et al 1994). Recent research suggests, however, that this might be only a piece of the entire picture. That is, according to the hedonic contingency position (Wegener & Petty 1994), happy moods can foster greater mood management efforts than sad or neutral moods. Given that most demonstrations of processing deficits in positive moods involved counterattitudinal and/or depressing messages, it is plausible that these effects were due to attempts by happy people to maintain their positive feelings. In fact, in a critical test of the hedonic contingency position, Wegener et al (1995) found that sad message recipients processed message arguments more than happy message recipients when the message advocated a counterattitudinal/depressing position, but happy message recipients processed message arguments more than sad message recipients when the same message advocated a proattitudinal/uplifting position. Consistent with the hedonic contingency framework, happy message recipients processed uplifting more than depressing messages, but processing by sad message recipients was unaffected by valence of the position being advocated (cf Howard & Barry 1994).

In addition to work on happiness and sadness, some work investigated the effects of fear on scrutiny of persuasive messages. Gleicher & Petty (1992) found that moderately fearful message recipients processed messages less than message recipients who were not fearful, but only when the solution in the message was presented as highly efficacious. Baron et al (1992) also found that fearful message recipients processed messages less than those who were not fearful (but see Baron et al 1994 for the opposite result).

One emerging theme in the mood literature is the contextual nature of mood effects. That is, mood effects on judgment, persuasion, and processing are not universal but depend on such factors as the baseline level of elaboration likelihood (Petty et al 1993b, Wegener et al 1994), framing of the message arguments (Wegener et al 1994), awareness of the source of the mood state (Gorn et al 1993, Martin et al 1990, Petty & Wegener 1993, Sinclair et al 1994), activated "stop rules" (Martin et al 1993), and the perceived valence of the processing task (Wegener et al 1995). Like the ELM perspective, Forgas's (1992, 1995a) recent Affect Infusion Model (AIM) also postulates that mood can influence attitudes through heuristic (peripheral) processes, by biasing information processing or by affecting the amount of processing of information. Evidence cited as supporting this model includes results suggesting that mood-congruent outcomes are stronger for atypical rather than for typical targets (Forgas 1993, 1995b). Unlike attitude models such as the ELM, however, the AIM posits a role for a previously stored evaluation only when the judgment task is perceived as unimportant [although attitudes perceived as important tend to persist longer and have greater impact on other judgments than attitudes perceived as unimportant (see Boninger et al 1995b)]. In addition, the AIM posits that the effect of mood on the amount of message processing is for negative states to instigate greater processing than positive states, although the empirical evidence shows that positive moods can sometimes instigate greater processing than negative states (Wegener et al 1995).

Continuing Research on Persuasion Variables

Within the ELM framework, many variables can influence persuasion through the multiple roles identified above. For most variables, the recent research has focused on just one or another of the possible roles, though eventually many of the variables might be shown to influence persuasion by serving as cues or arguments, biasing processing, and determining the amount of scrutiny given to a message.

SOURCE FACTORS The source factors receiving the most attention were credibility, attractiveness, and minority/majority status.

Credibility/attractiveness In recent work, a variety of effects of source credibility have been researched. Cue effects of source credibility have been investigated as a means of stereotype change, and they have been found to operate under conditions of low but not high task involvement (Johnston & Coolen 1995) [though credibility might also affect stereotypes through changing perceptions of stereotype-inconsistent behaviors, which would likely occur at a higher level of processing of those behaviors (see Macrae et al 1992)]. In addition, such source effects have been shown to be most likely when source perceptions are relatively accessible in memory (Roskos-Ewoldsen & Fazio 1992b). Researchers have also investigated the relations between perceptions of sources and other variables in the persuasion setting. For instance, Smith & Shaffer (1995) found that increases in speed of speech were associated with perceptions of higher source credibility, and that these source perceptions mediated persuasion effects of speed of speech when involvement was low rather than high.

Research has also expanded our knowledge of the effects of various source characteristics on the amount of scrutiny given to message arguments. For example, Priester & Petty (1995) showed that perceiving a source as low in trustworthiness increases message processing for people not intrinsically motivated to scrutinize messages (i.e. people low in need for cognition). Consistent with the notion that people high in need for cognition are intrinsically motivated to engage in effortful cognitive activities, these individuals effortfully processed the messages regardless of source trustworthiness. In another study, DeBono & Klein (1993) found that people low in dogmatism tended to process a message regardless of the expertise of the source, but people high in dogmatism tended to process only when the source was not an expert. Source attractiveness/likability can also influence the amount of message processing. White & Harkins (1994) showed that a disliked source can instigate greater processing than a liked source. In one study, White & Harkins provided Caucasian message recipients with a message presented by either a Caucasian or African-American source and found that message recipients processed the message more effortfully when presented by an African American. This increase of processing generalized to other ethnic minorities that this population disliked (e.g. Hispanic), but not to minorities that were not negatively evaluated (e.g. Asian).

Some research has explicitly addressed multiple roles of source characteristics within the same study. For example, Chaiken & Maheswaran (1994) showed that the impact of source credibility on attitudes was greater under low than high task importance conditions when message arguments were unambiguous (and effects of the source were more likely to serve as a persuasion cue). When message arguments were ambiguous, however, source credibility affected attitudes under both low and high task importance conditions—an effect that was mediated by a bias in thoughts about the attitude object under high but not low importance conditions. Such a result supports the idea that some level of message ambiguity is necessary for biased processing to occur.

In a study examining multiple roles for source attractiveness, Shavitt et al (1994) manipulated the attractiveness of an endorser in an ad, the salient (central) features of the product (either unrelated to attractiveness—taste and aroma—or related to attractiveness—public image), and motivation to process the ad. When endorser attractiveness was unrelated to the central merits of the product (and the ELM would predict that any impact of attractiveness would be due to its impact as a peripheral cue), endorser attractiveness had an impact on evaluations of the product under low but not high motivation (and had little impact on thoughts about the product). However, when endorser attractiveness was related to the central merits of the product (and thus could itself act as an argument), the same variation in endorser attractiveness influenced evaluations of the product under high but not low motivation (and under high motivation, influenced the favorability of cognitive responses to the ad).

Minority/majority status Research continues to show that message sources who are in the numerical minority create influence that could be characterized as "indirect," and they especially do so when they are consistent over time in their advocacy of a position (see Wood et al 1994).

In persuasion settings, some work has shown that minority influence is greater when the personal relevance of the message is low (Trost et al 1992), when much of the message is assumed to be censored (Clark 1994), or when the minority speaks to a highly cohesive group (Kozakai et al 1994). Some have recently suggested that the dichotomy of minority versus majority influence might be less extreme than has been the case in much of the theorizing in this area (Clark 1995; cf Perez et al 1995). Consistent with this notion, Baker & Petty (1994) showed that either majority or minority sources can instigate greater processing of message arguments, depending on the position advocated. When the position was counterattitudinal, majority sources fostered greater message elaboration, but when the position was proattitudinal, minority sources led to greater elaboration. This occurs, at least in part, because people are surprised when a majority disagrees or a minority agrees with them (both of which imply that the message recipient is in the numerical minority). Levine & Russo (1995) also found results consistent with the notion of similarities between majority and minority influence processes. Levine & Russo found that anticipation of disagreement creates greater seeking of information supporting (rather than opposing) one's view, and that this tendency was stronger when the disagreement was with a numerical majority rather than with a minority. However, seeking of supporting rather than opposing information was greater to the extent that the opposing side had more supporters, regardless of whether that opposition constituted a majority or minority (which could also account for the majority/minority difference). Although much of the existing work has used numerically defined majority/minority status in which the status of the person is related to the focal task itself (e.g. one is in the majority because most people agree with the person on the topic to be discussed in the focal experimental task), future work is likely to expand into majority/minority status identified separate from the focal experimental activity (see Crano & Hannula-Bral 1994).

Similar to the minority/majority literature, recent work on persuasive effects of in-group versus out-group sources has shown that sometimes out-group sources produce greater scrutiny of their statements [when their statements are inconsistent with the stereotype of the group (Vonk & van Knippenberg 1995)], but sometimes in-group sources produce greater scrutiny [when the in-group member is believed to be prototypical of the in-group (van Knippenberg & Wilke 1992) or when the position the prototypical in-group member would take was not known in advance (van Knippenberg et al 1994; see also Mackie et al 1992)].

MESSAGE FACTORS Message framing, scarcity, one- versus two-sided communications, and sporadic other features of persuasive messages were also studied.

Message framing Initial research tended to suggest that messages that use negatively framed arguments were more effective than messages that use positively framed arguments (e.g. Meyerowitz & Chaiken 1987). More recent studies indicate that which framing is more effective depends on various situational and dispositional factors. Recall that Wegener et al (1994) found that frame interacted with mood and processing motivation to influence attitudes. Rothman et al (1993) found that negative framing tended to be superior for influencing people with respect to high-risk behaviors, but that positive framing tended to be better for influencing low-risk behaviors. Tykocinski et al (1994) found that a positive outcome message was more effective than a negative outcome message for recipients with a chronic actual-ought discrepancy, but that the reverse was the case for recipients with an actual-ideal discrepancy (Higgins 1989). The authors argued that the appropriately framed messages were least likely to activate the vulnerability system of the recipient and cause distress. At the moment, there is no coherent framework for understanding the complex effects observed for different message frames. Integration of message framing research with multiprocess models of persuasion could prove productive.

Scarcity An entire issue of *Basic and Applied Social Psychology* was devoted to the psychology of scarcity (Lynn 1992), with a number of authors providing their conceptual analysis of the effects of scarcity on evaluation. For example, in an integration of commodity theory (Brock 1968) with the ELM (Petty & Cacioppo 1986), Brock & Brannon (1992) argued that scarcity has its impact on attitudes by increasing elaboration of messages. This hypothesis was supported in a study by Bozzolo & Brock (1992) but only for individuals low in need for cognition. High need for cognition individuals showed the reverse pattern. Worchel (1992) also argued that scarcity does not invariably lead to increased liking of objects. Specifically, when people do not have access to a commodity, their desire for it increases with the number of other people who have the commodity. Thus, the distribution of supply rather than supply per se is an important factor in determining the effects of scarcity on value.

One-sided versus two-sided and comparative messages Considerable interest was also shown in understanding when and why two-sided (e.g. Crowley & Hoyer 1994) and comparative (Snyder 1992, Rose et al 1993) advertising is more effective than one-sided and noncomparative ads. For example, in a study exploring multiple roles for upward comparative ads, Pechmann & Esteban (1994) established three levels of motivation to process an advertisement using a combination of instructions and situational distraction. Consistent with the ELM multiple roles notion, under low motivation conditions, argument quality did not influence purchase intentions, but comparative ads elicited more favorable intentions than noncomparative ads (cue effect). Under high motivation, only argument strength influenced intentions. Under moderate motivation, comparative ads elicited greater message scrutiny than noncomparative ads. The data further suggested that this enhanced scrutiny was biased in a favorable direction.

Other message factors Many other isolated message factors received treatment. For example, Frey & Eagly (1993) attempted to understand why vivid messages typically are either no more effective than pallid messages or are sometimes less effective (see Taylor & Thompson 1982). They argued that vivid elements in messages can interfere with recipients' cognitive elaboration of messages and appraisal of arguments they contain. This distraction should reduce persuasion when the arguments are strong (Petty et al 1976). To examine this, they exposed recipients to pallid and vivid messages designed to be persuasive. Under low processing conditions, vividness reduced persuasion, but under high elaboration conditions, vividness had no impact. A surprising result from this study was that in the pallid conditions, high elaboration recipients generated more counterarguments and were less persuaded than low elaboration recipients. This suggests that the messages were actually mixed or weak rather than strong as the authors intended (Petty & Cacioppo 1986). Thus, vividness may not have affected persuasion under low elaboration conditions by disrupting elaboration of strong arguments. Rather, if both vivid and pallid message recipients attempted to retrieve message arguments to form a memory based judgment (Hastie & Park 1986), and vividness interfered with reception, then use of a "more is better" heuristic would have produced the obtained result. Future work on vividness could vary argument quality to examine these issues.

Siero & Doosje (1993) measured recipients' motivation to think about the message topic and varied whether they received a message containing strong or weak arguments that fell in their latitude of acceptance, noncommitment, or rejection. Consistent with much work on social judgment theory (Sherif & Sherif 1967), the message falling in the latitude of noncommitment was most persuasive. Consistent with the ELM, high-motivation recipients were more influenced by argument quality than low-motivation recipients, but this was especially the case when the message fell in the latitude of noncommitment where message processing would be expected to be the most objective (Petty et al 1992).

Van Schie et al (1994) demonstrated that providing people with evaluatively biased words with which to construct a persuasive message could influence the nature of the essays written and attitudes formed (see also Eiser & Pancer 1979). Exposure to the words by having subjects copy them was insufficient to produce attitude change, however, which suggested that the effect of evaluatively biased language on attitudes requires active cognitive effort rather than passive exposure alone (Cialdini et al 1981). Finally, Simonson et al (1993) examined the effectiveness of using "irrelevant" arguments in a message. As would be expected if irrelevant arguments are weak for most people, this research showed that people are less likely to accept an option supported by irrelevant reasons and are less likely to reject an option discounted by irrelevant reasons.

RECIPIENT FACTORS Research examined a number of individual differences. Rhodes & Wood (1992) meta-analyzed the literature on intelligence and self-esteem. Much of this work was guided by McGuire's (1968) two-factor reception/yielding model of persuasion which predicts a curvilinear effect on persuasion of both variables. The meta-analysis revealed that intelligence showed a linear effect (more intelligence associated with less persuasion), whereas the latter showed the expected curvilinear effect (with moderate self-esteem individuals being most influenceable). The mediation of these effects is unclear, however, and work on these traditional variables has yet to be guided by the more recent multiprocess models. New primary research during the review period focused on recipient knowledge, and individual differences such as self-monitoring and need for cognition.

Prior knowledge/experience Like other variables, recipient knowledge should be capable of serving in multiple roles. For example, perceived knowledge could function as a peripheral cue (e.g. "I'm the expert so I already know what's best"), could affect the extent of information processing through either motivational ("I've never heard of that, so I'm curious about it" or "I've heard so much about that, I'm bored with it") or ability factors (e.g. providing sufficient background to discern the merits of strong arguments and the flaws in weak ones), or could bias information processing by motivating or enabling pro- or counterarguing (Petty & Cacioppo 1986, Petty et al 1994). Some of these possible roles for knowledge were documented empirically during the review period. In one study (DeBono 1992), people who had previously sampled a product were less attentive to the quality of the arguments in a subsequent message about the product than people who had no prior experience, which suggested that prior knowledge reduced the need for further information. In another study, Johnson (1994) found that prior knowledge interacted with message relevance to influence information processing. Under low-knowledge conditions, increased relevance enhanced message processing replicating prior work (Petty & Cacioppo 1990). When knowledge was high, however, people processed to a similar extent regardless of message relevance. Viewed differently, Johnson found that under low-relevance conditions, increased knowledge tended to increase message processing, but that under high-relevance conditions, increased knowledge tended to decrease message processing.

Much prior work has suggested that people with many issue-relevant beliefs tend to resist influence on a counterattitudinal issue but also process the message more (see Wood et al 1995). Consistent with this, Smith (1993) found that previous negative experience with a product produced more negative evaluations of a subsequent advertisement for the product. Johnson et al (1995a) found that high-knowledge individuals tended to process a proattitudinal message more, but that the more beliefs people could list about the issue, the more persuaded they were by the message. This work is consistent with the notion that prior knowledge can both foster thinking about a message and help people bolster their initial opinions (i.e. engage in biased processing). It is likely that to fully explicate the effects of knowledge on information processing and persuasion, future researchers will need to consider factors such as the extent and accessibility of the prior knowledge as well as its valence and relevance to evaluating the message information.

Matching messages A popular general hypothesis is that persuasion can be increased by matching messages to some aspect of the message recipient. For example, additional evidence was obtained for the view that matching messages to the psychological functions served by recipients' attitudes (e.g. value expressive, utilitarian) enhances persuasion (Clary et al 1994). In a variation of the typical function matching study, Shavitt et al (1992) had high and low self-monitors construct persuasive messages. When the attitude object could serve multiple attitude functions, high self-monitors tended to generate social arguments, and low self-monitors tended to generate utilitarian arguments. However, for objects that tend to serve just one function, both high and low self-monitors generated arguments consistent with that function. In other matching research, Edwards & von Hippel (1995) provided further evidence for the view that affective persuasive appeals are more effective in changing affectively rather than cognitively based attitudes. Han & Shavitt (1994) found that matching messages to one's culture enhanced persuasion, and Strathman et al (1994) found that people who chronically consider the future consequences of potential behaviors were more persuaded by a message that included such consequences than one that did not. Although these matching effects are robust, it is not entirely clear why they occur. For example, matching could work because of a peripheral process (e.g. "it speaks to my values, so I like it") or because matching enhances scrutiny of the information presented. If the information is cogent, matching would enhance persuasion, but if not, it could reduce persuasion. Future work should pay greater attention to the processes mediating matching effects and attempt to account for when mismatching is superior (Millar & Millar 1990).

Need for cognition In addition to the need for cognition effects mentioned earlier, research reinforced the view that people high in need for cognition engage in greater message processing than those low in need for cognition (for a thorough review, see Cacioppo et al 1996). Specifically, Haugtvedt et al (1992) found that high need for cognition individuals were more influenced by the substantive arguments in an advertisement and less influenced by peripheral cues than individuals low in need for cognition. Stayman & Kardes (1992) found that high need for cognition individuals were more likely to draw inferences about omitted conclusions in messages than were low need for cognition individuals. This study also revealed that inferences about omitted conclusions had a greater impact on the attitudinal judgments of low rather than high self-monitors, consistent with the view of these individuals as more guided by their internal reactions (Snyder 1979).

CONTEXT FACTORS In recent years, the most researched contextual factor concerned the effects of contextually induced mood. Although other context factors have received some attention, no cluster of studies on one topic appeared. Researchers have found, however, that a number of contextual factors can influence the amount of scrutiny given to persuasive messages. For example, faster speech in an orally presented message reduces scrutiny of the merits of the position [probably by making it more difficult to scrutinize the externally paced information (Smith & Shaffer 1995)]. Similarly, involvement in a television program decreases scrutiny of an advertising message [probably because of distraction from message content as the message recipient continues to think about the program content (Anand & Sternthal 1992)]. In addition, high levels of self-awareness (e.g. when in front of a mirror) encourages high levels of message scrutiny (Hutton & Baumeister 1992), as does deprivation of control before receipt of a persuasive appeal (Pittman 1994). Although repetition of a message can enhance message scrutiny, it can also be used to strengthen the association between a message and peripheral cues. This cue-repetition strategy can enhance attitude persistence though it has little effect on making attitudes more resistant to counterpersuasion (Haugtvedt et al 1994; for further discussion, see Petty et al 1995).

CONSEQUENCES OF ATTITUDES

Along with work on the underlying structure of attitudes and attitude change, a substantial amount of both basic and applied research continues to be conducted on the consequences of attitudes, especially the impact of attitudes on behavior and judgments.

The Impact of Attitudes on Behavior

THE MODERATING ROLE OF ATTITUDE STRENGTH One continuing theme in attitude strength research has been examining the moderating role of attitude strength in attitude-behavior consistency (for reviews of the moderating impact of numerous attitude strength variables, see Petty & Krosnick 1995). Of the different strength dimensions, attitude accessibility has received the most attention. For instance, Bassili (1993, 1995) obtained evidence from computer-assisted telephone interviewing (CATI) surveys that voting intentions became more predictive of self-reports of voting behavior as the accessibility of voting intentions increased. A meta-analysis by Kraus (1995) also found that increased accessibility was associated with greater attitude-behavior consistency. However, Doll & Ajzen (1992) failed to find evidence that attitude accessibility moderated attitude-behavior consistency for playing with video games. Fazio (1995) suggested that this failure might have been due to methodological problems in the way response latencies were measured as well as analyses that failed to fully control for individual differences in baseline speed of responding. Other research has found that attitude-behavior consistency is moderated by amount of cognitive elaboration (Pieters & Verplanken 1995; see also MacKenzie & Spreng 1992), certainty/confidence (Kraus 1995, Petkova et al 1995), attitudinal ambivalence (Sparks et al 1992), attitudinal stability (Doll & Ajzen

1992, Kraus 1995), affective-cognitive consistency (Kraus 1995), and direct experience (Kraus 1995).

PERSONALITY AS A MODERATOR OF ATTITUDE-BEHAVIOR CONSISTENCY Self-monitoring (Snyder 1979) is probably the most widely researched personality moderator of attitude-behavior consistency. Self-monitoring refers to how much people rely on internal cues such as attitudes (low self-monitoring) versus situational cues (high self-monitoring) as a guide to behavior. In a meta-analysis, Kraus (1995) found that low self-monitors showed higher attitude-behavior consistency than high self-monitors. DeBono & Snyder (1995) found that one's history of choosing attitude-relevant situations predicted willingness to engage in future behavior more for low than high self-monitors. They also found that repeated attitude expression had a greater impact on accessibility among low self-monitors than high self-monitors, and that people's history of choosing attitude-relevant situations predicted accessibility more among high than among low self-monitors. Along similar lines, other individual difference variables thought to reflect internal versus external focus such as autonomous-control behavioral self-regulation (Koestner et al 1992) and action-state orientation (Bagozzi et al 1992) have been found to moderate attitude-behavior consistency.

OTHER IMPACTS ON ATTITUDE-BEHAVIOR CONSISTENCY Many studies of attitude-behavior consistency have focused on factors that cannot readily be classified as dimensions of attitude strength or dimensions of personality. Some of these investigations have examined factors that moderate the impact of attitudes on behavior relative to other constructs such as subjective norms (Fishbein et al 1992, Trafimow 1994, Trafimow & Fishbein 1994), habitual behavioral tendencies (Verplanken et al 1994), and emotional reactions (Allen et al 1992). Other research has explored the impact of introspecting about the reasons for holding an attitude on attitude-behavior consistency. This work has found that introspection reduces postchoice satisfaction for those who generate evaluatively inconsistent rather than consistent reasons for their choice (Wilson et al 1993). Introspecting about behavior that is evaluatively inconsistent compared with consistent with one's attitude toward the object of the behavior has been found to cause poorer self-prediction of behavior related to the object (Wilson & LaFleur 1995). Finally, research has suggested that introspection causes people to focus on highly accessible thoughts (Wilson et al 1995) and that the disruptive impact of introspection on attitude-behavior consistency occurs primarily for attitudes low in accessibility (Hodges & Wilson 1993).

MODELS OF ATTITUDE-BEHAVIOR CONSISTENCY Research continues to be conducted on general models of attitude-behavior consistency. Among the various attitude-behavior theories, the Theory of Reasoned Action (TORA) (Fishbein

& Ajzen 1975, Ajzen & Fishbein 1980) and the Theory of Planned Behavior (TOPB) (Ajzen 1985) continue to generate the most research. New studies have applied these theories to a wide variety of domains. Perhaps the most common recent application has been in the area of AIDS-related sexual behavior, where both the TORA (e.g. Cochran et al 1992, Fishbein et al 1992) and the TOPB (e.g. Richard et al 1995, White et al 1994) have been examined.

Other research focused on comparing the effectiveness of the two models, which differ in that the TOPB includes perceived behavioral control as an antecedent of intentions and behaviors, whereas the TORA does not. Madden et al (1992) found that the TOPB predicted behaviors and intentions better than the TORA across 10 different types of behaviors varying in perceived control. This was particularly true when the behavior was perceived as difficult to control. Similar results have been obtained in other domains of behavior (Kurland 1995, Giles & Cairns 1995). However, some studies have failed to find improvements in prediction of intentions and/or behaviors when measures of perceived behavioral control were included in analyses (Chan & Fishbein 1993, Kelly & Breinlinger 1995). Thus, it is important to determine when behavioral control will be important and when it will not.

The Impact of Attitudes on Information Processing and Social Judgments

ATTITUDE STRENGTH AS A MODERATOR OF ATTITUDINAL CONSEQUENCES Recent research suggests that strong attitudes facilitate the ease and quality of decision making involving preferences. Fazio et al (1992) found that people showed less autonomic reactivity during a preference decision task when their attitudes toward the targets of judgment were high in accessibility compared with when they were low (see also Blascovich et al 1993). Decision choices also tended to be more stable when attitudes toward the judgment targets were relatively high in accessibility (Fazio et al 1992). Other research has suggested that attitude strength might moderate the extent to which attitudes serve an orienting function to stimuli in the environment. Roskos-Ewoldsen & Fazio (1992a) found that people devoted greater visual attention to objects for which they had attitudes high in accessibility. Finally, Fabrigar & Krosnick (1995) examined the extent to which attitude strength moderated the impact of attitudes on perceptions of others. They found a consistent false consensus effect (i.e. tendency to see one's own attitudes as common relative to attitudes one does not hold) but no evidence that this effect was influenced by the importance of the attitude.

PSYCHOLOGICAL MECHANISMS UNDERLYING ATTITUDINAL CONSEQUENCES Another theme in recent research on social judgment and information processing consequences of attitudes has been a focus on clarifying the underlying mechanisms of many well established attitudinal effects. One interesting development has been the work on implicit social cognition. Greenwald & Banaji (1995) noted that an attitude can have implicit effects on social judgments (i.e. effects on judgments of which a person is not consciously aware). They suggested that many well-known social judgment effects—including halo effects, mere exposure effects, subliminal attitude conditioning, and context effects in surveys—can be regarded as implicit effects of attitudes. They also argued that explicit measures of attitudes (i.e. direct self-reports of attitudes) might fail to capture many implicit effects and that researchers need to increasingly use implicit (i.e. indirect) measures of attitudes. Although increased use of implicit measures of attitudes has the potential to advance our understanding, it is worth noting that explicit attitude measures are not inherently unable to detect implicit effects. This is supported by the fact that most of the literature demonstrating implicit attitude effects reviewed by Greenwald & Banaji was based on explicit measures of attitudes. Finally, we note that work on implicit attitudes has much in common with work on implicit personality (McClelland et al 1989), and thus integration of this work seems potentially fruitful.

Other research on attitudinal consequences examined the extent to which the false consensus effect can truly be regarded as a judgmental bias or a result of sound statistical reasoning (Krueger & Clement 1994, Krueger & Zeiger 1993). This research suggested that the false consensus effect does in fact represent an overuse of self-information and thus should be regarded as a bias. Other research examined the mechanisms underlying the hostile media bias effect (Giner-Sorolla & Chaiken 1994) and the attitude similarity-interpersonal attraction effect (Drigotas 1993, Hoyle 1993, Tan & Singh 1995). Finally, Klauer & Stern (1992) reported evidence that attitudes bias judgments of the traits of objects in an evaluatively consistent manner. They found that this bias was particularly strong when judgments were made under time pressure.

CONCLUSIONS

Our examination of the past four years of research on attitudes clearly indicates that the field is robust. As predicted by McGuire (1985), research on attitude structure has become an indispensable and vibrant part of the literature. Much of this work is aimed at understanding what structural features of attitudes contribute to their strength (e.g. stable attitudes that predict behavior). There were two noteworthy trends. First, research has revealed new complexities in well-established effects in the attitude accessibility literature. The generality of accessibility as a moderator of the automatic activation effect has been debated, and the repeated attitude expression manipulation, once thought to only influence accessibility, has been shown to also influence other dimensions of attitudes. A second trend has been the (re)emergence of ambivalence and structural consistency as a major focus of theoretical and empirical investigation. The work on attitude structure and strength has made it abundantly clear that assessing features of attitudes other than the overall summary evaluation such as accessibility, affective-cognitive consistency, ambivalence, and so forth can be very informative.

In addition, work on attitude change continues to flourish. In the 1970s and 1980s researchers moved away from asking the first generation question of whether some variable (e.g. source expertise) was good or bad for persuasion and began to address the fundamental processes by which variables had their impact (Petty 1996). Questions such as whether variables increased or decreased cognitive elaboration, or served as positive or negative cues dominated research efforts. During the past four years, the manner in which variables bias information processing became a major theme. We anticipate that this theme will continue and that work on bias correction (e.g. Petty & Wegener 1993, Wilson & Brekke 1994) will become integrated with work on persuasion (Wegener & Petty 1997). For example, once people become aware that some variable has biased their information processing, or led to an inappropriate cue-based judgment, how are attitudes debiased? Of the work on biases in information processing, studies of dissonance effects were especially prolific. However, there are still several viable accounts for dissonance effects that assume different fundamental motivations are at work. Given the strong evidence for each of these motivations, we suspect that future research will not select one motivation as the correct one, but will specify when each motivation operates.

It is noteworthy that investigators have made considerable additional progress in recognizing the complexities of persuasion processes. For example, research has clearly demonstrated that the same variable that enhances message elaboration in one setting can reduce it in another (Baker & Petty 1994, Wegener et al 1995). Furthermore, researchers have moved away from asking which role (e.g. cue effect, influence processing, bias processing) a variable takes on in persuasion settings and toward asking when variables take on each role (Chaiken & Maheswaran 1994, Pechmann & Esteban 1994, Petty et al 1993a). In the future it is likely that even more attention will be paid to the multiple processes by which any one variable has an impact on persuasion.

Literature Cited

Aitken CK, McMahon TA, Wearing AJ, Finlayson BL. 1994. Residential water use: predicting and reducing consumption. *J. Appl. Soc. Psychol.* 24:136–58

Ajzen I. 1985. From intentions to actions: a theory of planned behavior. In *Action-control: From Cognition to Behavior,* ed. J Kuhl, J Beckmann, pp. 11–39. Heidelberg: Springer-Verlag

Ajzen I, Fishbein M. 1980. *Understanding Attitudes and Predicting Social Behavior.* Englewood Cliffs, NJ: Prentice-Hall

Allen CT, Machleit KA, Klein SS. 1992. A comparison of attitudes and emotions as predictors of behavior at diverse levels of behavioral experience. *J. Consum. Res.* 18: 493–504

Allport GW. 1935. Attitudes. In *Handbook of Social Psychology,* ed. C Murchison, pp. 798–844. Worchester, MA: Clark Univ. Press

Anand P, Sternthal B. 1992. The effects of program involvement and ease of message counterarguing on advertising persuasiveness. *J. Consum. Psychol.* 1:225–38

Aronson E. 1968. Dissonance theory: progress and problems. In *Theories of Cognitive Consistency: A Sourcebook,* ed. RP Abelson, E Aronson, WJ McGuire, MJ Rosenberg, PH Tannenbaum, pp. 5–28. Chicago: Rand McNally

Aronson E. 1992. The return of the repressed: dissonance theory makes a comeback. *Psychol. Inquiry* 3:303–11

Aronson J, Blanton H, Cooper J. 1995. From dissonance to disidentification: selectivity in the self-affirmation process. *J. Pers. Soc. Psychol.* 68:986–96

Bagozzi RP, Baumgartner H, Yi Y. 1992. State versus action orientation and the theory of reasoned action: an application to coupon usage. *J. Consum. Res.* 18:505–18

Baker SM, Petty RE. 1994. Majority and minority influence: source-position imbalance as a determinant of message scrutiny. *J. Pers. Soc. Psychol.* 67:5–19

Bargh JA, Chaiken S, Govender R, Pratto F. 1992. The generality of the automatic attitude activation effect. *J. Pers. Soc. Psychol.* 62:893–912

Bargh JA, Chaiken S, Raymond P, Hymes C. 1996. The automatic evaluation effect: unconditional automatic attitude activation with a pronunciation task. *J. Exp. Soc. Psychol.* 32:104–28

Baron RS, Inman M, Kao C, Logan H. 1992. Emotion and superficial social processing. *Motiv. Emot.* 16:323–45

Baron RS, Logan H, Lilly J, Inman M, Brennan M. 1994. Negative emotion and message processing. *J. Exp. Soc. Psychol.* 30: 181–201

Bassili JN. 1993. Response latency versus certainty as indexes of the strength of voting intentions in a CATI survey. *Public Opin. Q.* 57:54–61

Bassili JN. 1995. Response latency and the accessibility of voting intentions: what contributes to accessibility and how it affects vote choice. *Pers. Soc. Psychol. Bull.* 21: 686–95

Beauvois JL, Bungert M, Mariette P. 1995. Forced compliance: commitment to compliance and commitment to activity. *Eur. J. Soc. Psychol.* 25:17–26

Bem DJ. 1967. Self-perception: an alternative interpretation of cognitive dissonance phenomena. *Psychol. Rev.* 74:183–200

Blascovich J, Ernest JM, Tomaka J, Kelsey RM, Salomon KL, Fazio RH. 1993. Attitude accessibility as a moderator of autonomic reactivity during decision making. *J. Pers. Soc. Psychol.* 64:165–76

Bless H, Mackie DM, Schwarz N. 1992. Mood effects on attitude judgments: independent effects of mood before and after message elaboration. *J. Pers. Soc. Psychol.* 63:585–95

Bohner G, Chaiken S, Hunyadi P. 1994. The role of mood and message ambiguity in the interplay of heuristic and systematic processing. *Eur. J. Soc. Psychol.* 24: 207–21

Bohner G, Crow K, Erb H, Schwarz N. 1992. Affect and persuasion: mood effects on the processing of message content and context cues and on subsequent behaviour. *Eur. J. Soc. Psychol.* 22:511–30

Boninger DS, Krosnick JA, Berent MK. 1995a. Origins of attitude importance: self-interest, social identification, and value relevance. *J. Pers. Soc. Psychol.* 68:61–80

Boninger DS, Krosnick JA, Berent MK, Fabrigar LR. 1995b. The causes and consequences of attitude importance. See Petty & Krosnick 1995, pp. 159–89

Bornstein RF, D'Agostino PR. 1992. Stimulus recognition and the mere exposure effect. *J. Pers. Soc. Psychol.* 63:545–52

Bornstein RF, D'Agostino PR. 1994. The attribution and discounting of perceptual fluency: preliminary tests of a perceptual fluency/attributional model of the mere exposure effect. *Soc. Cogn.* 12:103–28

Bouchard TJ Jr, Arvey RD, Keller LM, Segal NL. Genetic influences on job satisfaction: a reply to Cropanzano and James. 1992. *J. Appl. Psychol.* 77:89–93

Bozzolo AM, Brock TC. 1992. Unavailability effects on message processing: a theoretical analysis and an empirical test. *Basic Appl. Soc. Psychol.* 13:93–101

Brauer M, Judd CM, Gliner MD. 1995. The effects of repeated expressions on attitude polarization during group discussions. *J. Pers. Soc. Psychol.* 68:1014–29

Breckler SJ. 1994. A comparison of numerical indexes for measuring attitude ambivalence. *Ed. Psychol. Meas.* 54:350–65

Breckler SJ, Fried HS. 1993. On knowing what you like and liking what you smell: attitudes depend on the form in which the object is represented. *Pers. Soc. Psychol. Bull.* 19:228–40

Brock TC. 1968. Implications of commodity theory for value change. See Greenwald et al 1968, pp. 243–75

Brock TC, Brannon LA. 1992. Liberalization

of commodity theory. *Basic Appl. Soc. Psychol.* 13:135–44

Broniarczyk SM, Alba JW. 1994. The role of consumers' intuitions in inference making. *J. Consum. Res. 21*:393–407

Cacioppo JT, Berntson GG. 1994. Relationship between attitudes and evaluative space: a critical review, with emphasis on the separability of positive and negative substrates. *Psychol. Bull.* 115:401–23

Cacioppo JT, Crites SL Jr, Gardner WL, Berntson GG. 1994. Bioelectrical echoes from evaluative categorizations. I. A late positive brain potential that varies as a function of trait negativity and extremity. *J. Pers. Soc. Psychol.* 67:115–25

Cacioppo JT, Marshall-Goodell BS, Tassinary LG, Petty RE. 1992. Rudimentary determinants of attitudes: classical conditioning is more effective when prior knowledge about the attitude stimulus is low than high. *J. Exp. Soc. Psychol.* 28:207–33

Cacioppo JT, Petty RE, Feinstein J, Jarvis B. 1996. Individual differences in cognitive motivation: the life and times of people varying in need for cognition. *Psychol. Bull.* 119:197–253

Cacioppo JT, Priester JR, Berntson GG. 1993. Rudimentary determinants of attitudes. II. Arm flexion and extension have differential effects on attitudes. *J. Pers. Soc. Psychol.* 65:5–17

Chaiken S, Bargh JA. 1993. Occurrence versus moderation of the automatic attitude activation effect: reply to Fazio. *J. Pers. Soc. Psychol.* 64:759–65

Chaiken S, Giner-Sorolla R, Chen S. 1996a. Beyond accuracy: defense and impression motives in heuristic and systematic information processing. In *The Psychology Of Action: Linking Motivation and Cognition to Behavior,* ed. PM Gollwitzer, JA Bargh, pp. 553–78. New York: Guilford

Chaiken S, Liberman A, Eagly AH. 1989. Heuristic and systematic processing within and beyond the persuasion context. In *Unintended Thought,* ed. JS Uleman, JA Bargh, pp. 212–52. New York: Guilford

Chaiken S, Maheswaran D. 1994. Heuristic processing can bias systematic processing: effects of source credibility, argument ambiguity, and task importance on attitude judgment. *J. Pers. Soc. Psychol.* 66:460–73

Chaiken S, Wood W, Eagly AH. 1996b. Principles of persuasion. In *Social Psychology: Handbook of Basic Principles,* ed. ET Higgins, AW Kruglanski, pp. 702–42. New York: Guilford

Chan DK-S, Fishbein M. 1993. Determinants of college women's intentions to tell their partners to use condoms. *J. Appl. Soc. Psychol.* 23:1455–70

Chen HC, Reardon R, Rea C, Moore DJ. 1992. Forewarning of content and involvement: consequences for persuasion and resistance to persuasion. *J. Exp. Soc. Psychol.* 28:523–41

Cialdini RB, Petty RE, Cacioppo JT. 1981. Attitude and attitude change. *Annu. Rev. Psychol.* 32:357–404

Cialdini RB, Trost MR, Newsom JT. 1995. Preference for consistency: the development of a valid measure and the discovery of surprising behavioral implications. *J. Pers. Soc. Psychol.* 69:318–28

Clark RD. 1994. The role of censorship in minority influence. *Eur. J. Soc. Psychol.* 24:331–38

Clark RD. 1995. On being excommunicated from the European view of minority influence: a reply to Perez et al. *Eur. J. Soc. Psychol.* 25:711–14

Clary EG, Snyder M, Ridge RD, Miene PK, Haugen JA. 1994. Matching messages to motives in persuasion: a functional approach to promoting volunteerism. *J. Appl. Soc. Psychol. 24:*1129–49

Cochran SD, Mays VM, Ciarletta J, Caruso C, Mallon D. 1992. Efficacy of the theory of reasoned action in predicting AIDS-related sexual risk reduction among gay men. *J. Appl. Soc. Psychol.* 22:1481–501

Cooper J. 1992. Dissonance and the return of the self-concept. *Psychol. Inq.* 3:320– 23

Cooper J, Fazio RH. 1984. A new look at dissonance theory. *Adv. Exp. Soc. Psychol.* 17:229–66

Crano WD, Hannula-Bral KA. 1994. Context/categorization model of social influence: minority and majority influence in the formation of a novel response norm. *J. Exp. Soc. Psychol.* 30:247–76

Crites SL Jr, Cacioppo JT, Gardner WL, Berntson GG. 1995. Bioelectrical echoes from evaluative categorization. II. A late positive brain potential that varies as a function of attitude registration rather than attitude report. *J. Pers. Soc. Psychol.* 68:997–1013

Crites SL Jr, Fabrigar LR, Petty RE. 1994. Measuring the affective and cognitive properties of attitudes: conceptual and methodological issues. *Pers. Soc. Psychol. Bull.* 20:619–34

Cropanzano R, James K. 1990. Some methodological considerations for the behavioral genetic analysis of work attitudes. *J. Appl. Psychol.* 75:433–39

Crowley AE, Hoyer WD. 1994. An integrative framework for understanding two-sided persuasion. *J. Consum. Res.* 20:561–74

Darke PR, Freedman JL, Chaiken S. 1995. Percentage discounts, initial price, and bargain hunting: a heuristic-systematic approach to price search behavior. *J. Appl. Psychol.* 80: 580–86

Davies MF. 1993. Dogmatism and the persistence of discredited beliefs. *Pers. Soc. Psychol. 19:*692–99

DeBono KG. 1992. Pleasant scents and persuasion: an information processing approach. *J. Appl. Soc. Psychol.* 22:910–20

DeBono KG, Klein C. 1993. Source expertise and persuasion: the moderating role of recipient dogmatism. *Pers. Soc. Psychol. Bull.* 19:167–73

DeBono KG, Snyder M. 1995. Acting on one's attitudes: the role of a history of choosing situations. *Pers. Soc. Psychol. Bull.* 21: 629–36

De Houwer J, Baeyens F, Eelen P. 1994. Verbal evaluative conditioning with undetected US presentations. *Behav. Res. Ther.* 32: 629–33

Dickerson CA, Thibodeau R, Aronson E, Miller D. 1992. Using cognitive dissonance to encourage water conservation. *J. Appl. Soc. Psychol.* 22:841–54

Doll J, Ajzen I. 1992. Accessibility and stability of predictors in the theory of planned behavior. *J. Pers. Soc. Psychol.* 63:754–65

Downing JW, Judd CM, Brauer M. 1992. Effects of repeated expressions on attitude extremity. *J. Pers. Soc. Psychol.* 63:17–29

Drigotas SM. 1993. Similarity revisited: a comparison of similarity-attractions versus dissimilarity-repulsion. *Br. J. Soc. Psychol.* 32:365–77

Eagly AH, Chaiken S. 1993. *The Psychology of Attitudes.* Fort Worth, TX: Harcourt Brace

Eagly AH, Mladinic A, Otto S. 1994. Cognitive and affective bases of attitudes toward social groups and social policies. *J. Exp. Soc. Psychol.* 30:113–37

Edwards K, von Hippel W. 1995. Hearts and minds: the priority of affective versus cognitive factors in person perception. *Pers. Soc. Psychol. Bull.* 21:996–1011

Eiser JR. 1994. Toward a dynamic conception of attitude consistency and change. See Vallaceher & Nowak 1994, pp. 197–218

Eiser JR, Eiser C, Sani F, Sell L, Casas RM. 1995. Skin cancer attitudes: a cross-national comparison. *Br. J. Soc. Psychol.* 34: 23–30

Eiser JR, Pancer SM. 1979. Attitudinal effects of the use of evaluatively biased language. *Eur. J. Soc. Psychol.* 9:39–47

Elliot AJ, Devine PG. 1994. On the motivational nature of cognitive dissonance: dissonance as psychological discomfort. *J. Pers. Soc. Psychol.* 67:382–94

Fabrigar LR, Krosnick JA. 1995. Attitude importance and the false consensus effect. *Pers. Soc. Psychol. Bull.* 21:468–79

Fazio RH. 1993. Variability in the likelihood of automatic attitude activation: data reanalysis and commentary on Bargh, Chaiken, Govender, and Pratto. *J. Pers. Soc. Psychol.* 64:753–58

Fazio RH. 1995. Attitudes as object-evaluation associations: determinants, consequences, and correlates of attitude accessibility. See Petty & Krosnick 1995, pp. 247–82

Fazio RH, Blascovich J, Driscoll DM. 1992. On the functional value of attitudes: the influence of accessible attitudes on the ease and quality of decision making. *Pers. Soc. Psychol. Bull.* 18:388–401

Fazio RH, Jackson JR, Dunton BC, Williams CJ. 1995. Variability in automatic attitude activation as an unobtrusive measure of racial attitudes: a bona fide pipeline. *J. Pers. Soc. Psychol.* 69:103–27

Fazio RH, Sanbonmatusu DM, Powell MC, Kardes FR. 1986. On the automatic activation of attitudes. *J. Pers. Soc. Psychol.* 50: 229–38

Feather NT. 1995. Values, valences, and choice: the influence of values on the perceived attractiveness and choice of alternatives. *J. Pers. Soc. Psychol.* 68:1135–51

Festinger L. 1957. *A Theory of Cognitive Dissonance.* Evanston, IL: Row Peterson

Fishbein M, Ajzen I. 1975. *Belief, Attitude, Intention, and Behavior.* Reading, MA: Addison-Wesley

Fishbein M, Chan DK-S, O'Reilly K, Schnell D, Wood R, et al. 1992. Attitudinal and normative factors as determinants of gay men's intentions to perform AIDS-related sexual behaviors: a multiple analysis. *J. Appl. Soc. Psychol.* 22:999–1011

Fishbein M, Middlestadt S. 1995. Noncognitive effects on attitude formation and change: fact or artifact? *J. Consum. Psychol.* 4:181–202

Forgas J. 1992. Affect in social judgments and decisions: a multiprocess model. *Adv. Exp. Soc. Psychol.* 25:227–76

Forgas J. 1993. On making sense of odd couples: mood effects on the perception of mismatched relationships. *Pers. Soc. Psychol. Bull.* 19:59–70

Forgas J. 1995a. Mood and judgment: the affect infusion model (AIM). *Psychol. Bull.* 117:39–66

Forgas J. 1995b. Strange couples: mood effects on judgments and memory about prototypical and atypical relationships. *Pers. Soc. Psychol. Bull.* 21:747–65

Frey KP, Eagly AH. 1993. Vividness can undermine the persuasiveness of messages. *J. Pers. Soc. Psychol.* 65:32–44

Fried CB, Aronson E. 1995. Hypocrisy, misattribution, and dissonance reduction. *Pers. Soc. Psychol. Bull. 21:*925–33

Friestad M, Wright P. 1994. The persuasion

knowledge model: how people cope with persuasion attempts. *J. Consum. Res.* 21: 1–31

Gastil J. 1992. Why we believe in democracy: testing theories of attitude functions and democracy. *J. Appl. Soc. Psychol.* 22: 423–50

Gerard HB, Blevans SA, Malcom T. 1964. Self-evaluation and the evaluation of choice alternatives. *J. Pers.* 32:395–410

Giles M, Cairns E. 1995. Blood donation and Ajzen's theory of planned behavior: an examination of perceived behavioral control. *Br. J. Soc. Psychol.* 34:173–88

Gilovich T, Medvec VH, Chen S. 1995. Commission, omission, and dissonance reduction: coping with regret in the "Monty Hall" problem. *Pers. Soc. Psychol. Bull.* 21:182–90

Giner-Sorolla R, Chaiken S. 1994. The causes of hostile media judgements. *J. Exp. Soc. Psychol.* 30:165–80

Gleicher G, Petty RE. 1992. Expectations of reassurance influence the nature of fear-stimulated attitude change. *J. Exp. Soc. Psychol.* 28:86–100

Gorn GJ, Goldberg ME, Basu K. 1993. Mood, awareness, and product evaluation. *J. Consum. Psychol.* 2:237–56

Greenwald AG. 1968. Cognitive learning, cognitive response to persuasion, and attitude change. See Greenwald et al 1968, pp. 147–70

Greenwald AG, Banaji MR. 1995. Implicit social cognition: attitudes, self-esteem, and stereotypes. *Psychol. Rev.* 102:4–27

Greenwald AG, Ostrom TM, Brock TC, eds. 1968. *Psychological Foundations of Attitudes.* New York: Academic

Haddock G, Zanna MP, Esses VM. 1993. Assessing the structure of prejudicial attitudes: the case of attitudes towards homosexuals. *J. Pers. Soc. Psychol.* 65:1105–18

Han SP, Shavitt S. 1994. Persuasion and culture: advertising appeals in individualistic and collectivistic societies. *J. Exp. Soc. Psychol.* 30:326–50

Hansen CH, Shantz CA. 1995. Emotion-specific priming: congruence effects on affect and recognition across negative emotions. *Pers. Soc. Psychol. Bull.* 21:548–57

Hastie R, Park B. 1986. The relationship between memory and judgment depends on whether the judgment task is memory-based or on-line. *Psychol. Rev.* 93:258–68

Haugtvedt CP, Petty RE. 1992. Personality and persuasion: need for cognition moderates the persistence and resistance of attitude changes. *J. Pers. Soc. Psychol.* 63: 308–19

Haugtvedt CP, Petty RE, Cacioppo JT. 1992. Need for cognition and advertising: understanding the role of personality variables in consumer behavior. *J. Consum. Psychol.* 1:239–60

Haugtvedt CP, Schumann DW, Schneier WL, Warren WL. 1994. Advertising repetition and variation strategies: implications for understanding attitude strength. *J. Consum. Res.* 21:176–89

Haugtvedt CP, Wegener DT. 1994. Message order effects in persuasion: an attitude strength perspective. *J. Consum. Res.* 21: 205–18

Heath TB, McCarthy MS, Mothersbaugh DL. 1994. Spokesperson fame and the vividness effects in the context of issue-relevant thinking: the moderating role of competitive setting. *J. Consum. Res.* 20:520–34

Heesacker M, Conner K, Prichard S. 1995. Individual counseling and psychotherapy: applications from the social psychology of attitude change. *Couns. Psychol.* 23: 611–32

Higgins ET. 1989. Self-discrepancy theory: What patterns of beliefs cause people to suffer? *Adv. Exp. Soc. Psychol.* 22:93–136

Hodges SD, Wilson TD. 1993. Effects of analyzing reasons on attitude change: the moderating role of attitude accessibility. *Soc. Cogn.* 11:353–66

Hovland CI, Janis IL, Kelley HH. 1953. *Communication and Persuasion: Psychological Studies of Opinion Change.* New Haven, CT: Yale Univ. Press

Howard DJ, Barry TE. 1994. The role of thematic congruence between a mood-inducing event and an advertised product in determining the effects of mood on brand attitudes. *J. Consum. Psychol.* 3:1–27

Hoyle R. 1993. Interpersonal attraction in the absence of explicit attitudinal information. *Soc. Cogn.* 11:309–20

Hurwitz SD, Miron MS, Johnson BT. 1992. Source credibility and the language of expert testimony. *J. Appl. Soc. Psychol.* 22: 1909–39

Hutton DG, Baumeister RF. 1992. Self-awareness and attitude change: seeing oneself on the central route to persuasion. *Pers. Soc. Psychol. Bull.* 18:68–75

Janiszewski C. 1993. Preattentive mere exposure effects. *J. Consum. Res.* 20:376–92

Johnson BT. 1994. Effects of outcome-relevant involvement and prior information on persuasion. *J. Exp. Soc. Psychol.* 30:556–79

Johnson BT, Lin HY, Symons CS, Campbell LA, Ekstein G. 1995a. Initial beliefs and attitudinal latitudes as factors in persuasion. *Pers. Soc. Psychol. Bull.* 21:502–11

Johnson RW, Kelly RJ, LeBlanc BA. 1995b. Motivational basis of dissonance: aversive consequences or inconsistency. *Pers. Soc. Psychol. Bull.* 21:850–55

Johnston L, Coolen P. 1995. A dual processing approach to stereotype change. *Pers. Soc. Psychol. Bull.* 21:660–73

Judd CM, Brauer M. 1995. Repetition and evaluative extremity. See Petty & Krosnick 1995, pp. 43–71

Kaplan KJ. 1972. On the ambivalence-indifference problem in attitude theory and measurement: a suggested modification of the semantic differential technique. *Psychol. Bull.* 77:361–72

Kelly C, Breinlinger S. 1995. Attitudes, intentions and behavior: a study of women's participation in collective action. *J. Appl. Soc. Psychol.* 25:1430–45

Klauer KC, Stern E. 1992. How attitudes guide memory-based judgments: a two-process model. *J. Exp. Soc. Psychol.* 28:186–206

Koestner R, Bernieri F, Zuckerman M. 1992. Self-regulation and consistency between attitudes, traits, and behaviors. *Pers. Soc. Psychol. Bull.* 18:52–59

Kover AJ. 1995. Copywriters' implicit theories of communication: an exploration. *J. Consum. Res.* 21:596–611

Kozakai T, Moscovici S, Personnaz B. 1994. Contrary effects of group cohesiveness in minority influence: intergroup categorization of the source and levels of influence. *Eur. J. Soc. Psychol.* 24:713–18

Kraus SJ. 1995. Attitudes and the prediction of behavior: a meta-analysis of the empirical literature. *Pers. Soc. Psychol. Bull.* 21: 58–75

Krosnick JA, Betz AL, Jussim LJ, Lynn AR. 1992. Subliminal conditioning of attitudes. *Pers. Soc. Psychol. Bull.* 18:152–62

Krosnick JA, Boninger DS, Chuang YC, Berent MK, Carnot CG. 1993. Attitude strength: one construct or many related constructs? *J. Pers. Soc. Psychol.* 65:1132–51

Krosnick JA, Petty RE. 1995. Attitude strength: an overview. See Petty & Krosnick 1995, pp. 247–82

Krueger J, Clement RW. 1994. The truly false consensus effect: an ineradicable and egocentric bias in social perception. *J. Pers. Soc. Psychol.* 67:596–610

Krueger J, Zeiger JS. 1993. Social categorization and the truly false consensus effect. *J. Pers. Soc. Psychol.* 65:670–80

Kruglanski AW, Webster DM, Klem A. 1993. Motivated resistance and openness to persuasion in the presence or absence of prior information. *J. Pers. Soc. Psychol.* 65:861–76

Kurland NB. 1995. Ethical intentions and the theories of reasoned action and planned behavior. *J. Appl. Soc. Psychol.* 25:297–313

Lammers HB. 1982. Effects of biased scanning and distraction on cognitive responses. *J. Soc. Psychol.* 116:99–105

Lammers HB, Becker LA. 1992. Distraction, choice and self-esteem effects on cognitive response facilitation. *Br. J. Soc. Psychol.* 31:189–200

Latané B, Nowak A. 1994. Attitudes as catastrophes: from dimensions to categories with increasing involvement. See Vallacher & Nowak 1994, pp. 197–218

Leippe MR, Eisenstadt D. 1994. Generalization of dissonance reduction: decreasing prejudice through induced compliance. *J. Pers. Soc. Psychol.* 67:395–413

Levine JM, Russo E. 1995. Impact of anticipated interaction on information acquisition. *Soc. Cogn.* 13:293–317

Liberman A, Chaiken S. 1992. Defensive processing of personally relevant health messages. *Pers. Soc. Psychol. Bull.* 18:669–79

Lord CG, Ross L, Lepper MR. 1979. Biased assimilation and attitude polarization: the effects of prior theories on subsequently considered evidence. *J. Pers. Soc. Psychol.* 37:2098–109

Lykken DT, Bouchard TJ, McGue M, Tellegen A. 1993. Heritability of interests: a twin study. *J. Appl. Psychol.* 78:649–61

Lynn M. 1992. Scarcity's enhancement of desirability: the role of naive economic theories. *Basic Appl. Soc. Psychol.* 13:67–78

MacKenzie SB, Spreng RA. 1992. How does motivation moderate the impact of central and peripheral processing on brand attitudes and intentions? *J. Consum. Res.* 18: 519–29

Mackie DM, Asuncion AG. 1990. On-line and memory-based modification of attitudes: determinants of message recall-attitude change correspondence. *J. Pers. Soc. Psychol.* 59:5–16

Mackie DM, Gastardo-Conaco CM, Skelly JJ. 1992. Knowledge of the advocated position and the processing of in-group and out-group persuasive messages. *Pers. Soc. Psychol. Bull.* 18:145–51

Macrae CN, Shepherd JW, Milne AB. 1992. The effects of source credibility on the dilution of stereotype-based judgments. *Pers. Soc. Psychol. Bull.* 18:765–75

Madden TJ, Ellen PS, Ajzen I. 1992. A comparison of the theory of planned behavior and the theory of reasoned action. *Pers. Soc. Psychol. Bull.* 18:3–9

Maheswaran D. 1994. Country of origin as a stereotype: consumer expertise and attribute strength on product evaluations. *J. Consum. Res.* 21:354–65

Maheswaran D, Mackie DM, Chaiken S. 1992. Brand name as a heuristic cue: the effects of task importance and expectancy confirmation on consumer judgments. *J. Consum. Psychol.* 1:317–36

Maio GR, Olson JM. 1994. Value-attitude-behavior relations: the moderating role of attitude functions. *Br. J. Soc. Psychol.* 33: 301–12

Maio GR, Olson JM. 1995a. The effect of attitude dissimulation on attitude accessibility. *Soc. Cogn.* 13:127–44

Maio GR, Olson JM. 1995b. Relations between values, attitudes, and behavioral intentions: the moderating role of attitude function. *J. Exp. Soc. Psychol.* 31:266–85

Mandler G, Nakamura Y, Van Zandt BJ. 1987. Nonspecific effects of exposure to stimuli that cannot be recognized. *J. Exp. Psychol. Learn. Mem. Cogn.* 13: 646–48

Martin LL, Seta JJ, Crelia RA. 1990. Assimilation and contrast as a function of people's willingness and ability to expend effort in forming an impression. *J. Pers. Soc. Psychol.* 59:27–37

Martin LL, Ward DW, Achee JW, Wyer RS. 1993. Mood as input: people have to interpret the motivational implications of their moods. *J. Pers. Soc. Psychol.* 64:317–26

Mayer JD, Gaschke YN, Bravermen DL, Evans TW. 1992. Mood-congruent judgment is a general effect. *J. Pers. Soc. Psychol.* 63:119–32

Mayer JD, Hanson E. 1995. Mood-congruent judgment over time. *Pers. Soc. Psychol. Bull.* 21:237–44

McClelland DC, Koestner R, Weinberger J. 1989. How do self-attributed and implicit motives differ? *Psychol. Rev.* 96:690–702

McGuire WJ. 1968. Personality and susceptibility to social influence. In *Handbook of Personality Theory and Research,* ed. EF Borgatta, WW Lambert, pp. 1130–87. Chicago: Rand-McNally

McGuire WJ. 1969. The nature of attitudes and attitude change. In *The Handbook of Social Psychology,* ed. G Lindzey, E Aronson, 3:136–314. Reading, MA: Addison-Wesley. 2nd ed.

McGuire WJ. 1985. Attitudes and attitude change. In *The Handbook of Social Psychology,* ed. G Lindzey, E Aronson, 2: 233–346. New York: Random House. 3rd ed.

Mellema A, Bassili JN. 1995. On the relationship between attitudes and values: exploring the moderating effects of self-monitoring and self-monitoring schemacity. *Pers. Soc. Psychol. Bull.* 21:885–92

Meyerowitz BE, Chaiken S. 1987. The effect of message framing on breast self-examination, attitudes, intentions, and behavior. *J. Pers. Soc. Psychol.* 52:500–10

Millar MG, Millar KU. 1990. Attitude change as a function of attitude type and argument type. *J. Pers. Soc. Psychol.* 59:217–28

Miller AG, McHoskey JW, Bane CM, Dowd TG. 1993. The attitude polarization phenomenon: role of response measure, attitude extremity, and behavioral consequences of reported attitude change. *J. Pers. Soc. Psychol.* 64:561–74

Miniard PW, Sirdeshmukh D, Innes DE. 1992. Peripheral persuasion and brand choice. *J. Consum. Res.* 19:226–39

Moreland RL, Beach SR. 1992. Exposure effects in the classroom: the development of affinity among students. *J. Exp. Soc. Psychol.* 28:255–76

Murphy ST, Monahan JL, Zajonc RB. 1995. Additivity of nonconscious affect: combined effects of priming and exposure. *J. Pers. Soc. Psychol.* 69:589–602

Murphy ST, Zajonc RB. 1993. Affect, cognition, and awareness: affective priming with optimal and suboptimal exposures. *J. Pers. Soc. Psychol.* 64:723–39

Olson JM, Zanna MP. 1993. Attitudes and attitude change. *Annu. Rev. Psychol.* 44: 117–54

Pechmann C, Esteban G. 1994. Persuasion processes associated with direct comparative and noncomparative advertising and implications for advertising effectiveness. *J. Consum. Psychol.* 2:403–32

Pelham BW, Neter E. 1995. The effect of motivation of judgment depends on the difficulty of the judgment. *J. Pers. Soc. Psychol.* 68:581–94

Perez JA, Papastamou S, Mugny G. 1995. Zeitgeist and minority influence—where is the causality: a comment on Clark (1990). *Eur. J. Soc. Psychol.* 25:703–10

Perloff RM. 1993. *The Dynamics of Persuasion.* Hillsdale, NJ: Erlbaum

Petkova KG, Ajzen I, Driver BL. 1995. Salience of anti-abortion beliefs and commitment to an attitudinal position: on the strength, structure, and predicative validity of anti-abortion attitudes. *J. Appl. Soc. Psychol.* 25:463–83

Petty RE. 1994. Two routes to persuasion: state of the art. In *International Perspectives on Psychological Science,* ed. G d'Ydewalle, P Eelen, P Bertelson, 2:229– 47. Hillsdale, NJ: Erlbaum

Petty RE. 1995. Attitude change. In *Advanced Social Psychology,* ed. A Tesser, pp. 195–255. New York: McGraw-Hill

Petty RE. 1996. Evolution of theory in social psychology: from single to multi-effect and process models of persuasion. In *The Message of Social Psychology: Perspectives on Mind in Society,* ed. A Haslam, C McGarty, pp. 268–90. Oxford: Blackwell

Petty RE, Cacioppo JT. 1979a. Effects of forewarning of persuasive intent and involvement on cognitive responses and persuasion. *J. Pers. Soc. Psychol.* 37:1915–26

Petty RE, Cacioppo JT. 1979b. Issue-involvement can increase or decrease persuasion by enhancing message-relevant cognitive responses. *J. Pers. Soc. Psychol.* 37: 1915–26

Petty RE, Cacioppo JT. 1986. The Elaboration

Likelihood Model of persuasion. *Adv. Exp. Soc. Psychol.* 19:123–205
Petty RE, Cacioppo JT. 1990. Involvement and persuasion: tradition versus integration. *Psychol. Bull.* 107:367–74
Petty RE, Cacioppo JT, Haugtvedt C. 1992. Involvement and persuasion: an appreciative look at the Sherifs' contribution to the study of self-relevance and attitude change. In *Social Judgment and Intergroup Relations: Essays in Honor of Muzafer Sherif,* ed. D. Granberg, G Sarup, pp. 147–74. New York: Springer-Verlag
Petty RE, Haugtvedt CP, Smith SM. 1995. Elaboration as a determinant of attitude strength: creating attitudes that are persistent, resistant, and predictive of behavior. See Petty & Krosnick 1995, pp. 93–130
Petty RE, Krosnick JA, eds. 1995. *Attitude Strength: Antecedents and Consequences.* Mahwah, NJ: Erlbaum
Petty RE, Priester JR, Wegener DT. 1994. Cognitive processes in attitude change. In *Handbook of Social Cognition,* ed. RS Wyer, TK Srull, 2:69–142. Hillsdale, NJ: Erlbaum. 2nd ed.
Petty RE, Schumann DW, Richman SA, Strathman AJ. 1993a. Positive mood and persuasion: different roles for affect under high- and low-elaboration conditions. *J. Pers. Soc. Psychol.* 64:5–20
Petty RE, Wegener DT. 1991. Thought systems, argument quality, and persuasion. In *Advances in Social Cognition,* ed. RS Wyer, TK Srull, 4:147–61. Hillsdale, NJ: Erlbaum
Petty RE, Wegener DT. 1993. Flexible correction processes in social judgment: correcting for context induced contrast. *J. Exp. Soc. Psychol.* 29:137–65
Petty RE, Wegener DT. 1997. Attitude change: multiple roles for persuasion variables. In *Handbook of Social Psychology,* ed. D Gilbert, S Fiske, G Lindzey. 4th ed. New York: McGraw-Hill
Petty RE, Wegener DT, Fabrigar LR, Priester JR, Cacioppo JT. 1993b. Conceptual and methodological issues in the elaboration likelihood model of persuasion: a reply to the Michigan State critics. *Comm. Theory* 3:336–63
Petty RE, Wells GL, Brock TC. 1976. Distraction can enhance or reduce yielding to propaganda: thought disruption versus effort justification. *J. Pers. Soc. Psychol.* 34: 874–84
Pieters RGM, Verplanken B. 1995. Intention-behavior consistency: effects of consideration set size, involvement and need for cognition. *Eur. J. Soc. Psychol.* 25:531–43
Pittman TS. 1994. Control motivation and attitude change. In *Control Motivation and Social Cognition,* ed. G Weary, F Gleicher, K Marsh. New York: Springer-Verlag
Pomerantz EM, Chaiken S, Tordesillas RS. 1995. Attitude strength and resistance processes. *J. Pers. Soc. Psychol.* 69:408–19
Powell MC, Fazio RH. 1984. Attitude accessibility as a function of repeated attitudinal expression. *Pers. Soc. Psychol. Bull.* 10: 139–48
Priester JR, Petty RE. 1995. Source attributions and persuasion: perceived honesty as a determinant of message scrutiny. *Pers. Soc. Psychol. Bull.* 21:637–54
Pyszcynski T, Greenberg J, Solomon S, Sideris J, Stubing MJ. 1993. Emotional expression and the reduction of motivated cognitive bias: evidence from cognitive dissonance and distancing from victims' paradigms. *J. Pers. Soc. Psychol.* 64:177–86
Rhodes N, Wood W. 1992. Self-esteem and intelligence affect influenceability: the mediating role of message reception. *Psychol. Bull.* 111:156–71
Richard R, van der Pligt J, de Vries N. 1995. Anticipated affective reactions and prevention of AIDS. *Br. J. Soc. Psychol.* 34: 9–21
Roese NJ, Jamieson DW. 1993. Twenty years of bogus pipeline research: a critical review and meta-analysis. *Psychol. Bull.* 114: 363–75
Roese NJ, Olson JM. 1994. Attitude importance as a function of repeated attitude expression. *J. Exp. Soc. Psychol.* 30:39–51
Rose RL, Miniard PW, Barone MJ, Manning KC, Till BD. 1993. When persuasion goes undetected: the case of comparative advertising. *J. Mark. Res.* 30:315–30
Roskos-Ewoldsen DR, Fazio RH. 1992a. On the orienting value of attitudes: attitude accessibility as a determinant of an object's attraction of visual attention. *J. Pers. Soc. Psychol.* 63:198–211
Roskos-Ewoldsen DR, Fazio RH. 1992b. The accessibility of source likability as a determinant of persuasion. *Pers. Soc. Psychol. Bull.* 18:19–25
Rosselli F, Skelly JJ, Mackie DM. 1995. Processing rational and emotional messages: the cognitive and affective mediation of persuasion. *J. Exp. Soc. Psychol.* 31:163–90
Rothman AJ, Salovey P, Antone C, Keough K, Martin CD. 1993. The influence of message framing on intentions to perform health behaviors. *J. Exp. Soc. Psychol.* 29: 408–33
Rule BG, Bisanz GL. 1987. Goals and strategies of persuasion: a cognitive schema for understanding social events. In *Social Influence: The Ontario Symposium,* ed. MP Zanna, JM Olson, CP Herman, 5:185–206. Hillsdale, NJ: Erlbaum

Schuette RA, Fazio RH. 1995. Attitude accessibility and motivation as determinants of biased processing: a test of the MODE model. *Pers. Soc. Psychol. Bull.* 21:704–10

Schwarz N, Sudman S, eds. 1996. *Answering Questions: Methodology for Determining Cognitive and Communicative Processess in Survey Research.* San Francisco: Jossey-Bass

Shavitt S, Brock TC, eds. 1994. *Persuasion: Psychological Insights and Perspectives.* Needham Heights, MA: Allyn-Bacon

Shavitt S, Lowrey TM, Han SP. 1992. Attitude functions in advertising: the interactive role of products and self-monitoring. *J. Consum. Psychol.* 1:337–64

Shavitt S, Swan S, Lowrey TM, Wanke M. 1994. The interaction of endorser attractiveness and involvement in persuasion depends on the goal that guides message processing. *J. Consum. Psychol.* 3:137–62

Sherif CW, Sherif M, eds. 1967. *Attitude, Ego-Involvement, and Change.* New York: Wiley

Siero FW, Doosje BJ. 1993. Attitude change following persuasive communication: integrating social judgment theory and the Elaboration Likelihood Model. *Eur. J. Soc. Psychol.* 23:541–54

Simon L, Greenberg J, Brehm J. 1995. Trivialization: the forgotten mode of dissonance reduction. *J. Pers. Soc. Psychol.* 68:247–60

Simonson I, Nowlis SM, Simonson Y. 1993. The effect of irrelevant preference arguments on consumer choice. *J. Consum. Psychol.* 2:287–306

Sinclair RC, Mark MM, Clore GL. 1994. Mood-related persuasion depends on (mis)attributions. *Soc. Cogn.* 12:309–26

Smith RE. 1993. Integrating information from advertising and trial: processes and effects on consumer response to product information. *J. Mark. Res.* 30:204–19

Smith SM, Shaffer DR. 1995. Speed of speech and persuasion: evidence for multiple effects. *Pers. Soc. Psychol. Bull.* 21:1051–60

Snell J, Gibbs BJ, Varey C. 1995. Intuitive hedonics: consumer beliefs about the dynamics of liking. *J. Consum. Psychol.* 4: 33–60

Snyder M. 1979. Self-monitoring processes. *Adv. Exp. Soc. Psychol.* 12:86–128

Snyder R. 1992. Comparative advertising and brand evaluation: toward developing a categorization approach. *J. Consum. Psychol.* 1:15–30

Solarz A. 1960. Latency of instrumental responses as a function of compatibility with the meaning of eliciting verbal signs. *J. Exp. Psychol.* 59:239–45

Sparks P, Hedderley D, Sheperd R. 1992. An investigation into the relationship between perceived control, attitude variability and the consumption of two common foods. *Eur. J. Soc. Psychol.* 22:55–71

Stayman DM, Kardes FR. 1992. Spontaneous inference processes in advertising: effects of need for cognition and self-monitoring on inference generation and utilization. *J. Consum. Psychol.* 1:125–42

Steele CM. 1988. The psychology of self-affirmation. *Adv. Exp. Soc. Psychol.* 21: 261–302

Steele CM, Spencer SJ, Lynch M. 1993. Self-image resilience and dissonance: the role of affirmational resources. *J. Pers. Soc. Psychol.* 64:885–96

Stern PC, Dietz T, Kalof L, Guagnano GA. 1995. Values, beliefs, and preenvironmental action: attitude formation toward emergent attitude objects. *J. Appl. Soc. Psychol.* 25:1611–36

Stiff JB. 1994. *Persuasive Communication.* New York: Guilford

Stone J, Aronson E, Crain AL, Winslow MP, Fried CB. 1994. Inducing hypocrisy as a means of encouraging young adults to use condoms. *Pers. Soc. Psychol. Bull.* 21: 116–28

Strathman A, Gleicher F, Boninger DS, Edwards CS. 1994. The consideration of future consequences: weighing immediate and distant outcomes of behavior. *J. Pers. Soc. Psychol.* 66:742–52

Struckman-Johnson C, Struckman-Johnson D, Gilland RC, Ausman A. 1994. Effect of persuasive appeals in AIDS PSAs and condom commercials on intentions to use condoms. *J. Appl. Soc. Psychol.* 24:2223–44

Tan DTY, Singh R. 1995. Attitudes and attraction: a developmental study of the similarity-attraction and dissimilarity-repulsion hypotheses. *Pers. Soc. Psychol. Bull.* 21: 975–86

Tanur JM. 1992. *Questions About Questions.* New York: Russell Sage Found.

Taylor SE, Thompson SC. 1982. Stalking the elusive "vividness" effect. *Psychol. Rev.* 89:155– 81

Tesser A. 1993. The importance of heritability in psychological research: the case of attitudes. *Psychol. Rev.* 100:129–42

Thibodeau R, Aronson E. 1992. Taking a closer look: reasserting the role of the self-concept in dissonance theory. *Pers. Soc. Psychol. Bull.* 18:591–602

Thompson MM, Zanna MP. 1995. The conflicted individual: personality-based and Domain-specific antecedents of ambivalent social attitudes. *J. Pers.* 63:259–88

Thompson MM, Zanna MP, Griffin DW. 1995. Let's not be indifferent about (attitudinal) ambivalence. See Petty & Krosnick 1995, pp. 361–86

Trafimow D. 1994. Predicting intentions to use

a condom from perceptions of normative pressure and confidence in those perceptions. *J. Appl. Soc. Psychol.* 24:2151–63

Trafimow D, Davis JH. 1993. The effects of anticipated informational and normative influence on perceptions of hypothetical opinion change. *Basic Appl. Soc. Psychol.* 14:487–96

Trafimow D, Fishbein M. 1994. The importance of risk in determining the extent to which attitudes affect intentions to wear seat belts. *J. Appl. Soc. Psychol.* 24:1–11

Tripp C, Jensen TD, Carlson L. 1994. The effects of multiple product endorsements by celebrities on consumers' attitudes and intentions. *J. Consum. Res.* 20:535–47

Trost MR, Maass A, Kenrick DT. 1992. Minority influence: personal relevance biases cognitive processes and reverses private acceptance. *J. Exp. Soc. Psychol.* 28: 234–54

Tykocinski O, Higgins ET, Chaiken S. 1994. Message framing, self-discrepancies, and yielding to persuasive messages: the motivational significance of psychological situations. *Pers. Soc. Psychol. Bull.* 20:107–15

Vallacher RR, Nowak A, eds. 1994. *Dynamical Systems in Social Psychology.* San Diego: Academic

Vallacher RR, Nowak A, Kaufman J. 1994. Intrinsic dynamics of social judgment. *J. Pers. Soc. Psychol.* 67:20–34

van Knippenberg D, Lossie N, Wilke H. 1994. In-group prototypicality and persuasion: determinants of heuristic and systematic message processing. *Br. J. Soc. Psychol.* 33:289–300

van Knippenberg D, Wilke H. 1992. Prototypicality of arguments and conformity to ingroup norms. *Eur. J. Soc. Psychol.* 22:141–55

van Schie ECM, Martijn C, van der Pligt J. 1994. Evaluative language, cognitive effort and attitude change. *Eur. J. Soc. Psychol.* 24:707–12

Verplanken B, Aarts H, van Knippenberg A. 1994. Attitude versus general habit: antecedents of travel mode choices. *J. Appl. Soc. Psychol.* 24:285–300

Vonk R, van Knippenberg A. 1995. Processing attitude statements from in-group and outgroup members: effects of within-group and within-person inconsistencies on reading times. *J. Pers. Soc. Psychol.* 68:215–27

Webster DM, Kruglanski AW. 1994. Individual differences in need for cognitive closure. *J. Pers. Soc. Psychol.* 67:1049–62

Wegener DT, Petty RE. 1994. Mood-management across affective states: the hedonic contingency hypothesis. *J. Pers. Soc. Psychol.* 66:1034–48

Wegener DT, Petty RE. 1996. Effects of mood on persuasion processes: enhancing, reducing, and biasing scrutiny of attitude-relevant information. In *Striving and Feeling: Interactions Between Goals and Affect,* ed. LL Martin, A Tesser, pp.329–62. Mahwah, NJ: Erlbaum

Wegener DT, Petty RE. 1997. The flexible correction model: the role of naive theories of bias in bias correction. *Adv. Exp. Soc. Psychol.*

Wegener DT, Petty RE, Klein DJ. 1994. Effects of mood on high elaboration attitude change: the mediating role of likelihood judgments. *Eur. J. Soc. Psychol.* 24:25–43

Wegener DT, Petty RE, Smith SM. 1995. Positive mood can increase or decrease message scrutiny: the hedonic contingency view of mood and message processing. *J. Pers. Soc. Psychol.* 69:5–15

White KM, Terry DJ, Hogg MA. 1994. Safer sex behavior: the role of attitudes, norms, and control factors. *J. Appl. Soc. Psychol.* 24:2164–92

White PH, Harkins SG. 1994. Race of source effects in the Elaboration Likelihood Model. *J. Pers. Soc. Psychol.* 67:790–807

Wilson TD, Brekke N. 1994. Mental contamination and mental correction: unwanted influences on judgments and evaluations. *Psychol. Bull.* 116:117–42

Wilson TD, Hodges SD, LaFleur SJ. 1995. Effects of introspecting about reasons: inferring attitudes from accessible thoughts. *J. Pers. Soc. Psychol.* 69:16–28

Wilson TD, LaFleur SJ. 1995. Knowing what you'll do: effects of analyzing reasons on self-prediction. *J. Pers. Soc. Psychol.* 68: 21–35

Wilson TD, Lisle DJ, Schooler JW, Hodges SD, Klaaren KJ, LaFleur SJ. 1993. Introspecting about reasons can reduce post-choice satisfaction. *Pers. Soc. Psychol. Bull.* 19:331–39

Wood W, Lundgren S, Ouellette JA, Busceme S, Blackstone T. 1994. Minority influence: a meta-analytic review of social influence processes. *Psychol. Bull.* 115:323–45

Wood W, Rhodes N, Biek M. 1995. Working knowledge and attitude strength: an information processing analysis. See Petty & Krosnick 1995, pp. 283–314

Worchel S. 1992. Beyond a commodity theory analysis of censorship: when abundance and personalism enhance scarcity effects. *Basic Appl. Soc. Psychol.* 13:79–92

Zajonc R. 1965. Social facilitation. *Science* 149:269–74

Annu. Rev. Psychol. 1997. 48:649–84

CENTRAL CHOLINERGIC SYSTEMS AND COGNITION

Barry J. Everitt and Trevor W. Robbins

Department of Experimental Psychology, University of Cambridge, Downing Street, Cambridge CB2 3EB, and the MRC Cambridge Centre for Brain Repair, United Kingdom

KEY WORDS: acetylcholine, basal forebrain, learning, memory, attention

ABSTRACT

The organization and possible functions of basal forebrain and pontine cholinergic systems are reviewed. Whereas the basal forebrain cholinergic neuronal projections likely subserve a common electrophysiological function, e.g. to boost signal-to-noise ratios in cortical target areas, this function has different effects on psychological processes dependent upon the neural network operations within these various cortical domains. Evidence is presented that (*a*) the nucleus basalis-neocortical cholinergic system contributes greatly to visual attentional function, but not to mnemonic processes per se; (*b*) the septohippocampal projection is involved in the modulation of short-term spatial (working) memory processes, perhaps by prolonging the neural representation of external stimuli within the hippocampus; and (*c*) the diagonal band–cingulate cortex cholinergic projection impacts on the ability to utilize response rules through conditional discrimination. We also suggest that nucleus basalis–amygdala cholinergic projections have a role in the retention of affective conditioning while brainstem cholinergic projections to the thalamus and midbrain dopamine neurons affect basic arousal processes (e.g. sleep-wake cycle) and behavioral activation, respectively. The possibilities and limitations of therapeutic interventions with procholinergic drugs in patients with Alzheimer's disease and other neurodegenerative disorders in which basal forebrain cholinergic neurons degenerate are also discussed.

CONTENTS

0084-6570/96/1015-0649$08.00

INTRODUCTION

Interest in the functions of the central cholinergic systems greatly increased with the neuropathological demonstrations that cholinergic markers in the cerebral cortex are reduced in people who die with Alzheimer's disease and that this decrease correlates with both cortical pathology and the degree of cognitive impairment (Bowen et al 1976, Perry et al 1978). Together with psychopharmacological literature revealing impairments in learning and memory following treatment with a variety of anticholinergic drugs, these demonstrations led to the cholinergic hypothesis of geriatric memory dysfunction (Bartus et al 1982). In modified form, this hypothesis still fuels studies investigating the mechanisms of action of systemically administered cholinergic drugs as they affect mnemonic function in animals and human beings (see reviews by Gallagher & Colombo 1995, Lawrence & Sahakian 1995, Mohammed 1993).

A wealth of data shows that drugs such as scopolamine can induce impairments in learning and memory and that procholinergic drugs, especially acetylcholinesterase inhibitors, can ameliorate such impairments (Fibiger 1991, Mohammed 1993). More recent experiments focus on specific acetylcholine receptor subtypes in mediating the effects of acetylcholine on cognition. There is an emerging consensus that blockade of the muscarinic M1 subtype of acetylcholine receptor is particularly associated with memory impairment (Bymaster et al 1993, Ohno et al 1994) and that M2 receptor antagonists may be associated with improvements in memory, including attenuating the effects of M1 receptor blockade, perhaps by increasing acetylcholine release (Baratti et al 1993, Bymaster et al 1993). Nicotinic receptor antagonists do not appear to impair cognitive function in the same way as antimuscarinic drugs, but nicotine itself has been shown to improve aspects of cognitive performance, such as attentional function, in human beings, including those with early stage Alzheimer's disease (Sahakian & Coull 1994, Sahakian et al 1989). Nicotine has also been shown to enhance short-term memory in a delayed matching-to-sample task in monkeys, an effect that was reversed by treatment with scopolamine (Terry et al 1993).

Such data support attempts to improve (generally by reducing side effects) systemic procholinergic therapies for neurological and perhaps other disorders associated with cognitive decline. Some cholinesterase inhibitors, such as tacrine, have been used with limited success in this regard in animals and patient groups (Jakala et al 1993, Sahakian et al 1993). New ways of enhancing brain cholinergic function are also in development. For example, β-carboline inverse agonists at the benzodiazepine receptor can disinhibit cholinergic neuronal activity in the basal forebrain by opposing the inhibitory effects of GABA at receptors on these neurons, thereby increasing acetylcholine release in the neocortex (Sarter et al 1988). More recently, antagonists at the galanin receptor have been reported to enhance both acetylcholine release and spatial learning in rats (Crawley 1993, Ogren et al 1993), though there are reports to the contrary (Aspley & Fone 1993). The approach follows from the demonstration of the coexistence of the neuropeptide galanin in some forebrain cholinergic neurons, especially in the medial septum (Pasqualotto & Vincent 1991). Molecular biology has also influenced this research. For example, fibroblasts have been genetically modified to express the acetylcholine biosynthetic enzyme, choline acetyltransferase (ChAT), to produce and release acetylcholine when implanted into the brain (Fisher et al 1991). Such transplanted cells can apparently restore cognitive functions in rats with forebrain lesions (see below) (Winkler et al 1995).

METHODOLOGICAL ADVANCES

While the cognitive effects of drugs having therapeutic potential must be explored after systemic administration—the most likely regimen in human beings—this psychopharmacological approach fails to indicate the sites at which such drugs exert their effects. Moreover, the psychological processes that are affected by altering cholinergic transmission in this way are not always clear, nor are the mechanisms by which these processes can be influenced within discrete areas of the cortical and subcortical brain. Not until the early 1980s were antibodies to ChAT developed (Levey et al 1983), enabling for the first time accurate description of the organization of cholinergic neurons in the brain and allowing direct experimental manipulation of central cholinergic neurons. Careful use of retrograde and anterograde tract-tracing techniques, and the regional measurement of cholinergic markers following localized lesions, have led to a clear understanding not only of the site of origin but of the projections of cholinergic neurons in the brain. Some general principles of organization have emerged, but disagreement remains about the functional organization of the brain cholinergic systems.

It is generally agreed that there are two major groups of cholinergic neurons. The first is in the basal forebrain within the medial septal nucleus (MS), vertical (vdB) and horizontal (hdB) limb nuclei of the diagonal band of Broca, and the nucleus basalis magnocellularis (nbm), also called the nucleus basalis of Meynert in human beings, a site associated with profound neurodegeneration in Alzheimer's disease. Although located in relatively discrete sites, this group of neurons is often referred to as a continuum: the magnocellular basal forebrain cholinergic system (Mesulam et al 1983a,b). The latter notation distinguishes these neurons from the second major group of cholinergic neurons, which are found in the brainstem (excluding the neurons found in cranial nerve motor nuclei) in the region of the pedunculopontine tegmental nucleus (PPTg) and laterodorsal pontine tegmentum (Mesulam et al 1983a, Rye et al 1987). Basal forebrain cholinergic neurons innervate neocortical, juxtallocortical (cingulate cortex), and allocortical sites (hippocampus, basolateral amygdala, and olfactory bulb), whereas brainstem cholinergic neurons, particularly PPTg neurons, innervate principally the thalamus (for an overview of cholinergic neurons in the rat brain, see Figure 1). There is disagreement, however, about whether the basal forebrain cholinergic neurons are a homogeneous group of neurons activated under common circumstances and having a unitary function (see e.g. Fibiger 1991, Hodges et al 1991, Richardson & DeLong 1988, Turner et al 1992) or whether they are, as we view them, separable groups with separable functions determined and constrained by their cortical projection targets.

Although we acknowledge that basal forebrain cholinergic neurons form a physical continuum and that they share many characteristics in common with the noradrenergic, dopaminergic, and serotoninergic neurons of the brainstem reticular core (see Robbins & Everitt 1995), we have undertaken our experimental approach with the conceptual framework that magnocellular cholinergic neurons in the MS, vdB, and nbm affect distinct psychological processes that are themselves dependent upon the cortical targets to which these groups of neurons more or less discretely project. Thus, the functions of the forebrain cholinergic neurons will best be defined through a clear understanding of the relationship between particular psychological processes (e.g. spatial or contextual learning, short-term memory, visual attention) and the cortical substrates of these processes that will be modulated by cholinergic (and other reticular, often called nonspecific) afferents to these cortical areas.

A major methodological problem has afflicted most studies on the behavioral and cognitive effects of manipulations of forebrain cholinergic neurons. Unlike the case with dopaminergic, noradrenergic, and serotoninergic neurons, a specific chemical neurotoxin for cholinergic neurons has become available for functional studies only recently. This has greatly limited the interpretability of the results of many experiments, in particular those involving lesions of the nbm (Everitt et al 1987) as well as the MS and vdB. The reason is simple. Cholinergic neurons of the nbm are interspersed with other neurons in the basal forebrain, especially GABA-containing neurons of the dorsal and ventral

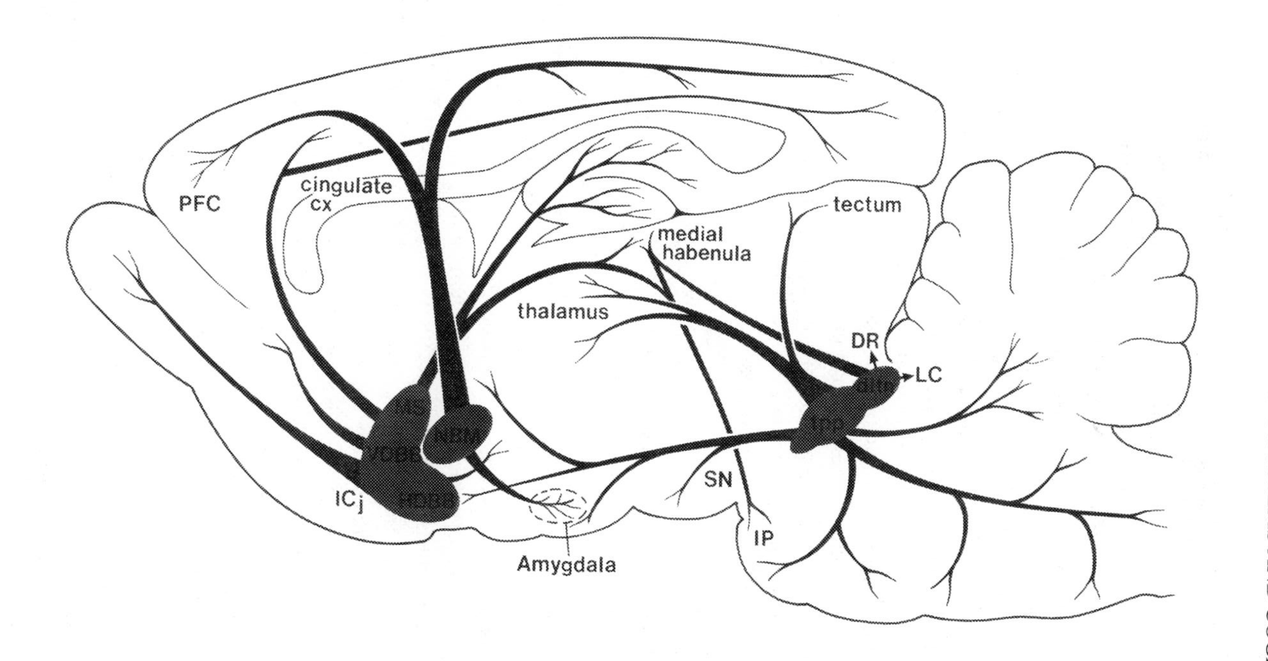

Figure 1 Schematic summary of the distribution of cholinergic neurons and their projections in the rat brain. Abbreviations: MS, medial septum (cell group Ch1); VDBB, vertical limb nucleus of the diagonal band of Broca (cell group Ch2); HDBB, horizontal limb nucleus of the diagonal band of Broca (cell group Ch3); NBM, nucleus basalis magnocellularis (cell group Ch4); tpp, pedunculopontine tegmental nucleus (cell group Ch5); dltn, laterodorsal tegmental nucleus (cell group Ch6); PFC, prefrontal cortex; ICj, islands of Calleja; SN, substantia nigra; IP, interpeduncular nucleus; DR, dorsal raphé; LC, locus ceruleus.

pallidum, the recently described "extended amygdala," and noncholinergic magnocellular corticopetal neurons (Alheid & Heimer 1988, Heimer et al 1995). Excluding dorsal pallidal neurons, the other cell populations have often been grouped together within the substantia innominata. Apart from a few studies using electrolytic lesions, which are very difficult to interpret because of their nonselectivity for fibers of passage as well as neuronal cell bodies, the most common lesioning approach used in functional studies has involved the infusion of excitatory amino acid analogues that produce what are usually described as cell body–specific, axon-sparing lesions. Excitotoxins are thus undoubtedly an improvement over physical lesioning methods, but even today there is doubt about the degree to which they truly spare axons of passage. They can certainly demyelinate axons; perhaps temporarily, but whether this may contribute to functional deficits has not yet been determined. Of much more concern is that many excitotoxins, especially those with efficacy at NMDA receptors, such as ibotenic acid (which has been by far the most commonly used) preferentially destroy noncholinergic pallidal and other neurons in the substantia innominata. Although this was demonstrated clearly in our own and other early studies (Dunnett et al 1987a, Everitt et al 1987), ibotenate continues to be used in contemporary studies of basal forebrain cholinergic function. This has led to interpretations of the effects of lesions as resulting from often somewhat minor cholinergic neuronal loss in the face of widespread and devastating destruction of the dorsal and ventral pallidum and other neurons in the substantia innominata (for a review, see Dunnett et al 1991).

Since our original observation of nonspecific neuroanatomical effects of NMDA receptor agonist–induced lesions, we embarked on a search for other excitotoxins that might have greater specificity for magnocellular cholinergic neurons, initially at a time when the diversity and complexity of excitatory amino acid receptors were not fully appreciated. We discovered that quisqualic acid (now known preferentially to affect non-NMDA AMPA and kainate receptors) more effectively, though not selectively, destroyed cholinergic nbm neurons than does ibotenate (see Figure 2), and that many behavioral and cognitive effects seen to follow ibotenate lesions were no longer seen following quisqualate lesions, despite larger reductions in cortical cholinergic markers (Dunnett et al 1987a, Etherington et al 1987). Finally, we discovered that AMPA itself (α-amino-3-hydroxy-5-methyl-4-propionic acid) when infused into the basal forebrain completely destroyed all magnocellular cholinergic neurons (see Figure 2) and resulted in greater than 70% reductions in ChAT activity in the neocortex (Page et al 1991). We have also demonstrated a cellular correlate of this greater efficacy of AMPA as a cholinergic toxin using c-*fos* activation techniques and by demonstrating the selective enrichment of the GluR-4 subtype of the AMPA receptor in this discrete population of nbm

1. Effects of Ibotenate, NMDA or Quinolinate infused into the basal forebrain

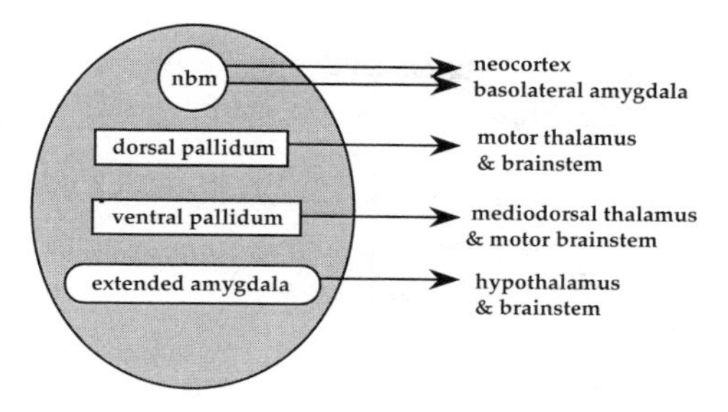

2. Effects of AMPA infusions into the basal forebrain

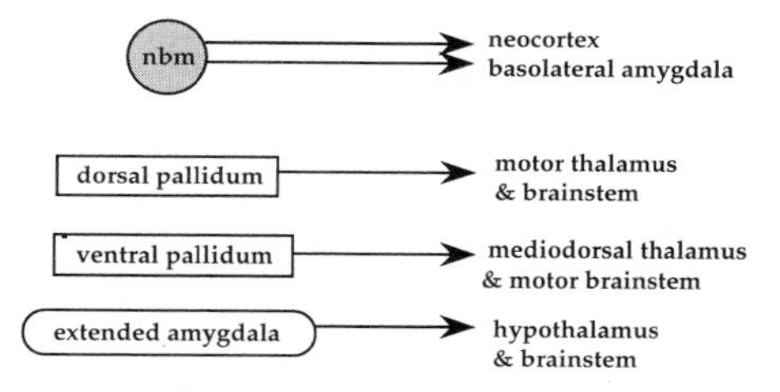

3. Effects of IgG-saporin infusions into the basal forebrain

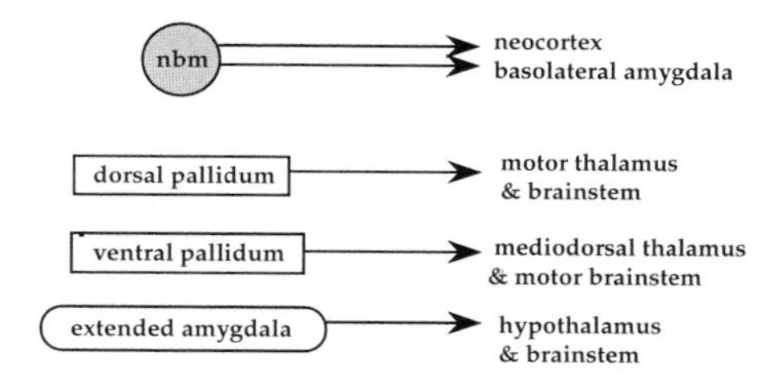

Figure 2 Schematic illustration of the neuronal cell groups damaged following infusion of various toxins into the basal forebrain. The shaded area denotes the lesion in each case. Note that ibotenate and other NMDA receptor agonists destroy nucleus basalis, dorsal and ventral pallidum, and also extended amygdala neurons. This is the most cholinergically nonselective lesion and also the least effective in terms of destruction of cholinergic neurons of the nbm. AMPA infusions destroy all nucleus basalis cholinergic neurons but in some cases can be associated with minor neuronal loss within the ventral pallidum and, presumably, the extended amygdala, although the latter has not been assessed directly in any study. IgG-saporin is selective for basal forebrain cholinergic neurons when infused locally into the basal forebrain but does not destroy those projecting to the amygdala.

neurons (Page & Everitt 1993, 1995; Page et al 1993, 1995). When used correctly, AMPA achieves this destruction of cholinergic neurons without appreciable damage to surrounding substantia innominata or pallidal neurons, but it cannot be called a selective cholinergic neurotoxin. Most importantly, use of this lesioning method emphasized even more that destroying nbm cholinergic neurons had few if any effects on learning and memory using test procedures employed (Dunnett et al 1991). As discussed below, the most consistent deficit after neocortical cholinergic depletion is one of visual attention (Muir et al 1994), not learning and memory—excluding passive avoidance retention that may be the consequence of cholinergic denervation of the amygdala (Page et al 1991b).

More recently, the immunotoxin ^{192}IgG-saporin has been developed (Wiley et al 1991) and employed in a growing number of studies of the cognitive effects of basal forebrain cholinergic neuron lesions. There seems little doubt that for these neurons, which are enriched in the low-affinity nerve growth factor (NGF) receptor, IgG-saporin is a powerful and selective lesioning tool. The antibody combines with this NGF receptor and is internalized into the cholinergic neurons that bear it, which allows the cytotoxin saporin then to destroy the neurons.

In the remainder of this review, we focus primarily on recent studies of the functions of the basal forebrain cholinergic system that have employed the most selective lesioning methods. In effect, this has been a search for those tasks that are sensitive to the more cholinergically specific lesions of MS, vdB, and nbm because this represents a most effective way of dissecting the psychological processes that are disrupted following cholinergic denervation, thereby resulting in impaired learning, memory, and attention. The search for an equally selective cholinergic toxin for the brainstem cholinergic neurons has not yet been successful (these neurons are not enriched in the NGF receptor). However, we briefly review some studies of the functional effects of manipulations of the PPTg. In vivo measures of cholinergic function, both neurochemical and electrophysiological, have also begun to clarify the conditions under which basal forebrain cholinergic neurons are activated, and these neurobiological clues to function are referred to in the context of lesion and psychopharmacological studies, below.

FUNCTIONS OF THE NUCLEUS BASALIS CORTICAL CHOLINERGIC SYSTEM

Studies of Learning and Memory: Rodents

Many experiments in the 1980s that investigated the effects of ibotenate- and other NMDA receptor agonist–induced lesions of the nbm (supposedly) confirmed the already widespread belief that this cortically projecting system subserved aspects of learning and memory. Almost every type of learning task, from working memory tasks such as delayed alternation to reference memory paradigms measuring spatial or conditional visual discrimination learning, is profoundly disrupted following such lesions (for a review, see Dunnett et al 1991). However, Dunnett et al raised concern about the cholinergic nature of these deficits when they described the massive destruction of dorsal and ventral pallidal neurons following ibotenate infusions into the basal forebrain and the often relatively minor loss of cortical cholinergic markers (Everitt et al 1987b). Moreover, Everitt et al (1987) demonstrated that pallidal lesions alone contributed to the marked deficit in conditional visual discrimination learning seen in our own experiments. Subsequently, in the search for more selective methods with which to lesion the nbm (described above), we demonstrated that in the face of more profound cholinergic neuronal and cortical marker loss following, initially, quisqualic acid– and then AMPA-induced nbm lesions, most of the learning deficits seen following NMDA agonist-induced lesions were no longer apparent (Dunnett et al 1991, Muir et al 1993, Page et al 1991b, Robbins et al 1989a). Others later confirmed these findings (Ammassari-Teule et al 1993, Markowska et al 1990, Olton et al 1992, Pang et al 1993, Wenk et al 1992) and began to share our view that the earlier, interpretation of lesion studies in terms of support for the hypothesis that cholinergic nbm neurons subserve learning and memory was generally unfounded. As discussed below, the introduction of IgG-saporin as a tool with which to lesion the nbm has generally confirmed the view that neocortical cholinergic depletion does not generally disrupt most forms of learning (Baxter et al 1995, Baxter & Gallagher 1996, Baxter et al 1996, Torres et al 1994, Wenk et al 1994; but see Berger-Sweeney et al 1994, Nilsson et al 1992). One task that was disrupted by NMDA-induced nbm lesions and that remained sensitive to nbm lesions made with AMPA was passive avoidance learning and retention (Page et al 1991). We argued that this may have been due to cholinergic denervation of the amygdala, a structure known to be important for this form of aversive conditioning (Page et al 1991). Lesions of the nbm made with IgG-saporin neither cholinergically denervate the amygdala (Heckers et al 1994) nor disrupt passive avoidance retention (Wenk et al 1994), a finding consistent with our earlier hypothesis.

There is less consensus about the impact on spatial learning of lesions of the cholinergic nbm (for a review, see McNamara & Skelton 1993). Many studies have shown that ibotenic acid– and other NMDA agonist–induced lesions of the basal forebrain result in often severe impairments in the acquisition of the Morris water maze (Connor et al 1991; Connor & Thal 1989; Dekker et al 1990; Dokla & Thal 1988; Mandel et al 1989a,b; Mandel & Thal 1988; Salamone et al 1987) and in radial maze performance (Hodges et al 1989,

Lerer & Warner 1986, Santucci & Haroutinian 1989, Turner et al 1992). However, more complete and selective lesions of the nbm made with quisqualic acid, and especially AMPA that reduced neocortical cholinergic markers to a much greater extent than was seen after lesions induced by ibotenate, were reported not to impair acquisition of the water maze (Ammassari-Teule et al 1993, Dunnett et al 1987b, Page et al 1991, Riekkinen & Sirvio 1990). Such observations led us to conclude that the deficits in spatial learning following nonspecific excitotoxic lesions of the basal forebrain are more related to pallidal cell loss and resultant disruption of one or more cortico-striato-pallidal loops that may subserve spatial cognition than to any disruption of cortical cholinergic projections. Synergistic effects of combined lesions of the nbm and MS (Turner et al 1992) could plausibly result from destruction of a hippocampal-ventral striato-pallidal pathway rather than damage to ascending cholinergic neurons, especially because ibotenate and high doses of quisqualic acid, which have nonselective excitotoxic effects in the basal forebrain, were used.

More recently, IgG-saporin has been used in increasing numbers of experiments on the role of nbm cholinergic neurons in spatial learning. Although intraventricular IgG-saporin does cause impairments in learning in the water maze (Berger-Sweeney et al 1994, Nilsson et al 1992), direct infusion into the nbm has no effect on such spatial learning, despite marked decreases in cortical acetylcholine but in concurrence with studies using AMPA and quisqualate (Baxter et al 1995, Torres et al 1994). Dornan et al (1995) reported a mild deficit in water maze acquisition following intra-nbm IgG-saporin, and Berger-Sweeney et al (1994) reported a deficit in acquisition, though one that is confounded by marked reductions in swim speed in the lesioned group (which would lead, of course, to increased escape latencies) and that is in any case a relatively minor deficit in learning compared with the effects of intraventricular infusions of the same toxin. The marked effects of intraventricular IgG-saporin on spatial learning may be related more to damage to striatal cholinergic neurons (reported in Berger-Sweeney et al 1994) than to neocortical cholinergic loss; it is well known that striatal damage produces deficits in the same task (Dunnett et al 1987b).

Together, these results suggest that nbm cortical cholinergic projections do not exert a major influence on spatial learning, an observation that, perhaps more surprisingly, also applies to the septo-hippocampal cholinergic projection (see below). However, this invites explanation of the marked paradox in Winkler et al (1995) and earlier studies (see Dunnett et al 1991) that deficits in learning tasks such as the water maze following the most nonselective of excitotoxic basal forebrain lesions (induced by ibotenic acid) can nevertheless be reversed by procholinergic treatments (Dunnett et al 1985, 1991; Fine et al 1985, Hodges et al 1991). In Winkler et al (1995), this cholinergic treatment was elegantly achieved by the implantation into neocortical sites of fibroblasts genetically modified to produce and release acetylcholine. Winkler et al concluded not only that acetylcholine is necessary for learning and memory but that its presence within the neocortex is sufficient to ameliorate spatial learning deficits and restore memory after damage to the nucleus basalis. This extraordinary claim is made on the basis of ibotenic acid–induced lesions that, even though they destroy some nbm cholinergic neurons, also destroy many pallidal neurons that are key elements in, for example, hippocampal-striatal loops central to the mechanisms underlying learning in the water maze (Annett et al 1989, Morris et al 1981, Sutherland et al 1983). Cholinergic reversal of a noncholinergic deficit, even when achieved through sophisticated molecular neurobiological innovations, should not really surprise us, because the ameliorative effects of the grafted cells could be mediated at cholinergic receptor sites other than the site of implantation or through other nonspecific mechanisms (including, possibly, other factors secreted by the modified cells (for a thorough discussion of this issue, see Dunnett et al 1991). At best, complete destruction of the nbm cholinergic neurons results in no—or only mild—deficits in spatial learning in tasks such as the Morris water maze, deficits that in any case are much less profound than those seen in attentional function following similar lesions.

Studies of Learning and Memory: Primates

Another approach to the difficult problem of the functions of the nbm is to study the effects of lesions of this structure in nonhuman primates. The advantages of this strategy are as follows: (*a*) the primate nbm is more spatially separated from the dorsal pallidum, and so it is more feasible to make lesions of the nbm without damaging the dorsal pallidum; (*b*) comparisons of cognitive deficits are more plausible between human beings and monkeys than rodents, especially because similar test paradigms can be used.

Early studies used ibotenic acid to make lesions of the nbm/substantia innominata region in Old World cynomolgus monkeys and employed delayed nonmatch-to-sample (DNMTS) tasks to quantify possible deficits in visual recognition memory. In fact, nbm lesions had little effect on relearning DNMTS tasks at 10-s delay, or when lists of stimuli were used to make the task more challenging (Aigner et al 1987). The lesioned animals were, however, more sensitive to the behaviorally disruptive effects of scopolamine, though this was true even for monkeys subsequently discovered not to have sustained major damage to the cortical cholinergic projections. One explanation may be that the monkeys' greater susceptibility to scopolamine resulted from damage to striatal outflow, as a consequence of damage to the globus pallidus. The lesioned monkeys were also less susceptible to beneficial effects of systemic physostigmine. A follow-up study investigated the effects of adding additional damage to the cholinergic basal forebrain by adding excitotoxic lesions to the medial septal and diagonal band of Broca (Aigner et al 1991). The study showed a deficit in the relearning of the DNMTS task at 10 s, but no convincing evidence could be provided for a recognition memory deficit that depended on cholinergic loss.

These findings on learning and memory contrasted with studies of a New World monkey, the common marmoset (Ridley et al 1985, 1986, 1988). Initial impairments in the retention of preoperatively acquired visual discriminations were observed, or impairments in visual discrimination reversal performance following ibotenic acid–induced lesions of the nbm were seen. These effects were also modulated by cholinergic drugs, suggesting, but not proving, that they resulted specifically from cholinergic cell loss. The transient nature of the deficits in visual discrimination retention and in visual discrimination learning was underlined by a further experiment that employed NMDA to induce lesions of the nbm (Roberts et al 1992). This study showed that serial reversal learning of visual discriminations was especially sensitive to the effects of nbm lesions, the progressive improvements in responding in sham-operated marmosets not occurring in animals with nbm lesions. The perseverative nature of this responding is similar to that seen after lesions of the prefrontal cortex, one of the regions most depleted of cholinergic markers in this study. Similar reversal learning deficits have also been observed in rats with nbm lesions (AC Roberts, unpublished observations). The cognitive inflexibility of the basal forebrain–lesioned monkeys could also be inferred from the relative lack of distractibility caused by changes to irrelevant stimuli in the discrimination tasks (Roberts et al 1994).

To resolve these apparent discrepancies in effects of basal forebrain lesions between Old World and New World monkeys, Voytko et al (1994) made combined lesions of the nbm, vdb, and medial septum in five cynomolgus monkeys and gave them a battery of tests of recognition memory (DNMTS), visual and spatial discrimination learning, and delayed-response and reversal learning. No deficits were observed on any of these tasks, except when scopolamine was used as a challenge treatment and the lesioned animals performed worst on the DNMTS task. However, in a subset of these lesioned monkeys, impairments were seen in a task measuring aspects of spatial attention (see below). Likely the major discrepancy with earlier results is the failure to observe deficits in visual discrimination reversal in the lesioned monkeys, with substantial reductions in cortical ChAT activity throughout the neocortex. This could have resulted from several differences in methodology between the two experiments. The visual discriminations employed in the experiments by Roberts et al (1992) were probably more difficult than the object discriminations employed by Voytko et al (1994) and so may have been more sensitive to detecting reversal deficits. Moreover, the lesions made by Roberts et al (1992) targeted the anterior nbm, which resulted in greater reductions of ChAT activity in the anterior than in the posterior neocortex. Thus, it is possible that the significant effects on reversal learning resulted from greater cholinergic depletions in the prefrontal cortex. However, it is also plausible that the impaired reversal learning in the experiments on the marmosets resulted from damage to noncholinergic neurons in the vicinity of the excitotoxin infusions into the basal forebrain. Whatever the final conclusions of these experiments, susbstantial damage to the cholinergic basal forebrain in monkeys fails to produce major learning and memory deficits, a result in basic agreement with the results of experiments in rodents (see above).

Studies of Attentional Function

Following the realization that increasingly selective and complete cholinergic nbm lesions did not generally impair learning, it was quite clear that further insight into the functions of the neocortical cholinergic system would be gained by defining tasks that are sensitive to nbm lesions induced by infusing AMPA or, in recent years, IgG-saporin. One such task measures aspects of visual attentional function using a five-choice serial reaction-time task based on a human test of continuous performance. In this task, rats are trained to detect brief 0.5-s flashes of light presented randomly in one of five discrete spatial locations in a curved array at one end of a specially designed apparatus (Carli et al 1983). Responses are made at the location of the just-presented stimulus, and if correct, the rat must move to the opposite end of the apparatus to collect earned food and turn rapidly to monitor the array for the next stimulus presentation. Robbins et al (1989) had demonstrated large impairments in this task following ibotenate-induced lesions of the nbm, but unlike the case with many learning tasks, these deficits were still seen following quisqualate- and AMPA-induced lesions of the nbm (Muir et al 1994, Robbins et al 1989). The deficit following AMPA-induced lesions that depleted the neocortex of ChAT by around 70% was long-lasting and primarily seen as an impairment in accuracy. The impairment in lesioned rats could be ameliorated by lengthening the stimulus duration, and in rats that had shown some recovery in their accuracy of performance after the cortical cholinergic depletion, their deficit could be reinstated by shortening the stimulus duration. These observations further strengthened the view that the deficit was one of visual attentional function. Other control procedures ruled out possible effects on motivation or sensory function (Muir et al 1994). Several additional converging lines of evidence support the view that lesions of the cholinergic nbm result rather specifically in attentional deficits (Muir et al 1992a, 1995). First, the impairment seen following AMPA-induced lesions can be reversed by treatment with physostigmine and nicotine but not other drugs such as a 5-HT3 receptor antagonist, ondansetron (Muir et al 1995). The transplantation of cholinergically enriched fetal neurons into the cortex of rats with quisqualate-induced nbm lesions also ameliorated the deficit in performance accuracy under certain conditions (Muir et al 1992a). Infusion of the GABA receptor agonist—muscimol—directly into the basal forebrain both decreased the activity of cortically projecting nbm neurons (Dudchenko & Sarter 1991) and impaired accuracy on the five-choice task, a deficit that was ameliorated by systemic physostigmine (Muir et al 1992b). It is important to note that performance of a conditional visual discrimination was also impaired by muscimol infusions into the basal forebrain, but this was not reversed by systemic physostigmine, which supports our finding that deficits in this task following ibotenate lesions were not because of cholinergic cell loss (Muir et al 1992a). Finally, intraventricular infusions of the choline uptake blocker hemicholinium, which is a cholinergically selective treatment that lacks neuroanatomical site specificity, resulted in impairments in visual attention that were identical to those seen following nbm lesions and were also reversed by systemic treatment with physostigmine (Muir et al 1992a).

Converging lines of evidence supporting our hypothesis that the cortically projecting cholinergic nbm system is involved in attentional function have also been reported by other laboratories. For example, in a two-choice reaction-time task, infusions of muscimol into the region of the nbm resulted in impairments of visual attention (Pang et al 1993), which is consistent with the results of our own study described above (Muir 1992b). Chiba et al (1995) have also shown that IgG-saporin lesions of the nbm disrupt incremental, but not decremental, attentional processes. In a series of studies involving both central and peripheral manipulation of cholinergic transmission, Sarter and colleagues have provided much evidence for a role for nbm neurons in attentional function (Holley & Sarter 1995, Holley et al 1995, Sarter 1994, Sarter & Bruno 1997, Wendelin et al 1995). In addition, in a novel test of vigilance, infusions of IgG-saporin into the basal forebrain were followed by a marked impairment in lesioned rats' abilities accurately to detect signals, although not in their abilities to correctly reject nonsignal trials (McGaughy et al 1996). In studies of the decline in attentional function in aged rats, clear evidence has been presented of increased sensitivity to the attention-improving effects of tacrine (a cholinesterase inhibitor) and attention-impairing effects of scopolamine (a muscarinic receptor antagonist) (Jones et al 1995). These results were interpreted as supportive of an attentional function of the nbm-cortical cholinergic projection, a conclusion also reached by Gallagher & Colombo (1995) in their review of the cholinergic hypothesis of cognitive decline in aging. Finally, experiments in which acetylcholine release has been measured in vivo in freely moving animals have also provided evidence supporting results of the lesion experiments reviewed above (Acquas et al 1996, Himmelheber et al 1995).

In the ambitious and impressive experiment on the effects of basal forebrain lesions targeted on the MS, vdB, and nbm in cynomolgus monkeys referred to above, further evidence of an important attentional function for cholinergic projections was found (Voytko et al 1994). In contrast with the lack of effects in several learning and memory tasks (see above), marked impairments were seen in a test of covert orienting used with human subjects in which a cue signaled target location in 80% of trials on a computer touch-screen. The impairments were expressed as significant increases in the latency to respond to peripheral cues, particularly when the spatial targets were invalidly cued. The lesioned monkeys were somewhat faster (though not significantly so) at responding to the target following the initiation of responding. The deficit was interpreted as one of focused attention that was independent of any alterations in motor ability and comparable to deficits seen in performance of a similar task in patients with Alzheimer's disease (Freed et al 1989, Parasuraman & Haxby 1993).

We have also demonstrated impaired attentional function in patients with Alzheimer's disease using the same or analogous (rapid visual information processing and five-choice serial reaction-time) tasks as employed in our animal experiments, and improvements in attention following treatment with tacrine also were evident (Eagger et al 1991, Sahakian & Coull 1994, Sahakian et al 1993). These deficits contrast with the relative sparing of attentional set-shifting in an analogue of the Wisconsin Card Sorting Test, termed an extradimensional shift task, in patients early in the course of probable Alzheimer's disease (Sahakian et al 1990). The relative selectivity of deficits in attention following basal forebrain damage is shown by the failure of nbm lesions to disrupt performance of the same extradimensional shift task in marmosets, even though reversal learning is impaired (Roberts et al 1992; see above). Thus, there are quite strong parallels between the attentional deficits in human patients with Alzheimer's disease and experimental animals with lesions of the cholinergic basal forebrain. In reviewing the sometimes complex literature on the functions of cholinergic systems in monkeys, Voytko (1996) concluded that the evidence strongly favors an important role for the nbm cholinergic system in certain aspects of attentional function.

FUNCTIONS OF THE SEPTO-HIPPOCAMPAL CHOLINERGIC SYSTEM

It has been apparent from the outset of investigations of the functions of the cholinergic medial septum that experiments should be undertaken within a conceptual framework determined by current understanding of the functions of the hippocampus, to which these neurons project. Although the precise role of the hippocampus in learning and memory is still debated, there are reliable examples of learning or memory deficits following lesions of this structure in rats, including impairments in the acquisition of the water maze (Morris et al 1981) and performance in the radial eight-arm maze (Olton et al 1979); both tests require forms of spatial processing. The hippocampus is probably essential for more than simply spatial tasks, but these may typify the nature of demands made on the hippocampus when numerous cues and their relations must be processed. Hippocampal damage also impairs contextual learning (Bouton 1992, Good & Honey 1991, Kim & Fanselow 1992, Selden et al 1991), a conclusion consistent with the view that space is an example of a context that contains and predicts, rather than competes with, explicit cues (Nadel & Willner 1980). Selden et al (1991), using a paradigm for simultaneously measuring aversive conditioning to explicit CSs and the background context (Marlin 1981), showed that excitotoxic lesions of the hippocampus impaired aversive contextual conditioning without affecting aversive conditioning to a CS, whereas similar lesions of the amygdala had the opposite pattern of effects.

Many paradigms for studying amnesia in rats and monkeys depend on short-term or so-called working memory rather than reference memory. One such classic working memory task, sensitive to hippocampal lesions, is the working memory version of the radial maze (Olton et al 1979). Simple analogues of this procedure include forced trial delayed alternation procedures (Rawlins & Olton 1982) and their operant counterpart, delayed nonmatching to position (DNMP) (Dunnett 1985, Rawlins & Olton 1982). Fornix lesions and lesions of the hippocampal formation reliably cause delay-dependent deficits (Aggleton et al 1992, Dunnett 1985). In other versions of spatial nonmatching, rats with hippocampal or fornix lesions have been reported to be impaired [spatial delayed nonmatching in the T-maze or in an operant chamber (Etherington et al 1987, Markowska et al 1989)], but in nonspatial delayed recognition tasks, apparently damage to the hippocampal system does not usually compromise performance, e.g. in delayed nonmatching to sample with trial unique objects (Aggleton et al 1986, Rothblat & Kromer 1991; but see Raffaele & Olton 1988, who employed nonspatial delayed matching to sample with repeated stimuli).

In our own experiments on this medial septal component of the basal forebrain cholinergic system, we have studied the effects of AMPA-induced MS lesions in three tasks sensitive to hippocampal damage, namely spatial learning in the Morris water maze, aversive contextual and CS trace conditioning (the procedure used by Selden et al 1991), and an operant delayed nonmatching-to-position task conducted in an apparatus that minimizes the adoption of mediating strategies (Etherington et al 1987). The results provide an intriguing and, in some cases, surprising indication of the functions of cholinergic modulation of hippocampal-dependent processes.

Spatial learning measured in the water maze was, in two replications of the study involving both large and small diameter mazes, generally unimpaired following AMPA-induced medial septal lesions that greatly reduced hippocampal extracellular acetylcholine levels, measured using in vivo microdialysis (McAlonan et al 1995a). Less selective excitotoxic and electrolytic lesions of the MS have been reported to cause appreciable deficits in the water maze (Hagan et al 1988, Kelsey & Vargas 1993, Marston et al 1993), but many studies report only mild and even no effects on this task of electrolytic, excitotoxic, or colchicine lesions of the MS (Barone et al 1991, Decker et al 1992, Sutherland & Rodriguez 1989). Moreover, it has been shown more recently that lesions of the cholinergic neurons in the MS induced by infusions of IgG-saporin are also without effect on the acquisition of the water maze (Baxter et al 1995, Berger-Sweeney et al 1994, Torres et al 1994). Whereas with AMPA-induced lesions of the medial septum, it was unclear as to the degree to which damage to the GABA-ergic innervation of the hippocampal formation may have compromised the consequences of cholinergic neuronal loss task (McAlonan et al 1995a), this difficulty does not apply to the effects of IgG-saporin lesions. Thus, it can be concluded that the septo-hippocampal cholinergic projection does not modulate to any significant degree spatial processing occurring in the hippocampus as assessed in the water maze task (McAlonan et al 1995a).

The perhaps surprising lack of effect of AMPA and IgG-saporin-induced cholinergic medial septal lesions on acquisition or performance of the water maze reflects the common assumption that disrupting the subcortical projection paths to a cortical target will result in deficits at least qualitatively similar to those observed following lesions of the target structure itself. In reconciling the apparent qualitative variation in effects of hippocampal and septal lesions on spatial learning in the water maze, it might be suggested that the reference memory requirements of this task require little modulation by the cholinergic innervation of the hippocampus. In addition, the role of the hippocampus itself in acquisition of the water maze is not as major as once thought. Thus, if excitotoxic damage is restricted to the hippocampus proper, sparing the subiculum and overlying neocortex, lesioned animals eventually acquire this task (Morris et al 1990). However, if damage extends to include the subiculum, the pattern of impairment is similar to that generated by conventional (aspirative) hippocampal lesions (Morris et al 1990). It seems that the water maze may not be sensitive enough to highlight the more subtle performance difficulties that accompany the more selective lesions. Moreover, a number of alternative strategies could be available to a lesioned animal that might compensate for restricted neural damage. For instance, recognition of where the hidden platform is could depend on a number of cues or just one, and aspects of procedural representation such as recall of a response could be important (Morris et al 1981).

In experiments on aversive contextual and discrete cue conditioning, AMPA-induced lesions of the cholinergic neurons enhanced contextual learning but impaired conditioning to a trace CS (McAlonan et al 1995b). There were no apparent differences between sham and lesioned animals in shock sensitivity, drinking patterns following water deprivation, or reaction to a novel stimulus in a familiar environment; therefore, the result showed behavioral selectivity within the task. Moreover, in these same lesioned subjects, spatial learning measured in the water maze was unimpaired (McAlonan et al 1995b). A striking finding was that AMPA-induced cholinergic medial septal lesions produced almost opposite effects on learning about an aversive context and spatial learning or memory in the water maze, enhanced in the former case and unaffected or mildly impaired late in acquisition in the latter case. In addition, deficits in CS trace conditioning were particularly evident at a longer, 30-s CS-US interval. Several issues arise from these effects of MS lesions. First, there is the paradox of how hippocampally mediated functions such as spatial learning or memory and contextual conditioning are either only mildly affected or actually enhanced following substantial cholinergic deafferentation, whereas hippocampal lesions impair both (Jarrard 1993, Selden et al 1991). Second, there is the issue of the more general theoretical significance of this pattern of results for understanding the nature of the relationship between spatial and contextual processing. Finally, the significance of impaired trace, or delayed conditioning following septal lesions, may be important for an understanding of the possible functions of the hippocampus in short-term working memory processes.

Clearly in the case of contextual conditioning, opposite effects of hippocampal cell body lesions and medial septal cholinergic cell body lesions have been shown in two studies from our own laboratory (McAlonan et al 1995b, Selden et al 1991). A similar problem has presented itself in interpreting the effects of dorsal noradrenergic bundle lesions, which produce profound noradrenergic loss in the hippocampus and yet also enhance contextual conditioning (Selden et al 1990). One way of explaining such contrasting results is to analyze the effect of these neurotransmitters on signal processing in the hippocampus and neocortex. Boosting noradrenergic activity in the hippocampus appears to enhance the processing of a salient CS and diminishes the processing of the same stimulus when insignificant (Segal & Bloom 1976). Thus, noradrenergic hippocampal denervation could enhance contextual conditioning by enhancing the processing of background stimuli at the expense of explicit CSs. In the hippocampus, acetylcholine can similarly have inhibitory and facilitatory effects depending on which synapses predominate (Krnjevic 1987, Krnjevic et al 1988). In general, however, electrophysiological evidence indicates that the septal cholinergic input to the hippocampus is inhibitory (Buzsáki 1989, Buzsáki et al 1989), which suggests that acetylcholine may increase "signal-to-noise" ratios by decreasing noise, that is, the processing of background or contextual stimuli.

The deficit in CS trace conditioning observed in our experiments (McAlonan et al 1995b) may possibly be considered in terms of an impairment in short-term memory. Nontrace CS conditioning depends critically on the amygdala rather than the hippocampus (Hiroi & White 1991, McDonald & White 1993, Selden et al 1991). However, trace conditioning is more sensitive to hippocampal lesions, e.g. in rabbit nictitating membrane preparation (Moyer et al 1990, Solomon et al 1986). Thus, the impairments in trace conditioning following septal cholinergic lesions were not altogether unexpected, although it is of considerable interest that the effects were much larger in the 30-s trace condition, where the load on short-term memory was greatest. These data suggest, therefore, that another role for the cholinergic input to the hippocampus related to that discussed above is in the prolongation of the pattern of neuronal activity subserving representation of the CS, or signal, thus optimizing associative conditioning to the US. In the neocortex, neurons give much stronger and more prolonged responses to various sensory inputs following iontophoresis of ACh (Krnjevic 1987). This is consistent with our observations described above that rats with cholinergic denervation of the anterior neocortex following AMPA-induced lesions of the nbm are maximally impaired in detecting brief flashes of light in a continuous performance paradigm and react normally to lengthened duration of the signals (see above; Muir et al 1994).

The possible involvement of hippocampal cholinergic mechanisms in short-term memory was further investigated in a spatial DNMP task using a specially constructed operant chamber. Such procedures have revealed delay-dependent effects of systemic anticholinergic drugs in some studies, and it has been a generally held assumption that these systemic drug effects were mediated by the hippocampus, given the effects of hippocampal lesions themselves in producing short-term memory impairments. Infusions of AMPA into the medial septal nucleus resulted in cholinergic deafferentation of the hippocampus, as assessed by both in vivo and ex vivo neurochemistry, and produced a delay-dependent deficit in spatial working memory (McAlonan et al 1995a). In contrast, in the same experiments it was shown that cholinergic deafferentation of the cingulate cortex induced by AMPA infusions into the vdB resulted in a delay-independent performance deficit. These latter rats also adopted biased response strategies during the imposition of a delay (discussed below; McAlonan et al 1995a). Together with our earlier work showing delay-independent effects of nbm lesions in the same DNMP task (Etherington et al 1987; see above), the results strongly implicate the septo-hippocampal cholinergic system in spatial short-term memory function. Such a conclusion is bolstered by the finding by Torres et al (1994) of impaired DNMP performance in rats having received infusions of IgG-saporin into the medial septum but not into the nbm, in a task similar to that used by McAlonan et al (1995a).

Overall, the pattern of results from our studies on the septo-hippocampal cholinergic system provide an interesting basis for speculation about the role of cholinergic hippocampal mechanisms in learning and memory. Hippocampal cholinergic depletion enhanced contextual learning processes at the expense of conditioning to a weak CS, and because hippocampal lesions impair contextual learning (see above), removing cholinergic afferents may possibly disinhibit hippocampal processing. Disinhibition in the hippocampus increases noise or contextual signals, and consequently the system is biased toward using contextual cues from which weak CS signals seem not to be distinguished (for further discussion of this point, see McAlonan et al 1995b). Such an interpretation might suggest that the cholinergic system innervating the hippocampal formation functions in part to keep selected cues in the foreground of a context. The impairment in visuospatial short-term memory following septal cholinergic lesions may be interpreted similarly because in the absence of cholinergic modulation of the hippocampus, sample information in the DNMP task may not be maintained in the foreground during delays, and hence a short-term memory deficit would be apparent.

FUNCTIONS OF THE VERTICAL DIAGONAL BAND OF BROCA CHOLINERGIC PROJECTION

The vdB and the MS are the main sources of the cholinergic innervation of the cingulate cortex. Both cholinergic nuclei, especially the MS, also innervate other structures implicated in certain forms of learning and memory—including the hippocampus and certain regions of limbic cortex—which are also compromised in Alzheimer's disease and related disorders. Relatively few studies have addressed the role of these projections (but see Hagan et al 1988, Hodges et al 1991, Olton et al 1991) in comparison with studies of the nbm, and hardly any have considered the problems of interpretation of the effects of fiber-sparing excitotoxins. In a recent series of studies, the visual conditional discrimination task previously employed in assessing the effects of nbm lesions (Everitt et al 1987, Robbins et al 1989a) was used to assess the effects of excitotoxic lesions of the MS and vdB neurons (Marston et al 1994). These lesions produced considerable reductions (about 50% on average) in ChAT activity in both the hippocampus and the cingulate cortex without effects on cortical monoamines. However, linear regression analysis showed that the reductions of ChAT activity in the cingulate cortex were most closely related to the deficit in performance. Specifically, when errors of commission made when asymptotic levels of performance had been attained were considered for both sham-operated controls and rats lesioned using quisqualic acid, the correlation was –0.82 ($p < 0.001$), which accounted for about 70% of the variance. When the controls and lesion animals were analyzed separately, the slopes of the lines were similar, which justified their incorporation into an overall analysis.

A second experiment confirmed the conclusion in rats receiving AMPA-induced lesions of the same region, which produced similar degrees of loss of cingulate and hippocampal cholinergic markers but with less nonspecific damage at the site of the infusion in the basal forebrain (Marston et al 1994). In this case, the correlation was –0.94 ($p < 0.001$). These relationships between accuracy of performance in the discrimination task and central cholinergic function are as strong as any we have observed in the literature to date. Clearly the presence of a correlation does not necessarily prove a causal relationship, but it seems unlikely that the very high values arise from an artifactual association with another, unmeasured neurochemical variable. There were also weaker associations between discrimination performance and ChAT activity in other brain regions, notably the hippocampus. However, a contribution from the hippocampus to this visual conditional discrimination task seems unlikely for at least two reasons. First, excitotoxic lesions of the entire hippocampal formation have relatively little effect on the acquisition or performance of this conditional discrimination task (Marston et al 1993). Therefore, it is difficult to see why cholinergic depletion of the same structure should have any major effect. Second, when the almost unavoidable correlation between ChAT activity in the cingulate cortex and the hippocampus was partialed out of the relationships between ChAT activity and errors of commission, the correlation with hippocampal reductions was reduced, becoming nonsignificant. This result is interesting given the very clear effects in the experiments by Ridley et al (1989) showing that excitotoxic lesions of the septum/vdB region produce impairments in learning visuoconditional discriminations in marmosets, which they attribute to loss of hippocampal acetylcholine, though ChAT activity was not measured in the cingulate cortex in that study. Nevertheless, these investigators do observe significant deficits in the task following fornix transection that can apparently be reversed by application of cholinergically enriched tissue transplanted into the hippocampus (Ridley & Baker 1993). Therefore, the exact contribution of the hippocampal cholinergic innervation to conditional learning remains in doubt.

The results in Marston et al (1994) add to the sparse published data on the functions of the cingulate cortex in the rat. Anatomical, behavioral, and electrophysiological evidence compels the conclusion that the functions of the anterior and posterior cingulate cortex are interactive though quite distinct, the latter linked to the functions of the hippocampal formation and posterior association cortex (Buchanan & Powell 1982, Gabriel 1990, Kolb 1984, Vogt 1985). Thus, in a notable series of experiments on discriminated avoidance conditioning in rabbits, discriminative neuronal activity developed earlier in training in the anterior rather than the posterior cingulate cortex, and the latter area has been suggested to be more concerned with the maintenance of the avoidance response than its acquisition (Gabriel 1990). This hypothesis could not be extended directly to the results of Marston et al (1994) because the dissection used to quantify the effects of the cholinergic lesion was more centered on the anterior cingulate cortex, with the most caudal tissue sample situated just posterior to the genu of the corpus callosum.

However, recent findings have shown possible relationships to the work of Gabriel and collaborators (Bussey et al 1996, Muir et al 1996). Separate excitotoxic lesions of the anterior and posterior cingulate cortex have revealed quite different effects on the conditional visual discrimination task. Although anterior cingulate cortex lesions facilitated learning during the early stages of training, posterior cingulate cortex lesions significantly impaired the attainment of asymptotic levels of performance, or "late learning" (Bussey et al 1996). Thus, the effects of discrete AMPA-induced lesions of the vdB were investigated. These produced small (30%) but significant reductions in ChAT activity in both the anterior and posterior portions of the cingulate cortex in the absence of decreases in other regions. The results revealed that the rats with vdB lesions were significantly facilitated in their ability to acquire the conditional visual discrimination task but showed significant impairment of late learning (Muir et al 1996). Therefore, it is plausible to hypothesize that the correlation between performance and the reduction in cingulate cortex ChAT activity previously observed (Marston et al 1994) arises from reductions of acetylcholine in the posterior cingulate cortex, and that the facilitated acquisition observed from effects of cholinergic depletion in the anterior cingulate cortex. These results are obviously also concordant with the general hypothesis of Gabriel and colleagues that these two sectors of the cingulate cortex participate in two interactive and competitive memory processes (Gabriel 1990), though the exact nature of the involvement of the cingulate cortex may depend on the form of motivation (appetitive vs aversive) associated with each learning task. More specifically, they agree with findings that training-stage neuronal plasticity in the limbic thalamus and cingulate cortex during discriminative avoidance learning corresponds with training-induced changes in muscarinic receptor binding in the anterior thalamus and cingulate cortex (Vogt et al 1991).

The deficits produced by cholinergic deafferentation of the cingulate cortex evidently differ from those produced by cholinergic depletion from other regions. Previous results argue against a major deficit in conditional discrimination performance following loss of cholinergic neurons from the nbm, which innervates frontal and sensorimotor regions of the lateral cortex (Robbins et al 1989). However, such lesions are effective in impairing performance of a test of visual attentional function described above in which rats have to detect brief flashes of light presented randomly in different spatial locations (Muir et al 1994, Robbins et al 1989), a capacity that is impaired by lesions of the prefrontal rather than the cingulate cortex (Muir et al 1996). Moreover, cholinergic depletion from the cingulate cortex has no major effect on performance on this test of visual attention. The comparison among the effects of cholinergic loss from the major cortical domains of the nbm, vdB, and MS has been further strengthened by using a spatial working memory task, delayed nonmatching to position (see above), which is sensitive to fornix lesions and to cholinergic loss from the hippocampus following excitotoxic lesions of the MS (McAlonan et al 1995a). As described above, this latter deficit is delay dependent, which suggests a mnemonic basis rather than an inability to use a decisional rule to guide responding, such as that implicated in conditional discriminations. However, as may have been predicted, rats with vdB lesions leading to cingulate cortical cholinergic loss were impaired at precisely these aspects of the task. Thus, their impairments in accuracy were delay independent, occurring at all values of delay, including the shortest ones (McAlonan et al 1995a). Therefore, the deficit might most parsimoniously be described as one of the ability to utilize response rules through conditional discrimination.

The deficits associated with cingulate cholinergic loss are quite specific and highly related to the functions of the cingulate cortex itself. However, what is the exact contribution of the cholinergic input, and under which circumstances is it most apparent? It is, of course, possible that a fundamentally similar attentional deficit underlies the different impairments produced by lesions to the nbm, MS, and vdB, but is expressed in different ways, according to the different functions of the cortical regions to which they project. Any differences between the effects of lesions to the ascending cholinergic systems and the cortical domains to which they project may help answer this question, though firm conclusions are compromised because the lesions may have nonspecific, noncholinergic effects. However, in the context of the cingulate cortex, it is noteworthy that the vdB lesions impaired the delayed retention of conditional discrimination performance, whereas the posterior cingulate cortex lesion itself had no such effect (Muir et al 1996). Moreover, whereas excitotoxic lesions of the anterior cingulate cortex lead to increases in impulsive responding (Muir et al 1996), these are not seen following cholinergic depletion from this region. It would be of considerable interest to determine the effects of manipulations of signal duration on the acquisition and performance of conditional discrimination tasks in rats with vdB lesions. Such experiments, together with the suggestion derived from the finding of impaired retention described above of a specific weakening of retrieval processes following vdB lesions, might further support the general hypothesis that cholinergic activity at the cortical level effectively enhances signal-to-noise values for processing of information in a number of cortical domains.

FUNCTIONS OF THE BRAINSTEM CHOLINERGIC NEURONS

The brainstem cholinergic system (see Figure 1), originating in the Ch5 group of cells in the pedunculopontine tegmental nucleus (PPTg), the subpeduncular tegmental nucleus (SPTg), and the Ch6 group of the laterodorsal tegmental nucleus (LTDg), has for some time been a topic of considerable interest at the neuroanatomical and electrophysiological levels of analysis (Mesulam et al 1983a,b, Rye et al 1987, Sato et al 1987, Steriade 1991; for a review, see Inglis & Winn 1995). However, only relatively recently have behavioral neuroscientists attempted to define the functions of this cell group.

Some clues to these functions come from considering the forebrain targets of the cholinergic cells. The Ch5 group provides a widespread ascending innervation of the thalamus, whereas the Ch6 group, like that of the basal forebrain (Ch4), targets only certain thalamic nuclei. There are also descending projections to regions thought to be associated with the induction of REM sleep, in the caudal pons (Semba 1993). These projections emphasize the important role of the brainstem cholinergic projections as a chemically specific component of the reticular core of the brain, with likely functions in arousal and regulation of the sleep/wake cycle. Specifically, they may participate in the processes by which there is a transition from burst-firing to single-spiking modes of operation, by inducing a prolonged depolarization of thalamocortical cells (Steriade 1993). The cholinergic projections may thus inhibit the development of spindles and delta waves characteristic of slow-wave sleep.

A second major set of cholinergic projections (possibly from both Ch5 and Ch6 cell groups) are those to the dopaminergic neurons in both the substantia nigra and the ventral tegmental area, which innervate the dorsal and ventral striatum, respectively. The environmental circumstances eliciting firing in the mesencephalic dopamine cells are now quite well documented (Schultz 1992), though there is a continuing controversy about whether they are active during aversive as well as appetitive situations (Robbins & Everitt 1992).

There are a few behavioral studies of effects of manipulations of these cholinergic inputs to the mesencephalic dopamine neurons (e.g. Winn 1990, Winn et al 1983). These investigations tend to confirm the hypothesis that cholinergic activation of the substantia nigra *pars compacta* produces some effects, such as eating, that are reminiscent of mild stimulation of dopaminergic neurones, although there is little convincing evidence of the behavioral stereotypy that is produced by high doses of dopaminergic agonists (see Inglis & Winn 1995).

A detailed appraisal of the functions of these cholinergic cell groups in behavior would be premature until the appropriate studies comparing them either with the other chemically defined neurotransmitter systems of the reticular core (e.g. the noradrenergic and serotoninergic systems) or the basal forebrain cholinergic neurons (i.e. Ch4 cell group) are carried out. However, it is intriguing that these brainstem cholinergic neurons seem to participate in processes involving both arousal (in electroencephalographic terms) and behavioral activation. It seems likely, therefore, that they have fundamental roles in behavioral regulation that are at a more basic level than the modulation of memory and cognitive functioning. This is considered further in the review by Steckler et al (1994).

At present there is no straightforward method for inducing selective neurotoxicity in the brain stem cholinergic cells. AMPA is not as selective as in the case of the basal forebrain neurons, and these cells are not vulnerable to the immunotoxin IgG-saporin because they do not express NGF receptors (Inglis et al 1993, Rugg et al 1992). Such selectivity is desirable because of the many noncholinergic cells in the pedunculopontine region and the complexity of their neural connections. Moreover, this lack of specificity has confounded the interpretation of the effects of lesions of the PPTg on behavior and cognitive function. While some studies have reported deficits (e.g. Dellu et al 1991) and others not (Steckler et al 1994), it remains unclear whether the impairments reflect specific loss of brainstem cholinergic neurons. Therefore, at present, progress in understanding the functions of these brainstem cholinergic cells is likely to depend on interpreting the effects of infusions of cholinergic compounds at the sites of their termination in the thalamus and brainstem.

CONCLUDING COMMENTS

The field of cholinergic mechanisms in relation to behavior and cognition has made some significant advances in the 1990s. Indeed, there are some substantial achievements we have surveyed from a number of laboratories that have begun with the objective of determining the effects of selective lesions of the forebrain cholinergic systems, particularly the nbm. These observations stemmed from a reappraisal of the role of this cholinergic cell group in learning and memory, to suggest a no less fundamental role in aspects of attentional function. The initial observations have been supplemented by more experiments in a multidisciplinary endeavor that has included the in vivo neurochemical monitoring of acetylcholine release in the cortex of rats, the use of nonhuman primates in a sophisticated paradigm for measuring changes in spatial attention, and the use of analogous paradigms in human patients with Alzheimer's disease receiving cholinergic medication. Experiments with rats have also employed a task with clear parallels to a test of sustained attention in human beings to show comparable improvements in performance with cholinergic drugs such as the anticholinesterases and nicotine, as well as with cholinergically enriched neural transplants and the promise of even more refined means of boosting cholinergic function based on experimentation in animals (Fisher et al 1993; Sarter et al 1988, 1990; Winkler et al 1995).

Although they may be surprising to many investigators, these advances are compatible with previous theorizing about the functions of the cholinergic system based on human and animal psychopharmacological studies and on neurobiological investigations. In the former instance, Drachman & Sahakian (1979) postulated that the cholinergic system boosted the signal-to-noise ratio for information processing in the cerebral cortex, whereas early experiments by Warburton (1977) showed that systemic treatment with cholinergic agents could enhance stimulus control in rats.

In the neurobiological sphere, microiontophoretic application of acetylcholine to the cortex has been shown to enhance the selectivity of firing in the visual, auditory, and somatosensory cortices, as well as in the prefrontal cortex in rats, cats, and monkeys (Metherate et al 1988, Sato et al 1987, Sillito & Kemp 1983, Tremblay et al 1990). Cellular discharges evoked by presentation of a specific sensory stimulus in anesthetized animals were enhanced when acetylcholine was applied during stimulus presentation. Similar observations were extended to the fully awake rat for auditory tone–evoked responses in the auditory cortex (Edeline et al 1994, Hars et al 1993).

Specifying the conditions under which the cholinergic neurons are normally active may provide an important clue to their functions. Two major investigations of the electrophysiological properties of the basal forebrain neurons in response to various environmental circumstances do not agree in all aspects but suggest that the cells are active during the presentation of arousing stimuli, e.g. because of their novelty or because of their association with reward (Richardson & DeLong 1988, Wilson & Rolls 1990). These results can be interpreted as indicating an important role for the basal forebrain cholinergic system in cortical arousal, a view consistent with the effects of basal forebrain lesions on the cortical electroencephalogram (Buzsaki et al 1988, Riekkinen & Aaltonen 1991). It will be important in future studies to differentiate this form of arousal from that depending on activity in the coeruleo-cortical noradrenergic system, the raphé-cortical serotoninergic system, and the meso-telencephalic dopamine systems (for a review, see Robbins & Everitt 1995). Because of their interconnectivity with limbic structures, it seems likely that the basal forebrain neurons are not simply responding to stressors but also to stimuli with motivational salience deriving from associative learning.

It will also be important to determine the relative roles of the basal forebrain cholinergic systems and the brainstem cholinergic systems which target in particular the thalamus and the substantia nigra. We have reviewed evidence suggesting important roles for these systems in the regulation of the sleep-waking cycle (see Steriade 1991). The existence of both a cortical and subcortical target for the cholinergic systems is a mode of organization that also appears to hold for the monoaminergic arousal systems. Of particular interest, however, for the cholinergic systems is their coordination in the regulation of thalamic function, especially because the thalamus itself also mediates aspects of cortical arousal and sensory processing.

The hypothesis that the basal forebrain cholinergic system has specific roles in attentional function, an obvious mode of expression of a subcortical arousal system, does not preclude, of course, any involvement of the cholinergic systems in aspects of learning and memory or processes of neuronal plasticity (Singer 1979). A more attractive hypothesis is that the cholinergic systems modulate many distinct forms of processing occurring in their main targets, the neocortex, hippocampus, and the amygdala. Thus the effects of manipulations of the cholinergic system will depend critically on which components of the system (e.g. nbm, vdB, and MS) have been manipulated and on which terminal domains are engaged in any particular test situation.

In the experiments reviewed above, evidence has been provided for specific roles of components of the basal forebrain system other than the nbm. We have observed clear evidence of cholinergic involvement in the acquisition and performance of visual discriminations within the cingulate cortex, following lesioning of the vdB. Moreover, lesions of the medial septal cholinergic system produce major deficits in a short-term spatial working memory task that is mediated by the hippocampus. A possible role for the amygdaloid cholinergic system has been suggested in the retention of affective conditioning. It is possible that other actions on specific memory or cognitive systems will be uncovered, e.g. following a means for effecting profound experimental depletion of acetylcholine in medial temporal lobe structures. The differentiation of effects of lesions to different parts of the cholinergic system on different aspects of cognitive performance is summarized in Figure 3. These effects may all be related to a common mode of action of the basal forebrain cholinergic system to enhance processing in the appropriate terminal domains (see discussions above). For example, memory retrieval can be conceived of as a form of processing that would also benefit from enhanced signal-to-noise ratios, and enhanced attention may facilitate memory encoding of stimulus material.

Whether the band of cholinergic neurons from the MS to the nbm through the vdB represents a unitary system whose action is governed by the principles of "Mass Action" seems more controversial. In practice, the modularity of the terminal systems to which the basal forebrain cholinergic system projects surely means that it will be rare for activity in different components of the cholinergic system to influence performance under the same circumstances, unless a task has many interactive and distinct components. This complexity may account for some findings in which there is an apparent synergy in the effects of combined lesions to different components of the cholinergic system (e.g. Hodges et al 1991, Turner et al 1992). However, the basal forebrain cholinergic system may be shown to function in a unitary mode in circumstances that engender a common activation of the system.

The identification of specific deficits that appear to respond to cholinergic therapy in patients with Alzheimer's disease is encouraging, but optimism should be tempered by the fact that many of these improvements are in rather limited domains. Given the profound cortical pathology in Alzheimer's disease, it is likely that many cognitive deficits will fail to respond to cholinergic therapy because of dysfunction of the basic processing networks that the cholinergic neurons modulate. In the absence of any form of normal activity, no amount of cholinergic "boosting" could help to amplify the products of deficient processing. It is notable therefore that in one study, tacrine only improved responding in a task in which the stimuli were simple and required little perceptual processing. In a more complex recognition memory task with complex visual stimuli, tacrine had little effect (Sahakian et al 1993). Such conditions may optimize the circumstances under which boosting cholinergic function may be beneficial to such patients. However, note that Alzheimer's disease is not the only condition in which there is malfunctioning of the cortical cholinergic system; both Parkinson's disease and olivo-pontine cerebellar atrophy, as well as possibly normal aging, are associated with loss of subcortical cholinergic neurons in the absence of profound cell loss from the cortex itself. Cognitive deficits in such conditions may benefit to a greater extent from appropriate forms of cholinergic therapy than advanced dementia.

Acknowledgments

The research reviewed here is supported by a Programme Grant from the Wellcome Trust.

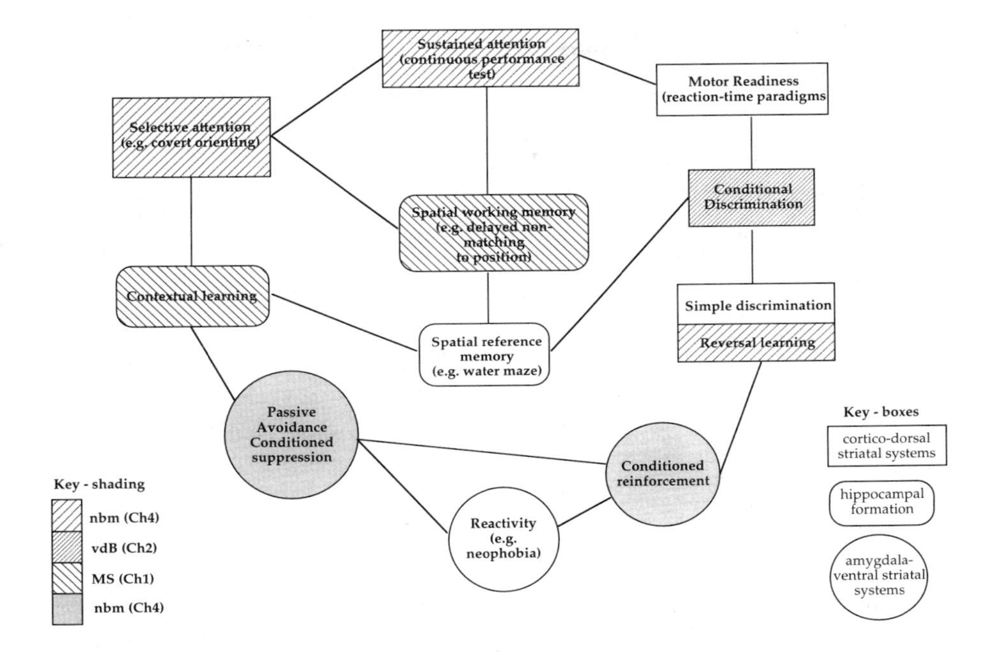

Figure 3 Summary of the main functional effects of lesions to various cholinergic cell groups. Cortical substrates of a variety of psychological processes are represented in differently shaped boxes. The innervation of these cortical targets is represented by different patterns of shading. For example, nbm lesions disrupt visual attentional function, which in rats is itself dependent upon the integrity of specific medial frontal cortical areas. To our knowledge, there is no data on the effects of cholinergic manipulations on simple discrimination learning or on reactivity to environmental stimuli. Spatial memory, which depends on the hippocampus, is unaffected by cholinergic deafferentation of this site. Full details are to be found in the text.

Literature Cited

Acquas E, Wilson C, Fibiger HC. 1996. Conditioned and unconditioned stimuli increase frontal cortical and hippocampal acetylcholine release: effects of novelty, habituation and fear. *J. Neurosci.* 16:3089–96

Aggleton JP, Hunt PR, Rawlins JNP. 1986. The effects of hippocampal lesions upon spatial and nonspatial tests of working memory. *Behav. Brain Res.* 19:133–46

Aggleton JP, Keith AB, Rawlins JNP, Hunt PR, Saghal A. 1992. Removal of the hippocampus and transection of the fornix produce comparable deficits on delayed nonmatching to position in rats. *Behav. Brain Res.* 52:61–71

Aigner TG, Mitchell SJ, Aggleton JP, DeLong MR, Struble RG, et al. 1987. Effects of scopolamine and physostigmine on recognition memory in monkeys with ibotenic acid lesions of the nucleus basalis of Meynert. *Psychopharmacology* 92:292–300

Aigner TG, Mitchell SJ, Aggleton JP, DeLong MR, Struble RG, et al. 1991. Transient impairment of recognition memory following ibotenic acid lesions of the basal forebrain in Macaques. *Brain Res.* 86:18–26

Alheid GF, Heimer L. 1988. New perspectives in basal forebrain organization of special relevance for neuropsychiatric disorders: the striatopallidal, amygdaloid and corticopetal components of the substantia innominata. *Neuroscience* 27:1–39

Ammassari-Teule M, Amoroso D, Forloni GL, Rossi-Arnaud C, Consolo S. 1993. Mechanical deafferentation of basal forebrain-cortical pathways and neurotoxic lesions of the nucleus basalis magnocellularis: comparative effect on spatial learning and cortical acetylcholine release in vivo. *Behav. Brain Res.* 54:145–52

Annett LE, McGregor A, Robbins TW. 1989. The effects of ibotenic acid lesions of the nucleus accumbens on spatial learning and extinction in the rat. *Behav. Brain Res.* 31: 231–42

Aspley S, Fone KCF. 1993. Galanin fails to alter both acquisition of a two trial per day water maze task and neurochemical markers of cholinergic or serotonergic neurones in adult rats. *Brain Res.* 622:330–36

Baratti CM, Opezzo JW, Kopf SR. 1993. Facilitation of memory storage by the acetylcholine M2 muscarinic receptor antagonist AF-DX 116. *Behav. Neural Biol.* 60:69–74

Barone S, Nanry KP, Mundy WR, McGinty JF, Tilson HA. 1991. Spatial learning deficits are not solely due to cholinergic deficits following medial septal lesions with cholchicine. *Psychobiology* 19:41–50

Bartus RT, Dean RLI, Beer B, Lippa AS. 1982. The cholinergic hypothesis of geriatric memory dysfunction. *Science* 217:408–17

Baxter MG, Bucci DJ, Gorman LK, Wiley RG, Gallagher M. 1995. Selective immunotoxic lesions of basal forebrain cholinergic cells: effects on learning and memory in rats. *Behav. Neurosci.* 109:714–22

Baxter MG, Bucci DJ, Sobel T, Williams MJ, Gorman LK, Gallagher M. 1996. Intact learning following lesions of basal forebrain cholinergic lesions. *NeuroReport.* In press

Baxter MG, Gallagher M. 1996. Intact spatial learning in both young and aged rats following selective removal of hippocampal cholinergic input. *Behav. Neurosci.* 110: 1–8

Berger-Sweeney J, Heckers S, Mesulam MM, Wiley RG, Lappi DA, Sharma M. 1994. Differential effects on spatial navigation of immunotoxin-induced cholinergic lesions of the medial septal area and nucleus basalis magnocellularis. *J. Neurosci.* 14: 4507–19

Bouton ME. 1992. Context and retrieval in extinction and in other examples of interference in simple associative learning. In *Current Topics in Animal Learning: Brain, Emotion and Cognition,* ed. L Dachowski, CF Flaherty, pp. 25–53. Hillsdale, NJ: Erlbaum

Bowen DM, Smith CB, White P, Davison AN. 1976. Neurotransmitter related enzymes and indices of hypoxia in senile dementia and other abiotrophies. *Brain* 99:459–96

Buchanan SL, Powell DA. 1982. Cingulate cortex: its role in Pavlovian conditioning. *J. Comp. Physiol. Psychol.* 96:745–54

Bussey TJ, Muir JL, Everitt BJ, Robbins TW. 1996. Dissociable effects of anterior and posterior cingulate cortex lesions on the acquisition of a conditional visual discrimination: facilitation of early learning vs. impairment of late learning. *Behav. Brain Res.* In press

Buzsáki G. 1989. Two stage model of memory trace formation: a role for noisy brain states. *Neuroscience* 31:551–70

Buzsáki G, Bickford RG, Ponomareff G, Thal LJ, Mandel R, Gage FH. 1988. Nucleus basalis and thalamic control of neocortical activity in the freely moving rat. *J. Neurosci.* 8:4007–26

Buzsáki G, Ponomareff GL, Bayardo F, Ruiz R, Gage FH. 1989. Neuronal activity in the subcortically denervated hippocampus: a chronic model for epilepsy. *Neuroscience* 28:527–38

Bymaster FP, Heath I, Hendrix JC, Shannon HE. 1993. Comparative behavioral and neurochemical activities of cholinergic antagonists in rats. *J. Pharmacol. Exp. Ther.* 267:16–24

Carli M, Robbins TW, Evenden JL, Everitt BJ. 1983. Effects of lesions to ascending noradrenergic neurons on performance of a 5-choice serial reaction time task in rats: implications for theories of dorsal bundle noradrenergic function based on selective attention and arousal. *Behav. Brain Res.* 9: 361–80

Chiba AA, Ducci DJ, Holland PC, Gallagher M. 1995. Basal forebrain cholinergic lesions disrupt increments but not decrements in conditioned stimulus processing. *J. Neurosci.* 15:7315–22

Connor DJ, Langlais PJ, Thal LJ. 1991. Behavioral impairments after lesions of the nucleus basalis by ibotenic acid and quisqualic acid. *Brain Res.* 555:84–90

Connor DJ, Thal LJ. 1989. Effect of ibotenate and quisqualate lesions of the nbM on water maze performance. *Soc. Neurosci.* 15, (Part 1):37.1–0

Crawley JN. 1993. Functional interactions of galanin and acetylcholine: relevance to memory and Alzheimer's disease. *Behav. Brain Res.* 57:133–41

Decker MW, Radek RJ, Majchrzak MJ, Anderson JD. 1992. Differential effects of medial septal lesions on spatial memory tasks. *Psychobiology* 20:9–19

Dekker AJAM, Connor DJ, Gage FH, Thal LJ. 1990. Chronic treatment with NGF improves spatial learning after NBM lesions. *Soc. Neurosci.* 16:207–17

Dellu F, Mayo W, Cherkaoui J, Le Moal M, Simon H. 1991. Learning disturbances following excitotoxic lesions of cholinergic pedunculo=pontine nucleus in the rat. *Brain Res.* 544:126–32

Dokla CPJ, Thal LJ. 1988. Effect of cholin esterase inhibitors on Morris water-task behavior following lesions of the nucleus basalis magnocellularis. *Behav. Neurosci.* 102:861–71

Dornan WA, McCampbell ARV, Tinkler GP, Hickman LJ. 1995. Selective acetylcholine neurotoxins, in combination with glucocorticoids, as a potential model of Alzheimer's disease: the effects of AF64A and saporin on spatial learning in the male rat. *Soc. Neurosci.* 21:773.5

Drachman DR, Sahakian BJ. 1979. The effects of cholinergic agents on human learning and memory. In *Nutrition in the Brain,* ed. A Barbeau, JH Growden, RJ Wurtman, pp. 351–66. New York: Raven

Dudchenko P, Sarter M. 1991. GABAergic control of basal forebrain cholinergic neurons and memory. *Behav. Brain Res.* 42: 33–41

Dunnett SB. 1985. Comparative effects of cholinergic drugs and lesions of nucleus basalis or fimbria-fornix on delayed matching in rats. *Psychopharmacology* 87:357–63

Dunnett SB, Everitt BJ, Robbins TW. 1991. The basal forebrain-cortical cholinergic system: interpreting the functional consequences of excitotoxic lesions. *Trends Neurosci.* 14(11):494–500

Dunnett SB, Toniolo G, Fine A, Ryan CN, Björklund A, Iversen SD. 1985. Transplantation of embryonic forebrain neurons to the neocortex of rats with lesions of nucleus basalis magnocellularis. II. Sensorimotor and learning impairments. *Neuroscience* 16:787–97

Dunnett SB, Whishaw IQ, Jones GH, Bunch ST. 1987. Behavioral biochemical and histochemical effects of different neurotoxic amino acids injected into nucleus basalis magnocellularis of rats. *Neuroscience* 20: 653–69

Eagger SA, Levy R, Sahakian BJ. 1991. Tacrine in Alzheimer's disease. *Lancet* 337: 989–92

Edeline J-M, Hars B, Maho C, Hennevin E. 1994. Transient and prolonged facilitation of tone-evoked responses induced by basal forebrain stimulations in the rat auditory cortex. *Exp. Brain Res.* 97:373–86

Etherington RE, Mittleman GM, Robbins TW. 1987. Comparative effects of nucleus basalis lesions and fimbria-fornix lesions on delayed matching and alternation in the rat. *Neurosci. Res. Commun.* 1:135–43

Everitt BJ, Robbins JL, Evenden JL, Marston HM, Jones GH, Sirkiä TE. 1987. The effects of excitotoxic lesions of the substantia innominata, ventral and dorsal globus pallidus on the acquisition and retention of a conditional visual discriminations: implications for cholinergic hypothesis of learning and memory. *Neuroscience* 22:441–69

Fibiger HC. 1991. Cholinergic mechanisms in learning, memory and dementia: a review of recent evidence. *Trends Neurosci.* 14: 220–23

Fine A, Dunnett SB, Björklund A, Iversen SD. 1985. Cholinergic ventral forebrain grafts into the neocortex improve passive avoidance memory in a rat model of Alzheimer's disease. *Proc. Natl. Acad. Sci. USA* 82: 5227–30

Fisher LJ, Jinnah HA, Kale LC, Higgins GA, Gage FH. 1991. Survival and function of intrastriatally grafted primary fibroblasts genetically modified to produce L-dopa. *Neuron* 6:371–80

Fisher LJ, Raymon HK, Gage FH. 1993. Cells engineered to produce acetylcholine: therapeutic potential for Alzheimer's disease. *Ann. NY Acad. Sci.* 695:278–84

Freed DM, Corkin S, Growdon JH, Nissen MJ. 1989. Selective attention in Alzheimer's disease: characterising cognitive subgroups of patients. *Neuropsychologia* 27:325–39

Gabriel M. 1990. Functions of anterior and posterior cingulate cortex during avoidance learning in rabbits. *Prog. Brain Res.* 85: 467–83

Gallagher M, Colombo PJ. 1995. Aging: the cholinergic hypothesis of cognitive decline. *Curr. Opin. Neurobiol.* 5:161–68

Good M, Honey RC. 1991. Conditioning and contextual retrieval in hippocampal rats. *Behav. Neurosci.* 4:499–509

Hagan JJ, Salamone JD, Simpson J, Iversen SD, Morris RGM. 1988. Place navigation in rats is impaired by lesions of medial septum and diagonal band but not nucleus basalis magnocellularis. *Behav. Brain Res.* 27:9–20

Hars B, Maho C, Edeline J-M, Hennevin E. 1993. Basal forebrain stimulation facilitates tone-evoked responses in the auditory cortex of awake rat. *Neuroscience* 56:61–74

Heckers S, Ohtake T, Wiley RG, Lappi DA, Geula C, Mesulam M-M. 1994. Complete and selective denervation of rat neocortex and hippocampus but not amygdala by an immunotoxin against the P75 NGF receptor. *J. Neurosci.* 14:1271–89

Heimer L, Zahm DS, Alheid GF. 1995. Basal ganglia. In *The Rat Nervous System,* ed. G

Paxinos, pp. 579–628. Sydney: Academic. 2nd ed.
Himmelheber A-M, Moore H, McGaughy J, Givens B, Sarter M. 1995. Cortical acetylcholine efflux and single unit activity in rats performing operant procedures assessing behavioral vigilance or sensorimotor and motivational task components. *Soc. Neurosci. Abstr.* 21:763.6
Hiroi N, White NM. 1991. The lateral nucleus of the amygdala mediates the expression of the amphetamine-produced conditioned place preference. *J. Neurosci.* 11:2107–16
Hodges H, Allen Y, Sinden J, Lantos PL, Gray JA. 1991. Effects of cholinergic rich neural grafts on radial maze performance of rats after excitotoxic lesions of the forebrain cholinergic system. II. Cholinergic drugs as probes to investigate lesion-induced deficits and transplantation-induced functional recovery. *Neuroscience* 43:609–23
Hodges H, Trasher S, Gray JA. 1989. Improved radial maze performance induced by the benzodiazepine receptor antagonist ZK 93 426 in lesioned and alcohol-treated rats. *Behav. Pharmacol.* 1:45–55
Holley LA, Sarter M. 1995. Functions of cholinergic inputs to visual cortical areas: effects of visual cortical cholinergic deafferentation on visual attention in rats. *Soc. Neurosci. Abstr.* 21:763.4
Holley LA, Turchi J, Apple C, Sarter M. 1995. Dissociation between the attentional effects of infusions of a benzodiazepine receptor agonist and an inverse agonist into the basal forebrain. *Psychopharmacology* 120: 99–108
Inglis WL, Dunbar JS, Winn P. 1993. Barbiturate anesthesia reduces the neurotoxic effects of quinolinate but not ibotenate in the rat pedunculopontine nucleus. *Neurosci. Lett.* 156:78–82
Inglis WL, Winn P. 1995. The pedunculopontine tegmental nucleus: where the striatum meets the reticular formation. *Prog. Neurobiol.* 47:1–29
Jakala P, Sirvio J, Riekkinen PJ. 1993. The effects of tacrine and zacopride on the performance of adult rats in the working memory task. *Gen. Pharmacol.* 24:675–79
Jarrard LE. 1993. On the role of the hippocampus in learning and memory in the rat. *Behav. Neur. Biol.* 60:9–26
Jones DNC, Barnes JC, Kirkby DL, Higgins GA. 1995. Age-associated impairments in a test of attention: evidence for involvement of cholinergic systems. *J. Neurosci.* 15:7282–92
Kelsey JE, Vargas H. 1993. Medial septal lesions disrupt spatial, but not nonspatial, working memory in rats. *Behav. Neurosci.* 107:565–74
Kim JJ, Fanselow MS. 1992. Modality specific retrograde amnesia of fear. *Science* 256: 675–76
Kolb B. 1984. Functions of the frontal cortex in the rat. *Brain Res. Rev.* 8:65–98
Krnjevic K. 1987. Role of acetlycholine in the cerebral cortex. In *Neurobiology of Memory,* ed. NJ Dun, RL Perlman, pp. 271–81. New York: Plenum
Krnjevic K, Ropert N, Casullo J. 1988. Septohippocampal disinhibition. *Brain Res.* 438: 182–92
Lawrence AD, Sahakian BJ. 1995. Alzheimer disease, attention and the cholinergic system. *Alzheimer Dis. Assoc. Disord.* 9:43–49
Lerer BE, Warner J. 1986. Radial maze performance deficits following lesions of rat basal forebrain. In *Advances in Behavioral Biology,* ed. A Fisher, I Hanin, C Lachman, 29:419–26. New York: Plenum
Levey AI, Armstrong DM, Atweh SF, Terry RD, Wainer BH. 1983. Monoclonal antibodies to choline acetyltransferase: specificity and immunohistochemistry. *Brain Res.* 218:313–87
Mandel RJ, Gage FH, Thal LJ. 1989a. Enhanced detection of nucleus basalis magnocellularis lesion-induced spatial learning deficit in rats by modification of training regimen. *Behav. Brain Res.* 31:221–29
Mandel RJ, Gage FH, Thal LJ. 1989b. Spatial-learning in rats: correlation with cortical choline acetyltransferase and improvement with NGF following NBM damage. *Exp. Neurol.* 104:208–17
Mandel RJ, Thal LJ. 1988. Physostigmine improves water maze performance following nucleus basalis magnocellularis lesions in rats. *Psychopharmacology* 96:421–25
Markowska AL, Olton DS, Murray EA, Gaffan D. 1989. A comparative analysis of the role of the fornix and cingulate cortex in rats. *Exp. Brain Res.* 74:187–201
Markowska AL, Wenk GL, Olton DS. 1990. Nucleus basalis magnocellularis and memory: differential effects of two neurotoxins. *Behav. Neur. Biol.* 54:13–26
Marlin NA. 1981. Contextual associations in trace conditioning. *Anim. Learn. Behav.* 9: 519–23
Marston HM, Everitt BJ, Robbins TW. 1993. Comparative effects of excitotoxic lesions of the hippocampus and septum/diagonal band on conditional visual discrimination and spatial learning. *Neuropsychologia* 31: 1099–118
Marston HM, West HL, Wilkinson LS, Everitt BJ, Robbins TW. 1994. Effects of excitotoxic lesions of the septum and vertical limb nucleus of the diagonal band of Broca on conditional visual discrimination: relationship between performance and choline

acetyltransferase activity in the cingulate cortex. *J. Neurosci.* 14:2009–19
McAlonan GM, Dawson GR, Wilkinson LO, Robbins TW, Everitt BJ. 1995a. The effects of AMPA-induced lesions of the medial septum and vertical limb nucleus of the diagonal band of Broca on spatial delayed non-matching to sample and spatial learning in the water maze. *Eur. J. Neurosci.* 7:1034–49
McAlonan GM, Wilkinson LS, Robbins TW, Everitt BJ. 1995b. The effects of AMPA-induced lesions of the septohippocampal cholinergic projection on aversive conditioning to explicit and contextual cues and spatial learning in the water maze. *Eur. J. Neurosci.* 7:281–92
McDonald RJ, White NM. 1993. A triple dissociation of memory systems: hippocampus, amygdala and dorsal striatum. *Behav. Neurosci.* 107:3–22
McGaughy J, Kaiser T, Sarter M. 1996. Behavioral vigilance following infusions of IgG-saporin into the basal forebrain: selectivity of the behavioral impairment and relation to cortical ACHE-positive fiber density. *Behav. Neurosci.* 110:247–65
McNamara RK, Skelton RW. 1993. The neuropharmacological and neurochemical basis of place learning in the Morris water maze. *Brain Res. Rev.* 18:33–49
Mesulam M-M, Mufson EJ, Wainer BH, Levey AI. 1983a. Central cholinergic pathways in the rat: an overview based on an alternative nomenclature (Ch1-Ch6). *Neuroscience* 10:1185–201
Mesulam M-M, Mufson EJ, Levey AI, Wainer BH. 1983b. Cholinergic innervation of cortex by the basal forebrain: cytochemistry and cortical connections of the septal area, diagonal band nuclei, nucleus basalis (substantia innominata) and hypothalamus in the rhesus monkey. *J. Comp. Neurol.* 214: 170–97
Metherate R, Tremblay N, Dykes RW. 1988. Transient and prolonged effects of acetylcholine on responsiveness of cat somatosensory cortical neurons. *J. Neurophysiol.* 59:1253–75
Mohammed AH. 1993. Effects of cholinesterase inhibitors on learning and memory in rats: a brief review with special reference to THA. *Acta Neurol. Scand. Suppl.* 88:13–15
Morris RGM, Garrud P, Rawlins JNP, O'Keefe J. 1981. Place navigation impaired in rats with hippocampal lesions. *Nature* 297:681–83
Morris RGM, Schenk F, Tweedie F, Jarrard LE. 1990. Ibotenate lesions of the hippocampus and/or subiculum: Dissociating the components of allocentric spatial learning. *Eur. J. Neurosci.* 2:1016–28
Moyer JR, Deyo RA, Disterhoft JF. 1990. Hippocampectomy disrupts trace eye-blink conditioning in rabbits. *Behav. Neurosci.* 104:243–52
Muir JL, Bussey TJ, Everitt BJ, Robbins TW. 1996. Dissociable effects of AMPA-induced lesions of the vertical limb nucleus of the diagonal band of Broca on performance of the 5-choice serial reaction time task and on acquisition of a conditional visual discrimination. *Behav. Brain Res.* In press
Muir JL, Dunnett SB, Robbins TW, Everitt BJ. 1992a. Attentional functions of the forebrain cholinergic systems: effects of intraventricular hemicholinium, physostigmine, basal forebrain lesions and intracortical grafts on a multiple-choice serial reaction time task. *Exp. Brain Res.* 89:611–22
Muir JL, Everitt BJ, Robbins TW. 1994. AMPA-induced excitotoxic lesions of the basal forebrain: a significant role for the cortical cholinergic system in attentional function. *J. Neurosci.* 14:2313–26
Muir JL, Everitt BJ, Robbins TW. 1995. Reversal of visual attentional dysfunction following lesions of the cholinergic basal forebrain by physostigmine and nicotine but not by the 5-HT3 receptor antagonist, ondansetron. *Psychopharmacology* 118: 82–92
Muir JL, Everitt BJ, Robbins TW. 1996. The cerebral cortex of the rat and visual attentional function: dissociable effects of mediofrontal, cingulate, anterior dorsolateral and parietal cortex lesions on a 5-choice serial reaction time task. *Cereb. Cortex.* In press
Muir JL, Page KJ, Sirinathsinghji DJS, Robbins TW, Everitt BJ. 1993. Excitotoxic lesions of basal forebrain cholinergic neurons: effects on learning, memory and attention. *Behav. Brain Res.* 57:123–31
Muir JL, Robbins TW, Everitt BJ. 1992b. Disruptive effects of muscimol infused into the basal forebrain: differential interaction with cholinergic mechanisms. *Psychopharmacology* 107:541–50
Nadel C, Willner J. 1980. Context and conditioning: a place for space. *Physiol. Psychol.* 8:218–28
Nilsson OG, Leanza G, Rosenblad C, Lappi DA, Wiley RG, Björklund A. 1992. Spatial learning impairments in rats with selective immunolesion of the forebrain cholinergic system. *NeuroReport* 3:1005–8
Ogren SO, Andersson P, Pramanik A. 1993. Galanin: potential role in learning and memory. *Eur. Neuropsychopharmacol.* 3: 195–96
Ohno M, Yamamoto T, Watanabe S. 1994. Blockade of hippocampal M1 muscarinic receptors impairs working memory performance of rats. *Brain Res.* 650:260–66

Olton DS, Becker JT, Handelmann JE. 1979. Hippocampus, space and memory. *Behav. Brain Sci.* 2:313–65

Olton DS, Markowska AL, Pang K, Golski S, Voytko ML, Gorman LK. 1992. Comparative cognition and assessment of cognitive processes in animals. *Behav. Pharmacol.* 3:307–18

Olton DS, Wenk GL, Markowska AL. 1991. Basal forebrain, memory and attention. In *Functional Aspects of the Basal Forebrain,* ed. R Richardson, pp. 247–62. Boston: Birkhauser

Page KJ, Everitt BJ. 1993. Transsynaptic induction of c-fos in basal forebrain, diencephalic and midbrain neurons following AMPA-induced activation of the dorsal and ventral striatum. *Exp. Brain Res.* 93: 399–411

Page KJ, Everitt BJ. 1995. The distribution of neurons coexpressing immunoreactivity to AMPA-sensitive glutamate receptor subtypes (GluR1–4) and nerve growth factor receptor in the rat basal forebrain. *Eur. J. Neurosci.* 7:1022–33

Page KJ, Everitt BJ, Robbins TW, Marston HM, Wilkinson LS. 1991. Dissociable effects on spatial maze and passive avoidance acquisition and retention following AMPA- and ibotenic acid-induced excitotoxic lesions of the basal forebrain in rats: differential dependence on cholinergic neuronal loss. *Neuroscience* 43:457–72

Page KJ, Saha A, Everitt BJ. 1993. Differential activation and survival of basal forebrain neurons following infusions of excitatory amino acids: studies with the immediate early gene c-fos. *Exp. Brain Res.* 93: 412–22

Page KJ, Sirinathsinghji DJS, Everitt BJ. 1995. AMPA-induced lesions of the basal forebrain differentially affect cholinergic and noncholinergic neurons: Lesion assessment using quantitative in situ hybridization histochemistry. *Eur. J. Neurosci.* 7:1012–21

Pang K, Williams MJ, Egeth H, Olton DS. 1993. Nucleus basalis magnocellularis and attention: effects of muscimol infusions. *Behav. Neurosci.* 107:1031–38

Parasuraman R, Haxby JV. 1993. Attention and brain function in Alzheimer's disease: a review. *Neuropsychology* 7:242–72

Pasqualotto BA, Vincent SR. 1991. Galanin and NADPH-diaphorase coexistence in cholinergic neurons of the basal forebrain. *Brain Res.* 551:78–86

Perry EK, Tomlinson BE, Blessed G, Bergmann K, Gibson PH, Perry RH. 1978. Correlation of cholinergic abnormalities with senile plaques and mental test scores in senile dementia. *Br. Med. J.* 2:1457–59

Raffaele KC, Olton DS. 1988. Hippocampal and amygdaloid involvement in working memory for nonspatial stimuli. *Behav. Neurosci.* 102(3):349–55

Rawlins JNP, Olton DS. 1982. The septohippocampal system and cognitive mapping. *Behav. Brain Res.* 5:331–58

Richardson RT, DeLong MR. 1988. A reappraisal of the functions of the nucleus basalis of Meynert. *Trends Neurosci.* 11: 264–67

Ridley RM, Aitken DM, Baker HF. 1989. Learning about rules but not about reward is impaired following lesions of the cholinergic projection to the hippocampus. *Brain Res.* 502:306–18

Ridley RM, Baker HF. 1993. Behavioral effects of cholinergic grafts. *Ann. NY Acad. Sci.* 695:274–77

Ridley RM, Baker HF, Drewett B, Johnson JA. 1985. Effects of ibotenic acid lesions of the basal forebrain on serial reversal-learning in the marmosets. *Psychopharmacology* 86:438–43

Ridley RM, Baker HF, Murray TK. 1988. Basal nucleus lesions in monkeys: recognition memory impairment or visual agnosia? *Psychopharmacology* 95:289–90

Ridley RM, Murray TK, Johnson JA, Baker HF. 1986. Learning impairment following lesion of the basal nucleus of Meynert in the marmoset: modification by cholinergic drugs. *Brain Res.* 376:108–16

Riekkinen P Jr, Sirvio J. 1990. Similar memory impairments found in medial septal-vertical diagonal band of Broca- and nucleus basalis lesioned rats: Are memory defects induced by nucleus basalis lesions related to the degree of nonspecific subcortical cell loss? *Behav. Brain Res.* 37:81–88

Riekkinen P Jr, Aaltonen M. 1991. Tetrahydro aminoacridine inhibits high-voltage spindle activity in aged rats after acute and chronic treatment. *Psychopharmacology* 103:265–67

Robbins TW, Everitt BJ. 1992. Functions of dopamine in the dorsal and ventral striatum. *Sem. Neurosci.* 4:119–28

Robbins TW, Everitt BJ. 1995. Arousal systems and attention. In *The Cognitive Neurosciences,* ed. MS Gazzaniga, pp. 703–20. Cambridge, MA: MIT Press

Robbins TW, Everitt BJ, Ryan CN, Marston HM, Jones GH, Page KJ. 1989a. Comparative effects of quisqualic and ibotenic acid-induced lesions of the substantia innominata and globus pallidus on the acquisition of a conditional visual discrimination: differential effects on cholinergic mechanisms. *Neuroscience* 28:337–52

Robbins TW, Everitt BJ, Marston HM, Wilkinson J, Jones GH, Page KJ. 1989b. Comparative effects of ibotenic acid- and quisqualic acid-induced lesions of the substantia innominata on attentional function in the rat: further implications for the role of the cholinergic neurons of the nucleus basalis in cognitive processes. *Behav. Brain Res.* 35:221–40

Roberts AC, De Salvia MA, Wilkinson LS, Collins P, Muir JL, et al. 1994. 6-Hydroxydopamine lesions of the prefrontal cortex in monkeys enhance performance on an analog of the Wisconsin card sort test: possible interactions with subcortical dopamine. *J. Neurosci.* 14:2531–44

Roberts AC, Robbins TW, Everitt BJ, Muir JL. 1992. A specific form of cognitive rigidity following excitotoxic lesions of the basal forebrain in marmosets. *Neuroscience* 47: 251–64

Rothblat LA, Kromer LF. 1991. Object recognition memory in the rat: the role of the hippocampus. *Behav. Brain Res.* 42:25–32

Rugg EL, Dunbar JS, Latimer M, Winn P. 1992. Excitotoxic lesions of the pedunculopontine tegmental nucleus of the rat 1. Comparison of the effects of various excitotoxins, with particular reference to the loss of immunohistochemically identified cholinergic neurons. *Brain Res.* 589: 181–93

Rye DB, Saper CB, Lee HJ, Wainer BH. 1987. Pedunculopontine tegmental nucleus in the rat: cytoarchitecture, cytochemistry and some extrapyramidal connections of the mesopontine tegmentum. *J. Comp. Neurol.* 259:483–528

Sahakian BJ, Coull JT. 1994. Nicotine and tetrahydroaminoacridine: evidence for improved attention in patients with dementia of the Alzheimer type. *Drug Dev. Res.* 31: 80–88

Sahakian BJ, Downes JJ, Eagger S, Evenden JL, Levy R, et al. 1990. Sparing of attentional relative to mnemonic function in a subgroup of patients with dementia of the Alzheimer type. *Neuropsychologia* 28: 1197–213

Sahakian BJ, Jones GMM, Levy R, Gray JA, Warburton DM. 1989. The effects of nicotine on attention, information processing and short-term memory in patients with dementia of the Alzheimer type. *Br. J. Psychiatry* 154:797–800

Sahakian BJ, Owen AM, Morant NJ, Eagger SA, Boddington S, et al. 1993. Further analysis of tetrahydroaminoacridine (THA) in Alzheimer's disease: assessment of attentional and mnemonic function using CANTAB. *Psychopharmacology* 110:395–401

Salamone JD, Channell SL, Welner SA, Gill R, Robbins TW, Iversen SD. 1987. Nucleus basalis lesions and anticholinergic drugs impair spatial memory and visual discrimination performance in the rat. In *Cellular and Molecular Basis of Cholinergic Function,* ed. MJ Dowdall, JN Hawthorn, pp. 835–40. Chichester: Ellis Horwood

Santucci AC, Haroutinian V. 1989. Nucleus basalis lesions impair memory in rats trained on nonspatial and spatial discrimination tasks. *Physiol. Behav.* 45:1025–31

Sarter M. 1994. Neuronal mechanisms of the attentional dysfunctions in senile dementia and schizophrenia. *Psychopharmacology* 114:539–50

Sarter M, Bruno JP. 1997. Trans-synaptic stimulation of cortical acetylcholine and enhancement of attentional functions: a rational approach for the development of cognitive enhancers. *Behav. Brain Res.* In press

Sarter M, Bruno JP, Dudchenko P. 1990. Activating the damaged basal forebrain system: tonic stimulation versus signal amplification. *Psychopharmacology* 101:1–17

Sarter M, Schneider HH, Stephens DN. 1988. Treatment strategies for senile dementia: antagonist beta-carbolines. *Trends Neurosci.* 11:13–17

Sato H, Hata Y, Masui H, Tsumoto T. 1987. A functional role of cholinergic innervation to neurons in cat visual cortex. *J. Neurophysiol.* 58:765–80

Schultz W. 1992. Activity of dopamine neurons in the behaving primate. *Semin. Neurosci.* 4:129–38

Segal M, Bloom FE. 1976. The action of norepinephrine in the rat hippocampus. IV. The effects of locus coeruleus stimulation on evoked hippocampal activity. *Brain Res.* 107:513–25

Selden NRW, Everitt BJ, Jarrard LE, Robbins TW. 1991. Complementary roles for the amygdala and hippocampus in aversive conditioning to explicit and contextual cues. *Neuroscience* 42:335–50

Selden NRW, Robbins TW, Everitt BJ. 1990. Enhanced behavioral conditioning to context and impaired behavioral and neuroendocrine responses to conditioned-stimuli following ceruleocortical noradrenergic lesions: support for an attentional theory of central noradrenergic function. *J. Neurosci.* 10:531–39

Semba K. 1993. Aminergic and cholinergic afferents to REM sleep induction regions of the pontine reticular formation in the rat. *J. Comp. Neurol.* 330:543–56

Sillito AM, Kemp JA. 1983. Cholinergic modulation of the functional organization of the cat visual cortex. *Brain Res.* 289: 143–55

Singer W. 1979. Central-core control of visual cortex function. In *The Neurosciences, Fourth Study Program,* ed. FO Schmitt, FG Worden, pp. 1093–109. Cambridge, MA: MIT Press

Solomon PR, Vander Schaaf ER, Thompson

RF, Weisz DJ. 1986. Hippocampus and trace conditioning of the rabbits classically conditioned nictitating membrane response. *Behav. Neurosci.* 100:729–44

Steckler T, Inglis W, Winn P, Sahgal A. 1994. The pedunculopontine tegmental nucleus: a role in cognitive processes? *Brain Res. Rev.* 19:298–318

Steriade M. 1991. Alertness, quiet sleep, dreaming. In *Cerebral Cortex,* ed. A Peters, 9:279–357. New York: Plenum

Steriade M. 1993. Central core modulation of spontaneous oscillations and sensory transmission in thalamocortical systems. *Curr. Opin. Neurobiol.* 3:619–25

Sutherland RJ, Rodriguez AJ. 1989. Role of the fornix/fimbria and some related subcortical structures in place learning and memory. *Behav. Brain Res.* 32:265–77

Sutherland RJ, Whishaw IQ, Kolb B. 1983. Abehavioural analysis of spatial localization following electrolytic, kainate- or colchicine-induced damage to the hippocampal formation in the rat. *Behav. Brain Res.* 7:133–53

Terry AV Jr, Buccafusco JJ, Jackson WJ. 1993. Scopolamine reversal of nicotine enhanced delayed matching-to-sample performance in monkeys. *Pharmacol. Biochem. Behav.* 45:925–29

Torres EM, Perry TA, Blokland A, Wilkinson LS, Wiley RG, et al. 1994. Behavioral, histochemical and biochemical consequences of selective immunolesions in discrete regions of the basal forebrain cholinergic system. *Neuroscience* 63:95–122

Tremblay N, Warren RA, Dykes RW. 1990. Electrophysiological studies of acetylcholine and the role of the basal forebrain in somatosensory cortex of the cat, I. Cortical neurons excited by somatic stimuli. *J. Neurophysiol.* 64:1199–211

Turner JJ, Hodges H, Sinden JD, Gray JA. 1992. Comparison of radial maze performance of rats after ibotenate and quisqualate lesions of the forebrain cholinergic projection system: effects of pharmacological challenge and changes in training regime. *Behav. Pharmacol.* 3:359–74

Vogt BA. 1985. Cingulate cortex. In *Cerebral Cortex,* ed. EG Jones, A Peters, pp. 89–149. New York: Plenum

Vogt BA, Gabriel M, Vogt LJ, Poremba A, Jensen EL, et al. 1991. Muscarinic receptor binding increases in anterior thalamus and cingulate cortex during discriminative avoidance learning. *J. Neurosci.* 11:1508–14

Voytko ML. 1996. Cognitive functions of the basal forebrain cholinergic system in monkeys: memory or attention. *Behav. Brain Res.* 75:13–25

Voytko ML, Olton DS, Richardson RT, Gorman LK, Tobin JR, Price DL. 1994. Basal forebrain lesions in monkeys disrupt attention but not learning and memory. *J. Neurosci.* 14:167–86

Warburton DM. 1977. Stimulus selection and behavioural inhibition. In *Handbook of Psychopharmacology,* ed. LL Iversen, SD Iversen, SH Snyder, 8:385–431. New York: Plenum

Wendelin D, McGaughy J, Smith BH, Sarter M. 1995. Comparison between the effects of infusions of 192 IgG-saporin into the basal forebrain or the cortex on behavioral vigilance. *Soc. Neurosci. Abstr.* 21:763.8

Wenk GL, Harrington CA, Tucker DA, Rance NE. 1992. Basal forebrain neurons and memory: a biochemical, histological and behavioral study of differential vulnerability to ibotenate and quisqualate. *Behav. Neurosci.* 106:909–23

Wenk GL, Stoehr JD, Quintana G, Mobley S, Wiley RG. 1994. Behavioral, biochemical, histological and electrophysiological effects of 192 IgG-saporin injections into the basal forebrain of rats. *J. Neurosci.* 14:5896–995

Wiley RG, Oeltmann TN, Lappi DA. 1991. Immunolesioning: selective destruction of neurons using immunotoxin to rat NGF receptor. *Brain Res.* 562:149–53

Wilson FAW, Rolls ET. 1990. Learning and memory is reflected in the responses of reinforcement-related neurons in the primate basal forebrain. *J. Neurosci.* 10:1254–67

Winkler J, Suhr ST, Gage FH, Thal LJ, Fisher LJ. 1995. Essential role of neocortical acetylcholine in spatial memory. *Nature* 375:484–87

Winn P. 1990. Cholinergic stimulation of substantia nigra: effects on feeding, drinking and sexual behavior in the male rat. *Psychopharmacology* 104:208–14

Winn P, Farrell A, Maconick A, Robbins TW. 1983. Behavioral and pharmacological specificity of the feeding elicited by cholinergic stimulation of the substantia nigra in the rat. *Behav. Neurosci.* 97:794–809

AUTHOR INDEX

A

B

C

D

F

H

K

L

P

Q

R

S

X

Y

Z

SUBJECT INDEX

A

B

D

N

O

Q

R

S

T

U

V

W

Y

Z

CUMULATIVE INDEXES

CONTRIBUTING AUTHORS, VOLUMES 38–48

CHAPTER TITLES, VOLUMES 38–48

SOCIAL PSYCHOLOGY

SPECIAL TOPICS

Annual Reviews

A nonprofit scientific publisher
4139 El Camino Way • P.O. Box 10139
Palo Alto, CA 94303-0139 USA

BB97

STEP 1: ENTER YOUR NAME & ADDRESS

NAME

ADDRESS

CITY STATE/PROVINCE COUNTRY POSTAL CODE

TODAY'S DATE DAYTIME PHONE

E-MAIL ADDRESS FAX NUMBER

Phone Orders **800-523-8635** *(U.S. or Canada)*
415-493-4400 ext. 1 *(worldwide)*
8 a.m. to 4 p.m. Pacific Time, Monday-Friday

FAX Orders **415-424-0910**
24 hours a day

Mention priority code **BB97** when placing phone orders

STEP 4: CHOOSE YOUR PAYMENT METHOD

❑ Check or Money Order Enclosed (US funds, made payable to "Annual Reviews")

❑ Bill Credit Card ❑ AmEx ❑ MasterCard ❑ VISA

Account No. ________

Signature ________

Exp. Date MO/YR Name ________
(print name exactly as it appears on credit card)

STEP 2: ENTER YOUR ORDER

QTY	ANNUAL REVIEW OF:	VOL.	Place on Standing Order? SAVE 10% NOW WITH PAYMENT	PRICE	TOTAL
		#	❑ Yes, save 10% ❑ No	$	$
		#	❑ Yes, save 10% ❑ No	$	$
		#	❑ Yes, save 10% ❑ No	$	$
		#	❑ Yes, save 10% ❑ No	$	$
		#	❑ Yes, save 10% ❑ No	$	$

30% STUDENT/RECENT GRADUATE DISCOUNT (past 3 years) *Not for standiung orders. Include proof of status.* $

CALIFORNIA CUSTOMERS: Add applicable California sales tax for your location. $

CANADIAN CUSTOMERS: Add 7% GST (Registration # 121449029 RT). $

STEP 3: CALCULATE YOUR SHIPPING & HANDLING

HANDLING CHARGE (Add $3 per volume, up to $9 max.). Applies to all orders. $

SHIPPING OPTIONS: U.S. Mail 4th Class Book Rate (surface). Standard option. FREE. $ **N/C**

(No UPS to P.O. boxes) UPS Ground Service ($3/ volume. 48 contiguous U.S. states.) $

Please note expedited shipping preference: ❑ UPS Next Day Air ❑ UPS Second Day Air ❑ US Airmail ❑ UPS Worldwide Express ❑ UPS Worldwide Expedited

Note option at left. We will calculate amount and add to your total

Abstracts and content lists available on the World Wide Web at www.annurev.org. **E-mail orders welcome: service@annurev.org**

TOTAL $

Orders may also be placed through booksellers or subscription agents or through our **Authorized Stockists.**
From Europe, the UK, the Middle East and Africa, contact: **Gazelle Book Service Ltd.**, Fax (0) 1524-63232.
From India, Pakistan, Bangladesh or Sri Lanka, contact: **SARAS Books**, Fax 91-11-941111.